ROTHMANS RUGBY UNION YEARBOOK 1995-96

Editors: Mick Cleary
and John Griffiths

ROTHMANS

HEADLINE

First published in 1995
by HEADLINE BOOK PUBLISHING

Cover photographs. Moments from the marvellous 1995 World Cup in South Africa. *Front:* The unstoppable Jonah Lomu, star of the tournament, leaves Tony Underwood floundering in his wake in New Zealand's semi-final demolition of England. *Back:* François Pienaar, captain of the victorious South Africans, receives the Webb Ellis Trophy from President Nelson Mandela, who is wearing an identical No 6 Springbok shirt in his honour.

All photographs by Colorsport

10 9 8 7 6 5 4 3 2

ISBN 0 7472 7816 4

Photoset by Cylinder Graphics Limited, London

Printed and bound in Great Britain by
The Bath Press, Avon

HEADLINE BOOK PUBLISHING
A division of Hodder Headline PLC
338 Euston Road
London NW1 3BH

CONTENTS

EDITORIAL PREFACE

As Rugby Union continues to expand apace, so does the scope of the Yearbook's coverage. The first *Rothmans Rugby Yearbook,* published in 1972, contained 368 pages. This, the 24th issue, is nearly 100 pages larger and the biggest ever compiled.

The third World Cup, held in the summer in South Africa, was of course the most important event of the past year. Our comprehensive reportage of the tournament includes full match details for every game, and complete squads and match appearances for each country. After careful deliberations our international panel of experts selected the two foremost personalities of that tournament, Jonah Lomu of New Zealand and François Pienaar of South Africa, together with Rob Andrew of England, Rob Wainwright of Scotland and Philippe Saint-André of France as our Five Players of the Year.

Once again, sincere thanks to our web of contributors and to all the readers who have written to us with ideas for improvements. Special thanks are due to Chris Rhys for his work on the extensive tours section, and to our house editor, Caroline North, without whose efficiency and cheerfulness under pressure our deadlines would never have been met. We should also like to acknowledge the help given by the administrators at the various unions, who have patiently answered our queries, and thank UNISYS, Michael Humphreys and Partners and the Jolyon Armstrong Network for a variety of statistical information.

Mick Cleary
John Griffiths

PLEASE NOTE: The principal statistical sections of the Yearbook are complete up to and including 31 March 1995. Full coverage of the tours which took place in the spring and summer of 1995 will be given in the next edition.

THE ASHES OF THE AMATEUR GAME

REVIEW OF THE 1994-95 SEASON
Mick Cleary

There can surely now be no turning back. Rupert Murdoch was the man finally to prod, cajole, boot, seduce, perhaps even bribe, the amateur game into the professional era. The announcement, in Johannesburg on the eve of the World Cup final, that Murdoch's News Corporation was willing to pay $550 million for broadcast rights to a new tri-nation competition between Australia, New Zealand and South Africa should have been the signal for the game's administrators to sweep away all the hypocrisy of the last few years and come clean in admitting that players should now be contracted and paid to play Rugby Union.

It is the only honest course left to those who run the game, and might even have been a step taken by the International Board at its summit meeting on amateurism in Paris at the end of August after the Yearbook went to press. Regrettably, the sense of anticipation of a momentous decision about to be taken was tempered for rugby writers by the experience of having attended so many epoque-making IB press conferences over the last decade at which precisely nothing of note has happened.

Well, if the IB themselves have not sanctioned professionalism, then it is a sure bet that the new southern alliance will do it themselves. For once, Louis Luyt kept his usually energetic lips sealed when quizzed as to what was in the deal for the players. Perhaps his reticence that day explains his outrageous behaviour at the microphone the following night at the World Cup banquet, when he insulted guest and host teams alike with his claim that the Springboks would have won the World Cup in 1987 and 1991 as well had they taken part. No one on the top table on the Friday (the presidents of the Australian and New Zealand unions, Leo Williams and Richie Guy, sat alongside Luyt) was prepared to admit that, at long last, the Rubicon had been crossed.

There are several possible reasons for this. One is that these men were conforming to the ostrich traditions of the game and burying their heads in the sand while money was being stuffed into the back pockets of all those around them. Now, while there is a long and shameful history of that sort of behaviour, it simply does not fit the bill as far as these three are concerned. Their unions have long been in the vanguard of a more progressive outlook on professionalism and certainly they carry to the debate none of the Corinthian baggage which so often seems to burden their northern hemisphere counterparts.

The only possible explanation for their silent posture can be that they wanted the others to climb into bed with them and were therefore giving the IB a clear two months to get its act together. (There were also, apparently, some finer points of tax law to sort out – aren't there always?) The view that the southern cousins were throwing down the gauntlet was one that was picked up by the RFU secretary elect, Tony Hallett. Hallett, who succeeded Dudley Wood on 14 July, had got wind of the press conference to announce the deal the previous evening and slipped in almost unnoticed as the news was being given out – *almost* unnoticed, for no sooner had the Gang of Three played a seriously straight bat to all questions than Hallett was surrounded and asked for his reaction.

'It does seem that they are saying, come with us or we'll go our own way,' he said, with a refreshing note of candour (wait until those committeemen get hold of him). 'It also appears obvious that, however you dress it up, you will now have the full-time employment of guys to play rugby. To talk of funds going to the development of the game is just concealing the point. Perhaps they mean the development of players' bank balances. It's no use talking about the death of amateurism any more. We passed that point long ago. The term is already in a state of rigor mortis. There is no doubt that this is a serious challenge to the countries in the northern hemisphere, one which I am fully prepared to take on board. Certainly I have no intention of pulling up the drawbridge on it, although I suspect that the discussion our end will go to the wire.'

Long may the Halletts of this side of the world be allowed to voice their significant opinions. What has been lacking for so long in the Home Unions has been a sense of realism about what is happening in the game and what ought to be done to protect those parts of the sport deemed to be worth preserving. To lose oneself in the ethical fog of money is to risk losing rugby to the entrepreneurs. With commercialism rampant in the sport (and the players didn't bring those forces to the table, remember), it has been obvious that there would come a point when the division of the spoils simply had to include those who are laying on the entertainment. Fortunately, in Vernon Pugh of Wales there has been another voice of sanity to inject into the debate which has been conducted among too many for too long.

There is nothing wrong with consultation. However, the chain of communication in most of the unions is far too long and unwieldy. Events now move at such a pace that, from the International Board downwards, there must be a full-time professional executive panel to react daily to the changing circumstances of the sport. That the Old Fartonians episode could so nearly jeopardise England's World Cup campaign is a minor example of how far removed from the realpolitik of the game some administrators are. The RFU's cabal of six who took the decision to sack Carling may well have thought they held the moral high ground and were right to act as they did. Which one of them, however, was going to break the news to Pilkington, the sponsors whose Cup final the following day they usurped, or to the gaggle of

England sponsors who had ploughed millions into the national cause? Principles are fine, just as long as you are not expecting your wallet to be looked after at the same time.

The Pughs and Halletts, men steeped in the traditions of the game but with an eye on the future, are the sort who must take hold of things now and map out where the game goes from here. The route will not be easy. It's quite straightforward to say that players ought to receive money for their labours, but at which point should they be contracted on a full-time basis? That is the real dilemma. The southern hemisphere will have to address that issue immediately, for the new arrangement creates, at the very least, six extra games a season – four Tests (the three are to play each other on a home-and-away basis) plus the extended commitment of the new Super-12 competition. These are no ordinary matches, either, for they involve extensive travel as well as preparation. And when there is so much prize-money – sorry, sporting glory – at stake, the pressure on players will be such that a quick flit into work the following Monday would be a ludicrous expectation.

The challenge for the adminstrators is to embrace the new order, not to reject or even to be suspicious of it. That is the weak-willed way, as well as the way to let television ride roughshod over your game. There is no way that Murdoch would dip that deeply into his purse if there were not a few strings attached. If these can be limited to tinkering with kick-off times or a few jazzy shirt designs, then all well and good. But if he wants wholesale changes to laws, schedules and personnel, then the rugby world needs to be strong in its resistance. It can only achieve that if it is united.

So much for the future. The year past was full of incident, delight, controversy and sadness. The shadow of Max Brito's injury will fall across the game for many years to come. The incident in the World Cup pool game against Tonga which led to the young Ivory Coast winger being rendered quadriplegic was innocuous in itself. 'There but for the grace of God...' must have been on the lips of many thousands of players round the world. If only they can keep the pressure on to ensure that Brito and his like are never forgotten, be it through the surveillance of adequate insurance schemes, support funds or continuing goodwill, then rugby can consider itself to be morally healthy. The signs are that, in this regard at least, its house is in order.

And perhaps, at long last, is its stance on violent play. The response to the brawl in Port Elizabeth (the second year running that the old ground has witnessed violent mayhem) in the World Cup pool match between South Africa and Canada was admirable. Gareth Rees and Rod Snow of Canada, along with James Dalton of South Africa, were sent off. Springbok Pieter Hendriks and Canada's Scott Stewart were later cited and banned for their part in the mass punch-up. There was a lot of ridiculous moral posturing in South Africa over the dismissal of Dalton as well as the citing of Hendriks. The authorities sent out the

Ivory Coast winger Max Brito is stretchered off after the tragic incident in the World Cup match against Tonga which left him paralysed for life. The world of rugby has already responded well but the authorities must ensure that they never forget his plight.

right message to the whole rugby world: raise your fists at your peril.

The wonderful achievements of François Pienaar's Springboks, crowning what was a memorable World Cup, are chronicled elsewhere. It was not memorable because the rugby itself was always scintillating and inventive, rather because the matches threw up an extraordinary number of dramatic occasions: the opening day; Jonah Lomu's first touch of the ball and almost every subsequent touch thereafter; Western Samoa-Argentina and the East London crowd; Italy-Argentina and the Pumas' failure to turn pressure into points in every one of their pool matches; France-Scotland and Ntamack's last-gasp and successful drive for the try-line; England-Australia and that right boot of Rob Andrew which nailed Wallaby hopes; the monsoon of Durban; the rout of Cape Town and the Mandela final. The catalogue of memories is rich. The good (one team, one nation; one World Cup in one country) far outweighed the bad (tickets too expensive and inaccessible; the violence of Johannesburg).

Domestically, England's proud achievement of their third Grand Slam in five years was overshadowed by the World Cup humbling by the All Blacks. Perhaps the subsequent showing of the northern hemisphere countries in the World Cup might have appeared to give substance to the theory that this was somehow an easy Grand Slam. There is no such thing as an easy Grand Slam. History simply does not toss them about like confetti. While it's true that the lessons of the World Cup suggest that once again the southern hemisphere is setting the pace in playing standards, the Five Nations, with its traditions and emotions, will never be a run-of-the-mill sideshow. England manager Jack Rowell, while he is to be applauded on the early success of his first year, will know that the critics will be on his case if England lose to the Springboks in November. He knows that England are some way from finding that elusive, dynamic, rounded pattern of play. Talking the game is one thing; playing it quite another.

Scotland regrouped magnificently after their dismal run through to heavy defeat by the Springboks at the start of the season. How well will they fare without their inspirational captain, Gavin Hastings, who bowed out after the World Cup? Scotland's Celtic cousins have less to look forward to. Ireland bumble along while Wales, who ousted the management team of Alan Davies, Robert Norster and Gareth Jenkins just days before the World Cup, are still drifting helplessly.

Leicester finally got their noses in front of Bath to take the Courage League Division 1 title, their first Championship since the inaugural year of the competition, 1987-88. Some were wondering whether Bath, after so many years of dominance, might be about to crumble. The sceptics had their answer on an afternoon of glorious rugby in the Pilkington Cup final, when Bath absorbed a spirited Wasps challenge before hitting them with an invigorating display of hard-nosed finishing. Some bloke called Carling had been sacked that morning. What a pity

The dropped goal from Rob Andrew which won England's World Cup quarter-final against the holders, Australia. It was to be their last moment of glory in the tournament.

such a match was overshadowed by off-field events. Saracens came charging back up from Division 2, a feat relegated Northampton, with their international contingent, hope to repeat within 12 months.

In Wales the sleeping giant of Cardiff finally stretched into life to win their first League title. No such joy and celebration for another famous name, Pontypool, who slipped out of the top flight. There was a sense of pain, too, at Pontypridd. They were bridesmaids in both competitions, losing out to Cardiff in the League and going out to Swansea in the final of the Cup. In Scotland, Stirling County won the League at a canter, while in Ireland, Shannon became the first club to win the All-Ireland League with a 100 per cent record.

There were a few farewells on the international stage. Michael Lynagh, that great ambassador of Australian rugby; Dewi Morris and Jon Hall in England, Gavin Hastings in Scotland, who made the national side believe in themselves once again, and Dudley Wood, who retired as secretary of the RFU after nine years of unstinting, productive and unfailingly good-humoured service.

A fledgling European club competition beckons this season: Sky television is set to beam Rugby Union from bedtime to breakfast-time; New Zealand tour France, South Africa and Western Samoa come to England. Once again there is scarcely time to draw breath. Imagine how the players must feel.

ROTHMANS FIVE PLAYERS OF THE YEAR

Most of the significant action last season seemed to involve South Africa. England toured there in 1994 before the Springboks set off for New Zealand. Within a couple of months they were in Britain, sweeping much before them in their tour of Wales, Scotland and, briefly, Ireland. France had an historic series win in New Zealand, Scotland rose from the ashes to regain respectability and England won their third Grand Slam in five seasons. And then came the World Cup. The choice of our panel reflects these helter-skelter months of rugby.

The five players are **François Pienaar,** the South African flanker and captain, who has led his country with such openness and distinction, taking them to a World Cup and into a new era; **Philippe Saint-André,** another captain, who helped put France into the record books when he steered them to that tumultuous first-ever series win in New Zealand; **Rob Andrew,** whose right boot won match after match for England, none more dramatically than the World Cup quarter-final against Australia; **Rob Wainwright,** for his straight-backed charges upfield, for his shrewd, influential line-out play and for the pride with which he wore the Scotland shirt, and **Jonah Lomu,** the 20-year-old All Black wing who proved to be the sensation of the World Cup.

NB: No player can be nominated more than once. Career details given are correct up to the end of the World Cup (30 June 1995).

Previous nominations
1989-90: **Will Carling, Patrice Lagisquet, Steve McDowell, David Sole, Paul Ackford**
1990-91: **Dean Richards, Gary Armstrong, Wade Dooley, Serge Blanco, Rory Underwood**
1991-92: **Peter Winterbottom, Jonathan Webb, David Campese, Simon Poidevin, Marc Cecillon**
1992-93: **Gavin Hastings, Laurent Cabannes, Phil Kearns, Jean-Baptiste Lafond, Waisale Serevi**
1993-94: **Philippe Sella, Phil Davies, Ben Clarke, Tim Horan, Nigel Redman**

FRANCOIS PIENAAR

He talked a good game throughout the year, and for once this was an admirable quality. François Pienaar was an enlightened choice as Springbok captain. After so many years of darkness and furtiveness, it was essential that the South Africans addressed their image around the globe. Pienaar was a front man of impeccable credentials, a player of note and honest in all his dealings. One other man thought so too – Nelson Mandela. What greater tribute could there have been to the South

François Pienaar.

African captain's importance to both his team and his country than to be presented with the World Cup trophy by the President, dressed in the No 6 Springbok shirt he had worn to the game?

When South Africa arrived in Cardiff for the start of their 13-match tour of Wales, Scotland and Ireland, they were given a very warm welcome – that is to say, they were nailed to the spit and roasted over accusations that they were a bunch of arrogant, drug-ridden, psychopathic racists. So much for South Africa being the land of the one-eyed bigot. Pienaar took all this in his stride, not denying the past but stating firmly his desire to live in the present. 'Our old assumptions were flawed,' he said. 'We have learned our lesson. From our new humility will come strength.'

He also endured a hostile reception in his own land. Such was the backbiting and sniping that he was at one point almost driven to resignation. On the tour here Pienaar formed a back row of considerable distinction alongside Rudolf Straeuli and Ruben Kruger. The trio made their mark with hard-hitting tackling and intelligent support play.

Pienaar was chosen to lead the Springboks in his very first Test match, against France in Durban in 1993. This honour came on the back of his successes with Transvaal, whom he captained to the Super-10 title in 1993 – their first Currie Cup for 21 years – and to significant domestic honours in the following two seasons. Pienaar is a law graduate and now runs a business with his national coach, Kitch Christie, just outside Johannesburg.

The coach for the England series, Ian McIntosh, called Pienaar 'an emancipated Afrikaner and excellent ambassador'. McIntosh did not survive the year; Pienaar did, and for that, the rest of the rugby world should be grateful.

François Pienaar *Born Port Elizabeth, South Africa, 2 January 1967; flanker; plays for Transvaal; 21 caps for South Africa since first cap against France in 1993.*

PHILIPPE SAINT-ANDRE

It used to be said that the French did not travel well, that in cold lands far from the summer warmth of their homeland and Mama's fine cooking, their heads would drop at the first sighting on the horizon of a spot of adversity. In the last two years they have won series victories in South Africa and New Zealand, a feat which was beyond the scope of, recently, both England and the British Lions. So much for the 'bad tourists' theory.

If there had been any danger of falling back into bad habits on the trip to New Zealand last year, then the captain, Philippe Saint-André, who was appointed only in March 1994, was just the man to yank spirits back up. The Montferrand winger is renowned for his free spirit, his laughter and his essential belief in the enjoyment of the game. He is also the man who launched the try from the end of the earth. In the Auckland Test, when all seemed lost, Saint-André fielded a ball in his own 22. He looked up to see four All Blacks closing in on him. 'I can kick only about as far as a sparrow,' he said, 'so the only thing to do was to run the ball.' And run he did. The ball flashed through eight pairs of hands, the New Zealanders stretched to the four corners of the field, before the move was rounded off by full-back Jean-Luc Sadourny, with his captain hard on his shoulder.

It was a moment to treasure and enough to warm Saint-André's memory on drab winter nights to come. There would be a cluster of other images vying for attention as well. Three years earlier, at Twickenham, Saint-André featured in yet another try of the century. In the Grand Slam decider of that year, when the high stakes might have inhibited natural instincts, he finished off the sweeping, breathtaking 100-metre movement, triggered by the magical Blanco, that took France to glory but not the ultimate honours.

Saint-André is not the most stylish of players – 'I run more like a wild boar than some feline creature' – but effective he certainly is. He was top try-scorer in this season's Championship with four. Once again the boar roared.

Philippe Saint-André *Born Romans-sur-Isère, France, 19 April 1967; wing; plays for Montferrand; 50 caps since first cap against Romania in 1990.*

Philippe Saint-André

ROB ANDREW

He's had his critics and he's had his own moments of doubt, but Rob Andrew has never let any external pressure weigh down his shoulders. There was no more telling and wonderfully uplifting illustration of this than his towering, last-ditch dropped goal against Australia in the World Cup quarter-final. The whole Newlands Stadium in Cape Town, and millions back home watching on television, were quivering with tension as the match looked to be heading into extra time. One last drive, one last line-out delivered faithfully by Martin Bayfield, and the opportunity for one last swing of the boot. Never did a ball sail more truly or sweetly. Even the hardened old souls in the press box foresook their customary cynicism and impartiality and rose to salute the dramatic winner.

Rob Andrew.

Andrew, who was awarded the MBE the week after that game, was to fall slightly from grace the following weekend, when Jonah Lomu left him floundering on his backside as New Zealand strode to victory. This would not have fazed Andrew at all. He knows the capricious hands that direct sporting destinies. Despite his head-prefect looks, the England fly-half is as hard and driven a competitive animal as Brian Moore. He would have been devastated by the manner as well as the size of the defeat by the All Blacks, but he would also have appreciated that, in sport, there is always another day. Andrew's equanimity has long been one of the rocks upon which the current England side has been based.

Andrew brings many qualities to the game – not least composure, reliability and application – all of which came into play last year. He was handed the position of principal goal-kicker towards the end of the 1993-94 season. He'd always dabbled with kicking, both for Wasps and England, but now the job was his he gave it his full attention. He travelled up and down the M4 for kicking tutorials with the Bristol-based coach Dave Alred. The result was a hatful of records: 27 in the First Test against South Africa in the summer of 1994; 10 out of 11 successes against Romania; and then a full house against Canada to equal the then world record of 30 points, held by Didier Camberabero. In the Grand Slam decider against Scotland, he also eased past Jon Webb's record aggregate of points for England.

Rob Andrew *Born Richmond, Yorkshire, England, 18 February 1963; fly-half; plays for Wasps; 70 caps for England since first cap against Romania in 1985.*

ROB WAINWRIGHT

Rob Wainwright's year bears striking resemblance to that of the man with whom he once shared a barracks, Tim Rodber. Both had inauspicious starts in the summer of 1994, Rodber with his dismissal in South Africa, Wainwright because he failed to even make it to the ball park. The 30-year-old army doctor was due to captain the Scottish tour party to Argentina but was forced to withdraw through injury. By the season's end, however, Wainwright was running Rodber close as the northern hemisphere's outstanding blindside.

If the tour to Argentina was a good one to miss (not that Wainwright would have seen it in those terms), then so too was Scotland's pitiful capitulation to South Africa in November. While many in these isles were being laid to waste by the Springboks, Wainwright had an unparalleled record of success against them: played 2, won 2. He was prominent in the Scotland A 17-15 win over South Africa at the Greenyards and then again for the Barbarians in the 23-15 victory in Dublin.

By now even the Scottish selectors had woken up to the error of their

Rob Wainwright.

ways and Wainwright was restored to the side for the first time since he fractured his jaw against England the previous season. The proud, upright stance, the long, straight-backed drive and the jolting tackle all became features of his own play and Scotland's stirring revival during the Championship. Like England, Scotland have made best use of the resources available to them in the back row, choosing Wainwright this season at blindside. In previous years he has won caps at openside, No 8 and even as a replacement lock. 'I don't think I could say I was ideally suited to any of the back-row positions, and you could say much the same about Ben Clarke,' he says.

A former captain of Glenalmond, David Sole's old school, Wainwright won three rugby Blues between 1986 and 1988 as well as a boxing Blue. Scotland's back row last season of Morrison, Peters and Wainwright was an all-Light Blue affair. Wainwright is now involved in general practice for the army in Catterick. 'If I was in the NHS,' he says, 'I wouldn't have had the time to try for an international place.' He left Edinburgh Academicals to join West Hartlepool last season. During the year he lost his pet hawk, but nothing else escaped his grasp.

Rob Wainwright *Born Perth, Scotland, 22 March 1965; back row; plays for West Hartlepool, 17 caps since winning first cap as a replacement against Ireland in 1992.*

JONAH LOMU

Colin Meads reckons that it takes at least two years of playing at international level before anyone can claim to be a 'great All Black'. Pinetree

Jonah Lomu.

had a point, for consistency is one of the hallmarks of greatness. Yet in evaluating a single season's play, the name of Jonah Lomu could simply not be omitted from its roll of honour. Lomu, who became the youngest-ever All Black when he was selected on the wing at the age of 19 to play against France in the summer of 1994, had a sensational World Cup, living up to every last syllable of his potential. Ironically, his inexperience (he played nearly all his schoolboy rugby as a back-row forward) had been shown up by the French, with the result that Lomu had been far from a certainty for New Zealand's World Cup squad. He had performed poorly in the fitness tests in their training camps – indeed, it was only a rigorous fitness programme that secured his place in the party for South Africa. He had made a massive impression in both his appearances at the Hong Kong Sevens but, inclined to laziness, could not keep himself in shape. Coach Laurie Mains confessed: 'We had to get inside Jonah's head.'

This they did to huge effect. Lomu, at 6ft 4ins and 19st, was the heaviest member of the squad, yet he had also recorded 10.8 seconds for the 100 metres. He was sharp, alert and quite devastating with the ball in his hands in all his World Cup matches. His four tries against England in the semi-final gave a vivid demonstration of his pace, power and massive self-belief. He is more than simply a demolition ball in a black shirt, however, for he showed when cutting inside Catt for his last try of that game that he has swerve and balance as well.

Rugby League clubs and the Dallas Cowboys American football club were all queueing up to sign the youngster. Lomu had played League from an early age, growing up with the sport in Mangere, a working-class suburb of South Auckland. His parents, worried about the gang lifestyle of the area, were able to get him enrolled at Wesley College, a Methodist boarding school. Lomu played in many positions for Wesley before going on to represent New Zealand schoolboys in 1992 and 1993.

Lomu is a Christian – his father, Semisi Lomu, is a Tongan Methodist lay preacher – who used to be banned from playing on Sundays. His father eventually relented. England, who played New Zealand on a Sunday, will not have thanked Lomu senior.

Jonah Lomu *Born Auckland, New Zealand, 12 May 1975; wing; plays for Counties; 7 caps since first cap against France in 1994.*

CROWNING GLORY FOR THE RAINBOW NATION

REVIEW OF THE 1995 WORLD CUP THIRD TOURNAMENT IN SOUTH AFRICA

South Africa claimed they could stage a magnificent World Cup, and they were right. Nearly all the pre-tournament fears about a country stretched to breaking-point by inadequate transport and accommodation systems proved to be more rumour than fact. Unfortunately, the threat of violence on the streets of Johannesburg was not the product of nervous imaginations. Eight journalists alone were mugged in the city, and two of them had guns held to their heads. Now, while it's true that there were many thousands of other tourists in the country who had a joyous time, most of these were on strict travel schedules and were wisely kept away from the mean streets. The teams, too, were closely monitored. One of the great joys of the sport is that the après-rugby should be free and easy. In Johannesburg, at any rate, that was not the case.

However, there were so many positives to bring into the overall equation. Worries that the rugby might be fierce but uninspiring proved to be groundless. Of course, there is still a huge gulf between the top and the bottom countries – a divide which makes the decision to increase the number of teams in the competition for 1999 absolutely crazy – but even though Japan were swamped by New Zealand in that afternoon of riotous rugby at Bloemfontein, who could say that their running and handling in defeat to both Ireland and Wales did not bring some pleasure? Western Samoa, Argentina and Italy were magnificent in battling for the runners-up spot behind England, while Canada, and, to a lesser extent, Romania, made sure that both Australia and South Africa knew that qualification for the knock-out stages was no formality.

South Africa got many things right in this tournament. The scriptwriter for the final was certainly one of them. It is doubtful that there can ever have been an occasion or a match so perfectly in tune with the backdrop, the people, the country and the event itself. Of course, there will be many a Kiwi out there who would point out, with great justification, that his team had played by far the best football in the tournament and therefore had a huge claim on the trophy. But if there is any merit in the argument that sport does sometimes transcend its own parochial boundaries, then it was surely demonstrated by this memorable afternoon. It was not so much the action in the game itself which lent it such status. Joel Stransky's dropped goal in the second minute of the second half of extra time was dramatic enough but, in itself, was no more gripping than many other sporting denouements. Rather it was the sense of the rainbow nation coming together in a celebration of their new-found freedom which brought a lump to the throats of even the most seasoned observers. Two men epitomised this spiritual marriage – Nelson Mandela and François Pienaar. No team in the competition was allowed to field two players wearing identical shirts, but for a man who has achieved miraculous things a bit of petty bureaucracy was going to be no obstacle. Thus Mandela and Pienaar together, both sporting No 6 shirts, in the wild frenzy of Ellis Park, was the image of the tournament. It doesn't need this Yearbook to record definitively that Mandela is some man, for his great deeds will be etched in historical stone the world over. But what other statesman could wear a loose-fitting rugby shirt flapping outside his trousers, punch his arms in the air, and *still* look dignified?

For Pienaar (and his management team of Kitch Christie and Morné du Plessis), victory was the crowning moment of a journey to win not just silverware but hearts and minds too. Oh, but this smiling rainbow image is contrived and forced, say the sceptics. Of course it is forced. How else do you punch through the barriers of 40 years' bigotry if you don't apply force? It was a PR act, but a genuine PR act. Pienaar and his team set out to show the world that good things can happen in South Africa, and for that they must be hugely congratulated. Their rugby too was all about collective effort. Sure, they had individual genius to offer in Van der Westhuizen, Chester Williams and André Joubert, but their hallmark was not single moments of magic but rather bonded belief in each other and their destiny. If they were to be beaten, if their last line of defence was to be breached (and, Lord knows, Canada, France and New Zealand gave it a fearful pounding), then it would be because every last man exhausted every last ounce of breath in his lungs. This is not to denigrate their talents; it is merely to explain why the All Blacks were unable to express themselves in the thrilling manner in which they had done throughout the tournament. The answer was simple: the odds were unequal. As Pienaar said just moments after the final whistle sounded, 'There were not 63,000 cheering us on out there. There were 43 million.'

If Pienaar and his squad were the enlightened face of South African rugby, one old fleshy visage continues to cast a shadow across it. Louis Luyt had an opportunity to salute a great moment in his country's history. Instead, at the closing banquet, he confirmed every prejudice the outside world had of the blinkered Afrikaner mentality. His speech boasting that South Africa's victory in the final proved that they would have won in 1987 and 1991 as well was in crass bad taste. Luyt may well have brought millions to South African rugby, but you can't measure respect by the size of a bank balance. Luyt's remarks should not be allowed to take the shine off a glorious five weeks during which (with the exception of the brawl in Port Elizabeth after which three men were sent off and two more were cited) the rugby world came together in a spirit of adventure and brotherhood. Few who were there will forget the opening and closing ceremonies in particular, and none, it is to be

The All Blacks' haka *was no idle threat to England in the second semi-final (above). The World Cup was over for Will Carling's men only minutes into the match. New Zealand were eventually defeated in the final by the collective effort of South Africa, who became world champions at their first attempt (below).*

hoped, will ever forget one man – Max Brito. The tragic fate which befell the young Ivory Coast player, a fall in the last pool match against Tonga leaving him paralysed for life, should never be forgotten. The immediate response was touching – monies were pledged by both the organisers and ad-hoc collections everywhere – but Brito's name must live on, for, in 40 years' time, he and his family will still be suffering. If this Rugby World Cup can ensure that he is remembered, then it truly will have been a success.

FINAL

SOUTH AFRICA 15 NEW ZEALAND 12

If the Boeing 747 with 'Good Luck Bokke' painted across its wingspan which rumbled just 50ft above the stands before the start gave a vivid image of danger and excitement, then the match itself created its sense of tension through less spectacular means. The roll of events themselves conjured up no great sense of theatre, for the action was more about shuddering defence than vivacious attack. But as the clock ticked into extra time there were few in the stadium far from the very edge of their seats.

Joel Stransky's two penalties and a dropped goal saw South Africa to a 9-6 half-time advantage, Andrew Mehrtens knocking over two penalties for the All Blacks. In the second half, as Ian Jones soared to greater and greater heights in the line-out, winning a stream of possession for New Zealand, it seemed inevitable that the All Blacks would eventually click into gear and lay the Springboks to waste in the same destructive manner they had used to deal with England the previous weekend. But Mehrtens' dropped goal in the 54th minute was the only score of the second half and the 'Boks held firm. Mehrtens missed his fourth drop at goal just before the final whistle and, with the match tied at 9-9, extra time arrived.

The New Zealand fly-half made partial amends for his lapses with a penalty goal in the first minute of extra time, only for Stransky to restore the balance in the last minute of the first period. Whose nerve would hold? Who would get the rub of the green? Would it come down to criteria such as who had had the most players sent off in the tournament to determine the winners? How on earth could the players keep going after five weeks of withering commitment? But keep going they did. A scrum wide on the New Zealand 22, the ball reaches Stransky, a swing of the boot and over it goes. New Zealand threw everything at the Springboks in those last desperate eight minutes. Bunce tried to put Ellis away but threw a poor pass; a minute later Lomu failed to gather a pass from Zinzan Brooke. How the wheel of sporting fortune can turn within the space of a few days.

Nelson Mandela, wearing a Springbok shirt, presented the William Webb Ellis Trophy. With him on your side, how could you lose?

Joel Stransky's celebrated dropped goal in extra time of the final, which won the World Cup for South Africa.

24 June, Johannesburg **FINAL**

SOUTH AFRICA 15 (3PG 2DG) **NEW ZEALAND 12** (3PG 1DG) *(aet)*

SOUTH AFRICA: A J Joubert; J T Small, J C Mulder, H P le Roux, C M Williams; J T Stransky, J H van der Westhuizen; J P du Randt, C L C Rossouw, I S Swart, J J Wiese, J J Strydom, J F Pienaar *(capt)*, M G Andrews, R J Kruger
Replacements G L Pagel for Swart (68 mins); R A W Straeuli for Andrews (90 mins); B Venter for Small (97 mins)
Scorer *Penalty Goals:* Stransky (3) *Dropped Goals:* Stransky (2)
NEW ZEALAND: G M Osborne; J W Wilson, F E Bunce, W K Little, J T Lomu; A P Mehrtens, G T M Bachop; C W Dowd, S B T Fitzpatrick *(capt)*, O M Brown, I D Jones, R M Brooke, M R Brewer, Z V Brooke, J A Kronfeld *Replacements* J W Joseph for Brewer (40 mins); M C G Ellis for Wilson (55 mins); R W Loe for Dowd (83 mins); A D Strachan for Bachop (temp)
Scorer *Penalty Goals:* Mehrtens (3) *Dropped Goal:* Mehrtens
Referee E F Morrison (England)

THIRD-PLACE PLAY-OFF 22 June, Pretoria

FRANCE 19 (3PG 2T) **ENGLAND 9** (3PG)

FRANCE: J-L Sadourny; E Ntamack, P Sella, T Lacroix, P Saint-André *(capt)*; F Mesnel, F Galthié; L Benezech, J-M Gonzalez, C Califano, O Merle, O Roumat, A Benazzi, A Cigagna, L Cabannes *Replacement* O Brouzet for Merle (temp)
Scorers *Tries:* Roumat, Ntamack *Penalty Goals:* Lacroix (3)
ENGLAND: M J Catt; I Hunter, W D C Carling *(capt)*, J C Guscott, R Underwood; C R Andrew, C D Morris; J Leonard, B C Moore, V E Ubogu, M O Johnson, M C Bayfield, T A K Rodber, S O Ojomoh, B B Clarke
Scorer *Penalty Goals:* Andrew (3)
Referee D J Bishop (New Zealand)

SEMI-FINALS

SOUTH AFRICA 19 FRANCE 15

Durban is renowned for its balmy winter weather. On the weekend of the World Cup semi-finals, however, it went completely barmy. The heavens opened on Friday evening and continued to dump their miserable load right through to Saturday morning. An hour before the scheduled kick-off at King's Park, as lightning flashed and thunder rumbled round the bay, one end of the pitch was a lake. It seemed that it would be impossible to start.

The organisers, in consultation with Welsh referee Derek Bevan, decided to delay the kick-off for an hour. They then pushed that further back by another 30 minutes. If there had been rain in that time the game would have been postponed. As it was, it began, only for the rains to come sweeping in nine minutes later. Somehow the match survived, a tribute to the willingness of the players to adapt and the nerve of Bevan in not panicking when the storm started again. Once the game had started it was up to him whether or not it should continue. This was a huge burden of responsibility, for if there had been no tries scored in the first half, and the match had had to be abandoned, then France would have gone through, the decisive criterion in those circumstances being the number of sendings-off in the tournament. If it had been halted in the second half, the score as it was would have stood.

The match itself was bravely fought. For scoring the only try, Kruger screwing through a forest of bodies after good forward build-up in the 26th minute, and for the resilience of the defence which, memorably, just held Benazzi near the end, South Africa deserved their victory. Stransky kicked a conversion and four penalties for the Springboks, Lacroix replying with five penalty goals for France.

17 June, Durban **Semi-Final**
SOUTH AFRICA 19 (1G 4PG) **FRANCE 15** (5PG)

SOUTH AFRICA: A J Joubert; J T Small, J C Mulder, H P le Roux, C M Williams; J T Stransky, J H van der Westhuizen; J P du Randt, C L C Rossouw, I S Swart, J J Wiese, J J Strydom, J F Pienaar (*capt*), M G Andrews, R J Kruger *Replacement* J P Roux for Van der Westhuizen (52 mins)
Scorers *Try:* Kruger *Conversion:* Stransky *Penalty Goals:* Stransky (4)
FRANCE: J-L Sadourny; E Ntamack, P Sella, T Lacroix, P Saint-André (*capt*); C Deylaud, F Galthié; L Armary, J-M Gonzalez, C Califano, O Merle, O Roumat, A Benazzi, M Cecillon, L Cabannes
Scorer *Penalty Goals:* Lacroix (5)
Referee W D Bevan (Wales)

NEW ZEALAND 45 ENGLAND 29

It took just 60 seconds for nightmare to become reality. With his first touch of the ball, Jonah Lomu confirmed England's every worst fear. He gathered a bouncing ball and then went through, round and over Tony Underwood, Will Carling and Mike Catt. The game was as good as finished before it had scarcely started, for there was panic in English eyes from that moment on. There were errors everywhere, all induced by the terror of possible humiliation. That England managed to finish within 16 points of the All Blacks was a minor miracle. The relative proximity of the scores gave a distorted perspective of events, however, for this, in truth, should have been a 40-point differential. It was not just Lomu and his four tries. All over the pitch, from Osborne at the back to Dowd at prop, New Zealand were faster in thought and in deed. Kronfeld and Bachop scored their other tries, with Brooke adding a dropped goal and Mehrtens three conversions, a penalty goal and a dropped goal to make him, in his fifth game, the fastest player in history to 100 points. Carling, with two, and Rory Underwood, with two, scored England's tries. Andrew added three conversions and a penalty. In victory New Zealand completed their fastest-ever Grand Slam over the home countries (three weeks and one day), while their 45 points was the highest score ever conceded by England.

18 June, Cape Town **Semi-Final**
NEW ZEALAND 45 (3G 1PG 2DG 3T) **ENGLAND 29** (3G 1PG 1T)

NEW ZEALAND: G M Osborne; J W Wilson, F E Bunce, W K Little, J T Lomu; A P Mehrtens, G T M Bachop; C W Dowd, S B T Fitzpatrick (*capt*), O M Brown, I D Jones, R M Brooke, M R Brewer, Z V Brooke, J A Kronfeld *Replacement* B P Larsen

for Z Brooke (64 mins)
Scorers *Tries:* Lomu (4), Kronfeld, Bachop *Conversions:* Mehrtens (3)
Penalty Goal: Mehrtens *Dropped Goals:* Z Brooke, Mehrtens
ENGLAND: M J Catt; T Underwood, W D C Carling (*capt*), J C Guscott, R Underwood; C R Andrew, C D Morris; J Leonard, B C Moore, V E Ubogu, M O Johnson, M C Bayfield, T A K Rodber, D Richards, B B Clarke
Scorers *Tries:* R Underwood (2), Carling (2) *Conversions:* Andrew (3)
Penalty Goal: Andrew
Referee S R Hilditch (Ireland)

KNOCK-OUT STAGES

QUARTER-FINALS

FRANCE 36 IRELAND 12

Ireland were not able to blow up their traditional storm of mayhem, as they had done to decent effect against the All Blacks. Instead they looked muted and rather forlorn as France trotted away unmolested to a comfortable victory. The boot of Thierry Lacroix kept French morale high, and his eight penalty goals were just reward for the greater French pressure. If he hadn't struck such form, perhaps Gallic heads might have dropped, for their two tries, by Saint-André and Ntamack, were not scored until the death. Benazzi and Cabannes rumbled throughout the game to great effect. Ireland did modestly well in the line-out through Francis, but were poorly supported at half-back by the service and distribution of Hogan and Elwood. Elwood did, however, score all Ireland's points with four penalties.

10 June, Durban **Quarter-Final**
FRANCE 36 (1G 8PG 1T) **IRELAND 12** (4PG)

FRANCE: J-L Sadourny; E Ntamack, P Sella, T Lacroix, P Saint-André (*capt*); C Deylaud, A Hueber; L Armary, J-M Gonzalez, C Califano, O Merle, O Roumat, A Benazzi, M Cecillon, L Cabannes
Scorers *Tries:* Saint-André, Ntamack *Conversion:* Lacroix *Penalty Goals:* Lacroix (8)
IRELAND: C M P O'Shea; D O'Mahony, B J Mullin, J C Bell, S P Geoghegan; E P Elwood, N A Hogan; N J Popplewell, T J Kingston (*capt*), G F Halpin, G M Fulcher, N P J Francis, D Corkery, P S Johns, W D McBride
Replacement E O Halvey for Fulcher (61 mins)
Scorer *Penalty Goals:* Elwood (4)
Referee E F Morrison (England)

SOUTH AFRICA 42 WESTERN SAMOA 14

This triumphant victory was marred by several factors. The Samoans, in their desperation to unsettle the 'Boks on their home turf, were too robust and, at times, downright dangerous. Full-back Mike Umaga was lucky to stay on the field after flattening Joubert and Van der Westhuizen with high and late tackles. Umaga was later cited by RWC and banned for 60 days. Van der Westhuizen did make a meal of one hard, but marginally fair, tackle by Umaga – indeed, the behaviour of the South African scrum-half throughout the match left a lot to be desired. It was alleged that he made racist comments, a charge which was emphatically denied. The third factor to impair the match was the refereeing of Jim Fleming. He missed a forward pass for one of Chester Williams' four tries and adjudged a touchdown for another when TV replays suggested that Williams had not grounded the ball. The 'Boks had too much power and control up front and a deadly finisher behind in Williams, recalled to the squad after the suspension of Pieter Hendriks. Williams' four tries, two in each half, were a South African record. Rossouw and Andrews scored the other Springbok tries, Johnson adding 12 points with the boot. Nu'uali'itia and Tatupu scored the Samoan tries in a late rally.

10 June, Johannesburg **Quarter-Final**
SOUTH AFRICA 42 (3G 2PG 3T) **WESTERN SAMOA 14** (2G)

SOUTH AFRICA: A J Joubert; G K Johnson, C P Scholtz, J C Mulder, C M Williams; H P le Roux, J H van der Westhuizen; J P du Randt, C L C Rossouw, I S Swart, J J Wiese, M G Andrews, J F Pienaar (*capt*), R A W Straeuli, R J Kruger
Replacements B Venter for Joubert (18 mins); A Richter for Kruger (48 mins); K Otto for Andrews (71 mins); A E Drotské for Wiese (78 mins)
Scorers *Tries:* Williams (4), Rossouw, Andrews *Conversions:* Johnson (3)
Penalty Goals: Johnson (2)
WESTERN SAMOA: M T Umaga; B Lima, T Vaega, T Fa'amasino, G Harder; F Sini, T Nu'uali'itia; M A N Mika, T Leiasamaivao, G Latu, L Falaniko, S Lemamea, S J Tatupu, P R Lam (*capt*), P J Paramore *Replacements* F Tuilagi for Harder (44 mins); P Fatialofa for Latu (65 mins); B P Reidy for Mika (71 mins); S L Vaifale for Tatupu (75 mins)
Scorers *Tries:* Nu'uali'itia, Tatupu *Conversions:* Fa'amasino (2)
Referee J M Fleming (Scotland)

ENGLAND 25 AUSTRALIA 22

Few who witnessed this dramatic match will ever forget the sense of sheer shock at the final whistle. Everyone in the ground, including the players, was busy racking his brains to try to remember exactly what the regulations were concerning extra time. The match moved into injury time with the scores locked at 22-22. From nowhere England drove to just inside Australia's half. Bayfield won a line-out, the ball was lashed to Andrew, the right boot swung and the ball sailed majestically through the posts from 45 metres. It was a stunning finale. England might well have closed down the game earlier. Their pack were magnificent in the first half, when they ought to have turned round better placed than 13-6. In the 20th minute Tony Underwood raced 50 metres and just outstripped Damian Smith after England had swooped on to an Australian fumble. Ironically, Andrew missed an easy drop-goal attempt in that half, but he did convert the try and two penalties. Lynagh struck two penalty goals for Australia. A wonderful up-and-under, gathered by Smith, put Australia right back in the match within 40 seconds of the restart. Lynagh and Andrew then traded kicks before that marvellous denouement.

England scrum-half Dewi Morris succumbs to Gregan and Wilson in the gripping quarter-final against Australia, in which England avenged their defeat in the 1991 World Cup final (above). Scotland's last match, their quarter-final against New Zealand, marked the retirement of their inspirational captain, Gavin Hastings, pictured leaving the field with Sean Fitzpatrick (below). Though the Scots lost, they scored 30 points against the All Blacks.

11 June, Cape Town **Quarter-Final**
ENGLAND 25 (1G 5PG 1DG) **AUSTRALIA** 22 (1G 5PG)

ENGLAND: M J Catt; T Underwood, W D C Carling (*capt*), J C Guscott, R Underwood; C R Andrew, C D Morris; J Leonard, B C Moore, V E Ubogu, M O Johnson, M C Bayfield, T A K Rodber, D Richards, B B Clarke
Replacement S O Ojomoh for Richards (temp – twice)
Scorers *Try:* T Underwood *Conversion:* Andrew *Penalty Goals:* Andrew (5)
Dropped Goal: Andrew
AUSTRALIA: M Burke; D I Campese, J S Little, T J Horan, D P Smith; M P Lynagh (*capt*), G M Gregan; D J Crowley, P N Kearns, E J A McKenzie, R J McCall, J A Eales, V Ofahengaue, B T Gavin, D J Wilson
Scorers *Try:* Smith *Conversion:* Lynagh *Penalty Goals:* Lynagh (5)
Referee D J Bishop (New Zealand)

NEW ZEALAND 48 SCOTLAND 30

The Scots were once again left to rue lost opportunities. They contributed to their own downfall in this match by making too many errors, several of which led directly to New Zealand scores, and conceded two soft tries at the start of the second half. Without these mistakes would they actually have recorded their first-ever victory over the All Blacks? Perhaps not, for the power of the New Zealand running in the open field was overwhelming. Jonah Lomu was again a riotous handful, scoring one try and wreaking havoc in the Scottish ranks on other occasions. The All Blacks seemed to let their concentration slip as they led 45-16. Their defence is not what it was, and Doddie Weir was able to drive through for two tries. Sean Fitzpatrick scored in his 100th game for his country, Mehrtens sprinted 60 metres for his try, while Little impressed for his brace. Bunce scored the other. Gavin Hastings' 15 points took him to 104 in the tournament. Brother Scott scored Scotland's other try.

11 June, Pretoria **Quarter-Final**
NEW ZEALAND 48 (6G 2PG) **SCOTLAND 30** (3G 3PG)

NEW ZEALAND: J W Wilson; M C G Ellis, F E Bunce, W K Little, J T Lomu; A P Mehrtens, G T M Bachop; R W Loe, S B T Fitzpatrick (*capt*), O M Brown, I D Jones, R M Brooke, J W Joseph, Z V Brooke, J A Kronfeld
Scorers *Tries:* Little (2), Lomu, Mehrtens, Bunce, Fitzpatrick
Conversions: Mehrtens (6) *Penalty Goals:* Mehrtens (2)
SCOTLAND: A G Hastings (*capt*); C A Joiner, S Hastings, A G Shiel, K M Logan; C M Chalmers, B W Redpath; D I W Hilton, K S Milne, P H Wright, D F Cronin, G W Weir, R I Wainwright, E W Peters, I R Morrison *Replacements* I C Jardine for Chalmers (40 mins); S J Campbell for Cronin (63 mins)
Scorers *Tries:* Weir (2), S Hastings *Conversions:* G Hastings (3)
Penalty Goals: G Hastings (3)
Referee W D Bevan (Wales)

Pool A

The so-called group of death had lost some of its venom by the time the competition kicked off. Both Romania and Canada had already fallen by the wayside, suffering heavy defeats to England, Scotland and New

Zealand, among others, in their build-up. All rested, then, on the first match between Australia and South Africa. Not only did it live up to expectations; it exceeded them. For passion, a sense of occasion and compelling commitment, the tournament could not have got off to a better start. On the day the Springboks had greater heart and a more definite sense of purpose. The 27-18 defeat consigned Australia to the tougher route in the knock-out stages.

For all their woes, in the event Canada and Romania performed superbly. Against Australia, after a disastrous opening ten minutes in which they conceded two tries, Canada pressed the Wallabies for much of the game. Their physical exuberance got the better of them against the Springboks in Port Elizabeth. The brawl at the end of the match saw Canadians Gareth Rees and Rod Snow sent off along with South African hooker James Dalton. Pieter Hendriks and Scott Stewart of Canada were later cited and banned by Rugby World Cup.

POOL A	*P*	*W*	*D*	*L*	*F*	*A*	*Pts*
South Africa	3	3	0	0	68	26	9
Australia	3	2	0	1	87	41	7
Canada	3	1	0	2	45	50	5
Romania	3	0	0	3	14	97	3

25 May, Cape Town
SOUTH AFRICA 27 (1G 4PG 1DG 1T) **AUSTRALIA 18** (1G 2PG 1T)

SOUTH AFRICA: A J Joubert; J T Small, J C Mulder, H P le Roux, P Hendriks; J T Stransky, J H van der Westhuizen; J P du Randt, J Dalton, I S Swart, M G Andrews, J J Strydom, J F Pienaar (*capt*), R A W Straeuli, R J Kruger *Replacement* G L Pagel for Swart (65 mins)
Scorers *Tries:* Hendriks, Stransky *Conversion:* Stransky *Penalty Goals:* Stransky (4) *Dropped Goal:* Stransky
AUSTRALIA: M J Pini; D I Campese, D J Herbert, J S Little, D P Smith; M P Lynagh (*capt*), G M Gregan; D J Crowley, P N Kearns, E J A McKenzie, R J McCall, J A Eales, V Ofahengaue, B T Gavin, D J Wilson
Scorers *Tries:* Lynagh, Kearns *Conversion:* Lynagh *Penalty Goals:* Lynagh (2)
Referee W D Bevan (Wales)

26 May, Port Elizabeth
CANADA 34 (2G 4PG 1DG 1T) **ROMANIA 3** (1PG)

CANADA: D S Stewart; W Stanley, C Stewart, S D Gray, D C Lougheed; G L Rees (*capt*), J D Graf; E A Evans, M E Cardinal, R Snow, G D Ennis, M James, A J Charron, C McKenzie, I Gordon
Scorers *Tries:* Snow, Charron, McKenzie *Conversions:* Rees (2) *Penalty Goals:* Rees (4) *Dropped Goal:* Rees
ROMANIA: G Solomie; L Colceriu, N Racean, R Gontineac, I Rotaru; N Nichitean, D Neaga; G Leonte, I Negreci, G Vlad, S Ciorascu (*capt*), C Cojocariu, T Oroian, O Slusariuc, A Gealapu *Replacements* V Flutur for Neaga (53 mins); I Ivanciuc for Nichitean (66 mins)
Scorer *Penalty Goal:* Nichitean
Referee C J Hawke (New Zealand)

Drama from Pool A. A try for Joel Stransky in the exciting opening match of the tournament, South Africa v Australia (above). The end of the World Cup for Gareth Rees of Canada and Springbok James Dalton, sent off, along with Canadian Rod Snow, for their part in the flare-up in the last game of the group (below).

30 May, Cape Town
SOUTH AFRICA 21 (1G 3PG 1T) **ROMANIA 8** (1PG 1T)

SOUTH AFRICA: G K Johnson; J T Small, C P Scholtz, B Venter, P Hendriks; H P le Roux, J P Roux; G L Pagel, C L C Rossouw, M H Hurter, J J Wiese, K Otto, R J Kruger, A Richter (*capt*), R Brink *Replacement* J T Stransky for Venter (temp)
Scorers *Tries:* Richter (2) *Conversion:* Johnson *Penalty Goals:* Johnson (3)
ROMANIA: V Brici; L Colceriu, N Racean, R Gontineac, G Solomie; I Ivanciuc, V Flutur; G Leonte, I Negreci, G Vlad, S Ciorascu, C Cojocariu, A Guranescu, T Brinza (*capt*), A Gealapu *Replacement* V Tufa for Negreci (62 mins)
Scorers *Try:* Guranescu *Penalty Goal:* Ivanciuc
Referee K W McCartney (Scotland)

31 May, Port Elizabeth
AUSTRALIA 27 (3G 2PG) **CANADA 11** (2PG 1T)

AUSTRALIA: M Burke; D I Campese, J S Little, T J Horan, J Roff; M P Lynagh (*capt*), P J Slattery; A J Daly, P N Kearns, M N Hartill, W W Waugh, J A Eales, V Ofahengaue, B T Gavin, I Tabua *Replacements* E J A McKenzie for Hartill (56 mins); M Foley for Kearns (70 mins); G M Gregan for Slattery (80 mins)
Scorers *Tries:* Tabua, Roff, Lynagh *Conversions:* Lynagh (3)
Penalty Goals: Lynagh (2)
CANADA: D S Stewart; W Stanley, C Stewart, S D Gray, D C Lougheed; G L Rees (*capt*), J D Graf; E A Evans, K F Svoboda, R Snow, M James, G Rowlands, J Hutchinson, A J Charron, G I MacKinnon *Replacement* G D Ennis for Rowlands (70 mins)
Scorers *Try:* Charron *Penalty Goals:* Rees (2)
Referee P Robin (France)

3 June, Stellenbosch
AUSTRALIA 42 (6G) **ROMANIA 3** (1DG)

AUSTRALIA: M Burke; D P Smith, D J Herbert, T J Horan, J Roff; S Bowen, G M Gregan; A J Daly, M Foley, E J A McKenzie, R J McCall (*capt*), J A Eales, I Tabua, B T Gavin, D J Wilson *Replacements* D Manu for Wilson (temp); M J Pini for Herbert (temp); P J Slattery for Gregan (71 mins)
Scorers *Tries:* Roff (2), Foley, Burke, Smith, Wilson *Conversions:* Burke (2), Eales (4)
ROMANIA: V Brici; L Colceriu, N Racean, R Gontineac, G Solomie; I Ivanciuc, V Flutur; G Leonte, I Negreci, G Vlad, S Ciorascu, C Cojocariu, A Guranescu, T Brinza (*capt*), A Gealapu *Replacements* A Lungu for Gontineac (56 mins); V Tufa for Negreci (73 mins)
Scorer *Dropped Goal:* Ivanciuc
Referee N Saito (Japan)

3 June, Port Elizabeth
SOUTH AFRICA 20 (2G 2PG) **CANADA 0**

SOUTH AFRICA: A J Joubert; G K Johnson, C P Scholtz, B Venter, P Hendriks; J T Stransky, J P Roux; G L Pagel, J Dalton, M H Hurter, J J Wiese, J J Strydom, J F Pienaar (*capt*), A Richter, R Brink *Replacements* J H van der Westhuizen for Johnson (17 mins); K Otto for Strydom (73 mins); H P le Roux for Stransky (59 mins)
Scorers *Tries:* Richter (2) *Conversions:* Stransky (2) *Penalty Goals:* Stransky (2)
CANADA: D S Stewart; W Stanley, C Stewart, S D Gray, D C Lougheed; G L Rees (*capt*), J D Graf; E A Evans, M E Cardinal, R Snow, A J Charron, G D Ennis, I Gordon, C McKenzie, G I MacKinnon *Replacements* C Michaluk for McKenzie (80 mins); J Hutchinson for Ennis (65 mins)
Referee D T M McHugh (Ireland)

Pool B

The tag of favourites seemed to weigh heavily on England. Having struggled to find form or fluency against either Argentina or Italy, they finally pulled it together in the last match, against Western Samoa. This was perhaps the most well balanced of all the groups. All three of the other teams – Western Samoa, Italy and Argentina – delighted crowds on the coast with their spirit, drive and collective strength. The nail-biter in East London between Western Samoa and Argentina will live in the memory. The Argentinians, through Corral, Mendez, Noriega and Llanes, had perhaps the best pack in the World Cup. They might have won all three matches; instead they lost the lot. Such are the vagaries of sport.

POOL B	*P*	*W*	*D*	*L*	*F*	*A*	*Pts*
England	3	3	0	0	95	60	9
Western Samoa	3	2	0	1	96	88	7
Italy	3	1	0	2	69	94	5
Argentina	3	0	0	3	69	87	3

27 May, East London
WESTERN SAMOA 42 (3G 2PG 3T) **ITALY 18** (1G 1PG 1DG 1T)

WESTERN SAMOA: M T Umaga; B Lima, T Vaega, T Fa'amasino, G Harder; D J Kellett, T Nu'uli'itia; M A N Mika, T Leiasamaivao, P Fatialofa (*capt*), L Falaniko, D R Williams, S L Vaifale, S J Tatupu, P J Paramore *Replacement* P L Leavasa for Falaniko (57 mins)
Scorers *Tries:* Lima (2), Harder (2), Tatupu, Kellett *Conversions:* Kellett (3) *Penalty Goals:* Kellett (2)
ITALY: P Vaccari; M Ravazzolo, I Francescato, M Bonomi, Marcello Cuttitta; D Dominguez, A Troncon; Massimo Cuttitta (*capt*), C Orlandi, F Properzi Curti, P Pedroni, R Favaro, O Arancio, C Checchinato, J M Gardner
Scorers *Tries:* Marcello Cuttitta, Vaccari *Conversion:* Dominguez *Penalty Goal:* Dominguez *Dropped Goal:* Dominguez
Referee J Dumé (France)

27 May, Durban
ENGLAND 24 (6PG 2DG) **ARGENTINA 18** (1G 2PG 1T)

ENGLAND: M J Catt; T Underwood, W D C Carling (*capt*), J C Guscott, R Underwood; C R Andrew, C D Morris; J Leonard, B C Moore, V E Ubogu, M O Johnson M C Bayfield, T A K Rodber, S O Ojomoh, B B Clarke *Replacements* N A Back for Ojomoh (temp – twice); P R de Glanville for Carling (79 mins)
Scorer *Penalty Goals:* Andrew (6) *Dropped Goals:* Andrew (2)
ARGENTINA: E Jurado; M J Teran, D Cuesta Silva, S Salvat (*capt*), D Albanese; L Arbizu, R H Crexell; M E Corral, F E Mendez, E P Noriega, G A Llanes, P L Sporleder, R Martin, J M Santamarina, C Viel *Replacement* S Irazoqui for Viel (70 mins)
Scorers *Tries:* Noriega, Arbizu *Conversion:* Arbizu *Penalty Goals:* Arbizu (2)
Referee J M Fleming (Scotland)

30 May, East London
WESTERN SAMOA 32 (1G 5PG 2T) **ARGENTINA 26** (2G 4PG)

WESTERN SAMOA: M T Umaga; B Lima, T Vaega, T Fa'amasino, G Harder; D J Kellett, T Nu'uali'itia; M A N Mika, T Leiasamaivao, G Latu, P L Leavasa,

L Falaniko, S J Tatupu, P R Lam (*capt*), P J Paramore *Replacements* P Fatialofa for Latu (temp & 45 mins); G E Leaupepe for Harder (51 mins); F Sini for Kellett (80 mins)
Scorers *Tries:* Harder, Leaupepe, Lam *Conversion:* Kellett *Penalty Goals:* Kellett (5)
ARGENTINA: E Jurado; D Cuesta Silva, L Arbizu, S Salvat (*capt*), M J Teran; J L Cilley, R H Crexell; M E Corral, F E Mendez, E P Noriega, G A Llanes, P L Sporleder, R Martin, J M Santamarina, C Viel
Scorers *Tries:* pen try, Crexell *Conversions:* Cilley (2) *Penalty Goals:* Cilley (4)
Referee D J Bishop (New Zealand)

31 May, Durban
ENGLAND 27 (1G 5PG 1T) **ITALY 20** (2G 2PG)

ENGLAND: M J Catt; T Underwood, P R de Glanville, J C Guscott, R Underwood; C R Andrew (*capt*), K P P Bracken; G C Rowntree, B C Moore, J Leonard, M O Johnson, M C Bayfield, T A K Rodber, B B Clarke, N A Back
Scorers *Tries:* R Underwood, T Underwood *Conversion:* Andrew
Penalty Goals: Andrew (5)
ITALY: L Troiani; P Vaccari, S Bordon, I Francescato, M Gerosa; D Dominguez, A Troncon; Massimo Cuttitta (*capt*), C Orlandi, F Properzi Curti, P Pedroni, M Giacheri, O Arancio, J M Gardner, A Sgorlon
Scorers *Tries:* Vaccari, Massimo Cuttitta *Conversions:* Dominguez (2)
Penalty Goals: Dominguez (2)
Referee S R Hilditch (Ireland)

4 June, East London
ITALY 31 (2G 4PG 1T) **ARGENTINA 25** (1G 1PG 3T)

ITALY: L Troiani; P Vaccari, I Francescato, S Bordon, M Gerosa; D Dominguez, A Troncon; Massimo Cuttitta (*capt*), C Orlandi, F Properzi Curti, P Pedroni, M Giacheri, O Arancio, J M Gardner, A Sgorlon
Scorers *Tries:* Vaccari, Gerosa, Dominguez *Conversions:* Dominguez (2)
Penalty Goals: Dominguez (4)
ARGENTINA: E Jurado; D Cuesta Silva, L Arbizu, S Salvat (*capt*), M J Teran; J L Cilley, R H Crexell; M E Corral, F E Mendez, E P Noriega, G A Llanes, P L Sporleder, R Martin, J M Santamarina, C Viel
Scorers *Tries:* Martin, Corral, Cilley, pen try *Conversion:* Cilley *Penalty Goal:* Cilley
Referee C Thomas (Wales)

4 June, Durban
ENGLAND 44 (3G 5PG 1DG 1T) **WESTERN SAMOA 22** (2G 1PG 1T)

ENGLAND: J E B Callard; I Hunter, W D C Carling (*capt*), P R de Glanville, R Underwood; M J Catt, C D Morris; G C Rowntree, R G R Dawe, V E Ubogu, M O Johnson, R West, S O Ojomoh, D Richards, N A Back *Replacements* J A Mallett for Rowntree (25 mins); T A K Rodber for Back (33 mins); D P Hopley for Carling (70 mins); B C Moore for Richards (73 mins); K P P Bracken for Rodber (temp)
Scorers *Tries:* Back, R Underwood (2), pen try *Conversions:* Callard (3)
Penalty Goals: Callard (5) *Dropped Goal:* Catt
WESTERN SAMOA: M T Umaga; B Lima, T Vaega, T Fa'amasino, G E Leaupepe, E Puleitu, T Nu'uali'itia; M A N Mika, T Leiasamaivo, G Latu, D R Williams, L Falaniko, P L Leavasa, P R Lam (*capt*), M Iupeli *Replacements* S J Tatupu for Leavasa (29 mins); F Sini for Puleitu (40 mins); S Lemamea for Tatupu (67 mins); P Fatialofa for Latu (74 mins)
Scorers *Tries:* Sini (2), Umaga *Conversions:* Fa'amasino (2) *Penalty Goal:* Fa'amasino
Referee P Robin (France)

Pool C

We all knew the All Blacks had been quiet – too quiet – in their build-up. When they unleashed their secret weapon, Jonah Lomu, on the World Cup, he made some impact. Lomu was essentially the difference between the sides in the All Blacks' 43-19 victory over Ireland. The giant winger scored two tries and made another. Ireland played with sustained passion but struggled to rediscover their appetite against Japan. Japan, even though they suffered the humiliation of a world-record 145-17 defeat, once again showed ingenuity and real class in their handling. If only for brief patches, they troubled all three sides. The qualification decider between Wales and Ireland was low in quality and high on tension. Ireland got off to an electric start, scoring two tries, and then defended well. Wales disappointed with their lack of ambition. A more courageous attitude might have brought victory.

POOL C	*P*	*W*	*D*	*L*	*F*	*A*	*Pts*
New Zealand	3	3	0	0	222	45	9
Ireland	3	2	0	1	93	94	7
Wales	3	1	0	2	89	68	5
Japan	3	0	0	3	55	252	3

27 May, Bloemfontein
WALES 57 (5G 4PG 2T) **JAPAN 10** (2T)

WALES: A Clement; I C Evans, M R Hall *(capt)*, N R Jenkins, G Thomas; A Davies, A P Moore; M Griffiths, G R Jenkins, J D Davies, D Jones, G O Llewellyn, S Davies, E W Lewis, H T Taylor *Replacements* D W Evans for A Davies (57 mins); W S Roy for Jones (72 mins)
Scorers *Tries:* I Evans (2), Thomas (3), Taylor, Moore *Conversions:* N Jenkins (5) *Penalty Goals:* N Jenkins (4)
JAPAN: T Matsuda; L Oto, A Yoshida, Y Motoki, T Masuho; S Hirao, M Horikoshi; O Ota, M Kunda *(capt)*, K Takahashi, Y Sakuraba, B Ferguson, H Kajihara, Sione Latu, Sinali Latu
Scorer *Tries:* Oto (2)
Referee E J Sklar (Argentina)

27 May, Johannesburg
NEW ZEALAND 43 (3G 4PG 2T) **IRELAND 19** (2G 1T)

NEW ZEALAND: G M Osborne; J W Wilson, F E Bunce, W K Little, J T Lomu; A P Mehrtens, G T M Bachop; C W Dowd, S B T Fitzpatrick *(capt)*, O M Brown, I D Jones, B P Larsen, J W Joseph, M R Brewer, J A Kronfeld *Replacements* M C G Ellis for Wilson (32 mins); K J Schuler for Brewer (78 mins); N J Hewitt for Fitzpatrick (temp)
Scorers *Tries:* Lomu (2), Bunce, Kronfeld, Osborne *Conversions:* Mehrtens (3) *Penalty Goals:* Mehrtens (4)
IRELAND: J E Staples; R M Wallace, B J Mullin, J C Bell, S P Geoghegan; E P Elwood, M T Bradley; N J Popplewell, T J Kingston *(capt)*, G F Halpin, G M Fulcher, N P J Francis, D Corkery, P S Johns, W D McBride *Replacement* M J Field for Bell (temp) and for Staples (36 mins)
Scorers *Tries:* Halpin, McBride, Corkery *Conversions:* Elwood (2)
Referee W J Erickson (Australia)

31 May, Bloemfontein
IRELAND 50 (6G 1PG 1T) **JAPAN 28** (4G)

IRELAND: C M P O'Shea; R M Wallace, B J Mullin, M J Field, S P Geoghegan; P A Burke, N A Hogan; N J Popplewell (*capt*), K G M Wood, P S Wallace, D A Tweed, N P J Francis, D Corkery, P S Johns, E O Halvey *Replacements* T J Kingston for Wood (9 mins); A G Foley for Halvey (temp – twice) and for Tweed (73 mins)
Scorers *Tries:* pen tries (2), Corkery, Francis, Geoghegan, Halvey, Hogan *Conversions:* Burke (6) *Penalty Goal:* Burke
JAPAN: T Matsuda; L Oto, A Yoshida, Y Motoki, Y Yoshida; S Hirao, M Horikoshi; O Ota, M Kunda (*capt*), M Takura, Y Sakuraba, B Ferguson, H Kajihara, Sione Latu, Sinali Latu *Replacement* K Izawa (temp) and for Sione Latu (20 mins)
Scorers *Tries:* Sinali Latu, Izawa, Hirao, Takura *Conversions:* Y Yoshida (4)
Referee S Neethling (South Africa)

31 May, Johannesburg

NEW ZEALAND 34 (2G 4PG 1DG 1T) **WALES 9** (2PG 1DG)
NEW ZEALAND: G M Osborne; J T Lomu, F E Bunce, W K Little, M C G Ellis; A P Mehrtens, G T M Bachop; C W Dowd, S B T Fitzpatrick (*capt*), O M Brown, I D Jones, B P Larsen, J W Joseph, M R Brewer, J A Kronfeld *Replacement* E J Rush for Lomu (71 mins)
Scorers *Tries:* Little, Ellis, Kronfeld *Conversions:* Mehrtens (2) *Penalty Goals:* Mehrtens (4) *Dropped Goal:* Mehrtens
WALES: A Clement; I C Evans, M R Hall (*capt*), G Thomas, W T Proctor; N R Jenkins, R N Jones; R L Evans, J Humphreys, J D Davies, D Jones, G Prosser, G O Llewellyn, H T Taylor, M Bennett
Scorers *Penalty Goals:* Jenkins (2) *Dropped Goal:* Jenkins
Referee E F Morrison (England)

4 June, Bloemfontein
NEW ZEALAND 145 (20G 1T) **JAPAN 17** (2G 1PG)

NEW ZEALAND: G M Osborne; J W Wilson, M C G Ellis, A I Ieremia, E J Rush; S D Culhane, A D Strachan; C W Dowd, N J Hewitt, R W Loe, R M Brooke, B P Larsen, K J Schuler, Z V Brooke, P W Henderson (*capt*) *Replacement* J W Joseph for Larsen (16 mins)
Scorers *Tries:* Ellis (6), Rush (3), Wilson (3), Osborne (2), R Brooke (2), Loe, Ieremia, Culhane, Dowd, Henderson *Conversions:* Culhane (20)
JAPAN: T Matsuda; L Oto, A Yoshida, Y Motoki, Y Yoshida; K Hirose, W Murata; O Ota, M Kunda (*capt*), K Takahashi, Y Sakuraba, B Ferguson, H Kajihara, Sinali Latu, K Izawa *Replacement* T Akatsuka for Latu (56 mins)
Scorers *Tries:* Kajihara (2) *Conversions:* Hirose (2) *Penalty Goal:* Hirose
Referee G Gadjovich (Canada)

4 June, Johannesburg
IRELAND 24 (3G 1PG) **WALES 23** (2G 2PG 1DG)

IRELAND: C M P O'Shea; R M Wallace, B J Mullin, J C Bell, S P Geoghegan; E P Elwood, N A Hogan; N J Popplewell, T J Kingston (*capt*), G F Halpin, G M Fulcher, N P J Francis, D Corkery, P S Johns, W D McBride *Replacement* E O Halvey for McBride (temp)
Scorers *Tries:* Popplewell, McBride, Halvey *Conversions:* Elwood (3) *Penalty Goal:* Elwood
WALES: A Clement; I C Evans, M R Hall (*capt*), N R Jenkins, G Thomas; A Davies, R N Jones; M Griffiths, J Humphreys, J D Davies, D Jones, G O Llewellyn, S Davies, E W Lewis, H T Taylor *Replacement* R L Evans for J Davies (84 mins)

Wales scrum-half Robert Jones gets his pass away as Nick Popplewell of Ireland looms in the last match of Pool C (above). Ireland won a scrappy battle for the remaining quarter-final place and Wales were on the plane home. In Pool D, Emile Ntamack scores for France in the last seconds to leave Scotland the short straw: a quarter-final against the All Blacks (below).

Scorers *Tries:* Humphreys, Taylor *Conversions:* Jenkins (2) *Penalty Goals:* Jenkins (2) *Dropped Goal:* A Davies
Referee I Rogers (South Africa)

Pool D

The shadow of tragic Max Brito hung heavy over this group. The fate of the Ivory Coast winger, paralysed after being tackled in the final pool match against Tonga, put everything else into perspective. Brito, however, would have been the first to salute the tremendous group decider between France and Scotland in Pretoria. Scotland thought they had it won when, with the last roll of the dice, France surged downfield yet again, launching a sweeping movement which saw Ntamack cross for a try which broke Scottish hearts. Gavin Hastings scored a record 44 points in the 89-0 victory over the Ivory Coast.

POOL D	*P*	*W*	*D*	*L*	*F*	*A*	*Pts*
France	3	3	0	0	114	47	9
Scotland	3	2	0	1	149	27	7
Tonga	3	1	0	2	44	90	5
Ivory Coast	3	0	0	3	29	172	3

26 May, Rustenburg
SCOTLAND 89 (9G 2PG 4T) **IVORY COAST 0**

SCOTLAND: A G Hastings (*capt*); C A Joiner, A G Stanger, A G Shiel, K M Logan; C M Chalmers, B W Redpath; A P Burnell, K D McKenzie, P H Wright, G W Weir, S J Campbell, P Walton, R I Wainwright, I R Smith
Scorers *Tries:* Hastings (4), Walton (2), Logan (2), Chalmers, Stanger, Burnell, Wright, Shiel *Conversions:* Hastings (9) *Penalty Goals:* Hastings (2)
IVORY COAST: V Kouassi; P Bouazo, J Sathicq, L Niakou, C N'Gbala; A Dali (*capt*), F Dupont; E Bley, E Angoran, T Djehi, G Bado, A Kone, P Pere, D Sanoko, I Lassissi *Replacements* A Camara for Dali (28 mins); M Brito for N'Gbala (40 mins); A Okou for Bado (71 mins)
Referee F Vito (Western Samoa)

26 May, Pretoria
FRANCE 38 (3G 3PG 1DG 1T) **TONGA 10** (1G 1PG)

FRANCE: J-L Sadourny; E Ntamack, P Sella, T Lacroix, P Saint-André (*capt*); Y Delaigue, A Hueber; L Armary, J-M Gonzalez, P Gallart, O Merle, O Brouzet, P Benetton, M Cecillon, A Benazzi *Replacement* L Cabannes for Cecillon (58 mins)
Scorers *Tries:* Lacroix (2), Hueber, Saint-André *Conversions:* Lacroix (3) *Penalty Goals:* Lacroix (3) *Dropped Goal:* Delaigue
TONGA: S Tu'ipulotu; A S Taufa, U Va'enuku, P Latu, T Va'enuku; 'E Vunipola, M Vunipola; S Fe'ao, F Masila, T Fukofuka, W K Lose, F Mafi, F Mahoni, K M F 'Otai (*capt*), I Fenukitau *Replacements* F Vunipola for Masila (9 mins); 'I U Afeaki for Mafi (76 mins)
Scorers *Try:* T Va'enuku *Conversion:* Tu'ipulotu *Penalty Goal:* Tu'ipulotu
Referee S Lander (England)

30 May, Rustenburg
FRANCE 54 (4G 2PG 4T) **IVORY COAST 18** (1G 2PG 1T)

FRANCE: S Viars; W Techoueyres, F Mesnel, T Lacroix, P Saint-André (*capt*); Y Delaigue, G Accoceberry; L Benezech, M de Rougemont, C Califano, O Brouzet,

O Roumat, A Costes, A Benazzi, L Cabannes *Replacements* C Deylaud for Delaigue (40 mins); P Benetton for Benazzi (71 mins)
Scorers *Tries:* Lacroix (2), Benazzi, Accoceberry, Viars, Costes, Techoueyres, Saint-André *Conversions:* Lacroix (2), Deylaud (2) *Penalty Goals:* Lacroix (2)
IVORY COAST: V Kouassi; A Soulama, J Sathicq (*capt*), L Niakou, M Brito; A Camara, F Dupont; J-P Ezoua, A Niamien, T Djehi, B Aka, D Sanoko, P Pere, I Lassissi, A Okou *Replacements* E Bley for Ezoua (47 mins); A Kone for Sanoko (56 mins); E Angoran for Djehi (74 mins); P Bouazo for Soulama (79 mins)
Scorers *Tries:* Camara, Soulama *Conversion:* Kouassi *Penalty Goals:* Kouassi (2)
Referee H Moon-Soo (South Korea)

30 May, Pretoria
SCOTLAND 41 (1G 8PG 2T) **TONGA** 5 (1T)

SCOTLAND: A G Hastings (*capt*); C A Joiner, S Hastings, I C Jardine, K M Logan; C M Chalmers, D W Patterson; D I W Hilton, K S Milne, P H Wright, D F Cronin, G W Weir, R I Wainwright, E W Peters, I R Morrison *Replacement* A P Burnell for Wright (76 mins)
Scorers *Tries:* Peters, G Hastings, S Hastings *Conversion:* G Hastings
Penalty Goals: G Hastings (8)
TONGA: S Tu'ipulotu; A S Taufa, U Va'enuku, P Latu, T Va'enuku; E Vunipola, M Vunipola; S Fe'ao, F Vunipola, T Fukofuka, W K Lose, P Latukefu, 'I U Afeaki, K M F 'Otai, I Fenukitau *Replacements* N Tufui for M Vunipola (57 mins); E Talakai for Fe'ao (75 mins)
Scorer *Try:* Fenukitau
Referee B Leask (Australia)

3 June, Rustenburg
TONGA 29 (3G 1PG 1T) **IVORY COAST 11** (2PG 1T)

TONGA: S Tu'ipulotu; P Latu, S Mafile'o, U Va'enuku, T Va'enuku; E Vunipola, N Tufui; T Fukofuka, F Vunipola, E Talakai, P Latukefu, F Mafi, 'I U Afeaki, K M F 'Otai (*capt*), W K Lose *Replacements* T Lutua for Fukofuka (51 mins); T Isitolo for U Va'enuku (68 mins); F Fakaongo for Afeaki (64 mins)
Scorers *Tries:* Tu'ipulotu, Latukefu, 'Otai, pen try *Conversions:* Tu'ipulotu (3)
Penalty Goal: Tu'ipulotu
IVORY COAST: V Kouassi; A Soulama, J Sathicq (*capt*), L Niakou, M Brito; A Camara, F Dupont; E Bley, E Angoran, T Djehi, G Bado, S Kone, P Pere, I Lassissi, A Okou *Replacements* T Kouame for Brito (6 mins); A Dali for Camara (39 mins); D Sanoko for Kone (40 mins); D Quansah for Bley (50 mins)
Scorers *Try:* Okou *Penalty Goals:* Dali (2)
Referee D Reordan (USA)

3 June, Pretoria
FRANCE 22 (1G 5PG) **SCOTLAND 19** (1G 4PG)

FRANCE: J-L Sadourny; E Ntamack, P Sella, T Lacroix, P Saint-André (*capt*); C Deylaud, G Accoceberry; L Benezech, J-M Gonzalez, C Califano, O Merle, O Roumat, A Benazzi, P Benetton, L Cabannes *Replacements* M Cecillon for Benetton (19 mins); A Hueber for Accoceberry (33 mins)
Scorers *Try:* Ntamack *Conversion:* Lacroix *Penalty Goals:* Lacroix (5)
SCOTLAND: A G Hastings (*capt*); C A Joiner, S Hastings, A G Shiel, K M Logan; C M Chalmers, B W Redpath; D I W Hilton, K S Milne, P H Wright, D F Cronin, G W Weir, R I Wainwright, E W Peters, I R Morrison *Replacements* I C Jardine for Shiel (temp & 44 mins); A P Burnell for Wright (70 mins)
Scorers *Try:* Wainwright *Conversion:* G Hastings *Penalty Goals:* G Hastings (4)
Referee W J Erickson (Australia)

WORLD CUP SQUADS

Abbreviations: *Arg – Argentina, A – Australia, C – Canada, E – England, F – France, I – Ireland, It – Italy, Iv – Ivory Coast, J – Japan, NZ – New Zealand, R – Romania, S – Scotland, SA – South Africa, Tg – Tonga, W – Wales, WS – Western Samoa,* (R) *– Replacement,* t *– temporary replacement,* * *– late replacement.*

AUSTRALIA Captain M Lynagh **Manager** P Falk **Coach** R Dwyer
POOL A Runners-up Lost 22-25 to England in quarter-final

Full-backs: M Burke (NSW) *C, R, E*; M J Pini (Queensland) *SA, R*(t). *Threequarters:* D I Campese (NSW) *SA, C, E*; D P Smith (Queensland) *SA, R, E*; D J Herbert (Queensland) *SA, R*; T J Horan (Queensland) *C, R, E*; J Roff (ACT) *C, R*; J S Little (Queensland) *SA, C, E*. *Half-backs:* S Bowen (NSW) *R*; M P Lynagh (Queensland) *SA, C, E*; G M Gregan (ACT) *SA, C*(R), *R, E*; P J Slattery (Queensland) *C, R*(R). *Forwards:* P N Kearns (NSW) *SA, C, E*; M Foley (Queensland) *C*(R), *R*; D J Crowley (Queensland) *SA, E*; A J Daly (NSW) *C, R*; M N Hartill (NSW) *C*; E J A McKenzie (NSW) *SA, C*(R), *R, E*; J A Eales (Queensland) *SA, C, R, E*; R J McCall (Queensland) *SA, R, E*; W W Waugh (NSW) *C*; T Coker (Queensland); V Ofahengaue (NSW) *SA, C, E*; I Tabua (Queensland) *C, R*; D J Wilson (Queensland) *SA, R, E*; B T Gavin (NSW) *SA, C, R, E*; *D Manu (NSW) *R*(t)

CANADA Captain G Rees **Manager** R Skett **Coach** I Birtwell
POOL A 3rd place

Full-back: D S Stewart (UBC Old Boys) *R, A, SA*. *Threequarters:* D C Lougheed (Toronto Welsh) *R, A, SA*; W Stanley (U of BC) *R, A, SA*; R Toews (Meralomas); S D Gray (Kats) *R, A, SA*; S Lytton (Meralomas); C Stewart (Western Province, SA) *R, A, SA*. *Half-backs:* G L Rees (Newport & Oak Bay Castaways) *R, A, SA*; B Ross (James Bay); J D Graf (UBC Old Boys) *R, A, SA*; A Tynan (Meralomas). *Forwards:* K F Svoboda (Ajax Wanderers) *A*; M E Cardinal (James Bay) *R, SA*; R Bice (Vancouver Rowing Club); E A Evans (IBM Tokyo & UBC Old Boys) *R, A, SA*; P LeBlanc (Kats); R Snow (Dogs) *R, A, SA*; G D Ennis (Suntory Tokyo & Kats) *R, A*(R), *SA*; I Gordon (James Bay) *R, SA*; M James (Burnaby Lake) *R, A*; G Rowlands (Velox Valhallians) *A*; A J Charron (Ottawa Irish) *R, A, SA*; J Hutchinson (UBC Old Boys) *A, SA*(R); G I MacKinnon (Ex-Britannia Lions) *A, SA*; C McKenzie (UBC Old Boys) *R, SA*; C Michaluk (Vancouver Rowing Club) *SA*(R).

ROMANIA Captain T Brinza **Manager** T Radulescu **Coaches** C Fugigi & M Paraschiv
POOL A 4th place

Full-back: V Brici (Farul Constanta) *SA, A*. *Threequarters:* I Rotaru (CSM Foresta Sibiu) *C*; G Solomie (Timisoara U) *C, SA, A*; A Lungu (Castres Olympique) *A*(R); L Colceriu (Steaua Bucharest) *C, SA, A*; N Racean (Cluj U) *C, SA, A*; R Gontineac (Cluj U) *C, SA, A*; R Fugigi (CSM Foresta Sibiu). *Half-backs:* N Nichitean (Cluj U) *C*; I Ivanciuc (Stinta Petrosani) *C*(R), *SA, A*; D Neaga (Dinamo Bucharest) *C*; V Flutur (Cluj U) *C*(R), *SA, A*. *Forwards:* I Negreci (CFR Constanta) *C, SA, A*; V Tufa (Dinamo Bucharest) *SA*(R), *A*(R); G Leonte (Vienne, France) *C, SA, A*; L Costea (Steaua Bucharest); V Lucaci (Baia Mare); G Vlad (Grivita Rosie) *C, SA, A*; C Cojocariu (Bayonne, France) *C, SA, A*; S Ciorascu (Auch, France) *C, SA, A*; A Guranescu (Dinamo Bucharest) *SA, A*; O Slusariuc (Dinamo Bucharest) *C*; A Gealapu (Steaua Bucharest) *C, SA, A*; T Oroian (Steaua Bucharest) *C*; C Draguceanu (Steaua Bucharest); T Brinza (Cluj U) *SA, A*.

SOUTH AFRICA Captain F Pienaar **Manager** M du Plessis **Coach** K Christie
POOL A Winners Winners World Cup

Full-backs: G K Johnson (Transvaal) *R, C, WS*; A J Joubert (Natal) *A, C, WS, F, NZ*. *Threequarters:* P Hendriks (Transvaal) *A, R, C*; J T Small (Natal) *A, R, F, NZ*; B Venter (OFS) *R, C, WS*(R), *NZ*(R); J C Mulder (Transvaal) *A, WS, F, NZ*; C P Scholtz (Transvaal) *R, C, WS*; *C M Williams (Western Province) *WS, F, NZ*. *Half-backs:* J T Stransky (Western Province) *A, R*(t), *C, F, NZ*; H P le Roux (Transvaal) *A, R, C*(R), *WS, F, NZ*; J P Roux (Transvaal) *R, C, F*(R); J H van der Westhuizen (Northern Transvaal) *A, C*(R), *WS, F, NZ*. *Forwards:* J Dalton (Transvaal) *A, C*; C L C Rossouw (Transvaal) *R, WS, F, NZ*; *A E Drotské (OFS) *WS*(R); G L Pagel (Western Province) *A*(R), *R, C, NZ*(R); I S Swart (Transvaal) *A, WS, F, NZ*; J P du Randt (OFS) *A, WS, F, NZ*; M H Hurter (Northern Transvaal) *R, C*; K Otto (Northern Transvaal) *R, C*(R), *WS*(R); J J Strydom (Transvaal) *A, C, F, NZ*; J J Wiese (Transvaal)

R, C, WS, F, NZ; M G Andrews (Natal) *A, WS, F, NZ*; J F Pienaar (Transvaal) *A, C, WS, F, NZ*; R Brink (Western Province) *R, C*; R J Kruger (Northern Transvaal) *A, R, WS, F, NZ*; A Richter (Northern Transvaal) *R, C, WS*(R); R A W Straeuli (Transvaal) *A, WS, NZ*(R).

ARGENTINA Captain S Salvat **Manager** L Chaluleu **Coaches** A Petra & R Paganini
POOL B 4th place

Full-back: E Jurado (Jockey Rosario) *E, WS, It. Threequarters:* D Albanese (San Isidro BA) *E*; D Cuesta Silva (San Isidro BA) *E, WS, It*; M J Teran (Tucumán RC) *E, WS, It*; S Salvat (Alumni BA) *E, WS, It*; F Garcia (Alumni BA); F del Castillo (Jockey Rosario); L Arbizu (Belgrano BA) *E, WS, It. Half-backs:* G J del Castillo (Jockey Rosario); J L Cilley (San Isidro BA) *WS, It*; R H Crexell (Jockey Rosario) *E, WS, It*; A Pichot (CA San Isidro BA). *Forwards:* F E Mendez (Mendoza RC) *E, WS, It*; R A le Fort (Tucumán RC); M Urbano (BAC&RC); E P Noriega (Hindu) *E, WS, It*; M E Corral (San Isidro BA) *E, WS, It*; P L Sporleder (Curupayti BA) *E, WS, It*; G A Llanes (La Plata RCBA) *E, WS, It*; N Bossicovich (Gimnasia Rosario); P M Buabsé (Los Tarcos Tucumán); C Viel (Newman BA) *E, WS, It*; M Sugasti (Jockey Rosario); R Martin (San Isidro BA) *E, WS, It*; S Irazoqui (Palermo Bajo Cordoba) *E*(R); J M Santamarina (Tucumán RC) *E, WS, It.*

ENGLAND Captain W Carling **Manager** J Rowell **Coach** L Cusworth
POOL B Winners Lost 29-45 to New Zealand in semi-final; lost 9-19 to France in 3rd-place play-off

Full-backs: J E B Callard (Bath) *WS*; M J Catt (Bath) *Arg, It, WS, A, NZ, F.*
Threequarters: T Underwood (Leicester) *Arg, It, A, NZ*; I Hunter (Northampton) *WS, F*; R Underwood (Leicester & RAF) *Arg, It, WS, A, NZ, F*; P R de Glanville (Bath) *Arg*(R), *It, WS*; W D C Carling (Harlequins) *Arg, WS, A, NZ, F*; J C Guscott (Bath) *Arg, It, A, NZ, F*; D P Hopley (Wasps) *WS*(R). *Half-backs:* C R Andrew (Wasps) *Arg, It, A, NZ, F*; C D Morris (Orrell) *Arg, WS, A, NZ, F*; K P P Bracken (Bristol) *It, WS*(t); *A Gomarsall (Wasps). *Forwards:* B C Moore (Harlequins) *Arg, It, WS*(R), *A, NZ, F*; R G R Dawe (Bath) *WS*; J Leonard (Harlequins) *Arg, It, A, NZ, F*; V E Ubogu (Bath) *Arg, WS, A, NZ, F*; J A Mallett (Bath) *WS*(R); G C Rowntree (Leicester) *It, WS*; M C Bayfield (Northampton) *Arg, It, A, NZ, F*; M O Johnson (Leicester) *Arg, It, WS, A, NZ, F*; R West (Gloucester) *WS*; N A Back (Leicester) *Arg*(t), *It, WS*; T A K Rodber (Northampton & Army) *Arg, It, WS*(R), *A, NZ, F*; B B Clarke (Bath) *Arg, It, A, NZ, F*; S O Ojomoh (Bath) *Arg, WS, A*(t), *F*; D Richards (Leicester) *WS, A, NZ.*

ITALY Captain Massimo Cuttitta **Manager** G Dondi **Coach** G Coste
POOL B 3rd place

Full-backs: L Troiani (L'Aquila) *E, Arg*; P Vaccari (Milan) *WS, E, Arg.*
Threequarters: Marcello Cuttitta (Milan) *WS*; M Gerosa (Piacenza) *E, Arg*; M Platania (Milan); M Ravazzolo (Calvisano) *WS*; F Mazzariol (Treviso); I Francescato (Treviso) *WS, E, Arg*; S Bordon (Rovigo) *E, Arg*; M Bonomi (Milan) *WS. Half-backs:* D Dominguez (Milan) *WS, E, Arg*; A Troncon (Treviso) *WS, E, Arg. Forwards:* M Trevisiol (Treviso); C Orlandi (Piacenza) *WS, E, Arg*; M Dal Sie (San Dona); Massimo Cuttitta (Milan) *WS, E, Arg*; F Properzi Curti (Milan) *WS, E, Arg*; P Pedroni (Milan) *WS, E, Arg*; M Giacheri (Treviso) *E, Arg*; R Favaro (Treviso) *WS*; A Castellani (L'Aquila); A Sgorlon (San Dona) *E, Arg*; J M Gardner (Roma) *WS, E, Arg*; M Capuzzoni (Milan); O Arancio (Catania) *WS, E, Arg*; C Checchinato (Rovigo) *WS.*

WESTERN SAMOA Captain P Fatialofa **Manager** T Simi **Coach** P Schuster
POOL B Runners-up Lost 14-42 to South Africa in quarter-finals

Full-back: M T Umaga (Wellington, NZ) *It, Arg, E, SA. Threequarters:* G Harder (Te Atatu, Auckland) *It, Arg, SA*; B Lima (Auckland, NZ) *It, Arg, E, SA*; G E Leaupepe (Auckland, NZ) *Arg*(R), *E*; T Vaega (Moata'a) *It, Arg, E, SA*; F Tuilagi (Marist St Joseph's) *SA*(R); T Fa'amasino (Vaimoso) *It, Arg, E, SA. Half-backs:* D J Kellett (Counties, NZ) *It, Arg*; E Puleitu (Inst of Technology, Auckland) *E*; F Sini (Marist Apia) *Arg*(R), *E*(R), *SA*; V Vitale (Vaiala); T Nu'uali'itia (Te Atatu, Auckland) *It, Arg, E, SA. Forwards:* T Leiasamaivao (Wellington, NZ) *It, Arg, E, SA*; B P Reidy (Wellington, NZ) *SA*(R); P Fatialofa (Counties, NZ) *It, Arg*(t & R), *E*(R), *SA*(R); G Latu (Vaimoso) *Arg, E, SA*; M A N Mika (Otago, NZ) *It, Arg, E, SA*; D R Williams (Colomiers, France) *It, E*; L Falaniko (Marist St Joseph's) *It, Arg, E, SA*;

P L Leavasa (Hawke's Bay, NZ) *It*(R), *Arg, E*; S Lemamea (Scopa) *E*(R), *SA*; M Iupeli (Marist St Joseph's) *E*; P J Paramore (Counties, NZ) *It, Arg, SA*; S L Vaifale (Hawke's Bay, NZ) *It, SA*(R); S J Tatupu (Auckland, NZ) *It, Arg, E*(R), *SA*; P R Lam (Auckland, NZ) *Arg, E, SA*; *S P Kaleta (Auckland, NZ).

IRELAND Captain T Kingston **Manager** N Murphy **Coach** G Murphy
POOL C Runners-up Lost 12-36 to France in quarter-final

Full-backs: C M P O'Shea (Lansdowne) *J, W, F*; J E Staples (Harlequins) *NZ*. *Threequarters:* R M Wallace (Garryowen) *NZ, J, W*; D O'Mahony (UC Dublin) *F*; S P Geoghegan (Bath) *NZ, J, W, F*; B J Mullin (Blackrock Coll) *NZ, J, W, F*; J C Bell (Ballymena) *NZ, W, F*; M J Field (Malone) *NZ*(t & R), *J*; *P P A Danaher (Garryowen). *Half-backs:* P A Burke (Cork Const) *J*; E P Elwood (Lansdowne) *NZ, W, F*; N A Hogan (Terenure Coll) *J, W, F*; M T Bradley (Cork Const) *NZ*. *Forwards:* T J Kingston (Dolphin) *NZ, J*(R), *W, F*; K G M Wood (Garryowen) *J*; *S J Byrne (Blackrock Coll); N J Popplewell (Wasps) *NZ, J, W, F*; G F Halpin (London Irish) *NZ, W, F*; H D Hurley (Old Wesley); P S Wallace (Blackrock Coll) *J*; D A Tweed (Ballymena) *J*; N P J Francis (Old Belvedere) *NZ, J, W, F*; G M Fulcher (Cork Const) *NZ, W, F*; A G Foley (Shannon) *J*(t & R); W D McBride (Malone) *NZ, W, F*; E O Halvey (Shannon) *J, W*(t), *F*(R); D Corkery (Cork Const) *NZ, J, W, F*; P S Johns (Dungannon) *NZ, J, W, F*.

JAPAN Captain M Kunda **Manager** Z Shirai **Coach** O Koyabu
POOL C 4th place

Full-backs: T Matsuda (Toshiba Fuchu) *W, I, NZ;* K Imaizumi (Suntory). *Threequarters:* L Oto (Daito Bunka U) *W, I, NZ*; T Masuho (Kobe Steel) *W*; Y Yoshida (Isetan) *I, NZ*; A Yoshida (Sanyo) *W, I, NZ*; Y Motoki (Kobe Steel) *W, I, NZ*. *Half-backs:* K Hirose (Kyoto Sangyo U) *NZ*; K Matsuo (World); S Hirao (Kobe Steel) *W, I*; M Horikoshi (Kobe Steel) *W, I*; W Murata (Toshiba Fuchu) *NZ*. *Forwards:* M Kunda (Toshiba Fuchu) *W, I, NZ*; E Hirotsu (Kobe Steel); M Takura (Mitsubishi) *I*; K Takahashi (Toyota) *W, NZ*; O Ota (NEC) *W, I, NZ*; K Hamabe (Kinki Nippon Railway); B Ferguson (Hino) *W, I, NZ*; Y Sakuraba (Nippon) *W, I, NZ*; T Akatsuka (Meiji U) *NZ*(R); H Kajihara (Katsunuma) *W, I, NZ*; Sinali Latu (Sanyo) *W, I, NZ*; K Izawa (Daito Bunka U) *I*(t & R), *NZ*; Sione Latu (Daito Bunka U) *W, I*; T Haneda (World).

NEW ZEALAND Captain S Fitzpatrick **Managers** B Lochore & C Meads
Coaches L Mains & E Kirton
POOL C Winners Lost 12-15 to South Africa in final

Full-back: G M Osborne (North Harbour) *I, W, J, E, SA*. *Threequarters:* J T Lomu (Counties) *I, W, S, E, SA*; E J Rush (North Harbour) *W*(R), *J*; J W Wilson (Otago) *I, J, S, E, SA*; M C G Ellis (Otago) *I*(R), *W, J, S, SA*(R); F E Bunce (North Harbour) *I, W, S, E, SA*; A I Ieremia (Wellington) *J*; W K Little (North Harbour) *I, W, S, E, SA*. *Half-backs:* S D Culhane (Southland) *J*; A P Mehrtens (Canterbury) *I, W, S, E, SA*; G T M Bachop (Canterbury) *I, W, S, E, SA*; A D Strachan (North Harbour) *J, SA*(t). *Forwards:* N J Hewitt (Southland) *I*(t), *J*; S B T Fitzpatrick (Auckland) *I, W, S, E, SA*; O M Brown (Auckland) *I, W, S, E, SA*; C W Dowd (Auckland) *I, W, J, E, SA*; R W Loe (Canterbury) *J, S, SA*(R); R M Brooke (Auckland) *J, S, E, SA*; I D Jones (North Harbour) *I, W, S, E, SA*; B P Larsen (North Harbour) *I, W, J, E*(R); M R Brewer (Canterbury) *I, W, E, SA*; P W Henderson (Southland) *J*; J W Joseph (Otago) *I, W, J*(R), *S, SA*(R); J A Kronfeld (Otago) *I, W, S, E, SA*; K J Schuler (North Harbour) *I*(R), *J*; Z V Brooke (Auckland) *J, S, E, SA*.

WALES Captain M Hall **Manager** G Evans **Coach** A Evans
POOL C 3rd place

Full-backs: A Clement (Swansea) *J, NZ, I*; W J L Thomas (Cardiff Inst). *Threequarters:* I C Evans (Llanelli) *J, NZ, I*; W T Proctor (Llanelli) *NZ*; S P Ford (Cardiff); G Thomas (Bridgend) *J, NZ, I*; M R Hall (Cardiff) *J, NZ, I*; D W Evans (Treorchy) *J*(R). *Half-backs:* A Davies (Cardiff) *J, I*; N R Jenkins (Pontypridd) *J, NZ, I*; R N Jones (Swansea) *NZ, I*; A P Moore (Cardiff) *J*. *Forwards:* J Humphreys (Cardiff) *NZ, I*; G R Jenkins (Swansea) *J*; J D Davies (Neath) *J, NZ, I*; R L Evans (Llanelli) *NZ, I*(R); M Griffiths (Cardiff) *J, I*; S C John (Llanelli); W S Roy (Cardiff) *J*(R); G Prosser (Pontypridd) *NZ*; D Jones (Cardiff) *J, NZ, I*; G O Llewellyn (Neath) *J, NZ, I*; M Bennett

(Cardiff) *NZ*; H T Taylor (Cardiff) *J, NZ, I*; S Davies (Swansea) *J, I*; E W Lewis (Cardiff) *J, I*.

FRANCE Captain P Saint-André **Manager** G Laporte **Coach** P Berbizier
POOL D Winners Lost 15-19 to South Africa in semi-final; beat England 19-9 in 3rd-place play-off

Full-backs: J-L Sadourny (Colomiers) *Tg, S, I, SA, E*; S Viars (Brive) *Iv*. *Threequarters:* E Ntamack (Toulouse) *Tg, S, I, SA, E*; P Saint-André (Montferrand) *Tg, Iv, S, I, SA, E*; W Techoueyres (SBUC) *Iv*; P Sella (Agen) *Tg, S, I, SA, E*; T Lacroix (Dax) *Tg, Iv, S, I, SA, E*; F Mesnel (Racing Club de France) *Iv, E*. *Half-backs:* C Deylaud (Toulouse) *Iv(R), S, I, SA*; Y Delaigue (Toulon) *Tg, Iv*; G Accoceberry (Bègles-Bordeaux) *Iv, S*; A Hueber (Toulon) *Tg, S*(R), *I*; *F Galthié (Colomiers) *SA, E*. *Forwards:* J-M Gonzalez (Bayonne) *Tg, S, I, SA, E*; M de Rougemont (Toulon) *Iv*; P Gallart (Béziers) *Tg*; L Armary (Lourdes) *Tg, I, SA*; L Benezech (Racing Club de France) *Iv, S, E*; C Califano (Toulouse) *Iv, S, I, SA, E*; O Roumat (Dax) *Iv, S, I, SA, E*; O Brouzet (Grenoble) *Tg, Iv, E*(t); O Merle (Montferrand) *Tg, S, I, SA, E*; A Costes (Montferrand) *Iv*; M Cecillon (Bourgoin) *Tg, S*(R), *I, SA*; L Cabannes (Racing Club de France) *Tg*(R), *Iv, S, I, SA, E*; A Benazzi (Agen) *Tg, Iv, S, I, SA, E*; P Benetton (Agen) *Tg, Iv*(R), *S*; *A Cigagna (Toulouse) *E*.

TONGA Captain M 'Otai **Manager** M Tuku'aho **Coach** F Valu
POOL D 3rd place

Full-backs: T 'Isitolo (Kolofo'ou) *Iv*(R); S Tu'ipulotu (Manly, NSW) *F, S, Iv*. *Threequarters:* U Va'enuku (Toloa OB) *F, S, Iv*; T Va'enuku (Police) *F, S, Iv*; A S Taufa (Wellington, NZ) *F, S*; P Latu (Vaheloto) *F, S, Iv*; F Manukia (Siutaka). *Half-backs:* S Mafile'o *Iv*; 'E Vunipola (Toako Ma'afu) *F, S, Iv*; N Tufui (Kolomotu'a) *S*(R), *Iv*; M Vunipola (Toako Ma'afu) *F, S*. *Forwards:* F Vunipola (Toako Ma'afu) *F*(R), *S, Iv*; F Masila (Kolomotu'a) *F*; T Lutua (Police) *Iv*(R); T Fukofuka (Grammar, Auckland) *F, S, Iv*; 'E Talakai (Siutaka) *S*(R), *Iv*; S Fe'ao (Queensland, Aus) *F, S*; P Latukefu (Canberra Royals, ACT) *S, Iv*; F Mafi (ACT, Aus) *F, Iv*; W K Lose (North Harbour, NZ) *F, S, Iv*; I Fenukitau (ACT, Aus) *F, S*; F Fakaongo (Toako Ma'afu) *Iv*(R); F Mahoni (Fasi Ma'ufanga) *F*; 'I U Afeaki (Wellington, NZ) *F*(R), *S, Iv*; K M F 'Otai (Manawatu, NZ) *F, S, Iv*; A Mafi (Queanbeyan, ACT).

IVORY COAST Captain A Dali **Manager** P Cassagnet **Coaches** D Davanier & C Ezoua
POOL D 4th place

Full-backs: V Koussi (Burotic) *S, F, Tg*. *Threequarters:* P Bouazo (Burotic) *S, F*(R); M Brito (Biscarosse) *S*(R), *F, Tg*; C N'Gbala (Cahors) *S*; A Soulama (Burotic) *F, Tg*; J Sathicq (CASG) *S, F, Tg*; L Niakou (Niort) *S, F, Tg*; T Kouame (ASPAA) *Tg*(R). *Half-backs:* A Dali (Clamart) *S, Tg*(R); A Camara (ASPAA) *S*(R), *F, Tg*; F Dago (ASPAA); F Dupont (Nîmes) *S, F, Tg*. *Forwards:* E Angoran (Rodez) *S, F*(R), *Tg*; A Niamien (Bouake) *F*; E Bley (ASPAA) *S, F*(R), *Tg*; T Djehi (Millau) *S, F, Tg*; J-P Ezoua (ASPAA) *F*; D Quansah (ASPAA) *Tg*(R); B Aka (Burotic) *F*; G Bado (Cognac) *S, Tg*; A Kone (Soustons) *S, F*(R); D Sanoko (Biarritz) *S, F, Tg*(R); S Kone (Burotic) *Tg*; I Lassissi (Burotic) *S, F, Tg*; A Okou (Poitiers) *S*(R), *F, Tg*; P Pere (ACBB) *S, F, Tg*.

SCOTLAND Captain G Hastings **Manager** D Paterson **Coach** D Morgan
POOL D Runners-up Lost 30-48 to New Zealand in quarter-final

Full-back: A G Hastings (Watsonians) *Iv, Tg, F, NZ*. *Threequarters:* I C Glasgow (Heriot's FP); C A Joiner (Melrose) *Iv, Tg, F, NZ*; K M Logan (Stirling County) *Iv, Tg, F, NZ*; A G Stanger (Hawick) *Iv*; S Hastings (Watsonians) *Tg, F, NZ*; I C Jardine (Stirling County) *Tg, F*(t & R), *NZ*(R). *Half-backs:* C M Chalmers (Melrose) *Iv, Tg, F, NZ*; A G Shiel (Melrose) *Iv, F, NZ*; D W Patterson (West Hartlepool) *Tg*; B W Redpath (Melrose) *Iv, F, NZ*. *Forwards:* K D McKenzie (Stirling County) *Iv*; K S Milne (Heriot's FP) *Tg, F, NZ*; A P Burnell (London Scottish) *Iv, Tg*(R), *F*(R); D I W Hilton (Bath) *Tg, F, NZ*; J J Manson (Dundee HSFP); P H Wright (Boroughmuir) *Iv, Tg, F, NZ*; S J Campbell (Dundee HSFP) *Iv, NZ*(R); D F Cronin (Bourges) *Tg, F, NZ*; J F Richardson (Edinburgh Acads); G W Weir (Melrose) *Iv, Tg, F, NZ*; I R Morrison (London Scottish) *Tg, F, NZ*; I R Smith (Gloucester) *Iv*; R I Wainwright (West Hartlepool) *Iv, Tg, F, NZ*; P Walton (Northampton) *Iv*; E W Peters (Bath) *Tg, F, NZ*.

WORLD CUP RECORDS

(Final stages only)

LEADING SCORERS

Most points in the competition

126	G J Fox	New Zealand	1987
112	T Lacroix	France	1995
104	A G Hastings	Scotland	1995
84	A P Mehrtens	New Zealand	1995
82	M P Lynagh	Australia	1987

Most tries in one competition

7	M C G Ellis	New Zealand	1995
	J T Lomu	New Zealand	1995

Most conversions in one competition

30	G J Fox	New Zealand	1987
20	S D Culhane	New Zealand	1995
	M P Lynagh	Australia	1987

Most penalty goals in one competition

26	T Lacroix	France	1995
21	G J Fox	New Zealand	1987
20	C R Andrew	England	1995

Most dropped goals in one competition

3	A P Mehrtens	New Zealand	1995
	J T Stransky	South Africa	1995
	C R Andrew	England	1995
	J Davies	Wales	1987

MOST POINTS IN A MATCH

By a team

145	New Zealand v Japan	1995
89	Scotland v Ivory Coast	1995
74	New Zealand v Fiji	1987
70	New Zealand v Italy	1987
	France v Zimbabwe	1987

By a player

45	S D Culhane	New Zealand v Japan	1995
44	A G Hastings	Scotland v Ivory Coast	1995
31	A G Hastings	Scotland v Tonga	1995
30	M C G Ellis	New Zealand v Japan	1995
	D Camberabero	France v Zimbabwe	1987

MOST TRIES IN A MATCH

By a team

21	New Zealand v Japan	1995
13	Scotland v Ivory Coast	1995
	France v Zimbabwe	1987
12	New Zealand v Italy	1987
	New Zealand v Fiji	1987

By a player

6	M C G Ellis	New Zealand v Japan	1995
4	A G Hastings	Scotland v Ivory Coast	1995
	C M Williams	South Africa v Western Samoa	1995
	J T Lomu	New Zealand v England	1995
	B F Robinson	Ireland v Zimbabwe	1991
	I C Evans	Wales v Canada	1987
	C I Green	New Zealand v Fiji	1987
	J A Gallagher	New Zealand v Fiji	1987

MOST CONVERSIONS IN A MATCH

By a team

20	New Zealand v Japan	1995
10	New Zealand v Fiji	1987
9	Scotland v Ivory Coast	1995
	France v Zimbabwe	1987

By a player

20	S D Culhane	New Zealand v Japan	1995
10	G J Fox	New Zealand v Fiji	1987
9	A G Hastings	Scotland v Ivory Coast	1995
	D Camberabero	France v Zimbabwe	1987

MOST PENALTY GOALS IN A MATCH

By a team

8	Scotland v Tonga	1995
	France v Ireland	1995

By a player

8	A G Hastings	Scotland v Tonga	1995
	T Lacroix	France v Ireland	1995

MOST DROPPED GOALS IN A MATCH

By a team

3	Fiji v Romania	1991

By a player

2	J T Stransky	South Africa v New Zealand	1995
	C R Andrew	England v Argentina	1995
	T Rabaka	Fiji v Romania	1991
	L Arbizu	Argentina v Australia	1991
	J Davies	Wales v Ireland	1987

WORLD CUP QUALIFIERS

Two World Cup qualifying tournaments took place in September and October 1994. Romania, Italy and Wales, the three qualifiers from the earlier European rounds, played a round robin to determine their seedings for South Africa, while in late October the 14th Asian Rugby Football Tournament doubled as the Asian Zone qualifying competition for the World Cup finals.

EUROPEAN SEEDING MATCHES

17 September 1994, Bucharest
ROMANIA 9 (3PG) WALES 16 (1G 3PG)

Wales had never previously beaten the Romanians in a cap match, though this was a far from convincing win. Yet their forwards did well to overcome the stifling heat and, despite being overwhelmed at the line-out, they rarely looked likely to concede a try. Ieuan Evans' brilliant touchline run for the only try of the match took him to the top of the all-time list of Welsh try-scorers. Moreover, it set up the win which gave Wales a good chance of claiming the coveted Pool C place in the least demanding group for the finals.

ROMANIA: V Brici (Farul Constanta); L Colceriu (Steaua Bucharest), N Racean (Brescia), N Fulina (Farul Constanta), G Solomie (Timisoara U); N Nichitean (Baia Mare), D Neaga (Dinamo Bucharest); G Leonte (Vienne), G Ion (Dinamo Bucharest), G Vlad (Grivita Rosie), S Ciorascu (Auch), C Cojocariu (Bayonne), T Oroian (Steaua Bucharest), T Brinza (Cluj) (*capt*), A Guranescu (Dinamo Bucharest) *Replacements* C Draguceanu (Steaua Bucharest) for Brinza (62 mins); C Gheorghe (Grivita Rosie) for Leonte (71 mins)
Scorer *Penalty Goals:* Nichitean (3)
WALES: M A Rayer (Cardiff); I C Evans (Llanelli) (*capt*), M R Hall (Cardiff), N G Davies (Llanelli), W T Proctor (Llanelli); N R Jenkins (Pontypridd), R H StJ B Moon (Llanelli); R L Evans (Llanelli), G R Jenkins (Swansea), J D Davies (Neath), P T Davies (Llanelli), G O Llewellyn (Neath), H T Taylor (Cardiff), E W Lewis (Cardiff), R G Collins (Pontypridd)
Scorers *Try:* I Evans *Conversion:* N Jenkins *Penalty Goals:* N Jenkins (3)
Referee D T M McHugh (Ireland)

1 October 1994, Catania
ITALY 24 (8PG) ROMANIA 6 (2PG)

The Romanian forwards looked a mere shadow of the pack which had so troubled the Welsh in Bucharest a fortnight earlier. They struggled to achieve parity in the rucks and mauls, and were unable to disrupt the Italians in the line-out. Diego Dominguez, the Argentinian-born Italy captain, became only the third kicker to place eight successful penalty shots in an international. By contrast Neculai Nichitean, Romania's kicker, missed six of his eight pots at goal.

ITALY: P Dotto (Benetton Treviso); P Vaccari (Milan), S Bordon (Ciabatta Rovigo), I Francescato (Benetton Treviso), M Gerosa (Lyons Piacenza); D Dominguez (Milan)

(*capt*), A Troncon (Benetton Treviso); M Dal Sie (Lafert San Dona), C Orlandi (Lyons Piacenza), G Grespan (Benetton Treviso), R Favaro (Benetton Treviso), D Scaglia (Tegolaia Tarvisium), O Arancio (Catania), C Checchinato (Ciabatta Rovigo), A Sgorlon (Lafert San Dona) *Replacements* C de Rossi (Benetton Treviso) for Sgorlon (61 mins); D Sesenna (Lyons Piacenza) for Scaglia (80 mins)
Scorer *Penalty Goals:* Dominguez (8)
ROMANIA: V Brici (Farul Constanta); L Colceriu (Steaua Bucharest), G Solomie (Timisoara U), N Fulina (Farul Constanta), R Cioca (Dinamo Bucharest), N Nichitean (Baia Mare), D Neaga (Dinamo Bucharest); G Leonte (Vienne), G Ion (Dinamo Bucharest) (*capt*), G Vlad (Grivita Rosie), C Branescu (Farul Constanta), C Cojocariu (Bayonne), T Oroian (Steaua Bucharest), C Draguceanu (Steaua Bucharest), A Gealapu (Steaua Bucharest) *Replacements* I S Tofan (Dinamo Bucharest) (temp) for Fulina; T Brinza (Cluj) for Branescu (56 mins)
Scorer *Penalty Goals:* Nichitean (2)
Referee E Sklar (Argentina)

12 October 1994, Cardiff
WALES 29 (7PG 1DG 1T) ITALY 19 (1G 4PG)

Wales achieved the seeding they wanted in a match which demonstrated the strides forward made by the Italians since the 1991 World Cup. Italy scored a dazzling try in the seventh minute when Ivan Francescato, a former scrum-half turned left wing, scuttled away for a corner score after the Welsh defence had muffed a garryowen. Moreover their forwards, gingered up by captain Massimo Cuttitta, made Wales struggle in the tight. The place-kickers turned out to be the protagonists in a low-key match. Neil Jenkins scored 24 points to equal the Welsh record he had set against Canada in 1993, and in so doing took his overall international tally past Paul Thorburn's previous Welsh record of 304. Diego Dominguez chipped in with another 14 points for the Italians.

WALES: M A Rayer (Cardiff); W T Proctor (Llanelli), M R Hall (Cardiff), N G Davies (Llanelli), A Clement (Swansea); N R Jenkins (Pontypridd), R H StJ B Moon (Llanelli); R L Evans (Llanelli), G R Jenkins (Swansea), J D Davies (Neath), P T Davies (Llanelli), G O Llewellyn (Neath) (*capt*), H T Taylor (Cardiff), E W Lewis (Llanelli), R G Collins (Pontypridd) *Replacement* H Williams-Jones (Llanelli) for Evans (temp)
Scorers *Try:* N Davies *Penalty Goals:* N Jenkins (7) *Dropped Goal:* N Jenkins
ITALY: P Vaccari (Milan); M Gerosa (Lyons Piacenza), S Bordon (Ciabatta Rovigo), M Bonomi (Milan), I Francescato (Benetton Treviso); D Dominguez (Milan), A Troncon (Benetton Treviso); Massimo Cuttitta (Milan) (*capt*), C Orlandi (Lyons Piacenza), G Grespan (Benetton Treviso), R Favaro (Benetton Treviso), D Scaglia (Tegolaia Tarvisium), O Arancio (Catania), C Checchinato (Ciabatta Rovigo), A Sgorlon (Lafert San Dona) *Replacement* M Dal Sie (Lafert San Dona) for Grespan (67 mins)
Scorers *Try:* Francescato *Conversion:* Dominguez *Penalty Goals:* Dominguez (4)
Referee K W McCartney (Scotland)

FINAL TABLE

	P	*W*	*D*	*L*	*F*	*A*	*Pts*
Wales	2	2	0	0	45	28	6
Italy	2	1	0	1	43	35	4
Romania	2	0	0	2	15	40	2

3 points for a win; 2 for a draw; 1 for a loss

Wales joined Pool C, Italy Pool B and Romania Pool A in the finals

ASIAN QUALIFYING TOURNAMENT

The 16th and final place for the 1995 World Cup was decided in Kuala Lumpur in the last week of October 1994. Japan, as expected, emerged with ease from their League A group, averaging more than 70 points a match.

The Koreans were the other finalists, beating a Hong Kong side of 15 expatriates in the tightest match of League B. Hong Kong led 14-10 at half-time but their misdirected kicking in the second half gave Korea scope to move the ball. At length, the superior fitness and slick handling of the Koreans brought them a relatively comfortable victory. Not that Hong Kong failed to leave a mark on the competition: in their final league match they overwhelmed Singapore by a world-record score, 164-13, with Ashley Billington (50 points from ten tries) and Jamie McKee (17 conversions) establishing individual world records for an international. Another three tries by Billington and 20 more points from McKee's boot were the major contributions to Hong Kong's win against Chinese Taipei in the third-fourth-place play-off staged as a curtain-raiser to the final.

GROUP A

Results

22 Oct 1994	Malaysia	23	Sri Lanka	18	(Cheras)
22 Oct 1994	Japan	56	Chinese Taipei	5	(Cheras)
24 Oct 1994	Sri Lanka	3	Japan	67	(Cheras)
24 Oct 1994	Chinese Taipei	23	Malaysia	15	(Cheras)
26 Oct 1994	Malaysia	9	Japan	103	(Cheras)
26 Oct 1994	Chinese Taipei	25	Sri Lanka	9	(Cheras)

FINAL TABLE

	P	*W*	*D*	*L*	*F*	*A*	*Pts*
Japan	3	3	0	0	226	17	9
Chinese Taipei	3	2	0	1	53	80	7
Malaysia	3	1	0	2	47	144	5
Sri Lanka	3	0	0	3	30	115	3

GROUP B

Results

23 Oct 1994	Singapore	5	Thailand	69	(Cheras)
23 Oct 1994	Hong Kong	17	Korea	28	(Cheras)
25 Oct 1994	Thailand	0	Hong Kong	93	(Cheras)
25 Oct 1994	Korea	90	Singapore	3	(Cheras)
27 Oct 1994	Singapore	13	Hong Kong	164	(Cheras)
27 Oct 1994	Korea	65	Thailand	11	(Cheras)

FINAL TABLE

	P	*W*	*D*	*L*	*F*	*A*	*Pts*
Korea	3	3	0	0	183	31	9
Hong Kong	3	2	0	1	274	41	7
Thailand	3	1	0	2	80	163	5
Singapore	3	0	0	3	21	323	3

Third-Fourth-Place Play-Off

29 Oct 1994	Hong Kong	80	Chinese Taipei	26	(Cheras)

29 October 1994, KL Football Stadium, Cheras **Final**
JAPAN 26 (2G 4PG) **KOREA 11** (2PG 1T)

Japan won a fast, furious final on a wet ground thanks to accurate place-kicking by Keiji Hirose and superior air power at the line-out provided by imports Bruce Ferguson from Fiji and the two unrelated Latus, Sinale and Sione, of Tonga. Hirose, whose six successful kicks from his eight attempts at goal were taken from difficult angles, also varied the Japanese tactics sensibly from fly-half.

Korean efforts to run the ball at their traditional rivals were invariably held up by the hard-tackling Japanese back row. Sadly, towards the end of the match, as victory slipped away, in frustration Korea were guilty of permitting their emotions to get the better of their rugby skills. Hirose gladly accepted opportunities to extend Japan's lead.

JAPAN: T Matsuda (Toshiba Fuchu); T Matsuho (Kobe Steel), T Takeyama (Suntory), Y Motoki (Kobe Steel), Y Yoshida (Isetan); K Hirose (Kyoto Sangyo U), M Horikoshi (Kobe Steel); O Ota (NEC), M Kunda (Toshiba Fuchu) (*capt*), M Takura (Mitsubishi Electric), Y Sakuraba (Nippon Steel), B Ferguson (Hino Motors), H Kajihara (Katsunuma), Sione Latu (Daito Bunka U), Sinali Latu (Sanyo Electric)
Scorers *Tries:* Yoshida (2) *Conversions:* Hirose (2) *Penalty Goals:* Hirose (4)
KOREA: Yung-Hyeon Yoo (Army); Chang-Ryul Choi (Army), Yoon-Ki Kim (Army), Doo-Hwan Cho (Korea Electric) (*capt*), Hwan-Myung Yong (Yon-Sei U); Young-Soo Song (Yon-Sei U), Cheol-Kee No (Army); Sung-Kyu Park (Kyoung-Hee U), Hyung-Joon Kim (Posco Chem), Kwan-Hee Lee (Korea Electric), Dong-Ho Kang (Army), Kwang-Je Kim (Korea Electric), Jin-Sik Cho (Army), Young-Choon Kim (Posco Chem), Keun-Wook Lee (Army) *Replacement* Jae-Hyoung Son (Posco Chem) for Young-Choon Kim
Scorers *Try:* Yung-Hyeon Yoo *Penalty Goals:* Yung-Soo Song (2)
Referee P O'Brien (New Zealand)

Japan joined Pool C in the finals

TOURS 1994-95

ENGLAND TO SOUTH AFRICA 1994

It's best to keep some sort of perspective on these things. That the tour went ahead at all was an achievement in itself: only a few weeks before England were due to arrive in South Africa, New South Wales pulled out of their Super-10 match against Natal, citing the volatile political situation as their excuse. England had no trouble off the field, and for that great credit must go to the South African authorities and their people. They were wonderful hosts.

Events on the field proved more troublesome for England. The wondrously spirited performance in the First Test apart, they struggled to get to grips with rugby on hard grounds. Their percentage game, which relied heavily on kicking, was shown to be inappropriate by a succession of provincial teams. The final tour record of only three wins in eight matches tells its own tale.

England also had problems with local refereeing interpretations. Their suffering here, however, was as nothing compared with the real pain inflicted down in Port Elizabeth in the penultimate match of the tour. The game will go down as one of the most brutal ever played. Tim Rodber became only the second Englishman ever to be dismissed playing for his country (Mike Burton was the first in 1975) when he retaliated. Rodber's patience snapped minutes after witnessing Jonathan Callard's right eye being sliced open by the boot of Elandre van der Bergh. Callard received 25 stitches and van der Bergh a ticking-off. Rodber escaped suspension, a disciplinary panel deeming the sending-off sufficient punishment. It was the wrong message to send to the rest of the world.

England did have the solace of discovering new talent. Bristol's Paul Hull proved outstanding in winning his first cap at full-back while Simon Shaw, a late arrival for the concussed Martin Johnson, and John Mallett both came of age in the dirt-trackers. The midweek side was well led by Dean Ryan.

THE TOURING PARTY

Manager J Rowell **Assistant Manager** J Elliott **Coaches** R Best & L Cusworth
Captain W D C Carling

FULL-BACKS

P A Hull (Bristol & RAF)
D Pears (Harlequins)
***J E B Callard** (Bath)

THREEQUARTERS

A A Adebayo (Bath)
T Underwood (Leicester)
R Underwood (Leicester & RAF)
D P Hopley (Wasps)
W D C Carling (Harlequins)
M J Catt (Bath)
P R de Glanville (Bath)
S Potter (Leicester)

HALF-BACKS

C R Andrew (Wasps)
S Barnes (Bath)
C D Morris (Orrell)
S M Bates (Wasps)

FORWARDS

J Leonard (Harlequins)
G C Rowntree (Leicester)
V E Ubogu (Bath)
J Mallett (Bath)
R G R Dawe (Bath)
B C Moore (Harlequins)
M C Bayfield (Northampton)
N C Redman (Bath)
M O Johnson (Leicester)
M D Poole (Leicester)
***S Shaw** (Bristol)
T A K Rodber (Northampton & Army)
S O Ojomoh (Bath)
L B N Dallaglio (Wasps)
B B Clarke (Bath)
D Richards (Leicester)
D Ryan (Wasps)

**Replacement during tour*

TOUR RECORD

All matches Played 8 Won 3 Lost 5 Points for 152 Against 165
International matches Played 2 Won 1 Lost 1 Points for 41 Against 42

SCORING DETAILS

All matches

For:	11T	8C	26PG	1DG	152 Pts
Against:	13T	5C	29PG	1DG	165 Pts

International matches

For:	2T	2C	8PG	1DG	41 Pts
Against:	2T	1C	10PG	–	42 Pts

MATCH DETAILS

1994	OPPONENTS	VENUE	RESULT
18 May	Orange Free State	Bloemfontein	L 11-22
21 May	Natal	Durban	L 6-21
25 May	Western Transvaal	Potchefstroom	W 26-24
28 May	Transvaal	Johannesburg	L 21-24
31 May	South Africa A	Kimberley	L 16-19
4 June	SOUTH AFRICA	Pretoria	W 32-15
7 June	Eastern Province	Port Elizabeth	W 31-13
11 June	SOUTH AFRICA	Cape Town	L 9-27

*Appearances: 7 – Ojomoh**; 6 – T Underwood*, Hull; 5 – Bates*, Carling, Redman, Clarke, R Underwood*, Ubogu*, Rodber*; 4 – Hopley, Potter, Rowntree, Dawe, Mallett, Ryan, De Glanville, Andrew, Morris, Leonard, Moore, Bayfield; 3 – Barnes, Richards, Catt, Adebayo, Poole, Dallaglio, Callard*; 2 – Johnson, Shaw; 1 – Pears *includes appearances as a replacement*
Scorers: 58 – Andrew (2T 3C 13PG 1DG); 22 – Barnes (2C 6PG); 17 – Callard (1C 5PG); 10 – T Underwood (2T), Hopley (2T), Hull (2T), Catt (2C 2PG); 5 – R Underwood, Clarke, Bates (all 1T)

MATCH 1 18 May, Springbok Park, Bloemfontein

Orange Free State 22 (1G 3T) **England XV 11** (2PG 1T)
Orange Free State: A Pawson; C Badenhorst, E Lubbe, B Venter, D van Rensburg; F Smith, H Martens; O le Roux, N Drotske (*capt*), D Heymans, R Opperman, B Els, A Venter, J von Solms, A Cloete *Replacements* C Marais for Drotske (2 mins); J Coetzee for A Venter (65 mins)
Scorers *Tries:* Badenhorst (2), A Venter, Coetzee *Conversion:* Van Rensburg
England XV: Hull; Hopley, Potter, Catt, Adebayo; Barnes, Bates; Rowntree, Dawe, Mallett, Poole, Bayfield, Dallaglio, Ryan (*capt*), Ojomoh *Replacement* T Underwood for Catt (65 mins)
Scorers *Try:* Hopley *Penalty Goals:* Barnes (2)
Referee P Lombard (Natal)

MATCH 2 21 May, King's Park, Durban

Natal 21 (7PG) **England XV 6** (2PG)
Natal: A Joubert; J Enslin, P Müller, R Muir, J F van der Westhuizen; H Honiball, K Putt; G Kebble, J Allan, A Garvey, S Atherton, M Andrews, W Bartmann (*capt*), G Teichmann, A Blakeway

Scorers *Penalty Goals:* Joubert (4), Honiball (3)
England XV: Pears; T Underwood, De Glanville, Carling (*capt*), R Underwood; Andrew, Morris; Leonard, Moore, Ubogu, Johnson, Redman, Rodber, Richards, Clarke *Replacements* Ojomoh for Richards (40 mins); Barnes for Pears (64 mins)
Scorer *Penalty Goals:* Andrew (2)
Referee M Franken (Griqualand West)

MATCH 3 25 May, Olen Park, Potchefstroom

Western Transvaal 24 (1G 4PG 1T) **England XV 26** (2G 4PG)
Western Transvaal: J Blaauw; A Vermeulen, D Swart, J van Wyck, D Basson; E Hare (*capt*), A Pretorius; E Grobler, L Boshoff, M Proudfoot, P Oosthuizen, P Herbst, A Kriek, M van Greunen, S Bekker
Scorers *Tries:* Basson, Van Greunen *Conversion:* Basson *Penalty Goals:* Basson (4)
England XV: Hull; Hopley, Carling, Potter, T Underwood; Barnes, Bates; Rowntree, Dawe, Mallett, Bayfield, Redman, Ryan, Clarke, Ojomoh *Replacement* Callard for Barnes (75 mins)
Scorers *Tries:* T Underwood (2) *Conversions:* Barnes (2) *Penalty Goals:* Barnes (4)
Referee N Heilbron (Cape Town)

MATCH 4 28 May, Ellis Park, Johannesburg

Transvaal 24 (1G 4PG 1T) **England XV 21** (1G 3PG 1T)
Transvaal: T van Rensburg; J Louw, J Mulder, C Scholtz, P Hendriks; H le Roux, J Roux; B Swart, J Dalton, J le Roux, K Wiese, H Strydom, F Pienaar (*capt*), R Straeuli, I Macdonald
Scorers *Tries:* H le Roux, Louw *Conversion:* Van Rensburg
Penalty Goals: Van Rensburg (4)
England XV: Hull; T Underwood, Carling (*capt*), De Glanville, R Underwood; Andrew, Morris; Leonard, Moore, Ubogu, Johnson, Redman, Rodber, Richards, Clarke
Replacement Bates for Morris (52 mins)
Scorers *Tries:* Andrew, R Underwood *Conversion:* Andrew *Penalty Goals:* Andrew (3)
Referee I Rogers (Natal)

MATCH 5 31 May, Hoffepark, Kimberley

South Africa A 19 (2PG 1DG 2T) **England XV 16** (1G 3PG)
South Africa A: C Dirks (Transvaal); S Berridge (Western Province), J Mulder (Transvaal), C Scholtz (Transvaal), J F van der Westhuizen (Natal); J Stransky (Western Province), J Roux (Transvaal); G Pagel (Western Province), J Dalton (Transvaal), J le Roux (Transvaal), K Wiese (Transvaal), K Otto (Northern Transvaal), A Venter (Orange Free State), A Richter (Northern Transvaal) (*capt*), F van Heerden (Western Province) *Replacement* F C Smit (Western Province) for Wiese (79 mins)
Scorers *Tries:* Scholtz, Stransky *Penalty Goals:* Stransky (2) *Dropped Goal:* Stransky
England XV: Callard; Hopley, Catt, Potter, Adebayo; Barnes, Bates; Rowntree, Dawe, Mallett, Shaw, Poole, Dallaglio, Ryan (*capt*), Ojomoh
Scorers *Try:* Hopley *Conversion:* Callard *Penalty Goals:* Callard (3)
Referee S Neethling (Boland)

MATCH 6 4 June, Loftus Versveld, Pretoria 1st Test

SOUTH AFRICA 15 (5PG) **ENGLAND 32** (2G 5PG 1DG)

It was an afternoon of high emotion on the high veld. The new President, Nelson Mandela, was given a tumultuous welcome by a capacity crowd. Their ecstasy lasted about a quarter of an hour, by which time England were 20 points to the good.

It was perhaps one of the most emphatic starts to any international match. Rob Andrew scored a record-breaking 27 points but it was Tim Rodber who really caught the eye with a staggering performance. Andrew nudged over two early penalties before Clarke rounded off a fine England movement with a try. Then, in the 15th minute, Andrew's chip and catch foxed the South African defence for the fly-half to score only his second international try. South Africa closed to within 11 points through Joubert's five penalties but Andrew, who had earlier added two more penalty goals, rounded things off in style with another penalty and a dropped goal.

SOUTH AFRICA: A J Joubert (Natal); J T Small (Natal), P G Müller (Natal), B Venter (Orange Free State), C M Williams (Western Province); H P le Roux (Transvaal), J H van der Westhuizen (Northern Transvaal); A-H le Roux (Orange Free State), J Allan (Natal), I S Swart (Natal), J J Strydom (Natal), S Atherton (Natal), J F Pienaar (Transvaal) *(capt)*, C P Strauss (Western Province), F J Van Heerden (Western Province)
Scorer *Penalty Goals:* Joubert (5)
ENGLAND: Hull; T Underwood, Carling *(capt)*, De Glanville, R Underwood; Andrew, Morris; Leonard, Moore, Ubogu, Bayfield, Redman, Rodber, Richards, Clarke
Replacement Ojomoh for Richards (55 mins)
Scorers *Tries:* Clarke, Andrew *Conversions:* Andrew (2) *Penalty Goals:* Andrew (5) *Dropped Goal:* Andrew
Referee C J Hawke (New Zealand)

MATCH 7 7 June, Boet Erasmus Stadium, Port Elizabeth

Eastern Province 13 (1G 2PG) **England XV 31** (2G 4PG 1T)
Eastern Province: A Fourie; A Markow, R Potgieter, F Crouse, M Van Vuuren; B Kruger, A Coetzee; G Halford, J Kirsten, W Meyer, A Geldenhuys, E van der Bergh, M Mastert *(capt)*, H Karele, S Tremain *Replacements* D Marshall for Markow (57 mins); N Meyer for Mastert (73 mins); R Lurie for Coetzee (79 mins)
Scorers *Try:* Fourie *Conversion:* Kruger *Penalty Goals:* Kruger (2)
England XV: Callard; Hull, Hopley, Potter, Adebayo; Catt, Bates; Rowntree, Dawe, Mallett, Poole, Shaw, Dallaglio, Ryan *(capt)*, Ojomoh *Replacements* Rodber for Ryan (12 mins); Ubogu for Rowntree (22 mins); R Underwood for Callard (28 mins)
Scorers *Tries:* Bates, Hull (2) *Conversions:* Catt (2) *Penalty Goals:* Callard (2), Catt (2)
Referee P van Blommenstein (Western Province)

MATCH 8 11 June, Newlands, Cape Town 2nd Test

SOUTH AFRICA 27 (1G 5PG 1T) ENGLAND 9 (3PG)

South Africa made five changes from the side taken apart by England a week earlier. Natal's Mark Andrews came in at second row and Transvaal's Johan Roux at scrum-half. The big lock won the ball and the No 9 used it.

It was not quite as simple as that of course, But South Africa certainly had far more about them in every department. There was more steel in their forwards and more intelligence in their back play. In the loose the Springboks rucked with sustained ferocity. Rodber, after his tribulations of midweek, was a shadow of his former self. Only Hull emerged with honours for England.

The scores were tied at half-time, Andrew and Le Roux having exchanged penalty goals. After the interval the kickers, Joubert aiding

England's Jason Leonard steams ahead in the First Test victory over South Africa in Pretoria.

Le Roux, kept things tight on the scoreboard. The English line had to give, though, and it did so 11 minutes from time when Hennie le Roux crossed for a try. Another penalty goal followed before a wonderful break from defence by Van der Westhuizen in the dying minutes sent Joubert to the line.

SOUTH AFRICA: A J Joubert (Natal); J T Small (Natal), P G Müller (Natal), B Venter (Orange Free State), C M Williams (Western Province); H P le Roux (Transvaal), J Roux (Transvaal); I S Swart (Transvaal), J Allan (Natal), J H S le Roux (Transvaal), M G Andrews (Natal), S Atherton (Natal), J F Pienaar (Transvaal) (*capt*), A Richter (Northern Transvaal), I Macdonald (Transvaal) *Replacements* J H van der Westhuizen (Northern Transvaal) for Williams (32 mins); F J van Heerden (Western Province) for Macdonald (69 mins)
Scorers *Tries:* H le Roux, Joubert *Conversion:* Joubert *Penalty Goals:* H le Roux (3), Joubert (2)
ENGLAND: Hull; T Underwood, Carling (*capt*), De Glanville, R Underwood; Andrew, Morris; Leonard, Moore, Ubogu, Bayfield, Redman, Rodber, Clarke, Ojomoh
Scorer *Penalty Goals:* Andrew (3)
Referee C J Hawke (New Zealand)

SCOTLAND TO ARGENTINA 1994

Argentinians speak like Spaniards, react like Italians, dress like the British and buy French furniture. So they say about themselves. They also play fine rugby in their own land, as the Scots found out when they toured Argentina with a squad minus a dozen unavailable capped players. Only a 24-24 draw with Buenos Aires and a 40-14 victory over Cordoba offset four defeats, including the loss of the two Test matches. It was Scotland's worst record in any but one of their 19 tours since 1960. Yet they would have won the Test series and at least one other game if they had taken the chances the forwards created, especially if they had had a reliable goal-kicker.

Scotland's forwards continued the good work they had been doing under Richie Dixon's guidance over the two previous seasons at home. After the dismal 25-11 defeat by Cuyo in Mendoza, the Scottish pack pulled their scrummaging together so well that they held their own in the Tests against a nation who still place heavy emphasis on that aspect of set-piece rugby. The forwards also asserted themselves in the line-out in the first four matches, though they lost their way in the 27-16 defeat by Rosario on the Tuesday between the Tests.

The backs had the wherewithal to follow the policy of 15-man rugby laid down by coach Douglas Morgan, but they achieved it only in the opening draw with Buenos Aires, the highly satisfying win over Cordoba and phases of the Second Test. It was also inhibiting that the four place-kickers used – Mike Dods, Duncan Hodge, Rowen Shepherd and Graham Shiel – managed a total of only 18 goals from 49 attempts, not to mention missed dropped goal attempts. It was a strike rate of less than 37 per cent, whereas their opponents scored 23 from 36, almost 84 per cent. Any one of Dods' five misses would have given the Scots a deserved victory in the opening match. The Gala full-back also missed five in the First Test, which Argentina won by 16-15, and he had only one from three to add to Shiel's two out of five when the Pumas took the series with the 19-17 victory in the Second Test.

Despite defeat in the thoroughly disappointing First Test, the Scots returned to the Ferro Carril Oeste Stadium in Buenos Aires with high hopes of winning the second match of the series, and at times they played pleasing rugby, with an aggressive forward game, collective support and swift movement of the ball. They led 6-0 after 11 minutes and 17-16 after 17 minutes of the second half, but they lost control when it mattered.

Yet the tour was not without benefits to Scottish rugby. Two youngsters, Craig Joiner and Duncan Hodge, emerged with credit and much promise. Joiner, the 20-year-old Melrose wing, played in both Tests, making his mark especially in the Second, when he helped to create Kenny Logan's try and pulled off a memorable try-saving tackle on Martin Teran. Hodge, Watsonians' 19-year-old fly-half, projected himself as a highly talented footballer against Cordoba. The accuracy and choice of his kicking from hand was exemplary, and he had fine judgement in his passing, especially a precisely weighted long ball to Scott Nichol for Logan's try. In that match, under the Cordoba University ground's floodlights, Jeremy Richardson, the Edinburgh Academicals lock, captaining Scotland for the first time, led the tourists with inspiration through an almost complete performance as they scored six tries to two, but he could not repeat the feat against Rosario the following week. Rosario, playing a 15-man game, were by far the best all-round provincial team the Scots met.

THE TOURING PARTY

Manager F C H McLeod **Coach** D W Morgan **Assistant Coach** J R Dixon
Captain A I Reed

FULL-BACK

M Dods (Gala)

THREEQUARTERS

C S Dalgleish (Gala)
I C Jardine (Stirling County)
C A Joiner (Melrose)
K M Logan (Stirling County)
S A Nichol (Selkirk)
R J S Shepherd (Edinburgh Acads)
A G Shiel (Melrose)

HALF-BACKS

D W Hodge (Watsonians)
G P J Townsend (Gala)
B W Redpath ((Melrose)
D W Patterson (West Hartlepool)

FORWARDS

S J Brotherstone (Melrose)
A P Burnell (London Scottish)
S J Campbell (Dundee HSFP)
S W Ferguson (Peebles)
C D Hogg (Melrose)
D J McIvor (Edinburgh Acads)
K D McKenzie (Stirling County)
D S Munro (Glasgow High/Kelvinside)
A I Reed (Bath)
S J Reid (Boroughmuir)
J F Richardson (Edinburgh Acads)
A V Sharp (Bristol)
I R Smith (Gloucester)
F D Wallace (Glasgow High/Kelvinside)
P Walton (Northampton)
A G J Watt (Glasgow High/Kelvinside)

TOUR RECORD

All matches Played 6 Won 1 Drawn 1 Lost 4 Points for 123 Against 125
International matches Played 2 Lost 2 Points for 32 Against 35

SCORING DETAILS

All matches						**International matches**					
For:	13T	2C	16PG	2DG	123 Pts	For:	1T	–	8PG	1DG	32 Pts
Against:	11T	8C	13PG	5DG	125 Pts	Against:	2T	2C	6PG	1DG	35 Pts

MATCH DETAILS

1994	OPPONENTS	VENUE	RESULT
25 May	Buenos Aires	Buenos Aires	D 24-24
28 May	Cuyo	Mendoza	L 11-25
31 May	Cordoba	Cordoba	W 40-14
4 June	ARGENTINA	Buenos Aires	L 15-16
7 June	Rosario	Rosario	L 16-27
11 June	ARGENTINA	Buenos Aires	L 17-19

Appearances: 5 – Joiner, Logan; 4 – Dalgleish, Jardine, Nichol*, Redpath, Sharp*, Townsend, Watt*; 3 – Brotherstone, Burnell, Campbell, Dods, Ferguson, Hodge, Hogg, McIvor, McKenzie, Munro, Reed, Reid, Richardson, Shepherd, Shiel, Smith, Wallace, Walton; 2 – Patterson *includes appearances as a replacement*
Scorers: 27 – Dods (9PG); 24 – Shepherd (1T 2C 5PG); 15 – Logan (3T); 8 – Hodge (1T 1DG); 10 – Dalgleish, Watt (both 2T); 6 – Shiel (2PG); 5 – Jardine, Joiner, McIvor, Nichol (all 1T); 3 – Townsend (1DG)

MATCH 1 25 May, Ferro Carril Oeste, Buenos Aires

Buenos Aires 24 (1G 4PG 1T) **Scotland XV 24** (3PG 3T)
Buenos Aires: R Bullrich; H Rivarola, E Laborde, F Garcia, D Albanese; D Forrester, F Salvat; M Grotte, M Bosch, G Holmgren, G Ugartemendia (*capt*), M Lerga, D Devries, P J Camerlinckx, P Traini
Scorers *Tries:* Rivarola, Lerga *Conversion:* Forrester *Penalty Goals:* Forrester (4)
Scotland XV: Dods; Joiner, Nichol, Shiel, Dalgleish; Townsend, Patterson; Sharp, McKenzie, Ferguson, Richardson, Reed (*capt*), Walton, Reid, Smith
Scorers *Tries:* Dalgleish (2), Nichol *Penalty Goals:* Dods (3)
Referee S Borsani (Rosario)

MATCH 2 28 May, Independiente Rivadavia, Mendoza

Cuyo 25 (2G 1PG 1DG 1T) **Scotland XV 11** (2PG 1T)
Cuyo: M Brandi; E Saurina, P Cremaschi, C Cipitelli (*capt*), M Roby; G Andia, M Diaz; R Grau, F Bartolini, M Miranda, P Pascual, P Lambert, M Cassone, G Correa Llano, M Bertranou
Scorers *Tries:* Bertranou, Cassone, Diaz *Conversions:* Cremaschi (2)
Penalty Goal: Cremaschi *Dropped Goal:* Andia
Scotland XV: Logan; Joiner, Jardine, Shepherd, Dalgleish; Hodge, Redpath; Watt, Brotherstone, Burnell (*capt*), Munro, Campbell, McIvor, Reid, Wallace
Replacement Sharp for Munro (temp)
Scorers *Try:* Hodge *Penalty Goals:* Shepherd (2)
Referee E Sklar (Buenos Aires)

MATCH 3 31 May, Cordoba University Stadium

Cordoba 14 (2G) **Scotland XV 40** (2G 1PG 1DG 4T)
Cordoba: J M Luna; G Tomalino, G Ussher, I Merlo, F Pereyra; F Grangetto, J Dragotto; F Zarate, I Ferreyra, P Sanchez, D Pereyra (*capt*), J Simes, G Piergentilli, D Rotondo, S Irazoqui *Replacement* M Caldo for Merlo (temp)
Scorers *Tries:* Dragotto (2) *Conversions:* Luna (2)
Scotland XV: Shepherd; Joiner, Nichol, Jardine, Logan; Hodge, Redpath; Watt,

Brotherstone, Ferguson, Richardson (*capt*), Campbell, McIvor, Hogg, Wallace
Replacement Dalgleish for Joiner (68 mins)
Scorers *Tries:* Jardine, Joiner, Logan, McIvor, Shepherd, Watt
Conversions: Shepherd (2) *Penalty Goal:* Shepherd *Dropped Goal:* Hodge
Referee E Casenave (Buenos Aires)

MATCH 4 4 June, Ferro Carril Oeste, Buenos Aires **1st Test**

ARGENTINA 16 (1G 3PG) **SCOTLAND 15** (5PG)
ARGENTINA: S E Meson (Tucumán); M J Teran Nougues (Tucumán), D Cuesta Silva (San Isidro), M H Loffreda (San Isidro) (*capt*), G M Jorge (Pucara); G J del Castillo (Jockey Club, Rosario), N Fernandez Miranda (Hindu); M Corral (San Isidro), J J Angelillo (San Isidro), E P Noriega (Hindu), G A Llanes (La Plata), P L Sporleder (Curupayti), R Martin (San Isidro), P J Camerlinckx (Regatas), C Viel Temperley (Newman)
Scorers *Try:* Teran *Conversion:* Meson *Penalty Goals:* Meson (3)
SCOTLAND: Dods; Joiner, Jardine, Shiel, Logan; Townsend, Redpath; Sharp, McKenzie, Burnell, Munro, Reed (*capt*), Walton, Hogg, Smith
Scorer *Penalty Goals:* Dods (5)
Referee W J Erickson (Australia)

MATCH 5 7 June, Jockey Club, Rosario

Rosario 27 (1G 2PG 3DG 1T) **Scotland XV 16** (2PG 2T)
Rosario: E Jurado; L Bouza, A Caffaro Rossi, F del Castillo, G Romero Acuna; G del Castillo, R Crexell (*capt*); H Cespedes, C Promancio, S Pietrobon, N Bosicovich, R Perez, M Carmona, C Ovieda, P Baraldi *Replacement* M Sugasti for Carmona
Scorers *Tries:* Caffaro Rossi, Crexell *Conversion:* Crexell *Penalty Goals:* Crexell (2)
Dropped Goals: G del Castillo (2), Jurado
Scotland XV: Shepherd; Dalgleish, Townsend, Nichol, Logan; Hodge, Patterson; Watt, Brotherstone, Ferguson, Richardson (*capt*), Campbell, McIvor, Reid, Wallace
Scorers *Tries:* Logan, Watt *Penalty Goals:* Shepherd (2)
Referee R Bordcoch (Cordoba)

MATCH 6 11 June, Ferro Carril Oeste, Buenos Aires **2nd Test**

ARGENTINA 19 (1G 3PG 1DG) **SCOTLAND 17** (3PG 1DG 1T)
ARGENTINA: S E Meson (Tucumán); M J Teran Nougues (Tucumán), D Cuesta Silva (San Isidro), M H Loffreda (San Isidro) (*capt*), G M Jorge (Pucara); G J del Castillo (Jockey Club, Rosario), N Fernandez Miranda (Hindu); F Mendez (Tucumán), J J Angelillo (San Isidro), E P Noriega (Hindu), G A Llanes (La Plata), P L Sporleder (Curupayti), R Martin (San Isidro), J M Santamarina (Tucumán), C Viel Temperley (Newman)
Scorers *Try:* Martin *Conversion:* Meson *Penalty Goals:* Meson (3)
Dropped Goal: Del Castillo
SCOTLAND: Dods; Joiner, Jardine, Shiel, Logan; Townsend, Redpath; Sharp, McKenzie, Burnell, Munro, Reed (*capt*), Watton, Hogg, Smith *Replacements* Watt (temp) and for Sharp (70 mins); Nichol for Logan (74 mins)
Scorers *Try:* Logan *Penalty Goals:* Dods, Shiel (2) *Dropped Goal:* Townsend
Referee W J Erickson (Australia)

IRELAND TO AUSTRALIA 1994

Ireland's third tour of Australia was daunting in prospect and disappointing in retrospect. For a start the itinerary was a tough one, involving warm-up matches against an Australian XV and both leading state sides as well as two Tests against the world champions. On top of that Richard Wallace and Nick Popplewell, two of Ireland's automatic choices for the 1994 International Championship, were unavailable because of injury.

At least the tourists went on a spree in the opening match, running up an Irish tour record with a 64-8 win against Western Australia, but thereafter it was a tale of disaster. New South Wales thrashed them 55-18, leaving coach Gerry Murphy 'appalled' at his team's lack of skill. Then ACT, Queensland (albeit winning only through a last-minute penalty from Michael Lynagh), and an Australian second XV exposed the visitors' shortcomings, forcing the Irish to go into the Test series on a platform of four successive defeats.

Losses in the Tests came as no surprise, therefore, but there were some crumbs of comfort for the Irish management. Of the 12 uncapped players who started the tour, five established serious challenges as contenders for places in Ireland's World Cup squad. Hooker Keith Wood, son of former Ireland and Lions prop Gordon, overtook Terry Kingston and impressed in the Tests with his all-round skills and pace in the loose. Ballymena's young redhead, Jonathan Bell, gave notice of his potential as an intelligent threequarter, and there were also tidy Test performances by two other newcomers, David Corkery and Gabriel Fulcher, in the pack. Nor did Niall Woods, standing in for Wallace at left wing, disgrace himself opposite David Campese in the internationals.

THE TOURING PARTY

Manager F Sowman **Assistant Manager** L G Butler **Coach** G Murphy
Captain M T Bradley

FULL-BACKS

C M P O'Shea (Lansdowne)
J E Staples (London Irish)

THREEQUARTERS

S P Geoghegan (London Irish)
J C Bell (Ballymena & Loughborough U)
N K P J Woods (Blackrock Coll)
P P A Danaher (Garryowen)
M J Field (Malone)
M P Ridge (Blackrock Coll)
B Walsh (Cork Const)

HALF-BACKS

E P Elwood (Lansdowne)
A N McGowan (Blackrock Coll)
M T Bradley (Cork Const)
A C P Rolland (Blackrock Coll)
***N A Hogan** (Terenure Coll)

FORWARDS

P J Soden (Cork Const)
P M Clohessy (Young Munster)
J J Fitzgerald (Young Munster)
G F Halpin (London Irish)
T J Kingston (Dolphin)
K G M Wood (Garryowen)
G M Fulcher (Cork Const)
M J Galwey (Shannon)
N P J Francis (Old Belvedere)
J Davidson (Dungannon)
P J Hogan (Garryowen)
W D McBride (Malone)
D Corkery (Cork Const)
B F Robinson (Ballymena)
V C P Costello (St Mary's Coll)
P S Johns (Dungannon)
R K Wilson (Instonians)
***B M Cronin** (Garryowen)
***S J Byrne** (Blackrock Coll)

**Replacement during tour*

TOUR RECORD

All matches Played 8 Won 2 Lost 6 Points for 177 Against 254
International matches Played 2 Lost 2 Points for 31 Against 65

SCORING DETAILS

All matches						**International matches**					
For:	17T	13C	20PG	2DG	177 Pts	For:	3T	2C	3PG	1DG	31 Pts
Against:	34T	15C	18PG	–	254 Pts	Against:	8T	2C	7PG	–	65 Pts

MATCH DETAILS

1994	OPPONENTS	VENUE	RESULT
18 May	Western Australia	Perth	W 64-8
22 May	New South Wales	Sydney	L 18-55
25 May	Australian Capital Territory	Canberra	L 9-22
29 May	Queensland	Brisbane	L 26-29
1 June	Australia XV	Mount Isa	L 9-57
5 June	AUSTRALIA	Brisbane	L 13-33
8 June	New South Wales Country	Lismore	W 20-18
11 June	AUSTRALIA	Brisbane	L 18-32

Appearances: 6 – Woods, Bradley, Bell*, Robinson**; 5 – Geoghegan, Staples, Elwood, Clohessy, Corkery, Johns, O'Shea*, Field*, Halpin*; 4 – Ridge, Fitzgerald, Wood, Davidson, Danaher, Fulcher, Francis, Galwey*, Costello*, Kingston*, McBride*; 3 – Walsh, McGowan, Soden; 2 – Rolland, O'Connell, Byrne*; 1 – Hogan, Wilson, Cronin, Hogan*
**includes appearances as a replacement*
Scorers: 35 – Elwood (10C 4PG 1DG); 33 – McGowan (11PG); 29 – O'Shea (1T 3C 5PG 1DG); 15 – Field (3T); 10 – Johns, Kingston, Francis (all 2T); 5 – Geoghegan, Staples, Wood, Clohessy, Davidson, Costello, Bell (all 1T)

MATCH 1 18 May, Perth

Western Australia 8 (1PG 1T) **Ireland XV 64** (8G 1PG 1T)
Western Australia: R Smith; G Hamilton, D Hamilton, S Bunce, D Dunbar; T Fearn, M Ryburn; J Tepania, P Roberts (*capt*), G Thompson, T Thomas, S Vitali, R Walters, D Gleghorn, J O'Callaghan *Replacement* G Johnson for Ryburn (40 mins)
Scorers *Try:* O'Callaghan *Penalty Goal:* Fearn
Ireland XV: O'Shea; Geoghegan, Field, Ridge, Staples; Elwood, Bradley (*capt*); Fitzgerald, Wood, Clohessy, Galwey, Davidson, Costello, Johns, Corkery
Replacements Kingston for Wood (31 mins); Robinson for Costello (39 mins)
Scorers *Tries:* Costello, Kingston (2), Davidson, Field (3), Johns, O'Shea
Conversions: Elwood (8) *Penalty Goal:* Elwood
Referee A Cole (Queensland)

MATCH 2 22 May, Waratah Stadium, Sydney

New South Wales 55 (6G 1PG 2T) **Ireland XV 18** (1G 2PG 1T)
New South Wales: T Kelaher; D Campese, M Burke, R Tombs, D Junee; T Wallace, S Payne; A Daly, P Kearns (*capt*), M Hartill, T Kava, W Waugh, T Dempsey, M Brial, S Domoni
Scorers *Tries:* Payne (2), Tombs (2), Campese (2), Brial, Waugh *Conversions:* Wallace (6)
Penalty Goal: Wallace
Ireland XV: Staples; Geoghegan, Bell, Danaher, Woods; Elwood, Bradley (*capt*); Soden, Kingston, Halpin, Francis, Fulcher, Robinson, Wilson, McBride *Replacement* Galwey for Wilson (38 mins)
Scorers *Tries:* Francis, Bell *Conversion:* Elwood *Penalty Goals:* Elwood (2)
Referee B Leask (Queensland)

MATCH 3 25 May, Manuka Oval, Canberra

Australian Capital Territory 22 (2G 1PG 1T) **Ireland XV 9** (3PG)
Australian Capital Territory: R Kafer; D McLachlan, J Swan, M O'Connor (*capt*),

D Grimmond; P Cornish, G Gregan; M Harley, M Caputo, T Hutchinson, F Mafi, C Sweeny, B Jones, C Bretton, I Fenukitau *Replacement* L O'Connor for Swan (38 mins)
Scorers *Tries:* Grimmond, M O'Connor, Swan *Conversions:* M O'Connor (2) *Penalty Goal:* M O'Connor
Ireland XV: Staples; Walsh, Field, Ridge, Woods; McGowan, Rolland; Halpin, Byrne, Clohessy, Galwey (*capt*), Davidson, Hogan, Johns, Corkery *Replacements* Costello for Galwey (temp); Costello for Hogan (38 mins); Bell for Field (51 mins)
Scorer *Penalty Goals:* McGowan (3)
Referee B Kinsey (New South Wales)

MATCH 4 29 May, Ballymore Oval, Brisbane

Queensland 29 (2G 5PG) **Ireland XV 26** (2G 3PG 1DG)
Queensland: M Pini; B Lea, A Herbert, D Herbert, D Smith; M Lynagh, P Slattery (*capt*); C Lillicrap, M Foley, A Skeggs, R McCall, G Morgan, J Eales, S Scott-Young, D Wilson *Replacements* M Connors for Morgan (temp); B Johnstone for Slattery (41 mins); P Carozza for Lea (56 mins)
Scorers *Tries:* Slattery, D Herbert *Conversions:* Lynagh (2) *Penalty Goals:* Lynagh (5)
Ireland XV: O'Shea; Geoghegan, Bell, Danaher, Woods; Elwood, Bradley (*capt*); Fitzgerald, Wood, Clohessy, Fulcher, Francis, Robinson, Johns, Corkery *Replacement* Halpin for Clohessy (75 mins)
Scorers *Tries:* Geoghegan, Wood *Conversions:* O'Shea (2) *Penalty Goals:* O'Shea (3) *Dropped Goal:* Elwood
Referee W Erickson (New South Wales)

MATCH 5 1 June, Mount Isa

Australian XV 57 (3G 2PG 6T) **Ireland XV 9** (3PG)
Australian XV: A Apps; A Murdoch, J Roff, P Cornish, R Constable; T Mandrusiak, M Catchpole; D Crowley (*capt*), T Dalton, G Websdale, J Nowlan, R Korst, W Ofahengaue, F Finau, B Robinson *Replacements* O Finegan for Finau (6 mins); R Harry for Ofahengaue (48 mins); P Howard for Cornish (67 mins)
Scorers *Tries:* Catchpole (3), Apps, Dalton, Howard, Mandrusiak, Murdoch, Ofahengaue *Conversions:* Mandrusiak (3) *Penalty Goals:* Mandrusiak (2)
Ireland XV: Staples; Walsh, Field, Ridge, Bell; McGowan, Rolland; Soden, Kingston (*capt*), Halpin, Fulcher, Davidson, O'Connell, Costello, McBride *Replacements* Bradley for Rolland (38 mins); O'Shea for Walsh (51 mins); Robinson for Fulcher (60 mins); Byrne for Robinson (70 mins)
Scorer *Penalty Goals:* McGowan (3)
Referee P Marshall (New South Wales)

MATCH 6 5 June, Ballymore, Brisbane 1st Test

AUSTRALIA 33 (1G 2PG 4T) IRELAND 13 (1G 2PG)

Ireland had never previously lost a tour Test in Australia. Even so, the ultra-conservative Aussie bookmakers had the home team as 8-1-on favourites to win the match, odds which never looked misplaced as the Wallabies, usually slow starters to their Test seasons, sailed to a comfortable victory by five tries to one.

Arithmetically, at least, Ireland were still in the hunt at 3-13 at the interval. Psychologically, however, the damage had already been inflicted on the Irish pack. Well before half-time Garrick Morgan and John Eales were on their way to establishing line-out supremacy by the ratio of 2:1, while elsewhere the entire pack was rucking and mauling with awesome efficiency.

Early on, Australia's threequarters clearly missed the effectiveness of Jason Little and Tim Horan, who were both injured, and in the first half the replacement centres struggled to cope with the greater pace of Test rugby. The four second-half tries scored by the backs, however, underlined the alacrity with which Australian players nowadays adapt to international sport.

AUSTRALIA: M Pini (Queensland); D I Campese (NSW), M Burke (NSW), M O'Connor (ACT), D Smith (Queensland); M P Lynagh (Queensland) (*capt*), P J Slattery (Queensland); A J Daly (NSW), P N Kearns (NSW), E J A McKenzie (NSW), J A Eales (Queensland), G J Morgan (Queensland), I Tabua (Queensland), B T Gavin (NSW), D J Wilson (Queensland)
Scorers *Tries:* Tabua, Lynagh, Campese, Burke, Smith *Conversion:* Lynagh
Penalty Goals: Lynagh (2)
IRELAND: O'Shea; Geoghegan, Bell, Danaher, Woods; Elwood, Bradley (*capt*); Fitzgerald, Wood, Clohessy, Galwey, Francis, Robinson, Johns, Corkery
Replacements McBride for Galwey (28 mins); Field for O'Shea (83 mins)
Scorers *Try:* Johns *Conversion:* Elwood *Penalty Goals:* Elwood, O'Shea
Referee J Dumé (France)

MATCH 7 8 June, Lismore

New South Wales Country 18 (1PG 3T) **Ireland XV 20** (5PG 1T)
New South Wales Country: T Eddy; M Sykes, P O'Brien, C Coffey, S Rutledge; S Salter, S Merrick; A Baldwin, J Ives, G Clarke, J Nowlan, J Langford, N Cobcroft, H Williams, A McCalman (*capt*) *Replacement* W Petty for Clarke (51 mins)
Scorers *Tries:* Sykes, Nowlan, Rutledge *Penalty Goal:* Salter
Ireland XV: Staples; Walsh, Field, Ridge, Woods; McGowan, Hogan; Soden, Kingston (*capt*), Halpin, Costello, Davidson, O'Connell, Cronin, McBride
Scorers *Try:* Staples *Penalty Goals:* McGowan (5)
Referee K O'Halloran (Queensland)

MATCH 8 11 June, Sydney Football Stadium 2nd Test

AUSTRALIA 32 (1G 5PG 2T) **IRELAND 18** (1G 1PG 1DG 1T)

Ireland were completely written off by the critics long before Joel Dumé set this last match of the tour in motion. Yet they emerged, albeit from another defeat, with their pride intact after Australian coach Bob Dwyer had complimented them on their dramatic improvement since Ballymore.

Australia, who stepped up a gear from their performance of six days earlier, rattled up a 21-6 lead by half-time. All credit to Ireland, therefore, for scoring two tries and staging a spirited recovery in which Keith Wood was prominent as a star of the first magnitude. The young Garryowen hooker was here, there and everywhere in both tight and loose and was, in the words of his coach, Gerry Murphy, 'the outstanding player on the pitch'.

The Irish, however, were guilty of frequently infringing and Michael Lynagh gratefully accepted opportunities to inflate his side's score. He kicked five penalty goals and collected 17 points altogether, bringing his points tally in Tests past 800.

AUSTRALIA: M Burke (NSW); D I Campese (NSW), R C Tombs (NSW), D Herbert (Queensland), D Smith (Queensland); M P Lynagh (Queensland) (*capt*), P J Slattery (Queensland); A J Daly (NSW), P N Kearns (NSW), E J A McKenzie (NSW), J A Eales (Queensland), G J Morgan (Queensland), I Tabua (Queensland), B T Gavin (NSW), D J Wilson (Queensland) *Replacement* R Constable (Queensland) for Campese (temp) and for Smith (75 mins)
Scorers *Tries:* Herbert, Wilson, Tabua *Conversion:* Lynagh *Penalty Goals:* Lynagh (5)
IRELAND: O'Shea; Geoghegan, Bell, Danaher, Woods; Elwood, Bradley (*capt*); Fitzgerald, Wood, Clohessy, Fulcher, Francis, Robinson, Johns, Corkery
Scorers *Tries:* Clohessy, Francis *Conversion:* O'Shea *Penalty Goal:* O'Shea *Dropped Goal:* O'Shea
Referee J Dumé (France)

WALES TO CANADA AND THE SOUTH SEAS 1994

For the first time since taking over as national coach in the autumn of 1991, Alan Davies had at his disposal a near to full-strength Welsh party for a summer tour (Lions demands had diluted the Welsh squad that toured Africa in 1993). True, Robert Jones was excused to play for Western Province in South Africa and three of the original choices withdrew owing to injury; nevertheless, the coach valued greatly the opportunity of working daily with a squad which achieved a creditable return of four wins in five games.

Several younger players who had been on the verge of honours for some time were finally blooded at Test level. Ian Buckett, Robin McBryde, Paul John, Steve Williams and Gwilym Wilkins came through their Test debuts with flying colours. Moreover, Richie Collins, a late replacement for Mark Perego, resumed his international career by promptly establishing himself as Wales' leading openside flanker.

The tour was a happy one – in sharp contrast to the ill-starred Welsh visit to Australia in 1991 that presaged Davies's arrival as coach. Much of the credit for the party's good spirit was due to the high regard the players held for their captain, Ieuan Evans, who set records every time he took the field.

THE TOURING PARTY

Manager R L Norster **Coach** A B C Davies **Captain** I C Evans

FULL-BACKS

M A Rayer (Cardiff)
A Clement (Swansea)

THREEQUARTERS

I C Evans (Llanelli)
G Wilkins (Bridgend)
D Manley (Pontypridd)
W T Proctor (Llanelli)
M R Hall (Cardiff)
N G Davies (Llanelli)
N Boobyer (Llanelli)

HALF-BACKS

A Davies (Cardiff)
N R Jenkins (Pontypridd)
R H StJ B Moon (Llanelli)
P John (Pontypridd)

FORWARDS

R L Evans (Llanelli)
I M Buckett (Swansea)
J D Davies (Neath)
H Williams-Jones (Llanelli)
R C McBryde (Swansea)

G R Jenkins (Swansea)
P Arnold (Swansea)
P T Davies (Llanelli)
G O Llewellyn (Neath)
A H Copsey (Llanelli)
H T Taylor (Cardiff)
E W Lewis (Llanelli)
R G Collins (Pontypridd)
L S Quinnell (Llanelli)
S M Williams (Neath)

TOUR RECORD

All matches Played 5 Won 4 Lost 1 Points for 111 Against 85
International matches Played 4 Won 3 Lost 1 Points for 83 Against 66

SCORING DETAILS

All matches

For:	8T	7C	19PG	–	111 Pts
Against:	5T	3C	18PG	–	85 Pts

International matches

For:	5T	5C	16PG	–	83 Pts
Against:	4T	2C	14PG	–	66 Pts

MATCH DETAILS

1994	OPPONENTS	VENUE	RESULT
8 June	Canadian Select XV	Hamilton	W 28-19
11 June	CANADA	Toronto	W 33-15
18 June	FIJI	Suva	W 23-8
22 June	TONGA	Nuku'alofa	W 18-9
25 June	WESTERN SAMOA	Apia	L 9-34

Appearances: 5 – Collins, N Davies, Taylor*; 4 – N Jenkins, G Jenkins, I Evans, P Davies*; 3 – Clement, Hall, J Davies, Quinnell, Rayer, Proctor, Moon, R Evans, Llewellyn, Williams-Jones*, Copsey*; 2 – John, Buckett, Arnold, Boobyer, Lewis, Wilkins, Williams*; 1 – Manley, A Davies, McBryde, Clement* *includes appearances as a replacement*
Scorers: 58 – N Jenkins (5C 16PG); 13 – A Davies (2C 3PG); 10 – Hall (2T); 5 – Arnold, Clement, Manley, I Evans, Rayer, Collins (all 1T)

MATCH 1 8 June, Hamilton

Canadian Select XV 19 (1G 4PG) **Wales XV 28** (2G 3PG 1T)
Canadian Select XV: L Subarana; W Stanley, S MacKinnon, D Clarke, C Smith; B Ross, I MacKay; K Wirachowski, D Nikkas, R Bice, G Ennis (*capt*), C Whittaker, J Hutchinson, M Schmid, B Breen
Scorers *Try:* MacKinnon *Conversion:* Rees *Penalty Goals:* Rees (4)
Wales XV: Clement; Manley, Hall, N Davies, Wilkins; N Jenkins, John; Buckett, G Jenkins, J Davies, P Davies (*capt*), Arnold, Taylor, Quinnell, Collins
Replacement Williams for Quinnell (25 mins)
Scorers *Tries:* Arnold, Clement, Manley *Conversions:* N Jenkins (2)
Penalty Goals: N Jenkins (3)
Referee D Mews (Calgary)

MATCH 2 11 June, Fletcher's Fields, Toronto 1st Test

CANADA 15 (5PG) **WALES 33** (3G 4PG)

Wales avenged their 24-26 defeat at Cardiff at the hands of the Canadians the previous November with an emphatic victory. It was also a suitable retort to some pretty unpleasant remarks made about Wales and the Welsh in a Canadian rugby magazine.

Canada, their confidence sky-high after beating the full French side a week earlier, had first use of a stiff wind and Gareth Rees quickly put them 9-0 ahead. But two Mike Hall tries, both converted by Neil Jenkins, who added a penalty into the wind, gave Wales a slim two-point lead at half-time.

Ieuan Evans inspired his men with a try early in the second half. It was the captain's 20th for Wales, equalling the career records set by Gerald Davies and Gareth Edwards in 1978, and heralded a Welsh scoring spree which brought 16 points without reply.

CANADA: D S Stewart (UBC Old Boys); R Toews (Vancouver Meralomas), S D Gray (Kats), I C Stuart (Vancouver RC) (*capt*), D C Lougheed (Toronto Welsh); G L Rees (Castaways & Oxford U), J D Graf (UBC Old Boys); E A Evans (UBC Old Boys & IBM Tokyo), K F Svoboda (Ajax Wands), D C Jackart (UBC Old Boys), A J Charron (Ottawa Irish), M James (Burnaby), G I MacKinnon (Ex-Britannia Lions), C McKenzie (UBC Old Boys), I Gordon (James Bay AA) *Replacement* G D Ennis (Kats & Suntory) for McKenzie (54 mins)
Scorer *Penalty Goals:* Rees (5)
WALES: Rayer; I Evans (*capt*), Hall, N Davies, Proctor; N Jenkins, Moon; R Evans, G Jenkins, J Davies, P Davies, Llewellyn, Taylor, Quinnell, Collins *Replacement* Clement for I Evans (57 mins)
Scorers *Tries:* Hall (2), I Evans *Conversions:* N Jenkins (3)
Penalty Goals: N Jenkins (4)
Referee I Rogers (South Africa)

MATCH 3 18 June, National Stadium, Suva 2nd Test

FIJI 8 (1PG 1T) **WALES 23** (2G 3PG)

Poor line-out play apart, this was a satisfactory display by a Welsh side understandably beginning to show signs of fatigue in the middle of a demanding rugby year. In winning their seventh international in eight games since January, Wales scarcely overstretched themselves against a side which was bolstered by the presence of eight New Zealand-based players.

Adrian Davies proved a capable stand-in at fly-half for Neil Jenkins, landing three of his four kicks at goal in the first half to contribute to Wales' 17-3 lead at the interval. Two more successful kicks stretched the tourists clear before massive prop Joe Veitayaki charged over for Fiji's only try in injury time.

Ieuan Evans played on the wing for Wales for the 45th time, passing the record set by the legendary Ken Jones of Newport between 1947 and 1957.

FIJI: R Bogisa; J Vidiri, J Toloi, E Nauga, P Tuidraki; P Rayasi, J McLennan; R Williams, E Batimala, J Veitayaki, I Tawake (*capt*), I Savai, S Matalulu, A Mocelutu, J Campbell *Replacement* M Korovou for Campbell (58 mins)
Scorers *Try:* Veitayaki *Penalty Goal:* Bogisa
WALES: Rayer; I Evans (*capt*), Boobyer, N Davies, Proctor; A Davies, Moon; R Evans, McBryde, Williams-Jones, Copsey, Arnold, Taylor, Lewis, Collins *Replacement* P Davies for Lewis (73 mins)
Scorers *Tries:* Rayer, Collins *Conversions:* A Davies (2) *Penalty Goals:* A Davies (3)
Referee E Sklar (Argentina)

MATCH 4 22 June, National Stadium, Nuku'alofa 3rd Test

TONGA 9 (3PG) **WALES 18** (6PG)

Wales came through an error-strewn match with their 100 per cent record intact. Once again they were unable to impose any design at the line-out, and even in rucks and mauls they were hustled off the ball by the energetic Tongans.

The islanders had warmed up for the Test with an unbeaten four-match visit to New Zealand, but their tendency to infringe gave Neil Jenkins the chances to kick Wales to victory. The Pontypridd man, paired with his club colleague Paul John at scrum-half, kicked immaculately to land penalty goals in the 2nd, 18th, 23rd, 38th, 44th and 82nd minutes. Sateki Tu'ipulotu kicked three from five attempts for Tonga.

Ieuan Evans thus led his team to their fifth successive away win, a new Welsh international record.

TONGA: S Tu'ipulotu ('Otu Felenite & Manly); T Va'enuku (Police), F Manukia (Siutaka), P Latu (Vaheloto), S Taupeaafu ('Otu Felenite); E Vunipola (Toakoma'afu), M Vunipola (Toakoma'afu); T Lutua (Police), F Vunipola (Siutaka) (*capt*), U Fa ('Otu Felenite), F Mafi ('Otu Felenite), V Taumoepeau (Kolomomotu'a), T Loto'ahea (Police), T Vikilani (Kolofo'ou), K Tu'ipulotu (Siutaka)
Replacement F Masila (Kolomotu'a) (temp) for Mafi
Scorer *Penalty Goals:* Tu'ipulotu (3)
WALES: Clement; I Evans (*capt*), Hall, Boobyer, Wilkins; N Jenkins, John; Buckett, G Jenkins, Williams-Jones, Copsey, Llewellyn, Taylor. Williams, Collins
Replacement N Davies for Hall (63 mins)
Scorer *Penalty Goals:* N Jenkins (6)
Referee E Sklar (Argentina)

MATCH 5 25 June, Chanel College, Moamoa, Apia 4th Test

WESTERN SAMOA 34 (2G 5PG 1T) WALES 9 (3PG)

Ieuan Evans became his country's most-capped threequarter and his clubmate Phil Davies set a new record for a Welsh forward, passing Graham Price's 41 appearances. But both, no doubt, would gladly have preferred to finish the tour by celebrating another win.

It was not to be. The Samoans repeated their Cardiff shock of 1991, resorting to the direct approach in attack and the aggressive defence that had characterised their famous World Cup win. In fairness, Wales did find the 100-degrees Fahrenheit conditions distressing. They were only 9-14 adrift at the interval, but the debilitating heat – described later as 'extraordinary and dangerous' by team doctor Rob Leyshon – took its toll on the players in the second half.

Pat Lam's chip-and-chase try after 71 minutes and Brian Lima's second try, scored in the sixth minute of injury time, slightly flattered the hosts. But the fact remained that Wales suffered the heaviest defeat ever inflicted by a so-called junior nation on a fully fledged senior International Board country.

WESTERN SAMOA: A Aiolupo (Moata'a); B Lima (Marist/St Joseph's), T M Vaega (Moata'a), F Tuilagi (Marist/St Joseph's), T Samania (Moata'a); D J Kellett (Ponsonby), V Vitale (Vaiala); P Fatialofa (Manurewa) (*capt*), T Leiasamaivao (Avalon), G Latu (Vaimoso), M L Birtwistle (Pukekohe), M Keenan (Pontypool), S L Vaifale

(Marist/St Joseph's), P R Lam (Marist & Auckland), M Iupeli (Marist/St Joseph's)
Replacements S Kaleta (Auckland) for Keenan (temp and 58 mins); D Mika (Marist/St Joseph's) for Lam (76 mins)
Scorers *Tries:* Lima (2), Lam *Conversions:* Kellett (2) *Penalty Goals:* Kellett (5)
WALES: Rayer; I Evans (*capt*), Clement, N Davies, Proctor; N Jenkins, Moon; R Evans, G Jenkins, J Davies, P Davies, Llewellyn, Lewis, Quinnell, Collins
Replacements Copsey for Davies (45 mins); Williams-Jones for R Evans (76 mins); Taylor for Quinnell (79 mins)
Scorer *Penalty Goals:* N Jenkins (3)
Referee B Leask (Australia)

FRANCE TO CANADA AND NEW ZEALAND 1994

There were elements of both the ridiculous and the sublime to the tour. Early on, France lost to Canada in Nepean, where Philippe Sella was dismissed for allegedly throwing a punch at an opponent. Then, in New Zealand, the visitors' unconvincing form continued when they were beaten by North Harbour, and their woes were compounded by the two-match suspension meted out to Xavier Blond, the acting captain, who was sent off in the Nelson Bays match.

The turning-point of the trip came one week before the first of the Tests against the All Blacks. France showed immense character, not to mention considerable restraint, in withstanding excessive physical aggression to defeat the New Zealand XV at Wanganui. Philippe Benetton was head-butted in an incident judged to be accidental and Laurent Benezech was on the receiving end of a nasty raking. Yet the French kept their cool to run out 33-25 winners after leading by one point at the break.

After that there was no stopping the tourists. New Zealand were routed in the First Test and a typically French try late in the Second left the All Blacks reflecting on a 2-0 defeat in a home series for the first time since 1949.

THE TOURING PARTY

Manager G Laporte **Coach** P Berbizier **Captain** P Saint-André

FULL-BACKS

J-L Sadourny (Colomiers)
S Viars (Brive)

THREEQUARTERS

P Saint-André (Montferrand)
E Ntamack (Toulouse)
W Téchoueyres (SBUC Bordeaux)
L Leflamand (Lyon)
P Sella (Agen)
Y Delaigue (Toulon)
F Mesnel (Racing Club de France)
T Lacroix (Dax)
***P Carbonneau** (Toulouse)

HALF-BACKS

B Bellot (Graulhet)
C Deylaud (Toulouse)
A Macabiau (Perpignan)
G Accoceberry (Bègles-Bordeaux)
***F Galthié** (Colomiers)

FORWARDS

L Seigne (Merignac)
L Benezech (Racing Club de France)
L Armary (Lourdes)
C Califano (Toulouse)
J-M Gonzalez (Bayonne)
J-F Tordo (Nice)

O Merle (Grenoble)
O Roumat (Dax)
O Brouzet (Grenoble)
A Benazzi (Agen)
X Blond (Racing Club de France)
L Cabannes (Racing Club de France)
P Benetton (Agen)
L Loppy (Toulon)
S Dispagne (Narbonne)
M Cecillon (Bourgoin)
** Replacement during tour*

TOUR RECORD

All matches Played 10 Won 7 Lost 3 Points for 303 Against 209
International matches Played 3 Won 2 Lost 1 Points for 61 Against 46

SCORING DETAILS

All matches

For:	34T	23C	23PG	6DG	303 Pts
Against:	15T	7C	38PG	2DG	209 Pts

International matches

For:	4T	4C	8PG	3DG	61 Pts
Against:	2T	–	12PG	–	46 Pts

MATCH DETAILS

1994	OPPONENTS	VENUE	RESULT
1 June	Canada A	Toronto	W 34-31
4 June	CANADA	Nepean	L 16-18
9 June	Northland	Whangarei	W 28-23
12 June	North Harbour	Auckland	L 23-27
15 June	Wairarapa Bush	Masterton	W 53-9
18 June	New Zealand XV	Wanganui	W 33-25
22 June	Nelson Bays	Nelson	W 46-18
26 June	NEW ZEALAND	Christchurch	W 22-8
29 June	Hawke's Bay	Napier	L 25-30
3 July	NEW ZEALAND	Auckland	W 23-20

Appearances: 7 – Gonzalez, Benezech, Accoceberry*; 6 – Seigne, Roumat, Cabannes, Sella, Lacroix, Ntamack, Sadourny, Merle*, Brouzet*, Benazzi*, Cecillon*, Deylaud*, Delaigue*, Viars*; 5 – Benetton, Loppy, Dispagne, Téchoueyres*, Saint-André, Leflamand, Armary*, Califano*, Blond**; 4 – Macabiau, Bellot; 3 – Tordo; 2 – Carbonneau; 1 – Mesnel; 0 – Galthié * includes appearances as a replacement*
Scorers: 64 – Lacroix (1T 10C 12PG 1DG); 55 – Bellot (1T 10C 9PG 1DG); 35 – Leflamand (7T); 20 – Ntamack (4T); 18 – Deylaud (3C 2PG 2DG); 15 – Benazzi, Viars, Carbonneau (all 3T); 13 – Sadourny (2T 1DG); 10 – Gonzalez, Tordo (both 2T); 5 – Merle, Benetton, Loppy, Téchoueyres, Delaigue, pen try; 3 – Macabiau (1DG)

MATCH 1 1 June, Fletcher's Fields, Toronto

Canada A 31 (1G 8PG) **France XV 34** (1G 4PG 3T)
Canada A: S MacKinnon (Ex-Britannia Lions); W Stanley (UBC), M Williams (Meralomas), D Clarke (Swilers), C Smith (Meralomas); B Ross (James Bay), I MacKay (Kats); R Bice (Vancouver RC), K Svoboda (Ajax Wands), K Wirachowski (Velox Valhallians), C Whittaker (James Bay), G Ennis (Suntory) (*capt*), M Schmid (UBC), B Breen (Meralomas), J Hutchinson (UBC Old Boys) *Replacements* R Cornish (Regina Campion Grads) for Wirachowski (42 mins); R Snow (Dogs) for Ennis (75 mins)
Scorers *Try:* Smith *Conversion:* Ross *Penalty Goals:* Ross (8)
France XV: Viars; Leflamand, Mesnel, Delaigue, Téchoueyres; Bellot, Accoceberry; Armary, Tordo (*capt*), Seigne, Cecillon, Brouzet, Loppy, Blond, Dispagne
Replacements Benazzi for Blond (44 mins); Benetton for Armary (78 mins)
Scorers *Tries:* Tordo, Viars, Leflamand, Bellot *Conversion:* Bellot
Penalty Goals: Bellot (4)
Referee D Steele (Canadian RU)

MATCH 2 4 June, Twin Elms Rugby Park, Nepean Test Match

CANADA 18 (6PG) **FRANCE 16** (1G 3PG)

Canada advanced their claim to be considered a major rugby power with a deserved victory against France. Besides expressing delight at the way his jumpers cleaned out the French in the line-out, Canada's coach Ian Birtwell was pleased with the effective rucking and mauling his pack practised at the breakdowns.

Despite the sending-off of their hooker, Mark Cardinal, for stamping, in the 30th minute, Canada led 12-6 at half-time, thanks to four penalties kicked by Gareth Rees. It should be added that, to minimise disruption to the front rows, the referee had permitted Colin McKenzie, the No 8, to withdraw from the game and be replaced by Karl Svoboda, an experienced Test hooker.

France did take the lead early in the second spell when Emile Ntamack raced after a chip-kick by his captain, Saint-André, and Thierry Lacroix converted. But Gareth Rees' fifth and sixth penalties for Canada to one from Lacroix, who also missed with an attempt near the end, completed the scoring.

Philippe Sella's expulsion ten minutes from time after a touch-judge intervened to accuse him of punching added to France's disappointment.

CANADA: D S Stewart (UBC Old Boys); R Toews (Meralomas), S D Gray (Kats), I C Stuart (Vancouver RC) (*capt*), D C Lougheed (Toronto Welsh); G L Rees (Oak Bay Castaways & Oxford U), J D Graf (UBC Old Boys); E A Evans (IBM Tokyo), M E Cardinal (James Bay), D C Jackart (UBC Old Boys), A J Charron (Ottawa Irish), M James (Burnaby), I Gordon (James Bay), C McKenzie (UBC Old Boys), G I MacKinnon (Ex-Britannia Lions) *Replacement* K F Svoboda (Ajax Wands) for McKenzie (35 mins)
Scorer *Penalty Goals:* Rees (6)
FRANCE: Sadourny; Ntamack, Sella, Lacroix, Saint-André (*capt*); Deylaud, Macabiau; Benezech, Gonzalez, Seigne, Merle, Roumat, Benetton, Benazzi, Cabannes *Replacement* Viars for Saint-André (68 mins)
Scorers *Try:* Ntamack *Conversion:* Lacroix *Penalty Goals:* Lacroix (3)
Referee I Rogers (South Africa)

MATCH 3 9 June, Lowe Walker Stadium, Whangarei

Northland 23 (6PG 1T) **France XV 28** (2G 3PG 1T)
Northland: N Berryman; R Watts, M Going, R Dunn, S Davis; W Johnston, A Goodhew; C Barrell, D Te Puni, J Barrell, G Crawford, J Pickering, G Taylor (*capt*), J Collins, A Going *Replacement* L Davies for C Barrell (27 mins)
Scorers *Try:* Davis *Penalty Goals:* Johnston (6)
France XV: Sadourny; Leflamand, Delaigue, Lacroix, Téchoueyres; Deylaud, Accoceberry; Benezech, Gonzalez, Califano, Benazzi, Roumat (*capt*), Cabannes, Dispagne, Loppy
Scorers *Tries:* Leflamand (2), Benazzi *Conversions:* Lacroix (2) *Penalty Goals:* Deylaud, Lacroix (2)
Referee G K Wahlstrom (Auckland)

MATCH 4 12 June, Eden Park, Auckland

North Harbour 27 (1G 5PG 1T) **France XV 23** (2G 1PG 2DG)
North Harbour: G M Osborne; P Woods, F E Bunce, W K Little, E J Rush; W J Burton, A D Strachan; R O Williams, S P McFarland, G L Walsh, D W Mayhew, I D Jones, L J Barry, R S Turner (*capt*), B P Larsen *Replacement* W Lose for Turner
Scorers *Tries:* Osborne, Strachan *Conversion:* Burton *Penalty Goals:* Burton (5)

France XV: Sadourny; Viars, Delaigue, Sella, Saint-André (*capt*); Bellot, Macabiau; Armary, Tordo, Califano, Brouzet, Merle, Cabannes, Cecillon, Benetton
Replacement Téchoueyres for Saint-André (temp)
Scorers *Tries:* Merle, Delaigue *Conversions:* Bellot (2) *Penalty Goal:* Bellot
Dropped Goals: Bellot, Macabiau
Referee S Walsh (Wellington)

MATCH 5 15 June, Memorial Park, Masterton

Wairarapa Bush 9 (2PG 1DG) **France XV 53** (5G 1DG 3T)
Wairarapa Bush: Q G O'Neale; D A Spicer, P Noble, S Brown, B Percy; P A Roache, N M Foote; M M Mason, M Hoggard, S C Coley, V M Boyce, J Hutchins, D A Bassett, J Cummings (*capt*), B Bowie *Replacements* N O'Neale for Hoggard (16 mins); R Guildford for Percy (40 mins); R Rutene for G O'Neale; M Percy for Spicer
Scorer *Penalty Goals:* Roache (2) *Dropped Goal:* Roache
France XV: Viars; Ntamack, Sella, Téchoueyres, Leflamand; Lacroix, Accoceberry; Benezech, Gonzalez, Seigne, Brouzet, Cecillon (*capt*), Loppy, Blond, Dispagne
Replacements Deylaud for Sella (40 mins); Armary for Seigne (57 mins)
Scorers *Tries:* Loppy, Ntamack (2), Leflamand (2), Lacroix, Gonzalez, Viars
Conversions: Lacroix (3), Deylaud (2) *Dropped Goal:* Lacroix
Referee R Hill (Wellington)

MATCH 6 18 June, Wanganui

New Zealand XV 25 (2G 2PG 1T) **France XV 33** (2G 3PG 2T)
New Zealand XV: S P Howarth (Auckland); J W Wilson (Otago), W K Little (North Harbour), A I Ieremia (Wellington), E J Rush (North Harbour); M C G Ellis (Otago), O F J Tonu'u (Auckland); C W Dowd (Auckland), N J Hewitt (Hawke's Bay), M R Allen (Taranaki), R T Fromont (Auckland), S B Gordon (Waikato), M N Jones (Auckland), J E P Mitchell (Waikato) (*capt*), J W Joseph (Otago) *Replacements* G Taylor (Northland) for Fromont (50 mins); G N Konia (Hawke's Bay) for Wilson (53 mins)
Scorers *Tries:* Little, pen try, Dowd *Conversions:* Howarth (2)
Penalty Goals: Howarth (2)
France XV: Sadourny; Ntamack, Sella, Lacroix, Saint-André (*capt*); Deylaud, Accoceberry; Benezech, Gonzalez, Seigne, Merle, Roumat, Cabannes, Benetton, Benazzi *Replacements* Califano for Seigne (53 mins); Blond for Benetton (temp and 65 mins); Armary for Benezech (temp)
Scorers *Tries:* Gonzalez, Benazzi (2), Sadourny *Conversions:* Lacroix (2)
Penalty Goals: Lacroix (3)
Referee P D O'Brien (Southland)

MATCH 7 22 June, Trafalgar Park, Nelson

Nelson Bays 18 (1G 2PG 1T) **France XV 46** (5G 2PG 1T)
Nelson Bays: R Hodgkinson; H Couper, C Benge, W Havili, K B Byers; C J Lott, B Calder; D Murcott, S Carter, P A Fitisemanu, T Matakaiongo, G Smith, D Cavaye, D G Inch (*capt*), B J Henderson *Replacement* S Maxwell for Henderson (78 mins)
Scorers *Tries:* Matakaiongo, Fitisemanu *Conversion:* Lott *Penalty Goals:* Lott (2)
France XV: Viars; Leflamand, Carbonneau, Delaigue, Téchoueyres; Bellot, Macabiau; Seigne, Gonzalez, Armary, Cecillon, Brouzet, Loppy, Dispagne, Blond (*capt*)
Scorers *Tries:* Carbonneau (3), Leflamand (2), Téchoueyres *Conversions:* Bellot (5)
Penalty Goals: Bellot (2)
Referee A G Riley (Waikato)

MATCH 8 26 June, Lancaster Park, Christchurch 1st Test

NEW ZEALAND 8 (1PG 1T) FRANCE 22 (1G 2PG 3DG)

France bounced back from the early traumas of the tour to outclass the

All Blacks with a brilliant display of controlled rugby, never allowing a predictable and ponderous New Zealand team to get into its stride. Despite winning only the minority of possession, the French pack worked constructively in the tight and loose to contain the home forwards, who seemed incapable of adjusting their game from some prearranged pattern. Laurent Benezech, France's loose head, had an outstanding all-round match.

France, 9-3 up at half-time, took an unassailable 19-3 lead when Philippe Benetton finished a run by his skipper with a corner try which Thierry Lacroix converted midway through the second half. A penalty by Lacroix and Frank Bunce's consolation try for the All Blacks wrapped up the scores.

It was only France's second Test win on New Zealand soil – a marvellous occasion for Philippe Sella to celebrate becoming the first player to reach 100 caps in major internationals. John Kirwan set an All Black record with his 59th Test appearance.

NEW ZEALAND: J K R Timu (Otago); J J Kirwan (Auckland), F E Bunce (North Harbour), M J A Cooper (Waikato), J Lomu (Counties); S J Mannix (Wellington), S T Forster (Otago); R W Loe (Canterbury), S B T Fitzpatrick (Auckland) (*capt*), O M Brown (Auckland), I D Jones (North Harbour), M S B Cooksley (Waikato), B P Larsen (North Harbour), A R B Pene (Otago), M R Brewer (Canterbury)
Scorers *Try:* Bunce *Penalty Goal:* Cooper
FRANCE: Sadourny; Ntamack, Sella, Lacroix, Saint-André (*capt*); Deylaud, Accoceberry; Benezech, Gonzalez, Califano, Merle, Roumat, Benazzi, Benetton, Cabannes *Replacements* Cecillon for Cabannes (80 mins); Viars for Sadourny (temp); Armary for Benezech (temp)
Scorers *Try:* Benetton *Conversion:* Lacroix *Penalty Goals:* Lacroix (2)
Dropped Goals: Deylaud (2), Sadourny
Referee W D Bevan (Wales)

MATCH 9 29 June, McLean Park, Napier

Hawke's Bay 30 (2G 1PG 1DG 2T) **France XV 25** (2G 2PG 1T)
Hawke's Bay: J B Cunningham; A R Hamilton, G N Konia, M R Paewai, T K Maidens; R McLeod, J A Bradbrook; W Maere, N J Hewitt, O H Crawford, C Gibbs, M Atkinson, D J Watts, G J Falcon, D J Seymour (*capt*)
Scorers *Tries:* Falcon (2), Hewitt, pen try *Conversions:* McLeod (2)
Penalty Goal: Cunningham *Dropped Goal:* McLeod
France XV: Viars; Leflamand, Carbonneau, Delaigue, Ntamack; Bellot, Macabiau; Armary, Tordo (*capt*), Seigne, Brouzet, Roumat, Loppy, Cecillon, Dispagne
Replacements Accoceberry for Macabiau (40 mins); Merle for Roumat (47 mins)
Scorers *Tries:* Tordo, Viars, pen try *Conversions:* Bellot (2) *Penalty Goals:* Bellot (2)
Referee C J Hawke (South Canterbury)

MATCH 10 3 July, Eden Park, Auckland — 2nd Test

NEW ZEALAND 20 (5PG 1T) **FRANCE 23** (2G 3PG)

In the wake of defeat at Christchurch, New Zealand dropped Simon Mannix and Arran Pene while France were unchanged. There was a big improvement by the All Blacks, but it was France who won, thanks to a sublime move which produced a try by Jean-Luc Sadourny.

The tourists led, rather luckily, at half-time after Emile Ntamack had intercepted to score an opportunist try. Then, early in the second half, Sean Fitzpatrick put his side ahead with a touchdown after a powerful forward drive. The All Blacks stretched their lead to 20-16 and appeared to be in control as the Test moved to its dramatic conclusion.

Two minutes from the end, however, Philippe Saint-André gathered a loose ball 15 metres from his goal-line. Instead of clearing to touch, he initiated a counter-attack which saw the ball pass through nine pairs of hands before Sadourny dotted it down for a score described as 'from the end of the world', by Saint-André, the French captain.

France had never previously beaten New Zealand in a Test series and it was only the fifth time that the All Blacks had lost a rubber on their own soil.

NEW ZEALAND: J K R Timu (Otago); J J Kirwan (Auckland), F E Bunce (North Harbour), M J A Cooper (Waikato), J Lomu (Counties); S J Bachop (Otago), S T Forster (Otago); R W Loe (Canterbury), S B T Fitzpatrick (Auckland) (*capt*), O M Brown (Auckland), I D Jones (North Harbour), M S B Cooksley (Waikato), B P Larsen (North Harbour), Z V Brooke (Auckland), M R Brewer (Canterbury)
Replacement A R B Pene (Otago) for Brooke (76 mins)
Scorers *Try:* Fitzpatrick *Penalty Goals:* Cooper (5)
FRANCE: Sadourny; Ntamack, Sella, Lacroix, Saint-André (*capt*); Deylaud, Accoceberry; Benezech, Gonzalez, Califano, Merle, Roumat, Benazzi, Benetton, Cabannes *Replacements* Armary for Califano (temp); Delaigue for Lacroix (48 mins); Blond for Benetton (72 mins); Brouzet for Blond (81 mins)
Scorers *Tries:* Ntamack, Sadourny *Conversions:* Lacroix, Deylaud
Penalty Goals: Lacroix (2), Deylaud
Referee W D Bevan (Wales)

ITALY TO AUSTRALIA 1994

May and June 1994 were two of the busiest months yet for Italian international rugby. Two qualifying matches (both won) for the 1995 World Cup and a disappointing defeat by Romania in the FIRA competition were followed by an eight-match tour of Australia in June.

Many would have forgiven the Italians for believing that it was better to travel in hope than to arrive in the land of the world champions. On the previous Test visit to Australia in 1986, the Azzurri were easily beaten in the international and won only two of their other matches. This time, however, they enjoyed a marvellous trip, winning all six of the provincial matches and giving the Wallabies a scare or two in the Tests to boot.

The only blot on the tourists' copybook was the sending off of Franco Properzi-Curti for retaliation in the ill-tempered opening match against Northern Territory. Two particularly good wins – against a strong Sydney side which included seven Wallabies, and over a Queensland XV – gave notice that the Italians would be no pushover for Australia in the Tests. Unfortunately, Diego Dominguez, who kicked the winning penalty against Queensland six minutes from time, broke a bone in his hand during the match and missed the rest of the tour. Italy's Julian Gardner, the ex-Australian flanker who now plays in Rovigo, damaged medial ligaments in the same game and was denied the chance of playing in the internationals against his former team-mates.

In the First Test Italy played skilfully and led 17-13 as the game entered its last quarter. Only a late penalty by Tim Wallace – on as replacement for Michael Lynagh, who had injured a thigh muscle – permitted Australia to escape with a narrow victory. The score was more clear-cut in teeming rain in Melbourne a week later. Even so, there was an element of doubt about the late score awarded to David Campese, who plays club rugby in Italy: afterwards he himself admitted that he did not believe he had grounded the ball for a try. In addition, Massimo Cuttitta, the South African-educated Italian prop, appeared to have a valid try disallowed in the second half.

THE TOURING PARTY

Manager G Dondi **Assistant Manager** F Hostie **Coach** G Coste
Captain M Giovanelli

FULL-BACK

P Vaccari (Milan)

THREEQUARTERS

M Gerosa (Piacenza)
E G Filizzola (Roma)
M Bonomi (Milan)
Marcello Cuttitta (Milan)
N Aldrovandi (Bologna)
S Bordon (Rovigo)
H de Marco (Padova)
R Crotti (Milan)

HALF-BACKS

D Dominguez (Milan)
L Troiani (L'Aquila)
A Troncon (Treviso)
I Francescato (Treviso)

FORWARDS

G Grespan (Treviso)
M Trevisiol (Treviso)
F Properzi-Curti (Milan)
Massimo Cuttitta (Milan)
C Orlandi (Piacenza)
A Castellani (L'Aquila)
R Favaro (Treviso)
M Giacheri (Treviso)
P Pedroni (Milan)
M Giovanelli (Milan)
A Sgorlon (San Dona)
J M Gardner (Rovigo)
C de Rossi (Treviso)
O Arancio (Catania)
C Checchinato (Rovigo)
***D Sesenna** (Piacenza)

**Replacement during tour*

TOUR RECORD

All matches Played 8 Won 6 Lost 2 Points for 268 Against 139
International matches Played 2 Lost 2 Points for 27 Against 43

SCORING DETAILS

All matches

For:	30T	23C	24PG	–	268 Pts
Against:	10T	7C	25PG	–	139 Pts

International matches

For:	2T	1C	5PG	–	27 Pts
Against:	3T	2C	8PG	–	43 Pts

MATCH DETAILS

1994	OPPONENTS	VENUE	RESULT
1 June	Northern Territory	Darwin	W 37-6
4 June	South Australia	Adelaide	W 60-12

8 June	Sydney	Sydney	W 36-26
12 June	Queensland XV	Ballymore	W 21-19
15 June	Queensland Country	Toowoomba	W 57-13
18 June	AUSTRALIA	Brisbane	L 20-23
21 June	New South Wales Country	Nowra	W 30-20
25 June	AUSTRALIA	Melbourne	L 7-20

MATCH 1 1 June, Darwin

Northern Territory 6 (2PG) **Italy XV 37** (2G 6PG 1T)
Northern Territory: *Penalty Goals:* Lingman (2)
Italy XV: *Tries:* Troncon, Vaccari, pen try *Conversions:* Dominguez (2)
Penalty Goals: Dominguez (6)

MATCH 2 4 June, Adelaide

South Australia 12 (1G 1T) **Italy XV 60** (6G 1PG 3T)
South Australia: *Tries:* Fanua, Smith *Conversion:* Elliot
Italy XV: *Tries:* Aldrovandi (3), Checchinato (2), Gerosa (2), Orlandi, Vaccari
Conversions: Troiani (6) *Penalty Goal:* Troiani

MATCH 3 8 June, Sydney

Sydney 26 (2G 4PG) **Italy XV 36** (3G 5PG)
Sydney: *Tries:* Junee (2) *Conversions:* Knox (2) *Penalty Goals:* Knox (4)
Italy XV: *Tries:* Troncon, Filizzola, Giovanelli *Conversions:* Dominguez (3)
Penalty Goals: Dominguez (5)

MATCH 4 12 June, Ballymore, Brisbane

Queensland XV 19 (1G 4PG) **Italy XV 21** (1G 3PG 1T)
Queensland XV: *Try:* Connors *Conversion:* Kahl *Penalty Goals:* Kahl (4)
Italy XV: *Tries:* Massimo Cuttitta, Arancio *Conversion:* Dominguez
Penalty Goals: Dominguez (3)

MATCH 5 15 June, Toowoomba

Queensland Country 13 (1G 2PG) **Italy XV 57** (7G 1PG 1T)
Queensland Country: *Try:* Kasey *Conversion:* Berlett *Penalty Goals:* Berlett (2)
Italy XV: *Tries:* Sgorlon (2), Troncon (2), Gerosa, Trevisiol, Checchinato, Castellani
Conversions: Troiani (7) *Penalty Goal:* Troiani

MATCH 6 18 June, Ballymore, Brisbane **1st Test**

AUSTRALIA 23 (2G 3PG) **ITALY 20** (5PG 1T)
AUSTRALIA: M Burke (NSW); D I Campese (NSW), D Herbert (Queensland), R C Tombs (NSW), D Smith (Queensland); M P Lynagh (Queensland) (*capt*), G Gregan (ACT); A J Daly (NSW), P N Kearns (NSW), E J A McKenzie (NSW), G J Morgan (Queensland), J A Eales (Queensland), I Tabua (Queensland), B T Gavin (NSW), D J Wilson (Queensland) *Replacements* T M Wallace (NSW) for Lynagh (52 mins); P J Slattery (Queensland) for Gregan (60 mins)
Scorers *Tries:* Herbert, Burke *Conversions:* Lynagh, Wallace
Penalty Goals: Lynagh (2), Wallace
ITALY: Vaccari; Gerosa, Filizzola, Bonomi, Marcello Cuttitta; Troiani, Troncon; Massimo Cuttitta, Orlandi, Properzi-Curti, Favoro, Giacheri, Arancio, Checchinato, Giovanelli (*capt*) *Replacement* Bordon for Filizzola (3 mins)
Scorers *Try:* Bonomi *Penalty Goals:* Troiani (5)
Referee I Rogers (South Africa)

MATCH 7 **22 June, Nowra**

New South Wales Country 20 (5PG 1T) **Italy XV 30** (3G 3PG)
New South Wales Country: *Try:* Ives *Penalty Goals:* Eddy (5)
Italy XV: *Tries:* Gerosa (2), Checchinato *Conversions:* Troiani (3)
Penalty Goals: Troiani (3)

MATCH 8 **25 June, Melbourne** **2nd Test**

AUSTRALIA 20 (5PG 1T) **ITALY 7** (1G)
AUSTRALIA: M Pini (Queensland); D I Campese (NSW), D Herbert (Queensland), M Burke (NSW), D Smith (Queensland); T M Wallace (NSW), G Gregan (ACT), A J Daly (NSW), P N Kearns (NSW) (*capt*), E J A McKenzie (NSW), R J McCall (Queensland), J A Eales (Queensland), I Tabua (Queensland), B T Gavin (NSW), D J Wilson (Queensland)
Scorers *Try:* Campese *Penalty Goals:* Wallace (5)
ITALY: Vaccari; Gerosa, Bordon, Bonomi, Marcello Cuttitta; Troiani, Troncon; Properzi-Curti, Orlandi, Massimo Cuttitta, Favaro, Giacheri, Arancio, Checchinato, Giovanelli (*capt*)
Scorers *Try:* Orlandi *Conversion:* Troiani
Referee I Rogers (South Africa)

SOUTH AFRICA TO NEW ZEALAND 1994

Although this was South Africa's sixth tour of New Zealand since 1921, it was their first there for 13 years. Moreover, it was the first visit on which they failed to win a Test against the All Blacks.

In the past, the rubber would have been billed as a world-championship decider, but this latest meeting of rugby's former superpowers was a dreadful anti-climax – just another dreary series between nations more desperate to avoid defeat than to fashion exciting victories.

The tour was a huge disappointment for South Africa. Not only was it tainted by allegations of foul play, it was also followed by bitter recriminations between Louis Luyt, SARFU's all-powerful president, and the tour's management team. James Small, the abrasive wing, was cited for a kneeing incident in the Waikato match, though subsequently exonerated; Adri Geldenhuys was dismissed for punching in the Manawatu game and Johan le Roux bit Sean Fitzpatrick's ear in the Second Test. Le Roux was immediately sent home for his misdemeanour.

It was the management's handling of disciplinary matters which sparked off the very public verbal fireworks from Louis Luyt. Not even the draw in the final Test of the series, which saved South Africa from a whitewash, prevented him from promising manager Jannie Engelbrecht and coach Ian McIntosh that their days with South African rugby teams were numbered.

THE TOURING PARTY

Manager J P Engelbrecht **Coach** I B McIntosh **Captain** J F Pienaar

FULL-BACKS

A J Joubert (Natal)
J T J van Rensburg (Transvaal)
***G K Johnson** (Transvaal)

THREEQUARTERS

J T Small (Natal)
C M Williams (Western Province)
C Badenhorst (Orange Free State)

J F van der Westhuizen (Natal)
P G Müller (Natal)
B Venter (Orange Free State)
J P Claassens (Northern Transvaal)
F A Meiring (Northern Transvaal)
***J C Mulder** (Transvaal)

HALF-BACKS

H P le Roux (Transvaal)
L R Sherrell (Natal)
J P Roux (Tranvaal)
J H van der Westhuizen (Northern Transvaal)

FORWARDS

I S Swart (Transvaal)
K S Andrews (Western Province)
J H S le Roux (Transvaal)
G R Kebble (Natal)
J Allan (Natal)
J Dalton (Transvaal)
S Atherton (Natal)
M G Andrews (Natal)
J J Wiese (Transvaal)
K Otto (Northern Transvaal)
I Macdonald (Transvaal)
***R J Kruger** (Northern Transvaal)
F J van Heerden (Western Province)
J F Pienaar (Transvaal)
W J Bartmann (Natal)
C P Strauss (Western Province)
A Richter (Northern Transvaal)
***R A W Straeuli** (Transvaal)
***A-H le Roux** (Orange Free State)
***A Geldenhuys** (Eastern Province)
***G N Wegner** (Western Province)

**Replacement during tour*

TOUR RECORD

All matches Played 14 Won 10 Drawn 1 Lost 3 Points for 445 Against 241
International matches Played 3 Drawn 1 Lost 2 Points for 41 Against 53

SCORING DETAILS

All matches

For:	58T	34C	28PG	1DG	445 Pts
Against:	22T	13C	34PG	1DG	241 Pts

International matches

For:	3T	1C	8PG	–	41 Pts
Against:	3T	1C	12PG	–	53 Pts

MATCH DETAILS

1994	OPPONENTS	VENUE	RESULT
23 June	King Country	Taupo	W 46-10
25 June	Counties	Pukekohe	W 37-26
28 June	Wellington	Wellington	W 36-26
2 July	Southland	Invercargill	W 51-15
5 July	Hanan Shield Districts	Timaru	W 67-19
9 July	NEW ZEALAND	Dunedin	L 14-22
13 July	Taranaki	New Plymouth	W 16-12
16 July	Waikato	Hamilton	W 38-17
19 July	Manawatu	Palmerston	W 47-21
23 July	NEW ZEALAND	Wellington	L 9-13
27 July	Otago	Dunedin	L 12-19
30 July	Canterbury	Christchurch	W 21-11
2 Aug	Bay of Plenty	Rotorua	W 33-12
6 Aug	NEW ZEALAND	Auckland	D 18-18

Appearances: 9 – Strauss, van Heerden*, J H van der Westhuizen**; 8 – H P le Roux, Richter, Joubert*, Allan*, J Roux*, Atherton*, Kebble*, Dalton*, K Andrews*, Straeuli**; 7 – Badenhorst, Venter, Claassens, J F van der Westhuizen, Williams, M Andrews, Meiring*, van Rensburg*, Small*; 6 – Sherrell, Kruger, J H S le Roux, Pienaar; 5 – Mulder, Otto, Swart, Geldenhuys*; 4 – A-H le Roux*; 3 – Müller; 2 – Johnson, Wiese, Wegner; 1 – Bartmann *includes appearances as a replacement*
Scorers: 85 – Van Rensburg (5T 12C 11PG 1DG); 56 – Joubert (13C 10PG); 35 – Badenhorst (7T); 31 – Sherrell (3T 5C 2PG); 26 – Johnson (1T 3C 5PG); 20 – J H van der Westhuizen, Venter (both 4T); 15 – Strauss, Straeuli, Claassens, Small, Mulder (all 3T); 12 – H P le Roux (2T 1C); 10 – Richter, Allan, J Roux, J F van der Westhuizen, Meiring (all 2T); 5 – Atherton, Kebble, Williams, Otto, A-H le Roux, Kruger, pen try (all 1T)

MATCH 1 23 June, Taupo

King Country 10 (1G 1PG) **South Africa XV 46** (5G 2PG 1T)
King Country: W Te Huia; M S Seavill, L Langkilde, J M Wells, J Sim; R Daly, C N Wills; J Veitayaki, P L Mitchell, P N Coffin (*capt*), F Fakaongo, G Stanton, H J Morgan, H Nelson, W D Anglesey *Replacements* W Parkes for Sim; M Heke for Seavill; C J Herbert for Mitchell (temp)
Scorers *Try:* pen try *Conversion:* Te Huia *Penalty Goal:* Daly
South Africa XV: Van Rensburg; Small, Claassens, Meiring, J F van der Westhuizen; Sherrell, J H van der Westhuizen; Swart, Dalton, J H S le Roux, Otto, Wiese, Straeuli, Strauss, Pienaar (*capt*)
Scorers *Tries:* Wiese, Otto, J F van der Westhuizen, Straeuli, Small, pen try
Conversions: Van Rensburg (3), Sherrell (2) *Penalty Goals:* Sherrell (2)
Referee D J Bishop (Otago)

MATCH 2 25 June, Pukekohe

Counties 26 (2G 4PG) **South Africa XV 37** (3G 2PG 2T)
Counties: D R Sheppard; L Foai, T Marsh, G L Millington, D Henare; D A Love, M W Scott; T R Barchard, A T Roose, L Lidgard, C Rose, J N Coe, J J Ahuativa, E F Brain (*capt*), J Paramore
Scorers *Tries:* Foai, Barchard *Conversions:* Love (2) *Penalty Goals:* Love (4)
South Africa XV: Joubert; Badenhorst, Müller, Venter, J F van der Westhuizen; H P le Roux, J Roux; Kebble, Allan, K Andrews, M Andrews, Atherton, Bartmann (*capt*), Richter, van Heerden *Replacements* Straeuli for Bartmann; J H van der Westhuizen for Roux
Scorers *Tries:* Roux (2), H P le Roux, Venter, Straeuli *Conversions:* Joubert (3)
Penalty Goals: Joubert (2)
Referee R Hill (Wellington)

MATCH 3 28 June, Athletic Park, Wellington

Wellington 26 (1G 3PG 2T) **South Africa XV 36** (1G 3PG 4T)
Wellington: S Doyle; A S Taufa, S R Cottrell, A I Ieremia, M T Umaga; S J Mannix (*capt*), E A Moncrieff; M R W Edwards, T P Mannix, S C McDowell, C D Tregaskis, M Russell, D Tuiavi'i, F I Tiatia, G Simpson
Scorers *Tries:* Doyle (2), Umaga *Conversion:* Moncrieff *Penalty Goals:* Moncrieff (3)
South Africa XV: Van Rensburg; Small, Müller, Venter, J F van der Westhuizen; H P le Roux, J Roux; Swart, Dalton, J H S le Roux, M Andrews, Atherton, Straeuli, Strauss, Pienaar (*capt*) *Replacements* Meiring for Müller; Van Heerden for Pienaar; K Andrews for J H S le Roux; Allan for Dalton
Scorers *Tries:* Van Rensburg (2), Venter, Strauss, Allan *Conversion:* Van Rensburg
Penalty Goals: Van Rensburg (3)
Referee P D O'Brien (Southland)

MATCH 4 2 July, Homestead Rugby Stadium, Invercargill

Southland 15 (1G 1PG 1T) **South Africa XV 51** (4G 1PG 4T)
Southland: E S Todd; P Dynes, P J Johnston, G J Beardsley, R Stodart; S D Culhane, J Marshall; R Borland, D Heaps, C C Corbett, W A Miller, M Tinnock, B J Morton, S Harvey (*capt*), B Shepherd *Replacement* S P Hayes for Corbett (temp) and for Borland
Scorers *Tries:* Todd, Stodart *Conversion:* Culhane *Penalty Goal:* Culhane
South Africa XV: Joubert; Badenhorst, Claassens, Meiring, Williams; Sherrell, J H van der Westhuizen; Kebble, Allan, K Andrews, Otto, Wiese, Kruger, Richter (*capt*), van Heerden *Replacements* Van Rensburg for Joubert; Atherton for Wiese
Scorers *Tries:* Badenhorst (3), Richter (2), Claassens, Kruger, Atherton
Conversions: Joubert (4) *Penalty Goal:* Joubert
Referee J A E Taylor (Counties)

MATCH 5 **5 July, Fraser Park, Timaru**

Hanan Shield Districts 19 (2G 1T) **South Africa XV 67** (6G 5T)
Hanan Shield Districts: D Hunter; S Todd, B Laney, S Tarrant (*capt*), H Hunt; C Gard, B Matthews; D McCrea, R McArthur, R Morgan, J Simpson, T Gresham, V Muir, J Mawhinney, S Wills *Replacements* S Hewson for Tarrant; J Smitheram for Mawhinney; J Gregan for Gresham; N Walsh for McArthur (temp)
Scorers *Tries:* Todd (2), pen try *Conversions:* Laney (2)
South Africa XV: Van Rensburg; Badenhorst, Claassens, Meiring, Williams; Sherrell, J H van der Westhuizen; Kebble, Dalton, J H S le Roux, Otto, Van Heerden, Kruger, Strauss (*capt*), Richter *Replacement* Straeuli for Strauss (temp)
Scorers *Tries:* Sherrell (2), Badenhorst (2), Van Rensburg (2), Williams, J H van der Westhuizen, Claassens, Meiring, Strauss *Conversions:* Sherrell (3), Van Rensburg (3)
Referee R T A Ross (North Harbour)

MATCH 6 9 July, Carisbrook, Dunedin 1st Test

NEW ZEALAND 22 (1G 5PG) **SOUTH AFRICA 14** (3PG 1T)

After defeats by the French, New Zealand were happy to win a rough, undistinguished match and thus to avoid losing three successive home Tests for the first time. Balie Swart (concussion), Pieter Müller (torn neck ligaments) and Ian Jones (hairline cheekbone fracture) were wounded in action, while Richard Loe, Johan le Roux and Johan Roux were reprimanded by the referee for foul play.

South Africa, who had never won a Dunedin Test, were optimistic after a try by Rudi Straeuli brought them to within a point of the All Blacks early in the second half. But later, with 15 minutes remaining, Zinzan Brooke and Mark Brewer provided a rare moment of creativity to work John Kirwan clear for the try which proved to be the game-breaker. It was the wing's 35th and last in Tests: he announced his retirement at the end of the season.

NEW ZEALAND: S P Howarth (Auckland); J J Kirwan (Auckland), F E Bunce (North Harbour), A I Ieremia (Wellington), J K R Timu (Otago); S J Bachop (Otago), G T M Bachop (Canterbury); R W Loe (Canterbury), S B T Fitzpatrick (Auckland) (*capt*), O M Brown (Auckland), I D Jones (North Harbour), M S B Cooksley (Counties), B P Larsen (North Harbour), Z V Brooke (Auckland), M R Brewer (Canterbury) *Replacements* A R B Pene (Otago) for Jones (9 mins); C W Dowd (Auckland) for Pene (75 mins)
Scorers *Try:* Kirwan *Conversion:* Howarth *Penalty Goals:* Howarth (5)
SOUTH AFRICA: Joubert; Small, Venter, Müller, Williams; H P le Roux, J Roux, Swart, Allan, J H S le Roux, M Andrews, Atherton, Strauss (*capt*), Richter, Straeuli *Replacement* Kebble for Swart (23 mins)
Scorers *Try:* Straeuli *Penalty Goals:* Joubert (3)
Referee B W Stirling (Ireland)

MATCH 7 **13 July, Rugby Park, New Plymouth**

Taranaki 12 (4PG) **South Africa XV 16** (1G 2PG 1DG)
Taranaki: K J Crowley; F Mahoni, K W Eynon, D Asi, T W N Wolfe; J B Cameron, R A Jarman; M R Allen (*capt*), S R McDonald, G L Slater, J Roche, S Lines, R Wheeler, A W Slater, S T Tiatia
Scorer *Penalty Goals:* Crowley (4)

South Africa XV: Van Rensburg; Badenhorst, Meiring, Claassens, J H van der Westhuizen; Sherrell, J F van der Westhuizen; Kebble, Dalton, K Andrews, Otto, Geldenhuys, Kruger, Straeuli (*capt*), van Heerden *Replacement* Strauss for Kruger
Scorer *Try:* Van Rensburg *Conversion:* Van Rensburg *Penalty Goals:* Van Rensburg (2) *Dropped Goal:* Van Rensburg
Referee B R Smallridge (Auckland)

MATCH 8 16 July, Rugby Park, Hamilton

Waikato 17 (2G 1PG) **South Africa XV 38** (5G 1PG)
Waikato: A H Strawbridge; J W Walters, M J A Cooper, D R Ellison, W S Warlow; I D Foster, S J Crabb; C M Stevenson, W D Gatland, P G Martin, M S B Cooksley, S B Gordon, R M Jerram, J E P Mitchell (*capt*), D I Monkley *Replacements* T J Coventry for Gordon; M Driver for Martin; I Calder for Warlow (temp)
Scorers *Tries:* Warlow, Cooksley *Conversions:* Cooper (2) *Penalty Goal:* Cooper
South Africa XV: Joubert; Small, Mulder, Venter, Williams; H P le Roux, J Roux; Kebble, Allan, J H S le Roux, Otto, M Andrews, Straeuli, Strauss (*capt*), Van Heerden *Replacements* Dalton for Otto; Geldenhuys for Straeuli; J H van der Westhuizen for Allan; A le Roux for Kebble
Scorers *Tries:* Small (2), Mulder, Venter, Allan *Conversions:* Joubert (5) *Penalty Goal:* Joubert
Referee C J Hawke (South Canterbury)

MATCH 9 19 July, Showgrounds Oval, Palmerston North

Manawatu 21 (1G 2PG 1DG 1T) **South Africa XV 47** (4G 3PG 2T)
Manawatu: J M Smith; J W Whyte, C S Izatt, W M Furnell, C W Gowler; J J Holland, G Baines; G M Hurunui, P J Doyle (*capt*), G J Nesdale, A B McKellar, K M F Otai, B Hansen, K J Williams, D J Rowe *Replacement* S J Halford for Nesdale (temp)
Scorers *Tries:* Hurunui, Izatt *Conversion:* Holland *Penalty Goals:* Holland (2) *Dropped Goal:* Holland
South Africa XV: Van Rensburg; Badenhorst, Claassens, Meiring, J F van der Westhuizen; Sherrell, J H van der Westhuizen; K Andrews, Dalton, A-H le Roux, Atherton, Geldenhuys, Kruger, Richter, Pienaar (*capt*)
Scorers *Tries:* Badenhorst (2), J F van der Westhuizen, Claassens, J H van der Westhuizen, Le Roux *Conversions:* Van Rensburg (4) *Penalty Goals:* Van Rensburg (3)
Referee S Walsh (Wellington)

MATCH 10 23 July, Athletic Park, Wellington 2nd Test

NEW ZEALAND 13 (1PG 2T) SOUTH AFRICA 9 (3PG)

New Zealand won an exciting match to put themselves two up in the series with one to go. By playing more open rugby than in the First Test, they scored two tries in the opening 20 minutes and, despite giving away kickable penalties through carelessness, were better value for their victory than the result suggests.

The afternoon, however, was darkened by the unsavoury second-half incident in which All Black captain Sean Fitzpatrick had his ear bitten by Johan le Roux. As the pair went to ground on the fringes of a ruck, le Roux was clearly seen to bend over and lower his head towards the prostrate Fitzpatrick. The All Black, blood streaming from his ear, immediately reacted by protesting to the referee, who had not seen the incident. Next day, le Roux was ordered home by the tourists' manager.

NEW ZEALAND: S P Howarth (Auckland); J J Kirwan (Auckland), F E Bunce (North Harbour), A I Ieremia (Wellington), J K R Timu (Otago); S J Bachop (Otago), G T M Bachop (Canterbury); R W Loe (Canterbury), S B T Fitzpatrick (Auckland) (*capt*), O M Brown (Auckland), R M Brooke (Auckland), M S B Cooksley (Waikato), B P Larsen (North Harbour), Z V Brooke (Auckland), M R Brewer (Canterbury)
Replacements W K Little (North Harbour) for Bunce (74 mins); J W Joseph (Otago) for Z Brooke (temp)
Scorers *Tries:* Timu, Z Brooke *Penalty Goal:* Howarth
SOUTH AFRICA: Van Rensburg; Small, Mulder, Venter, Williams; H P le Roux, J Roux; Kebble, Allan, J H S le Roux, Atherton, M Andrews, Strauss, Richter, Pienaar (*capt*) *Replacement* Joubert for Van Rensburg
Scorer *Penalty Goals:* Van Rensburg (3)
Referee B W Stirling (Ireland)

MATCH 11 27 July, Carisbrook, Dunedin

Otago 19 (1G 4PG) **South Africa XV 12** (1G 1T)
Otago: J K R Timu; J W Wilson, M C G Ellis, J A Leslie, P J Cooke; S J Bachop, S T Forster; R Lawton, D E Latta (*capt*), N S Moore, A M Rich, A Campbell, J W Joseph, A R B Pene, J A Kronfeld
Scorers *Try:* Leslie *Conversion:* Wilson *Penalty Goals:* Wilson (4)
South Africa XV: Joubert; Badenhorst, Mulder, Claassens, J F van der Westhuizen; H P le Roux, J H van der Westhuizen; A-H le Roux, Dalton, K Andrews, Geldenhuys, Wegner, Kruger, Strauss (*capt*), Van Heerden *Replacement* J Roux for J H van der Westhuizen
Scorers *Tries:* J H van der Westhuizen, H P le Roux *Conversion:* H P le Roux
Referee G K Wahlstrom (Auckland)

MATCH 12 30 July, Lancaster Park, Christchurch

Canterbury 11 (2PG 1T) **South Africa XV 21** (1G 3PG 1T)
Canterbury: S Forrest; P Bale, T Matson, M Mayerhofler, A Prince; A P Mehrtens, G T M Bachop; R W Loe, M R Sexton, S Loe, M R McAtamney, G N Kelly, T J Blackadder, R H Penney, M R Brewer (*capt*)
Scorers *Try:* Mayerhofler *Penalty Goals:* Mehrtens (2)
South Africa XV: Joubert; Small, Mulder, Venter, Williams; H P le Roux, J Roux; K Andrews, Allan, Swart, Atherton, M Andrews, Straeuli, Richter, Pienaar (*capt*)
Scorers *Tries:* Mulder (2) *Conversion:* Joubert *Penalty Goals:* Joubert (3)
Referee A G Riley (Waikato)

MATCH 13 2 August, Rotorua International Stadium

Bay of Plenty 12 (1G 1T) **South Africa XV 33** (2G 3PG 2T)
Bay of Plenty: D A Kaui; D Menzies, C Bidois, W Clarke, S Whareaorere; D Stone, J J Tauiwi; S A Simpkins, R George (*capt*), W Morehu, P Weedon, S R Axtens, J Winiata, M R McGregor, B D Sinkinson *Replacement* K F Pryor for Clarke
Scorers *Tries:* Winiata, Sinkinson *Conversion:* Stone
South Africa XV: Johnson; Badenhorst, Meiring, Claassens, J F van der Westhuizen; Sherrell, J H van der Westhuizen; A-H le Roux, Dalton, Kebble, Geldenhuys, Wegner, Kruger, Strauss (*capt*), Van Heerden
Scorers *Tries:* J H van der Westhuizen, Kebble, Sherrell, Meiring
Conversions: Johnson (2) *Penalty Goals:* Johnson (3)
Referee M L Fitzgibbon (Canterbury)

MATCH 14 6 August, Eden Park, Auckland 3rd Test

NEW ZEALAND 18 (6PG) SOUTH AFRICA 18 (1G 2PG 1T)

The South Africans, who had lost their only provincial match (against

Otago) between the second and third internationals, put up their best Test display of the tour to salvage some respect from the series with a draw.

Two splendid first-half tries, both the products of crisp handling by the Springbok backs, took them to a 12-6 lead. Unfortunately, their well-deserved advantage was frittered away through indiscipline. Overall, Mr Yeman awarded 18 penalties to New Zealand – six of which Shane Howarth converted into goals – to their opponents' five.

As a result, Laurie Mains, whose job as New Zealand's coach had been on the line at the outset of the series, survived to mastermind the All Blacks' bid to wrest the Rugby World Cup from Australia at the 1995 finals in South Africa. Ian McIntosh, on the other hand, would not be so lucky: his reign as South African coach came to an abrupt end.

NEW ZEALAND: S P Howarth (Auckland); J J Kirwan (Auckland), F E Bunce (North Harbour), A I Ieremia (Wellington), J K R Timu (Otago); S J Bachop (Otago), G T M Bachop (Canterbury); R W Loe (Canterbury), S B T Fitzpatrick (Auckland) (*capt*), O M Brown (Auckland), R M Brooke (Auckland), I D Jones (North Harbour), B P Larsen (North Harbour), Z V Brooke (Auckland), M R Brewer (Canterbury)
Replacement M N Jones (Canterbury) for Larsen (45 mins)
Scorer *Penalty Goals:* Howarth (6)
SOUTH AFRICA: Joubert; Johnson, Mulder, Venter, Williams; H P le Roux, J Roux; Swart, Allan, K Andrews, Atherton, M Andrews, Pienaar (*capt*), Richter, Van Heerden
Replacement Small for Johnson (temp)
Scorers *Tries:* Johnson, Venter *Conversion:* Johnson *Penalty Goals:* Johnson (2)
Referee R Yeman (Wales)

WESTERN SAMOA TO AUSTRALIA 1994

Nobody could accuse Western Samoa of resting on their laurels since taking the rugby community by surprise at the 1991 World Cup. After reaching the quarter-finals and so guaranteeing their place at the 1995 tournament, the ambitious islanders toured New Zealand in 1993 and made their first Test tour of Australia in 1994.

They began their trip in a state of shock, having failed to win their annual three-nation Pacific tournament. Although they beat Tonga 32-19, a surprise 20-13 defeat in Fiji left the Samoans, like Tonga and Fiji, with one win from two games. Tonga were declared champions by virtue of having scored most tries in the games, and so supplanted the Samoans at the prestigious 1995 Super-10 Championship.

It was with a determination to re-establish their standing as the leading power among the Pacific rugby nations, therefore, that Western Samoa undertook their tour of Australia. They comfortably disposed of Victoria in Melbourne, but only squeezed home against both Queensland and a New South Wales XV by the margin of a single score. In doing so, however, they managed to thrill good crowds with their readiness to throw the ball about and attack from all corners of the pitch.

In the Test, though, they were annihilated under the Sydney Football Stadium's floodlights by an Aussie team for whom everything was all right on the night. The Wallabies, reinforced by the return from injury of both Jason Little and Willie Ofahengaue, registered their record win for a major international, scoring 50 points in an exhilarating second half.

'I wonder if Polynesian Airlines will fly us home,' mused Pita Fatialofa, the Samoan captain, after the defeat. 'If not, we'll have to row.'

THE TOURING PARTY

Manager T Simi **Technical Adviser** B G Williams **Coach** P Schuster
Captain P Fatialofa

FULL-BACK

A Aiolupo (Moata'a)

THREEQUARTERS

T Samania (Moata'a)
R Koko (Wests, Wellington, NZ)
B Lima (Marist/St Joseph's)
T M Vaega (Moata'a)
G Leaupepe (Marist, Auckland, NZ)
K Sio (Scopa)
F Tuilagi (Marist/St Joseph's)

HALF-BACKS

D J Kellett (Ponsonby, NZ)
P Faoagali (Moata'a)
T Nuualitiia (Auckland, NZ)
V Vitale (Vaiala)

FORWARDS

P Fatialofa (Manurewa, NZ)
G Latu (Vaimoso)
R Ale (Marist/St Joseph's)
T Leiasamaivao (Avalon, NZ)
S Toomalatai (Vaiala)
M L Birtwistle (Pukekohe, NZ)
M G Keenan (Pontypool, Wales)
T Curtis (Suburbs, NZ)
M Iupeli (Marist/St Joseph's)
S Vaifale (Marist/St Joseph's)
P Lam (Marist, Auckland, NZ)
D Mika (Marist/St Joseph's)
M Kolomatangi (Marist, Auckland, NZ)
S Lemamea (Scopa)

TOUR RECORD

All matches Played 5 Won 4 Lost 1 Points for 147 Against 152
International matches Played 1 Lost 1 Points for 3 Against 73

SCORING DETAILS

All matches

For:	16T	11C	14PG	1DG	147 Pts
Against:	21T	7C	11PG	–	152 Pts

International matches

For:	–	–	1PG	–	3 Pts
Against:	11T	6C	2PG	–	73 Pts

MATCH DETAILS

1994	OPPONENTS	VENUE	RESULT
23 July	Victoria	Melbourne	W 60-26
27 July	ACT	Canberra	W 39-13
31 July	Queensland	Brisbane	W 24-22
3 Aug	NSW XV	Newcastle	W 21-18
6 Aug	AUSTRALIA	Sydney	L 3-73

MATCH 1 23 July, Olympic Park, Melbourne

Victoria 26 (2PG 4T) **Western Samoa XV 60** (6G 1PG 3T)
Victoria *Tries:* Hammond (2), Strauss, Scott *Penalty Goals:* Goodman (2)
Western Samoa XV *Tries:* Aiolupo (3), Leaupepe (3), Sio, Mika, Samania
Conversions: Samania (3), Faoagali (2), Kellett *Penalty Goal:* Kellett

MATCH 2 27 July, Canberra

Australian Capital Territory 13 (1G 2PG) **Western Samoa XV 39** (3G 5PG 1DG)
Australian Capital Territory *Try:* Didier *Conversion:* O'Connor
Penalty Goals: O'Connor (2)
Western Samoa XV *Tries:* Vaega (2), Lima *Conversions:* Kellett (3)
Penalty Goals: Kellett (5) *Dropped Goal:* Kellett

MATCH 3 31 July, Ballymore, Brisbane

Queensland 22 (4PG 2T) **Western Samoa XV 24** (1G 4PG 1T)
Queensland *Tries:* Connors, Wilson *Penalty Goals:* Pini (4)
Western Samoa XV *Tries:* Keenan, Tuilagi *Conversion:* Kellett
Penalty Goals: Kellett (4)

MATCH 4 3 August, Newcastle

New South Wales XV 18 (1PG 3T) **Western Samoa XV 21** (1G 3PG 1T)
New South Wales XV *Tries:* Sykes, Magro, Scarr *Penalty Goal:* Wallace
Western Samoa XV *Tries:* Leaupepe, Vaega *Conversion:* Samania
Penalty Goals: Kellett (3)

MATCH 5 6 August, Sydney Football Stadium

AUSTRALIA 73 (6G 2PG 5T) **WESTERN SAMOA 3** (1PG)
AUSTRALIA: M Pini (Queensland); D I Campese (NSW), J S Little (Queensland), P W Howard (Queensland), D Smith (Queensland); D J Knox (NSW), G Gregan (ACT); A J Daly (NSW), P N Kearns (NSW) (*capt*), E J A McKenzie (NSW), J A Eales (Queensland), G J Morgan (Queensland), V Ofahengaue (NSW), B T Gavin (NSW), D J Wilson (Queensland) *Replacements* D K Junee (NSW) for Pini (61 mins); D Herbert (Queensland) for Little (70 mins)
Scorers *Tries:* Smith (2), Little (2), Pini, Howard, Campese, Gregan, Junee, Gavin, Ofahengaue *Conversions:* Knox (6) *Penalty Goals:* Knox (2)
WESTERN SAMOA: Aiolupo; Lima, Vaega, Tuilagi, Samania; Kellett, Vitale; Fatialofa (*capt*), To'omalatai, Latu, Birtwistle, Keenan, Mika, Lam, Vaifale
Replacements Iupeli for Lam (52 mins); Nu'uali'itia for Vitale (71 mins)
Scorer *Penalty Goal:* Kellett
Referee G K Wahlstrom (New Zealand)

ARGENTINA TO SOUTH AFRICA 1994

The strict interpretation of amateurism by the Argentinian Rugby Union (UAR) has precipitated a mass exodus of its leading players, mainly to Italy, in recent years. The high turnover of international personnel has left the Pumas with little continuity to their style of play. A strong scrummage supported by a good tactical kicker able to place goals have been the principal sources of recent Test successes.

The pack lived up to its reputation on this tour, with Paul Ackford's old sparring partner, Féderico Mendez, moving from prop to establish himself as a Test-class hooker. But the Pumas' lack of a decent kicker reduced their credibility as a potential threat to a Springbok side gearing itself up for the World Cup. Poor Hugo Porta, the former Argentinian captain and champion kicker who is now his country's ambassador in South Africa, must have had tears in his eyes as he watched his successors miss kick after kick on tour.

South Africa comfortably won the series. At Port Elizabeth, Johan Roux became the first South African scrum-half to score a brace of tries in a Test, but his celebrations were curtailed when an injury ruled him out for the Second Test and the imminent tour of Britain. For the second international, the Pumas, beset by injuries, had to make an emergency call for replacement fly-half José Cilley. He flew into Johannesburg only four hours before making his Test debut, but left his mark on an otherwise unenterprising performance by his colleagues, scoring 21 points.

After the tour, the coaching team of Hector Mendez and José Javier Fernandez, having made strident criticisms of several UAR officials, were relieved of their responsibilities.

THE TOURING PARTY

Manager L Chaluleu **Coach** H Mendez **Assistant Coach** J Javier Fernandez
Captain M Loffreda

FULL-BACK

S Salvat (Buenos Aires)

THREEQUARTERS

M Pfister (Tucumán)
M J Teran (Tucumán)
D Cuesta Silva (Buenos Aires)
F del Castillo (Rosario)
F Garcia (Buenos Aires)
M H Loffreda (Buenos Aires)

HALF-BACKS

L Bouza (Rosario)
G J del Castillo (Rosario)
C O Barrea (Cordoba)
R Bullrich (Buenos Aires)
G F Camardon (Buenos Aires)
***J Cilley** (Buenos Aires)

FORWARDS

M Corral (Buenos Aires)
R Grau (Mendoza)
M Grotto (Buenos Aires)
F E Mendez (Mendoza)
E P Noriega (Buenos Aires)
C Promanzio (Rosario)
G A Llanes (Buenos Aires)
P L Sporleder (Buenos Aires)
G Ugartemendia (Buenos Aires)
N Bossicovich (Rosario)
S Irazoqui (Cordoba)
R Martin (Buenos Aires)
C Viel-Temperley (Buenos Aires)

**Replacement during tour*

TOUR RECORD

All matches Played 6 Won 3 Lost 3 Points for 216 Against 216
International matches Played 2 Lost 2 Points for 48 Against 88

SCORING DETAILS

All matches

For:	27T	18C	15PG	–	216 Pts
Against:	28T	20C	12PG	–	216 Pts

International matches

For:	5T	4C	5PG	–	48 Pts
Against:	12T	8C	4PG	–	88 Pts

MATCH DETAILS

1994	OPPONENTS	VENUE	RESULT
27 Sept	South African Development XV	Wellington	W 51-20
30 Sept	Border	East London	W 41-25
4 Oct	South Africa A	Brakpan	L 12-56
8 Oct	SOUTH AFRICA	Port Elizabeth	L 22-42
11 Oct	Northern Orange Free State	Welkom	W 64-27
15 Oct	SOUTH AFRICA	Johannesburg	L 26-46

MATCH 1 27 September, Boland Stadium, Wellington

South African Development XV 20 (1G 1PG 2T) **Argentina XV 51** (4G 1PG 4T)
South African Development XV *Tries:* Breda, O'Neil, Thomson *Conversion:* O'Neil
Penalty Goal: O'Neil
Argentina XV *Tries:* Noriega, Corral, Mendez, Camardon (2), Bullrich, pen tries (2)
Conversions: Bouza (4) *Penalty Goal:* Bouza

MATCH 2 30 September, Basil Kenyon Stadium, East London

Border 25 (2G 2PG 1T) **Argentina XV 41** (3G 5PG 1T)
Border *Tries:* Gelderbloom, Claassen, Alexander *Conversions:* Henry (2)
Penalty Goals: Henry (2)
Argentina XV *Tries:* Pfister (2), Salvat, Martin *Conversions:* G del Castillo (3)
Penalty Goals: G del Castillo (5)

MATCH 3 4 October, Bosman Stadium, Brakpan

South Africa A 56 (6G 3PG 1T) **Argentina XV 12** (4PG)
South Africa A *Tries:* Badenhorst (2), Joubert (2), Swart, Kruger, Linee
Conversions: Herbert (6) *Penalty Goals:* Herbert (3)
Argentina XV *Penalty Goals:* Garcia (4)

MATCH 4 8 October, Boet Erasmus Stadium, Port Elizabeth 1st Test

SOUTH AFRICA 42 (4G 3PG 1T) **ARGENTINA 22** (2G 1PG 1T)
SOUTH AFRICA: G K Johnson (Transvaal); J T Small (Natal), C P Scholtz (Transvaal), B Venter (Orange Free State), C M Williams (Western Province); J T Stransky (Western Province), J Roux (Transvaal); J P du Randt (Orange Free State), U L Schmidt (Transvaal), T G Laubscher (Western Province), M G Andrews (Natal), H Hattingh (Northern Transvaal), J F Pienaar (Transvaal) (*capt*), C P Strauss (Western Province), R A W Straeuli (Transvaal) *Replacement* J Dalton (Transvaal) for Schmidt (75 mins)
Scorers *Tries:* Roux (2), Stransky, Strauss, Williams *Conversions:* Stransky (4)
Penalty Goals: Stransky (3)
ARGENTINA: Salvat; Teran, Loffreda (*capt*), Cuesta Silva, Pfister; G del Castillo, Bullrich; Corral, Mendez, Noriega, Sporleder, Llanes, Martin, Ugartemendia, Viel-Temperley *Replacement* F del Castillo for Cuesta Silva (60 mins)
Scorers *Tries:* Loffreda, Pfister, Teran *Conversions:* G del Castillo (2)
Penalty Goal: G del Castillo
Referee G K Wahlstrom (New Zealand)

MATCH 5 11 October, North West Stadium, Welkom

Northern Orange Free State 27 (3G 2PG) **Argentina XV 64** (7G 3T)
Northern Orange Free State *Tries:* Badenhorst, Jerling, Fouche
Conversions: Roeland (3) *Penalty Goals:* Roeland (2)
Argentina XV *Tries:* Teran (2), Ugartemendia, Bossicovich, Corral, Martin (2), Bullrich, Loffreda, Camardon *Conversions:* G del Castillo (4), Garcia, Loffreda (2)

MATCH 6 15 October, Ellis Park, Johannesburg 2nd Test

SOUTH AFRICA 46 (4G 1PG 3T) **ARGENTINA 26** (2G 4PG)
SOUTH AFRICA: A J Joubert (Natal); C Badenhorst (Orange Free State), H P le Roux (Transvaal), B Venter (Orange Free State), C M Williams (Western Province); J T Stransky (Western Province), J H van der Westhuizen (Northern Transvaal); J P du Randt (Orange Free State), U L Schmidt (Transvaal), T G Laubscher (Western Province), M G Andrews (Natal), H Hattingh (Northern Transvaal), J F Pienaar (Transvaal) (*capt*), C P Strauss (Western Province), R A W Straeuli

(Transvaal) *Replacements* E van der Bergh (Eastern Province) temp for Pienaar and for Strauss (42 mins); I S Swart (Transvaal) for Laubscher (63 mins)
Scorers *Tries:* Badenhorst (2), Stransky, Andrews, Straeuli, Williams, van der Westhuizen *Conversions:* Stransky (4) *Penalty Goal:* Stransky
ARGENTINA: Salvat; Teran, Garcia, Loffreda (*capt*), Pfister; Cilley, Bullrich; Corral, Mendez, Noriega, Llanes, Sporleder, Martin, Ugartemendia, Viel-Temperley
Scorers *Tries:* Llanes, Cilley *Conversions:* Cilley (2) *Penalty Goals:* Cilley (4)
Referee G K Wahlstrom (New Zealand)

SOUTH AFRICA TO WALES, SCOTLAND AND IRELAND 1994

The tour was the end of a long road for the South Africans. Some doubted the wisdom of coming to the wet fields of Europe when every other international team, with an eye on the World Cup, was anxious about getting in some practice on hard grounds.

By the end, though, the decision was vindicated. The team had gelled on the field, winning both Tests and losing only twice in 13 games. They averaged almost 30 points a match. The tourists were also a great hit off the field, captain François Pienaar representing his country with dignity and honour. A squalid evening at Neath apart, the tour passed off without major incident, showing that the South Africans are getting to grips at long last with discipline.

South Africa gave further proof that they can run with the best of them. The backs, André Joubert, Chester Williams and Joost van der Westhuizen in particular, had tremendous tours. Joubert, after several lean years through injury, looks to have made the full-back berth his own. He scored six tries and finished with 75 points in all.

The forwards, though, did not make quite the same impact. In full flow, as shown in that stunning 78-7 win against Swansea, the Springbok forwards handle and run with ease. Challenged at close quarters, however, they quickly lose that aura of invincibility. Wales proved that, as to a lesser extent did Neath and Scotland A. The South Africans have yet to find a middle jumper to supplement Andrews. The back row of Straeuli, Kruger and Pienaar, on the other hand, was outstanding.

THE TOURING PARTY

Manager J P Engelbrecht **Coach** G M Christie **Assistant Coach** Z M J Pienaar
Captain J F Pienaar

FULL-BACKS

G K Johnson (Transvaal)
A J Joubert (Natal)

THREEQUARTERS

C M Williams (Western Province)
P Hendriks (Transvaal)
J Olivier (Northern Transvaal)
C Badenhorst (Orange Free State)
P G Müller (Natal)
B Venter (Orange Free State)
M Linee (Western Province)
J C Mulder (Transvaal)
***J F van der Westhuizen** (Natal)
***J P Claassens** (Northern Transvaal)
***H L Müller** (Orange Free State)

HALF-BACKS

J T Stransky (Western Province)

H P le Roux (Transvaal)
J H van der Westhuizen (Northern Transvaal)
K B Putt (Natal)

FORWARDS

J P du Randt (Orange Free State)
I S Swart (Transvaal)
T G Laubscher (Western Province)
S J Hattingh (Transvaal)
U L Schmidt (Transvaal)
J Dalton (Transvaal)
M G Andrews (Natal)
J J Wiese (Transvaal)
H Hattingh (Northern Transvaal)
P J W Schutte (Transvaal)
J F Pienaar (Transvaal)
R J Kruger (Northern Transvaal)
R A W Straeuli (Transvaal)
C P Strauss (Western Province)
E van der Bergh (Eastern Province)
G H Teichmann (Natal)
***K Otto** (Northern Transvaal)
**Replacement during tour*

TOUR RECORD

All matches Played 13 Won 11 Lost 2 Points for 375 Against 151
International matches Played 2 Won 2 Points for 54 Against 22

SCORING DETAILS

All matches

For:	50T	31C	21PG	–	375 Pts
Against:	12T	8C	22PG	3DG	151 Pts

International matches

For:	8T	4C	2PG	–	54 Pts
Against:	1T	1C	5PG	–	22 Pts

MATCH DETAILS

1994	OPPONENTS	VENUE	RESULT
22 Oct	Cardiff	Cardiff	W 11-6
26 Oct	Wales A	Newport	W 25-13
29 Oct	Llanelli	Llanelli	W 30-12
2 Nov	Neath	Neath	W 16-13
5 Nov	Swansea	Swansea	W 78-7
9 Nov	Scotland A	Melrose	L 15-17
12 Nov	Scottish Combined Districts	Glasgow	W 33-6
15 Nov	Scottish Select	Aberdeen	W 35-10
19 Nov	SCOTLAND	Murrayfield	W 34-10
22 Nov	Pontypridd	Pontypridd	W 9-3
26 Nov	WALES	Cardiff	W 20-12
29 Nov	Combined Provinces	Belfast	W 54-19
3 Dec	Barbarians	Dublin	L 15-23

*Appearances: 9 – Stransky**; 8 – Joubert*, Teichmann*, Straeuli*, Johnson*, Laubscher**; 7 – P Müller, Williams, J H van der Westhuizen, Schmidt, S Hattingh, Andrews, Kruger, Du Randt, Van der Bergh; 6 – Swart, Mulder, Hendriks, Le Roux, Putt, Dalton, Wiese, Schutte, Pienaar; 5 – Venter, Olivier, Strauss; 4 – H Hattingh, Linee, J F van der Westhuizen; 3 – Badenhorst, H Müller, Otto; 1 – Claassens * includes appearances as a replacement*
Scorers: 75 – Joubert (6T 18C 3PG); 69 – Johnson (3T 9C 12PG); 26 – Stransky (3T 1C 3PG); 25 – J H van der Westhuizen (5T), Straeuli (5T); 20 – Le Roux (1T 3C 3PG); 15 – Williams (3T), Schmidt (3T), Kruger (3T), P Müller (3T), Otto (3T); 10 – Hendriks (2T), S Hattingh (2T); 5 – Putt (1T), Linee (1T), Venter (1T), H Hattingh (1T), Strauss (1T), Pienaar (1T), Van der Bergh (1T), Mulder (1T)

MATCH 1 22 October, Cardiff Arms Park

Cardiff 6 (2PG) **South African XV 11** (2PG 1T)
Cardiff: C John; S Ford, M Hall (*capt*), C Laity, N Walker; A Davies, A Moore; M Griffiths, J Humphreys, L Mustoe, S Roy, D Jones, H Taylor, O Williams, E Lewis
Replacement A Booth for Moore (temp)
Scorers *Penalty Goals:* Davies, John
South African XV: Joubert; Badenhorst, Venter, P Müller, Williams; Stransky, J H van der Westhuizen; Swart, Schmidt, S Hattingh, Andrews, H Hattingh, Kruger,

Teichmann, Straeuli (*capt*)
Scorers *Try:* J H van der Westhuizen *Penalty Goals:* Stransky (2)
Referee J M Fleming (Scotland)

MATCH 2 26 October, Rodney Parade, Newport

Wales A 13 (1G 2PG) **South African XV 25** (2G 2PG 1T)
Wales A: M Back (Bridgend); D Manley (Pontypridd), S Lewis (Pontypridd), M Taylor (Pontypool), N Walker (Cardiff); A Davies (Cardiff), P John (Pontypridd) (*capt*); I Buckett (Swansea), B Williams (Neath), L Mustoe (Cardiff), P Arnold (Swansea), D Jones (Cardiff), S Davies (Swansea), S Williams (Neath), R Appleyard (Swansea)
Replacement M Griffiths (Cardiff) for Mustoe (66 mins)
Scorers *Try:* Walker *Conversion:* A Davies *Penalty Goals:* A Davies (2)
South African XV: Johnson; Olivier, Mulder, Linee, Hendriks; Le Roux, Putt; Du Randt, Dalton, Laubscher, Wiese, Schutte, Kruger, Straeuli (*capt*), Van der Bergh
Replacement Teichmann for Kruger (56 mins)
Scorers *Tries:* Putt, Linee, Straeuli *Conversions:* Le Roux (2) *Penalty Goals:* Le Roux (2)
Referee A J Spreadbury (England)

MATCH 3 29 October, Stradey Park, Llanelli

Llanelli 12 (1G 1T) **South African XV 30** (2G 2PG 2T)
Llanelli: I Jones; W Proctor, N Boobyer, N Davies, M Wintle; C Stephens, R Moon (*capt*); R Evans, R McBryde, S John, P Davies, A Copsey, P Jones, J Williams, M Perego
Replacements J Strange for Stephens (61 mins); H Harries for Proctor (76 mins)
Scorers *Tries:* Wintle, Proctor *Conversion:* Stephens
South African XV: Joubert; Badenhorst, Mulder, Venter, Williams; Stransky, J H van der Westhuizen; Swart, Schmidt, S Hattingh, Andrews, H Hattingh, Pienaar (*capt*), Teichmann, Van der Bergh *Replacement* Laubscher for Swart (40 mins)
Scorers *Tries:* Stransky, Van der Bergh, Joubert, Pienaar *Conversions:* Joubert (2)
Penalty Goals: Stransky, Joubert
Referee D McHugh (Ireland)

MATCH 4 2 November, The Gnoll, Neath

Neath 13 (1G 2PG) **South African XV 16** (1G 3PG)
Neath: P Thorburn; C Higgs, J Bird, H Woodland, L Davies; A Thomas, R Jones; Brian Williams, Barry Williams, J Davies, G O Llewellyn (*capt*), C Wyatt, A Kembury, S Williams, C Scott *Replacements* S Bowling for Woodland (temp); M Morgan for Brian Williams (temp); R Morris for S Williams (70 mins)
Scorers *Try:* Jones *Conversion:* Thomas *Penalty Goals:* Thomas (2)
South African XV: Johnson; Badenhorst, P Müller, Venter, Olivier; Stransky, Putt; Du Randt, Dalton, S Hattingh, Wiese, H Hattingh, Teichmann, Strauss (*capt*), Van der Bergh *Replacement* Joubert for Badenhorst (21 mins)
Scorers *Try:* Strauss *Conversion:* Joubert *Penalty Goals:* Johnson (2), Joubert
Referee R J Megson (Scotland)

MATCH 5 5 November, St Helen's, Swansea

Swansea 7 (1G) **South African XV 78** (9G 3T)
Swansea: A Clement (*capt*); Simon Davies, R Boobyer, D Weatherley, S Marshall; A Williams, R Jones; I Buckett, G Jenkins, K Colclough, P Arnold, R Moriarty, A Reynolds, I Davies, R Appleyard *Replacements* M Evans for Moriarty (53 mins); Stuart Davies for Appleyard (63 mins)
Scorers *Try:* Simon Davies *Conversion:* Williams
South African XV: Joubert; Hendriks, Mulder, P Müller, Williams; Le Roux, J H van der Westhuizen; Du Randt, Schmidt, Laubscher, Andrews, Schutte, Pienaar (*capt*), Straeuli, Kruger

Scorers *Tries:* Joubert (4), Hendriks (2), Williams, Le Roux, Schmidt, J H van der Westhuizen, Straeuli, Kruger *Conversions:* Joubert (9)
Referee S R Hilditch (Ireland)

MATCH 6 9 November, The Greenyards, Melrose

Scotland A 17 (2PG 2DG 1T) **South African XV 15** (1G 1PG 1T)
Scotland A: R Shepherd (Edinburgh Acads); C Joiner (Melrose), S Nichol (Selkirk), I Jardine (Stirling County), C Glasgow (Heriot's FP); D Hodge (Watsonians), B Redpath (Melrose); D Hilton (Bath), K McKenzie (Stirling County) (*capt*), P Wright (Boroughmuir), D Cronin (Bourges), S Campbell (Dundee HSFP), F Wallace (Glasgow High/Kelvinside), R Wainwright (West Hartlepool), I Smith (Gloucester)
Scorers *Try:* Wallace *Penalty Goals:* Shepherd (2) *Dropped Goals:* Hodge (2)
South African XV: Johnson; Olivier, Linee, Venter, J F van der Westhuizen; Stransky, Putt; S Hattingh, Dalton, Swart, Wiese, H Hattingh, Teichmann, Strauss (*capt*), Van der Bergh
Scorers *Tries:* Venter, H Hattingh *Conversion:* Stransky *Penalty Goal:* Johnson
Referee P Thomas (France)

MATCH 7 12 November, Old Anniesland, Glasgow

Scottish Combined Districts 6 (2PG) **South African XV 33** (4G 1T)
Scottish Combined Districts: N Mardon (Boroughmuir); H Gilmour (Heriot's FP), A McRobbie (Heriot's FP), S Lineen (Boroughmuir) (*capt*), J Kerr (Watsonians); M McKenzie (Stirling County), G Burns (Stewart's-Melville FP); G Wilson (Boroughmuir), G Ellis (Currie), B Robertson (Stirling County), A Watt (Glasgow High/Kelvinside), S Munro (Glasgow High/Kelvinside), B Ward (Currie), S Reid (Boroughmuir), G Mackay (Stirling County)
Scorer *Penalty Goals:* McKenzie (2)
South African XV: Joubert; Hendriks, P Müller, Venter, Williams; Le Roux, J H van der Westhuizen; Du Randt, Schmidt, Laubscher, Andrews, Schutte, Pienaar (*capt*), Straeuli, Kruger *Replacements* Johnson for Joubert (60 mins); Stransky for Venter (74 mins)
Scorers *Tries:* J H van der Westhuizen, Müller (2), Straeuli, Kruger *Conversions:* Joubert (3), Johnson
Referee C Thomas (Wales)

MATCH 8 15 November, Rubislaw Playing Fields, Aberdeen

Scottish Select 10 (1G 1PG) **South African XV 35** (1G 6PG 2T)
Scottish Select: M Dods (Gala); G Sharp (Bristol), F Harrold (London Scottish), R Eriksson (London Scottish), M Appleson (Sale); S Welsh (Hawick), G Oliver (Hawick) (*capt*); J Manson (Dundee HSFP), M Scott (Dunfermline), D Herrington (Dundee HSFP), R Brown (Melrose), R Scott (London Scottish), D Turnbull (Hawick), E Peters (Bath), R Kirkpatrick (Jedforest) *Replacement* B Renwick (Hawick) for Turnbull (44 mins)
Scorers *Try:* Oliver *Conversion:* Welsh *Penalty Goal:* Welsh
South African XV: Johnson; Olivier, H Müller, Linee, J F van der Westhuizen; Stransky, Putt; Swart, Dalton, S Hattingh, Otto, Wiese, Teichmann, Strauss (*capt*), Van der Bergh *Replacement* Laubscher for Hattingh (temp)
Scorers *Tries:* Otto, Johnson, Hattingh *Conversion:* Johnson *Penalty Goals:* Johnson (6)
Referee G Simmonds (Wales)

MATCH 9 19 November, Murrayfield 1st Test

SCOTLAND 10 (1G 1PG) SOUTH AFRICA 34 (3G 1PG 2T)

South Africa blew Scotland away at the beginning of the second half with an awesome display of power rugby, scoring three tries within six minutes of the restart. It was only a lapse of concentration in the last quarter which spared the Scots further humiliation in front of a crowd of 63,500 who had earlier seen the new £44 million Murrayfield opened by the Princess Royal.

Schutte made his debut for South Africa in the second row. Van der Westhuizen brazenly bolted clear round the base of a 22-metre scrum to score South Africa's only try of the first half. The scrum-half was first on the scoresheet after the break, selling a huge dummy to Gavin Hastings. South Africa probed the blind side time and again, a tactic which brought tries for Williams and Straeuli, while Mulder forced his way over on the hour. There was small consolation for Scotland in a late try by Stanger.

SCOTLAND: A G Hastings (Watsonians) (*capt*); A G Stanger (Melrose), S Hastings (Watsonians), A G Shiel (Melrose), K M Logan (Stirling County); C M Chalmers (Melrose), D W Patterson (West Hartlepool); A V Sharp (Bristol), K S Milne (Heriot's FP), A P Burnell (London Scottish), J F Richardson (Edinburgh Acads), A I Reed (Bath), D J McIvor (Edinburgh Acads), G W Weir (Melrose), I R Morrison (London Scottish)
Scorers *Try:* Stanger *Conversion:* A G Hastings *Penalty Goal:* A G Hastings
SOUTH AFRICA: Joubert; Hendriks, P Müller, Mulder, Williams; Le Roux, J H van der Westhuizen; Du Randt, Schmidt, Laubscher, Andrews, Schutte, Pienaar (*capt*), Straeuli, Kruger
Scorers *Tries:* J H van der Westhuizen (2), Williams, Straeuli, Mulder
Conversions: Joubert (3) *Penalty Goal:* Joubert
Referee O E Doyle (Ireland)

MATCH 10 22 November, Sardis Road, Pontypridd

Pontypridd 3 (1PG) **South African XV 9** (3PG)
Pontypridd: G Jones; D Manley, J Lewis, S Lewis, O Robbins; C Cormack, Paul John; N Bezani (*capt*), Phil John, A Metcalfe, G Prosser, M Rowley, M Spiller, M Lloyd, P Thomas *Replacement* C Jones for J Lewis (72 mins)
Scorer *Penalty Goal:* Cormack
South African XV: Johnson; Olivier, H Müller, Linee, J F van der Westhuizen; Stransky, Putt; Swart, Dalton, S Hattingh, Wiese, Otto, Teichmann, Strauss (*capt*), Van der Bergh
Scorer *Penalty Goals:* Johnson (3)
Referee B Campsall (Halifax)

MATCH 11 26 November, Cardiff Arms Park 2nd Test

WALES 12 (4PG) SOUTH AFRICA 20 (1G 1PG 2T)

Wales have still never beaten South Africa but there were times here when the Springboks were under severe pressure. In the end three tries to nil is an emphatic enough victory. South Africa had a decisive edge behind the scrum with Joubert and Williams a constant threat. Wales prospered through one of their two new caps, 6ft 10in lock Derwyn Jones. He helped his side dominate the line-out.

A soft try by Straeuli in the eighth minute following a tap penalty boded ill for Wales. Jenkins nudged over a penalty in the 20th minute before Joubert rounded off a flourishing movement involving 14 pairs of hands just two minutes later. Jenkins kept swinging the boot, however, succeeding once more before half-time and twice afterwards. Le Roux replied for South Africa with a penalty goal before Williams' try in the 69th minute put Wales beyond contention.

WALES: A Clement (Swansea); W T Proctor (Llanelli), M R Hall (Cardiff), M Taylor (Pontypool), S D Hill (Cardiff); N R Jenkins (Pontypridd), R H StJ B Moon (Llanelli); R L Evans (Llanelli), G R Jenkins (Swansea), J D Davies (Neath), D Jones (Cardiff), G O Llewellyn (Neath) (*capt*), H T Taylor (Cardiff), E W Lewis (Cardiff), R G Collins (Pontypridd) *Replacement* R C McBryde (Llanelli) for G R Jenkins (temp)
Scorer *Penalty Goals:* N R Jenkins (4)
SOUTH AFRICA: Joubert; Hendriks, P Müller, Mulder, Williams; Le Roux, J H van der Westhuizen; Du Randt, Schmidt, Laubscher, Andrews, Schutte, Pienaar (*capt*), Straeuli, Kruger
Scorers *Tries:* Straeuli, Joubert, Williams *Conversion:* Le Roux
Penalty Goal: Le Roux
Referee D Mene (France)

MATCH 12 29 November, Ravenhill, Belfast

Combined Provinces 19 (3PG 2T) **South African XV 54** (7G 1T)
Combined Provinces: J Bell (Ballymena); P Gavin (Old Belvedere), P Danaher (Garryowen), M Field (Malone), R Wallace (Garryowen); A McGowan (Blackrock), A Rolland (Blackrock); J Fitzgerald (Young Munster), T Kingston (Dolphin) (*capt*), G Halpin (London Irish), M Galwey (Shannon), N Francis (Old Belvedere), E Halvey (Shannon), S McKinty (Bangor), D Corkery (Cork Const)
Scorers *Tries:* Bell, Fitzgerald *Penalty Goals:* McGowan (3)
South African XV: Johnson; Hendriks, H Müller, Claassens, J F van der Westhuizen; Stransky, Putt; S Hattingh, Schmidt, Laubscher, Otto, Schutte, Teichmann, Straeuli (*capt*), Van der Bergh
Scorers *Tries:* Stransky (2), Otto (2), Schmidt (2), Hattingh, Johnson
Conversions: Johnson (7)
Referee R Yeman (Wales)

MATCH 13 3 December, Lansdowne Road, Dublin

Barbarians 23 (2G 2PG 1DG) **South Africa 15** (3T)
Barbarians: J E B Callard (Bath & England); S P Geoghegan (Bath & Ireland), M R Hall (Cardiff & Wales), S Hastings (Watsonians & Scotland), P Saint-André (Montferrand & France); C M Chalmers (Melrose & Scotland), R N Jones (Swansea & Wales) (*capt*); N J Popplewell (Wasps & Ireland), K G M Wood (Garryowen & Ireland), P M Clohessy (Young Munster & Ireland), I D Jones (North Harbour & New Zealand), S D Shaw (Bristol), A J Charron (Ottawa Irish & Canada), R I Wainwright (West Hartlepool & Scotland), N A Back (Leicester & England)
Replacements G Manson-Bishop (Newport) for Charron (26 mins); P W Howard (Queensland & Australia) for Hastings (46 mins)
Scorers *Tries:* Saint-André, Geoghegan *Conversions:* Callard (2)
Penalty Goals: Callard (2) *Dropped Goal:* Chalmers
South Africa: Joubert; Johnson, P Müller, Mulder, Williams; Le Roux, J H van der Westhuizen; Du Randt, Dalton, Swart, Wiese, Andrews, Pienaar (*capt*), Strauss, Kruger *Replacements* Stransky for Williams (22 mins); Straeuli for Pienaar (79 mins)
Scorers *Tries:* Kruger, Müller, Johnson
Referee W D Bevan (Wales)

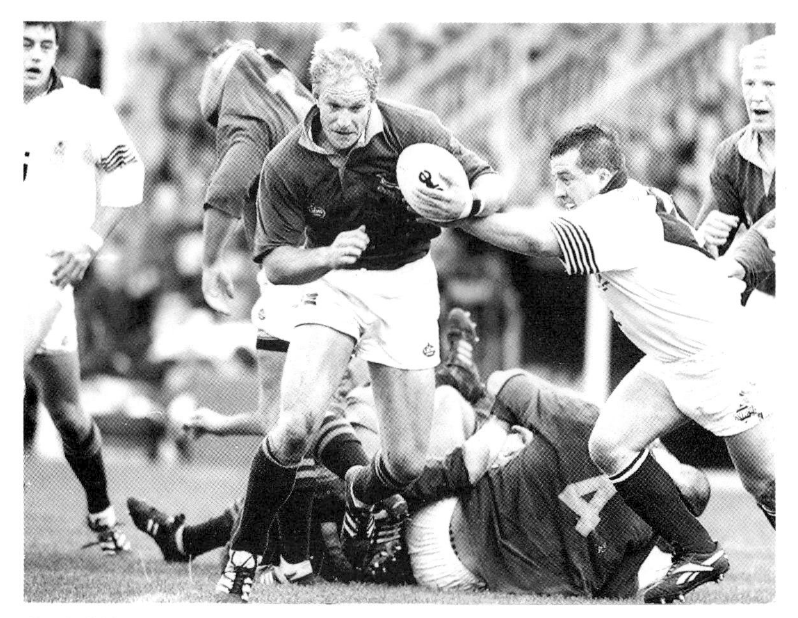

South African captain François Pienaar powers past Garin Jenkins in the Springboks' 78-7 demolition of Swansea.

Rob Andrew tackles Steve Gray of Canada in England's emphatic victory at Twickenham. Andrew equalled the world record for most points scored in an international with 30 in this match.

CANADA TO EUROPE 1994

In the early 1990s, Canada emerged as a rugby-playing nation capable of taking on and pressing the best in the world. Witness their performances in the 1991 World Cup, where they gave New Zealand a tough time in the quarter-finals, as well as subsequent victories in full internationals against both Wales and France. The 1994 tour, therefore, gave Canada the opportunity of testing their mettle against two of the world's best teams and measuring their rugby progress.

It has to be said that the results made disappointing reading for the Canadians. A 100 per cent record of defeats suggested that they had reached a crossroads on their path to glory. The tour showed that an ageing side was desperately in need of an injection of youth to add strength and depth to the national squad, while extra pace outside the scrum would have increased tactical options on the field.

The loss of Al Charron, who dislocated a shoulder playing for the Barbarians against South Africa in Dublin, was unfortunate, but hardly went any way towards explaining heavy defeats in both Tests, where the Canadians were bereft of attacking ideas. Except for a ten-minute purple patch at Twickenham, during which Dave Lougheed twice showed England's cover a clean pair of heels, their only chances of scoring were when Gareth Rees was lining up kicks at goal.

On the evidence of this tour, Canada had an awful lot of preparation ahead before Monty Heald's eve-of-tour prophecy that they would win the World Cup in South Africa stood a chance of coming true. This tour showed that the Canadian Rugby Union's president was highly unlikely to see his team reach the quarter-finals.

THE TOURING PARTY

Managers D Whidden, R Skett **Coach** I Birtwell **Assistant Coach** R Holloway
Captain I C Stuart

FULL-BACK

D S Stewart (UBC Old Boys)

THREEQUARTERS

D C Lougheed (Toronto Welsh)
C Smith (Meralomas & Balmy Beach)
W Stanley (U of BC)
S MacKinnon (Ex-Britannia Lions)
C Stewart (Rovigo & Western Province)
S D Gray (Kats)
R Toews (Meralomas)
I C Stuart (Vancouver RC)
D Clarke (Swilers)

HALF-BACKS

G L Rees (Oxford U & Oak Bay Castaways)
J D Graf (UBC Old Boys)
I MacKay (Kats)
C J C Tynan (Cambridge U & Meralomas)
***B Ross** (James Bay)

FORWARDS

E A Evans (IBM Tokyo & UBC Old Boys)
D C Jackart (UBC Old Boys)
P le Blanc (Kats)
R Snow (Dogs)
M E Cardinal (James Bay)
K F Svoboda (Ajax Wanderers)
N Hadley (Wasps & UBC Old Boys)
J R Robertsen (UBC Old Boys)
K Whitley (Calgary Irish & Capilano)
M James (Burnaby Lake)
A J Charron (Ottawa Irish)
I Gordon (James Bay)
G I MacKinnon (Ex-Britannia Lions)
B Breen (Meralomas)
J Hutchinson (UBC Old Boys)

C McKenzie (UBC Old Boys)
***C Michaluk** (Vancouver RC)
***I Cooper** (Vancouver RC)
**Replacement during tour*

TOUR RECORD

All matches Played 6 Lost 6 Points for 86 Against 185
International matches Played 2 Lost 2 Points for 28 Against 88

SCORING DETAILS

All matches

For:	8T	5C	12PG	–	86 Pts
Against:	18T	13C	21PG	2DG	185 Pts

International matches

For:	3T	2C	3PG	–	28 Pts
Against:	9T	8C	8PG	1DG	88 Pts

MATCH DETAILS

1994	OPPONENTS	VENUE	RESULT
30 Nov	Italy A	Rovigo	L 11-18
3 Dec	Combined Services	Devonport	L 20-21
6 Dec	Emerging England XV	Bath	L 6-34
10 Dec	ENGLAND	Twickenham	L 19-60
13 Dec	Mediterranean XV	Toulon	L 21-24
17 Dec	FRANCE	Besançon	L 9-28

*Appearances: 5 – Gray**; 4 – Toews, Stanley, Ross, Jackart, James, Hadley*, Gordon, Le Blanc*, Hutchinson*, Cardinal*, McKenzie; 3 – S MacKinnon, Smith, S Stewart, C Stewart, Lougheed, MacKay, Graf, Svoboda, G MacKinnon, Robertsen, Evans; 2 – Clarke, Stuart, Snow, Whitley, Michaluk, Rees; 1 – Charron, Cooper *includes appearances as a replacement*
Scorers: 33 – Ross (9PG 3C); 15 – Lougheed (3T); 13 – Rees (3PG 2C); 5 – McKenzie, Gordon, Evans, Hutchinson, Stanley (all 1T)

MATCH 1 30 November, Rovigo

Italy A 18 (5PG 1DG) **Canada XV 11** (2PG 1T)
Italy A: C Pilat (Bologna); P-F Donati (Treviso), F Mazzariol (Treviso), M Piovene (Padova), L Manteri (Treviso); S Brolis (Piacenza), G Faltiba (San Dona); A Castellani (L'Aquila), T Ravasini (Parma), A Piazza (San Dona), D Sesenna (Piacenza), G Croci (Milan), W Cristofoletto (Treviso), M Capuzzoni (Milan), D Scaglia (Tarvisium) (*capt*)
Replacement G Cicino (L'Aquila) for Capuzzoni (3 mins)
Scorers *Penalty Goals:* Pilat (5) *Dropped Goal:* Mazzariol
Canada XV: D Stewart; Stanley, C Stewart, Stuart (*capt*), Lougheed; Ross, Graf; Snow, Svoboda, Jackart, James, Hadley, Charron, G MacKinnon, Gordon
Replacements Hutchinson for Charron (63 mins); Gray for Stuart (77 mins)
Scorers *Try:* Lougheed *Penalty Goals:* Ross (2)
Referee S Giacomel (Italian RU)

MATCH 2 3 December, Devonport

Combined Services 21 (1G 3PG 1T) **Canada XV 20** (2G 2PG)
Combined Services: S Lazenby (RAF); S Bartliff (Army), D Sibson (RN), G Sharp (RAF), S Crossland (RAF); E Rayner (RAF), S Worrall (RAF) (*capt*); B Williams (RAF), J Brammer (Army), J Fowers (Army), D Dahinton (Army), G Harrison (RN), D Williams (RAF), R Armstrong (RN), I Dixon (RN)
Scorers *Tries:* Sharp, Brammer *Conversion:* Worrall *Penalty Goals:* Worrall (3)
Canada XV: S MacKinnon; Smith, Clarke, Gray, Toews; Ross, Mackay; Le Blanc, Cardinal, Jackart, Robertsen, Whitley, Gordon, McKenzie (*capt*), Hutchinson
Scorers *Tries:* McKenzie, Gordon *Conversions:* Ross (2) *Penalty Goals:* Ross (2)
Referee H Lewis (Wales)

MATCH 3 6 December, Recreation Ground, Bath

Emerging England XV 34 (4G 2PG) **Canada XV 6** (2PG)

Emerging England XV: W Greenwood (Harlequins); J Sleightholme (Bath), G Childs (Wasps), N Greenstock (Wasps), H Thorneycroft (Northampton); G Gregory (Wasps), R Kitchin (Harlequins); R Hardwick (Coventry), G Adams (Bath), D Hinkins (Bristol); G Archer (Newcastle Gosforth), R West (Gloucester), A Diprose (Saracens), R Hill (Saracens), D Eves (Bristol) *(capt)* *Replacement* M Haag (Bath) for West (67 mins)
Scorers *Tries:* Greenstock (2), Sleightholme, Childs *Conversions:* Gregory (4)
Penalty Goals: Gregory (2)
Canada XV: S MacKinnon; Smith, Toews, Gray, Stanley; Ross, Mackay; Evans, Svoboda, Le Blanc, Robertsen, James, Michaluk, McKenzie *(capt)*, Hutchinson
Scorer *Penalty Goals:* Ross (2)
Referee P Bolland (Wales)

MATCH 4 10 December, Twickenham — 1st Test

ENGLAND 60 (6G 6PG) CANADA 19 (2G 1T)

Canada crashed to their heaviest defeat for nine years and conceded 60 points in an international for the first time. England were simply unstoppable at times, and Rob Andrew's immaculate conversion and penalty kicks – he landed 12 goals from 12 attempts on a blustery day – equalled the world record for most points (30) in a major international.

It was 15-0 at the break (all penalties) before Jack Rowell's grand designs, in the form of all-out attack, brought England the rich reward of six second-half tries. Yet full credit was due to Canada, whose defence against wave after wave of attack remained brave. Moreover, they drew consolation from the determined running of Dave Lougheed. His dashes along the left touchline and fine finishing early in the second half added respectability to Canada's score.

ENGLAND: P A Hull (Bristol & RAF); T Underwood (Leicester), W D C Carling (Harlequins) *(capt)*, J C Guscott (Bath), R Underwood (Leicester & RAF); C R Andrew (Wasps), K P P Bracken (Bristol); J Leonard (Harlequins), B C Moore (Harlequins), V E Ubogu (Bath), M O Johnson (Leicester), M C Bayfield (Northampton), T A K Rodber (Northampton & Army), D Richards (Leicester), B B Clarke (Bath)
Replacements M J Catt (Bath) for Hull (26 mins); P R de Glanville (Bath) for T Underwood (65 mins)
Scorers *Tries:* T Underwood, R Underwood (2), Bracken, Catt (2)
Conversions: Andrew (6) *Penalty Goals:* Andrew (6)
CANADA: S Stewart; Toews, C Stewart, Stuart *(capt)*, Lougheed; Rees, Graf; Evans, Cardinal, Jackart, James, Hadley, Gordon, McKenzie, G MacKinnon
Replacement Gray for Stuart (65 mins)
Scorers *Tries:* Lougheed (2), Evans *Conversions:* Rees (2)
Referee W J Erickson (Australia)

MATCH 5 13 December, Stade Mayol, Toulon

Mediterranean XV 24 (3PG 3T) **Canada XV 21** (1G 3PG 1T)
Mediterranean XV: E Berdeu (Nice); P Fabre (Perpignan), P Arlettaz (Perpignan), P Bondouy (Narbonne), C Dominici (Toulon); C Poumeaud (Mandelieu), A Hueber (Toulon) *(capt)*; M Perie (Toulon), H Guiraud (Nîmes), P Gallart (Béziers), G Orsoni (Toulon), Y Theron (Bourgoin), C Moni (Nice), M Delpoux (Perpignan), C Labit (Narbonne) *Replacement* M Marfaing (Narbonne) for Arlettaz (10 mins)
Scorers *Tries:* Fabre, Delpoux (2) *Penalty Goals:* Bondouy (3)
Canada XV: S MacKinnon; Smith, Clarke, Toews, Stanley; Ross, Mackay; Snow,

Cardinal, Le Blanc, Cooper, Whitley, Michaluk, Robertsen (*capt*), Hutchinson
Replacement Hadley for Cooper (63 mins)
Scorers *Tries:* Hutchinson, Stanley *Conversion:* Ross *Penalty Goals:* Ross (3)
Referee D Mene (Provence)

MATCH 6 17 December, Stade Leo Lagrange, Besançon 2nd Test

FRANCE 28 (2G 2PG 1DG 1T) **CANADA 9** (3PG)

This was France's first-ever international at Besançon in the lee of the Jura Mountains and it was played in bitterly cold weather. Canada lost again, though there were performances which gave their management team grounds for optimism at the end of a gruelling tour.

Gareth Rees, enjoying better-quality possession – and more of it – than at Twickenham, tried admirably to involve a back line in which Chris Stewart and Dave Lougheed ran with purpose. At the final whistle, however, all Canada had to show for their efforts were three Rees penalty goals.

There was a pleasing moment at the end of the match for Philippe Sella, who was winning his 102nd cap. He called for a pass from a quick tap penalty and crossed unchallenged at the corner for the last try of the game, helping to erase the memory of his sending-off earlier in the year in Nepean for allegedly punching an opponent.

FRANCE: J-L Sadourny (Colomiers); E Ntamack (Toulouse), P Sella (Agen), T Lacroix (Dax), P Saint-André (Montferrand) (*capt*); Y Delaigue (Toulon), G Accoceberry (Bègles-Bordeaux); L Benezech (Racing Club de France), J-L Gonzalez (Bayonne), C Califano (Toulouse), O Merle (Montferrand), O Roumat (Dax), A Costes (Montferrand), P Benetton (Agen), A Benazzi (Agen)
Scorers *Tries:* Benetton, Sadourny, Sella *Conversions:* Lacroix (2)
Penalty Goals: Lacroix (2) *Dropped Goal:* Delaigue
CANADA: S Stewart; Stanley, C Stewart, Gray, Lougheed; Rees (*capt*), Graf; Evans, Svoboda, Jackart, James, Hadley, Gordon, McKenzie, G MacKinnon
Replacement Le Blanc for Jackart (temp); Cardinal for Svoboda (78 mins)
Scorer *Penalty Goals:* Rees (3)
Referee B Leask (Australia)

USA TO IRELAND 1994

Namibia were due to visit Ireland in the autumn of 1994, but their unexpected failure to qualify for the World Cup led to their withdrawal from the tour. Instead, the American Eagles jumped at the opportunity of picking up the itinerary at late notice to give Ireland a pre-season Test.

The Eagles, like Namibia, had failed to qualify for South Africa, but their rugby authorities have never lacked ambition and, as soon as they were knocked out of the 1995 tournament, began planning for the 1999 event. The trip to Ireland was seen as an ideal chance to develop the talents of a new generation of players.

The tour showed the benefits of coach Jack Clark's far-sighted plans to fast-track leading American sportsmen into his rugby side. Take Dan Lyle, a former all-American gridiron star, for instance. He made the tour to Ireland only 12 months after converting to rugby. At 17st 2lb and 6ft 5ins he is typical of the new breed of dynamic forward sought by Clark. Lyle acquitted himself well on his Test debut at Lansdowne Road and, in tandem with Richard Tardits, a Frenchman, formed an outstanding flank to the American scrum.

For Ireland, the Test was a disappointment. Despite Brendan Mullin's return after a couple of years of retirement from international rugby, the Irish were rusty and unimaginative against a side which tackled and matched them try for try. Only the accurate goal-kicking of Alan McGowan gave them a comfortable cushion of points. The fly-half landed five of his nine kicks at goal for 13 points on his Test debut.

THE TOURING PARTY

Manager E Schram **Coaches** J Clark, D Porter **Captain** A Bachelet

FULL-BACKS

M K Sika (Rhinos)
S J Hiatt (Old Blues)

THREEQUARTERS

T Z Takau (Rhinos)
R E Schurfield (Belmont Shore)
C J Schlereth (St Louis Bombers)
R Green (California)
M A Scharrenberg (Golden Gate)
E C Schram (OMBAC)
V N Anitoni (Olympic Club)

HALF-BACKS

J McVeigh (OMBAC)
M A Williams (Olympic Club)
A Bachelet (Old Blues)
B Howard (Life College)

FORWARDS

S Allen (OMBAC)
T W Billups (Old Blues)
S M Bracken (OMBAC)
D W James (Old Blues)
R P Lehner (Old Blues)
C Lippert (OMBAC)
P Codevilla (California)
W N Leversee (OMBAC)
C King (Olympic Club)
D J Lyle (Aspen)
R R Randell (United)
J Walker (Aspen)
J P Wilkerson (Belmont Shore)
R A Lumkong (Old Blues)
R Tardits (Mystic River)

TOUR RECORD

All matches Played 4 Won 1 Lost 3 Points for 50 Against 59
International matches Played 1 Lost 1 Points for 15 Against 26

SCORING DETAILS

All matches

For:	4T	3C	7PG	1DG	50 Pts
Against:	5T	2C	9PG	1DG	59 Pts

International matches

For:	2T	1C	1PG	–	15 Pts
Against:	2T	2C	4PG	–	26 Pts

MATCH DETAILS

1994	OPPONENTS	VENUE	RESULT
1 Nov	Irish Development XV	Galway	W 20-13
5 Nov	IRELAND	Dublin	L 15-26
9 Nov	Irish Universities	Cork	L 9-11
12 Nov	Leinster	Dublin	L 6-9

MATCH 1 1 November, Sports Ground, Galway

Irish Development XV 13 (1PG 2T) **USA XV 20** (2G 1PG 1DG)
Irish Development XV: C Clarke (Terenure); I Gray (Oxford U), S McCahill (Sunday's Well), M McCall (Bangor) (*capt*), D Wall (St Mary's); D Humphreys (Ballymena), S McIvor (Garryowen); N Donovan (London Irish), S Byrne (Blackrock), A McKeen (Lansdowne), B Cusack (Bective Rangers), M Galwey (Shannon), A Foley (Shannon), R Wilson (Instonians), K McKee (Instonians) *Replacements* M McDermott (Lansdowne) for Byrne (18 mins); P Burke (Cork Const) for Humphreys (70 mins)
Scorers *Tries:* Wall, McCall *Penalty Goal:* Humphreys
USA XV: Sika; Schlereth, Takau, Green, Schurfield; Williams, Bachelet (*capt*); Bracken, Billups, James, Randell, Leversee, Lyle, Lumkong, Tardits
Replacement Lippert for James (64 mins)
Scorers *Tries:* Tardits, Schurfield *Conversions:* Williams (2) *Penalty Goal:* Williams
Dropped Goal: Williams
Referee B Campsall (England)

MATCH 2 5 November, Lansdowne Road, Dublin **Test Match**

IRELAND 26 (2G 4PG) **USA 15** (1G 1PG 1T)
IRELAND: C M P O'Shea (Lansdowne); S P Geoghegan (Bath), B J Mullin (Blackrock Coll), P P A Danaher (Garryowen), J C Bell (Ballymena); A N McGowan (Blackrock Coll), M T Bradley (Cork Const) (*capt*); N J Popplewell (Wasps), K G M Wood (Garryowen), P M Clohessy (Young Munster), G M Fulcher (Cork Const), N P J Francis (Old Belvedere), P T J O'Hara (Cork Const), P S Johns (Dungannon), D Corkery (Cork Const) *Replacements* N G Malone (Leicester) for Mullin (39 mins); A C Rolland (Blackrock Coll) for Bradley (73 mins); M J Galwey (Shannon) for Johns (78 mins)
Scorers *Tries:* Geoghegan, Bradley *Conversions:* McGowan (2)
Penalty Goals: McGowan (3), O'Shea
USA: Sika; Schlereth, Takau, Green, Anitoni; Williams, Bachelet (*capt*); Lippert, Billups, James, Leversee, Randell, Lyle, Lumkong, Tardits
Scorers *Tries:* Anitoni, Bachelet *Conversion:* Williams *Penalty Goal:* Williams
Referee J-L Rolandi (Argentina)

MATCH 3 9 November, Cork

Irish Universities 11 (2PG 1T) **USA XV 9** (3PG)
Irish Universities: D Crotty (UC Cork); J Kelly (UC Cork), S Tynan (Dublin U), K M McCarthy (UC Dublin), D O'Mahony (UC Dublin); B Carey (UC Dublin), J Kenefick (UC Cork); D Cole (Dublin U), A Donovan (UC Dublin) (*capt*), J O'Driscoll (UC Cork), H Kos (UC Dublin), G Heaslip (UC Galway), G Tuohy (UC Cork), M Reilly (Dublin U), G McConkey (UC Dublin) *Replacement* D Hickie (UC Dublin) for Tynan
Scorers *Try:* O'Mahony *Penalty Goals:* Carey (2)
USA XV: Hiatt; Anitoni, Schram, Scharrenberg, Schurfield; McVeigh, Howard; Bracken, Allen, Lehner (*capt*), Codevilla, Leversee, Wilkerson, King, Walker
Replacement Takau for Scharrenberg
Scorer *Penalty Goals:* McVeigh (3)
Referee B Wallace (Wales)

MATCH 4 12 November, Donnybrook, Dublin

Leinster 9 (2PG 1DG) **USA XV 6** (2PG)
Leinster: C M P O'Shea (Lansdowne); P Gavin (Old Belvedere), B T Glennon (Lansdowne), R Moloney (Old Wesley), D Wall (St Mary's); A N McGowan (Blackrock Coll), A C Rolland (Blackrock Coll) (*capt*); H Hurley (Old Wesley), S Byrne (Blackrock Coll), J Feehan (Old Wesley), B J Rigney (Shannon), J O'Callaghan

(Wanderers), C Pim (Old Wesley), K Potts (St Mary's Coll), R Love (Old Wesley)
Replacement C Clarke (Terenure) for O'Shea (36 mins)
Scorer *Penalty Goals:* McGowan (2) *Dropped Goal:* McGowan
USA XV: Sika; Anitoni, Takau, Green, Schurfield; Williams, Bachelet (*capt*); Lippert, Billups, James, Randell, Leversee, Lyle, Walker, Tardits
Scorer *Penalty Goals:* Williams (2)
Referee E Murray (Scotland)

ROMANIA TO ENGLAND 1994

Romania's approach to the three-match tour which culminated with the international against England was puzzling. Several of the hard-core forwards who had given the Welsh pack such a roasting in Bucharest six weeks earlier were left at home. Instead, the Romanian management turned to inexperienced youngsters, hoping to find new players with the potential to stiffen the side's challenge in the so-called 'group of death' at the World Cup finals.

The experiment was, as everyone had predicted, an utter disaster. The tourists were so short on basic skills that their passionless displays in two warm-up matches against Oxford and Cambridge universities caused few worries to an England side preparing for its first Test of the season. There was a lacklustre win against Cambridge, but Oxford thoroughly deserved their 26-16 victory. England duly overwhelmed the visitors in a mismatch which clearly exposed the Romanians' folly in taking untried players into an international against one of the world's foremost rugby powers.

THE TOURING PARTY

Manager V G Moraru **Assistant Manager and Coach** T P Radulescu
Assistant Coaches C Fugigi, M Paraschiv **Captain** T Brinza

FULL-BACK

V Brici (Farul Constanta)

THREEQUARTERS

I S Tofan (Dinamo Bucharest)
R Cioca (Dinamo Bucharest)
L Colceriu (Steaua Bucharest)
G Solomie (Timisoara U)
R Fugigi (CSM Foresta Sibiu)
M Vioreanu (Timisoara U)

HALF-BACKS

I Ivanciuc (CSM Suceava)
C Patrichi (Minerul Lupini)
E Apjoc (Baia Mare U)
V Flutur (Minerul Lupini)
D Neaga (Dinamo Bucharest)
S Tranca (Farul Constanta)

FORWARDS

L Costea (Steaua Bucharest)
C Stan (Dinamo Bucharest)
G Vlad (Grivita Bucharest)
F Marioara (Dinamo Bucharest)
G Christian (Grivita Bucharest)
I Negreci (CFR Constanta)
M Radoi (Dinamo Bucharest)
C Bransecu (Farul Constanta)
C Cojocariu (Bayonne, France)
T Oroian (Steaua Bucharest)
O Slusariuc (Dinamo Bucharest)
C Draguceanu (Steaua Bucharest)
A Guranescu (Dinamo Bucharest)
A Gealapu (Steaua Bucharest)
T Brinza (Cluj U)

TOUR RECORD

All matches Played 3 Won 1 Lost 1 Points for 46 Against 98
International matches Played 1 Lost 1 Points for 3 Against 54

SCORING DETAILS

All matches						**International matches**					
For:	4T	1C	6PG	2DG	46 Pts	For:	–	–	1PG	–	3 Pts
Against:	8T	8C	13PG	1DG	98 Pts	Against:	6T	6C	4PG	–	54 Pts

MATCH DETAILS

1994	**OPPONENTS**	**VENUE**	**RESULT**
5 Nov	Oxford University XV	Oxford	L 16-26
8 Nov	Cambridge University XV	Cambridge	W 27-18
11 Nov	ENGLAND	Twickenham	L 3-54

MATCH 1 5 November, Iffley Road, Oxford

Oxford University XV 26 (2G 3PG 1DG) **Romania XV 16** (1G 2PG 1DG)
Oxford University XV: M T Joy; I R H Gray, S P Bromley, M S Nolan, T G Howe; G L Rees, J M Kirsten; A N S Bryce, D S Henderson (*capt*), S C Thompson, P F Coveney, J B B Daniell, G V Allison, R S Yeabsley, N F C Martin
Replacement E J Nasser for Daniell (68 mins)
Scorers *Tries:* Joy, Nolan *Conversions:* Rees (2) *Penalty Goals:* Rees (3)
Dropped Goal: Rees
Romania XV: Brici; Cioca, Solomie, Tofan, Colceriu; Ivanciuc, Flutur; Stan, Gheorghe, Vlad, Cojocariu, Branescu, Oroian, Draguceanu (*capt*), Gealapu *Replacements* Brinza for Branescu (55 mins); Neaga for Flutur (60 mins)
Scorers *Try:* Oroian *Conversion:* Ivanciuc *Penalty Goals:* Ivanciuc (2)
Dropped Goal: Colceriu
Referee N Lasaga (France)

MATCH 2 8 November, Grange Road, Cambridge

Cambridge University XV 18 (6PG) **Romania XV 27** (3PG 1DG 3T)
Cambridge University XV: S Phillips; A Richards, A J Palfrey, S R Cottrell (*capt*), A J Reynolds; A Kennedy, R J Davies; L T Mooney, I MacKenzie, M Q Cox, R A Bramley, A J Meadows, A F M Metcalfe, E D Rollitt, A Jones
Scorer *Penalty Goals:* Richards (6)
Romania XV: Brici; Colceriu, Solomie, Tofan, Cioca; Ivanciuc, Neaga; Costea, Negreci, Marioara, Oroian, Bransecu, Guranescu, Brinza (*capt*), Gealapu *Replacements* Cojocariu for Branescu (29 mins); Tranca for Colceriu (40 mins); Draguceanu for Guranescu (68 mins)
Scorers *Tries:* Negreci, Gealapu, Brinza *Penalty Goals:* Ivanciuc (3)
Dropped Goal: Ivanciuc
Referee C Muir (Scotland)

MATCH 3 12 November, Twickenham — Test Match

ENGLAND 54 (6G 4PG) ROMANIA 3 (1PG)

This was England's first home international under Jack Rowell. The new coach, who promised a fresh approach, was true to his word: England played with a commitment to continuity and, against weak opposition, chose to move the ball at every opportunity. Yet critics and spectators were left wondering whether they had found the style and gained the expertise that would make the big guns of the southern hemisphere quake in their boots as the World Cup loomed.

Jeremy Guscott looked rusty on his return to Test rugby – he and Will Carling were paired for a world-record 29th time in major internationals – and the flat alignment of the England threequarters nullified the off-the-ball running of a back division that was clearly eager for work.

On the credit side, Rob Andrew began his international season with the tidy return of 24 points – ten goals from 11 place-kicks.

ENGLAND: P A Hull (Bristol & RAF); T Underwood (Leicester), W D C Carling (Harlequins) (*capt*), J C Guscott (Bath), R Underwood (Leicester & RAF); C R Andrew (Wasps), C D Morris (Orrell); J Leonard (Harlequins), B C Moore (Harlequins), V E Ubogu (Bath), M O Johnson (Leicester), M C Bayfield (Northampton), T A K Rodber (Northampton & Army), B B Clarke (Bath), S O Ojomoh (Bath)
Scorers *Tries:* T Underwood (2), Carling, pen try, Rodber, R Underwood
Conversions: Andrew (6) *Penalty Goals:* Andrew (4)
ROMANIA: Brici; Solomie, Vioreanu, Tofan, Cioca; Ivanciuc, Neaga; Costea, Negreci,

The Romanians join forces in an attempt to check danger man Tony Underwood, who scored two tries in England's 54-3 victory.

Vlad, Cojocariu, Branescu, Oroian, Brinza (*capt*), Gealapu *Replacements* Draguceanu for Oroian (51 mins); Marioara for Costea (52 mins); Gheorghe for Negreci (65 mins); Guranescu for Branescu (78 mins)
Scorer *Penalty Goal:* Ivanciuc
Referee S Neethling (South Africa)

ITALY TO ENGLAND AND SCOTLAND 1994-95

As England headed for dry-weather pre-season Test preparation in Lanzarote, Italy turned up in cold, wet Britain for a mini-tour. The purpose of the visit was to prepare physically, mentally and technically for the challenges which lay ahead in 1995, according to their manager, Giancarlo Dondi.

Certainly the Italians adapted well to the awful conditions at the Stoop Memorial Ground against Middlesex in the tour opener. In rain and mud they swamped the county to the tune of seven tries to nil. More significantly, the match demonstrated that two of their leading players, Diego Dominguez and Julian Gardner, were fully restored to fitness after suffering injuries in Australia six months earlier.

A frozen pitch at Sunbury caused the cancellation of the planned match against Surrey four days later, but the Italians were in good spirits as they set off for their annual New Year fixture with Scotland A. At Perth their desire to play expansive rugby was offset by a propensity to give away penalties – a failing which marred their 1991 World Cup match against England. The Scots were thus presented with ample opportunities to grind out a narrow two-point win. Even so, as nine of the Scotland A side went on to feature prominently in the nation's subsequent bid for the Grand Slam, Italy's performance began to assume a greater significance.

THE TOURING PARTY

Manager G Dondi **Coach** G Costes
Captain Massimo Cuttitta

FULL-BACKS

L Troiani (L'Aquila)
J Pertile (Roma)

THREEQUARTERS

M Gerosa (Piacenza)
M Bonomi (Milan)
S Bordon (Rovigo)
Marcello Cuttitta (Milan)
I Francescato (Treviso)
M Ravazzolo (Calvisano)

HALF-BACKS

D Dominguez (Milan)
A Troncon (Treviso)
G Faltiba (San Dona)

FORWARDS

M Trevisiol (Treviso)
M Dal Sie (San Dona)
F Properzi-Curti (Milan)
Massimo Cuttitta (Milan)
C Orlandi (Piacenza)
R Favaro (Treviso)
M Giacheri (Treviso)
P Pedroni (Milan)
M Capuzzoni (Milan)
D Scaglia (Tarvisium)
A Sgorlon (San Dona)
J M Gardner (Rovigo)
O Arancio (Catania)

TOUR RECORD

All matches Played 2 Won 1 Lost 1 Cancelled 1 Points for 66 Against 21

SCORING DETAILS

All matches
For: 8T 7C 4PG 66 Pts
Against: 2T 1C 3PG 21 Pts

MATCH DETAILS

1994	OPPONENTS	VENUE	RESULT
29 Dec	Middlesex	Stoop Memorial Ground	W 50-3
1995			
2 Jan	Surrey	Sunbury	*cancelled*
7 Jan	Scotland A	Perth	L 16-18

MATCH 1 29 December, Stoop Memorial Ground, Twickenham

Middlesex 3 (1PG) **Italy XV 50** (6G 1PG 1T)
Middlesex: J Ufton (Wasps); C Henderson (London Scottish), A James (Wasps), D Millard (London Scottish), P Hopley (Wasps); S Howard (Blackheath), A Gomersall (Wasps); M Hobley (Henley), D Macer (Wasps), W Green (Wasps), R Scott (London Scottish), S Shortland (Wasps), D Peters (London Irish), E Rollitt (Cambridge U), A Fox (Harlequins) (*capt*) *Replacements* J Hamilton-Smith (Harlequins) for Macer (40 mins); C Braithwaite (Wasps) for Howard (67 mins)
Scorer *Penalty Goal:* Ufton
Italy XV: Pertile; Ravazzolo, Francescato, Bonomi, Marcello Cuttitta; Dominguez, Troncon; Massimo Cuttitta (*capt*), Orlandi, Properzi-Curti, Favaro, Giacheri, Gardner, Scaglia, Sgorlon *Replacements* Bordon for Bonomi (40 mins); Troiani for Ravazzolo (53 mins)
Scorers *Tries:* Ravazzolo (2), Massimo Cuttitta, Gardner, Marcello Cuttitta, pen try, Troiani *Conversions:* Dominguez (6) *Penalty Goal:* Dominguez
Referee J Wallis (Somerset)

MATCH 2 2 January, London Irish RFC, Sunbury

Surrey v Italy XV – *cancelled due to frozen pitch*

MATCH 3 7 January, McDiarmid Park, Perth

Scotland A 18 (1G 2PG 1T) **Italy 16** (1G 3PG)
Scotland A: R J S Shepherd (Edinburgh Acads); C A Joiner (Melrose), I C Jardine (Stirling County), B R S Eriksson (London Scottish), I C Glasgow (Heriot's FP); D W Hodge (Watsonians), B W Redpath (Melrose); D I W Hilton (Bath), K D McKenzie (Stirling County) (*capt*), P H Wright (Boroughmuir), D F Cronin (Bourges), S J Campbell (Dundee HSFP), F D Wallace (Glasgow High/Kelvinside), E W Peters (Bath), I R Smith (Gloucester) *Replacement* G W Weir (Melrose) for Wallace (79 mins); J J Manson (Dundee HSFP) for Wright (temp)
Scorers *Tries:* Peters, Redpath *Conversion:* Glasgow *Penalty Goals:* Shepherd, Glasgow
Italy: Troiani; Ravazzolo, Francescato, Bonomi, Marcello Cuttitta; Dominguez, Troncon; Massimo Cuttitta (*capt*), Orlandi, Properzi-Curti, Favaro, Giacheri, Arancio, Scaglia, Sgorlon *Replacement* Gardner for Sgorlon (60 mins)
Scorers *Try:* Troiani *Conversion:* Dominguez *Penalty Goals:* Dominguez (3)
Referee G Black (Ireland)

THE FIVE NATIONS STILL TOPS THE BILL

THE INTERNATIONAL CHAMPIONSHIP 1995

This was billed as no more than a gentle warm-up, a loosener before the really serious stuff began down in Cape Town in the summer; simply a means for spectators to keep warm and happy during the bleak winter months and for teams to meddle a bit here and fine-tune a bit there. The Five Nations Championship become a sideshow in World Cup year? There was never any danger of it. There is too much rich tradition underpinning the whole competition, too many deep-rooted rivalries and, quite simply, too much fun to be had by fan and player alike, for that ever to happen.

If the outcome was predictable in that the pre-Championship favourites, England, took not just the title but their third Grand Slam in five years, then little else was. The other short-odds lot, the French, on the back of a glorious series victory in New Zealand, failed to get anywhere near a decent stride. They faltered and fretted, obsessed, it seemed, by trying to get the better of perfidious Albion. They lost for the eighth time in succession to England and went down, for the first time in 26 years, to Scotland too, in Paris and succeeded only in losing rhythm, morale and personnel along the way. Olivier Merle was dropped after headbutting Welsh prop Ricky Evans, and only their captain, Philippe Saint-André, came through with any sort of honour, his four tries once again again helping to put France on top of the Championship try-pile with ten. The overall total of 31 tries came as a refreshing relief after the drought of recent years.

England went through the Championship unchanged, only the sixth side ever to do so, and Will Carling became the first captain to lead a country to three Grand Slams – Billy Trew of Wales (in 1909 and 1911) and 'Dave' Davies of England (1921 and 1923) are the only captains to have managed two. Mike Catt emerged as a strike full-back of the highest order. Every side in the Championship threatened to expose his lack of experience in the position by bombarding him with high kicks. Catt is still waiting.

Scotland flourished beyond anyone's wildest expectations – except those of their talisman, Gavin Hastings. After a run of nine matches without a win, they beat Canada and then went storming through the Championship, riding their luck for all it was worth. Hastings' match-winning try in Paris was scripted in Hollywood. Damian Cronin re-emerged from his exile in Bourges, France as a force in the second row while Logan and Townsend were jewels in the back line.

Ireland came in with decent hopes only to fall away badly. Selection was to blame for some of their woes, the bright stars of the Australian tour, Keith Wood and David Corkery, being summarily dropped after the England game. The half-backs chopped and changed throughout. The only light came in the invigorating debut at the age of 35 of lock Dave Tweed and the promise of blindside flanker Tony Foley.

How steep was the fall for Wales, from champions to a whitewash – only their second ever – within 12 months. The management team resigned at the end, prop John Davies was sent off against England, and Ieuan Evans was a shadow of the player he was before injury. The clouds hung low over Wales.

FINAL TABLE

	P	*W*	*D*	*L*	*F*	*A*	*Pts*
England	4	4	0	0	98	39	8
Scotland	4	3	0	1	87	71	6
France	4	2	0	2	77	70	4
Ireland	4	1	0	3	44	83	2
Wales	4	0	0	4	43	86	0

England captain Will Carling tackles Philippe Bernat-Salles of France in the Twickenham match billed once again as 'Le Crunch' as the Championship began. England beat the French for the eighth time in succession – a sequence which was to be broken in the World Cup.

21 January, Lansdowne Road
IRELAND 8 (1PG 1T) **ENGLAND 20** (1G 1PG 2T)

The winds blew, the goalposts rocked, the crowd swayed – only England stood firm. This was a classic of its kind. If you wanted fast and loose rugby you had to go elsewhere, but in the wild conditions England played the perfect game.

It was every bit as compelling as any free-flowing encounter; every bit as impressive as those match-winning displays of recent times in Paris. There was an engaging intensity about their commitment, and more than just the huge English contingent in the crowd wondered at the exactness of their control. If only their finishing had been up to scratch – Guscott failed to pass on to Rory Underwood on one notable occasion – they would have posted a record score. It was, nonetheless, their highest Championship score in Dublin since 1938.

Ireland fielded debutant half-backs Hogan and Burke (a former England Schools and Colts captain) and another new cap on the flank; Tony Foley, son of the former Lions prop the late Brendan Foley. Rory Underwood was playing his 70th match for England, a new Home Unions record, passing Mike Gibson's 69 for Ireland.

Such was the composure and authority of England that the match was over as a contest after six minutes. By then Carling had corkscrewed his way over the line from a line-out for his ninth international try and Ireland had had barely a look-in. In the 23rd minute Clarke crashed over following grafting work by Rodber but his joy was tempered later when he became the first player in international rugby to be shown the yellow card after he stamped on Geoghegan. Burke scored a penalty for Ireland in the 17th minute, while Rob Andrew's first-half miss ended a run of 22 successful international place-kicks. He did convert a penalty five minutes after the interval, however. Tony Underwood completed England's scoring after great build-up work from Rodber. Foley scored a try from a tapped penalty in injury time. It was the only mark made on England all day.

IRELAND: C M P O'Shea (Lansdowne); S P Geoghegan (Bath), B J Mullin (Blackrock Coll), P P A Danaher (Garryowen), N K P Woods (Blackrock Coll); P A Burke (Cork Const), N A Hogan (Terenure Coll); N J Popplewell (Wasps), K G M Wood (Garryowen), P M Clohessy (Young Munster), M Galwey (Shannon), N P J Francis (Old Belvedere), A Foley (Shannon), P S Johns (Dungannon), D Corkery (Cork Const) *Replacement* G Fulcher (Cork Const) for Francis (40 mins)
Scorers *Try:* Foley *Penalty Goal:* Burke
ENGLAND: M J Catt (Bath); T Underwood (Leicester), W D C Carling (Harlequins) (*capt*), J C Guscott (Bath), R Underwood (Leicester & RAF); C R Andrew (Wasps), K P P Bracken (Bristol); J Leonard (Harlequins), B C Moore (Harlequins), V E Ubogu (Bath), M O Johnson (Leicester), M C Bayfield (Northampton), T A K Rodber (Northampton), D Richards (Leicester), B B Clarke (Bath)
Scorers *Tries:* Carling, Clarke, T Underwood *Conversion:* Andrew
Penalty Goal: Andrew
Referee P Thomas (France)

21 January, Parc des Princes
FRANCE 21 (1G 3PG 1T) **WALES 9** (3PG)

If there is solace to be had in keeping a score within acceptable limits, then Wales were in reasonable mood after this wholly expected defeat, which continued a losing run in Paris dating back to 1975. France had more firepower when it mattered, even if they did not switch on the burner until after the first quarter. By then the Welsh fire had fizzled out, Ricky Evans had left the field with a broken leg after being disgracefully headbutted by Merle, and attacking options were restricted to high bomb-kicks by Jenkins.

Even though they came into the match as Five Nations champions, Wales had modest hopes. They had been hit by an appalling run of injuries which had robbed them of five front-line players – Ieuan Evans, Emyr Lewis, Mike Rayer, Nigel Davies and Hemi Taylor. On the eve of the game, Mike Proctor withdrew with a chest infection to be replaced by Cardiff's Simon Hill.

There was one bright spot on the horizon for Welsh supporters. Little bloke by the name of Jones, Robert, scrum-half, a genius on the day – a fact not always recognised by Welsh selectors down the years. He was recalled to the colours for the sixth time in his nine-year career to win his 49th cap. There were three other changes from the Welsh side which lost to the Springboks earlier in the season.

France had great hopes for both this match and the Championship itself. They were slow to get into their stride and were pinned to their line for the first 20 minutes. Wales' only return was a Jenkins penalty. Then, on their first visit to the Welsh 22, France scored. They moved the ball from one side of the field to the other for Toulouse wing Ntamack to go in unopposed.

Sella was always purposeful in midfield, even though the distribution of Deylaud, making his Championship debut, was shaky. Saint-André scored France's second try in the 28th minute, taking advantage of Hill's absence from the field with an injury. Lacroix and Jenkins kicked penalties for each side in the second half.

FRANCE: J-L Sadourny (Colomiers); E Ntamack (Toulouse), P Sella (Agen), T Lacroix (Dax), P Saint-André (Montferrand) (*capt*); C Deylaud (Toulouse), G Accoceberry (Bègles); L Benezech (Racing Club de France), J-M Gonzalez (Bayonne), C Califano (Toulouse), O Merle (Montferrand), O Roumat (Dax), A Benazzi (Agen), P Benetton (Agen), L Cabannes (Racing Club de France)
Scorers *Tries:* Ntamack, Saint-André *Conversion:* Lacroix *Penalty Goals:* Lacroix (3)
WALES: A Clement (Swansea); S D Hill (Cardiff), M R Hall (Cardiff), M Taylor (Pontypool), N Walker (Cardiff); N R Jenkins (Pontypridd), R N Jones (Swansea); R L Evans (Llanelli), G R Jenkins (Swansea), J D Davies (Neath), D Jones (Cardiff), G O Llewellyn (Neath) (*capt*), S Davies (Swansea), P T Davies (Llanelli), R Collins (Pontypridd) *Replacements* M Griffiths (Cardiff) for Evans (9 mins); M Back (Bridgend) for Hill (32 mins)
Scorer *Penalty Goals:* Jenkins (3)
Referee J Pearson (England)

4 February, Murrayfield
SCOTLAND 26 (2G 4PG) **IRELAND 13** (1PG 2T)

The pitch looked a mess, and so too did Scotland in the first half. The threadbare surface was a legacy of the rebuilding of Murrayfield, which did wonders for the concrete stands and wreaked havoc with the grass. The team was a legacy of the one that had gone nine matches without a win, a losing sequence broken by victory over Canada a fortnight earlier.

And then it all changed – in playing terms, that is. Scotland, who had been fortunate to hit the interval 9-8 ahead after Ireland monopolised the play, began to assert themselves, and this despite conceding a try just four minutes after the restart. They began to dominate the line-outs through the marvellously rejuvenated Cronin – who, in the 63rd minute, scored his second successive international try here – the emerging Campbell and the fine efforts of Wainwright at the tail. The forwards gelled and put together some stirring rucks and mauls, while behind, Gavin Hastings lorded over proceedings as only he can.

The Watsonians full-back was winning his 53rd cap, breaking the Scottish record of 52 held jointly by Jim Renwick and Colin Deans. He had a tear in his eye when he was presented with his shirt by coach Dougie Morgan beforehand. Hastings, with six successful kicks at goal, four penalty goals and two conversions, also became the first European to break through the 500-point mark for his country. It was his delightful chip-kick which Joiner followed up for Scotland's first try in the 50th minute. Geoghegan appeared to baulk Logan, and Welsh referee Derek Bevan, setting a new world record in officiating his 26th international, played an excellent advantage to enable Joiner to touch down.

Ireland lacked a kicker – Paul Burke missed four out of five attempts – and ran out of steam badly in the last quarter. In contrast, their two tries were crisply executed. Mullin went over after 31 minutes and then, four minutes into second half, a tap penalty on halfway saw the ball worked to Jonathan Bell. The Ballymena youngster, who made an impressive Five Nations debut, scooted down the left wing to score brilliantly in the corner. It was the last time the Irish had cause to celebrate in the match.

SCOTLAND: A G Hastings (Watsonians) (*capt*); C A Joiner (Melrose), G P J Townsend (Gala), I C Jardine (Stirling County), K M Logan (Stirling County); C M Chalmers (Melrose), B W Redpath (Melrose); D I W Hilton (Bath), K S Milne (Heriot's FP), P H Wright (Boroughmuir), D F Cronin (Bourges), S J Campbell (Dundee HSFP), R I Wainwright (West Hartlepool), E W Peters (Bath), I R Morrison (London Scottish)
Scorers *Tries:* Joiner, Cronin *Conversions:* Hastings (2) *Penalty Goals:* Hastings (4)
IRELAND: C M P O'Shea (Lansdowne); S P Geoghegan (Bath), B J Mullin (Blackrock Coll), P P A Danaher (Garryowen), J C Bell (Ballymena); P A Burke (Cork Const), M T Bradley (Cork Const) (*capt*); N J Popplewell (Wasps), K G M Wood (Garryowen), P M Clohessy (Young Munster), P S Johns (Dungannon), G M Fulcher (Cork Const), A G Foley (Shannon), B M Cronin (Garryowen), W D McBride (Malone)
Scorers *Tries:* Mullin, Bell *Penalty Goal:* Burke
Referee W D Bevan (Wales)

4 February, Twickenham
ENGLAND 31 (2G 4PG 1T) **FRANCE 10** (1G 1PG)

These two sides have collided so often and so memorably in recent years that the pre-match billing of Le Crunch (Part 8) was always in danger of producing an anti-climax. While there was much to admire in both teams, the reason for the slight flatness at the final whistle was easy to detect: England had never looked like losing.

Not even when the gods decided to pop down to Twickenham and play a bit of rugby. The French, as only they can, flowed out of defence shortly after the interval with a burst from Saint-André, carried on by Bernat-Salles; a chip, a knock-down by Catt regathered by France; Accoceberry, Cabannes and, finally, Viars. If it took the spectator's breath away it did nothing to knock England out of their stride. Once again they were composed and controlled. Rodber, Richards and Clarke swamped their much-vaunted counterparts, Ubogu made great dents at close quarters and, even though the line-out return was below par, there was order and precision in nearly everything England did.

France appeared neutered, as if intimidated by their overblown reputation as the hard men of European rugby. In searching for discipline, their coach, Pierre Berbizier, who had dropped lock Olivier Merle after his headbutt on Ricky Evans of Wales, might well have quelled some of his team's instinctive passion. After Andrew (two) and Lacroix traded penalty goals, England's pressure paid off eight minutes before half-time, when Guscott dummied through to score under the posts.

The two second-half tries by Tony Underwood may have lacked the élan of Viars' effort but, in their different ways, they were commendable. For the first, in the 73rd minute, Underwood warded off Saint-André in chasing Rob Andrew's diagonal; then, on the stroke of full-time, a brilliant incursion by Catt set up Underwood for the run-in. This was England's eighth win in succession against France, and their biggest victory over that country since 1914.

ENGLAND: M J Catt (Bath); T Underwood (Leicester), W D C Carling (Harlequins) (*capt*), J C Guscott (Bath), R Underwood (Leicester & RAF); C R Andrew (Wasps), K P P Bracken (Bristol); J Leonard (Harlequins), B C Moore (Harlequins), V E Ubogu (Bath), M O Johnson (Leicester), M C Bayfield (Northampton), T A K Rodber (Northampton), D Richards (Leicester), B B Clarke (Bath)
Scorers *Tries:* T Underwood (2), Guscott *Conversions:* Andrew (2)
Penalty Goals: Andrew (4)
FRANCE: J-L Sadourny (Colomiers); P Bernat-Salles (Pau), P Sella (Agen), T Lacroix (Dax), P Saint-André (Montferrand) (*capt*); C Deylaud (Toulouse), G Accoceberry (Bègles); L Benezech (Racing Club de France), J-M Gonzalez (Bayonne), C Califano (Toulouse), O Brouzet (Grenoble), O Roumat (Dax), A Benazzi (Agen), P Benetton (Agen), L Cabannes (Racing Club de France) *Replacements* S Viars (Brive) for J-L Sadourny (38 mins); L Seigne (Brive) for Benezech (23 mins); M de Rougemont (Toulon) for J-M Gonzalez (temp)
Scorers *Try:* Viars *Conversion:* Lacroix *Penalty Goal:* Lacroix
Referee K W McCartney (Scotland)

18 February, Cardiff Arms Park
WALES 9 (3PG) **ENGLAND 23** (1G 2PG 2T)

The signposts to hell no longer line the route England take as they cross into Wales. This was their second victory in three visits, consigning to rich folklore those deeds of *hwyl* and heroes which saw Wales unbeaten here against their historic enemy for 28 years.

The most daunting aspect of this win for England's future opponents was that they were far from at their best. There was a lack of fluency at half-back, where Bracken struggled to get the ball away cleanly and Andrew slipped from his season's peak of excellence in his distribution. As expected, Wales gave England a hard, and occasionally torrid, time in the tight phases of the game. And yet they still came off the park well beaten, which tells you everything you need to know about their cohesion and continuity throughout.

The Welsh were also embarrassed by the dismissal of tight-head prop John Davies in the 64th minute for stamping on Ben Clarke. It was a marginal decision, but correct. Davies was banned for 60 days. But the sending-off produced high farce when back-row forward Hemi Taylor was press-ganged into duty as a makeshift prop. Ieuan Evans asked Will Carling if a replacement prop, Hugh Williams-Jones, could be called from the bench. The laws forbid this, but common sense prevailed and the laws were amended at the IB meeting the following month.

Ubogu punched over for England's first try in the 19th minute after Jenkins had put Wales into the lead with a penalty. The two kickers then swung their boots to good effect and England were 13-6 ahead nine minutes into second half. Three minutes later, a poor Jenkins 22 saw Clarke drive the ball on for England. It was recycled and moved wide for Underwood to come off his left foot and score. Superb handling by Carling and Catt put Rory Underwood over for his second on the stroke of full-time. Dean Richards broke the world record (41 for England, six for the Lions) for most appearances as a No 8 and Gareth Llewellyn became Wales' most-capped lock.

WALES: A Clement (Swansea); I C Evans (Llanelli) (*capt*), M Taylor (Pontypool), N G Davies (Llanelli), N Walker (Cardiff); N R Jenkins (Pontypridd), R N Jones (Swansea); M Griffiths (Cardiff), G R Jenkins (Swansea), J D Davies (Neath), D Jones (Cardiff), G O Llewellyn (Neath), H T Taylor (Cardiff), E W Lewis (Cardiff), R Collins (Pontypridd) *Replacements* M Back (Bridgend) for A Clement (11 mins); R Moon (Llanelli) for N Walker (46 mins); H Williams-Jones (Llanelli) for H Taylor (65 mins)
Scorer *Penalty Goals:* Jenkins (3)
ENGLAND: M J Catt (Bath); T Underwood (Leicester), W D C Carling (Harlequins) (*capt*), J C Guscott (Bath), R Underwood (Leicester & RAF); C R Andrew (Wasps), K P P Bracken (Bristol); J Leonard (Harlequins), B C Moore (Harlequins), V E Ubogu (Bath), M O Johnson (Leicester), M C Bayfield (Northampton), T A K Rodber (Northampton), D Richards (Leicester), B B Clarke (Bath)
Scorers *Tries:* R Underwood (2), Ubogu *Conversion:* Andrew
Penalty Goals: Andrew (2)
Referee D Mene (France)

18 February, Parc des Princes
FRANCE 21 (1PG 1DG 3T) **SCOTLAND 23** (2G 3PG)

There were reported sightings of Gavin Hastings scorching through the depths of France late on Saturday evening. Certainly when he raced on to the deftly flicked reverse pass from Gregor Townsend two minutes from the end of this riveting match, he looked as if he would never stop running.

The celebrations – the Scottish team returned to the pitch here ten minutes after the final whistle to sing and dance with their fans – might have been a long time coming but they were thoroughly deserved nonetheless. This was Scotland's first victory in Paris for 26 years and their first ever at the Parc des Princes. They recovered from an appalling start during which they conceded a try to Saint-André in the third minute, and then once again climbed out of the pit when the French captain scored his second try of the match with barely seven minutes left to give France an undeserved 21-16 lead.

Behind the posts, with the seconds ticking away, the indefatigable Gavin Hastings simply told a distraught Gregor Townsend, the man whose fluffed clearance kick had triggered the French counter-attack, to get them back down the other end in position for a try under the posts. Message received loud and clear. Hastings, one of only five Scots to have played in Paris before, finished with 18 points in all to equal the record for the series he himself set back in his very first match in 1986. He landed five of his place-kicks, including one from 54 metres. Cronin, until he departed injured at half-time, was immense in the pack, as was Wainwright. Behind, Townsend and Jardine posed all sorts of problems for the French. It was Townsend's try in the 24th minute which signalled the Scottish revival, the Gala centre rounding off a great length-of-the-field sequence by twinkling through a gap from 15 metres out. Lacroix missed five of his six shots at goal. Deylaud nudged over a dropped goal in the 55th minute, while Sadourny's blindside try ten minutes later set up the dramatic finale.

FRANCE: J-L Sadourny (Colomiers); P Bernat-Salles (Pau), P Sella (Agen), T Lacroix (Dax), P Saint-André (Montferrand) (*capt*); C Deylaud (Toulouse), G Accoceberry (Bègles); C Califano (Toulouse), J-M Gonzalez (Bayonne), L Seigne (Brive), O Brouzet (Grenoble), O Roumat (Dax), A Benazzi (Agen), P Benetton (Agen), L Cabannes (Racing Club de France)
Scorers *Tries:* Saint-André (2), Sadourny *Penalty Goal:* Lacroix
Dropped Goal: Deylaud
SCOTLAND: A G Hastings (Watsonians) (*capt*); C A Joiner (Melrose), G P J Townsend (Gala), I C Jardine (Stirling County), K M Logan (Stirling County); C M Chalmers (Melrose), B W Redpath (Melrose); D I W Hilton (Bath), K S Milne (Heriot's FP), P H Wright (Boroughmuir), D F Cronin (Bourges), S J Campbell (Dundee HSFP), R I Wainwright (West Hartlepool), E W Peters (Bath), I R Morrison (London Scottish)
Replacement G Weir (Melrose) for Cronin (40 mins)
Scorers *Tries:* Townsend, Hastings *Conversions:* Hastings (2)
Penalty Goals: Hastings (3)
Referee D McHugh (Ireland)

4 March, Murrayfield
SCOTLAND 26 (2G 4PG) **WALES 13** (1G 2PG)

There was snow driving across Murrayfield by the time referee Steve Lander blew his whistle to signal the end of this match. The Welsh supporters, who have not seen victory here for ten years, had been chilled to the bone long before the elements turned, however. The Scots? They felt as snug and warm as if it were a summer's day.

Their team was heading south for the Grand Slam decider, the first to do so since Charlie Usher's set off in hope back in 1920. They witnessed a victory based not on elaboration or sophistication but on guts, determination and simplicity. The Scots proved once again that they had found that intangible, elusive quality called team spirit, a mood which means that the sum of the parts is much greater than the parts themselves. Wales fell apart after a promising opening burst which saw Robert Jones shoot over for a try after just three minutes. Even though the front five once again had at least parity in the tight phases, their back row was skinned alive, every 50-50 ball went Scotland's way and there was simply no sense of unity or purpose in the loose play.

Scotland made two changes for the match due to injuries. Scott Hastings came back for Jardine and Doddie Weir deputised for Cronin. After the early setback, so reminiscent of the French match, Gavin Hastings steadied the ship with two penalties in the first quarter. Then Scotland hit Wales with two tries within six minutes on the half-hour. The first was a stunner. Wales attacked, Scotland scrambled clear, Wales returned and Wainwright fielded Proctor's kick. Out of defence came Scotland, Gavin Hastings to Weir to Logan. The wing danced along the touchline with barely an inch to spare. Fifty metres later, he found Peters with an inside pass and the Bath man roared in from the 22. A few minutes later another bout of sustained play ended with his Bath colleague Hilton, the butcher of Bedminster, blasting over.

At 20-7 at half-time, Wales were out of it. Jenkins, who succeeded with all three of his kicks for goal, and Gavin Hastings, six from ten, completed the scoring in the second half, the Scotland captain again landing one from inside his own half.

SCOTLAND: A G Hastings (Watsonians) (*capt*); C A Joiner (Melrose), G P J Townsend (Gala), S Hastings (Watsonians), K M Logan (Stirling County); C M Chalmers (Melrose), B W Redpath (Melrose); D I W Hilton (Bath), K S Milne (Heriot's FP), P H Wright (Boroughmuir), G Weir (Melrose), S J Campbell (Dundee HSFP), R I Wainwright (West Hartlepool), E W Peters (Bath), I R Morrison (London Scottish)
Scorers *Tries:* Peters, Hilton *Conversions:* G Hastings (2) *Penalty Goals:* G Hastings (4)
WALES: M Back (Bridgend); I C Evans (Llanelli) (*capt*), M R Hall (Cardiff), N Davies (Llanelli), M Proctor (Llanelli); N R Jenkins (Pontypridd), R N Jones (Swansea); M Griffiths (Cardiff), G R Jenkins (Swansea), S John (Llanelli), D Jones (Cardiff), G O Llewellyn (Neath), H Taylor (Cardiff), E Lewis (Cardiff), R Collins (Pontypridd)
Scorers *Try:* R Jones *Conversion:* Jenkins *Penalty Goals:* Jenkins (2)
Referee S Lander (England)

4 March, Lansdowne Road
IRELAND 7 (1G) **FRANCE** 25 (1G 1PG 3T)

No one could rip a piece of paper to shreds, toss it into the air and expect it to fall complete and perfect. Yet sometimes you feel that selection committees operate along such lines. Here France made six changes from the side which lost to Scotland, while Ireland made three. (They were further disrupted by three late drop-outs through injury and illness.) So much for the master plan at the start of the season.

France at least seemed to be moving towards more shape and cohesion. The return of the old warhorses, Mesnel in the centre and Cecillon at No 8, gave them more solidity in the loose and in midfield.

Two very late tries by France lent a proper perspective to the scoreboard. They had more to offer throughout, but simply lacked someone to pull the trigger to finish off the moves. In fact, neither side found much rhythm in what was a fitful, albeit lively, encounter. Ireland, who had dropped their much-heralded hooker, Wood, as well as fly-half Burke, were again shackled by woeful distribution and decision-making at half-back. Even the return of Elwood did not enhance Ireland's goal-kicking fortunes. He missed two out of three and also fluffed a dropped goal attempt. France, too, suffered in this department. Ntamack sent four from six attempts wide, Sadourny flunked his only pot and Delaigue failed with a drop at goal.

Tweed, making his debut at the age of 35, and Fulcher gave Ireland a massive, if unexpected, advantage in the line-out. France had a solitary penalty goal on the board at half-time; then, within 35 seconds of the restart, they were over. A great catch and drive from the kick-off was rounded off by the scampering Delaigue. Cecillon drove over from the base of a scrum in the 57th minute before Geoghegan's try, scored from a lovely chip from Field, briefly raised Irish hopes six minutes later. Then, almost into injury time, France scored twice. Ntamack took a blindside pass from Accoceberry to cross and Saint-André squeezed in at the corner.

IRELAND: J E Staples (Harlequins); S P Geoghegan (Bath), B J Mullin (Blackrock Coll), P P A Danaher (Garryowen), N K P Woods (Blackrock Coll); E P Elwood (Lansdowne), M T Bradley (Cork Const) (*capt*); N J Popplewell (Wasps), T J Kingston (Dolphin), P M Clohessy (Young Munster), D A Tweed (Ballymena), G M Fulcher (Cork Const), E O Halvey (Shannon), A Foley (Shannon), D McBride (Malone) *Replacement* M Field (Malone) for Mullin (40 mins)
Scorers *Try:* Geoghegan *Conversion:* Elwood
FRANCE: J-L Sadourny (Colomiers); E Ntamack (Toulouse), P Sella (Agen), F Mesnel (Racing Club de France), P Saint-André (Montferrand) (*capt*); Y Delaigue (Toulon), G Accoceberry (Bègles); L Armary (Lourdes), J-M Gonzalez (Bayonne), C Califano (Toulouse), O Merle (Montferrand), O Brouzet (Grenoble), A Benazzi (Agen), M Cecillon (Bourgoin), P Benetton (Agen)
Scorers *Tries:* Delaigue, Cecillon, Ntamack, Saint-André *Conversion:* Ntamack *Penalty Goal:* Ntamack
Referee C Thomas (Wales)

18 March, Cardiff Arms Park
WALES 12 (4PG) **IRELAND 16** (1G 2PG 1DG)

The wooden spoon was a suitable utensil for Wales to pick up here: they needed something with which to stir the simmering discontent that had entrapped the team all season. Days later, the entire management team – coaches Alan Davies and Gareth Jenkins and manager Robert Norster – were to resign in the wake of what was only Wales' second whitewash ever and their fifth defeat by Ireland in succession.

Not all the blame can be laid at the management's door, but it was evident that the team had lost confidence. When that goes, morale evaporates and skills break down. Selection for the game was also puzzling. There were two principal changes: giant lock Derwyn Jones was dropped, as was Hemi Taylor, who lost out to debutant Andrew Gibbs. Veteran Phil Davies was brought in to bolster the pack. Ireland, too, made changes, finally giving in to the clamour for Michael Bradley's head. The Irish scrum-half and skipper was demoted to the bench, and the captaincy passed to hooker Terry Kingston.

Ireland had not lost at the Arms Park since 1983. In the fractured opening quarter precious little was created by either side. Jenkins knocked over a penalty goal for Wales in the 15th minute. Richie Collins flattened Elwood with a late tackle and was lucky to stay on the field. Elwood was not so fortunate, and was replaced by Burke. Within five minutes Burke put over a dropped goal followed by a penalty on the half-hour. Irish heads lifted, so much so that two minutes before the interval the elegant Mullin glided over after Wallace came in from his wing to set up the centre.

Jenkins reduced the ten-point deficit with a penalty in injury time at the end of the first half and closed the gap still further with two more successful kicks within 11 minutes of the restart. In such a loose game so littered with mistakes, anything might have happened. Eventually, 13 minutes from time, Burke settled matters with a penalty goal awarded after he had been late-tackled on the Welsh 22.

WALES: M Back (Bridgend); I C Evans (Llanelli) (*capt*), M R Hall (Cardiff), N G Davies (Llanelli), M Proctor (Llanelli); N R Jenkins (Pontypridd), R N Jones (Swansea); M Griffiths (Cardiff), G R Jenkins (Swansea), S C John (Llanelli), P T Davies (Llanelli), G O Llewellyn (Neath), A Gibbs (Newbridge), E Lewis (Cardiff), R Collins (Pontypridd)
Scorer *Penalty Goals:* Jenkins (4)
IRELAND: J E Staples (Harlequins); R M Wallace (Garryowen), B J Mullin (Blackrock Coll), P P A Danaher (Garryowen), S P Geoghegan (Bath); E P Elwood (Lansdowne), N A Hogan (Terenure); N J Popplewell (Wasps), T J Kingston (Dolphin) (*capt*), P M Clohessy (Young Munster), D A Tweed (Ballymena), G M Fulcher (Cork Const), A G Foley (Shannon), P S Johns (Dungannon), E O Halvey (Shannon)
Replacement P Burke (Cork Const) for Elwood (20 mins)
Scorers *Try:* Mullin *Conversion:* Burke *Penalty Goals:* Burke (2)
Dropped Goal: Burke
Referee R J Megson (Scotland)

The wooden spoon decider in which Ireland sealed misery for Wales by 16-12. Ireland's Niall Hogan (left) and Paul Burke halt Nigel Davies.

18 March, Twickenham
ENGLAND 24 (7PG 1DG) **SCOTLAND 12** (2PG 2DG)

The stands were full, the car parks were packed, the tickets were changing hands at a reputed £1,500 a pair and what did we get for it? There was scarcely a try in sight and much of the play was disjointed. Even the post-match mood was flat. Brian Moore sounded off about what he deemed to be the negative spoiling tactics of the Scots, while Will Carling attempted a lap of honour which he aborted halfway round when he was mobbed. Apart from all this, it was not a bad day.

It was unrealistic to expect too much. With such a lot at stake – take your pick from the real and the mythical of Grand Slam, Triple Crown, Five Nations Championship and Calcutta Cup – neither side was likely to throw caution to the winds. A final penalty tally of 19-9 suggests that Moore may have had a point, but it's far too late after the final whistle has been blown to be wondering what to do about it. England need to learn to impose themselves on troublesome opponents.

The Scots again showed that they have bonded together well up front. Doddie Weir had a magnificent opening quarter, although by the end Bayfield and Johnson had reclaimed the line-out honours for England. Bayfield, in fact, enjoyed a great afternoon all over the park. Neither back line managed to create much of note behind. Catt once again looked to be the England danger-man. He also saved a certain try when he knocked the ball from Gavin Hastings' grasp in the tackle.

There were two early and smartly taken dropped goals for Scotland from Craig Chalmers, while England once more turned to the boot of Rob Andrew. He finished with 24 points in all to equal the record set by Sebastien Viars in 1992. Andrew also passed Jon Webb's aggregate record for England. By the end of the Championship he had 317 points in internationals. Gavin Hastings finished with 56 from the four games to break his own Championship record, set back in 1986. Jason Leonard became England's most-capped prop and Scott Hastings Scotland's most-capped centre. If nothing else, it was a day of records.

ENGLAND: M J Catt (Bath); T Underwood (Leicester), W D C Carling (Harlequins) (*capt*), J C Guscott (Bath), R Underwood (Leicester & RAF); C R Andrew (Wasps), K P P Bracken (Bristol); J Leonard (Harlequins), B C Moore (Harlequins), V E Ubogu (Bath), M O Johnson (Leicester), M C Bayfield (Northampton), T A K Rodber (Northampton), D Richards (Leicester), B B Clarke (Bath) *Replacements* S O Ojomoh (Bath) for D Richards (50 mins); C D Morris (Orrell) for K Bracken (temp); G C Rowntree (Leicester) for Leonard (temp)
Scorer *Penalty Goals:* Andrew (7) *Dropped Goal:* Andrew
SCOTLAND: A G Hastings (Watsonians) (*capt*); C A Joiner (Melrose), G P J Townsend (Gala), S Hastings (Watsonians), K M Logan (Stirling County); C M Chalmers (Melrose), B W Redpath (Melrose); D I W Hilton (Bath), K S Milne (Heriot's FP), P H Wright (Boroughmuir), G W Weir (Melrose), S J Campbell (Dundee HSFP), R I Wainwright (West Hartlepool), E W Peters (Bath), I R Morrison (London Scottish)
Replacement J J Manson (Dundee HSFP) for Hilton (44 mins)
Scorers *Penalty Goals:* G Hastings (2) *Dropped Goals:* Chalmers (2)
Referee B W Stirling (Ireland)

Martin Johnson, supported by Jason Leonard, wins a line-out for England in the match which brought them their third Grand Slam in five years. Martin Bayfield keeps Scotland's Doddie Weir out of harm's way.

RESULTS OF INTERNATIONAL MATCHES *(up to 31 March 1995)*

Cap matches only.

Years for Five Nations' matches are for the second half of the season: eg 1972 means season 1971-72. Years for matches against touring teams from the Southern Hemisphere refer to the actual year of the match.

Points-scoring was first introduced in 1886, when an International Board was formed by Scotland, Ireland and Wales. Points values varied between countries until 1890, when England agreed to join the Board, and uniform values were adopted.

WC indicates a fixture played during the Rugby World Cup finals.

Northern Hemisphere seasons	*Try*	*Conversion*	*Penalty goal*	*Dropped goal*	*Goal from mark*
1890-91	1	2	2	3	3
1891-92 to 1892-93	2	3	3	4	4
1893-94 to 1904-05	3	2	3	4	4
1905-06 to 1947-48	3	2	3	4	3
1948-49 to 1970-71	3	2	3	3	3
1971-72 to 1991-92	4	2	3	3	3*
1992-93 onwards	5	2	3	3	–

**The goal from mark ceased to exist when free kick clause was introduced, 1977-78.*

ENGLAND v SCOTLAND

Played 112 England won 56, Scotland won 39, Drawn 17

1871 Raeburn Place (Edinburgh) **Scotland** 1G 1T to 1T
1872 The Oval (London) **England** 1G 1DG 2T to 1DG
1873 Glasgow **Drawn** no score
1874 The Oval **England** 1DG to 1T
1875 Raeburn Place **Drawn** no score
1876 The Oval **England** 1G 1T to 0
1877 Raeburn Place **Scotland** 1 DG to 0
1878 The Oval **Drawn** no score
1879 Raeburn Place **Drawn** Scotland 1DG England 1G
1880 Manchester **England** 2G 3T to 1G
1881 Raeburn Place **Drawn** Scotland 1G 1T England 1DG 1T
1882 Manchester **Scotland** 2T to 0
1883 Raeburn Place **England** 2T to 1T
1884 Blackheath (London) **England** 1G to 1T
1885 No Match
1886 Raeburn Place **Drawn** no score
1887 Manchester **Drawn** 1T each
1888 No Match
1889 No Match
1890 Raeburn Place **England** 1G 1T to 0
1891 Richmond (London) **Scotland** 9-3
1892 Raeburn Place **England** 5-0
1893 Leeds **Scotland** 8-0
1894 Raeburn Place **Scotland** 6-0
1895 Richmond **Scotland** 6-3
1896 Glasgow **Scotland** 11-0
1897 Manchester **England** 12-3
1898 Powderhall (Edinburgh) **Drawn** 3-3
1899 Blackheath **Scotland** 5-0
1900 Inverleith (Edinburgh) **Drawn** 0-0
1901 Blackheath **Scotland** 18-3
1902 Inverleith **England** 6-3
1903 Richmond **Scotland** 10-6
1904 Inverleith **Scotland** 6-3
1905 Richmond **Scotland** 8-0
1906 Inverleith **England** 9-3
1907 Blackheath **Scotland** 8-3
1908 Inverleith **Scotland** 16-10
1909 Richmond **Scotland** 18-8
1910 Inverleith **England** 14-5
1911 Twickenham **England** 13-8
1912 Inverleith **Scotland** 8-3
1913 Twickenham **England** 3-0
1914 Inverleith **England** 16-15
1920 Twickenham **England** 13-4
1921 Inverleith **England** 18-0
1922 Twickenham **England** 11-5
1923 Inverleith **England** 8-6
1924 Twickenham **England** 19-0
1925 Murrayfield **Scotland** 14-11
1926 Twickenham **Scotland** 17-9
1927 Murrayfield **Scotland** 21-13
1928 Twickenham **England** 6-0
1929 Murrayfield **Scotland** 12-6
1930 Twickenham **Drawn** 0-0
1931 Murrayfield **Scotland** 28-19
1932 Twickenham **England** 16-3
1933 Murrayfield **Scotland** 3-0
1934 Twickenham **England** 6-3

1935 Murrayfield **Scotland** 10-7
1936 Twickenham **England** 9-8
1937 Murrayfield **England** 6-3
1938 Twickenham **Scotland** 21-16
1939 Murrayfield **England** 9-6
1947 Twickenham **England** 24-5
1948 Murrayfield **Scotland** 6-3
1949 Twickenham **England** 19-3

Craig Chalmers and Eric Peters feel the force of a challenge by Tim Rodber and Ben Clarke in the 112th international between England and Scotland, the Grand Slam decider at Twickenham in 1995. England's 24-12 victory gave them the Grand Slam, Championship, Triple Crown and Calcutta Cup.

1950 Murrayfield **Scotland** 13-11
1951 Twickenham **England** 5-3
1952 Murrayfield **England** 19-3
1953 Twickenham **England** 26-8
1954 Murrayfield **England** 13-3
1955 Twickenham **England** 9-6
1956 Murrayfield **England** 11-6
1957 Twickenham **England** 16-3
1958 Murrayfield **Drawn** 3-3
1959 Twickenham **Drawn** 3-3
1960 Murrayfield **England** 21-12
1961 Twickenham **England** 6-0
1962 Murrayfield **Drawn** 3-3
1963 Twickenham **England** 10-8
1964 Murrayfield **Scotland** 15-6
1965 Twickenham **Drawn** 3-3
1966 Murrayfield **Scotland** 6-3
1967 Twickenham **England** 27-14
1968 Murrayfield **England** 8-6
1969 Twickenham **England** 8-3
1970 Murrayfield **Scotland** 14-5
1971 Twickenham **Scotland** 16-15
1971 Murrayfield **Scotland** 26-6
Special Centenary match – non-championship
1972 Murrayfield **Scotland** 23-9
1973 Twickenham **England** 20-13
1974 Murrayfield **Scotland** 16-14
1975 Twickenham **England** 7-6
1976 Murrayfield **Scotland** 22-12
1977 Twickenham **England** 26-6
1978 Murrayfield **England** 15-0
1979 Twickenham **Drawn** 7-7
1980 Murrayfield **England** 30-18
1981 Twickenham **England** 23-17
1982 Murrayfield **Drawn** 9-9
1983 Twickenham **Scotland** 22-12
1984 Murrayfield **Scotland** 18-6
1985 Twickenham **England** 10-7
1986 Murrayfield **Scotland** 33-6
1987 Twickenham **England** 21-12
1988 Murrayfield **England** 9-6
1989 Twickenham **Drawn** 12-12
1990 Murrayfield **Scotland** 13-7
1991 Twickenham **England** 21-12
1991 Murrayfield *WC* **England** 9-6
1992 Murrayfield **England** 25-7
1993 Twickenham **England** 26-12
1994 Murrayfield **England** 15-14
1995 Twickenham **England** 24-12

ENGLAND v IRELAND

Played 108 England won 62, Ireland won 38, Drawn 8

1875 The Oval (London) **England** 1G 1DG 1T to 0
1876 Dublin **England** 1G 1T to 0
1877 The Oval **England** 2G 2T to 0
1878 Dublin **England** 2G 1T to 0
1879 The Oval **England** 2G 1DG 2T to 0
1880 Dublin **England** 1G 1T to 1T
1881 Manchester **England** 2G 2T to 0
1882 Dublin **Drawn** 2T each
1883 Manchester **England** 1G 3T to 1T
1884 Dublin **England** 1G to 0
1885 Manchester **England** 2T to 1T
1886 Dublin **England** 1T to 0
1887 Dublin **Ireland** 2G to 0
1888 No Match
1889 No Match
1890 Blackheath (London) **England** 3T to 0
1891 Dublin **England** 9-0
1892 Manchester **England** 7-0
1893 Dublin **England** 4-0
1894 Blackheath **Ireland** 7-5
1895 Dublin **England** 6-3
1896 Leeds **Ireland** 10-4
1897 Dublin **Ireland** 13-9
1898 Richmond (London) **Ireland** 9-6
1899 Dublin **Ireland** 6-0
1900 Richmond **England** 15-4
1901 Dublin **Ireland** 10-6
1902 Leicester **England** 6-3
1903 Dublin **Ireland** 6-0
1904 Blackheath **England** 19-0
1905 Cork **Ireland** 17-3
1906 Leicester **Ireland** 16-6
1907 Dublin **Ireland** 17-9
1908 Richmond **England** 13-3
1909 Dublin **England** 11-5
1910 Twickenham **Drawn** 0-0
1911 Dublin **Ireland** 3-0
1912 Twickenham **England** 15-0
1913 Dublin **England** 15-4
1914 Twickenham **England** 17-12
1920 Dublin **England** 14-11
1921 Twickenham **England** 15-0
1922 Dublin **England** 12-3
1923 Leicester **England** 23-5
1924 Belfast **England** 14-3
1925 Twickenham **Drawn** 6-6
1926 Dublin **Ireland** 19-15
1927 Twickenham **England** 8-6
1928 Dublin **England** 7-6
1929 Twickenham **Ireland** 6-5
1930 Dublin **Ireland** 4-3
1931 Twickenham **Ireland** 6-5
1932 Dublin **England** 11-8
1933 Twickenham **England** 17-6
1934 Dublin **England** 13-3
1935 Twickenham **England** 14-3
1936 Dublin **Ireland** 6-3
1937 Twickenham **England** 9-8
1938 Dublin **England** 36-14
1939 Twickenham **Ireland** 5-0
1947 Dublin **Ireland** 22-0
1948 Twickenham **Ireland** 11-10
1949 Dublin **Ireland** 14-5
1950 Twickenham **England** 3-0
1951 Dublin **Ireland** 3-0
1952 Twickenham **England** 3-0

1953 Dublin **Drawn** 9-9
1954 Twickenham **England** 14-3
1955 Dublin **Drawn** 6-6
1956 Twickenham **England** 20-0
1957 Dublin **England** 6-0
1958 Twickenham **England** 6-0
1959 Dublin **England** 3-0
1960 Twickenham **England** 8-5
1961 Dublin **Ireland** 11-8
1962 Twickenham **England** 16-0
1963 Dublin **Drawn** 0-0
1964 Twickenham **Ireland** 18-5
1965 Dublin **Ireland** 5-0
1966 Twickenham **Drawn** 6-6
1967 Dublin **England** 8-3
1968 Twickenham **Drawn** 9-9
1969 Dublin **Ireland** 17-15
1970 Twickenham **England** 9-3
1971 Dublin **England** 9-6
1972 Twickenham **Ireland** 16-12
1973 Dublin **Ireland** 18-9
1974 Twickenham **Ireland** 26-21
1975 Dublin **Ireland** 12-9
1976 Twickenham **Ireland** 13-12
1977 Dublin **England** 4-0
1978 Twickenham **England** 15-9
1979 Dublin **Ireland** 12-7
1980 Twickenham **England** 24-9
1981 Dublin **England** 10-6
1982 Twickenham **Ireland** 16-15
1983 Dublin **Ireland** 25-15
1984 Twickenham **England** 12-9
1985 Dublin **Ireland** 13-10
1986 Twickenham **England** 25-20
1987 Dublin **Ireland** 17-0
1988 Twickenham **England** 35-3
1988 Dublin **England** 21-10
Non-championship match
1989 Dublin **England** 16-3
1990 Twickenham **England** 23-0
1991 Dublin **England** 16-7
1992 Twickenham **England** 38-9
1993 Dublin **Ireland** 17-3
1994 Twickenham **Ireland** 13-12
1995 Dublin **England** 20-8

ENGLAND v WALES

Played 101 England won 41, Wales won 48, Drawn 12

1881 Blackheath (London) **England** 7G 1DG 6T to 0
1882 No Match
1883 Swansea **England** 2G 4T to 0
1884 Leeds **England** 1G 2T to 1G
1885 Swansea **England** 1G 4T to 1G 1T
1886 Blackheath **England** 1GM 2T to 1G
1887 Llanelli **Drawn** no score
1888 No Match
1889 No Match
1890 Dewsbury **Wales** 1T to 0
1891 Newport **England** 7-3
1892 Blackheath **England** 17-0
1893 Cardiff **Wales** 12-11
1894 Birkenhead **England** 24-3
1895 Swansea **England** 14-6
1896 Blackheath **England** 25-0
1897 Newport **Wales** 11-0
1898 Blackheath **England** 14-7
1899 Swansea **Wales** 26-3
1900 Gloucester **Wales** 13-3
1901 Cardiff **Wales** 13-0
1902 Blackheath **Wales** 9-8
1903 Swansea **Wales** 21-5
1904 Leicester **Drawn** 14-14
1905 Cardiff **Wales** 25-0
1906 Richmond (London) **Wales** 16-3
1907 Swansea **Wales** 22-0
1908 Bristol **Wales** 28-18
1909 Cardiff **Wales** 8-0
1910 Twickenham **England** 11-6
1911 Swansea **Wales** 15-11
1912 Twickenham **England** 8-0
1913 Cardiff **England** 12-0
1914 Twickenham **England** 10-9
1920 Swansea **Wales** 19-5
1921 Twickenham **England** 18-3
1922 Cardiff **Wales** 28-6
1923 Twickenham **England** 7-3
1924 Swansea **England** 17-9
1925 Twickenham **England** 12-6
1926 Cardiff **Drawn** 3-3
1927 Twickenham **England** 11-9
1928 Swansea **England** 10-8
1929 Twickenham **England** 8-3
1930 Cardiff **England** 11-3
1931 Twickenham **Drawn** 11-11
1932 Swansea **Wales** 12-5
1933 Twickenham **Wales** 7-3
1934 Cardiff **England** 9-0
1935 Twickenham **Drawn** 3-3
1936 Swansea **Drawn** 0-0
1937 Twickenham **England** 4-3
1938 Cardiff **Wales** 14-8
1939 Twickenham **England** 3-0
1947 Cardiff **England** 9-6
1948 Twickenham **Drawn** 3-3
1949 Cardiff **Wales** 9-3
1950 Twickenham **Wales** 11-5
1951 Swansea **Wales** 23-5
1952 Twickenham **Wales** 8-6
1953 Cardiff **England** 8-3
1954 Twickenham **England** 9-6
1955 Cardiff **Wales** 3-0
1956 Twickenham **Wales** 8-3
1957 Cardiff **England** 3-0
1958 Twickenham **Drawn** 3-3
1959 Cardiff **Wales** 5-0
1960 Twickenham **England** 14-6
1961 Cardiff **Wales** 6-3
1962 Twickenham **Drawn** 0-0
1963 Cardiff **England** 13-6

1964 Twickenham **Drawn** 6-6
1965 Cardiff **Wales** 14-3
1966 Twickenham **Wales** 11-6
1967 Cardiff **Wales** 34-21
1968 Twickenham **Drawn** 11-11
1969 Cardiff **Wales** 30-9
1970 Twickenham **Wales** 17-13
1971 Cardiff **Wales** 22-6
1972 Twickenham **Wales** 12-3
1973 Cardiff **Wales** 25-9
1974 Twickenham **England** 16-12
1975 Cardiff **Wales** 20-4
1976 Twickenham **Wales** 21-9
1977 Cardiff **Wales** 14-9
1978 Twickenham **Wales** 9-6
1979 Cardiff **Wales** 27-3
1980 Twickenham **England** 9-8
1981 Cardiff **Wales** 21-19
1982 Twickenham **England** 17-7
1983 Cardiff **Drawn** 13-13
1984 Twickenham **Wales** 24-15
1985 Cardiff **Wales** 24-15
1986 Twickenham **England** 21-18
1987 Cardiff **Wales** 19-12
1987 Brisbane *WC* **Wales** 16-3
1988 Twickenham **Wales** 11-3
1989 Cardiff **Wales** 12-9
1990 Twickenham **England** 34-6
1991 Cardiff **England** 25-6
1992 Twickenham **England** 24-0
1993 Cardiff **Wales** 10-9
1994 Twickenham **England** 15-8
1995 Cardiff **England** 23-9

ENGLAND v FRANCE

Played 71 England won 40, France won 24, Drawn 7

1906 Paris **England** 35-8
1907 Richmond (London) **England** 41-13
1908 Paris **England** 19-0
1909 Leicester **England** 22-0
1910 Paris **England** 11-3
1911 Twickenham **England** 37-0
1912 Paris **England** 18-8
1913 Twickenham **England** 20-0
1914 Paris **England** 39-13
1920 Twickenham **England** 8-3
1921 Paris **England** 10-6
1922 Twickenham **Drawn** 11-11
1923 Paris **England** 12-3
1924 Twickenham **England** 19-7
1925 Paris **England** 13-11
1926 Twickenham **England** 11-0
1927 Paris **France** 3-0
1928 Twickenham **England** 18-8
1929 Paris **England** 16-6
1930 Twickenham **England** 11-5
1931 Paris **France** 14-13
1947 Twickenham **England** 6-3
1948 Paris **France** 15-0
1949 Twickenham **England** 8-3
1950 Paris **France** 6-3
1951 Twickenham **France** 11-3
1952 Paris **England** 6-3
1953 Twickenham **England** 11-0
1954 Paris **France** 11-3
1955 Twickenham **France** 16-9
1956 Paris **France** 14-9
1957 Twickenham **England** 9-5
1958 Paris **England** 14-0
1959 Twickenham **Drawn** 3-3
1960 Paris **Drawn** 3-3
1961 Twickenham **Drawn** 5-5
1962 Paris **France** 13-0
1963 Twickenham **England** 6-5
1964 Paris **England** 6-3
1965 Twickenham **England** 9-6
1966 Paris **France** 13-0
1967 Twickenham **France** 16-12
1968 Paris **France** 14-9
1969 Twickenham **England** 22-8
1970 Paris **France** 35-13
1971 Twickenham **Drawn** 14-14
1972 Paris **France** 37-12
1973 Twickenham **England** 14-6
1974 Paris **Drawn** 12-12
1975 Twickenham **France** 27-20
1976 Paris **France** 30-9
1977 Twickenham **France** 4-3
1978 Paris **France** 15-6
1979 Twickenham **England** 7-6
1980 Paris **England** 17-13
1981 Twickenham **France** 16-12
1982 Paris **England** 27-15
1983 Twickenham **France** 19-15
1984 Paris **France** 32-18
1985 Twickenham **Drawn** 9-9
1986 Paris **France** 29-10
1987 Twickenham **France** 19-15
1988 Paris **France** 10-9
1989 Twickenham **England** 11-0
1990 Paris **England** 26-7
1991 Twickenham **England** 21-19
1991 Paris *WC* **England** 19-10
1992 Paris **England** 31-13
1993 Twickenham **England** 16-15
1994 Paris **England** 18-14
1995 Twickenham **England** 31-10

ENGLAND v NEW ZEALAND

Played 17 England won 4, New Zealand won 13, Drawn 0

1905 Crystal Palace (London) **New Zealand** 15-0
1925 Twickenham **New Zealand** 17-11

1936 Twickenham **England** 13-0
1954 Twickenham **New Zealand** 5-0
1963 *1* Auckland **New Zealand** 21-11
2 Christchurch **New Zealand** 9- 6
New Zealand won series 2-0
1964 Twickenham **New Zealand** 14-0
1967 Twickenham **New Zealand** 23-11
1973 Twickenham **New Zealand** 9-0
1973 Auckland **England** 16-10
1978 Twickenham **New Zealand** 16-6
1979 Twickenham **New Zealand** 10-9
1983 Twickenham **England** 15-9
1985 *1* Christchurch **New Zealand** 18-13
2 Wellington **New Zealand** 42-15
New Zealand won series 2-0
1991 Twickenham *WC* **New Zealand** 18-12
1993 Twickenham **England** 15-9

ENGLAND v SOUTH AFRICA

Played 12 England won 4, South Africa won 7, Drawn 1

1906 Crystal Palace (London) **Drawn** 3-3
1913 Twickenham **South Africa** 9-3
1932 Twickenham **South Africa** 7-0
1952 Twickenham **South Africa** 8-3
1961 Twickenham **South Africa** 5-0
1969 Twickenham **England** 11-8
1972 Johannesburg **England** 18-9
1984 *1* Port Elizabeth **South Africa** 33-15
2 Johannesburg **South Africa** 35-9
South Africa won series 2-0
1992 Twickenham **England** 33-16
1994 *1* Pretoria **England** 32-15
2 Cape Town **South Africa** 27-9
Series drawn 1-1

ENGLAND v AUSTRALIA

Played 18 England won 6, Australia won 12, Drawn 0

1909 Blackheath (London) **Australia** 9-3
1928 Twickenham **England** 18-11
1948 Twickenham **Australia** 11-0
1958 Twickenham **England** 9-6
1963 Sydney **Australia** 18-9
1967 Twickenham **Australia** 23-11
1973 Twickenham **England** 20-3
1975 *1* Sydney **Australia** 16-9
2 Brisbane **Australia** 30-21
Australia won series 2-0
1976 Twickenham **England** 23-6
1982 Twickenham **England** 15-11
1984 Twickenham **Australia** 19-3
1987 Sydney *WC* **Australia** 19-6
1988 *1* Brisbane **Australia** 22-16
2 Sydney **Australia** 28-8
Australia won series 2-0
1988 Twickenham **England** 28-19
1991 Sydney **Australia** 40-15
1991 Twickenham *WC* **Australia** 12-6

ENGLAND v NEW ZEALAND NATIVES

Played 1 England won 1

1889 Blackheath **England** 1G 4T to 0

ENGLAND v RFU PRESIDENT'S XV

Played 1 President's XV won 1

1971 Twickenham **President's XV** 28-11

ENGLAND v ARGENTINA

Played 5 England won 3, Argentina won 1, Drawn 1

1981 *1* Buenos Aires **Drawn** 19-19
2 Buenos Aires **England** 12-6
England won series 1-0 with 1 draw
1990 *1* Buenos Aires **England** 25-12
2 Buenos Aires **Argentina** 15-13
Series drawn 1-1
1990 Twickenham **England** 51-0

ENGLAND v ROMANIA

Played 3 England won 3

1985 Twickenham **England** 22-15
1989 Bucharest **England** 58-3
1994 Twickenham **England** 54-3

ENGLAND v JAPAN

Played 1 England won 1

1987 Sydney *WC* **England** 60-7

ENGLAND v UNITED STATES

Played 2 England won 2

1987 Sydney *WC* **England** 34-6
1991 Twickenham *WC* **England** 37-9

ENGLAND v FIJI

Played 3 England won 3

1988 Suva **England** 25-12
1989 Twickenham **England** 58-23
1991 Suva **England** 28-12

ENGLAND v ITALY

Played 1 England won 1

1991 Twickenham *WC* **England** 36-6

ENGLAND v CANADA

Played 2 England won 2

1992 Wembley **England** 26-13
1994 Twickenham **England** 60-19

SCOTLAND v IRELAND

Played 107 Scotland won 56, Ireland won 45, Drawn 5, Abandoned 1

1877 Belfast **Scotland** 4G 2DG 2T to 0
1878 No Match
1879 Belfast **Scotland** 1G 1DG 1T to 0
1880 Glasgow **Scotland** 1G 2DG 2T to 0
1881 Belfast **Ireland** 1DG to 1T
1882 Glasgow **Scotland** 2T to 0
1883 Belfast **Scotland** 1G 1T to 0
1884 Raeburn Place (Edinburgh) **Scotland** 2G 2T to 1T
1885 Belfast **Abandoned** Ireland 0 Scotland 1T
1885 Raeburn Place **Scotland** 1G 2T to 0
1886 Raeburn Place **Scotland** 3G 1DG 2T to 0
1887 Belfast **Scotland** 1G 1GM 2T to 0
1888 Raeburn Place **Scotland** 1G to 0
1889 Belfast **Scotland** 1DG to 0
1890 Raeburn Place **Scotland** 1DG 1T to 0
1891 Belfast **Scotland** 14-0
1892 Raeburn Place **Scotland** 2-0
1893 Belfast **Drawn** 0-0
1894 Dublin **Ireland** 5-0
1895 Raeburn Place **Scotland** 6-0
1896 Dublin **Drawn** 0-0
1897 Powderhall (Edinburgh) **Scotland** 8-3
1898 Belfast **Scotland** 8-0
1899 Inverleith (Edinburgh) **Ireland** 9-3
1900 Dublin **Drawn** 0-0
1901 Inverleith **Scotland** 9-5
1902 Belfast **Ireland** 5-0
1903 Inverleith **Scotland** 3-0
1904 Dublin **Scotland** 19-3
1905 Inverleith **Ireland** 11-5
1906 Dublin **Scotland** 13-6
1907 Inverleith **Scotland** 15-3
1908 Dublin **Ireland** 16-11
1909 Inverleith **Scotland** 9-3
1910 Belfast **Scotland** 14-0
1911 Inverleith **Ireland** 16-10
1912 Dublin **Ireland** 10-8
1913 Inverleith **Scotland** 29-14
1914 Dublin **Ireland** 6-0
1920 Inverleith **Scotland** 19-0
1921 Dublin **Ireland** 9-8
1922 Inverleith **Scotland** 6-3
1923 Dublin **Scotland** 13-3
1924 Inverleith **Scotland** 13-8
1925 Dublin **Scotland** 14-8
1926 Murrayfield **Ireland** 3-0
1927 Dublin **Ireland** 6-0
1928 Murrayfield **Ireland** 13-5
1929 Dublin **Scotland** 16-7
1930 Murrayfield **Ireland** 14-11
1931 Dublin **Ireland** 8-5
1932 Murrayfield **Ireland** 20-8
1933 Dublin **Scotland** 8-6
1934 Murrayfield **Scotland** 16-9
1935 Dublin **Ireland** 12-5
1936 Murrayfield **Ireland** 10-4
1937 Dublin **Ireland** 11-4
1938 Murrayfield **Scotland** 23-14
1939 Dublin **Ireland** 12-3
1947 Murrayfield **Ireland** 3-0
1948 Dublin **Ireland** 6-0
1949 Murrayfield **Ireland** 13-3
1950 Dublin **Ireland** 21-0
1951 Murrayfield **Ireland** 6-5
1952 Dublin **Ireland** 12-8
1953 Murrayfield **Ireland** 26-8
1954 Belfast **Ireland** 6-0
1955 Murrayfield **Scotland** 12-3
1956 Dublin **Ireland** 14-10
1957 Murrayfield **Ireland** 5-3
1958 Dublin **Ireland** 12-6
1959 Murrayfield **Ireland** 8-3
1960 Dublin **Scotland** 6-5
1961 Murrayfield **Scotland** 16-8

1962 Dublin **Scotland** 20-6
1963 Murrayfield **Scotland** 3-0
1964 Dublin **Scotland** 6-3
1965 Murrayfield **Ireland** 16-6
1966 Dublin **Scotland** 11-3
1967 Murrayfield **Ireland** 5-3
1968 Dublin **Ireland** 14-6
1969 Murrayfield **Ireland** 16-0
1970 Dublin **Ireland** 16-11
1971 Murrayfield **Ireland** 17-5
1972 No Match
1973 Murrayfield **Scotland** 19-14
1974 Dublin **Ireland** 9-6
1975 Murrayfield **Scotland** 20-13
1976 Dublin **Scotland** 15-6
1977 Murrayfield **Scotland** 21-18
1978 Dublin **Ireland** 12-9
1979 Murrayfield **Drawn** 11-11
1980 Dublin **Ireland** 22-15
1981 Murrayfield **Scotland** 10-9
1982 Dublin **Ireland** 21-12
1983 Murrayfield **Ireland** 15-13
1984 Dublin **Scotland** 32-9
1985 Murrayfield **Ireland** 18-15
1986 Dublin **Scotland** 10-9
1987 Murrayfield **Scotland** 16-12
1988 Dublin **Ireland** 22-18
1989 Murrayfield **Scotland** 37-21
1990 Dublin **Scotland** 13-10
1991 Murrayfield **Scotland** 28-25
1991 Murrayfield *WC* **Scotland** 24-15
1992 Dublin **Scotland** 18-10
1993 Murrayfield **Scotland** 15-3
1994 Dublin **Drawn** 6-6
1995 Murrayfield **Scotland** 26-13

SCOTLAND v WALES

Played 99 Scotland won 43, Wales won 54, Drawn 2

1883 Raeburn Place (Edinburgh) **Scotland** (3G to 1G
1884 Newport **Scotland** 1DG 1T to 0
1885 Glasgow **Drawn** no score
1886 Cardiff **Scotland** 2G 8T to 0
1887 Raeburn Place **Scotland** 4G 8T to 0
1888 Newport **Wales** 1T to 0
1889 Raeburn Place **Scotland** 2T to 0
1890 Cardiff **Scotland** 1G 2T to 1T
1891 Raeburn Place **Scotland** 15-0
1892 Swansea **Scotland** 7-2
1893 Raeburn Place **Wales** 9-0
1894 Newport **Wales** 7-0
1895 Raeburn Place **Scotland** 5-4
1896 Cardiff **Wales** 6-0
1897 No Match
1898 No Match
1899 Inverleith (Edinburgh) **Scotland** 21-10
1900 Swansea **Wales** 12-3
1901 Inverleith **Scotland** 18-8
1902 Cardiff **Wales** 14-5
1903 Inverleith **Scotland** 6-0
1904 Swansea **Wales** 21-3
1905 Inverleith **Wales** 6-3
1906 Cardiff **Wales** 9-3
1907 Inverleith **Scotland** 6-3
1908 Swansea **Wales** 6-5
1909 Inverleith **Wales** 5-3
1910 Cardiff **Wales** 14-0
1911 Inverleith **Wales** 32-10
1912 Swansea **Wales** 21-6
1913 Inverleith **Wales** 8-0
1914 Cardiff **Wales** 24-5
1920 Inverleith **Scotland** 9-5
1921 Swansea **Scotland** 14-8
1922 Inverleith **Drawn** 9-9
1923 Cardiff **Scotland** 11-8
1924 Inverleith **Scotland** 35-10
1925 Swansea **Scotland** 24-14
1926 Murrayfield **Scotland** 8-5
1927 Cardiff **Scotland** 5-0
1928 Murrayfield **Wales** 13-0
1929 Swansea **Wales** 14-7
1930 Murrayfield **Scotland** 12-9
1931 Cardiff **Wales** 13-8
1932 Murrayfield **Wales** 6-0
1933 Swansea **Scotland** 11-3
1934 Murrayfield **Wales** 13-6
1935 Cardiff **Wales** 10-6
1936 Murrayfield **Wales** 13-3
1937 Swansea **Scotland** 13-6
1938 Murrayfield **Scotland** 8-6
1939 Cardiff **Wales** 11-3
1947 Murrayfield **Wales** 22-8
1948 Cardiff **Wales** 14-0
1949 Murrayfield **Scotland** 6-5
1950 Swansea **Wales** 12-0
1951 Murrayfield **Scotland** 19-0
1952 Cardiff **Wales** 11-0
1953 Murrayfield **Wales** 12-0
1954 Swansea **Wales** 15-3
1955 Murrayfield **Scotland** 14-8
1956 Cardiff **Wales** 9-3
1957 Murrayfield **Scotland** 9-6
1958 Cardiff **Wales** 8-3
1959 Murrayfield **Scotland** 6-5
1960 Cardiff **Wales** 8-0
1961 Murrayfield **Scotland** 3-0
1962 Cardiff **Scotland** 8-3
1963 Murrayfield **Wales** 6-0
1964 Cardiff **Wales** 11-3
1965 Murrayfield **Wales** 14-12
1966 Cardiff **Wales** 8-3
1967 Murrayfield **Scotland** 11-5
1968 Cardiff **Wales** 5-0
1969 Murrayfield **Wales** 17-3
1970 Cardiff **Wales** 18-9
1971 Murrayfield **Wales** 19-18
1972 Cardiff **Wales** 35-12
1973 Murrayfield **Scotland** 10-9
1974 Cardiff **Wales** 6-0

1975 Murrayfield **Scotland** 12-10
1976 Cardiff **Wales** 28-6
1977 Murrayfield **Wales** 18-9
1978 Cardiff **Wales** 22-14
1979 Murrayfield **Wales** 19-13
1980 Cardiff **Wales** 17-6
1981 Murrayfield **Scotland** 15-6
1982 Cardiff **Scotland** 34-18
1983 Murrayfield **Wales** 19-15
1984 Cardiff **Scotland** 15-9
1985 Murrayfield **Wales** 25-21
1986 Cardiff **Wales** 22-15
1987 Murrayfield **Scotland** 21-15
1988 Cardiff **Wales** 25-20
1989 Murrayfield **Scotland** 23-7
1990 Cardiff **Scotland** 13-9
1991 Murrayfield **Scotland** 32-12
1992 Cardiff **Wales** 15-12
1993 Murrayfield **Scotland** 20-0
1994 Cardiff **Wales** 29-6
1995 Murrayfield **Scotland** 26-13

SCOTLAND v FRANCE

Played 66 Scotland won 31, France won 32, Drawn 3

1910 Inverleith (Edinburgh) **Scotland** 27-0
1911 Paris **France** 16-15
1912 Inverleith **Scotland** 31-3
1913 Paris **Scotland** 21-3
1914 No Match
1920 Paris **Scotland** 5-0
1921 Inverleith **France** 3-0
1922 Paris **Drawn** 3-3
1923 Inverleith **Scotland** 16-3
1924 Paris **France** 12-10
1925 Inverleith **Scotland** 25-4
1926 Paris **Scotland** 20-6
1927 Murrayfield **Scotland** 23-6
1928 Paris **Scotland** 15-6
1929 Murrayfield **Scotland** 6-3
1930 Paris **France** 7-3
1931 Murrayfield **Scotland** 6-4
1947 Paris **France** 8-3
1948 Murrayfield **Scotland** 9-8
1949 Paris **Scotland** 8-0
1950 Murrayfield **Scotland** 8-5
1951 Paris **France** 14-12
1952 Murrayfield **France** 13-11
1953 Paris **France** 11-5
1954 Murrayfield **France** 3-0
1955 Paris **France** 15-0
1956 Murrayfield **Scotland** 12-0
1957 Paris **Scotland** 6-0
1958 Murrayfield **Scotland** 11-9
1959 Paris **France** 9-0
1960 Murrayfield **France** 13-11
1961 Paris **France** 11-0
1962 Murrayfield **France** 11-3
1963 Paris **Scotland** 11-6
1964 Murrayfield **Scotland** 10-0
1965 Paris **France** 16-8
1966 Murrayfield **Drawn** 3-3
1967 Paris **Scotland** 9-8
1968 Murrayfield **France** 8-6
1969 Paris **Scotland** 6-3
1970 Murrayfield **France** 11-9
1971 Paris **France** 13-8
1972 Murrayfield **Scotland** 20-9
1973 Paris **France** 16-13
1974 Murrayfield **Scotland** 19-6
1975 Paris **France** 10-9
1976 Murrayfield **France** 13-6
1977 Paris **France** 23-3
1978 Murrayfield **France** 19-16
1979 Paris **France** 21-17
1980 Murrayfield **Scotland** 22-14
1981 Paris **France** 16-9
1982 Murrayfield **Scotland** 16-7
1983 Paris **France** 19-15
1984 Murrayfield **Scotland** 21-12
1985 Paris **France** 11-3
1986 Murrayfield **Scotland** 18-17
1987 Paris **France** 28-22
1987 Christchurch *WC* **Drawn** 20-20
1988 Murrayfield **Scotland** 23-12
1989 Paris **France** 19-3
1990 Murrayfield **Scotland** 21-0
1991 Paris **France** 15-9
1992 Murrayfield **Scotland** 10-6
1993 Paris **France** 11-3
1994 Murrayfield **France** 20-12
1995 Paris **Scotland** 23-21

SCOTLAND v NEW ZEALAND

Played 17 Scotland won 0, New Zealand won 15, Drawn 2

1905 Inverleith (Edinburgh) **New Zealand** 12-7
1935 Murrayfield **New Zealand** 18-8
1954 Murrayfield **New Zealand** 3-0
1964 Murrayfield **Drawn** 0-0
1967 Murrayfield **New Zealand** 14-3
1972 Murrayfield **New Zealand** 14-9
1975 Auckland **New Zealand** 24-0
1978 Murrayfield **New Zealand** 18-9
1979 Murrayfield **New Zealand** 20-6
1981 *1* Dunedin **New Zealand** 11-4
2 Auckland **New Zealand** 40-15
New Zealand won series 2-0
1983 Murrayfield **Drawn** 25-25
1987 Christchurch *WC* **New Zealand** 30-3
1990 *1* Dunedin **New Zealand** 31-16
2 Auckland **New Zealand** 21-18
New Zealand won series 2-0
1991 Cardiff *WC* **New Zealand** 13-6
1993 Murrayfield **New Zealand** 51-15

SCOTLAND v SOUTH AFRICA

Played 9 Scotland won 3, South Africa won 6, Drawn 0

1906 Glasgow **Scotland** 6-0
1912 Inverleith **South Africa** 16-0
1932 Murrayfield **South Africa** 6-3
1951 Murrayfield **South Africa** 44-0
1960 Port Elizabeth **South Africa** 18-10
1961 Murrayfield **South Africa** 12-5
1965 Murrayfield **Scotland** 8-5
1969 Murrayfield **Scotland** 6-3
1994 Murrayfield **South Africa** 34-10

SCOTLAND v AUSTRALIA

Played 14 Scotland won 7, Australia won 7, Drawn 0

1927 Murrayfield **Scotland** 10-8
1947 Murrayfield **Australia** 16-7
1958 Murrayfield **Scotland** 12-8
1966 Murrayfield **Scotland** 11-5
1968 Murrayfield **Scotland** 9-3
1970 Sydney **Australia** 23-3
1975 Murrayfield **Scotland** 10-3
1981 Murrayfield **Scotland** 24-15
1982 *1* Brisbane **Scotland** 12-7
2 Sydney **Australia** 33-9
Series drawn 1-1
1984 Murrayfield **Australia** 37-12
1988 Murrayfield **Australia** 32-13
1992 *1* Sydney **Australia** 27-12
2 Brisbane **Australia** 37-13
Australia won series 2-0

SCOTLAND v SRU PRESIDENT'S XV

Played 1 Scotland won 1

1973 Murrayfield **Scotland** 27-16

SCOTLAND v ROMANIA

Played 6 Scotland won 4, Romania won 2

1981 Murrayfield **Scotland** 12-6
1984 Bucharest **Romania** 28-22
1986 Bucharest **Scotland** 33-18
1987 Dunedin *WC* **Scotland** 55-28
1989 Murrayfield **Scotland** 32-0
1991 Bucharest **Romania** 18-12

SCOTLAND v ZIMBABWE

Played 2 Scotland won 2

1987 Wellington *WC* **Scotland** 60-21
1991 Murrayfield *WC* **Scotland** 51-12

SCOTLAND v FIJI

Played 1 Scotland won 1

1989 Murrayfield **Scotland** 38-17

SCOTLAND v ARGENTINA

Played 3 Scotland won 1, Argentina won 2

1990 Murrayfield **Scotland** 49-3
1994 *1* Buenos Aires **Argentina** 16-15
2 Buenos Aires **Argentina** 19-17
Argentina won series 2-0

SCOTLAND v JAPAN

Played 1 Scotland won 1

1991 Murrayfield *WC* **Scotland** 47-9

SCOTLAND v WESTERN SAMOA

Played 1 Scotland won 1

1991 Murrayfield *WC* **Scotland** 28-6

SCOTLAND v CANADA

Played 1 Scotland won 1

1995 Murrayfield **Scotland** 22-6

IRELAND v WALES

Played 98 Ireland won 34, Wales won 58, Drawn 6

1882 Dublin **Wales** 2G 2T to 0
1883 No Match
1884 Cardiff **Wales** 1DG 2T to 0
1885 No Match
1886 No Match
1887 Birkenhead **Wales** 1DG 1T to 3T
1888 Dublin **Ireland** 1G 1DG 1T to 0
1889 Swansea **Ireland** 2T to 0
1890 Dublin **Drawn** 1G each
1891 Llanelli **Wales** 6-4
1892 Dublin **Ireland** 9-0
1893 Llanelli **Wales** 2-0
1894 Belfast **Ireland** 3-0
1895 Cardiff **Wales** 5-3
1896 Dublin **Ireland** 8-4
1897 No Match
1898 Limerick **Wales** 11-3
1899 Cardiff **Ireland** 3-0
1900 Belfast **Wales** 3-0
1901 Swansea **Wales** 10-9
1902 Dublin **Wales** 15-0
1903 Cardiff **Wales** 18-0
1904 Belfast **Ireland** 14-12
1905 Swansea **Wales** 10-3
1906 Belfast **Ireland** 11-6
1907 Cardiff **Wales** 29-0
1908 Belfast **Wales** 11-5
1909 Swansea **Wales** 18-5
1910 Dublin **Wales** 19-3
1911 Cardiff **Wales** 16-0
1912 Belfast **Ireland** 12-5
1913 Swansea **Wales** 16-13
1914 Belfast **Wales** 11-3
1920 Cardiff **Wales** 28-4
1921 Belfast **Wales** 6-0
1922 Swansea **Wales** 11-5
1923 Dublin **Ireland** 5-4
1924 Cardiff **Ireland** 13-10
1925 Belfast **Ireland** 19-3
1926 Swansea **Wales** 11-8
1927 Dublin **Ireland** 19-9
1928 Cardiff **Ireland** 13-10
1929 Belfast **Drawn** 5-5
1930 Swansea **Wales** 12-7
1931 Belfast **Wales** 15-3
1932 Cardiff **Ireland** 12-10
1933 Belfast **Ireland** 10-5
1934 Swansea **Wales** 13-0
1935 Belfast **Ireland** 9-3
1936 Cardiff **Wales** 3-0
1937 Belfast **Ireland** 5-3
1938 Swansea **Wales** 11-5
1939 Belfast **Wales** 7-0
1947 Swansea **Wales** 6-0
1948 Belfast **Ireland** 6-3
1949 Swansea **Ireland** 5-0
1950 Belfast **Wales** 6-3
1951 Cardiff **Drawn** 3-3
1952 Dublin **Wales** 14-3
1953 Swansea **Wales** 5-3
1954 Dublin **Wales** 12-9
1955 Cardiff **Wales** 21-3
1956 Dublin **Ireland** 11-3
1957 Cardiff **Wales** 6-5
1958 Dublin **Wales** 9-6
1959 Cardiff **Wales** 8-6
1960 Dublin **Wales** 10-9
1961 Cardiff **Wales** 9-0
1962 Dublin **Drawn** 3-3
1963 Cardiff **Ireland** 14-6
1964 Dublin **Wales** 15-6
1965 Cardiff **Wales** 14-8
1966 Dublin **Ireland** 9-6
1967 Cardiff **Ireland** 3-0
1968 Dublin **Ireland** 9-6
1969 Cardiff **Wales** 24-11
1970 Dublin **Ireland** 14-0
1971 Cardiff **Wales** 23-9
1972 No Match
1973 Cardiff **Wales** 16-12
1974 Dublin **Drawn** 9-9
1975 Cardiff **Wales** 32-4
1976 Dublin **Wales** 34-9
1977 Cardiff **Wales** 25-9
1978 Dublin **Wales** 20-16
1979 Cardiff **Wales** 24-21
1980 Dublin **Ireland** 21-7
1981 Cardiff **Wales** 9-8
1982 Dublin **Ireland** 20-12
1983 Cardiff **Wales** 23-9
1984 Dublin **Wales** 18-9
1985 Cardiff **Ireland** 21-9
1986 Dublin **Wales** 19-12
1987 Cardiff **Ireland** 15-11
1987 Wellington *WC* **Wales** 13-6
1988 Dublin **Wales** 12-9
1989 Cardiff **Ireland** 19-13
1990 Dublin **Ireland** 14-8
1991 Cardiff **Drawn** 21-21
1992 Dublin **Wales** 16-15
1993 Cardiff **Ireland** 19-14
1994 Dublin **Wales** 17-15
1995 Cardiff **Ireland** 16-12

IRELAND v FRANCE

Played 68 Ireland won 25, France won 38, Drawn 5

1909 Dublin **Ireland** 19-8
1910 Paris **Ireland** 19-8
1911 Cork **Ireland** 25-5
1912 Paris **Ireland** 11-6
1913 Cork **Ireland** 24-0
1914 Paris **Ireland** 8-6

1920 Dublin **France** 15-7
1921 Paris **France** 20-10
1922 Dublin **Ireland** 8-3
1923 Paris **France** 14-8
1924 Dublin **Ireland** 6-0
1925 Paris **Ireland** 9-3
1926 Belfast **Ireland** 11-0
1927 Paris **Ireland** 8-3
1928 Belfast **Ireland** 12-8
1929 Paris **Ireland** 6-0
1930 Belfast **France** 5-0
1931 Paris **France** 3-0
1947 Dublin **France** 12-8
1948 Paris **Ireland** 13-6
1949 Dublin **France** 16-9
1950 Paris **Drawn** 3-3
1951 Dublin **Ireland** 9-8
1952 Paris **Ireland** 11-8
1953 Belfast **Ireland** 16-3
1954 Paris **France** 8-0
1955 Dublin **France** 5-3
1956 Paris **France** 14-8
1957 Dublin **Ireland** 11-6
1958 Paris **France** 11-6
1959 Dublin **Ireland** 9-5
1960 Paris **France** 23-6
1961 Dublin **France** 15-3
1962 Paris **France** 11-0
1963 Dublin **France** 24-5
1964 Paris **France** 27-6
1965 Dublin **Drawn** 3-3
1966 Paris **France** 11-6
1967 Dublin **France** 11-6
1968 Paris **France** 16-6
1969 Dublin **Ireland** 17-9
1970 Paris **France** 8-0
1971 Dublin **Drawn** 9-9
1972 Paris **Ireland** 14-9
1972 Dublin **Ireland** 24-14
Non-championship match
1973 Dublin **Ireland** 6-4
1974 Paris **France** 9-6
1975 Dublin **Ireland** 25-6
1976 Paris **France** 26-3
1977 Dublin **France** 15-6
1978 Paris **France** 10-9
1979 Dublin **Drawn** 9-9
1980 Paris **France** 19-18
1981 Dublin **France** 19-13
1982 Paris **France** 22-9
1983 Dublin **Ireland** 22-16
1984 Paris **France** 25-12
1985 Dublin **Drawn** 15-15
1986 Paris **France** 29-9
1987 Dublin **France** 19-13
1988 Paris **France** 25-6
1989 Dublin **France** 26-21
1990 Paris **France** 31-12
1991 Dublin **France** 21-13
1992 Paris **France** 44-12
1993 Dublin **France** 21-6
1994 Paris **France** 35-15
1995 Dublin **France** 25-7

IRELAND v NEW ZEALAND

Played 12 Ireland won 0, New Zealand won 11, Drawn 1

1905 Dublin **New Zealand** 15-0
1924 Dublin **New Zealand** 6-0
1935 Dublin **New Zealand** 17-9
1954 Dublin **New Zealand** 14-3
1963 Dublin **New Zealand** 6-5
1973 Dublin **Drawn** 10-10
1974 Dublin **New Zealand** 15-6
1976 Wellington **New Zealand** 11-3
1978 Dublin **New Zealand** 10-6
1989 Dublin **New Zealand** 23-6
1992 *1* Dunedin **New Zealand** 24-21
2 Wellington **New Zealand** 59-6
New Zealand won series 2-0

IRELAND v SOUTH AFRICA

Played 10 Ireland won 1, South Africa won 8, Drawn 1

1906 Belfast **South Africa** 15-12
1912 Dublin **South Africa** 38-0
1931 Dublin **South Africa** 8-3
1951 Dublin **South Africa** 17-5
1960 Dublin **South Africa** 8-3
1961 Cape Town **South Africa** 24-8
1965 Dublin **Ireland** 9-6
1970 Dublin **Drawn** 8-8
1981 *1* Cape Town **South Africa** 23-15
2 Durban **South Africa** 12-10
South Africa won series 2-0

IRELAND v AUSTRALIA

Played 16 Ireland won 6, Australia won 10, Drawn 0

1927 Dublin **Australia** 5-3
1947 Dublin **Australia** 16-3
1958 Dublin **Ireland** 9-6
1967 Dublin **Ireland** 15-8
1967 Sydney **Ireland** 11-5
1968 Dublin **Ireland** 10-3
1976 Dublin **Australia** 20-10
1979 *1* Brisbane **Ireland** 27-12
2 Sydney **Ireland** 9-3
Ireland won series 2-0
1981 Dublin **Australia** 16-12
1984 Dublin **Australia** 16-9

1987 Sydney *WC* **Australia** 33-15
1991 Dublin *WC* **Australia** 19-18
1992 Dublin **Australia** 42-17
1994 *1* Brisbane **Australia** 33-13
2 Sydney **Australia** 32-18
Australia won series 2-0

IRELAND v NEW ZEALAND NATIVES

Played 1 New Zealand Natives won 1

1888 Dublin **New Zealand Natives**
4G 1T to 1G 1T

IRELAND v IRU PRESIDENT'S XV

Played 1 Drawn 1

1974 Dublin **Drawn** 18-18

IRELAND v ROMANIA

Played 2 Ireland won 2

1986 Dublin **Ireland** 60-0
1993 Dublin **Ireland** 25-3

IRELAND v CANADA

Played 1 Ireland won 1

1987 Dunedin *WC* **Ireland** 46-19

IRELAND v TONGA

Played 1 Ireland won 1

1987 Brisbane *WC* **Ireland** 32-9

IRELAND v WESTERN SAMOA

Played 1 Ireland won 1

1988 Dublin **Ireland** 49-22

IRELAND v ITALY

Played 1 Ireland won 1

1988 Dublin **Ireland** 31-15

IRELAND v ARGENTINA

Played 1 Ireland won 1

1990 Dublin **Ireland** 20-18

IRELAND v NAMIBIA

Played 2 Namibia won 2

1991 *1* Windhoek **Namibia** 15-6
2 Windhoek **Namibia** 26-15
Namibia won series 2-0

IRELAND v ZIMBABWE

Played 1 Ireland won 1

1991 Dublin *WC* **Ireland** 55-11

IRELAND v JAPAN

Played 1 Ireland won 1

1991 Dublin *WC* **Ireland** 32-16

IRELAND v UNITED STATES

Played 1 Ireland won 1

1994 Dublin **Ireland** 26-15

WALES v FRANCE

Played 69 Wales won 37, France won 29, Drawn 3

1908 Cardiff **Wales** 36-4
1909 Paris **Wales** 47-5
1910 Swansea **Wales** 49-14
1911 Paris **Wales** 15-0
1912 Newport **Wales** 14-8
1913 Paris **Wales** 11-8
1914 Swansea **Wales** 31-0
1920 Paris **Wales** 6-5
1921 Cardiff **Wales** 12-4
1922 Paris **Wales** 11-3
1923 Swansea **Wales** 16-8
1924 Paris **Wales** 10-6
1925 Cardiff **Wales** 11-5
1926 Paris **Wales** 7-5
1927 Swansea **Wales** 25-7
1928 Paris **France** 8-3
1929 Cardiff **Wales** 8-3
1930 Paris **Wales** 11-0
1931 Swansea **Wales** 35-3
1947 Paris **Wales** 3-0
1948 Swansea **France** 11-3
1949 Paris **France** 5-3
1950 Cardiff **Wales** 21-0
1951 Paris **France** 8-3
1952 Swansea **Wales** 9-5
1953 Paris **Wales** 6-3
1954 Cardiff **Wales** 19-13
1955 Paris **Wales** 16-11
1956 Cardiff **Wales** 5-3
1957 Paris **Wales** 19-13
1958 Cardiff **France** 16-6
1959 Paris **France** 11-3
1960 Cardiff **France** 16-8
1961 Paris **France** 8-6
1962 Cardiff **Wales** 3-0
1963 Paris **France** 5-3
1964 Cardiff **Drawn** 11-11
1965 Paris **France** 22-13
1966 Cardiff **Wales** 9-8
1967 Paris **France** 20-14
1968 Cardiff **France** 14-9
1969 Paris **Drawn** 8-8
1970 Cardiff **Wales** 11-6
1971 Paris **Wales** 9-5
1972 Cardiff **Wales** 20-6
1973 Paris **France** 12-3
1974 Cardiff **Drawn** 16-16
1975 Paris **Wales** 25-10
1976 Cardiff **Wales** 19-13
1977 Paris **France** 16-9
1978 Cardiff **Wales** 16-7
1979 Paris **France** 14-13
1980 Cardiff **Wales** 18-9
1981 Paris **France** 19-15
1982 Cardiff **Wales** 22-12
1983 Paris **France** 16-9
1984 Cardiff **France** 21-16
1985 Paris **France** 14-3
1986 Cardiff **France** 23-15
1987 Paris **France** 16-9
1988 Cardiff **France** 10-9
1989 Paris **France** 31-12
1990 Cardiff **France** 29-19
1991 Paris **France** 36-3
1991 Cardiff **France** 22-9
Non-championship match
1992 Cardiff **France** 12-9
1993 Paris **France** 26-10
1994 Cardiff **Wales** 24-15
1995 Paris **France** 21-9

WALES v NEW ZEALAND

Played 15 Wales won 3, New Zealand won 12, Drawn 0

1905 Cardiff **Wales** 3-0
1924 Swansea **New Zealand** 19-0
1935 Cardiff **Wales** 13-12
1953 Cardiff **Wales** 13-8
1963 Cardiff **New Zealand** 6-0
1967 Cardiff **New Zealand** 13-6
1969 *1* Christchurch **New Zealand** 19-0
2 Auckland **New Zealand** 33-12
New Zealand won series 2-0
1972 Cardiff **New Zealand** 19-16
1978 Cardiff **New Zealand** 13-12
1980 Cardiff **New Zealand** 23-3
1987 Brisbane *WC* **New Zealand** 49-6
1988 *1* Christchurch **New Zealand** 52-3
2 Auckland **New Zealand** 54-9
New Zealand won series 2-0
1989 Cardiff **New Zealand** 34-9

WALES v SOUTH AFRICA

Played 8 Wales won 0, South Africa won 7, Drawn 1

1906 Swansea **South Africa** 11-0
1912 Cardiff **South Africa** 3-0
1931 Swansea **South Africa** 8-3
1951 Cardiff **South Africa** 6-3
1960 Cardiff **South Africa** 3-0
1964 Durban **South Africa** 24-3
1970 Cardiff **Drawn** 6-6
1994 Cardiff **South Africa** 20-12

WALES v AUSTRALIA

Played 16 Wales won 8, Australia won 8, Drawn 0

1908 Cardiff **Wales** 9-6
1927 Cardiff **Australia** 18-8

1947 Cardiff **Wales** 6-0
1958 Cardiff **Wales** 9-3
1966 Cardiff **Australia** 14-11
1969 Sydney **Wales** 19-16
1973 Cardiff **Wales** 24-0
1975 Cardiff **Wales** 28-3
1978 *1* Brisbane **Australia** 18-8
2 Sydney **Australia** 19-17
Australia won series 2-0
1981 Cardiff **Wales** 18-13
1984 Cardiff **Australia** 28-9
1987 Rotorua *WC* **Wales** 22-21
1991 Brisbane **Australia** 63-6
1991 Cardiff *WC* **Australia** 38-3
1992 Cardiff **Australia** 23-6

WALES v NEW ZEALAND NATIVES

Played 1 Wales won 1

1888 Swansea **Wales** 1G 2T to 0

WALES v NEW ZEALAND ARMY

Played 1 New Zealand Army won 1

1919 Swansea **New Zealand Army** 6-3

WALES v ROMANIA

Played 3 Romania won 2, Wales won 1

1983 Bucharest **Romania** 24-6
1988 Cardiff **Romania** 15-9
1994 Bucharest **Wales** 16-9

WALES v FIJI

Played 3 Wales won 3

1985 Cardiff **Wales** 40-3
1986 Suva **Wales** 22-15
1994 Suva **Wales** 23-8

WALES v TONGA

Played 3 Wales won 3

1986 Nuku'Alofa **Wales** 15-7
1987 Palmerston North *WC* **Wales** 29-16
1994 Nuku'Alofa **Wales** 18-9

WALES v WESTERN SAMOA

Played 4 Wales won 2, Western Samoa won 2

1986 Apia **Wales** 32-14
1988 Cardiff **Wales** 28-6
1991 Cardiff *WC* **Western Samoa** 16-13
1994 Moamoa **Western Samoa** 34-9

WALES v CANADA

Played 3 Wales won 2, Canada won 1

1987 Invercargill *WC* **Wales** 40-9
1993 Cardiff **Canada** 26-24
1994 Toronto **Wales** 33-15

WALES v UNITED STATES

Played 1 Wales won 1

1987 Cardiff **Wales** 46-0

WALES v NAMIBIA

Played 3 Wales won 3

1990 *1* Windhoek **Wales** 18-9
2 Windhoek **Wales** 34-30
Wales won series 2-0
1993 Windhoek **Wales** 38-23

WALES v BARBARIANS

Played 1 Barbarians won 1

1990 Cardiff **Barbarians** 31-24

WALES v ARGENTINA

Played 1 Wales won 1

1991 Cardiff *WC* **Wales** 16-7

WALES v ZIMBABWE

Played 2 Wales won 2

1993 *1* Bulawayo **Wales** 35-14
2 Harare **Wales** 42-13
Wales won series 2-0

WALES v JAPAN

Played 1 Wales won 1

1993 Cardiff **Wales** 55-5

WALES v PORTUGAL

Played 1 Wales won 1

1994 Lisbon **Wales** 102-11

WALES v SPAIN

Played 1 Wales won 1

1994 Madrid **Wales** 54-0

WALES v ITALY

Played 1 Wales won 1

1994 Cardiff **Wales** 29-19

FRANCE v NEW ZEALAND

Played 30 France won 7, New Zealand won 23, Drawn 0

1906 Paris **New Zealand** 38-8
1925 Toulouse **New Zealand** 30-6
1954 Paris **France** 3-0
1961 *1* Auckland **New Zealand** 13-6
2 Wellington **New Zealand** 5-3
3 Christchurch **New Zealand** 32- 3
New Zealand won series 3-0
1964 Paris **New Zealand** 12-3
1967 Paris **New Zealand** 21-15
1968 *1* Christchurch **New Zealand** 12-9
2 Wellington **New Zealand** 9-3
3 Auckland **New Zealand** 19-12
New Zealand won series 3-0
1973 Paris **France** 13-6
1977 *1* Toulouse **France** 18-13
2 Paris **New Zealand** 15-3
Series drawn 1-1
1979 *1* Christchurch **New Zealand** 23-9
2 Auckland **France** 24-19
Series drawn 1-1
1981 *1* Toulouse **New Zealand** 13-9
2 Paris **New Zealand** 18-6
New Zealand won series 2-0
1984 *1* Christchurch **New Zealand** 10-9
2 Auckland **New Zealand** 31-18
New Zealand won series 2-0
1986 Christchurch **New Zealand** 18-9
1986 *1* Toulouse **New Zealand** 19-7
2 Nantes **France** 16-3
Series drawn 1-1
1987 Auckland *WC* **New Zealand** 29-9
1989 *1* Christchurch **New Zealand** 25-17
2 Auckland **New Zealand** 34-20
New Zealand won series 2-0
1990 *1* Nantes **New Zealand** 24-3
2 Paris **New Zealand** 30-12
New Zealand won series 2-0
1994 *1* Christchurch **France** 22-8
2 Auckland **France** 23-20
France won series 2-0

FRANCE v SOUTH AFRICA

Played 23 France won 5, South Africa won 13, Drawn 5

1913 Bordeaux **South Africa** 38-5
1952 Paris **South Africa** 25-3
1958 *1* Cape Town **Drawn** 3-3
2 Johannesburg **France** 9-5
France won series 1-0, with 1 draw
1961 Paris **Drawn** 0-0
1964 Springs (SA) **France** 8-6
1967 *1* Durban **South Africa** 26-3
2 Bloemfontein **South Africa** 16-3
3 Johannesburg **France** 19-14
4 Cape Town **Drawn** 6-6
South Africa won series 2-1, with 1 draw

1968 *1* Bordeaux **South Africa** 12-9
2 Paris **South Africa** 16-11
South Africa won series 2-0
1971 *1* Bloemfontein **South Africa** 22-9
2 Durban **Drawn** 8-8
South Africa won series 1-0, with 1 draw
1974 *1* Toulouse **South Africa** 13-4
2 Paris **South Africa** 10-8
South Africa won series 2-0
1975 *1* Bloemfontein **South Africa** 38-25
2 Pretoria **South Africa** 33-18
South Africa won series 2-0
1980 Pretoria **South Africa** 37-15
1992 *1* Lyons **South Africa** 20-15
2 Paris **France** 29-16
Series drawn 1-1
1993 *1* Durban **Drawn** 20-20
2 Johannesburg **France** 18-17
France won series 1-0 with 1 draw

FRANCE v AUSTRALIA

Played 25 France won 13, Australia won 10, Drawn 2

1928 Paris **Australia** 11-8
1948 Paris **France** 13-6
1958 Paris **France** 19-0
1961 Sydney **France** 15-8
1967 Paris **France** 20-14
1968 Sydney **Australia** 11-10
1971 *1* Toulouse **Australia** 13-11
2 Paris **France** 18-9
Series drawn 1-1
1972 *1* Sydney **Drawn** 14-14
2 Brisbane **France** 16-15
France won series 1-0, with 1 draw
1976 *1* Bordeaux **France** 18-15
2 Paris **France** 34-6
France won series 2-0
1981 *1* Brisbane **Australia** 17-15
2 Sydney **Australia** 24-14
Australia won series 2-0
1983 *1* Clermont-Ferrand **Drawn** 15-15
2 Paris **France** 15-6
France won series 1-0, with 1 draw
1986 Sydney **Australia** 27-14
1987 Sydney *WC* **France** 30-24
1989 *1* Strasbourg **Australia** 32-15
2 Lille **France** 25-19
Series drawn 1-1
1990 *1* Sydney **Australia** 21-9
2 Brisbane **Australia** 48-31
3 Sydney **France** 28-19
Australia won series 2-1
1993 *1* Bordeaux **France** 16-13
2 Paris **Australia** 24-3
Series drawn 1-1

FRANCE v UNITED STATES

Played 5 France won 4, United States won 1

1920 Paris **France** 14-5
1924 Paris **United States** 17-3
1976 Chicago **France** 33-14
1991 *1* Denver **France** 41-9
2 Colorado Springs **France** 10-3*
**Abandoned after 43 mins*
France won series 2-0

FRANCE v ROMANIA

Played 40 France won 30, Romania won 8, Drawn 2

1924 Paris **France** 59-3
1938 Bucharest **France** 11-8
1957 Bucharest **France** 18-15
1957 Bordeaux **France** 39-0
1960 Bucharest **Romania** 11-5
1961 Bayonne **Drawn** 5-5
1962 Bucharest **Romania** 3-0
1963 Toulouse **Drawn** 6-6
1964 Bucharest **France** 9-6
1965 Lyons **France** 8-3
1966 Bucharest **France** 9-3
1967 Nantes **France** 11-3
1968 Bucharest **Romania** 15-14
1969 Tarbes **France** 14-9
1970 Bucharest **France** 14-3
1971 Béziers **France** 31-12
1972 Constanza **France** 15-6
1973 Valence **France** 7-6
1974 Bucharest **Romania** 15-10
1975 Bordeaux **France** 36-12
1976 Bucharest **Romania** 15-12
1977 Clermont-Ferrand **France** 9-6
1978 Bucharest **France** 9-6
1979 Montauban **France** 30-12
1980 Bucharest **Romania** 15-0
1981 Narbonne **France** 17-9
1982 Bucharest **Romania** 13-9
1983 Toulouse **France** 26-15
1984 Bucharest **France** 18-3
1986 Lille **France** 25-13
1986 Bucharest **France** 20-3
1987 Wellington *WC* **France** 55-12
1987 Agen **France** 49-3
1988 Bucharest **France** 16-12
1990 Auch **Romania** 12-6
1991 Bucharest **France** 33-21
1991 Béziers *WC* **France** 30-3
1992 Le Havre **France** 25-6
1993 Bucharest **France** 37-20
1993 Brive **France** 51-0

FRANCE v NEW ZEALAND MAORIS

Played 1 New Zealand Maoris won 1

1926 Paris **New Zealand Maoris** 12-3

FRANCE v GERMANY

Played 15 France won 13, Germany won 2

1927 Paris **France** 30-5
1927 Frankfurt **Germany** 17-16
1928 Hanover **France** 14-3
1929 Paris **France** 24-0
1930 Berlin **France** 31-0
1931 Paris **France** 34-0
1932 Frankfurt **France** 20-4
1933 Paris **France** 38-17
1934 Hanover **France** 13-9
1935 Paris **France** 18-3
1936 *1* Berlin **France** 19-14
2 Hanover **France** 6-3
France won series 2-0
1937 Paris **France** 27-6
1938 Frankfurt **Germany** 3-0
1938 Bucharest **France** 8-5

FRANCE v ITALY

Played 17 France won 17

1937 Paris **France** 43-5
1952 Milan **France** 17-8
1953 Lyons **France** 22-8
1954 Rome **France** 39-12
1955 Grenoble **France** 24-0
1956 Padua **France** 16-3
1957 Agen **France** 38-6
1958 Naples **France** 11-3
1959 Nantes **France** 22-0
1960 Treviso **France** 26-0
1961 Chambéry **France** 17-0
1962 Brescia **France** 6-3
1963 Grenoble **France** 14-12
1964 Parma **France** 12-3
1965 Pau **France** 21-0
1966 Naples **France** 21-0
1967 Toulon **France** 60-13

FRANCE v BRITISH XVs

Played 5 France won 2, British XVs won 3

1940 Paris **British XV** 36-3
1945 Paris **France** 21-9
1945 Richmond **British XV** 27-6
1946 Paris **France** 10-0
1989 Paris **British XV** 29-27

FRANCE v NEW ZEALAND ARMY

Played 1 New Zealand Army won 1

1946 Paris **New Zealand Army** 14-9

FRANCE v ARGENTINA

Played 26 France won 21, Argentina won 4, Drawn 1

1949 *1* Buenos Aires **France** 5-0
2 Buenos Aires **France** 12-3
France won series 2-0
1954 *1* Buenos Aires **France** 22-8
2 Buenos Aires **France** 30-3
France won series 2-0
1960 *1* Buenos Aires **France** 37-3
2 Buenos Aires **France** 12-3
3 Buenos Aires **France** 29-6
France won series 3-0
1974 *1* Buenos Aires **France** 20-15
2 Buenos Aires **France** 31-27
France won series 2-0
1975 *1* Lyons **France** 29-6
2 Paris **France** 36-21
France won series 2-0
1977 *1* Buenos Aires **France** 26-3
2 Buenos Aires **Drawn** 18-18
France won series 1-0, with 1 draw
1982 *1* Toulouse **France** 25-12
2 Paris **France** 13-6
France won series 2-0
1985 *1* Buenos Aires **Argentina** 24-16
2 Buenos Aires **France** 23-15
Series drawn 1-1
1986 *1* Buenos Aires **Argentina** 15-13
2 Buenos Aires **France** 22-9
Series drawn 1-1
1988 *1* Buenos Aires **France** 18-15
2 Buenos Aires **Argentina** 18-6
Series drawn 1-1
1988 *1* Nantes **France** 29-9
2 Lille **France** 28-18
France won series 2-0
1992 *1* Buenos Aires **France** 27-12
2 Buenos Aires **France** 33-9
France won series 2-0
1992 Nantes **Argentina** 24-20

FRANCE v CZECHOSLOVAKIA

Played 2 France won 2

1956 Toulouse **France** 28-3
1968 Prague **France** 19-6

FRANCE v FIJI

Played 3 France won 3

1964 Paris **France** 21-3
1987 Auckland *WC* **France** 31-16
1991 Grenoble *WC* **France** 33-9

FRANCE v JAPAN

Played 1 France won 1

1973 Bordeaux **France** 30-18

FRANCE v ZIMBABWE

Played 1 France won 1

1987 Auckland *WC* **France** 70-12

FRANCE v CANADA

Played 3 France won 2, Canada won 1

1991 Agen *WC* **France** 19-13
1994 Nepean **Canada** 18-16
1994 Besançon **France** 28-9

NEW ZEALAND v SOUTH AFRICA

Played 41 New Zealand won 18, South Africa won 20, Drawn 3

1921 *1* Dunedin **New Zealand** 13-5
2 Auckland **South Africa** 9-5
3 Wellington **Drawn** 0-0
Series drawn 1-1, with 1 draw
1928 *1* Durban **South Africa** 17-0
2 Johannesburg **New Zealand** 7-6
3 Port Elizabeth **South Africa** 11-6
4 Cape Town **New Zealand** 13-5
Series drawn 2-2
1937 *1* Wellington **New Zealand** 13-7
2 Christchurch **South Africa** 13-6
3 Auckland **South Africa** 17-6
South Africa won series 2-1
1949 *1* Cape Town **South Africa** 15-11
2 Johannesburg **South Africa** 12-6
3 Durban **South Africa** 9-3
4 Port Elizabeth **South Africa** 11-8
South Africa won series 4-0
1956 *1* Dunedin **New Zealand** 10-6
2 Wellington **South Africa** 8-3
3 Christchurch **New Zealand** 17-10
4 Auckland **New Zealand** 11-5
New Zealand won series 3-1
1960 *1* Johannesburg **South Africa** 13-0
2 Cape Town **New Zealand** 11-3
3 Bloemfontein **Drawn** 11-11
4 Port Elizabeth **South Africa** 8-3
South Africa won series 2-1, with 1 draw
1965 *1* Wellington **New Zealand** 6-3
2 Dunedin **New Zealand** 13-0
3 Christchurch **South Africa** 19-16
4 Auckland **New Zealand** 20-3
New Zealand won series 3-1
1970 *1* Pretoria **South Africa** 17-5
2 Cape Town **New Zealand** 9-8
3 Port Elizabeth **South Africa** 14-3
4 Johannesburg **South Africa** 20-17
South Africa won series 3-1
1976 *1* Durban **South Africa** 16-7
2 Bloemfontein **New Zealand** 15-9
3 Cape Town **South Africa** 15-10
4 Johannesburg **South Africa** 15-14
South Africa won series 3-1
1981 *1* Christchurch **New Zealand** 14-9
2 Wellington **South Africa** 24-12
3 Auckland **New Zealand** 25-22
New Zealand won series 2-1
1992 Johannesburg **New Zealand** 27-24
1994 *1* Dunedin **New Zealand** 22-14
2 Wellington **New Zealand** 13-9
3 Auckland **Drawn** 18-18
New Zealand won series 2-0, with 1 draw

NEW ZEALAND v AUSTRALIA

Played 98 New Zealand won 66, Australia won 27, Drawn 5

1903 Sydney **New Zealand** 22-3
1905 Dunedin **New Zealand** 14-3
1907 *1* Sydney **New Zealand** 26-6
2 Brisbane **New Zealand** 14-5

3 Sydney **Drawn** 5-5
New Zealand won series 2-0, with 1 draw
1910 *1* Sydney **New Zealand** 6-0
2 Sydney **Australia** 11-0
3 Sydney **New Zealand** 28-13
New Zealand won series 2-1
1913 *1* Wellington **New Zealand** 30-5
2 Dunedin **New Zealand** 25-13
3 Christchurch **Australia** 16-5
New Zealand won series 2-1
1914 *1* Sydney **New Zealand** 5-0
2 Brisbane **New Zealand** 17-0
3 Sydney **New Zealand** 22-7
New Zealand won series 3-0
1929 *1* Sydney **Australia** 9-8
2 Brisbane **Australia** 17-9
3 Sydney **Australia** 15-13
Australia won series 3-0
1931 Auckland **New Zealand** 20-13
1932 *1* Sydney **Australia** 22-17
2 Brisbane **New Zealand** 21-3
3 Sydney **New Zealand** 21-13
New Zealand won series 2-1
1934 *1* Sydney **Australia** 25-11
2 Sydney **Drawn** 3-3
Australia won series 1-0, with 1 draw
1936 *1* Wellington **New Zealand** 11-6
2 Dunedin **New Zealand** 38-13
New Zealand won series 2-0
1938 *1* Sydney **New Zealand** 24-9
2 Brisbane **New Zealand** 20-14
3 Sydney **New Zealand** 14-6
New Zealand won series 3-0
1946 *1* Dunedin **New Zealand** 31-8
2 Auckland **New Zealand** 14-10
New Zealand won series 2-0
1947 *1* Brisbane **New Zealand** 13-5
2 Sydney **New Zealand** 27-14
New Zealand won series 2-0
1949 *1* Wellington **Australia** 11-6
2 Auckland **Australia** 16-9
Australia won series 2-0
1951 *1* Sydney **New Zealand** 8-0
2 Sydney **New Zealand** 17-11
3 Brisbane **New Zealand** 16-6
New Zealand won series 3-0
1952 *1* Christchurch **Australia** 14-9
2 Wellington **New Zealand** 15-8
Series drawn 1-1
1955 *1* Wellington **New Zealand** 16-8
2 Dunedin **New Zealand** 8-0
3 Auckland **Australia** 8-3
New Zealand won series 2-1
1957 *1* Sydney **New Zealand** 25-11
2 Brisbane **New Zealand** 22-9
New Zealand won series 2-0
1958 *1* Wellington **New Zealand** 25-3
2 Christchurch **Australia** 6-3
3 Auckland **New Zealand** 17-8
New Zealand won series 2-1
1962 *1* Brisbane **New Zealand** 20-6
2 Sydney **New Zealand** 14-5
New Zealand won series 2-0
1962 *1* Wellington **Drawn** 9-9
2 Dunedin **New Zealand** 3-0
3 Auckland **New Zealand** 16-8
New Zealand won series 2-0, with 1 draw
1964 *1* Dunedin **New Zealand** 14-9
2 Christchurch **New Zealand** 18- 3
3 Wellington **Australia** 20-5
New Zealand won series 2-1
1967 Wellington **New Zealand** 29-9
1968 *1* Sydney **New Zealand** 27-11
2 Brisbane **New Zealand** 19-18
New Zealand won series 2-0
1972 *1* Wellington **New Zealand** 29-6
2 Christchurch **New Zealand** 30-17
3 Auckland **New Zealand** 38-3
New Zealand won series 3-0
1974 *1* Sydney **New Zealand** 11-6
2 Brisbane **Drawn** 16-16
3 Sydney **New Zealand** 16-6
New Zealand won series 2-0, with 1 draw
1978 *1* Wellington **New Zealand** 13-12
2 Christchurch **New Zealand** 22-6
3 Auckland **Australia** 30-16
New Zealand won series 2-1
1979 Sydney **Australia** 12-6
1980 *1* Sydney **Australia** 13-9
2 Brisbane **New Zealand** 12-9
3 Sydney **Australia** 26-10
Australia won series 2-1
1982 *1* Christchurch **New Zealand** 23-16
2 Wellington **Australia** 19-16
3 Auckland **New Zealand** 33-18
New Zealand won series 2-1
1983 Sydney **New Zealand** 18-8
1984 *1* Sydney **Australia** 16-9
2 Brisbane **New Zealand** 19-15
3 Sydney **New Zealand** 25-24
New Zealand won series 2-1
1985 Auckland **New Zealand** 10-9
1986 *1* Wellington **Australia** 13-12
2 Dunedin **New Zealand** 13-12
3 Auckland **Australia** 22-9
Australia won series 2-1
1987 Sydney **New Zealand** 30-16
1988 *1* Sydney **New Zealand** 32-7
2 Brisbane **Drawn** 19-19
3 Sydney **New Zealand** 30-9
New Zealand won series 2-0, with 1 draw
1989 Auckland **New Zealand** 24-12
1990 *1* Christchurch **New Zealand** 21-6
2 Auckland **New Zealand** 27-17
3 Wellington **Australia** 21-9
New Zealand won series 2-1
1991 *1* Sydney **Australia** 21-12
2 Auckland **New Zealand** 6-3
1991 Dublin *WC* **Australia** 16-6
1992 *1* Sydney **Australia** 16-15
2 Brisbane **Australia** 19-17
3 Sydney **New Zealand** 26-23
Australia won series 2-1
1993 Dunedin **New Zealand** 25-10
1994 Sydney **Australia** 20-16

NEW ZEALAND v UNITED STATES

Played 2 New Zealand won 2

1913 Berkeley **New Zealand** 51-3
1991 Gloucester *WC* **New Zealand** 46-6

NEW ZEALAND v ROMANIA

Played 1 New Zealand won 1

1981 Bucharest **New Zealand** 14-6

NEW ZEALAND v ARGENTINA

Played 7 New Zealand won 6, Drawn 1

1985 *1* Buenos Aires **New Zealand** 33-20
2 Buenos Aires **Drawn** 21-21
New Zealand won series 1-0, with 1 draw
1987 Wellington *WC* **New Zealand** 46-15
1989 *1* Dunedin **New Zealand** 60-9
2 Wellington **New Zealand** 49-12
New Zealand won series 2-0
1991 *1* Buenos Aires **New Zealand** 28-14
2 Buenos Aires **New Zealand** 36-6
New Zealand won series 2-0

NEW ZEALAND v ITALY

Played 2 New Zealand won 2

1987 Auckland *WC* **New Zealand** 70-6
1991 Leicester *WC* **New Zealand** 31-21

NEW ZEALAND v FIJI

Played 1 New Zealand won 1

1987 Christchurch *WC* **New Zealand** 74-13

NEW ZEALAND v CANADA

Played 1 New Zealand won 1

1991 Lille *WC* **New Zealand** 29-13

NEW ZEALAND v WORLD XVs

Played 3 New Zealand won 2, World XV won 1

1992 *1* Christchurch **World XV** 28-14
2 Wellington **New Zealand** 54-26
3 Auckland **New Zealand** 26-15
New Zealand won series 2-1

NEW ZEALAND v WESTERN SAMOA

Played 1 New Zealand won 1

1993 Auckland **New Zealand** 35-13

SOUTH AFRICA v AUSTRALIA

Played 32 South Africa won 22, Australia won 10, Drawn 0

1933 *1* Cape Town **South Africa** 17-3
2 Durban **Australia** 21-6
3 Johannesburg **South Africa** 12-3
4 Port Elizabeth **South Africa** 11-0
5 Bloemfontein **Australia** 15-4
South Africa won series 3-2
1937 *1* Sydney **South Africa** 9-5
2 Sydney **South Africa** 26-17
South Africa won series 2-0
1953 *1* Johannesburg **South Africa** 25-3
2 Cape Town **Australia** 18-14
3 Durban **South Africa** 18-8
4 Port Elizabeth **South Africa** 22-9
South Africa won series 3-1
1956 *1* Sydney **South Africa** 9-0
2 Brisbane **South Africa** 9-0
South Africa won series 2-0
1961 *1* Johannesburg **South Africa** 28-3
2 Port Elizabeth **South Africa** 23-11
South Africa won series 2-0
1963 *1* Pretoria **South Africa** 14-3
2 Cape Town **Australia** 9-5
3 Johannesburg **Australia** 11-9
4 Port Elizabeth **South Africa** 22-6
Series drawn 2-2
1965 *1* Sydney **Australia** 18-11
2 Brisbane **Australia** 12-8
Australia won series 2-0

1969 *1* Johannesburg **South Africa** 30-11
2 Durban **South Africa** 16-9
3 Cape Town **South Africa** 11-3
4 Bloemfontein **South Africa** 19-8
South Africa won series 4-0
1971 *1* Sydney **South Africa** 19-11
2 Brisbane **South Africa** 14-6
3 Sydney **South Africa** 18-6
South Africa won series 3-0
1992 Cape Town **Australia** 26-3
1993 *1* Sydney **South Africa** 19-12
2 Brisbane **Australia** 28-20
3 Sydney **Australia** 19-12
Australia won series 2-1

SOUTH AFRICA v WORLD XVs

Played 3 South Africa won 3

1977 Pretoria **South Africa** 45-24
1989 *1* Cape Town **South Africa** 20-19
2 Johannesburg **South Africa** 22-16
South Africa won series 2-0

SOUTH AFRICA v SOUTH AMERICA

Played 8 South Africa won 7, South America won 1

1980 *1* Johannesburg **South Africa** 24-9
2 Durban **South Africa** 18-9
South Africa won series 2-0
1980 *1* Montevideo **South Africa** 22-13
2 Santiago **South Africa** 30-16
South Africa won series 2-0
1982 *1* Pretoria **South Africa** 50-18
2 Bloemfontein **South America** 21-12
Series drawn 1-1
1984 *1* Pretoria **South Africa** 32-15
2 Cape Town **South Africa** 22-13
South Africa won series 2-0

SOUTH AFRICA v UNITED STATES

Played 1 South Africa won 1

1981 Glenville **South Africa** 38-7

SOUTH AFRICA v NEW ZEALAND CAVALIERS

Played 4 South Africa won 3, New Zealand Cavaliers won 1

1986 *1* Cape Town **South Africa** 21-15
2 Durban **New Zealand Cavaliers** 19-18
3 Pretoria **South Africa** 33-18
4 Johannesburg **South Africa** 24-10
South Africa won series 3-1

SOUTH AFRICA v ARGENTINA

Played 4 South Africa won 4

1993 *1* Buenos Aires **South Africa** 29-26
2 Buenos Aires **South Africa** 52-23
South Africa won series 2-0
1994 *1* Port Elizabeth **South Africa** 42-22
2 Johannesburg **South Africa** 46-26
South Africa won series 2-0

AUSTRALIA v UNITED STATES

Played 5 Australia won 5

1912 Berkeley **Australia** 12-8
1976 Los Angeles **Australia** 24-12
1983 Sydney **Australia** 49-3
1987 Brisbane *WC* **Australia** 47-12
1990 Brisbane **Australia** 67-9

AUSTRALIA v NEW ZEALAND MAORIS

Played 10 Australia won 4, New Zealand Maoris won 4, Drawn 2

1928 Wellington **New Zealand Maoris** 9-8
1931 Palmerston North **Australia** 14-3
1936 Palmerston North **Australia** 31-6
1946 Hamilton **New Zealand Maoris** 20-0
1949 *1* Sydney **New Zealand Maoris** 12-3
2 Brisbane **Drawn** 8-8
3 Sydney **Australia** 18-3
Series drawn 1-1, with 1 draw
1958 *1* Brisbane **Australia** 15-14
2 Sydney **Drawn** 3-3
3 Melbourne **New Zealand Maoris** 13-6
Series drawn 1-1, with 1 draw

AUSTRALIA v FIJI

Played 15 Australia won 12, Fiji won 2, Drawn 1

1952 *1* Sydney **Australia** 15-9
2 Sydney **Fiji** 17-15
Series drawn 1-1
1954 *1* Brisbane **Australia** 22-19
2 Sydney **Fiji** 18-16
Series drawn 1-1
1961 *1* Brisbane **Australia** 24-6
2 Sydney **Australia** 20-14
3 Melbourne **Drawn** 3-3
Australia won series 2-0, with 1 draw
1972 Suva **Australia** 21-19
1976 *1* Sydney **Australia** 22-6
2 Brisbane **Australia** 21-9
3 Sydney **Australia** 27-17
Australia won series 3-0
1980 Suva **Australia** 22-9
1984 Suva **Australia** 16-3
1985 *1* Brisbane **Australia** 52-28
2 Sydney **Australia** 31-9
Australia won series 2-0

AUSTRALIA v TONGA

Played 3 Australia won 2, Tonga won 1

1973 *1* Sydney **Australia** 30-12
2 Brisbane **Tonga** 16-11
Series drawn 1-1
1993 Brisbane **Australia** 52-14

AUSTRALIA v JAPAN

Played 3 Australia won 3

1975 *1* Sydney **Australia** 37-7
2 Brisbane **Australia** 50-25
Australia won series 2-0
1987 Sydney *WC* **Australia** 42-23

AUSTRALIA v ARGENTINA

Played 9 Australia won 5, Argentina won 3, Drawn 1

1979 *1* Buenos Aires **Argentina** 24-13
2 Buenos Aires **Australia** 17-12
Series drawn 1-1
1983 *1* Brisbane **Argentina** 18-3
2 Sydney **Australia** 29-13
Series drawn 1-1
1986 *1* Brisbane **Australia** 39-19
2 Sydney **Australia** 26-0
Australia won series 2-0
1987 *1* Buenos Aires **Drawn** 19-19
2 Buenos Aires **Argentina** 27-19
Argentina won series 1-0, with 1 draw
1991 Llanelli *WC* **Australia** 32-19

AUSTRALIA v WESTERN SAMOA

Played 2 Australia won 2

1991 Pontypool *WC* **Australia** 9-3
1994 Sydney **Australia** 73-3

AUSTRALIA v ITALY

Played 5 Australia won 5

1983 Rovigo **Australia** 29-7
1986 Brisbane **Australia** 39-18
1988 Rome **Australia** 55-6
1994 *1* Brisbane **Australia** 23-20
2 Melbourne **Australia** 20-7
Australia won series 2-0

AUSTRALIA v CANADA

Played 3 Australia won 3

1985 *1* Sydney **Australia** 59-3
2 Brisbane **Australia** 43-15
Australia won series 2-0
1993 Calgary **Australia** 43-16

AUSTRALIA v KOREA

Played 1 Australia won 1

1987 Brisbane **Australia** 65-18

INTERNATIONAL HONOURS

WORLD CUP WINNERS

New Zealand once: 1987
Australia once: 1991

GRAND SLAM WINNERS

England 11 times: 1913, 1914, 1921, 1923, 1924, 1928, 1957, 1980, 1991, 1992, 1995.
Wales 8 times: 1908, 1909, 1911, 1950, 1952, 1971, 1976, 1978.
France 4 times: 1968, 1977, 1981, 1987. **Scotland** 3 times: 1925, 1984, 1990.
Ireland once: 1948.

TRIPLE CROWN WINNERS

England 18 times: 1883, 1884, 1892, 1913, 1914, 1921, 1923, 1924, 1928, 1934, 1937, 1954, 1957, 1960, 1980, 1991, 1992, 1995. **Wales** 17 times: 1893, 1900, 1902, 1905, 1908, 1909, 1911, 1950, 1952, 1965, 1969, 1971, 1976, 1977, 1978, 1979, 1988.
Scotland 10 times: 1891, 1895, 1901, 1903, 1907, 1925, 1933, 1938, 1984, 1990.
Ireland 6 times: 1894, 1899, 1948, 1949, 1982, 1985.

INTERNATIONAL CHAMPIONSHIP WINNERS

Year	Winner
1883	**England**
1884	**England**
1885*	——
1886	**England** / **Scotland**
1887	**Scotland**
1888*	——
1889*	——
1890	**England** / **Scotland**
1891	**Scotland**
1892	**England**
1893	**Wales**
1894	**Ireland**
1895	**Scotland**
1896	**Ireland**
1897*	——
1898*	——
1899	**Ireland**
1900	**Wales**
1901	**Scotland**
1902	**Wales**
1903	**Scotland**
1904	**Scotland**
1905	**Wales**
1906	**Ireland** / **Wales**
1907	**Scotland**
1908	**Wales**
1909	**Wales**
1910	**England**
1911	**Wales**
1912	**England** / **Ireland**
1913	**England**
1914	**England**
1920	**England** / **Scotland** / **Wales**
1921	**England**
1922	**Wales**
1923	**England**
1924	**England**
1925	**Scotland**
1926	**Scotland** / **Ireland**
1927	**Scotland** / **Ireland**
1928	**England**
1929	**Scotland**
1930	**England**
1931	**Wales**
1932	**England** / **Wales** / **Ireland**
1933	**Scotland**
1934	**England**
1935	**Ireland**
1936	**Wales**
1937	**England**
1938	**Scotland**
1939	**England** / **Wales** / **Ireland**
1947	**Wales** / **England**
1948	**Ireland**
1949	**Ireland**
1950	**Wales**
1951	**Ireland**
1952	**Wales**
1953	**England**
1954	**England** / **France** / **Wales**
1955	**France** / **Wales**
1956	**Wales**
1957	**England**
1958	**England**
1959	**France**
1960	**France** / **England**
1961	**France**
1962	**France**
1963	**England**
1964	**Scotland** / **Wales**
1965	**Wales**
1966	**Wales**
1967	**France**
1968	**France**
1969	**Wales**
1970	**France** / **Wales**
1971	**Wales**
1972*	——
1973	**Quintuple tie**
1974	**Ireland**
1975	**Wales**
1976	**Wales**
1977	**France**
1978	**Wales**
1979	**Wales**
1980	**England**
1981	**France**
1982	**Ireland**
1983	**France** / **Ireland**
1984	**Scotland**
1985	**Ireland**
1986	**France** / **Scotland**
1987	**France**
1988	**Wales** / **France**
1989	**France**
1990	**Scotland**
1991	**England**
1992	**England**
1993	**France**
1994**	**Wales**
1995	**England**

**Matches not completed, for various reasons*
***Indicates winners of the Five Nations Trophy (introduced 1993) on points difference.*

Wales have won the title outright most times, 22; England have won it 21 times, Scotland 13, Ireland 10, and France 10.

A INTERNATIONALS 1994-95

20 January 1995, Donnybrook
Ireland A 20 (2G 2PG) England A 21 (1G 2PG 1DG 1T)

Ireland A: J Staples (Harlequins); R Wallace (Garryowen), M McCall (Bangor), M Field (Malone), Darragh O'Mahony (UC Dublin); A McGowan (Blackrock Coll), David O'Mahony (Cork Const); J Fitzgerald (Young Munster), W Mulcahy (Skerries), P Wallace (Blackrock Coll), D Tweed (Ballymena), R Costello (Garryowen), E Halvey (Shannon), B Cronin (Garryowen), D McBride (Malone) (*capt*) *Replacement* R Wilson (Instonians) for Cronin (temp)
Scorers *Tries:* David O'Mahony, Mulcahy *Conversions:* McGowan (2)
Penalty Goals: McGowan (2)
England A: A Tunningley (Saracens); D Hopley (Wasps), N Greenstock (Wasps), S Potter (Leicester), J Sleightholme (Bath); P Grayson (Northampton), S Bates (Wasps) (*capt*); R Hardwick (Coventry), M Regan (Bristol), J Mallett (Bath), S Shaw (Bristol), G Archer (Newcastle Gosforth), L Dallaglio (Wasps), A Diprose (Saracens), N Back (Leicester)
Scorers *Tries:* Diprose, Back *Conversion:* Grayson *Penalty Goals:* Grayson (2)
Dropped Goal: Grayson
Referee N Lasaga (France)

20 January 1995, Balgray, Glasgow
Scotland A 9 (3PG) France A 13 (1G 2PG)

Scotland A: R Shepherd (Edinburgh Acads)); H Gilmour (Heriot's FP), S Hastings (Watsonians), R Eriksson (London Scottish), C Dalgleish (Gala); S Laing (Instonians), G Burns (Stewart's-Melville FP); J Manson (Dundee HSFP), J Hay (Hawick), D Herrington (Dundee HSFP), R Scott (London Scottish), J Richardson (Edinburgh Acads), F Wallace (Glasgow High/Kelvinside), S Reid (Boroughmuir), I Smith (Gloucester)
Scorer *Penalty Goals:* Laing (3)
France A: O Campan (Agen); D Venditti (Bourgoin), P Carbonneau (Toulouse), T Castaignede (Toulouse), P Bernat-Salles (Pau); B Bellot (Graulhet), A Hueber (Toulon) (*capt*); E Menieu (Montferrand), F Landreau (Grenoble), P Gallart (Béziers), O Brouzet (Grenoble), A Berthozat (Bègles), N Hallinger (Colomiers), S Dispagne (Narbonne), A Costes (Montferrand) *Replacement* S Loubsens (Bègles) for Bernat-Salles
Scorers *Try:* Hallinger *Conversion:* Bellot *Penalty Goals:* Bellot (2)
Referee G Gadjovich (Canada)

21 January 1995, Stade Jean Bouin, Paris
French Combined Services 15 (5PG) Wales A 21 (1G 3PG 1T)

French Combined Services: P Bondouy (Narbonne); S Rouch (Graulhet), S Detuncq (ASB Herault), G Bouic (Agen), P Labeyrie (Dax); F Duberger (Agen), B Marty (Brive); S Trybusch (Brive), S Begon (Grenoble), L Metelenbos (Aurillac), E Joliveau (Dijon) (*capt*), S Larue (Rumilly), O Magne (Dax), C Donjieu (Bayonne), R Sonnes (Toulouse)
Scorer *Penalty Goals:* Labeyrie (5)
Wales A: I Jones (Llanelli); D Manley (Pontypridd), S Lewis (Pontypridd), D Edwards (Leicester), G Wilkins (Bridgend); A Davies (Cardiff), P John (Pontypridd) (*capt*); A Dibble (Treorchy), J Humphreys (Cardiff), L Mustoe (Cardiff), G Prosser (Pontypool), M Rowley (Pontypridd), A Gibbs (Newbridge), G Taylor (Pontypool), P Crane (Newbridge) *Replacement* B Williams for Humphreys (temp)
Scorers *Tries:* Taylor, John *Conversion:* Davies *Penalty Goals:* Davies (3)
Referee B Stirling (Ireland)

3 February 1995, Myreside, Edinburgh
Scotland A 24 (1G 4PG 1T) Ireland A 18 (1G 1PG 1DG 1T)

Scotland A: R Shepherd (Edinburgh Acads); H Gilmour (Heriot's FP), A Stanger (Hawick), S Hastings (Watsonians), D Stark (Boroughmuir); S Laing (Instonians), G Burns (Stewart's-Melville FP); J Manson (Dundee HSFP), M Scott (Orrell), S Paul (Heriot's FP), J Richardson (Edinburgh Acads) (*capt*), R Scott (London Scottish), F Wallace (Glasgow High/Kelvinside), S Reid (Boroughmuir), I Smith (Gloucester)
Scorers *Tries:* Stanger (2) *Conversion:* Laing *Penalty Goals:* Laing (4)
Ireland A: P Murray (Shannon); R Wallace (Garryowen), L Boyle (Harlequins), M McCall (Bangor) (*capt*), Darragh O'Mahony (UC Dublin); A McGowan (Blackrock Coll), David O'Mahony (Cork Const); J Fitzgerald (Young Munster), W Mulcahy (Skerries), P Wallace (Blackrock Coll), D Tweed (Ballymena), R Costello (Garryowen), E Halvey (Shannon), R Wilson (Instonians), D Corkery (Cork Const)
Replacements N Malone (Leicester) for Boyle; C Clarke (Lansdowne) for McGowan
Scorers *Tries:* Darragh O'Mahony, McCall *Conversion:* Malone
Penalty Goal: McGowan *Dropped Goal:* McGowan
Referee B Campsall (England)

3 February 1995, Leicester
England A 29 (2G 3PG 2DG) France A 9 (3PG)

England A: P Hull (Bristol); D Hopley (Wasps), N Greenstock (Wasps), S Potter (Leicester), J Sleightholme (Bath); J Harris (Leicester), S Bates (Wasps) (*capt*); R Hardwick (Coventry), M Regan (Bristol), D Garforth (Leicester), G Archer (Newcastle Gosforth), S Shaw (Bristol), L Dallaglio (Wasps), A Diprose (Saracens), N Back (Leicester) *Replacements* H Thorneycroft (Northampton) for Hopley; C Clark (Bath) for Garforth (temp)
Scorers *Tries:* Regan, Sleightholme *Conversions:* Harris (2) *Penalty Goals:* Harris (3) *Dropped Goals:* Harris (2)
France A: O Campan (Agen); W Techouèyres (Bordeaux U), S Loubsens (Mont-de-Marsan), P Carbonneau (Toulouse), L Arbo (Perpignan); D Charvet (Racing Club de France), A Hueber (Toulon) (*capt*); E Menieu (Montferrand), F Landreau (Grenoble), P Gallart (Béziers), A Berthozat (Bègles), C Deslandes (Racing Club de France), L Loppy (Toulon), S Dispagne (Narbonne), A Costes (Montferrand) *Replacement* G Orsoni (Toulon) for Loppy (temp)
Scorer *Penalty Goals:* Charvet (3)
Referee A Lewis (Ireland)

17 February 1995, Brierton Lane, West Hartlepool
England Emerging Players 97 (11G 4T) Romania A 14 (2G)

England Emerging Players: W Greenwood (Harlequins); S Hackney (Leicester), G Childs (Wasps), P Mensah (Harlequins), N Beal (Northampton); P Grayson (Northampton), R Kitchin (Harlequins); D Molloy (Wasps), G Adams (Bath), D Hinkins (Bristol), R West (Gloucester), M Haag (Bath), R Jenkins (Harlequins), C Sheasby (Harlequins), D Eves (Bristol) (*capt*) *Replacement* P Holford (Gloucester) for Mensah
Scorers *Tries:* Hackney (5), Greenwood (3), Beal (2), Mensah, Grayson, Adams, Childs, Haag *Conversions:* Grayson (11)
Romania A: C Patrichi; O Rotaru, M Stan, R Fugigi, E Florea; E Apjok, V Flutur (*capt*); C Constantin, V Tufa, G Voicu, N Branescu, A Stanca, F Scafariu, N Marin, I Ruxanda
Replacements C Fugigi for Flutur; V Maftei for Florea; R Gontineac for Apjok; D Chiriac for Marin
Scorers *Tries:* Stan, Fugigi *Conversions:* Apjok (2)
Referee E Murray (Scotland)

19 February 1995, Gloucester
England A 33 (2G 3PG 2T) Italy A 9 (3PG)

England A: P Hull (Bristol); J Sleightholme (Bath), S Potter (Leicester), N Greenstock (Wasps), H Thorneycroft (Northampton); J Harris (Leicester), S Bates (Wasps) (*capt*); R Hardwick (Coventry), R Cockerill (Leicester), D Garforth (Leicester), G Archer (Newcastle Gosforth), S Shaw (Bristol), L Dallaglio (Wasps), A Diprose (Saracens), R Hill (Saracens) *Replacements* C Wilkins (Wasps) for Shaw; C Clark (Bath) for Garforth (temp)
Scorers *Tries:* Thorneycroft, Bates, Sleightholme, Hill *Conversions:* Harris (2) *Penalty Goals:* Harris (3)
Italy A: J Pertile; R Crotti, S Bordon, M Piovene, F Mazzariol; L Troiani (*capt*), G Faltiba; G Grespan, G de Carli, A Castellani, R Cassina, M Giacheri, M Capuzzoni, D Scaglia, A Sgorlon *Replacement* G Cicino for Scaglia
Scorer *Penalty Goals:* Troiani (3)
Referee D Gillet (France)

17 March 1995, Sardis Road, Pontypridd
Wales A 30 (2G 2PG 2T) Ireland A 19 (3PG 2T)

Wales A: J Thomas (Cardiff Inst); D Manley (Pontypridd), M Taylor (Pontypool), D Edwards (Leicester), S Hill (Cardiff); D Evans (Treorchy), P John (Pontypridd) (*capt*); A Dibble (Treorchy), J Humphreys (Cardiff), L Mustoe (Cardiff), G Prosser (Pontypridd), A Copsey (Llanelli), C Wyatt (Neath), O Williams (Cardiff), M Bennett (Cardiff)
Scorers *Tries:* Williams (2), Taylor, Thomas *Conversions:* Evans (2) *Penalty Goals:* Evans (2)
Ireland A: C O'Shea (Lansdowne); Darragh O'Mahony (UC Dublin), L Boyle (Harlequins), M McCall (Bangor) (*capt*), N Woods (Blackrock Coll); A McGowan (Blackrock Coll), David O'Mahony (Cork Const); J Fitzgerald (Young Munster), W Mulcahy (Skerries), P Wallace (Blackrock Coll), M Galwey (Shannon), N Francis (Old Belvedere), S Rooney (Lansdowne), R Wilson (Instonians), L Toland (Old Crescent)
Scorers *Tries:* Darragh O'Mahony, Wilson *Penalty Goals:* O'Shea (3)
Referee E Morrison (England)

18 March 1995, Durban
Natal 33 (1G 6PG 1DG 1T) England A 25 (4PG 1DG 2T)

Natal: H Reece-Edwards; C van der Westhuizen, D Muir, P Müller, J Small; H Honiball, K Putt; R Kempson, J Allan, A Garvey, M Andrews, S Atherton, W Bartman (*capt*), G Teichmann, D Kriese *Replacements* J Thompson for Müller; W van Heerden for Kriese
Scorers *Tries:* Allan, Small *Conversion:* Honiball *Penalty Goals:* Honiball (6) *Dropped Goal:* Honiball
England A: P Hull (Bristol); I Hunter (Northampton), S Potter (Leicester), D Hopley (Wasps), J Sleightholme (Bath); P Grayson (Northampton), M Dawson (Northampton); R Hardwick (Coventry), M Regan (Bristol), D Garforth (Leicester), G Archer (Newcastle Gosforth), R West (Gloucester), J Hall (Bath) (*capt*), A Diprose (Saracens), N Back (Leicester)
Scorers *Tries:* Hunter, Potter *Penalty Goals:* Grayson (4) *Dropped Goal:* Grayson
Referee S Neethling (South Africa)

OTHER INTERNATIONAL MATCHES 1994-95

17 August 1994, Sydney Football Stadium — Bledisloe Cup
AUSTRALIA 20 (2G 2PG) NEW ZEALAND 16 (1G 3PG)

AUSTRALIA: M Pini (Queensland); D I Campese (New South Wales), J S Little (Queensland), P W Howard (Queensland), D Smith (Queensland); D J Knox (New South Wales), G Gregan (Australian Capital Territory); A J Daly (New South Wales), P N Kearns (New South Wales) (*capt*), E J A McKenzie (New South Wales), G J Morgan (Queensland), J A Eales (Queensland), V Ofahengaue (New South Wales), B T Gavin (New South Wales), D J Wilson (Queensland) *Replacement* D K Junee (New South Wales) for Pini (73 mins)
Scorers *Tries:* Little, Kearns *Conversions:* Knox (2) *Penalty Goals:* Knox (2)
NEW ZEALAND: S P Howarth (Auckland); J W Wilson (Otago), F E Bunce (North Harbour), W K Little (North Harbour), J K R Timu (Otago); S J Bachop (Otago), G T M Bachop (Canterbury); R W Loe (Canterbury), S B T Fitzpatrick (Auckland) (*capt*), O M Brown (Auckland), M S B Cooksley (Waikato), I D Jones (North Harbour), M R Brewer (Canterbury), Z V Brooke (Auckland), M N Jones (Auckland) *Replacement* B P Larsen (North Harbour) for Brooke (temp)
Scorers *Try:* Howarth *Conversion:* Howarth *Penalty Goals:* Howarth (3)
Referee E F Morrison (England)

21 May 1994, Long Beach — 18th Can-Am Test
USA 10 (1G 1PG) CANADA 15 (5PG)

USA: M Sika (Rhinos); V Anitoni (Olympic Club), E Schram (Old Blues), M Scharrenberg (Golden Gate), R Schurfield (Belmont Shore); M Williams (Olympic Club), A Bachelet (Old Blues); C Lippert (OMBAC), T Billups (Old Blues), D James (Old Blues), K Swords (Beacon Hill) (*capt*), R Randell (United), C Campbell (Washington), R Lumkong (Old Blues), R Tardits (Mystic River) *Replacement* J Wilkerson (Belmont Shore) for Randall (76 mins)
Scorers *Try:* Anitoni *Conversion:* Williams *Penalty Goal:* Williams
CANADA: S Stewart (UBC Old Boys); W Stanley (UBC), S Gray (Kats), I Stuart (Vancouver Rowing Club) (*capt*), R Toews (Meralomas); G Rees (Oak Bay Castaways), J Graf (UBC Old Boys); E Evans (UBC Old Boys), M Cardinal (James Bay), D Jackart (UBC Old Boys), M James (Burnaby), G Ennis (Kats), A Charron (Ottawa Irish), C McKenzie (UBC Old Boys), G MacKinnon (Ex-Britannia Lions)
Scorer *Penalty Goals:* Rees (5)
Referee B Campsall (England)

21 January 1995, Murrayfield
SCOTLAND 22 (1G 5PG) CANADA 6 (2PG)

SCOTLAND: A G Hastings (Watsonians) (*capt*); C A Joiner (Melrose), G P J Townsend (Gala), I C Jardine (Stirling County), K M Logan (Stirling County); C M Chalmers (Melrose), B W Redpath (Melrose); D I W Hilton (Bath), K S Milne (Heriot's FP), P H Wright (Boroughmuir), D F Cronin (Bourges), S J Campbell (Dundee HSFP), R I Wainwright (West Hartlepool), E W Peters (Bath), I R Morrison (London Scottish)
Scorers *Try:* Cronin *Conversion:* G Hastings *Penalty Goals:* G Hastings (5)
CANADA: D S Stewart (UBC Old Boys); W Stanley (UBC), C Stewart (Rovigo & Western Province), S D Gray (Kats), R Toews (Meralomas); G L Rees (Oak Bay Castaways & Newport) (*capt*), J D Graf (UBC Old Boys); E A Evans (UBC Old Boys & IBM Tokyo), M E Cardinal (James Bay), D C Jackart (UBC Old Boys), M James (Burnaby), K Whitley (Capilano), I Gordon (James Bay), C McKenzie (UBC Old Boys),

G I MacKinnon (ex-Britannia Lions) *Replacement* J Hutchinson (UBC Old Boys) for Whitley (40 mins)
Referee C Thomas (Wales)

8 April, National Stadium, Bucharest
FRANCE 24 (1G 4PG 1T) ROMANIA 15 (2PG 3DG)

ROMANIA: V Brici (Farul Constanta); L Colceriu (Steaua Bucharest), N Racean (Cluj U), R Gontineac (Cluj U), G Solomie (Timisoara U); N Nichitean (Cluj U), D Neaga (Dinamo Bucharest); G Leonte (Vienne), I Negreci (CFR Constanta), L Costea (Steaua Bucharest), S Ciorascu (Auch), C Cojocariu (Bayonne), T Oroian (Steaua Bucharest), T Brinza (Cluj U) (*capt*), A Gealapu (Steaua Bucharest) *Replacement* V Tufa (Dinamo Bucharest) for Negreci (57 mins)
Scorer *Penalty Goals:* Nichitean (2) *Dropped Goals:* Nichitean (3)
FRANCE: J-L Sadourny (Colomiers); E Ntamack (Toulouse), F Mesnel (Racing Club de France), T Lacroix (Dax), P Saint-André (Montferrand) (*capt*); Y Delaigue (Toulon), G Accoceberry (Bègles-Bordeaux); L Armary (Lourdes), J-M Gonzalez (Bayonne), P Gallart (Béziers), O Merle (Montferrand), O Brouzet (Grenoble), A Costes (Montferrand), M Cecillon (Bourgoin), L Cabannes (Racing Club de France) *Replacement* M de Rougemont (Toulon) for Gallart (temp)
Scorers *Tries:* pen try, Sadourny *Conversion:* Lacroix *Penalty Goals:* Lacroix (4)
Referee G Simmonds (Wales)

13 April, Ellis Park, Johannesburg
SOUTH AFRICA 60 (6G 1PG 3T) WESTERN SAMOA 8 (1PG 1T)

SOUTH AFRICA: G K Johnson (Transvaal); J T Small (Natal), J C Mulder (Transvaal), H P le Roux (Transvaal), C M Williams (Western Province); J T Stransky (Western Province), J H van der Westhuizen (Northern Transvaal); J P du Randt (Orange Free State), C L C Rossouw (Transvaal), I S Swart (Transvaal), J J Wiese (Transvaal), M G Andrews (Natal), J F Pienaar (Transvaal) (*capt*), R A W Straeuli (Transvaal), R J Kruger (Northern Transvaal) *Replacements* C Badenhorst (Orange Free State) for Williams (55 mins); H W Honiball (Natal) for Johnson (66 mins); M Visser (Western Province) for Rossouw (72 mins); I Macdonald (Transvaal) for Wiese (80 mins)
Scorers *Tries:* Johnson (3), Williams (2), Stransky, Small, Rossouw, Andrews *Conversions:* Johnson (5), Stransky *Penalty Goal:* Johnson
WESTERN SAMOA: M T Umaga (Wellington); B Lima (Auckland), T M Vaega (Moata'a), G E Leaupepe (Auckland), G Harder (Te Atatu); E Puleitu (Auckland Inst of Technology), T Nu'uali'itia (Te Atatu); P Fatialofa (Counties) (*capt*), T Leiasamaivao (Wellington), M A N Mika (Otago), L Falaniko (Marist St Joseph's), D R Williams (Colomiers), S L Vaifale (Hawke's Bay), P R Lam (Auckland), M Iupeli (Marist St Joseph's) *Replacements* G Latu (Vaimoso) for Mika; P J Paramore (Counties) for Vaifale; F Sini (Marist Apia) for Vaega
Scorers *Try:* Lima *Penalty Goal:* Umaga
Referee J Meuwesen (Namibia)

22 April, Eden Park Auckland
NEW ZEALAND 73 (7G 3PG 3T) CANADA 7 (1G)

NEW ZEALAND: G M Osborne (North Harbour); M C G Ellis (Otago), F E Bunce (North Harbour), W K Little (North Harbour), J W Wilson (Otago); A P Mehrtens (Canterbury), G T M Bachop (Canterbury); C W Dowd (Auckland), S B T Fitzpatrick (Auckland) (*capt*), O M Brown (Auckland), I D Jones (North Harbour), R M Brooke (Auckland), J W Joseph (Otago), M R Brewer (Canterbury), J A Kronfeld (Otago)

Scorers *Tries:* Osborne (2), Bunce (2), Ellis (2), Brown, Mehrtens, Bachop, Wilson *Conversions:* Mehrtens (7) *Penalty Goals:* Mehrtens (3)
CANADA: D S Stewart (UBC Old Boys); B Ebl (Kats), S D Gray (Kats), G L Rees (Newport & Oak Bay Castaways) (*capt*), D C Lougheed (Toronto Welsh); B Ross (James Bay), J D Graf (UBC Old Boys); E A Evans (IBM Tokyo & UBC Old Boys), M E Cardinal (James Bay), P LeBlanc (Kats), M James (Burnaby Lake), G D Ennis (Suntory Tokyo & Kats), A J Charron (Ottawa Irish), C McKenzie (UBC Old Boys), G I MacKinnon (Ex-Britannia Lions) *Replacements* C Stewart (Western Province) for Gray (25 mins); A Tynan (Meralomas) for Ebl (27 mins); G Rowlands (Velox Valhallians) for James (46 mins); R Snow (Dogs) for LeBlanc (52 mins)
Scorers *Try:* C Stewart *Conversion:* Ross
Referee W J Erickson (Australia)

22 April, Murrayfield
SCOTLAND 49 (4G 2PG 3T) ROMANIA 16 (1G 3PG)

SCOTLAND: A G Hastings (Watsonians) (*capt*); C A Joiner (Melrose), A G Stanger (Hawick), A G Shiel (Melrose), K M Logan (Stirling County); C M Chalmers (Melrose), B W Redpath (Melrose); D I W Hilton (Bath), K D McKenzie (Stirling County), P H Wright (Boroughmuir), G W Weir (Melrose), S J Campbell (Dundee HSFP), R I Wainwright (West Hartlepool), E W Peters (Bath), I R Morrison (London Scottish) *Replacement* S Hastings (Watsonians) for A G Hastings (78 mins)
Scorers *Tries:* Stanger (2), G Hastings, Shiel, Peters, Joiner, Logan *Conversions:* G Hastings (4) *Penalty Goals:* G Hastings (2)
ROMANIA: V Brici (Farul Constanta); R Cioca (Dinamo Bucharest), N Racean (Cluj U), R Gontineac (Cluj U), G Solomie (Timisoara U); N Nichitean (Cluj U), D Neaga (Dinamo Bucharest); G Leonte (Vienne), V Tufa (Dinamo Bucharest), L Costea (Steaua Bucharest), S Ciorascu (Auch), C Cojocariu (Bayonne), T Oroian (Steaua Bucharest), T Brinza (Cluj U) (*capt*), A Gealapu (Steaua Bucharest) *Replacement* C Draguceanu (Steaua Bucharest) for Gealapu (48 mins)
Scorers *Try:* Racean *Conversion:* Nichitean *Penalty Goals:* Nichitean (3)
Referee N Lasaga (France)

30 April, Ballymore, Brisbane
AUSTRALIA 53 (3G 4PG 4T) ARGENTINA 7 (1G)

AUSTRALIA: M J Pini (Queensland); D I Campese (New South Wales), J S Little (Queensland), D J Herbert (Queensland), D P Smith (Queensland); M P Lynagh (Queensland) (*capt*), G M Gregan (Australian Capital Territory); D J Crowley (Queensland), P N Kearns (New South Wales), E J A McKenzie (New South Wales), R J McCall (Queensland), J A Eales (Queensland), V Ofahengaue (New South Wales), B T Gavin (New South Wales), D J Wilson (Queensland) *Replacement* M N Hartill (New South Wales) for McKenzie (65 mins)
Scorers *Tries:* Lynagh (2), Eales, Ofahengaue, Pini, Smith, Campese *Conversions:* Lynagh (3) *Penalty Goals:* Lynagh (4)
ARGENTINA: S E Meson (San Isidro); M J Teran (Tucumán), S Salvat (Alumni) (*capt*), F Garcia (Alumni), G F Camardon (Alumni); L Arbizu (Belgrano), A Pichot (CA San Isidro); M E Corral (San Isidro), F E Mendez (Mendoza), E P Noriega (Hindu), P L Sporleder (Curupayti), G A Llanes (La Plata), R A Martin (San Isidro), J M Santamarina (Tucumán), C E Viel (Newman) *Replacement* P M Buabsé (Tarcos) for Llanes (48 mins)
Scorers *Try:* Pichot *Conversion:* Arbizu
Referee C J Hawke (New Zealand)

6 May, Sydney Football Stadium
AUSTRALIA 30 (5PG 3T) ARGENTINA 13 (1G 2PG)

AUSTRALIA: M J Pini (Queensland); D I Campese (New South Wales), J S Little (Queensland), D J Herbert (Queensland), D P Smith (Queensland); M P Lynagh (Queensland) (*capt*), G M Gregan (Australian Capital Territory); D J Crowley (Queensland), P N Kearns (New South Wales), E J A McKenzie (New South Wales), R J McCall (Queensland), J A Eales (Queensland), T Coker (Queensland), B T Gavin (New South Wales), D J Wilson (Queensland) *Replacements* V Ofahengaue (New South Wales) for Coker (40 mins); M N Hartill (New South Wales) for McKenzie (65 mins)
Scorers *Tries:* Campese (2), Wilson *Penalty Goals:* Lynagh (5)
ARGENTINA: S E Meson (San Isidro); M J Teran (Tucumán), F Garcia (Alumni), S Salvat (Alumni) (*capt*), E Jurado (Jockey Rosario); G J del Castillo (Jockey Rosario), R H Crexell (Jockey Rosario); M E Corral (San Isidro), F E Mendez (Mendoza), E P Noriega (Hindu), G A Llanes (La Plata), P L Sporleder (Curupayti), R A Martin (San Isidro), J M Santamarina (Tucumán), C E Viel (Newman) *Replacement* L Arbizu (Belgrano) for Meson (13 mins)
Scorers *Try:* Arbizu *Conversion:* Crexell *Penalty Goals:* Meson, Crexell
Referee D J Bishop (New Zealand)

6 May, Stadio Communale Rugby, Monigo, Treviso
ITALY 22 (1G 4PG 1DG) IRELAND 12 (4PG)

ITALY: P Vaccari (Milan); M Ravazzolo (Calvisano), I Francescato (Treviso), M Bonomi (Milan), Marcello Cuttitta (Milan); D Dominguez (Milan), A Troncon (Treviso); Massimo Cuttitta (Milan) (*capt*), C Orlandi (Piacenza), F Properzi Curti (Milan), R Favaro (Treviso), M Giacheri (Treviso), O Arancio (Catania), P Pedroni (Milan), J M Gardner (Roma) *Replacements* M Capuzzoni (Milan) for Giacheri (1 min); S Bordon (Rovigo) for Bonomi (76 mins)
Scorers *Try:* Vaccari *Conversion:* Dominguez *Penalty Goals:* Dominguez (4) *Dropped Goal:* Dominguez
IRELAND: J E Staples (Harlequins); R M Wallace (Garryowen), B J Mullin (Blackrock Coll), J C Bell (Ballymena), Darragh O'Mahony (UC Dublin); P A Burke (Cork Const), David O'Mahony (Cork Const); N J Popplewell (Wasps), T J Kingston (Dolphin) (*capt*), G F Halpin (London Irish), G M Fulcher (Cork Const), D A Tweed (Ballymena), A G Foley (Shannon), P S Johns (Dungannon), E O Halvey (Shannon) *Replacements* A C Rolland (Blackrock Coll) for David O'Mahony (41 mins); M J Field (Malone) for Staples (79 mins)
Scorer *Penalty Goals:* Burke (4)
Referee A J Spreadbury (England)

SUPER-10 SERIES 1995

8 April, Ellis Park, Johannesburg
Transvaal 16 (1G 3DG) **Queensland 30** (2G 1PG 1DG 2T)

Queensland sent tremors through South African rugby on the eve of the World Cup with this emphatic victory. It was not just the margin of defeat which disturbed locals; it was the manner of it, too. Queensland, who fielded nine of the players likely to be in the Wallaby starting line-up, had more bite up front and more thrust behind, attributes which enabled them to score four tries and become the first team to retain the title. Transvaal, who had won the inaugural Championship three years before, were a pale imitation of that outfit and could only reply with three dropped goals and a soft try in the last minute of play.

Queensland were much sharper all round the field, more committed in the close-quarter exchanges and far more organised in the loose phases, where their ball retention was exemplary. Leading the way in every sense was the Queensland lock John Eales. He towered above everyone in the line-out, was the core of so many clattering forward drives and, if that weren't enough to earn him his post-match pie 'n' beans, he struck two conversions and a penalty goal with all the nonchalance of a golfer taking a practice swing on the first tee. Behind, the forceful punch of Little and Herbert in the centre, allied to their shrewd positioning, was far too much for the opposition to cope with.

Eales opened the scoring in the second minute with a penalty, only for Transvaal to hit back immediately with a dropped goal from de Beer. Just after the half-hour Little swept through the Transvaal defence, and linked with Wilson. He fed Connors, who then had a free run to the line. De Beer's two dropped goals kept the scores close at the interval. However, Johnstone's interception of le Roux's pass in the 56th minute began the final softening-up process. Kahl dropped a goal six minutes later, and Little and Herbert finished things off for Queensland with a two-try flourish. There was a consolation try for Roux in the dying seconds.

Transvaal: G Johnson; J van der Watt, C Scholtz, H le Roux, P Hendriks; J de Beer, J Roux; B Swart, Chris Rossouw, I Hattingh, K Wiese, H Strydom, G Combrinck, Charles Rossouw, R Straeuli *Replacement* J Mulder for Scholtz (1 min)
Scorers *Try:* J Roux *Conversion:* De Beer *Dropped Goals:* De Beer (3)
Queensland: M Pini; D Smith, D Herbert, J Little, P Carozza; P Kahl, P Slattery; D Crowley, M Foley, A Blades, R McCall, J Eales, I Tabua, T Coker, D Wilson *Replacements* M Connors for Coker (9 mins); Johnstone for Slattery (54 mins); M Ryan for Crowley (temp); D Barrett for Foley (temp)
Scorers *Tries:* Connors, Johnstone, Little, Herbert *Conversions:* Eales (2) *Penalty Goal:* Eales *Dropped Goal:* Kahl
Referee E O'Brien (New Zealand)

SEVENS TOURNAMENTS 1994-95
Michael Austin

THE 1995 CATHAY PACIFIC-HONG KONG BANK SEVENS

25-26 March 1995, Hong Kong
NEW ZEALAND 35 (5G) **FIJI 17** (1G 2T)

Eric Rush led New Zealand to a second successive triumph at the Hong Kong Sevens as they beat seven-times champions Fiji 35-17 in a top-quality final watched by a crowd of 40,000. They reached the last stage by eliminating Western Samoa, the side which had inflicted their most recent tournament defeat in the semi-final of 1993.

New Zealand were the leading side throughout the tournament, discovering yet another talented young player, Tongan-born Jonah Lomu, along the way. Lomu was to become the sensation of the World Cup later in the year. Aged 19 and powerfully built, in Hong Kong he caused consternation for Fiji every time he was in possession and scored two tries in the final to complement others by Rush, wing Peter Woods and centre Adrian Cashmore, who also kicked five conversions. Lomu confirmed the impression he had made in the previous year's competition and was the tournament's top player.

Rush said afterwards that New Zealand had a youthful team and that it had been the younger members who had pulled the older fellows through. His unbeatable side had all the classic sevens skills, notably blistering pace, flawless handling, support play and determined tackling.

Fiji, beaten finalists two years earlier, also excelled in overpowering Australia 35-5 in the second semi-final, Waisale Serevi scoring 25 points. The talents of Serevi, one of the world's leading exponents of the sevens game, were already well known in Hong Kong, as he had led Fiji to three consecutive wins over New Zealand in finals between 1990 and 1992. The size of the defeat shocked Australia, because they had amassed 28 points without reply from England in the quarter-finals.

England competed in the tournament for the first time on a March weekend when there was a full Courage Leagues programme at home. Managed by Andrew Harriman, captain of the Rugby World Cup Sevens-winning England team in 1993, and coached by Les Cusworth, the side was geared to preparing for the defence of the world title in 1997, and thus relied heavily on youth. Australia had played in several top-level events; England's hastily assembled squad had had only two training sessions and had played in a single tournament, in which they lost warm-up games to Twickenham and Edinburgh Wanderers.

Members of the 1995 World Cup squad were unavailable and the side was led by Derek Eves, the Bristol flanker, who operated as a hooker. They lacked a sharp edge of pace in the forwards, but there were rich

New Zealand and Fiji contest the Hong Kong Sevens final. Andrew Cashmore, who scored a try and five conversions, is in possession, with rising star Jonah Lomu in support.

benefits, as Harriman stressed: 'Sevens have become a cog in the developmental process of players in which important skills can be learned.' Cusworth, a past master of the sevens art, was also convinced of the merits of England recognising the event for the first time. 'There is no hiding place out there. You have to come to tournaments like this, both to learn and to develop players. You can immediately see a player's strengths and weaknesses. We have to show our youngsters the world stage.' He believed that the investment in bringing Richard Hill and Tony Diprose of Saracens, Nick Greenstock of Wasps, and Orrell's Austin Healey to Hong Kong was 'worth the trip five times over'. His view was supported by the rise of Australia's George Gregan, who had been an unknown student at the previous year's competition and had afterwards rapidly become a pivotal member of their squad for the 1995 World Cup.

England's leading performers were David Scully, a member of the World Cup Sevens-winning team in 1993, and Greenstock, who moved to fly-half when Healey limped off to be replaced by Chris Yates of Sale.

While England at least reached the last eight in the Cup competition, their fellow Five Nations teams Ireland and France finished in the Plate tournament with discouraging results. France lost 17-12 to Korea and Ireland were squeezed out 22-14 by Japan. Canada, beaten 19-5 by England in the qualifying round, went on to win the Plate, scoring five tries in beating Argentina, while Hong Kong were highly popular winners of the Bowl. They overwhelmed Papua New Guinea, who had also lost to England in the main competition.

As a joyous celebration of the game, the tournament has few peers. The combination of sun and fun is always laced with a try-scoring bonanza. Australia achieved the biggest victory, by 63 points over the Ivory Coast, while the competition threw together teams which could only have dreamed of meeting each other in the past. South Africa playing Sri Lanka and Canada vying with Papua New Guinea were examples of the global game rugby has become.

Group matches: New Zealand 42, Kwang-Hua Taipei 5; South Africa 35, Sri Lanka 14; Hong Kong 19, France 14; Western Samoa 31, Singapore 0; Fiji 35, Thailand 7; Ireland 12, Portugal 12; England 26, Papua New Guinea 7; Australia 27, Malaysia 7; USA 38, Kwang-Hua Taipei 7; Argentina 19, Sri Lanka 0; Tonga 19, Hong Kong 10; Korea 49, Singapore 5; Japan 35, Thailand 12; Namibia 24, Portugal 7; Canada 26, Papua New Guinea 12; Ivory Coast 17, Malaysia 7; New Zealand 40, USA 7; South Africa 35, Argentina 17; France 21, Tonga 19; Western Samoa 35, Korea 7; Fiji 42, Japan 7; Namibia 26, Ireland 19; England 19, Canada 5; Australia 63, Ivory Coast 0

BOWL:
Semi-finals: Hong Kong 33, Kwang-Hua Taipei 0; Papua New Guinea 40, Thailand 0
Final: Hong Kong 45, Papua New Guinea 7

PLATE:
Semi-finals: Argentina 10, Korea 7; Canada 28, Japan 5
Final: Canada 35, Argentina 12

CUP:
Quarter-finals: New Zealand 26, South Africa 0; Western Samoa 28, Tonga 5; Fiji 47, Namibia 0; Australia 26, England 0
Semi-finals: New Zealand 26, Western Samoa 0; Fiji 35, Australia 5
Final: New Zealand 35, Fiji 17

Teams in the Final
NEW ZEALAND: J Lomu, E Rush, D Seymour, J Vidiri; P Woods, A Cashmore, J Tauiwi
Scorers *Tries:* Lomu (2), Rush, Woods, Cashmore *Conversions:* Cashmore (5)
FIJI: W Masirewa, S Vonolagi, J Tuikabe, S Rabaka; W Serevi, M Bari, E R Bolobolo
Scorers *Tries:* Vonolagi, Bari, Bolobolo *Conversion:* Serevi

THE MIDDLESEX SEVENS 1995

(Sponsored by Save & Prosper)

13 May 1995, Twickenham
Leicester 38 (4G 2T) **Ithuba 19** (2G 1T)

Leicester lifted the Russell Cargill Memorial Cup as winners of the Middlesex Sevens for the first time but Ithuba, a side representing 69 clubs in the townships of western Cape Province, South Africa, won the hearts of a record 53,000 crowd in reaching the final.

Roughly translated from the Xhosa, Ithuba means 'chance', and theirs was taken with victories over Haywards Heath, Harlequins and Rosslyn Park on the way to the final, which they lost 38-19 to the more bulky and powerful Tigers side. Ithuba had not even played sevens until they set foot in Britain, but they were quick learners on their first visit abroad. They would have competed in the tournament the previous year but for a South African domestic ruling that teams cannot tour overseas unless permission is granted a year in advance.

Leicester are not usually noted for their sevens expertise, preferring to reserve their energies and skills for the 15-a-side game, but with John Liley leading by example, they consigned West Sussex Institute, Selkirk, Blackheath and finally Ithuba to defeat. Fittingly, Liley was the tournament's leading scorer with 38 points, comprising 14 conversions and two tries, while 'Percy' Booysen of Ithuba and Leicester's Nigel Richardson ran in four tries each.

Rosslyn Park eliminated Bath, the holders, in the first round and led Ithuba by 14 points before being brushed aside 24-14. Harlequins, who had won the competition a record 13 times, lost 28-7 to Ithuba and even Leicester trailed in the final to a third-minute breakaway try by Booysen. Liley rallied his team with an exemplary performance of tackling, creating and scoring tries and kicking goals. They scored six tries to three, two of Ithuba's coming from the speedy Julian Visser.

Orrell won the Plate competition, beating Reading after defeating Northampton 19-0 in the semi-finals. Reading qualified for the final with a 21-7 victory over London Scottish on an afternoon of rich entertainment.

RESULTS
Sixth round: Orrell 17, Blackheath 27; Wasps 31, Gloucester 10; Leicester 40, West Sussex Institute 12; Northampton 14, Selkirk 17; Ithuba (SA) 31, Haywards Heath 7; Harlequins 19, London Scottish 14; Bristol 28, Reading 7; Rosslyn Park 17, Bath 14
Seventh round: Blackheath 19, Wasps 12; Leicester 31, Selkirk 7; Ithuba 28, Harlequins 7; Bristol 14, Rosslyn Park 24
Semi-finals: Blackheath 5, Leicester 21; Ithuba 24, Rosslyn Park 14
Final: Leicester 38, Ithuba 19
Plate final: Orrell 15, Reading 12

Teams in the final
Leicester: T Reynolds, J Liley (*capt*), N Malone, J Hamilton; C Tarbuck, C Johnson, N Richardson
Scorers *Tries:* Liley, Hamilton, Johnson, Reynolds, Richardson, Malone
Conversions: Liley (4)
Ithuba: W Louw, J Visser, I October (*capt*), L Booysen; S Langenhoven, K January, N Witbooli
Scorers *Tries:* Visser (2), Booysen *Conversions:* October (2)
Referee N Cousins (London Society)

WINNERS

1926 **Harlequins**
1927 **Harlequins**
1928 **Harlequins**
1929 **Harlequins**
1930 **London Welsh**
1931 **London Welsh**
1932 **Blackheath**
1933 **Harlequins**
1934 **Barbarians**
1935 **Harlequins**
1936 **Sale**
1937 **London Scottish**
1938 **Metropolitan Police**
1939 **Cardiff**
1940 **St Mary's Hospital**
1941 **Cambridge University**
1942 **St Mary's Hospital**
1943 **St Mary's Hospital**
1944 **St Mary's Hospital**
1945 **Notts**
1946 **St Mary's Hospital**
1947 **Rosslyn Park**
1948 **Wasps**
1949 **Heriot's FP**
1950 **Rosslyn Park**
1951 **Richmond II**
1952 **Wasps**
1953 **Richmond**
1954 **Rosslyn Park**
1955 **Richmond**
1956 **London Welsh**
1957 **St Luke's College**
1958 **Blackheath**
1959 **Loughborough Colls**
1960 **London Scottish**
1961 **London Scottish**
1962 **London Scottish**
1963 **London Scottish**
1964 **Loughborough Colls**
1965 **London Scottish**
1966 **Loughborough Colls**
1967 **Harlequins**
1968 **London Welsh**
1969 **St Luke's College**
1970 **Loughborough Colls**
1971 **London Welsh**
1972 **London Welsh**
1973 **London Welsh**
1974 **Richmond**
1975 **Richmond**
1976 **Loughborough Colls**
1977 **Richmond**
1978 **Harlequins**
1979 **Richmond**
1980 **Richmond**
1981 **Rosslyn Park**
1982 **Stewart's-Melville FP**
1983 **Richmond**
1984 **London Welsh**
1985 **Wasps**
1986 **Harlequins**
1987 **Harlequins**
1988 **Harlequins**
1989 **Harlequins**
1990 **Harlequins**
1991 **London Scottish**
1992 **Western Samoa**
1993 **Wasps**
1994 **Bath**
1995 **Leicester**

Harlequins have won the title 13 times, Richmond 9 (including one by their second VII), London Welsh 8, London Scottish 7, St Mary's Hospital and Loughborough Colleges 5 each, Rosslyn Park and Wasps 4 each, Blackheath and St Luke's College (now Exeter University) twice, Barbarians, Sale, Met Police, Cardiff, Cambridge University, Notts (now Nottingham), Heriot's FP, Stewart's-Melville FP, Western Samoa, Bath and Leicester once each

WORTHINGTON WELSH SEVENS 1994-95

(for the Snelling Trophy)

13 August 1994, Cardiff Arms Park

Bath 42 (6G) **Cardiff 5** (1T)

Bath completed a notable double in the 40th anniversary Worthington Welsh tournament, adding to their success at the previous season's Middlesex Sevens and becoming the first English club to win the Snelling Trophy.

Cardiff and Bridgend had won the tournament 15 times between them and entered their strongest available squads, but Bath, with Ireland wing Simon Geoghegan making his club debut, scored a six-try runaway win over Cardiff in the final.

Preliminary round: Treorchy 40, Glamorgan Wanderers 7; Aberavon 10, Neath 21
First round: Abertillery 7, Pontypool 31; Tredegar 12, Penarth 10; Maesteg 19, Newbridge 17; Ebbw Vale 26, Llanharan 12; Cardiff 33, Bristol 7; Treorchy 19, Neath 12
Second round: Moseley 14, Newport 17; Swansea 12, Llanelli 40; Abercynon 7, Bridgend 24; South Wales Police 21, Cross Keys 24; Bath 24, Pontypridd 5; Ebbw Vale 12, Cardiff 27; Tredegar 7, Maesteg 31; Treorchy 24, Pontypool 21 (*aet*)
Quarter-finals: Cross Keys 0, Bath 47; Llanelli 7, Bridgend 43; Cardiff 42, Newport 7; Treorchy 19, Maesteg 5
Semi-finals: Bath 26, Bridgend 14; Cardiff 24, Treorchy 7
Final: Bath 42, Cardiff 5

Teams in the final
Bath: M Haag, G Adams, E Peters, J Callard (*capt*); M Catt, A Lumsden, S Geoghegan
Scorers *Tries:* Lumsden (2), Haag, Geoghegan, Callard, Adams *Conversions:* Callard (6)
Cardiff: H Stone, M Budd, O Williams (*capt*), A Moore; C John, S Hill, S Ford
Scorer *Try:* Hill
Bill Everett Player of the Competition: A Lumsden (Bath)

COMMITTEE PUT BACK LABEL ON CARLING

THE 1994-95 SEASON IN ENGLAND
Mick Cleary

Regrettably, the season may well be remembered for what was said rather than what was done. The Carling affair, which exploded on the day of the Pilkington Cup final, was the biggest rugby, if not sports, story of the year. The next sponsorship negotiations might be interesting considering that the RFU's outrageous stance stole all the publicity from what was a magnificent match.

For Carling to be hauled over the coals in the manner that he was for a juvenile remark in a television programme – he said, as the world now knows, that the RFU committee were no more than 57 'old farts' – was an absurd overreaction. The decision to sack the most successful captain the sport has ever known was taken behind the closed doors of the East India Club in London. Present were the president, Dennis Easby, along with president elect Bill Bishop, honorary treasurer and chairman of the new executive Peter Bromage; assistant treasurer John Motum, immediate past president Ian Beer and, technically, at any rate, junior vice-president John Richardson, who was in phone contact from Coventry. They considered that Carling had brought the game, his country and the sport into disrepute. Goodness knows what punishment might have befallen him if he'd actually punched an opponent on the field.

The shockwaves went far and wide. Easby confirmed on the Sunday morning that there was no way back for Carling. By mid-afternoon, after a radio link with Carling's agent, Jon Holmes, there was a suggestion that an olive branch might be accepted. The peace talks took place on Monday morning at Twickenham. Carling then drove to Marlow, where the England squad were training, reinstated as England captain.

What was all that about? the general public asked. The small group on the RFU committee who took the decision should have resigned immediately. A point of principle is either worth making or it isn't. Whether or not they were right to object to Carling's remark is not the issue. They considered it a point of honour, and so they should have stepped down when they saw the general reaction against them.

That this ludicrous storm should have have occurred in the last moments of one of England's most successful seasons made it all the more ironic. The campaign had begun with the sacking of coach Dick Best. The manner of his dismissal was tawdry: he had been given little inkling of it and was busy preparing some tactical videos when the call came. This is no slight on England manager Jack Rowell. It is the RFU's responsibility to handle these matters more diplomatically. Rowell wasted no time in asserting that he wanted England to play a more dynamic, rounded game. The autumn warm-up matches against Romania and Canada suggested that the side might be heeding what he was saying. A cruel minor injury to Bristol full-back Paul Hull in the Canada match was all it took for Mike Catt to grasp opportunity with both hands and clench it tightly. He played superbly as a replacement and held his place at full-back throughout the season. Hull did not even have the consolation of a World Cup place – Ian Hunter and Jon Callard were taken as the cover full-backs.

The tone for the Five Nations campaign was set within the first ten minutes of the opening match at Lansdowne Road. England, playing into the teeth of a gale and facing the customary passionate onslaught from the Irish, both crowd and team, had worked their way downfield with control, precision and absolute conviction, eventually sending Will Carling over the try-line. Although there were occasional moments of waivering during the season, England nonetheless always had that edge of power and organisation on any side they played. Kyran Bracken made the scrum-half position his own during the Championship, although that great fighter Dewi Morris pledged to be back. As the World Cup showed, he was true to his word.

The World Cup loomed large over the season, and at no time more so than in the final stages of the Courage Leagues. The ridiculous pressure on players to turn out for club and still be fresh for country had been pointed out as far back as the beginning of the season. The RFU, though, did nothing to alleviate the fixture congestion, throwing the problem back on to the players. At an early-season meeting the England squad decided that they would limit themselves to two out of four matches in the final month. Little did the likes of Brian Moore and Tim Rodber, captains at Harlequins and Northampton respectively, think that, come April, their two clubs would be fighting for survival.

The absence of the England players in those last key matches undoubtedly devalued the competition. The sponsors, Courage, may well have kept a diplomatic silence on the RFU's inability to restructure the season to meaningful effect, but as it turned out, they got their money's worth in that Division 1 went to the wire and, for the first time in many moons, was competitive throughout. Leicester were crowned champions, their second Championship in seven years, while Harlequins' victory at Gloucester ensured their survival. At the final whistle, an emotional Brian Moore, who had announced his retirement the day before the game, a decision he was later to reconsider, hugged another fellow traveller, Gloucester's Mike Teague, who was also bowing out. Other magnificent servants of the game also took the final curtain: Orrell's Dewi Morris, and Jon Hall and Tony Swift of Bath. They were wished well by friend and rival alike.

Sale were a great addition to the ranks, not just for the silly old romantic reason that northern rugby needs to be supported and promoted – ultimately, such thinking can only be patronising. Teams

The England team which beat Scotland at Twickenham for the Grand Slam. L-R, back row: B W Stirling (referee), O E Doyle (touch-judge), G C Rowntree (replacement), M J Catt, V E Ubogu, D Richards, B B Clarke, M C Bayfield, M O Johnson, T A K Rodber, S O Ojomoh (replacement), J Leonard, S R Hilditch (touch-judge); front row: K P P Bracken, G Botterman (replacement), J E B Callard, T Underwood, J C Guscott, C R Andrew, W D C Carling (capt), B C Moore, R Underwood, P R de Glanville (replacement), C D Morris (replacement).

are either good enough or they're not. Sale were. Inspired by the twinkling touches of their fly-half and player-coach, former Welsh international Paul Turner, Sale not only played pretty rugby, they played positive, effective rugby with it. They troubled sides throughout the season with the inventiveness of their back play. They also had muscle up front, No 8 Charlie Vyvyan enjoying a great return to the high echelons. They thoroughly deserved their fourth place.

Wasps had threatened to cruise through the League season scoring tries at will. They beat Gloucester by 45-8 on the first Saturday, then took Harlequins apart by 57-26 the week afterwards. Unfortunately, a cold dose of northern reality hit them between the eyes the following week when, in the driving rain, their bubble burst, 20-15 at West Hartlepool. Wasps regrouped, though, and, with Damian Hopley, Dean Ryan, Lawrence Dallaglio and the half-backs, Steve Bates and Rob Andrew, in ebullient mood all season, they mixed a little bit of calculation into their free-and-easy rugby to finish strongly in third place.

Saracens romped to the Second Division title, eventually finishing six points clear of Wakefield. Spare a thought for Fylde. They began the last Saturday in fourth place in the division. By 4.30 pm they had been relegated along with Coventry. Three other clubs had been on 16 points along with Fylde, and two more on 15. The only losers among the six were Fylde and Waterloo, Fylde on inferior points difference. Bedford and Blackheath finished comfortably ahead of the pack in Division 3.

Disappointing as Bath's season had been by their standards, they still had a trophy to put on the mantelpiece at the end. Their defeat of Wasps in the Pilkington Cup final was yet another vivid illustration of the huge heart which, for all the occasional murmurs, continues to beat strongly at the club.

ENGLISH INTERNATIONAL PLAYERS
(up to 31 March 1995)

ABBREVIATIONS

A – Australia; *Arg* – Argentina; *C* – Canada; *F* – France; *Fj* – Fiji; *I* – Ireland; *It* – Italy; *J* – Japan; *M* – Maoris; *NZ* – New Zealand; *R* – Romania; *S* – Scotland; *SA* – South Africa; *US* – United States; *W* – Wales; (C) – Centenary match v Scotland at Murrayfield, 1971 (non-championship); *P* – England v President's Overseas XV at Twickenham in RFU's Centenary season, 1970-71; (R) – Replacement; (t) – temporary replacement. Entries in square brackets [ ] indicate appearances in the World Cup.

Note: Years given for Five Nations' matches are for second half of season; eg 1972 means season 1971-72. Years for all other matches refer to the actual year of the match. When a series has taken place, figures have been used to denote the particular matches in which players have featured. Thus 1984 *SA* 2 indicates that a player appeared in the second Test of the series.

Aarvold, C D (Cambridge U, W Hartlepool, Headingley, Blackheath) 1928 *A, W, I, F, S*, 1929 *W, I, F*, 1931 *W, S, F*, 1932 *SA, W, I, S*, 1933 *W*
Ackford, P J (Harlequins) 1988 *A*, 1989 *S, I, F, W, R, Fj*, 1990 *I, F, W, S, Arg* 3, 1991 *W, S, I, F, A*, [*NZ, It, F, S, A*]
Adams, A A (London Hospital) 1910 *F*
Adams, F R (Richmond) 1875 *I, S*, 1876 *S*, 1877 *I*, 1878 *S*, 1879 *S, I*
Adey, G J (Leicester) 1976 *I, F*
Adkins, S J (Coventry) 1950 *I, F, S*, 1953 *W, I, F, S*
Agar, A E (Harlequins) 1952 *SA, W, S, I, F*, 1953 *W, I*
Alcock, A (Guy's Hospital) 1906 *SA*
Alderson, F H R (Hartlepool R) 1891 *W, I, S*, 1892 *W, S*, 1893 *W*
Alexander, H (Richmond) 1900 *I, S*, 1901 *W, I, S*, 1902 *W, I*
Alexander, W (Northern) 1927 *F*
Allison, D F (Coventry) 1956 *W, I, S, F*, 1957 *W*, 1958 *W, S*
Allport, A (Blackheath) 1892 *W*, 1893 *I*, 1894 *W, I, S*
Anderson, S (Rockcliff) 1899 *I*
Anderson, W F (Orrell) 1973 *NZ* 1
Anderton, C (Manchester FW) 1889 *M*
Andrew, C R (Cambridge U, Nottingham, Wasps, Toulouse) 1985 *R, F, S, I, W*, 1986 *W, S, I, F*, 1987 *I, F, W*, [*J* (R), *US*], 1988 *S, I* 1,2, *A* 1,2, *Fj, A*, 1989 *S, I, F, W, R, Fj*, 1990 *I, F, W, S, Arg* 3, 1991 *W, S, I, F, Fj, A*, [*NZ, It, US, F, S, A*], 1992 *S, I, F, W, C, SA*, 1993 *F, W, NZ*, 1994 *S, I, F, W, SA* 1,2, *R, C*, 1995 *I, F, W, S*
Archer, H (Bridgwater A) 1909 *W, F, I*
Armstrong, R (Northern) 1925 *W*
Arthur, T G (Wasps) 1966 *W, I*
Ashby, R C (Wasps) 1966 *I, F*, 1967 *A*
Ashcroft, A (Waterloo) 1956 *W, I, S, F*, 1957 *W, I, F, S*, 1958 *W, A, I, F, S*, 1959 *I, F, S*
Ashcroft, A H (Birkenhead Park) 1909 *A*
Ashford, W (Richmond) 1897 *W, I*, 1898 *S, W*
Ashworth, A (Oldham) 1892 *I*
Askew, J G (Cambridge U) 1930 *W, I, F*
Aslett, A R (Richmond) 1926 *W, I, F, S*, 1929 *S, F*
Assinder, E W (O Edwardians) 1909 *A, W*
Aston, R L (Blackheath) 1890 *S, I*
Auty, J R (Headingley) 1935 *S*

Back, N A (Leicester) 1994 *S, I*
Bailey, M D (Cambridge U, Wasps) 1984 *SA* 1,2, 1987 [*US*], 1989 *Fj*, 1990 *I, F, S* (R)
Bainbridge, S (Gosforth, Fylde) 1982 *F, W*, 1983 *F, W, S, I, NZ*, 1984 *S, I, F, W*, 1985 *NZ* 1,2, 1987 *F, W, S*, [*J, US*]
Baker, D G S (OMTs) 1955 *W, I, F, S*
Baker, E M (Moseley) 1895 *W, I, S*, 1896 *W, I, S*, 1897 *W*
Baker, H C (Clifton) 1887 *W*
Bance, J F (Bedford) 1954 *S*
Barley, B (Wakefield) 1984 *I, F, W, A*, 1988 *A* 1,2, *Fj*
Barnes, S (Bristol, Bath) 1984 *A*, 1985 *R* (R), *NZ* 1,2, 1986 *S* (R), *F* (R), 1987 *I* (R), 1988 *Fj*, 1993 *S, I*
Barr, R J (Leicester) 1932 *SA, W, I*
Barrett, E I M (Lennox) 1903 *S*
Barrington, T J M (Bristol) 1931 *W, I*
Barrington-Ward, L E (Edinburgh U) 1910 *W, I, F, S*
Barron, J H (Bingley) 1896 *S*, 1897 *W, I*
Bartlett, J T (Waterloo) 1951 *W*
Bartlett, R M (Harlequins) 1957 *W, I, F, S*, 1958 *I, F, S*
Barton, J (Coventry) 1967 *I, F, W*, 1972 *F*
Batchelor, T B (Oxford U) 1907 *F*
Bates, S M (Wasps) 1989 *R*
Bateson, A H (Otley) 1930 *W, I, F, S*
Bateson, H D (Liverpool) 1879 *I*
Batson, T (Blackheath) 1872 *S*, 1874 *S*, 1875 *I*
Batten, J M (Cambridge U) 1874 *S*
Baume, J L (Northern) 1950 *S*
Baxter, J (Birkenhead Park) 1900 *W, I, S*
Bayfield, M C (Northampton) 1991 *Fj, A*, 1992 *S, I, F, W, C, SA*, 1993 *F, W, S, I*, 1994 *S, I, SA* 1,2, *R, C*, 1995 *I, F, W, S*
Bazley, R C (Waterloo) 1952 *I, F*, 1953 *W, I, F, S*, 1955 *W, I, F, S*
Beaumont, W B (Fylde) 1975 *I, A* 1(R),2, 1976 *A, W, S, I, F*, 1977 *S, I, F, W*, 1978 *F, W, S, I, NZ*, 1979 *S, I, F, W, NZ*, 1980 *I, F, W, S*, 1981 *W, S, I, F, Arg* 1,2, 1982 *A, S*
Bedford, H (Morley) 1889 *M*, 1890 *S, I*
Bedford, L L (Headingley) 1931 *W, I*
Beer, I D S (Harlequins) 1955 *F, S*
Beese, M C (Liverpool) 1972 *W, I, F*
Bell, F J (Northern) 1900 *W*
Bell, H (New Brighton) 1884 *I*
Bell, J L (Darlington) 1878 *I*
Bell, P J (Blackheath) 1968 *W, I, F, S*
Bell, R W (Northern) 1900 *W, I, S*
Bendon, G J (Wasps) 1959 *W, I, F, S*
Bennett, N O (St Mary's Hospital, Waterloo) 1947 *W, S, F*, 1948 *A, W, I, S*
Bennett, W N (Bedford, London Welsh) 1975 *S, A* 1, 1976 *S* (R), 1979 *S, I, F, W*
Bennetts, B B (Penzance) 1909 *A, W*
Bentley, J (Sale) 1988 *I* 2, *A* 1
Bentley, J E (Gipsies) 1871 *S*, 1872 *S*
Berridge, M J (Northampton) 1949 *W, I*
Berry, H (Gloucester) 1910 *W, I, F, S*
Berry, J (Tyldesley) 1891 *W, I, S*
Berry, J T W (Leicester) 1939 *W, I, S*
Beswick, E (Swinton) 1882 *I, S*
Biggs, J M (UCH) 1878 *S*, 1879 *I*
Birkett, J G G (Harlequins) 1906 *S, F, SA*, 1907 *F, W, S*, 1908 *F, W, I, S*, 1910 *W, I, S*, 1911 *W, F, I, S*, 1912 *W, I, S, F*
Birkett, L (Clapham R) 1875 *S*, 1877 *I, S*
Birkett, R H (Clapham R) 1871 *S*, 1875 *S*, 1876 *S*, 1877 *I*
Bishop, C C (Blackheath) 1927 *F*
Black, B H (Blackheath) 1930 *W, I, F, S*, 1931 *W, I, S, F*, 1932 *S*, 1933 *W*
Blacklock, J H (Aspatria) 1898 *I*, 1899 *I*
Blakeway, P J (Gloucester) 1980 *I, F, W, S*, 1981 *W, S, I, F*, 1982 *I, F, W*, 1984 *I, F, W, SA* 1, 1985 *R, F, S, I*
Blakiston, A F (Northampton) 1920 *S*, 1921 *W, I, S, F*, 1922 *W*, 1923 *S, F*, 1924 *W, I, F, S*, 1925 *NZ, W, I, S, F*
Blatherwick, T (Manchester) 1878 *I*
Body, J A (Gipsies) 1872 *S*, 1873 *S*
Bolton, C A (United Services) 1909 *F*
Bolton, R (Harlequins) 1933 *W*, 1936 *S*, 1937 *S*, 1938 *W, I*
Bolton, W N (Blackheath) 1882 *I, S*, 1883 *W, I, S*, 1884

W, I, S, 1885 *I*, 1887 *I, S*
Bonaventura, M S (Blackheath) 1931 *W*
Bond, A M (Sale) 1978 *NZ*, 1979 *S, I, NZ*, 1980 *I*, 1982 *I*
Bonham-Carter, E (Oxford U) 1891 *S*
Bonsor, F (Bradford) 1886 *W, I, S*, 1887 *W, S*, 1889 *M*
Boobbyer, B (Rosslyn Park) 1950 *W, I, F, S*, 1951 *W, F*, 1952 *S, I, F*
Booth, L A (Headingley) 1933 *W, I, S*, 1934 *S*, 1935 *W, I, S*
Botting, I J (Oxford U) 1950 *W, I*
Boughton, H J (Gloucester) 1935 *W, I, S*
Boyle, C W (Oxford U) 1873 *S*
Boyle, S B (Gloucester) 1983 *W, S, I*
Boylen, F (Hartlepool R) 1908 *F, W, I, S*
Bracken, K P P (Bristol) 1993 *NZ*, 1994 *S, I, C*, 1995 *I, F, W, S*
Bradby, M S (United Services) 1922 *I, F*
Bradley, R (W Hartlepool) 1903 *W*
Bradshaw, H (Bramley) 1892 *S*, 1893 *W, I, S*, 1894 *W, I, S*
Brain, S E (Coventry) 1984 *SA* 2, *A* (R), 1985 *R, F, S, I, W, NZ* 1,2, 1986 *W, S, I, F*
Braithwaite, J (Leicester) 1905 *NZ*
Braithwaite-Exley, B (Headingley) 1949 *W*
Brettargh, A T (Liverpool OB) 1900 *W*, 1903 *I, S*, 1904 *W, I, S*, 1905 *I, S*
Brewer, J (Gipsies) 1876 *I*
Briggs, A (Bradford) 1892 *W, I, S*
Brinn, A (Gloucester) 1972 *W, I, S*
Broadley, T (Bingley) 1893 *W, S*, 1894 *W, I, S*, 1896 *S*
Bromet, W E (Richmond) 1891 *W, I*, 1892 *W, I, S*, 1893 *W, I, S*, 1895 *W, I, S*, 1896 *I*
Brook, P W P (Harlequins) 1930 *S*, 1931 *F*, 1936 *S*
Brooke, T J (Richmond) 1968 *F, S*
Brooks, F G (Bedford) 1906 *SA*
Brooks, M J (Oxford U) 1874 *S*
Brophy, T J (Liverpool) 1964 *I, F, S*, 1965 *W, I*, 1966 *W, I, F*
Brough, J W (Silloth) 1925 *NZ, W*
Brougham, H (Harlequins) 1912 *W, I, S, F*
Brown, A A (Exeter) 1938 *S*
Brown, L G (Oxford U, Blackheath) 1911 *W, F, I, S*, 1913 *SA, W, F, I, S*, 1914 *W, I, S, F*, 1921 *W, I, S, F*, 1922 *W*
Brown, T W (Bristol) 1928 *S*, 1929 *W, I, S, F*, 1932 *S*, 1933 *W, I, S*
Brunton, J (N Durham) 1914 *W, I, S*
Brutton, E B (Cambridge U) 1886 *S*
Bryden, C C (Clapham R) 1876 *I*, 1877 *S*
Bryden, H A (Clapham R) 1874 *S*
Buckingham, R A (Leicester) 1927 *F*
Bucknall, A L (Richmond) 1969 *SA*, 1970 *I, W, S, F*, 1971 *W, I, F, S* (2[1C])
Buckton, J R D (Saracens) 1988 *A* (R), 1990 *Arg* 1,2
Budd, A (Blackheath) 1878 *I*, 1879 *S, I*, 1881 *W, S*
Budworth, R T D (Blackheath) 1890 *W*, 1891 *W, S*
Bull, A G (Northampton) 1914 *W*
Bullough, E (Wigan) 1892 *W, I, S*
Bulpitt, M P (Blackheath) 1970 *S*
Bulteel, A J (Manchester) 1876 *I*
Bunting, W L (Moseley) 1897 *I, S*, 1898 *I, S, W*, 1899 *S*, 1900 *S*, 1901 *I, S*
Burland, D W (Bristol) 1931 *W, I, F*, 1932 *I, S*, 1933 *W, I, S*
Burns, B H (Blackheath) 1871 *S*
Burton, G W (Blackheath) 1879 *S, I*, 1880 *S*, 1881 *I, W, S*
Burton, H C (Richmond) 1926 *W*
Burton, M A (Gloucester) 1972 *W, I, F, S, SA*, 1974 *F, W*, 1975 *S, A* 1,2, 1976 *A, W, S, I, F*, 1978 *F, W*
Bush, J A (Clifton) 1872 *S*, 1873 *S*, 1875 *S*, 1876 *I, S*
Butcher, C J S (Harlequins) 1984 *SA* 1,2, *A*
Butcher, W V (Streatham) 1903 *S*, 1904 *W, I, S*, 1905 *W, I, S*
Butler, A G (Harlequins) 1937 *W, I*
Butler, P E (Gloucester) 1975 *A* 1, 1976 *F*
Butterfield, J (Northampton) 1953 *F, S*, 1954 *W, NZ, I, S, F*, 1955 *W, I, F, S*, 1956 *W, I, S, F*, 1957 *W, I, F,*

Rob Andrew clears the ball against Scotland in 1995, the match in which he equalled the record for most penalty goals with seven.

S, 1958 *W*, *A*, *I*, *F*, *S*, 1959 *W*, *I*, *F*, *S*
Byrne, F A (Moseley) 1897 *W*
Byrne, J F (Moseley) 1894 *W*, *I*, *S*, 1895 *I*, *S*, 1896 *I*, 1897 *W*, *I*, *S*, 1898 *I*, *S*, *W*, 1899 *I*

Cain, J J (Waterloo) 1950 *W*
Callard, J E B (Bath) 1993 *NZ*, 1994 *S*, *I*
Campbell, D A (Cambridge U) 1937 *W*, *I*
Candler, P L (St Bart's Hospital) 1935 *W*, 1936 *NZ*, *W*, *I*, *S*, 1937 *W*, *I*, *S*, 1938 *W*, *S*
Cannell, L B (Oxford U, St Mary's Hospital) 1948 *F*, 1949 *W*, *I*, *F*, *S*, 1950 *W*, *I*, *F*, *S*, 1952 *SA*, *W*, 1953 *W*, *I*, *F*, 1956 *I*, *S*, *F*,1957 *W*, *I*
Caplan, D W N (Headingley) 1978 *S*, *I*
Cardus, R M (Roundhay) 1979 *F*, *W*
Carey, G M (Blackheath) 1895 *W*, *I*, *S*, 1896 *W*, *I*
Carleton, J (Orrell) 1979 *NZ*, 1980 *I*, *F*, *W*, *S*, 1981 *W*, *S*, *I*, *F*, *Arg* 1,2, 1982 *A*, *S*, *I*, *F*, *W*, 1983 *F*, *W*, *S*, *I*, *NZ*, 1984 *S*, *I*, *F*, *W*, *A*
Carling, W D C (Durham U, Harlequins) 1988 *F*, *W*, *S*, *I* 1,2, *A*2, *Fj*, *A*, 1989 *S*, *I*, *F*, *W*, *Fj*, 1990 *I*, *F*, *W*, *S*, *Arg* 1,2,3, 1991 *W*, *S*, *I*, *F*, *Fj*, *A*, [*NZ*, *It*, *US*, *F*, *S*, *A*], 1992 *S*, *I*, *F*, *W*, *C*, *SA*, 1993 *F*, *W*, *S*, *I*, *NZ*, 1994 *S*, *I*, *F*, *W*, *SA* 1,2, *R*, *C*, 1995 *I*, *F*, *W*, *S*
Carpenter, A D (Gloucester) 1932 *SA*
Carr, R S L (Manchester) 1939 *W*, *I*, *S*
Cartwright, V H (Nottingham) 1903 *W*, *I*, *S*, 1904 *W*, *S*, 1905 *W*, *I*, *S*, *NZ*, 1906 *W*, *I*, *S*, *F*, *SA*
Catcheside, H C (Percy Park) 1924 *W*, *I*, *F*, *S*, 1926 *W*, *I*, 1927 *I*, *S*
Catt, M J (Bath) 1994 *W*(R), *C*(R), 1995 *I*, *F*, *W*, *S*
Cattell, R H B (Blackheath) 1895 *W*, *I*, *S*, 1896 *W*, *I*, *S*, 1900 *W*
Cave, J W (Richmond) 1889 *M*
Cave, W T C (Blackheath) 1905 *W*
Challis, R (Bristol) 1957 *I*, *F*, *S*
Chambers, E L (Bedford) 1908 *F*, 1910 *W*, *I*
Chantrill, B S (Bristol) 1924 *W*, *I*, *F*, *S*
Chapman, C E (Cambridge U) 1884 *W*
Chapman, F E (Hartlepool) 1910 *W*, *I*, *F*, *S*, 1912 *W*, 1914 *W*, *I*
Cheesman, W I (OMTs) 1913 *SA*, *W*, *F*, *I*
Cheston, E C (Richmond) 1873 *S*, 1874 *S*, 1875 *I*, *S*, 1876 *S*
Chilcott, G J (Bath) 1984 *A*, 1986 *I*, *F*, 1987 *F* (R), *W*, [*J*, *US*, *W*(R)], 1988 *I* 2(R), *Fj*, 1989 *I* (R), *F*, *W*, *R*
Christopherson, P (Blackheath) 1891 *W*, *S*
Clark, C W H (Liverpool) 1876 *I*
Clarke, A J (Coventry) 1935 *W*, *I*, *S*, 1936 *NZ*, *W*, *I*
Clarke, B B (Bath) 1992 *SA*, 1993 *F*, *W*, *S*, *I*, *NZ*, 1994 *S*, *F*, *W*, *SA* 1,2, *R*, *C*, 1995 *I*, *F*, *W*, *S*
Clarke, S J S (Cambridge U, Blackheath) 1963 *W*, *I*, *F*, *S*, *NZ* 1,2, *A*, 1964 *NZ*, *W*, *I*, 1965 *I*, *F*, *S*
Clayton, J H (Liverpool) 1871 *S*
Clements, J W (O Cranleighans) 1959 *I*, *F*, *S*
Cleveland, C R (Blackheath) 1887 *W*, *S*
Clibborn, W G (Richmond) 1886 *W*, *I*, *S*, 1887 *W*, *I*, *S*
Clough, F J (Cambridge U, Orrell) 1986 *I*, *F*, 1987 [*J*(R), *US*]
Coates, C H (Yorkshire W) 1880 *S*, 1881 *S*, 1882 *S*
Coates, V H M (Bath) 1913 *SA*, *W*, *F*, *I*, *S*
Cobby, W (Hull) 1900 *W*
Cockerham, A (Bradford Olicana) 1900 *W*
Colclough, M J (Angoulême, Wasps, Swansea) 1978 *S*, *I*, 1979 *NZ*, 1980 *F*, *W*, *S*, 1981 *W*, *S*, *I*, *F*, 1982 *A*, *S*, *I*, *F*, *W*, 1983 *F*, *NZ*, 1984 *S*, *I*, *F*, *W*, 1986 *W*, *S*, *I*, *F*
Coley, E (Northampton) 1929 *F*, 1932 *W*
Collins, P J (Camborne) 1952 *S*, *I*, *F*
Collins, W E (O Cheltonians) 1874 *S*, 1875 *I*, *S*, 1876 *I*, *S*
Considine, S G U (Bath) 1925 *F*
Conway, G S (Cambridge U, Rugby, Manchester) 1920 *F*, *I*, *S*, 1921 *F*, 1922 *W*, *I*, *F*, *S*, 1923 *W*, *I*, *S*, *F*, 1924 *W*, *I*, *F*, *S*, 1925 *NZ*, 1927 *W*
Cook, J G (Bedford) 1937 *S*
Cook, P W (Richmond) 1965 *I*, *F*
Cooke, D A (Harlequins) 1976 *W*, *S*, *I*, *F*
Cooke, D H (Harlequins) 1981 *W*, *S*, *I*, *F*, 1984 *I*, 1985 *R*, *F*, *S*, *I*, *W*, *NZ* 1,2
Cooke, P (Richmond) 1939 *W*, *I*
Coop, T (Leigh) 1892 *S*
Cooper, J G (Moseley) 1909 *A*, *W*
Cooper, M J (Moseley) 1973 *F*, *S*, *NZ* 2 (R), 1975 *F*, *W*, 1976 *A*, *W*, 1977 *S*, *I*, *F*, *W*
Coopper, S F (Blackheath) 1900 *W*, 1902 *W*, *I*, 1905 *W*, *I*, *S*, 1907 *W*
Corbett, L J (Bristol) 1921 *F*, 1923 *W*, *I*, 1924 *W*, *I*, *F*, *S*, 1925 *NZ*, *W*, *I*, *S*, *F*, 1927 *W*, *I*, *S*, *F*
Corless, B J (Coventry, Moseley) 1976 *A*, *I* (R), 1977 *S*, *I*, *F*, *W*, 1978 *F*, *W*, *S*, *I*
Cotton, F E (Loughborough Colls, Coventry, Sale) 1971 *S* (2[1C]), *P*, 1973 *W*, *I*, *F*, *S*, *NZ* 2, *A*, 1974 *S*, *I*, 1975 *I*, *F*, *W*, 1976 *A*, *W*, *S*, *I*, *F*, 1977 *S*, *I*, *F*, *W*, 1978 *S*, *I*, 1979 *NZ*, 1980 *I*, *F*, *W*, *S*, 1981 *W*
Coulman, M J (Moseley) 1967 *A*, *I*, *F*, *S*, *W*, 1968 *W*, *I*, *F*, *S*
Coulson, T J (Coventry) 1927 *W*, 1928 *A*, *W*
Court, E D (Blackheath) 1885 *W*
Coverdale, H (Blackheath) 1910 *F*, 1912 *I*, *F*, 1920 *W*
Cove-Smith, R (OMTs)1921 *S*, *F*, 1922 *I*, *F*, *S*, 1923 *W*, *I*, *S*, *F*, 1924 *W*, *I*, *S*, *F*, 1925 *NZ*, *W*, *I*, *S*, *F*, 1927 *W*, *I*, *S*, *F*,1928 *A*, *W*, *I*, *F*, *S*, 1929 *W*, *I*
Cowling, R J (Leicester) 1977 *S*, *I*, *F*, *W*, 1978 *F*, *NZ*, 1979 *S*, *I*
Cowman, A R (Loughborough Colls, Coventry) 1971 *S* (2[1C]), *P*, 1973 *W*, *I*
Cox, N S (Sunderland) 1901 *S*
Cranmer, P (Richmond, Moseley) 1934 *W*, *I*, *S*, 1935 *W*, *I*, *S*, 1936 *NZ*, *W*, *I*, *S*, 1937 *W*, *I*, *S*, 1938 *W*, *I*, *S*
Creed, R N (Coventry) 1971 *P*
Cridlan, A G (Blackheath) 1935 *W*, *I*, *S*
Crompton, C A (Blackheath) 1871 *S*
Crosse, C W (Oxford U) 1874 *S*, 1875 *I*
Cumberlege, B S (Blackheath) 1920 *W*, *I*, *S*, 1921 *W*, *I*, *S*, *F*, 1922 *W*
Cumming, D C (Blackheath) 1925 *S*, *F*
Cunliffe, F L (RMA) 1874 *S*
Currey, F I (Marlborough N) 1872 *S*
Currie, J D (Oxford U, Harlequins, Bristol) 1956 *W*, *I*, *S*, *F*, 1957 *W*, *I*, *F*, *S*, 1958 *W*, *A*, *I*, *F*, *S*, 1959 *W*, *I*, *F*, *S*, 1960 *W*, *I*, *F*, *S*, 1961 *SA*, 1962 *W*, *I*, *F*
Cusani, D A (Orrell) 1987 *I*
Cusworth, L (Leicester) 1979 *NZ*, 1982 *F*, *W*, 1983 *F*, *W*, *NZ*, 1984 *S*, *I*, *F*, *W*, 1988 *F*, *W*

D'Aguilar, F B G (Royal Engineers) 1872 *S*
Dalton, T J (Coventry) 1969 *S* (R)
Danby, T (Harlequins) 1949 *W*
Daniell, J (Richmond) 1899 *W*, 1900 *I*, *S*, 1902 *I*, *S*, 1904 *I*, *S*
Darby, A J L (Birkenhead Park) 1899 *I*
Davenport, A (Ravenscourt Park) 1871 *S*
Davey, J (Redruth) 1908 *S*, 1909 *W*
Davey, R F (Teignmouth) 1931 *W*
Davidson, Jas (Aspatria) 1897 *S*, 1898 *S*, *W*, 1899 *I*, *S*
Davidson, Jos (Aspatria) 1899 *W*, *S*
Davies, G H (Cambridge U, Coventry, Wasps) 1981 *S*, *I*, *F*, *Arg* 1,2, 1982 *A*, *S*, *I*, 1983 *F*, *W*, *S*, 1984 *S*, *SA* 1,2, 1985 *R* (R), *NZ* 1,2, 1986 *W*, *S*, *I*, *F*
Davies, P H (Sale) 1927 *I*
Davies, V G (Harlequins) 1922 *W*, 1925 *NZ*
Davies, W J A (United Services, RN) 1913 *SA*, *W*, *F*, *I*, *S*, 1914 *I*, *S*, *F*,1920 *F*, *I*, *S*, 1921 *W*, *I*, *S*, *F*, 1922 *I*, *F*, *S*, 1923 *W*, *I*, *S*, *F*
Davies, W P C (Harlequins) 1953 *S*, 1954 *NZ*, *I*, 1955 *W*, *I*, *F*, *S*, 1956 *W*, 1957 *F*, *S*, 1958 *W*
Davis, A M (Harlequins) 1963 *W*, *I*, *S*, *NZ* 1,2, 1964 *NZ*, *W*, *I*, *F*, *S*, 1966 *W*, 1967 *A*, 1969 *SA*, 1970 *I*, *W*, *S*
Dawe, R G R (Bath) 1987 *I*, *F*, *W*, [*US*]
Dawson, E F (RIEC) 1878 *I*
Day, H L V (Leicester) 1920 *W*, 1922 *W*, *F*, 1926 *S*
Dean, G J (Harlequins) 1931 *I*
Dee, J M (Hartlepool R) 1962 *S*, 1963 *NZ* 1
Devitt, Sir T G (Blackheath) 1926 *I*, *F*, 1928 *A*, *W*
Dewhurst, J H (Richmond) 1887 *W*, *I*, *S*, 1890 *W*
De Glanville, P R (Bath) 1992 *SA*(R), 1993 *W*(R), *NZ*, 1994 *S*, *I*, *F*, *W*, *SA* 1,2, *C*(R)
De Winton, R F C (Marlborough N) 1893 *W*
Dibble, R (Bridgwater A) 1906 *S*, *F*, *SA*, 1908 *F*, *W*, *I*, *S*, 1909 *A*, *W*, *F*, *I*, *S*, 1910 *S*, 1911 *W*, *F*, *S*, 1912 *W*, *I*, *S*
Dicks, J (Northampton) 1934 *W*, *I*, *S*, 1935 *W*, *I*, *S*, 1936 *S*, 1937 *I*
Dillon, E W (Blackheath) 1904 *W*, *I*, *S*, 1905 *W*
Dingle, A J (Hartlepool R) 1913 *I*, 1914 *S*, *F*
Dixon, P J (Harlequins, Gosforth) 1971 *P*, 1972 *W*, *I*, *F*, *S*, 1973 *I*, *F*, *S*, 1974 *S*, *I*, *F*, *W*, 1975 *I*, 1976 *F*, 1977 *S*, *I*, *F*, *W*, 1978 *F*, *S*, *I*, *NZ*

Dobbs, G E B (Devonport A) 1906 *W, I*
Doble, S A (Moseley) 1972 *SA*, 1973 *NZ* 1, *W*
Dobson, D D (Newton Abbot) 1902 *W, I, S*, 1903 *W, I, S*
Dobson, T H (Bradford) 1895 *S*
Dodge, P W (Leicester) 1978 *W, S, I, NZ*, 1979 *S, I, F, W*, 1980 *W, S*, 1981 *W, S, I, F, Arg* 1,2, 1982 *A, S, F, W*, 1983 *F, W, S, I, NZ*, 1985 *R, F, S, I, W, NZ* 1,2
Donnelly, M P (Oxford U) 1947 *I*
Dooley, W A (Preston Grasshoppers, Fylde) 1985 *R, F, S, I, W, NZ* 2 (R), 1986 *W, S, I, F*, 1987 *F, W*, [*A, US, W*], 1988 *F, W, S, I* 1,2, *A* 1,2, *Fj, A*, 1989 *S, I, F, W, R, Fj*, 1990 *I, F, W, S, Arg* 1,2,3, 1991 *W, S, I, F*, [*NZ, US, F, S, A*], 1992 *S, I, F, W, C, SA*, 1993 *W, S, I*
Dovey, B A (Rosslyn Park) 1963 *W, I*
Down, P J (Bristol) 1909 *A*
Dowson, A O (Moseley) 1899 *S*
Drake-Lee, N J (Cambridge U, Leicester) 1963 *W, I, F, S*, 1964 *NZ, W, I*, 1965 *W*
Duckett, H (Bradford) 1893 *I, S*
Duckham, D J (Coventry) 1969 *I, F, S, W, SA*, 1970 *I, W, S, F*, 1971 *W, I, F, S* (2[1C]), *P*, 1972 *W, I, F, S*, 1973 *NZ* 1, *W, I, F, S, NZ* 2, *A*, 1974 *S, I, F, W*, 1975 *I, F, W*, 1976 *A, W, S*
Dudgeon, H W (Richmond) 1897 *S*, 1898 *I, S, W*, 1899 *W, I, S*
Dugdale, J M (Ravenscourt Park) 1871 *S*
Dun, A F (Wasps) 1984 *W*
Duncan, R F H (Guy's Hospital) 1922 *I, F, S*
Dunkley, P E (Harlequins) 1931 *I, S*, 1936 *NZ, W, I, S*
Duthie, J (W Hartlepool) 1903 *W*
Dyson, J W (Huddersfield) 1890 *S*, 1892 *S*, 1893 *I, S*

Ebdon, P J (Wellington) 1897 *W, I*
Eddison, J H (Headingley) 1912 *W, I, S, F*
Edgar, C S (Birkenhead Park) 1901 *S*
Edwards, R (Newport) 1921 *W, I, S, F*, 1922 *W, F*, 1923 *W*, 1924 *W, F, S*, 1925 *NZ*
Egerton, D W (Bath) 1988 *I* 2, *A* 1, *Fj* (R), *A*, 1989 *Fj*, 1990 *I, Arg* 2 (R)
Elliot, C H (Sunderland) 1886 *W*
Elliot, E W (Sunderland) 1901 *W, I, S*, 1904 *W*
Elliot, W (United Services, RN) 1932 *I, S*, 1933 *W, I, S*, 1934 *W, I*
Elliott, A E (St Thomas's Hospital) 1894 *S*
Ellis, J (Wakefield) 1939 *S*
Ellis, S S (Queen's House) 1880 *I*
Emmott, C (Bradford) 1892 *W*
Enthoven, H J (Richmond) 1878 *I*
Estcourt, N S D (Blackheath) 1955 *S*
Evans, B J (Leicester) 1988 *A* 2, *Fj*
Evans, E (Sale) 1948 *A*, 1950 *W*, 1951 *I, F, S*, 1952 *SA, W, S, I, F*, 1953 *I, F, S*, 1954 *W, NZ, I, F*, 1956 *W, I, S, F*, 1957 *W, I, F, S*, 1958 *W, A, I, F, S*
Evans, G W (Coventry) 1972 *S*, 1973 *W* (R), *F, S, NZ* 2, 1974 *S, I, F, W*
Evans, N L (RNEC) 1932 *W, I, S*, 1933 *W, I*
Evanson, A M (Richmond) 1883 *W, I, S*, 1884 *S*
Evanson, W A D (Richmond) 1875 *S*, 1877 *S*, 1878 *S*, 1879 *S, I*
Evershed, F (Blackheath) 1889 *M*, 1890 *W, S, I*, 1892 *W, I, S*, 1893 *W, I, S*
Eyres, W C T (Richmond) 1927 *I*

Fagan, A R St L (Richmond) 1887 *I*
Fairbrother, K E (Coventry) 1969 *I, F, S, W, SA*, 1970 *I, W, S, F*, 1971 *W, I, F*
Faithfull, C K T (Harlequins) 1924 *I*, 1926 *F, S*
Fallas, H (Wakefield T) 1884 *I*
Fegan, J H C (Blackheath) 1895 *W, I, S*
Fernandes, C W L (Leeds) 1881 *I, W, S*
Fidler, J H (Gloucester) 1981 *Arg* 1,2, 1984 *SA* 1,2
Field, E (Middlesex W) 1893 *W, I*
Fielding, K J (Moseley, Loughborough Colls) 1969 *I, F, S, SA*, 1970 *I, F*, 1972 *W, I, F, S*
Finch, R T (Cambridge U) 1880 *S*
Finlan, J F (Moseley) 1967 *I, F, S, W, NZ*, 1968 *W, I*, 1969 *I, F, S, W*, 1970 *F*, 1973 *NZ* 1
Finlinson, H W (Blackheath) 1895 *W, I, S*
Finney, S (RIE Coll) 1872 *S*, 1873 *S*
Firth, F (Halifax) 1894 *W, I, S*
Fletcher, N C (OMTs) 1901 *W, I, S*, 1903 *S*
Fletcher, T (Seaton) 1897 *W*
Fletcher, W R B (Marlborough N) 1873 *S*, 1875 *S*
Fookes, E F (Sowerby Bridge) 1896 *W, I, S*, 1897 *W, I, S*, 1898 *I, W*, 1899 *I, S*
Ford, P J (Gloucester) 1964 *W, I, F, S*
Forrest, J W (United Services, RN) 1930 *W, I, F, S*, 1931 *W, I, S, F*, 1934 *I, S*
Forrest, R (Wellington) 1899 *W*, 1900 *S*, 1902 *I, S*, 1903 *I, S*
Foulds, R T (Waterloo) 1929 *W, I*
Fowler, F D (Manchester) 1878 *S*, 1879 *S*
Fowler, H (Oxford U) 1878 *S*, 1881 *W, S*
Fowler, R H (Leeds) 1877 *I*
Fox, F H (Wellington) 1890 *W, S*
Francis, T E S (Cambridge U) 1926 *W, I, F, S*
Frankcom, G P (Cambridge U, Bedford) 1965 *W, I, F, S*
Fraser, E C (Blackheath) 1875 *I*
Fraser, G (Richmond) 1902 *W, I, S*, 1903 *W, I*
Freakes, H D (Oxford U) 1938 *W*, 1939 *W, I*
Freeman, H (Marlborough N) 1872 *S*, 1873 *S*, 1874 *S*
French, R J (St Helens) 1961 *W, I, F, S*
Fry, H A (Liverpool) 1934 *W, I, S*
Fry, T W (Queen's House) 1880 *I, S*, 1881 *W*
Fuller, H G (Bath) 1882 *I, S*, 1883 *W, I, S*, 1884 W

Gadney, B C (Leicester, Headingley) 1932 *I, S*, 1933 *I, S*, 1934 *W, I, S*, 1935 *S*, 1936 *NZ, W, I, S*, 1937 *S*, 1938 *W*
Gamlin, H T (Blackheath) 1899 *W, S*, 1900 *W, I, S*, 1901 *S*, 1902 *W, I, S*, 1903 *W, I, S*, 1904 *W, I, S*
Gardner, E R (Devonport Services) 1921 *W, I, S*, 1922 *W, I, F*, 1923 *W, I, S, F*
Gardner, H P (Richmond) 1878 *I*
Garnett, H W T (Bradford) 1877 *S*
Gavins, M N (Leicester) 1961 *W*
Gay, D J (Bath) 1968 *W, I, F, S*
Gent, D R (Gloucester) 1905 *NZ*, 1906 *W, I*, 1910 *W, I*
Genth, J S M (Manchester) 1874 *S*, 1875 *S*
George, J T (Falmouth) 1947 *S, F*, 1949 *I*
Gerrard, R A (Bath) 1932 *SA, W, I, S*, 1933 *W, I, S*, 1934 *W, I, S*, 1936 *NZ, W, I, S*
Gibbs, G A (Bristol) 1947 *F*, 1948 *I*
Gibbs, J C (Harlequins) 1925 *NZ, W*, 1926 *F*, 1927 *W, I, S, F*
Gibbs, N (Harlequins) 1954 *S, F*
Giblin, L F (Blackheath) 1896 *W, I*, 1897 *S*
Gibson, A S (Manchester) 1871 *S*
Gibson, C O P (Northern) 1901 *W*
Gibson, G R (Northern) 1899 *W*, 1901 *S*
Gibson, T A (Northern) 1905 *W, S*
Gilbert, F G (Devonport Services) 1923 *W, I*
Gilbert, R (Devonport A) 1908 *W, I, S*
Giles, J L (Coventry) 1935 *W, I*, 1937 *W, I*, 1938 *I, S*
Gittings, W J (Coventry) 1967 *NZ*
Glover, P B (Bath) 1967 *A*, 1971 *F, P*
Godfray, R E (Richmond) 1905 *NZ*
Godwin, H O (Coventry) 1959 *F, S*, 1963 *S, NZ* 1,2, *A*, 1964 *NZ, I, F, S*, 1967 *NZ*
Gordon-Smith, G W (Blackheath) 1900 *W, I, S*
Gotley, A L H (Oxford U) 1910 *F, S*, 1911 *W, F, I, S*
Graham, D (Aspatria) 1901 *W*
Graham, H J (Wimbledon H) 1875 *I, S*, 1876 *I, S*
Graham, J D G (Wimbledon H) 1876 *I*
Gray, A (Otley) 1947 *W, I, S*
Green, J (Skipton) 1905 *I*, 1906 *S, F, SA*, 1907 *F, W, I, S*
Green, J F (West Kent) 1871 *S*
Greenwell, J H (Rockcliff) 1893 *W, I*
Greenwood, J E (Cambridge U, Leicester) 1912 *F*, 1913 *SA, W, F, I, S*, 1914 *W, S, F*, 1920 *W, F, I, S*
Greenwood, J R H (Waterloo) 1966 *I, F, S*, 1967 *A*, 1969 *I*
Greg, W (Manchester) 1876 *I, S*
Gregory, G G (Bristol) 1931 *I, S, F*, 1932 *SA, W, I, S*, 1933 *W, I, S*, 1934 *W, I, S*
Gregory, J A (Blackheath) 1949 *W*
Grylls, W M (Redruth) 1905 *I*
Guest, R H (Waterloo) 1939 *W, I, S*, 1947 *W, I, S, F*, 1948 *A, W, I, S*, 1949 *F, S*
Guillemard, A G (West Kent) 1871 *S*, 1872 *S*
Gummer, C H A (Plymouth A) 1929 *F*
Gunner, C R (Marlborough N) 1876 *I*
Gurdon, C (Richmond) 1880 *I, S*, 1881 *I, W, S*, 1882 *I, S*, 1883 *S*, 1884 *W, S*, 1885 *I*, 1886 *W, I, S*

Gurdon, E T (Richmond) 1878 *S*, 1879 *I*, 1880 *S*, 1881 *I*, *W*, *S*, 1882 *S*, 1883 *W*, *I*, *S*, 1884 *W*, *I*, *S*, 1885 *W*, *I*, 1886 *S*
Guscott, J C (Bath) 1989 *R*, *Fj*, 1990 *I*, *F*, *W*, *S*, *Arg* 3, 1991 *W*, *S*, *I*, *F*, *Fj*, *A*, [*NZ*, *It*, *F*, *S*, *A*], 1992 *S*, *I*, *F*, *W*, *C*, *SA*, 1993 *F*, *W*, *S*, *I*, 1994 *R*, *C*, 1995 *I*, *F*, *W*, *S*

Haigh, L (Manchester) 1910 *W*, *I*, *S*, 1911 *W*, *F*, *I*, *S*
Hale, P M (Moseley) 1969 *SA*, 1970 *I*, *W*
Hall, C (Gloucester) 1901 *I*, *S*
Hall, J (N Durham) 1894 *W*, *I*, *S*
Hall, J P (Bath) 1984 *S* (R), *I*, *F*, *SA* 1,2, *A*, 1985 *R*, *F*, *S*, *I*, *W*, *NZ* 1,2, 1986 *W*, *S*, 1987 *I*, *F*, *W*, *S*, 1990 *Arg* 3, 1994 *S*
Hall, N M (Richmond) 1947 *W*, *I*, *S*, *F*, 1949 *W*, *I*, 1952 *SA*, *W*, *S*, *I*, *F*, 1953 *W*, *I*, *F*, *S*, 1955 *W*, *I*
Halliday, S J (Bath, Harlequins) 1986 *W*, *S*, 1987 *S*, 1988 *S*, *I* 1,2, *A* 1, *A*, 1989 *S*, *I*, *F*, *W*, *R*, *Fj* (R), 1990 *W*, *S*, 1991 [*US*, *S*, *A*], 1992 *S*, *I*, *F*, *W*
Hamersley, A St G (Marlborough N) 1871 *S*, 1872 *S*, 1873 *S*, 1874 *S*
Hamilton-Hill, E A (Harlequins) 1936 *NZ*, *W*, *I*
Hamilton-Wickes, R H (Cambridge U) 1924 *I*, 1925 *NZ*, *W*, *I*, *S*, *F*, 1926 *W*, *I*, *S*, 1927 *W*
Hammett, E D G (Newport) 1920 *W*, *F*, *S*, 1921 *W*, *I*, *S*, *F*, 1922 *W*
Hammond, C E L (Harlequins) 1905 *S*, *NZ*, 1906 *W*, *I*, *S*, *F*, 1908 *W*, *I*
Hancock, A W (Northampton) 1965 *F*, *S*, 1966 *F*
Hancock, G E (Birkenhead Park) 1939 *W*, *I*, *S*
Hancock, J H (Newport) 1955 *W*, *I*
Hancock, P F (Blackheath) 1886 *W*, *I*, 1890 *W*
Hancock, P S (Richmond) 1904 *W*, *I*, *S*
Handford, F G (Manchester) 1909 *W*, *F*, *I*, *S*
Hands, R H M (Blackheath) 1910 *F*, *S*
Hanley, J (Plymouth A) 1927 *W*, *S*, *F*, 1928 *W*, *I*, *F*, *S*
Hannaford, R C (Bristol) 1971 *W*, *I*, *F*
Hanvey, R J (Aspatria) 1926 *W*, *I*, *F*, *S*
Harding, E H (Devonport Services) 1931 *I*
Harding, R M (Bristol) 1985 *R*, *F*, *S*, 1987 S, [*A*, *J*, *W*], 1988 *I* 1(R),2, *A* 1,2, *Fj*
Harding, V S J (Saracens) 1961 *F*, *S*, 1962 *W*, *I*, *F*, *S*
Hardwick, P F (Percy Park) 1902 *I*, *S*, 1903 *W*, *I*, *S*, 1904 *W*, *I*, *S*
Hardy, E M P (Blackheath) 1951 *I*, *F*, *S*
Hare, W H (Nottingham, Leicester) 1974 *W*, 1978 *F*, *NZ*, 1979 *NZ*, 1980 *I*, *F*, *W*, *S*, 1981 *W*, *S*, *Arg* 1,2, 1982 *F*, *W*, 1983 *F*, *W*, *S*, *I*, *NZ*, 1984 *S*, *I*, *F*, *W*, *SA* 1,2
Harper, C H (Exeter) 1899 *W*
Harriman, A T (Harlequins) 1988 *A*
Harris, S W (Blackheath) 1920 *I*, *S*
Harris, T W (Northampton) 1929 *S*, 1932 *I*
Harrison, A C (Hartlepool R) 1931 *I*, *S*
Harrison, A L (United Services, RN) 1914 *I*, *F*
Harrison, G (Hull) 1877 *I*, *S*, 1879 *S*, *I*, 1880 *S*, 1885 *W*, *I*
Harrison, H C (United Services, RN) 1909 *S*, 1914 *I*, *S*, *F*
Harrison, M E (Wakefield) 1985 *NZ* 1,2, 1986 *S*, *I*, *F*, 1987 *I*, *F*, *W*, *S*, [*A*, *J*, *US*, *W*], 1988 *F*, *W*
Hartley, B C (Blackheath) 1901 *S*, 1902 *S*
Haslett, L W (Birkenhead Park) 1926 *I*, *F*
Hastings, G W D (Gloucester) 1955 *W*, *I*, *F*, *S*, 1957 *W*, *I*, *F*, *S*, 1958 *W*, *A*, *I*, *F*, *S*
Havelock, H (Hartlepool R) 1908 *F*, *W*, *I*
Hawcridge, J J (Bradford) 1885 *W*, *I*
Hayward, L W (Cheltenham) 1910 *I*
Hazell, D St G (Leicester) 1955 *W*, *I*, *F*, *S*
Hearn, R D (Bedford) 1966 *F*, *S*, 1967 *I*, *F*, *S*, *W*
Heath, A H (Oxford U) 1876 *S*
Heaton, J (Waterloo) 1935 *W*, *I*, *S*, 1939 *W*, *I*, *S*, 1947 *I*, *S*, *F*
Henderson, A P (Edinburgh Wands) 1947 *W*, *I*, *S*, *F*, 1948 *I*, *S*, *F*, 1949 *W*, *I*
Henderson, R S F (Blackheath) 1883 *W*, *S*, 1884 *W*, *S*, 1885 *W*
Heppell, W G (Devonport A) 1903 *I*
Herbert, A J (Wasps) 1958 *F*, *S*, 1959 *W*, *I*, *F*, *S*
Hesford, R (Bristol) 1981 *S* (R), 1982 *A*, *S*, *F* (R), 1983 *F* (R), 1985 *R*, *F*, *S*, *I*, *W*
Heslop, N J (Orrell) 1990 *Arg* 1,2,3, 1991 *W*, *S*, *I*, *F*, [*US*, *F*], 1992 *W*(R)
Hetherington, J G G (Northampton) 1958 *A*, *I*, 1959 *W*, *I*, *F*, *S*
Hewitt, E N (Coventry) 1951 *W*, *I*, *F*
Hewitt, W W (Queen's House) 1881 *I*, *W*, *S*, 1882 *I*
Hickson, J L (Bradford) 1887 *W*, *I*, *S*, 1890 *W*, *S*, *I*
Higgins, R (Liverpool) 1954 *W*, *NZ*, *I*, *S*, 1955 *W*, *I*, *F*, *S*, 1957 *W*, *I*, *F*, *S*, 1959 *W*
Hignell, A J (Cambridge U, Bristol) 1975 *A* 2, 1976 *A*, *W*, *S*, *I*, 1977 *S*, *I*, *F*, *W*, 1978 *W*, 1979 *S*, *I*, *F*, *W*
Hill, B A ((Blackheath) 1903 *I*, *S*, 1904 *W*, *I*, 1905 *W*, *NZ*, 1906 *SA*, 1907 *F*, *W*
Hill, R J (Bath) 1984 *SA* 1,2, 1985 *I* (R), *NZ* 2 (R), 1986 *F* (R), 1987 *I*, *F*, *W*, [*US*], 1989 *Fj*, 1990 *I*, *F*, *W*, *S*, *Arg* 1,2,3, 1991 *W*, *S*, *I*, *F*, *Fj*, *A*, [*NZ*, *It*, *US*, *F*, *S*, *A*]
Hillard, R J (Oxford U) 1925 *NZ*
Hiller, R (Harlequins) 1968 *W*, *I*, *F*, *S*, 1969 *I*, *F*, *S*, *W*, *SA*, 1970 *I*, *W*, *S*, 1971 *I*, *F*, *S* (2[1C]), *P*, 1972 *W*, *I*
Hind, A E (Leicester) 1905 *NZ*, 1906 *W*
Hind, G R (Blackheath) 1910 *S*, 1911 *I*
Hobbs, R F A (Blackheath) 1899 *S*, 1903 *W*
Hobbs, R G S (Richmond) 1932 *SA*, *W*, *I*, *S*
Hodges, H A (Nottingham) 1906 *W*, *I*
Hodgkinson, S D (Nottingham) 1989 *R*, *Fj*, 1990 *I*, *F*, *W*, *S*, *Arg* 1,2,3, 1991 *W*, *S*, *I*, *F*, [*US*]
Hodgson, J McD (Northern) 1932 *SA*, *W*, *I*, *S*, 1934 *W*, *I*, 1936 *I*
Hodgson, S A M (Durham City) 1960 *W*, *I*, *F*, *S*, 1961 *SA*, *W*, 1962 *W*, *I*, *F*, *S*, 1964 *W*
Hofmeyr, M B (Oxford U) 1950 *W*, *F*, *S*
Hogarth, T B (Hartlepool R) 1906 *F*
Holford, G (Gloucester) 1920 *W*, *F*
Holland, D (Devonport A) 1912 *W*, *I*, *S*
Holliday, T E (Aspatria) 1923 *S*, *F*, 1925 *I*, *S*, *F*, 1926 *F*, *S*
Holmes, C B (Manchester) 1947 *S*, 1948 *I*, *F*
Holmes, E (Manningham) 1890 *S*, *I*
Holmes, W A (Nuneaton) 1950 *W*, *I*, *F*, *S*, 1951 *W*, *I*, *F*, *S*, *1952 SA*, *S*, *I*, *F*, 1953 *W*, *I*, *F*, *S*
Holmes, W B (Cambridge U) 1949 *W*, *I*, *F*, *S*
Hook, W G (Gloucester) 1951 *S*, 1952 *SA*, *W*
Hooper, C A (Middlesex W) 1894 *W*, *I*, *S*
Hopley, F J V (Blackheath) 1907 *F*, *W*, 1908 *I*
Hordern, P C (Gloucester) 1931 *I*, *S*, *F*, 1934 *W*
Horley, C H (Swinton) 1885 *I*
Hornby, A N (Manchester) 1877 *I*, *S*, 1878 *S*, *I*, 1880 *I*, 1881 *I*, *S*, 1882 *I*, *S*
Horrocks-Taylor, J P (Cambridge U, Leicester, Middlesbrough) 1958 *W*, *A*, 1961 *S*, 1962 *S*, 1963 *NZ* 1,2, *A*, 1964 *NZ*, *W*
Horsfall, E L (Harlequins) 1949 *W*
Horton, A L (Blackheath) 1965 *W*, *I*, *F*, *S*, 1966 *F*, *S*, 1967 *NZ*
Horton, J P (Bath) 1978 *W*, *S*, *I*, *NZ*, 1980 *I*, *F*, *W*, *S*, 1981 *W*, 1983 *S*, *I*, 1984 *SA* 1,2
Horton, N E (Moseley, Toulouse) 1969 *I*, *F*, *S*, *W*, 1971 *I*, *F*, *S*, 1974 *S*, 1975 *W*, 1977 *S*, *I*, *F*, *W*, 1978 *F*, *W*, 1979 *S*, *I*, *F*, *W*, 1980 *I*
Hosen, R W (Bristol, Northampton) 1963 *NZ* 1,2, *A*, 1964 *F*, *S*, 1967 *A*, *I*, *F*, *S*, *W*
Hosking, G R d'A (Devonport Services) 1949 *W*, *I*, *F*, *S*, 1950 *W*
Houghton, S (Runcorn) 1892 *I*, 1896 *W*
Howard, P D (O Millhillians) 1930 *W*, *I*, *F*, *S*, 1931 *W*, *I*, *S*, *F*
Hubbard, G C (Blackheath) 1892 *W*, *I*
Hubbard, J C (Harlequins) 1930 *S*
Hudson, A (Gloucester) 1906 *W*, *I*, *F*, 1908 *F*, *W*, *I*, *S*, 1910 *F*
Hughes, G E (Barrow) 1896 *S*
Hull, P A (Bristol & RAF) 1994 *SA* 1,2, *R*, *C*
Hulme, F C (Birkenhead Park) 1903 *W*, *I*, 1905 *W*, *I*
Hunt, J T (Manchester) 1882 *I*, *S*, 1884 *W*
Hunt, R (Manchester) 1880 *I*, 1881 *W*, *S*, 1882 *I*
Hunt, W H (Manchester) 1876 *S*, 1877 *I*, *S*, 1878 *I*
Hunter, I (Northampton) 1992 *C*, 1993 *F*, *W*, 1994 *F*, *W*
Huntsman, R P (Headingley) 1985 *NZ* 1,2
Hurst, A C B (Wasps) 1962 *S*
Huskisson, T F (OMTs) 1937 *W*, *I*, *S*, 1938 *W*, *I*, 1939 *W*, *I*, *S*
Hutchinson, F (Headingley) 1909 *F*, *I*, *S*
Hutchinson, J E (Durham City) 1906 *I*
Hutchinson, W C (RIE Coll) 1876 *S* 1877 *I*
Hutchinson, W H H (Hull) 1875 *I*, 1876 *I*
Huth, H (Huddersfield) 1879 *S*
Hyde, J P (Northampton) 1950 *F*, *S*
Hynes, W B (United Services, RN) 1912 *F*

Ibbitson, E D (Headingley) 1909 *W, F, I, S*
Imrie, H M (Durham City) 1906 *NZ*, 1907 *I*
Inglis, R E (Blackheath) 1886 *W, I, S*
Irvin, S H (Devonport A) 1905 *W*
Isherwood, F W (Ravenscourt Park) 1872 *S*

Jackett, E J (Leicester, Falmouth) 1905 *NZ*, 1906 *W, I, S, F, SA*, 1907 *W, I, S*, 1909 *W, F, I, S*
Jackson, A H (Blackheath) 1878 *I*, 1880 *I*
Jackson, B S (Broughton Park) 1970 *S* (R), *F*
Jackson, P B (Coventry) 1956 *W, I, F*, 1957 *W, I, F, S*, 1958 *W, A, F, S*, 1959 *W, I, F, S*, 1961 *S*, 1963 *W, I, F, S*
Jackson, W J (Halifax) 1894 *S*
Jacob, F (Cambridge U) 1897 *W, I, S*, 1898 *I, S, W*, 1899 *W, I*
Jacob, H P (Blackheath) 1924 *W, I, F, S*, 1930 *F*
Jacob, P G (Blackheath) 1898 *I*
Jacobs, C R (Northampton) 1956 *W, I, S, F*, 1957 *W, I, F, S*, 1958 *W, A, I, F, S*, 1960 *W, I, F, S*, 1961 *SA, W, I, F, S*, 1963 *NZ* 1,2, *A*, 1964 *W, I, F, S*
Jago, R A (Devonport A) 1906 *W, I, SA*, 1907 *W, I*
Janion, J P A G (Bedford) 1971 *W, I, F, S* (2[1C]), *P*, 1972 *W, S, SA*, 1973 *A*, 1975 *A* 1,2
Jarman, J W (Bristol) 1900 *W*
Jeavons, N C (Moseley) 1981 *S, I, F, Arg* 1,2, 1982 *A, S, I, F, W*, 1983 *F, W, S, I*
Jeeps, R E G (Northampton) 1956 *W*, 1957 *W, I, F, S*, 1958 *W, A, I, F, S*, 1959 *I*, 1960 *W, I, F, S*, 1961 *SA, W, I, F, S*, 1962 *W, I, F, S*
Jeffery, G L (Blackheath) 1886 *W, I, S*, 1887 *W, I, S*
Jennins, C R (Waterloo) 1967 *A, I, F*
Jewitt, J (Hartlepool R) 1902 *W*
Johns, W A (Gloucester) 1909 *W, F, I, S*, 1910 *W, I, F*
Johnson, M O (Leicester) 1993 *F, NZ*, 1994 *S, I, F, W, R, C*, 1995 *I, F, W, S*
Johnston, W R (Bristol) 1910 *W, I, S*, 1912 *W, I, S, F*, 1913 *SA, W, F, I, S*, 1914 *W, I, S, F*
Jones, F P (N Brighton) 1893 *S*
Jones, H A (Barnstaple) 1950 *W, I, F*
Jorden, A M (Cambridge U, Blackheath, Bedford) 1970 *F*, 1973 *I, F, S*, 1974 *F*, 1975 *W, S*
Jowett, D (Heckmondwike) 1889 *M*, 1890 *S, I*, 1891 *W, I, S*
Judd, P E (Coventry) 1962 *W, I, F, S*, 1963 *S, NZ* 1,2, *A*, 1964 *NZ*, 1965 *I, F, S*, 1966 *W, I, F, S*, 1967 *A, I, F, S, W, NZ*

Kayll, H E (Sunderland) 1878 *S*
Keeling, J H (Guy's Hospital) 1948 *A, W*
Keen, B W (Newcastle U) 1968 *W, I, F, S*
Keeton, G H (Leicester) 1904 *W, I, S*
Kelly, G A (Bedford) 1947 *W, I, S*, 1948 *W*
Kelly, T S (London Devonians) 1906 *W, I, S, F, SA*, 1907 *F, W, I, S*, 1908 *F, I, S*
Kemble, A T (Liverpool) 1885 *W, I*, 1887 *I*
Kemp, D T (Blackheath) 1935 *W*
Kemp, T A (Richmond) 1937 *W, I*, 1939 *S*, 1948 *A, W*
Kendall, P D (Birkenhead Park) 1901 *S*, 1902 *W*, 1903 *S*
Kendall-Carpenter, J MacG K (Oxford U, Bath) 1949 *I, F, S*, 1950 *W, I, F, S*, 1951 *I, F, S*, 1952 *SA, W, S, I, F*, 1953 *W, I, F, S*, 1954 *W, NZ, I, F*
Kendrew, D A (Leicester) 1930 *W, I*, 1933 *I, S*, 1934 *S*, 1935 *W, I*, 1936 *NZ, W, I*
Kennedy, R D (Camborne S of M) 1949 *I, F, S*
Kent, C P (Rosslyn Park) 1977 *S, I, F, W*, 1978 *F* (R)
Kent, T (Salford) 1891 *W, I, S*, 1892 *W, I, S*
Kershaw, C A (United Services, RN) 1920 *W, F, I, S*, 1921 *W, I, S, F*, 1922 *W, I, F, S*, 1923 *W, I, S, F*
Kewley, E (Liverpool) 1874 *S*, 1875 *S*, 1876 *I, S*, 1877 *I, S*, 1878 *S*
Kewney, A L (Leicester) 1906 *W, I, S, F*, 1909 *A, W, F, I, S*, 1911 *W, F, I, S*, 1912 *I, S*, 1913 *SA*
Key, A (O Cranleighans) 1930 *I*, 1933 *W*
Keyworth, M (Swansea) 1976 *A, W, S, I*
Kilner, B (Wakefield T) 1880 *I*
Kindersley, R S (Exeter) 1883 *W*, 1884 *S*, 1885 *W*
King, I (Harrogate) 1954 *W, NZ, I*
King, J A (Headingley) 1911 *W, F, I, S*, 1912 *W, I, S*, 1913 *SA, W, F, I, S*
King, Q E M A (Army) 1921 *S*
Kingston, P (Gloucester) 1975 *A*, 1,2, 1979 *I, F, W*
Kitching, A E (Blackheath) 1913 *I*
Kittermaster, H J (Harlequins) 1925 *NZ, W, I*, 1926 *W, I, F, S*
Knight, F (Plymouth) 1909 *A*
Knight, P M (Bristol) 1972 *F, S, SA*
Knowles, E (Millom) 1896 *S*, 1897 *S*
Knowles, T C (Birkenhead Park) 1931 *S*
Krige, J A (Guy's Hospital) 1920 *W*

Labuschagne, N A (Harlequins, Guy's Hospital) 1953 *W*, 1955 *W, I, F, S*
Lagden, R O (Richmond) 1911 *S*
Laird, H C C (Harlequins) 1927 *W, I, S*, 1928 *A, W, I, F, S*, 1929 *W, I*
Lambert, D (Harlequins) 1907 *F*, 1908 *F, W, S*, 1911 *W, F, I*
Lampkowski, M S (Headingley) 1976 *A, W, S, I*
Lapage, W N (United Services, RN) 1908 *F, W, I, S*
Larter, P J (Northampton, RAF) 1967 *A, NZ*, 1968 *W, I, F, S*, 1969 *I, F, S, W, SA*, 1970 *I, W, F, S*, 1971 *W, I, F, S* (2[1C]), *P*, 1972 *SA*, 1973 *NZ* 1, *W*
Law, A F (Richmond) 1877 *S*
Law, D E (Birkenhead Park) 1927 *I*
Lawrence, Hon H A (Richmond) 1873 *S*, 1874 *S*, 1875 *I, S*
Lawrie, P W (Leicester) 1910 *S*, 1911 *S*
Lawson, R G (Workington) 1925 *I*
Lawson, T M (Workington) 1928 *A, W*
Leadbetter, M M (Broughton Park) 1970 *F*
Leadbetter, V H (Edinburgh Wands) 1954 *S, F*
Leake, W R M (Harlequins) 1891 *W, I, S*
Leather, G (Liverpool) 1907 *I*
Lee, F H (Marlborough N) 1876 *S*, 1877 *I*
Lee, H (Blackheath) 1907 *F*
Le Fleming, J (Blackheath) 1887 *W*
Leonard, J (Saracens, Harlequins) 1990 *Arg* 1,2,3, 1991 *W, S, I, F, Fj, A*, [*NZ, It, US, F, S, A*], 1992 *S, I, F, W, C, SA*, 1993 *F, W, S, I, NZ* 1994 *S, I, F, W, SA* 1,2, *R, C*, 1995 *I, F, W, S*
Leslie-Jones, F A (Richmond) 1895 *W, I*
Lewis, A O (Bath) 1952 *SA, W, S, I, F*, 1953 *W, I, F, S*, 1954 *F*
Leyland, R (Waterloo) 1935 *W, I, S*
Linnett, M S (Moseley) 1989 *Fj*
Livesay, R O'H (Blackheath) 1898 *W*, 1899 *W*
Lloyd, R H (Harlequins) 1967 *NZ*, 1968 *W, I, F, S*
Locke, H M (Birkenhead Park) 1923 *S, F*, 1924 *W, F, S*, 1925 *W, I, S, F*, 1927 *W, I, S*
Lockwood, R E (Heckmondwike) 1887 *W, I, S*, 1889 *M*, 1891 *W, I, S*, 1892 *W, I, S*, 1893 *W, I*, 1894 *W, I*
Login, S H M (RN Coll) 1876 *I*
Lohden, F C (Blackheath) 1893 *W*
Longland, R J (Northampton) 1932 *S*, 1933 *W, S*, 1934 *W, I, S*, 1935 *W, I, S*, 1936 *NZ, W, I, S*, 1937 *W, I, S*, 1938 *W, I, S*
Lowe, C N (Cambridge U, Blackheath) 1913 *SA, W, F, I, S*, 1914 *W, I, S, F*, 1920 *W, F, I, S*, 1921 *W, I, S, F*, 1922 *W, I, F, S*, 1923 *W, I, S, F*
Lowrie, F (Wakefield T) 1889 *M*, 1890 *W*
Lowry, W M (Birkenhead Park) 1920 *F*
Lozowski, R A P (Wasps) 1984 *A*
Luddington, W G E (Devonport Services) 1923 *W, I, S, F*, 1924 *W, I, F, S*, 1925 *W, I, S, F*, 1926 *W*
Luscombe, F (Gipsies) 1872 *S*, 1873 *S*, 1875 *I, S*, 1876 *I, S*
Luscombe, J H (Gipsies) 1871 *S*
Luxmoore, A F C C (Richmond) 1900 *S*, 1901 *W*
Luya, H F (Waterloo, Headingley) 1948 *W, I, S, F*, 1949 *W*
Lyon, A (Liverpool) 1871 *S*
Lyon, G H d'O (United Services, RN) 1908 *S*, 1909 *A*

McCanlis, M A (Gloucester) 1931 *W, I*
McFadyean, C W (Moseley) 1966 *I, F, S*, 1967 *A, I, F, S, W, NZ*, 1968 *W, I*
MacIlwaine, A H (United Services, Hull & E Riding) 1912 *W, I, S, F*, 1920 *I*
Mackie, O G (Wakefield T, Cambridge U) 1897 *S*, 1898 *I*
Mackinlay, J E H (St George's Hospital) 1872 *S*, 1873 *S*, 1875 *I*
MacLaren, W (Manchester) 1871 *S*
MacLennan, R R F (OMTs) 1925 *I, S, F*
McLeod, N F (RIE Coll) 1879 *S, I*
Madge, R J P (Exeter) 1948 *A, W, I, S*
Malir, F W S (Otley) 1930 *W, I, S*
Mangles, R H (Richmond) 1897 *W, I*

Manley, D C (Exeter) 1963 *W, I, F, S*
Mann, W E (United Services, Army) 1911 *W, F, I*
Mantell, N D (Rosslyn Park) 1975 *A* 1
Markendale, E T (Manchester R) 1880 *I*
Marques, R W D (Cambridge U, Harlequins) 1956 *W, I, S, F,* 1957 *W, I, F, S,* 1958 *W, A, I, F, S,* 1959 *W, I, F, S,* 1960 *W, I, F, S,* 1961 *SA, W*
Marquis, J C (Birkenhead Park) 1900 *I, S*
Marriott, C J B (Blackheath) 1884 *W, I, S,* 1886 *W, I, S,* 1887 *I*
Marriott, E E (Manchester) 1876 *I*
Marriott, V R (Harlequins) 1963 *NZ* 1,2, *A,* 1964 *NZ*
Marsden, G H (Morley) 1900 *W, I, S*
Marsh, H (RIE Coll) 1873 *S*
Marsh, J (Swinton) 1892 *I*
Marshall, H (Blackheath) 1893 *W*
Marshall, M W (Blackheath) 1873 *S,* 1874 *S,* 1875 *I, S,* 1876 *I, S,* 1877 *I, S,* 1878 *S, I*
Marshall, R M (Oxford U) 1938 *I, S,* 1939 *W, I, S*
Martin, C R (Bath) 1985 *F, S, I, W*
Martin, N O (Harlequins) 1972 *F* (R)
Martindale, S A (Kendal) 1929 *F*
Massey, E J (Leicester) 1925 *W, I, S*
Mathias, J L (Bristol) 1905 *W, I, S, NZ*
Matters, J C (RNE Coll) 1899 *S*
Matthews, J R C (Harlequins) 1949 *F, S,* 1950 *I, F, S,* 1952 *SA, W, S, I, F*
Maud, P (Blackheath) 1893 *W, I*
Maxwell, A W (New Brighton, Headingley) 1975 *A* 1, 1976 *A, W, S, I, F,* 1978 *F*
Maxwell-Hyslop, J E (Oxford U) 1922 *I, F, S*
Maynard, A F (Cambridge U) 1914 *W, I, S*
Meikle, G W C (Waterloo) 1934 *W, I, S*
Meikle, S S C (Waterloo) 1929 *S*
Mellish, F W (Blackheath) 1920 *W, F, I, S,* 1921 *W, I*
Melville, N D (Wasps) 1984 *A,* 1985 *I, W, NZ* 1,2, 1986 *W, S, I, F,* 1988 *F, W, S, I* 1
Merriam, L P B (Blackheath) 1920 *W, F*
Michell, A T (Oxford U) 1875 *I, S,* 1876 *I*
Middleton, B B (Birkenhead Park) 1882 *I,* 1883 *I*
Middleton, J A (Richmond) 1922 *S*
Miles, J H (Leicester) 1903 *W*
Millett, H (Richmond) 1920 *F*
Mills, F W (Marlborough N) 1872 *S,* 1873 *S*
Mills, S G F (Gloucester) 1981 *Arg* 1,2, 1983 *W,* 1984 *SA* 1, *A*
Mills, W A (Devonport A) 1906 *W, I, S, F, SA,* 1907 *F, W, I, S,* 1908 *F, W*
Milman, D L K (Bedford) 1937 *W,* 1938 *W, I, S*
Milton, C H (Camborne S of M) 1906 *I*
Milton, J G (Camborne S of M) 1904 *W, I, S,* 1905 *S,* 1907 *I*
Milton, W H (Marlborough N) 1874 *S,* 1875 *I*
Mitchell, F (Blackheath) 1895 *W, I, S,* 1896 *W, I, S*
Mitchell, W G (Richmond) 1890 *W, S, I,* 1891 *W, I, S,* 1893 *S*
Mobbs, E R (Northampton) 1909 *A, W, F, I, S,* 1910 *I, F*
Moberly, W O (Ravenscourt Park) 1872 *S*
Moore, B C (Nottingham, Harlequins) 1987 *S,* [*A, J, W*], 1988 *F, W, S, I* 1,2, *A* 1,2, *Fj, A,* 1989 *S, I, F, W, R, Fj,* 1990 *I, F, W, S, Arg* 1,2, 1991 *W, S, I, F, Fj, A,* [*NZ, It, F, S, A*], 1992 *S, I, F, W, SA,* 1993 *F, W, S, I, NZ,* 1994 *S, I, F, W, SA* 1,2, *R, C,* 1995 *I, F, W, S*
Moore, E J (Blackheath) 1883 *I, S*
Moore, N J N H (Bristol) 1904 *W, I, S*
Moore, P B C (Blackheath) 1951 *W*
Moore, W K T (Leicester) 1947 *W, I,* 1949 *F, S,* 1950 *I, F, S*
Mordell, R J (Rosslyn Park) 1978 *W*
Morfitt, S (W Hartlepool) 1894 *W, I, S,* 1896 *W, I, S*
Morgan, J R (Hawick) 1920 *W*
Morgan, W G D (Medicals, Newcastle) 1960 *W, I, F, S,* 1961 *SA, W, I, F, S*
Morley, A J (Bristol) 1972 *SA,* 1973 *NZ* 1, *W, I,* 1975 *S, A* 1,2
Morris, A D W (United Services, RN) 1909 *A, W, F*
Morris, C D (Liverpool St Helens, Orrell) 1988 *A,* 1989 *S, I, F, W,* 1992 *S, I, F, W, C, SA,* 1993 *F, W, S, I,* 1994 *F, W, SA* 1,2, *R,* 1995 *S*(t)
Morrison, P H (Cambridge U) 1890 *W, S, I,* 1891 *I*
Morse, S (Marlborough N) 1873 *S,* 1874 *S,* 1875 *S*
Mortimer, W (Marlborough N) 1899 *W*
Morton, H J S (Blackheath) 1909 *I, S,* 1910 *W, I*
Moss, F (Broughton) 1885 *W, I,* 1886 *W*
Mullins, A R (Harlequins) 1989 *Fj*
Mycock, J (Sale) 1947 *W, I, S, F,* 1948 *A*
Myers, E (Bradford) 1920 *I, S,* 1921 *W, I,* 1922 *W, I, F, S,* 1923 *W, I, S, F,* 1924 *W, I, F, S,* 1925 *S, F*
Myers, H (Keighley) 1898 *I*

Nanson, W M B (Carlisle) 1907 *F, W*
Nash, E H (Richmond) 1875 *I*
Neale, B A (Rosslyn Park) 1951 *I, F, S*
Neale, M E (Blackheath) 1912 *F*
Neame, S (O Cheltonians) 1879 *S, I,* 1880 *I, S*
Neary, A (Broughton Park) 1971 *W, I, F, S* (2[1C]), *P,* 1972 *W, I, F, S, SA,* 1973 *NZ* 1, *W, I, F, S, NZ* 2, *A,* 1974 *S, I, F, W,* 1975 *I, F, W, S, A* 1, 1976 *A, W, S, I, F,* 1977 *I,* 1978 *F* (R), 1979 *S, I, F, W, NZ,* 1980 *I, F, W, S*
Nelmes, B G (Cardiff) 1975 *A* 1,2, 1978 *W, S, I, NZ*
Newbold, C J (Blackheath) 1904 *W, I, S,* 1905 *W, I, S*
Newman, S C (Oxford U) 1947 *F,* 1948 *A, W*
Newton, A W (Blackheath) 1907 *S*
Newton, P A (Blackheath) 1882 *S*
Newton-Thompson, J O (Oxford U) 1947 *S, F*
Nichol, W (Brighouse R) 1892 *W, S*
Nicholas, P L (Exeter) 1902 *W*
Nicholson, B E (Harlequins) 1938 *W, I*
Nicholson, E S (Leicester) 1935 *W, I, S,* 1936 *NZ, W*
Nicholson, E T (Birkenhead Park) 1900 *W, I*
Nicholson, T (Rockcliff) 1893 *I*
Ninnes, B F (Coventry) 1971 *W*
Norman, D J (Leicester) 1932 *SA, W*
North, E H G (Blackheath) 1891 *W, I, S*
Northmore, S (Millom) 1897 *I*
Novak, M J (Harlequins) 1970 *W, S, F*
Novis, A L (Blackheath) 1929 *S, F,* 1930 *W, I, F,* 1933 *I, S*

Oakeley, F E (United Services, RN) 1913 *S,* 1914 *I, S, F*
Oakes, R F (Hartlepool R) 1897 *W, I, S,* 1898 *I, S, W,* 1899 *W, S*
Oakley, L F L (Bedford) 1951 *W*
Obolensky, A (Oxford U) 1936 *NZ, W, I, S*
Ojomoh, S O (Bath) 1994 *I, F, SA* 1(R),2, *R,* 1995 *S*(R)
Old, A G B (Middlesbrough, Leicester, Sheffield) 1972 *W, I, F, S, SA,* 1973 *NZ* 2, *A,* 1974 *S, I, F, W,* 1975 *I, A* 2, 1976 *S, I,* 1978 *F*
Oldham, W L (Coventry) 1908 *S,* 1909 *A*
Olver, C J (Northampton) 1990 *Arg* 3, 1991 [*US*], 1992 *C*
O'Neill, A (Teignmouth, Torquay A) 1901 *W, I, S*
Openshaw, W E (Manchester) 1879 *I*
Orwin, J (Gloucester, RAF, Bedford) 1985 *R, F, S, I, W, NZ* 1,2, 1988 *F, W, S, I* 1,2, *A* 1,2
Osborne, R R (Manchester) 1871 *S*
Osborne, S H (Oxford U) 1905 *S*
Oti, C (Cambridge U, Nottingham, Wasps) 1988 *S, I* 1, 1989 *S, I, F, W, R,* 1990 *Arg* 1,2, 1991 *Fj, A,* [*NZ, It,*]
Oughtred, B (Hartlepool R) 1901 *S,* 1902 *W, I, S,* 1903 *W, I*
Owen, J E (Coventry) 1963 *W, I, F, S, A,* 1964 *NZ,* 1965 *W, I, F, S,* 1966 *I, F, S,* 1967 *NZ*
Owen-Smith, H G O (St Mary's Hospital) 1934 *W, I, S,* 1936 *NZ, W, I, S,* 1937 *W, I, S*

Page, J J (Bedford, Northampton) 1971 *W, I, F, S,* 1975 *S*
Pallant, J N (Notts) 1967 *I, F, S*
Palmer, A C (London Hospital) 1909 *I, S*
Palmer, F H (Richmond) 1905 *W*
Palmer, G V (Richmond) 1928 *I, F, S*
Palmer, J A (Bath) 1984 *SA* 1,2, 1986 *I* (R)
Pargetter, T A (Coventry) 1962 *S,* 1963 *F, NZ* 1
Parker, G W (Gloucester) 1938 *I, S*
Parker, Hon S (Liverpool) 1874 *S,* 1875 *S*
Parsons, E I (RAF) 1939 *S*
Parsons, M J (Northampton) 1968 *W, I, F, S*
Patterson, W M (Sale) 1961 *SA, S*
Pattisson, R M (Blackheath) 1883 *I, S*
Paul, J E (RIE Coll) 1875 *S*
Payne, A T (Bristol) 1935 *I, S*
Payne, C M (Harlequins) 1964 *I, F, S,* 1965 *I, F, S,* 1966 *W, I, F, S*
Payne, J H (Broughton) 1882 *S,* 1883 *W, I, S,* 1884 *I,* 1885 *W, I*
Pearce, G S (Northampton) 1979 *S, I, F, W,* 1981 *Arg*

1,2, 1982 *A, S*, 1983 *F, W, S, I, NZ*, 1984 *S, SA* 2, A, 1985 *R, F, S, I, W, NZ* 1,2, 1986 *W, S, I, F*, 1987 *I, F, W, S*, [*A, US, W*], 1988 *Fj*, 1991 [*US*]
Pears, D (Harlequins) 1990 *Arg* 1,2, 1992 *F*(R), 1994 *F*
Pearson, A W (Blackheath) 1875 *I, S*, 1876 *I, S*, 1877 *S*, 1878 *S, I*
Peart, T G A H (Hartlepool R) 1964 *F, S*
Pease, F E (Hartlepool R) 1887 *I*
Penny, S H (Leicester) 1909 *A*
Penny, W J (United Hospitals) 1878 *I*, 1879 *S, I*
Percival, L J (Rugby) 1891 *I*, 1892 *I*, 1893 *S*
Periton, H G (Waterloo) 1925 *W*, 1926 *W, I, F, S*, 1927 *W, I, S, F*, 1928 *A, I, F, S*, 1929 *W, I, S, F*, 1930 *W, I, F, S*
Perrott, E S (O Cheltonians) 1875 *I*
Perry, D G (Bedford) 1963 *F, S, NZ* 1,2, *A* 1964 *NZ, W, I*, 1965 *W, I, F, S*, 1966 *W, I, F*
Perry, S V (Cambridge U, Waterloo) 1947 *W, I*, 1948 *A, W, I, S, F*
Peters, J (Plymouth) 1906 *S, F*, 1907 *I, S*, 1908 *W*
Phillips, C (Birkenhead Park) 1880 *S*, 1881 *I, S*
Phillips, M S (Fylde) 1958 *A, I, F, S*, 1959 *W, I, F, S*, 1960 *W, I, F, S*, 1961 *W*, 1963 *W, I, F, S, NZ* 1,2, *A*, 1964 *NZ, W, I, F, S*
Pickering, A S (Harrogate) 1907 *I*
Pickering, R D A (Bradford) 1967 *I, F, S, W*, 1968 *F, S*
Pickles, R C W (Bristol) 1922 *I, F*
Pierce, R (Liverpool) 1898 *I*, 1903 *S*
Pilkington, W N (Cambridge U) 1898 *S*
Pillman, C H (Blackheath) 1910 *W, I, F, S*, 1911 *W, F, I, S*, 1912 *W, F*, 1913 *SA, W, F, I, S*, 1914 *W, I, S*
Pillman, R L (Blackheath) 1914 *F*
Pinch, J (Lancaster) 1896 *W, I*, 1897 *S*
Pinching, W W (Guy's Hospital) 1872 *S*
Pitman, I J (Oxford U) 1922 *S*
Plummer, K C (Bristol) 1969 *W*, 1976 *S, I, F*
Poole, F O (Oxford U) 1895 *W, I, S*
Poole, R W (Hartlepool R) 1896 *S*
Pope, E B (Blackheath) 1931 *W, S, F*
Portus, G V (Blackheath) 1908 *F, I*
Poulton, R W (later **Poulton Palmer**) (Oxford U, Harlequins, Liverpool) 1909 *F, I, S*, 1910 *W*, 1911 *S*, 1912 *W, I, S*, 1913 *SA, W, F, I, S*, 1914 *W, I, S, F*
Powell, D L (Northampton) 1966 *W, I*, 1969 *I, F, S, W*, 1971 *W, I, F, S* (2[1C])
Pratten, W E (Blackheath) 1927 *S, F*
Preece, I (Coventry) 1948 *I, S, F*, 1949 *F, S*, 1950 *W, I, F, S*, 1951 *W, I, F*
Preece, P S (Coventry) 1972 *SA*, 1973 *NZ* 1, *W, I, F, S, NZ* 2, 1975 *I, F, W, A* 2, 1976 *W* (R)
Preedy, M (Gloucester) 1984 *SA* 1
Prentice, F D (Leicester) 1928 *I, F, S*
Prescott, R E (Harlequins) 1937 *W, I*, 1938 *I*, 1939 *W, I, S*
Preston, N J (Richmond) 1979 *NZ*, 1980 *I, F*
Price, H L (Harlequins) 1922 *I, S*, 1923 *W, I*
Price, J (Coventry) 1961 *I*
Price, P L A (RIE Coll) 1877 *I, S*, 1878 *S*
Price, T W (Cheltenham) 1948 *S, F*, 1949 *W, I, F, S*
Probyn, J A (Wasps, Askeans) 1988 *F, W, S, I* 1,2, *A* 1,2, *A*, 1989 *S, I, R* (R), 1990 *I, F, W, S, Arg* 1,2,3, 1991 *W, S, I, F, Fj, A*, [*NZ, It, F, S, A*], 1992 *S, I, F, W*, 1993 *F, W, S, I*
Prout, D H (Northampton) 1968 *W, I*
Pullin, J V (Bristol) 1966 *W*, 1968 *W, I, F, S*, 1969 *I, F, S, W, SA*, 1970 *I, W, S, F*, 1971 *W, I, F, S* (2[1C]), *P*, 1972 *W, I, F, S, SA*, 1973 *NZ* 1, *W, I, F, S, NZ* 2, *A*, 1974 *S, I, F, W*, 1975 *I, W* (R), *S, A* 1,2, 1976 *F*
Purdy, S J (Rugby) 1962 *S*
Pyke, J (St Helens Recreation) 1892 *W*
Pym, J A (Blackheath) 1912 *W, I, S, F*

Quinn, J P (New Brighton) 1954 *W, NZ, I, S, F*

Rafter, M (Bristol) 1977 *S, F, W*, 1978 *F, W, S, I, NZ*, 1979 *S, I, F, W, NZ*, 1980 *W* (R), 1981 *W, Arg* 1,2
Ralston, C W (Richmond) 1971 *S* (C), *P*, 1972 *W, I, F, S, SA*, 1973 *NZ* 1, *W, I, F, S, NZ* 2, *A*, 1974 *S, I, F, W*, 1975 *I, F, W, S*
Ramsden, H E (Bingley) 1898 *W, S*
Ranson, J M (Rosslyn Park) 1963 *NZ* 1,2, *A*, 1964 *W, I, F, S*
Raphael, J E (OMTs) 1902 *W, I, S*, 1905 *W, S, NZ*, 1906 *W, S, F*
Ravenscroft, J (Birkenhead Park) 1881 *I*
Rawlinson, W C W (Blackheath) 1876 *S*
Redfern, S (Leicester) 1984 *I* (R)
Redman, N C (Bath) 1984 *A*, 1986 *S* (R), 1987 *I, S*, [*A, J, W*], 1988 *Fj*, 1990 *Arg* 1,2, 1991 *Fj*, [*It, US*], 1993 *NZ*, 1994 *F, W, SA* 1,2
Redmond, G F (Cambridge U) 1970 *F*
Redwood, B W (Bristol) 1968 *W, I*
Rees, G W (Nottingham) 1984 *SA* 2 (R), *A*, 1986 *I, F*, 1987 *F, W, S*, [*A, J, US, W*], 1988 *S* (R), *I* 1,2, *A* 1,2, *Fj*, 1989 *W* (R), *R* (R), *Fj* (R), 1990 *Arg* 3 (R), 1991 *Fj*, [*US*]
Reeve, J S R (Harlequins) 1929 *F*, 1930 *W, I, F, S*, 1931 *W, I, S*
Regan, M (Liverpool) 1953 *W, I, F, S*, 1954 *W, NZ, I, S, F*, 1956 *I, S, F*
Rendall, P A G (Wasps, Askeans) 1984 *W, SA* 2, 1986 *W, S*, 1987 *I, F, S*, [*A, J, W*], 1988 *F, W, S, I* 1,2, *A* 1,2, *A*, 1989 *S, I, F, W, R*, 1990 *I, F, W, S*, 1991 [*It* (R)]
Rew, H (Blackheath) 1929 *S, F*, 1930 *F, S*, 1931 *W, S, F*, 1934 *W, I, S*
Reynolds, F J (O Cranleighans) 1937 *S*, 1938 *I, S*
Reynolds, S (Richmond) 1900 *W, I, S*, 1901 *I*
Rhodes, J (Castleford) 1896 *W, I, S*
Richards, D (Leicester) 1986 *I, F*, 1987 *S*, [*A, J, US, W*], 1988 *F, W, S, I* 1, *A* 1,2, *Fj, A*, 1989 *S, I, F, W, R*, 1990 *Arg* 3, 1991 *W, S, I, F, Fj, A*, [*NZ, It, US*], 1992 *S*(R), *F, W, C*, 1993 *NZ*, 1994 *W, SA* 1, *C*, 1995 *I, F, W, S*
Richards, E E (Plymouth A) 1929 *S, F*
Richards, J (Bradford) 1891 *W, I, S*
Richards, S B (Richmond) 1965 *W, I, F, S*, 1967 *A, I, F, S, W*
Richardson, J V (Birkenhead Park) 1928 *A, W, I, F, S*
Richardson, W R (Manchester) 1881 *I*
Rickards, C H (Gipsies) 1873 *S*
Rimmer, G (Waterloo) 1949 *W, I*, 1950 *W*, 1951 *W, I, F*, 1952 *SA, W*, 1954 *W, NZ, I, S*
Rimmer, L I (Bath) 1961 *SA, W, I, F, S*
Ripley, A G (Rosslyn Park) 1972 *W, I, F, S, SA*, 1973 *NZ* 1, *W, I, F, S, NZ* 2, *A*, 1974 *S, I, F, W*, 1975 *I, F, S, A* 1,2, 1976 *A, W, S*
Risman, A B W (Loughborough Coll) 1959 *W, I, F, S*, 1961 *SA, W, I, F*
Ritson, J A S (Northern) 1910 *F, S*, 1912 *F*, 1913 *SA, W, F, I, S*
Rittson-Thomas, G C (Oxford U) 1951 *W, I, F*
Robbins, G L (Coventry) 1986 *W, S*
Robbins, P G D (Oxford U, Moseley, Coventry) 1956 *W, I, S, F*, 1957 *W, I, F, S*, 1958 *W, A, I, S*, 1960 *W, I, F, S*, 1961 *SA, W*, 1962 *S*
Roberts, A D (Northern) 1911 *W, F, I, S*, 1912 *I, S, F*, 1914 *I*
Roberts, E W (RNE Coll) 1901 *W, I*, 1905 *NZ*, 1906 *W, I*, 1907 *S*
Roberts, G D (Harlequins) 1907 *S*, 1908 *F, W*
Roberts, J (Sale) 1960 *W, I, F, S*, 1961 *SA, W, I, F, S*, 1962 *W, I, F, S*, 1963 *W, I, F, S*, 1964 *NZ*
Roberts, R S (Coventry) 1932 *I*
Roberts, S (Swinton) 1887 *W, I*
Roberts, V G (Penryn, Harlequins) 1947 *F*, 1949 *W, I, F, S*, 1950 *I, F, S*, 1951 *W, I, F, S*, 1956 *W, I, S, F*
Robertshaw, A R (Bradford) 1886 *W, I, S*, 1887 *W, S*
Robinson, A (Blackheath) 1889 *M*, 1890 *W, S, I*
Robinson, E T (Coventry) 1954 *S*, 1961 *I, F, S*
Robinson, G C (Percy Park) 1897 *I, S*, 1898 *I*, 1899 *W*, 1900 *I, S*, 1901 *I, S*
Robinson, J J (Headingley) 1893 *S*, 1902 *W, I, S*
Robinson, R A (Bath) 1988 *A* 2, *Fj, A*, 1989 *S, I, F, W*
Robson, A (Northern) 1924 *W, I, F, S*, 1926 *W*
Robson, M (Oxford U) 1930 *W, I, F, S*
Rodber, T A K (Army, Northampton) 1992 *S, I*, 1993 *NZ*, 1994 *I, F, W, SA* 1,2, *R, C*, 1995 *I, F, W, S*
Rogers, D P (Bedford) 1961 *I, F, S*, 1962 *W, I, F*, 1963 *W, I, F, S, NZ* 1,2, *A*, 1964 *NZ, W, I, F, S*, 1965 *W, I, F, S*, 1966 *W, I, F, S*, 1967 *A, S, W, NZ*, 1969 *I, F, S, W*
Rogers, J H (Moseley) 1890 *W, S, I*, 1891 *S*
Rogers, W L Y (Blackheath) 1905 *W, I*
Rollitt, D M (Bristol) 1967 *I, F, S, W*, 1969 *I, F, S, W*, 1975 *S, A* 1,2
Roncoroni, A D S (West Herts, Richmond) 1933 *W, I, S*
Rose, W M H (Cambridge U, Coventry, Harlequins) 1981 *I, F*, 1982 *A, S, I*, 1987 *I, F, W, S*, [*A*]
Rossborough, P A (Coventry) 1971 *W*, 1973 *NZ* 2, *A*,

1974 *S, I,* 1975 *I, F*
Rosser, D W A (Wasps) 1965 *W, I, F, S,* 1966 *W*
Rotherham, Alan (Richmond) 1883 *W, S,* 1884 *W, S,* 1885 *W, I,* 1886 *W, I, S,* 1887 *W, I, S*
Rotherham, Arthur (Richmond) 1898 *S, W,* 1899 *W, I, S*
Roughley, D (Liverpool) 1973 *A,* 1974 *S, I*
Rowell, R E (Leicester) 1964 *W,* 1965 *W*
Rowley, A J (Coventry) 1932 *SA*
Rowley, H C (Manchester) 1879 *S, I,* 1880 *I, S,* 1881 *I, W, S,* 1882 *I, S*
Rowntree, G C (Leicester) 1995 *S*(t)
Royds, P M R (Blackheath) 1898 *S, W,* 1899 *W*
Royle, A V (Broughton R) 1889 *M*
Rudd, E L (Liverpool) 1965 *W, I, S,* 1966 *W, I, S*
Russell, R F (Leicester) 1905 *NZ*
Rutherford, D (Percy Park, Gloucester) 1960 *W, I, F, S,* 1961 *SA,* 1965 *W, I, F, S,* 1966 *W, I, F, S,* 1967 *NZ*
Ryalls, H J (N Brighton) 1885 *W, I*
Ryan, D (Wasps) 1990 *Arg* 1,2, 1992 *C*
Ryan, P H (Richmond) 1955 *W, I*

Sadler, E H (Army) 1933 *I, S*
Sagar, J W (Cambridge U) 1901 *W, I*
Salmon, J L B (Harlequins) 1985 *NZ* 1,2, 1986 *W, S,* 1987 *I, F, W, S,* [*A, J, US, W*]
Sample, C H (Cambridge U) 1884 *I,* 1885 *I,* 1886 *S*
Sanders, D L (Harlequins) 1954 *W, NZ, I, S, F,* 1956 *W, I, S, F*
Sanders, F W (Plymouth A) 1923 *I, S, F*
Sandford, J R P (Marlborough N) 1906 *I*
Sangwin, R D (Hull and E Riding) 1964 *NZ, W*
Sargent, G A F (Gloucester) 1981 *I* (R)
Savage, K F (Northampton) 1966 *W, I, F, S,* 1967 *A, I, F, S, W, NZ,* 1968 *W, F, S*
Sawyer, C M (Broughton) 1880 *S,* 1881 *I*
Saxby, L E (Gloucester) 1932 *SA, W*
Schofield, J W (Manchester) 1880 *I*
Scholfield, J A (Preston Grasshoppers) 1911 *W*
Schwarz, R O (Richmond) 1899 *S,* 1901 *W, I*
Scorfield, E S (Percy Park) 1910 *F*
Scott, C T (Blackheath) 1900 *W, I,* 1901 *I, W*
Scott, E K (St Mary's Hospital, Redruth) 1947 *W,* 1948 *A, W, I, S*
Scott, F S (Bristol) 1907 *W*
Scott, H (Manchester) 1955 *F*
Scott, J P (Rosslyn Park, Cardiff) 1978 *F, W, S, I, NZ,* 1979 *S* (R), *I, F, W, NZ,* 1980 *I, F, W, S,* 1981 *W, S, I, F, Arg* 1,2, 1982 *I, F, W,* 1983 *F, W, S, I, NZ,* 1984 *S, I, F, W, SA* 1,2
Scott, J S M (Oxford U) 1958 *F*
Scott, M T (Cambridge U) 1887 *I,* 1890 *S, I*
Scott, W M (Cambridge U) 1889 *M*
Seddon, R L (Broughton R) 1887 *W, I, S*
Sellar, K A (United Services, RN) 1927 *W, I, S,* 1928 *A, W, I, F*
Sever, H S (Sale) 1936 *NZ, W, I, S,* 1937 *W, I, S,* 1938 *W, I, S*
Shackleton, I R (Cambridge U) 1969 *SA,* 1970 *I, W, S*
Sharp, R A W (Oxford U, Wasps, Redruth) 1960 *W, I, F, S,* 1961 *I, F,* 1962 *W, I, F,* 1963 *W, I, F, S,* 1967 *A*
Shaw, C H (Moseley) 1906 *S, SA,* 1907 *F, W, I, S*
Shaw, F (Cleckheaton) 1898 *I*
Shaw, J F (RNE Coll) 1898 *S, W*
Sheppard, A (Bristol) 1981 *W* (R), 1985 *W*
Sherrard, C W (Blackheath) 1871 *S,* 1872 *S*
Sherriff, G A (Saracens) 1966 *S,* 1967 *A, NZ*
Shewring, H E (Bristol) 1905 *I, NZ,* 1906 *W, S, F, SA,* 1907 *F, W, I, S*
Shooter, J H (Morley) 1899 *I, S,* 1900 *I, S*
Shuttleworth, D W (Headingley) 1951 *S,* 1953 *S*
Sibree, H J H (Harlequins) 1908 *F,* 1909 *I, S*
Silk, N (Harlequins) 1965 *W, I, F, S*
Simms, K G (Cambridge U, Liverpool, Wasps) 1985 *R, F, S, I, W,* 1986 *I, F,* 1987 *I, F, W,* [*A, J, W*], 1988 *F, W*
Simpson, C P (Harlequins) 1965 *W*
Simpson, P D (Bath) 1983 *NZ,* 1984 *S,* 1987 *I*
Simpson, T (Rockcliff) 1902 *S,* 1903 *W, I, S,* 1904 *I, S,* 1905 *I, S,* 1906 *S, SA,* 1909 *F*
Skinner, M G (Harlequins) 1988 *F, W, S, I* 1,2, 1989 *Fj,* 1990 *I, F, W, S, Arg* 1,2, 1991 *Fj* (R), [*US, F, S, A*], 1992 *S, I, F, W*
Sladen, G M (United Services, RN) 1929 *W, I, S*
Slemen, M A C (Liverpool) 1976 *I, F,* 1977 *S, I, F, W,* 1978 *F, W, S, I, NZ,* 1979 *S, I, F, W, NZ,* 1980 *I, F, W, S,* 1981 *W, S, I, F,* 1982 *A, S, I, F, W,* 1983 *NZ,* 1984 *S*
Slocock, L A N (Liverpool) 1907 *F, W, I, S,* 1908 *F, W, I, S*
Slow, C F (Leicester) 1934 *S*
Small, H D (Oxford U) 1950 *W, I, F, S*
Smallwood, A M (Leicester) 1920 *F, I,* 1921 *W, I, S, F,* 1922 *I, S,* 1923 *W, I, S, F,* 1925 *I, S*
Smart, C E (Newport) 1979 *F, W, NZ,* 1981 *S, I, F, Arg* 1,2, 1982 *A, S, I, F, W,* 1983 *F, W, S, I*
Smart, S E J (Gloucester) 1913 *SA, W, F, I, S,* 1914 *W, I, S, F,* 1920 *W, I, S*
Smeddle, R W (Cambridge U) 1929 *W, I, S,* 1931 *F*
Smith, C C (Gloucester) 1901 *W*
Smith, D F (Richmond) 1910 *W, I*
Smith, J V (Cambridge U, Rosslyn Park) 1950 *W, I, F, S*
Smith, K (Roundhay) 1974 *F, W,* 1975 *W, S*
Smith, M J K (Oxford U) 1956 *W*
Smith, S J (Sale) 1973 *I, F, S, A,* 1974 *I, F,* 1975 *W* (R), 1976 *F,* 1977 *F* (R), 1979 *NZ,* 1980 *I, F, W, S,* 1981 *W, S, I, F, Arg* 1,2, 1982 *A, S, I, F, W,* 1983 *F, W, S*
Smith, S R (Richmond) 1959 *W, F, S,* 1964 *F, S*
Smith, S T (Wasps) 1985 *R, F, S, I, W, NZ* 1,2, 1986 *W, S*
Smith, T H (Northampton) 1951 *W*
Soane, F (Bath) 1893 *S,* 1894 *W, I, S*
Sobey, W H (O Millhillians) 1930 *W, F, S,* 1932 *SA, W*
Solomon, B (Redruth) 1910 *W*
Sparks, R H W (Plymouth A) 1928 *I, F, S,* 1929 *W, I, S,* 1931 *I, S, F*
Speed, H (Castleford) 1894 *W, I, S,* 1896 *S*
Spence, F W (Birkenhead Park) 1890 *I*
Spencer, J (Harlequins) 1966 *W*
Spencer, J S (Cambridge U, Headingley) 1969 *I, F, S, W, SA,* 1970 *I, W, S, F,* 1971 *W, I, S* (2[1C]), *P*
Spong, R S (O Millhillians) 1929 *F,* 1930 *W, I, F, S,* 1931 *F,* 1932 *SA, W*
Spooner, R H (Liverpool) 1903 *W*
Springman, H H (Liverpool) 1879 *S,* 1887 *S*
Spurling, A (Blackheath) 1882 *I*
Spurling, N (Blackheath) 1886 *I, S,* 1887 *W*
Squires, P J (Harrogate) 1973 *F, S, NZ* 2, *A,* 1974 *S, I, F, W,* 1975 *I, F, W, S, A* 1,2, 1976 *A, W,* 1977 *S, I, F, W,* 1978 *F, W, S, I, NZ,* 1979 *S, I, F, W*
Stafford, R C (Bedford) 1912 *W, I, S, F*
Stafford, W F H (RE) 1874 *S*
Stanbury, E (Plymouth A) 1926 *W, I, S,* 1927 *W, I, S, F,* 1928 *A, W, I, F, S,* 1929 *W, I, S, F*
Standing, G (Blackheath) 1883 *W, I*
Stanger-Leathes, C F (Northern) 1905 *I*
Stark, K J (O Alleynians) 1927 *W, I, S, F,* 1928 *A, W, I, F, S*
Starks, A (Castleford) 1896 *W, I*
Starmer-Smith, N C (Harlequins) 1969 *SA,* 1970 *I, W, S, F,* 1971 *S* (C), *P*
Start, S P (United Services, RN) 1907 *S*
Steeds, J H (Saracens) 1949 *F, S,* 1950 *I, F, S*
Steele-Bodger, M R (Cambridge U) 1947 *W, I, S, F,* 1948 *A, W, I, S, F*
Steinthal, F E (Ilkley) 1913 *W, F*
Stevens, C B (Penzance-Newlyn, Harlequins) 1969 *SA,* 1970 *I, W, S,* 1971 *P,* 1972 *W, I, F, S, SA,* 1973 *NZ* 1, *W, I, F, S, NZ* 2, *A,* 1974 *S, I, F, W,* 1975 *I, F, W, S*
Still, E R (Oxford U, Ravenscourt P) 1873 *S*
Stirling, R V (Leicester, RAF, Wasps) 1951 *W, I, F, S,* 1952 *SA, W, S, I, F,* 1953 *W, I, F, S,* 1954 *W, NZ, I, S, F*
Stoddart, A E (Blackheath) 1885 *W, I,* 1886 *W, I, S,* 1889 *M,* 1890 *W, I,* 1893 *W, S*
Stoddart, W B (Liverpool) 1897 *W, I, S*
Stokes, F (Blackheath) 1871 *S,* 1872 *S,* 1873 *S*
Stokes, L (Blackheath) 1875 *I,* 1876 *S,* 1877 *I, S,* 1878 *S,* 1879 *S, I,* 1880 *I, S,* 1881 *I, W, S*
Stone, F le S (Blackheath) 1914 *F*
Stoop, A D (Harlequins) 1905 *S,* 1906 *S, F, SA,* 1907 *F, W,* 1910 *W, I, S,* 1911 *W, F, I, S,* 1912 *W, S*
Stoop, F M (Harlequins) 1910 *S,* 1911 *F, I,* 1913 *SA*
Stout, F M (Richmond) 1897 *W, I,* 1898 *I, S, W,* 1899 *I, S,* 1903 *S,* 1904 *W, I, S,* 1905 *W, I, S*
Stout, P W (Richmond) 1898 *S, W,* 1899 *W, I, S*
Stringer, N C (Wasps) 1982 *A* (R), 1983 *NZ* (R), 1984 *SA* 1 (R), *A,* 1985 *R*

Strong, E L (Oxford U) 1884 *W, I, S*
Summerscales, G E (Durham City) 1905 *NZ*
Sutcliffe, J W (Heckmondwike) 1889 *M*
Swarbrick, D W (Oxford U) 1947 *W, I, F*, 1948 *A, W*, 1949 *I*
Swayne, D H (Oxford U) 1931 *W*
Swayne, J W R (Bridgwater) 1929 *W*
Swift, A H (Swansea) 1981 *Arg* 1,2, 1983 *F, W, S*, 1984 *SA* 2
Syddall, J P (Waterloo) 1982 *I*, 1984 *A*
Sykes, A R V (Blackheath) 1914 *F*
Sykes, F D (Northampton) 1955 *F, S*, 1963 *NZ* 2, *A*
Sykes, P W (Wasps) 1948 *F*, 1952 *S, I, F*, 1953 *W, I, F*
Syrett, R E (Wasps) 1958 *W, A, I, F*, 1960 *W, I, F, S*, 1962 *W, I, F*

Tallent, J A (Cambridge U, Blackheath) 1931 *S, F*, 1932 *SA, W*, 1935 *I*
Tanner, C C (Cambridge U, Gloucester) 1930 *S*, 1932 *SA, W, I, S*
Tarr, F N (Leicester) 1909 *A, W, F*, 1913 *S*
Tatham, W M (Oxford U) 1882 *S*, 1883 *W, I, S*, 1884 *W, I, S*
Taylor, A S (Blackheath) 1883 *W, I*, 1886 *W, I*
Taylor, E W (Rockcliff) 1892 *I*, 1893 *I*, 1894 *W, I, S*, 1895 *W, I, S*, 1896 *W, I*, 1897 *W, I, S*, 1899 *I*
Taylor, F (Leicester) 1920 *F, I*
Taylor, F M (Leicester) 1914 *W*
Taylor, H H (Blackheath) 1879 *S*, 1880 *S*, 1881 *I, W*, 1882 *S*
Taylor, J T (W Hartlepool) 1897 *I*, 1899 *I*, 1900 *I*, 1901 *W, I*, 1902 *W, I, S*, 1903 *W, I*, 1905 *S*
Taylor, P J (Northampton) 1955 *W, I*, 1962 *W, I, F, S*
Taylor, R B (Northampton) 1966 *W*, 1967 *I, F, S, W, NZ*, 1969 *F, S, W, SA*, 1970 *I, W, S, F*, 1971 *S* (2[1C])
Taylor, W J (Blackheath) 1928 *A, W, I, F, S*
Teague, M C (Gloucester, Moseley) 1985 *F* (R), *NZ* 1,2, 1989 *S, I, F, W, R*, 1990 *F, W, S*, 1991 *W, S, I, F, Fj, A*, [*NZ, It, F, S, A*], 1992 *SA*, 1993 *F, W, S, I*
Teden, D E (Richmond) 1939 *W, I, S*
Teggin, A (Broughton R) 1884 *I*, 1885 *W*, 1886 *I, S*, 1887 *I, S*
Tetley, T S (Bradford) 1876 *S*
Thomas, C (Barnstaple) 1895 *W, I, S*, 1899 *I*
Thompson, P H (Headingley, Waterloo) 1956 *W, I, S, F*, 1957 *W, I, F, S*, 1958 *W, A, I, F, S*, 1959 *W, I, F, S*
Thomson, G T (Halifax) 1878 *S*, 1882 *I, S*, 1883 *W, I, S*, 1884 *I, S*, 1885 *I*
Thomson, W B (Blackheath) 1892 *W*, 1895 *W, I, S*
Thorne, J D (Bristol) 1963 *W, I, F*
Tindall, V R (Liverpool U) 1951 *W, I, F, S*
Tobin, F (Liverpool) 1871 *S*
Todd, A F (Blackheath) 1900 *I, S*
Todd, R (Manchester) 1877 *S*
Toft, H B (Waterloo) 1936 *S*, 1937 *W, I, S*, 1938 *W, I, S*, 1939 *W, I, S*
Toothill, J T (Bradford) 1890 *S, I*, 1891 *W, I*, 1892 *W, I, S*, 1893 *W, I, S*, 1894 *W, I*
Tosswill, L R (Exeter) 1902 *W, I, S*
Touzel, C J C (Liverpool) 1877 *I, S*
Towell, A C (Bedford) 1948 *F*, 1951 *S*
Travers, B H (Harlequins) 1947 *W, I*, 1948 *A, W*, 1949 *F, S*
Treadwell, W T (Wasps) 1966 *I, F, S*
Trick, D M (Bath) 1983 *I*, 1984 *SA* 1
Tristram, H B (Oxford U) 1883 *S*, 1884 *W, S*, 1885 *W*, 1887 *S*
Troop, C L (Aldershot S) 1933 *I, S*
Tucker, J S (Bristol) 1922 *W*, 1925 *NZ, W, I, S, F*, 1926 *W, I, F, S*, 1927 *W, I, S, F*, 1928 *A, W, I, F, S*, 1929 *W, I, F*, 1930 *W, I, F, S*, 1931 *W*
Tucker, W E (Blackheath) 1894 *W, I*, 1895 *W, I, S*
Tucker, W E (Blackheath) 1926 *I*, 1930 *W, I*
Turner, D P (Richmond) 1871 *S*, 1872 *S*, 1873 *S*, 1874 *S*, 1875 *I, S*
Turner, E B (St George's Hospital) 1876 *I*, 1877 *I*, 1878 *I*
Turner, G R (St George's Hospital) 1876 *S*
Turner, H J C (Manchester) 1871 *S*
Turner, M F (Blackheath) 1948 *S, F*
Turquand-Young, D (Richmond) 1928 *A, W*, 1929 *I, S, F*
Twynam, H T (Richmond) 1879 *I*, 1880 *I*, 1881 *W*, 1882 *I*, 1883 *I*, 1884 *W, I, S*

Ubogu, V E (Bath) 1992 *C, SA*, 1993 *NZ*, 1994 *S, I, F, W, SA* 1,2, *R, C*, 1995 *I, F, W, S*
Underwood, A M (Exeter) 1962 *W, I, F, S*, 1964 *I*
Underwood, R (Leicester, RAF) 1984 *I, F, W, A*, 1985 *R, F, S, I, W*, 1986 *W, I, F*, 1987 *I, F, W, S*, [*A, J, W*], 1988 *F, W, S, I* 1,2, *A* 1,2, *Fj, A*, 1989 *S, I, F, W, R, Fj*, 1990 *I, F, W, S, Arg* 3, 1991 *W, S, I, F, Fj, A*, [*NZ, It, US, F, S, A*], 1992 *S, I, F, W, SA*, 1993 *F, W, S, I, NZ*, 1994 *S, I, F, W, SA* 1,2, *R, C*, 1995 *I, F, W, S*
Underwood, T (Leicester) 1992 *C, SA*, 1993 *S, I, NZ*, 1994 *S, I, W, SA* 1,2, *R, C*, 1995 *I, F, W, S*
Unwin, E J (Rosslyn Park, Army) 1937 *S*, 1938 *W, I, S*
Unwin, G T (Blackheath) 1898 *S*
Uren, R (Waterloo) 1948 *I, S, F*, 1950 *I*
Uttley, R M (Gosforth) 1973 *I, F, S, NZ* 2, *A*, 1974 *I, F, W*, 1975 *F, W, S, A* 1,2, 1977 *S, I, F, W*, 1978 *NZ*, 1979 *S*, 1980 *I, F, W, S*

Valentine, J (Swinton) 1890 *W*, 1896 *W, I, S*
Vanderspar, C H R (Richmond) 1873 *S*
Van Ryneveld, C B (Oxford U) 1949 *W, I, F, S*
Varley, H (Liversedge) 1892 *S*
Vassall, H (Blackheath) 1881 *W, S*, 1882 *I, S*, 1883 *W*
Vassall, H H (Blackheath) 1908 *I*
Vaughan, D B (Headingley) 1948 *A, W, I, S*, 1949 *I, F, S*, 1950 *W*
Vaughan-Jones, A (Army) 1932 *I, S*, 1933 *W*
Verelst, C L (Liverpool) 1876 *I*, 1878 *I*
Vernon, G F (Blackheath) 1878 *S, I*, 1880 *I, S*, 1881 *I*
Vickery, G (Aberavon) 1905 *I*
Vivyan, E J (Devonport A) 1901 *W*, 1904 *W, I, S*
Voyce, A T (Gloucester) 1920 *I, S*, 1921 *W, I, S, F*, 1922 *W, I, F, S*, 1923 *W, I, S, F*, 1924 *W, I, F, S*, 1925 *NZ, W, I, S, F*, 1926 *W, I, F, S*

Wackett, J A S (Rosslyn Park) 1959 *W, I*
Wade, C G (Richmond) 1883 *W, I, S*, 1884 *W, S*, 1885 *W*, 1886 *W, I*
Wade, M R (Cambridge U) 1962 *W, I, F*
Wakefield, W W (Harlequins) 1920 *W, F, I, S*, 1921 *W, I, S, F*, 1922 *W, I, F, S*, 1923 *W, I, S, F*, 1924 *W, I, F, S*, 1925 *NZ, W, I, S, F*, 1926 *W, I, F, S*, 1927 *S, F*
Walker, G A (Blackheath) 1939 *W, I*
Walker, H W (Coventry) 1947 *W, I, S, F*, 1948 *A, W, I, S, F*
Walker, R (Manchester) 1874 *S*, 1875 *I*, 1876 *S*, 1879 *S*, 1880 *S*
Wallens, J N S (Waterloo) 1927 *F*
Walton, E J (Castleford) 1901 *W, I*, 1902 *I, S*
Walton, W (Castleford) 1894 *S*
Ward, G (Leicester) 1913 *W, F, S*, 1914 *W, I, S*
Ward, H (Bradford) 1895 *W*
Ward, J I (Richmond) 1881 *I*, 1882 *I*
Ward, J W (Castleford) 1896 *W, I, S*
Wardlow, C S (Northampton) 1969 *SA* (R), 1971 *W, I, F, S* (2[1C])
Warfield, P J (Rosslyn Park, Durham U) 1973 *NZ* 1, *W, I*, 1975 *I, F, S*
Warr, A L (Oxford U) 1934 *W, I*
Watkins, J A (Gloucester) 1972 *SA*, 1973 *NZ* 1, *W, NZ* 2, *A*, 1975 *F, W*
Watkins, J K (United Services, RN) 1939 *W, I, S*
Watson, F B (United Services, RN) 1908 *S*, 1909 *S*
Watson, J H D (Blackheath) 1914 *W, S, F*
Watt, D E J (Bristol) 1967 *I, F, S, W*
Webb, C S H (Devonport Services, RN) 1932 *SA, W, I, S*, 1933 *W, I, S*, 1935 *S*, 1936 *NZ, W, I, S*
Webb, J M (Bristol, Bath) 1987 [*A*(R), *J, US, W*], 1988 *F, W, S, I* 1,2, *A* 1,2, *A*, 1989 *S, I, F, W*, 1991 *Fj, A*, [*NZ, It, F, S, A*], 1992 *S, I, F, W, C, SA*, 1993 *F, W, S, I*
Webb, J W G (Northampton) 1926 *F, S*, 1929 *S*
Webb, R E (Coventry) 1967 *S, W, NZ*, 1968 *I, F, S*, 1969 *I, F, S, W*, 1972 *I, F*
Webb, St L H (Bedford) 1959 *W, I, F, S*
Webster, J G (Moseley) 1972 *W, I, SA*, 1973 *NZ* 1, *W, NZ* 2, 1974 *S, W*, 1975 *I, F, W*
Wedge, T G (St Ives) 1907 *F*, 1909 *W*
Weighill, R H G (RAF, Harlequins) 1947 *S, F*, 1948 *S, F*
Wells, C M (Cambridge U, Harlequins) 1893 *S*, 1894 *W, S*, 1896 *S*, 1897 *W, S*
West, B R (Loughborough Colls, Northampton) 1968 *W, I, F, S*, 1969 *SA*, 1970 *I, W, S*
Weston, H T F (Northampton) 1901 *S*
Weston, L E (W of Scotland) 1972 *F, S*

Weston, M P (Richmond, Durham City) 1960 *W, I, F, S*, 1961 *SA, W, I, F, S*, 1962 *W, I, F*, 1963 *W, I, F, S, NZ* 1,2, *A*, 1964 *NZ, W, I, F, S*, 1965 *F, S*, 1966 *S*, 1968 *F, S*
Weston, W H (Northampton) 1933 *I, S*, 1934 *I, S*, 1935 *W, I, S*, 1936 *NZ, W, S*, 1937 *W, I, S*, 1938 *W, I, S*
Wheatley, A A (Coventry) 1937 *W, I, S*, 1938 *W, S*
Wheatley, H F (Coventry) 1936 *I*, 1937 *S*, 1938 *W, S*, 1939 *W, I, S*
Wheeler, P J (Leicester) 1975 *F, W*, 1976 *A, W, S, I*, 1977 *S, I, F, W*, 1978 *F, W, S, I, NZ*, 1979 *S, I, F, W, NZ*, 1980 *I, F, W, S*, 1981 *W, S, I, F*, 1982 *A, S, I, F, W*, 1983 *F, S, I, NZ*, 1984 *S, I, F, W*
White, C (Gosforth) 1983 *NZ*, 1984 *S, I, F*
White, D F (Northampton) 1947 *W, I, S*, 1948 *I, F*, 1951 *S*, 1952 *SA, W, S, I, F*, 1953 *W, I, S*
Whiteley, E C P (O Alleynians) 1931 *S, F*
Whiteley, W (Bramley) 1896 *W*
Whitley, H (Northern) 1929 *W*
Wightman, B J (Moseley, Coventry) 1959 *W*, 1963 *W, I, NZ* 2, *A*
Wigglesworth, H J (Thornes) 1884 *I*
Wilkins, D T (United Services, RN, Roundhay) 1951 *W, I, F, S*, 1952 *SA, W, S, I, F*, 1953 *W, I, F, S*
Wilkinson, E (Bradford) 1886 *W, I, S*, 1887 *W, S*
Wilkinson, H (Halifax) 1929 *W, I, S*, 1930 *F*
Wilkinson, H J (Halifax) 1889 *M*
Wilkinson, P (Law Club) 1872 *S*
Wilkinson, R M (Bedford) 1975 *A* 2, 1976 *A, W, S, I, F*
Willcocks, T J (Plymouth) 1902 *W*
Willcox, J G (Oxford U, Harlequins) 1961 *I, F, S*, 1962 *W, I, F, S*, 1963 *W, I, F, S*, 1964 *NZ, W, I, F, S*
William-Powlett, P B R W (United Services, RN) 1922 *S*
Williams, C G (Gloucester, RAF) 1976 *F*
Williams, C S (Manchester) 1910 *F*
Williams, J E (O Millhillians, Sale) 1954 *F*, 1955 *W, I, F, S*, 1956 *I, S, F*, 1965 *W*
Williams, J M (Penzance-Newlyn) 1951 *I, S*
Williams, P N (Orrell) 1987 *S*, [*A, J, W*]
Williams, S G (Devonport A) 1902 *W, I, S*, 1903 *I, S*, 1907 *I, S*
Williams, S H (Newport) 1911 *W, F, I, S*
Williamson, R H (Oxford U) 1908 *W, I, S*, 1909 *A, F*
Wilson, A J (Camborne S of M) 1909 *I*
Wilson, C E (Blackheath) 1898 *I*
Wilson, C P (Cambridge U, Marlborough N) 1881 *W*
Wilson, D S (Met Police, Harlequins) 1953 *F*, 1954 *W, NZ, I, S, F*, 1955 *F, S*
Wilson, G S (Tyldesley) 1929 *W, I*
Wilson, K J (Gloucester) 1963 *F*
Wilson, R P (Liverpool OB) 1891 *W, I, S*
Wilson, W C (Richmond) 1907 *I, S*
Winn, C E (Rosslyn Park) 1952 *SA, W, S, I, F*, 1954 *W, S, F*
Winterbottom, P J (Headingley, Harlequins) 1982 *A, S, I, F, W*, 1983 *F, W, S, I, NZ*, 1984 *S, F, W, SA* 1,2, 1986 *W, S, I, F*, 1987 *I, F, W*, [*A, J, US, W*], 1988 *F, W, S*, 1989 *R, Fj*, 1990 *I, F, W, S, Arg* 1,2,3, 1991 *W, S, I, F, A*, [*NZ, It, F, S, A*], 1992 *S, I, F, W, C, SA*, 1993 *F, W, S, I*
Wintle, T C (Northampton) 1966 *S*, 1969 *I, F, S, W*
Wodehouse, N A (United Services, RN) 1910 *F*, 1911 *W, F, I, S*, 1912 *W, I, S, F*, 1913 *SA, W, F, I, S*
Wood, A (Halifax) 1884 *I*
Wood, A E (Gloucester, Cheltenham) 1908 *F, W, I*
Wood, G W (Leicester) 1914 *W*
Wood, R (Liversedge) 1894 *I*
Wood, R D (Liverpool OB) 1901 *I*, 1903 *W, I*
Woodgate, E E (Paignton) 1952 *W*
Woodhead, E (Huddersfield) 1880 *I*
Woodruff, C G (Harlequins) 1951 *W, I, F, S*
Woods, S M J (Cambridge U, Wellington) 1890 *W, S, I*, 1891 *W, I, S*, 1892 *I, S*, 1893 *W, I*, 1895 *W, I, S*
Woods, T (Bridgwater) 1908 *S*
Woods, T (United Services, RN) 1920 *S*, 1921 *W, I, S, F*
Woodward, C R (Leicester) 1980 *I* (R), *F, W, S*, 1981 *W, S, I, F, Arg* 1,2, 1982 *A, S, I, F, W*, 1983 *I, NZ*, 1984 *S, I, F, W*
Woodward, J E (Wasps) 1952 *SA, W, S*, 1953 *W, I, F, S*, 1954 *W, NZ, I, S, F*, 1955 *W, I*, 1956 *S*
Wooldridge, C S (Oxford U, Blackheath) 1883 *W, I, S*, 1884 *W, I, S*, 1885 *I*
Wordsworth, A J (Cambridge U) 1975 *A* 1 (R)
Worton, J R B (Harlequins, Army) 1926 *W*, 1927 *W*
Wrench, D F B (Harlequins) 1964 *F, S*
Wright, C C G (Cambridge U, Blackheath) 1909 *I, S*
Wright, F T (Edinburgh Acady, Manchester) 1881 *S*
Wright, I D (Northampton) 1971 *W, I, F, S* (R)
Wright, J C (Met Police) 1934 *W*
Wright, J F (Bradford) 1890 *W*
Wright, T P (Blackheath) 1960 *W, I, F, S*, 1961 *SA, W, I, F, S*, 1962 *W, I, F, S*
Wright, W H G (Plymouth) 1920 *W, F*
Wyatt, D M (Bedford) 1976 *S* (R)

Yarranton, P G (RAF, Wasps) 1954 *W, NZ, I*, 1955 *F, S*
Yiend, W (Hartlepool R, Gloucester) 1889 *M*, 1892 *W, I, S*, 1893 *I, S*
Young, A T (Cambridge U, Blackheath, Army) 1924 *W, I, F, S*, 1925 *NZ, F*, 1926 *I, F, S*, 1927 *I, S, F*, 1928 *A, W, I, F, S*, 1929 *I*
Young, J R C (Oxford U, Harlequins) 1958 *I*, 1960 *W, I, F, S*, 1961 *SA, W, I, F*
Young, M (Gosforth) 1977 *S, I, F, W*, 1978 *F, W, S, I, NZ*, 1979 *S*
Young, P D (Dublin Wands) 1954 *W, NZ, I, S, F*, 1955 *W, I, F, S*
Youngs, N G (Leicester) 1983 *I, NZ*, 1984 *S, I, F, W*

ENGLISH INTERNATIONAL RECORDS

Both team and individual records are for official England international matches up to 31 March 1995.

TEAM RECORDS

Highest score

60 { v Japan (60-7) 1987 Sydney
60 { v Canada (60-19) 1994 Twickenham

v individual countries

51 v Argentina (51-0) 1990 Twickenham
28 v Australia (28-19) 1988 Twickenham
60 v Canada (60-19) 1994 Twickenham
58 v Fiji (58-23) 1989 Twickenham
41 v France (41-13) 1907 Richmond
38 v Ireland (38-9) 1992 Twickenham
36 v Italy (36-6) 1991 Twickenham
60 v Japan (60-7) 1987 Sydney
16 v N Zealand (16-10) 1973 Auckland
58 v Romania (58-3) 1989 Bucharest
30 v Scotland (30-18) 1980 Murrayfield
33 v S Africa (33-16) 1992 Twickenham
37 v US (37-9) 1991 Twickenham
34 v Wales (34-6) 1990 Twickenham

Biggest winning points margin
55 v Romania (58-3) 1989 Bucharest
v individual countries
51 v Argentina (51-0) 1990 Twickenham
17 v Australia { (20-3) 1973 Twickenham / (23-6) 1976 Twickenham }
41 v Canada (60-19) 1994 Twickenham
35 v Fiji (58-23) 1989 Twickenham
37 v France (37-0) 1911 Twickenham
32 v Ireland (35-3) 1988 Twickenham
30 v Italy (36-6) 1991 Twickenham
53 v Japan (60-7) 1987 Sydney
13 v N Zealand (13-0) 1936 Twickenham
55 v Romania (58-3) 1989 Bucharest
20 v Scotland (26-6) 1977 Twickenham
17 v S Africa { (33-16) 1992 Twickenham / (32-15) 1994 Pretoria }
28 v US { (34-6) 1987 Sydney / (37-9) 1991 Twickenham }
28 v Wales (34-6) 1990 Twickenham

Longest winning sequence
10 matches – 1882-86

Highest score by opposing team
42 N Zealand (15-42) 1985 Wellington
by individual countries
19 Argentina (19-19) 1981 Buenos Aires
40 Australia (15-40) 1991 Sydney
19 Canada (60-19) 1994 Twickenham
23 Fiji (58-23) 1989 Twickenham
37 France (12-37) 1972 Colombes
26 Ireland (21-26) 1974 Twickenham
6 Italy (36-6) 1991 Twickenham
7 Japan (60-7) 1987 Sydney
42 N Zealand (15-42) 1985 Wellington
15 Romania (22-15) 1985 Twickenham
33 Scotland (6-33) 1986 Murrayfield
35 S Africa (9-35) 1984 Johannesburg
9 United States (37-9) 1991 Twickenham
34 Wales (21-34) 1967 Cardiff

Biggest losing points margin
27 v N Zealand (15-42) 1985 Wellington
27 v Scotland (6-33) 1986 Murrayfield
v individual countries
2 v Argentina (13-15) 1990 Buenos Aires
25 v Australia (15-40) 1991 Sydney
25 v France (12-37) 1972 Colombes
22 v Ireland (0-22) 1947 Dublin
27 v N Zealand (15-42) 1985 Wellington
27 v Scotland (6-33) 1986 Murrayfield
26 v S Africa (9-35) 1984 Johannesburg
25 v Wales (0-25) 1905 Cardiff

No defeats v Canada, Fiji, Italy, Japan, Romania or United States

---

Longest losing sequence
7 matches – 1904-06
and 1971-72

Most tries by England in an international
13 v Wales 1881 Blackheath

Most tries against England in an international
8 by Wales (6-28) 1922 Cardiff

Most points by England in International Championship in a season – 118
in season 1991-92

Most tries by England in International Championship in a season – 20
in season 1913-14

INDIVIDUAL RECORDS

Most capped player
R Underwood 73 1984-95
in individual positions
Full-back
J M Webb 33 1987-93
Wing
R Underwood 73 1984-95
Centre
W D C Carling 55 1988-95
Fly-half
C R Andrew 64(65)[1] 1985-95
Scrum-half
R J Hill 29 1984-91
Prop
J Leonard 38 1990-95
Hooker
B C Moore 58 1987-95
Lock
W A Dooley 55 1985-93
Flanker
P J Winterbottom 58 1982-93
No 8
D Richards 42 1986-95

[1]*Andrew has played once as a full-back*

Longest international career
G S Pearce 14 seasons 1978-79 to 1991-92

Most consecutive internationals – 43
W D C Carling 1989-95

Most internationals as captain – 48
W D C Carling 1988-95

Most points in internationals – 317
C R Andrew (65 matches) 1985-95

Most points in International Championship in a season – 67
J M Webb (4 matches) 1991-92

Most points in an international – 30
C R Andrew v Canada 1994 Twickenham

Most tries in internationals – 42
R Underwood (73 matches) 1984-95

Most tries in International Championship in a season – 8
C N Lowe (4 matches) 1913-14

Most tries in an international – 5
D Lambert v France 1907 Richmond
R Underwood v Fiji 1989 Twickenham

Most conversions in internationals – 41
J M Webb (33 matches) 1987-93

Most conversions in International Championship in a season – 11
J M Webb (4 matches) 1991-92

Most conversions in an international – 8
S D Hodgkinson v Romania 1989 Bucharest

Most dropped goals in internationals – 18
C R Andrew (65 matches) 1985-95

Most dropped goals in an international – 2
R Hiller v Ireland 1970 Twickenham
A G B Old v France 1978 Paris
A G B Old v France 1980 Paris
C R Andrew v Romania 1985 Twickenham
C R Andrew v Fiji 1991 Suva

Most penalty goals in internationals – 67
W H Hare (25 matches) 1974-84

Most penalty goals in International Championship in a season – 18
S D Hodgkinson (4 matches) 1990-91

Most penalty goals in an international – 7
S D Hodgkinson v Wales 1991 Cardiff
C R Andrew v Scotland 1995 Twickenham

Most points on major tour – 58
C R Andrew (4 matches) South Africa 1994
W H Hare scored 79 points on the N American tour of 1982, but this was not a major tour

Most points in a tour match – 36
W N Bennett v Western Australia 1975 Perth

Most tries in a tour match – 4
A J Morley v Western Australia 1975 Perth
P S Preece v New South Wales 1975 Sydney
R E Webb scored 4 tries v Canada in 1967, and J Carleton scored 4 against Mid-West at Cleveland in 1982, but these were not on major tours

MIDLANDS WIN CAUSES CONTROVERSY

CIS INSURANCE DIVISIONAL CHAMPIONSHIP 1994-95

Michael Austin

Love it or loathe it – and many do – the Divisional Championship still has a role in the game, if only as a vital development competition, signposting the route to England Emerging Players, thence to England A and the full national side. The Co-operative Insurance Society nailed their colours to the RFU's mast with a £750,000 sponsorship, which also embraced the County Championship, over three years, of which this was the second.

Led by 34-year-old Gary Rees, the Nottingham and former England flanker, the Midlands won the Championship even though they played only one of their three matches at home, repeating their successes of 1985 and 1991. In doing so they became the first side since London five years earlier to take the title for a third time. Underdogs from the start, they clinched the Championship with their first win in the competition's history in London, by 17-15 at Sudbury, scoring two tries to none. They almost threw away the title as Richard Angell missed five kicks at goal while Guy Gregory of London landed five for a 15-0 lead. Angell, the Welsh-born Coventry utility back, converted a second try by Harvey Thorneycroft with the last kick of the match. If he had missed and the match had been drawn, London would have won the Championship on their superior points difference.

Before this dramatic about-turn, Bob Coward of the Midlands had been invited by his London hosts, 'as the losing divisional chairman', to leave his stand seat and make his way towards the clubhouse to attend the presentations. He was amused and pleased to find that by the time he got there, his team had won.

The title was not won without controversy, which stemmed at least in part from the disenchantment of the losing divisions. Both David Scully of the North and Steve Bates of London heavily criticised the Midlands' style of play after their respective much-fancied sides, both of which prepared seriously for the competition, lost to the eventual winners. The North and London had been on summer tours; the Midlands went nowhere. Scully was reported as saying: 'The Midlands won because they were very good at cheating. That's basically the only word I can use, and the referee just allowed them to get away with it.' Later, he suggested that some of his words had been taken out of context. Bates claimed that the Midlands made a premeditated attempt to stop London playing.

The subject was not closed there. Stan Purdy, chairman of the Midlands selectors, said in his annual report to his divisional committee: 'Unfavourable comments about the Midlands' style and play were deplored.' The counter-argument from the Midlands was that London had collapsed mauls because they did not have the upper-body strength to withstand the efforts of such players as Chris Tarbuck, and that they 'dropped' scrums to defend their heel.

Meanwhile, the value of the competition was summed up by Michael Harrison, manager of the England Emerging Players, who captained the North when they last won the Championship in 1987. 'I know that the purpose of the divisionals is to see how newcomers face up to established internationals, but with no England senior squad members available this year, it had given us an opportunity to look at all sorts of players who would not otherwise have been seen.'

The South and South-West finished bottom for the fifth time, but Richard Hill, the Saracens back-row forward, made progress, along with Nick Greenstock, the Wasps and London centre, and Rob Hardwick, the Coventry prop, who went on to play for England A against Natal in Durban and joined the summer tour to Australia and Fiji. Hardwick, playing for a club now relegated to Courage League 3, would probably have gone unnoticed without the divisional platform. Hill created a competition record for tries in a season, running in five to overtake the four each scored by Ben Clarke (for London) and Jim Fallon (for the South-West) in 1989. In the South and South-West's 33-26 defeat by the North, Hill also became the fifth player to score a hat-trick of tries since the competition's inception.

The North have won the Divisional Championship 4 times, London and the Midlands 3 times, and the South & South-West twice.

19 November, Otley RFC

Northern Division 10 (1G 1PG) **Midlands Division 12** (4PG)
Northern Division: W Greenwood (Harlequins); J Sleightholme (Bath), P Johnson (Orrell), S Ravenscroft (Saracens), A Healey (Orrell); N Ryan (Waterloo), D Scully (Wakefield) (*capt*); P Smith (Sale), S Mitchell (West Hartlepool), A Smith (Sale), D Baldwin (Sale), J Fowler (Sale), C Vyvyan (Sale), M Watson (West Hartlepool), C Manley (Orrell)
Scorers *Try:* Vyvyan *Conversion:* Scully *Penalty Goal:* Greenwood
Midlands Division: M Mapletoft (Gloucester); S Hackney (Leicester), S Potter (Leicester), D Edwards (Leicester), H Thorneycroft (Northampton); R Angell (Coventry), A Kardooni (Leicester); R Hardwick (Coventry), R Cockerill (Leicester), D Garforth (Leicester), R West (Gloucester), J Phillips (Northampton), C Tarbuck (Leicester), I Skingsley (Bedford), G Rees (Nottingham) (*capt*) *Replacement* A Kerr (Moseley) for Mapletoft (40 mins)
Scorer *Penalty Goals:* Angell (4)
Referee J Bacigalupo (Scotland)

19 November, Bristol RFC

South & South-West Division 18 (1G 2PG 1T) **London Division 23** (2G 3PG)
South & South-West Division: A Lumsden (Bath); N Beal (Northampton), M Denney (Bristol), S Morris (Gloucester), P Holford (Gloucester); M Tainton (Bristol), R Kitchin (Harlequins) (*capt*); C Clark (Bath), M Regan (Bristol), D Hinkins (Bristol), D Sims (Gloucester), A Blackmore (Bristol), R Armstrong (Bristol), D Eves (Bristol),

R Hill (Saracens)
Scorers *Tries:* Hill (2) *Conversion:* Tainton *Penalty Goals:* Tainton (2)
London Division: A Tunningley (Saracens); J Keyter (Harlequins), N Greenstock (Wasps), G Childs (Wasps), D O'Leary (Harlequins); G Gregory (Wasps), S Bates (Wasps) (*capt*); D Molloy (Wasps), G Botterman (Saracens), I Dunston (Wasps), A Diprose (Saracens), S Shaw (Bristol), C Wilkins (Wasps), D Ryan (Wasps), L Dallaglio (Wasps)
Scorers *Tries:* Bates, Dallaglio *Conversions:* Gregory (2) *Penalty Goals:* Gregory (3)
Referee S Piercy (Yorkshire Society)

26 November, Wasps RFC

London Division 38 (2G 3PG 3T) **Northern Division 16** (1G 3PG)
London Division: A Tunningley (Saracens); S Roiser (Wasps), N Greenstock (Wasps), G Childs (Wasps), D O'Leary (Harlequins); G Gregory (Wasps), S Bates (Wasps) (*capt*); D Molloy (Wasps), G Botterman (Saracens), I Dunston (Wasps), M Greenwood (Wasps), S Shaw (Bristol), A Diprose (Saracens), C Sheasby (Harlequins), L Dallaglio (Wasps)
Scorers *Tries:* Sheasby (3), Roiser, Gregory *Conversions:* Gregory (2)
Penalty Goals: Gregory (3)
Northern Division: W Greenwood (Harlequins); J Sleightholme (Bath), P Johnson (Orrell), S Ravenscroft (Saracens), A Healey (Orrell); N Ryan (Waterloo), D Scully (Wakefield) (*capt*); P Smith (Sale), S Mitchell (West Hartlepool), A Smith (Sale), D Baldwin (Sale), J Fowler (Sale), C Vyvyan (Sale), M Watson (West Hartlepool), P Manley (Orrell) *Replacement* A Brown (West Hartlepool) for Manley (49 mins)
Scorers *Try:* Baldwin *Conversion:* Greenwood *Penalty Goals:* Greenwood (2), Scully
Referee B Stirling (Ireland)

26 November, Leicester RFC

Midlands Division 43 (3G 4PG 2T) **South & South-West Division 23** (2G 3PG)
Midlands Division: R Angell (Coventry); S Hackney (Leicester), S Potter (Leicester), D Edwards (Leicester), H Thorneycroft (Northampton); J Harris (Leicester), A Kardooni (Leicester); R Hardwick (Coventry), R Cockerill (Leicester), D Garforth (Leicester), R West (Gloucester), J Phillips (Northampton), I Skingsley (Bedford), C Tarbuck (Leicester), G Rees (Nottingham) (*capt*) *Replacement* D Bishop (Rugby Lions) for Kardooni (72 mins)
Scorers *Tries:* Potter, Hackney, Tarbuck, Skingsley, Hardwick *Conversions:* Harris (3)
Penalty Goals: Harris (4)
South & South-West Division: L Anson (Narberth); N Beal (Northampton), M Denney (Bristol), S Morris (Gloucester), P Holford (Gloucester); R Dix (Cambridge U), R Kitchin (Harlequins) (*capt*); D Crompton (Bath), J Hawker (Gloucester), D Hinkins (Bristol), D Sims (Gloucester), C Yandell (Narberth), D Eves (Bristol), R Hill (Saracens), I Patten (Bristol) *Replacements* A Turner (Exeter) for Anson (52 mins); M Olsen (Bath) for Beal (75 mins)
Scorers *Tries:* Eves (2) *Conversions:* Dix (2) *Penalty Goals:* Dix (3)
Referee S Lander (Liverpool Society)

3 December, Wasps RFC

London Division 15 (5PG) **Midlands Division 17** (2G 1PG)
London Division: A Tunningley (Saracens); S Roiser (Wasps), H Davies (Wasps), G Childs (Wasps), D O'Leary (Harlequins); G Gregory (Wasps), S Bates (Wasps) (*capt*); D Molloy (Wasps), G Botterman (Saracens), I Dunston (Wasps), M Greenwood (Wasps), D Ryan (Wasps), A Diprose (Saracens), C Sheasby (Harlequins), C Wilkins (Wasps)
Replacement A Snow (Harlequins) for Ryan (42 mins)
Scorer *Penalty Goals:* Gregory (5)

Andy Tunningley and Graham Childs (No 12) of London take out Stuart Potter in the match against the Midlands. The Midlands won by 17-15 only in the closing seconds to take the title.

Midlands Division: W Kilford (Leicester); S Hackney (Leicester), S Potter (Leicester), D Edwards (Leicester), H Thorneycroft (Northampton); R Angell (Coventry), A Kardooni (Leicester); R Hardwick (Coventry), R Cockerill (Leicester), D Garforth (Leicester), R West (Gloucester), J Phillips (Northampton), I Skingsley (Bedford), C Tarbuck (Leicester), G Rees (Nottingham) (*capt*) *Replacement* J Flood (Rosslyn Park) for Hackney (40 mins)
Scorers *Tries:* Thorneycroft (2) *Conversions:* Angell (2) *Penalty Goal:* Angell
Referee W Erickson (Australia)

3 December, Sale RFC

Northern Division 33 (1G 2PG 4T) **South & South-West Division 26** (3G 1T)
Northern Division: W Greenwood (Harlequins); J Naylor (Orrell), A Northey (Waterloo), P Johnson (Orrell), A Healey (Orrell); N Ryan (Waterloo), D Scully (Wakefield) (*capt*); P Winstanley (Orrell), G French (Bath), A Smith (Sale), D Baldwin (Sale), J Fowler (Sale), P Manley (Orrell), M Watson (West Hartlepool), A Brown (West Hartlepool)
Scorers *Tries:* Greenwood, Naylor, Johnson, Fowler, Watson *Conversion:* Scully *Penalty Goals:* Scully (2)
South & South-West Division: P Belshaw (Reading); P Holford (Gloucester), S Morris (Gloucester), M Denney (Bristol), A Adebayo (Bath); R Dix (Cambridge U), R Kitchin (Harlequins) (*capt*); C Clark (Bath), J Hawker (Gloucester), D Crompton (Bath), D Sims (Gloucester), C Yandell (Narberth), P Glanville (Gloucester), R White (Loughborough U), R Hill (Saracens) *Replacement* A Turner (Exeter) for Morris (75 mins)
Scorers *Tries:* Hill (3), Holford *Conversions:* Dix (2), Belshaw
Referee P Robin (France)

TIGERS FINALLY TWEAK BATH'S TAIL

THE COURAGE LEAGUES 1994-95

They always said that they would do it, but it was not until the last few minutes of a rather tame finale that everyone at Welford Road really believed Leicester had beaten the curse of Bath. In fact, it was only the neutral supporter (of which there were very few) at that last match against Bristol who gave a hoot that the game itself was scrappy and disjointed. Everyone else was riding the wave of emotion which swept round the packed ground from kick-off. How fitting that it was the Tigers' totem, Dean Richards, who was to lift the trophy in acclaim of Leicester's first League triumph since the inaugural year of the competition, 1988.

Bath had run them to the final Saturday, when they surprisingly lost at home to Sale. But in taking three points from the previous champions, Leicester fully merited their crown. Their rugby was not always wondrous but it was spirited, considered and consistent, prompted by the best club front five in the competition and, when necessary, galvanised by the flying Underwoods. The goal-kicking of Liley and Harris was absolutely critical.

Wasps had threatened to sweep away all teams and all theories. They rattled up the points in their early games, belying the contention that open rugby is not suited to England's conditions. Then came defeat in the rain at West Hartlepool, and old theories were back in fashion. Wasps, though, were a breath of fresh air, as were Sale. The Division 2 champions of the previous year were a magnificent addition to the top league, prompted by the enduring skills of fly-half and coach Paul Turner.

At the bottom, the battle to avoid the drop was fierce. The world wanted the Harlequins to suffer the indiginity of relegation. Again it went to the wire, Harlequins' victory at Gloucester meaning that Northampton's win away to West Hartlepool was in vain.

All these great sporting endeavours were undermined by the administrators, who had failed to reorganise the fixture list in World Cup year. England players were restricted to playing two out of four of the final games, and other countries also called upon their players. The competition was devalued as a result.

In Division 2, Saracens romped home. Hanging on to their players will not prove as easy. Relegation was a furiously fought affair. Fylde started the last Saturday in fourth place but by 4.30 pm they were sunk. It's a harsh world in the Leagues.

PREVIOUS WINNERS OF THE COURAGE TROPHY

1987-88: **Leicester** (runners-up: Wasps); 1988-89: **Bath** (runners-up: Gloucester); 1989-90: **Wasps** (runners-up: Gloucester); 1990-91: **Bath** (runners-up: Wasps); 1991-92: **Bath** (runners-up: Orrell); 1992-93: **Bath** (runners-up: Wasps); 1993-94: **Bath** (runners-up: Leicester)

A celebratory soaking for Leicester captain Dean Richards as the Tigers show off the Courage Trophy after their home win against Bristol on the last Saturday of the competition.

** points deducted for various reasons*

NATIONAL DIVISION

National 1

	P	W	D	L	F	A	Pts
Leicester	18	15	1	2	400	239	31
Bath	18	12	3	3	373	245	27
Wasps	18	13	0	5	470	313	26
Sale	18	7	2	9	327	343	16
Orrell	18	6	3	9	256	326	15
Bristol	18	7	0	11	301	353	14
Gloucester	18	6	1	11	269	336	13
Harlequins	18	6	1	11	275	348	13
W Hartlepool	18	6	1	11	312	412	13
Northampton	18	6	0	12	267	335	12

National 2

	P	W	D	L	F	A	Pts
Saracens	18	15	1	2	389	213	31
Wakefield	18	12	1	5	354	261	25
N Gosforth	18	8	2	8	373	281	18
L Scottish	18	9	0	9	351	321	18
L Irish	18	9	0	9	363	381	18
Moseley	18	8	1	9	299	303	17
Nottingham	18	8	1	9	299	322	17
Waterloo	18	8	0	10	287	331	16
Fylde	18	8	0	10	250	329	16
Coventry	18	2	0	16	213	436	4

National 3

	P	W	D	L	F	A	Pts
Bedford	18	13	1	4	421	238	27
Blackheath	18	12	2	4	299	190	26
Rugby	18	11	0	7	333	271	22
Rosslyn Pk	18	10	0	8	313	280	20
Morley	18	9	2	7	277	326	20
Otley	18	9	0	9	278	248	18
Harrogate	18	7	2	9	275	404	16
Richmond	18	6	1	11	319	290	13
Clifton	18	5	1	12	242	344	11
Exeter	18	3	1	14	153	319	7

National 4

	P	W	D	L	F	A	Pts
Rotherham	18	17	0	1	576	267	34
Reading	18	14	1	3	435	319	29
Liverpool St H	18	10	3	5	374	243	23
Havant	18	10	2	6	390	330	22
Aspatria	18	7	1	10	265	378	15
Leeds*	18	8	0	10	335	291	14
Redruth	18	6	2	10	309	387	14
Plymouth Alb	18	4	2	12	324	381	10
Askeans	18	4	1	13	257	451	9
Broughton Pk	18	4	0	14	217	435	8

National 5 North

	P	W	D	L	F	A	Pts
Walsall	12	10	1	1	389	110	21
Kendal	12	9	1	2	226	162	19
Preston Grass	12	8	1	3	187	137	17
Wharfedale	12	6	1	5	209	198	13
Lichfield	12	6	0	6	217	208	12
Stourbridge	12	6	0	6	166	174	12
Stoke-on-Trent	12	5	1	6	154	154	11
Winnington Pk	12	5	1	6	173	214	11
Sheffield	12	5	0	7	156	197	10
B'ham S'hull	12	5	0	7	167	226	10
Nuneaton	12	4	0	8	129	161	8
Barker's Butts	12	4	0	8	98	233	8
Hereford	12	1	2	9	153	250	4

National 5 South

	P	W	D	L	F	A	Pts
L Welsh	12	10	2	0	409	126	22
Lydney	12	10	1	1	263	131	21
Weston-s-Mare	12	8	0	4	194	160	16
North Walsham	12	7	1	4	233	190	15
Barking	12	7	0	5	223	173	14
Tabard	12	7	0	5	207	208	14
Met Police	12	5	0	7	183	175	10
Camborne	12	4	2	6	174	188	10
Henley	12	5	0	7	190	299	10
High Wycombe	12	4	0	8	192	261	8
Berry Hill	12	3	0	9	133	229	6
Sudbury	12	3	0	9	150	352	6
Basingstoke	12	2	0	10	122	181	4

SOUTH-WEST DIVISION

South-West 1

	P	W	D	L	F	A	Pts
Cheltenham*	12	11	1	0	275	112	21
Newbury	12	9	1	2	376	113	19
Barnstaple	12	9	0	3	226	115	18
Gloucester OB	12	9	0	3	222	147	18
Brixham	12	5	2	5	177	180	12
St Ives*	12	7	0	5	151	170	12
Maidenhead	12	5	1	6	198	159	11
Salisbury	12	4	1	7	183	296	9
Cinderford	12	3	2	7	141	178	8
Torquay	12	3	1	8	134	244	7
Sherborne*	12	4	0	8	168	257	6
Taunton	12	2	1	9	193	285	5
Stroud	12	2	0	10	136	324	4

South-West 2

	P	W	D	L	F	A	Pts
Matson	12	10	1	1	279	130	21
Bridgwater	12	10	0	2	238	127	20
Gordon League	12	8	1	3	173	131	17
Clevedon	12	8	0	4	266	168	16
O Patesians*	12	7	0	5	288	167	12

Nick Greenstock of Wasps avoids Rob Glenister's attempted tackle in the early-season 57-26 defeat of Harlequins at the Stoop. Greenstock scored two tries in the match. Wasps finished third in Division 1.

	P	W	D	L	F	A	Pts
Combe Down	12	6	0	6	202	208	12
Bournemouth	12	5	1	6	166	163	11
Oxford	12	5	0	7	157	237	10
Swanage	12	4	1	7	212	288	9
Aylesbury	12	4	0	8	143	186	8
Banbury	12	4	0	8	170	289	8
Penryn	12	3	0	9	181	295	6
Marlow*	12	2	0	10	156	242	2

Southern Counties

	P	W	D	L	F	A	Pts
Dorchester	12	10	1	1	257	119	21
Bracknell	12	10	0	2	365	80	20
Chippenham	12	9	0	3	229	156	18
Olney	12	8	0	4	229	164	16
Bicester*	12	9	1	2	248	149	15
Amersham & C	12	7	0	5	238	154	14
Devizes	12	5	0	7	138	215	10
Wimborne	12	4	0	8	126	186	8
Bletchley	12	4	0	8	158	253	8
Abbey	12	3	1	8	178	228	7
Windsor	12	3	1	8	158	251	7
Oxford Marathon	12	3	0	9	126	275	6
Slough	12	1	0	11	92	312	2

Western Counties

	P	W	D	L	F	A	Pts
Launceston	12	12	0	0	438	90	24
D'port Services	12	9	1	2	272	111	19
Dings Crusaders	12	9	0	3	335	124	18
Penzance-Newlyn	12	8	0	4	287	160	16
Spartans*	12	9	0	3	253	152	16
Okehampton	12	7	0	5	172	168	14
O Culverhaysians	12	5	0	7	167	226	10
Tiverton	12	4	1	7	143	232	9
Crediton	12	3	2	7	141	205	8
Drybrook	12	3	1	8	136	391	7
Bideford	12	3	0	9	118	238	6
Dev & C'wall Pol	12	3	0	9	104	313	6
Avonmouth	12	0	1	11	91	247	1

Cornwall & Devon

	P	W	D	L	F	A	Pts
Paignton	12	11	0	1	216	111	22
Sidmouth	12	8	0	4	244	153	16
Exmouth	12	8	0	4	225	157	16
Hayle	12	6	2	4	174	143	14
Truro	12	6	2	4	148	154	14
Saltash	12	6	1	5	156	140	13
Honiton	12	6	0	6	171	227	12
Ivybridge*	12	8	1	3	190	123	11
Teignmouth*	12	6	0	6	245	173	10
S Molton	12	4	0	8	179	185	8
Veor	12	4	0	8	176	245	8
Plymouth CS	12	2	0	10	144	289	4
Newquay*	12	0	0	12	114	282	-2

Gloucestershire & Somerset

	P	W	D	L	F	A	Pts
Keynsham	12	10	0	2	344	140	20
Whitehall	12	10	0	2	252	164	20
Hornets	12	9	1	2	213	146	19
St Mary's OB	12	9	0	3	251	153	18
Stow-on-the-W	12	6	0	6	209	160	12
Thornbury	12	5	1	6	226	218	11
Oldfield OB*	12	6	0	6	203	181	10
Bristol Har'quins	12	5	0	7	180	211	10
North Bristol	12	5	0	7	171	258	10
Cirencester	12	4	0	8	178	217	8
O Redcliffians	12	3	1	8	92	192	7
Wiveliscombe	12	3	0	9	183	306	6
M'somer Norton	12	1	1	10	127	283	3

Cornwall 1

	P	W	D	L	F	A	Pts
St Austell	10	10	0	0	321	111	20
Liskeard-Looe	10	9	0	1	225	99	18
Bude	10	7	0	3	286	73	14
Falmouth	10	6	0	4	260	137	12
St Agnes	10	5	0	5	177	190	10
Helston*	10	6	0	4	193	141	8
Perranporth	10	3	0	7	133	243	6
Stithians	10	2	0	8	152	239	4
Wadebridge*	10	3	0	7	95	204	4
Bodmin*	10	3	0	7	73	271	4
Illogan Pk	10	1	0	9	65	272	2

Illogan Park v Stithians: referee did not turn up

Cornwall 2

	P	W	D	L	F	A	Pts
Redruth Albany	10	10	0	0	502	49	20
St Day	10	6	0	4	133	176	12
Camborne SoM	10	5	1	4	270	172	11
St Just	10	5	0	5	198	172	10
Roseland	10	2	1	7	135	308	5
Lankelly Fowey	10	1	0	9	62	423	2

Devon 1

	P	W	D	L	F	A	Pts
O Plymothian	12	11	0	1	314	86	22
Newton Abbot	12	11	0	1	295	84	22
Kingsbridge	12	10	0	2	281	128	20
O Public Oaks	12	8	0	4	155	161	16
Withycombe	12	6	0	6	160	165	12
Ilfracombe*	12	6	1	5	214	117	11
O Technicians*	12	6	1	5	216	128	11
Tavistock*	12	7	0	5	244	169	10
Topsham*	12	5	0	7	208	254	8
Salcombe	12	3	1	8	71	244	7
Exeter Saracens*	12	2	1	9	96	195	3
Dartmouth	12	1	0	11	104	306	2
Prince Rock	12	0	0	12	71	392	0

Devon 2

	P	W	D	L	F	A	Pts
Totnes	11	9	0	2	373	90	18
Cullompton	11	9	0	2	247	81	18
Tamar Saracens	11	9	0	2	204	74	18
Jesters*	11	7	1	3	129	105	13
Plymstock*	11	6	1	4	174	136	11
Torrington*	11	6	0	5	378	157	10
P'mouth Argaum*	11	6	0	5	197	152	10
St Columba*	11	4	0	7	173	194	6
N Tawton	11	3	0	8	143	268	6
Axminster*	11	3	1	7	72	287	3
Plympton-Vic	11	1	1	9	79	342	3
Plymouth YMCA*	11	1	0	10	71	354	-2

Devonport HSOB have withdrawn. Their fixtures have been removed

Gloucester 1

	P	W	D	L	F	A	Pts
Cleve*	12	11	1	0	314	112	21
Longlevens	12	7	1	4	173	163	15
Barton Hill	12	7	0	5	217	157	14
O Cryptians	12	7	0	5	206	173	14
Cheltenham N	12	6	0	6	241	200	12
F'pton Cotterell*	12	7	0	5	226	233	12
Hucclecote	12	5	2	5	163	170	12
O Richians*	12	6	0	6	232	207	10
Brockworth*	12	6	0	6	228	224	10
Bream*	12	5	1	6	221	177	9
Widden OB	12	4	1	7	137	175	9
Coney Hill	12	3	0	9	143	279	6
Painswick	12	1	0	11	115	346	2

Gloucester 2

	P	W	D	L	F	A	Pts
Tredworth	12	9	0	3	219	158	18
Bristol Saracens	12	8	1	3	243	110	17
Cheltenham CS	12	8	1	3	162	137	17
C'ham Saracens*	12	9	0	3	218	129	16
Ashley Down OB	12	8	0	4	217	148	16
Saintbridge	12	7	0	5	161	130	14
Bishopston	12	5	0	7	162	170	10
O Bristolians	12	5	0	7	186	214	10
Bristol Tele	12	5	0	7	123	171	10
Tetbury*	12	5	2	5	154	216	10
Cotham Pk	12	3	0	9	100	157	6
Chosen Hill FP*	12	3	0	9	147	207	4
Kingswood*	12	1	0	11	118	263	0

Gloucester 3

	P	W	D	L	F	A	Pts
Cainscross*	12	12	0	0	304	94	22
Broad Plain*	12	10	0	2	229	110	18
Southmead	12	9	0	3	254	160	18
Smiths (Ind)	12	8	0	4	245	176	16
Aretians	12	8	0	4	154	140	16
Chipping Sodbury	12	6	0	6	222	157	12
W'bury-o-Sev	12	6	0	6	171	156	12
Tewkesbury	12	5	0	7	131	159	10
Dursley	12	5	0	7	168	197	10
O Colstonians	12	3	0	9	125	264	6
Gloucester CS*	12	3	0	9	130	205	4
O Elizabethans*	12	2	0	10	102	271	2
Minchinhampton*	12	1	0	11	112	258	0

Gloucester 4

	P	W	D	L	F	A	Pts
Gloucs Police	12	11	0	1	333	62	22
Bristol Aero	12	8	1	3	204	82	17
Gloucester AB*	12	7	0	5	159	143	12
Pilning*	12	6	2	4	130	138	12
Newent	12	3	0	9	111	195	6
Dowty*	12	5	1	6	103	136	3
Wotton-u-Edge*	12	0	0	12	45	329	-2

Somerset 1

	P	W	D	L	F	A	Pts
Wellington	12	12	0	0	332	127	24
Walcot OB	12	9	0	3	203	126	18
Yatton*	12	9	0	3	181	157	16
Chard	12	8	0	4	162	166	16
Tor	12	6	1	5	213	161	13
Old Sulians	12	6	0	6	166	189	12
St Bernadettes OB	12	5	0	7	157	177	10
Gordano	12	5	0	7	182	221	10
Minehead Barbs	12	5	0	7	150	275	10
Frome*	12	5	1	6	253	182	9
Wells	12	3	0	9	165	197	6
N Petherton	12	2	0	10	136	192	4
Yeovil*	12	2	0	10	121	251	2

St Bernadettes v Walcot OB: game void as Walcot couldn't field a front row

Somerset 2

	P	W	D	L	F	A	Pts
Imperial	12	10	0	2	299	120	20
Stothert & Pitt	12	9	0	3	271	145	18
Chew Valley	12	9	0	3	209	108	18
Winscombe*	12	9	0	3	214	102	16
Blagdon*	12	6	1	5	189	119	11
Crewkerne*	12	6	0	6	194	144	10
O Ashtonians*	12	6	0	6	172	159	10
Avon*	12	6	0	6	155	190	10
Backwell	12	5	0	7	157	208	10
Bath O Edwards	12	4	1	7	133	212	9
St Brendans OB	12	3	0	9	147	233	6
Westlands	12	1	1	10	90	231	3
Cheddar Valley*	12	2	1	9	68	327	3

Somerset 3

	P	W	D	L	F	A	Pts
Avonvale	16	15	0	1	725	103	30
Bath Saracens*	16	14	1	1	646	119	27

Burnham-o-Sea	16	10	0	6	315	207	20
Castle Cary	16	7	2	7	227	218	16
Morganians	16	7	2	7	199	291	16
British Gas*	16	8	0	8	318	235	12
Wincanton	16	4	0	12	179	411	8
Aller	16	3	1	12	133	531	7
Martock	16	1	0	15	82	709	2

Berks/Dorset/Wilts 1

	P	*W*	*D*	*L*	*F*	*A*	*Pts*
Swindon	12	12	0	0	356	80	24
Melksham	12	9	1	2	241	151	19
Marlborough	12	8	1	3	256	165	17
Wootton Bass	12	8	0	4	343	137	16
Redingensians	12	6	1	5	254	185	13
Aldermaston	12	3	3	6	88	135	9
Thatcham	12	4	1	7	149	227	9
Corsham	12	4	1	7	124	206	9
Weymouth	12	4	1	7	149	263	9
Blandford	12	4	1	7	131	252	9
Supermarine	12	4	0	8	143	182	8
Lytchett Minster	12	3	1	8	135	282	7
Swindon Coll*	12	3	1	8	165	269	5

Berks/Dorset/Wilts 2

	P	*W*	*D*	*L*	*F*	*A*	*Pts*
Bournemouth U	12	11	0	1	453	139	22
N Dorset	12	9	0	3	412	120	16
Bradford-on-A	12	9	0	3	192	144	16
Bridport	12	8	0	4	284	159	16
Calne	12	7	1	4	220	83	15
Berkshire SH	12	7	0	5	156	210	14
Trowbridge	12	6	0	6	240	193	12
Westbury	12	5	0	7	177	214	10
Pewsey Vale	12	3	1	8	136	313	7
Oakmeadians*	12	6	0	6	229	140	6
Warminster	12	3	0	9	139	280	6
Puddletown	12	3	0	9	110	335	6
Poole*	12	0	0	12	71	489	-6

Berks/Dorset/Wilts 3

	P	*W*	*D*	*L*	*F*	*A*	*Pts*
Portcastrians	14	12	0	2	246	89	24
Tadley	14	11	0	3	347	94	22
Dorset Police	14	11	0	3	236	90	22
Minety	14	6	1	7	167	186	13
Colerne*	14	6	0	8	249	222	10
Christchurch	14	4	1	9	217	226	9
Hungerford	14	4	0	10	122	273	8
Cricklade	14	0	2	12	35	439	2

Bucks/Oxon 1

	P	*W*	*D*	*L*	*F*	*A*	*Pts*
Chinnor	12	12	0	0	437	106	24
Oxford OB	12	8	0	4	342	186	16
Phoenix	12	8	0	4	154	178	16
Witney	12	7	0	5	217	157	14
Buckingham	12	6	0	6	207	199	12
Grove	12	6	0	6	194	227	12
Chesham*	12	6	1	5	133	184	11
Beaconsfield	12	5	0	7	224	213	10
Milton Keynes*	12	5	2	5	148	150	10
Pennanians	12	5	0	7	175	208	10
Drifters	12	4	0	8	162	203	8
Littlemore	12	3	1	8	149	210	7
Abingdon	12	1	0	11	143	464	2

Bucks/Oxon 2

	P	*W*	*D*	*L*	*F*	*A*	*Pts*
Wheatley	14	11	1	2	463	74	23
Chipping Norton*	14	12	0	2	320	89	22
Didcot	14	8	2	4	177	213	18
Gosford AB*	14	8	1	5	215	169	15
Thames V Police	14	5	1	8	112	140	11
Winslow	14	5	1	8	127	285	11
Cholsey*	14	3	0	11	97	311	4
Harwell	14	1	0	13	92	322	2

LONDON DIVISION

London 1

	P	*W*	*D*	*L*	*F*	*A*	*Pts*
Camberley	11	11	0	0	335	103	22
Esher	12	10	0	2	344	132	20
Ruislip	11	10	0	1	236	135	20
Harlow	11	7	0	4	329	193	14
G'ford & G'ming	12	7	0	5	294	184	14
Ealing	10	6	0	4	147	132	12
Southend	12	6	0	6	243	249	12
O Mid Whitgift	12	6	0	6	207	225	12
Sutton & Epsom	11	4	0	7	153	177	8
Old Colfeians	12	4	0	8	202	256	8
Streatham-Croy	12	2	0	10	99	325	4
Eton Manor*	12	2	0	10	129	259	2
Maidstone*	12	0	0	12	106	454	-2

London 2 North

	P	*W*	*D*	*L*	*F*	*A*	*Pts*
Staines	12	11	0	1	318	107	22
O Verulamians	12	9	0	3	239	178	18
Cheshunt	11	8	0	3	200	150	16
Norwich	11	6	1	4	185	120	13
Cambridge	11	5	2	4	154	125	12
Bishop's Stort	11	5	2	4	196	193	12
Thurrock	12	5	0	7	201	204	10
Finchley*	12	5	2	5	165	192	10
Brentwood	12	4	2	6	140	171	10
Romford & G Pk	12	3	1	8	119	212	7
O Gaytonians	12	3	0	9	149	216	6
Chingford	12	3	0	9	141	240	6
Woodford	10	3	0	7	128	227	6

London 2 South

	P	W	D	L	F	A	Pts
Charlton Pk	12	11	1	0	332	125	23
O Blues	12	9	0	3	229	158	18
O Wimbledonians	12	7	1	4	228	177	15
Westcombe Pk	12	7	0	5	271	182	14
Dorking	12	6	1	5	216	199	13
Thanet Wands	12	6	0	6	181	200	12
Gravesend	12	6	0	6	222	267	12
O Juddian	12	5	0	7	217	189	10
Horsham	12	5	0	7	159	205	10
O Reigatian	12	4	1	7	119	225	9
Sidcup	12	4	0	8	177	169	8
O Alleynian	12	4	0	8	167	250	8
Portsmouth	12	2	0	10	165	337	4

London 3 North-East

	P	W	D	L	F	A	Pts
Colchester	11	10	0	1	273	87	20
Rochford	12	10	0	2	198	80	20
Ipswich	12	9	0	3	237	115	18
Bury St Eds	12	7	0	5	153	160	14
Braintree	12	6	0	6	236	186	12
O Edwardians	11	4	2	5	163	180	10
Maldon	12	4	1	7	129	166	9
Chelmsford	12	4	1	7	96	177	9
Shelford	12	4	0	8	169	210	8
W Norfolk	12	4	0	8	146	213	8
Campion	12	4	0	8	159	233	8
Basildon	12	4	0	8	109	183	8
Woodbridge*	12	5	0	7	133	211	8

London 3 North-West

	P	W	D	L	F	A	Pts
Hertford	12	11	0	1	207	105	22
Grasshoppers	11	9	0	2	187	89	18
Lensbury	12	9	0	3	246	169	18
O Albanians	12	8	0	4	210	138	16
O Merchant Ts	12	7	0	5	231	153	14
O Elizabethans	11	6	1	4	165	139	13
Letchworth	11	6	0	5	209	148	12
O Millhillians	12	5	1	6	191	158	11
Welwyn	11	5	1	5	189	219	11
Barnet	12	4	0	8	174	224	8
Kingsburians	12	2	1	9	112	213	5
Upper Clapton	12	1	0	11	114	256	2
London NZ	12	1	0	11	69	293	2

London 3 South-East

	P	W	D	L	F	A	Pts
Brockleians	12	12	0	0	282	118	24
Beckenham	12	10	0	2	300	100	20
Worthing	12	9	1	2	262	126	19
Canterbury	12	9	0	3	217	126	18
Park House	12	7	0	5	167	146	14
Lewes	12	5	1	6	183	145	11
O Beccehamian	12	5	0	7	177	140	10
Chichester	12	5	0	7	196	206	10
Haywards Hth	12	5	0	7	183	214	10
Brighton	11	3	0	8	157	183	6
H'field & Waldren*	12	3	0	9	156	324	4
E Grinstead	11	1	1	9	137	281	3
Erith	12	1	1	10	86	394	3

London 3 South-West

	P	W	D	L	F	A	Pts
Wimbledon	11	11	0	0	255	64	22
Alton	11	9	0	2	263	97	18
O Emanuel	11	6	0	5	196	174	12
Gosport	11	6	0	5	171	152	12
Warlingham	11	6	0	5	145	201	12
Cranleigh	11	5	1	5	138	149	11
Purley	11	5	0	6	164	161	10
O Guildfordians	11	5	0	6	151	200	10
Guy's Hosp	11	4	0	7	181	195	8
O Walcountians	11	4	0	7	137	209	8
Southampton	11	2	1	8	130	224	5
Eastleigh	11	2	0	9	106	211	4
KCS OB*	0	0	0	0	0	0	-1

Eastern Counties 1

	P	W	D	L	F	A	Pts
Lowestoft & Yar	12	11	0	1	424	92	22
Canvey Island	12	9	1	2	286	151	19
Diss	11	8	0	3	255	97	16
Wymondham	12	8	0	4	277	129	16
Ely	12	7	0	5	204	177	14
Saffron Walden	12	5	1	6	183	205	11
Newmarket	12	5	1	6	141	194	11
Bancroft	12	4	1	7	152	173	9
Harwich & Dov	12	4	1	7	126	236	9
Holt	11	4	0	7	115	218	8
Upminster	12	3	0	9	98	309	6
Ravens*	12	3	1	8	125	280	5
Westcliff*	12	2	2	8	100	225	4

Eastern Counties 2

	P	W	D	L	F	A	Pts
Ilford Wands	11	9	0	2	216	52	18
Loughton*	11	9	0	2	257	110	16
Wanstead*	11	8	2	1	153	56	16
O Palmerians	10	6	1	3	121	109	13
Cantabrigian	11	6	0	5	149	144	12
Thetford	10	5	0	5	137	170	10
O Cooperians	11	5	0	6	156	222	10
Met Pol Chigwell	11	4	0	7	118	161	8
O Bealonians	11	4	0	7	127	177	8
Lakenham Hew	10	3	0	7	101	238	6
Thames	10	2	0	8	114	135	4
East London	11	1	1	9	118	193	3
Clacton*	0	0	0	0	0	0	-4

Eastern Counties 3

	P	W	D	L	F	A	Pts
Fakenham	11	9	0	2	203	93	18
Southwold	12	7	1	4	201	123	15
Ipswich YMCA	12	7	1	4	170	122	15
S Woodham Ferr	12	7	0	5	166	139	14
Hadleigh	11	6	0	5	211	129	12
Stowmarket	11	6	0	5	172	100	12
Felixstowe*	11	6	0	5	124	89	10
Crusaders	11	5	0	6	139	124	10
Thurston	12	5	0	7	155	202	10
Haverhill*	10	5	1	4	135	101	9
Broadland	12	4	1	7	117	221	9
Beccles	12	4	0	8	169	168	8

Eastern Counties 4

	P	W	D	L	F	A	Pts
Billericay	9	8	0	1	216	40	16
Burnham-on-C*	10	7	1	2	161	74	13
Brightlingsea	10	6	0	4	217	129	12
Wisbech	9	6	0	3	160	75	12
Witham	9	5	0	4	150	141	10
May & Baker	10	5	0	5	180	196	10
Ongar	9	4	0	5	104	122	8
Mersea Island	9	3	0	6	108	122	6
Dereham	8	3	0	5	61	205	6
March*	9	3	1	5	110	95	5
Essex Police	0	0	0	0	0	0	-1

Eastern Counties 5

	P	W	D	L	F	A	Pts
Sawston	6	5	0	1	166	36	10
Rayleigh	6	5	0	1	131	88	10
Swaffham	5	3	0	2	112	85	6
Stanford*	6	3	0	3	91	71	4
Essex CC	5	2	0	3	49	63	4
Norwich U	6	1	0	5	73	130	2
Dagenham	6	1	0	5	62	211	2

Hampshire 1

	P	W	D	L	F	A	Pts
Jersey	12	12	0	0	401	89	24
US Portsmouth	12	11	0	1	374	70	22
Winchester	12	8	0	4	328	156	16
Millbrook	11	7	0	4	273	156	14
Petersfield*	12	7	1	4	203	219	13
Trojans	12	5	0	7	141	242	10
Esso	11	4	1	6	177	177	9
Tottonians	12	4	0	8	203	209	8
Guernsey	9	4	0	5	143	150	8
Farnborough*	12	4	1	7	161	228	7
Sandown & Sh'n	11	1	0	10	78	372	2
New Milton	12	0	1	11	97	493	1
Isle of Wight*	12	6	0	6	184	202	-4

Hampshire 2

	P	W	D	L	F	A	Pts
Andover*	12	12	0	0	373	57	22
Fordingbridge	12	7	0	5	186	151	14
Ventnor*	12	7	0	5	195	142	12
F'ham Heaths*	12	6	0	6	179	213	10
Romsey*	12	5	0	7	171	197	8
AC Delco*	12	4	0	8	133	288	6
Overton*	12	1	0	11	84	273	0

Hampshire 3

	P	W	D	L	F	A	Pts
Fleet*	9	7	0	2	183	69	12
Nomads	9	6	0	3	121	79	12
Alresford*	9	6	0	3	159	89	10
Basingstoke Ws	7	4	0	3	97	81	8
Waterlooville*	8	2	0	6	66	145	2
Ellingham	10	1	0	9	47	210	2

Hertfordshire 1

	P	W	D	L	F	A	Pts
Tring	9	9	0	0	255	51	18
Stevenage	9	7	0	2	155	73	14
Datchworth*	9	7	0	2	144	81	12
Royston	9	5	1	3	176	106	11
O Stanfordians	9	4	1	4	87	83	9
O Ashmoleans	9	3	1	5	151	134	7
Hatfield	9	3	0	6	94	210	6
Bacavians*	9	4	1	4	144	151	3
Watford*	9	1	0	8	91	216	-2
QE II Hosp*	9	0	0	9	41	233	-2

Herts/Middlesex 1

	P	W	D	L	F	A	Pts
Mill Hill	12	10	0	2	342	145	20
Fullerians	12	10	0	2	302	118	20
St Albans	12	9	1	2	282	168	19
O Meadonians	11	8	1	2	208	102	17
Hampstead	12	6	1	5	246	154	13
Haringey*	12	5	2	5	252	225	10
Centaurs*	12	6	0	6	202	219	10
Hendon	12	5	0	7	128	229	10
Hemel Hemps	11	4	0	7	137	217	8
St Mary's Hosp	11	3	1	7	162	231	7
Uxbridge*	12	4	0	8	166	212	6
Hitchin	11	2	0	9	126	387	4
Harpenden	12	1	0	11	131	277	2

Kent 1

	P	W	D	L	F	A	Pts
Sevenoaks	12	12	0	0	503	116	24
Tunbridge Wells	12	11	0	1	332	106	18
Dartfordians	12	9	0	3	201	183	18
Met Pol Hayes	12	7	0	5	192	151	14
Sheppey	12	6	1	5	209	145	13
Bromley	12	5	0	7	251	201	10

O Dunstonians	12	5	0	7	181	169	10
O Sho'hillians	12	5	0	7	195	186	10
Medway*	12	5	2	5	194	214	10
Gillingham Anch	12	4	2	6	153	212	10
O Elthamians	12	3	1	8	181	344	7
Betteshanger	12	3	0	9	146	324	6
Thames Poly	12	0	0	12	65	452	0

Kent 2

	P	W	D	L	F	A	Pts
Ashford	12	10	0	2	248	75	20
Dover	12	10	0	2	249	130	20
Cranbrook	12	9	1	2	282	97	19
O Gravesendians	12	7	1	4	267	206	15
Folkestone	12	6	1	5	212	151	13
Snowdown CW	12	6	0	6	149	173	12
Whitstable	12	6	0	6	159	197	12
Vigo	12	5	1	6	151	153	11
Nat West Bank	12	5	0	7	179	168	10
Sittingbourne	12	2	2	8	101	175	6
Deal*	12	4	1	7	183	206	5
New Ash Green	12	2	0	10	128	322	4
Midland Bank*	12	2	1	9	110	365	3

Kent 3

	P	W	D	L	F	A	Pts
Lordswood	9	8	0	1	249	74	16
O Williamsonians	9	7	1	1	133	75	15
Tonbridge	9	6	2	1	285	51	14
Bexley	9	6	0	3	189	93	12
Darenth Valley	9	4	0	5	186	114	8
O Olavians	9	4	0	5	129	137	8
Linton (Aylesford)	9	3	2	4	79	105	8
Citizens	9	3	0	6	97	178	6
Greenwich	9	1	1	7	55	264	3
Lloyds Bank	9	0	0	9	19	330	0

Kent 4

	P	W	D	L	F	A	Pts
Orpington	8	6	0	2	158	68	12
STC Footscray	8	5	1	2	76	50	11
Faversham	8	3	1	4	71	78	7
Edenbridge	7	2	2	3	49	96	6
Westerham	7	1	0	6	39	101	2

Middlesex 1

	P	W	D	L	F	A	Pts
O Hamptonians	12	11	0	1	336	125	22
Wembley	11	9	1	1	223	109	19
O Paulines	12	7	1	4	192	129	15
Hackney	12	7	1	4	180	124	15
Harrow	11	7	0	4	195	105	14
Twickenham	12	7	0	5	244	189	14
Civil Service	12	6	2	4	176	184	14
O Actonians	12	6	0	6	172	137	12
O Haberdashers	12	4	1	7	136	248	9
Roxeth Manor OB*	12	4	1	7	130	213	7
Belsize Pk	12	2	0	10	167	306	4
Sudbury Court	12	2	0	10	117	266	4
Antlers	12	1	1	10	118	251	3

Middlesex 2

	P	W	D	L	F	A	Pts
L Nigerians	11	10	1	0	374	67	21
HAC	11	8	2	1	249	91	18
Enfield Ignats	11	9	0	2	234	134	18
Barclays Bank	11	7	0	4	190	187	14
H'smith & Ful	11	6	0	5	193	182	12
Bank of England	11	5	1	5	171	156	11
O Abbotstonians	10	4	0	6	181	153	8
O Isleworthians	11	4	0	7	118	217	8
Thamesians	10	4	0	6	101	202	8
Feltham	11	3	0	8	212	193	6
Hayes	11	3	0	8	114	210	6
Pinner & Grams	11	0	0	11	61	406	0
O Grammarians*	0	0	0	0	0	0	-2

Middlesex 3

	P	W	D	L	F	A	Pts
L Exiles	9	8	0	1	333	79	16
L French	9	6	0	2	243	78	13
O Tottonians	8	5	1	2	116	91	11
UCS OB	9	5	0	4	202	177	10
St Nicholas OB*	8	6	0	2	207	86	8
Orleans FP	9	4	0	5	130	239	8
Southgate	9	3	0	6	114	204	6
L Cornish	8	2	0	6	150	120	4
Northolt*	9	3	0	6	97	168	2
Osterley*	8	0	0	8	21	371	-2

Middlesex 4

	P	W	D	L	F	A	Pts
Quintin	5	5	0	0	123	34	10
BA	7	5	0	2	98	75	10
GWR	7	4	0	3	167	115	8
St George's Hosp	5	3	0	2	64	171	6
St Bart's Hosp	4	2	0	2	90	41	4
Kodak	5	2	0	3	121	88	4
Middlesex Hosp	4	0	0	4	41	98	0
Meadhurst	5	0	0	5	24	106	0

Surrey 1

	P	W	D	L	F	A	Pts
O Whitgiftians	12	11	1	0	283	111	23
Barnes	12	8	1	3	243	150	17
Effingham	12	8	0	4	115	104	16
O Reedonians	12	7	2	3	124	134	16
O Cranleighans	12	6	1	5	126	129	13
John Fisher OB*	12	6	1	5	126	103	11
University Vands	12	5	1	6	164	182	11
Chobham	12	5	1	6	137	175	11
Kingston*	12	6	0	6	147	150	10

	P	W	D	L	F	A	Pts
Shirley Wands	12	5	0	7	116	125	10
Farnham	12	4	0	8	140	179	8
O Rutlishians	12	2	1	9	133	219	5
Raynes Pk	12	0	1	11	80	173	1

Surrey 2

	P	W	D	L	F	A	Pts
O Caterhamians	12	11	0	1	334	114	22
Woking	11	10	1	0	361	76	21
Chipstead	12	9	1	2	216	167	19
O Tiffinians	12	8	0	4	206	194	16
Bec OB	10	6	0	4	146	112	12
Merton	10	5	0	5	111	101	10
Cobham	10	5	0	5	126	121	10
Mitcham	12	4	1	7	142	152	9
Wandsworthians	11	4	1	6	117	192	9
Law Society	12	3	1	8	164	273	7
O Haileyburians	12	3	0	9	219	273	6
L Fire Brigade*	12	2	1	9	102	202	3
Reigate & Redhill*	12	1	0	11	81	348	0

Surrey 3

	P	W	D	L	F	A	Pts
O Suttonians	10	9	0	1	217	65	18
Battersea Irons	10	8	1	1	169	53	17
Egham	10	6	1	3	113	123	13
O Freemans	10	5	1	4	155	95	11
O Bevonians	10	4	2	4	123	133	10
London Media	10	4	1	5	152	148	9
O Pelhamians	10	4	1	5	123	157	9
O Johnians	9	3	0	6	95	156	6
Croydon	10	3	0	7	83	172	6
Lightwater	9	2	1	6	95	157	5
Haslemere	10	2	0	8	98	164	4

Surrey 4

	P	W	D	L	F	A	Pts
Kew Occas	8	8	0	0	322	59	16
O Wellingtonian	8	7	0	1	283	72	14
King's Coll Hosp	8	5	0	3	144	129	10
Surrey U	7	4	1	2	84	99	9
Economicals	7	4	0	3	81	77	8
R Holloway Coll	7	3	0	4	201	162	6
Oxted	9	2	1	6	85	166	5
Surrey Police	8	2	1	5	78	208	5
Racal-Decca	8	1	1	6	88	182	3
O Epsomians	8	1	0	7	35	247	2

Sussex 1

	P	W	D	L	F	A	Pts
Uckfield	12	11	0	1	309	87	22
Seaford	12	10	0	2	218	144	20
Hastings & Bex	12	9	0	3	331	92	18
Crawley	12	8	0	4	270	109	16
Burgess Hill	12	6	1	5	166	202	13
Bognor	11	6	0	5	193	125	12
Hove	11	6	0	5	222	172	12
O Brightonians	12	5	0	7	167	268	10
Sun All Horsham	12	4	0	8	130	202	8
Pulborough	12	4	0	8	135	262	8
Eastbourne	12	3	2	7	164	342	8
Crowborough	12	3	1	8	151	184	7
Ditchling	12	0	0	12	64	331	0

Sussex 2

	P	W	D	L	F	A	Pts
BA Wingspan	10	10	0	0	387	63	20
Hellingly	10	7	0	3	223	103	14
St Francis	10	5	1	4	230	192	11
Newick	10	3	2	5	58	152	8
Sussex Police	10	2	1	7	64	243	5
Plumpton	10	1	0	9	53	262	2

Sussex 3

	P	W	D	L	F	A	Pts
Rye	8	6	2	0	125	82	14
Shoreham	8	4	0	4	110	78	8
Arun	8	4	0	4	79	91	8
Midhurst	8	2	2	4	92	98	6
Robertsbridge	8	2	0	6	68	125	4

NORTH DIVISION

North 1

	P	W	D	L	F	A	Pts
Sandal	12	8	3	1	227	126	19
Stockton	12	8	2	2	196	111	18
Manchester	12	7	3	2	217	166	17
Bradford & Bing	12	8	0	4	230	166	16
Hull Ionians	12	5	1	6	198	196	11
Huddersfield	12	5	1	6	163	167	11
Widnes	12	5	1	6	163	188	11
York	12	5	1	6	157	198	11
Middlesbro	12	5	1	6	162	206	11
W Pk Bramhope	12	5	1	6	197	162	9
Tynedale	12	4	1	7	184	154	9
Wigton	12	3	1	8	132	238	7
Durham C	12	2	0	10	124	272	4

North 2

	P	W	D	L	F	A	Pts
Macclesfield	12	12	0	0	314	106	24
Bridlington	12	11	0	1	232	101	22
N Brighton	12	9	0	3	376	140	18
W Pk St Helens	12	8	1	3	316	205	17
Northern	12	8	0	4	206	115	16
Doncaster	12	7	0	5	136	155	14
Birkenhead	12	4	1	7	177	188	9
O Crossleyans*	12	4	2	6	141	240	8
H'pool Rovers	12	4	0	8	110	212	8
Alnwick	12	3	0	9	155	276	6
Halifax*	12	4	0	8	146	229	4

	P	W	D	L	F	A	Pts
Vale of Lune	12	2	0	10	146	293	4
Northwich	12	0	0	12	65	260	0

North-West 1

	P	W	D	L	F	A	Pts
Sedgley Pk	12	12	0	0	421	60	24
Lymm	12	7	1	4	215	192	15
Chester	11	7	1	3	149	134	15
Netherhall	12	7	1	4	220	208	15
Oldershaw*	12	7	0	5	259	172	12
Wilmslow	11	6	0	5	204	130	12
Ashton-o-Mersey*	12	6	1	5	133	171	11
Sandbach	12	5	0	7	191	240	10
Carlisle	12	5	0	7	132	190	10
Cockermouth*	12	5	1	6	134	156	9
Blackburn	12	3	1	8	138	208	7
Stockport	12	2	0	10	135	243	4
Wigan	12	2	0	10	84	311	4

North-West 2

	P	W	D	L	F	A	Pts
Leigh	12	11	0	1	231	130	22
Penrith	12	9	1	2	285	131	19
O Salians	12	7	2	3	142	120	16
Fleetwood	12	7	1	4	211	144	15
Kirkby Lonsdale	11	7	0	4	193	161	14
Merseyside Pol	11	7	0	4	142	126	14
O Aldwinians	12	5	0	7	190	177	10
Vagabonds (IoM)	12	5	0	7	124	175	10
Rossendale	12	5	0	7	132	193	10
Caldy	12	3	1	8	186	191	7
Egremont	12	2	1	9	118	205	5
St Edward's OB	12	3	1	8	138	265	5
Ruskin Pk*	12	2	1	9	134	208	3

Cumbria/Lancashire North

	P	W	D	L	F	A	Pts
Windermere	12	12	0	0	316	97	24
Workington	12	10	0	2	223	125	20
Calder Vale	12	8	0	4	230	67	16
Upper Eden	12	7	1	4	163	141	15
Rochdale	12	7	0	5	127	138	14
Vickers	12	5	1	6	139	124	11
St Benedicts	12	5	0	7	148	155	10
Moresby	12	5	0	7	144	182	10
Tyldesley	12	4	0	8	145	200	8
Furness	12	4	0	8	111	174	8
Keswick	12	4	0	8	144	211	8
Ormskirk	12	4	0	8	137	234	8
De La S (Salford)	12	2	0	10	87	266	4

Cumbria

	P	W	D	L	F	A	Pts
Carnforth	8	7	0	1	226	37	14
Creighton	8	6	1	1	118	51	13
Millom	8	6	0	2	191	66	12
Whitehaven	8	5	0	3	144	53	10
Smith Bros	8	4	1	3	103	142	9
Ambleside	8	3	0	5	140	83	6
Green Garth	8	3	0	5	71	95	6
British Steel	8	1	0	7	35	277	2
Silloth	8	0	0	8	48	272	0

Lancashire North 1

	P	W	D	L	F	A	Pts
Metrovick	12	11	1	0	235	77	23
Oldham	12	8	2	2	154	128	18
Thornton Cleve	12	8	1	3	196	100	17
Blackpool	11	8	0	3	209	128	16
Bolton	11	8	0	3	168	115	16
Ashton-u-Lyne	12	6	1	5	173	180	13
Bury	11	5	2	4	112	154	12
Heaton Moor	12	5	0	7	130	155	10
Dukinfield	12	3	1	8	151	151	7
Colne & Nelson	12	3	0	9	115	143	6
N Manchester	12	3	0	9	115	211	6
Chorley	12	2	0	10	109	206	4
Burnage	11	2	0	9	75	194	4

Lancashire North 2

	P	W	D	L	F	A	Pts
Eccles	8	7	0	1	113	40	14
Littleborough	8	6	1	1	166	68	13
Marple	8	6	0	2	213	44	12
O Bedians	8	6	0	2	171	25	12
British Aero	8	4	0	4	34	162	8
Broughton	8	2	1	5	138	96	5
Shell Carrington*	8	3	0	5	85	163	2
Clitheroe*	8	1	0	7	53	124	0
Lostock*	8	0	0	8	24	275	-2

Cheshire/Lancashire South

	P	W	D	L	F	A	Pts
Aspull	12	12	0	0	280	45	24
Eagle	12	8	0	4	183	161	16
S Liverpool	12	7	0	5	209	144	14
Crewe & Nantwich	12	7	0	5	193	177	14
Wirral*	12	8	0	4	133	127	14
Altrincham Kers	12	6	1	5	142	138	13
Warrington	12	5	0	7	152	146	10
Sefton	12	5	0	7	156	186	10
Port Sunlight	12	5	0	7	86	147	10
O Parkonians*	12	5	0	7	157	146	8
Southport	12	4	0	8	137	176	8
O Anselmians	12	3	1	8	112	213	7
Vulcan	12	2	0	10	88	222	4

Cheshire

	P	W	D	L	F	A	Pts
Congleton	9	9	0	0	265	66	18
Wallasey	8	7	0	1	210	77	14
Shell Stanlow	9	6	0	3	156	99	12

	P	W	D	L	F	A	Pts
Bowdon	9	5	1	3	198	117	11
Prenton	9	4	0	5	127	115	8
Helsby	9	2	2	5	73	72	6
Holmes Chapel	9	2	0	7	67	250	4
Whitehouse Pk*	8	2	0	6	59	196	2
Hoylake*	8	2	1	5	97	173	-1
Moore*	8	2	0	6	81	168	-4

Lancashire South

	P	W	D	L	F	A	Pts
Newton-le-Will	9	9	0	0	423	74	18
Liverpool Coll	9	7	0	2	146	60	14
St Mary's OB	9	6	0	3	189	84	12
Didsbury Toc H	9	4	1	4	163	150	9
Birchfield*	9	5	0	4	189	160	8
Douglas	9	4	0	5	135	128	8
Mossley Hill	9	3	1	5	94	178	7
Lucas	9	1	0	8	60	359	2
Halton*	9	4	0	5	146	199	0
Hightown*	9	1	0	8	100	253	-2

North-East 1

	P	W	D	L	F	A	Pts
Blaydon	12	11	0	1	212	116	22
Horden	12	9	0	3	248	135	18
Keighley	12	9	0	3	233	162	18
Driffield	12	8	0	4	213	115	16
Gateshead Fell	12	8	0	4	235	159	16
O Brodleians	12	7	0	5	218	216	14
Morpeth	12	6	0	6	156	174	12
Cleckheaton	12	5	0	7	169	166	10
Pontefract	12	5	0	7	159	182	10
Roundhegians	12	3	1	8	126	227	7
Selby*	12	3	1	8	177	232	5
Redcar	12	2	0	10	96	281	4
Thornensians	12	1	0	11	114	191	2

North-East 2

	P	W	D	L	F	A	Pts
Ashington	12	8	1	3	209	112	17
N Ribblesdale	12	8	1	3	161	129	17
Westoe	12	7	2	3	245	135	16
Darl Mowden Pk	12	7	1	4	168	106	15
Hull	12	7	1	4	171	116	15
Blyth	12	6	0	6	160	176	12
Bramley	12	6	0	6	150	238	12
Ripon	12	4	2	6	136	131	10
Whitby	12	5	0	7	142	144	10
Goole	12	4	2	6	129	150	10
Beverley	12	5	0	7	145	168	10
Whitley Bay Rock	12	4	0	8	73	200	8
Novocastrians	12	2	0	10	112	196	4

Durham & Northumberland 1

	P	W	D	L	F	A	Pts
Percy Pk	12	11	0	1	396	63	22
Sunderland	12	10	1	1	301	89	21
Acklam	12	10	1	1	203	100	21
Darlington	12	9	0	3	333	76	18
Ryton	12	8	0	4	244	208	16
W Hart TDSOB*	12	7	0	5	207	177	12
N Durham	12	5	1	6	164	219	11
N Shields	12	3	2	7	165	125	8
Darlington RA	12	3	1	8	105	275	7
Bishop Auck	12	3	0	9	142	284	6
Ponteland	12	3	0	9	88	255	6
Guisborough	12	2	0	10	87	326	4
Wallsend	12	1	0	11	77	315	2

Durham & Northumberland 2

	P	W	D	L	F	A	Pts
Winlaton Vs	12	11	0	1	341	55	22
Medicals	12	10	0	2	278	71	20
Wensleydale	12	8	1	3	186	140	17
Hartlepool	12	8	0	4	231	117	16
Chester-le-St	12	7	1	4	164	94	15
Seaham*	12	7	0	5	152	153	12
Billingham	12	5	1	6	106	150	11
Hartlepool BBOB	12	5	0	7	125	231	10
Richmondshire	12	4	0	8	80	212	8
Houghton	12	3	1	8	103	220	7
Consett*	12	4	0	8	117	194	6
Seghill	12	2	2	8	108	189	6
Seaton Carew	12	1	0	11	93	258	2

Durham & Northumberland 3

	P	W	D	L	F	A	Pts
Barnard Castle	9	9	0	0	286	48	18
Sedgefield	9	8	0	1	211	75	16
Jarrovians	9	6	1	2	195	83	13
Newton Aycliffe	9	6	0	3	153	96	12
Wearside	9	5	0	4	143	125	10
Hartlepool Ath	9	3	0	6	93	177	6
Belmont	9	3	0	6	92	241	6
Benton	9	2	0	7	32	157	4
Prudhoe	9	1	1	7	52	169	3
Washington*	9	1	0	8	46	132	0

Yorkshire 1

	P	W	D	L	F	A	Pts
Wheatley Hills	12	12	0	0	343	90	24
Wath	12	10	0	2	255	119	20
Ikley	12	7	1	4	171	122	15
Yarnbury	12	7	1	4	149	121	15
Barnsley	12	7	1	4	139	129	15
Malton & Norton	12	6	1	5	178	198	13
Leodiensians	12	6	0	6	179	197	12
Sheffield Oaks	12	5	0	7	128	201	10
Bradford Salem	12	4	0	8	171	179	8
Pocklington	12	4	0	8	155	204	8
Castleford	12	3	2	7	125	210	8

	P	W	D	L	F	A	Pts
O Otliensians	12	2	0	10	115	200	4
Hemsworth*	12	2	0	10	138	276	2

Yorkshire 2

	P	W	D	L	F	A	Pts
Wibsey	12	12	0	0	272	95	24
Halifax Vands	12	9	0	3	222	143	18
Northallerton	12	8	0	4	147	120	16
O Modernians*	12	8	1	3	172	104	15
W Leeds	12	6	0	6	158	161	12
Aireborough	12	6	0	6	201	215	12
Hud'field YMCA	12	5	1	6	109	181	11
Moortown	11	4	2	5	123	127	10
Sheffield Tigers	12	5	0	7	164	222	10
Dinnington	11	4	1	6	167	167	9
Hessle	12	3	1	8	111	132	7
Scarborough	12	1	3	8	114	187	5
York RI	12	1	1	10	129	235	3

Yorkshire 3

	P	W	D	L	F	A	Pts
Wetherby	12	10	0	2	243	88	20
Skipton	12	9	2	1	237	114	20
O Rishworthians	12	8	2	2	195	103	18
Stanley Rodillians	12	7	1	4	150	140	15
Heath	12	7	0	5	155	156	14
Phoenix Pk	12	6	1	5	148	135	13
Marist	12	6	1	5	156	163	13
Ossett	12	5	1	6	132	231	11
Knottingley	12	3	3	6	118	130	9
Hullensians	12	4	0	8	115	124	8
Lawnswood	12	3	1	8	123	187	7
Leeds Corinthians	12	3	1	8	59	125	7
Burley	12	0	1	11	85	220	1

Yorkshire 4

	P	W	D	L	F	A	Pts
Mosborough	12	11	1	0	250	43	23
Baildon	12	10	0	2	271	74	20
Stockbridge	12	9	1	2	190	83	19
Hornsea*	12	9	0	3	195	79	16
Rowntrees	12	7	1	4	161	141	15
BP Chemicals	12	5	0	7	108	141	10
Withernsea	12	5	0	7	131	200	10
Yorkshire Main*	12	4	3	5	87	162	9
De La S (Sheff)	12	4	0	8	90	170	8
Adwick le Street	12	3	0	9	82	154	6
Danum Phoenix*	12	3	1	8	97	185	5
Garforth	12	2	1	9	99	204	5
Knaresborough*	12	2	0	10	71	196	2

Yorkshire 5

	P	W	D	L	F	A	Pts
Rawmarsh	5	4	0	1	108	49	8
N Earswick	5	3	0	2	80	67	6
Yorkshire CW*	5	3	0	2	61	44	4
Harlow Nomads*	5	3	0	2	63	59	4
Menwith Hill Qs	5	2	0	3	80	88	4
Armthorpe M'ham*	5	0	0	5	50	135	-2

MIDLANDS DIVISION

Midlands 1

	P	W	D	L	F	A	Pts
Worcester	12	11	1	0	278	82	23
Burton	12	10	0	2	209	156	20
Whitchurch	12	7	1	4	240	157	15
Westleigh	12	6	2	4	135	114	14
Mansfield	12	5	1	6	167	197	11
Stafford	12	5	1	6	155	209	11
Wolverhampton	12	5	0	7	215	173	10
Camp Hill	12	4	2	6	157	175	10
Leamington	12	4	2	6	157	200	10
Syston	12	5	0	7	169	227	10
Bedworth	12	3	2	7	135	200	8
Towcestrians	12	3	1	8	177	229	7
Derby	12	3	1	8	116	191	7

Midlands 2

	P	W	D	L	F	A	Pts
Leighton Buzz	12	11	0	1	210	131	22
Broad St	12	10	0	2	291	129	20
Stockwood Pk	12	9	0	3	208	153	18
Hinckley	12	8	1	3	286	134	17
Belgrave	12	7	0	5	225	163	14
Paviors	12	6	0	6	153	134	12
Matlock	12	5	1	6	170	176	11
Bedford Ath	12	5	0	7	177	204	10
Keresley	12	4	1	7	125	198	9
Sutton Coldfield*	12	5	0	7	162	177	8
Peterborough	12	3	0	9	149	242	6
Newark	12	1	1	10	109	249	3
Willenhall*	12	2	0	10	98	273	2

Midlands East 1

	P	W	D	L	F	A	Pts
Scunthorpe	12	11	0	1	366	86	22
Long Buckby	12	11	0	1	285	83	22
Spalding	12	7	1	4	137	185	15
Kettering	12	7	0	5	172	99	14
Ampthill	12	7	0	5	189	141	14
Stoneygate	12	6	1	5	163	125	13
Stewarts & Lloyds	12	5	1	6	124	146	11
Biggleswade	12	5	1	6	131	165	11
Vipers	12	5	0	7	135	152	10
Amber Valley	12	4	1	7	72	121	9
Wellingborough	12	4	0	8	133	141	8
Northampton BB	12	2	0	10	85	207	4
Chesterfield	12	1	1	10	66	407	3

Midlands West 1

	P	W	D	L	F	A	Pts
Newport	12	11	1	0	248	103	23
Longton	12	9	0	3	227	92	18
O Laurentians	12	8	0	4	191	96	16
Bromsgrove	12	8	0	4	153	109	16
Dudley*	12	8	0	4	157	107	14
Aston O Eds	12	6	1	5	208	207	13
Newbold*	12	6	1	5	220	123	11
King's Norton	12	4	0	8	99	196	8
Leek	12	4	0	8	113	218	8
O Halesonians	12	3	1	8	128	186	7
O Leam'tonians	12	3	0	9	150	211	6
Newcastle (Staffs)	12	3	0	9	73	228	6
Ludlow*	12	2	2	8	67	158	4

Midlands East 2

	P	W	D	L	F	A	Pts
Ilkeston	12	10	0	2	230	113	20
Huntingdon	12	9	0	3	275	151	18
W Bridgford	12	8	0	4	223	177	16
Lutterworth	12	7	1	4	189	136	15
Moderns	12	7	0	5	265	188	14
Kibworth	12	7	0	5	223	153	14
Coalville	12	7	0	5	126	125	14
S Leicester	12	6	1	5	205	144	13
Lincoln	12	5	0	7	174	199	10
Mellish	12	4	1	7	118	209	9
Luton	12	3	0	9	98	153	6
Grimsby	12	2	1	9	107	223	5
Worksop*	12	1	0	11	86	348	-2

Midlands West 2

	P	W	D	L	F	A	Pts
Luctonians	12	12	0	0	591	61	24
Kenilworth	12	10	0	2	422	132	20
O Coventrians	12	8	1	3	238	225	17
Tamworth	12	7	1	4	181	113	15
Dixonians	12	6	1	5	179	158	13
Nuneaton O Eds	12	6	0	6	195	211	12
Selly Oak*	12	6	1	5	250	200	11
Stratford-o-Avon	12	5	0	7	184	184	10
O Yardleians	12	4	1	7	142	244	9
Woodrush	12	4	0	8	159	238	8
Shrewsbury	12	3	1	8	154	329	7
Dunlop	12	3	0	9	99	259	6
Cov Welsh	12	1	0	11	42	482	2

East Midlands/Leicestershire 1

	P	W	D	L	F	A	Pts
O N'ptonians	12	10	1	1	280	127	21
Bedford Queens	12	10	1	1	254	114	21
Northampton OS	12	9	0	3	295	166	18
Northampton MO	12	7	0	5	205	156	14
St Neots	12	7	0	5	179	149	14
Dunstablians	12	6	0	6	229	180	12
Oadby Wygges	12	5	1	6	165	173	11
M Mowbray	12	5	1	6	149	161	11
Loughborough	12	4	2	6	134	219	10
Market Bosworth	12	4	0	8	167	168	8
Aylestone St J	12	4	0	8	87	218	8
O Bosworthians	12	3	0	9	160	230	6
Daventry	12	1	0	11	86	329	2

East Midlands/Leicestershire 2

	P	W	D	L	F	A	Pts
Rushden & High	12	12	0	0	293	63	24
Oakham	12	11	0	1	307	58	22
Bedford Swifts	12	10	0	2	283	100	20
St Ives	12	7	0	5	224	118	14
Wellingboro OG	12	7	0	5	114	87	14
Brackley	12	6	1	5	103	104	13
Colworth House	12	5	0	7	163	183	10
Birstall*	12	6	0	6	135	187	10
O Ashbeians	12	4	2	6	113	216	10
Bugbrooke	12	3	1	8	120	169	7
N'pton Casuals	12	2	2	8	116	200	6
Aylestonians	12	2	0	10	99	233	4
Wigston*	12	0	0	12	53	405	-2

East Midlands/Leicestershire 3

	P	W	D	L	F	A	Pts
Kempston	11	9	0	2	278	82	18
New Pks	11	8	0	3	314	104	16
Oundle	11	8	0	3	221	92	16
Corby	11	8	0	3	219	92	16
O Newtonians	11	6	0	5	219	106	12
N'pton Heathens	11	6	0	5	204	169	12
Westwood	11	6	0	5	175	181	12
Vauxhall Motors	11	5	0	6	101	164	10
Deepings	11	5	0	6	133	199	10
Anstey	11	3	0	8	118	213	6
W Leicester	11	2	0	9	114	263	4
O Wellingburians	11	0	0	11	47	478	0

East Midlands/Leicestershire 4

	P	W	D	L	F	A	Pts
Burbage	12	11	0	1	286	78	22
Thorney*	12	11	0	1	380	58	20
Braunstone T	12	7	0	5	132	169	14
Cosby	12	6	0	6	136	231	12
Biddenham	12	3	0	9	122	179	6
Shepshed	12	3	0	9	78	217	6
Clapham Twins	12	1	0	11	78	280	2

North Midlands 1

	P	W	D	L	F	A	Pts
Malvern	12	11	1	0	329	85	23
Telford	12	11	0	1	269	101	22
Edwardians	12	8	1	3	215	141	17
Evesham	12	8	1	3	187	134	17
Five Ways O Eds	12	6	0	6	220	211	12

	P	W	D	L	F	A	Pts
O Griffinians	12	6	0	6	208	213	12
O Centrals	12	6	0	6	205	217	12
Veseyans	12	6	0	6	168	220	12
Pershore	12	4	0	8	192	197	8
Bridgnorth	12	3	2	7	141	265	8
Warley	12	3	1	8	132	206	7
Kidderminster	12	3	0	9	182	213	6
Droitwich	12	0	0	12	115	360	0

North Midlands 2

	P	*W*	*D*	*L*	*F*	*A*	*Pts*
Erdington	12	12	0	0	327	60	24
Bromyard	12	9	1	2	368	105	19
Birmingham CO	12	9	0	3	282	96	18
Birmingham CS	12	9	0	3	158	117	18
Redditch	12	7	0	5	159	133	14
O Saltleians	12	7	0	5	127	158	14
Tenbury	12	6	0	6	164	153	12
Kynoch	12	5	1	6	180	218	11
Ross-o-Wye	12	5	0	7	157	282	10
Upton-o-Severn	12	4	0	8	159	162	8
B'ham Welsh	12	3	0	9	149	208	6
Bournville	12	1	0	11	78	278	2
Market Drayton*	12	0	0	12	63	401	-2

North Midlands 3

	P	*W*	*D*	*L*	*F*	*A*	*Pts*
Wulfrun	10	9	0	1	225	71	18
Stourport	10	8	0	2	141	96	16
Bishops Castle*	10	8	0	2	244	105	14
Yardley & Dist*	10	8	0	2	185	72	14
Ledbury*	10	6	1	3	276	92	11
Birchfield	10	4	1	5	184	144	9
Oswestry	10	4	0	6	79	190	8
Witton	10	2	0	8	127	200	4
O Mosleians*	10	3	0	7	109	176	2
Cleobury Mortimer*	10	2	0	8	120	196	2
Bredon Star	10	0	0	10	31	379	0

Notts, Lincs & Derbys 1

	P	*W*	*D*	*L*	*F*	*A*	*Pts*
Ashbourne	12	10	0	2	196	113	20
Stamford	12	8	0	4	247	134	16
Glossop	12	7	1	4	186	116	15
Kesteven*	12	7	2	3	186	118	14
N'ham Casuals	12	6	1	5	241	170	13
Long Eaton	12	6	1	5	150	140	13
Southwell	12	6	1	5	141	141	13
East Leake	12	6	0	6	164	158	12
Sleaford	12	5	0	7	166	183	10
Melbourne	12	5	0	7	128	174	10
Leesbrook	12	4	1	7	158	205	9
Bakewell Mans	12	2	1	9	102	271	5
Dronfield	12	2	0	10	93	235	4

Notts, Lincs & Derbys 2

	P	*W*	*D*	*L*	*F*	*A*	*Pts*
Buxton	12	11	0	1	288	95	22
E Retford	12	10	1	1	409	148	21
M Rasen & Louth	12	8	0	4	254	130	16
Keyworth	12	8	0	4	167	109	16
Ashfield Swans	12	8	0	4	173	116	16
All Spartans	12	7	0	5	173	140	14
Boston	12	6	0	6	133	173	12
Rolls-Royce*	12	6	0	6	117	190	10
N'hamshire Cons*	12	5	1	6	105	115	9
N Kesteven*	12	5	0	7	173	138	8
Bingham	12	1	1	10	75	333	3
Barton & Dist	12	0	2	10	86	295	2
Meden Vale	12	0	1	11	78	249	1

Notts, Lincs & Derbys 3

	P	*W*	*D*	*L*	*F*	*A*	*Pts*
Castle Don	12	9	2	1	313	107	20
Boots Ath	12	9	1	2	217	118	19
Derby U	12	9	1	2	253	151	19
Stamford Coll	12	9	0	3	240	101	18
Nottinghamians	12	8	1	3	204	150	17
Cotgrave	12	7	2	3	290	139	16
Tupton	12	7	0	5	198	137	14
Belper	12	5	1	6	179	131	11
Horncastle	12	4	0	8	145	233	8
Ollerton & B'coat	12	3	0	9	158	336	6
Skegness	12	2	0	10	113	203	4
Bolsover*	12	2	0	10	113	189	2
Gainsborough	12	0	0	12	57	485	0

Notts, Lincs & Derbys 4

	P	*W*	*D*	*L*	*F*	*A*	*Pts*
Cleethorpes	12	9	0	3	293	117	18
Yarboro Bees	12	7	2	3	239	81	16
S Bonnington S	12	7	2	3	172	86	16
Bourne*	12	8	1	3	194	88	15
Whitwell	12	3	1	8	94	165	7
Hope Valley	12	3	0	9	54	378	6
Bilsthorpe	12	2	0	10	114	245	4

Staffs/Warwickshire 1

	P	*W*	*D*	*L*	*F*	*A*	*Pts*
Stoke OB	12	11	0	1	362	88	22
Southam	12	9	0	3	225	89	18
Coventry Saras	12	8	0	4	229	118	16
Rugby St Andrews	12	8	0	4	273	166	16
Trinity Guild	12	8	0	4	261	168	16
GEC Coventry	12	8	0	4	188	121	16
Manor Pk	12	6	0	6	141	163	12
Atherstone	12	5	1	6	205	149	11
GEC St Leonards*	12	5	1	6	140	201	9
Eccleshall*	12	3	2	7	141	316	6
Uttoxeter	12	2	2	8	107	358	6

	P	W	D	L	F	A	Pts
Trentham	12	1	1	10	75	248	3
O Wheatleyans	12	0	1	11	83	245	1

Staffs/Warwickshire 2

	P	*W*	*D*	*L*	*F*	*A*	*Pts*
Silhillians	12	9	0	3	207	128	18
Coventrians	12	9	0	3	161	89	18
Berks & Bals	12	8	1	3	213	80	17
Pinley	12	7	2	3	218	131	16
Cannock	12	8	0	4	168	154	16
Handsworth	12	7	0	5	172	102	14
Spartans	12	6	1	5	238	112	13
Wednesbury	12	6	1	5	126	179	13
Shipston-o-Stour	12	6	0	6	173	119	12
Earlsdon	12	5	1	6	167	96	11
Linley	12	2	0	10	129	211	4
Warwicks Police	12	2	0	10	85	198	4
Harbury	12	0	0	12	35	493	0

Staffs/Warwickshire 3

	P	*W*	*D*	*L*	*F*	*A*	*Pts*
O Warwickians	11	10	0	1	334	73	20
Alcester	11	9	1	1	250	44	19
Bloxwich	11	9	0	2	167	90	18
Rubery Owen	11	7	1	3	194	81	15
Claverdon	11	6	0	5	132	119	12
Burntwood	11	5	0	6	160	123	10
Rugeley	11	4	1	6	125	173	9
Wheaton Aston*	11	5	0	6	143	138	8
Coventry Tech*	11	5	0	6	151	202	8
Standard	11	3	1	7	171	169	7
O Oaks	11	0	0	11	67	356	0
Warwick*	11	1	0	10	55	381	-2

Staffs/Warwickshire 4

	P	*W*	*D*	*L*	*F*	*A*	*Pts*
Rugby Welsh	7	7	0	0	235	50	14
Shottery	7	6	0	1	229	36	12
Ford	7	4	0	3	127	54	8
Stone	7	4	0	3	91	127	8
Michelin*	7	4	0	3	146	93	4
Jaguar (Coventry)	7	2	0	5	78	104	4
Onley Pk*	7	0	0	7	31	243	-2
Fife St*	7	1	0	6	43	273	-2

BATH BACK TO FULL STEAM

PILKINGTON CUP 1994-95

6 May, Twickenham
Bath 36 (4G 1PG 1T) **Wasps 16** (2PG 2T)

Just when you thought it was safe to write them off... Bath had ceded their League title the previous week to Leicester in the most inglorious fashion, losing at home to Sale. Their outgoing talismanic captain, Jon Hall, cried off through injury two days before the final, a decision which must have caused him more pain than any blow received on a rugby field throughout his long and illustrious career. Mike Catt was also missing, as were internationals Dave Hilton, Simon Geoghegan, Nick Popplewell – the list went on. Bath were up against it.

Yet if you had to stake your life on any one club in the world triumphing against the odds, it would still be Bath. For all the pains of transition they experienced when the power base of Rowell and Barnes moved on to other things, there is still plenty of residual spirit and sheer fight left in the club, as was amply proved in this wonderful final. For long stretches Bath were pinned back in their own half and often on their own line, bearing the full brunt of a spirited Wasps assault. Wave after wave of black shirts headed towards the Bath shore: scarcely any reached land, rebuffed by some magnificent rearguard tackling by de Glanville and Robinson in particular, and also, it must be said, hampered by some Wasps failings. As any competitor in any sport will tell you, it ain't what you do in the build-up that counts, it's what you do at the death. In that critical area of the field and of the mind, there was only one team in it.

By that criterion Bath richly deserved their ninth title in eleven years – they have never been beaten in a final – continuing a marvellous run of success which dates back to 1988, the last time they finished a season without a trophy of one sort of another. It was this level of experience which ultimately divided the teams. Wasps had been here before – in 1986 and 1987, losing to Bath on both occasions – but not often enough to be familiar with the special pressures and needs that games at this exalted level bring. Bath were almost perfect in their execution of chances, turning pressure into points, glimmers of opportunity into gilt-edged rewards.

If one man epitomised this difference it was Tony Swift. The veteran winger won the last of his six caps in 1984, which is a staggering indictment of selection policy in the mid-1980s. Here, just a few days short of his 36th birthday and in his last game for the club he has served so fulsomely since 1985, he showed all his skills. Of course he has pace, but more than that, Swift has balance, timing and awareness. In scoring his try in the 52nd minute he combined all these attributes. There was nothing much on as Bath scrummed near the Wasps' 22. The ball went right, Swift was off one foot, then swaying off the other, leaving Greenstock, Ufton and Bates clutching thin air as he crossed the line.

Bath lock Martin Haag left it late to score his first try of the season, peeling off a forward scrum drive in the fourth minute. He must have liked the taste, for he was over again 20 minutes later, after great work down the narrow side by, amongst others, Clarke, Callard and Robinson.

Tony Swift (left), playing his last game for Bath in the Cup final at Twickenham, acknowledges Jon Callard's congratulations for his second-half try.

In between times Rob Andrew kicked two penalty goals for Wasps, rare successes on a day when he missed five kicks in all. Ben Clarke widened the gap just before half-time when he galloped on to a pass from Swift as Wasps complained bitterly back in midfield that they had been illegally turned over. Dunston closed it to 19-11 on the stroke of half-time when he spearheaded the thrust from a line-out.

Callard set the tone for the second half when he kicked an early penalty. Then came Swift's try, followed in the 62nd minute by one from Callard himself after a glorious burst upfield by Guscott. Damian Hopley pulled one back for Wasps, but the old order was back in place. Fittingly, Jon Hall went up to collect the trophy.

Bath: J E B Callard; A H Swift, P R de Glanville (*capt*), J C Guscott, A Adebayo; R Butland, I Sanders; K Yates, G Adams, V E Ubogu, M Haag, N C Redman, R A Robinson, B B Clarke, S O Ojomoh *Replacement* J Mallett for Ubogu (73 mins)
Scorers *Tries:* Haag (2), Clarke, Swift, Callard *Conversions:* Callard (4)
Penalty Goal: Callard
Wasps: J Ufton; P Hopley, D P Hopley, G Childs, N Greenstock; C R Andrew, S M Bates; D Molloy, K A Dunn, I Dunston, M Greenwood, N Hadley, L B N Dallaglio, D Ryan (*capt*), M White
Scorers *Tries:* Dunston, D Hopley *Penalty Goals:* Andrew (2)
Referee J Pearson (Durham)

The magic fingers of the RFU president and sundry others made this an unusual cup competition in that the fancied teams all avoided each other along the way. Every fourth Monday or so the media all trooped along to Twickenham for the draw, hoping that perhaps two of the big guns might be drawn together to allow one of the little teams to sneak through on the outside. It just never happened. Bath, Harlequins, Wasps and Leicester were all kept apart until the semi-finals: a sponsor's dream, a romantic's nightmare.

One of the great joys of the season was the form of Sale, flying the standard for the game in Manchester, who came so close to edging into the last four. They almost saw off Leicester, only to be thwarted in the cruellest fashion. They were clinging to a single-point lead when Leicester were awarded a dubious put-in to a scrum. Time and again the scrum was reset as the packs wheeled. The fourth time it collapsed, referee Chris Rees blew the whistle of doom for Sale. John Liley made no mistake in slotting the penalty which sent Leicester into the semi-finals. Paul Turner, the Sale player-coach, was distraught. At least he kept his anger in check, which is more than can be said for former Sale and England scrum-half Steve Smith, who let fly a volley of abuse.

There was no such controversy hanging over the semi-finals. In a tense, engrossing game at Welford Road Wasps ended Leicester's record run of 23 home wins. A full house of 13,750 saw a match of fluctuating fortunes in which Wasps put some of their fancy-free rugby on ice, playing with the head rather than the heart. Rob Andrew picked up 20 points in all, from three dropped goals, three penalty goals and a conversion. He also hit everything that moved in the tackle, perfectly capturing the tenacious mood which accompanied Wasps throughout their season of wild-roving rugby. Adventure always works better with a bit of steel behind it. At times, though, Wasps do overstep the mark. Here both Dean Ryan and Norm Hadley were shown the yellow card. Leicester missed the injured Dean Richards, the man who might have called the game better for them, particularly when they had the wind behind them in the second half. Even so, a spilled pass by Stuart Potter with the line at his mercy in the closing minutes might otherwise have taken the spoils for the Tigers.

Bath had an easier ride at the Stoop, where they had featured in one of the great Cup ties of all time the previous season. This time they ran out comfortable winners, 31-13, the ubiquitous Tony Swift running in two tries. Harlequins threw off the dilettante image that has followed them around but had a poor afternoon with goal-kickers, seven kicks being missed in all by three different players. Harlequins had accounted for Wakefield, the last of the Division 2 representatives, in the quarter-finals by 13-8. Further down-country Wasps were seeing off Division 3's last hope, Exeter, 31-0. The glutinous surface of the pitch drained some of the Wasps' energy. They were also checked by sterling tackling from Exeter, superbly led by scrum-half Andy Maunder. Northampton went down rather tamely, 26-6, in the other quarter-final to Bath.

The Cup-holders' only real scare came in the fifth round, when they struggled to overcome a doughty Orrell side. How often have you read this script? Orrell led deep into the second half, when a contested penalty award gave Bath an opening. Callard took it, and Bath rubbed it in with a last-minute try by Guscott. Some call it luck; others the stuff of champions.

RESULTS

First Round

North Walsham 27, Okehampton 3; Sherborne 16, Tabard 26; Ealing 7, Basingstoke 26; Southend 8, Metropolitan Police 20; Alton 9, Lydney 28; Launceston 38, Banbury 3; Weston-super-Mare 19, Berry Hill 3; Ruislip 28, Ipswich 3; Old Albanians 3, Barking 22; Camborne 23, Old Colfeians 15; London Welsh 20, Gloucester Old Boys 15; Henley 10, Sudbury 6; Maidenhead 3, Horsham 0; Aylesbury 10, High Wycombe 38; Esher 11, Bridgwater & Albion 0; Wharfedale 20, Stoke-on-Trent 11; Stourbridge 15, New Brighton 10; Loughborough Students 11, Winnington Park 40; Sheffield 11, Birmingham/Solihull 5; Hereford 14, Nuneaton 6; Preston Grasshoppers 31, Stockwood Park 3; Scunthorpe 27, Kendal 21; Old Coventrians 6, Camp Hill 13; Tynedale 35, Barker's Butts 21; West Park 38, Old Crossleyans 5; Walsall 56, Stafford 8; Sandal 18, Wigton 3; Lichfield 20, Stockton 12

Second Round

Askeans 12, Redruth 19; Lydney 17, Esher 15; Metropolitan Police 10, Havant 16; Rosslyn Park 12, Blackheath 24; Ruislip 19, Clifton 20; Henley 5, Launceston 27; Basingstoke 13, Plymouth Albion 10; Reading 26, Barking 15; Tabard 13, Weston-super-Mare 5; Maidenhead 14, High Wycombe 18; North Walsham 7, Exeter 32;

Richmond 47, Camborne 22; West Park 20, Broughton Park 0; Sandal 23, Winnington Park 10; Tynedale 29, Otley 28; Stourbridge 17, Bedford 35; Camp Hill 15, Liverpool St Helens 10; Aspatria 23, Leeds 0; Lichfield 24, Preston Grasshoppers 12; Harrogate 46, Sheffield 10; Rugby Lions 23, London Welsh 10; Morley 11, Rotherham 15; Scunthorpe 17, Hereford 16; Wharfedale 32, Walsall 16

Third Round
Basingstoke 29, Clifton 26; Lydney 16, Reading 6; Blackheath 31, Redruth 0; Havant 13, Richmond 15; High Wycombe 22, Tabard 36; Launceston 7, Exeter 30; Tynedale 16, Rugby Lions 23; Camp Hill 8, Sandal 17; West Park 14, Bedford 40; Aspatria 14, Scunthorpe 9; Harrogate 22, Lichfield 14; Rotherham 33, Wharfedale 30

Fourth Round
Wakefield 19, Gloucester 9; Aspatria 32, Bedford 6; Rotherham 19, Waterloo 21; London Scottish 6, Bath 31; Sale 33, Harrogate 0; Newcastle Gosforth 12, Wasps 58; Coventry 7, Fylde 45; Richmond 24, Tabard 16; Harlequins 9, Saracens 5; Basingstoke 3, London Irish 18; Sandal 5, Lydney 17; Leicester 56, Blackheath 11; Moseley 6, Northampton 16; Bristol 41, Nottingham 10; Exeter 9, Rugby Lions 7; Orrell 28, West Hartlepool 7

Fifth Round
Bristol 8, Leicester 16; Waterloo 13, Wasps 54; Northampton 27, Richmond 6; Sale 55, Fylde 13; Orrell 19, Bath 25; London Irish 15, Harlequins 40; Lydney 10, Wakefield 23; Exeter 18, Aspatria 6

Quarter-finals
Sale 12, Leicester 14; Harlequins 13, Wakefield 8; Bath 26, Northampton 6; Exeter 0, Wasps 31

Semi-finals
Leicester 22, Wasps 25; Harlequins 13, Bath 31

Previous finals *(all at Twickenham)*
1972 Gloucester 17 Moseley 6
1973 Coventry 27 Bristol 15
1974 Coventry 26 London Scottish 6
1975 Bedford 28 Rosslyn Park 12
1976 Gosforth 23 Rosslyn Park 14
1977 Gosforth 27 Waterloo 11
1978 Gloucester 6 Leicester 3
1979 Leicester 15 Moseley 12
1980 Leicester 21 London Irish 9
1981 Leicester 22 Gosforth 15
1982 Gloucester 12 Moseley 12 *(title shared)*
1983 Bristol 28 Leicester 22
1984 Bath 10 Bristol 9
1985 Bath 24 London Welsh 15
1986 Bath 25 Wasps 17
1987 Bath 19 Wasps 12
1988 Harlequins 28 Bristol 22
1989 Bath 10 Leicester 6
1990 Bath 48 Gloucester 6
1991 Harlequins 25, Northampton 13 *(aet)*
1992 Harlequins 12, Bath 15 *(aet)*
1993 Leicester 23, Harlequins 16
1994 Bath 21, Leicester 9

COUNTY CUP WINNERS 1994-95

Berkshire	**Abbey**
Buckinghamshire	**Olney**
Cheshire	**Macclesfield**
Cornwall	**Launceston**
Cumbria	**Netherall**
Devon	**Brixham**
Dorset/Wilts	**Bournemouth**
Durham	**Stockton**
Eastern Counties	**Harlow**
East Midlands	**Leighton Buzzard**
Gloucestershire	**Gloucester Old Boys**
Hampshire	**Basingstoke**
Hertfordshire	**Letchworth**
Kent	**Westcombe Park**
Lancashire	**Manchester**
Leicestershire	**Syston**
Middlesex	**Ruislip**
North Midlands	**Selly Oak**
Northumberland	**Northern**
Notts, Lincs & Derbys	**Scunthorpe**
Oxfordshire	**Oxford**
Somerset	**Hornets**
Staffordshire	**Stafford**
Surrey	**Old Blues**
Sussex	**Lewes**
Warwickshire	**Broad Street**
Yorkshire	**Rotherham**

WARWICKSHIRE STIR FROM THEIR SLUMBER

CIS INSURANCE COUNTY CHAMPIONSHIP 1994-95
Michael Austin

22 April, Twickenham
Northumberland 9 (3PG) **Warwickshire 15** (5PG)

One of the old giants, Warwickshire, stirred from its torpor to take the County Championship title for the tenth time after a nine-year gap. The competition, in its second season of sponsorship by the Co-operative Insurance Society, provided many players with the chance to make their first appearance at Twickenham, among them Jim Quantrill, a bank management trainee in Nottingham. Quantrill, the Warwickshire full-back, managed only one practice kick before the match and missed that. But when it came to the real thing, he landed all of his five penalty attempts in a game which failed to produce a try for a crowd of 8,000.

Both sides had missed opportunities upon which to reflect. Northumberland believed that both David Rees, their wing, and Michael Old, the full-back, had scored legitimate tries, but Matt Bayliss, the Gloucester referee – officiating in his final match before retiring on the eve of his 50th birthday – ruled that they had been held up on the line.

The game produced some valiant tackling, notably from Andy Smallwood, the Nottingham wing, who, along with club-mate Matt Gallagher, had opted to play for Warwickshire in the County final rather than in a Courage League Division 2 relegation match. Smallwood twice prevented tries and Northumberland were restricted to three penalty goals from five attempts by David Johnson, the seasoned former Newcastle Gosforth and England B player.

The best moments were reserved for the final minutes, but the whistle brought joy and relief for Warwickshire, and especially for captain Gareth Tregilgas, who had also skippered Coventry, relegated to Division 3, and was making his Twickenham debut.

Warwickshire, coached by Jim Robinson, had won all their previous five matches, scoring 194 points in the process, under the benign influence of Mark Warr, the Sale and former Barker's Butts scrum-half. Their 70-3 win over East Midlands was the biggest in their history. Northumberland's only blemish en route to Twickenham was defeat in their opening game against Cumbria by 15-10. Northumberland had won the title twice, in 1898 and in 1981, their centenary year.

The beaten semi-finalists had vastly different past records. Berkshire, founded in 1931 and admitted to the competition in 1947-48, reached the last four for the first time before losing to Warwickshire, who were new opponents. Before this triumphant run, Berkshire had won only one match in four years. Going down in a second successive semi-final by a single point was a big disappointment for Gloucestershire. They had been beaten 13-12 at Otley the previous year and still stand one Championship short of equalling Lancashire's record 16 titles.

TEAMS IN THE FINAL

Northumberland: M Old (Tynedale); G Ward (Novocastrians), R Wilkinson (Newcastle Gosforth), I Chandler (Newcastle Gosforth), D Rees (Sale); D Johnson (Blaydon), S Clayton-Hibbott (Tynedale); R Parker (Tynedale) (*capt*), E Parker (Tynedale), D Clark (Morpeth), K Westgarth (West Hartlepool), R Metcalfe (Newcastle Gosforth), R Hoole (Edinburgh Acads), D Guthrie (Blaydon), N Frankland (Newcastle Gosforth) *Replacement* S Turnbull (Tynedale) for Guthrie (temp)
Scorer *Penalty Goals:* Johnson (3)
Warwickshire: J Quantrill (Rugby Lions); A Smallwood (Nottingham), A Gillooly (Rugby Lions), M Palmer (Rugby Lions), D Watson (Rugby Lions); M Gallagher (Nottingham), M Warr (Sale); G Tregilgas (Coventry) (*capt*), D Addleton (Coventry), T Revan (Rugby Lions), S Smith (Rugby Lions), P Bowman (Rugby Lions), D Oram (Rugby Lions), S Carter (Coventry), M Ellis (Kenilworth)
Scorer *Penalty Goals:* Quantrill (5)
Referee M Bayliss (Gloucester Society)

TEAMS IN THE SEMI-FINALS

11 March, Rugby Lions RFC
Warwickshire 31 (1G 3PG 3T) **Berkshire 5** (1T)

Warwickshire: J Quantrill (Rugby Lions); A Smallwood (Nottingham), A Gillooly (Rugby Lions), M Palmer (Rugby Lions), D Watson (Rugby Lions); M Gallagher (Nottingham), M Warr (Sale); G Tregilgas (Coventry) (*capt*), D Addleton (Coventry), T Revan (Rugby Lions), S Smith (Rugby Lions), P Bowman (Rugby Lions), A Ruddlesdin (Long Buckby), S Carter (Coventry), M Ellis (Kenilworth)
Scorers *Tries:* Smallwood, Revan, Watson, Ruddlesdin *Conversion:* Quantrill *Penalty Goals:* Quantrill (3)
Berkshire: S Smith (Reading); M Richmond (Reading), S Kearns (Reading) (*capt*), L Fanning (Reading), St J Ford (Maidenhead); S Rogers (Reading), C Phillips (Reading); A Greene (Maidenhead), R Kellam (London Irish), N Collins (Harlequins), M Atherton (Reading), D Pratt (Reading), M Hart (Maidenhead), C Hutson (Reading), I Armstrong (Reading)
Scorer *Try:* Hart
Referee D Reordan (USA)

11 March, Tynedale RFC
Northumberland 14 (2G) **Gloucestershire 13** (1G 2PG)

Northumberland: A Blyth (Tynedale); G Ward (Novocastrians), R Wilkinson (Newcastle Gosforth), I Chandler (Newcastle Gosforth), D Rees (Sale); D Johnson (Blaydon), S Clayton-Hibbott (Tynedale); R Parker (Tynedale) (*capt*), E Parker (Tynedale), D Clark (Morpeth), K Westgarth (West Hartlepool), R Metcalfe (Newcastle Gosforth), N Frankland (Newcastle Gosforth), D Guthrie (Blaydon), R Hoole (Edinburgh Acads)
Scorers *Tries:* Wilkinson (2) *Conversions:* Johnson (2)
Gloucestershire: T Smith (Gloucester); D John (Bristol), A Williams (Bristol), I Morgan (Gloucester), D Morgan (Cheltenham); M Hamlin (Gloucester) (*capt*), J Davis (Lydney); G Williams (Lydney), N Nelmes (Lydney), S Baldwin (Gloucester Old Boys),

T Clink (Cheltenham), R Blake (Clifton), R Fowke (Gloucester), I Patten (Bristol), A Stanley (Gloucester)
Scorers *Try:* D Morgan *Conversion:* Smith *Penalty Goals:* Smith (2)
Referee B Campsall (Yorkshire Society)

DIVISIONAL ROUNDS

North Division

Durham 5, Yorkshire 13; Cheshire 3, Lancashire 16; Cumbria 15, Northumberland 10; Cheshire 10, Cumbria 6; Lancashire 43, Durham 8; Northumberland 30, Yorkshire 14; Cumbria 6, Durham 5; Cheshire 17, Northumberland 19; Yorkshire 27, Lancashire 27; Cumbria 24, Lancashire 17; Northumberland 11, Durham 3; Yorkshire 49, Cheshire 19; Durham 5, Cheshire 6; Lancashire 8, Northumberland 17; Yorkshire 25, Cumbria 18

	P	*W*	*D*	*L*	*F*	*A*	*Pts*
Northumberland	5	4	0	1	87	57	8
Yorkshire	5	3	1	1	128	99	7
Cumbria	5	3	0	2	69	67	6
Lancashire	5	2	1	2	111	79	5
Cheshire	5	2	0	3	55	95	4
Durham	5	0	0	5	26	79	0

Midland Division

Group A

Staffordshire 12, Leicestershire 15; Leicestershire 13, North Midlands 14; North Midlands 17, Staffordshire 25

	P	*W*	*D*	*L*	*F*	*A*	*Pts*
Staffordshire	2	1	0	1	37	32	2
Leicestershire	2	1	0	1	28	26	2
North Midlands	2	1	0	1	31	38	2

Group B

East Midlands 29, Notts, Lincs & Derbys 31; Notts, Lincs & Derbys 8, Warwickshire 42; Warwickshire 70, East Midlands 3

	P	*W*	*D*	*L*	*F*	*A*	*Pts*
Warwickshire	2	2	0	0	112	11	4
East Midlands	2	0	0	2	32	101	0

Play-Off Matches

Semi-finals: Staffordshire 18, Notts, Lincs & Derbys 8; Warwickshire 21, Leicestershire 8
Divisional final: Warwickshire 30, Staffordshire 3

London & South-West

Group 1

Surrey 42, Hertfordshire 7; Hertfordshire 18, Somerset 14; Somerset 27, Surrey 20

	P	*W*	*D*	*L*	*F*	*A*	*Pts*
Surrey	2	1	0	1	62	34	2
Somerset	2	1	0	1	41	38	2
Hertfordshire	2	1	0	1	25	56	2

Group 2

Buckinghamshire 16, Sussex 18; Gloucestershire 25, Devon 12; Devon 16, Sussex 13; Gloucestershire 41, Buckinghamshire 13; Buckinghamshire 3, Devon 3; Sussex 19, Gloucestershire 42

	P	*W*	*D*	*L*	*F*	*A*	*Pts*
Gloucestershire	3	3	0	0	108	44	6
Devon	3	1	1	1	31	41	3
Sussex	3	1	0	2	50	74	2
Buckinghamshire	3	0	1	2	32	62	1

Group 3

Hampshire 40, Oxfordshire 15; Kent 49, Eastern Counties 32; Hampshire 20, Kent 24; Oxfordshire 19, Eastern Counties 37; Eastern Counties 18, Hampshire 21; Kent 62, Oxfordshire 0

	P	*W*	*D*	*L*	*F*	*A*	*Pts*
Kent	3	3	0	0	135	52	6
Hampshire	3	2	0	1	81	57	4
Eastern Counties	3	1	0	2	87	89	2
Oxfordshire	3	0	0	3	34	134	0

Group 4
Cornwall 16, Middlesex 17; Dorset & Wilts 13, Berkshire 28; Cornwall 39, Dorset & Wilts 15; Middlesex 13, Berkshire 18; Berkshire 22, Cornwall 11; Dorset & Wilts 6, Middlesex 58

	P	*W*	*D*	*L*	*F*	*A*	*Pts*
Berkshire	3	3	0	0	68	37	6
Middlesex	3	2	0	1	88	40	4
Cornwall	3	1	0	2	66	54	2
Dorset & Wilts	3	0	0	3	34	125	0

Quarter-finals:
Gloucestershire 23, Surrey 6; Berkshire 25, Kent 12

ENGLISH COUNTY CHAMPIONS 1889-1994

1889 **Yorkshire,** undefeated, declared champions by RU (scored 18G 17T to 1G 3T)

1890 **Yorkshire,** undefeated, declared champions (scored 10G 16T to 2G 4T)

1891	**Lancashire** champions.	Group Winners — Yorkshire, Surrey, Gloucestershire.
1892	**Yorkshire** champions.	Group Winners — Lancashire, Kent, Midlands.
1893	**Yorkshire** champions.	Group Winners — Cumberland, Devon, Middlesex.
1894	**Yorkshire** champions.	Group Winners — Lancashire, Gloucestershire, Midlands.
1895	**Yorkshire** champions.	Group Winners — Cumberland, Devon, Midlands.

	Champions	*Runners-up*	*Played at*
1896	**Yorkshire**	Surrey	Richmond
1897	**Kent**	Cumberland	Carlisle
1898	**Northumberland**	Midlands	Coventry
1899	**Devon**	Northumberland	Newcastle
1900	**Durham**	Devon	Exeter
1901	**Devon**	Durham	W Hartlepool
1902	**Durham**	Gloucestershire	Gloucester
1903	**Durham**	Kent	W Hartlepool
1904	**Kent**	Durham	Blackheath (2nd meeting)
1905	**Durham**	Middlesex	W Hartlepool
1906	**Devon**	Durham	Exeter
1907	**Devon** and **Durham** joint champions after drawn games at W Hartlepool and Exeter		
1908	**Cornwall**	Durham	Redruth
1909	**Durham**	Cornwall	W Hartlepool
1910	**Gloucestershire**	Yorkshire	Gloucester
1911	**Devon**	Yorkshire	Headingley
1912	**Devon**	Northumberland	Devonport
1913	**Gloucestershire**	Cumberland	Carlisle
1914	**Midlands**	Durham	Leicester
1920	**Gloucestershire**	Yorkshire	Bradford
1921	**Gloucestershire (31)**	Leicester (4)	Gloucester
1922	**Gloucestershire (19)**	N Midlands (0)	Birmingham
1923	**Somerset (8)**	Leicester (6)	Bridgwater
1924	**Cumberland (14)**	Kent (3)	Carlisle
1925	**Leicestershire (14)**	Gloucestershire (6)	Bristol
1926	**Yorkshire (15)**	Hampshire (14)	Bradford
1927	**Kent (22)**	Leicestershire (12)	Blackheath
1928	**Yorkshire (12)**	Cornwall (8)	Bradford
1929	***Middlesex (9)**	Lancashire (8)	Blundellsands
1930	**Gloucestershire (13)**	Lancashire (7)	Blundellsands
1931	**Gloucestershire (10)**	Warwickshire (9)	Gloucester
1932	**Gloucestershire (9)**	Durham (3)	Blaydon
1933	**Hampshire (18)**	Lancashire (7)	Boscombe
1934	**E Midlands (10)**	Gloucester (0)	Northampton
1935	**Lancashire (14)**	Somerset (0)	Bath

1936	**Hampshire (13)**	Northumberland (6)	Gosforth
1937	**Gloucestershire** (5)	E Midlands (0)	Bristol
1938	**Lancashire (24)**	Surrey (12)	Blundellsands
1939	**Warwickshire (8)**	Somerset (3)	Weston
1947	†**Lancashire (14)**	Gloucestershire (3)	Gloucester
1948	**Lancashire (5)**	E Counties (0)	Cambridge
1949	**Lancashire (9)**	Gloucestershire (3)	Blundellsands
1950	**Cheshire (5)**	E Midlands (0)	Birkenhead Park
1951	**E Midlands (10)**	Middlesex (0)	Northampton
1952	**Middlesex (9)**	Lancashire (6)	Twickenham
1953	**Yorkshire (11)**	E Midlands (3)	Bradford
1954	**Middlesex (24)**	Lancashire (6)	Blundellsands
1955	**Lancashire (14)**	Middlesex (8)	Twickenham
1956	**Middlesex (13)**	Devon (9)	Twickenham
1957	**Devon (12)**	Yorkshire (3)	Plymouth
1958	**Warwickshire (16)**	Cornwall (8)	Coventry
1959	**Warwickshire (14)**	Gloucestershire (9)	Bristol
1960	**Warwickshire (9)**	Surrey (6)	Coventry
1961	o**Cheshire (5)**	Devon (3)	Birkenhead Park
1962	**Warwickshire (11)**	Hampshire (6)	Twickenham
1963	**Warwickshire (13)**	Yorkshire (10)	Coventry
1964	**Warwickshire (8)**	Lancashire (6)	Coventry
1965	**Warwickshire (15)**	Durham (9)	Hartlepool
1966	**Middlesex (6)**	Lancashire (0)	Blundellsands
1967	****Surrey** and **Durham**		
1968	**Middlesex (9)**	Warwickshire (6)	Twickenham
1969	**Lancashire (11)**	Cornwall (9)	Redruth
1970	**Staffordshire (11)**	Gloucestershire (9)	Burton-on-Trent
1971	**Surrey (14)**	Gloucestershire (3)	Gloucester
1972	**Gloucestershire (11)**	Warwickshire (6)	Coventry
1973	**Lancashire (17)**	Gloucestershire (12)	Bristol
1974	**Gloucestershire (22)**	Lancashire (12)	Blundellsands
1975	**Gloucestershire (13)**	E Counties (9)	Gloucester
1976	**Gloucester (24)**	Middlesex (9)	Richmond
1977	**Lancashire (17)**	Middlesex (6)	Blundellsands
1978	**N Midlands (10)**	Gloucestershire (7)	Moseley
1979	**Middlesex (19)**	Northumberland (6)	Twickenham
1980	**Lancashire (21)**	Gloucestershire (15)	Vale of Lune
1981	**Northumberland (15)**	Gloucestershire (6)	Gloucester
1982	**Lancashire (7)**	North Midlands (3)	Moseley
1983	**Gloucestershire (19)**	Yorkshire (7)	Bristol
1984	**Gloucestershire (36)**	Somerset (18)	Twickenham
1985	**Middlesex (12)**	Notts, Lincs and Derbys (9)	Twickenham
1986	**Warwickshire (16)**	Kent (6)	Twickenham
1987	**Yorkshire (22)**	Middlesex (11	Twickenham
1988	**Lancashire (23)**	Warwickshire (18)	Twickenham
1989	**Durham (13)**	Cornwall (9)	Twickenham
1990	**Lancashire (32)**	Middlesex (9)	Twickenham
1991	**Cornwall (29**	Yorkshire (20) (*aet*)	Twickenham
1992	**Lancashire (9)**	Cornwall (6)	Twickenham
1993	**Lancashire (9)**	Yorkshire (6)	Twickenham
1994	**Yorkshire (26)**	Durham (3)	Twickenham
1995	**Warwickshire (15)**	Northumberland (9)	Twickenham

**After a draw at Twickenham. †After a draw, 8-8, at Blundellsands. oAfter a draw 0-0, at Plymouth. **Surrey and Durham drew 14 each at Twickenham and no score at Hartlepool and thus became joint champions. Lancashire have won the title 16 times, Gloucestershire 15, Yorkshire 12, Warwickshire 10, Middlesex 8, Durham 8 (twice jointly), Devon 7 (once jointly), Kent 3 times, Hampshire, East Midlands, Cheshire, Northumberland and Cornwall twice each, Surrey twice (once jointly), and Midlands (3rd System), Somerset, Cumberland, Leicestershire, Staffordshire and North Midlands once each.*

QUEENS RISE TO ROYAL OCCASION

PILKINGTON SHIELD 1994-95
Michael Austin

6 May 1995, Twickenham
Bedford Queens 11 (1PG 1DG 1T) **St Albans 10** (1G 1PG)

Tim Clarke, a No 8 with a happy knack of scoring tries, ran in his 11th and probably most treasured in the competition as Bedford Queens, a club close to extinction six years earlier, won the Pilkington Shield. Lack of funds and a shortage of interest in 1989, the year before this highly popular competition began, left Queens only one vote away from being disbanded. In 1995, by contrast, they estimated that their victory over St Albans was worth £20,000 in sponsorship and revenue.

Clarke's try, together with a dropped goal from Andy Moffat, guided Queens to an 8-3 lead before St Albans launched a rally in which wing James Dickinson raced between the posts for Adrian King to convert, putting St Albans ahead with ten minutes remaining. Queens hooker Darren Stapleton then calmly responded with the penalty goal that won the match for the Bedford club.

Dickinson, captain of St Albans School the previous season, scored in all but one of the nine rounds on the path to Twickenham – and that exception was because he missed a match through a prior commitment with Hertfordshire Colts.

Queens, founded in 1919 by the staff of Queens Engineering of Bedford, went open in 1972. Players were attracted from local schools and colleges, many of them progressing to higher levels with clubs such as Bedford, Harlequins and Richmond. Since the Leagues were introduced, Queens have advanced from East Midlands 3 to East Midlands/Leicestershire 1. They qualified for the Shield final with a 21-16 win over Kingsbridge, a farming village club 12 miles east of Plymouth, while St Albans triumphed 21-8 over North Shields.

St Albans scored three tries to one but their disappointment in losing narrowly in the final was compounded by a marginal failure to win promotion from the Hertfordshire/Middlesex League.

North Shields produced quality performances in becoming the first Northumberland club to reach such an advanced stage of the competition. They have a new £600,000 clubhouse, having begun with just a shed on a windswept field. Peter Hardwick, the North Shields-born England forward of the turn of the century, would have been proud. He founded the club as Smiths Dock, a team of ship repairers. They have added to the rapidly growing folklore of a competition designed for the lowest-placed 512 clubs and, in the second year of new sponsorship, worth £300,000 over three seasons.

Fly-half Darryl Fale, captain of 1994-95 Pilkington Shield winners Bedford Queens, gives chase in the final at Twickenham.

Bedford Queens: A Moffat; K McMillin, J Kitchener, D Twigden, J Smith; D Fale *(capt)*, J Cunningham; J Matthews, D Stapleton, I Mortimer, A Radnor, S Pearce-Roberts, R Millard, T Clarke, T Dean *Replacement* C Holloway for Smith (62 mins)
Scorers *Try:* Clarke *Penalty Goal:* Stapleton *Dropped Goal:* Moffat
St Albans: N Lister; D Falvey, D Morete, W Cox, J Dickinson; A King, T Andrews *(capt)*; M Millar, R Hume, D Batchelor, A Smith, R Doggett, D Patrick, J Sayers, D Stanford
Scorers *Try:* Dickinson *Conversion:* King *Penalty Goal:* King
Referee B Campsall (Yorkshire Society)

Third Round
London Division: Region 1 – Eastern Counties, Hertfordshire, Middlesex London Cornish 0, Ilford Wanderers 10; Barclays Bank 10, Hadleigh 23; Stowmarket 15, Datchworth 7; London Nigerians 29, Haverhill 5; Ongar 19, Belsize Park 16; St Albans 30, Quintin 10; Witham 6, Enfield Ignatians 5; Tring 20, St Nicholas Old Boys 7; HAC 55, Hayes 6; Wisbech 18, Fakenham 3
Region 2 – Hampshire, Surrey, Kent, Sussex Ventnor 16, Aylesford 8; Old Gravesendians 17, Cobham 3; Crowborough 17, Chipstead 6; Old Tiffinians 9, Deal Wanderers 6; Esso 3, Tonbridge 43; Woking 49, Overton 0; London Media 7, Old Bevonians 24; Orpington 3, Cranbrook 29; Ditchling 3, Darenth Valley 12; Whitstable 6, Ashford 3
Midland Division: Region 1 – North Midlands, Staffordshire, Warwickshire Birmingham City Officials 12, Berkswell & Balsall 6; Bishop's Castle & Onny Valley 13, Handsworth 5; Coventry Technical College 0, Burntwood 11; Erdington 7, Edwardians 3; Shipston-on-Stour 11, Wednesbury 17; Standard 13, Bromyard 22; Warley 26, Coventrians 11
Region 2 – East Midlands, Leicestershire, Notts, Lincs, & Derbys Boots Athletic 5, Melton Mowbray 30; Corby 8, Rushden & Higham 14; Northampton Casuals 15, Vauxhall Motors 3; North Kesteven 7, Kempston 8; Oakham 24, Colworth House 6; Warwickshire Police 12, Buxton 18; Wellingborough Old Grammarians 10, All Spartans 5; Bedford Queens 21, St Ives (Cambs) 6
South-West Division: Region 1 – Berkshire, Buckinghamshire, Dorset & Wilts, Oxfordshire Beaconsfield 20, Bridport 3; Buckingham 7, Calne 0; Thatcham 17, Gosford All Blacks 3; Pennanians 26, Portcastrians 5
Region 2 – Cornwall, Gloucestershire, Devon, Somerset Totnes 6, Old Plymouthians 42; Exeter Saracens 7, Kingsbridge 15; St Agnes 13, Wadebridge 10; Plymouth Argaum 12, Salcombe 20; Cotham Park 6, Bristol Saracens 16; Blagdon 7, Tredworth 30; Avon 0, Crewkerne 15; Gloucestershire Police 8, Bishopston 17; Cheltenham Civil Service 9, Cainscross 17; Bristol Telephones 14, Broad Plain 19
North Division: Region 1 – East of Pennines Hessle 0, Medicals 19; Knottingley 16, Dinnington 3; Moortown 17, Marist 11; Newton Aycliffe 7, Winlaton Vulcans 14; North Shields 11, Stanley Rodillians 0; Phoenix Park 3, Huddersfield YMCA 14; Ponteland 27, Richmondshire 10; Stocksbridge 0, Wibsey 34
Region 2 – West of Pennines Birchfield 6, Newton-le-Willows 39; Crewe & Nantwich 12, Port Sunlight 9; Didsbury Toc H 12, Blackpool 13; Marple 17, Millom 5; Mossley Hill 3, Eccles 0; Old Parkonians 22, Keswick 10; Wallasey 14, Bolton 3

Fourth Round
London Division: Crowborough 0, HAC 39; Old Bevonians 25, Witham 3; Ongar 18, Darenth Valley 25; St Albans 11, London Nigerians 3; Stowmarket 18, Cranbrook 10; Tonbridge 0, Ilford Wanderers 3; Tring 19, Hadleigh 14; Ventnor 24, Old Gravesendians 22; Whitstable 21, Woking 13; Wisbech 11, Old Tiffinians 3
Midland Division: Birmingham City Officials 41, Buxton 11; Bromyard 15, Warley 13; Erdington 8, Wellingborough Old Grammarians 3; Melton Mowbray 6,

Bedford Queens 11; Oakham 30, Kempston 13; Rushden & Higham 13, Bishop's Castle & Onny Valley 0; Wednesbury 0, Burntwood 10
South-West Division: Beaconsfield 37, Thatcham 7; Bristol Saracens 36, Pennanians 20; Buckingham 21, Salcombe 3; Cainscross 24, St Agnes 10; Crewkerne 50, Broad Plain 0; Kingsbridge 21, Bishopston 0; Old Plymouthians 8, Tredworth 12
North Division: Blackpool 6, Newton-le-Willows 5; Medicals 5, Marple 7; Moortown 8, North Shields 9; Mossley Hill 5, Ponteland 8; Northampton Casuals 5, Huddersfield YMCA 14; Wallasey 22, Crewe & Nantwich 18; Wibsey 20, Old Parkonians 10; Winlaton Vulcans 23, Knottingley 5

Fifth Round
London Division: Ilford Wanderers 11, Tring 0; St Albans 11, HAC 6; Old Bevonians 13, Ventnor 16; Derenth Valley 6, Whitstable 12; Wisbech 19, Stowmarket 12
Midland Division: Rushden & Higham 16, Birmingham City Officials 6; Bromyard 10, Oakham 9; Bedford Queens 14, Erdington 6
South-West Division: Beaconsfield 20, Burntwood 6; Tredworth 15, Cainscross 8; Kingsbridge 17, Crewkerne 7; Buckingham 24, Bristol Saracens 19
North Division: Huddersfield YMCA 14, Winlaton Vulcans 3; Wibsey 22, Ponteland 0; Blackpool 9, North Shields 17; Wallasey 32, Marple 5

Sixth Round
North & Midlands: Bromyard 0, North Shields 11; Rushden & Higham 8, Buckingham 0; Wallasey 19, Bedford Queens 33; Wibsey 12, Huddersfield YMCA 8
London & South-West: Tredworth 5, Wisbech 0; Kingsbridge 23, Ventnor 3; St Albans 15, Whitstable 5; Ilford Wanderers 16, Beaconsfield 11

Quarter-finals
North & Midlands: Rushden & Higham 3, Bedford Queens 14; Wibsey 6, North Shields 15
London & South-West: Ilford Wanderers 11, St Albans 20; Tredworth 3, Kingsbridge 6

Semi-finals
North Shields 8, St Albans 21 (*at Harrogate*); Bedford Queens 21, Kingsbridge 15 (*at Bristol*)

SPRINGBOKS LOSE IN DUBLIN TO SPIRITED BAA-BAAS

THE BARBARIANS 1994-95

Geoff Windsor-Lewis

Barbaria put itself back on the map in beating the Springboks 23-15 in Dublin on an afternoon rich in spectacle, vigour and significance. In a team selected from seven different countries, Robert Jones led by example, establishing a spirit within the players which was to be so important. The Barbarians played with bone-shuddering commitment, tactical nous and a blazing desire for victory. The all-Irish front row of Wood, Clohessy and Popplewell rose to the occasion on their home ground, producing some rousing charges. Only 70 seconds into the match, sponsored by Scottish Amicable, South Africa showed all the hallmarks of their strength on this tour when Kruger strolled over the try-line before the Barbarians had even gained possession. After half an hour the Baa-Baas began to take the game to the opposition. They were rewarded when Philippe Saint-André pounced and fly-hacked a loose ball over the line for an opportunist try which Jon Callard converted. Callard added a penalty goal, and at half-time the score was 10-5 to the Barbarians.

Within ten minutes of the interval Müller and Johnson had scored impressive tries. The Barbarians responded with some superb attacking rugby, seizing the initiative when Pat Howard, a young Australian who had come on for the hamstrung Scott Hastings, cleverly intercepted a midfield pass, escaped clutching tackles and, racing away, found Simon Geoghegan in support. As Geoghegan scored, a deafening noise rang round the ground. Callard converted and suddenly it was 17-15 to the Baa-Baas. After another Callard penalty and a dropped goal by Craig Chalmers, the Barbarians defence held out for the last few minutes and a fine victory was achieved.

The season had started with a double celebration. The Barbarians paid their first visit to Bath since the 1890s to commemorate 100 years of rugby at the Recreation Ground, and in front of a full house the home team won a close game by 23-18. Paul Hull and André Joubert produced glimpses of their attacking prowess and were well supported by a strong pack of forwards.

The following day the Barbarians flew to Paris to take part in the celebration of the 50th anniversary of the Liberation of Paris. A special match had been arranged with their French counterparts, the first ever, to open the new Stade Charlety, the home of the Paris University Club. A strong French team included the two Australian stalwarts, David Campese and Nick Farr-Jones. Charvet, Sella and Lagisquet all had their moments, but perhaps the outstanding corner tackle by André Joubert on Campese will remain longest in the memory.

In October the Barbarians played Newport, winning 54-45, and Swansea, losing 39-17. Leicester at Christmas time has become a strong tradition, and this year the game was notable for Dean Richards' 100th try for his club. A crowd of 15,000 endured the cold drizzle and were rewarded when the home side took the spoils, 31-18. The Mobbs Match produced another high-scoring game with eight tries for the Baa-Baas in an emphatic 56-19 victory.

On Easter Saturday Cardiff scored their highest number of points, 75, in the history of the fixture. It was a great result for a club celebrating winning the League for the first time.

RESULTS 1994-95

Played 11 Won 5 Lost 6 Drawn 0 Points for 346 (32G 16PG 3DG 13T) **Against 337** (30G 13PG 1DG 17T)

1994	
28 May	**Beat Zimbabwe Goshawks** at Mutare Sports Club 53 (6G 2PG 1T) to 9 (3PG)
2 June	**Beat Matabeleland** at Hartsfield 35 (5PG 4T) to 23 (2G 3PG)
4 June	**Lost to Zimbabwe** at Police Ground, Harare 21 (1G 2PG 1DG 1T) to 23 (2G 2PG 1DG)
3 Sept	**Lost to Bath** at Recreation Ground, Bath 18 (1G 2PG 1T) to 23 (1G 2PG 2T)
6 Sept	**Lost to French Barbarians** at Stade Charlety, Paris 18 (1G 1PG 1DG 1T) to 35 (1G 1PG 5T)
4 Oct	**Beat Newport** at Rodney Parade, Newport 54 (7G 1T) to 45 (5G 2T)
18 Oct	**Lost to Swansea** at St Helen's, Swansea 17 (1G 2T) to 39 (3G 1PG 3T)
3 Dec	**Beat South Africa** at Lansdowne Road, Dublin 23 (2G 2PG 1DG) to 15 (3T)
27 Dec	**Lost to Leicester** at Welford Road 18 (1G 2PG 1T) to 31 (4G 1PG)
1995	
8 Mar	**Beat East Midlands** at Franklins Gardens, Northampton 56 (8G) to 19 (2G 1T)
15 Apr	**Lost to Cardiff** at Cardiff Arms Park 33 (4G 1T) to 75 (10G 1T)

PLAYERS 1994-95

Abbreviations: *B* – Bath; *FB* – French Barbarians; *N* – Newport; *S* – Swansea; *SA* – South Africa; *L* – Leicester; *EM* – East Midlands; *C* – Cardiff;
Zimbabwe tour: *Z1* – Goshawks; *Z2* – Matabeleland; *Z3* – Zimbabwe;
(R) – Replacement; * – New Barbarian

Full-backs: I C Glasgow (Heriot's FP) [*Z1, Z2, Z3*]; A J Joubert (Natal & South Africa) [*B, FB*]; S D Hodgkinson (Moseley & England) [*N*]; *J E B Callard (Bath & England) [*S, SA, L*]; *M J Back (Bridgend & Wales) [*EM*]; A Williams (Swansea & Wales) [*Z2*(R)]; *E J Rayner (Bath) [*B*(R), *S*]; *A Penaud (Brive & France) [*C*]
Wings: S J Davies (Swansea) [*Z1, Z2, Z3*]; S J Hackney (Leicester) [*Z1, Z2, Z3*]; *S B Burnhill (Cleckheaton) [*Z1*(R)]; *D Manley (Pontypridd) [*B*]; M Dods (Gala & Scotland) [*B, FB*]; *K P P Bracken (Bristol & England) [*B*(R)]; N T Walker (Cardiff & Wales) [*FB*]; A Gomersall (Wasps) [*N, L*(R)]; D A Stark (Boroughmuir & Scotland) [*N, EM*]; *G M C Webbe (Bridgend & Wales) [*S*]; *B Taylor (Pontypool) [*S*]; S P Geoghegan (Bath & Ireland) [*SA*]; *P Saint-André (Montferrand & France) [*SA*]; I C Glasgow (Heriot's FP) [*L*]; *K M Logan (Stirling County & Scotland) [*L*]; N K P Woods (Blackrock Coll & Ireland) [*EM, C*]; J M Sleightholme (Bath) [*C*]
Centres: *N D Beal (Northampton) [*Z1, Z2, B*]; R A Bidgood (Newport & Wales) [*Z1, Z3*]; S B Burnhill (Cleckheaton) [*Z2, Z3*]; A G Shiel (Melrose & Scotland) [*B, FB*]; *D P Hopley (Wasps) [*FB, L*];*M Taylor (Pontypool) [*N, L*]; *J C Bell (Ballymena) [*N*]; *J Lewis (Pontypridd) [*S*]; E J Rayner (Bath) [*B*(R), *S*]; M R Hall (Cardiff & Wales) [*SA*]; S Hastings (Watsonians & Scotland) [*SA*]; *P W Howard (Queensland) [*SA*(R)]; *N J J Greenstock (Wasps) [*EM*]; P R de Glanville (Bath & England) [*EM*]; *S R Cottrell (Cambridge U) [*C*]; P P A Danaher (Garryowen & Ireland) [*C*]
Fly-halves: A Williams (Swansea & Wales) [*Z1, Z3*]; C J Stephens (Llanelli & Wales) [*Z2*]; *P A Hull (Bristol & England) [*B, FB*]; I L Evans (Treorchy & Wales) [*N*]; *M Lewis (Bridgend) [*S*]; C M Chalmers (Melrose & Scotland) [*SA*]; G W Rees (Oxford U, Newport & Canada) [*L*]; *P A Burke (Cork Const & Ireland) [*EM*]; D Charvet (Racing Club de France & France) [*C*]
Scrum-halves: *R Jones (Neath) [*Z1, Z2, C*]; *M J S Dawson (Northampton & England) [*Z2*]; *A Gomarsall (Wasps) [*B*]; K P P Bracken (Bristol & England) [*FB*]; *A Booth (Cardiff) [*N*]; M de Maid (Pontypool) [*S*]; R N Jones (Swansea & Wales) [*SA*]; R Howley (Bridgend) [*L*]; *S Worrall (RAF) [*EM*]; R H Q B Moon (Walsall) [*C*(R)]
Forwards: *D I W Hilton (Bath) [*Z1, Z2*]; *R Cockerill (Leicester) [*Z1, B*]; *D J Garforth (Leicester) [*Z1, Z3*]; N G B Edwards (Northampton & Scotland) [*Z1, Z2, Z3*]; *D J Jones (Cardiff) [*Z1, N*]; *M Haag (Bath) [*Z1, Z3*]; *C B Vyvyan (Upper Wharfedale) [*Z1, Z2, S, EM*]; N A Back (Leicester & England) [*Z1, Z2*(R), *Z3, B, FB, SA*]; N N Meek (Pontypool & Wales) [*Z1*(R), *Z2, Z3*]; D J Eves (Bristol) [*Z1*(R), *Z2, Z3, S, L*]; *C J Clark (Oxford U & Bath) [*Z2, Z3, FB*(R)]; R West (Gloucester) [*Z2, Z3, N*]; D W Egerton (Bath & England) [*Z2, N*]; *C Lippert (San Diego & USA) [*B, FB, C*]; P M Clohessy (Young Munster & Ireland) [*B, FB, SA, C*]; M Poole (Leicester) [*B*]; *C Tregaskis (Wellington, NZ) [*B, FB, S*]; *A J Charron (Ottawa Irish & Canada) [*B, FB, SA*]; R I Wainwright (West Hartlepool & Scotland) [*B, FB, SA*]; *K P Yates (Bath) [*B*(R), *N*]; R G R Dawe (Bath & England) [*FB, L*]; *J A Eales (Brothers, Brisbane & Australia) [*FB*]; E W Peters (Bath) [*FB*(R), *L*]; *J Humphries (Cardiff), [*N*]; M Griffiths (Cardiff & Wales) [*N*]; *S O Ojomoh (Bath & England) [*N, S*]; *D Corkery (Cork Const & Ireland) [*N*]; *N Bezani (Pontypridd) [*N*(R), *S*(R)]; *M Budd (Bridgend) [*N*(R)]; N J Popplewell (Wasps & Ireland) [*S, SA*]; *S Mitchell (West Hartlepool) [*S*]; M S Linnett (Moseley & England) [*S, L*(R)]; R Goodey (Newport) [*S*]; *K G M Wood (Garryowen & Ireland) [*SA*]; I D Jones (North Harbour & New Zealand) [*SA*]; *S D Shaw (Bristol) [*SA, L*]; *G Manson-Bishop (Newport) [*SA*(R), *L*]; *R L Evans (Llanelli) [*L*]; A P Burnell (London Scottish & Scotland) [*L*]; *A Blackmore (Bristol) [*L*]; *M Thomas (Swansea) [*L*(R)]; *K Colclough (Swansea) [*EM*]; *S Byrne (Blackrock Coll) [*EM, C*]; *G F Halpin (London Irish & Ireland) [*EM*]; *J F Richardson (Edinburgh Acads & Scotland) [*EM*]; *R Appleyard (Swansea) [*EM*]; *A Foley (Shannon & Ireland) [*EM*]; N Hadley (Wasps & Canada) [*EM*]; *D N Baldwin (Sale) [*C*]; A E D Macdonald (Heriot's FP & Scotland) [*C*]; *P Alston (Bedford) [*C*]; M J Galwey (Shannon & Ireland) [*C*]; *R Hill (Saracens) [*C*]; *M Davis (Newbridge) [*C*(R)]

MAGNIFICENT GAME MATCHES THE OCCASION

THE VARSITY MATCH 1994 *(for the Bowring Bowl)*

6 December, Twickenham
Oxford University 21 (1G 2PG 1DG 1T)
Cambridge University 26 (1G 1PG 2DG 2T)

Those in the capacity crowd of 55,000 who were attending the Varsity Match for the first time left Twickenham rather bemused. They'd been promised a good day out, which had been dutifully delivered in the packed car parks, but what was this cracking game that had been laid on for them? No one had said anything about that. The 113th University Match will surely go down as one of the finest ever, and not just because of the record number of points scored. It was the richness of the play itself which impressed: full of wit, invention, courage and, let's say it long and loud, skill. In recent years many critics had quite rightly wondered aloud why such a gathering should go along to watch such a pitifully limited offering.

Here there was no opting for caution. Oxford had sailed into the match on a wave of optimism, stirred by their season's buoyant form of 12 victories in 16 matches with 621 points scored. In fact Cambridge were not far behind them, with 11 victories in 18 matches and 502 points to their credit. So much for the book: the pundits had really been beguiled by Oxford's slick back line, coached once again in the build-up by Pierre Villepreux. On the day, too, they had another master at the helm, Canadian fly-half Gareth Rees, the only international on either side. The former Harrow schoolboy was to turn out again at Twickenham four days later when Canada faced England.

Cambridge, though, were not overawed. They had four Blues on show, including Palfrey in the centre, a late call-up to replace New Zealand trialist Cottrell. Oxford had five Blues, the most celebrated of whom, Rees, opened the scoring after just 56 seconds with a dropped goal. If that score was supposed to settle nerves in the Oxford ranks, it failed. Throughout they showed little composure, were erratic in their passing and wasted several good chances to score. They were eclipsed by the Cambridge middle five. The Light Blue back row of Rollitt, Metcalfe and Richardson punched great holes round the fringes, creating space and opportunity which Davies and McCarthy at half-back exploited shrewdly.

Three of these players were involved in the move which led to Reynolds' try in the 11th minute. The Neath winger went on to celebrate his 22nd birthday in style, scoring again 14 minutes into the second half. McCarthy dropped the first of his two goals in the 25th minute but Rees narrowed the gap with a penalty goal for Oxford two minutes later.

The second half was every bit as invigorating as the first. Harrison of Cambridge raced away for an interception try 11 minutes after the interval, McCarthy converting. Reynolds' second try gave the Light Blues a comfortable 20-6 lead. Rees galvanised his troops, spiralling over for a try midway through the half and adding the conversion as well as a later penalty goal. In between Martin barged through for another Oxford try. McCarthy, though, maintained the gap between the sides with a penalty and his second dropped goal, becoming in the

Oxford full-back Michael Joy impedes the progress of Eben Rollitt, the Cambridge No 8, in the marvellous 1994 Varsity Match.

process the first Light Blue ever to drop two goals in the Varsity Match. Rees finished with 16 points, a record for an Oxford player. On the day it was scant consolation.

Oxford University: M T Joy (Marling School, Stroud & Keble); I R H Gray (Royal Belfast Academical Institute & St Catherine's), S P Bromley (Cardinal Langley HS & Keble), M S Nolan (Tonbridge & Pembroke), T G Howe (Banbridge Academy & Keble); G L Rees (St Michael's University School, British Columbia, Harrow & Keble), J M Kirsten (Diocesan College, Cape Town & Keble); A N S Bryce (Glenalmond & Keble), D S Henderson (Glenalmond & Keble) (*capt*), S C Thompson (Durham & St Cross), P F Coveney (Clongowes Wood College & New College), J B B Daniell (Wanganui Collegiate School, NZ, Eton & St Catherine's), N F C Martin (King Edward's School, Birmingham & Keble), R S Yeabsley (Haberdashers' Aske's & Keble), G V Allison (St Paul's & Templeton) *Replacement* N J Marval (QEH, Bristol & St Catherine's) for Bromley (66 mins)
Scorers *Tries:* Rees, Martin *Conversion:* Rees *Penalty Goals:* Rees (2)
Dropped Goal: Rees
Cambridge University: A L Dalwood (St Albans School & St Edmund's); N J Walne (Caerleon CS & St Catharine's), R G Harrison (Ermysted's GS, Skipton & Christ's), A J Palfrey (St Cyres CS & Hughes Hall), A J Reynolds (Christ's College, Brecon & Homerton); M McCarthy (Mount St Mary's, Sheffield & Hughes Hall), R J Davies (Gresham's & Downing); L T Mooney (St Boniface, Plymouth & Hughes Hall), I Mackenzie (Brentwood County HS & Homerton), M Q Cox (St Columba's, Dublin & Hughes Hall), A J Meadows (Sedbergh & St Edmund's), R A Bramley (Queen Elizabeth GS, Wakefield & St Edmund's), A F M Metcalfe (Sedbergh & Homerton), E D Rollitt (St Paul's & Magdalene), N D Richardson (King's, Worcester & St Edmund's) (*capt*) *Replacements* R S Dix (Millfield & Homerton) for Palfrey (82 mins); A Spencer (Priestly SFC & St John's) for Harrison (57 mins)
Scorers *Tries:* Reynolds (2), Harrison *Conversion:* McCarthy *Penalty Goal:* McCarthy
Dropped Goals: McCarthy (2)
Referee S R Hilditch (Ireland)

6 December, Stoop Memorial Ground

Oxford University Under-21s 19 (2G 1T) **Cambridge University Under-21s 21** (1G 3PG 1T)
Oxford University Under-21s: M Dumbell (Brasenose); M Djaba (Pembroke), J Wyatt (Pembroke), J Cameron (St Peter's), J Tiley (Pembroke); J Dargie (Brasenose) (*capt*), N Street (Worcester); H Slack (St Hugh's), N Hockley (Worcester), N Sharp (Brasenose), C Smith (Keble), M Fanning (Exeter), J Bevan (St John's), J Britton (New College), M Hutchinson (Keble)
Scorers *Tries:* Dargie (2), Djaba *Conversions:* Dargie (2)
Cambridge University Under-21s: A Janisch (Trinity); S Lippett (Corpus Christi), J Hurst (Homerton), D Clark (Fitzwilliam) (*capt*), M Cooksley (Emanuel); O Clayton (Magdalene), S Young (Pembroke); N Studer (St John's), R Sugden (St Catharine's), N Holgate (Robinson), D Sommers (Gonville & Caius), C Courtnay (St John's), J Hammill (Trinity), M Holmes (Peterhouse), R Earnshaw (St John's)
Scorers *Tries:* pen try, Clark *Conversion:* Lippett *Penalty Goals:* Lippett (3)
Referee R Rees (London)

1 December, Grange Road, Cambridge

Cambridge University LX Club 19 (1G 3PG 1DG) **Oxford University Greyhounds 11** (2PG 1T)
Cambridge University LX Club: R Dix (Homerton); A Richards (Hughes Hall), D Moore (Trinity Hall), A Spencer (St John's), J Rutter (St John's); A Kennedy (St John's), D Maslen (Girton); D Brandt (Downing), J Edwards (St Catharine's), E Simpson (Clare), G Fury (Hughes Hall), L Longstaff (Downing), M Wright (Hughes Hall), R Earnshaw (St John's), H Jones (Caius) (*capt*) *Replacement* O Clayton (Magdalene) for Richards (40 mins)
Scorers *Try:* Rutter *Conversion:* Kennedy *Penalty Goals:* Richards (2), Kennedy *Dropped Goal:* Kennedy
Oxford University Greyhounds: A Macrobert (Keble); C Bailey (Oriel), J Lloyd (Keble), A Enthoven (St Peter's), J Burcell (New College); M Mermagen (Keble), C Jones (University) (*capt*); J Bothwell (Merton), A Logan (St Anne's), D Grant (Worcester), R Underhill (Queen's), J Reader (University), P Harrison (New), M Orsler (Christ Church), M Davies (St Anne's)
Scorers *Try:* Burcell *Penalty Goals:* Mermagen (2)
Referee D Grasshoff (East Midlands)

VARSITY MATCH RESULTS

113 Matches played Oxford 48 wins Cambridge 52 wins 13 Draws

*Match played at Oxford 1871-72; Cambridge 1872-73; The Oval 1873-74 to 1879-80; Blackheath 1880-81 to 1886-87; Queen's Club 1887-88 to 1920-21; then Twickenham. *At this date no match could be won unless a goal was scored.*

Season	Result	Score
1871-72	**Oxford**	1G 1T to 0
1872-73	**Cambridge**	1G 2T to 0
1873-74	Drawn	1T each
1874-75*	Drawn	Oxford 2T to 0
1875-76	**Oxford**	1T to 0
1876-77	**Cambridge**	1G 2T to 0
1877-78	**Oxford**	2T to 0
1878-79	Drawn	No score
1879-80	**Cambridge**	1G 1DG to 1DG
1880-81	Drawn	1T each
1881-82	**Oxford**	2G 1T to 1G
1882-83	**Oxford**	1T to 0
1883-84	**Oxford**	3G 4T to 1G
1884-85	**Oxford**	3G 1T to 1T
1885-86	**Cambridge**	2T to 0
1886-87	**Cambridge**	3T to 0
1887-88	**Cambridge**	1DG 2T to 0
1888-89	**Cambridge**	1G 2T to 0
1889-90	**Oxford**	1G 1T to 0
1890-91	Drawn	1G each
1891-92	**Cambridge**	2T to 0
1892-93	Drawn	No score
1893-94	**Oxford**	1T to 0
1894-95	Drawn	1G each
1895-96	**Cambridge**	1G to 0
1896-97	**Oxford**	1G 1DG to 1G 1T
1897-98	**Oxford**	2T to 0
1898-99	**Cambridge**	1G 2T to 0
1899-1900	**Cambridge**	2G 4T to 0
1900-01	**Oxford**	2G to 1G 1T
1901-02	**Oxford**	1G 1T to 0
1902-03	Drawn	1G 1T each
1903-04	**Oxford**	3G 1T to 2G 1T
1904-05	**Cambridge**	3G to 2G
1905-06	**Cambridge**	3G (15) to 2G 1T (13)
1906-07	**Oxford**	4T (12) to 1G 1T (8)
1907-08	**Oxford**	1G 4T (17) to 0
1908-09	Drawn	1G (5) each
1909-10	**Oxford**	4G 5T (35) to 1T (3)
1910-11	**Oxford**	4G 1T (23) to 3G 1T (18)
1911-12	**Oxford**	2G 3T (19) to 0
1912-13	**Cambridge**	2G (10) to 1T (3)
1913-14	**Cambridge**	1DG 3T (13) to 1T (3)
1914-18	*No matches*	
1919-20	**Cambridge**	1PG 1DG (7) to 1G (5)
1920-21	**Oxford**	1G 4T (17) to 1G 3T (14)
1921-22	**Oxford**	1G 2T (11) to 1G (5)
1922-23	**Cambridge**	3G 2T (21) to 1G 1T (8)
1923-24	**Oxford**	3G 2T (21) to 1G 1PG 2T (14)
1924-25	**Oxford**	1G 2T (11) to 2T (6)
1925-26	**Cambridge**	3G 6T (33) to 1T (3)
1926-27	**Cambridge**	3G 5T (30) to 1G (5)
1927-28	**Cambridge**	2G 2PG 2T (22) to 1G 3T (14)
1928-29	**Cambridge**	1G 3T (14) to
		1PG 1DG 1T (10)
1929-30	**Oxford**	1G 1DG (9) to 0
1930-31	Drawn	Oxford 1PG (3)
		Cambridge 1T (3)
1931-32	**Oxford**	1DG 2T (10) to 1T (3)
1932-33	**Oxford**	1G 1T (8) to 1T (3)
1933-34	**Oxford**	1G (5) to 1T (3)
1934-35	**Cambridge**	2G 1PG 1DG 4T (29) to
		1DG (4)
1935-36	Drawn	No score
1936-37	**Cambridge**	2T (6) to 1G (5)
1937-38	**Oxford**	1G 4T (17) to 1DG (4)
1938-39	**Cambridge**	1G 1PG (8) to 2PG (6)
1939-45	*War-time series*	
1945-46	**Cambridge**	1G 2T (11) to 1G 1PG (8)
1946-47	**Oxford**	1G 1DG 2T (15) to 1G (5)
1947-48	**Cambridge**	2PG (6) to 0
1948-49	**Oxford**	1G 1DG 2T (14) to 1G 1PG (8)
1949-50	**Oxford**	1T (3) to 0
1950-51	**Oxford**	1G 1PG (8) to 0
1951-52	**Oxford**	2G 1T (13) to 0
1952-53	**Cambridge**	1PG 1T (6) to 1G (5)
1953-54	Drawn	Oxford 1PG 1T (6)
		Cambridge 2PG (6)
1954-55	**Cambridge**	1PG(3) to 0
1955-56	**Oxford**	1PG 2T (9) to 1G (5)
1956-57	**Cambridge**	1G 1PG 1DG 1T (14) to
		2PG 1T (9)
1957-58	**Oxford**	1T (3) to 0
1958-59	**Cambridge**	1G 1PG 3T (17) to 1PG 1T (6)
1959-60	**Oxford**	3PG (9) to 1PG (3)
1960-61	**Cambridge**	2G 1T (13) to 0
1961-62	**Cambridge**	1DG 2T (9) to 1DG (3)
1962-63	**Cambridge**	1G 1PG 1DG 1T (14) to 0
1963-64	**Cambridge**	2G 1PG 2T (19) to
		1G 1PG 1DG (11)
1964-65	**Oxford**	2G 1PG 2T (19) to 1PG 1GM (6)
1965-66	Drawn	1G (5) each
1966-67	**Oxford**	1G 1T (8) to 1DG 1T (6)
1967-68	**Cambridge**	1T 1PG (6) to 0
1968-69	**Cambridge**	1T 1PG 1DG (9) to 2T (6)
1969-70	**Oxford**	3PG (9) to 2PG (6)
1970-71	**Oxford**	1G 1DG 2T (14) to 1PG (3)
1971-72	**Oxford**	3PG 3T (21) to 1PG (3)
1972-73	**Cambridge**	1G 1PG 1DG 1T (16) to
		2PG (6)
1973-74	**Cambridge**	1PG 1DG 2T (14) to
		1G 2PG (12)
1974-75	**Cambridge**	1G 2PG 1T (16) to 5PG (15)
1975-76	**Cambridge**	2G 5PG 1DG 1T (34) to
		3PG 1DG (12)
1976-77	**Cambridge**	1G 3PG (15) to 0
1977-78	**Oxford**	4PG 1T (16) to 2PG 1T (10)
1978-79	**Cambridge**	2G 3PG 1T (25) to
		1PG 1T (7)
1979-80	**Oxford**	2PG 1DG (9) to 1PG (3)
1980-81	**Cambridge**	3PG 1T (13) to 3PG (9)
1981-82	**Cambridge**	3PG (9) to 2PG (6)
1982-83	**Cambridge**	3PG 1DG 2T (20) to
		1G 1PG 1T (13)
1983-84	**Cambridge**	4PG 2T (20) to 3PG (9)
1984-85	**Cambridge**	4G 2T (32) to 2PG (6)
1985-86	**Oxford**	1PG 1T (7) to 2PG (6)
1986-87	**Oxford**	3PG 2DG (15) to 1PG 1DG 1T (10)
1987-88	**Cambridge**	1DG 3T (15) to 2PG 1T (10)
1988-89	**Oxford**	2G 1DG 3T (27) to 1DG 1T (7)
1989-90	**Cambridge**	2G 2PG 1T (22) to
		1G 1PG 1T (13)
1990-91	**Oxford**	2G 2PG 1DG (21) to 1G 2PG (12)
1991-92	**Cambridge**	2PG 1DG 2T (17) to
		1DG 2T (11)
1992-93	**Cambridge**	1G 2PG 2DG (19) to
		1PG 1DG 1T (11)
1993-94	**Oxford**	3PG 2DG 1T (20) to 1DG 1T (8)
1994-95	**Cambridge**	1G 1PG 2DG 2T (26)
		to 1G 2PG 1DG 1T (21)

THE WAR-TIME MATCHES

Season	Result	Score
1939-40	**Oxford**	1G 1DG 2T (15) to
		1T (3) (at Cambridge)
	Cambridge	1G 3T (14) to
		2G 1T (13) (at Oxford)
1940-41	**Cambridge**	1G 2T (11) to
		1G 1DG (9) (at Oxford)
	Cambridge	2G 1T (13) to 0
		(at Cambridge)
1941-42	**Cambridge**	1PG 2T (9) to
		1PG 1T (6) (at Cambridge)
	Cambridge	1G 2PG 2T (17) to
		1G 1T (8) (at Oxford)

Season	Winner	Score
1942-43	Cambridge	1G 1DG (9) to 0 (at Oxford)
	Cambridge	2G 2T (16) to 1T (3) (at Cambridge)
1943-44	Cambridge	2G 1T (13) to 1DG (4) (at Cambridge)
	Oxford	2T (6) to 1G (5) (at Oxford)
1944-45	Drawn	1T (3) each (at Oxford)
	Cambridge	2G 2T (16) to 1DG (4) (at Cambridge)

OXFORD and CAMBRIDGE BLUES 1872-1994

(Each year indicates a separate appearance, and refers to the first half of the season. Thus 1879 refers to the match played in the 1879-80 season.) (R) indicates an appearance as a replacement; (t) denotes an appearance as a temporary replacement.

OXFORD

Name	Years
Abbott, J S	1954-55
Abell, G E B	1923-24-25-26
Adamson, J A	1928-29-31
Adcock, J R L	1961
Aitken, A D	1993
Aitken, G G	1922-24
Aldridge, J E	1888
Alexander, H	1897-98
Alexander, P C	1930
Allaway, R C P	1953-54-55
Allen, C P	1881-82-83
Allen, T	1909
Allen, W C	1910
Allison, G V	1994
Allison, M G	1955
Almond, R G P	1937
Ashby, C J	1973
Asher, A G G	1881-82-83-84
Asquith, P R	1974
Atkinson, C C	1876
Back, A	1878
Badenoch, D F	1971
Baden-Powell, F S	1873
Baggaley, J C	1953-54
Bain, D McL	1910-11-12-13
Bainbrigge, J H	1874-76-77
Baird, J S	1966-67
Baiss, R S H	1894-95
Baker, C D	1891-93
Baker, D G S	1951-52
Baker, E M	1893-94-95-96
Baker, P	1980(R)
Baker, R T	1968
Balfour, E R	1893-94-95
Bannerman, J MacD	1927-28
Barclay, S L	1990-91
Barker, A C	1966-67
Barnes, S	1981-82-83
Barr, D C A	1980
Barry, C E	1897-98-99
Barry, D M	1968-69-70
Barwick, W M	1880-81
Bass, R G	1961
Batchelor, T B	1906
Bateson, H D	1874-75-77
Baxter, T J	1958-59
Beamish, S H	1971
Beare, A	1982
Bedford, T P	1965-66-67
Behn, A R	1968-69
Bell, D L	1970
Benson, E T	1928
Bentley, P J	1960
Berkeley, W V	1924-25-26
Berry, C W	1883-84
Bettington, R H B	1920-22
Bevan, J H	1946
Bibby, A J	1980-81
Binham, P A	1971
Birrell, H B	1953
Black, B H	1929
Blair, A S	1884
Blencowe, L C	1907-08
Bloxham, C T	1934-35-36-37
Blyth, P H	1885-86
Bolton, W H	1873-74-75
Bonham-Carter, C R	1990
Bonham-Carter, E	1890-91
Boobbyer, B	1949-50-51
Booker, J L	1880
Booth, J L	1956
Bos, F H ten	1958-59-60
Boswell, J D	1885-86-87
Botfield, A S G	1871
Botting, I J	1949-50
Bourdillon, H	1873-74-75
Bourns, C	1903
Bowers, J B	1932-34
Boyce, A W	1952-53
Boyd, A de H	1924
Boyd, E F	1912
Boyle, D S	1967-68-69
Boyle, L S	1993
Brace, D O	1955-56
Bradby, G F	1882-85
Bradford, C C	1887
Branfoot, E P	1878-79
Bray, C N	1979
Bray, K A	1989
Bremridge, H	1876-77
Brett, J A	1935-36-37
Brett, P V	1978
Brewer, R J	1965
Brewer, T J	1951
Bridge, D J W	1946-47-48
Brierley, H	1871
Britton, R B	1963-64
Bromet, W E	1889
Bromley, S P	1994
Brooks, A W	1980-81-82
Brooks, M J	1873
Brooks, W	1872
Broster, L R	1912
Broughton, R C	1965
Brown, L G	1910-11-12
Brown, M E O	1988
Brunskill, R F	1873-74
Bryan, T A	1975-76-77
Bryce, A N S	1994
Bryer, L W	1953
Buchanan, F G	1909-10
Buckett, I M	1992
Bucknall, A L	1965-66
Budge, K J	1977-78-79
Budworth, R T D	1887-88-89
Bullard, G L	1950-51
Bullock, H	1910-11
Bulpett, C W L	1871
Burnet, P J	1960
Burrow, K C	1933
Burse, R M	1974
Bush, A	1934
Bussell, J G	1903-04
Butcher, W M	1954
Butler, F E R	1959-60
Button, E L	1936
Byers, R M	1926
Caccia, H A	1926
Cadell, P R	1890
Cairns, A G	1899-1900-01
Calcraft, W J	1986-87
Cameron, A J	1988
Campbell, E	1919-20-21
Campbell, W	1987
Cannell, L B	1948-49-50
Cardale, C F	1929-30
Carey, G M	1891-92-94
Carey, W J	1894-95-96-97
Carlyon, H B	1871
Carroll, B M	1970-71
Carroll, P R	1968-69-70
Carter, C R	1885
Cartwright, V H	1901-02-03-04
Cass, T	1961
Castens, H H	1886-87
Cattell, R H B	1893
Cave, H W	1881
Cawkwell, G L	1946-47
Chadwick, A J	1898-99
Chambers, J C	1921
Champain, F H B	1897-98-99
Champneys, F W	1874-75-76
Charles, A E S	1932
Cheesman, W I	1910-11
Cheyne, H	1903-04
Chislett, J	1986-87
Cholmondeley, F G	1871-73
Christopherson, P	1886-87-88
Clark, C J	1993
Clark, R B	1978-79
Clarke, E J D	1973
Clarke, I A	1913
Clauss, P R	1889-90-91
Clements, B S	1975
Cleveland, C R	1885-86
Cochran, P C	1889-91
Cohen, B A	1884
Coker, J B H	1965
Coker, T	1988-89
Cole, B W	1945
Coleman, D J	1982-83
Coles, D G G	1937-38
Coles, P	1884-85-86
Coles, S C	1954-56-57
Collingwood, J A	1961-62
Colville, A H	1892-93
Conway-Rees, J	1891-92-93
Cook, D J	1988(R)-89
Cooke, J L	1968-69
Cooke, P	1936-37
Cooke, W R	1976
Cookson, G H F	1891-92
Cooper, A H	1951
Cooper, M McG	1934-35-36
Cooper, R A	1937
Cooper, R M	1946
Cornish, W H	1876
Couper, T	1899-1900
Court, E D	1882-83
Cousins, F C	1885-86
Coutts, I D F	1951
Coveney, P F	1994
Coventry, R G T	1889-90-91
Cowen, T J	1938
Cowlishaw, F I	1890-91
Cox, G V	1878
Cozens-Hardy, B	1904-05-06
Crabbie, J E	1898-99-1900-01
Craig, F J R	1963-64-65
Crane, C M	1985-86-87
Cranmer, P	1933-34
Crawfurd, J W F A	1900
Creese, N A H	1951
Cridlan, A G	1928-29-30
Croker, J R	1966-67

Name	Years
Crole, G B	1913-19
Cronje, S N	1907-08
Crosse, C W	1874
Crowe, P J	1981-82-83
Crump, L M	1896
Cuff, T W	1945
Cunningham, G	1907-08-09
Currie, D S	1992 (R)
Currie, J D	1954-55-56-57
Curry, J A H	1961
Curtis, A B	1949
Curtis, D M	1989
Dalby, C	1923
Daniell, J B B	1992-93-94
Davey, P	1967
Davey, R A E	1972
David, A M	1921-22
Davies, D B	1905-06-07
Davies, D E	1951
Davies, D M	1958-59-60
Davies, J A B	1920
Davies, L L J	1927
Davies, R	1969
Davies, R H	1955-56-57
Davies, S J T	1972-73
Davies, W G	1977
Davis, R A	1974-75
Davis, T M E	1978-79-80
Dawkins, P M	1959-60-61
Deacon, E A	1871-72
De Glanville, P R	1990
De Winton, R F C	1888-89-90
Dew, C J	1978
Diamond, A J	1957
Dickson, M R	1903
Dickson, W M	1912
Diggle, P R	1908-09
Dingemans, J M	1985
Dingle, A J	1911
Disney, P C W	1935
Dixon, P J	1967-68-69-70
Dobson, D D	1899-1900-01
Donald, D G	1911-12-13
Donaldson, C L	1895
Donaldson, D W	1893
Donaldson, W P	1892-93-94
Donnelly, M P	1946
Donovan, T J	1971
Douglas, A I	1970-71
Dorman, J M A	1964
Dowson, A O	1896
Druitt, W A H	1929-30-31
Dryburgh, D J W	1926
Drysdale, D	1925
Dunbar, I T	1970-71-73
Duncan, D D	1919-20
Dunn, L B	1897
Durand, J J	1990
Duthie, A L	1986-87
Du Toit, S F	1991-92-93
Eberle, G S J F	1901-02
Edgell, E M R	1871-73
Edmiston, J H F	1926-27
Edmonds, J N	1978
Egan, M S	1988-89-90
Egerton, R H	1987-88
Elliot, J R	1989
Ellis, A W	1975
Elwes, A C	1892-93
Emms, D A	1949-50
Enevoldson, T P	1976-77-78-79-80
Evans, A H	1877-78
Evans, C D	1984
Evans, C H	1919-20
Evans, D P	1959
Evans, D R	1991-92-93
Evans, D W	1887-88
Evans, D W	1988
Evanson, A M	1880-81
Everett, A E	1990-91
Evers, C P	1897-98
Evers, R W	1909

Name	Years
Ewart, C B	1982
Ewing, M H O	1886
Faktor, S J	1977
Fallon, T J	1953-55
Farquharson, J C L	1903
Fearenside, E	1903
Fellows-Smith, J P	1953-54
Fennell, B	1993
Ferguson, S M	1986
Fergusson, E A J	1952-53
Fewtrell, J C	1989
Field, H	1873
Filby, L L	1960
Fildes, D G	1922-25
Finch, C J	1978
Findlay, A C	1983
Fisher, C D C	1902
Fisher, S J	1976
Fitzwater, N J	1991
Fleming, C J N	1887-88-89-90
Flemmer, W K	1906
Fletcher, K R	1871
Fletcher, W R B	1871-73-74
Forman, J	1875-76
Forsayth, H H	1920-21
Forster, F M McL	1937
Fowler, H	1877-78
Francis, C K	1871
Francis, D G	1919
Franklin, H W F	1923
Fraser, E C	1872-73-74-75
Freakes, H D	1936-37-38
Furnival, A G D	1987
Gabitass, J R	1965-66
Gaisford, R B	1876
Galbraith, J H	1947
Game, W H	1872-73-74
Gardner, C J	1905-06
Gardner, J W	1871
Gargan, M F	1980-82-83
Gedge, H T S	1893
Geen, W P	1910-11-12
Gent, G N	1949
German, G J	1922
Gibson, A G	1894-95
Gibson, C H	1927
Gill, R D	1947-48
Gilmour, A	1911
Gilray, C M	1908-09
Gilthorpe, C G	1946-47
Glover, J	1959-60
Glover, T R	1973-74
Glubb, J M	1887
Glynn, R I	1985
Gooding, W F	1872-73
Goold, A N	1927
Gordon, P F C	1970
Gotley, A L H	1909
Gould, E J H	1963-64-65-66
Grant, A D	1922
Grant, A H	1892
Gray, I R H	1994
Green, R	1948-49-50
Greenhalgh, J E	1984
Gregson, R E S	1903
Grellet, R C	1899-1900-01-02
Grenfell, W T	1888
Grieve, C F	1934-35-36
Griffin, S J M	1985-86
Griffith, C J L	1950-51-52
Griffiths, D A	1969-70
Griffiths, R L	1969
Grischotti, W	1899
Gubb, T W	1926-27-28-29
Gush, E P	1963
Guy, J C	1934
Habergham, W D R	1980-82
Hadman, W G	1964-65-66
Hall, J D	1885-86
Halliday, S J	1979-80-81
Hamilton, C W	1872

Name	Years
Hammond, C E L	1899-1900
Hands, K C M	1912
Hands, P A M	1910
Hands, R H M	1908-09
Harcourt, A B	1945-46
Harding, R F	1935
Harper, C H	1897-98
Harrison, C F	1873-74-75
Hartley, J C	1894-95-96
Harvey, R C M	1886
Havard, W T	1919
Hawkesworth, C J	1970-71-72
Hayashi, T	1990
Heal, M G	1971
Hearn, R D	1964
Heath, A H	1875-77-78-79
Hefer, W J	1949-50
Hein, G M	1989-90
Henderson, D S	1993-94
Henderson, J H	1952
Henderson, N F	1886
Henderson, W M C	1991
Henley, W E	1929-30-31
Heppenstall, A F	1926-27
Herring, D G	1909
Herrod, N J	1981-82-83
Higham, J R S	1959
Hillard, R J	1923-24
Hiller, R	1965
Hines, G W	1961-62
Hirst, E T	1877-78-79
Hoadley, A A	1905-06
Hoare, A H M	1956-57
Hobart, A H	1981
Hockley, M	1975
Hodges, H A	1905-06-07-08
Hodgson, F W	1881
Hofmeyr, K de J	1927
Hofmeyr, M B	1948-49-50
Hofmeyr, S J	1928-29-30
Hofmeyr, S M	1979
Hollis, G	1938
Holroyd, C A	1966
Honey, R	1909-10
Hood, R K	1976
Hoolahan, R M C	1976-77-78
Hopkins, K M	1977
Hordern, P C	1928
Horne, E C	1975-76-77
Horrocks-Taylor, R	1989
Hoskin, W W	1904-05-06-07
Houston, K J	1964
Hovde, F L	1931
Howard, A	1907
Howard, P D	1929-30
Howe, T G	1994
Howe-Browne, N R F G	1905-06
Hoyer-Millar, G C	1952
Hughes, H M	1935-36
Hughes, R A	1978
Hugo-Hamman, C T	1981-82
Hume, J W G	1927-28
Humfrey, L C	1892-93
Humphrey, M W	1923
Hunt, R W	1890
Hunter, R S	1888-89
Hutchinson, J M	1972-73
Hutchison, R O	1902
Ilett, N L	1947
Inglis, R E	1883-84
Irwin, H	1880
Isherwood, F W	1871
Jackson, K L T	1932-33
Jackson, W M	1938
Jacob, G O	1878-79
Jacob, H P	1923-24-25
Jacot, B L	1920
James, A I	1934
James, D W	1989
James, J	1875-76-77
James, S	1970-71
James, S J B	1966
Jenkin, J M	1952

Jenkins, A 1971
Jenkins, O 1913-19
Jenkins, P 1980
Jenkins, V G J 1930-31-32
Jesson, D 1957-58-59
Johnson, A M 1985-86-87
Johnson, P M 1968-70
Johnson, T F 1875
Johnstone, P G 1952-53-54
Jones, A M 1989
Jones, D K 1963
Jones, D R R 1972
Jones, G S A 1896
Jones, I C 1962-63-64
Jones, K W J 1931-32
Jones, L E 1991
Jones, R M 1991
Jones, R O P 1969-70-71
Jones, T O 1898
Jones, T W 1978-79
Jones, V W 1954
Joy, M T 1992-93-94
Joyce, A L 1984
Jupp, H B 1873

Kay, A R 1889-90-91
Kay, D C 1972-73
Kelly, H M 1932
Kendall-Carpenter, J MacG K 1948-49-50
Kennedy, A P 1985
Kennedy, N 1901
Kennedy, W D 1904
Kent, C P 1972-73-74-75
Kent, P C 1970
Kershaw, F 1898-99-1900-01
Key, K J 1885-86
Kindersley, R S 1882-83
King, B B H 1963
King, P E 1975
King, T W 1929
Kininmonth, P W 1947-48
Kirk, D E 1987-88
Kirsten, J M 1994
Kitson, J A 1895
Kittermaster, H J 1922-24
Kitto, R C M 1884-85-86-87
Knight, R L 1879
Knott, F H 1910-11-12-13
Koe, A P 1886
Kyrke, G V 1902-03
Kyrke-Smith, P St L 1973-74-75(R)

Lagden, R O 1909-10-11
Laidlaw, C R 1968-69
Lamb, R H 1962-63-64
Lamport, N K 1930-31-32
Landale, D F 1925-26
Lane, R O B 1887-88-89
Langley, P J 1949
Latham, H E 1907
Latter, A 1892
Law, A F 1875
Lawrence, W S 1954-56
Lawrie, A A 1903-05
Lawton, T 1921-22-23
Lee, F H 1874-75-76-77
Lee, J W 1973-74
Lee, R J 1972
Legge, D 1897
Lennox-Cook, J M 1945
Leslie, C F H 1880-81
Leslie, R E 1954
Leslie-Jones, F A 1894-95-96
Lewin, A J A 1962-63
Lewis, A K 1888
Lewis, D J 1950
Lewis, S M 1973
Light, B 1977
Lindsay, G C 1882-83-84-85
Lion-Cachet, C C 1992-93
Littlechild, E J F 1972
Littlewood, R B 1893
Lloyd, E A 1964-65-66
Lloyd, J E 1872-74
Lloyd, R 1908
Lombard, L T 1956-57-58
Longdon, J S 1889
Lorraine, H D B 1932-33-34
Loudoun-Shand, E G 1913-19
Love, R D 1972
Low, R C S 1933
Luce, F M 1899-1900
Luddington, R S 1980-81-82
Lumsden, A E 1992
Lusty, W 1927
Luyt, R E 1938
Lyle, A M P 1902-04-05

McBain, N S 1986-87
McCanlis, M A 1926-27
McClure, R N 1973
Macdonald, C P 1985-86
Macdonald, D A 1975-76
Macdonald, D S M 1974-75-76
Macdonald, G E 1922
Macdonald, N L 1926
Macdonald, N W 1984-85
MacEwen, G L 1895
McFarland, P R E 1967
MacGibbon, R R 1930-31
McGlashan, J R C 1945
McGrath, N F 1934-35-36
MacGregor, A 1871
Mackenzie, A O M 1880-81
Mackenzie, D W 1974
Mackenzie, F J C 1882-83
Mackintosh, C E W C 1925
MacLachlan, L P 1953
Maclachlan, N 1879-80
Macmillan, M 1876
McNeill, A 1884
MacNeill, H P 1982-83-84
McPartlin, J J 1960-61-62
Macpherson, G P S 1922-23-24
Macpherson, N M S 1928
McQuaid, A S J 1983
McShane, J M S 1933-35
Maddock, W P 1972
Mallalieu, J P W 1927
Mallett, N V H 1979
Malone, N G 1992
Marshall, H P 1921
Marshall, R M 1936-37-38
Martin, H 1907-08-09
Martin, N F C 1993-94
Marval, N J 1994(R)
Marvin, T G R 1984-85
Mather, E G S 1933
Maxwell-Hyslop, J E 1920-21-22
Mayhew, P K 1937
Mead, B D 1972-73
Meadows, H J 1948
Merivale, G M 1874
Merriam, L P B 1913
Michell, A T 1871-72-73-74
Millerchip, C J 1981-82
Mills, D J 1983-84
Milton, N W 1905-06-07
Milward, A W 1991
Minns, P C 1930-31-32
Mitchell, M D 1977
Moberly, W O 1871-72-73
Moir, M J P 1977
Molohan, M J B 1928
Moloney, R J 1990
Monteath, J G 1912
Montgomery, J R 1958
Moorcroft, E K 1966
Moore, A P 1990
Moore, E J 1882-83
Moore, H B 1912-13
Moore, H R 1956
Moore, P B C 1945-46
Moresby-White, J M 1913-19
Morgan, A K 1963-64
Morgan, D J 1979
Morgan, F 1888
Morgan, R de R 1983
Morris, E G 1904
Morrison, W E A 1979-80
Mortimer, L 1892
Moubray, J J 1876-77-78
Muller, H 1938
Mullin, B J 1986-87
Mullins, R C 1894
Mulvey, R S 1968
Munro, P 1903-04-05
Murray, G C 1959

Nash, E H 1874-75
Nasser, B P 1992
Nelson, T A 1897-98
Nesbitt, J V 1904-05
Neser, V H 1919-20
Neville, T B 1971-72
Newman, A P 1973
Newman, S C 1946-47
Newton, H F 1895-96-97
Newton, P A 1879-80
Newton-Thompson, J O 1945-46
Nicholas, P L 1897-98-99
Nicholson, E S 1931-32-33-34
Nolan, M S 1994
North, E G H 1888-89-90
Norwitz, E R 1988-89-90
Novis, A L 1927
Nunn, J A 1925-26

Obolensky, A 1935-37
O'Brien, T S 1983-84
O'Connor, A 1958
O'Mahony, B G 1992
O'Mahony, D P 1992
Odgers, W B 1901-02
Orpen, L J J 1898
Osborn, E C 1969
Osborne, S H 1900-01-02
Osler, S G 1931
Owen-Smith, H G O 1932-33

Page, H V 1884-85
Painter, P A 1967
Palmer, M S 1960
Parker, L 1905
Parker, T 1888
Parkin, W H 1890
Pask, R A 1991
Paterson, A M 1889-90
Paterson, L R 1886-87
Patterson, A R 1879-80-81
Patton, M B 1991-92
Payne, C M 1960
Peacock, M B 1880
Peacock, M F 1932-33
Peacock, N C 1987
Peake, H W 1871
Pearce, J K 1945
Pearson, S B 1983-84-85
Pearson, T S 1871
Peat, W H 1898
Peck, A Q 1981
Pennington, H H 1937-38
Percival, L J 1889-91
Percy, H R G 1936-38
Pether, S 1938
Phillips, C 1876-77-78-79
Phillips, E L 1933
Phillips, L R L 1984
Phillips, M S 1956-57-58-59
Phillips, P C 1938
Phillips, R H 1966-67-68
Pienaar, J H 1933-34-35
Pitman, I J 1921
Plant, W I 1958
Pleydell-Bouverie, Hon B 1923
Plumbridge, R A 1954-55-56
Podmore, G 1872
Pollard, D 1952
Poole, F O 1891-92-93-94
Poulton, R W 1909-10-11

Prescott, A E C 1928
Prescott, R E 1932
Preston, B W 1925
Price, H L 1920-21
Price, V R 1919-20-21
Pritchard, N S M 1985(R)
Prodger, J A 1955

Quinnen, P N 1974-75
Quist-Arcton, E A K 1978-79

Rahmatallah, F J 1976
Ramsay, A W 1952-53
Ramsden, J E 1945
Raphael, J E 1901-02-03-04
Rashleigh, W 1887-88
Ravenscroft, J 1877-78
Raymond, R L 1924
Rayner, E J 1993
Rayner-Wood, A C 1895-96
Read, R F 1965
Reed, D K 1984
Reeler, I L 1955-56
Rees, G L 1993-94
Rees, H 1930
Rees, H J V 1913
Rees, P S 1974-75-78
Rees-Jones, G R 1933-34-35
Reid, C J 1896
Reid, G A 1935-36
Reid, N 1912-13
Renwick, W N 1936-37
Rice-Evans, W 1890
Richards, C A L 1932
Richards, S B 1962
Richardson, J V 1925
Richardson, W R 1881
Rigby, J P 1955-56
Rimmer, L I 1958
Risman, J M 1984-85-86
Rittson-Thomas, G C 1949-50
Robbins, P G D 1954-55-56-57
Roberts, D G 1990
Roberts, G D 1907-08
Roberts, M G 1968
Roberts, N T 1979-80-81
Roberts, S N J 1985-86
Roberts, W 1928-29-30-31
Robertson, A M 1903
Robertson, J W 1921
Robertson, M A 1894-96
Robinson, D A B 1952-53
Robinson, R G 1976-77
Robson, M 1929
Rogers, W L Y 1898-1900
Rolfe, A J 1987
Roos, G D 1936
Rosier, J R H 1983
Ross, W S 1980
Rotherham, A 1882-83-84
Roughead, W N 1924-25-26
Rousseau, W P 1929
Row, A W L 1921
Rowley, J V D'A 1929
Rucker, R W 1874-76
Rudd, E L 1963-64
Russell, H 1872-73-74-75
Russell, J H 1929
Russell-Roberts, F D 1931
Rydon, R A 1985-86

Sachs, D M 1962
Sampson, D H 1945
Sampson, H F 1910-11
Sanctuary, C F S 1879-80
Sandford, J R P 1902-03
Saunders, C J 1951
Sawtell, P R 1972
Sayer, J 1871
Sayer, J B 1887
Scholefield, B G 1920-21
Scott, J S M 1957-58
Searle, J P 1981-82
Seccombe, L S 1925
Selby, E 1891
Sexton, C M 1976
Seymour, T M 1971-73
Shacksnovis, A 1922-23
Sharp, H S 1910-11
Sharp, R A W 1959-60-61
Sharp, R G 1919
Shaw, C 1974-75
Shearman, M 1878-79
Sheffield, R W 1873-74
Sheil, A G R 1958
Shillito, G V 1930
Sidgwick, A 1872
Siepmann, C A 1921
Silk, N 1961-62-63
Sim, A C 1876
Simmie, M S 1965-66
Simonet, P M 1984
Simpson, E P 1887
Simpson, H B 1920
Skipper, D J 1952
Slater, N T 1960
Sloan, T 1908
Sloane, A D 1902
Small, H D 1949-50
Smith, A R 1894-95-96-97
Smith, B A 1988-89
Smith, I S 1923
Smith, J A 1892-93
Smith, M J K 1954-55
Southee, E A 1913
Speed, R R 1967-68-69
Spence, D O 1992
Spence, K M 1951-52
Spencer, B L 1960
Spragg, F F 1926
Springman, P 1877-78
Squire, W H S 1882-83-84
Stafford, P M W 1961-62
Stagg, P K 1961-62
Starmer-Smith, N C 1965-66
Steel, J J 1953
Steinthal, F E 1906
Stevens, D T 1959
Stewart, A 1947-48
Stewart, W B 1892
Steyn, S S L 1911-12
Stileman, W M C 1988-90
Still, E R 1871-73
Stobie, A M 1945
Stobie, W D K 1947
Stone, T 1897
Stoneman, B M 1962
Stoop, A D 1902-03-04
Strand-Jones, J 1899-1900-01
Stratton, J W 1897
Street, K P 1991-92
Strong, E L 1881-83
Strong, W I N 1924-25
Stuart-Watson, J L 1935
Summerskill, W H J 1945
Surtees, E A 1885
Sutherland, I W 1938
Sutherland, J G B 1885
Sutton, M A 1945-46
Swan, M W 1957
Swanston, J F A 1897-98-99-1900
Swanzy, A J 1901-02
Swarbrick, D W 1946-47-48
Swayne, D H 1930-31
Sweatman, E A 1927

Taberer, H M 1892
Tahany, M P 1945
Tanner, T L 1931
Tapper, A D 1991
Tarr, F N 1907-08-09
Tatham, W M 1881-82-83
Taylor, E G 1926-27-28
Taylor, G C 1990
Taylor, J A 1974
Taylor, S C 1989
Terry, H F 1900-01
Theron, T P 1923
Thomas, A C 1979
Thomas, T R 1938
Thomas, W E 1911-12
Thomas, W L 1893-94
Thompson, S C 1994
Thomson, B E 1951-52
Thomson, C 1896
Thomson, F W 1912-13
Thomson, J B 1983
Thomson, W J 1895-96
Thorburn, C W 1964
Thorniley-Walker, M J 1967
Thresher, P R 1991
Tongue, P K 1975
Torry, P J 1968-69
Travers, B H 1946-47
Tristram, H B 1882-83-84
Troup, D S 1928
Tudor, H A 1878-79-80-81
Turcan, H H 1928
Turner, A B 1884
Turner, F H 1908-09-10

Ubogu, V E 1987
Unwin, G T 1894-95-96

Valentine, A C 1923-24-25
Van Der Merwe, W M 1989
Van Der Riet, E F 1920-21
Van Ryneveld, A J 1946-47-48
Van Ryneveld, C B 1947-48-49
Vassall, H 1879-80-81-82
Vassall, H H 1906-07-08
Vecqueray, A H 1877-78
Vecqueray, G C 1873
Vessey, S J R 1984-85-86-87-88
Vidal, R W S 1872
Vincent, A N 1948-49

Wade, C G 1882-83-84
Waide, S L 1932
Wake, H B L 1922
Wakefield, W H 1891-92
Wakelin, W S 1964
Waldock, F A 1919
Waldock, H F 1919-20
Waldron, O C 1965-67
Walford, M M 1935-36-37
Walker, A 1880
Walker, J C 1955
Walker, J G 1879-80-81
Walker, M 1950-51
Wall, T W 1875-76-77
Wallace, A C 1922-23-24-25
Walton, E J 1900-01
Ward, J M 1972
Ware, M A 1961-62
Warr, A L 1933-34
Waterman, J S 1974
Wates, C S 1961
Watkins, L 1879
Watkinson, A F 1977-78
Watson, P W 1954-55
Watson, T C S 1993
Watt, K A 1976
Watts, I H 1937-38
Watts, L D 1957-58
Webster, J G M 1980-81
Webster, J P 1982-83
Welsh, A R 1984
Wensley, S C 1988
Wesche, V V G 1924
Weston, B A G 1957
Weston, J W 1871
White, G L 1976-77
White, N T 1905-06
Whiteside, S D 1991
Whyte, A G D 1963
Whyte, D J 1963
Wilcock, R M 1962
Wilcock, S H 1957-58-59
Wilkinson, J V S 1904
Wilkinson, W E 1891
Willcox, J G 1959-60-61-62

Williams, A D 1988-92
Williams, C D 1945
Williams, I M 1988
Williams, J R 1969
Williams, S R 1988(R)
Williamson, A C 1913
Williamson, R H 1906-07-08
Willis, D C 1975-76-77
Willis, T G 1985-86-88
Wilson, C T M 1948
Wilson, D B 1874
Wilson, G A 1946-48
Wilson, J 1967-68
Wilson, J H G 1888-89-90
Wilson, N G C 1967
Wilson, R W 1956
Wilson, S 1963-64
Wilson, S E 1890
Wilson, W G 1887
Wimperis, E J 1951
Winn, C E 1950
Winn, R R 1953
Wintle, R V 1993
Witney, N K J 1970-71
Wix, R S 1904-05-06-07
Wood, A E 1904
Wood, D E 1952-53
Wood, G F 1919
Woodhead, P G 1974
Woodrow, D K 1978-79-80
Wooldridge, C S 1882
Wordsworth, C R 1922-23-24
Wordsworth, C W 1902
Wordsworth, J R 1885
Wray, M O 1933-34
Wyatt, D M 1981
Wydell, H A 1951
Wynter, E C C 1947

Yeabsley, R S 1994
Young, J R C 1957-58

CAMBRIDGE

Aarvold, C D 1925-26-27-28
Ackford, P J 1979
Adams, G C A 1929
Adams, H F S 1884-85
Agnew, C M 1875-76
Agnew, G W 1871-72-73
Agnew, W L 1876-77-78
Albright, G S 1877
Alderson, F H R 1887-88
Alexander, E P 1884-85-86
Alexander, J W 1905-06
Allan, C J 1962
Allan, J L F 1956
Allchurch, T J 1980-81
Allen, A D 1925-26-27
Allen, D B 1975
Allen, J 1875-76
Anderson, W T 1931-32
Andrew, C R 1982-83-84
Anthony, A J 1967
Archer, G M D 1950-51
Arentsen, A N 1993
Arthur, T G 1962
Ashcroft, A H 1908-09
Ashford, C L 1929
Ashworth, J 1988-89
Askew, J G 1929-30-31
Asquith, J P K 1953
Aston, R L 1889-90
Atkinson, M L 1908-09
Attfield, S J W 1982-84

Back, F F 1871-72
Bailey, G H 1931
Bailey, M D 1982-83-84-85
Bailey, R C 1982-83
Balding, I A 1961
Balfour, A 1896-97
Bance, J F 1945
Bannerman, C M 1990
Barker, R E 1966
Barlow, C S 1923-24-25-26
Barlow, R M M 1925
Barrow, C 1950
Barter, A F 1954-55-56
Bartlett, R M 1951
Bateman-Champain, P J C 1937
Bates, C S 1991
Batstone, G R D 1992
Batten, J M 1871-72-73-74
Batty, P A 1919-20
Baxter, R 1871-72-73
Baxter, W H B 1912-13
Bealey, R J 1874
Beard, P L 1987
Bearne, K R F 1957-58-59
Beazley, T A G 1971
Bedell-Sivright, D R 1899-1900-01-02
Bedell-Sivright, J V 1900-01-02-03
Beer, I D S 1952-53-54
Bell, D S 1989
Bell, R W 1897-98-99
Bell, S P 1894-95-96
Bennett, G M 1897-98
Bennett, N J 1981
Benthall, E C 1912
Beringer, F R 1951-52
Beringer, G G 1975-76
Berman, J V 1966
Berry, S P 1971
Bevan, G A J 1951
Bevan, J A 1877-80
Bevan, W 1887
Bickle, D J 1992
Biddell, C W 1980-81
Biggar, M A 1971
Bird, D R J 1958-59
Birdwood, C R B 1932
Bishop, C C 1925
Black, M A 1897-98
Blair, P C B 1910-11-12-13
Blake, W H 1875
Boggon, R P 1956
Bole, E 1945-46-47
Bonham-Carter, J 1873
Booth, A H 1989-90
Bordass, J H 1923-24
Borthwick, T J L 1985
Boughton-Leigh, C E W 1878
Boulding, P V 1975-76
Bowcott, H M 1927-28
Bowcott, J E 1933
Bowen, R W 1968
Bowhill, J W 1888-89
Bowman, J H 1933-34
Boyd, A 1993
Boyd, C W 1909
Boyd-Moss, R J 1980-81-82
Bramley, R A 1993-94
Brandram, R A 1896
Brash, J C 1959-60-61
Brathwaite, G A 1934
Breakey, J N F 1974-75(R)-77
Bree-Frink, F C 1888-89-90
Briggs, P D 1962
Bromet, E 1887-88
Brook, P W P 1928-29-30-31
Brookstein, R 1969
Brooman, R J 1977-78
Browell, H H 1877-78
Brown, A C 1920-21
Brown, S L 1975-76
Browning, O C 1934
Bruce Lockhart, J H 1910
Bruce Lockhart, L 1945-46
Bruce Lockhart, R B 1937-38
Brutton, E B 1883-85-86
Bryant, S S 1988
Bryce, R D H 1965
Bull, H A 1874-75
Bunting, W L 1894-95
Burns, S A 1992
Burt-Marshall, J 1905
Burton, B C 1882-83
Bush, J D 1983
Bussey, W M 1960-61-62
Butler, E T 1976-77-78
Buzza, A J 1988-89

Cake, J J 1988
Callow, P G 1992-93
Campbell, D A 1936
Campbell, H H 1946
Campbell, J A 1897-98-99
Campbell, J D 1927
Campbell, J W 1973-74
Campbell, R C C 1907
Candler, P L 1934
Cangley, B T G 1946
Carey, G V 1907-08
Carpmael, W P 1885
Carris, H E 1929
Carter, C P 1965
Cave, J W 1887-88
Cave, W T C 1902-03-04
Chadwick, W O 1936-37-38
Chalmers, P S 1979
Chambers, E L 1904
Chapman, C E 1881-84
Chapman, E S 1879-80
Chapman, G M 1907-08-09
Chapman, J M 1873
Chapple, M A 1991
Chilcott, E W 1883
Child, H H 1875-76
Clarke, B D F 1978
Clarke, S J S 1962-63
Clayton, H R 1876-77-78
Clayton, J R W 1971
Clements, J W 1953-54-55
Clifford, P H 1876-77-78
Clough, F J 1984-85-86-87
Coates, C H 1877-78-79
Coates, V H M 1907
Cobby, W 1900
Cock, T A 1899
Cocks, F W 1935
Coghlan, G B 1926-27-28
Cohen, A S 1922
Colbourne, G L 1883
Coley, M 1964
Collett, G F 1898
Collier, R B 1960-61
Collin, T 1871
Collins, W O H 1931
Collis, W R F 1919-20
Collison, L H 1930
Combe, P H 1984-85
Considine, W C D 1919
Conway, G S 1919-20-21
Cook, D D B 1920-21
Cook, S 1920-21
Cooke, S J 1981
Cooper, H S 1881

Name	Years
Cooper, P T	1927-28
Cope, W	1891
Corry, T M	1966
Cosh, N J	1966
Covell, G A B	1949
Cove-Smith, R	1919-20-21
Cox, F L	1879
Cox, M Q	1994
Craig, H J	1891
Craigmile, H W C	1920
Crichton-Miller, D	1928
Crothers, G	1977(R)
Crow, W A M	1961-62
Cullen, J C	1980-81-82
Cumberlege, B S	1910-11-12-13
Cumberlege, R F	1897
Cumming, D C	1922-23-24
Currie, W C	1905
Cushing, A	1986
Dalgleish, K J	1951-52-53
Dalton, E R	1872-73-74
Dalton, W L T	1875-76
Dalwood, A L	1993-94
Daniell, J	1898-99-1900
Darby, A J L	1896-97-98
Darch, W J	1875
David, P W	1983
Davies, A	1988-89-90-91
Davies, B P	1991
Davies, G	1988-89
Davies, G	1948-49-50
Davies, G H	1980-81
Davies, H J	1958
Davies, J C	1949
Davies, J S	1977
Davies, L	1991-92
Davies, P M	1952-53-54
Davies, R J	1994
Davies, T G R	1968-69-70
Davies, W G	1946-47
Deakin, J E	1871
Delafield, G E	1932
De Maid, M W	1991-92
De Nobriga, A P	1948
De Villiers, D I	1913
Devitt, Sir T G	1923-24-25
Dewhurst, J H	1885-86
Dick, R C S	1933
Dickins, J P	1972-73
Dickson, J W	1881
Dinwiddy, H P	1934-35
Dix, D P A	1991-92
Dix, R S	1994(R)
Dixon, A M	1928
Dixon, C	1894
Dods, M	1938
Doherty, H D	1950
Doherty, W D	1913
Don Wauchope, A R	1880-81
Dorward, A F	1947-48-49
Douglas, E A	1882-83-84
Douglas, R N	1891
Douty, P S	1924
Dovey, B A	1960
Downes, K D	1936-37-38
Downey, W J	1954-55-56-57
Doyle, M G	1965
Drake-Lee, N J	1961-62-63
Drake, T R	1965
Druce, W G	1893-94
Drummond, N W	1971
Drysdale, T	1900-01
Duckworth, J F	1993 (t)
Dudgeon, R F	1871
Duncan, C	1966
Duncan, M M	1885-86-87
Duthie, M B	1991-92
Dutson, C S	1963
Edlmann, S R R	1974-75
Edmonds, G A	1976
Edwards, E F	1971
Edwards, R J	1971-72
Elliott, A E	1891
Ellis, P R	1975
Ellison, J F	1983-84
Embleton, J J E	1928-29-30
Evans, A E	1906-07
Evans, D P	1922
Evans, E D	1903-04
Evans, M R M	1955
Evans, W R	1955
Ewbank, C F	1983
Fairbanks, W	1873-74
Fairgrieve, J	1945
Falcon, W	1894-95
Fasson, F H	1897-98-99
Fforde, A B	1891
Fiddian, J V	1908-09
Field, E	1892-93-94
Finch, R T	1876-77-78-79
Fitch, C E	1889
Fleming, R S	1964
Fletcher, N C	1897-98-99
Flood, J P	1992-93
Fogg-Elliott, J W	1887
Folker, E L A	1937
Folwell, A J S	1967-68
Forbes, A S	1873
Ford, J N	1977-78-79
Fordham, J G	1898
Forman, A	1904-05
Forrest, J G S	1936-37-38
Fosh, M K	1977-78
Foster, J	1988-89
Fowler, T G	1911-12
Fox, S	1945
Francis, T E S	1922-23-24-25
Frankcom, G P	1961-63-64
Fraser, R	1908-09-10
Freeman, J P	1987
French, N J	1973
French, R B	1969
Fuller, H G	1878-79-80-81-82-83
Fyfe, K C	1932-33-34-35
Gardiner, F A	1921-22-23
Gatford, H J H	1946
Geddes, K I	1938
Gegg, B G	1991
Geoghegan, K F	1977
Gethin, D	1965-66
Gibbins, R B	1905-06
Gibbons, J F	1882
Gibbs, J D	1965
Giblin, L F	1894-95-96
Gibson, C M H	1963-64-65
Gibson, E	1925-26
Gibson, T A	1901-02
Gilchrist, B W	1986-87
Gill, S M	1980-81
Gilliland, W D	1979
Given, R A	1990-91
Glanvill, S F	1977-79-80
Glasgow, I C	1988
Gloag, I S	1949-50-52
Gloag, L G	1948
Godby, T A	1906-07
Godson, A	1959-60
Golightly, C H	1879
Goodhue, F W J	1885-86
Gover, J J	1879
Gowans, J J	1892-93
Grant, A R	1975-76
Grant, J J H	1978
Green, M J	1965-66-67
Green, P A	1984-85
Greenlees, J R C	1898-99-1900-01
Greenwood, G M	1929-30
Greenwood, J E	1910-11-12-13-19
Greenwood, J R H	1962-63
Greg, A H	1893
Greig, I A	1977-78
Griffin, J F	1990
Griffith, J M	1933
Griffith, R	1894-95
Griffiths, H B	1953
Gurdon, C	1877
Gurdon, E T	1874-75-76
Guthrie, G B	1883
Gwilliam, J A	1947-48
Hacking, A	1898-99
Hall, M R	1987-88
Hamilton, G A C	1925-26
Hamilton, H A	1871-73
Hamilton-Smythe, A F	1926
Hamilton-Wickes, R H	1920-21-22-23
Hammond, J	1881
Hampel, A K R	1982
Hamp-Ferguson, A J C	1964-65
Hancock, M E	1987-88
Hannaford, C	1967
Harding, R	1973-74
Harding, V S J	1958-59-60
Harding, W R	1924-25-26-27
Harper, A G R	1983
Harriman, A T	1985
Harris, B G	1904-05-06
Harrison, R B	1951
Harrison, R G	1994
Hartley, B C	1900
Hartley, J J	1974
Harvey, M J	1957
Harvey, J R W	1963-64
Hastings, A G	1984-85
Hearfield, J	1901
Hearson, H F P	1904-06
Heath, F M N	1936-37
Heath, N R M	1977-78
Heginbotham, R C	1984
Henderson, A P	1945-46-47
Herbert, A J	1954-55-56
Herrod, N J	1985-86-87
Heslip, M R	1967
Hetherington, J G G	1955
Hewett, B J	1963
Heywood, F M	1928
Higham, C F W	1961-62
Hignell, A J	1974-75-76-77
Hill, D B	1892
Hind, A E	1900
Hinton, N P	1969-70
Hobbs, A R	1986-87
Hockey, J R	1957
Hodges, E C	1903-04-05
Hodgson, J T	1955
Hodgson, M E	1973
Holloway, B H	1907-09
Holmes, S D	1989-90
Holmes, W B	1947-48
Hooper, C A	1890
Hopkins, A A	1874
Hopkins, W D B	1929
Hopley, D P	1992
Hopper, L B	1897
Hornby, J J	1873-74-76
Horner, P J	1982
Horrocks-Taylor, J P	1956-57
Horsfall, J	1903-04
Horsley, S	1901-02-03
Howard, J M	1971-72
Howell, R G B	1924
Hughes, K	1968-69
Hughes, T J	1993
Hull, F M	1871-72-73
Hunt, N	1986
Hunter, J M	1946
Illingworth, P H	1889-90
Inglis, F C	1959
Inglis, W M	1935-36
Irons, P C M	1993
Irving, K G	1935
Isaac, T W D	1986
Jackson, A L	1889
Jackson, T L	1892
Jacob, F	1895-96

Jacob, P G 1894-95-96
Jagger, D 1954
James, A M 1948-49
James, J H H 1962-63-64
James, S R 1876-77-78
Jameson, A 1874
Jeffcock, C E 1877
Jeffrey, G L 1884-85
Jenkins, J D 1964
Jenkins, J M 1949-51
Jenkins, R H J 1992
Jenkins, W G 1948
Jessop, A W 1972
Johnson, J N 1981
Johnston, D 1897
Johnston, W G S 1932-33-34
Johnstone, H B L 1931
Jolliffe, R L K 1965
Jones, B M 1949
Jones, C W 1933-34-35
Jones, D G H 1951-52
Jones, E A A 1895
Jones, F H 1898-99-1900
Jones, J S 1908-09
Jones, R B 1931-32-33
Jones, S E 1878
Jones, T R K 1921
Jones, W I 1923-24-25
Jones, W W A 1968-69-70-72
Jorden, A M 1968-69
Juckes, R 1913
Juckes, T R 1938

Keeton, G H 1899-1900
Keith-Roach, P d'A 1969-70-71
Kelly, S R 1985-86-87
Kemp, T A 1936
Kennedy, A J S 1993
Kennedy, C M 1877-78
Kennedy, R S 1907-09
Kershaw, M E 1955
Killick, S E 1978
Kimberley, H M 1945-46-47-48
King, R H 1950
Kingston, C J 1980-81-82
Kirby, T K M 1945
Kitchin, P A 1965
Kitching, A E 1910-11
Koop, G G 1905

Laborde, C D 1933-34-35-36
Laing, H 1893
Lambert, I C 1871
Langton, E C 1888-89
Lawry, S J 1894-95
Laxon, H 1903-04
Laycock, A M 1979
Leadbetter, V H 1951-52
Leake, W R M 1885-86-87
Leather, W H 1931-32
Leather, W J 1931-32-33-34
Lee, H 1904
Lees, J 1883
Le Fanu, V C 1884-85-86
Le Fleming, J 1884-85-86
Leishman, F J 1938
Lely, W G 1906-07-08
Leonard, R J N 1957
Lewis, A D 1975-76
Lewis, A R 1874-75
Lewis, A R 1959
Lewis, B R 1909-10-11
Lewis, G A 1872-73-75
Lewis, G G 1976
Lewis, G W 1956-57-58
Lewis, J M C 1913-19
Lewis, W H 1926-27
Lewthwaithe, W 1872-73
Lillington, P M 1981-82
Lindsay, P A R 1937-38
Linnecar, R J D 1970
Lintott, T M R 1974
Lister, R C 1969
Lloyd-Davies, R H 1947
Lord, J R C 1933-34-35
Lord, M 1960
Lord, T M 1986
Loveday, B R 1956-57
Low, J D 1935-36-37
Lowden, G S 1945
Lowe, C N 1911-12-13
Lowry, R H W 1923
Loxdale, J W 1874
Lucas, P M 1882
Luscombe, R P 1871-72-73-74
Lushington, A J 1872
Luxmoore, A F C C 1896-97
Lyon, C E 1871
Lyon, D W 1967-68

McAfee, L A 1910
McCarthy, M 1994
McClung, T 1954
McCosh, E 1910
McCosh, R 1905-06-07
MacDonald, A 1871
Macdonald, A 1989
MacDonald, J A 1936-37
MacDonnell, J C 1889
MacEwen, D L 1887
MacEwen, R K G 1953-54
McGahey, A M J 1979-80-81
McGown, T M W 1896
MacGregor, G 1889-90
McIlwaine, G A 1926-27-28
Mackenzie, I 1994
Mackenzie, W G B 1922
McKenzie, M R 1968
Mackie, O G 1895-96-97
Macklin, A J 1979-80-82
Maclay, J P 1920
MacLeod, K G 1905-06-07-08
MacLeod, L M 1903-04-05
Macleod, W M 1880-82
McMorris, L 1963
MacMyn, D J 1921-22-23-24
McNeill, A H 1902-03
McRoberts, T S 1946-47-48
MacSweeney, D A 1957-58-59
Mainprice, H 1902-03-04-05
Makin, R L 1959
Malik, N A 1975
Mann, F T 1910
Marburg, C L H 1909-10
Margerison, R 1871-72-73
Marques, R W D 1954-55-56-57
Marr, D M 1929-30-31-32
Marr, T C K 1945
Marriott, C J B 1881-82-83
Marsden, E W 1950
Marshall, T R 1950
Martin, A W 1983-84
Martin, N O 1965-66-67
Martin, S A 1961-62-63
Massey, D G 1952-53
Massey, M J O 1951-52-53
Maxwell, D M W 1922
Mayfield, E 1891
Maynard, A F 1912-13
Mayne, W N 1888
Meadows, A J 1993-94
Mellor, J E 1906
Melluish, R K 1922
Metcalfe, A F M 1994
Metcalfe, I R 1978-79
Methuen, A 1886-87-88
Michaelson, R C B 1960-61-62
Michell, W G 1873-75-76
Middlemas, P 1912
Miliffe, M J 1964
Millard, D E S 1956
Miller, J L H 1920
Mills, D C 1958
Mills, H H 1947-48
Mills, P R 1958-59
Milne, C J B 1882-83-84
Mitchell, F 1893-94-95
Mitchell, W G 1886
Monahan, J D 1967-68
Monro, A H 1973
Monteith, H G 1903-04-05
Montgomery, R 1891
Moon, R H Q B 1984
Mooney, L T 1994
Moore, A W 1874
Moore, P J de A 1947-48
Morel, T E 1920-22
Morgan, H P 1952-53
Morgan, W G 1926-27-28-29
Moriarty, S P 1980
Morpeth, G 1925
Morrison, B J 1965
Morrison, I R 1983-84
Morrison, P H 1887-88-89-90
Morse, E St J 1871
Mortimer, W 1895-96
Morton, H J S 1908
Moyes, J L 1974-75
Mulligan, A A 1955-56-57
Murray, R A 1982
Murray, R O 1933-34

Napier, Hon M F 1871
Neild, W C 1911-12
Neilson, H 1884
Neilson, W 1891-92-93
Nelson, W E 1892
Newbold, C J 1902-03
Newman, C H 1882
Newton-Thompson, C L 1937-38
Nicholl, C B 1890-91-92-93
Nixon, P J L 1976

O'Brien, T S 1981-82
O'Callaghan, C 1978
O'Callaghan, J J 1989-90
O'Callaghan, M W 1974-75-76-77
O'Leary, S T 1984-85
Odgers, F W 1901
Ogilvy, F J L 1887
Onyett, P S 1966-67
Orr, J C S 1891
Orr-Ewing, D 1919
Oswald, G B R 1945
Oti, C 1986-87
Oulton, E V 1901
Ovens, A B 1910-11
Owen, A V 1945
Owen, J E 1961

Page, J J 1968-69-70
Page, R S 1972-73
Palfrey, A J 1993-94
Palmer, H R 1899
Parker, G W 1932-33-34-35
Parr, M F 1978
Parry, T R 1936-37-38
Parsons, J 1938
Parton, A R 1990-91
Pater, S 1880-81
Paterson-Brown, T 1983
Patterson, H W T 1890
Patterson, W M 1956
Pattisson, R M 1881-82
Payne, J H 1879
Payne, O V 1900
Pearce, D 1873-74
Pearson, T C 1952-53
Peck, I G 1979
Pender, A R 1963
Penny, W M 1906
Perrett, D R 1992
Perry, D G 1958
Perry, S V 1946-47
Peters, E W 1991-92
Phillips, G P 1971-72
Phillips, J H L 1930-32
Phillips, R J 1964
Pienaar, L L 1911
Pierce, D J 1985(R)
Pilkington, L E 1893-94
Pilkington, W N 1896-97

Name	Years
Pinkham, C	1910
Pitt, T G	1905-06
Plews, W J	1884
Pool-Jones, R J	1989-90
Pope, E B	1932
Powell, P	1900
Pratt, S R G	1973-74
Price, K L	1991-92
Price, P R	1967
Pringle, A S	1897-98
Pringle, J S	1902
Prosser-Harries, A	1957
Pumphrey, C E	1902
Purves, W D C L	1907-08-09
Pyman, F C	1907-08
Rae, A J	1901
Raffle, N C G	1954-55
Raikes, W A	1872-74
Raine, J B	1947
Rainforth, J J	1958-59
Ramsay, A R	1930
Ransome, H F	1882-83-84
Rawlence, J R	1935-36
Raybould, W H	1966
Read, A J G	1992-93
Redmond, G F	1969-70-71
Reed, E D E	1937
Reed, P N	1989-90
Rees, A M	1933-34
Rees, B I	1963-64-65-66
Rees, G	1972-73
Rees, J I	1931-32
Reeve, P B	1950-51
Reid, J L P	1932
Rendall, H D	1892-93
Reynolds, A J	1994
Reynolds, E P	1909
Rice, E	1880-81
Richards, T B	1955
Richardson, N D	1993-94
Richardson, W P	1883
Rigby, J C A	1982
Riley, H	1871-72-73
Risman, M A	1987(R)
Ritchie, W T	1903-04
Robbie, J C	1977-78
Roberts, A F	1901-02
Roberts, A J R	1901-02
Roberts, J	1952-53-54
Roberts, J	1927-28
Roberts, S N J	1983
Robertson, A J	1990
Robertson, D D	1892
Robertson, I	1967
Robinson, A	1886-87
Robinson, B F	1891-92-93
Robinson, J J	1892
Robinson, N J	1990
Robinson, P J	1962
Rocyn-Jones, D N	1923
Roden, W H	1936-37
Rodgers, A K	1968-69-70
Roffey, D B	1874-75
Rollitt, E D	1994
Rose, H	1872
Rose, W M H	1979-80-81
Rosser, D W A	1962-63-64
Rosser, M F	1972-73
Ross-Skinner, W M	1924
Rotherham, A	1890-91
Rottenburg, H	1898
Rowell, W I	1890
Roy, W S	1993
Ryan, C J	1966
Ryan, P H	1952-53
Ryder, D C D	1921-23
Sagar, J W	1899-1900
Salmon, W B	1883
Sample, C H	1882-83-84
Sample, H W	1884
Sanderson, A B	1901
Saunders-Jacobs, S M	1929

Name	Years
Saville, C D	1967-68-69-70
Sawyer, B T C	1910
Saxon, K R J	1919-21
Scholfield, J A	1909-10
Schwarz, R O	1893
Scotland, K J F	1958-59-60
Scott, A W	1945-48
Scott, C T	1899
Scott, J M	1927
Scott, M T	1885-86-87
Scott, R R F	1957
Scott, W B	1923-24
Scott, W M	1888
Scoular, J G	1905-06
Seddon, E R H	1921
Shackleton, I R	1968-69-70
Shaw, P A V	1977
Sheasby, C M A	1990-91
Shepherd, J K	1950
Sherrard, P	1938
Shipsides, J	1970
Shirer, J A	1885
Silk, D R W	1953-54
Sim, R G	1966-67
Simms, K G	1983-84-85
Simms, N J	1989
Simpson, C P	1890
Simpson, F W	1930-31
Sisson, J P	1871
Skinner, R C O	1970-71
Slater, K J P	1964
Smallwood, A M	1919
Smeddle, R W	1928-29-30-31
Smith, A F	1873-74
Smith, A R	1954-55-56-57
Smith, H K P	1920
Smith, H Y L	1878-79-80-81
Smith, J	1889
Smith, J J E	1926
Smith, J M	1972
Smith, J V	1948-49-50
Smith, K P	1919
Smith, M A	1966-67
Smith, P K	1970
Smith, S R	1958-59
Smith, S T	1982-83
Sobey, W H	1925-26
Spencer, A	1994(R)
Spencer, J S	1967-68-69
Spicer, N	1901-02
Spray, K A N	1946-47
Sprot, A	1871
Stauton, H	1891
Stead, R J	1977
Steeds, J H	1938
Steel, D Q	1877
Steele, H K	1970
Steele, J T	1879-80
Steele-Bodger, M R	1945-46
Stevenson, H J	1977(R)-79
Stevenson, L E	1884-85
Steward, R	1875-76
Stewart, A A	1975-76
Stewart, J R	1935
Stileman, W M C	1985
Stokes, R R	1921
Stone, R J	1901
Storey, E	1878-79-80
Storey, L H T	1909
Storey, T W P	1889-90-91-92
Stothard, N A	1979
Style, H B	1921
Surtees, A A	1886
Sutherland, J F	1908
Sutton, A J	1987-88
Swanson, J C	1938
Swayne, F G	1884-85-86
Symington, A W	1911-12-13
Synge, J S	1927
Tait, J G	1880-82
Talbot, S C	1900
Tallent, J A	1929-30-31
Tanner, C C	1930

Name	Years
Tarrant, J M	1990
Tarsh, D N	1955
Taylor, A S	1879-80-81
Taylor, D G	1982
Taylor, H B J	1894-96
Taylor, W J	1926
Templer, J L	1881-82
Thomas, B E	1960-61-62
Thomas, D R	1972-73-74
Thomas, H W	1912
Thomas, J	1945
Thomas, M D C	1986-87
Thomas, N B	1966
Thomas, R C C	1949
Thomas, T J	1895-96
Thomas, W H	1886-87
Thompson, C W	1993 (R)
Thompson, M J M	1950
Thompson, R	1890
Thompson, R V	1948-49
Thorman, W H	1890
Thorne, C	1911
Thornton, J F	1976-78-79
Threlfall, R	1881-83
Timmons, F J	1983
Todd, A F	1893-94-95
Todd, T	1888
Topping, N P	1986-87
Touzel, C J C	1874-75-76
Tredwell, J R	1968
Trethewy, A	1888
Trubshaw, A R	1919
Tucker, W E	1892-93-94
Tucker, W E	1922-23-24-25
Tudsbery, F C T	1907-08
Tunningley, A J	1988(R)
Turnbull, B R	1924-25
Turner, J A	1956
Turner, J M P C	1985
Turner, M F	1946
Tyler, R H	1978-79-80
Tynan, C J C	1993
Umbers, R H	1954
Underwood, T	1990-91
Ure, C McG	1911
Valentine, G E	1930
Van Schalkwijk, J	1906
Vaughan, G P	1949
Vaux, J G	1957
Vickerstaff, M	1988
Vincent, C A	1913
Vivian, J M	1976
Vyvyan, C B	1987-88
Wace, H	1873-74
Waddell, G H	1958-60-61
Wade, M R	1958-59-60-61
Wainwright, J F	1956
Wainwright, M A	1980
Wainwright, R I	1986-87-88
Wakefield, W W	1921-22
Walker, A W	1929-30
Walker, D R	1980-81
Walker, E E	1899-1900
Walker, R M	1963
Walkey, J R	1902
Wallace, W M	1912-13
Waller, G S	1932
Wallis, H T	1895-96
Walne, N J	1994
Ward, R O C	1903
Ware, C H	1882
Warfield, P J	1974
Warlow, S	1972-74
Waters, F H	1927-28-29
Waters, J B	1902-03-04
Watherston, J G	1931
Watson, C F K	1919-20
Watt, J R	1970
Webb, G K M	1964-65
Webster, A P	1971
Wells, C M	1891-92
Wells, T U	1951

Weston, M T	1958-59-60
Wheeler, P J F	1951-52-53
White, J B	1922
White, W N	1947
Whiteway, S E A	1893
Wiggins, C E M	1928
Wiggins, C M	1964
Wilby, J B	1989
Wilkinson, R M	1971-72-73
Will, J G	1911-12-13
Williams, A G	1926-27
Williams, C C U	1950
Williams, C H	1930
Williams, C R	1971-72-73
Williams, D B	1973
Williams, E J H	1946
Williams, H A	1876
Williams, J M	1949
Williams, L T	1874-75
Williams, N E	1950
Williams, P T	1888-89
Williamson, I S	1972
Williamson, P R	1984
Willis, H	1949-50-51
Wilson, A H	1911-12-13
Wilson, C P	1877-78-79-80
Wilton, C W	1936
Winthrop, W Y	1871
Wintle, T C	1960-61
Withyman, T A	1985-86
Wood, G E	1974-75-76
Wood, G E C	1919
Woodall, B J C	1951
Woodroffe, O P	1952
Woods, S M J	1888-89-90
Wooller, W	1933-34-35
Wordley, S A	1988-89
Wordsworth, A J	1973-75
Wotherspoon, W	1888-89
Wrench, D F B	1960
Wright, C C G	1907-08
Wrigley, P T	1877-78-79-80
Wyles, K T	1985-86
Wynne, E H	1887
Yetts, R M	1879-80-81
Young, A B S	1919-20
Young, A T	1922-23-24
Young, J S	1935
Young, J V	1906
Young, P D	1949
Young, S K	1974
Young, W B	1935-36-37

VARSITY MATCH REFEREES

(From 1881, when referees first officiated at the match. Prior to this date, the match was controlled by a pair of umpires elected by the Universities.) Each year indicates a separate appearance, and refers to the first half of the season. Thus 1881 refers to the match played in the 1881-82 season.

Allan, M A	1933-34
Ashmore, H L	1891-92-93-95-96
Bean, A S	1948-49
Bevan, W D	1993
Bolton, W N	1882
Boundy, L M	1958
Burnett, D I H	1980-82
Burrell, R P	1963
Clark, K H	1973
Cooper, Dr P F	1951-53
Crawford, S H	1920
Currey, F I	1885
Dallas, J D	1910-12
D'Arcy, D P	1968
David, I	1954-55
Doyle, O E	1990
Evans, G	1907
Findlay, J C	1904-08
Fleming, J M	1991
Freethy, A E	1923-25-27-29-31-32
Gadney, C H	1935-36-37-38-45-47
Gillespie, J I	1905
Harnett, G H	1897-98-99-1900-01-02
Hilditch, S R	1994
Hill, G R	1883-84-86-87-88-89-90
Hosie, A M	1979
Howard, F A	1986
Jeffares, R W	1930
John, K S	1956-67
Johnson, R F	1972
Jones, T	1950
Lamb, Air Cdre G C	1970
Lambert, N H	1946
Lawrence, Capt H D	1894
Lewis, R	1971
Marsh, F W	1906
Morrison, E F	1992
Murdoch, W C W	1952
Norling, C	1977-78-81-88-89
Pattinson, K A	1974
Potter-Irwin, F C	1909-11-13-19
Prideaux, L	1984
Quittenton, R C	1985-87
Sanson, N R	1976
Sturrock, J C	1921
Taylor, H H	1881
Titcombe, M H	1969
Trigg, J A F	1983
Vile, T H	1922-24-26-28
Walters, D G	1957-60-61-62-64-65-66
Welsby, A	1975
Williams, R C	1959
Williams, T	1903

STUDENT POWER FUELS RUGBY OF THE FUTURE

RUGBY IN THE STUDENT SECTOR 1994-95

Harry Townsend

More and more students each year are attending IHEs (institutes of higher education). The current figure, 1,177,100, compares with 50,636 60 years ago. Within five years, one third of the age group 18 to 22 will be in higher education. If half are female, and even if only 2 per cent of the remainder play rugby, that still means almost 12,000 men, plus an increasing number of women, playing the game. Students are the lifeblood of rugby: they are not just the stars, but the club players and administrators of the future. The 'universitisation' of former polytechnics and colleges has meant fewer representative stages on which the enormous numbers of talented student players can be more widely noticed.

The one-day Divisional Championship serves a purpose for the selection of the English University (BUSA) team, but that's patently not enough. It will be interesting to see the conclusions of the imminent and eagerly awaited Richardson report on student rugby. The RFU development pyramid caters for those players who have progressed within the system from Under-16 to senior levels, but students within this pyramid are in a dilemma. While they have commitments to their own IHEs, where they inevitably have loyalties to friends and tutors, they are also courted by first-class clubs, county, division and country at any or all of Colts, Under-21, Emerging Player, University, Student, A and senior levels.

Many senior clubs don't play fair: they are interested only in the short term. The answer is to keep pressure off the 'stars' and provide a good rugby environment in which others can develop without recourse to the lower levels of senior club rugby. Meagre Student Union finances must of necessity be spread thinly, but why can't more RFU money be forthcoming to support the game at this grass-roots level? More investment in coaching and training referees is also required. A meaningful student league is essential, outside the often one-sided Cup competition. Area matches are needed to augment these and to provide stepping-stones to a national universities team. A couple of universities and students Under-21 fixtures would encourage the freshmen, and a full four (or even five) nations tournament at both student and university levels is vital now that the World Students Cup is established on a four-year rotation and rugby will be included in 1997 for the first time (with a British team) in the World Student Games in Sicily.

The infrastructure for the 1996 Student World Cup team is confirmed, with Pat Briggs as manager, assisted by former England Under-21 coach Tony Lannaway and coaches Ian Smith and John Horton.

Representative matches: Irish Students 3, England Students 40 (Portlaoise); England Students 14, France Students 10 (Blackheath); Wales Students 10, England Students 27 (Swansea); England Students 56, Italy Students 18 (Leicester); Wales Students 18, France Students 9 (Paris); England Students Under-21s 13, Anglo-Irish Under-21s 11 (Castlecroft); England Students Under-21s 43, Combined Services Under-21s 12 (Twickenham); Scottish Universities 14, Welsh Universities 23 (Peffermill); Welsh Universities 6, Irish Universities 12 (BSC Llanwern); Scottish Universities 17, Irish Universities 22 (Peffermill); Welsh Universities 32, English Universities 7 (Newport); Edinburgh Under-21s 74, Scottish Universities 13 (Meggetland); South of Scotland Under-21s 18, Scottish Universities 30 (Jedburgh); North & Midlands Under-21s 3, Scottish Universities 44 (Cupar); Glasgow Under-21s 25, Scottish Universities 24 (Ayr); Nottinghamshire 37, Midlands Universities 10 (Newark RFC); Yorkshire Under-21s 14, Midlands Universities 13 (Sheffield RFC); Shropshire 3, Midlands Universities 17 (Harper Adams); Cornwall Development XV 29, South-West Universities 27 (St Austell RFC); Northumberland Development XV 22, North-East Universities 20 (Newcastle/Gosforth RFC)

BRITISH UNIVERSITIES SPORTS ASSOCIATION CHAMPIONSHIP 1994-95

Sponsored by Lucozade Sport

22 March, Twickenham
West London Institute 31 (1G 7PG 1DG)
University of Wales, Swansea 30 (2G 1PG 1DG 2T)

The Student Rugby Cup final always seems to produce a match that a scriptwriter would dismiss as too far-fetched, and this, the first under the new name of BUSA, surpassed most of its predecessors. Swansea, six times beaten finalists since 1970, had ridden their luck throughout the competition, and had Cardiff Institute not been disqualified, it is likely that Swansea would have faced a potentially harder run. Instead, they progressed against De Montfort 71-17, Gwent 39-0, West Sussex Institute 41-11 and Brighton 39-10 to a semi-final against Durham, which they won 29-17.

West London Institute, once Borough Road College, are next to be known as Brunel University College. Ironically, they had defeated namesakes Brunel 77-0 as they steamrollered their way through the five group matches. They then beat the Royal Agricultural College 30-0, but Roehampton Institute (29-18) pushed them hard. Bath (29-5), Exeter (46-10) and Loughborough (27-12) paved their way to the final.

Swansea began the final in spectacular fashion: many of the Twickenham spectators had not even taken their seats before wing Gerry Williams pounced on a towering up-and-under from Lee Davies to score the first Swansea try. Duncan Hughes scythed through the centre for a second, and two further touchdowns were disallowed for a double movement by punctilious American referee Don Reordan. Davies added two conversions and a penalty, and West London trailed 17-3, reeling under the free-running Swansea onslaught, with only a penalty by Saracens fly-half Andy Lee in reply.

Yet Lee soldiered metronomically on, and five more penalties gave West London the lead early in the second half. Swansea regained it with a blindside try by skipper and No 8 Rhodri Griffiths, but then a Malcolm Kemp score, converted by Lee, put West London ahead. The lead changed yet again when Wales Under-21 flanker Paul Beard scored Swansea's fourth try, only for Lee to restore it for West London with a dropped goal which struck the post on the way. Hughes snatched it back with a dropped goal in reply after two Swansea penalty attempts had hit the post. It all depended on the last play of the game, just as it had done two years previously. Lee notched up his seventh penalty goal as the advantage changed for the eighth time.

Drama apart, it was a superb exhibition of running rugby and a wonderful advertisement for the student game. Non-partisan spectators must have felt for Swansea, who were bridesmaids for the seventh time in 24 years.

West London Institute: R Hennessey; A Clarke, M Kemp, S Thompson, R Francis; A Lee, A Down; E Cripps, S Rodgers (*capt*), I Peel, D Ruffell, D Zaltzman, C Clements, R Hill, N Jones
Scorers *Try:* Kemp *Conversion:* A Lee *Penalty Goals:* A Lee (7) *Dropped Goal:* A Lee
University of Wales, Swansea: N Ferns; G Williams, D Hughes, D Fitzgerald, A Harris; L Davies, S Powell; A Lewis, D Robbins, A Collins, R Heal, C Yandell, A Little, P Beard, R Griffiths (*capt*) *Replacement* B Martin for Little (78 mins)
Scorer *Tries:* Williams, Hughes, Griffiths, Beard *Conversions:* Davies (2)
Penalty Goal: Davies *Dropped Goal:* Hughes
Referee D Reordan (USA)

Loughborough have won the title 25 times, Durham 8, Liverpool and Swansea 7, Bristol 5, Cardiff and Manchester 4, Bangor and UWIST 2, Aberystwyth, Birmingham, Leeds, Newcastle, Northumbria and West London Institute once each.

Second XV final: West London Institute 19, Loughborough 16
Third XV final: Durham 14, West London Institute 3

More IHEs than ever took part in the BUSA rugby competition this year. The group matches contained the inevitable mismatches with the odd century break being registered, but overall, standards were higher and fewer teams withdrew from potentially embarrassing encounters. The most extraordinary lapse was the failure of Cardiff Institute to honour their fixture with bottom-of-the-table Bangor, a match which would almost certainly have handed Cardiff Institute the Welsh Championship on points difference ahead of Swansea, and a potentially similar route to Twickenham in their place. But teams which withdraw from their last group match are disqualified should they be in contention for the play-off rounds (although points and results are allowed to stand in calculating other placings), and that was that.

Roehampton Institute overturned one of the favourites by beating Bristol 6-3 in the first play-off round through their heroic defence, and ultimate winners West London Institute beat them 29-18 only after extra time in the next round. Holders Northumbria traced an erratic route to the quarter-finals, where they lost to Loughborough by 36-10.

They had lost to Durham 33-0 and progressed as group runners-up thanks only to victory over Newcastle by 16-12 – their other two matches went their way on default – while Bristol went through only in third place in the South-West. Such inconsistencies are invariably due to the relative availabilities of 'star' players, and it could be argued that this is not what student rugby is all about.

Loughborough recorded 369 points to 40 against in six matches and West London Institute 310 to 33 in five, and it was encouraging to note the impressive progress of Manchester Metropolitan and Brighton, who both reached the last eight, and West Sussex Institute (Sussex RFU seven-a-side champions), who lost to Swansea 41-11 in the previous round.

GROUP TABLES

An agreed number of places in the first play-off round are allocated to each division, which decides the number of teams to progress from each group within the division.

The qualifier from Scotland, who entered the competition in the third round, was the winner of a knock-out competition. Leagues were organised in Scotland during the spring term, but had no bearing on the BUSA competition.

LONDON DIVISION: Group A

	P	*W*	*D*	*L*	*F*	*A*	*Pts*
RHBNC	5	5	0	0	120	27	10
UCL	5	4	0	1	175	51	8
King's College	5	3	0	2	100	122	6
Imperial College	5	2	0	3	73	78	4
Q Mary Westfield	5	1	0	4	60	113	2
LSE	5	0	0	5	32	169	0

LONDON DIVISION: Group B

	P	*W*	*D*	*L*	*F*	*A*	*Pts*
Charing X/West	5	5	0	0	197	15	10
R Ldn Hosp MS	5	3	0	2	90	26	6
UMDS	5	3	0	2	55	39	6
St George's Hosp	5	2	0	3	41	156	4
St Mary's Hosp	5	1	0	4	26	85	2
Goldsmith's	5	1	0	4	12	97	2

LONDON DIVISION: Group C

	P	*W*	*D*	*L*	*F*	*A*	*Pts*
St Bart's Hosp	4	4	0	0	134	10	8
Royal Free Hosp	4	2	1	1	29	28	5
UCHMS	4	2	0	2	20	56	4
Wye College	4	1	1	2	20	53	3
SEES & SOAS	4	0	0	4	5	61	0

SOUTH-EAST DIVISION: Group A

	P	*W*	*D*	*L*	*F*	*A*	*Pts*
West London Inst	5	5	0	0	310	33	10
Portsmouth	5	3	0	2	149	105	6
Reading	5	3	0	2	68	133	6
Brunel	5	2	0	3	116	154	4
Surrey	5	2	0	3	88	130	4
Thames Valley	5	0	0	5	37	210	0

SOUTH-EAST DIVISION: Group B

	P	*W*	*D*	*L*	*F*	*A*	*Pts*
Brighton	5	5	0	0	147	30	10
West Sussex	5	3	1	1	121	44	7
Kent	5	3	1	1	100	103	7
Greenwich	5	2	0	3	84	105	4
Can'bury Christ C	5	1	0	4	34	130	2
Sussex	5	0	0	5	67	141	0

SOUTH-EAST DIVISION: Group C

	P	*W*	*D*	*L*	*F*	*A*	*Pts*
North London	6	5	0	1	179	51	10
Essex	6	4	1	1	126	100	9
Hertfordshire	6	4	0	2	143	50	8
Middlesex	6	3	1	2	139	111	7
East Anglia	6	3	0	3	96	58	6
Cranfield (Beds)	6	1	0	5	27	145	2
East London	6	0	0	6	18	213	0

SOUTH-EAST DIVISION: Group D

	P	*W*	*D*	*L*	*F*	*A*	*Pts*
Roehampton	5	5	0	0	219	51	10
St Mary's Coll	5	4	0	1	178	28	8
South Bank	5	3	0	2	76	107	6
Westminster	5	2	0	3	77	64	4
Kingston	5	1	0	4	50	111	2
City	5	0	0	5	22	261	0

SOUTH-WEST DIVISION: Group A

	P	*W*	*D*	*L*	*F*	*A*	*Pts*
Bath	5	5	0	0	168	48	10
Exeter	5	4	0	1	109	35	8
Bristol	5	3	0	2	144	40	6
West of England	5	2	0	3	34	161	4

	P	W	D	L	F	A	Pts
Southampton	5	1	0	4	75	134	2
Plymouth	5	0	0	5	38	160	0

SOUTH-WEST DIVISION: Group B

	P	*W*	*D*	*L*	*F*	*A*	*Pts*
St Mark & St John	5	4	0	1	125	58	8
Cranfield (Sh'ham)	5	3	0	2	119	50	6
Royal Agric Coll	5	3	0	2	69	44	6
Seal Hayne	5	3	0	2	48	56	6
Bournemouth	5	2	0	3	56	75	4
Southampton Inst	5	0	0	5	38	172	0

MIDLANDS DIVISION: Group A

	P	*W*	*D*	*L*	*F*	*A*	*Pts*
Loughborough	6	6	0	0	369	40	12
Nottingham	6	4	0	2	128	138	8
Sheffield Hallam	6	4	0	2	85	117	8
Birmingham	6	3	0	3	115	147	6
Harper Adams	6	2	0	4	80	88	4
Cheltenham & Glos	6	1	0	5	87	184	2
Sheffield	6	1	0	5	63	213	2

MIDLANDS DIVISION: Group B

	P	*W*	*D*	*L*	*F*	*A*	*Pts*
Warwick	6	5	0	1	173	31	10
Leicester	6	4	0	2	130	72	8
Wolverhampton	6	4	0	2	101	51	8
Bedford	6	3	0	3	91	118	6
Coventry	6	3	0	3	76	115	6
Oxford Brookes	6	2	0	4	47	100	4
Central England	6	0	0	6	47	178	0

MIDLANDS DIVISION: Group C

	P	*W*	*D*	*L*	*F*	*A*	*Pts*
De Montfort Leics	5	4	0	1	128	56	8
Aston	5	4	0	1	97	62	8
Nott'ham Trent	5	2	0	3	65	42	4
Stoke	5	2	0	3	110	96	4
Derby	5	2	0	3	86	115	4
Worcester	5	0	0	5	43	158	0

MIDLANDS DIVISION: Group D

	P	*W*	*D*	*L*	*F*	*A*	*Pts*
Nene	4	4	0	0	274	21	8
Newman	4	3	0	1	103	53	6
Birmingham Coll	4	2	0	2	44	58	4
De Montfort MK	4	1	0	3	23	105	2
Staffordshire	4	0	0	4	27	234	0

NORTH-EAST DIVISION: Group A

	P	*W*	*D*	*L*	*F*	*A*	*Pts*
Durham	4	4	0	0	122	36	8
Northumbria	4	3	0	1	16	45	6
Newcastle	4	2	0	2	81	51	4
Leeds	4	1	0	3	38	67	2
Leeds Metro	4	0	0	4	27	85	0

NORTH-EAST DIVISION: Group B

	P	*W*	*D*	*L*	*F*	*A*	*Pts*
Hull	1	1	0	0	28	14	2
Humberside	1	0	0	1	14	28	0

NORTH-WEST DIVISION: Group A

	P	*W*	*D*	*L*	*F*	*A*	*Pts*
Liverpool	5	5	0	0	161	8	10
L'pool J Moores	5	3	0	2	56	79	6
Keele	5	2	0	3	58	72	4
Chester	5	2	0	3	72	96	4
Central Lancs	5	2	0	3	53	121	4
Lancaster	5	1	0	4	62	86	2

NORTH-WEST DIVISION: Group B

	P	*W*	*D*	*L*	*F*	*A*	*Pts*
Manchester Met	5	5	0	0	184	28	10
Manchester	5	4	0	1	113	75	8
Crewe & Alsager	5	3	0	2	97	50	6
UMIST	5	1	0	4	28	91	2
Bradford	5	1	0	4	43	128	2
Salford	5	1	0	4	43	136	2

NORTH-WEST DIVISION: Group C

	P	*W*	*D*	*L*	*F*	*A*	*Pts*
Edge Hill	4	4	0	0	155	29	8
St Martin's	4	3	0	1	123	49	6
Warrington	4	2	0	2	64	87	4
Bolton Inst	4	1	0	3	42	79	2
Northumbria (C)	4	0	0	4	22	162	0

WALES: Group A

	P	*W*	*D*	*L*	*F*	*A*	*Pts*
Swansea	6	5	0	1	202	85	10
Cardiff Inst	6	4	0	2	246	43	8
UWCM	6	4	0	2	232	121	8
Cardiff	6	4	0	2	113	157	8
Aberystwyth	6	2	0	4	63	259	4
Bangor	6	1	0	5	46	106	2
Glamorgan	6	1	0	5	63	194	2

Cardiff Institute were disqualified for failing to fulfil their fixture with Bangor.

WALES: Group B

	P	*W*	*D*	*L*	*F*	*A*	*Pts*
Trinity Coll	5	5	0	0	303	38	10
Gwent	5	3	0	2	117	51	6
Normal (Bangor)	5	2	0	3	125	104	4
St David's Coll	5	2	0	3	127	153	4
Swansea Inst	5	1	0	4	70	115	2
NE Wales Inst	5	0	0	5	0	286	0

SCOTLAND:

Preliminary round: St Andrew's 79, Robert Gordon 15; Edinburgh w/o Stirling
Quarter-finals: St Andrew's 10, Edinburgh 29; Aberdeen 50, Napier 7; Strathclyde 11,

Glasgow 34; Dundee 46, Heriot-Watt 3 **Semi-finals:** Edinburgh 14, Aberdeen 27; Glasgow 8, Dundee 11 **Final:** Aberdeen 29, Dundee 15

BUSA CHAMPIONSHIPS
Sponsored by Lucozade Sport
Knock-out Rounds
1st play-off round: Crewe and Alsager 51, Edge Hill 10; Manchester Metropolitan w/o Wye; Liverpool 36, Humberside 0; Hull 3, Keele 5; Leeds 54, St Martin's 6; Newcastle 32, Manchester 17; Liverpool John Moores 11, Northumbria 13; Sheffield Hallam 37, Aston 10; Trinity Coll 18, Harper Adams 14; Nottingham 31, Leicester 5; Aberystwyth 0, Loughborough 59; Birmingham 12, Warwick 6; Wolverhampton 6, Cardiff 26; Gwent 15, Cheltenham & Gloucester 13; Swansea 71, De Montfort (Leicester) 17; Nene 33, North London 0; West Sussex 24, King's College 0; RHBNC 21, Kent 18; UCL 14, Essex 5; Brighton 20, Hertfordshire 7; London Hospital 15, St Mary's Hospital 11; South Bank 7, Bath 48; Cranfield (Shrivenham) 9, Portsmouth 20; Roehampton Institute 6, Bristol 3; West London Institute 33, RAC 0; UWCM (Coll of Medicine) 63, West of England 3; St Mary's Coll 18, St Mark & St John 15; Exeter 60, Reading 6; Charing X/Westminster Hospital 22, Royal Free Hospital 6
2nd play-off round: Durham 26, Crewe and Alsager 12; Manchester Metropolitan 26, Liverpool 3; Keele 16, Leeds 0; Newcastle 7, Northumbria 21; Sheffield Hallam 11, Trinity College 7; Nottingham 6, Loughborough 37; Birmingham 18, Cardiff 9; Gwent 0, Swansea 39; Nene 3, West Sussex 5; RHBNC 17, Essex 19; Brighton w/o London Hospital; Bath 53, Portsmouth 9; Roehampton Institute 18, West London Institute 29 (*aet*); UWCM (Coll of Medicine) 5, St Mary's Coll 7; Exeter 49, Charing X/Westminster Hospital 7
3rd play-off round: Aberdeen 20, Durham 33; Manchester Metropolitan 10, Keele 3; Northumbria w/o Sheffield Hallam; Loughborough 41, Birmingham 12; Swansea 41, West Sussex 11; Essex 13, Brighton 31; Bath 5, West London Institute 29; St Mary's Coll 0, Exeter 26
Quarter-finals: Durham 11, Manchester Metropolitan 3; Northumbria 10, Loughborough 36; Swansea 39, Brighton 10; West London Institute 46, Exeter 10
Semi-finals: Durham 17, Swansea 29; Loughborough 12, West London Institute 27

ENGLISH UNIVERSITIES INTER-DIVISIONAL TOURNAMENT
14 December 1994, Nottingham RUFC
Final: South-West 32, North 26
SCOTTISH UNIVERSITIES CHAMPIONSHIP
Spring Term 1995
Semi-finals: Aberdeen w/o Edinburgh; Dundee 20, St Andrew's 16 **Final:** Dundee 31, Aberdeen 21 (St Andrew's)
BUSA SEVEN-A-SIDE TOURNAMENT
29 March 1995, Preston Grasshoppers RFC
Final: Bristol 12, Exeter 10 **3rd & 4th Place:** Swansea 33, Northumbria 14
SCOTTISH UNIVERSITIES SEVEN-A-SIDE TOURNAMENT
3 May 1995, Peffermill
Semi-finals: Dundee 26, Stirling 7; Glasgow Caledonian 7, Edinburgh 47
Final: Edinburgh 21, Dundee 7 **Plate Final:** Aberdeen 21, President's VII 19
YORKSHIRE UNIVERSITIES CUP
1st XV Semi-finals: Leeds Metropolitan 11, Huddersfield 10; Sheffield Hallam 12, Hull 13 (*Hull subsequently withdrew*); **1st XV Final:** (*26 April 1995, Sandal RFC*): Sheffield Hallam 22, Leeds Metropolitan 16 **2nd XV Final** (*26 April 1995, Sandal RFC*): Sheffield 27, Leeds Metropolitan 5

NAVY END RAF SUPREMACY

THE SERVICES 1994-95

John Mace *Daily Telegraph*

Inter-Services Tournament

Having previously won only one inter-service match since they took the title outright in 1987, the Royal Navy emerged as clear winners of this season's tournament and the Willis Corroon Bowl, thus raising morale throughout the fleet and revitalising the competition. They played direct and effective rugby founded upon their traditionally rumbustious forwards – spearheaded by their outstanding Royal Marine back row of Bob Armstrong, Corin Palmer and Mick Reece – supplemented by some forthright running and tackling from their backs. They also benefited from two influential performances by their long-serving scrum-half Paul Livingstone.

They did not start as favourites against the Army, but such was the sustained ferocity of their assault that the soldiers were unable to establish a platform from which to launch any coherent attacks. As a result they were forced to try to run indifferent possession, which proved an unprofitable option against the Navy's well-organised and committed defence. The longer the game progressed, the better the senior service played, and, with Dale Cross and Gerard Harrison dominating the line-outs, they outscored the Army by five tries to two.

The RAF failed in their attempt to record their first hat-trick of successive outright titles when they lost to a rejuvenated Army side who showed little evidence of the mauling they had received from the Navy. Although not overhauled until the 70th minute, the RAF seldom functioned smoothly and, had it not been for four penalty goals by Steve Worrall, playing in his 25th inter-service game, they would not have remained in contention for so long. Their pack's inability to subdue the fiery Army forwards, energetically led by Julian Brammer, meant they were unable to provide consistent quality possession for their talented backs. Nevertheless, the airmen had enough chances to win the game, but their composure often deserted them and they fell prey to the hard-tackling Army threequarters, who invariably nailed their man to give their lively back row of Rob Hunter, Gary Knight and Chris Rushworth the opportunity of setting up some telling counter-attacks.

In the final game, the RAF were hoping to secure a fair share of possession and tie in the Navy breakaways with heavy scrummaging and effective ball retention. But although they were more cohesive than they had been against the Army, and did well territorially, they again had to rely on four penalty goals, this time from Steve Lazenby, to keep them in touch. In the end the Navy's skill and relentless commitment proved too much, as with a final broadside of 19 points in the last ten minutes they condemned the airmen to losing both matches for the first time since 1981.

1 April, Twickenham
Royal Navy 34 (2PG 1DG 5T) **Army 17** (2G 1PG)
for the Willis Corroon Trophy

Royal Navy: Sub Lt J R Coulton (RNAS Culdrose); Mne C White (HMS Deal), LS D Sibson (HMS London), Surg Lt B Powell (CTCRM), Mne Musn S Brown (RM Deal); PO I Fletcher (HMS Repulse), Cpl P Livingstone (RM Stonehouse); LWEM S J Burns (HMS Collingwood), Cpl M Wooltorton (45 Cdo RM), WEM D R Parkes (HMS Drake), LRO G Harrison (HMS Warrior), LCpl D Cross (RM Stonehouse), Cpl R W Armstrong (CTCRM), Lt C B Palmer RM (HMS Warrior) (*capt*), CSgt M Reece (CTCRM)
Scorers *Tries:* Fletcher, Powell, Burns, Livingstone, White *Penalty Goals:* Coulton (2) *Dropped Goal:* Sibson
Army: Lt M Abernethy (RGR); Lt H G Graham (RHA), Capt A Glasgow (RE), Capt A Deans (AGC), Lt B G W Johnson (R Sigs); Sgt D J Hammond (REME), Capt S Pinder (DWR); LCpl M Stewart (PWRR), Capt J S Brammer (RE) (*capt*), Sgt J Fowers (RHA), Sig G Archer (R Sigs), Spr R S Hunter (RE), Cpl P R Curtis (R Sigs), Capt G C Knight (DWR), Sgt C Rushworth (REME) *Replacement* Cpl A J Sanger (RE) for Deans (64 mins)
Scorers *Tries:* Graham, Sanger *Conversions:* Hammond (2) *Penalty Goal:* Hammond
Referee J Pearson (Durham Society)

12 April, Twickenham
Army 28 (1G 2PG 3T) **Royal Air Force 26** (2G 4PG)
for the Willis Corroon Shield

Army: Lt M Abernethy (RGR); Cpl S P Bartliff (R Sigs), Capt A Glasgow (RE), Capt A Deans (AGC), Lt B G W Johnson (R Sigs); 2/Lt P Knowles (RRF), Capt S Pinder (DWR); LCpl M Stewart (PWRR), Capt J S Brammer (RE) (*capt*), Sgt J Fowers (RHA), Sig G Archer (R Sigs), Lt D A Dahinten (RHA), Spr R S Hunter (RE), Capt G C Knight (DWR), Sgt C Rushworth (REME)
Scorers *Tries:* Deans, Johnson, Dahinten, Knight *Conversion:* Abernethy *Penalty Goals:* Abernethy (2)
Royal Air Force: Sgt S Lazenby (Cosford); SAC S Crossland (Innsworth), Cpl S Roke (Wittering), SAC G Sharp (Rudloe Manor) Flt Lt R Underwood (Finningley); Cpl P Hull (Innsworth), Sgt S Worrall (Cottesmore) (*capt*); CT D Robson (Odiham), Sqn Ldr R Miller (Wyton), Cpl A Billett (St Athan), Sgt B Richardson (CIO Bradford), Cpl P Taylor (Northolt), Flt Lt D Watkins (Locking), Flt Lt D Williams (Locking), Flt Lt C Moore (Lyneham) *Replacements* Flt Lt J Dearing (Halton) for Miller (40 mins); Flt Lt R Burn (Scampton) (temp); Cpl S Carbutt (Linton-on-Ouse) (temp)
Scorers *Tries:* Williams, Hull *Conversions:* Worrall (2) *Penalty Goals:* Worrall (4)
Referee S Lander (Liverpool Society)

26 April, Twickenham
Royal Navy 43 (4G 3T) **Royal Air Force 19** (1G 4PG)
for the Willis Corroon Hibernia Cup

Royal Navy: Sub Lt J R Coulton (RNAS Culdrose); Mne C White (RM Deal), LS D Sibson (HMS London), Surg Lt B Powell (CTCRM), Mne Musn S Brown (RM Deal); PO I Fletcher (HMS Repulse), Cpl P Livingstone (RM Stonehouse); Maj W Dunham RM (ASC Camberley), Cpl M Wooltorton (45 Cdo RM), PO E Cowie (RNAS Culdrose), LRO G Harrison (HMS Warrior), LCpl D Cross (RM Stonehouse), Cpl R W Armstrong (CTCRM), Lt C B Palmer RM (HMS Warrior) (*capt*), CSgt M Reece (CTCRM) *Replacements* Sub Lt M Jarrett (HMS Dryad) for Powell (55 mins); PO N Jones (HMS Heron) (temp); LPT R Packer (HMS Dryad) (temp)

Scorers *Tries:* White, Powell, Harrison, Sibson, Armstrong, Livingstone, pen try *Conversions:* Coulton (4)
Royal Air Force: Cpl P Hull (Innsworth); SAC G Sharp (Rudloe Manor), Cpl S Roke (Wittering), Sgt S Lazenby (Cosford), SAC S Crossland (Innsworth); Cpl N James (St Athan), Sgt S Worrall (Cottesmore) (*capt*); Cpl A Billett (St Athan), Sqn Ldr R Miller (Wyton), CT D Robson (Odiham), Sgt B Richardson (CIO Bradford), Flt Lt R Burn, (Scampton), Flt Lt D Watkins (Locking), Flt Lt C Moore (Lyneham), Cpl A Nesbit (Halton) *Replacements* Sgt R Wadmore (Brize Norton) for Worrall (76 mins); Cpl R Alexander (Boulmer) (temp)
Scorers *Try:* Watkins *Conversion:* Lazenby *Penalty Goals:* Lazenby (4)
Referee J Wallis (Somerset Society)

Inter-Services Tournament Champions

The Army have won the tournament outright 28 times, the Royal Navy 17 times and the Royal Air Force 14 times. The Army and the Royal Air Force have shared it on 2 occasions and there have been 9 triple ties.

1920 **RN**
1921 **RN**
1922 **RN**
1923 **RAF**
1924 Triple Tie
1925 **Army and RAF**
1926 **Army**
1927 **RN**
1928 **Army**
1929 **Army**
1930 **Army**
1931 **RN**
1932 **Army**
1933 **Army**
1934 **Army**
1935 Triple Tie
1936 **Army**
1937 **Army**
1938 **RN**
1939 **RN**
1946 **Army**
1947 **RAF**
1948 Triple Tie
1949 **Army and RAF**
1950 **Army**
1951 **RN**
1952 **Army**
1953 **Army**
1954 Triple Tie
1955 **RAF**
1956 Triple Tie
1957 **Army**
1958 **RAF**
1959 **RAF**
1960 **Army**
1961 **RN**
1962 **RAF**
1963 **Army**
1964 **Army**
1965 **Army**
1966 **RN**
1967 **Army**
1968 **Army**
1969 **Army**
1970 **RN**
1971 **RAF**
1972 **Army**
1973 **RN**
1974 **RN**
1975 Triple Tie
1976 **Army**
1977 **RN**
1978 Triple Tie
1979 **RAF**
1980 **Army**
1981 **RN**
1982 **RAF**
1983 **Army**
1984 Triple Tie
1985 **RAF**
1986 **RAF**
1987 **RN**
1988 **Army**
1989 **Army**
1990 **Army**
1991 **RAF**
1992 Triple Tie
1993 **RAF**
1994 **RAF**
1995 **RN**

Royal Navy v Army The Royal Navy have won 32, the Army 43, and 3 matches have been drawn (including matches before 1920) **Royal Navy v Royal Air Force** The Royal Navy have won 38, the Royal Air Force 28, and 4 matches have been drawn **Army v Royal Air Force** The Army have won 39, the Royal Air Force 23, and 8 matches have been drawn.

Other Fixtures, Competitions and Tours

The Combined Services again fielded a weakened team against the British Police, who retained the Securicor Trophy by 25-12. However, they beat Canada 21-20 and the Australian Services 12-9 at Devonport, which is fast becoming their favourite venue. The Australians, on their first tour to England, won five of their seven fixtures.

The Royal Navy did well to share the Inter-Services Under-21 title with the Army, but there was no Colts (Under-19) tournament. Royal

Marines Stonehouse won the Royal Navy Cup and HMS Raleigh triumphed in the Navy Sevens tournament.

The Royal Artillery headed Division 1 of the Army Inter-Corps Merit Table and the Adjutant General's Corps won Division 2. The 7th Parachute Regiment Royal Horse Artillery recorded their seventh win in nine seasons in the final of the Army Major Units Cup competition as well as capturing the Army Sevens title. The 15th Regiment Royal Logistics Corps won the Minor Units Cup.

Strike won the RAF Inter-Command tournament, Brize Norton retained the RAF Inter-Station Cup and Innsworth took the Inter-Station Shield for units eliminated in the first round of the Cup competition. Lyneham emerged as winners of the Binbrook Bomb in the RAF Sevens tournament.

On 10 November 1994, the Royal Air Force played the French Air Force in Paris to commemorate a match in the city 50 years previously against a Paris XV, which was credited with making a major contribution to France's reinstatement following the 1931 ban. Although the RAF won the original game 26-6, they were unable to field any of their potent back division in the second encounter and lost 59-23.

Inter-Services Under-21 Tournament
Royal Navy 16, Royal Air Force 15; Royal Navy 13, Army 13; Army 11, Royal Air Force 0
Winners: Royal Navy and Army

Combined Services Matches
Senior: Combined Services 12, British Police 25 (*for the Securicor Trophy*); Combined Services 21, Canada 20; Combined Services 12, Australian Services 9
Under-21s: Combined Services 8, New Zealand *Rugby News* XV 20; Combined Services 12, England Students 43
Under-20s: Combined Services 12, Cardiff 0; Combined Services 12, Ogmore and District 0

Individual Service Competitions
ROYAL NAVY
Inter-Command Matches: Royal Marines 23, Naval Air Command 15; Plymouth Command 0, Royal Marines 39; Portsmouth Command 25, Naval Air Command 16 (*Portsmouth's matches against Plymouth and the Royal Marines were cancelled*)
Inter-Unit Cup: Royal Marines Stonehouse 24, HMS Nelson 0
Inter-Unit Sevens: HMS Raleigh 17, RM Lympstone 14
ARMY
Inter Corps Merit Table: Division 1 winners: Royal Artillery **Division 2 winners:** Adjutant General's Corps **Major Units Cup:** 7th Parachute Regiment Royal Horse Artillery 15, 2nd Signal Regiment 9 **Minor Units Cup:** Infantry Training Battalion Strensall 19, 15th Regiment Royal Logistics Corps 28; **Inter-Unit Sevens:** 7th Parachute Regiment Royal Horse Artillery 30, 2nd Signal Regiment 15
RAF
Inter-Command Matches: Logistics Command 14, Personnel & Training Command 17; Logistics Command 22, Strike Command 27; Personnel & Training Command 17, Strike Command 22 **Inter-Station Shield:** RAF Brize Norton 17, RAF Laarbruch 8 **Inter-Station Shield:** RAF Innsworth 37, RAF Odiham 19 **Inter-Station Sevens:** RAF Lyneham 38, RAF St Athan 12

DETERMINED ENGLAND DOMINATE

SCHOOLS RUGBY 1994-95
Brendan Gallagher

England, whose collective will to win overcame any shortcomings in natural ability, claimed a second consecutive junior Grand Slam and a first home victory over Australia in 21 years during a season of conspicuous success under the guidance of coach Geoff Wappett. Only a 23-12 defeat against an exceptional New Zealand Schools side at Welford Road prevented a remarkable clean sweep. England produced their best performance in their opening game, against Australia at Kingsholm, destroying Australia by 30-3 after the break with three tries in seven minutes from wing Nick Booth, centre Joe Ewens and scrum-half Martyn Wood.

And so to the Junior Five Nations, which began with a hard-fought 19-14 victory over a lively Scotland at Twickenham, the highlight of the successful *Daily Mail* National Schools Day. Next came a narrow 9-6 win over Wales at Llanelli, where England soaked up continuous pressure, and a convincing 17-6 triumph over Ireland in Galway. A memorable season was concluded at Grange Road, Cambridge, where tries from Ewens, Beardshaw and the outstanding Joe Worsley ensured a 22-6 win over France. Jerry Cook landed two conversions and a penalty to hoist his season's total to 69.

Wales, both talented and erratic, achieved a strange mix of results. They lost heavily to New Zealand (42-6) and slipped to defeat against Scotland and England, but bounced back with heartening victories over Wales Youth (42-7), Ireland (28-20) and Japanese Schools (21-18).

Ireland, always very competitive at this level, endured a disappointing season with defeats against Australia, Wales and England and just one solitary victory, against Scotland (29-23) at Balgray. The Scots, too, tasted victory just once – 20-18 against Wales at Goldenacre – but rarely can a side have played so well and lost so often. A 25-13 defeat against France in Paris was followed by an unlucky 18-17 reverse against Australia at Murrayfield where, by common consent, the Scots deserved to win. There was a brave performance in defeat against New Zealand, and narrow failures away to England and at home to Ireland.

On the domestic scene, Colston's College, Bristol crowned an unbeaten season by winning the *Daily Mail* Under-18s Cup at Twickenham, beating QEGS Wakefield 23-0 in the final. A 10-10 draw against local rivals Bristol GS was the only blemish on an otherwise perfect record. A 33-21 away win to the top Scottish school, Merchiston Castle, was possibly their finest moment. The *Daily Mail* Under-15s final was won by Dulwich College, who have never lost as a year group and comprehensively defeated Bristol GS 36-0.

The Shell Rosslyn Park National Schools Sevens resulted in well-deserved trophies for St Cyres Comprehensive in the open section and Wellington College (Berks) in the festival event which begins the tournament. Wellington convincingly beat Blundell's in the final by 27-5 for their third title in five years. The Berkshire school, splendidly led by captain Jim Brownrigg, overcame highly rated Monmouth by 14-12 in the qualifying group and then accounted for Oakham (33-0), Loughborough GS (17-14), Rossall (35-7) and King's, Canterbury (26-7). St Cyres, from Penarth, defeated Tiffin 19-14 in an exciting final.

Royal Belfast Academical Institution claimed their 24th Ulster Schools Cup, but only their first since 1970, when they defeated Bangor GS 18-9. To reach the final, RBAI beat favourites Methodist College, Belfast 14-7 and Bangor overcame holders Regent House 10-9. St Aloysius College defeated Queen Victoria College, Dunblane by 44-10 in the Bank of Scotland Schools Cup final.

RGS Lancaster were unbeaten in the regular season for the first time since 1969, recording pleasing victories over Stonyhurst, King's, Macclesfield, Arnold and Bradford GS. Bradford were badly disrupted by injury. They won 18 of their 24 fixtures.

Stonyhurst College returned to top form after a couple of mediocre seasons, winning 14 of their 15 games. Their sole defeat came at RGS Lancaster, where they lost an entertaining game by 25-15. Pangbourne College have worked hard to improved their fixture list and playing standards and will be well pleased with a season that yielded 12 victories in 14 games. QEGS Wakefield, fielding seven Yorkshire caps, produced an adventurous style of rugby all season to win 16 of their 18 fixtures.

Campion Hornchurch, a fertile breeding-ground for senior clubs, maintained their high standards with 21 victories and just three defeats. Epsom College completed a fourth unbeaten season in 12 years. Only a 9-9 draw against Cranleigh prevented a 100 per cent record. In the second half of the season they registered emphatic wins over King's, Canterbury, Merchant Taylor's, Reigate and South African tourists Hottentots.

Rugby began with convincing victories over Lawrence Sheriff and Uppingham but played erratically thereafter and finished with just four victories in 12 games. Clifton were also inconsistent, but an excellent side when roused. Millfield scored 90 in 14 victories in 15 games. Wellington College ended a tough season with defeats against St Edward's, Oxford, Sherborne, Haileybury, Harrow, Radley, Tonbridge and Marlborough, but never lost their enthusiasm for running rugby. Radley finished with a flurry of victories after an indifferent start.

St David's College, Cardiff, provided the upset of the season in Wales in defeating five-times winners Neath College by 22-15 in the Welsh Schools Under-18s Cup final. Ysgol Glantaf played some thrilling rugby in winning 21 of their 25 games. The only Welsh team to lower their colours were Monmouth, who enjoyed a fine season, losing just five of their 21 fixtures. The much-improved Hawthorn HS lost only one game, while Cowbridge CS went close to toppling Neath in the Cup semi-final. Rydal and Christ College were generally disappointing by their own high standards, but Llandovery College managed 13 victories on their difficult circuit.

In Scotland, Merchiston Castle from Edinburgh were again the pick, winning 14 games out of 17 during their most testing season on record. They began by winning the early-season tournament at Bradford GS and subsequently recorded notable victories over Edinburgh Academy (27-20), Loretto (35-24), Stewart's-Melville (23-14) and 1994 Ulster Schools champions Regent House (27-12).

MATCH DETAILS

19 December 1994, Paris

FRANCE 25 SCOTLAND 13 (1G 2PG)
SCOTLAND *Try:* Craig *Conversion:* Mallinson *Penalty Goals:* Mallinson (2)

23 December 1994, Lansdowne Road

IRELAND 3 (1DG) **AUSTRALIA 27**
IRELAND *Dropped Goal:* Farrell

31 December 1994, Murrayfield

SCOTLAND 17 (3PG 1DG 1T) **AUSTRALIA 18**
SCOTLAND *Try:* Keenan *Penalty Goals:* Mallinson (3) *Dropped Goal:* Ross

7 January 1995, Goldenacre

SCOTLAND 20 (1G 1PG 2T) **WALES 18** (1G 2PG 1T)
SCOTLAND *Tries:* Barnes, Keenan, Bulloch *Conversion:* Mallinson
Penalty Goal: Ross
WALES *Tries:* Young, Field *Conversion:* Jarvis *Penalty Goals:* Jarvis (2)

14 January 1995, Cardiff Arms Park

WALES 6 (2PG) **NEW ZEALAND 42**
WALES *Penalty Goals:* Hawkins (2)

21 January 1995, Murrayfield

SCOTLAND 7 (1G) **NEW ZEALAND 19**
SCOTLAND *Try:* Bulloch *Conversion:* Mallinson

23 January 1995, Kingsholm, Gloucester

ENGLAND 30 (3G 3PG) **AUSTRALIA 3** (1PG)
ENGLAND *Tries:* Booth, Ewens, Wood *Conversions:* Cook (3)
Penalty Goals: Cook (3)
AUSTRALIA *Penalty Goal:* Flatley

1 February 1995, Welford Road, Leicester

ENGLAND 12 (4PG) **NEW ZEALAND 23** (1G 2PG 2T)
ENGLAND *Penalty Goals:* Cook (4)

NEW ZEALAND *Tries:* Willis, Patelo, Howlett *Conversion:* Carrington
Penalty Goals: Carrington (2)

23 February 1995, Paris

FRANCE 10 WALES 15 (1G 1DG 1T)
WALES *Tries:* Cook, Jarvis *Conversion:* Jarvis *Dropped Goal:* Roberts

5 March 1995, Aberavon

WALES 21 (1G 3PG 1T) **JAPANESE HIGH SCHOOLS 18**
WALES *Tries:* Young, Davies *Conversion:* Jarvis *Penalty Goals:* Jarvis (3)

23 March 1995, Twickenham

ENGLAND 19 (1G 4PG) **SCOTLAND 14** (3PG 1T)
ENGLAND *Try:* Worsley *Conversion:* Cook *Penalty Goals:* Cook
SCOTLAND *Try:* Outlaw *Penalty Goals:* Mallinson (3)

29 March 1995, Stradey Park, Llanelli

WALES 6 (2PG) **ENGLAND 9** (3PG)
WALES *Penalty Goals:* Hawkins (2)
ENGLAND *Penalty Goals:* Cook (3)

8 April 1995, Balgray

SCOTLAND 23 (1G 2PG 2T) **IRELAND 29** (1G 4PG 2T)
SCOTLAND *Tries:* Craig (2), Bulloch *Conversion:* Ross *Penalty Goals:* Ross (2)
IRELAND *Tries:* Moran, Girvan, Keenan *Conversion:* Ormond
Penalty Goals: Ormond (4)

15 April 1995, Dunvant

WALES 28 (2G 3PG 1T) **IRELAND 20** (2G 2PG)
WALES *Tries:* Jarvis (3) *Conversions:* Jarvis (2) *Penalty Goals:* Jarvis (3)
IRELAND *Tries:* Girvan, Leahy *Conversions:* Ormond (2) *Penalty Goals:* Ormond (2)

15 April 1995, Galway

IRELAND 6 (2PG) **ENGLAND 17** (4PG 1T)
IRELAND *Penalty Goals:* Ormond (2)
ENGLAND *Try:* Ewens *Penalty Goals:* Cook (4)

19 April 1995, Grange Road, Cambridge

ENGLAND 22 (2G 1PG 1T) **FRANCE 6** (2PG)
ENGLAND *Tries:* Ewens, Beardshaw, Worsley *Conversions:* Cook (2)
Penalty Goal: Cook
FRANCE *Penalty Goals:* Barrau (2)

The following players took part in the 18 Group international matches. Countries played against are shown in square brackets.
Abbreviations: *A* – Australia, *E* – England, *F* – France, *I* – Ireland, *J* – Japanese High Schools, *NZ* – New Zealand, *S* – Scotland, *W* – Wales, (R) – Replacement.

ENGLAND

Threequarters: P Sampson (Woodhouse Grove) [*A, NZ, S, W, I, F*]; N Booth (Lytham HS) [*A, NZ, S*]; J Ewens (Colston's) [*A, NZ, W, I, F*]; O Jones (Marlborough) [*A*]; C Pawson (Skinners) [*S*]; M Dobson (RGS Lancaster) [*NZ*]; K Sorrell (Campion) [*S, W, I, F*]; J Cook (Millfield) [*A, NZ, S, W, I, F*]
Half-backs: T Barlow (Rossall) [*NZ*(R), *F*(R)]; J Hurst (Stonyhurst) [*A, NZ, S, W, I, F*]; I McLennan (Hall Cross) [*I, F*]; M Wood (Harrogate GS) [*A, NZ, S, W, I, F*]; S Conley (Durham) [*F*(R)]

Forwards: M Worsley (St Ambrose) [*A, NZ, S, W, I, F*]; R Protherough (King's, Worcester) [*A, NZ, S, W, I, F*]; C Cano (Thomas Alleyne) [*A, NZ, S, W, I, F*]; C Codo (QE Barnet) [*F*(R)]; A Bell (Colston's) [*A, NZ, S*]; J Beardshaw (Gresham's) [*W, I, F*]; W Fuller (Wallington HS) [*A, NZ, S, W, I, F*]; J Cockle (Prior Park) [*A, NZ, S, W, I, F*]; M Cornish (Ivybridge) [*A, NZ, S, W*(R)]; J Worsley (Hitchin) [*W, I, F*]; G Wappett (Bradford GS) [*A, NZ, S, W, F*]; P Ogilvie (Tonbridge) [*I*]
G Wappett was captain against Australia, New Zealand, Scotland, Wales and France; J Cockle against Ireland.

SCOTLAND

Threequarters: D Mallinson (George Watson's) [*F, A, W, NZ, E, I*]; J Moffatt (Edinburgh Acads) [*NZ, E*]; J Craig (St Aloysius) [*F, A, W, NZ, E, I*]; A Bulloch (Hutchesons' GS) [*F, A, W, NZ, E, I*]; S Hannah (Merchiston Castle) [*F, A, W*]; M Mayer (Merchiston Castle) [*NZ, E, I*]; C Keenan (Fettes) [*F, A, W, I*]
Half-backs: G Ross (George Heriot's) [*F, A, W, NZ, E, I*]; C Black (Merchiston Castle) [*F, A, W*]; S Hannah (Merchiston Castle) [*NZ, E, I*]
Forwards: P Fitzgerald (Dollar Academy) [*F, A, W, NZ, E, I*]; M Laudale (Loretto) [*F, A, W, NZ, E, I*]; L Walter (Strathallan) [*F, A, W, NZ*]; G Hoyle (Stewart's-Melville) [*E, I*]; J White (Cutts Academy) [*F, A, W, NZ, E, I*]; A Barnes (Stewart's-Melville) [*F, A, W, NZ, E, I*]; A Gladstone (Gordonstoun) [*F, A, W, NZ, E, I*]; N Outlaw (Loretto) [*F, A, W, NZ, E, I*]; A Dall (George Heriot's) [*F, A, W, NZ, E, I*]
S Hannah was captain in all matches.

WALES

Threequarters: D Case (Neath) [*S, NZ, J, E, I, F*]; P Hallett (St Albans) [*S, NZ, J, E, I, F*]; T Davies (Neath) [*S, NZ, J, E, I, F*]; D Hawkins (Neath) [*E, I*]; G Roberts (Treorchy) [*S, NZ, J, E, I, F*]; J Young (Neath) [*S, NZ, J, F*]; M Williams (Glantaf) [*E*]; R Jones (Bassaleg) [*I*(R)]
Half-backs: L Jarvis (Hawthorne) [*S, NZ, J, I, F*]; G Downs (Rhydfelen) [*S, NZ, J, E, I, F*]; M Lewis (Llandovery Coll) [*I*(R)]
Forwards: E Fear (Llanhari) [*S, NZ, J, E, I, F*]; C Wells (Neath) [*E, I, F*]; G Thomas (Llanhari) [*S, NZ, J*]; S Lee (Llanhari) [*S, NZ, I, F*]; M Gibbs (Pontypool) [*J, E*]; A Grabham (Glantaf) [*S, NZ, J, E, I, F*]; R Edwards (Tregaron) [*S, NZ, J, E, I, F*]; E Lewis (Tregaron) [*I*(R)]; M Cook (Neath) [*S, NZ, J, E, I, F*]; D Coates (Neath) [*S, NZ*]; R Field (St David's Coll) [*S, NZ, J, E, I, F*]; M Thomas (Christ's Coll) [*NZ*(R)]; G Newman (Neath) [*NZ*(R), *J, e, I, F*]; R Parkes (Monmouth School) [*J*(R)]
R Field was captain in all matches.

IRELAND

Threequarters: K Johnson (Methodist Coll, Belfast) [*S*]; D O'Brien [PBC Cork) [*A*]; C Kilroy (Crescent Coll) [*E, W*(R)]; S Doggett (St Mary's Coll) [*A, S, E*]; S Coulter (Belfast Royal Acads) [*A, S, E, W*]; R O'Donovan (CBC Cork) [*A*]; C Mahony (CBC Cork) [*A, S, E, W*]; J Keenan (St Munchin's Coll) [*S, E, W*]; D Johnson (Blackrock Coll) [*W*]
Half-backs: E Farrell (Blackrock Coll) [*A, E, W*]; R Ormond (St Mary's Coll) [*A*(R), *S, E, W*]; G McCullough (Royal Belfast Academy) [*A, E*(R)]; K Murphy (CBC Cork) [*S, E*]; M Finlay (Methodist Coll, Belfast) [*E*(R), *W*]
Forwards: R McCormack (St Mary's Coll) [*A, S, E, W*]; P Smyth (Blackrock Coll) [*A, S, E, W*]; J Spence (RS Dungannon) [*A*]; M Horan (St Munchin's Coll) [*S, E, W*]; P Murphy (Methodist Coll, Belfast) [*A, S, E, W*]; R Leahy (Crescent Coll) [*A, S, E, W*]; I Girvan (RS Dungannon) [*A, S, E, W*]; D Blaney (Terenure Coll) [*A, S, E, W*]; D Shanley (St Michael's Coll) [*A*]; L Cullen (Blackrock Coll) [*S, E, W*]; J Lane (St Mary's Coll) [*W*(R)]
L Girvan was captain against Australia; D Blaney against Scotland, England and Wales.

BRITAIN JOINS THE WORLD

COLTS AND YOUTH RUGBY 1994-95
Harry Townsend

Wales and Scotland found their first venture into the FIRA Youth Tournament in Romania a sobering experience. Welsh Youth, winners of the junior Grand Slam by virtue of beating Italy (33-7), England (22-12), France (26-0) and Scotland (36-8), must have expected to do well despite the FIRA age restriction of 1 January. This meant combining with their Under-18 team.

The FIRA Youth Tournament is an annual World Cup in which the venue tends to dictate the participants. The 12 participating nations in the Youth First Division in Bucharest reflected the priorities of several 'minor' rugby countries. Wales were grouped with the eventual winners, France, and Romania, to whom they lost 22-15 and 36-10 respectively. South Africa were grouped with Spain and Poland; Italy with Uruguay and Portugal. Scotland are never backward at being innovative in youth rugby – they are still the only British country with national youth leagues culminating in a knock-out competition. They shared their next notable 'first' with Wales by taking part in the tournament. They beat Russia 35-0 before losing to finalists Argentina, a highly skilled ball-handling team, by 43-3.

Play-offs for final placings saw Wales defeat Portugal 28-8 and Russia 43-10. Scotland were placed sixth, beating Spain 41-7 but losing to Romania 17-5. Both retained their FIRA First Division status. Romania, level with France in their group, were perhaps the best team on view, but disciplinary problems saw them demoted. Argentina ran a huge South Africa team to a standstill in their semi-final, but with a man sent off after only three minutes, they lost to France in the final. Ireland are considering taking part in FIRA next year: England, we are told, must await the conclusions of the Horner report.

The Sun Alliance Divisional Colts Festival at Castlecroft was won by London and the South-East, who beat the South-West 8-6 in the final, the North defeating the Midlands 14-10 for third place. England Colts beat North and Midlands (38-26), London and the South-West (41-6) and Loughborough University Freshmen (35-6). Italy Youth were defeated 29-0 at Camborne. England's success was halted by Wales (22-12), but victory over Scotland by 32-13 followed. France were defeated, 25-10, for the first time for ten years to conclude a very good season. Ireland, Wales and Scotland all place considerable emphasis on Under-18 rugby. Ireland lost only in the closing stages to Wales (18-12) and defeated Scotland by 15-11.

Surrey won the Sun Alliance Colts County Championship at Twickenham, the curtain-raiser to the England-Canada senior international. 1993 champions Yorkshire trod a charmed path to the semi-finals, where Surrey ended their run by 21-11; free-running Durham disposed of East Midlands by 33-5 in the other semi-final.

A month later, skipper and scrum-half Mark Percival (Harlequins) captained London and the South-East to the divisional title. Cardiff dominated the season in Wales. They were undefeated in 27 matches, scoring 1,375 points to 135 against.

The following players took part in the Colts/Youth international matches. Countries played against are shown in square brackets.
Abbreviations: *A* – Argentina, *E* – England, *F* – France, *It* – Italy, *J* – Japan Schools, *NZ* – New Zealand Schools, *P*– Portugal, *Ro* – Romania, *Ru* – Russia, *Sp* – Spain, *W* – Wales, *WSch* – Welsh Schools, (R) – Replacement

ENGLAND
Colts
Full-back: R Ashforth (Wakefield) [*It, W, S, F*];
Threequarters: G Truelove (Saracens) [*It, W, S*]; F Waters (Bristol U) [*It, W, S, F*]; A Blyth (Tynedale) [*It, W, S, F*]; G Smith (Orrell) [*It, W, S, F*]; B Stafford (Bath) [*It*(R), *F*]
Half-backs: P Belgian (Bath) [*It,W, S, F*]; P Harvey (Bath) [*It, W, S, F*]
Forwards: T Woodman (Bath) [*It, W, S, F*(R)]; P Greening (Gloucester) [*It, W, S, F*]; P Vickery (Redruth) [*It, W, S, F*]; M Fitzgerald (Durham U) [*W*(R), *S, F*]; C Murphy (West Hartlepool) [*It, W, S, F*]; D Zaltzman (Saracens) [*W*(R), *S, F*]; C Gillies (Bath) [*It, W*]; E Pearce (Bath) [*It, W, S, F*]; N Spence (Leicester) [*It, W, S, F*]; R Winters (Haywards Heath) [*It, W, S, F*]; G Chuter (Old Mid-Whigiftians) [*S*(R)]; M Orsler (Oxford U) [*It*(R)]
Greening was captain in all four matches.

IRELAND
Under-18s
Full-back: K Mullen (Clonakilty) [*W, S*]
Threequarters: J Finegan (Drogheda) [*W, S*]; K O'Riordan (Youghal) [*W, S*]; I Dunne (Tullamore) [*W, S*]; N Johnston (Dromore) [*W, S*]
Half-backs: M Maguire (Banbridge) [*W S*]; T Tierney (Richmond) [*W, S*]
Forwards: T Clifford (Bohemians) [*W, S*]; I Ryan (Richmond) [*W, S*]; M Cahill (Bohemians) [*W, S*]; P Bracken (Tullamore) [*W, S*]; J Wilson (Ballinahinch) [*W, S*]; P Hehir (Kilkenny) [*W, S*]; R Dickson (Banbridge) [*W, S*]; D Duggan (Thurles) [*W, S*]; B Buckley (Thomond) [*S*,(R)]
Tierney was captain in both matches.

SCOTLAND
Under-19s
Full-backs: K Baillie (Edinburgh Acads) [*W*]; S Tomlinson (Selkirk) [E]
Threequarters: G Caldwell (Ayr) [*W*]; C Murray (Edinburgh Acads) [*W, E*]; A Bulloch (Hutcheson's Grammar School) [*W*]; R Kennedy (Stirling County [*E*]; A McLean (Boroughmuir) [*W, E*]; D Bull (Stewart's-Melville) [*E*]
Half-backs: M Duncan (Blaydon) [*W*]; G Hay (Watsonians) [*E*]; G Beveridge (Peebles) [*W, E*]
Forwards: G Talac (Musselburgh) [*W*]; D Butcher (Middlesbrough) [*E*]; C Docherty (Glasgow High/Kelvinside) [*W, E*]; J Kelly (Harlequins) [*W, E*]; S Murray (Edinburgh Acads) [*W, E*]; C Hunter (Currie) [*E*]; A Barnes (Stewart's-Melville) [*W*]; I Fullerton (Kelso) [*E*]; S McNeil (Ross High) [*W, E*]; W Spencer (Aberdeen U) [*W*]; I Sinclair (Dundee HSFP) [*E*]; S Wands (Edinburgh Acads) [*W*]
Beveridge was captain against Wales; Sinclair against England.

FIRA Tournament
Full-backs: S Tomlinson (Selkirk) [*Ru*(R), *A, Sp, Ro*]; R Williams (Stewartry) [*Ru*]
Threequarters: G Caldwell (Ayr) [*Ru, A*(R), *Sp, Ro*]; S Jenkins (Kilmarnock) [*Ru*];

A Bulloch (Hutcheson's Grammar School) [*A, Sp, Ro*]; R Kennedy (Stirling County) [*Ru, A, Sp, Ro*]; A McLean (Boroughmuir) [*A, Sp, Ro*]; D Bull (Stewart's-Melville) [*Ru, A*]; G Dalgleish (Galashiels) [*Ru, Sp, Ro*]; G Hay (Watsonians) [*A*]; G Beveridge (Peebles) [*A, Sp, Ro*]; J Weston (Watsonians) [*Ru*]; M Smith (Watsonians) [*Ru, A, Sp*(R)]
Forwards: G Talac (Musselburgh) [*Ru*(R), *Sp, Ro*]; C Docherty (Glasgow High/Kelvinside) [*A, Sp, Ro*]; G Hodgson (Newcastle Gosforth) [*Ru*]; J Kelly (Harlequins) [*Ru, A*(R), *Sp, Ro*]; G Lambie (Edinburgh Wands) [*Ru*(R), *A*]; E Boyd (Boroughmuir) [*Ru, Sp*]; S Murray (Edinburgh Acads) [*Ru*(R), *A, Sp, Ro*]; C Hunter (Currie) [*A, Sp*(R), *Ro*]; I Fullerton (Kelso) [*Ru, A*]; S McNeil (Ross High) [*Ru, A, Sp, Ro*]; A Cadzow (Boroughmuir) [*Ru, Sp, Ro*]; I Sinclair (Dundee HSFP) [*Ru, A, Sp, Ro*]; E McDonald (Edinburgh Acads) [*Ru*]
Sinclair was captain in all four matches.

WALES
Under-19s
Full-back: A Durston (Bridgend) [*It, F, E, S*]
Threequarters: R Saddler (Cardiff) [*It, F, E, S*]; L Davies (Neath) [*It, F, E, S*]; T Edwards (Salford U) [*F*(R)]; J Funnell (Aberavon) [*It, F, E, S*]; N Walne (Cambridge U) [*F, E, S*]; M Garfield (Bridgend) [*It*]; G Watts (Llanelli) [*It*(R), *F*(R), *E*(R)]
Half-backs: D Morris (Maesteg Celtic) [*It, F, E, S*]; A Thomas (Llanelli) [*It*(R), *S*(R)]; D Hawkins (Swansea) [*It, F, E, S*]
Forwards: P Booth (Cardiff) [*It, F, E, S*]; I Evans (New Tredegar) [*E*(R), *S*(R)]; J Richards (Llanelli) [*It, F, E, S*]; J Kemble (Cardiff) [*S*(R)]; C Anthony (Swansea) [*It, F, E, S*]; J Lewis (Cardiff) [*S*(R)]; V Cooper (Ystradgynlais) [*It*]; N Watkins (Pencoed) [*It, F, E, S*]; S Gardner (Cardiff) [*It*(R), *F, E, S*]; G Green (Pontypool) [*It*]; D Thomas (Swansea) [*It*]; M Williams (Pontypridd) [*F, E, S*]; N Thomas (Bridgend) [*It, F, E, S*]; H Jenkins (Bedwas) [*It*(R), *F, E, S*]
Hawkins was captain in all four matches.

FIRA Tournament
Full-backs: S Hill (Maesteg Celtic) [*Ro, F, Ru*]; A James (Seven Sisters) [*Ro*(R), *F, P, Ru*]
Threequarters: S Winn (Maesteg Celtic) [*Ro, F, P*]; A Davies (Llanharan) [*P, Ru*(R)]; L Davies (Neath) [*Ro, F, P, Ru*]; G Bowen (Carmarthen Quins) [*F*(R), *P*(R), *Ru*]; A Henderson (New Tredegar) [*Ro, F, P*]; A Thomas (Llanelli) [*Ro, F*(R), *Ru*]
Half-backs: V Jervis (Llanharan) [*Ro, F, P, Ru*]; D Hawkins (Swansea) [*Ro, F, P, Ru*]
Forwards: P Booth (Cardiff) [*Ro, F*(R), *P, Ru*(R)]; I Evans (New Tredegar) [*F*]; J Lewis (Cardiff) [*P*(R), *Ru*]; P Grunewald (Llanharan) [*Ro, F, Ru*]; L Murray (Pontypool) [*P, Ru*(R)]; C Anthony (Swansea) [*Ro, F, P, Ru*]; V Cooper (Ystradgynlais) [*Ro, F, P, Ru*(R)]; P Williams (Blackpool) [*F*(R), *Ru*]; H Jenkins (Bedwas) [*Ro, F, Ru*]; C Gittings (Tonna) [*F, P*]; D Thomas (Swansea) [*Ro, F, P, Ru*(R)]; J Griffiths (Swansea) [*Ro*(R), *P*(R), *Ru*]; J Ringer (Cardiff) [*Ro, P, Ru*(R)]; N Thomas (Bridgend) [*Ro, F, Ru*(R)]; G Green (Pontypool) [*P, Ru*]
Hawkins was captain in all four matches.

MATCH DETAILS 1994-95

21 December 1994, The Gnoll, Neath

WELSH YOUTH UNDER-18 7 (1G) **WELSH SCHOOLS 42**
WELSH YOUTH *Try:* Gough *Conversion:* Wyatt
Referee D Bevan (Wales)

8 January 1995, St Helens, Swansea

WELSH YOUTH UNDER-18 3 (1DG) **NEW ZEALAND SCHOOLS 29**
WALES *Dropped Goal:* Piles
Referee E Morrison (England)

25 February 1995, Stadio Albricci, Naples

ITALIAN YOUTH 7 (1G) **WELSH YOUTH 33** (2G 3PG 2T)
ITALY *Try:* Dagnolo *Conversion:* Zarrillo
WALES *Tries:* Durston, Garfield, Saddler, Davies *Conversions:* Morris (2)
Penalty Goals: Morris (3)
Referee L Mayne (Ireland)

4 March 1995, Camborne

ENGLAND COLTS 29 (3PG 4T) **ITALIAN YOUTH 0**
ENGLAND *Tries:* Truelove (2), Waters, Vickery *Penalty Goals:* Belgian (2), Blyth
Referee R G Davies (Wales)

12 March 1995, Cardiff Arms Park

WELSH YOUTH 26 (2PG 4T) **FRANCE JUNIORS 0**
WALES *Tries:* Walne, Booth, Williams, Anthony *Penalty Goals:* Morris (2)
Referee I Ramage (Scotland)

19 March 1995, The Gnoll, Neath

WELSH YOUTH UNDER-18 17 (4PG 1T) **JAPAN SCHOOLS 11** (2PG 1T)
WALES *Try:* Thomas *Penalty Goals:* Jervis (4)
Referee S Buggy (Ireland)

26 March 1995, The Stoop, Twickenham

ENGLAND COLTS 12 (1G 1T) **WELSH YOUTH 22** (4PG 2T)
ENGLAND *Tries:* Blyth, Vickery *Conversion:* Belgian
WALES *Tries:* Saddler, Walne *Penalty Goals:* Watts (4)
Referee R McDowell (Ireland)

1 April 1995, Bridgehaven, Stirling

SCOTLAND UNDER-19 13 (1PG 2T) **ENGLAND COLTS 32** (2G 1PG 3T)
SCOTLAND *Tries:* Bull (2) *Penalty Goal:* Tomlinson
ENGLAND *Tries:* Smith, Ashforth, Zaltzman, Winters, Waters
Conversions: Belgian (2) *Penalty Goal:* Belgian
Referee D Pruvot (France)

2 April 1995, Thomond Park, Limerick

IRELAND YOUTH UNDER-18 12 (3PG 1DG)
WELSH YOUTH UNDER-18 17 (1G 2T)
IRELAND *Penalty Goals:* Maguire (3) *Dropped Goal:* Maguire
WALES *Tries:* Driscoll, Harley, Piles *Conversion:* Wyatt
Referee S Piercy (England)

2 April 1995, Madrid

SPAIN UNDER-19 32 **SCOTLAND UNDER-18 3** (1PG)
SCOTLAND *Penalty Goal:* Banks

8 April 1995, Millbrae, Ayr

SCOTLAND UNDER-18 11 (2PG 1T) **IRELAND UNDER-18 15** (1G 1PG 1T)
SCOTLAND *Try:* Melvin *Penalty Goals:* Melvin (2)
IRELAND *Tries:* Wilson, Tierney *Conversion:* Maguire *Penalty Goal:* Maguire
Referee A Malartic (France)

22 April 1995, La Teste

FRANCE JUNIORS 10 (1G 1PG) **ENGLAND COLTS 25** (2G 1PG 1DG 1T)
ENGLAND *Tries:* Smith, Murphy, Fitzgerald *Conversions:* Belgian (2)

Penalty Goal: Belgian *Dropped Goal:* Blyth
Referee I Ramage (Scotland)

30 April 1995, Stradey Park, Llanelli

WALES UNDER-18 29 (2G 3T) **SCOTLAND UNDER-18 22** (2G 1PG 1T)
WALES *Tries:* Hughes, Williams, Winn, Yarnton, Griffiths *Conversions:* Wyatt (2)
SCOTLAND *Tries:* Bull, Hunter, Steele *Conversions:* Tomlinson (2)
Penalty Goal: Tomlinson
Referee A Rowden (England)

30 April 1995, Stradey Park, Llanelli

WALES YOUTH 36 (3G 3T) **SCOTLAND UNDER-19 8** (1PG 1T)
WALES *Tries:* Davies, Evans, Saddler, Durston, Gardner, Hawkins
Conversions: Morris (3)
SCOTLAND *Try:* Wands *Penalty Goal:* Duncan
Referee J Pearson (England)

FIRA YOUTH TOURNAMENT, ROMANIA
11 April 1995, Tei Stadium, Bucharest

SCOTLAND 35 (2G 2PG 3T) **RUSSIA 0**
SCOTLAND *Tries:* Bull (2), Calder, Weston, Dalgleish *Conversions:* Dalgleish (2)
Penalty Goals: Dalgleish (2)

12 April 1995, Steaua Stadium, Bucharest

SCOTLAND 3 (1PG) **ARGENTINA 43**
SCOTLAND *Penalty Goal:* Hay

14 April 1995, Tei Stadium, Bucharest

SCOTLAND 41 (4G 1PG 2T) **SPAIN 7** (1G)
SCOTLAND *Tries:* Caldwell (3), Bulloch, Smith, McLean *Conversions:* Dalgleish (4)
Penalty Goal: Dalgleish

16 April 1995, Steaua Stadium, Bucharest

SCOTLAND 5 (1T) **ROMANIA 17**
SCOTLAND *Try:* Caldwell

11 April 1995, Tei Stadium, Bucharest

WELSH YOUTH 15 (1G 1PG 1T) **ROMANIA 22**
WALES *Tries:* Winn, Jenkins *Conversion:* Jervis *Penalty Goal:* Jervis
Referee Sr Borsani (Argentina)

12 April 1995, Ghencea Stadium, Bucharest

WELSH YOUTH 10 (1G 1PG) **FRANCE 36**
WALES *Try:* Hawkins *Conversion:* Jervis *Penalty Goal:* Jervis
Referee Sr Atorasagasi (Spain)

14 April 1995, Tei Stadium, Bucharest

WELSH YOUTH 28 (2G 3PG 1T) **PORTUGAL 8**
WALES *Tries:* Winn, Booth, Ringer *Conversions:* Jervis (2) *Penalty Goals:* Jervis (3)

16 April 1995, Parcul Copilului, Bucharest

WALES YOUTH 43 (5G 1PG 1T) **RUSSIA 10**
WALES *Tries:* Davies (2), Bowen, Thomas, Hill, Jervis *Conversions:* Jervis (5)
Penalty Goal: Jervis
Referee Sr Borsani (Argentina)

THE SCOTS RETURN FROM THE DEAD

THE 1994-95 SEASON IN SCOTLAND
Bill McMurtrie

Scotland, inspired by captain Gavin Hastings, came back from the dead in 1995. Their run of nine successive internationals without a win was almost forgiven as they beat Canada and Ireland, France and Wales to set up a Grand Slam decider against England. Although the Scots could not pull off the miracle at Twickenham, they tuned up for the World Cup with another Murrayfield victory, beating Romania by 49-16 in April.

Such an international season had seemed far beyond Scotland when they lost to South Africa by 34-10 at Murrayfield in November, exactly a year after an even heavier drubbing by New Zealand, again on home ground. The prophets of doom were forecasting further disasters: a Scottish magazine cover even portrayed a coffin draped with a saltire, the death knell for the Flower of Scotland. Yet even after the hammering by South Africa, Gavin Hastings proclaimed confidence. His belief was that Scotland could still challenge England for the Triple Crown at Twickenham. He did not mention the Grand Slam: after all Scotland had to visit Paris, and they had not won there since 1969.

While the four other countries were starting their Five Nations Championship campaigns, Scotland warmed up against Canada. It was the ideal opportunity for coach Douglas Morgan and his fellow selectors to ring the changes. Only six players survived in the original selection from the defeat by South Africa, and there was a further change when David Hilton, the Bath prop, deputising for the injured Alan Sharp, was called up as the third new cap in the team. Like the other newcomers, Stewart Campbell and Eric Peters, Hilton was promoted from Scotland's successful A team. Gavin Hastings, playing in his 52nd international, joined the Hawick pair Jim Renwick and Colin Deans as Scotland's most-capped players. It was an occasion for double celebration as Scotland ended their dismal run by beating Canada 22-6. It may not have been the most marvellous of performances, but it was a win in dreadful conditions – in a chilling downpour on a sodden pitch. Confidence was restored: Hastings, Morgan et al could breathe more easily again.

A fortnight later, back at Murrayfield, Hastings overtook Renwick and Deans, and his team started their Championship campaign against Ireland, pulling their game together in the second half to win by 26-13. Scottish rugby could truly believe in itself again.

It was with new confidence and enthusiasm that the Scots went to Parc des Princes, where they had never won in the modern stadium. Their last success in Paris had been at the old Stade Colombes 26 years earlier, when, as witnessed by grey film footage, Jim Telfer scored a captain's try for victory. So it was that history was recast on 18 February

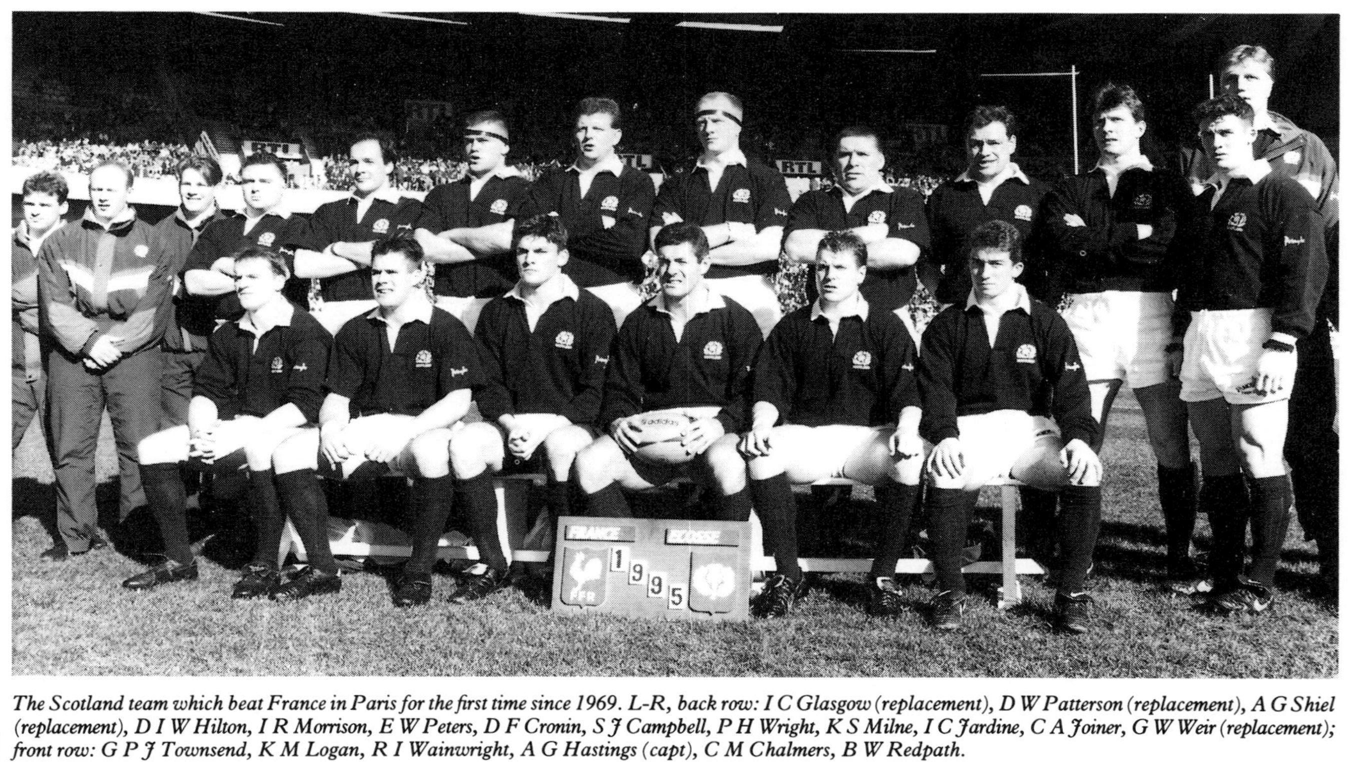

The Scotland team which beat France in Paris for the first time since 1969. L-R, back row: I C Glasgow (replacement), D W Patterson (replacement), A G Shiel (replacement), D I W Hilton, I R Morrison, E W Peters, D F Cronin, S J Campbell, P H Wright, K S Milne, I C Jardine, C A Joiner, G W Weir (replacement); front row: G P J Townsend, K M Logan, R I Wainwright, A G Hastings (capt), C M Chalmers, B W Redpath.

1995: in the dying seconds of a memorable, fluctuating encounter, Gregor Townsend slipped away a deft one-handed pass to release Gavin Hastings on a run of fully 40 metres to touch down between the posts and level the scores. It was another captain's try for posterity, and his conversion, which gave Scotland their 23-21 win, was a formality.

Scotland were on a high, and they went on to a 26-13 victory over Wales at Murrayfield, with tries by two forwards, Hilton and Peters, international newcomers less than two months earlier. Peters' was a try out of the top bracket, instigated deep in their own half by Rob Wainwright, Gavin Hastings and Doddie Weir and promoted up the west touchline by Kenny Logan, who found Peters in eager support. Murrayfield was rapturous.

So to Twickenham and the Grand Slam decider, but the match did not live up to the occasion. It was decided by goal-kicks, 24-12 to England. Even the aftermath left an unpleasant taste, soured by England hooker Brian Moore's remarks about the Scots' tactics.

Scotland's win against Romania in April was Hastings' last Murrayfield international. After 57 caps, all that remained was his third World Cup. He scored 19 of Scotland's points against the Romanians, raising his national tally to 563. Scotland scored seven tries in that match, including one by Hastings – his 12th, a record for a Scottish full-back in internationals. Even more remarkable, it was the first time that all four Scottish threequarters scored in a Test.

Scotland's rebirth owed much to their A XV, led by Kevin McKenzie. When Scotland's selectors recast the national team for the match against Canada, they promoted no fewer than eight of those who had played for Scotland A in the 18-16 victory over Italy two weeks earlier at the St Johnstone football ground, McDiarmid Park, in Perth. Under the command of the Stirling County hooker Scotland A won four of their three matches, beating even South Africa as well as Italy and Ireland A. McKenzie was otherwise engaged with the national squad when the team lost to France in Glasgow.

Scotland's Under-21 team, too, found a winning way at last. After 17 successive defeats they beat Wales by 15-9 at Inverleith, Edinburgh, albeit in a tryless match, and then went on to a more comprehensive win over Italy, by 36-10 at Bridgehaugh, Stirling. New champions emerged in district and club rugby. The Scottish Exiles took the district title for the first time, beating all four home teams, and not only did Stirling County win the McEwan's 70/- National League, but their youngsters took the national youth title as well.

In winning the District Championship, the Exiles owed much to their fly-half, Stuart Laing, from the Belfast club Instonians, who scored 64 of their 119 points, converting all 11 of their tries. But the Exiles' success also reflected credit on the captain, Andy Reed, the Bath lock who had led Scotland in Argentina in 1994, and coach Alastair McHarg. Injury prevented Reed from participating in the International Championship.

STIRLING COUNTY REACH THE SUMMIT

McEWAN'S 70/- NATIONAL LEAGUE REVIEW

Stirling County's achievement in 1994-95 was unique. Not only did they break the Edinburgh-Borders stranglehold on Scottish rugby's club championship, but in taking the McEwan's 70/- National League trophy for the first time they had come all the way up through the Leagues from the lower reaches to the very top. When the Championship was instituted in 1973, Stirling were in the bottom division. But even then the Bridgehaugh club had a strong youth policy. They bred their own talent, and that has been their strength as they have climbed from the Seventh Division to achieve the ultimate. They transplanted the Border principles of town identity to their own benefit. Most of their first-choice Championship XV were local lads.

Winning the title reflected credit also on Stirling's team hierarchy – Brian Edwards and Muff Scobie, the coaches, and Stewart Hamilton, the 38-year-old lock who led County to the Championship. By that age most have left the playing ranks to sit in committee or to coach or referee, but Hamilton's enthusiasm for the game and his confidence in his own ability were such that he refused to give up district rugby. When Glasgow did not need him he turned to the North and Midlands for further representative honours. His self-confidence has rubbed off on his young colleagues. It helped, too, that Stirling had three international players in their ranks. That trio – Kenny Logan, Ian Jardine and Kevin McKenzie – inspired others to challenge the established mould of Scottish rugby. Stirling believed in themselves and in their ability to play the wider game that Edwards and Scobie knew was possible.

Such rugby was not evident early in the season, however. Stirling stuttered through an opening 17-9 win against West of Scotland at Bridgehaugh, and had an even closer call a week later: they won by only 19-18 away to Dundee High School FP. Stirling set themselves on their true course with a 20-3 victory against Jedforest at Bridgehaugh, and they went on to see off most of the other challengers. They won by 22-15 at home against Melrose, champions for the previous three seasons, and a week later went to Edinburgh and beat Watsonians by 23-19. Kenny Logan, County's international wing, was in trenchant mood in both games, running in two tries against Melrose and three against Watsonians.

There were eight wins under the Stirling belt before they stumbled for the first time, beaten 14-10 by Hawick, but their only other hiccup was an 11-11 draw with Heriot's at Goldenacre. By then, Stirling were champions: they had won the title before playing their last two League matches.

Watsonians, the Hastings brothers' home club, were five points behind Stirling in the runners-up spot, again their best finishing position in 22 years of League rugby. The Edinburgh club were unbeaten before they lost to Stirling, but further defeats followed at the hands of Hawick, Boroughmuir and West of Scotland. Edinburgh Academicals won their last six League matches to climb into third place, and they were followed by five past champions – Hawick, Boroughmuir, Gala, Melrose and Heriot's. Those eight will make up the First Division of the 1995-96 Premier League in the recast Championship.

Glasgow High/Kelvinside, Jedforest, West of Scotland, Dundee, Currie and Stewart's-Melville FP, the others in the 1994-95 First Division, make up the new Premier Second with Kelso and Selkirk. As consolation, Jed won the Border League title. Kelso, with John Jeffrey still going strong, won the national Second Division Championship, though only on points difference. Selkirk gave themselves a chance of the title by beating Kelso 17-13 at Philiphaugh in February, but not even a 58-16 win over Corstorphine was enough to allow Selkirk to sneak ahead.

Ayr took the Third Division title, losing only to Langholm after the Championship had been won. Only Garnock, Seventh Division champions, went through the League season without defeat.

McEWAN'S 70/- NATIONAL LEAGUE 1994-95

Division 1	*P*	*W*	*D*	*L*	*F*	*A*	*Pts*
Stirling County	13	11	1	1	234	162	23
Watsonians	13	9	0	4	296	212	18
Edinburgh Acs	13	7	2	4	214	141	16
Hawick	13	7	2	4	215	199	16
Boroughmuir	13	7	1	5	325	226	15
Heriot's FP	13	7	1	5	199	195	15
Gala	13	7	1	5	226	245	15
Melrose	13	7	0	6	308	261	14
Glasgow H/K	13	6	1	6	228	183	13
Jedforest	13	6	0	7	221	256	12
W of Scotland	13	5	0	8	166	233	10
Dundee HSFP	13	3	1	9	200	264	7
Currie	13	3	0	10	188	280	6
Stewart's-Mel	13	1	0	12	158	321	2

Previous champions: Hawick 10 times, 1973-74 to 1977-78, 1981-82, 1983-84 to 1986-87; Melrose 4 times, 1989-90, 1991-92 to 1993-94; Gala 3 times, 1979-80, 1980-81, 1982-83; Kelso twice, 1987-88, 1988-89; Heriot's FP 1979-80; Boroughmuir 1990-91.

Division 2	*P*	*W*	*D*	*L*	*F*	*A*	*Pts*
Kelso	13	11	0	2	318	159	22
Selkirk	13	10	2	1	336	184	22
Kirkcaldy	13	8	1	4	271	230	17
Biggar	13	7	2	4	180	173	16
Preston Lodge	13	7	1	5	269	214	15
Glasgow Acs	13	7	0	6	299	239	14
Peebles	13	7	0	6	175	204	14
Musselburgh	13	6	1	6	203	196	13
Grangemouth	13	6	0	7	223	246	12
Corstorphine	13	5	1	7	180	212	11
Edinburgh W	13	5	0	8	210	261	10
Wigtownshire	13	3	0	10	173	265	6
Gordonians	13	3	0	10	145	300	6
Haddington	13	2	0	11	178	277	4

Division 3	*P*	*W*	*D*	*L*	*F*	*A*	*Pts*
Ayr	13	12	0	1	464	126	24
Kilmarnock	13	11	0	2	449	162	22
Clarkston	13	10	1	2	261	120	21
Langholm	13	9	0	4	204	152	18
Hillhead/J'hill	13	8	0	5	240	147	16
Dunfermline	13	7	0	6	237	261	14
Dumfries	13	6	1	6	209	293	13
Trinity Acs	13	6	0	7	233	272	12
Portobello FP	13	6	0	7	151	270	12
Stewartry	13	5	0	8	164	201	10
Edinburgh U	13	4	0	9	206	252	8
Royal High	13	3	1	9	145	358	7
East Kilbride	13	1	1	11	191	318	3
Hutchesons'/Al	13	1	0	12	151	373	2

Division 4	*P*	*W*	*D*	*L*	*F*	*A*	*Pts*
Glenrothes	13	12	0	1	317	99	24
Duns	13	10	1	2	316	166	21
Livingston	13	10	1	2	266	174	21

	P	W	D	L	F	A	Pts
Aberdeen GSFP	13	8	0	5	452	144	16
Ardrossan Acs	13	8	0	5	177	157	16
Cambuslang	13	7	0	6	165	148	14
Perthshire	13	6	1	6	163	184	13
St Boswell's	13	6	0	7	145	249	12
Howe of Fife	13	5	1	7	178	208	11
Dalziel HSFP	12	5	0	7	152	211	10
Highland	13	4	0	9	193	254	8
North Berwick	13	3	1	9	101	319	7
Alloa	12	2	0	10	116	239	4
Morgan FP	13	1	1	11	124	313	3

Division 5	*P*	*W*	*D*	*L*	*F*	*A*	*Pts*
Berwick	13	10	1	2	380	141	21
Allan Glen's	13	9	0	4	256	135	18
Cartha QP	13	9	0	4	259	195	18
Linlithgow	13	8	1	4	259	154	17
Leith Acs	13	8	0	5	233	199	16
Cumbernauld	13	7	1	5	186	163	15
Madras FP	13	7	0	6	157	216	14
Irvine	13	6	1	6	195	247	13
Hillfoots	13	6	0	7	176	153	12
Lismore	13	6	0	7	247	252	12
Clydebank	13	5	0	8	160	191	10
Penicuik	13	4	0	9	151	198	8
Paisley	13	3	0	10	164	280	6
Falkirk	13	1	0	12	120	419	2

Division 6	*P*	*W*	*D*	*L*	*F*	*A*	*Pts*
Annan	13	11	1	1	505	114	23
Waysiders/Dr	13	11	0	2	283	124	22
Dunbar	13	8	2	3	181	141	18
Forrester FP	13	8	0	5	193	165	16
Aberdeenshire	13	7	0	6	268	132	14
Lenzie	13	7	0	6	288	240	14
Greenock W	13	6	2	5	195	255	14
Murrayfield	13	6	0	7	254	222	12
Ross High	13	5	1	7	292	187	11
Marr	13	4	1	8	153	293	9
Earlston	13	4	1	8	150	344	9
Aberdeen U	13	4	0	9	260	335	8
St Andrew's U	13	3	2	8	190	334	8
Harris FP	13	2	0	11	114	440	4

Division 7	*P*	*W*	*D*	*L*	*F*	*A*	*Pts*
Garnock	13	12	1	0	425	47	25
Whitecraigs	13	10	0	3	273	146	20
Cumnock	13	9	1	3	262	153	19
Lochaber	12	8	2	2	228	94	18
Walkerburn	13	8	0	5	250	137	16
Holy Cross	12	8	0	4	207	161	16
RAF Kinloss	13	6	1	6	163	132	13
Broughton FP	13	6	0	7	148	194	12
Moray	13	5	1	7	177	269	11
Lasswade	13	5	0	8	174	186	10
Edinburgh N	13	4	0	9	134	171	8
Hyndland FP	13	2	0	11	124	341	4
Waid FP	13	2	0	11	120	372	4
Panmure	13	2	0	11	112	394	4

District League champions *(promoted to National League)*:
Edinburgh: Dalkeith
Glasgow: Hamilton Academicals
Midlands: Rosyth and District
North: RAF Lossiemouth

For season 1995-96, the Club Championship has been recast to comprise a Premier League of four divisions, each of eight clubs, and a National League of seven divisions, each of ten clubs, all playing home and away.

BANK OF SCOTLAND BORDER LEAGUE

	P	*W*	*D*	*L*	*F*	*A*	*Pts*
Jedforest	12	9	1	2	249	129	19
Gala	12	9	0	3	319	156	18
Hawick	12	8	1	3	192	140	17
Melrose	12	6	0	6	271	221	12
Selkirk	12	4	2	5	162	205	10
Kelso	11	3	0	8	156	189	6
Langholm	11	0	0	11	55	364	0

McEWAN'S 70/- DISTRICT CHAMPIONSHIP 1994-95

	P	*W*	*D*	*L*	*F*	*A*	*Pts*
Scottish Exiles	4	4	0	0	119	51	8
Edinburgh	4	1	2	1	62	62	4
N & Midlands	4	1	1	2	69	84	3
South	4	1	1	2	61	81	3
Glasgow	4	1	0	3	62	95	2

McEWAN'S 70/- DISTRICT CHAMPIONSHIP 1994-95

3 December, Hughenden
Glasgow 25 (1G 5PG 1DG) **North & Midlands 19** (1G 4PG)

Glasgow *(Stirling County unless otherwise stated):* D N Barrett (West of Scotland); M N McGrandles, C T Simmers (Edinburgh Acads), I C Jardine, K M Logan; M McKenzie, F H Stott (West of Scotland); J T Gibson, K D McKenzie *(capt)*, G B Robertson, A G J Watt (Glasgow High/Kelvinside), D S Munro (Glasgow High/Kelvinside), F D Wallace (Glasgow High/Kelvinside), J Brough, M I Wallace (Glasgow High/Kelvinside) *Replacement* C E Little (Glasgow High/Kelvinside) for Stott
Scorers *Try:* Jardine *Conversion:* Barrett *Penalty Goals:* Barrett (5) *Dropped Goal:* M McKenzie
North & Midlands: R J S Shepherd (Edinburgh Acads); M A Cousin (Dundee HSFP), P R Rouse (Dundee HSFP),

J W Thomson (Kirkcaldy), S A D Burns (Edinburgh Acads); J R Newton (Dundee HSFP), K G M Harper (Stirling County); J J Manson (Dundee HSFP), M W Scott (Dunfermline), D J Herrington (Dundee HSFP), J S Hamilton (Stirling County), S J Campbell (Dundee HSFP), D J McIvor (Edinburgh Acads) (*capt*), G N Flockhart (Stirling County), C J Allan (Dundee HSFP) *Replacements* W D Anderson (Kirkcaldy) for Herrington; A K Carruthers (Kirkcaldy) for Shepherd; M Waite (Edinburgh Acads) (temp)
Scorers *Try:* Cousin *Conversion:* Newton *Penalty Goals:* Newton (4)
Referee C B Muir (Langholm)

3 December, Murrayfield

Scottish Exiles 25 (1G 6PG) **South 9** (3PG)
Scottish Exiles: G Fraser (Waterloo); M Kemp (Saracens), M P Craig (Waterloo), B R S Eriksson (London Scottish), M E Appleson (Sale); S R Laing (Instonians), D W Patterson (West Hartlepool); D I W Hilton (Bristol), L M Mair (London Scottish), A P Burnell (London Scottish), D F Cronin (Bourges), A I Reed (Bath) (*capt*), D Blyth (Waterloo), E W Peters (Bath), S D Holmes (London Scottish) *Replacement* K A Whitaker (West Hartlepool) for Eriksson
Scorers *Try:* Fraser *Conversion:* Laing *Penalty Goals:* Laing (6)
South: M Dods (Gala); C A Joiner (Melrose), S A Nichol (Selkirk), B A J Swan (Gala), K L Suddon (Hawick); A G Shiel (Melrose) (*capt*), G C Farquharson (Gala); M G Browne (Melrose), J A Hay (Hawick), D Lunn (Melrose), R R Brown (Melrose), G W Weir (Melrose), R M Kirkpatrick (Jedforest), B L Renwick (Hawick), S A Aitken (Melrose) *Replacements* A J Roxburgh (Kelso) for Renwick; J R S McColm (Selkirk) for Lunn
Scorer *Penalty Goals:* Dods (3)
Referee J M Fleming (Boroughmuir)

10 December, Murrayfield

Scottish Exiles 34 (4G 2PG) **Glasgow 13** (1G 2PG)
Scottish Exiles: G Fraser (Waterloo); M Kemp (Saracens), M P Craig (Waterloo), B R S Eriksson (London Scottish), M E Appleson (Sale); S R Laing (Instonians), D W Patterson (West Hartlepool); D I W Hilton (Bristol), B W Gilchrist (London Scottish), A P Burnell (London Scottish), D F Cronin (Bourges), A I Reed (Bath) (*capt*), D Blyth (Waterloo), E W Peters (Bath), I R Morrison (London Scottish) *Replacement* R Scott (London Scottish) for Cronin
Scorers *Tries:* Kemp (2), Patterson, Peters *Conversions:* Laing (4) *Penalty Goals:* Laing (2)
Glasgow *(Stirling County unless otherwise stated):* D N Barrett (West of Scotland); M N McGrandles, C T Simmers (Edinburgh Acads), I C Jardine, K M Logan; M McKenzie, C E Little (Glasgow High/Kelvinside); J T Gibson, K D McKenzie (*capt*), G B Robertson, A G J Watt (Glasgow High/Kelvinside), D S Munro (Glasgow High/Kelvinside), G T Mackay, J Brough, B Ireland
Scorer *Try:* pen try *Conversion:* Barrett *Penalty Goals:* Barrett (2)
Referee R J Megson (Edinburgh Wands)

10 December, Duffus Park, Cupar

North & Midlands 11 (2PG 1T) **Edinburgh 11** (2PG 1T)
North & Midlands: A K Carruthers (Kirkcaldy); M A Cousin (Dundee HSFP), P R Rouse (Dundee HSFP), J W Thomson (Kirkcaldy), S A D Burns (Edinburgh Acads); J R Newton (Dundee HSFP), K G M Harper (Stirling County); J J Manson (Dundee HSFP), M W Scott (Dunfermline), W D Anderson (Kirkcaldy), J S Hamilton (Stirling County), S J Campbell (Dundee HSFP), D J McIvor (Edinburgh Acads) (*capt*), G N Flockhart (Stirling County), R I Wainwright (West Hartlepool)
Scorers *Try:* Rouse *Penalty Goals:* Newton (2)
Edinburgh: A G Hastings (Watsonians); H R Gilmour (Heriot's FP), A R McRobbie (Heriot's FP), P W B Flockhart (Stewart's-Melville FP), I C Glasgow (Heriot's FP); D W Hodge (Watsonians), G G Burns (Stewart's-Melville FP); G D Wilson (Boroughmuir), K S Milne (Heriot's FP), S W Paul (Heriot's FP), J F Richardson (Edinburgh Acads) (*capt*), P T Jennings (Boroughmuir), G J Drummond (Boroughmuir), S J Reid (Boroughmuir), G F Dall (Heriot's FP)
Scorer *Try:* Hastings *Penalty Goals:* Hastings (2)
Referee E Murray (Greenock Wands)

14 December, Riverside Park, Jedburgh
South 19 (1G 3PG 1DG) **Edinburgh 19** (1G 4PG)

South: M Dods (Gala); C A Joiner (Melrose), A G Stanger (Hawick), A G Shiel (Melrose), K L Suddon (Hawick); C M Chalmers (Melrose) (*capt*), B W Redpath (Melrose); G R Isaac (Gala), J A Hay (Hawick), J R S McColm (Selkirk), R R Brown (Melrose), G W Weir (Melrose), A J Roxburgh (Kelso), R M Kirkpatrick (Jedforest), J P Amos (Gala)
Scorers *Try:* Dods *Conversion:* Dods *Penalty Goals:* Dods (3) *Dropped Goal:* Chalmers
Edinburgh: A G Hastings (Watsonians); J A Kerr (Watsonians), A R McRobbie (Heriot's FP), P W B Flockhart (Stewart's-Melville FP), I C Glasgow (Heriot's FP); D W Hodge (Watsonians), G G Burns (Stewart's-Melville FP); R B McNulty (Stewart's-Melville FP), K S Milne (Heriot's FP), S W Paul (Heriot's FP), J F Richardson (Edinburgh Acads) (*capt*), A E D Macdonald (Heriot's FP), B W Ward (Currie), G A R Simpson (Heriot's FP), S J Reid (Boroughmuir) *Replacement* H R Gilmour (Heriot's FP) for Flockhart
Scorer *Try:* pen try *Conversion:* Hastings *Penalty Goals:* Hastings (4)
Referee S W Piercy (England)

17 December, Myreside

Edinburgh 16 (1G 3PG) **Glasgow 13** (1PG 2T)
Edinburgh: A G Hastings (Watsonians); H R Gilmour (Heriot's FP), J A Kerr (Watsonians), A R McRobbie (Heriot's FP), I C Glasgow (Heriot's FP); D W Hodge (Watsonians), G G Burns (Stewart's-Melville FP); G D Wilson (Boroughmuir), K S Milne (Heriot's FP), S W Paul (Heriot's FP), J F Richardson (Edinburgh Acads) (*capt*), A E D Macdonald (Heriot's FP), B W Ward (Currie), D G Burns (Boroughmuir), G F Dall (Heriot's FP)

Scorers *Try:* Richardson *Conversion:* Hastings *Penalty Goals:* Hastings (3)
Glasgow *(Stirling County unless otherwise stated):* D N Barrett (West of Scotland); G M Breckenridge (Glasgow High/Kelvinside), M N McGrandles, I C Jardine, K M Logan; M McKenzie, C E Little (Glasgow High/Kelvinside); J T Gibson, K D McKenzie *(capt)*, G B Robertson, A G J Watt (Glasgow High/Kelvinside), D S Munro (Glasgow High/Kelvinside), F D Wallace (Glasgow High/Kelvinside), J Lonergan (West of Scotland), G T Mackay
Scorers *Tries:* Logan, Wallace *Penalty Goal:* Barrett
Referee K W McCartney (Hawick)

17 December, Rubislaw, Aberdeen

North & Midlands 26 (1G 3PG 2T) **South 7** (1G)
North & Midlands: S A D Burns (Edinburgh Acads); M A Cousin (Dundee HSFP), P R Rouse (Dundee HSFP), J W Thomson (Kirkcaldy), J F Swanson (Edinburgh Acads); J R Newton (Dundee HSFP), K G M Harper (Stirling County); J J Manson (Dundee HSFP), M W Scott (Dunfermline), D J Herrington (Dundee HSFP) J S Hamilton (Stirling County), S J Campbell (Dundee HSFP), D J McIvor (Edinburgh Acads) *(capt)*, G N Flockhart (Stirling County), R I Wainwright (West Hartlepool) *Replacements* A K Carruthers (Kirkcaldy) for Thomson; W D Anderson (Kirkcaldy) for Herrington
Scorers *Tries:* Wainwright (2), Flockhart *Conversion:* Newton *Penalty Goals:* Newton (3)
South: M Dods (Gala); C A Joiner (Melrose), A D Stanger (Hawick), A G Shiel (Melrose), K L Suddon (Hawick); C M Chalmers (Melrose) *(capt)*, B W Redpath (Melrose); J R S McColm (Selkirk), J A Hay (Hawick), D Lunn (Melrose), R R Brown (Melrose), G W Weir (Melrose), A J Roxburgh (Kelso), R M Kirkpatrick (Jedforest), J P Amos (Gala) *Replacements* S A Nichol (Selkirk) for Stanger; S A Aitken (Melrose) for Amos
Scorers *Try:* Hay *Conversion:* Dods
Referee J M Fleming (Boroughmuir)

21 December, Murrayfield

Scottish Exiles 41 (5G 2PG) **North & Midlands 13** (1G 2PG)
Scottish Exiles: G Fraser (Waterloo); M Kemp (Saracens), M P Craig (Waterloo), B R S Eriksson (London Scottish), M E Appleson (Sale); S R Laing (Instonians), K Trump (London Scottish); D I W Hilton (Bristol), L M Mair (London Scottish), A P Burnell (London Scottish), D F Cronin (Bourges), A I Reed (Bath) *(capt)*, D Blyth (Waterloo), E W Peters (Bath), I R Morrison (London Scottish)
Scorers *Tries:* Craig (3), Appleson (2) *Conversions:* Laing (5) *Penalty Goals:* Laing (2)
North & Midlands: S A D Burns (Edinburgh Acads); M A Cousin (Dundee HSFP), P R Rouse (Dundee HSFP), R J S Shepherd (Edinburgh Acads), J F Swanson (Edinburgh Acads); J R Newton (Dundee HSFP), K G M Harper (Stirling County); J J Manson (Dundee HSFP), M W Scott (Dunfermline), D J Herrington (Dundee HSFP), J S Hamilton (Stirling County), S J Campbell (Dundee HSFP), D J McIvor (Edinburgh Acads) *(capt)*, G N Flockhart (Stirling County), R I Wainwright (West Hartlepool)
Scorers *Try:* Rouse *Conversion:* Newton *Penalty Goals:* Newton (2)
Referee E Murray (Greenock Wands)

23 December, Murrayfield

Edinburgh 16 (1G 3PG) **Scottish Exiles 19** (1G 3PG 1DG)
Edinburgh: A G Hastings (Watsonians); H R Gilmour (Heriot's FP), A R McRobbie (Heriot's FP), P W B Flockhart (Stewart's-Melville FP), I C Glasgow (Heriot's FP); D W Hodge (Watsonians), G G Burns (Stewart's-Melville FP); G D Wilson (Boroughmuir), K S Milne (Heriot's FP), S W Paul (Heriot's FP), J F Richardson (Edinburgh Acads) *(capt)*, A E D Macdonald (Heriot's FP), B W Ward (Currie), S J Reid (Boroughmuir), G F Dall (Heriot's FP)
Scorers *Try:* Gilmour *Conversion:* Hastings *Penalty Goals:* Hastings (3)
Scottish Exiles: G Fraser (Waterloo); M Kemp (Saracens), M P Craig (Waterloo), B R S Eriksson (London Scottish), M E Appleson (Sale); S R Laing (Instonians), K Troup (London Scottish); D I W Hilton (Bristol), L M Mair (London Scottish), A P Burnell (London Scottish), D F Cronin (Bourges), A I Reed (Bath) *(capt)*, D Blyth (Waterloo), E W Peters (Bath), I R Smith (Gloucester)
Scorers *Try:* Appleson *Conversion:* Laing *Penalty Goals:* Laing (3) *Dropped Goal:* Laing
Referee C B Muir (Langholm)

24 December, Bridgehaugh, Stirling

Glasgow 11 (2PG 1T) **South 26** (1G 3PG 2T)
Glasgow *(Stirling County unless otherwise stated):* D N Barrett (West of Scotland); G M Breckenridge (Glasgow High/Kelvinside), C T Simmers (Edinburgh Acads), I C Jardine, K M Logan; M McKenzie, C E Little (Glasgow High/Kelvinside); J T Gibson, K D McKenzie *(capt)*, G B Robertson, A G J Watt (Glasgow High/Kelvinside), D S Munro (Glasgow High/Kelvinside), F D Wallace (Glasgow High/Kelvinside), J Lonergan (West of Scotland), G T Mackay
Scorer *Try:* Barrett *Penalty Goals:* Barrett (2)
South: M Dods (Gala); C A Joiner (Melrose), A G Stanger (Hawick), A G Shiel (Melrose), K L Suddon (Hawick); C M Chalmers (Melrose) *(capt)*, B W Redpath (Melrose); G R Isaac (Gala), J A Hay (Hawick), D Lunn (Melrose), R R Brown (Melrose), I Elliot (Hawick), S Bennet (Kelso), G W Weir (Melrose), R M Kirkpatrick (Jedforest)
Scorers *Tries:* Suddon (2), pen try *Conversion:* Chalmers *Penalty Goals:* Chalmers (3)
Referee J L Bacigalupo (Edinburgh Wands)

SCOTTISH INTERNATIONAL PLAYERS
(up to 31 March 1995)

ABBREVIATIONS

A – Australia; *Arg* – Argentina; *C* – Canada; *E* – England; *F* – France; *Fj* – Fiji; *I* – Ireland; *J* – Japan; *NZ* – New Zealand; *R* – Romania; *SA* – South Africa; *W* – Wales; *WS* – Western Samoa; *Z* – Zimbabwe; (C) – Centenary match v England at Murrayfield, 1971 (non-championship); P – Scotland v President's Overseas XV at Murrayfield in SRU's Centenary season, 1972-73; (R) Replacement; (t) – temporary replacement. Entries in square brackets [ ] indicate appearances in the World Cup.

Note: Years given for Five Nations' matches are for second half of season; eg 1972 means season 1971-72. Years for all other matches refer to the actual year of the match. When a series has taken place, figures have been used to denote the particular matches in which players have featured. Thus 1981 *NZ* 1,2 indicates that a player appeared in the first and second Tests of the series. The abandoned game with Ireland at Belfast in 1885 is now included as a cap-match.

Abercrombie, C H (United Services) 1910 *I*, *E*, 1911 *F*, *W*, 1913 *F*, *W*
Abercrombie, J G (Edinburgh U) 1949 *F*, *W*, *I*, 1950 *F*, *W*, *I*, *E*
Agnew, W C C (Stewart's Coll FP) 1930 *W*, *I*
Ainslie, R (Edinburgh Inst FP) 1879 *I*, *E*, 1880 *I*, *E*, 1881 *E*, 1882 *I*, *E*
Ainslie, T (Edinburgh Inst FP) 1881 *E*, 1882 *I*, *E*, 1883 *W*, *I*, *E*, 1884 *W*, *I*, *E*, 1885 *W*, *I*1,2
Aitchison, G R (Edinburgh Wands) 1883 *I*
Aitchison, T G (Gala) 1929 *W*, *I*, *E*
Aitken, A I (Edinburgh Inst FP) 1889 *I*
Aitken, G G (Oxford U) 1924 *W*, *I*, *E*, 1925 *F*, *W*, *I*, *E*, 1929 *F*
Aitken, J (Gala) 1977 *E*, *I*, *F*, 1981 *F*, *W*, *E*, *I*, *NZ*1,2, *R*, *A*, 1982 *E*, *I*, *F*, *W*, 1983 *F*, *W*, *E*, *NZ*,1984 *W*, *E*, *I*, *F*, *R*
Aitken, R (London Scottish) 1947 *W*
Allan, B (Glasgow Acads) 1881 *I*
Allan, J (Edinburgh Acads) 1990 *NZ*1, 1991 *W*, *I*, *R*, [*J*, *I*, *WS*, *E*, *NZ*]
Allan, J L (Melrose) 1952 *F*, *W*, *I*, 1953 *W*
Allan, J L F (Cambridge U) 1957 *I*, *E*
Allan, J W (Melrose) 1927 *F*, 1928 *I*, 1929 *F*, *W*, *I*, *E*, 1930 *F*, *E*, 1931 *F*, *W*, *I*, *E*, 1932 *SA*, *W*, *I*, 1934 *I*, *E*
Allan, R C (Hutchesons' GSFP) 1969 *I*
Allardice, W D (Aberdeen GSFP) 1947 *A*, 1948 *F*, *W*, *I*, 1949 *F*, *W*, *I*, *E*
Allen, H W (Glasgow Acads) 1873 *E*
Anderson, A H (Glasgow Acads) 1894 *I*
Anderson, D G (London Scottish) 1889 *I*, 1890 *W*, *I*, *E*, 1891 *W*, *E*, 1892 *W*, *E*
Anderson, E (Stewart's Coll FP) 1947 *I*, *E*
Anderson, J W (W of Scotland) 1872 *E*
Anderson, T (Merchiston) 1882 *I*
Angus, A W (Watsonians) 1909 *W*, 1910 *F*, *W*, *E*, 1911 *W*, *I*, 1912 *F*, *W*, *I*, *E*, *SA*, 1913 *F*, *W*, 1914 *E*, 1920 *F*, *W*, *I*, *E*
Anton, P A (St Andrew's U) 1873 *E*
Armstrong, G (Jedforest) 1988 *A*, 1989 *W*, *E*, *I*, *F*, *Fj*, *R*, 1990 *I*, *F*, *W*, *E*, *NZ* 1,2, *Arg*, 1991 *F*, *W*, *E*, *I*, *R*, [*J*, *I*, *WS*, *E*, *NZ*], 1993 *I*, *F*, *W*, *E*, 1994 *E*, *I*
Arneil, R J (Edinburgh Acads, Leicester and Northampton) 1968 *I*, *E*, *A*,1969 *F*, *W*, *I*, *E*, *SA*, 1970 *F*, *W*, *I*, *E*, *A*, 1971 *F*, *W*, *I*, *E*(2[1C]), 1972 *F*, *W*, *E*, *NZ*
Arthur, A (Glasgow Acads) 1875 *E*, 1876 *E*
Arthur, J W (Glasgow Acads) 1871 *E*, 1872 *E*
Asher, A G G (Oxford U) 1882 *I*, 1884 *W*, *I*, *E*, 1885 *W*, 1886 *I*, *E*
Auld, W (W of Scotland) 1889 *W*, 1890 *W*
Auldjo, L J (Abertay) 1878 *E*

Bain, D McL (Oxford U) 1911 *E*, 1912 *F*, *W*, *E*, *SA*, 1913 *F*, *W*, *I*, *E*, 1914 *W*, *I*
Baird, G R T (Kelso) 1981 *A*, 1982 *E*, *I*, *F*, *W*, *A* 1,2, 1983 *I*, *F*, *W*, *E*, *NZ*, 1984 *W*, *E*, *I*, *F*, *A*, 1985 *I*, *W*, *E*, 1986 *F*, *W*, *E*, *I*, *R*, 1987 *E*, 1988 *I*
Balfour, A (Watsonians) 1896 *W*, *I*, *E*, 1897 *E*
Balfour, L M (Edinburgh Acads) 1872 *E*
Bannerman, E M (Edinburgh Acads) 1872 *E*, 1873 *E*
Bannerman, J M (Glasgow HSFP) 1921 *F*, *W*, *I*, *E*, 1922 *F*, *W*, *I*, *E*, 1923 *F*, *W*, *I*, *E*, 1924 *F*, *W*, *I*, *E*, 1925 *F*, *W*, *I*, *E*, 1926 *F*, *W*, *I*, *E*, 1927 *F*, *W*, *I*, *E*, *A*, 1928 *F*, *W*, *I*, *E*, 1929 *F*, *W*, *I*, *E*
Barnes, I A (Hawick) 1972 *W*, 1974 *F* (R), 1975 *E* (R), *NZ*, 1977 *I*, *F*, *W*
Barrie, R W (Hawick) 1936 *E*
Bearne, K R F (Cambridge U, London Scottish) 1960 *F*, *W*
Beattie, J A (Hawick) 1929 *F*, *W*, 1930 *W*, 1931 *F*, *W*, *I*, *E*, 1932 *SA*, *W*, *I*, *E*, 1933 *W*, *E*, *I*, 1934 *I*, *E*, 1935 *W*, *I*, *E*, *NZ*, 1936 *W*, *I*, *E*
Beattie, J R (Glasgow Acads) 1980 *I*, *F*, *W*, *E*, 1981 *F*, *W*, *E*, *I*, 1983 *F*, *W*, *E*, *NZ*, 1984 *E* (R), *R*, *A*, 1985 *I*, 1986 *F*, *W*, *E*, *I*, *R*, 1987 *I*, *F*, *W*, *E*
Bedell-Sivright, D R (Cambridge U, Edinburgh U) 1900 *W*, 1901 *W*, *I*, *E*, 1902 *W*, *I*, *E*, 1903 *W*, *I*, 1904 *W*, *I*, *E*, 1905 *NZ*, 1906 *W*, *I*, *E*, *SA*, 1907 *W*, *I*, *E*, 1908 *W*, *I*
Bedell-Sivright, J V (Cambridge U) 1902 *W*
Begbie, T A (Edinburgh Wands) 1881 *I*, *E*
Bell, D L (Watsonians) 1975 *I*, *F*, *W*, *E*
Bell, J A (Clydesdale) 1901 *W*, *I*, *E*, 1902 *W*, *I*, *E*
Bell, L H I (Edinburgh Acads) 1900 *E*, 1904 *W*, *I*
Berkeley, W V (Oxford U) 1926 *F*, 1929 *F*, *W*, *I*
Berry, C W (Fettesian-Lorettonians) 1884 *I*, *E*, 1885 *W*, *I* 1, 1887 *I*, *W*, *E*, 1888 *W*, *I*
Bertram, D M (Watsonians) 1922 *F*, *W*, *I*, *E*, 1923 *F*, *W*, *I*, *E*, 1924 *W*, *I*, *E*
Biggar, A G (London Scottish) 1969 *SA*, 1970 *F*, *I*, *E*, *A*, 1971 *F*, *W*, *I*, *E* (2[1C]), 1972 *F*, *W*
Biggar, M A (London Scottish) 1975 *I*, *F*, *W*, *E*, 1976 *W*, *E*, *I*, 1977 *I*, *F*, *W*, 1978 *I*, *F*, *W*, *E*, *NZ*, 1979 *W*, *E*, *I*, *F*, *NZ*, 1980 *I*, *F*, *W*, *E*
Birkett, G A (Harlequins, London Scottish) 1975 *NZ*
Bishop, J M (Glasgow Acads) 1893 *I*
Bisset, A A (RIE Coll) 1904 *W*
Black, A W (Edinburgh U) 1947 *F*, *W*, 1948 *E*, 1950 *W*, *I*, *E*
Black, W P (Glasgow HSFP) 1948 *F*, *W*, *I*, *E*, 1951 *E*
Blackadder, W F (W of Scotland) 1938 *E*
Blaikie, C F (Heriot's FP) 1963 *I*, *E*, 1966 *E*, 1968 *A*, 1969 *F*, *W*, *I*, *E*
Blair, P C B (Cambridge U) 1912 *SA*, 1913 *F*, *W*, *I*, *E*
Bolton, W H (W of Scotland) 1876 *E*
Borthwick, J B (Stewart's Coll FP) 1938 *W*, *I*
Bos, F H ten (Oxford U, London Scottish) 1959 *E*, 1960 *F*, *W*, *SA*, 1961 *F*, *SA*, *W*, *I*, *E*, 1962 *F*, *W*, *I*, *E*, 1963 *F*, *W*, *I*, *E*
Boswell, J D (W of Scotland) 1889 *W*, *I*, 1890 *W*, *I*, *E*, 1891 *W*, *I*, *E*, 1892 *W*, *I*, *E*, 1893 *I*, *E*, 1894 *I*, *E*
Bowie, T C (Watsonians) 1913 *I*, *E*, 1914 *I*, *E*
Boyd, G M (Glasgow HSFP) 1926 *E*
Boyd, J L (United Services) 1912 *E*, *SA*
Boyle, A C W (London Scottish) 1963 *F*, *W*, *I*
Boyle, A H W (St Thomas's Hospital, London Scottish) 1966 *A*, 1967 *F*, *NZ*, 1968 *F*, *W*, *I*
Brash, J C (Cambridge U) 1961 *E*
Breakey, R W (Gosforth) 1978 *E*
Brewis, N T (Edinburgh Inst FP) 1876 *E*, 1878 *E*, 1879 *I*, *E*, 1880 *I*, *E*
Brewster, A K (Stewart's-Melville FP) 1977 *E*, 1980 *I*, *F*, 1986 *E*, *I*, *R*
Brown, A H (Heriot's FP) 1928 *E*, 1929 *F*, *W*
Brown, A R (Gala) 1971 *E* (2[1C]), 1972 *F*, *W*, *E*

Brown, C H C (Dunfermline) 1929 *E*
Brown, D I (Cambridge U) 1933 *W, E, I*
Brown, G L (W of Scotland) 1969 *SA*, 1970 *F, W* (R), *I, E, A*, 1971 *F, W, I, E* (2[1C]), 1972 *F, W, E, NZ*, 1973 *E* (R), *P*, 1974 *W, E, I, F*, 1975 *I, F, W, E, A*, 1976 *F, W, E, I*
Brown, J A (Glasgow Acads) 1908 *W, I*
Brown, J B (Glasgow Acads) 1879 *I, E*, 1880 *I, E*, 1881 *I, E*, 1882 *I, E*, 1883 *W, I, E*, 1884 *W, I, E*, 1885 *I* 1,2, 1886 *W, I, E*
Brown, P C (W of Scotland, Gala) 1964 *F, NZ, W, I, E*, 1965 *I, E, SA*, 1966 *A*, 1969 *I, E*, 1970 *W, E*, 1971 *F, W, I, E* (2[1C]), 1972 *F, W, E, NZ*, 1973 *F, W, I, E, P*
Brown, T G (Heriot's FP) 1929 *W*
Brown, W D (Glasgow Acads) 1871 *E*, 1872 *E*, 1873 *E*, 1874 *E*, 1875 *E*
Brown, W S (Edinburgh Inst FP) 1880 *I, E*, 1882 *I, E*, 1883 *W, E*
Browning, A (Glasgow HSFP) 1920 *I*, 1922 *F, W, I*, 1923 *W, I, E*
Bruce, C R (Glasgow Acads) 1947 *F, W, I, E*, 1949 *F, W, I, E*
Bruce, N S (Blackheath, Army and London Scottish) 1958 *F, A, I, E*, 1959 *F, W, I, E*, 1960 *F, W, I, E, SA*, 1961 *F, SA, W, I, E*, 1962 *F, W, I, E*, 1963 *F, W, I, E*, 1964 *F, NZ, W, I, E*
Bruce, R M (Gordonians) 1947 *A*, 1948 *F, W, I*
Bruce-Lockhart, J H (London Scottish) 1913 *W*, 1920 *E*
Bruce-Lockhart, L (London Scottish) 1948 *E*, 1950 *F, W*, 1953 *I, E*
Bruce-Lockhart, R B (Cambridge U and London Scottish) 1937 *I*, 1939 *I, E*
Bryce, C C (Glasgow Acads) 1873 *E*, 1874 *E*
Bryce, R D H (W of Scotland) 1973 *I* (R)
Bryce, W E (Selkirk) 1922 *W, I, E*, 1923 *F, W, I, E*, 1924 *F, W, I, E*
Brydon, W R C (Heriot's FP) 1939 *W*
Buchanan, A (Royal HSFP) 1871 *E*
Buchanan, F G (Kelvinside Acads and Oxford U) 1910 *F*, 1911 *F, W*
Buchanan, J C R (Stewart's Coll FP) 1921 *W, I, E*, 1922 *W, I, E*, 1923 *F, W, I, E*, 1924 *F, W, I, E*, 1925 *F, I*
Buchanan-Smith, G A E (London Scottish, Heriot's FP) 1989 *Fj* (R), 1990 *Arg*
Bucher, A M (Edinburgh Acads) 1897 *E*
Budge, G M (Edinburgh Wands) 1950 *F, W, I, E*
Bullmore, H H (Edinburgh U) 1902 *I*
Burnell, A P (London Scottish) 1989 *E, I, F, Fj, R*, 1990 *I, F, W, E, Arg*, 1991 *F, W, E, I, R*, [*J, Z, I, WS, E, NZ*], 1992 *E, I, F, W*, 1993 *I, F, W, E, NZ*, 1994 *W, E, I, F, Arg* 1,2, *SA*
Burnet, P J (London Scottish and Edinburgh Acads) 1960 *SA*
Burnet, W (Hawick) 1912 *E*
Burnet, W A (W of Scotland) 1934 *W*, 1935 *W, I, E, NZ*, 1936 *W, I, E*
Burnett, J N (Heriot's FP) 1980 *I, F, W, E*
Burrell, G (Gala) 1950 *F, W, I*, 1951 *SA*

Cairns, A G (Watsonians) 1903 *W, I, E*, 1904 *W, I, E*, 1905 *W, I, E*, 1906 *W, I, E*
Calder, F (Stewart's-Melville FP) 1986 *F, W, E, I, R*, 1987 *I, F, W, E*, [*F, Z, R, NZ*], 1988 *I, F, W, E*, 1989 *W, E, I, F, R*, 1990 *I, F, W, E, NZ* 1,2, 1991 *R*, [*J, I, WS, E, NZ*]
Calder, J H (Stewart's-Melville FP) 1981 *F, W, E, I, NZ* 1,2, *R, A*, 1982 *E, I, F, W, A* 1,2, 1983 *I, F, W, E, NZ*, 1984 *W, E, I, F, A*, 1985 *I, F, W*
Callander, G J (Kelso) 1984 *R*, 1988 *I, F, W, E, A*
Cameron, A (Glasgow HSFP) 1948 *W*, 1950 *I, E*, 1951 *F, W, I, E, SA*, 1953 *I, E*, 1955 *F, W, I, E*, 1956 *F, W, I*
Cameron, A D (Hillhead HSFP) 1951 *F*, 1954 *F, W*
Cameron, A W (Watsonians) 1887 *W*, 1893 *W*, 1894 *I*
Cameron, D (Glasgow HSFP) 1953 *I, E*, 1954 *F, NZ, I, E*
Cameron, N W (Glasgow U) 1952 *E*, 1953 *F, W*
Campbell, A J (Hawick) 1984 *I, F, R*, 1985 *I, F, W, E*, 1986 *F, W, E, I, R*, 1988 *F, W, A*
Campbell, G T (London Scottish) 1892 *W, I, E*, 1893 *I, E*, 1894 *W, I, E*, 1895 *W, I, E*, 1896 *W, I, E*, 1897 *I*, 1899 *I*, 1900 *E*
Campbell, H H (Cambridge U, London Scottish) 1947 *I, E*, 1948 *I, E*
Campbell, J A (W of Scotland) 1878 *E*, 1879 *I, E*, 1881 *I, E*
Campbell, J A (Cambridge U) 1900 *I*
Campbell, N M (London Scottish) 1956 *F, W*
Campbell, S J (Dundee HSFP) 1995 *C, I, F, W, E*
Campbell-Lamerton, J R E (London Scottish) 1986 *F*, 1987 [*Z, R*(R)]
Campbell-Lamerton, M J (Halifax, Army, London Scottish) 1961 *F, SA, W, I*, 1962 *F, W, I, E*, 1963 *F, W, I, E*, 1964 *I, E*, 1965 *F, W, I, E, SA*, 1966 *F, W, I, E*
Carmichael, A B (W of Scotland) 1967 *I, NZ*, 1968 *F, W, I, E, A*, 1969 *F, W, I, E, SA*, 1970 *F, W, I, E, A*, 1971 *F, W, I, E*(2[1C]), 1972 *F, W, E, NZ*, 1973 *F, W, I, E, P*, 1974 *W, E, I, F*, 1975 *I, F, W, E, NZ, A*, 1976 *F, W, E, I*, 1977 *E, I*(R), *F, W*, 1978 *I*
Carmichael, J H (Watsonians) 1921 *F, W, I*
Carrick, J S (Glasgow Acads) 1876 *E*, 1877 *E*
Cassels, D Y (W of Scotland) 1880 *E*, 1881 *I*, 1882 *I, E*, 1883 *W, I, E*
Cathcart, C W (Edinburgh U) 1872 *E*, 1873 *E*, 1876 *E*
Cawkwell, G L (Oxford U) 1947 *F*
Chalmers, C M (Melrose) 1989 *W, E, I, F, Fj*, 1990 *I, F, W, E, NZ* 1,2, *Arg*, 1991 *F, W, E, I, R*, [*J, Z*(R), *I, WS, E, NZ*], 1992 *E, I, F, W, A* 1,2, 1993 *I, F, W, E, NZ*, 1994 *W, SA*, 1995 *C, I, F, W, E*
Chalmers, T (Glasgow Acads) 1871 *E*, 1872 *E*, 1873 *E*, 1874 *E*, 1875 *E*, 1876 *E*
Chambers, H F T (Edinburgh U) 1888 *W, I*, 1889 *W, I*
Charters, R G (Hawick) 1955 *W, I, E*
Chisholm, D H (Melrose) 1964 *I, E*, 1965 *E, SA*, 1966 *F, I, E, A*, 1967 *F, W, NZ*, 1968 *F, W, I*
Chisholm, R W T (Melrose) 1955 *I, E*, 1956 *F, W, I, E*, 1958 *F, W, A, I*, 1960 *SA*
Church, W C (Glasgow Acads) 1906 *W*
Clark, R L (Edinburgh Wands, Royal Navy) 1972 *F, W, E, NZ*, 1973 *F, W, I, E, P*
Clauss, P R A (Oxford U) 1891 *W, I, E*, 1892 *W, E*, 1895 *I*
Clay, A T (Edinburgh Acads) 1886 *W, I, E*, 1887 *I, W, E*, 1888 *W*
Clunies-Ross, A (St Andrews U) 1871 *E*
Coltman, S (Hawick) 1948 *I*, 1949 *F, W, I, E*
Colville, A G (Merchistonians, Blackheath) 1871 *E*, 1872 *E*
Connell, G C (Trinity Acads and London Scottish) 1968 *E, A*, 1969 *F, E*, 1970 *F*
Cooper, M McG (Oxford U) 1936 *W, I*
Corcoran, I (Gala) 1992 *A* 1(R)
Cordial, I F (Edinburgh Wands) 1952 *F, W, I, E*
Cotter, J L (Hillhead HSFP) 1934 *I, E*
Cottington, G S (Kelso) 1934 *I, E*, 1935 *W, I*, 1936 *E*
Coughtrie, S (Edinburgh Acads) 1959 *F, W, I, E*, 1962 *W, I, E*, 1963 *F, W, I, E*
Couper, J H (W of Scotland) 1896 *W, I*, 1899 *I*
Coutts, F H (Melrose, Army) 1947 *W, I, E*
Coutts, I D F (Old Alleynians) 1951 *F*, 1952 *E*
Cowan, R C (Selkirk) 1961 *F*, 1962 *F, W, I, E*
Cowie, W L K (Edinburgh Wands) 1953 *E*
Cownie, W B (Watsonians) 1893 *W, I, E*, 1894 *W, I, E*, 1895 *W, I, E*
Crabbie, G E (Edinburgh Acads) 1904 *W*
Crabbie, J E (Edinburgh Acads, Oxford U) 1900 *W*, 1902 *I*, 1903 *W, I*, 1904 *E*, 1905 *W*
Craig, J B (Heriot's FP) 1939 *W*
Cramb, R I (Harlequins) 1987 [*R*(R)], 1988 *I, F, A*
Cranston, A G (Hawick) 1976 *W, E, I*, 1977 *E, W*, 1978 *F* (R), *W, E, NZ*, 1981 *NZ* 1,2
Crawford, J A (Army, London Scottish) 1934 *I*
Crawford, W H (United Services, RN) 1938 *W, I, E*, 1939 *W, E*
Crichton-Miller, D (Gloucester) 1931 *W, I, E*
Crole, G B (Oxford U) 1920 *F, W, I, E*
Cronin, D F (Bath, London Scottish, Bourges) 1988 *I, F, W, E, A*, 1989 *W, E, I, F, Fj, R*, 1990 *I, F, W, E, NZ* 1,2, 1991 *F, W, E, I, R*, [*Z*], 1992 *A* 2, 1993 *I, F, W, E, NZ*, 1995 *C, I, F*
Cross, M (Merchistonians) 1875 *E*, 1876 *E*, 1877 *I, E*, 1878 *E*, 1879 *I, E*, 1880 *I, E*
Cross, W (Merchistonians) 1871 *E*, 1872 *E*
Cumming, R S (Aberdeen U) 1921 *F, W*
Cunningham, G (Oxford U) 1908 *W, I*, 1909 *W, E*, 1910 *F, I, E*, 1911 *E*
Cunningham, R F (Gala) 1978 *NZ*, 1979 *W, E*
Currie, L R (Dunfermline) 1947 *A*, 1948 *F, W, I*, 1949

F, W, I, E
Cuthbertson, W (Kilmarnock, Harlequins) 1980 *I*, 1981 *W, E, I, NZ* 1,2, *R, A*, 1982 *E, I, F, W, A* 1,2, 1983 *I, F, W, NZ*, 1984 *W, E, A*

Dalgleish, A (Gala) 1890 *W, E*, 1891 *W, I*, 1892 *W*, 1893 *W*, 1894 *W, I*
Dalgleish, K J (Edinburgh Wands, Cambridge U) 1951 *I, E*, 1953 *F, W*
Dallas, J D (Watsonians) 1903 *E*
Davidson, J A (London Scottish, Edinburgh Wands) 1959 *E*, 1960 *I, E*
Davidson, J N G (Edinburgh U) 1952 *F, W, I, E*, 1953 *F, W*, 1954 *F*
Davidson, J P (RIE Coll) 1873 *E*, 1874 *E*
Davidson, R S (Royal HSFP) 1893 *E*
Davies, D S (Hawick) 1922 *F, W, I, E*, 1923 *F, W, I, E*, 1924 *F, E*, 1925 *W, I, E*, 1926 *F, W, I, E*, 1927 *F, W, I*
Dawson, J C (Glasgow Acads) 1947 *A*, 1948 *F, W*, 1949 *F, W, I*, 1950 *F, W, I, E*, 1951 *F, W, I, E, SA*, 1952 *F, W, I, E*, 1953 *E*
Deans, C T (Hawick) 1978 *F, W, E, NZ*, 1979 *W, E, I, F, NZ*, 1980 *I, F*, 1981 *F, W, E, I, NZ* 1,2, *R, A*, 1982 *E, I, F, W, A* 1,2, 1983 *I, F, W, E, NZ*, 1984 *W, E, I, F, A*, 1985 *I, F, W, E*, 1986 *F, W, E, I, R*, 1987 *I, F, W, E*, [*F, Z, R, NZ*]
Deans, D T (Hawick) 1968 *E*
Deas, D W (Heriot's FP) 1947 *F, W*
Dick, L G (Loughborough Colls, Jordanhill, Swansea) 1972 *W* (R), *E*, 1974 *W, E, I, F*, 1975 *I, F, W, E, NZ, A*, 1976 *F*, 1977 *E*
Dick, R C S (Cambridge U, Guy's Hospital) 1934 *W, I, E*, 1935 *W, I, E, NZ*, 1936 *W, I, E*, 1937 *W*, 1938 *W, I, E*
Dickson, G (Gala) 1978 *NZ*, 1979 *W, E, I, F, NZ*, 1980 *W*, 1981 *F*, 1982 *W* (R)
Dickson, M R (Edinburgh U) 1905 *I*
Dickson, W M (Blackheath, Oxford U) 1912 *F, W, E, SA*, 1913 *F, W, I*
Dobson, J (Glasgow Acads) 1911 *E*, 1912 *F, W, I, E, SA*
Dobson, J D (Glasgow Acads) 1910 *I*
Dobson, W G (Heriot's FP) 1922 *W, I, E*,
Docherty, J T (Glasgow HSFP) 1955 *F, W*, 1956 *E*, 1958 *F, W, A, I, E*
Dods, F P (Edinburgh Acads) 1901 *I*
Dods, J H (Edinburgh Acads) 1895 *W, I, E*, 1896 *W, I, E*, 1897 *I, E*
Dods, M (Gala) 1994 *I*(t), *Arg* 1,2
Dods, P W (Gala) 1983 *I, F, W, E, NZ*, 1984 *W, E, I, F, R, A*, 1985 *I, F, W, E*, 1989 *W, E, I, F*, 1991 *I*(R), *R*, [*Z, NZ*(R)]
Donald, D G (Oxford U) 1914 *W, I*
Donald, R L H (Glasgow HSFP) 1921 *W, I, E*
Donaldson, W P (Oxford U, W of Scotland) 1893 *I*, 1894 *I*, 1895 *E*, 1896 *I, E*, 1899 *I*
Don-Wauchope, A R (Fettesian-Lorettonians) 1881 *E*, 1882 *E*, 1883 *W*, 1884 *W, I, E*, 1885 *W, I* 1,2, 1886 *W, I, E*, 1888 *I*
Don-Wauchope, P H (Fettesian-Lorettonians) 1885 *I* 1,2, 1886 *W*, 1887 *I, W, E*
Dorward, A F (Cambridge U, Gala) 1950 *F*, 1951 *SA*, 1952 *W, I, E*, 1953 *F, W, E*, 1955 *F*, 1956 *I, E*, 1957 *F, W, I, E*
Dorward, T F (Gala) 1938 *W, I, E*, 1939 *I, E*
Douglas, G (Jedforest) 1921 *W*
Douglas, J (Stewart's Coll FP) 1961 *F, SA, W, I, E*, 1962 *F, W, I, E*, 1963 *F, W, I*
Douty, P S (London Scottish) 1927 *A*, 1928 *F, W*
Drew, D (Glasgow Acads) 1871 *E*, 1876 *E*
Druitt, W A H (London Scottish) 1936 *W, I, E*
Drummond, A H (Kelvinside Acads) 1938 *W, I*
Drummond, C W (Melrose) 1947 *F, W, I, E*, 1948 *F, I, E*, 1950 *F, W, I, E*
Drybrough, A S (Edinburgh Wands, Merchistonians) 1902 *I*, 1903 *I*
Dryden, R H (Watsonians) 1937 *E*
Drysdale, D (Heriot's FP) 1923 *F, W, I, E*, 1924 *F, W, I, E*, 1925 *F, W, I, E*, 1926 *F, W, I, E*, 1927 *F, W, I, E, A*, 1928 *F, W, I, E*, 1929 *F*
Duff, P L (Glasgow Acads) 1936 *W, I*, 1938 *W, I, E*, 1939 *W*
Duffy, H (Jedforest) 1955 *F*
Duke, A (Royal HSFP) 1888 *W, I*, 1889 *W, I*, 1890 *W, I*
Duncan, A W (Edinburgh U) 1901 *W, I, E*, 1902 *W, I, E*
Duncan, D D (Oxford U) 1920 *F, W, I, E*
Duncan, M D F (W of Scotland) 1986 *F, W, E, R*, 1987 *I, F, W, E*, [*F, Z, R, NZ*], 1988 *I, F, W, E, A*, 1989 *W*
Duncan, M M (Fettesian-Lorettonians) 1888 *W*
Dunlop, J W (W of Scotland) 1875 *E*
Dunlop, Q (W of Scotland) 1971 *E* (2[1C])
Dykes, A S (Glasgow Acads) 1932 *E*
Dykes, J C (Glasgow Acads) 1922 *F, E*, 1924 *I*, 1925 *F, W, I*, 1926 *F, W, I, E*, 1927 *F, W, I, E, A*, 1928 *F, I*, 1929 *F, W, I*
Dykes, J M (Clydesdale, Glasgow HSFP) 1898 *I, E*, 1899 *W, E*, 1900 *W, I*, 1901 *W, I, E*, 1902 *E*

Edwards, D B (Heriot's FP) 1960 *I, E, SA*
Edwards, N G B (Harlequins, Northampton) 1992 *E, I, F, W, A* 1, 1994 *W*
Elgie, M K (London Scottish) 1954 *NZ, I, E, W*, 1955 *F, W, I, E*
Elliot, C (Langholm) 1958 *E*, 1959 *F*, 1960 *F*, 1963 *E*, 1964 *F, NZ, W, I, E*, 1965 *F, W, I*
Elliot, M (Hawick) 1895 *W*, 1896 *E*, 1897 *I, E*, 1898 *I, E*
Elliot, T (Gala) 1905 *E*
Elliot, T (Gala) 1955 *W, I, E*, 1956 *F, W, I, E*, 1957 *F, W, I, E*, 1958 *W, A, I*
Elliot, T G (Langholm) 1968 *W, A*, 1969 *F, W*, 1970 *E*
Elliot, W I D (Edinburgh Acads) 1947 *F, W, E, A*, 1948 *F, W, I, E*, 1949 *F, W, I, E*, 1950 *F, W, I, E*, 1951 *F, W, I, E, SA*, 1952 *F, W, I, E*, 1954 *NZ, I, E, W*
Emslie, W D (Royal HSFP) 1930 *F*, 1932 *I*
Evans, H L (Edinburgh U) 1885 *I* 1,2
Ewart, E N (Glasgow Acads) 1879 *E*, 1880 *I, E*

Fahmy, Dr E C (Abertillery) 1920 *F, W, I, E*
Fasson, F H (London Scottish, Edinburgh Wands) 1900 *W*, 1901 *W, I*, 1902 *W, E*
Fell, A N (Edinburgh U) 1901 *W, I, E*, 1902 *W, E*, 1903 *W, E*
Ferguson, J H (Gala) 1928 *W*
Ferguson, W G (Royal HSFP) 1927 *A*, 1928 *F, W, I, E*
Fergusson, E A J (Oxford U) 1954 *F, NZ, I, E, W*
Finlay, A B (Edinburgh Acads) 1875 *E*
Finlay, J F (Edinburgh Acads) 1871 *E*, 1872 *E*, 1874 *E*, 1875 *E*
Finlay, N J (Edinburgh Acads) 1875 *E*, 1876 *E*, 1878 *E*, 1879 *I, E*, 1880 *I, E*, 1881 *I, E*
Finlay, R (Watsonians) 1948 *E*
Fisher, A T (Waterloo, Watsonians) 1947 *I, E*
Fisher, C D (Waterloo) 1975 *NZ, A*, 1976 *W, E, I*
Fisher, D (W of Scotland) 1893 *I*
Fisher, J P (Royal HSFP, London Scottish) 1963 *E*, 1964 *F, NZ, W, I, E*, 1965 *F, W, I, E, SA*, 1966 *F, W, I, E, A*, 1967 *F, W, I, E, NZ*, 1968 *F, W, I, E*
Fleming, C J N (Edinburgh Wands) 1896 *I, E*, 1897 *I*
Fleming, G R (Glasgow Acads) 1875 *E*, 1876 *E*
Fletcher, H N (Edinburgh U) 1904 *E*, 1905 *W*
Flett, A B (Edinburgh U) 1901 *W, I, E*, 1902 *W, I*
Forbes, J L (Watsonians) 1905 *W*, 1906 *I, E*
Ford, D St C (United Services, RN) 1930 *I, E*, 1931 *E*, 1932 *W, I*
Ford, J R (Gala) 1893 *I*
Forrest, J E (Glasgow Acads) 1932 *SA*, 1935 *E, NZ*
Forrest, J G S (Cambridge U) 1938 *W, I, E*
Forrest, W T (Hawick) 1903 *W, I, E*, 1904 *W, I, E*, 1905 *W, I*
Forsayth, H H (Oxford U) 1921 *F, W, I, E*, 1922 *W, I, E*
Forsyth, I W (Stewart's Coll FP) 1972 *NZ*, 1973 *F, W, I, E, P*
Forsyth, J (Edinburgh U) 1871 *E*
Foster, R A (Hawick) 1930 *W*, 1932 *SA, I, E*
Fox, J (Gala) 1952 *F, W*, I, *E*
Frame, J N M (Edinburgh U, Gala) 1967 *NZ*, 1968 *F, W, I, E*, 1969 *W, I, E, SA*, 1970 *F, W, I, E, A*, 1971 *F, W, I, E* (2[1C]), 1972 *F, W, E*, 1973 *P* (R)
France, C (Kelvinside Acads) 1903 *I*
Fraser, C F P (Glasgow U) 1888 *W*, 1889 *W*
Fraser, J W (Edinburgh Inst FP) 1881 *E*
Fraser, R (Cambridge U) 1911 *F, W, I, E*
French, J (Glasgow Acads) 1886 *W*, 1887 *I, W, E*
Frew, A (Edinburgh U) 1901 *W, I, E*

Frew, G M (Glasgow HSFP) 1906 *SA*, 1907 *W*, *I*, *E*, 1908 *W*, *I*, *E*, 1909 *W*, *I*, *E*, 1910 *F*, *W*, *I*, 1911 *I*, *E*
Friebe, J P (Glasgow HSFP) 1952 *E*
Fulton, A K (Edinburgh U, Dollar Acads) 1952 *F*, 1954 *F*
Fyfe, K C (Cambridge U, Sale, London Scottish) 1933 *W*, *E*, 1934 *E*, 1935 *W*, *I*, *E*, *NZ*, 1936 *W*, *E*, 1939 *I*

Gallie, G H (Edinburgh Acads) 1939 *W*
Gallie, R A (Glasgow Acads) 1920 *F*, *W*, *I*, *E*, 1921 *F*, *W*, *I*, *E*
Gammell, W B B (Edinburgh Wands) 1977 *I*, *F*, *W*, 1978 *W*, *E*
Geddes, I C (London Scottish) 1906 *SA*, 1907 *W*, *I*, *E*, 1908 *W*, *E*
Geddes, K I (London Scottish) 1947 *F*, *W*, *I*, *E*
Gedge, H T S (Oxford U, London Scottish, Edinburgh Wands) 1894 *W*, *I*, *E*, 1896 *E*, 1899 *W*, *E*
Gedge, P M S (Edinburgh Wands) 1933 *I*
Gemmill, R (Glasgow HSFP) 1950 *F*, *W*, *I*, *E*, 1951 *F*, *W*, *I*
Gibson, W R (Royal HSFP) 1891 *I*, *E*, 1892 *W*, *I*, *E*, 1893 *W*, *I*, *E*, 1894 *W*, *I*, *E*, 1895 *W*, *I*, *E*
Gilbert-Smith, D S (London Scottish) 1952 *E*
Gilchrist, J (Glasgow Acads) 1925 *F*
Gill, A D (Gala) 1973 *P*, 1974 *W*, *E*, *I*, *F*
Gillespie, J I (Edinburgh Acads) 1899 *E*, 1900 *W*, *E*, 1901 *W*, *I*, *E*, 1902 *W*, *I*, 1904 *I*, *E*
Gillies, A C (Watsonians) 1924 *W*, *I*, *E*, 1925 *F*, *W*, *E*, 1926 *F*, *W*, 1927 *F*, *W*, *I*, *E*
Gilray, C M (Oxford U, London Scottish) 1908 *E*, 1909 *W*, *E*, 1912 *I*
Glasgow, R J C (Dunfermline) 1962 *F*, *W*, *I*, *E*, 1963 *I*, *E*, 1964 *I*, *E*, 1965 *W*, *I*
Glen, W S (Edinburgh Wands) 1955 *W*
Gloag, L G (Cambridge U) 1949 *F*, *W*, *I*, *E*
Goodfellow, J (Langholm) 1928 *W*, *I*, *E*
Goodhue, F W J (London Scottish) 1890 *W*, *I*, *E*, 1891 *W*, *I*, *E*, 1892 *W*, *I*, *E*
Gordon, R (Edinburgh Wands) 1951 *W*, 1952 *F*, *W*, *I*, *E*, 1953 *W*
Gordon, R E (Royal Artillery) 1913 *F*, *W*, *I*
Gordon, R J (London Scottish) 1982 *A* 1,2
Gore, A C (London Scottish) 1882 *I*
Gossman, B M (W of Scotland) 1980 *W*, 1983 *F*, *W*
Gossman, J S (W of Scotland) 1980 *E* (R)
Gowans, J J (Cambridge U, London Scottish) 1893 *W*, 1894 *W*, *E*, 1895 *W*, *I*, *E*, 1896 *I*, *E*
Gowland, G C (London Scottish) 1908 *W*, 1909 *W*, *E*, 1910 *F*, *W*, *I*, *E*
Gracie, A L (Harlequins) 1921 *F*, *W*, *I*, *E*, 1922 *F*, *W*, *I*, *E*, 1923 *F*, *W*, *I*, *E*, 1924 *F*
Graham, I N (Edinburgh Acads) 1939 *I*, *E*
Graham, J (Kelso) 1926 *I*, *E*, 1927 *F*, *W*, *I*, *E*, *A*, 1928 *F*, *W*, *I*, *E*, 1930 *I*, *E*, 1932 *SA*, *W*
Graham, J H S (Edinburgh Acads) 1876 *E*, 1877 *I*, *E*, 1878 *E*, 1879 *I*, *E*, 1880 *I*, *E*, 1881 *I*, *E*
Grant, D (Hawick) 1965 *F*, *E*, *SA*, 1966 *F*, *W*, *I*, *E*, *A*, 1967 *F*, *W*, *I*, *E*, *NZ*, 1968 *F*
Grant, D M (East Midlands) 1911 *W*, *I*
Grant, M L (Harlequins) 1955 *F*, 1956 *F*, *W*, 1957 *F*
Grant, T O (Hawick) 1960 *I*, *E*, *SA*, 1964 *F*, *NZ*, *W*
Grant, W St C (Craigmount) 1873 *E*, 1874 *E*
Gray, C A (Nottingham) 1989 *W*, *E*, *I*, *F*, *Fj*, *R*, 1990 *I*, *F*, *W*, *E*, *NZ* 1,2, *Arg*, 1991 *F*, *W*, *E*, *I*, [*J*, *I*, *WS*, *E*, *NZ*]
Gray, D (W of Scotland) 1978 *E*, 1979 *I*, *F*, *NZ*, 1980 *I*, *F*, *W*, *E*, 1981 *F*
Gray, G L (Gala) 1935 *NZ*, 1937 *W*, *I*, *E*
Gray, T (Northampton, Heriot's FP) 1950 *E*, 1951 *F*, *E*
Greenlees, H D (Leicester) 1927 *A*, 1928 *F*, *W*, 1929 *I*, *E*, 1930 *E*
Greenlees, J R C (Cambridge U, Kelvinside Acads) 1900 *I*, 1902 *W*, *I*, *E*, 1903 *W*, *I*, *E*
Greenwood, J T (Dunfermline and Perthshire Acads) 1952 *F*, 1955 *F*, *W*, *I*, *E*, 1956 *F*, *W*, *I*, *E*, 1957 *F*, *W*, *E*, 1958 *F*, *W*, *A*, *I*, *E*, 1959 *F*, *W*, *I*
Greig, A (Glasgow HSFP) 1911 *I*
Greig, L L (Glasgow Acads, United Services) 1905 *NZ*, 1906 *SA*, 1907 *W*, 1908 *W*, *I*
Greig, R C (Glasgow Acads) 1893 *W*, 1897 *I*
Grieve, C F (Oxford U) 1935 *W*, 1936 *E*
Grieve, R M (Kelso) 1935 *W*, *I*, *E*, *NZ*, 1936 *W*, *I*, *E*
Gunn, A W (Royal HSFP) 1912 *F*, *W*, *I*, *SA*, 1913 *F*

Scott Hastings, who became Scotland's most-capped centre in 1994-95, accelerates away from England captain Will Carling in the Grand Slam showdown at Twickenham.

Hamilton, A S (Headingley) 1914 *W*, 1920 *F*
Hamilton, H M (W of Scotland) 1874 *E*, 1875 *E*
Hannah, R S M (W of Scotland) 1971 *I*
Harrower, P R (London Scottish) 1885 *W*
Hart, J G M (London Scottish) 1951 *SA*
Hart, T M (Glasgow U) 1930 *W*, *I*
Hart, W (Melrose) 1960 *SA*
Harvey, L (Greenock Wands) 1899 *I*
Hastie, A J (Melrose) 1961 *W*, *I*, *E*, 1964 *I*, *E*, 1965 *E*, *SA*, 1966 *F*, *W*, *I*, *E*, *A*, 1967 *F*, *W*, *I*, *NZ*, 1968 *F*, *W*
Hastie, I R (Kelso) 1955 *F*, 1958 *F*, *E*, 1959 *F*, *W*, *I*
Hastie, J D H (Melrose) 1938 *W*, *I*, *E*
Hastings, A G (Cambridge U, Watsonians, London Scottish) 1986 *F*, *W*, *E*, *I*, *R*, 1987 *I*, *F*, *W*, *E*, [*F*, *Z*, *R*, *NZ*], 1988 *I*, *F*, *W*, *E*, *A*, 1989 *Fj*, *R*, 1990 *I*, *F*, *W*, *E*, *NZ* 1,2, *Arg*, 1991 *F*, *W*, *E*, *I*, [*J*, *I*, *WS*, *E*, *NZ*], 1992 *E*, *I*, *F*, *W*, *A* 1, 1993 *I*, *F*, *W*, *E*, *NZ*, 1994 *W*, *E*, *I*, *F*, *SA*, 1995 *C*, *I*, *F*, *W*, *E*
Hastings, S (Watsonians) 1986 *F*, *W*, *E*, *I*, *R*, 1987 *I*, *F*, *W*, [*R*], 1988 *I*, *F*, *W*, *A*, 1989 *W*, *E*, *I*, *F*, *Fj*, *R*, 1990 *I*, *F*, *W*, *E*, *NZ* 1,2, *Arg*, 1991 *F*, *W*, *E*, *I*, [*J*, *Z*, *I*, *WS*, *E*, *NZ*], 1992 *E*, *I*, *F*, *W*, *A* 1,2, 1993 *I*, *F*, *W*, *E*, *NZ*, 1994 *E*, *I*, *F*, *SA*, 1995 *W*, *E*
Hay, B H (Boroughmuir) 1975 *NZ*, *A*, 1976 *F*, 1978 *I*, *F*, *W*, *E*, *NZ*, 1979 *W*, *E*, *I*, *F*, *NZ*, 1980 *I*, *F*, *W*, *E*, 1981 *F*, *W*, *E*, *I*, *NZ* 1,2
Hay-Gordon, J R (Edinburgh Acads) 1875 *E*, 1877 *I*, *E*
Hegarty, C B (Hawick) 1978 *I*, *F*, *W*, *E*
Hegarty, J J (Hawick) 1951 *F*, 1953 *F*, *W*, *I*, *E*, 1955 *F*
Henderson, B C (Edinburgh Wands) 1963 *E*, 1964 *F*, *I*, *E*, 1965 *F*, *W*, *I*, *E*, 1966 *F*, *W*, *I*, *E*
Henderson, F W (London Scottish) 1900 *W*, *I*,
Henderson, I C (Edinburgh Acads) 1939 *I*, *E*, 1947 *F*, *W*, *E*, *A*, 1948 *I*, *E*
Henderson, J H (Oxford U, Richmond) 1953 *F*, *W*, *I*, *E*, 1954 *F*, *NZ*, *I*, *E*, *W*
Henderson, J M (Edinburgh Acads) 1933 *W*, *E*, *I*
Henderson, J Y M (Watsonians) 1911 *E*
Henderson, M M (Dunfermline) 1937 *W*, *I*, *E*
Henderson, N F (London Scottish) 1892 *I*
Henderson, R G (Newcastle Northern) 1924 *I*, *E*
Hendrie, K G P (Heriot's FP) 1924 *F*, *W*, *I*
Hendry, T L (Clydesdale) 1893 *W*, *I*, *E*, 1895 *I*
Henriksen, E H (Royal HSFP) 1953 *I*
Hepburn, D P (Woodford) 1947 *A*, 1948 *F*, *W*, *I*, *E*, 1949 *F*, *W*, *I*, *E*
Heron, G (Glasgow Acads) 1874 *E*, 1875 *E*
Hill, C C P (St Andrew's U) 1912 *F*, *I*
Hilton, D I W (Bath) 1995 *C*, *I*, *F*, *W*, *E*
Hinshelwood, A J W (London Scottish) 1966 *F*, *W*, *I*, *E*, *A*, 1967 *F*, *W*, *I*, *E*, *NZ*, 1968 *F*, *W*, *I*, *E*, *A*, 1969 *F*, *W*, *I*, *SA*, 1970 *F*, *W*
Hodgson, C G (London Scottish) 1968 *I*, *E*
Hogg, C D (Melrose) 1992 *A* 1,2, 1993 *NZ*(R), 1994 *Arg* 1,2
Hogg, C G (Boroughmuir) 1978 *F* (R), *W* (R)
Holms, W F (RIE Coll) 1886 *W*, *E*, 1887 *I*, *E*, 1889 *W*, *I*
Horsburgh, G B (London Scottish) 1937 *W*, *I*, *E*, 1938 *W*, *I*, *E*, 1939 *W*, *I*, *E*
Howie, D D (Kirkcaldy) 1912 *F*, *W*, *I*, *E*, *SA*, 1913 *F*, *W*
Howie, R A (Kirkcaldy) 1924 *F*, *W*, *I*, *E*, 1925 *W*, *I*, *E*
Hoyer-Millar, G C (Oxford U) 1953 *I*
Huggan, J L (London Scottish) 1914 *E*
Hume, J (Royal HSFP) 1912 *F*, 1920 *F*, 1921 *F*, *W*, *I*, *E*, 1922 *F*
Hume, J W G (Oxford U, Edinburgh Wands) 1928 *I*, 1930 *F*
Hunter, F (Edinburgh U) 1882 *I*
Hunter, I G (Selkirk) 1984 *I* (R), 1985 *F* (R), *W*, *E*
Hunter, J M (Cambridge U) 1947 *F*
Hunter, M D (Glasgow High) 1974 *F*
Hunter, W J (Hawick) 1964 *F*, *NZ*, *W*, 1967 *F*, *W*, *I*, *E*
Hutchison, W R (Glasgow HSFP) 1911 *E*
Hutton, A H M (Dunfermline) 1932 *I*
Hutton, J E (Harlequins) 1930 *E*, 1931 *F*

Inglis, H M (Edinburgh Acads) 1951 *F*, *W*, *I*, *E*, *SA*, 1952 *W*, *I*
Inglis, J M (Selkirk) 1952 *E*
Inglis, W M (Cambridge U, Royal Engineers) 1937 *W*, *I*, *E*, 1938 *W*, *I*, *E*
Innes, J R S (Aberdeen GSFP) 1939 *W*, *I*, *E*, 1947 *A*, 1948 *F*, *W*, *I*, *E*
Ireland, J C H (Glasgow HSFP) 1925 *W*, *I*, *E*, 1926 *F*, *W*, *I*, *E*, 1927 *F*, *W*, *I*, *E*
Irvine, A R (Heriot's FP) 1972 *NZ*, 1973 *F*, *W*, *I*, *E*, *P*, 1974 *W*, *E*, *I*, *F*, 1975 *I*, *F*, *W*, *E*, *NZ*, *A*, 1976 *F*, *W*, *E*, *I*, 1977 *E*, *I*, *F*, *W*, 1978 *I*, *F*, *E*, *NZ*, 1979 *W*, *E*, *I*, *F*, *NZ*, 1980 *I*, *F*, *W*, *E*, 1981 *F*, *W*, *E*, *I*, *NZ* 1,2, *R*, *A*, 1982 *E*, *I*, *F*, *W*, *A* 1,2
Irvine, D R (Edinburgh Acads) 1878 *E*, 1879 *I*, *E*
Irvine, R W (Edinburgh Acads) 1871 *E*, 1872 *E*, 1873 *E*, 1874 *E*, 1875 *E*, 1876 *E*, 1877 *I*, *E*, 1878 *E*, 1879 *I*, *E*, 1880 *I*, *E*
Irvine, T W (Edinburgh Acads) 1885 *I* 1,2, 1886 *W*, *I*, *E*, 1887 *I*, *W*, *E*, 1888 *W*, *I*, 1889 *I*

Jackson, K L T (Oxford U) 1933 *W*, *E*, *I*, 1934 *W*
Jackson, T G H (Army) 1947 *F*, *W*, *E*, *A*, 1948 *F*, *W*, *I*, *E*, 1949 *F*, *W*, *I*, *E*
Jackson, W D (Hawick) 1964 *I*, 1965 *E*, *SA*, 1968 *A*, 1969 *F*, *W*, *I*, *E*
Jamieson, J (W of Scotland) 1883 *W*, *I*, *E*, 1884 *W*, *I*, *E*, 1885 *W*, *I* 1,2
Jardine, I C (Stirling County) 1993 *NZ*, 1994 *W*, *E*(R), *Arg* 1,2, 1995 *C*, *I*, *F*
Jeffrey, J (Kelso) 1984 *A*, 1985 *I*, *E*, 1986 *F*, *W*, *E*, *I*, *R*, 1987 *I*, *F*, *W*, *E*, [*F*, *Z*, *R*], 1988 *I*, *W*, *A*, 1989 *W*, *E*, *I*, *F*, *Fj*, *R*, 1990 *I*, *F*, *W*, *E*, *NZ* 1,2, *Arg*, 1991 *F*, *W*, *E*, *I*, [*J*, *I*, *WS*, *E*, *NZ*]
Johnston, D I (Watsonians) 1979 *NZ*, 1980 *I*, *F*, *W*, *E*, 1981 *R*, *A*, 1982 *E*, *I*, *F*, *W*, *A* 1,2, 1983 *I*, *F*, *W*, *NZ*, 1984 *W*, *E*, *I*, *F*, *R*, 1986 *F*, *W*, *E*, *I*, *R*
Johnston, H H (Edinburgh Collegian FP) 1877 *I*, *E*
Johnston, J (Melrose) 1951 *SA*, 1952 *F*, *W*, *I*, *E*
Johnston, W C (Glasgow HSFP) 1922 *F*
Johnston, W G S (Cambridge U) 1935 *W*, *I*, 1937 *W*, *I*, *E*
Joiner, C A (Melrose) 1994 *Arg* 1,2, 1995 *C*, *I*, *F*, *W*, *E*
Jones, P M (Gloucester) 1992 *W*(R)
Junor, J E (Glasgow Acads) 1876 *E*, 1877 *I*, *E*, 1878 *E*, 1879 *E*, 1881 *I*

Keddie, R R (Watsonians) 1967 *NZ*
Keith, G J (Wasps) 1968 *F*, *W*
Keller, D H (London Scottish) 1949 *F*, *W*, *I*, *E*, 1950 *F*, *W*, *I*
Kelly, R F (Watsonians) 1927 *A*, 1928 *F*, *W*, *E*
Kemp, J W Y (Glasgow HSFP) 1954 *W*, 1955 *F*, *W*, *I*, *E*, 1956 *F*, *W*, *I*, *E*, 1957 *F*, *W*, *I*, *E*, 1958 *F*, *W*, *A*, *I*, *E*, 1959 *F*, *W*, *I*, *E*, 1960 *F*, *W*, *I*, *E*, *SA*
Kennedy, A E (Watsonians) 1983 *NZ*, 1984 *W*, *E*, *A*
Kennedy, F (Stewart's Coll FP) 1920 *F*, *W*, *I*, *E*, 1921 *E*
Kennedy, N (W of Scotland) 1903 *W*, *I*, *E*
Ker, A B M (Kelso) 1988 *W*, *E*
Ker, H T (Glasgow Acads) 1887 *I*, *W*, *E*, 1888 *I*, 1889 *W*, 1890 *I*, *E*
Kerr, D S (Heriot's FP) 1923 *F*, *W*, 1924 *F*, 1926 *I*, *E*, 1927 *W*, *I*, *E*, 1928 *I*, *E*
Kerr, G C (Old Dunelmians, Edinburgh Wands) 1898 *I*, *E*, 1899 *I*, *W*, *E*, 1900 *W*, *I*, *E*
Kerr, J M (Heriot's FP) 1935 *NZ*, 1936 *I*, *E*, 1937 *W*, *I*
Kerr, W (London Scottish) 1953 *E*
Kidston, D W (Glasgow Acads) 1883 *W*, *E*
Kidston, W H (W of Scotland) 1874 *E*
Kilgour, I J (RMC Sandhurst) 1921 *F*
King, J H F (Selkirk) 1953 *F*, *W*, *E*, 1954 *E*
Kininmonth, P W (Oxford U, Richmond) 1949 *F*, *W*, *I*, *E*, 1950 *F*, *W*, *I*, *E*, 1951 *F*, *W*, *I*, *E*, *SA*, 1952 *F*, *W*, *I*, 1954 *F*, *NZ*, *I*, *E*, *W*
Kinnear, R M (Heriot's FP) 1926 *F*, *W*, *I*
Knox, J (Kelvinside Acads) 1903 *W*, *I*, *E*
Kyle, W E (Hawick) 1902 *W*, *I*, *E*, 1903 *W*, *I*, *E*, 1904 *W*, *I*, *E*, 1905 *W*, *I*, *E*, *NZ*, 1906 *W*, *I*, *E*, 1908 *E*, 1909 *W*, *I*, *E*, 1910 *W*

Laidlaw, A S (Hawick) 1897 *I*
Laidlaw, F A L (Melrose) 1965 *F*, *W*, *I*, *E*, *SA*, 1966 *F*, *W*, *I*, *E*, *A*, 1967 *F*, *W*, *I*, *E*, *NZ*, 1968 *F*, *W*, *I*, *A*, 1969 *F*, *W*, *I*, *E*, *SA*, 1970 *F*, *W*, *I*, *E*, *A*, 1971 *F*, *W*, *I*
Laidlaw, R J (Jedforest) 1980 *I*, *F*, *W*, *E*, 1981 *F*, *W*, *E*, *I*, *NZ* 1,2, *R*, *A*, 1982 *E*, *I*, *F*, *W*, *A* 1,2, 1983 *I*, *F*, *W*, *E*, *NZ*, 1984 *W*, *E*, *I*, *F*, *R*, *A*, 1985 *I*, *F*, 1986 *F*, *W*, *E*, *I*, *R*, 1987 *I*, *F*, *W*, *E*, [*F*, *R*, *NZ*], 1988 *I*, *F*, *W*, *E*
Laing, A D (Royal HSFP) 1914 *W*, *I*, *E*, 1920 *F*, *W*, *I*, 1921 *F*
Lambie, I K (Watsonians) 1978 *NZ* (R), 1979 *W*, *E*, *NZ*

Lambie, L B (Glasgow HSFP) 1934 *W, I, E*, 1935 *W, I, E, NZ*
Lamond, G A W (Kelvinside Acads) 1899 *W, E*, 1905 *E*
Lang, D (Paisley) 1876 *E*, 1877 *I*
Langrish, R W (London Scottish) 1930 *F*, 1931 *F, W, I*
Lauder, W (Neath) 1969 *I, E, SA*, 1970 *F, W, I, A*, 1973 *F*, 1974 *W, E, I, F*, 1975 *I, F, NZ, A*, 1976 *F*, 1977 *E*
Laughland, I H P (London Scottish) 1959 *F*, 1960 *F, W, I, E*, 1961 *SA, W, I, E*, 1962 *F, W, I, E*, 1963 *F, W, I*, 1964 *F, NZ, W, I, E*, 1965 *F, W, I, E, SA*, 1966 *F, W, I, E*, 1967 *E*
Lawrie, J R (Melrose) 1922 *F, W, I, E*, 1923 *F, W, I, E*, 1924 *W, I, E*
Lawrie, K G (Gala) 1980 *F* (R), *W, E*
Lawson, A J M (Edinburgh Wands, London Scottish) 1972 *F* (R), *E*, 1973 *F*, 1974 *W, E*, 1976 *E, I*, 1977 *E*, 1978 *NZ*, 1979 *W, E, I, F, NZ*, 1980 *W* (R)
Lawther, T H B (Old Millhillians) 1932 *SA, W*
Ledingham, G A (Aberdeen GSFP) 1913 *F*
Lees, J B (Gala) 1947 *I, A*, 1948 *F, W, E*
Leggatt, H T O (Watsonians) 1891 *W, I, E*, 1892 *W, I*, 1893 *W, E*, 1894 *I, E*
Lely, W G (Cambridge U, London Scottish) 1909 *I*
Leslie, D G (Dundee HSFP, W of Scotland, Gala) 1975 *I, F, W, E, NZ, A*, 1976 *F, W, E, I*, 1978 *NZ*, 1980 *E*, 1981 *W, E, I, NZ* 1,2, *R, A*, 1982 *E*, 1983 *I, F, W, E*, 1984 *W, E, I, F, R*, 1985 *F, W, E*
Liddell, E H (Edinburgh U) 1922 *F, W, I*, 1923 *F, W, I, E*
Lind, H (Dunfermline) 1928 *I*, 1931 *F, W, I, E*, 1932 *SA, W, E*, 1933 *W, E, I*, 1934 *W, I, E*, 1935 *I*, 1936 *E*
Lindsay, A B (London Hospital) 1910 *I*, 1911 *I*
Lindsay, G C (London Scottish) 1884 *W*, 1885 *I* 1, 1887 *W, E*
Lindsay-Watson, R H (Hawick) 1909 *I*
Lineen, S R P (Boroughmuir) 1989 *W, E, I, F, Fj, R*, 1990 *I, F, W, E, NZ* 1,2, *Arg*, 1991 *F, W, E, I, R*, [*J, Z, I, E, NZ*], 1992 *E, I, F, W, A* 1,2
Little, A W (Hawick) 1905 *W*
Logan, K M (Stirling County) 1992 *A* 2, 1993 *E*(R), *NZ*(t), 1994 *W, E, I, F, Arg* 1,2, *SA*, 1995 *C, I, F, W, E*
Logan, W R (Edinburgh U, Edinburgh Wands) 1931 *E*, 1932 *SA, W, I*, 1933 *W, E, I*, 1934 *W, I, E*, 1935 *W, I, E, NZ*, 1936 *W, I, E*, 1937 *W, I, E*
Lorraine, H D B (Oxford U) 1933 *W, E, I*
Loudoun-Shand, E G (Oxford U) 1913 *E*
Lowe, J D (Heriot's FP) 1934 *W*
Lumsden, I J M (Bath, Watsonians) 1947 *F, W, A*, 1949 *F, W, I, E*
Lyall, G G (Gala) 1947 *A*, 1948 *F, W, I, E*
Lyall, W J C (Edinburgh Acads) 1871 *E*

Mabon, J T (Jedforest) 1898 *I, E*, 1899 *I*, 1900 *I*
Macarthur, J P (Waterloo) 1932 *E*
MacCallum, J C (Watsonians) 1905 *E, NZ*, 1906 *W, I, E, SA*, 1907 *W, I, E*, 1908 *W, I, E*, 1909 *W, I, E*, 1910 *F, W, I, E*, 1911 *F, I, E*, 1912 *F, W, I, E*
McClung, T (Edinburgh Acads) 1956 *I, E*, 1957 *W, I, E*, 1959 *F, W, I*, 1960 *W*
McClure, G B (W of Scotland) 1873 *E*
McClure, J H (W of Scotland) 1872 *E*
McCowan, D (W of Scotland) 1880 *I, E*, 1881 *I, E*, 1882 *I, E*, 1883 *I, E*, 1884 *I, E*
McCowat, R H (Glasgow Acads) 1905 *I*
McCrae, I G (Gordonians) 1967 *E*, 1968 *I*, 1969 *F* (R), *W*, 1972 *F, NZ*
McCrow, J W S (Edinburgh Acads) 1921 *I*
Macdonald, A E D (Heriot's FP) 1993 *NZ*
McDonald, C (Jedforest) 1947 *A*
Macdonald, D C (Edinburgh U) 1953 *F, W*, 1958 *I, E*
Macdonald, D S M (Oxford U, London Scottish, W of Scotland) 1977 *E, I, F, W*, 1978 *I, W, E*
Macdonald, J D (London Scottish, Army) 1966 *F, W, I, E*, 1967 *F, W, I, E*
Macdonald, J M (Edinburgh Wands) 1911 *W*
Macdonald, J S (Edinburgh U) 1903 *E*, 1904 *W, I, E*, 1905 *W*
Macdonald, K R (Stewart's Coll FP) 1956 *F, W, I*, 1957 *W, I, E*
Macdonald, R (Edinburgh U) 1950 *F, W, I, E*
McDonald, W A (Glasgow U) 1889 *W*, 1892 *I, E*
Macdonald, W G (London Scottish) 1969 *I* (R)
Macdougall, J B (Greenock Wands, Wakefield) 1913 *F*, 1914 *I*, 1921 *F, I, E*
McEwan, M C (Edinburgh Acads) 1886 *E*, 1887 *I, W, E*, 1888 *W, I*, 1889 *W, I*, 1890 *W, I, E*, 1891 *W, I, E*, 1892 *E*
MacEwan, N A (Gala, Highland) 1971 *F, W, I, E* (2[1C]), 1972 *F, W, E, NZ*, 1973 *F, W, I, E, P*, 1974 *W, E, I, F*, 1975 *W, E*
McEwan, W M C (Edinburgh Acads) 1894 *W, E*, 1895 *W, E*, 1896 *W, I, E*, 1897 *I, E*, 1898 *I, E*, 1889 *I, W, E*, 1900 *W, E*
MacEwen, R K G (Cambridge U, London Scottish) 1954 *F, NZ, I, W*, 1956 *F, W, I, E*, 1957 *F, W, I, E*, 1958 *W*
Macfarlan, D J (London Scottish) 1883 *W*, 1884 *W, I, E*, 1886 *W, I*, 1887 *I*, 1888 *I*
McFarlane, J L H (Edinburgh U) 1871 *E*, 1872 *E*, 1873 *E*
McGaughey, S K (Hawick) 1984 *R*
McGeechan, I R (Headingley) 1972 *NZ*, 1973 *F, W, I, E, P*, 1974 *W, E, I, F*, 1975 *I, F, W, E, NZ, A*, 1976 *F, W, E, I*, 1977 *E, I, F, W*, 1978 *I, F, W, NZ*, 1979 *W, E, I, F*
McGlashan, T P L (Royal HSFP) 1947 *F, I, E*, 1954 *F, NZ, I, E, W*
MacGregor, D G (Watsonians, Pontypridd) 1907 *W, I, E*
MacGregor, G (Cambridge U) 1890 *W, I, E*, 1891 *W, I, E*, 1893 *W, I, E*, 1894 *W, I, E*, 1896 *E*
MacGregor, I A A (Hillhead HSFP, Llanelli) 1955 *I, E*, 1956 *F, W, I, E*, 1957 *F, W, I*
MacGregor, J R (Edinburgh U) 1909 *I*
McGuinness, G M (W of Scotland) 1982 *A* 1,2, 1983 *I*, 1985 *I, F, W, E*
McHarg, A F (W of Scotland, London Scottish) 1968 *I, E, A*, 1969 *F, W, I, E*, 1971 *F, W, I, E* (2[1C]), 1972 *F, E, NZ*, 1973 *F, W, I, E, P*, 1974 *W, E, I, F*, 1975 *I, F, W, E, NZ, A*, 1976 *F, W, E, I*, 1977 *E, I, F, W*, 1978 *I, F, W, NZ*, 1979 *W, E*
McIndoe, F (Glasgow Acads) 1886 *W, I*
MacIntyre, I (Edinburgh Wands) 1890 *W, I, E*, 1891 *W, I, E*
McIvor, D J (Edinburgh Acads) 1992 *E, I, F, W*, 1993 *NZ*, 1994 *SA*
Mackay, E B (Glasgow Acads) 1920 *W*, 1922 *E*
McKeating, E (Heriot's FP) 1957 *F, W*, 1961 *SA, W, I, E*
McKendrick, J G (W of Scotland) 1889 *I*
Mackenzie, A D G (Selkirk) 1984 *A*
Mackenzie, C J G (United Services) 1921 *E*
Mackenzie, D D (Edinburgh U) 1947 *W, I, E*, 1948 *F, W, I*
Mackenzie, D K A (Edinburgh Wands) 1939 *I, E*
Mackenzie, J M (Edinburgh U) 1905 *NZ*, 1909 *W, I, E*, 1910 *W, I, E*, 1911 *W, I*
McKenzie, K D (Stirling County) 1994 *Arg* 1,2
Mackenzie, R C (Glasgow Acads) 1877 *I, E*, 1881 *I, E*
Mackie, G Y (Highland) 1975 *A*, 1976 *F, W*, 1978 *F*
MacKinnon, A (London Scottish) 1898 *I, E*, 1899 *I, W, E*, 1900 *E*
Mackintosh, C E W C (London Scottish) 1924 *F*
Mackintosh, H S (Glasgow U, W of Scotland) 1929 *F, W, I, E*, 1930 *F, W, I, E*, 1931 *F, W, I, E*, 1932 *SA, W, I, E*
MacLachlan, L P (Oxford U, London Scottish) 1954 *NZ, I, E, W*
Maclagan, W E (Edinburgh Acads) 1878 *E*, 1879 *I, E*, 1880 *I, E*, 1881 *I, E*, 1882 *I, E*, 1883 *W, I, E*, 1884 *W, I, E*, 1885 *W, I* 1,2, 1887 *I, W, E*, 1888 *W, I*, 1890 *W, I, E*
McLaren, A (Durham County) 1931 *F*
McLaren, E (London Scottish, Royal HSFP) 1923 *F, W, I, E*, 1924 *F*
McLauchlan, J (Jordanhill) 1969 *E, SA*, 1970 *F, W*, 1971 *F, W, I, E* (2[1C]), 1972 *F, W, E, NZ*, 1973 *F, W, I, E, P*, 1974 *W, E, I, F*, 1975 *I, F, W, E, NZ, A*, 1976 *F, W, E, I*, 1977 *W*, 1978 *I, F, W, E, NZ*, 1979 *W, E, I, F, NZ*
McLean, D I (Royal HSFP) 1947 *I, E*
Maclennan, W D (Watsonians) 1947 *F, I*
MacLeod, D A (Glasgow U) 1886 *I, E*
MacLeod, G (Edinburgh Acads) 1878 *E*, 1882 *I*
McLeod, H F (Hawick) 1954 *F, NZ, I, E, W*, 1955 *F, W, I, E*, 1956 *F, W, I, E*, 1957 *F, W, I, E*, 1958 *F, W, A, I, E*, 1959 *F, W, I, E*, 1960 *F, W, I, E, SA*, 1961 *F*,

SA, W, I, E, 1962 *F, W, I, E*
MacLeod, K G (Cambridge U) 1905 *NZ*, 1906 *W, I, E, SA*, 1907 *W, I, E*, 1908 *I, E*
MacLeod, L M (Cambridge U) 1904 *W, I, E*, 1905 *W, I, NZ*
Macleod, W M (Fettesian-Lorettonians, Edinburgh Wands) 1886 *W, I*
McMillan, K H D (Sale) 1953 *F, W, I, E*
MacMillan, R G (London Scottish) 1887 *W, I, E*, 1890 *W, I, E*, 1891 *W, E*, 1892 *W, I, E*, 1893 *W, E*, 1894 *W, I, E*, 1895 *W, I, E*, 1897 *I, E*
MacMyn, D J (Cambridge U, London Scottish) 1925 *F, W, I, E*, 1926 *F, W, I, E*, 1927 *E, A*, 1928 *F*
McNeil, A S B (Watsonians) 1935 *I*
McPartlin, J J (Harlequins, Oxford U) 1960 *F, W*, 1962 *F, W, I, E*
Macphail, J A R (Edinburgh Acads) 1949 *E*, 1951 *SA*
Macpherson, D G (London Hospital) 1910 *I, E*
Macpherson, G P S (Oxford U, Edinburgh Acads) 1922 *F, W, I, E*, 1924 *W, E*, 1925 *F, W, E*, 1927 *F, W, I, E*, 1928 *F, W, E*, 1929 *I, E*, 1930 *F, W, I, E*, 1931 *W, E*, 1932 *SA, E*
Macpherson, N C (Newport, Mon) 1920 *W, I, E*, 1921 *F, E*, 1923 *I, E*
McQueen, S B (Waterloo) 1923 *F, W, I, E*
Macrae, D J (St Andrews U) 1937 *W, I, E*, 1938 *W, I, E*, 1939 *W, I, E*
Madsen, D F (Gosforth) 1974 *W, E, I, F*, 1975 *I, F, W, E*, 1976 *F*, 1977 *E, I, F, W*, 1978 *I*
Mair, N G R (Edinburgh U) 1951 *F, W, I, E*
Maitland, G (Edinburgh Inst FP) 1885 *W, I* 2
Maitland, R (Edinburgh Inst FP) 1881 *E*, 1882 *I, E*, 1884 *W*, 1885 *W*
Maitland, R P (Royal Artillery) 1872 *E*
Malcolm, A G (Glasgow U) 1888 *I*
Manson, J J (Dundee HSFP) 1995 *E*(R)
Marsh, J (Edinburgh Inst FP) 1889 *W, I*
Marshall, A (Edinburgh Acads) 1875 *E*
Marshall, G R (Selkirk) 1988 *A* (R), 1989 *Fj*, 1990 *Arg*, 1991 [*Z*]
Marshall, J C (London Scottish) 1954 *F, NZ, I, E, W*
Marshall, K W (Edinburgh Acads) 1934 *W, I, E*, 1935 *W, I, E*, 1936 *W*, 1937 *E*
Marshall, T R (Edinburgh Acads) 1871 *E*, 1872 *E*, 1873 *E*, 1874 *E*
Marshall, W (Edinburgh Acads) 1872 *E*
Martin, H (Edinburgh Acads, Oxford U) 1908 *W, I, E*, 1909 *W, E*
Masters, W H (Edinburgh Inst FP) 1879 *I*, 1880 *I, E*
Maxwell, F T (Royal Engineers) 1872 *E*
Maxwell, G H H P (Edinburgh Acads, RAF, London Scottish) 1913 *I, E*, 1914 *W, I, E*, 1920 *W, E*, 1921 *F, W, I, E*, 1922 *F, E*
Maxwell, J M (Langholm) 1957 *I*
Mein, J (Edinburgh Acads) 1871 *E*, 1872 *E*, 1873 *E*, 1874 *E*, 1875 *E*
Melville, C L (Army) 1937 *W, I, E*
Menzies, H F (W of Scotland) 1893 *W, I*, 1894 *W, E*
Methuen, A (London Scottish) 1889 *W, I*
Michie, E J S (Aberdeen U, Aberdeen GSFP) 1954 *F, NZ, I, E*, 1955 *W, I, E*, 1956 *F, W, I, E*, 1957 *F, W, I, E*
Millar, J N (W of Scotland) 1892 *W, I, E*, 1893 *W*, 1895 *I, E*
Millar, R K (London Scottish) 1924 *I*
Millican, J G (Edinburgh U) 1973 *W, I, E*
Milne, C J B (Fettesian-Lorettonians, W of Scotland) 1886 *W, I, E*
Milne, D F (Heriot's FP) 1991 [*J*(R)]
Milne, I G (Heriot's FP, Harlequins) 1979 *I, F, NZ*, 1980 *I, F*, 1981 *NZ* 1,2, *R, A*, 1982 *E, I, F, W, A* 1,2, 1983 *I, F, W, E, NZ*, 1984 *W, E, I, F, A*, 1985 *F, W, E*, 1986 *F, W, E, I, R*, 1987 *I, F, W, E*, [*F, Z, NZ*], 1988 *A*, 1989 *W*, 1990 *NZ* 1,2
Milne, K S (Heriot's FP) 1989 *W, E, I, F, Fj, R*, 1990 *I, F, W, E*, 1990 *NZ* 2, *Arg*, 1991 *F, W*(R), *E*, [*Z*], 1992 *E, I, F, W, A* 1, 1993 *I, F, W, E, NZ*, 1994 *W, E, I, F, SA*, 1995 *C, I, F, W, E*
Milne, W M (Glasgow Acads) 1904 *I, E*, 1905 *W, I*
Milroy, E (Watsonians) 1910 *W*, 1911 *E*, 1912 *W, I, E, SA*, 1913 *F, W, I, E*, 1914 *I, E*
Mitchell, G W E (Edinburgh Wands) 1967 *NZ*, 1968 *F, W*
Mitchell, J G (W of Scotland) 1885 *W, I* 1,2
Moncreiff, F J (Edinburgh Acads) 1871 *E*, 1872 *E*, 1873 *E*
Monteith, H G (Cambridge U, London Scottish) 1905 *E*, 1906 *W, I, E, SA*, 1907 *W, I*, 1908 *E*
Monypenny, D B (London Scottish) 1899 *I, W, E*
Moodie, A R (St Andrew's U) 1909 *E*, 1910 *F*, 1911 *F*
Moore, A (Edinburgh Acads) 1990 *NZ* 2, *Arg*, 1991 *F, W, E*
Morgan, D W (Stewart's-Melville FP) 1973 *W, I, E, P*, 1974 *I, F*, 1975 *I, F, W, E, NZ, A*, 1976 *F, W*, 1977 *I, F, W*, 1978 *I, F, W, E*
Morrison, I R (London Scottish) 1993 *I, F, W, E*, 1994 *W, SA*, 1995 *C, I, F, W, E*
Morrison, M C (Royal HSFP) 1896 *W, I, E*, 1897 *I, E*, 1898 *I, E*, 1899 *I, W, E*, 1900 *W, E*, 1901 *W, I, E*, 1902 *W, I, E*, 1903 *W, I*, 1904 *W, I, E*
Morrison, R H (Edinburgh U) 1886 *W, I, E*
Morrison, W H (Edinburgh Acads) 1900 *W*
Morton, D S (W of Scotland) 1887 *I, W, E*, 1888 *W, I*, 1889 *W, I*, 1890 *I, E*
Mowat, J G (Glasgow Acads) 1883 *W, E*
Muir, D E (Heriot's FP) 1950 *F, W, I, E*, 1952 *W, I, E*
Munnoch, N M (Watsonians) 1952 *F, W, I*
Munro, D S (Glasgow High Kelvinside) 1994 *W, E, I, F, Arg* 1,2
Munro, P (Oxford, London Scottish) 1905 *W, I, E, NZ*, 1906 *W, I, E, SA*, 1907 *I, E*, 1911 *F, W, I*
Munro, R (St Andrews U) 1871 *E*
Munro, S (Ayr, W of Scotland) 1980 *I, F*, 1981 *F, W, E, I, NZ* 1,2, *R*, 1984 *W*
Munro, W H (Glasgow HSFP) 1947 *I, E*
Murdoch, W C W (Hillhead HSFP) 1935 *E, NZ*, 1936 *W, I*, 1939 *E*, 1948 *F, W, I, E*
Murray, G M (Glasgow Acads) 1921 *I*, 1926 *W*
Murray, H M (Glasgow U) 1936 *W, I*
Murray, K T (Hawick) 1985 *I, F, W*
Murray, R O (Cambridge U) 1935 *W, E*
Murray, W A K (London Scottish) 1920 *F, I*, 1921 *F*

Napier, H M (W of Scotland) 1877 *I, E*, 1878 *E*, 1879 *I, E*
Neill, J B (Edinburgh Acads) 1963 *E*, 1964 *F, NZ, W, I, E*, 1965 *F*
Neill, R M (Edinburgh Acads) 1901 *E*, 1902 *I*
Neilson, G T (W of Scotland) 1891 *W, I, E*, 1892 *W, E*, 1893 *W*, 1894 *W, I*, 1895 *W, I, E*, 1896 *W, I, E*
Neilson, J A (Glasgow Acads) 1878 *E*, 1879 *E*
Neilson, R T (W of Scotland) 1898 *I, E*, 1899 *I, W*, 1900 *I, E*
Neilson, T (W of Scotland) 1874 *E*
Neilson, W (Merchiston, Cambridge U, London Scottish) 1891 *W, E*, 1892 *W, I, E*, 1893 *I, E*, 1894 *E*, 1895 *W, I, E*, 1896 *I*, 1897 *I, E*
Neilson, W G (Merchistonians) 1894 *E*
Nelson, J B (Glasgow Acads) 1925 *F, W, I, E*, 1926 *F, W, I, E*, 1927 *F, W, I, E*, 1928 *I, E*, 1929 *F, W, I, E*, 1930 *F, W, I, E*, 1931 *F, W, I*
Nelson, T A (Oxford U) 1898 *E*
Nichol, J A (Royal HSFP) 1955 *W, I, E*
Nichol, S A (Selkirk) 1994 *Arg* 2(R)
Nicol, A D (Dundee HSFP) 1992 *E, I, F, W, A* 1,2, 1993 *NZ*, 1994 *W*
Nimmo, C S (Watsonians) 1920 *E*

Ogilvy, C (Hawick) 1911 *I, E*, 1912 *I*
Oliver, G H (Hawick) 1987 [*Z*], 1990 *NZ* 2 (R), 1991 [*Z*]
Oliver, G K (Gala) 1970 *A*
Orr, C E (W of Scotland) 1887 *I, E, W*, 1888 *W, I*, 1889 *W, I*, 1890 *W, I, E*, 1891 *W, I, E*, 1892 *W, I, E*
Orr, H J (London Scottish) 1903 *W, I, E*, 1904 *W, I*
Orr, J E (W of Scotland) 1889 *I*, 1890 *W, I, E*, 1891 *W, I, E*, 1892 *W, I, E*, 1893 *I, E*
Orr, J H (Edinburgh City Police) 1947 *F, W*
Osler, F L (Edinburgh U) 1911 *F, W*

Park, J (Royal HSFP) 1934 *W*
Paterson, D S (Gala) 1969 *SA*, 1970 *I, E, A*, 1971 *F, W, I, E* (2[1C]), 1972 *W*
Paterson, G Q (Edinburgh Acads) 1876 *E*
Paterson, J R (Birkenhead Park) 1924 *F, W, I, E*, 1926 *F, W, I, E*, 1927 *F, W, I, E, A*, 1928 *F, W, I, E*, 1929 *F, W, I, E*
Patterson, D (Hawick) 1896 *W*

Patterson, D W (West Hartlepool) 1994 *SA*
Pattullo, G L (Panmure) 1920 *F, W, I, E*
Paxton, I A M (Selkirk) 1981 *NZ* 1,2, *R, A*, 1982 *E, I, F, W, A* 1,2, 1983 *I, E, NZ*, 1984 *W, E, I, F*, 1985 *I* (R), *F, W, E*, 1986 *W, E, I, R*, 1987 *I, F, W, E*, [*F, Z, R, NZ*], 1988 *I, E, A*
Paxton, R E (Kelso) 1982 *I, A* 2 (R)
Pearson, J (Watsonians) 1909 *I, E*, 1910 *F, W, I, E*, 1911 *F*, 1912 *F, W, SA*, 1913 *I, E*
Pender, I M (London Scottish) 1914 *E*
Pender, N E K (Hawick) 1977 *I*, 1978 *F, W, E*
Penman, W M (RAF) 1939 *I*
Peterkin, W A (Edinburgh U) 1881 *E*, 1883 *I*, 1884 *W, I, E*, 1885 *W, I* 1,2
Peters, E W (Bath) 1995 *C, I, F, W, E*
Petrie, A G (Royal HSFP) 1873 *E*, 1874 *E*, 1875 *E*, 1876 *E*, 1877 *I, E*, 1878 *E*, 1879 *I, E*, 1880 *I, E*
Philp, A (Edinburgh Inst FP) 1882 *E*
Pocock, E I (Edinburgh Wands) 1877 *I, E*
Pollock, J A (Gosforth) 1982 *W*, 1983 *E, NZ*, 1984 *E* (R), *I, F, R*, 1985 *F*
Polson, A H (Gala) 1930 *E*
Purdie, W (Jedforest) 1939 *W, I, E*
Purves, A B H L (London Scottish) 1906 *W, I, E, SA*, 1907 *W, I, E*, 1908 *W, I, E*
Purves, W D C L (London Scottish) 1912 *F, W, I, SA*, 1913 *I, E*

Rea, C W W (W of Scotland, Headingley) 1968 *A*, 1969 *F, W, I, SA*, 1970 *F, W, I, A*, 1971 *F, W, E* (2[1C])
Redpath, B W (Melrose) 1993 *NZ*(t), 1994 *E*(t), *F, Arg* 1,2, 1995 *C, I, F, W, E*
Reed, A I (Bath) 1993 *I, F, W, E*, 1994 *E, I, F, Arg* 1,2, *SA*
Reid, C (Edinburgh Acads) 1881 *I, E*, 1882 *I, E*, 1883 *W, I, E*, 1884 *W, I, E*, 1885 *W, I* 1,2, 1886 *W, I, E*, 1887 *I, W, E*, 1888 *W, I*
Reid, J (Edinburgh Wands) 1874 *E*, 1875 *E*, 1876 *E*, 1877 *I, E*
Reid, J M (Edinburgh Acads) 1898 *I, E*, 1899 *I*
Reid, M F (Loretto) 1883 *I, E*
Reid-Kerr, J (Greenock Wand) 1909 *E*
Relph, W K L (Stewart's Coll FP) 1955 *F, W, I, E*
Renny-Tailyour, H W (Royal Engineers) 1872 *E*
Renwick, J M (Hawick) 1972 *F, W, E, NZ*, 1973 *F*, 1974 *W, E, I, F*, 1975 *I, F, W, E, NZ, A*, 1976 *F, W, E*(R), 1977 *I, F, W*, 1978 *I, F, W, E, NZ*, 1979 *W, E, I, F, NZ*, 1980 *I, F, W, E*, 1981 *F, W, E, I, NZ* 1,2, *R, A*, 1982 *E, I, F, W*, 1983 *I, F, W, E*, 1984 *R*
Renwick, W L (London Scottish) 1989 *R*
Renwick, W N (London Scottish, Edinburgh Wands) 1938 *E*, 1939 *W*
Richardson, J F (Edinburgh Acads) 1994 *SA*
Ritchie, G (Merchistonians) 1871 *E*
Ritchie, G F (Dundee HSFP) 1932 *E*
Ritchie, J M (Watsonians) 1933 *W, E, I*, 1934 *W, I, E*
Ritchie, W T (Cambridge U) 1905 *I, E*
Robb, G H (Glasgow U) 1881 *I*, 1885 *W*
Roberts, G (Watsonians) 1938 *W, I, E*, 1939 *W, E*
Robertson, A H (W of Scotland) 1871 *E*
Robertson, A W (Edinburgh Acads) 1897 *E*
Robertson, D (Edinburgh Acads) 1875 *E*
Robertson, D D (Cambridge U) 1893 *W*
Robertson, I (London Scottish, Watsonians) 1968 *E*, 1969 *E, SA*, 1970 *F, W, I, E, A*
Robertson, I P M (Watsonians) 1910 *F*
Robertson, J (Clydesdale) 1908 *E*
Robertson, K W (Melrose) 1978 *NZ*, 1979 *W, E, I, F, NZ*, 1980 *W, E*, 1981 *F, W, E, I, R, A*, 1982 *E, I, F, A* 1,2, 1983 *I, F, W, E*, 1984 *E, I, F, R, A*, 1985 *I, F, W, E*, 1986 *I*, 1987 *F* (R), *W, E*, [*F, Z, NZ*], 1988 *E, A*, 1989 *E, I, F*
Robertson, L (London Scottish, United Services) 1908 *E*, 1911 *W*, 1912 *W, I, E, SA*, 1913 *W, I, E*
Robertson, M A (Gala) 1958 *F*
Robertson, R D (London Scottish) 1912 *F*
Robson, A (Hawick) 1954 *F*, 1955 *F, W, I, E*, 1956 *F, W, I, E*, 1957 *F, W, I, E*, 1958 *W, A, I, E*, 1959 *F, W, I, E*, 1960 *F*
Rodd, J A T (United Services, RN, London Scottish) 1958 *F, W, A, I, E*, 1960 *F, W*, 1962 *F*, 1964 *F, NZ, W*, 1965 *F, W, I*
Rogerson, J (Kelvinside Acads) 1894 *W*
Roland, E T (Edinburgh Acads) 1884 *I, E*
Rollo, D M D (Howe of Fife) 1959 *E*, 1960 *F, W, I, E, SA*, 1961 *F, SA, W, I, E*, 1962 *F, W, E*, 1963 *F, W, I, E*, 1964 *F, NZ, W, I, E*, 1965 *F, W, I, E, SA*, 1966 *F, W, I, E, A*, 1967 *F, W, E, NZ*, 1968 *F, W, I*
Rose, D M (Jedforest) 1951 *F, W, I, E, SA*, 1953 *F, W*
Ross, A (Kilmarnock) 1924 *F, W*
Ross, A (Royal HSFP) 1905 *W, I, E*, 1909 *W, I*
Ross, A R (Edinburgh U) 1911 *W*, 1914 *W, I, E*
Ross, E J (London Scottish) 1904 *W*
Ross, G T (Watsonians) 1954 *NZ, I, E, W*
Ross, I A (Hillhead HSFP) 1951 *F, W, I, E*
Ross, J (London Scottish) 1901 *W, I, E*, 1902 *W*, 1903 *E*
Ross, K I (Boroughmuir FP) 1961 *SA, W, I, E*, 1962 *F, W, I, E*, 1963 *F, W, E*
Ross, W A (Hillhead HSFP) 1937 *W, E*
Rottenburg, H (Cambridge U, London Scottish) 1899 *W, E*, 1900 *W, I, E*
Roughead, W N (Edinburgh Acads, London Scottish) 1927 *A*, 1928 *F, W, I, E*, 1930 *I, E*, 1931 *F, W, I, E*, 1932 *W*
Rowan, N A (Boroughmuir) 1980 *W, E*, 1981 *F, W, E, I*, 1984 *R*, 1985 *I*, 1987 [*R*], 1988 *I, F, W, E*
Rowand, R (Glasgow HSFP) 1930 *F, W*, 1932 *E*, 1933 *W, E, I*, 1934 *W*
Roy, A (Waterloo) 1938 *W, I, E*, 1939 *W, I, E*
Russell, W L (Glasgow Acads) 1905 *NZ*, 1906 *W, I, E*
Rutherford, J Y (Selkirk) 1979 *W, E, I, F, NZ*, 1980 *I, F, E*, 1981 *F, W, E, I, NZ* 1,2, *A*, 1982 *E, I, F, W, A* 1,2, 1983 *E, NZ*, 1984 *W, E, I, F, R*, 1985 *I, F, W, E*, 1986 *F, W, E, I, R*, 1987 *I, F, W, E*, [*F*]

Sampson, R W F (London Scottish) 1939 *W*, 1947 *W*
Sanderson, G A (Royal HSFP) 1907 *W, I, E*, 1908 *I*
Sanderson, J L P (Edinburgh Acads) 1873 *E*
Schulze, D G (London Scottish) 1905 *E*, 1907 *I, E*, 1908 *W, I, E*, 1909 *W, I, E*, 1910 *W, I, E*, 1911 *W*
Scobie, R M (Royal Military Coll) 1914 *W, I, E*
Scotland, K J F (Heriot's FP, Cambridge U, Leicester) 1957 *F, W, I, E*, 1958 *E*, 1959 *F, W, I, E*, 1960 *F, W, I, E*, 1961 *F, SA, W, I, E*, 1962 *F, W, I, E*, 1963 *F, W, I, E*, 1965 *F*
Scott, D M (Langholm, Watsonians) 1950 *I, E*, 1951 *W, I, E, SA*, 1952 *F, W, I*, 1953 *F*
Scott, J M B (Edinburgh Acads) 1907 *E*, 1908 *W, I, E*, 1909 *W, I, E*, 1910 *F, W, I, E*, 1911 *F, W, I*, 1912 *W, I, E, SA*, 1913 *W, I, E*
Scott, J S (St Andrews U) 1950 *E*
Scott, J W (Stewart's Coll FP) 1925 *F, W, I, E*, 1926 *F, W, I, E*, 1927 *F, W, I, E, A*, 1928 *F, W, E*, 1929 *E*, 1930 *F*
Scott, M (Dunfermline) 1992 *A* 2
Scott, R (Hawick) 1898 *I*, 1900 *I, E*
Scott, T (Langholm, Hawick) 1896 *W*, 1897 *I, E*, 1898 *I, E*, 1899 *I, W, E*, 1900 *W, I, E*
Scott, T M (Hawick) 1893 *E*, 1895 *W, I, E*, 1896 *W, E*, 1897 *I, E*, 1898 *I, E*, 1900 *W, I*
Scott, W P (W of Scotland) 1900 *I, E*, 1902 *I, E*, 1903 *W, I, E*, 1904 *W, I, E*, 1905 *W, I, E, NZ*, 1906 *W, I, E, SA*, 1907 *W, I, E*
Scoular, J G (Cambridge U) 1905 *NZ*, 1906 *W, I, E, SA*
Selby, J A R (Watsonians) 1920 *W, I*
Shackleton, J A P (London Scottish) 1959 *E*, 1963 *F, W*, 1964 *NZ, W*, 1965 *I, SA*
Sharp, A V (Bristol) 1994 *E, I, F, Arg* 1,2, *SA*
Sharp, G (Stewart's FP, Army) 1960 *F*, 1964 *F, NZ, W*
Shaw, G D (Sale) 1935 *NZ*, 1936 *W*, 1937 *W, I, E*, 1939 *I*
Shaw, I (Glasgow HSFP) 1937 *I*
Shaw, J N (Edinburgh Acads) 1921 *W, I*
Shaw, R W (Glasgow HSFP) 1934 *W, I, E*, 1935 *W, I, E, NZ*, 1936 *W, I, E*, 1937 *W, I, E*, 1938 *W, I, E*, 1939 *W, I, E*
Shedden, D (W of Scotland) 1972 *NZ*, 1973 *F, W, I, E, P*, 1976 *W, E, I*, 1977 *I, F, W*, 1978 *I, F, W*
Shiel, A G (Melrose) 1991 [*I*(R), *WS*], 1993 *I, F, W, E, NZ*, 1994 *Arg* 1,2, *SA*
Shillinglaw, R B (Gala, Army) 1960 *I, E, SA*, 1961 *F, SA*
Simmers, B M (Glasgow Acads) 1965 *F, W*, 1966 *A*, 1967 *F, W, I*, 1971 *F* (R)
Simmers, W M (Glasgow Acads) 1926 *W, I, E*, 1927 *F, W, I, E, A*, 1928 *F, W, I, E*, 1929 *F, W, I, E*, 1930 *F, W, I, E*, 1931 *F, W, I, E*, 1932 *SA, W, I, E*

Simpson, J W (Royal HSFP) 1893 *I, E*, 1894 *W, I, E*, 1895 *W, I, E*, 1896 *W, I*, 1897 *E*, 1899 *W, E*
Simpson, R S (Glasgow Acads) 1923 *I*
Simson, E D (Edinburgh U, London Scottish) 1902 *E*, 1903 *W, I, E*, 1904 *W, I, E*, 1905 *W, I, E, NZ*, 1906 *W, I, E*, 1907 *W, I, E*
Simson, J T (Watsonians) 1905 *NZ*, 1909 *W, I, E*, 1910 *F, W*, 1911 *I*
Simson, R F (London Scottish) 1911 *E*
Sloan, A T (Edinburgh Acads) 1914 *W*, 1920 *F, W, I, E*, 1921 *F, W, I, E*
Sloan, D A (Edinburgh Acads, London Scottish) 1950 *F, W, E*, 1951 *W, I, E*, 1953 *F*
Sloan, T (Glasgow Acads, Oxford U) 1905 *NZ*, 1906 *W, SA*, 1907 *W, E*, 1908 *W*, 1909 *I*
Smeaton, P W (Edinburgh Acads) 1881 *I*, 1883 *I, E*
Smith, A R (Oxford U) 1895 *W, I, E*, 1896 *W, I*, 1897 *I, E*, 1898 *I, E*, 1900 *I, E*
Smith, A R (Cambridge U, Gosforth, Ebbw Vale, Edinburgh Wands) 1955 *W, I, E*, 1956 *F, W, I, E*, 1957 *F, W, I, E*, 1958 *F, W, A, I*, 1959 *F, W, I, E*, 1960 *F, W, I, E, SA*, 1961 *F, SA, W, I, E*, 1962 *F, W, I, E*
Smith, D W C (London Scottish) 1949 *F, W, I, E*, 1950 *F, W, I*, 1953 *I*
Smith, E R (Edinburgh Acads) 1879 *I*
Smith, G K (Kelso) 1957 *I, E*, 1958 *F, W, A*, 1959 *F, W, I, E*, 1960 *F, W, I, E*, 1961 *F, SA, W, I, E*
Smith, H O (Watsonians) 1895 *W*, 1896 *W, I, E*, 1898 *I, E*, 1899 *W, I, E*, 1900 *E*, 1902 *E*
Smith, I R (Gloucester) 1992 *E, I, W, A* 1,2, 1994 *E*(R), *I, F, Arg* 1,2
Smith, I S (Oxford U, Edinburgh U) 1924 *W, I, E*, 1925 *F, W, I, E*, 1926 *F, W, I, E*, 1927 *F, I, E*, 1929 *F, W, I, E*, 1930 *F, W, I*, 1931 *F, W, I, E*, 1932 *SA, W, I, E*, 1933 *W, E, I*
Smith, I S G (London Scottish) 1969 *SA*, 1970 *F, W, I, E*, 1971 *F, W, I*
Smith, M A (London Scottish) 1970 *W, I, E, A*
Smith, R T (Kelso) 1929 *F, W, I, E*, 1930 *F, W, I*
Smith, S H (Glasgow Acads) 1877 *I*, 1878 *E*
Smith, T J (Gala) 1983 *E, NZ*, 1985 *I, F*
Sole, D M B (Bath, Edinburgh Acads) 1986 *F, W*, 1987 *I, F, W, E*, [*F, Z, R, NZ*], 1988 *I, F, W, E, A*, 1989 *W, E, I, F, Fj, R*, 1990 *I, F, W, E, NZ* 1,2, *Arg*, 1991 *F, W, E, I, R*, [*J, I, WS, E, NZ*], 1992 *E, I, F, W, A* 1,2
Somerville, D (Edinburgh Inst FP) 1879 *I*, 1882 *I*, 1883 *W, I, E*, 1884 *W*
Speirs, L M (Watsonians) 1906 *SA*, 1907 *W, I, E*, 1908 *W, I, E*, 1910 *F, W, E*
Spence, K M (Oxford U) 1953 *I*
Spencer, E (Clydedale) 1898 *I*
Stagg, P K (Sale) 1965 *F, W, E, SA*, 1966 *F, W, I, E, A*, 1967 *F, W, I, E, NZ*, 1968 *F, W, I, E, A*, 1969 *F, W, I* (R), *SA*, 1970 *F, W, I, E, A*
Stanger, A G (Hawick) 1989 *Fj, R*, 1990 *I, F, W, E, NZ* 1,2, *Arg*, 1991 *F, W, E, I, R*, [*J, Z, I, WS, E, NZ*], 1992 *E, I, F, W, A* 1,2, 1993 *I, F, W, E, NZ*, 1994 *W, E, I, F, SA*
Stark, D A (Boroughmuir) 1993 *I, F, W, E*
Steele, W C C (Langholm, Bedford, RAF, London Scottish) 1969 *E*, 1971 *F, W, I, E* (2[1C]), 1972 *F, W, E, NZ*, 1973 *F, W, I, E*, 1975 *I, F, W, E, NZ* (R), 1976 *W, E, I*, 1977 *E*
Stephen, A E (W of Scotland) 1885 *W*, 1886 *I*
Steven, P D (Heriot's FP) 1984 *A*, 1985 *F, W, E*
Steven, R (Edinburgh Wands) 1962 *I*
Stevenson, A K (Glasgow Acads) 1922 *F*, 1923 *F, W, E*
Stevenson, A M (Glasgow U) 1911 *F*
Stevenson, G D (Hawick) 1956 *E*, 1957 *F*, 1958 *F, W, A, I, E*, 1959 *W, I, E*, 1960 *W, I, E, SA*, 1961 *F, SA, W, I, E*, 1963 *F, W, I*, 1964 *E*, 1965 *F*
Stevenson, H J (Edinburgh Acads) 1888 *W, I*, 1889 *W, I*, 1890 *W, I, E*, 1891 *W, I, E*, 1892 *W, I, E*, 1893 *I, E*
Stevenson, L E (Edinburgh U) 1888 *W*
Stevenson, R C (London Scottish) 1897 *I, E*, 1898 *E*, 1899 *I, W, E*
Stevenson, R C (St Andrews U) 1910 *F, I, E*, 1911 *F, W, I*
Stevenson, W H (Glasgow Acads) 1925 *F*
Stewart, A K (Edinburgh U) 1874 *E*, 1876 *E*
Stewart, A M (Edinburgh Acads) 1914 *W*
Stewart, C A R (W of Scotland) 1880 *I, E*
Stewart, C E B (Kelso) 1960 *W*, 1961 *F*
Stewart, J (Glasgow HSFP) 1930 *F*
Stewart, J L (Edinburgh Acads) 1921 *I*
Stewart, M S (Stewart's Coll FP) 1932 *SA, W, I*, 1933 *W, E, I*, 1934 *W, I, E*
Stewart, W A (London Hospital) 1913 *F, W, I*, 1914 *W*
Steyn, S S L (Oxford U) 1911 *E*, 1912 *I*
Strachan, G M (Jordanhill) 1971 *E* (C) (R), 1973 *W, I, E, P*
Stronach, R S (Glasgow Acads) 1901 *W, E*, 1905 *W, I, E*
Stuart, C D (W of Scotland) 1909 *I*, 1910 *F, W, I, E*, 1911 *I, E*
Stuart, L M (Glasgow HSFP) 1923 *F, W, I, E*, 1924 *F*, 1928 *E*, 1930 *I, E*
Suddon, N (Hawick) 1965 *W, I, E, SA*, 1966 *A*, 1968 *E, A*, 1969 *F, W, I*, 1970 *I, E, A*
Sutherland, W R (Hawick) 1910 *W, E*, 1911 *F, E*, 1912 *F, W, E, SA*, 1913 *F, W, I, E*, 1914 *W*
Swan, J S (Army, London Scottish, Leicester) 1953 *E*, 1954 *F, NZ, I, E, W*, 1955 *F, W, I, E*, 1956 *F, W, I, E*, 1957 *F, W*, 1958 *F*
Swan, M W (Oxford U, London Scottish) 1958 *F, W, A, I, E*, 1959 *F, W, I*
Sweet, J B (Glasgow HSFP) 1913 *E*, 1914 *I*
Symington, A W (Cambridge U) 1914 *W, E*

Tait, A V (Kelso) 1987 [*F*(R), *Z, R, NZ*], 1988 *I, F, W, E*
Tait, J G (Edinburgh Acads) 1880 *I*, 1885 *I* 2
Tait, P W (Royal HSFP) 1935 *E*
Taylor, E G (Oxford U) 1927 *W, A*
Taylor, R C (Kelvinside-West) 1951 *W, I, E, SA*
Telfer, C M (Hawick) 1968 *A*, 1969 *F, W, I, E*, 1972 *F, W, E*, 1973 *W, I, E, P*, 1974 *W, E, I*, 1975 *A*, 1976 *F*
Telfer, J W (Melrose) 1964 *F, NZ, W, I, E*, 1965 *F, W, I*, 1966 *F, W, I, E*, 1967 *W, I, E*, 1968 *E, A*, 1969 *F, W, I, E, SA*, 1970 *F, W, I*
Tennent, J M (W of Scotland) 1909 *W, I, E*, 1910 *F, W, E*
Thom, D A (London Scottish) 1934 *W*, 1935 *W, I, E, NZ*
Thom, G (Kirkcaldy) 1920 *F, W, I, E*
Thom, J R (Watsonians) 1933 *W, E, I*
Thomson, A E (United Services) 1921 *F, W, E*
Thomson, A M (St Andrews U) 1949 *I*
Thomson, B E (Oxford U) 1953 *F, W, I*
Thomson, I H M (Heriot's FP, Army) 1951 *W, I*, 1952 *F, W, I*, 1953 *I, E*
Thomson, J S (Glasgow Acads) 1871 *E*
Thomson, R H (London Scottish, PUC) 1960 *I, E, SA*, 1961 *F, SA, W, I, E*, 1963 *F, W, I, E*, 1964 *F, NZ, W*
Thomson, W H (W of Scotland) 1906 *SA*
Thomson, W J (W of Scotland) 1899 *W, E*, 1900 *W*
Timms, A B (Edinburgh U, Edinburgh Wands) 1896 *W*, 1900 *W, I*, 1901 *W, I, E*, 1902 *W, E*, 1903 *W, E*, 1904 *I, E*, 1905 *I, E*
Tod, H B (Gala) 1911 *F*
Tod, J (Watsonians) 1884 *W, I, E*, 1885 *W, I* 1,2, 1886 *W, I, E*
Todd, J K (Glasgow Acads) 1874 *E*, 1875 *E*
Tolmie, J M (Glasgow HSFP) 1922 *E*
Tomes, A J (Hawick) 1976 *E, I*, 1977 *E*, 1978 *I, F, W, E, NZ*, 1979 *W, E, I, F, NZ*, 1980 *F, W, E*, 1981 *F, W, E, I, NZ* 1,2, *R, A*, 1982 *E, I, F, W, A* 1,2, 1983 *I, F, W*, 1984 *W, E, I, F, R, A*, 1985 *W, E*, 1987 *I, F, E*(R), [*F, Z, R, NZ*]
Torrie, T J (Edinburgh Acads) 1877 *E*
Townsend, G P J (Gala) 1993 *E*(R), 1994 *W, E, I, F, Arg* 1,2, 1995 *C, I, F, W, E*
Tukalo, I (Selkirk) 1985 *I*, 1987 *I, F, W, E*, [*F, Z, R, NZ*], 1988 *F, W, E, A*, 1989 *W, E, I, F, Fj*, 1990 *I, F, W, E, NZ* 1, 1991 *I, R*, [*J, Z, I, WS, E, NZ*], 1992 *E, I, F, W, A* 1,2
Turk, A S (Langholm) 1971 *E* (R)
Turnbull, D J (Hawick) 1987 [*NZ*], 1988 *F, E*, 1990 *E* (R), 1991 *F, W, E, I, R*, [*Z*], 1993 *I, F, W, E*, 1994 *W*
Turnbull, F O (Kelso) 1951 *F, SA*
Turnbull, G O (W of Scotland) 1896 *I, E*, 1897 *I, E*, 1904 *W*
Turnbull, P (Edinburgh Acads) 1901 *W, I, E*, 1902 *W, I, E*
Turner, F H (Oxford U, Liverpool) 1911 *F, W, I, E*, 1912 *F, W, I, E, SA*, 1913 *F, W, I, E*, 1914 *I, E*
Turner, J W C (Gala) 1966 *W, A*, 1967 *F, W, I, E, NZ*,

1968 *F*, *W*, *I*, *E*, *A*, 1969 *F*, 1970 *E*, *A*, 1971 *F*, *W*, *I*, *E* (2[1C])

Usher, C M (United Services, Edinburgh Wands) 1912 *E*, 1913 *F*, *W*, *I*, *E*, 1914 *E*, 1920 *F*, *W*, *I*, *E*, 1921 *W*, *E*, 1922 *F*, *W*, *I*, *E*

Valentine, A R (RNAS, Anthorn) 1953 *F*, *W*, *I*
Valentine, D D (Hawick) 1947 *I*, *E*
Veitch, J P (Royal HSFP) 1882 *E*, 1883 *I*, 1884 *W*, *I*, *E*, 1885 *I* 1,2, 1886 *E*
Villar, C (Edinburgh Wands) 1876 *E*, 1877 *I*, *E*

Waddell, G H (London Scottish, Cambridge U) 1957 *E*, 1958 *F*, *W*, *A*, *I*, *E*, 1959 *F*, *W*, *I*, *E*, 1960 *I*, *E*, *SA*, 1961 *F*, 1962 *F*, *W*, *I*, *E*
Waddell, H (Glasgow Acads) 1924 *F*, *W*, *I*, *E*, 1925 *I*, *E*, 1926 *F*, *W*, *I*, *E*, 1927 *F*, *W*, *I*, *E*, 1930 *W*
Wade, A L (London Scottish) 1908 *E*
Wainwright, R I (Edinburgh Acads, West Hartlepool) 1992 *I*(R), *F*, *A* 1,2, 1993 *NZ*, 1994 *W*, *E*, 1995 *C*, *I*, *F*, *W*, *E*
Walker, A (W of Scotland) 1881 *I*, 1882 *E*, 1883 *W*, *I*, *E*
Walker, A W (Cambridge U, Birkenhead Park) 1931 *F*, *W*, *I*, *E*, 1932 *I*
Walker, J G (W of Scotland) 1882 *E*, 1883 *W*
Walker, M (Oxford U) 1952 *F*
Wallace, A C (Oxford U) 1923 *F*, 1924 *F*, *W*, *E*, 1925 *F*, *W*, *I*, *E*, 1926 *F*
Wallace, W M (Cambridge U) 1913 *E*, 1914 *W*, *I*, *E*
Walls, W A (Glasgow Acads) 1882 *E*, 1883 *W*, *I*, *E*, 1884 *W*, *I*, *E*, 1886 *W*, *I*, *E*
Walter, M W (London Scottish) 1906 *I*, *E*, *SA*, 1907 *W*, *I*, 1908 *W*, *I*, 1910 *I*
Walton, P (Northampton) 1994 *E*, *I*, *F*, *Arg* 1,2
Warren, J R (Glasgow Acads) 1914 *I*
Warren, R C (Glasgow Acads) 1922 *W*, *I*, 1930 *W*, *I*, *E*
Waters, F H (Cambridge U, London Scottish) 1930 *F*, *W*, *I*, *E*, 1932 *SA*, *W*, *I*
Waters, J A (Selkirk) 1933 *W*, *E*, *I*, 1934 *W*, *I*, *E*, 1935 *W*, *I*, *E*, *NZ*, 1936 *W*, *I*, *E*, 1937 *W*, *I*, *E*
Waters, J B (Cambridge U) 1904 *I*, *E*
Watherston, J G (Edinburgh Wands) 1934 *I*, *E*
Watherston, W R A (London Scottish) 1963 *F*, *W*, *I*
Watson, D H (Glasgow Acads) 1876 *E*, 1877 *I*, *E*
Watson, W S (Boroughmuir) 1974 *W*, *E*, *I*, *F*, 1975 *NZ*, 1977 *I*, *F*, *W*, 1979 *I*, *F*
Watt, A G J (Glasgow High Kelvinside) 1991 [*Z*], 1993 *I*, *NZ*, 1994 *Arg* 2(t & R)
Watt, A G M (Edinburgh Acads) 1947 *F*, *W*, *I*, *A*, 1948 *F*, *W*
Weatherstone, T G (Stewart's Coll FP) 1952 *E*, 1953 *I*, *E*, 1954 *F*, *NZ*, *I*, *E*, *W*, 1955 *F*, 1958 *W*, *A*, *I*, *E*, 1959 *W*, *I*, *E*
Weir, G W (Melrose) 1990 *Arg*, 1991 *R*, [*J*, *Z*, *I*, *WS*, *E*, *NZ*], 1992 *E*, *I*, *F*, *W*, *A* 1,2, 1993 *I*, *F*, *W*, *E*, *NZ*, 1994 *W*(R), *E*, *I*, *F*, *SA*, 1995 *F*(R), *W*, *E*
Welsh, R (Watsonians) 1895 *W*, *I*, *E*, 1896 *W*
Welsh, R B (Hawick) 1967 *I*, *E*
Welsh, W B (Hawick) 1927 *A*, 1928 *F*, *W*, *I*, 1929 *I*, *E*, 1930 *F*, *W*, *I*, *E*, 1931 *F*, *W*, *I*, *E*, 1932 *SA*, *W*, *I*, *E*, 1933 *W*, *E*, *I*
Welsh, W H (Edinburgh U) 1900 *I*, *E*, 1901 *W*, *I*, *E*, 1902 *W*, *I*, *E*
Wemyss, A (Gala, Edinburgh Wands) 1914 *W*, *I*, 1920 *F*, *E*, 1922 *F*, *W*, *I*
West, L (Edinburgh U, West Hartlepool) 1903 *W*, *I*, *E*, 1905 *I*, *E*, *NZ*, 1906 *W*, *I*, *E*
Weston, V G (Kelvinside Acads) 1936 *I*, *E*
White, D B (Gala, London Scottish) 1982 *F*, *W*, *A* 1,2, 1987 *W*, *E*, [*F*, *R*, *NZ*], 1988 *I*, *F*, *W*, *E*, *A*, 1989 *W*, *E*, *I*, *F*, *Fj*, *R*, 1990 *I*, *F*, *W*, *E*, *NZ* 1,2, 1991 *F*, *W*, *E*, *I*, *R*, [*J*, *Z*, *I*, *WS*, *E*, *NZ*], 1992 *E*, *I*, *F*, *W*
White, D M (Kelvinside Acads) 1963 *F*, *W*, *I*, *E*
White, T B (Edinburgh Acads) 1888 *W*, *I*, 1889 *W*
Whittington, T P (Merchistonians) 1873 *E*
Whitworth, R J E (London Scottish) 1936 *I*
Whyte, D J (Edinburgh Wands) 1965 *W*, *I*, *E*, *SA*, 1966 *F*, *W*, *I*, *E*, *A*, 1967 *F*, *W*, *I*, *E*
Will, J G (Cambridge U) 1912 *F*, *W*, *I*, *E*, 1914 *W*, *I*, *E*
Wilson, A W (Dunfermline) 1931 *F*, *I*, *E*
Wilson, G A (Oxford U) 1949 *F*, *W*, *E*
Wilson, G R (Royal HSFP) 1886 *E*, 1890 *W*, *I*, *E*, 1891 *I*
Wilson, J H (Watsonians) 1953 *I*
Wilson, J S (St Andrews U) 1931 *F*, *W*, *I*, *E*, 1932 *E*
Wilson, J S (United Services, London Scottish) 1908 *I*, 1909 *W*
Wilson, R (London Scottish) 1976 *E*, *I*, 1977 *E*, *I*, *F*, 1978 *I*, *F*, 1981 *R*, 1983 *I*
Wilson, R L (Gala) 1951 *F*, *W*, *I*, *E*, *SA*, 1953 *F*, *W*, *E*
Wilson, R W (W of Scotland) 1873 *E*, 1874 *E*
Wilson, S (Oxford U, London Scottish) 1964 *F*, *NZ*, *W*, *I*, *E*, 1965 *W*, *I*, *E*, *SA*, 1966 *F*, *W*, *I*, *A*, 1967 *F*, *W*, *I*, *E*, *NZ*, 1968 *F*, *W*, *I*, *E*
Wood, A (Royal HSFP) 1873 *E*, 1874 *E*, 1875 *E*
Wood, G (Gala) 1931 *W*, *I*, 1932 *W*, *I*, *E*
Woodburn, J C (Kelvinside Acads) 1892 *I*
Woodrow, A N (Glasgow Acads) 1887 *I*, *W*, *E*
Wotherspoon, W (W of Scotland) 1891 *I*, 1892 *I*, 1893 *W*, *E*, 1894 *W*, *I*, *E*
Wright, F A (Edinburgh Acads) 1932 *E*
Wright, H B (Watsonians) 1894 *W*
Wright, K M (London Scottish) 1929 *F*, *W*, *I*, *E*
Wright, P H (Boroughmuir) 1992 *A* 1,2, 1993 *F*, *W*, *E*, 1994 *W*, 1995 *C*, *I*, *F*, *W*, *E*
Wright, R W J (Edinburgh Wands) 1973 *F*
Wright, S T H (Stewart's Coll FP) 1949 *E*
Wright, T (Hawick) 1947 *A*
Wyllie, D S (Stewart's-Melville FP) 1984 *A*, 1985 *W* (R), *E*, 1987 *I*, *F*, [*F*, *Z*, *R*, *NZ*], 1989 *R*, 1991 *R*, [*J*(R), *Z*], 1993 *NZ*(R), 1994 *W*(R), *E*, *I*, *F*

Young, A H (Edinburgh Acads) 1874 *E*
Young, E T (Glasgow Acads) 1914 *E*
Young, R G (Watsonians) 1970 *W*
Young, T E B (Durham) 1911 *F*
Young, W B (Cambridge U, London Scottish) 1937 *W*, *I*, *E*, 1938 *W*, *I*, *E*, 1939 *W*, *I*, *E*, 1948 *E*

SCOTTISH INTERNATIONAL RECORDS

Both team and individual records are for official Scotland international matches, up to 31 March 1995.

TEAM RECORDS

Highest score

60 v Zimbabwe (60-21) 1987 Wellington

v individual countries

49 v Argentina (49-3) 1990 Murrayfield
24 v Australia (24-15) 1981 Murrayfield
22 v Canada (22-6) 1995 Murrayfield
33 v England (33-6) 1986 Murrayfield
38 v Fiji (38-17) 1989 Murrayfield
31 v France (31-3) 1912 Inverleith
37 v Ireland (37-21) 1989 Murrayfield
47 v Japan (47-9) 1991 Murrayfield
25 v N Zealand (25-25) 1983 Murrayfield
55 v Romania (55-28) 1987 Dunedin
10 v S Africa { (10-18) 1960 Port Elizabeth; (10-34) 1994 Murrayfield }
35 v Wales (35-10) 1924 Inverleith
28 v W Samoa (28-6) 1991 Murrayfield
60 v Zimbabwe (60-21) 1987 Wellington

Biggest winning points margin
46 v Argentina (49-3) 1990 Murrayfield
v individual countries
46 v Argentina (49-3) 1990 Murrayfield
9 v Australia (24-15) 1981 Murrayfield
16 v Canada (22-6) 1995 Murrayfield
27 v England (33-6) 1986 Murrayfield
21 v Fiji (38-17) 1989 Murrayfield
28 v France (31-3) 1912 Inverleith
23 v Ireland (32-9) 1984 Dublin
38 v Japan (47-9) 1991 Murrayfield
No win v N Zealand
32 v Romania (32-0) 1989 Murrayfield
6 v S Africa (6-0) 1906 Glasgow
25 v Wales (35-10) 1924 Inverleith
22 v W Samoa (28-6) 1991 Murrayfield
39 v Zimbabwe { (60-21) 1987 Wellington
(51-12) 1991 Murrayfield }

Longest winning sequence
6 matches – 1925-26 and 1989-90

Highest score by opposing team
51 N Zealand (15-51) 1993 Murrayfield
by individual countries
19 Argentina (17-19) 1994 Buenos Aires
37 Australia { (12-37) 1984 Murrayfield
(13-37) 1992 Brisbane }
6 Canada (22-6) 1995 Murrayfield
30 England (18-30) 1980 Murrayfield
17 Fiji (38-17) 1989 Murrayfield
28 France (22-28) 1987 Parc de Princes
26 Ireland (8-26) 1953 Murrayfield
9 Japan (47-9) 1991 Murrayfield
51 N Zealand (15-51) 1993 Murrayfield
28 Romania { (22-28) 1984 Bucharest
(55-28) 1987 Dunedin }
44 S Africa (0-44) 1951 Murrayfield
35 Wales (12-35) 1972 Cardiff
6 W Samoa (28-6) 1991 Murrayfield
21 Zimbabwe (60-21) 1987 Wellington

Biggest losing points margin
44 v S Africa (0-44) 1951 Murrayfield
v individual countries
2 v Argentina (17-19) 1994 Buenos Aires
25 v Australia (12-37) 1984 Murrayfield
20 v England (6-26) 1977 Twickenham
20 v France (3-23) 1977 Parc des Princes
21 v Ireland (0-21) 1950 Dublin
36 v N Zealand (15-51) 1993 Murrayfield
6 v Romania { (22-28) 1984 Bucharest
(12-18) 1991 Bucharest }
44 v S Africa (0-44) 1951 Murrayfield
23 v Wales { (12-35) 1972 Cardiff
(6-29) 1994 Cardiff }
No defeats v Canada, Fiji, Japan, Western Samoa or Zimbabwe

Longest losing sequence
17 matches – 1951-54

Most tries by Scotland in an international
12 v Wales 1887 Raeburn Place (Edinburgh)

Most tries against Scotland in an international
9 by S Africa (0-44) 1951 Murrayfield

Most points by Scotland in International Championship in a season – 87
in season 1994-95

Most tries by Scotland in International Championship in a season – 17
in season 1924-25

INDIVIDUAL RECORDS

Most capped player
A G Hastings 56 1986-95
in individual positions
Full-back
A G Hastings 56 1986-95
Wing
I Tukalo 37 1985-92
Centre
S Hastings 52(53)[1] 1986-95
Fly-half
J Y Rutherford 42 1979-87
Scrum-half
R J Laidlaw 47 1980-88
Prop
A B Carmichael 50 1967-78
Hooker
C T Deans 52 1978-87
Lock
A J Tomes 48 1976-87
Flanker
J Jeffrey 40 1984-91
No 8
D B White 29(41)[2] 1982-92

[1]J M Renwick, 52 caps, won 51 as a centre and one as a replacement wing. Hastings has been capped once as a wing
[2]White won 5 caps as a flanker and 7 as a lock

Longest international career
W C W Murdoch 14 seasons 1935-48

Most consecutive internationals – 49
A B Carmichael 1967-78

Most internationals as captain – 25
D M B Sole 1989-92

Most points in internationals – 544
A G Hastings (56 matches) 1986-95

Most points in International Championship in a season – 56
A G Hastings (4 matches) 1994-95

Most points in an international – 27
A G Hastings v Romania 1987 Dunedin

Most tries in internationals – 24
I S Smith (32 matches) 1924-33

Most tries in International Championship in a season – 8
I S Smith (4 matches) 1924-25

Most tries in an international – 5
G C Lindsay v Wales 1887 Raeburn Place (Edinburgh)

Most conversions in internationals – 68
A G Hastings (56 matches) 1986-95

Most conversions in International Championship in a season – 8
P W Dods (4 matches) 1983-84

Most conversions in an international – 8
A G Hastings v Zimbabwe 1987 Wellington
A G Hastings v Romania 1987 Dunedin

Most dropped goals in internationals – 12
J Y Rutherford (42 matches) 1972-82

Most dropped goals in an international – 2
R C MacKenzie v Ireland 1877 Belfast
N J Finlay v Ireland 1880 Glasgow
B M Simmers v Wales 1965 Murrayfield
D W Morgan v Ireland 1973 Murrayfield
B M Gossman v France 1983 Paris
J Y Rutherford v N Zealand 1983 Murrayfield
J Y Rutherford v Wales 1985 Murrayfield
J Y Rutherford v Ireland 1987 Murrayfield
C M Chalmers v England 1995 Twickenham

Most penalty goals in internationals – 121
A G Hastings (56 matches) 1986-95

Most penalty goals in International Championship in a season – 14
A G Hastings (4 matches) 1985-86

Most penalty goals in an international – 6
A G Hastings v France 1986 Murrayfield

Most points on major tour – 58
P W Dods (4 matches) N Zealand 1990
C D R Mair scored 100 points in the Far East in 1977, but this was not on a major tour

Most points in a tour match – 24
D W Morgan v Wellington 1975 Wellington, NZ
A R Irvine v King Country 1981 Taumarunui, NZ
A R Irvine v Wairarapa-Bush 1981 Masterton, NZ
P W Dods scored 43 points v Alberta in 1985, but this was not on a major tour

Most tries in a tour match – 3
A R Smith v Eastern Transvaal 1960 Springs, SA
K R F Bearne scored 5 tries v Ontario U in 1964, A J W Hinshelwood scored 5 v Quebec in 1964, and D E W Leckie scored 5 v Goshawks (Zimbabwe) in 1988, but these were not on a major tour

ELITE SQUAD NEEDED TO SAVE IRELAND FROM DIRE STRAITS

THE 1994-95 SEASON IN IRELAND

Sean Diffley *Irish Independent*

It's very difficult indeed to portray the condition of Irish rugby, on an international level, as being anything but in dire straits. Even the single victory in the Five Nations, over Wales in Cardiff, was secured in a game of poor quality. Criticism has been virulent, and not just in the media. Willie Anderson, who resigned during the season as an IRFU development officer, and who had been acting as assistant coach to Gerry Murphy, was later quoted as saying: 'The truth is that Irish rugby is experiencing one of its lowest points, if not the lowest, in its international history.' And former Ireland coach Mick Doyle kept up a stinging succession of critical newspaper columns, aimed mainly at the manager, Noel Murphy, alleging poor selectorial judgements .

It all reached the stage where legal writs were being brandished and, of course, the inflammatory atmosphere could only have a bad effect on the morale of the players. In all four Championship games the traditional Irish spirit managed to arouse itself only for short periods. Few players could feel all that happy with their performances and in the circumstances that was not really surprising.

There were selectorial mistakes. The half-back situation took a long time to resolve, with four players – Michael Bradley, Niall Hogan, Eric Elwood and Paul Burke – falling in and out of favour. The back five of the pack was another area for the selectors' games of ducks and drakes. But, in fairness to the selectors, the season presented the greatest number of injuries that anyone can remember. It almost reached the bizarre levels of Bill Beaumont's Lions in South Africa in 1980, when a horrendous total of eight replacements had to be sent for.

Ireland began their International Championship campaign with two of their sheet-anchors out of consideration because of injuries: back-row forwards Pat O'Hara and Brian Robinson. In the course of the tournament no fewer than 11 players selected for the national side had to withdraw: Jim Staples, Jonathan Bell, Niall Hogan, Keith Wood, Neil Francis, Denis McBride, Paddy Johns, Ben Cronin, Mick Galwey, Michael Bradley and Eric Elwood. Not even countries with large rugby populations could soldier on successfully after a purge like that. It certainly explains a lot, but nonetheless it is hardly a real excuse for the squad's lacklustre aura. Sooner or later, the IRFU will have to accept that if Ireland are to keep up with the major nations, the national squad will have to be treated as an élite and the demands of clubs will – as in New Zealand, in particular – have to take a very definite back seat.

At lower international levels, Schools, Under-21 and Youth, Ireland does remarkably well. Clearly, the talent is there. At ground level the

The Ireland team which beat Wales in Cardiff. L-R, back row: D Corkery (replacement), S J Byrne (replacement), E P Elwood, A G Foley, G M Fulcher, P S Johns, D A Tweed, E O Halvey, J E Staples, P M Clohessy, G F Halpin (replacement), M J Field (replacement); front row: M T Bradley (replacement), S P Geoghegan, P P A Danaher, N J Popplewell, T J Kingston (capt), B J Mullin, R M Wallace, N A Hogan, P A Burke (replacement).

game is strong, but at that standard rugby must make up its mind that it must take second place to the demands of the national squad.

The Insurance Corporation All-Ireland League completed its fifth season and retained its Munster accent. Shannon won all ten of their League games, the first time that a winning club managed a clean sheet. Their last game, at home at Thomond Park before an attendance of 6,000 (there for the occasion – the League was already won), was against Instonians, and a very sporting encounter it was, too. It culminated in the whole crowd giving the most spirited rendering of the Shannon anthem, 'There is an Isle', on an incredible afternoon of celebration.

So, since the inauguration of the League in 1991, when Cork Constitution were the winners of Division 1, the honours have remained solidly in Limerick. Garryowen were the victors in 1992 and 1994, Young Munster in 1993, and now Shannon were triumphant.

The Inter-Provincial Championship also went south. Ulster had dominated for a decade, but their run came to an end and Munster were clearly the best and most committed side this time.

INSURANCE CORPORATION ALL-IRELAND LEAGUE 1994-95

Division 1	*P*	*W*	*D*	*L*	*F*	*A*	*Pts*
Shannon	10	10	0	0	162	60	20
Blackrock Coll	10	7	0	3	228	135	14
St Mary's Coll	10	7	0	3	151	134	14
Garryowen	10	6	0	4	160	113	12
Cork Const	10	6	0	4	148	129	12
Old Wesley	10	5	0	5	131	171	10
Lansdowne	10	3	1	6	150	225	7
Young Munster	10	3	0	7	115	153	6
Instonians	10	3	0	7	108	160	6
Sunday's Well	10	2	1	7	119	165	5
Dungannon	10	2	0	8	114	141	4

Division 2	*P*	*W*	*D*	*L*	*F*	*A*	*Pts*
Old Belvedere	10	8	0	2	157	123	16
Ballymena	10	7	1	2	191	122	15
Wanderers	10	6	1	3	151	133	13
Terenure Coll	10	6	0	4	187	171	12
Bective Rangers	10	5	1	4	181	135	11
Malone	10	5	0	5	140	141	10
Old Crescent	10	4	1	5	179	173	9
Greystones	10	4	1	5	173	188	9
Dolphin	10	3	1	6	99	144	7
UC Dublin	10	2	2	6	141	157	6
Bangor	10	1	0	9	90	205	2

Division 3	*P*	*W*	*D*	*L*	*F*	*A*	*Pts*
NIFC	11	9	0	2	210	135	18
Clontarf	11	8	0	3	187	126	16
Highfield	11	7	0	4	172	147	14
City of Derry	11	6	1	4	140	117	13
DLS Palmerston	11	5	1	5	135	125	11
Buccaneers	11	6	0	5	179	142	12
Monkstown	11	5	1	5	138	137	11
Waterpark	11	5	0	6	160	183	10
Galwegians	11	4	1	6	121	128	9
UC Cork	11	3	3	5	129	141	9
Corinthians	11	3	1	7	116	174	7
Ballina	11	1	0	10	115	247	2

Division 4	*P*	*W*	*D*	*L*	*F*	*A*	*Pts*
Bohemians	10	9	0	1	213	92	18
Skerries	10	8	1	1	254	74	17
Portadown	10	8	1	1	166	92	17
Dublin U	10	7	2	1	329	108	16
Queen's U, Belfast	10	5	1	4	183	163	11
CIYMS	10	4	0	6	145	134	8
Ards	10	3	1	6	90	143	7
Collegians	10	2	1	7	110	207	5
Armagh	10	2	1	7	112	246	5
Sligo	10	2	0	8	95	196	4
UC Galway	10	0	2	8	60	302	2

INTER-PROVINCIAL TOURNAMENT 1994

12 November, Musgrave Park, Cork

Munster 17 (3PG 1DG 1T) **Ulster 16** (1G 2PG 1DG)
Munster: P Murray (Shannon); K Smith (Garryowen), S McCahill (Sunday's Well), P P A Danaher (Garryowen), B Roche (Sunday's Well); P A Burke (Cork Const), D O'Mahony (Cork Const); J J Fitzgerald (Young Munster), K G M Wood (Garryowen), P M Clohessy (Young Munster), M J Galwey (Shannon), G M Fulcher (Cork Const), E O Halvey (Shannon), A G Foley (Shannon), D Corkery (Cork Const) *Replacements* D Larkin (Garryowen) for Roche; B Toland (Old Crescent) for Fulcher
Scorers *Try:* Smith *Penalty Goals:* Burke (3) *Dropped Goal:* Burke
Ulster: J C Bell (Ballymena); R W Carey (Dungannon), M J Field (Malone), M C McCall (Bangor), D Smyth (Ballymena); D Humphreys (Ballymena), A Matchett (Ballymena); S Booth (Ballymena), J P McDonald (Malone), G Bell (Instonians), G Longwell (Ballymena), D A Tweed (Ballymena), D Erskine (Sale), S McKinty (Bangor), W D McBride (Malone)
Scorers *Try:* Matchett *Conversion:* McCall *Penalty Goals:* Humphreys (2) *Dropped Goal:* Humphreys
Referee A Lewis

12 November, Galway

Exiles 35 (1G 1PG 5T) **Connacht 9** (2PG 1DG)
Connacht: A White (Garryowen); C Leahy (Wanderers), G Lavin (St Mary's Coll), S Tormey (Old Belvedere), G Curley (Buccaneers); H Carolan (Old Crescent), D Reddan (Old Crescent); T P J Clancy (Blackrock Coll), W Mulcahy (Skerries), P Flavin (Blackrock Coll), S Jameson (St Mary's Coll), J Etheridge (Blackrock Coll), V Costello (St Mary's Coll), N P Mannion (Buccaneers), K Devlin (St Mary's Coll) *Replacement* M Murphy (Galwegians) for Leahy
Scorer *Penalty Goals:* Carolan (2) *Dropped Goal:* Carolan
Exiles: J E Staples (Harlequins); M Corcoran (London Irish), D Dooley (Saracens), L Boyle (Harlequins), S P Geoghegan (Bath); N G Malone (Leicester), G Easterby (Harrogate); N Donovan (London Irish), D Addleton (Coventry), G F Halpin (London Irish), K Gallagher (Treorchy), A Verling (London Irish), D O'Grady (Sale), D McCartney (Pau), M Dobson (Sale) *Replacements* B Wellens (Liverpool St Helen's) for Malone; A Higgins (London Irish) for O'Grady
Referee A Watson

19 November, Ravenhill

Ulster 20 (2G 1PG 1DG) **Connacht 6** (1PG 1DG)
Ulster: J C Bell (Ballymena); R W Carey (Dungannon), M C McCall (Bangor), M J Field (Malone), G McCluskey (Instonians); D Humphreys (Ballymena), A Matchett (Ballymena); S Booth (Ballymena), J P McDonald (Malone), G Bell (Instonians), G Longwell (Ballymena), D A Tweed (Ballymena), D Erskine (Sale), S McKinty (Bangor), W D McBride (Malone) *Replacements* A Adair (Instonians) for McDonald; J Hastings (Dungannon) for Erskine
Scorers *Tries:* Tweed (2) *Conversions:* McCall (2) *Penalty Goal:* McCall *Dropped Goal:* Humphreys
Connacht: H Carolan (Old Crescent); M Devine (Buccaneers), S Tormey (Old Belvedere), M Cosgrave (Wanderers), M O'Reilly (Old Belvedere); A White (Garryowen), D Reddan (Old Crescent); T P J Clancy (Blackrock Coll), W Mulcahy (Skerries), P Flavin (Blackrock Coll), S Jameson (St Mary's Coll), J Etheridge (Blackrock Coll), V Costello (St Mary's Coll), N P Mannion (Buccaneers), K Devlin (St Mary's Coll) *Replacement* B Gavin (St Mary's Coll) for Costello
Scorers *Penalty Goal:* Carolan *Dropped Goal:* White
Referee G Black

20 November, Donnybrook, Dublin

Leinster 20 (2G 1PG 1DG) **Exiles 18** (1G 2PG 1T)
Leinster: C P Clarke (Terenure Coll); P Gavin (Old Belvedere), B T Glennon (Lansdowne), R Moloney (Old Wesley), D Wall (St Mary's Coll); A N McGowan (Blackrock Coll), A C Rolland (Blackrock Coll); H Hurley (Old Wesley), S Byrne (Blackrock Coll), B Keane (St Mary's Coll), B Cusack (Bective Rangers), N P J Francis (Old Belvedere), C Pim (Old Wesley), K Potts (St Mary's Coll), R Love (Old Wesley) *Replacement* M Carney (Greystones) for Clarke
Scorers *Tries:* Rolland, Francis *Conversions:* McGowan (2) *Penalty Goal:* McGowan *Dropped Goal:* Moloney
Exiles: J E Staples (Harlequins); M Corcoran (London Irish), L Boyle (Harlequins), D Dooley (Saracens), S P Geoghegan (Bath); N G Malone (Leicester), G Easterby (Harlequins); N Donovan (London Irish), D Addleton (Coventry), G F Halpin (London Irish), K Gallagher (Treorchy), A Verling (London Irish), J Green (Saracens), D O'Grady (Sale), M Dobson (Sale)
Scorers *Tries:* Staples, Halpin *Conversion:* Corcoran *Penalty Goals:* Corcoran (2)
Referee D McHugh

26 November, Sportsground, Galway

Connacht 20 (2G 2PG) **Leinster 19** (1G 4PG)
Connacht: H Carolan (Old Crescent); M Devine (Buccaneers), M Cosgrave (Wanderers), M Murphy (Galwegians), M O'Reilly (Old Belvedere); A White (Garryowen), D Reddan (Old Crescent); T P J Clancy (Blackrock Coll), W Mulcahy (Skerries), P Flavin (Blackrock Coll), S Jameson (St Mary's Coll), J Etheridge (Blackrock Coll), B Gavin (Blackrock Coll), K Devlin (St Mary's Coll), N P Mannion (Buccaneers) *Replacements* T Coughlin (Old Belvedere) for Devlin; D Henshaw (Buccaneers) for Flavin
Scorers *Tries:* Etheridge, Mannion *Conversions:* Carolan (2) *Penalty Goals:* Carolan (2)
Leinster: M Carney (Greystones); P Gavin (Old Belvedere), B T Glennon (Lansdowne), R Moloney (Old Wesley), D Finnegan (Wanderers); A N McGowan (Blackrock Coll), A C Rolland (Blackrock Coll); H Hurley (Old Wesley),

S Byrne (Blackrock Coll), J Feehan (Old Wesley), B J Rigney (Shannon), N P J Francis (Old Belvedere), C Pim (Old Wesley), R Love (Old Wesley), P J Lawlor (Bective Rangers) *Replacement* F Campion (St Mary's Coll) for McGowan
Scorers *Try:* Carney *Conversion:* Campion *Penalty Goals:* McGowan (2), Campion (2)
Referee L Mayne

26 November, Sunbury

Exiles 8 (1PG 1T) **Munster 46** (4G 6PG)
Exiles: J E Staples (Harlequins); P Hopley (Wasps), R Henderson (London Irish), L Boyle (Harlequins), S P Geoghegan (Bath); N G Malone (Leicester), G Easterby (Harrogate); N Donovan (London Irish), T Garnett (Wakefield), G F Halpin (London Irish), S Smith (Rugby), A Verling (London Irish), J Green (Saracens), M Dobson (Ballymena), D O'Grady (Sale)
Scorers *Try:* Henderson *Penalty Goal:* Malone
Munster: P Murray (Shannon); B O'Shea (Shannon), S McCahill (Sunday's Well), P P A Danaher (Garryowen), K Smith (Garryowen); P A Burke (Cork Const), D O'Mahony (Cork Const); J J Fitzgerald (Young Munster), K G M Wood (Garryowen), P M Clohessy (Young Munster), M J Galwey (Shannon), G M Fulcher (Cork Const), E O Halvey (Shannon), D Corkery (Cork Const), A G Foley (Shannon) *Replacements* R A Costello (Garryowen) for Fulcher; D Larkin (Garryowen) for Murray
Scorers *Tries:* Burke, Foley, Halvey, Smith *Conversions:* Smith (4) *Penalty Goals:* Smith (6)
Referee G Black

10 December, Donnybrook, Dublin

Leinster 14 (3PG 1T) **Munster 36** (4G 1PG 1T)
Leinster: M Carney (Greystones); P Gavin (Old Belvedere), R Moloney (Old Wesley), M Ridge (Blackrock Coll), N K P J Woods (Blackrock Coll); A N McGowan (Blackrock Coll), A C Rolland (Blackrock Coll); H Hurley (Old Wesley), S Byrne (Blackrock Coll), J Feehan (Old Wesley), B J Rigney (Shannon), N P J Francis (Old Belvedere), C Pim (Old Wesley), P J Lawlor (Bective Rangers), R Love (Old Wesley) *Replacement* B Keane (St Mary's Coll) for Love
Scorers *Try:* Rigney *Penalty Goals:* McGowan (3)
Munster: P Murray (Shannon); B O'Shea (Shannon), S McCahill (Sunday's Well), P P A Danaher (Garryowen), K Smith (Garryowen); P A Burke (Cork Const), D O'Mahony (Cork Const); J J Fitzgerald (Young Munster), T J Kingston (Dolphin), P M Clohessy (Young Munster), M J Galwey (Shannon), R A Costello (Garryowen), E O Halvey (Shannon), A G Foley (Shannon), D Corkery (Cork Const)
Scorers *Tries:* O'Shea, Corkery, O'Mahony, Danaher, Foley *Conversions:* Smith (4) *Penalty Goal:* Smith
Referee S Hilditch

10 December, Sale

Exiles 16 (1G 3PG) **Ulster 42** (1G 5PG 4T)
Exiles: J E Staples (Harlequins); D Casado (Newcastle Gosforth), B Wellens (Liverpool St Helen's), L Boyle (Harlequins), J Reynolds (Cambridge U); N G Malone (Leicester), G Easterby (Harrogate); N Donovan (London Irish), D Addleton (Coventry), G F Halpin (London Irish), F Smith (Rugby), A Verling (London Irish), D McCartney (Pau), D O'Grady (Sale), D Adams (Racing Club de France) *Replacement* O Cobbe (London Irish) for Reynolds
Scorers *Try:* Smith *Conversion:* Malone *Penalty Goals:* Malone (3)
Ulster: J C Bell (Ballymena); I Gray (Oxford U), M C McCall (Bangor), M J Field (Malone), T Howe (Oxford U); D Humphreys (Ballymena), A Matchett (Ballymena); S Booth (Ballymena), J P McDonald (Malone), G Bell (Instonians), G Longwell (Ballymena), D A Tweed (Ballymena), S McKinty (Bangor), W D McBride (Malone), R Wilson (Instonians)
Scorers *Tries:* Bell (2), Howe (2), Wilson *Conversion:* McCall *Penalty Goals:* McCall (4), Humphreys
Referee B Smith

17 December, Ravenhill

Ulster 6 (2PG) **Leinster 12** (4PG)
Ulster: J C Bell (Ballymena); I Gray (Oxford U), M C McCall (Bangor), M J Field (Malone), T Howe (Oxford U); D Humphreys (Ballymena), A Matchett (Ballymena); S Booth (Ballymena), J P McDonald (Malone), G Bell (Instonians), D A Tweed (Ballymena), J Davidson (Dungannon), S McKinty (Bangor), R Wilson (Instonians), W D McBride (Malone) *Replacements* S McDowell (Dungannon) for Bell; G Longwell (Ballymena) for Davidson
Scorers *Penalty Goals:* Humphreys, McCall
Leinster: C M P O'Shea (Lansdowne); P Gavin (Old Belvedere), R Moloney (Old Wesley), M Ridge (Blackrock Coll), N K P J Woods (Blackrock Coll); A N McGowan (Blackrock Coll), N A Hogan (Terenure Coll); B Keane (St Mary's Coll), S Byrne (Blackrock Coll), A McKeen (Lansdowne), B J Rigney (Shannon), N P J Francis (Blackrock Coll), C Pim (Old Wesley), S Rooney (Lansdowne), P J Lawlor (Bective Rangers) *Replacement* K Potts (St Mary's Coll) for Lawlor
Scorer *Penalty Goals:* McGowan (4)
Referee A Spreadbury (RFU)

17 December, Thomond Park, Limerick

Munster 60 (4G 3PG 1DG 4T) **Connacht 20** (1G 1PG 2T)
Munster: P Murray (Shannon); B O'Shea (Shannon), P P A Danaher (Garryowen), S McCahill (Sunday's Well), K Smith (Garryowen); P A Burke (Cork Const), D O'Mahony (Cork Const); J J Fitzgerald (Young Munster), T J Kingston (Dolphin), P M Clohessy (Young Munster), M J Galwey (Shannon), R A Costello (Garryowen), E O Halvey (Shannon), A G Foley (Shannon), D Corkery (Cork Const)

Scorers *Tries:* Foley (3), Murray, O'Shea, Corkery, Danaher, pen try *Conversions:* Smith (4) *Penalty Goals:* Smith (3) *Dropped Goal:* Burke
Connacht: H Carolan (Old Crescent); M Devine (Buccaneers), S Tormey (Old Belvedere), M Cosgrave (Wanderers), M O'Reilly (Old Belvedere); E P Elwood (Lansdowne), D Reddan (Old Crescent); T P J Clancy (Blackrock Coll), B Mulcahy (Skerries), P Flavin (Blackrock Coll), S Jameson (St Mary's Coll), J Etheridge (Blackrock Coll), B Gavin (Blackrock Coll), N P Mannion (Buccaneers), R Rogers (Blackrock Coll)
Scorers *Tries:* Devine (3) *Conversion:* Carolan *Penalty Goal:* Carolan
Referee A Lewis

Richard Wallace and Brendan Mullin with a cause for celebration – a rarity during Ireland's season – Mullin's try against Wales in the Five Nations, Ireland's sole victory in the tournament.

IRISH INTERNATIONAL PLAYERS
(up to 31 March 1995)

ABBREVIATIONS

A – Australia; *Arg* – Argentina; *C* – Canada; *E* – England; *F* – France; *It* – Italy; *J* – Japan; *M* – Maoris; *Nm* – Namibia; *NZ* – New Zealand; *R* – Romania; *S* – Scotland; *SA* – South Africa; *Tg* – Tonga; *US* – United States; *W* – Wales; *WS* – Western Samoa; *Z* – Zimbabwe; *P* – Ireland v IRFU President's XV at Lansdowne Road in IRFU centenary season, 1974-75; (R) – Replacement; (t) – temporary replacement. Entries in square brackets [ ] indicate appearances in the World Cup. NIFC – North of Ireland Football Club; CIYMS – Church of Ireland Young Men's Society; KCH – King's College Hospital

Note: Years given for Five Nations' matches are for second half of season; eg 1972 means season 1971-72. Years for all other matches refer to the actual year of the match. When a series has taken place, figures have been used to denote the particular matches in which players have featured. Thus 1981 *SA* 2 indicates that a player appeared in the second Test of the series. The abandoned game with Scotland at Belfast in 1885 is now included as a cap match.

NB – The second of Ireland's two matches against France in 1972 was a non-championship match.

Abraham, M (Bective Rangers) 1912 *E, S, W, SA*, 1914 *W*
Adams, C (Old Wesley) 1908 *E*, 1909 *E, F*, 1910 *F*, 1911 *E, S, W, F*, 1912 *S, W, SA*, 1913 *W, F*, 1914 *F, E, S*
Agar, R D (Malone) 1947 *F, E, S, W*, 1948 *F*, 1949 *S, W*, 1950 *F, E , W*
Agnew, P J (CIYMS) 1974 *F* (R), 1976 *A*
Ahearne, T (Queen's Coll, Cork) 1899 *E*
Aherne, L F P (Dolphin, Lansdowne) 1988 *E* 2, *WS, It*, 1989 *F, W, E, S, NZ*, 1990 *E, S, F, W*(R), 1992 *E, S, F, A*
Alexander, R (NIFC, Police Union) 1936 *E, S, W*, 1937 *E, S, W*, 1938 *E, S*, 1939 *E, S, W*
Allen, C E (Derry, Liverpool) 1900 *E, S, W*, 1901 *E, S, W*, 1903 *S, W*, 1904 *E, S, W*, 1905 *E, S, W, NZ*, 1906 *E, S, W, SA*, 1907 *S, W*
Allen, G G (Derry, Liverpool) 1896 *E, S, W*, 1897 *E, S*, 1898 *E, S*, 1899 *E, W*
Allen, T C (NIFC) 1885 *E, S* 1
Allen, W S (Wanderers) 1875 *E*
Allison, J B (Edinburgh U) 1899 *E, S*, 1900 *E, S, W*, 1901 *E, S, W*, 1902 *E, S, W*, 1903 *S*
Anderson, F E (Queen's U, Belfast, NIFC) 1953 *F, E, S, W*, 1954 *NZ, F, E, S, W*, 1955 *F, E, S, W*
Anderson, H J (Old Wesley) 1903 *E, S*, 1906 *E, S*
Anderson, W A (Dungannon) 1984 *A*, 1985 *S, F, W, E*, 1986 *F, S, R*, 1987 *E, S, F, W*, [*W, C, Tg, A*], 1988 *S, F, W, E* 1,2, 1989 *F, W, E, NZ*, 1990 *E, S*
Andrews, G (NIFC) 1875 *E*, 1876 *E*
Andrews, H W (NIFC) 1888 *M*, 1889 *S, W*
Archer, A M (Dublin U, NIFC) 1879 *S*
Arigho, J E (Lansdowne) 1928 *F, E, W*, 1929 *F, E, S, W*, 1930 *F, E, S, W*, 1931 *F, E, S, W, SA*
Armstrong, W K (NIFC) 1960 *SA*, 1961 *E*
Arnott, D T (Lansdowne) 1876 *E*
Ash, W H (NIFC) 1875 *E*, 1876 *E*, 1877 *S*
Aston, H R (Dublin U) 1908 *E, W*
Atkins, A P (Bective Rangers) 1924 *F*
Atkinson, J M (NIFC) 1927 *F, A*
Atkinson, J R (Dublin U) 1882 *W, S*

Bagot, J C (Dublin U, Lansdowne) 1879 *S, E*, 1880 *E, S*, 1881 *S*
Bailey, A H (UC Dublin, Lansdowne) 1934 *W*, 1935 *E, S, W, NZ*, 1936 *E, S, W*, 1937 *E, S, W*, 1938 *E, S*
Bailey, N (Northampton) 1952 *E*
Bardon, M E (Bohemians) 1934 *E*
Barlow, M (Wanderers) 1875 *E*
Barnes, R J (Dublin U, Armagh) 1933 *W*
Barr, A (Methodist Coll, Belfast) 1898 *W*, 1899 *S*, 1901 *E, S*
Barry, N J (Garryowen) 1991 *Nm*2(R)
Beamish, C E St J (RAF, Leicester) 1933 *W, S*, 1934 *S, W*, 1935 *E, S, W, NZ*, 1936 *E, S, W*, 1938 *W*
Beamish, G R (RAF, Leicester) 1925 *E, S, W*, 1928 *F, E, S, W*, 1929 *F, E, S, W*, 1930 *F, S, W*, 1931 *F, E, S, W, SA*, 1932 *E, S, W*, 1933 *E, W, S*
Beatty, W J (NIFC, Richmond) 1910 *F*, 1912 *F, W*
Becker, V A (Lansdowne) 1974 *F, W*
Beckett, G G P (Dublin U) 1908 *E, S, W*
Bell, J C (Ballymena) 1994 *A* 1,2, *US*, 1995 *S*
Bell, R J (NIFC) 1875 *E*, 1876 *E*
Bell, W E (Belfast Collegians) 1953 *F, E, S, W*
Bennett, F (Belfast Collegians) 1913 *S*
Bent, G C (Dublin U) 1882 *W, E*
Berkery, P J (Lansdowne) 1954 *W*, 1955 *W*, 1956 *S, W*, 1957 *F, E, S, W*, 1958 *A, E, S*
Bermingham, J J C (Blackrock Coll) 1921 *E, S, W, F*
Blackham, J C (Queen's Coll, Cork) 1909 *S, W, F*, 1910 *E, S, W*
Blake-Knox, S E F (NIFC) 1976 *E, S*, 1977 *F* (R)
Blayney, J J (Wanderers) 1950 *S*
Bond, A T W (Derry) 1894 *S, W*
Bornemann, W W (Wanderers) 1960 *E, S, W, SA*
Bowen, D St J (Cork Const) 1977 *W, E, S*
Boyd, C A (Dublin U) 1900 *S*, 1901 *S, W*
Boyle, C V (Dublin U) 1935 *NZ*, 1936 *E, S, W*, 1937 *E, S, W*, 1938 *W*, 1939 *W*
Brabazon, H M (Dublin U) 1884 *E*, 1885 *S* 1, 1886 *E*
Bradley, M J (Dolphin) 1920 *W, F*, 1922 *E, S, W, F*, 1923 *E, S, W, F*, 1925 *F, S, W*, 1926 *F, E, S, W*, 1927 *F, W*
Bradley, M T (Cork Constitution) 1984 *A*, 1985 *S, F, W, E*, 1986 *F, W, E, S, R*, 1987 *E, S, F, W*, [*W, C, Tg, A*], 1988 *S, F, W, E* 1, 1990 *W*, 1992 *NZ* 1,2, 1993 *S, F, W, E, R*, 1994 *F, W, E, S, A* 1,2, *US*, 1995 *S, F*
Bradshaw, G (Belfast Collegians) 1903 *W*
Bradshaw, R M (Wanderers) 1885 *E, S* 1,2
Brady, A M (UC Dublin, Malone) 1966 *S*, 1968 *E, S, W*
Brady, J A (Wanderers) 1976 *E, S*
Brady, J R (CIYMS) 1951 *S, W*, 1953 *F, E, S, W*, 1954 *W*, 1956 *W*, 1957 *F, E, S, W*
Bramwell, T (NIFC) 1928 *F*
Brand, T N (NIFC) 1924 *NZ*
Brennan, J I (CIYMS) 1957 *S, W*
Bresnihan, F P K (UC Dublin, Lansdowne, London Irish) 1966 *E, W*, 1967 *A* 1, *E, S, W, F*, 1968 *F, E, S, W, A*, 1969 *F, E, S, W*, 1970 *SA, F, E, S, W*, 1971 *F, E, S, W*
Brett, J T (Monkstown) 1914 *W*
Bristow, J R (NIFC) 1879 *E*
Brophy, N H (Blackrock Coll, UC Dublin, London Irish) 1957 *F, E*, 1959 *E, S, W, F*, 1960 *F, SA*, 1961 *S, W*, 1962 *E, S, W*, 1963 *E, W*, 1967 *E, S, W, F, A* 2
Brown, E L (Instonians) 1958 *F*
Brown, G S (Monkstown, United Services) 1912 *S, W, SA*
Brown, H (Windsor) 1877 *E*
Brown, T (Windsor) 1877 *E, S*
Brown, W H (Dublin U) 1899 *E*
Brown, W J (Malone) 1970 *SA, F, S, W*
Brown, W S (Dublin U) 1893 *S, W*, 1894 *E, S, W*
Browne, A W (Dublin U) 1951 *SA*
Browne, D (Blackrock Coll) 1920 *F*
Browne, H C (United Services and RN) 1929 *E, S, W*
Browne, W F (United Services and Army) 1925 *E, S, W*, 1926 *S, W*, 1927 *F, E, S, W, A*, 1928 *E, S*
Browning, D R (Wanderers) 1881 *E, S*
Bruce, S A M (NIFC) 1883 *E, S*, 1884 *E*

Brunker, A A (Lansdowne) 1895 *E, W*
Bryant, C H (Cardiff) 1920 *E, S*
Buchanan, A McM (Dublin U) 1926 *E, S, W*, 1927 *S, W, A*
Buchanan, J W B (Dublin U) 1882 *S*, 1884 *E, S*
Buckley, J H (Sunday's Well) 1973 *E, S*
Bulger, L Q (Lansdowne) 1896 *E, S, W*, 1897 *E, S*, 1898 *E, S, W*
Bulger, M J (Dublin U) 1888 *M*
Burges, J H (Rosslyn Park) 1950 *F, E*
Burgess, R B (Dublin U) 1912 *SA*
Burke, P A (Cork Constitution) 1995 *E, S, W*(R)
Burkitt, J C S (Queen's Coll, Cork) 1881 *E*
Burns, I J (Wanderers) 1980 *E* (R)
Butler, L G (Blackrock Coll) 1960 *W*
Butler, N (Bective Rangers) 1920 *E*
Byers, R M (NIFC) 1928 *S, W*, 1929 *E, S, W*
Byrne, E M J (Blackrock Coll) 1977 *S, F*, 1978 *F, W, E, NZ*
Byrne, N F (UC Dublin) 1962 *F*
Byrne, S J (UC Dublin, Lansdowne) 1953 *S, W*, 1955 *F*
Byron, W G (NIFC) 1896 *E, S, W*, 1897 *E, S*, 1898 *E, S, W*, 1899 *E, S, W*

Caddell, E D (Dublin U, Wanderers) 1904 *S*, 1905 *E, S, W, NZ*, 1906 *E, S, W, SA*, 1907 *E, S*, 1908 *S, W*
Cagney, S J (London Irish) 1925 *W*, 1926 *F, E, S, W*, 1927 *F*, 1928 *E, S, W*, 1929 *F, E, S, W*
Callan, C P (Lansdowne) 1947 *F, E, S, W*, 1948 *F, E, S, W*, 1949 *F, E*
Cameron, E D (Bective Rangers) 1891 *S, W*
Campbell, C E (Old Wesley) 1970 *SA*
Campbell, E F (Monkstown) 1899 *S, W*, 1900 *E, W*
Campbell, S B B (Derry) 1911 *E, S, W, F*, 1912 *F, E, S, W, SA*, 1913 *E, S, F*
Campbell, S O (Old Belvedere) 1976 *A*, 1979 *A* 1,2, 1980 *E, S, F, W*, 1981 *F, W, E, S, SA* 1, 1982 *W, E, S, F*, 1983 *S, F, W, E*, 1984 *F, W*
Canniffe, D M (Lansdowne) 1976 *W, E*
Cantrell, J L (UC Dublin, Blackrock Coll) 1976 *A, F, W, E, S*, 1981 *S, SA* 1,2, *A*
Carey, R W (Dungannon) 1992 *NZ* 1,2
Carpendale, M J (Monkstown) 1886 *S*, 1887 *W*, 1888 *W, S*
Carr, N J (Ards) 1985 *S, F, W, E*, 1986 *W, E, S, R*, 1987 *E, S, W*
Carroll, C (Bective Rangers) 1930 *F*
Carroll, R (Lansdowne) 1947 *F*, 1950 *S, W*
Casement, B N (Dublin U) 1875 *E*, 1876 *E*, 1879 *E*
Casement, F (Dublin U) 1906 *E, S, W*
Casey, J C (Young Munster) 1930 *S*, 1932 *E*
Casey, P J (UC Dublin, Lansdowne) 1963 *F, E, S, W*,

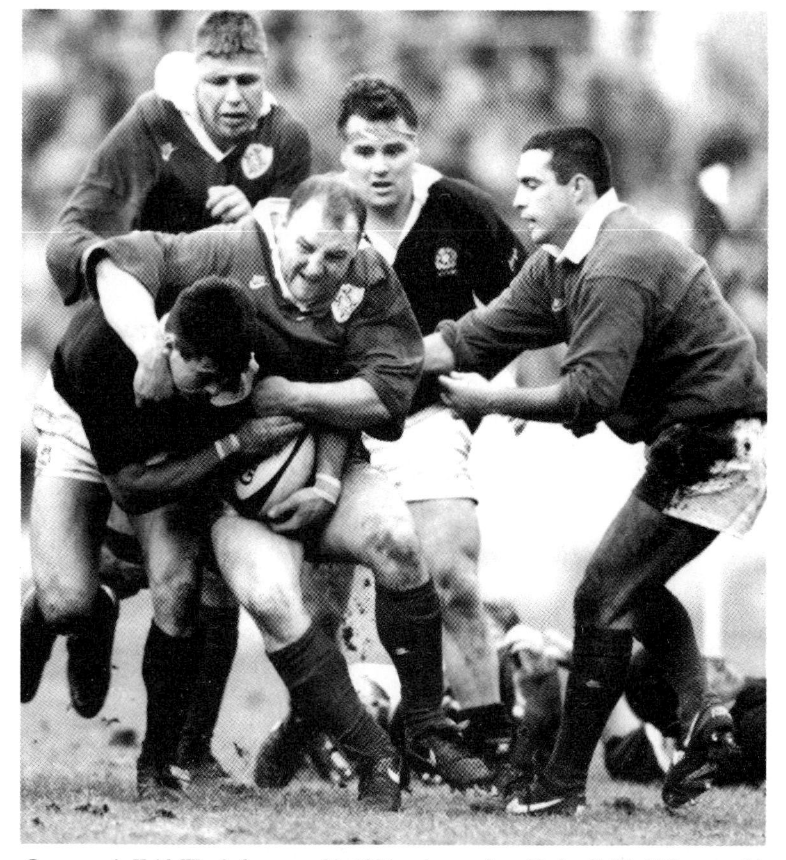

Garryowen's Keith Wood, first capped in 1994 and a member of Ireland's World Cup squad in 1995, tackles Kenny Logan in the Five Nations match against Scotland at Murrayfield.

NZ, 1964 *E*, *S*, *W*, *F*, 1965 *F*, *E*, *S*
Chambers, J (Dublin U) 1886 *E*, *S*, 1887 *E*, *S*, *W*
Chambers, R R (Instonians) 1951 *F*, *E*, *S*, *W*, 1952 *F*, *W*
Clancy, T P J (Lansdowne) 1988 *W*, *E* 1,2, *WS*, *It*, 1989 *F*, *W*, *E*, *S*
Clarke, C P (Terenure Coll) 1993 *F*, *W*, *E*
Clarke, D J (Dolphin) 1991 *W*, *Nm* 1,2, [*J*, *A*], 1992 *NZ* 2(R)
Clarke, J A B (Bective Rangers) 1922 *S*, *W*, *F*, 1923 *F*, 1924 *E*, *S*, *W*
Clegg, R J (Bangor) 1973 *F*, 1975 *E*, *S*, *F*, *W*
Clifford, J T (Young Munster) 1949 *F*, *E*, *S*, *W*, 1950 *F*, *E*, *S*, *W*, 1951 *F*, *E*, *SA*, 1952 *F*, *S*, *W*
Clinch, A D (Dublin U, Wanderers) 1892 *S*, 1893 *W*, 1895 *E*, *S*, *W*, 1896 *E*, *S*, *W*, 1897 *E*, *S*
Clinch, J D (Wanderers, Dublin U) 1923 *W*, 1924 *F*, *E*, *S*, *W*, *NZ*, 1925 *F*, *E*, *S*, 1926 *E*, *S*, *W*, 1927 *F*, 1928 *F*, *E*, *S*, *W*, 1929 *F*, *E*, *S*, *W*, 1930 *F*, *E*, *S*, *W*, 1931 *F*, *E*, *S*, *W*, *SA*
Clohessy, P M (Young Munster) 1993 *F*, *W*, *E*, 1994 *F*, *W*, *E*, *S*, *A* 1,2, *US*, 1995 *E*, *S*, *F*, *W*
Clune, J J (Blackrock Coll) 1912 *SA*, 1913 *W*, *F*, 1914 *F*, *E*, *W*
Coffey, J J (Lansdowne) 1900 *E*, 1901 *W*, 1902 *E*, *S*, *W*, 1903 *E*, *S*, *W*, 1905 *E*, *S*, *W*, *NZ*, 1906 *E*, *S*, *W*, *SA*, 1907 *E*, 1908 *W*, 1910 *F*
Cogan, W St J (Queen's Coll, Cork) 1907 *E*, *S*
Collier, S R (Queen's Coll, Belfast) 1883 *S*
Collins, P C (Lansdowne, London Irish) 1987 [*C*], 1990 *S* (R)
Collis, W R F (KCH, Harlequins) 1924 *F*, *W*, *NZ*, 1925 *F*, *E*, *S*, 1926 *F*
Collis, W S (Wanderers) 1884 *W*
Collopy, G (Bective Rangers) 1891 *S*, 1892 *S*
Collopy, R (Bective Rangers) 1923 *E*, *S*, *W*, *F*, 1924 *F*, *E*, *S*, *W*, *NZ*, 1925 *F*, *E*, *S*, *W*
Collopy, W P (Bective Rangers) 1914 *F*, *E*, *S*, *W*, 1921 *E*, *S*, *W*, *F*, 1922 *E*, *S*, *W*, *F*, 1923 *S*, *W*, *F*, 1924 *F*, *E*, *S*, *W*
Combe, A (NIFC) 1875 *E*
Condon, H C (London Irish) 1984 *S* (R)
Cook, H G (Lansdowne) 1884 *W*
Coote, P B (RAF, Leicester) 1933 *S*
Corcoran, J C (London Irish) 1947 *A*, 1948 *F*
Corken, T S (Belfast Collegians) 1937 *E*, *S*, *W*
Corkery, D (Cork Constitution) 1994 *A* 1,2, *US*, 1995 *E*
Corley, H H (Dublin U, Wanderers) 1902 *E*, *S*, *W*, 1903 *E*, *S*, *W*, 1904 *E*, *S*
Cormac, H S T (Clontarf) 1921 *E*, *S*, *W*
Costello, P (Bective Rangers) 1960 *F*
Costello, R A (Garryowen) 1993 *S*
Cotton, J (Wanderers) 1889 *W*
Coulter, H H (Queen's U, Belfast) 1920 *E*, *S*, *W*
Courtney, A W (UC Dublin) 1920 *S*, *W*, *F*, 1921 *E*, *S*, *W*, *F*
Cox, H L (Dublin U) 1875 *E*, 1876 *E*, 1877 *E*, *S*
Craig, R G (Queen's U, Belfast) 1938 *S*, *W*
Crawford, E C (Dublin U) 1885 *E*, *S* 1
Crawford, W E (Lansdowne) 1920 *E*, *S*, *W*, *F*, 1921 *E*, *S*, *W*, *F*, 1922 *E*, *S*, 1923 *E*, *S*, *W*, *F*, 1924 *F*, *E*, *W*, *NZ*, 1925 *F*, *E*, *S*, *W*, 1926 *F*, *E*, *S*, *W*, 1927 *F*, *E*, *S*, *W*
Crean, T J (Wanderers) 1894 *E*, *S*, *W*, 1895 *E*, *S*, *W*, 1896 *E*, *S*, *W*
Crichton, R Y (Dublin U) 1920 *E*, *S*, *W*, *F*, 1921 *F*, 1922 *E*, 1923 *W*, *F*, 1924 *F*, *E*, *S*, *W*, *NZ*, 1925 *E*, *S*
Croker, E W D (Limerick) 1878 *E*
Cromey, G E (Queen's U, Belfast) 1937 *E*, *S*, *W*, 1938 *E*, *S*, *W*, 1939 *E*, *S*, *W*
Cronin, B M (Garryowen) 1995 *S*
Cronyn, A P (Dublin U, Lansdowne) 1875 *E*, 1876 *E*, 1880 *S*
Crossan, K D (Instonians) 1982 *S*, 1984 *F*, *W*, *E*, *S*, 1985 *S*, *F*, *W*, *E*, 1986 *E*, *S*, *R*, 1987 *E*, *S*, *F*, *W*, [*W*, *C*, *Tg*, *A*], 1988 *S*, *F*, *W*, *E* 1, *WS*, *It*, 1989 *W*, *S*, *NZ*, 1990 *E*, *S*, *F*, *W*, *Arg*, 1991 *E*, *S* , *Nm* 2, [*Z*, *J*, *S*], 1992 *W*
Crowe, J F (UC Dublin) 1974 *NZ*
Crowe, L (Old Belvedere) 1950 *E*, *S*, *W*
Crowe, M P (Lansdowne) 1929 *W*, 1930 *E*, *S*, *W*, 1931 *F*, *S*, *W*, *SA*, 1932 *S*, *W*, 1933 *W*, *S*, 1934 *E*
Crowe, P M (Blackrock Coll) 1935 *E*, 1938 *E*
Cullen, T J (UC Dublin) 1949 *F*
Cullen, W J (Monkstown and Manchester) 1920 *E*
Culliton, M G (Wanderers) 1959 *E*, *S*, *W*, *F*, 1960 *E*, *S*, *W*, *F*, *SA*, 1961 *E*, *S*, *W*, *F*, 1962 *S*, *F*, 1964 *E*, *S*, *W*, *F*
Cummins, W E A (Queen's Coll, Cork) 1879 *S*, 1881 *E*, 1882 *E*
Cunningham, D McC (NIFC) 1923 *E*, *S*, *W*, 1925 *F*, *E*, *W*
Cunningham, M J (UC Cork) 1955 *F*, *E*, *S*, *W*, 1956 *F*, *S*, *W*
Cunningham, V J G (St Mary's Coll) 1988 *E* 2, *It* 1990 *Arg* (R), 1991 *Nm* 1,2, [*Z*, *J*(R)], 1992 *NZ* 1,2, *A*, 1993 *S*, *F*, *W*, *E*, *R*, 1994 *F*
Cunningham, W A (Lansdowne) 1920 *W*, 1921 *E*, *S*, *W*, *F*, 1922 *E*, 1923 *S*, *W*
Cuppaidge, J L (Dublin U) 1879 *E*, 1880 *E*, *S*
Currell, J (NIFC) 1877 *S*
Curtis, A B (Oxford U) 1950 *F*, *E*, *S*
Curtis, D M (London Irish) 1991 *W*, *E*, *S*, *Nm* 1,2, [*Z*, *J*, *S*, *A*], 1992 *W*, *E*, *S*(R), *F*
Cuscaden, W A (Dublin U, Bray) 1876 *E*
Cussen, D J (Dublin U) 1921 *E*, *S*, *W*, *F*, 1922 *E*, 1923 *E*, *S*, *W*, *F*, 1926 *F*, *E*, *S*, *W*, 1927 *F*, *E*

Daly, J C (London Irish) 1947 *F*, *E*, *S*, *W*, 1948 *E*, *S*, *W*
Daly, M J (Harlequins) 1938 *E*
Danaher, P P A (Lansdowne, Garryowen) 1988 *S*, *F*, *W*, *WS*, *It*, 1989 *F*, *NZ* (R), 1990 *F*, 1992 *S*, *F*, *NZ* 1, *A*, 1993 *S*, *F*, *W*, *E*, *R*, 1994 *F*, *W*, *E*, *S*, *A* 1,2, *US*, 1995 *E*, *S*, *F*, *W*
Dargan, M J (Old Belvedere) 1952 *S*, *W*
Davidson, C T (NIFC) 1921 *F*
Davidson, I G (NIFC) 1899 *E*, 1900 *S*, *W*, 1901 *E*, *S*, *W*, 1902 *E*, *S*, *W*
Davidson, J C (Dungannon) 1969 *F*, *E*, *S*, *W*, 1973 *NZ*, 1976 *NZ*
Davies, F E (Lansdowne) 1892 *S*, *W*, 1893 *E*, *S*, *W*
Davis, J L (Monkstown) 1898 *E*, *S*
Davis, W J N (Edinburgh U, Bessbrook) 1890 *S*, *W*, *E*, 1891 *E*, *S*, *W*, 1892 *E*, *S*, 1895 *S*
Davison, W (Belfast Academy) 1887 *W*
Davy, E O'D (UC Dublin, Lansdowne) 1925 *W*, 1926 *F*, *E*, *S*, *W*, 1927 *F*, *E*, *S*, *W*, *A*, 1928 *F*, *E*, *S*, *W*, 1929 *F*, *E*, *S*, *W*, 1930 *F*, *E*, *S*, *W*, 1931 *F*, *E*, *S*, *W*, *SA*, 1932 *E*, *S*, *W*, 1933 *E*, *W*, *S*, 1934 *E*
Dawson, A R (Wanderers) 1958 *A*, *E*, *S*, *W*, *F*, 1959 *E*, *S*, *W*, *F*, 1960 *F*, *SA*, 1961 *E*, *S*, *W*, *F*, *SA*, 1962 *S*, *F*, *W*, 1963 *F*, *E*, *S*, *W*, *NZ*, 1964 *E*, *S*, *F*
Dean, P M (St Mary's Coll) 1981 *SA* 1,2, *A*, 1982 *W*, *E*, *S*, *F*, 1984 *A*, 1985 *S*, *F*, *W*, *E*, 1986 *F*, *W*, *R*, 1987 *E*, *S*, *F*, *W*, [*W*, *A*], 1988 *S*, *F*, *W*, *E* 1,2, *WS*, *It*, 1989 *F*, *W*, *E*, *S*
Deane, E C (Monkstown) 1909 *E*
Deering, M J (Bective Rangers) 1929 *W*
Deering, S J (Bective Rangers) 1935 *E*, *S*, *W*, *NZ*, 1936 *E*, *S*, *W*, 1937 *E*, *S*
Deering, S M (Garryowen, St Mary's Coll) 1974 *W*, 1976 *F*, *W*, *E*, *S*, 1977 *W*, *E*, 1978 *NZ*
de Lacy, H (Harlequins) 1948 *E*, *S*
Delaney, M G (Bective Rangers) 1895 *W*
Dennison, S P (Garryowen) 1973 *F*, 1975 *E*, *S*
Dick, C J (Ballymena) 1961 *W*, *F*, *SA*, 1962 *W*, 1963 *F*, *E*, *S*, *W*
Dick, J S (Queen's U, Belfast) 1962 *E*
Dick, J S (Queen's U, Cork) 1887 *E*, *S*, *W*
Dickson, J A N (Dublin U) 1920 *E*, *W*, *F*
Doherty, A E (Old Wesley) 1974 *P* (R)
Doherty, W D (Guy's Hospital) 1920 *E*, *S*, *W*, 1921 *E*, *S*, *W*, *F*
Donaldson, J A (Belfast Collegians) 1958 *A*, *E*, *S*, *W*
Donovan, T M (Queen's Coll, Cork) 1889 *S*
Dooley, J F (Galwegians) 1959 *E*, *S*, *W*
Doran, B R W (Lansdowne) 1900 *S*, *W*, 1901 *E*, *S*, *W*, 1902 *E*, *S*, *W*
Doran, E F (Lansdowne) 1890 *S*, *W*
Doran, G P (Lansdowne) 1899 *S*, *W*, 1900 *E*, *S*, 1902 *S*, *W*, 1903 *W*, 1904 *E*
Douglas, A C (Instonians) 1923 *F*, 1924 *E*, *S*, 1927 *A*, 1928 *S*
Downing, A J (Dublin U) 1882 *W*
Dowse, J C A (Monkstown) 1914 *F*, *S*, *W*
Doyle, J A P (Greystones) 1984 *E*, *S*
Doyle, J T (Bective Rangers) 1935 *W*
Doyle, M G (Blackrock Coll, UC Dublin, Cambridge U, Edinburgh Wands) 1965 *F*, *E*, *S*, *W*, *SA*, 1966 *F*, *E*, *S*, *W*, 1967 *A* 1, *E*, *S*, *W*, *F*, *A* 2, 1968 *F*, *E*, *S*, *W*, *A*
Doyle, T J (Wanderers) 1968 *E*, *S*, *W*

Duggan, A T A (Lansdowne) 1963 *NZ*, 1964 *F*, 1966 *W*, 1967 *A* 1, *S, W, A* 2, 1968 *F, E, S, W*, 1969 *F, E, S, W*, 1970 *SA, F, E, S, W*, 1971 *F, E, S, W*, 1972 *F* 2
Duggan, W (UC Cork) 1920 *S, W*
Duggan, W P (Blackrock Coll) 1975 *E, S, F, W*, 1976 *A, F, W, S, NZ*, 1977 *W, E, S, F*, 1978 *S, F, W, E, NZ*, 1979 *E, S, A* 1,2, 1980 *E*, 1981 *F, W, E, S, SA* 1,2, *A*, 1982 *W, E, S*, 1983 *S, F, W, E*, 1984 *F, W, E, S*
Duncan, W R (Malone) 1984 *W, E*
Dunlea, F J (Lansdowne) 1989 *W, E, S*
Dunlop, R (Dublin U) 1889 *W*, 1890 *S, W, E*, 1891 *E, S, W*, 1892 *E, S*, 1893 *W*, 1894 *W*
Dunn, P E F (Bective Rangers) 1923 *S*
Dunn, T B (NIFC) 1935 *NZ*
Dunne, M J (Lansdowne) 1929 *F, E, S*, 1930 *F, E, S, W*, 1932 *E, S, W*, 1933 *E, W, S*, 1934 *E, S, W*
Dwyer, P J (UC Dublin) 1962 *W*, 1963 *F, NZ*, 1964 *S, W*

Edwards, H G (Dublin U) 1877 *E*, 1878 *E*
Edwards, R W (Malone) 1904 *W*
Edwards, T (Lansdowne) 1888 *M*, 1890 *S, W, E*, 1892 *W*, 1893 *E*
Edwards, W V (Malone) 1912 *F, E*
Egan, J D (Bective Rangers) 1922 *S*
Egan, J T (Cork Constitution) 1931 *F, E, SA*
Egan, M S (Garryowen) 1893 *E*, 1895 *S*
Ekin, W (Queen's Coll, Belfast) 1888 *W, S*
Elliott, W R J (Bangor) 1979 *S*
Elwood, E P (Lansdowne) 1993 *W, E, R*, 1994 *F, W, E, S, A* 1,2, 1995 *F, W*
English, M A F (Lansdowne, Limerick Bohemians) 1958 *W, F*, 1959 *E, S, F*, 1960 *E, S*, 1961 *S, W, F*, 1962 *F, W*, 1963 *E, S, W, NZ*
Ennis, F N G (Wanderers) 1979 *A* 1 (R)
Ensor, A H (Wanderers) 1973 *W, F*, 1974 *F, W, E, S, P, NZ*, 1975 *E, S, F, W*, 1976 *A, F, W, E, NZ*, 1977 *E*, 1978 *S, F, W, E*
Entrican, J C (Queen's U, Belfast) 1931 *S*

Fagan, G L (Kingstown School) 1878 *E*
Fagan, W B C (Wanderers) 1956 *F, E, S*
Farrell, J L (Bective Rangers) 1926 *F, E, S, W*, 1927 *F, E, S, W, A*, 1928 *F, E, S, W*, 1929 *F, E, S, W*, 1930 *F, E, S, W*, 1931 *F, E, S, W, SA*, 1932 *E, S, W*
Feddis, N (Lansdowne) 1956 *E*
Feighery, C F P (Lansdowne) 1972 *F* 1, *E, F* 2
Feighery, T A O (St Mary's Coll) 1977 *W, E*
Ferris, H H (Queen's Coll, Belfast) 1901 *W*
Ferris, J H (Queen's Coll, Belfast) 1900 *E, S, W*
Field, M J (Malone) 1994 *E, S, A* 1(R), 1995 *F*(R), *W*(t)
Finlay, J E (Queen's Coll, Belfast) 1913 *E, S, W*, 1920 *E, S, W*
Finlay, W (NIFC) 1876 *E*, 1877 *E, S*, 1878 *E*, 1879 *S, E*, 1880 *S*, 1882 *S*
Finn, M C (UC Cork, Cork Constitution) 1979 *E*, 1982 *W, E, S, F*, 1983 *S, F, W, E*, 1984 *E, S, A*, 1986 *F, W*
Finn, R G A (UC Dublin) 1977 *F*
Fitzgerald, C C (Glasgow U, Dungannon) 1902 *E*, 1903 *E, S*
Fitzgerald, C F (St Mary's Coll) 1979 *A* 1,2, 1980 *E, S, F, W*, 1982 *W, E, S, F*, 1983 *S, F, W, E*, 1984 *F, W, A*, 1985 *S, F, W, E*, 1986 *F, W, E, S*
Fitzgerald, D C (Lansdowne, De La Salle Palmerston) 1984 *E, S*, 1986 *W, E, S, R*, 1987 *E, S, F, W*, [*W, C, A*], 1988 *S, F, W, E* 1, 1989 *NZ* (R), 1990 *E, S, F, W, Arg*, 1991 *F, W, E, S, Nm* 1,2, [*Z, S, A*], 1992 *W, S*(R)
Fitzgerald, J (Wanderers) 1884 *W*
Fitzgerald, J J (Young Munster) 1988 *S, F*, 1990 *S, F, W*, 1991 *F, W, E, S*, [*J*], 1994 *A* 1,2
Fitzgibbon, M J J (Shannon) 1992 *W, E, S, F, NZ* 1,2
Fitzpatrick, M P (Wanderers) 1978 *S*, 1980 *S, F, W*, 1981 *F, W, E, S, A*, 1985 *F* (R)
Fletcher, W W (Kingstown) 1882 *W, S*, 1883 *E*
Flood, R S (Dublin U) 1925 *W*
Flynn, M K (Wanderers) 1959 *F*, 1960 *F*, 1962 *E, S, F, W*, 1964 *E, S, W, F*, 1965 *F, E, S, W, SA*, 1966 *F, E, S*, 1972 *F* 1, *E, F* 2, 1973 *NZ*
Fogarty, T (Garryowen) 1891 *W*
Foley, A G (Shannon) 1995 *E, S, F, W*
Foley, B O (Shannon) 1976 *F, E*, 1977 *W* (R), 1980 *F, W*, 1981 *F, E, S, SA*, 1,2, *A*
Forbes, R E (Malone) 1907 *E*
Forrest, A J (Wanderers) 1880 *E, S*, 1881 *E, S*, 1882 *W, E*, 1883 *E*, 1885 *S* 2
Forrest, E G (Wanderers) 1888 *M*, 1889 *S, W*, 1890 *S, E*, 1891 *E*, 1893 *S*, 1894 *E, S, W*, 1895 *W*, 1897 *E, S*
Forrest, H (Wanderers) 1893 *S, W*
Fortune, J J (Clontarf) 1963 *NZ*, 1964 *E*
Foster, A R (Derry) 1910 *E, S, F*, 1911 *E, S, W, F*, 1912 *F, E, S, W*, 1914 *E, S, W*, 1921 *E, S, W*
Francis, N P J (Blackrock Coll, London Irish, Old Belvedere) 1987 [*Tg, A*], 1988 *WS, It*, 1989 *S*, 1990 *E, F, W*, 1991 *E, S, Nm* 1,2, [*Z, J, S, A*], 1992 *W, E, S*, 1993 *F, R*, 1994 *F, W, E, S, A* 1,2, *US*, 1995 *E*
Franks, J G (Dublin U) 1898 *E, S, W*
Frazer, E F (Bective Rangers) 1891 *S*, 1892 *S*
Freer, A E (Lansdowne) 1901 *E, S, W*
Fulcher, G M (Cork Constitution) 1994 *A* 2, *US*, 1995 *E*(R), *S, F, W*
Fulton, J (NIFC) 1895 *S, W*, 1896 *E*, 1897 *E*, 1898 *W*, 1899 *E*, 1900 *W*, 1901 *E*, 1902 *E, S, W*, 1903 *E, S, W*, 1904 *E, S*
Furlong, J N (UC Galway) 1992 *NZ* 1,2

Gaffikin, W (Windsor) 1875 *E*
Gage, J H (Queen's U, Belfast) 1926 *S, W*, 1927 *S, W*
Galbraith, E (Dublin U) 1875 *E*
Galbraith, H T (Belfast Acad) 1890 *W*
Galbraith, R (Dublin U) 1875 *E*, 1876 *E*, 1877 *E*
Galwey, M J (Shannon) 1991 *F, W, Nm* 2(R), [*J*], 1992 *E, S, F, NZ* 1,2, *A*, 1993 *F, W, E, R*, 1994 *F, W, E, S, A* 1, *US*(R), 1995 *E*
Ganly, J B (Monkstown) 1927 *F, E, S, W, A*, 1928 *F, E, S, W*, 1929 *F, S*, 1930 *F*
Gardiner, F (NIFC) 1900 *E, S*, 1901 *E, W*, 1902 *E, S, W*, 1903 *E, W*, 1904 *E, S, W*, 1906 *E, S, W*, 1907 *S, W*, 1908 *S, W*, 1909 *E, S, F*
Gardiner, J B (NIFC) 1923 *E, S, W, F*, 1924 *F, E, S, W, NZ*, 1925 *F, E, S, W*
Gardiner, S (Belfast Albion) 1893 *E, S*
Gardiner, W (NIFC) 1892 *E, S*, 1893 *E, S, W*, 1894 *E, S, W*, 1895 *E, S, W*, 1896 *E, S, W*, 1897 *E, S*, 1898 *W*
Garry, M G (Bective Rangers) 1909 *E, S, W, F*, 1911 *E, S, W*
Gaston, J T (Dublin U) 1954 *NZ, F, E, S, W*, 1955 *W*, 1956 *F, E*
Gavin, T J (Moseley, London Irish) 1949 *F, E*
Geoghegan, S P (London Irish, Bath) 1991 *F, W, E, S, Nm* 1, [*Z, S, A*], 1992 *E, S, F, A*, 1993 *S, F, W, E, R*, 1994 *F, W, E, S, A* 1,2, *US*, 1995 *E, S, F, W*
Gibson, C M H (Cambridge U, NIFC) 1964 *E, S, W, F*, 1965 *F, E, S, W, SA*, 1966 *F, E, S, W*, 1967 *A* 1, *E, S, W, F, A* 2, 1968 *E, S, W, A*, 1969 *E, S, W*, 1970 *SA, F, E, S, W*, 1971 *F, E, S, W*, 1972 *F* 1, *E, F* 2, 1973 *NZ, E, S, W, F*, 1974 *F, W, E, S, P*, 1975 *E, S, F, W*, 1976 *A, F, W, E, S, NZ*, 1977 *W, E, S, F*, 1978 *F, W, E, NZ*, 1979 *S, A* 1,2
Gibson, M E (Lansdowne, London Irish) 1979 *F, W, E, S*, 1981 *W* (R), 1986 *R*, 1988 *S, F, W, E* 2
Gifford, H P (Wanderers) 1890 *S*
Gillespie, J C (Dublin U) 1922 *W, F*
Gilpin, F G (Queen's U, Belfast) 1962 *E, S, F*
Glass, D C (Belfast Collegians) 1958 *F*, 1960 *W*, 1961 *W, SA*
Glennon, B T (Lansdowne) 1993 *F*(R)
Glennon, J J (Skerries) 1980 *E, S*, 1987 *E, S, F*, [*W*(R)]
Godfrey, R P (UC Dublin) 1954 *S, W*
Goodall, K G (City of Derry, Newcastle U) 1967 *A* 1, *E, S, W, F, A* 2, 1968 *F, E, S, W, A*, 1969 *F, E, S*, 1970 *SA, F, E, S, W*
Gordon, A (Dublin U) 1884 *S*
Gordon, T G (NIFC) 1877 *E, S*, 1878 *E*
Gotto, R P C (NIFC) 1906 *SA*
Goulding, W J (Cork) 1879 *S*
Grace, T O (UC Dublin, St Mary's Coll) 1972 *F* 1, *E*, 1973 *NZ, E, S, W*, 1974 *E, S, P, NZ*, 1975 *E, S, F, W*, 1976 *A, F, W, E, S, NZ*, 1977 *W, E, S, F*, 1978 *S*
Graham, R I (Dublin U) 1911 *F*
Grant, E L (CIYMS) 1971 *F, E, S, W*
Grant, P J (Bective Rangers) 1894 *S, W*
Graves, C R A (Wanderers) 1934 *E, S, W*, 1935 *E, S, W, NZ*, 1936 *E, S, W*, 1937 *E, S*, 1938 *E, S, W*
Gray, R D (Old Wesley) 1923 *E, S*, 1925 *F*, 1926 *F*
Greene, E H (Dublin U, Kingstown) 1882 *W*, 1884 *W*, 1885 *E, S* 2, 1886 *E*
Greer, R (Kingstown) 1876 *E*
Greeves, T J (NIFC) 1907 *E, S, W*, 1909 *W, F*
Gregg, R J (Queen's U, Belfast) 1953 *F, E, S, W*, 1954 *F, E, S*

Griffin, C S (London Irish) 1951 *F, E*
Griffin, J L (Wanderers) 1949 *S, W*
Griffiths, W (Limerick) 1878 *E*
Grimshaw, C (Queen's U, Belfast) 1969 *E* (R)
Guerin, B N (Galwegians) 1956 *S*
Gwynn, A P (Dublin U) 1895 *W*
Gwynn, L H (Dublin U) 1893 *S*, 1894 *E, S, W*, 1897 *S*, 1898 *E, S*

Hakin, R F (CIYMS) 1976 *W, S, NZ*, 1977 *W, E, F*
Hall, R O N (Dublin U) 1884 *W*
Hall, W H (Instonians) 1923 *E, S, W, F*, 1924 *F, S*
Hallaran, C F G T (Royal Navy) 1921 *E, S, W*, 1922 *E, S, W*, 1923 *E, F*, 1924 *F, E, S, W*, 1925 *F*, 1926 *F, E*
Halpin, G F (Wanderers, London Irish) 1990 *E*, 1991 [*J*], 1992 *E, S, F*, 1993 *R*, 1994 *F*(R)
Halpin, T (Garryowen) 1909 *S, W, F*, 1910 *E, S, W*, 1911 *E, S, W, F*, 1912 *F, E, S*
Halvey, E O (Shannon) 1995 *F, W*
Hamilton, A J (Lansdowne) 1884 *W*
Hamilton, G F (NIFC) 1991 *F, W, E, S, Nm* 2, [*Z, J, S, A*], 1992 *A*
Hamilton, R L (NIFC) 1926 *F*
Hamilton, R W (Wanderers) 1893 *W*
Hamilton, W J (Dublin U) 1877 *E*
Hamlet, G T (Old Wesley) 1902 *E, S, W*, 1903 *E, S, W*, 1904 *S, W*, 1905 *E, S, W, NZ*, 1906 *SA*, 1907 *E, S, W*, 1908 *E, S, W*, 1909 *E, S, W, F*, 1910 *E, S, F*, 1911 *E, S, W, F*
Hanrahan, C J (Dolphin) 1926 *S, W*, 1927 *E, S, W, A*, 1928 *F, E, S*, 1929 *F, E, S, W*, 1930 *F, E, S, W*, 1931 *F*, 1932 *S, W*
Harbison, H T (Bective Rangers) 1984 *W* (R), *E, S*, 1986 *R*, 1987 *E, S, F, W*
Hardy, G G (Bective Rangers) 1962 *S*
Harman, G R A (Dublin U) 1899 *E, W*
Harper, J (Instonians) 1947 *F, E, S*
Harpur, T G (Dublin U) 1908 *E, S, W*
Harrison, T (Cork) 1879 *S*, 1880 *S*, 1881 *E*
Harvey, F M W (Wanderers) 1907 *W*, 1911 *F*
Harvey, G A D (Wanderers) 1903 *E, S*, 1904 *W*, 1905 *E, S*
Harvey, T A (Dublin U) 1900 *W*, 1901 *S, W*, 1902 *E, S, W*, 1903 *E, W*
Haycock, P P (Terenure Coll) 1989 *E*
Headon, T A (UC Dublin) 1939 *S, W*
Healey, P (Limerick) 1901 *E, S, W*, 1902 *E, S, W*, 1903 *E, S, W*, 1904 *S*
Heffernan, M R (Cork Constitution) 1911 *E, S, W, F*
Hemphill, R (Dublin U) 1912 *F, E, S, W*
Henderson, N J (Queen's U, Belfast, NIFC) 1949 *S, W*, 1950 *F*, 1951 *F, E, S, W, SA*, 1952 *F, S, W, E*, 1953 *F, E, S, W*, 1954 *NZ, F, E, S, W*, 1955 *F, E, S, W*, 1956 *S, W*, 1957 *F, E, S, W*, 1958 *A, E, S, W, F*, 1959 *E, S, W, F*
Henebrey, G J (Garryowen) 1906 *E, S, W, SA*, 1909 *W, F*
Heron, A G (Queen's Coll, Belfast) 1901 *E*
Heron, J (NIFC) 1877 *S*, 1879 *E*
Heron, W T (NIFC) 1880 *E, S*
Herrick, R W (Dublin U) 1886 *S*
Heuston, F S (Kingstown) 1882 *W*, 1883 *E, S*
Hewitt, D (Queen's U, Belfast, Instonians) 1958 *A, E, S, F*, 1959 *S, W, F*, 1960 *E, S, W, F*, 1961 *E, S, W, F*, 1962 *S, F*, 1965 *W*
Hewitt, F S (Instonians) 1924 *W, NZ*, 1925 *F, E, S*, 1926 *E*, 1927 *E, S, W*
Hewitt, J A (NIFC) 1981 *SA* 1 (R), 2 (R)
Hewitt, T R (Queen's U, Belfast) 1924 *W, NZ*, 1925 *F, E, S*, 1926 *F, E, S, W*
Hewitt, V A (Instonians) 1935 *S, W, NZ*, 1936 *E, S, W*
Hewitt, W J (Instonians) 1954 *E*, 1956 *S*, 1959 *W*, 1961 *SA*
Hewson, F T (Wanderers) 1875 *E*
Hickie, D J (St Mary's Coll) 1971 *F, E, S, W*, 1972 *F* 1, *E*
Higgins, J A D (Civil Service) 1947 *S, W, A*, 1948 *F, S, W*
Higgins, W W (NIFC) 1884 *E, S*
Hillary, M F (UC Dublin) 1952 *E*
Hingerty, D J (UC Dublin) 1947 *F, E, S, W*
Hinton, W P (Old Wesley) 1907 *W*, 1908 *E, S, W*, 1909 *E, S*, 1910 *E, S, W, F*, 1911 *E, S, W*, 1912 *F, E, W*
Hipwell, M L (Terenure Coll) 1962 *E, S*, 1968 *F, A*, 1969 *F* (R), *S* (R), *W*, 1971 *F, E, S, W*, 1972 *F* 2
Hobbs, T H M (Dublin U) 1884 *S*, 1885 *E*
Hobson, E W (Dublin U) 1876 *E*
Hogan, N A (Terenure Coll) 1995 *E, W*
Hogan, P (Garryowen) 1992 *F*
Hogg, W (Dublin U) 1885 *S* 2
Holland, J J (Wanderers) 1981 *SA* 1,2, 1986 *W*
Holmes, G W (Dublin U) 1912 *SA*, 1913 *E, S*
Holmes, L J (Lisburn) 1889 *S, W*
Hooks, K J (Queen's U, Belfast, Ards, Bangor) 1981 *S*, 1989 *NZ*, 1990 *F, W, Arg*, 1991 *F*
Horan, A K (Blackheath) 1920 *E, W*
Houston, K J (Oxford U, London Irish) 1961 *SA*, 1964 *S, W*, 1965 *F, E, SA*
Hughes, R W (NIFC) 1878 *E*, 1880 *E, S*, 1881 *S*, 1882 *E, S*, 1883 *E, S*, 1884 *E, S*, 1885 *E*, 1886 *E*
Hunt, E W F de Vere (Army, Rosslyn Park) 1930 *F*, 1932 *E, S, W*, 1933 *E*
Hunter, D V (Dublin U) 1885 *S* 2
Hunter, L (Civil Service) 1968 *W, A*
Hunter, W R (CIYMS) 1962 *E, S, W, F*, 1963 *F, E, S*, 1966 *F, E, S*
Hutton, S A (Malone) 1967 *S, W, F, A* 2

Ireland, J (Windsor) 1876 *E*, 1877 *E*
Irvine, H A S (Collegians) 1901 *S*
Irwin, D G (Queen's U, Belfast, Instonians) 1980 *F, W*, 1981 *F, W, E, S, SA* 1,2, *A*, 1982 *W*, 1983 *S, F, W, E*, 1984 *F, W*, 1987 [*Tg, A*(R)], 1989 *F, W, E, S, NZ*, 1990 *E, S*
Irwin, J W S (NIFC) 1938 *E, S*, 1939 *E, S, W*
Irwin, S T (Queen's Coll, Belfast) 1900 *E, S, W*, 1901 *E, W*, 1902 *E, S, W*, 1903 *S*

Jack, H W (UC Cork) 1914 *S, W*, 1921 *W*
Jackson, A R V (Wanderers) 1911 *E, S, W, F*, 1913 *W, F*, 1914 *F, E, S, W*
Jackson, F (NIFC) 1923 *E*
Jackson, H W (Dublin U) 1877 *E*
Jameson, J S (Lansdowne) 1888 *M*, 1889 *S, W*, 1891 *W*, 1892 *E, W*, 1893 *S*
Jeffares, E W (Wanderers) 1913 *E, S*
Johns, P S (Dublin U, Dungannon) 1990 *Arg*, 1992 *NZ* 1,2, *A*, 1993 *S, F, W, E, R*, 1994 *F, W, E, S, A* 1,2, *US*, 1995 *E, S, W*
Johnston, J (Belfast Acad) 1881 *S*, 1882 *S*, 1884 *S*, 1885 *S* 1,2, 1886 *E*, 1887 *E, S, W*
Johnston, M (Dublin U) 1880 *E, S*, 1881 *E, S*, 1882 *E*, 1884 *E, S*, 1886 *E*
Johnston, R (Wanderers) 1893 *E, W*
Johnston, R W (Dublin U) 1890 *S, W, E*
Johnston, T J (Queen's Coll, Belfast) 1892 *E, S, W*, 1893 *E, S*, 1895 *E*
Johnstone, W E (Dublin U) 1884 *W*
Johnstone-Smyth, T R (Lansdowne) 1882 *E*

Kavanagh, J R (UC Dublin, Wanderers) 1953 *F, E, S, W*, 1954 *NZ, S, W*, 1955 *F, E*, 1956 *E, S, W*, 1957 *F, E, S, W*, 1958 *A, E, S, W*, 1959 *E, S, W, F*, 1960 *E, S, W, F, SA*, 1961 *E, S, W, F, SA*, 1962 *F*
Kavanagh, P J (UC Dublin, Wanderers) 1952 *E*, 1955 *W*
Keane, M I (Lansdowne) 1974 *F, W, E, S, P, NZ*, 1975 *E, S, F, W*, 1976 *A, F, W, E, S, NZ*, 1977 *W, E, S, F*, 1978 *S, F, W, E, NZ*, 1979 *F, W, E, S, A* 1,2, 1980 *E, S, F, W*, 1981 *F, W, E, S*, 1982 *W, E, S, F*, 1983 *S, F, W, E*, 1984 *F, W, E, S*
Kearney, R K (Wanderers) 1982 *F*, 1984 *A*, 1986 *F, W*
Keeffe, E (Sunday's Well) 1947 *F, E, S, W, A*, 1948 *F*
Kelly, H C (NIFC) 1877 *E, S*, 1878 *E*, 1879 *S*, 1880 *E, S*
Kelly, J C (UC Dublin) 1962 *F, W*, 1963 *F, E, S, W, NZ*, 1964 *E, S, W, F*
Kelly, S (Lansdowne) 1954 *S, W*, 1955 *S*, 1960 *W, F*
Kelly, W (Wanderers) 1884 *S*
Kennedy, A G (Belfast Collegians) 1956 *F*
Kennedy, A P (London Irish) 1986 *W, E*
Kennedy, F (Wanderers) 1880 *E*, 1881 *E*, 1882 *W*
Kennedy, F A (Wanderers) 1904 *E, W*
Kennedy, H (Bradford) 1938 *S, W*
Kennedy, J M (Wanderers) 1882 *W*, 1884 *W*
Kennedy, K W (Queen's U, Belfast, London Irish) 1965 *F, E, S, W, SA*, 1966 *F, E, W*, 1967 *A* 1, *E, S, W, F, A* 2, 1968 *F, A*, 1969 *F, E, S, W*, 1970 *SA, F, E, S, W*, 1971 *F, E, S, W*, 1972 *F* 1, *E, F* 2, 1973 *NZ, E, S, W, F*, 1974 *F, W, E, S, P, NZ*, 1975 *F, W*
Kennedy, T J (St Mary's Coll) 1978 *NZ*, 1979 *F, W, E*

(R), *A* 1,2, 1980 *E, S, F, W,* 1981 *SA* 1,2, *A*
Kenny, P (Wanderers) 1992 *NZ* 2(R)
Keogh, F S (Bective Rangers) 1964 *W, F*
Keon, J J (Limerick) 1879 *E*
Keyes, R P (Cork Constitution) 1986 *E,* 1991 [*Z, J, S, A*], 1992 *W, E, S*
Kidd, F W (Dublin U, Lansdowne) 1877 *E, S,* 1878 *E*
Kiely, M D (Lansdowne) 1962 *W,* 1963 *F, E, S, W*
Kiernan, M J (Dolphin, Lansdowne) 1982 *W*(R), *E, S, F,* 1983 *S, F, W, E,* 1984 *E, S, A,* 1985 *S, F, W, E,* 1986 *F, W, E, S, R,* 1987 *E, S, F, W,* [*W, C, A*], 1988 *S, F, W, E* 1,2, *WS,* 1989 *F, W, E, S,* 1990 *E, S, F, W, Arg,* 1991 *F*
Kiernan, T J (UC Cork, Cork Const) 1960 *E, S, W, F, SA,* 1961 *E, S, W, F, SA,* 1962 *E, W,* 1963 *F, S, W, NZ,* 1964 *E, S,* 1965 *F, E, S, W, SA,* 1966 *F, E, S, W,* 1967 *A* 1, *E, S, W, F, A* 2, 1968 *F, E, S, W, A,* 1969 *F, E, S, W,* 1970 *SA, F, E, S, W,* 1971 *F,* 1972 *F* 1, *E, F* 2, 1973 *NZ, E, S*
Killeen, G V (Garryowen) 1912 *E, S, W,* 1913 *E, S, W, F,* 1914 *E, S, W*
King, H (Dublin U) 1883 *E, S*
Kingston, T J (Dolphin) 1987 [*W, Tg, A*], 1988 *S, F, W, E* 1, 1990 *F, W,* 1991 [*J*], 1993 *F, W, E, R,* 1994 *F, W, E, S,* 1995 *F, W*
Knox, J H (Dublin U, Lansdowne) 1904 *W,* 1905 *E, S, W, NZ,* 1906 *E, S, W,* 1907 *W,* 1908 *S*
Kyle, J W (Queen's U, Belfast, NIFC) 1947 *F, E, S, W, A,* 1948 *F, E, S, W,* 1949 *F, E, S, W,* 1950 *F, E, S, W,* 1951 *F, E, S, W, SA,* 1952 *F, S, W, E,* 1953 *F, E, S, W,* 1954 *NZ, F,* 1955 *F, E, W,* 1956 *F, E, S, W,* 1957 *F, E, S, W,* 1958 *A, E, S*

Lambert, N H (Lansdowne) 1934 *S, W*
Lamont, R A (Instonians) 1965 *F, E, SA,* 1966 *F, E, S, W,* 1970 *SA, F, E, S, W*
Landers, M F (Cork Const) 1904 *W,* 1905 *E, S, W, NZ*
Lane, D (UC Cork) 1934 *S, W,* 1935 *E, S*
Lane, M F (UC Cork) 1947 *W,* 1949 *F, E, S, W,* 1950 *F, E, S, W,* 1951 *F, S, W, SA,* 1952 *F, S,* 1953 *F, E*
Lane, P (Old Crescent) 1964 *W*
Langan, D J (Clontarf) 1934 *W*
Langbroek, J A (Blackrock Coll) 1987 [*Tg*]
Lavery, P (London Irish) 1974 *W,* 1976 *W*
Lawlor, P J (Clontarf) 1951 *S, SA,* 1952 *F, S, W, E,* 1953 *F,* 1954 *NZ, E, S,* 1956 *F, E*
Lawlor, P J (Bective Rangers) 1935 *E, S, W,* 1937 *E, S, W*
Lawlor, P J (Bective Rangers) 1990 *Arg,* 1992 *A,* 1993 *S*
Leahy, K T (Wanderers) 1992 *NZ* 1
Leahy, M W (UC Cork) 1964 *W*
Lee, S (NIFC) 1891 *E, S, W,* 1892 *E, S, W,* 1893 *E, S, W,* 1894 *E, S, W,* 1895 *E, W,* 1896 *E, S, W,* 1897 *E,* 1898 *E*
Le Fanu, V C (Cambridge U, Lansdowne) 1886 *E, S,* 1887 *E, W,* 1888 *S,* 1889 *W,* 1890 *E,* 1891 *E,* 1892 *E, S, W*
Lenihan, D G (UC Cork, Cork Const) 1981 *A,* 1982 *W, E, S, F,* 1983 *S, F, W, E,* 1984 *F, W, E, S, A,* 1985 *S, F, W, E,* 1986 *F, W, E, S, R,* 1987 *E, S, F, W,* [*W, C, Tg, A*], 1988 *S, F, W, E* 1,2, *WS, It,* 1989 *F, W, E, S, NZ,* 1990 *S, F, W, Arg,* 1991 *Nm* 2, [*Z, S, A*], 1992 *W*
L'Estrange, L P F (Dublin U) 1962 *E*
Levis, F H (Wanderers) 1884 *E*
Lightfoot, E J (Lansdowne) 1931 *F, E, S, W, SA,* 1932 *E, S, W,* 1933 *E, W, S*
Lindsay, H (Dublin U, Armagh) 1893 *E, S, W,* 1894 *E, S, W,* 1895 *E,* 1896 *E, S, W,* 1898 *E, S, W*
Little, T J (Bective Rangers) 1898 *W,* 1899 *S, W,* 1900 *S, W,* 1901 *E, S*
Lloyd, R A (Dublin U, Liverpool) 1910 *E, S,* 1911 *E, S, W, F,* 1912 *F, E, S, W, SA,* 1913 *E, S, W, F,* 1914 *F, E,* 1920 *E, F*
Lydon, C T J (Galwegians) 1956 *S*
Lyle, R K (Dublin U) 1910 *W, F*
Lyle, T R (Dublin U) 1885 *E, S* 1,2, 1886 *E,* 1887 *E, S*
Lynch, J F (St Mary's Coll) 1971 *F, E, S, W,* 1972 *F* 1, *E, F* 2, 1973 *NZ, E, S, W,* 1974 *F, W, E, S, P, NZ*
Lynch, L (Lansdowne) 1956 *S*
Lytle, J H (NIFC) 1894 *E, S, W,* 1895 *W,* 1896 *E, S, W,* 1897 *E, S,* 1898 *E, S,* 1899 *S*
Lytle, J N (NIFC) 1888 *M,* 1889 *W,* 1890 *E,* 1891 *E, S,* 1894 *E, S, W*
Lyttle, V J (Collegians, Bedford) 1938 *E,* 1939 *E, S*

McAleese, D R (Ballymena) 1992 *F*
McAllan, G H (Dungannon) 1896 *S, W*
Macaulay, J (Limerick) 1887 *E, S*
McBride, W D (Malone) 1988 *W, E* 1, *WS, It,* 1989 *S,* 1990 *F, W, Arg,* 1993 *S, F, W, E, R,* 1994 *W, E, S, A* 1(R), 1995 *S, F*
McBride, W J (Ballymena) 1962 *E, S, F, W,* 1963 *F, E, S, W, NZ,* 1964 *E, S, F,* 1965 *F, E, S, W, SA,* 1966 *F, E, S, W,* 1967 *A* 1, *E, S, W, F, A* 2, 1968 *F, E, S, W, A,* 1969 *F, E, S, W,* 1970 *SA, F, E, S, W,* 1971 *F, E, S, W,* 1972 *F* 1, *E, F* 2, 1973 *NZ, E, S, W, F,* 1974 *F, W, E, S, P, NZ,* 1975 *E, S, F, W*
McCall, B W (London Irish) 1985 *F* (R), 1986 *E, S*
McCall, M C (Bangor) 1992 *NZ* 1(R),2, 1994 *W*
McCallan, B (Ballymena) 1960 *E, S*
McCarten, R J (London Irish) 1961 *E, W, F*
McCarthy, E A (Kingstown) 1882 *W*
McCarthy, J S (Dolphin) 1948 *F, E, S, W,* 1949 *F, E, S, W,* 1950 *W,* 1951 *F, E, S, W, SA,* 1952 *F, S, W, E,* 1953 *F, E, S,* 1954 *NZ, F, E, S, W,* 1955 *F, E*
McCarthy, P D (Cork Const) 1992 *NZ* 1,2, *A,* 1993 *S, R*(R)
MacCarthy, St G (Dublin U) 1882 *W*
McCarthy, T (Cork) 1898 *W*
McClelland, T A (Queen's U, Belfast) 1921 *E, S, W, F,* 1922 *E, W, F,* 1923 *E, S, W, F,* 1924 *F, E, S, W, NZ*
McClenahan, R O (Instonians) 1923 *E, S, W*
McClinton, A N (NIFC) 1910 *W, F*
McCombe, W McM (Dublin U, Bangor) 1968 *F,* 1975 *E, S, F, W*
McConnell, A A (Collegians) 1947 *A,* 1948 *F, E, S, W,* 1949 *F, E*
McConnell, G (Derry, Edinburgh U) 1912 *F, E,* 1913 *W, F*
McConnell, J W (Lansdowne) 1913 *S*
McCormac, F M (Wanderers) 1909 *W,* 1910 *W, F*
McCormick, W J (Wanderers) 1930 *E*
McCoull, H C (Belfast Albion) 1895 *E, S, W,* 1899 *E*
McCourt, D (Queen's U, Belfast) 1947 *A*
McCoy, J J (Dungannon, Bangor, Ballymena) 1984 *W, A,* 1985 *S, F, W, E,* 1986 *F,* 1987 [*Tg*], 1988 *E* 2, *WS, It,* 1989 *F, W, E, S, NZ*
McCracken, H (NIFC) 1954 *W*
McDermott, S J (London Irish) 1955 *S, W*
Macdonald, J A (Methodist Coll, Belfast) 1875 *E,* 1876 *E,* 1877 *S,* 1878 *E,* 1879 *S,* 1880 *E,* 1881 *S,* 1882 *E, S,* 1883 *E, S,* 1884 *E, S*
McDonald, J P (Malone) 1987 [*C*], 1990 *E* (R), *S, Arg*
McDonnell, A C (Dublin U) 1889 *W,* 1890 *S, W,* 1891 *E*
McDowell, J C (Instonians) 1924 *F, NZ*
McFarland, B A T (Derry) 1920 *S, W, F,* 1922 *W*
McGann, B J (Lansdowne) 1969 *F, E, S, W,* 1970 *SA, F, E, S, W,* 1971 *F, E, S, W,* 1972 *F* 1, *E, F* 2, 1973 *NZ, E, S, W,* 1976 *F, W, E, S, NZ*
McGowan, A N (Blackrock Coll) 1994 *US*
McGown, T M W (NIFC) 1899 *E, S,* 1901 *S*
McGrath, D G (UC Dublin, Cork Const) 1984 *S,* 1987 [*W, C, Tg, A*]
McGrath, N F (Oxford U, London Irish) 1934 *W*
McGrath, P J (UC Cork) 1965 *E, S, W, SA,* 1966 *F, E, S, W,* 1967 *A* 1, *A* 2
McGrath, R J M (Wanderers) 1977 *W, E, F* (R), 1981 *SA* 1,2, *A,* 1982 *W, E, S, F,* 1983 *S, F, W, E,* 1984 *F, W*
McGrath, T (Garryowen) 1956 *W,* 1958 *F,* 1960 *E, S, W, F,* 1961 *SA*
McGuire, E P (UC Galway) 1963 *E, S, W, NZ,* 1964 *E, S, W, F*
MacHale, S (Lansdowne) 1965 *F, E, S, W, SA,* 1966 *F, E, S, W,* 1967 *S, W, F*
McIldowie, G (Malone) 1906 *SA,* 1910 *E, S, W*
McIlrath, J A (Ballymena) 1976 *A, F, NZ,* 1977 *W, E*
McIlwaine, E H (NIFC) 1895 *S, W*
McIlwaine, E N (NIFC) 1875 *E,* 1876 *E*
McIlwaine, J E (NIFC) 1897 *E, S,* 1898 *E, S, W,* 1899 *E, W*
McIntosh, L M (Dublin U) 1884 *S*
MacIvor, C V (Dublin U) 1912 *F, E, S, W,* 1913 *E, S, F*
McKay, J W (Queen's U, Belfast) 1947 *F, E, S, W, A,* 1948 *F, E, S, W,* 1949 *F, E, S, W,* 1950 *F, E, S, W,* 1951 *F, E, S, W, SA,* 1952 *F*
McKee, W D (NIFC) 1947 *A,* 1948 *F, E, S, W,* 1949 *F, E, S, W,* 1950 *F, E,* 1951 *SA*
McKelvey, J M (Queen's U, Belfast) 1956 *F, E*
McKibbin, A R (Instonians, London Irish) 1977 *W, E,*

S, 1978 *S*, *F*, *W*, *E*, *NZ*, 1979 *F*, *W*, *E*, *S*, 1980 *E*, *S*
McKibbin, C H (Instonians) 1976 *S* (R)
McKibbin, D (Instonians) 1950 *F*, *E*, *S*, *W*, 1951 *F*, *E*, *S*, *W*
McKibbin, H R (Queen's U, Belfast) 1938 *W*, 1939 *E*, *S*, *W*
McKinney, S A (Dungannon) 1972 *F* 1, *E*, *F* 2, 1973 *W*, *F*, 1974 *F*, *E*, *S*, *P*, *NZ*, 1975 *E*, *S*, 1976 *A*, *F*, *W*, *E*, *S*, *NZ*, 1977 *W*, *E*, *S*, 1978 *S* (R), *F*, *W*, *E*
McLaughlin, J H (Derry) 1887 *E*, *S*, 1888 *W*, *S*
McLean, R E (Dublin U) 1881 *S*, 1882 *W*, *E*, *S*, 1883 *E*, *S*, 1884 *E*, *S*, 1885 *E*, *S* 1
Maclear, B (Cork County, Monkstown) 1905 *E*, *S*, *W*, *NZ*, 1906 *E*, *S*, *W*, *SA*, 1907 *E*, *S*, *W*
McLennan, A C (Wanderers) 1977 *F*, 1978 *S*, *F*, *W*, *E*, *NZ*, 1979 *F*, *W*, *E*, *S*, 1980 *E*, *F*, 1981 *F*, *W*, *E*, *S*, *SA* 1,2
McLoughlin, F M (Northern) 1976 *A*
McLoughlin, G A J (Shannon) 1979 *F*, *W*, *E*, *S*, *A* 1,2, 1980 *E*, 1981 *SA* 1,2, 1982 *W*, *E*, *S*, *F*, 1983 *S*, *F*, *W*, *E*, 1984 *F*
McLoughlin, R J (UC Dublin, Blackrock Coll, Gosforth) 1962 *E*, *S*, *F*, 1963 *E*, *S*, *W*, *NZ*, 1964 *E*, *S*, 1965 *F*, *E*, *S*, *W*, *SA*, 1966 *F*, *E*, *S*, *W*, 1971 *F*, *E*, *S*, *W*, 1972 *F* 1, *E*, *F* 2, 1973 *NZ*, *E*, *S*, *W*, *F*, 1974 *F*, *W*, *E*, *S*, *P*, *NZ*, 1975 *E*, *S*, *F*, *W*
McMahon, L B (Blackrock Coll, UC Dublin) 1931 *E*, *SA*, 1933 *E*, 1934 *E*, 1936 *E*, *S*, *W*, 1937 *E*, *S*, *W*, 1938 *E*, *S*
McMaster, A W (Ballymena) 1972 *F* 1, *E*, *F* 2, 1973 *NZ*, *E*, *S*, *W*, *F*, 1974 *F*, *E*, *S*, *P*, 1975 *F*, *W*, 1976 *A*, *F*, *W*, *NZ*
McMordie, J (Queen's Coll, Belfast) 1886 *S*
McMorrow, A (Garryowen) 1951 *W*
McMullen, A R (Cork) 1881 *E*, *S*
McNamara, V (UC Cork) 1914 *E*, *S*, *W*
McNaughton, P P (Greystones) 1978 *S*, *F*, *W*, *E*, 1979 *F*, *W*, *E*, *S*, *A* 1,2, 1980 *E*, *S*, *F*, *W*, 1981 *F*
MacNeill, H P (Dublin U, Oxford U, Blackrock Coll, London Irish) 1981 *F*, *W*, *E*, *S*, *A*, 1982 *W*, *E*, *S*, *F*, 1983 *S*, *F*, *W*, *E*, 1984 *F*, *W*, *E*, *A*, 1985 *S*, *F*, *W*, *E*, 1986 *F*, *W*, *E*, *S*, *R*, 1987 *E*, *S*, *F*, *W*, [*W*, *C*, *Tg*, *A*], 1988 *S*(R), *E* 1,2
MacSweeney, D A (Blackrock Coll) 1955 *S*
McVicker, H (Army, Richmond) 1927 *E*, *S*, *W*, *A*, 1928 *F*
McVicker, J (Collegians) 1924 *F*, *E*, *S*, *W*, *NZ*, 1925 *F*, *E*, *S*, *W*, 1926 *F*, *E*, *S*, *W*, 1927 *F*, *E*, *S*, *W*, *A*, 1928 *W*, 1930 *F*
McVicker, S (Queen's U, Belfast) 1922 *E*, *S*, *W*, *F*
Madden, M N (Sunday's Well) 1955 *E*, *S*, *W*
Magee, J T (Bective Rangers) 1895 *E*, *S*
Magee, A M (Louis) (Bective Rangers, London Irish) 1895 *E*, *S*, *W*, 1896 *E*, *S*, *W*, 1897 *E*, *S*, 1898 *E*, *S*, *W*, 1899 *E*, *S*, *W*, 1900 *E*, *S*, *W*, 1901 *E*, *S*, *W*, 1902 *E*, *S*, *W*, 1903 *E*, *S*, *W*, 1904 *W*
Maginiss, R M (Dublin U) 1875 *E*, 1876 *E*
Magrath, R M (Cork Constitution) 1909 *S*
Maguire, J F (Cork) 1884 *S*
Mahoney, J (Dolphin) 1923 *E*
Malcolmson, G L (RAF, NIFC) 1935 *NZ*, 1936 *E*, *S*, *W*, 1937 *E*, *S*, *W*
Malone, N G (Oxford U, Leicester) 1993 *S*, *F*, 1994 *US*(R)
Mannion, N P (Corinthians, Lansdowne, Wanderers) 1988 *WS*, *It*, 1989 *F*, *W*, *E*, *S*, *NZ*, 1990 *E*, *S*, *F*, *W*, *Arg*, 1991 *Nm* 1(R),2, [*J*], 1993 *S*
Marshall, B D E (Queen's U, Belfast) 1963 *E*
Massey-Westropp, R H (Limerick, Monkstown) 1886 *E*
Matier, R N (NIFC) 1878 *E*, 1879 *S*
Matthews, P M (Ards, Wanderers) 1984 *A*, 1985 *S*, *F*, *W*, *E*, 1986 *R*, 1987 *E*, *S*, *F*, *W*, [*W*, *Tg*, *A*], 1988 *S*, *F*, *W*, *E* 1,2, *WS*, *It*, 1989 *F*, *W*, *E*, *S*, *NZ*, 1990 *E*, *S*, 1991 *F*, *W*, *E*, *S*, *Nm* 1, [*Z*, *S*, *A*], 1992 *W*, *E*, *S*
Mattsson, J (Wanderers) 1948 *E*
Mayne, R B (Queen's U, Belfast) 1937 *W*, 1938 *E*, *W*, 1939 *E*, *S*, *W*
Mayne, R H (Belfast Academy) 1888 *W*, *S*
Mayne, T (NIFC) 1921 *E*, *S*, *F*
Mays, K M A (UC Dublin) 1973 *NZ*, *E*, *S*, *W*
Meares, A W D (Dublin U) 1899 *S*, *W*, 1900 *E*, *W*
Megaw, J (Richmond, Instonians) 1934 *W*, 1938*E*
Millar, A (Kingstown) 1880 *E*, *S*, 1883 *E*
Millar, H J (Monkstown) 1904 *W*, 1905 *E*, *S*, *W*
Millar, S (Ballymena) 1958 *F*, 1959 *E*, *S*, *W*, *F*, 1960 *E*, *S*, *W*, *F*, *SA*, 1961 *E*, *S*, *W*, *F*, *SA*, 1962 *E*, *S*, *F*, 1963 *F*, *E*, *S*, *W*, 1964 *F*, 1968 *F*, *E*, *S*, *W*, *A*, 1969 *F*, *E*, *S*, *W*, 1970 *SA*, *F*, *E*, *S*, *W*
Millar, W H J (Queen's U, Belfast) 1951 *E*, *S*, *W*, 1952 *S*, *W*
Miller, F H (Wanderers) 1886 *S*
Milliken, R A (Bangor) 1973 *E*, *S*, *W*, *F*, 1974 *F*, *W*, *E*, *S*, *P*, *NZ*, 1975 *E*, *S*, *F*, *W*
Millin, T J (Dublin U) 1925 *W*
Minch, J B (Bective Rangers) 1912 *SA*, 1913 *E*, *S*, 1914 *E*, *S*
Moffat, J (Belfast Academy) 1888 *W*, *S*, *M*, 1889 *S*, 1890 *S*, *W*, 1891 *S*
Moffatt, J E (Old Wesley) 1904 *S*, 1905 *E*, *S*, *W*
Moffett, J W (Ballymena) 1961 *E*, *S*
Molloy, M G (UC Galway, London Irish) 1966 *F*, *E*, 1967 *A* 1, *E*, *S*, *W*, *F*, *A* 2, 1968 *F*, *E*, *S*, *W*, *A*, 1969 *F*, *E*, *S*, *W*, 1970 *F*, *E*, *S*, *W*, 1971 *F*, *E*, *S*, *W*, 1973 *F*, 1976 *A*
Moloney, J J (St Mary's Coll) 1972 *F* 1, *E*, *F* 2, 1973 *NZ*, *E*, *S*, *W*, *F*, 1974 *F*, *W*, *E*, *S*, *P*, *NZ*, 1975 *E*, *S*, *F*, *W*, 1976 *S*, 1978 *S*, *F*, *W*, *E*, 1979 *A* 1,2, 1980 *S*, *W*
Moloney, L A (Garryowen) 1976 *W* (R), *S*, 1978 *S* (R), *NZ*
Molony, J U (UC Dublin) 1950 *S*
Monteith, J D E (Queen's U, Belfast) 1947 *E*, *S*, *W*
Montgomery, A (NIFC) 1895 *S*
Montgomery, F P (Queen's U, Belfast) 1914 *E*, *S*, *W*
Montgomery, R (Cambridge U) 1887 *E*, *S*, *W*, 1891 *E*, 1892 *W*
Moore, C M (Dublin U) 1887 *S*, 1888 *W*, *S*
Moore, D F (Wanderers) 1883 *E*, *S*, 1884 *E*, *W*
Moore, F W (Wanderers) 1884 *W*, 1885 *E*, *S* 2, 1886 *S*
Moore, H (Windsor) 1876 *E*, 1877 *S*
Moore, H (Queen's U, Belfast) 1910 *S*, 1911 *W*, *F*, 1912 *F*, *E*, *S*, *W*, *SA*
Moore, T A P (Highfield) 1967 *A* 2, 1973 *NZ*, *E*, *S*, *W*, *F*, 1974 *F*, *W*, *E*, *S*, *P*, *NZ*
Moore, W D (Queen's Coll, Belfast) 1878 *E*
Moran, F G (Clontarf) 1936 *E*, 1937 *E*, *S*, *W*, 1938 *S*, *W*, 1939 *E*, *S*, *W*
Morell, H B (Dublin U) 1881 *E*, *S*, 1882 *W*, *E*
Morgan, G J (Clontarf) 1934 *E*, *S*, *W*, 1935 *E*, *S*, *W*, *NZ*, 1936 *E*, *S*, *W*, 1937 *E*, *S*, *W*, 1938 *E*, *S*, *W*, 1939 *E*, *S*, *W*
Moriarty, C C H (Monkstown) 1899 *W*
Moroney, J C M (Garryowen) 1968 *W*, *A*, 1969 *F*, *E*, *S*, *W*
Moroney, R J M (Lansdowne) 1984 *F*, *W*, 1985 *F*
Moroney, T A (UC Dublin) 1964 *W*, 1967 *A* 1, *E*
Morphy, E McG (Dublin U) 1908 *E*
Morris, D P (Bective Rangers) 1931 *W*, 1932 *E*, 1935 *E*, *S*, *W*, *NZ*
Morrow, J W R (Queen's Coll, Belfast) 1882 *S*, 1883 *E*, *S*, 1884 *E*, *W*, 1885 *S* 1,2, 1886 *E*, *S*, 1888 *S*
Morrow, R D (Bangor) 1986 *F*, *E*, *S*
Mortell, M (Bective Rangers, Dolphin) 1953 *F*, *E*, *S*, *W*, 1954 *NZ*, *F*, *E*, *S*, *W*
Morton, W A (Dublin U) 1888 *S*
Moyers, L W (Dublin U) 1884 *W*
Moylett, M M F (Shannon) 1988 *E* 1
Mulcahy, W A (UC Dublin, Bective Rangers, Bohemians) 1958 *A*, *E*, *S*, *W*, *F*, 1959 *E*, *S*, *W*, *F*, 1960 *E*, *S*, *W*, *SA*, 1961 *E*, *S*, *W*, *SA*, 1962 *E*, *S*, *F*, *W*, 1963 *F*, *E*, *S*, *W*, *NZ*, 1964 *E*, *S*, *W*, *F*, 1965 *F*, *E*, *S*, *W*, *SA*
Mullan, B (Clontarf) 1947 *F*, *E*, *S*, *W*, 1948 *F*, *E*, *S*, *W*
Mullane, J P (Limerick Bohemians) 1928 *W*, 1929 *F*
Mullen, K D (Old Belvedere) 1947 *F*, *E*, *S*, *W*, *A*, 1948 *F*, *E*, *S*, *W*, 1949 *F*, *E*, *S*, *W*, 1950 *F*, *E*, *S*, *W*, 1951 *F*, *E*, *S*, *W*, *SA*, 1952 *F*, *S*, *W*
Mulligan, A A (Wanderers) 1956 *F*, *E*, 1957 *F*, *E*, *S*, *W*, 1958 *A*, *E*, *S*, *F*, 1959 *E*, *S*, *W*, *F*, 1960 *E*, *S*, *W*, *F*, *SA*, 1961 *W*, *F*, *SA*
Mullin, B J (Dublin U, Oxford U, Blackrock Coll, London Irish) 1984 *A*, 1985 *S*, *W*, *E*, 1986 *F*, *W*, *E*, *S*, *R*, 1987 *E*, *S*, *F*, *W*, [*W*, *C*, *Tg*, *A*], 1988 *S*, *F*, *W*, *E* 1,2, *WS*, *It*, 1989 *F*, *W*, *E*, *S*, *NZ*, 1990 *E*, *S*, *W*, *Arg*, 1991 *F*, *W*, *E*, *S*, *Nm* 1,2, [*J*, *S*, *A*], 1992 *W*, *E*, *S*, 1994 *US*, 1995 *E*, *S*, *F*, *W*
Murphy, C J (Lansdowne) 1939 *E*, *S*, *W*, 1947 *F*, *E*
Murphy, J G M W (London Irish) 1951 *SA*, 1952 *S*, *W*, *E*, 1954 *NZ*, 1958 *W*
Murphy, J J (Greystones) 1981 *SA* 1, 1982 *W* (R), 1984 *S*

Murphy, J N (Greystones) 1992 *A*
Murphy, K J (Cork Constitution) 1990 *E, S, F, W, Arg*, 1991 *F, W*(R), *S*(R), 1992 *S, F, NZ* 2(R)
Murphy, N A A (Cork Constitution) 1958 *A, E, S, W, F*, 1959 *E, S, W, F*, 1960 *E, S, W, F, SA*, 1961 *E, S, W*, 1962 *E*, 1963 *NZ*, 1964 *E, S, W, F*, 1965 *F, E, S, W, SA*, 1966 *F, E, S, W*, 1967 *A* 1, *E, S, W, F*, 1969 *F, E, S, W*
Murphy, N F (Cork Constitution) 1930 *E, W*, 1931 *F, E, S, W, SA*, 1932 *E, S, W*, 1933 *E*
Murphy-O'Connor, J (Bective Rangers) 1954 *E*
Murray, H W (Dublin) 1877 *S*, 1878 *E*, 1879 *E*
Murray, J B (UC Dublin) 1963 *F*
Murray, P F (Wanderers) 1927 *F*, 1929 *F, E, S*, 1930 *F, E, S, W*, 1931 *F, E, S, W, SA*, 1932 *E, S, W*, 1933 *E, W, S*
Murtagh, C W (Portadown) 1977 *S*
Myles, J (Dublin U) 1875 *E*

Nash, L C (Queen's Coll, Cork) 1889 *S*, 1890 *W, E*, 1891 *E, S, W*
Neely, M R (Collegians) 1947 *F, E, S, W*
Neill, H J (NIFC) 1885 *E, S* 1,2, 1886 *S*, 1887 *E, S, W*, 1888 *W, S*
Neill, J McF (Instonians) 1926 *F*
Nelson, J E (Malone) 1947 *A*, 1948 *E, S, W*, 1949 *F, E, S, W*, 1950 *F, E, S, W*, 1951 *F, E, W*, 1954 *F*
Nelson, R (Queen's Coll, Belfast) 1882 *E, S*, 1883 *S*, 1886 *S*
Nesdale, T J (Garryowen) 1961 *F*
Neville, W C (Dublin U) 1879 *S, E*
Nicholson, P C (Dublin U) 1900 *E, S, W*
Norton, G W (Bective Rangers) 1949 *F, E, S, W*, 1950 *F, E, S, W*, 1951 *F, E, S*
Notley, J R (Wanderers) 1952 *F, S*

O'Brien, B (Derry) 1893 *S, W*
O'Brien, B A P (Shannon) 1968 *F, E, S*
O'Brien, D J (London Irish, Cardiff, Old Belvedere) 1948 *E, S, W*, 1949 *F, E, S, W*, 1950 *F, E, S, W*, 1951 *F, E, S, W, SA*, 1952 *F, S, W, E*
O'Brien, K A (Broughton Park) 1980 *E*, 1981 *SA* 1 (R), 2
O'Brien-Bulter, P E (Monkstown) 1897 *S*, 1898 *E, S*, 1899 *S, W*, 1900 *E*
O'Callaghan, C T (Carlow) 1910 *W, F*, 1911 *E, S, W, F*, 1912 *F*
O'Callaghan, M P (Sunday's Well) 1962 *W*, 1964 *E, F*
O'Callaghan, P (Dolphin) 1967 *A* 1, *E, A* 2, 1968 *F, E, S, W*, 1969 *F, E, S, W*, 1970 *SA, F, E, S, W*, 1976 *F, W, E, S, NZ*
O'Connell, K D (Sunday's Well) 1994 *F, E*(t)
O'Connell, P (Bective Rangers) 1913 *W, F*, 1914 *F, E, S, W*
O'Connell, W J (Lansdowne) 1955 *F*
O'Connor, H S (Dublin U) 1957 *F, E, S, W*
O'Connor, J (Garryowen) 1895 *S*
O'Connor, J H (Bective Rangers) 1888 *M*, 1890 *S, W, E*, 1891 *E, S*, 1892 *E, W*, 1893 *E, S*, 1894 *E, S, W*, 1895 *E*, 1896 *E, S, W*
O'Connor, J J (Garryowen) 1909 *F*
O'Connor, J J (UC Cork) 1933 *S*, 1934 *E, S, W*, 1935 *E, S, W, NZ*, 1936 *S, W*, 1938 *S*
O'Connor, P J (Lansdowne) 1887 *W*
Odbert, R V M (RAF) 1928 *F*
O'Donnell, R C (St Mary's Coll) 1979 *A* 1,2, 1980 *S, F, W*
O'Donoghue, P J (Bective Rangers) 1955 *F, E, S, W*, 1956 *W*, 1957 *F, E*, 1958 *A, E, S, W*
O'Driscoll, B J (Manchester) 1971 *F* (R), *E, S, W*
O'Driscoll, J B (London Irish, Manchester) 1978 *S*, 1979 *A* 1,2, 1980 *E, S, F, W*, 1981 *F, W, E, S, SA* 1,2, *A*, 1982 *W, E, S, F*, 1983 *S, F, W, E*, 1984 *F, W, E, S*
O'Flanagan, K P (London Irish) 1947 *A*
O'Flanagan, M (Lansdowne) 1948 *S*
O'Hanlon, B (Dolphin) 1947 *E, S, W*, 1948 *F, E, S, W*, 1949 *F, E, S, W*, 1950 *F*
O'Hara, P T J (Sunday's Well, Cork Const) 1988 *WS* (R), 1989 *F, W, E, NZ*, 1990 *E, S, F, W*, 1991 *Nm* 1, [*J*], 1993 *F, W, E*, 1994 *US*
O'Leary, A (Cork Constitution) 1952 *S, W, E*
O'Loughlin, D B (UC Cork) 1938 *E, S, W*, 1939 *E, S, W*
O'Meara, J A (UC Cork, Dolphin) 1951 *F, E, S, W, SA*, 1952 *F, S, W, E*, 1953 *F, E, S, W*, 1954 *NZ, F, E, S*, 1955 *F, E*, 1956 *S, W*, 1958 *W*
O'Neill, H O'H (Queen's U, Belfast, UC Cork) 1930 *E, S, W*, 1933 *E, S, W*
O'Neill, J B (Queen's U, Belfast) 1920 *S*
O'Neill, W A (UC Dublin, Wanderers) 1952 *E*, 1953 *F, E, S, W*, 1954 *NZ*
O'Reilly, A J F (Old Belvedere, Leicester) 1955 *F, E, S, W*, 1956 *F, E, S, W*, 1957 *F, E, S, W*, 1958 *A, E, S, W, F*, 1959 *E, S, W, F*, 1960 *E*, 1961 *E, F, SA*, 1963 *F, S, W*, 1970 *E*
Orr, P A (Old Wesley) 1976 *F, W, E, S, NZ*, 1977 *W, E, S, F*, 1978 *S, F, W, E, NZ*, 1979 *F, W, E, S, A* 1,2, 1980 *E, S, F, W*, 1981 *F, W, E, S, SA* 1,2, *A*, 1982 *W, E, S, F*, 1983 *S, F, W, E*, 1984 *F, W, E, S, A*, 1985 *S, F, W, E*, 1986 *F, S, R*, 1987 *E, S, F, W*, [*W, C, A*]
O'Shea, C M P (Lansdowne) 1993 *R*, 1994 *F, W, E, S, A* 1,2, *US*, 1995 *E, S*
O'Sullivan, A C (Dublin U) 1882 *S*
O'Sullivan, J M (Limerick) 1884 *S*, 1887 *S*
O'Sullivan, P J A (Galwegians) 1957 *F, E, S, W*, 1959 *E, S, W, F*, 1960 *SA*, 1961 *E, S*, 1962 *F, W*, 1963 *F, NZ*
O'Sullivan, W (Queen's Coll, Cork) 1895 *S*
Owens, R H (Dublin U) 1922 *E, S*

Parfrey, P (UC Cork) 1974 *NZ*
Parke, J C (Monkstown) 1903 *W*, 1904 *E, S, W*, 1905 *W, NZ*, 1906 *E, S, W, SA*, 1907 *E, S, W*, 1908 *E, S, W*, 1909 *E, S, W, F*
Parr, J S (Wanderers) 1914 *F, E, S, W*
Patterson, C S (Instonians) 1978 *NZ*, 1979 *F, W, E, S, A* 1,2, 1980 *E, S, F, W*
Patterson, R d'A (Wanderers) 1912 *F, S, W, SA*, 1913 *E, S, W, F*
Payne, C T (NIFC) 1926 *E*, 1927 *F, E, S, A*, 1928 *F, E, S, W*, 1929 *F, E, W*, 1930 *F, E, S, W*
Pedlow, A C (CIYMS) 1953 *W*, 1954 *NZ, F, E*, 1955 *F, E, S, W*, 1956 *F, E, S, W*, 1957 *F, E, S, W*, 1958 *A, E, S, W, F*, 1959 *E*, 1960 *E, S, W, F, SA*, 1961 *S*, 1962 *W*, 1963 *F*
Pedlow, J (Bessbrook) 1882 *S*, 1884 *W*
Pedlow, R (Bessbrook) 1891 *W*
Pedlow, T B (Queen's Coll, Belfast) 1889 *S, W*
Peel, T (Limerick) 1892 *E, S, W*
Peirce, W (Cork) 1881 *E*
Phipps, G C (Army) 1950 *E, W*, 1952 *F, W, E*
Pike, T O (Lansdowne) 1927 *E, S, W, A*, 1928 *F, E, S, W*
Pike, V J (Lansdowne) 1931 *E, S, W, SA*, 1932 *E, S, W*, 1933 *E, W, S*, 1934 *E, S, W*
Pike, W W (Kingstown) 1879 *E*, 1881 *E, S*, 1882 *E*, 1883 *S*
Pinion, G (Belfast Collegians) 1909 *E, S, W, F*
Piper, O J S (Cork Constitution) 1909 *E, S, W, F*, 1910 *E, S, W, F*
Polden, S E (Clontarf) 1913 *W, F*, 1914 *F*, 1920 *F*
Popham, I (Cork Constitution) 1922 *S, W, F*, 1923 *F*
Popplewell, N J (Greystones, Wasps) 1989 *NZ*, 1990 *Arg*, 1991 *Nm* 1,2, [*Z, S, A*], 1992 *W, E, S, F, NZ* 1,2, *A*, 1993 *S, F, W, E, R*, 1994 *F, W, E, S, US*, 1995 *E, S, F, W*
Potterton, H N (Wanderers) 1920 *W*
Pratt, R H (Dublin U) 1933 *E, W, S*, 1934 *E, S*
Price, A H (Dublin U) 1920 *S, F*
Pringle, J C (NIFC) 1902 *S, W*
Purcell, N M (Lansdowne) 1921 *E, S, W, F*
Purdon, H (NIFC) 1879 *S, E*, 1880 *E*, 1881 *E, S*
Purdon, W B (Queen's Coll, Belfast) 1906 *E, S, W*
Purser, F C (Dublin U) 1898 *E, S, W*

Quinlan, S V J (Blackrock Coll) 1956 *F, E, W*, 1958 *W*
Quinn, B T (Old Belvedere) 1947 *F*
Quinn, F P (Old Belvedere) 1981 *F, W, E*
Quinn, J P (Dublin U) 1910 *E, S*, 1911 *E, S, W, F*, 1912 *E, S, W*, 1913 *E, W, F*, 1914 *F, E, S*
Quinn, K (Old Belvedere) 1947 *F, A*, 1953 *F, E, S*
Quinn, M A M (Lansdowne) 1973 *F*, 1974 *F, W, E, S, P, NZ*, 1977 *S, F*, 1981 *SA* 2
Quirke, J M T (Blackrock Coll) 1962 *E, S*, 1968 *S*

Rainey, P I (Ballymena) 1989 *NZ*
Rambaut, D F (Dublin U) 1887 *E, S, W*, 1888 *W*
Rea, H H (Edinburgh U) 1967 *A* 1, 1969 *F*
Read, H M (Dublin U) 1910 *E, S*, 1911 *E, S, W, F*,

1912 *F, E, S, W, SA*, 1913 *E, S*
Rearden, J V (Cork Constitution) 1934 *E, S*
Reid, C (NIFC) 1899 *S, W*, 1900 *E*, 1903 *W*
Reid, J L (Richmond) 1934 *S, W*
Reid, P J (Garryowen) 1947 *A*, 1948 *F, E, W*
Reid, T E (Garryowen) 1953 *E, S, W*, 1954 *NZ, F*, 1955 *E, S*, 1956 *F, E*, 1957 *F, E, S, W*
Reidy, C J (London Irish) 1937 *W*
Reidy, G F (Dolphin, Lansdowne) 1953 *W*, 1954 *F, E, S, W*
Richey, H A (Dublin U) 1889 *W*, 1890 *S*
Ridgeway, E C (Wanderers) 1932 *S, W*, 1935 *E, S, W*
Rigney, B J (Greystones) 1991 *F, W, E, S, Nm* 1, 1992 *F, NZ* 1(R),2
Ringland, T M (Queen's U, Belfast, Ballymena) 1981 *A*, 1982 *W, E, F*, 1983 *S, F, W, E*, 1984 *F, W, E, S, A*, 1985 *S, F, W, E*, 1986 *F, W, E, S, R*, 1987 *E, S, F, W*, [*W, C, Tg, A*], 1988 *S, F, W, E* 1
Riordan, W F (Cork Constitution) 1910 *E*
Ritchie, J S (London Irish) 1956 *F, E*
Robb, C G (Queen's Coll, Belfast) 1904 *E, S, W*, 1905 *NZ*, 1906 *S*
Robbie, J C (Dublin U, Greystones) 1976 *A, F, NZ*, 1977 *S, F*, 1981 *F, W, E, S*
Robinson, B F (Ballymena, London Irish) 1991 *F, W, E, S, Nm* 1,2, [*Z, S, A*], 1992 *W, E, S, F, NZ* 1,2, *A*, 1993 *W, E, R*, 1994 *F, W, E, S, A* 1,2
Robinson, T T H (Wanderers) 1904 *E, S*, 1905 *E, S, W, NZ*, 1906 *SA*, 1907 *E, S, W*
Roche, J (Wanderers) 1890 *S, W, E*, 1891 *E, S, W*, 1892 *W*
Roche, R E (UC Galway) 1955 *E, S*, 1957 *S, W*
Roche, W J (UC Cork) 1920 *E, S, F*
Roddy, P J (Bective Rangers) 1920 *S, F*
Roe, R (Lansdowne) 1952 *E*, 1953 *F, E, S, W*, 1954 *F, E, S, W*, 1955 *F, E, S, W*, 1956 *F, E, S, W*, 1957 *F, E, S, W*
Rolland, A C (Blackrock Coll) 1990 *Arg*, 1994 *US*(R)
Rooke, C V (Dublin U) 1891 *E, W*, 1892 *E, S, W*, 1893 *E, S, W*, 1894 *E, S, W*, 1895 *E, S, W*, 1896 *E, S, W*, 1897 *E, S*
Ross, D J (Belfast Academy) 1884 *E*, 1885 *S* 1,2, 1886 *E, S*
Ross, G R P (CIYMS) 1955 *W*
Ross, J F (NIFC) 1886 *S*
Ross, J P (Lansdowne) 1885 *E, S* 1,2, 1886 *E, S*
Ross, N G (Malone) 1927 *F, E*
Ross, W McC (Queen's U, Belfast) 1932 *E, S, W*, 1933 *E, W, S*, 1934 *E, S*, 1935 *NZ*
Russell, J (UC Cork) 1931 *F, E, S, W, SA*, 1933 *E, W, S*, 1934 *E, S, W*, 1935 *E, S, W*, 1936 *E, S, W*, 1937 *E, S*
Russell, P (Instonians) 1990 *E*, 1992 *NZ* 1,2, *A*
Rutherford, W G (Tipperary) 1884 *E, S*, 1885 *E, S* 1, 1886 *E*, 1888 *W*
Ryan, E (Dolphin) 1937 *W*, 1938 *E, S*
Ryan, J (Rockwell Coll) 1897 *E*, 1898 *E, S, W*, 1899 *E, S, W*, 1900 *S, W*, 1901 *E, S, W*, 1902 *E*, 1904 *E*
Ryan, J G (UC Dublin) 1939 *E, S, W*
Ryan, M (Rockwell Coll) 1897 *E, S*, 1898 *E, S, W*, 1899 *E, S, W*, 1900 *E, S, W*, 1901 *E, S, W*, 1903 *E*, 1904 *E, S*

Saunders, R (London Irish) 1991 *F, W, E, S, Nm* 1,2, [*Z, J, S, A*], 1992 *W*, 1994 *F*(t)
Sayers, H J M (Lansdowne) 1935 *E, S, W*, 1936 *E, S, W*, 1938 *W*, 1939 *E, S, W*
Schute, F (Wanderers) 1878 *E*, 1879 *E*
Schute, F G (Dublin U) 1912 *SA*, 1913 *E, S*
Scott, D (Malone) 1961 *F, SA*, 1962 *S*
Scott, R D (Queen's U, Belfast) 1967 *E, F*, 1968 *F, E, S*
Scovell, R H (Kingstown) 1883 *E*, 1884 *E*
Scriven, G (Dublin U) 1879 *S, E*, 1880 *E, S*, 1881 *E*, 1882 *S*, 1883 *E, S*
Sealy, J (Dublin U) 1896 *E, S, W*, 1897 *S*, 1899 *E, S, W*, 1900 *E, S*
Sexton, J F (Dublin U, Lansdowne) 1988 *E* 2, *WS, It*, 1989 *F*
Sexton, W J (Garryowen) 1984 *A*, 1988 *S, E* 2
Shanahan, T (Lansdowne) 1885 *E, S* 1,2, 1886 *E*, 1888 *S, W*
Shaw, G M (Windsor) 1877 *S*
Sheehan, M D (London Irish) 1932 *E*
Sherry, B F (Terenure Coll) 1967 *A* 1, *E, S, A* 2, 1968 *F, E*
Sherry, M J A (Lansdowne) 1975 *F, W*
Siggins, J A E (Belfast Collegians) 1931 *F, E, S, W, SA*, 1932 *E, S, W*, 1933 *E, W, S*, 1934 *E, S, W*, 1935 *E, S, W, NZ*, 1936 *E, S, W*, 1937 *E, S, W*
Slattery, J F (UC Dublin, Blackrock Coll) 1970 *SA, F, E, S, W*, 1971 *F, E, S, W*, 1972 *F* 1, *E, F* 2, 1973 *NZ, E, S, W, F*, 1974 *F, W, E, S, P, NZ*, 1975 *E, S, F, W*, 1976 *A*, 1977 *S, F*, 1978 *S, F, W, E, NZ*, 1979 *F, W, E, S, A* 1,2, 1980 *E, S, F, W*, 1981 *F, W, E, S, SA* 1,2, *A*, 1982 *W E, S, F*, 1983 *S, F, W, E*, 1984 *F*
Smartt, F N B (Dublin U) 1908 *E, S*, 1909 *E*
Smith, B A (Oxford U, Leicester) 1989 *NZ*, 1990 *S, F, W, Arg*, 1991 *F, W, E, S*
Smith, J H (London Irish) 1951 *F, E, S, W, SA*, 1952 *F, S, W, E*, 1954 *NZ, W, F*
Smith, R E (Lansdowne) 1892 *E*
Smith, S J (Ballymena) 1988 *E* 2, *WS, It*, 1989 *F, W, E, S, NZ*, 1990 *E*, 1991 *F, W, E, S, Nm* 1,2, [*Z, S, A*], 1992 *W, E, S, F, NZ* 1,2, 1993 *S*
Smithwick, F F S (Monkstown) 1898 *S, W*
Smyth, J T (Queen's U, Belfast) 1920 *F*
Smyth, P J (Belfast Collegians) 1911 *E, S, F*
Smyth, R S (Dublin U) 1903 *E, S*, 1904 *E*
Smyth, T (Malone, Newport) 1908 *E, S, W*, 1909 *E, S, W*, 1910 *E, S, W, F*, 1911 *E, S, W*, 1912 *E*
Smyth, W S (Belfast Collegians) 1910 *W, F*, 1920 *E*
Solomons, B A H (Dublin U) 1908 *E, S, W*, 1909 *E, S, W, F*, 1910 *E, S, W*
Spain, A W (UC Dublin) 1924 *NZ*
Sparrow, W (Dublin U) 1893 *W*, 1894 *E*
Spillane, B J (Bohemians) 1985 *S, F, W, E*, 1986 *F, W, E*, 1987 *F, W*, [*W, C, A*(R)], 1989 *E* (R)
Spring, D E (Dublin U) 1978 *S, NZ*, 1979 *S*, 1980 *S, F, W*, 1981 *W*
Spring, R M (Lansdowne) 1979 *F, W, E*
Spunner, H F (Wanderers) 1881 *E, S*, 1884 *W*
Stack, C R R (Dublin U) 1889 *S*
Stack, G H (Dublin U) 1875 *E*
Staples, J E (London Irish, Harlequins) 1991 *W, E, S, Nm* 1,2, [*Z, J, S, A*], 1992 *W, E, NZ* 1,2, *A*, 1995 *F, W*
Steele, H W (Ballymena) 1976 *E*, 1977 *F*, 1978 *F, W, E*, 1979 *F, W, E, A* 1,2
Stephenson, G V (Queen's U, Belfast, London Hosp) 1920 *F*, 1921 *E, S, W, F*, 1922 *E, S, W, F*, 1923 *E, S, W, F*, 1924 *F, E, S, W, NZ*, 1925 *F, E, S, W*, 1926 *F, E, S, W*, 1927 *F, E, S, W, A*, 1928 *F, E, S, W*, 1929 *F, E, W*, 1930 *F, E, S, W*
Stephenson, H W V (United Services) 1922 *S, W, F*, 1924 *F, E, S, W, NZ*, 1925 *F, E, S, W*, 1927 *A*, 1928 *E*
Stevenson, J (Dungannon) 1888 *M*, 1889 *S*
Stevenson, J B (Instonians) 1958 *A, E, S, W, F*
Stevenson, R (Dungannon) 1887 *E, S, W*, 1888 *M*, 1889 *S, W*, 1890 *S, W, E*, 1891 *W*, 1892 *W*, 1893 *E, S, W*
Stevenson, T H (Belfast Acad) 1895 *E, W*, 1896 *E, S, W*, 1897 *E, S*
Stewart, A L (NIFC) 1913 *W, F*, 1914 *F*
Stewart, W J (Queen's U, Belfast, NIFC) 1922 *F*, 1924 *S*, 1928 *F, E, S, W*, 1929 *F, E, S, W*
Stoker, E W (Wanderers) 1888 *W, S*
Stoker, F O (Wanderers) 1886 *S*, 1888 *W, M*, 1889 *S*, 1891 *W*
Stokes, O S (Cork Bankers) 1882 *E*, 1884 *E*
Stokes, P (Garryowen) 1913 *E, S*, 1914 *F*, 1920 *E, S, W, F*, 1921 *E, S, F*, 1922 *W, F*
Stokes, R D (Queen's Coll, Cork) 1891 *S, W*
Strathdee, E (Queen's U, Belfast) 1947 *E, S, W, A*, 1948 *W, F*, 1949 *E, S, W*
Stuart, C P (Clontarf) 1912 *SA*
Stuart, I M B (Dublin U) 1924 *E, S*
Sugars, H S (Dublin U) 1905 *NZ*, 1906 *SA*, 1907 *S*
Sugden, M (Wanderers) 1925 *F, E, S, W*, 1926 *F, E, S, W*, 1927 *E, S, W, A*, 1928 *F, E, S, W*, 1929 *F, E, S, W*, 1930 *F, E, S, W*, 1931 *F, E, S, W*
Sullivan, D B (UC Dublin) 1922 *E, S, W, F*
Sweeney, J A (Blackrock Coll) 1907 *E, S, W*
Symes, G R (Monkstown) 1895 *E*
Synge, J S (Lansdowne) 1929 *S*

Taggart, T (Dublin U) 1887 *W*
Taylor, A S (Queen's Coll, Belfast) 1910 *E, S, W*, 1912 *F*
Taylor, D R (Queen's Coll, Belfast) 1903 *E*
Taylor, J (Belfast Collegians) 1914 *E, S, W*
Taylor, J W (NIFC) 1879 *S*, 1880 *E, S*, 1881 *S*, 1882 *E, S*, 1883 *E, S*

Tector, W R (Wanderers) 1955 *F, E, S*
Tedford, A (Malone) 1902 *E, S, W*, 1903 *E, S, W*, 1904 *E, S, W*, 1905 *E, S, W, NZ*, 1906 *E, S, W, SA*, 1907 *E, S, W*, 1908 *E, S, W*
Teehan, C (UC Cork) 1939 *E, S, W*
Thompson, C (Belfast Collegians) 1907 *E, S*, 1908 *E, S, W*, 1909 *E, S, W, F*, 1910 *E, S, W, F*
Thompson, J A (Queen's Coll, Belfast) 1885 *S* 1,2
Thompson, J K S (Dublin U) 1921 *W*, 1922 *E, S, F*, 1923 *E, S, W, F*
Thompson, R G (Lansdowne) 1882 *W*
Thompson, R H (Instonians) 1951 *SA*, 1952 *F*, 1954 *NZ, F, E, S, W*, 1955 *F, S, W*, 1956 *W*
Thornhill, T (Wanderers) 1892 *E, S, W*, 1893 *E*
Thrift, H (Dublin U) 1904 *W*, 1905 *E, S, W, NZ*, 1906 *E, W, SA*, 1907 *E, S, W*, 1908 *E, S, W*, 1909 *E, S, W, F*
Tierney, D (UC Cork) 1938 *S, W*, 1939 *E*
Tillie, C R (Dublin U) 1887 *E, S*, 1888 *W, S*
Todd, A W P (Dublin U) 1913 *W, F*, 1914 *F*
Torrens, J D (Bohemians) 1938 *W*, 1939 *E, S, W*
Tucker, C C (Shannon) 1979 *F, W*, 1980 *F* (R)
Tuke, B B (Bective Rangers) 1890 *E*, 1891 *E, S*, 1892 *E*, 1894 *E, S, W*, 1895 *E, S*
Turley, N (Blackrock Coll) 1962 *E*
Tweed, D A (Ballymena) 1995 *F, W*
Tydings, J J (Young Munster) 1968 *A*
Tyrrell, W (Queen's U, Belfast) 1910 *F*, 1913 *E, S, W, F*, 1914 *F, E, S, W*

Uprichard, R J H (Harlequins, RAF) 1950 *S, W*

Waide, S L (Oxford U, NIFC) 1932 *E, S, W*, 1933 *E, W*
Waites, J (Bective Rangers) 1886 *S*, 1888 *M*, 1889 *W*, 1890 *S, W, E*, 1891 *E*
Waldron, O C (Oxford U, London Irish) 1966 *S, W*, 1968 *A*
Walker, S (Instonians) 1934 *E, S*, 1935 *E, S, W, NZ*, 1936 *E, S, W*, 1937 *E, S, W*, 1938 *E, S, W*
Walkington, D B (NIFC) 1887 *E, W*, 1888 *W*, 1890 *W, E*, 1891 *E, S, W*
Walkington, R B (NIFC) 1875 *E*, 1876 *E*, 1877 *E, S*, 1878 *E*, 1879 *S*, 1880 *E, S*, 1882 *E, S*
Wall, H (Dolphin) 1965 *S, W*
Wallace, Jas (Wanderers) 1904 *E, S*
Wallace, Jos (Wanderers) 1903 *S, W*, 1904 *E, S, W*, 1905 *E, S, W, NZ*, 1906 *W*
Wallace R M (Garryowen) 1991 *Nm* 1(R), 1992 *W, E, S, F, A*, 1993 *S, F, W, E, R*, 1994 *F, W, E, S*, 1995 *W*
Wallace, T H (Cardiff) 1920 *E, S, W*
Wallis, A K (Wanderers) 1892 *E, S, W*, 1893 *E, W*
Wallis, C O'N (Old Cranleighans, Wanderers) 1935 *NZ*
Wallis, T G (Wanderers) 1921 *F*, 1922 *E, S, W, F*
Wallis, W A (Wanderers) 1880 *S*, 1881 *E, S*, 1882 *W*, 1883 *S*
Walmsley, G (Bective Rangers) 1894 *E*
Walpole, A (Dublin U) 1888 *S, M*
Walsh, E J (Lansdowne) 1887 *E, S, W*, 1892 *E, S, W*, 1893 *E*
Walsh, H D (Dublin U) 1875 *E*, 1876 *E*
Walsh, J C (UC Cork, Sunday's Well) 1960 *S, SA*, 1961 *E, S, F, SA*, 1963 *E, S, W, NZ*, 1964 *E, S, W, F*, 1965 *F, S, W, SA*, 1966 *F, S, W*, 1967 *E, S, W, F, A* 2
Ward, A J P (Garryowen, St Mary's Coll, Greystones) 1978 *S, F, W, E, NZ*, 1979 *F, W, E, S*, 1981 *W, E, S, A*, 1983 *E* (R), 1984 *E, S*, 1986 *S*, 1987 [*C, Tg*]
Warren, J P (Kingstown) 1883 *E*
Warren, R G (Lansdowne) 1884 *W*, 1885 *E, S* 1,2, 1886 *E*, 1887 *E, S, W*, 1888 *W, S, M*, 1889 *S, W*, 1890 *S, W, E*
Watson, R (Wanderers) 1912 *SA*
Wells, H G (Bective Rangers) 1891 *S, W*, 1894 *E, S*
Westby, A J (Dublin U) 1876 *E*
Wheeler, G H (Queen's Coll, Belfast) 1884 *S*, 1885 *E*
Wheeler, J R (Queen's U, Belfast) 1922 *E, S, W, F*, 1924 *E*
Whelan, P C (Garryowen) 1975 *E, S*, 1976 *NZ*, 1977 *W, E, S, F*, 1978 *S, F, W, E, NZ*, 1979 *F, W, E, S*, 1981 *F, W, E*
White, M (Queen's Coll, Cork) 1906 *E, S, W, SA*, 1907 *E, W*
Whitestone, A M (Dublin U) 1877 *E*, 1879 *S, E*, 1880 *E*, 1883 *S*
Whittle, D (Bangor) 1988 *F*
Wilkinson, C R (Malone) 1993 *S*
Wilkinson, R W (Wanderers) 1947 *A*
Williamson, F W (Dolphin) 1930 *E, S, W*
Willis, W J (Lansdowne) 1879 *E*
Wilson, F (CIYMS) 1977 *W, E, S*
Wilson, H G (Glasgow U, Malone) 1905 *E, S, W, NZ*, 1906 *E, S, W, SA*, 1907 *E, S, W*, 1908 *E, S, W*, 1909 *E, S, W*, 1910 *W*
Wilson, W H (Bray) 1877 *E, S*
Withers, H H C (Army, Blackheath) 1931 *F, E, S, W, SA*
Wolfe, E J (Armagh) 1882 *E*
Wood, G H (Dublin U) 1913 *W*, 1914 *F*
Wood, B G M (Garryowen) 1954 *E, S*, 1956 *F, E, S, W*, 1957 *F, E, S, W*, 1958 *A, E, S, W, F*, 1959 *E, S, W, F*, 1960 *E, S, W, F, SA*, 1961 *E, S, W, F, SA*
Wood, K G M (Garryowen) 1994 *A* 1,2, *US*, 1995 *E, S*
Woods, D C (Bessbrook) 1888 *M*, 1889 *S*
Woods, N K P J (Blackrock Coll) 1994 *A* 1,2, 1995 *E, F*
Wright, R A (Monkstown) 1912 *S*

Yeates, R A (Dublin U) 1889 *S, W*
Young, G (UC Cork) 1913 *E*
Young, R M (Collegians) 1965 *F, E, S, W, SA*, 1966 *F, E, S, W*, 1967 *W, F*, 1968 *W, A*, 1969 *F, E, S, W*, 1970 *SA, F, E, S, W*, 1971 *F, E, S, W*

IRISH INTERNATIONAL RECORDS

Both team and individual records are for official Ireland international matches up to 31 March 1995.

TEAM RECORDS

Highest score

60 v Romania (60-0) 1986 Dublin
v individual countries
20 v Argentina (20-18) 1990 Dublin
27 v Australia (27-12) 1979 Brisbane
46 v Canada (46-19) 1987 Dunedin
26 v England (26-21) 1974 Twickenham
25 v France { (25-5) 1911 Cork; (25-6) 1975 Dublin }
31 v Italy (31-15) 1988 Dublin
32 v Japan (32-16) 1991 Dublin
15 v Namibia (15-26) 1991 Windhoek
21 v N Zealand (21-24) 1992 Dunedin
60 v Romania (60-0) 1986 Dublin
15 v S Africa (15-23) 1981 Cape Town
26 v Scotland (26-8) 1953 Murrayfield
32 v Tonga (32-9) 1987 Brisbane

26 v United States (26-15) 1994 Dublin
21 v Wales (21-24) 1979 Cardiff
21 v Wales (21-7) 1980 Dublin
21 v Wales (21-9) 1985 Cardiff
21 v Wales (21-21) 1991 Cardiff
49 v W Samoa (49-22) 1988 Dublin
55 v Zimbabwe (55-11) 1991 Dublin

Biggest winning points margin
60 v Romania (60-0) 1986 Dublin
v individual countries
2 v Argentina (20-18) 1990 Dublin
15 v Australia (27-12) 1979 Brisbane
27 v Canada (46-19) 1987 Dunedin
22 v England (22-0) 1947 Dublin
24 v France (24-0) 1913 Cork
16 v Italy (31-15) 1988 Dublin
16 v Japan (32-16) 1991 Dublin
No win v Namibia
No win v N Zealand
60 v Romania (60-0) 1986 Dublin
3 v S Africa (9-6) 1965 Dublin
21 v Scotland (21-0) 1950 Dublin
23 v Tonga (32-9) 1987 Brisbane
11 v United States (26-15) 1994 Dublin
16 v Wales (19-3) 1925 Belfast
27 v W Samoa (49-22) 1988 Dublin
44 v Zimbabwe (55-11) 1991 Dublin

Longest winning sequence
6 matches 1968-69

Highest score by opposing team
59 N Zealand (6-59) 1992 Wellington
by individual countries
18 Argentina (20-18) 1990 Dublin
42 Australia (17-42) 1992 Dublin
19 Canada (46-19) 1987 Dunedin
38 England (9-38) 1992 Twickenham
44 France (12-44) 1992 Paris
15 Italy (31-15) 1988 Dublin
16 Japan (32-16) 1991 Dublin
26 Namibia (15-26) 1991 Windhoek
59 N Zealand (6-59) 1992 Wellington
3 Romania (25-3) 1993 Dublin
38 S Africa (0-38) 1912 Dublin
37 Scotland (21-37) 1989 Murrayfield
9 Tonga (32-9) 1987 Brisbane
15 United States (26-15) 1994 Dublin
34 Wales (9-34) 1976 Dublin
22 W Samoa (49-22) 1988 Dublin
11 Zimbabwe (55-11) 1991 Dublin

Biggest losing points margin
53 v N Zealand (6-59) 1992 Wellington
v individual countries
25 v Australia (17-42) 1992 Dublin
32 v England (3-35) 1988 Twickenham
32 v France (12-44) 1992 Paris
11 v Namibia (15-26) 1991 Windhoek
53 v N Zealand (6-59) 1992 Wellington
38 v S Africa (0-38) 1912 Dublin
23 v Scotland (9-32) 1984 Dublin
29 v Wales (0-29) 1907 Cardiff
No defeats v Argentina, Canada, Italy, Japan, Romania, Tonga, United States, W Samoa or Zimbabwe

Longest losing sequence
11 matches 1991-93

Most tries by Ireland in an international
10 v Romania (60-0) 1986 Dublin

Most tries against Ireland in an international
10 by S Africa (0-38) 1912 Dublin

Most points by Ireland in International Championship in a season – 71
in season 1982-83

Most tries by Ireland in International Championship in a season – 12
in seasons 1927-28 and 1952-53

INDIVIDUAL RECORDS

Most capped player
C M H Gibson 69 1964-79
in individual positions
Full-back
T J Kiernan 54 1960-73
Wing
K D Crossan 41 1982-92
Centre
B J Mullin 50[1] 1984-95
Fly-half
J W Kyle 46 1947-58
Scrum-half
M T Bradley 39 1984-95
Prop
P A Orr 58 1976-87
Hooker
K W Kennedy 45 1965-75

Lock
W J McBride 63 1962-75
Flanker
J F Slattery 61 1970-84
No 8
W P Duggan 39(41)[2] 1975-84

[1]C M H Gibson won 40 caps as a centre, 25 at fly-half and 4 as a wing
[2]Duggan won 39 caps at No 8 and 2 as a flanker

Longest international career
A J F O'Reilly 16 seasons 1955-70
C M H Gibson 16 seasons 1964-79
Gibson's career ended during a Southern Hemisphere season

Most consecutive Tests – 52
W J McBride 1964-75

Most internationals as captain – 24
T J Kiernan 1963-73

Most points in internationals – 308
M J Kiernan (43 matches) 1982-91

Most points in International Championship in a season – 52
S O Campbell (4 matches) 1982-83

Most points in an international – 23
R P Keyes v Zimbabwe 1991 Dublin

Most tries in internationals – 17
B J Mullin (50 matches) 1984-95

Most tries in International Championship in a season – 5
J E Arigho (3 matches) 1927-28

Most tries in an international – 4
B F Robinson v Zimbabwe 1991 Dublin

Most conversions in internationals – 40
M J Kiernan (43 matches) 1982-91

Most conversions in International Championship in a season – 7
R A Lloyd (4 matches) 1912-13

Most conversions in an international – 7
M J Kiernan v Romania 1986 Dublin

Most dropped goals in internationals – 7
R A Lloyd (19 matches) 1910-20
S O Campbell (22 matches) 1976-84

Most dropped goals in an international – 2
C M H Gibson v Australia 1967 Dublin
W M McCombe v France 1975 Dublin
S O Campbell v Australia 1979 Sydney
E P Elwood v England 1993 Dublin

Most penalty goals in internationals – 62
M J Kiernan (43 matches) 1982-91

Most penalty goals in International Championship in a season – 14
S O Campbell (4 matches) 1982-83
E P Elwood (4 matches) 1993-94

Most penalty goals in an international – 6
S O Campbell v Scotland 1982 Dublin
E P Elwood v Romania 1993 Dublin

Most points for Ireland on overseas tour – 60
S O Campbell (5 appearances) 1979 Australia
M J Kiernan scored 65 points in Japan 1985, but this was not on a major tour

Most points in any match on tour – 19
A J P Ward v Australian Capital Territory 1979 Canberra
S O Campbell v Australia 1979 Brisbane
E P Elwood v Western Australia 1994 Perth
M J Kiernan scored 25 points in the second match against Japan 1985, but this was not on a major tour

Most tries in any match on tour – 3
A T A Duggan v Victoria 1967 Melbourne
J F Slattery v SA President's XV 1981 East London
M J Kiernan v Gold Cup XV 1981 Oudtshoorn, SA
M J Field v Western Australia 1994 Perth
T M Ringland scored 3 tries v Japan at Osaka 1985, but this was not on a major tour

HEADS HAD TO ROLL FOR LACK OF STYLE

THE 1994-95 SEASON IN WALES

John Billot *Western Mail*

Many disillusioned followers believed Wales had become a wilderness of heroes; talented players desperately seeking a destiny they were denied by uninspired selection of the national team and a definite absence of tactical adventure. Lack of style caused considerable heartache and undeniably mirrored much of the general League scene. The collapse from Five Nations champions to the tournament's paupers was a bitter experience indeed. The aftermath was inevitable: a cleansing of manager and coaches in a drastic reshuffle.

In March, after the final humiliation of losing to Ireland, it was obvious that heads would roll. Alan Davies, the coach, attempted to stall the approach of the tumbril: 'I hope my position is not under threat because of this defeat,' he said. 'The players are to blame. They let him down,' stressed Robert Jones, who was recalled at scrum-half and showed he was still a potent force at the highest level. But the aridity of tactical thought brought widespread dissatisfaction and the whispering campaign for change became a clamour. New players must be given their chance: too many of the élite squad seemed to be granted immunity from accountability. Unimaginative selection has been the curse of Welsh rugby for many years, and it could not be overlooked after this season of disaster.

The team management of coach Davies, assistant Gareth Jenkins and manager Robert Norster asked to put to the WRU general committee their case for why Wales suffered a whitewash in the Five Nations for only the second time. Then it was announced that the WRU had accepted their resignation. This meant a major upheaval with little time left before the World Cup, but a purge or two had been known to be beneficial in the history of mankind and there were hopes that it might help this particular rugby problem.

The new command structure consisted of Australian Alex Evans, forwards coach to the 1984 Grand Slam Wallabies in the UK, with Dennis John (backs) and Mike Ruddock (forwards) as assistants, under the managership of former London Welsh and Lions lock Geoff Evans. Could they inject fresh freedom of expression into a fettered back division and rediscover the passion that the pack had shown in a fighting display against the Springboks? Wales' exit from Pool C of the World Cup showed that there was no positive answer in the short term.

The only uplifting news in a bleak season was the successful campaign to stage the 1999 World Cup against the formidable challenge from Australia. At least Wales will qualify for the next tournament as host nation. South Africa tipped a close-run contest in Wales' favour with their vote as the national team lurched from crisis to catastrophe on the

The Wales team which lost to Ireland in Cardiff. L-R, back row: H T Taylor (replacement), R C McBryde (replacement), N G Davies, W T Proctor, R G Collins, A Gibbs, G O Llewellyn, P T Davies, E W Lewis, D Jones (replacement), H Williams-Jones (replacement); front row: R H StJ B Moon (replacement), M R Hall, N R Jenkins, M Back, I C Evans (capt), S C John, G R Jenkins, M Griffiths, R N Jones, A Davies (replacement).

playing field. They had made no tactical advancement, while ball retention proved an insoluble problem. A driving display behind a creeping barrage of towering punts from Neil Jenkins certainly troubled the Springboks, but the tourists' superiority in attack was demonstrated by a 3-0 try-count.

The try famine – Wales scored only one in the International Championship – was to haunt Ieuan Evans and his team throughout the season. Injuries certainly hampered plans, especially the one which kept out Mike Rayer, a visionary attacker from full-back. The absence at various times of Ieuan Evans, Nigel Walker and Nigel Davies dictated limited tactics. Kicking possession away was a criminal negation of the Welsh way of expression. Paris, a mausoleum of Welsh hopes for 20 years, brought no respite. Next Wales were subordinated to the will of England's giant back row at the Arms Park before the disaster at Murrayfield, where Robert Jones scored that elusive try. Ireland, impoverished themselves, nevertheless won at Cardiff with a try that was the envy of every Welshman in the land.

The talent drain to Rugby League continued, with Llanelli's Scott Quinnell, aged 22, moving to Wigan in a deal reputedly worth around £400,000. On the same September day, the WRU held a meeting to clarify what payments were permitted to players. Winning bonuses were banned and cash inducements to transfer pronounced illegal. Then, on 4 April, the WRU announced plans for a new 80,000-seater national ground, incorporating a retractable skydome, in time for the 1999 World Cup. The £100 million project would swing the current stadium through 90 degrees and dispatch Cardiff RFC to find another site in the city – if their members sanction what many consider to be sacrilege, that is. Otherwise, the WRU may have to build near Bridgend.

CARDIFF BREAK THE WEST'S GRIP

THE HEINEKEN LEAGUES 1994-95

Cardiff's first success as champions ended the domination of the western clubs. Neath, Swansea (twice) and Llanelli had enjoyed their moments of triumph, but this time the top three positions were filled by clubs from the east. Pontypridd came second, while Treorchy, thanks to Swansea and Pontypridd fielding shadow teams before the Cup final, took third place. Cardiff's Steve Ford was the League's leading try-scorer with 19, but his team did not always play the wide game as convincingly as expected.

Treorchy, in the First Division for the first time, were the romance story of the season. They recruited widely and lost just one of their last nine League games. But the most dramatic moment involved Abertillery, who were doomed to relegation if they lost at Swansea (where only

Neath had succeeded all season) in their final League match. The home side, fielding virtually their entire Cup final team, led 21-6 at half-time. Incredibly, Swansea fell apart: the green and whites hit them with four tries and stole a sensational 35-29 victory to retain their place in Division 1. It was just reward for moving the ball into space throughout the season with almost reckless adventure.

Neath, with their worst try aggregate in five years, were the only club from the west in the top five. Coach David Pickering quit, but saw his side turn a 26-3 deficit into an astonishing 35-33 victory at Llanelli in their final match, which also marked the retirement of two notable international players, Paul Thorburn and Brian Williams. Llanelli had two points deducted for keeping a bigger-than-stipulated squad, but the penalty was rescinded on appeal. More wounding to the Scarlets was the loss of back-row stars Emyr Lewis (to Cardiff), Scott Quinnell (to Wigan) and Mark Perego (to contemplate his loss of enthusiasm for the game). For the first time, the Stradey club lost more games than they won.

Newport took a long time to recover from the drift of their players to other clubs – not to mention that of coach Roger Powell to Rumney – but recruited Canadian international Gareth Rees to fill their problem position at outside-half. Relegation threatened, but they pulled off home successes against Neath and Llanelli and were saved by four victories in their last five games. Dunvant went down after two seasons in the First Division, and Pontypool went with them. Mark Ring, the Pontypool captain, was sacked in January without explanation, and, suffering the effects of the pernicious player-drain, the club managed only four victories. Although they defeated Llanelli (twice), Swansea and Treorchy, they lost to all the teams in the lower reaches of the division.

Aberavon were champions of Division 2 and will return to the top flight after a season's absence. Promoted with them, for the first time, were Ebbw Vale, who pipped Abercynon with a superior try-count. Ebbw finished with a flourish, winning their last nine matches. Alas for Penarth, they dropped for the first time into Division 3 to join their fellow ex-major clubs Glamorgan Wanderers and Tredegar. Ystradgynlais, champions of Division 3, were promoted along with Caerphilly. Cardiff Institute of Education became Division 4 champions, going up with Pyle to replace the demoted Pontypool United and Aberavon Quins.

The new Division 5 brought Rumney promotion as champions. They attracted a number of leading players, such as Welsh international Glen George, as did Merthyr, who acquired Mark Titley and Steve Sutton and join Rumney in Division 4. Division 5 status came for Abergavenny, Pontyberem and Ystrad Rhondda from the feeder leagues.

HEINEKEN LEAGUES

Division 1	P	W	D	L	F	A	Pts
Cardiff	22	18	0	4	672	269	36
Pontypridd	22	17	0	5	555	255	34
Treorchy	22	13	0	9	479	312	26
Neath	22	12	2	8	379	398	26
Bridgend	22	12	1	9	518	451	25
Swansea	22	12	0	10	475	400	24
Llanelli	22	10	0	12	459	409	20
Newport	22	9	0	13	366	433	18
Newbridge	22	8	0	14	302	452	16
Abertillery	22	8	0	14	349	604	16
Dunvant	22	7	1	14	333	542	15
Pontypool	22	4	0	18	293	655	8

Division 2	P	W	D	L	F	A	Pts
Aberavon	22	17	0	5	506	263	34
Ebbw Vale	22	16	1	5	447	283	33
Abercynon	22	16	1	5	380	260	33
SW Police	22	12	2	8	413	357	26
Bonymaen	22	11	1	10	370	312	23
Maesteg	22	10	1	11	365	388	21
Tenby Utd	22	10	0	12	290	374	20
Llandovery	22	9	0	13	313	363	18
Llanharan	22	9	0	13	316	319	18
Cross Keys	22	8	0	14	292	438	16
Narberth	22	6	2	14	299	446	14
Penarth	22	4	0	18	289	477	8

Division 3	P	W	D	L	F	A	Pts
Ystradgynlais	22	19	0	3	411	192	38
Caerphilly	22	18	1	3	424	210	37
Tredegar	22	14	0	8	375	339	28
Mountain Ash	22	13	1	8	372	253	27
Builth Wells	22	11	0	11	297	300	22
Blaina	22	10	2	10	248	252	22
Kenfig Hill	22	10	0	12	384	360	20
Blackwood	22	9	2	11	268	291	20
Glam Wands	22	9	0	13	293	356	18
Tondu	22	7	1	14	304	316	15
Aberavon Qs	22	6	2	14	196	357	14
Pontypool Utd	22	1	1	20	238	584	3

Division 4	P	W	D	L	F	A	Pts
Cardiff Inst	22	18	0	4	447	256	36
Pyle	22	16	1	5	443	246	33
Whitland	22	14	0	8	379	249	28
Carmarthen Qs	22	13	0	9	414	273	26
Glynneath	22	11	1	10	305	274	23
St Peters	22	10	0	12	326	301	20
Tumble	22	9	1	12	318	351	19
Rhymney	22	9	0	13	275	376	18
Vardre	22	8	0	14	208	385	16
Llantrisant	22	8	0	14	256	354	16
Oakdale	22	7	1	14	270	366	15
Kidwelly	22	7	0	15	250	460	14

Division 5	P	W	D	L	F	A	Pts
Rumney	22	19	1	2	583	148	39
Merthyr	22	16	1	5	538	266	33
Seven Sisters	22	12	1	9	334	255	25
Hendy	22	11	1	10	322	457	23
Abercarn	22	10	3	9	306	357	23
Tonmawr	22	11	1	10	263	262	23
Cardiff Qns	22	11	0	11	342	281	22
Felinfoel	22	10	1	11	340	383	21
Garndiffaith	22	10	1	11	318	293	21
Cardigan	22	9	3	10	301	329	21
Pwllheli	22	4	0	18	162	382	8
Wrexham	22	2	1	19	185	581	5

NATIONAL LEAGUE TABLES

Division 6 East	P	W	D	L	Pts
Abergavenny	22	20	0	2	40
Old Illtydians	22	16	1	5	33
Mold	22	14	1	7	29
Pencoed	22	13	0	9	26
Bedwas	22	12	1	9	25
Croesyceiliog	22	11	1	10	23
O Penarthians	22	11	0	11	22
Talywain	22	9	0	13	18
Blaenau Gwent	22	8	0	14	16
Rhiwbina	22	7	0	15	14
Pill Harriers	22	5	0	17	10
Tredegar I'sides	22	4	0	18	8

Division 7 East	P	W	D	L	Pts
Brynmawr	22	18	1	3	37
Dinas Powys	22	16	0	6	32
Newport Saracens	22	15	2	5	32
Rhyl	22	13	0	9	26
RTB (Ebbw Vale)	22	12	2	8	26
Ruthin	22	12	0	10	24
Fleur de Lys	22	10	2	10	22
Pentyrch	22	9	3	10	21
Newport HSOB	22	7	2	13	16
Llandaff	22	6	3	13	15
Monmouth	22	4	0	18	8
Llandaff North	22	2	1	19	5

Division 8A East finishing order: Chepstow, St Joseph's, Cowbridge, Caldicot, Ynysddu, Cwmbran, Barry, Machen, Usk, Llantwit Major, Nantyglo, Cardiff U

Division 8B East finishing order: Llanhilleth, Blaenavon, Risca,

Heol-y-Cyw, Llanishen, Crumlin, Taff's Well, Trinant, Llandudno, Pontyclun, Caernarfon, Denbigh

Division 6 Central	*P*	*W*	*D*	*L*	*Pts*
Ystrad Rhondda	22	20	0	2	40
Tonyrefail	22	18	0	4	36
Nelson	22	15	0	7	30
Beddau	22	13	2	7	26
Cwmgwrach	22	13	0	9	26
Abercrave	22	10	2	10	22
Hirwaun	22	10	2	10	22
Ynysybwl	22	8	2	12	18
Maesteg Celtic	22	6	1	15	13
Nantymoel	22	6	0	16	12
Bridgend Ath	22	4	1	17	9
Bridgend Sports	22	4	0	18	8

Division 7 Central	*P*	*W*	*D*	*L*	*Pts*
Resolven	22	18	1	3	37
Gilfach Goch	22	18	0	4	36
Skewen	22	17	1	4	35
Senghenydd	22	12	1	9	25
Cilfynydd	22	12	0	10	24
Neath Athletic	21	11	2	8	24
Newtown	22	9	1	12	19
Rhydyfelin	21	7	2	12	16
Nantyffyllon	22	7	1	14	15
Aberavon G Stars	22	6	0	16	12
Porthcawl	21	5	1	15	11
Colwyn Bay	19	2	0	17	4

Division 8A Central finishing order: Llantwit Fardre, Treherbert, Blaengarw, Dolgellau, Tylorstown, Ystalyfera, Cwmavon, Crynant, Maesteg Quins, Welshpool, Brecon, Bangor
Division 8B Central finishing order: Penygraig, Bargoed, Cefn Coed, Aberaman, Bryncoch, Pontycymmer, Cefn Cribbwr, British Steel, Taibach, Tonna, Briton Ferry, Ogmore Vale

Division 6 West	*P*	*W*	*D*	*L*	*Pts*
Pontyberem	22	18	0	4	36
Morriston	22	16	1	5	33
Pembroke Dock Qs	22	12	3	7	27
New Dock Stars	22	12	0	10	24
Waunarlwydd	22	11	1	10	23
Brynamman	22	10	0	12	20
Llandybie	22	9	2	11	20
Carmarthen Ath	22	9	2	11	20
Pembroke	22	9	1	12	19
Llandeilo	22	9	1	12	19
Pontarddulais	22	7	0	15	14
Trimsaran	22	4	1	17	9

Division 7 West	*P*	*W*	*D*	*L*	*Pts*
Penygroes	22	19	1	2	39
Ammanford	22	16	1	5	33
Neyland	22	14	1	7	29
Trebanos	22	14	0	7	28
Gowerton	22	13	0	9	26
Cwmgors	22	12	2	8	26
Amman Utd	22	10	2	10	22
Loughor	22	9	2	11	20
Gorseinon	22	8	0	14	16
Milford Haven	22	5	1	16	11
Laugharne	22	4	1	17	9
Haverfordwest	22	1	1	20	3

Division 8A West finishing order: Llangennech, Aberystwyth, Newcastle Emlyn, Lampeter, Llanelli Wands, Burry Port, Fishguard, Pontyates, St Davids, Llangwm, Llanybydder
Division 8B West finishing order: Glais, Mumbles, Bynea, Furnace Utd, Cefneithin, Alltwen, Penclawdd, Cwmllynfell, Swansea Uplands, Tycroes, Pontardawe, BP Llandarcy

THE DAY JENKINS MISSED

SWALEC CUP 1994-95
6 May, Cardiff Arms Park
Swansea 17 (2G 1PG) **Pontypridd 12** (1G 1T)

First is glory; second is nowhere. That cruel modern sentiment was the fate of Pontypridd in both their campaigns this season: they were runners-up to Cardiff in the Heineken Leagues and then defeated finalists in the SWALEC Cup. It rather upset the theory that the team with the best goal-kicker ruled the roost. Yet the situation could easily have been reversed. Pontypridd lost away to Dunvant, who were relegated, and suffered their only home League defeat, 6-12, by Cardiff. Had those games been won, Ponty would have captured the title. Even more significantly, if Neil Jenkins, the greatest kicker of points for both club and country, had not missed four penalty chances in perfect conditions at the sun-baked National Stadium, the Cup could well have been theirs for the first time.

'Don't blame Neil for us losing,' stressed Nigel Bezani, the 38-year-old Pontypridd captain. 'He has been a wonder man for us and Wales. When he puts his kicks over we go up a gear, but even the best of kickers can sometimes have an off day. Then the rest of the team have to do the job.' Stuart Davies, the Swansea No 8 and scorer of the decisive try, remarked succinctly: 'Missing those kicks showed Neil is only human – and we are thankful for that!'

Swansea's second Cup triumph, their first for 17 years, was forged by the drive of their back row, the jumping of Paul Arnold and the perception of Aled Williams. 'At half-time we had a mountain to climb,' admitted Mike Ruddock, the Swansea coaching supremo. 'But we were confident that we could absorb their pressure, move our game up a gear, tie them in and let our forward strength settle it.'

That was exactly how it unfolded after Manley's 40-yard interception try, converted by Jenkins, gave Pontypridd a 7-0 lead into the second half. Williams narrowed the gap with a penalty goal for Swansea and then his sharp probe and in-pass sent the powerful Appleyard charging across. Williams converted and added the points to a close-up try by Stuart Davies eight minutes from the end. In injury time, Manley scored again, but the day had been lost on the business end of Jenkins' boot as far as Ponty fans were concerned.

Swansea: A Clement (*capt*); A Harris, R Boobyer, D Weatherley, Simon Davies; A Williams, R N Jones; C Loader, G R Jenkins, K Colclough, P Arnold, A Moore, A D Reynolds, Stuart Davies, R Appleyard
Scorers *Tries:* Appleyard, Stuart Davies *Conversions:* Williams (2)
Penalty Goal: Williams
Pontypridd: C Cormack; D Manley, J Lewis, S Lewis, O Robbins; N R Jenkins, Paul John; N Bezani (*capt*), Phil John, A Metcalfe, G Prosser, M Rowley, M Lloyd, D McIntosh, R G Collins *Replacements* G Jones for Robbins (6 mins); M Spiller for Lloyd (66 mins)
Scorers *Tries:* Manley (2) *Conversion:* Jenkins
Referee C Thomas (Neath)

Cardiff, considered favourites for the Cup, produced a doleful, tryless display in icy rain during their semi-final at Stradey and departed the competition in extra time, losing 9-16. Aled Williams kicked three penalty goals for Swansea and then surged through to put Roddy Boobyer over two minutes into the first period of extra time. Williams converted and was acclaimed the outstanding player. Once again,

Greg Prosser of Pontypridd beats Paul Arnold in the SWALEC Cup final, won 17-12 by Swansea. Arnold received the Lloyd Lewis Memorial Award as the outstanding player.

Arnold dominated the line-out and the Cup-holders faded after Adrian Davies' two penalty goals and a slanted drop-shot were scored.

The other semi-final saw Pontypridd, having all lost previous seven of their Cup encounters with Llanelli, at last end the Scarlets' domination by 20-14. At a muddy Cardiff RFC ground Neil Jenkins was inevitably a dynamic influence: he put over five penalty goals and stormed through to open a clear passage for Manley to scud in for a try. Llanelli had led 5-3 through a try by Robin McBryde, and added penalty goals through Colin Stephens (who then broke his left ankle), Rupert Moon and Jason Strange.

The quarter-final stage featured Cardiff's record Cup score of 73 points, including ten tries, three of them by Simon Hill. Their victims, Aberavon, could manage only three points in reply. Pontypridd also registered their most convincing Cup tally, 76-3, Paul John whisking through the Mountain Ash defence for four of their 12 tries. Llanelli lost their captain, the bubbling Moon, with a sprung shoulder, but fought back spiritedly from 0-8 arrears to defeat Bridgend 18-11 at Stradey. Swansea had not a moment's respite at Newbridge before Aled Williams' three penalty goals enabled them to shade the issue 19-11.

Swansea's most anxious experience came at the Gnoll in the sixth round. Neath appeared destined for victory with five penalty goals by Matthew McCarthy and a try by David Llewellyn, but Swansea toughed it out and were able to snatch a dramatic verdict, 22-20, through a penalty goal in injury time by Aled Williams. Neil Jenkins also found the target and fired over all ten of his kicks to help crush Old Illtydians by 66-0 at Sardis Road.

The fifth round featured Jenkins again: his 29 points doomed Pontypool to their most horrendous Cup defeat, 69-12. There were shocks at this stage for Ebbw Vale and South Wales Police. Ebbw lost on their home ground, 11-14, to Illtydians, who celebrated on the pitch with champagne, while the Police, also with home advantage, fell glumly by 3-20 to Old Penarthians.

Abercynon marked the fourth round by repeating their giant-killing performance of 17 years earlier, again winning at Abertillery. Bridgend recorded their highest Cup score, 80-5, against Cross Keys with three tries by the exciting new centre, Gareth Thomas, who won a place in the Wales World Cup squad in his first season in senior rugby. McCarthy supplied 24 points in Neath's record 79-12 victory against Aberaman, in which Chris Higgs collected four tries. Newport crashed to their worst Cup defeat, 0-56, at Pontypridd, where Manley sniped in for three tries. In the first round, Nelson humiliated Bangor Normal College 105-0, 26 of those points coming from Mike Kelleher.

RESULTS

Third Round

Aberaman 17, Rhymney 9; Aberavon Green Stars 11, Oakdale 6; Aberavon Quins 22, Felinfoel 11; Abergavenny 17, Blaina 20; Aberystwyth 8, Old Illtydians

14; Amman Utd 17, Tonyrefail 29; Blackwood 5, Brynmawr 3; Caerphilly 27, Trebanos 5; Cardiff Institute of Education 47, Tredegar 0; Cardigan 7, Nelson 19; Carmarthen Quins 43, Wattstown 0; Croesyceiliog 0, Glamorgan Wanderers 27; Garndiffaith 15, Fleur de Lys 16; Glyncoch 3, Morriston 20; Glynneath 12, Pontycymmer 3; Hartridge HSOB (Newport) 31, Ynysybwl 10; Hendy 6, Abercrave 13; Hirwaun 0, Gilfach Goch 3; Llandybie 3, Llantwit Fardre 8; Merthyr 48, Pill Harriers 8; Mountain Ash 8, Llandeilo 7; Neyland 22, Ystalyfera 13; Old Penarthians 26, New Dock Stars 18; Pentyrch 8, Risca 3; Penygraig 25, Treherbert 11; Pwllheli 21, Pontypool Utd 13; Pyle 30, Tredegar Ironsides 0; Resolven 12, Mold 0; Rhyl 11, Llantrisant 10; Ruthin 29, Kidwelly 9; Seven Sisters 25, Kenfig Hill 12; St Peter's (Cardiff) 9, Bargoed 10; Tondu 31, Neath Ath 0; Tonmawr 0, Builth Wells 5; Tylorstown 16, Lampeter 10; Vardre 15, Tumble 13; Whitland 28, Ammanford 13; Ystrad Rhondda 28, Abercarn 3

Fourth Round

Aberavon Green Stars 15, Tenby Utd 22; Aberavon Quins 17, Tonyrefail 23; Abercrave 6, Aberavon 21; Abertillery 6, Abercynon 29; Blackwood 23, Glamorgan Wanderers 3; Blaina 0, Bonymaen 21; Bridgend 80, Cross Keys 5; Cardiff 63, Merthyr 8; Cardiff Institute of Education 32, Llandovery 3; Carmarthen Quins 18, S W Police 32; Glynneath 26, Vardre Utd 0; Hartridge HSOB 12, Old Illtydians 14; Llanelli 51, Caerphilly 0; Maesteg 9, Ebbw Vale 14; Maesteg Celtic 8, Penygraig 22; Morriston 21, Gilfach Goch 8; Narberth 10, Mountain Ash 15; Neath 79, Aberaman 12; Nelson 5, Fleur de Lys 0; Newbridge 25, Treorchy 20; Neyland 8, Dunvant 34; Old Penarthians 24, Bargoed 11; Pentyrch 7, Whitland 25; Pontypridd 56, Newport 0; Pyle 29, Tylorstown 8; Resolven 6, Pontypool 13; Rhyl 14, Llantwit Fardre 3; Ruthin 7, Builth Wells 30; Seven Sisters 14, Ystradgynlais 6; Swansea 22, Llanharan 12; Tondu 40, Pwllheli 9; Ystrad Rhondda 19; Penarth 8

Fifth Round

Builth Wells 10, Bonymaen 0; Dunvant 28, Tonyrefail 7; Ebbw Vale 11, Old Illtydians 14; Glynneath 0, Llanelli 27; Morriston 13, Neath 40; Nelson 0, Newbridge 20; Penygraig 13, Rhyl 10; Pontypridd 69, Pontypool 12; Pyle 7, Cardiff 36; Seven Sisters 13, Blackwood 15; S W Police 3, Old Penarthians 20; Swansea 58, Abercynon 24; Tenby Utd 3, Aberavon 6; Tondu 5, Cardiff Institute of Education 22; Whitland 14, Mountain Ash 14 (*aet – Mountain Ash through on away-team ruling*); Ystrad Rhondda 0, Bridgend 39

Sixth Round

Aberavon 21, Cardiff Institute of Education 15; Blackwood 6, Newbridge 14; Bridgend 25, Penygraig 10; Builth Wells 13, Mountain Ash 18; Llanelli 29, Dunvant 8; Neath 20, Swansea 22; Old Penarthians 9, Cardiff 45; Pontypridd 66, Old Illtydians 0

Seventh Round

Cardiff 73, Aberavon 3; Llanelli 18, Bridgend 11; Newbridge 11, Swansea 19; Pontypridd 76, Mountain Ash 3

Semi-finals

Pontypridd 20, Llanelli 14 (*at Cardiff RFC*); Swansea 16, Cardiff 9 (*at Llanelli*)

FINAL (*at Cardiff Arms Park*)

Swansea 17 Pontypridd 12

Previous finals

(*all at Cardiff Arms Park*)

1972	Neath 15 Llanelli 9
1973	Llanelli 30 Cardiff 7
1974	Llanelli 12 Aberavon 10
1975	Llanelli 15 Aberavon 6
1976	Llanelli 15 Swansea 4
1977	Newport 16 Cardiff 15
1978	Swansea 13 Newport 9
1979	Bridgend 18 Pontypridd 12
1980	Bridgend 15 Swansea 9
1981	Cardiff 14 Bridgend 6
1982*	Cardiff 12 Bridgend 12
1983	Pontypool 18 Swansea 6
1984	Cardiff 24 Neath 19
1985	Llanelli 15 Cardiff 14
1986	Cardiff 28 Newport 21
1987	Cardiff 16 Swansea 15
1988	Llanelli 28 Neath 13
1989	Neath 14 Llanelli 13
1990	Neath 16 Bridgend 10
1991	Llanelli 24 Pontypool 9
1992	Llanelli 16 Swansea 7
1993	Llanelli 21 Neath 18
1994	Cardiff 15 Llanelli 8

* *Winners on 'most tries' rule*

WELSH INTERNATIONAL PLAYERS
(up to 31 March 1995)

ABBREVIATIONS

A – Australia; *Arg* – Argentina; *Bb* – Barbarians; *C* – Canada; *E* – England; *F* – France; *Fj* – Fiji; *I* – Ireland; *It* – Italy; *J* – Japan; *M* – Maoris; *Nm* – Namibia; *NZ* – New Zealand; *NZA* – New Zealand Army; *Pt* – Portugal; *R* – Romania; *S* – Scotland; *SA* – South Africa; *Sp* – Spain; *Tg* – Tonga; *US* – United States; *WS* – Western Samoa; *Z* – Zimbabwe; (R) – Replacement; (t) – temporary replacement. Entries in square brackets [ ] indicate appearances in the World Cup.

Note: Years given for Five Nations' matches are for second half of season; eg 1972 means season 1971-72. Years for all other matches refer to the actual year of the match. When a series has taken place, figures have been used to denote the particular matches in which players have featured. Thus 1969 *NZ* 2 indicates that a player appeared in the second Test of the series.

Ackerman, R A (Newport, London Welsh) 1980 *NZ*, 1981 *E, S, A*, 1982 *I, F, E, S*, 1983 *S, I, F, R*, 1984 *S, I, F, E, A*, 1985 *S, I, F, E, Fj*
Alexander, E P (Llandovery Coll, Cambridge U) 1885 *S*, 1886 *E, S*, 1887 *E, I*
Alexander, W H (Llwynypia) 1898 *I, E*, 1899 *E, S, I*, 1901 *S, I*
Allen, A G (Newbridge) 1990 *F, E, I*
Allen, C P (Oxford U, Beaumaris) 1884 *E, S*
Andrews, F (Pontypool) 1912 *SA*, 1913 *E, S, I*
Andrews, F G (Swansea) 1884 *E, S*
Andrews, G E (Newport) 1926 *E, S*, 1927 *E, F, I*
Anthony, L (Neath) 1948 *E, S, F*
Arnold, P (Swansea) 1990 *Nm* 1,2, *Bb*, 1991 *E, S, I, F*1, *A*, [*Arg, A*], 1993 *F*(R), *Z*2, 1994 *Sp, Fj*
Arnold, W R (Swansea) 1903 *S*
Arthur, C S (Cardiff) 1888 *I, M*, 1891 *E*
Arthur, T (Neath) 1927 *S, F, I*, 1929 *E, S, F, I*, 1930 *E, S, I, F*, 1931 *E, S, F, I, SA*, 1933 *E, S*
Ashton, C (Aberavon) 1959 *E, S, I*, 1960 *E, S, I*, 1962 *I*
Attewell, S L (Newport) 1921 *E, S, F*

Back, M J (Bridgend) 1995 *F*(R), *E*(R), *S, I*
Badger, O (Llanelli) 1895 *E, S, I*, 1896 *E*
Baker, A (Neath) 1921 *I*, 1923 *E, S, F, I*
Baker, A M (Newport) 1909 *S, F*, 1910 *S*
Bancroft, J (Swansea) 1909 *E, S, F, I*, 1910 *F, E, S, I*, 1911 *E, F, I*, 1912 *E, S, I*, 1913 *I*, 1914 *E, S, F*
Bancroft, W J (Swansea) 1890 *S, E, I*, 1891 *E, S, I*, 1892 *E, S, I*, 1893 *E, S, I*, 1894 *E, S, I*, 1895 *E, S, I*, 1896 *E, S, I*, 1897 *E*, 1898 *I, E*, 1899 *E, S, I*, 1900 *E, S, I*, 1901 *E, S, I*
Barlow, T M (Cardiff) 1884 *I*
Barrell, R J (Cardiff) 1929 *S, F, I*, 1933 *I*
Bartlett, J D (Llanelli) 1927 *S*, 1928 *E, S*
Bassett, A (Cardiff) 1934 *I*, 1935 *E, S, I*, 1938 *E, S*
Bassett, J A (Penarth) 1929 *E, S, F, I*, 1930 *E, S, I*, 1931 *E, S, F, I, SA*, 1932 *E, S, I*
Bateman, A G (Neath) 1990 *S, I, Nm* 1,2
Bayliss, G (Pontypool) 1933 *S*
Bebb, D I E (Carmarthen TC, Swansea) 1959 *E, S, I, F*, 1960 *E, S, I, F, SA*, 1961 *E, S, I, F*, 1962 *E, S, F, I*, 1963 *E, F, NZ*, 1964 *E, S, F, SA*, 1965 *E, S, I, F*, 1966 *F, A*, 1967 *S, I, F, E*
Beckingham, G (Cardiff) 1953 *E, S*, 1958 *F*
Bennett, I (Aberavon) 1937 *I*
Bennett, P (Cardiff Harlequins) 1891 *E, S*, 1892 *S, I*
Bennett, P (Llanelli) 1969 *F* (R), 1970 *SA, S, F*, 1972 *S* (R), *NZ*, 1973 *E, S, I, F, A*, 1974 *S, I, F, E*, 1975 *S* (R), *I*, 1976 *E, S, I, F*, 1977 *I, F, E, S*, 1978 *E, S, I, F*
Bergiers, R T E (Cardiff Coll of Ed, Llanelli) 1972 *E, S, F, NZ*, 1973 *E, S, I, F, A*, 1974 *E*, 1975 *I*
Bevan, G W (Llanelli) 1947 *E*
Bevan, J A (Cambridge U) 1881 *E*
Bevan, J C (Cardiff, Cardiff Coll of Ed) 1971 *E, S, I, F*, 1972 *E, S, F, NZ*, 1973 *E, S*
Bevan, J D (Aberavon) 1975 *F, E, S, A*
Bevan, S (Swansea) 1904 *I*
Beynon, B (Swansea) 1920 *E, S*
Beynon, G E (Swansea) 1925 *F, I*
Bidgood, R A (Newport) 1992 *S*, 1993 *Z*1,2, *Nm, J*(R)
Biggs, N W (Cardiff) 1888 *M*, 1889 *I*, 1892 *I*, 1893 *E, S, I*, 1894 *E, I*
Biggs, S H (Cardiff) 1895 *E, S*, 1896 *S*, 1897 *E*, 1898 *I, E*, 1899 *S, I*, 1900 *I*
Birch, J (Neath) 1911 *S, F*
Birt, F W (Newport) 1911 *E, S*, 1912 *E, S, I, SA*, 1913 *E*
Bishop, D J (Pontypool) 1984 *A*
Bishop, E H (Swansea) 1889 *S*
Blackmore, J H (Abertillery) 1909 *E*
Blackmore, S W (Cardiff) 1987 *I*, [*Tg* (R), *C, A*]
Blake, J (Cardiff) 1899 *E, S, I*, 1900 *E, S, I*, 1901 *E, S, I*
Blakemore, R E (Newport) 1947 *E*
Bland, A F (Cardiff) 1887 *E, S, I*, 1888 *S, I, M*, 1890 *S, E, I*
Blyth, L (Swansea) 1951 *SA*, 1952 *E, S*
Blyth, W R (Swansea) 1974 *E*, 1975 *S* (R), 1980 *F, E, S, I*
Boobyer, N (Llanelli) 1993 *Z*1(R), 2, *Nm*, 1994 *Fj, Tg*
Boon, R W (Cardiff) 1930 *S, F*, 1931 *E, S, F, I, SA*, 1932 *E, S, I*, 1933 *E, I*
Booth, J (Pontymister) 1898 *I*
Boots, J G (Newport) 1898 *I, E*, 1899 *I*, 1900 *E, S, I*, 1901 *E, S, I*, 1902 *E, S, I*, 1903 *E, S, I*, 1904 *E*
Boucher, A W (Newport) 1892 *E, S, I*, 1893 *E, S, I*, 1894 *E*, 1895 *E, S, I*, 1896 *E, I*, 1897 *E*
Bowcott, H M (Cardiff, Cambridge U) 1929 *S, F, I*, 1930 *E*, 1931 *E, S*, 1933 *E, I*
Bowdler, F A (Cross Keys) 1927 *A*, 1928 *E, S, I, F*, 1929 *E, S, F, I*, 1930 *E*, 1931 *SA*, 1932 *E, S, I*, 1933 *I*
Bowen, B (S Wales Police, Swansea) 1983 *R*, 1984 *S, I, F, E*, 1985 *Fj*, 1986 *E, S, I, F, Fj, Tg, WS*, 1987 [*C, E, NZ*], *US*, 1988 *E, S, I, F, WS*, 1989 *S, I*
Bowen, C A (Llanelli) 1896 *E, S, I*, 1897 *E*
Bowen, D H (Llanelli) 1883 *E*, 1886 *E, S*, 1887 *E*
Bowen, G E (Swansea) 1887 *S, I*, 1888 *S, I*
Bowen, W (Swansea) 1921 *S, F*, 1922 *E, S, I, F*
Bowen, Wm A (Swansea) 1886 *E, S*, 1887 *E, S, I*, 1888 *M*, 1889 *S, I*, 1890 *S, E, I*, 1891 *E, S*
Brace, D O (Llanelli, Oxford U) 1956 *E, S, I, F*, 1957 *E*, 1960 *S, I, F*, 1961 *I*
Braddock, K J (Newbridge) 1966 *A*, 1967 *S, I*
Bradshaw, K (Bridgend) 1964 *E, S, I, F, SA*, 1966 *E, S, I, F*
Brewer, T J (Newport) 1950 *E*, 1955 *E, S*
Brice, A B (Aberavon) 1899 *E, S, I*, 1900 *E, S, I*, 1901 *E, S, I*, 1902 *E, S, I*, 1903 *E, S, I*, 1904 *E, S, I*
Bridges, C J (Neath) 1990 *Nm* 1,2, *Bb*, 1991 *E*(R), *I, F*1, *A*
Bridie, R H (Newport) 1882 *I*
Britton, G R (Newport) 1961 *S*
Broughton, A S (Treorchy) 1927 *A*, 1929 *S*
Brown, A (Newport) 1921 *I*
Brown, J (Cardiff) 1925 *I*
Brown, J A (Cardiff) 1907 *E, S, I*, 1908 *E, S, F*, 1909 *E*
Brown, M (Pontypool) 1983 *R*, 1986 *E, S, Fj* (R), *Tg, WS*
Bryant, D J (Bridgend) 1988 *NZ* 1,2, *WS, R*, 1989 *S, I, F, E*
Buchanan, A (Llanelli) 1987 [*Tg, E, NZ, A*], 1988 *I*
Buckett, I M (Swansea) 1994 *Tg*
Burcher, D H (Newport) 1977 *I, F, E, S*
Burgess, R C (Ebbw Vale) 1977 *I, F, E, S*, 1981 *I, F*, 1982 *F, E, S*
Burnett, R (Newport) 1953 *E*
Burns, J (Cardiff) 1927 *F, I*
Bush, P F (Cardiff) 1905 *NZ*, 1906 *E, SA*, 1907 *I*, 1908 *E, S*, 1910 *S, I*
Butler, E T (Pontypool) 1980 *F, E, S, I, NZ* (R), 1982 *S*, 1983 *E, S, I, F, R*, 1984 *S, I, F, E, A*

Cale, W R (Newbridge, Pontypool) 1949 *E, S, I*, 1950 *E, S, I, F*
Carter, A J (Newport) 1991 *E, S*
Cattell, A (Llanelli) 1883 *E, S*
Challinor, C (Neath) 1939 *E*
Clapp, T J S (Newport) 1882 *I*, 1883 *E, S*, 1884 *E, S, I*, 1885 *E, S*, 1886 *S*, 1887 *E, S, I*, 1888 *S, I*
Clare, J (Cardiff) 1883 *E*
Clark, S S (Neath) 1882 *I*, 1887 I
Cleaver, W B (Cardiff) 1947 *E, S, F, I, A*, 1948 *E, S, F, I*, 1949 *I*, 1950 *E, S, I, F*
Clegg, B G (Swansea) 1979 *F*
Clement, A (Swansea) 1987 *US* (R), 1988 *E, NZ* 1, *WS* (R), *R*, 1989 *NZ*, 1990 *S* (R), *I* (R), *Nm* 1,2, 1991 *S*(R), *A*(R), *F*2, [*WS, A*], 1992 *I, F, E, S*, 1993 *I*(R), *F, J, C*, 1994 *S, I, F, Sp, C*(R), *Tg, WS, It, SA*, 1995 *F, E*
Clement, W H (Llanelli) 1937 *E, S, I*, 1938 *E, S, I*
Cobner, T J (Pontypool) 1974 *S, I, F, E*, 1975 *F, E, S, I, A*, 1976 *E, S*, 1977 *F, E, S*, 1978 *E, S, I, F, A* 1
Coldrick, A P (Newport) 1911 *E, S, I*, 1912 *E, S, F*
Coleman, E (Newport) 1949 *E, S, I*
Coles, F C (Pontypool) 1960 *S, I, F*
Collins, J (Aberavon) 1958 *A, E, S, F*, 1959 *E, S, I, F*, 1960 *E*, 1961 *F*
Collins, R G (S Wales Police, Cardiff, Pontypridd) 1987 *E* (R), *I*, [*I, E, NZ*], *US*, 1988 *E, S, I, F, R*, 1990 *E, S, I*, 1991 *A, F*2, [*WS*], 1994 *C, Fj, Tg, WS, R, It, SA*, 1995 *F, E, S, I*
Collins, T (Mountain Ash) 1923 *I*
Conway-Rees, J (Llanelli) 1892 *S*, 1893 *E*, 1894 *E*
Cook, T (Cardiff) 1949 *S, I*
Cope, W (Cardiff, Blackheath) 1896 *S*
Copsey, A H (Llanelli) 1992 *I, F, E, S, A*, 1993 *E, S, I, J, C*, 1994 *E*(R), *Pt, Sp*(R), *Fj, Tg, WS*(R)
Cornish, F H (Cardiff) 1897 *E*, 1898 *I, E*, 1899 *I*
Cornish, R A (Cardiff) 1923 *E, S*, 1924 *E*, 1925 *E, S, F*, 1926 *E, S, I, F*
Coslett, K (Aberavon) 1962 *E, S, F*
Cowey, B T V (Welch Regt, Newport) 1934 *E, S, I*, 1935 *E*
Cresswell, B (Newport) 1960 *E, S, I, F*
Cummins, W (Treorchy) 1922 *E, S, I, F*
Cunningham, L J (Aberavon) 1960 *E, S, I, F*, 1962 *E, S, F, I*, 1963 *NZ*, 1964 *E, S, I, F, SA*

Dacey, M (Swansea) 1983 *E, S, I, F, R*, 1984 *S, I, F, E, A*, 1986 *Fj, Tg, WS*, 1987 *F* (R), [*Tg*]
Daniel, D J (Llanelli) 1891 *S*, 1894 *E, S, I*, 1898 *I, E*, 1899 *E, I*
Daniel, L T D (Newport) 1970 *S*
Daniels, P C T (Cardiff) 1981 *A*, 1982 *I*
Darbishire, G (Bangor) 1881 *E*
Dauncey, F H (Newport) 1896 *E, S, I*
Davey, C (Swansea) 1930 *F*, 1931 *E, S, F, I, SA*, 1932 *E, S, I*, 1933 *E, S*, 1934 *E, S, I*, 1935 *E, S, I, NZ*, 1936 *S*, 1937 *E, I*, 1938 *E, I*
David, R J (Cardiff) 1907 *I*
David, T P (Llanelli, Pontypridd) 1973 *F, A*, 1976 *I, F*
Davidge, G D (Newport) 1959 *F*, 1960 *S, I, F, SA*, 1961 *E, S, I*, 1962 *F*
Davies, A (Cambridge U, Neath, Cardiff) 1990 *Bb*(R), 1991 *A*, 1993 *Z*1,2, *J, C*, 1994 *Fj*
Davies, A C (London Welsh) 1889 *I*
Davies, A E (Llanelli) 1984 *A*
Davies, B (Llanelli) 1895 *E*, 1896 *E*
Davies, C (Cardiff) 1947 *S, F, I, A*, 1948 *E, S, F, I*, 1949 *F*, 1950 *E, S, I, F*, 1951 *E, S, I*
Davies, C (Llanelli) 1988 *WS*, 1989 *S, I* (R), *F*
Davies, C H A (Llanelli, Cardiff) 1957 *I*, 1958 *A, E, S, I*, 1960 *SA*, 1961 *E*
Davies, C L (Cardiff) 1956 *E, S, I*
Davies, C R (Bedford, RAF) 1934 *E*
Davies, D (Bridgend) 1921 *I*, 1925 *I*
Davies, D B (Llanelli) 1907 *E*
Davies, D B (Llanelli) 1962 *I*, 1963 *E, S*
Davies, D G (Cardiff) 1923 *E, S*
Davies, D H (Neath) 1904 *S*
Davies, D H (Aberavon) 1924 *E*
Davies, D I (Swansea) 1939 *E*
Davies, D J (Neath) 1962 *I*
Davies, D M (Somerset Police) 1950 *E, S, I, F*, 1951 *E, S, I, F, SA*, 1952 *E, S, I, F*, 1953 *I, F, NZ*, 1954 *E*
Davies, E (Aberavon) 1947 *A*, 1948 *I*
Davies, E (Maesteg) 1919 *NZA*
Davies, E G (Cardiff) 1912 *E, F*
Davies, E G (Cardiff) 1928 *F*, 1929 *E*, 1930 *S*
Davies, G (Swansea) 1900 *E, S, I*, 1901 *E, S, I*, 1905 *E, S, I*
Davies, G (Cambridge U, Pontypridd) 1947 *S, A*, 1948 *E, S, F, I*, 1949 *E, S, F*, 1951 *E, S*
Davies, G (Llanelli) 1921 *F, I*, 1925 *F*
Davies, H (Swansea) 1898 *I, E*, 1901 *S, I*
Davies, H (Swansea, Llanelli) 1939 *S, I*, 1947 *E, S, F, I*
Davies, H (Neath) 1912 *E, S*
Davies, H (Bridgend) 1984 *S, I, F, E*
Davies, H J (Cambridge U, Aberavon) 1959 *E, S*
Davies, H J (Newport) 1924 *S*
Davies, I T (Llanelli) 1914 *S, F, I*
Davies, J (Neath, Llanelli) 1985 *E, Fj*, 1986 *E, S, I, F, Fj, Tg, WS*, 1987 *F, E, S, I*, [*I, Tg* (R), *C, E, NZ, A*], 1988 *E, S, I, F, NZ* 1,2, *WS, R*
Davies, Rev J A (Swansea) 1913 *S, F, I*, 1914 *E, S, F, I*
Davies, J D (Neath) 1991 *I, F*1, 1993 *F*(R), *Z*2, *J, C*, 1994 *S, I, F, E, Pt, Sp, C, WS, R, It, SA*, 1995 *F, E*
Davies, J H (Aberavon) 1923 *I*
Davies, L (Swansea) 1939 *S, I*
Davies, L (Bridgend) 1966 *E, S, I*
Davies, L M (Llanelli) 1954 *F, S*, 1955 *I*
Davies, M (Swansea) 1981 *A*, 1982 *I*, 1985 *Fj*
Davies, M J (Blackheath) 1939 *S, I*
Davies, N G (London Welsh) 1955 *E*
Davies, N G (Llanelli) 1988 *NZ* 2, *WS*, 1989 *S, I*, 1993 *F*, 1994 *S, I, E, Pt, Sp, C, Fj, Tg*(R), *WS, R, It*, 1995 *E, S, I*
Davies, P T (Llanelli) 1985 *E, Fj*, 1986 *E, S, I, F, Fj, Tg, WS*, 1987 *F, E, I*, [*Tg, C, NZ*], 1988 *WS, R*, 1989 *S, I, F, E, NZ*, 1990 *F, E, S*, 1991 *I, F*1, *A, F*2, [*WS, Arg, A*], 1993 *F, Z*1, *Nm*, 1994 *S, I, F, E, C, Fj*(R), *WS, R, It*, 1995 *F, I*
Davies, R H (Oxford U, London Welsh) 1957 *S, I, F*, 1958 *A*, 1962 *E, S*
Davies, S (Treherbert) 1923 *I*
Davies, S (Swansea) 1992 *I, F, E, S, A*, 1993 *E, S, I, Z*1(R), 2, *Nm, J*, 1995 *F*
Davies, T G R (Cardiff, London Welsh) 1966 *A*, 1967 *S, I, F, E*, 1968 *E, S*, 1969 *S, I, F, NZ* 1,2, *A*, 1971 *E, S, I, F*, 1972 *E, S, F, NZ*, 1973 *E, S, I, F, A*, 1974 *S, F, E*, 1975 *F, E, S, I*, 1976 *E, S, I, F*, 1977 *I, F, E, S*, 1978 *E, S, I, A* 1,2
Davies, T J (Devonport Services, Swansea, Llanelli) 1953 *E, S, I, F*, 1957 *E, S, I, F*, 1958 *A, E, S, F*, 1959 *E, S, I, F*, 1960 *E, SA*, 1961 *E, S, F*
Davies, T M (London Welsh, Swansea) 1969 *S, I, F, E, NZ* 1,2, *A*, 1970 *SA, S, E, I, F*, 1971 *E, S, I, F*, 1972 *E, S, F, NZ*, 1973 *E, S, I, F, A*, 1974 *S, I, F, E*, 1975 *F, E, S, I, A*, 1976 *E, S, I, F*
Davies, W (Cardiff) 1896 *S*
Davies, W (Swansea) 1931 *SA*, 1932 *E, S, I*
Davies, W A (Aberavon) 1912 *S, I*
Davies, W G (Cardiff) 1978 *A* 1,2, *NZ*, 1979 *S, I, F, E*, 1980 *F, E, S, NZ*, 1981 *E, S, A*, 1982 *I, F, E, S*, 1985 *S, I, F*
Davies, W T H (Swansea) 1936 *I*, 1937 *E, I*, 1939 *E, S, I*
Davis, C E (Newbridge) 1978 *A* 2, 1981 *E, S*
Davis, M (Newport) 1991 *A*
Davis, W E N (Cardiff) 1939 *E, S, I*
Dawes, S J (London Welsh) 1964 *I, F, SA*, 1965 *E, S, I, F*, 1966 *A*, 1968 *I, F*, 1969 *E, NZ* 2, *A*, 1970 *SA, S, E, I, F*, 1971 *E, S, I, F*
Day, H C (Newport) 1930 *S, I, F*, 1931 *E, S*
Day, H T (Newport) 1892 *I*, 1893 *E, S*, 1894 *S, I*
Day, T B (Swansea) 1931 *E, S, F, I, SA*, 1932 *E, S, I*, 1934 *S, I*, 1935 *E, S, I*
Deacon, J T (Swansea) 1891 *I*, 1892 *E, S, I*
Delahay, W J (Bridgend) 1922 *E, S, I, F*, 1923 *E, S, F, I*, 1924 *NZ*, 1925 *E, S, F, I*, 1926 *E, S, I, F*, 1927 *S*
Delaney, L (Llanelli) 1989 *I, F, E*, 1990 *E*, 1991 *F*2, [*WS, Arg, A*], 1992 *I, F, E*
Devereux, D (Neath) 1958 *A, E, S*
Devereux, J A (S Glamorgan Inst, Bridgend) 1986 *E, S, I, F, Fj, Tg, WS*, 1987 *F, E, S, I*, [*I, C, E, NZ, A*], 1988 *NZ* 1,2, *R*, 1989 *S, I*
Diplock, R (Bridgend) 1988 *R*
Dobson, G (Cardiff) 1900 *S*
Dobson, T (Cardiff) 1898 *I, E*, 1899 *E, S*
Donovan, A J (Swansea) 1978 *A* 2, 1981 *I* (R), *A*, 1982 *E, S*

Donovan, R (S Wales Police) 1983 *F* (R)
Douglas, M H J (Llanelli) 1984 *S, I, F*
Douglas, W M (Cardiff) 1886 *E, S*, 1887 *E, S*
Dowell, W H (Newport) 1907 *E, S, I*, 1908 *E, S, F, I*
Dyke, J C M (Penarth) 1906 *SA*
Dyke, L M (Penarth, Cardiff) 1910 *I*, 1911 *S, F, I*

Edmunds, D A (Neath) 1990 *I* (R), *Bb*
Edwards, A B (London Welsh, Army) 1955 *E, S*
Edwards, B O (Newport) 1951 *I*
Edwards, D (Glynneath) 1921 *E*
Edwards, G O (Cardiff, Cardiff Coll of Ed) 1967 *F, E, NZ*, 1968 *E, S, I, F*, 1969 *S, I, F, E, NZ* 1,2, *A*, 1970 *SA, S, E, I, F*, 1971 *E, S, I, F*, 1972 *E, S, F, NZ*, 1973 *E, S, I, F, A*, 1974 *S, I, F, E*, 1975 *F, E, S, I, A*, 1976 *E, S, I, F*, 1977 *I, F, E, S*, 1978 *E, S, I, F*
Eidman, I H (Cardiff) 1983 *S, R*, 1984 *I, F, E, A*, 1985 *S, I, Fj*, 1986 *E, S, I, F*
Elliott, J E (Cardiff) 1894 *I*, 1898 *I, E*
Elsey, W J (Cardiff) 1895 *E*
Emyr, Arthur (Swansea) 1989 *E, NZ*, 1990 *F, E, S, I, Nm* 1,2, 1991 *F* 1,2, [*WS, Arg, A*]
Evans, A C (Pontypool) 1924 *E, I, F*
Evans, B (Swansea) 1933 *S*
Evans, B (Llanelli) 1933 *E, S*, 1936 *E, S, I*, 1937 *E*
Evans, B S (Llanelli) 1920 *E*, 1922 *E, S, I, F*
Evans, C (Pontypool) 1960 *E*
Evans, D (Penygraig) 1896 *S, I*, 1897 *E*, 1898 *E*
Evans, D B (Swansea) 1926 *E*
Evans, D D (Cheshire, Cardiff U) 1934 *E*
Evans, D P (Llanelli) 1960 *SA*
Evans, D W (Cardiff) 1889 *S, I*, 1890 *E, I*, 1891 *E*
Evans, D W (Oxford U, Cardiff) 1989 *F, E, NZ*, 1990 *F, E, S, I, Bb*, 1991 *A*(R), *F*2(R), [*A*(R)]
Evans, E (Llanelli) 1937 *E*, 1939 *S, I*
Evans, F (Llanelli) 1921 *S*
Evans, G (Cardiff) 1947 *E, S, F, I, A*, 1948 *E, S, F, I*, 1949 *E, S, I*
Evans, G (Maesteg) 1981 *S* (R), *I, F, A*, 1982 *I, F, E, S*, 1983 *F, R*
Evans, G L (Newport) 1977 *F* (R), 1978 *F, A* 2 (R)
Evans, I (London Welsh) 1934 *S, I*
Evans, I (Swansea) 1922 *E, S, I, F*
Evans, I C (Llanelli) 1987 *F, E, S, I*, [*I, C, E, NZ, A*], 1988 *E, S, I, F, NZ* 1,2, 1989 *I, F, E*, 1991 *E, S, I, F*1, *A, F*2, [*WS, Arg, A*], 1992 *I, F, E, S, A*, 1993 *E, S, I, F, J, C*, 1994 *S, I, E, Pt, Sp, C, Fj, Tg, WS, R*, 1995 *E, S, I*
Evans, I L (Llanelli) 1991 *F*2(R)
Evans, J (Llanelli) 1896 *S, I*, 1897 *E*
Evans, J (Blaina) 1904 *E*
Evans, J (Pontypool) 1907 *E, S, I*
Evans, J D (Cardiff) 1958 *I, F*
Evans, J E (Llanelli) 1924 *S*
Evans, J R (Newport) 1934 *E*
Evans, O J (Cardiff) 1887 *E, S*, 1888 *S, I*
Evans, P D (Llanelli) 1951 *E, F*
Evans, R (Cardiff) 1889 *S*
Evans, R (Bridgend) 1963 *S, I, F*
Evans, R L (Llanelli) 1993 *E, S, I, F*, 1994 *S, I, F, E, Pt, Sp, C, Fj, WS, R, It, SA*, 1995 *F*
Evans, R T (Newport) 1947 *F, I*, 1950 *E, S, I, F*, 1951 *E, S, I, F*
Evans, S (Swansea, Neath) 1985 *F, E*, 1986 *Fj, Tg, WS*, 1987 *F, E*, [*I, Tg*]
Evans, T (Swansea) 1924 *I*
Evans, T G (London Welsh) 1970 *SA, S, E, I*, 1972 *E, S, F*
Evans, T H (Llanelli) 1906 *I*, 1907 *E, S, I*, 1908 *I, A*, 1909 *E, S, F, I*, 1910 *F, E, S, I*, 1911 *E, S, F, I*
Evans, T P (Swansea) 1975 *F, E, S, I, A*, 1976 *E, S, I, F*, 1977 *I*
Evans, V (Neath) 1954 *I, F, S*
Evans, W (Llanelli) 1958 *A*
Evans, W F (Rhymney) 1882 *I*, 1883 *S*
Evans, W G (Brynmawr) 1911 *I*
Evans, W H (Llwynypia) 1914 *E, S, F, I*
Evans, W J (Pontypool) 1947 *S*
Evans, W R (Bridgend) 1958 *A, E, S, I, F*, 1960 *SA*, 1961 *E, S, I, F*, 1962 *E, S, I*
Everson, W A (Newport) 1926 *S*

Faulkner, A G (Pontypool) 1975 *F, E, S, I, A*, 1976 *E, S, I, F*, 1978 *E, S, I, F, A* 1,2, *NZ*, 1979 *S, I, F*
Faull, J (Swansea) 1957 *I, F*, 1958 *A, E, S, I, F*, 1959 *E, S, I*, 1960 *E, F*
Fauvel, T J (Aberavon) 1988 *NZ* 1 (R)
Fear, A G (Newport) 1934 *S, I*, 1935 *S, I*
Fender, N H (Cardiff) 1930 *I, F*, 1931 *E, S, F, I*
Fenwick, S P (Bridgend) 1975 *F, E, S, A*, 1976 *E, S, I, F*, 1977 *I, F, E, S*, 1978 *E, S, I, F, A* 1,2, *NZ*, 1979 *S, I, F, E*, 1980 *F, E, S, I, NZ*, 1981 *E, S*
Finch, E (Llanelli) 1924 *F, NZ*, 1925 *F, I*, 1926 *F*, 1927 *A*, 1928 *I*
Finlayson, A A J (Cardiff) 1974 *I, F, E*
Fitzgerald, D (Cardiff) 1894 *S, I*
Ford, F J V (Welch Regt, Newport) 1939 *E*
Ford, I (Newport) 1959 *E, S*
Ford, S P (Cardiff) 1990 *I, Nm* 1,2, *Bb*, 1991 *E, S, I, A*
Forward, A (Pontypool, Mon Police) 1951 *S, SA*, 1952 *E, S, I, F*
Fowler, I J (Llanelli) 1919 *NZA*
Francis, D G (Llanelli) 1919 *NZA*, 1924 *S*
Francis, P (Maesteg) 1987 *S*

Gabe, R T (Cardiff, Llanelli) 1901 *I*, 1902 *E, S, I*, 1903 *E, S, I*, 1904 *E, S, I*, 1905 *E, S, I, NZ*, 1906 *E, I, SA*, 1907 *E, S, I*, 1908 *E, S, F, I*
Gale, N R (Swansea, Llanelli) 1960 *I*, 1963 *E, S, I, NZ*, 1964 *E, S, I, F, SA*, 1965 *E, S, I, F*, 1966 *E, S, I, F, A*, 1967 *E, NZ*, 1968 *E*, 1969 *NZ* 1 (R), 2, *A*
Gallacher, I S (Llanelli) 1970 *F*
Garrett, R M (Penarth) 1888 *M*, 1889 *S*, 1890 *S, E, I*, 1891 *S, I*, 1892 *E*
Geen, W P (Oxford U, Newport) 1912 *SA*, 1913 *E, I*
George, E E (Pontypridd, Cardiff) 1895 *S, I*, 1896 *E*
George, G M (Newport) 1991 *E, S*
Gething, G I (Neath) 1913 *F*
Gibbs, A (Newbridge) 1995 *I*
Gibbs, I S (Neath, Swansea) 1991 *E, S, I, F*1, *A, F*2, [*WS, Arg, A*], 1992 *I, F, E, S, A*, 1993 *E, S, I, F, J, C*
Gibbs, R A (Cardiff) 1906 *S, I*, 1907 *E, S*, 1908 *E, S, F, I*, 1910 *F, E, S, I*, 1911 *E, S, F, I*
Giles, R (Aberavon) 1983 *R*, 1985 *Fj* (R), 1987 [*C*]
Girling, B E (Cardiff) 1881 *E*
Goldsworthy, S J (Swansea) 1884 *I*, 1885 *E, S*
Gore, J H (Blaina) 1924 *I, F, NZ*, 1925 *E*
Gore, W (Newbridge) 1947 *S, F, I*
Gould, A J (Newport) 1885 *E, S*, 1886 *E, S*, 1887 *E, S, I*, 1888 *S*, 1889 *I*, 1890 *S, E, I*, 1892 *E, S, I*, 1893 *E, S, I*, 1894 *E, S*, 1895 *E, S, I*, 1896 *E, S, I*, 1897 *E*
Gould, G H (Newport) 1892 *I*, 1893 *S, I*
Gould, R (Newport) 1882 *I*, 1883 *E, S*, 1884 *E, S, I*, 1885 *E, S*, 1886 *E*, 1887 *E, S*
Graham, T C (Newport) 1890 *I*, 1891 *S, I*, 1892 *E, S*, 1893 *E, S, I*, 1894 *E, S*, 1895 *E, S*
Gravell, R W R (Llanelli) 1975 *F, E, S, I, A*, 1976 *E, S, I, F*, 1978 *E, S, I, F, A* 1,2, *NZ*, 1979 *S, I*, 1981 *I, F*, 1982 *F, E, S*
Gray, A J (London Welsh) 1968 *E, S*
Greenslade, D (Newport) 1962 *S*
Greville, H G (Llanelli) 1947 *A*
Griffin, Dr J (Edinburgh U) 1883 *S*
Griffiths, C (Llanelli) 1979 *E* (R)
Griffiths, D (Llanelli) 1888 *M*, 1889 *I*
Griffiths, G (Llanelli) 1889 *I*
Griffiths, G M (Cardiff) 1953 *E, S, I, F, NZ*, 1954 *I, F, S*, 1955 *I, F*, 1957 *E, S*
Griffiths, J L (Llanelli) 1988 *NZ* 2, 1989 *S*
Griffiths, M (Bridgend, Cardiff) 1988 *WS, R*, 1989 *S, I, F, E, NZ*, 1990 *F, E, Nm* 1,2, *Bb*, 1991 *I, F*1,2, [*WS, Arg, A*], 1992 *I, F, E, S, A*, 1993 *Z*1,2, *Nm, J, C*, 1995 *F*(R), *E, S, I*
Griffiths, V M (Newport) 1924 *S, I, F*
Gronow, B (Bridgend) 1910 *F, E, S, I*
Gwilliam, J A (Cambridge U, Newport) 1947 *A*, 1948 *I*, 1949 *E, S, I, F*, 1950 *E, S, I, F*, 1951 *E, S, I, SA*, 1952 *E, S, I, F*, 1953 *E, I, F, NZ*, 1954 *E*
Gwynn, D (Swansea) 1883 *E*, 1887 *S*, 1890 *E, I*, 1891 *E, S*
Gwynn, W H (Swansea) 1884 *E, S, I*, 1885 *E, S*

Hadley, A M (Cardiff) 1983 *R*, 1984 *S, I, F, E*, 1985 *F, E, Fj*, 1986 *E, S, I, F, Fj, Tg*, 1987 *S* (R), *I*, [*I, Tg, C, E, NZ, A*], *US*, 1988 *E, S, I, F*
Hall, I (Aberavon) 1967 *NZ*, 1970 *SA, S, E*, 1971 *S*, 1974 *S, I, F*
Hall, M R (Cambridge U, Bridgend, Cardiff) 1988 *NZ*

1 (R) 2, *WS*, *R*, 1989 *S*, *I*, *F*, *E*, *NZ*, 1990 *F*, *E*, *S*, 1991 *A*, *F*2, [*WS*, *Arg*, *A*], 1992 *I*, *F*, *E*, *S*, *A*, 1993 *E*, *S*, *I*, 1994 *S*, *I*, *F*, *E*, *Pt*, *Sp*, *C*, *Tg*, *R*, *It*, *SA*, 1995 *F*, *S*, *I*
Hall, W H (Bridgend) 1988 *WS*
Hancock, F E (Cardiff) 1884 *I*, 1885 *E*, *S*, 1886 *S*
Hannan, J (Newport) 1888 *M*, 1889 *S*, *I*, 1890 *S*, *E*, *I*, 1891 *E*, 1892 *E*, *S*, *I*, 1893 *E*, *S*, *I*, 1894 *E*, *S*, *I*, 1895 *E*, *S*, *I*
Harding, A F (London Welsh) 1902 *E*, *S*, *I*, 1903 *E*, *S*, *I*, 1904 *E*, *S*, *I*, 1905 *E*, *S*, *I*, *NZ*, 1906 *E*, *S*, *I*, *SA*, 1907 *I*, 1908 *E*, *S*
Harding, G F (Newport) 1881 *E*, 1882 *I*, 1883 *E*, *S*
Harding, R (Swansea, Cambridge U) 1923 *E*, *S*, *F*, *I*, 1924 *I*, *F*, *NZ*, 1925 *F*, *I*, 1926 *E*, *I*, *F*, 1927 *E*, *S*, *F*, *I*, 1928 *E*
Harding, T (Newport) 1888 *M*, 1889 *S*, *I*
Harris, D J E (Pontypridd, Cardiff) 1959 *I*, *F*, 1960 *S*, *I*, *F*, *SA*, 1961 *E*, *S*
Harris, T (Aberavon) 1927 *A*
Hathway, G F (Newport) 1924 *I*, *F*
Havard, Rev W T (Llanelli) 1919 *NZA*
Hawkins, F (Pontypridd) 1912 *I*, *F*
Hayward, D (Newbridge) 1949 *E*, *F*, 1950 *E*, *S*, *I*, *F*, 1951 *E*, *S*, *I*, *F*, *SA*, 1952 *E*, *S*, *I*, *F*
Hayward, D J (Cardiff) 1963 *E*, *NZ*, 1964 *S*, *I*, *F*, *SA*
Hayward, G (Swansea) 1908 *S*, *F*, *I*, *A*, 1909 *E*
Hellings, R (Llwynypia) 1897 *E*, 1898 *I*, *E*, 1899 *S*, *I*, 1900 *E*, *I*, 1901 *E*, *S*
Herrerá, R C (Cross Keys) 1925 *S*, *F*, *I*, 1926 *E*, *S*, *I*, *F*, 1927 *E*
Hiams, H (Swansea) 1912 *I*, *F*
Hickman, A (Neath) 1930 *E*, 1933 *S*
Hiddlestone, D D (Neath) 1922 *E*, *S*, *I*, *F*, 1924 *NZ*
Hill, A F (Cardiff) 1885 *S*, 1886 *E*, *S*, 1888 *S*, *I*, *M*, 1889 *S*, 1890 *S*, *I*, 1893 *E*, *S*, *I*, 1894 *E*, *S*, *I*
Hill, S D (Cardiff) 1993 *Z*1,2, *Nm*, 1994 *I*(R), *F*, *SA*, 1995 *F*
Hinam, S (Cardiff) 1925 *I*, 1926 *E*, *S*, *I*, *F*
Hinton, J T (Cardiff) 1884 *I*
Hirst, G L (Newport) 1912 *S*, 1913 *S*, 1914 *E*, *S*, *F*, *I*
Hodder, W (Pontypool) 1921 *E*, *S*, *F*
Hodges, J J (Newport) 1899 *E*, *S*, *I*, 1900 *E*, *S*, *I*, 1901 *E*, *S*, 1902 *E*, *S*, *I*, 1903 *E*, *S*, *I*, 1904 *E*, *S*, 1905 *E*, *S*, *I*, *NZ*, 1906 *E*, *S*, *I*
Hodgson, G T R (Neath) 1962 *I*, 1963 *E*, *S*, *I*, *F*, *NZ*, 1964 *E*, *S*, *I*, *F*, *SA*, 1966 *S*, *I*, *F*, 1967 *I*
Hollingdale, H (Swansea) 1912 *SA*, 1913 *E*
Hollingdale, T H (Neath) 1927 *A*, 1928 *E*, *S*, *I*, *F*, 1930 *E*
Holmes, T D (Cardiff) 1978 *A* 2, *NZ*, 1979 *S*, *I*, *F*, *E*, 1980 *F*, *E*, *S*, *I*, *NZ*, 1981 *A*, 1982 *I*, *F*, *E*, 1983 *E*, *S*, *I*, *F*, 1984 *E*, 1985 *S*, *I*, *F*, *E*, *Fj*
Hopkin, W H (Newport) 1937 *S*
Hopkins, K (Cardiff, Swansea) 1985 *E*, 1987 *F*, *E*, *S*, [*Tg*, *C*(R)], *US*
Hopkins, P L (Swansea) 1908 *A*, 1909 *E*, *I*, 1910 *E*
Hopkins, R (Maesteg) 1970 *E* (R)
Hopkins, T (Swansea) 1926 *E*, *S*, *I*, *F*
Hopkins, W J (Aberavon) 1925 *E*, *S*
Howells, B (Llanelli) 1934 *E*
Howells, W G (Llanelli) 1957 *E*, *S*, *I*, *F*
Howells, W H (Swansea) 1888 *S*, *I*
Hughes, D (Newbridge) 1967 *NZ*, 1969 *NZ* 2, 1970 *SA*, *S*, *E*, *I*
Hughes, G (Penarth) 1934 *E*, *S*, *I*
Hughes, H (Cardiff) 1887 *S*, 1889 *S*
Hughes, K (Cambridge U, London Welsh) 1970 *I*, 1973 *A*, 1974 *S*
Hullin, W (Cardiff) 1967 *S*
Hurrell, J (Newport) 1959 *F*
Hutchinson, F (Neath) 1894 *I*, 1896 *S*, *I*
Huxtable, R (Swansea) 1920 *F*, *I*
Huzzey, H V P (Cardiff) 1898 *I*, *E*, 1899 *E*, *S*, *I*
Hybart, A J (Cardiff) 1887 *E*

Ingledew, H M (Cardiff) 1890 *I*, 1891 *E*, *S*
Isaacs, I (Cardiff) 1933 *E*, *S*

Jackson, T H (Swansea) 1895 *E*
James, B (Bridgend) 1968 *E*
James, C R (Llanelli) 1958 *A*, *F*
James, D (Swansea) 1891 *I*, 1892 *S*, *I*, 1899 *E*
James, D R (Treorchy) 1931 *F*, *I*
James, E (Swansea) 1890 *S*, 1891 *I*, 1892 *S*, *I*, 1899 *E*
James, M (Cardiff) 1947 *A*, 1948 *E*, *S*, *F*, *I*
James, T O (Aberavon) 1935 *I*, 1937 *S*
James, W J (Aberavon) 1983 *E*, *S*, *I*, *F*, *R*, 1984 *S*, 1985 *S*, *I*, *F*, *E*, *Fj*, 1986 *E*, *S*, *I*, *F*, *Fj*, *Tg*, *WS*, 1987 *E*, *S*, *I*
James, W P (Aberavon) 1925 *E*, *S*
Jarman, H (Newport) 1910 *E*, *S*, *I*, 1911 *E*
Jarrett, K S (Newport) 1967 *E*, 1968 *E*, *S*, 1969 *S*, *I*, *F*, *E*, *NZ* 1,2, *A*
Jeffery, J J (Cardiff Coll of Ed, Newport) 1967 *NZ*
Jenkin, A M (Swansea) 1895 *I*, 1896 *E*
Jenkins, A (Llanelli) 1920 *E*, *S*, *F*, *I*, 1921 *S*, *F*, 1922 *F*, 1923 *E*, *S*, *F*, *I*, 1924 *NZ*, 1928 *S*, *I*
Jenkins, D M (Treorchy) 1926 *E*, *S*, *I*, *F*
Jenkins, D R (Swansea) 1927 *A*, 1929 *E*
Jenkins, E (Newport) 1910 *S*, *I*
Jenkins, E M (Aberavon) 1927 *S*, *F*, *I*, *A*, 1928 *E*, *S*, *I*, *F*, 1929 *F*, 1930 *E*, *S*, *I*, *F*, 1931 *E*, *S*, *F*, *I*, *SA*, 1932 *E*, *S*, *I*
Jenkins, G R (Pontypool, Swansea) 1991 *F*2, [*WS*(R), *Arg*, *A*], 1992 *I*, *F*, *E*, *S*, *A*, 1993 *C*, 1994 *S*, *I*, *F*, *E*, *Pt*, *Sp*, *C*, *Tg*, *WS*, *R*, *It*, *SA*, 1995 *F*, *E*, *S*, *I*
Jenkins, J C (London Welsh) 1906 *SA*
Jenkins, J L (Aberavon) 1923 *S*, *F*
Jenkins, L H (Mon TC, Newport) 1954 *I*, 1956 *E*, *S*, *I*, *F*
Jenkins, N R (Pontypridd) 1991 *E*, *S*, *I*, *F*1, 1992 *I*, *F*, *E*, *S*, 1993 *E*, *S*, *I*, *F*, *Z*1,2, *Nm*, *J*, *C*, 1994 *S*, *I*, *F*, *E*, *Pt*, *Sp*, *C*, *Tg*, *WS*, *R*, *It*, *SA*, 1995 *F*, *E*, *S*, *I*
Jenkins, V G J (Oxford U, Bridgend, London Welsh) 1933 *E*, *I*, 1934 *S*, *I*, 1935 *E*, *S*, *NZ*, 1936 *E*, *S*, *I*, 1937 *E*, 1938 *E*, *S*, 1939 *E*
Jenkins, W (Cardiff) 1912 *I*, *F*, 1913 *S*, *I*
John, B (Llanelli, Cardiff) 1966 *A*, 1967 *S*, *NZ*, 1968 *E*, *S*, *I*, *F*, 1969 *S*, *I*, *F*, *E*, *NZ* 1,2, *A*, 1970 *SA*, *S*, *E*, *I*, 1971 *E*, *S*, *I*, *F*, 1972 *E*, *S*, *F*
John, D A (Llanelli) 1925 *I*, 1928 *E*, *S*, *I*
John, D E (Llanelli) 1923 *F*, *I*, 1928 *E*, *S*, *I*
John, E R (Neath) 1950 *E*, *S*, *I*, *F*, 1951 *E*, *S*, *I*, *F*, *SA*, 1952 *E*, *S*, *I*, *F*, 1953 *E*, *S*, *I*, *F*, *NZ*, 1954 *E*
John, G (St Luke's Coll, Exeter) 1954 *E*, *F*
John, J H (Swansea) 1926 *E*, *S*, *I*, *F*, 1927 *E*, *S*, *F*, *I*
John, P (Pontypridd) 1994 *Tg*
John, S C (Llanelli) 1995 *S*, *I*
Johnson, T A (Cardiff) 1921 *E*, *F*, *I*, 1923 *E*, *S*, *F*, 1924 *E*, *S*, *NZ*, 1925 *E*, *S*, *F*
Johnson, W D (Swansea) 1953 *E*
Jones, A H (Cardiff) 1933 *E*, *S*
Jones, B (Abertillery) 1914 *E*, *S*, *F*, *I*
Jones, Bert (Llanelli) 1934 *S*, *I*
Jones, Bob (Llwynypia) 1901 *I*
Jones, B J (Newport) 1960 *I*, *F*
Jones, B Lewis (Devonport Services, Llanelli) 1950 *E*, *S*, *I*, *F*, 1951 *E*, *S*, *SA*, 1952 *E*, *I*, *F*
Jones, C W (Cambridge U, Cardiff) 1934 *E*, *S*, *I*, 1935 *E*, *S*, *I*, *NZ*, 1936 *E*, *S*, *I*, 1938 *E*, *S*, *I*
Jones, C W (Bridgend) 1920 *E*, *S*, *F*
Jones, D (Neath) 1927 *A*
Jones, D (Aberavon) 1897 *E*
Jones, D (Swansea) 1947 *E*, *F*, *I*, 1949 *E*, *S*, *I*, *F*
Jones, D (Treherbert) 1902 *E*, *S*, *I*, 1903 *E*, *S*, *I*, 1905 *E*, *S*, *I*, *NZ*, 1906 *E*, *S*, *SA*
Jones, D (Newport) 1926 *E*, *S*, *I*, *F*, 1927 *E*
Jones, D (Llanelli) 1948 *E*
Jones, D (Cardiff) 1994 *SA*, 1995 *F*, *E*, *S*
Jones, D K (Llanelli, Cardiff) 1962 *E*, *S*, *F*, *I*, 1963 *E*, *F*, *NZ*, 1964 *E*, *S*, *SA*, 1966 *E*, *S*, *I*, *F*
Jones, D P (Pontypool) 1907 *I*
Jones, E H (Neath) 1929 *E*, *S*
Jones, E L (Llanelli) 1930 *F*, 1933 *E*, *S*, *I*, 1935 *E*
Jones, Elvet L (Llanelli) 1939 *S*
Jones, G (Ebbw Vale) 1963 *S*, *I*, *F*
Jones, G (Llanelli) 1988 *NZ* 2, 1989 *F*, *E*, *NZ*, 1990 *F*
Jones, G G (Cardiff) 1930 *S*, 1933 *I*
Jones, H (Penygraig) 1902 *S*, *I*
Jones, H (Neath) 1904 *I*
Jones, H (Swansea) 1930 *I*, *F*
Jones, Iorwerth (Llanelli) 1927 *A*, 1928 *E*, *S*, *I*, *F*
Jones, I C (London Welsh) 1968 *I*
Jones, Ivor E (Llanelli) 1924 *E*, *S*, 1927 *S*, *F*, *I*, *A*, 1928 *E*, *S*, *I*, *F*, 1929 *E*, *S*, *F*, *I*, 1930 *E*, *S*
Jones, J (Aberavon) 1901 *E*
Jones, J (Swansea) 1924 *F*
Jones, Jim (Aberavon) 1919 *NZA*, 1920 *E*,*S*, 1921 *S*,

F, *I*
Jones, J A (Cardiff) 1883 *S*
Jones, J P (Tuan) (Pontypool) 1913 *S*
Jones, J P (Pontypool) 1908 *A*, 1909 *E*, *S*, *F*, *I*, 1910 *F*, *E*, 1912 *E*, *F*, 1913 *F*, *I*, 1920 *F*, *I*, 1921 *E*
Jones, K D (Cardiff) 1960 *SA*, 1961 *E*, *S*, *I*, 1962 *E*, *F*, 1963 *E*, *S*, *I*, *NZ*
Jones, K J (Newport) 1947 *E*, *S*, *F*, *I*, *A*, 1948 *E*, *S*, *F*, *I*, 1949 *E*, *S*, *I*, *F*, 1950 *E*, *S*, *I*, *F*, 1951 *E*, *S*, *I*, *F*, *SA*, 1952 *E*, *S*, *I*, *F*, 1953 *E*, *S*, *I*, *F*, *NZ*, 1954 *E*, *I*, *F*, *S*, 1955 *E*, *S*, *I*, *F*, 1956 *E*, *S*, *I*, *F*, 1957 *S*
Jones, K W J (Oxford U, London Welsh) 1934 *E*
Jones, M A (Neath) 1987 *S*, 1988 *NZ* 2 (R), 1989 *S*, *I*, *F*, *E*, *NZ*, 1990 *F*, *E*, *S*, *I*, *Nm* 1,2, *Bb*
Jones, P (Newport) 1912 *SA*, 1913 *E*, *S*, *F*, 1914 *E*, *S*, *F*, *I*
Jones, P B (Newport) 1921 *S*
Jones, R (Swansea) 1901 *I*, 1902 *E*, 1904 *E*, *S*, *I*, 1905 *E*, 1908 *F*, *I*, *A*, 1909 *E*, *S*, *F*, *I*, 1910 *F*, *E*
Jones, R (London Welsh) 1929 *E*
Jones, R (Northampton) 1926 *E*, *S*, *F*
Jones, R (Swansea) 1927 *A*, 1928 *F*
Jones, R B (Cambridge U) 1933 *E*, *S*
Jones, R E (Coventry) 1967 *F*, *E*, 1968 *S*, *I*, *F*
Jones, R L (Llanelli) 1993 *Z*1,2, *Nm*, *J*, *C*
Jones, R N (Swansea) 1986 *E*, *S*, *I*, *F*, *Fj*, *Tg*, *WS*, 1987 *F*, *E*, *S*, *I*, [*I*, *Tg*, *E*, *NZ*, *A*], *US*, 1988 *E*, *S*, *I*, *F*, *NZ* 1, *WS*, *R*, 1989 *I*, *F*, *E*, *NZ*, 1990 *F*, *E*, *S*, *I*, 1991 *E*, *S*, *F*2, [*WS*, *Arg*, *A*], 1992 *I*, *F*, *E*, *S*, *A*, 1993 *E*, *S*, *I*, 1994 *I*(R), *Pt*, 1995 *F*, *E*, *S*, *I*
Jones, S T (Pontypool) 1983 *S*, *I*, *F*, *R*, 1984*S*, 1988 *E*, *S*, *F*, *NZ* 1,2
Jones, Tom (Newport) 1922 *E*, *S*, *I*, *F*, 1924 *E*, *S*
Jones, T B (Newport) 1882 *I*, 1883 *E*, *S*, 1884 *S*, 1885 *E*, *S*
Jones, W (Cardiff) 1898 *I*, *E*
Jones, W (Mountain Ash) 1905 *I*
Jones, W I (Llanelli, Cambridge U) 1925 *E*, *S*, *F*, *I*
Jones, W J (Llanelli) 1924 *I*
Jones, W K (Cardiff) 1967 *NZ*, 1968 *E*, *S*, *I*, *F*
Jones-Davies, T E (London Welsh) 1930 *E*, *I*, 1931 *E*, *S*
Jordan, H M (Newport) 1885 *E*, *S*, 1889 *S*
Joseph, W (Swansea) 1902 *E*, *S*, *I*, 1903 *E*, *S*, *I*, 1904 *E*, *S*, 1905 *E*, *S*, *I*, *NZ*, 1906 *E*, *S*, *I*, *SA*
Jowett, W F (Swansea) 1903 *E*
Judd, S (Cardiff) 1953 *E*, *S*, *I*, *F*, *NZ*, 1954 *E*, *F*, *S*, 1955 *E*, *S*
Judson, J H (Llanelli) 1883 *E*, *S*

Kedzlie, Q D (Cardiff) 1888 *S*, *I*
Keen, L (Aberavon) 1980 *F*, *E*, *S*, *I*
Knight, P (Pontypridd) 1990 *Nm* 1,2, *Bb*(R), 1991 *E*, *S*
Knill, F M D (Cardiff) 1976 *F* (R)

Lamerton, A E H (Llanelli) 1993 *F*, *Z*1,2, *Nm*, *J*
Lane, S M (Cardiff) 1978 *A* 1 (R), 2, 1979 *I* (R), 1980 *S*, *I*
Lang, J (Llanelli) 1931 *F*, *I*, 1934 *S*, *I*, 1935 *E*, *S*, *I*, *NZ*, 1936 *E*, *S*, *I*, 1937 *E*
Lawrence, S (Bridgend) 1925 *S*, *I*, 1926 *S*, *I*, *F*, 1927 *E*
Law, V J (Newport) 1939 *I*
Legge, W S G (Newport) 1937 *I*, 1938 *I*
Leleu, J (London Welsh, Swansea) 1959 *E*, *S*, 1960 *F*, *SA*
Lemon, A (Neath) 1929 *I*, 1930 *S*, *I*, *F*, 1931 *E*, *S*, *F*, *I*, *SA*, 1932 *E*, *S*, *I*, 1933 *I*
Lewis, A J L (Ebbw Vale) 1970 *F*, 1971 *E*, *I*, *F*, 1972 *E*, *S*, *F*, 1973 *E*, *S*, *I*, *F*
Lewis, A R (Abertillery) 1966 *E*, *S*, *I*, *F*, *A*, 1967 *I*
Lewis, B R (Swansea, Cambridge U) 1912 *I*, 1913 *I*
Lewis, C P (Llandovery Coll) 1882 *I*, 1883 *E*, *S*, 1884 *E*, *S*
Lewis, D H (Cardiff) 1886 *E*, *S*
Lewis, E J (Llandovery) 1881 *E*
Lewis, E W (Llanelli, Cardiff) 1991 *I*, *F*1, *A*, *F*2, [*WS*, *Arg*, *A*], 1992 *I*, *F*, *S*, *A*, 1993 *E*, *S*, *I*, *F*, *Z*1,2, *Nm*, *J*, *C*, 1994 *S*, *I*, *F*, *E*, *Pt*, *Sp*, *Fj*, *WS*, *R*, *It*, *SA*, 1995 *E*, *S*, *I*
Lewis, G W (Richmond) 1960 *E*, *S*
Lewis, H (Swansea) 1913 *S*, *F*, *I*, 1914 *E*
Lewis, J G (Llanelli) 1887 *I*
Lewis, J M C (Cardiff, Cambridge U) 1912 *E*, 1913 *S*, *F*, *I*, 1914 *E*, *S*, *F*, *I*, 1921 *I*, 1923 *E*, *S*
Lewis, J R (S Glam Inst, Cardiff) 1981 *E*, *S*, *I*, *F*, 1982 *F*, *E*, *S*
Lewis, M (Treorchy) 1913 *F*
Lewis, P I (Llanelli) 1984 *A*, 1985 *S*, *I*, *F*, *E*, 1986 *E*, *S*, *I*
Lewis, T W (Cardiff) 1926 *E*, 1927 *E*, *S*
Lewis, W (Llanelli) 1925 *F*
Lewis, W H (London Welsh, Cambridge U) 1926 *I*, 1927 *E*, *F*, *I*, *A*, 1928 *F*
Llewelyn, D B (Newport, Llanelli) 1970 *SA*, *S*, *E*, *I*, *F*, 1971 *E*, *S*, *I*, *F*, 1972 *E*, *S*, *F*, *NZ*
Llewellyn, G D (Neath) 1990 *Nm* 1,2, *Bb*, 1991 *E*, *S*, *I*, *F*1, *A*, *F*2
Llewellyn, G O (Neath) 1989 *NZ*, 1990 *E*, *S*, *I*, 1991 *E*, *S*, *A*(R), 1992 *I*, *F*, *E*, *S*, *A*, 1993 *E*, *S*, *I*, *F*, *Z*1,2, *Nm*, *J*, *C*, 1994 *S*, *I*, *F*, *E*, *Pt*, *Sp*, *C*, *Tg*, *WS*, *R*, *It*, *SA*, 1995 *F*, *E*, *S*, *I*
Llewellyn, P D (Swansea) 1973 *I*, *F*, *A*, 1974 *S*, *E*
Llewellyn, W (Llwynypia) 1899 *E*, *S*, *I*, 1900 *E*, *S*, *I*, 1901 *E*, *S*, *I*, 1902 *E*, *S*, *I*, 1903 *I*, 1904 *E*, *S*, *I*, 1905 *E*, *S*, *I*, *NZ*
Lloyd, D J (Bridgend) 1966 *E*, *S*, *I*, *F*, *A*, 1967 *S*, *I*, *F*, *E*, 1968 *S*, *I*, *F*, 1969 *S*, *I*, *F*, *E*, *NZ* 1, *A*, 1970 *F*, 1972 *E*, *S*, *F*, 1973 *E*, *S*
Lloyd, E (Llanelli) 1895 *S*
Lloyd, G L (Newport) 1896 *I*, 1899 *S*, *I*, 1900 *E*, *S*, 1901 *E*, *S*, 1902 *S*, *I*, 1903 *E*, *S*, *I*
Lloyd, P (Llanelli) 1890 *S*, *E*, 1891 *E*, *I*
Lloyd, R A (Pontypool) 1913 *S*, *F*, *I*, 1914 *E*, *S*, *F*, *I*
Lloyd, T (Maesteg) 1953 *I*, *F*
Lloyd, T C (Neath) 1909 *F*, 1913 *F*, *I*, 1914 *E*, *S*, *F*, *I*
Lockwood, T W (Newport) 1887 *E*, *S*, *I*
Long, E C (Swansea) 1936 *E*, *S*, *I*, 1937 *E*, *S*, 1939 *S*, *I*
Lyne, H S (Newport) 1883 *S*, 1884 *E*, *S*, *I*, 1885 *E*

McBryde, R C (Swansea, Llanelli) 1994 *Fj*, *SA*(t)
McCall, B E W (Welch Regt, Newport) 1936 *E*, *S*, *I*
McCarley, A (Neath) 1938 *E*, *S*, *I*
McCutcheon, W M (Swansea) 1891 *S*, 1892 *E*, *S*, 1893 *E*, *S*, *I*, 1894 *E*
Maddock, H T (London Welsh) 1906 *E*, *S*, *I*, 1907 *E*, *S*, 1910 *F*
Maddocks, K (Neath) 1957 *E*
Main, D R (London Welsh) 1959 *E*, *S*, *I*, *F*
Mainwaring, H J (Swansea) 1961 *F*
Mainwaring, W T (Aberavon) 1967 *S*, *I*, *F*, *E*, *NZ*, 1968 *E*
Major, W C (Maesteg) 1949 *F*, 1950 *S*
Male, B O (Cardiff) 1921 *F*, 1923 *S*, 1924 *S*, *I*, 1927 *E*, *S*, *F*, *I*, 1928 *S*, *I*, *F*
Manfield, L (Mountain Ash, Cardiff) 1939 *S*, *I*, 1947 *A*, 1948 *E*, *S*, *F*, *I*
Mann, B B (Cardiff) 1881 *E*
Mantle, J T (Loughborough Colls, Newport) 1964 *E*, *SA*
Margrave, F L (Llanelli) 1884 *E*, *S*
Marsden-Jones, D (Cardiff) 1921 *E*, 1924 *NZ*
Martin, A J (Aberavon) 1973 *A*, 1974 *S*, *I*, 1975 *F*, *E*, *S*, *I*, *A*, 1976 *E*, *S*, *I*, *F*, 1977 *I*, *F*, *E*, *S*, 1978 *E*, *S*, *I*, *F*, *A* 1,2, *NZ*, 1979 *S*, *I*, *F*, *E*, 1980 *F*, *E*, *S*, *I*, *NZ*, 1981 *I*, *F*
Martin, W J (Newport) 1912 *I*, *F*, 1919 *NZA*
Mason, J (Pontypridd) 1988 *NZ* 2 (R)
Mathews, Rev A A (Lampeter) 1886 *S*
Mathias, R (Llanelli) 1970 *F*
Matthews, C (Bridgend) 1939 *I*
Matthews, J (Cardiff) 1947 *E*, *A*, 1948 *E*, *S*, *F*, 1949 *E*, *S*, *I*, *F*, 1950 *E*, *S*, *I*, *F*, 1951 *E*, *S*, *I*, *F*
May, P S (Llanelli) 1988 *E*, *S*, *I*, *F*, *NZ* 1,2, 1991 [*WS*]
Meek, N N (Pontypool) 1993 *E*, *S*, *I*
Meredith, A (Devonport Services) 1949 *E*, *S*, *I*
Meredith, B V (St Luke's Coll, London Welsh, Newport) 1954 *I*, *F*, *S*, 1955 *E*, *S*, *I*, *F*, 1956 *E*, *S*, *I*, *F*, 1957 *E*, *S*, *I*, *F*, 1958 *A*, *E*, *S*, *I*, 1959 *E*, *S*, *I*, *F*, 1960 *E*, *S*, *F*, *SA*, 1961 *E*, *S*, *I*, 1962 *E*, *S*, *F*, *I*
Meredith, C C (Neath) 1953 *S*, *NZ*, 1954 *E*, *I*, *F*, *S*, 1955 *E*, *S*, *I*, *F*, 1956 *E*, *I*, 1957 *E*, *S*
Meredith, J (Swansea) 1888 *S*, *I*, 1890 *S*, *E*
Merry, A E (Pill Harriers) 1912 *I*, *F*
Michael, G (Swansea) 1923 *E*, *S*, *F*
Michaelson, R C B (Aberavon, Cambridge U) 1963 *E*
Miller, F (Mountain Ash) 1896 *I*, 1900 *E*, *S*, *I*, 1901 *E*, *S*, *I*
Mills, F M (Swansea, Cardiff) 1892 *E*, *S*, *I*, 1893 *E*, *S*,

I, 1894 *E*, *S*, *I*, 1895 *E*, *S*, *I*, 1896 *E*
Moon, R H StJ B (Llanelli) 1993 *F*, *Z*1,2, *Nm*, *J*, *C*, 1994 *S*, *I*, *F*, *E*, *Sp*, *C*, *Fj*, *WS*, *R*, *It*, *SA*, 1995 *E*(R)
Moore, W J (Bridgend) 1933 *I*
Morgan, C H (Llanelli) 1957 *I*, *F*
Morgan, C I (Cardiff) 1951 *I*, *F*, *SA*, 1952 *E*, *S*, *I*, 1953 *S*, *I*, *F*, *NZ*, 1954 *E*, *I*, *S*, 1955 *E*, *S*, *I*, *F*, 1956 *E*, *S*, *I*, *F*, 1957 *E*, *S*, *I*, *F*, 1958 *E*, *S*, *I*, *F*
Morgan, D (Swansea) 1885 *S*, 1886 *E*, *S*, 1887 *E*, *S*, *I*, 1889 *I*
Morgan, D (Llanelli) 1895 *I*, 1896 *E*
Morgan, D R R (Llanelli) 1962 *E*, *S*, *F*, *I*, 1963 *E*, *S*, *I*, *F*, *NZ*
Morgan, E (Llanelli) 1920 *I*, 1921 *E*, *S*, *F*
Morgan, Edgar (Swansea) 1914 *E*, *S*, *F*, *I*
Morgan, E T (London Welsh) 1902 *E*, *S*, *I*, 1903 *I*, 1904 *E*, *S*, *I*, 1905 *E*, *S*, *I*, *NZ*, 1906 *E*, *S*, *I*, *SA*, 1908 *F*
Morgan, F L (Llanelli) 1938 *E*, *S*, *I*, 1939 *E*
Morgan, H J (Abertillery) 1958 *E*, *S*, *I*, *F*, 1959 *I*, *F*, 1960 *E*, 1961 *E*, *S*, *I*, *F*, 1962 *E*, *S*, *F*, *I*, 1963 *S*, *I*, *F*, 1965 *E*, *S*, *I*, *F*, 1966 *E*, *S*, *I*, *F*, *A*
Morgan, H P (Newport) 1956 *E*, *S*, *I*, *F*
Morgan, I (Swansea) 1908 *A*, 1909 *E*, *S*, *F*, *I*, 1910 *F*, *E*, *S*, *I*, 1911 *E*, *F*, *I*, 1912 S
Morgan, J L (Llanelli) 1912 *SA*, 1913 *E*
Morgan, M E (Swansea) 1938 *E*, *S*, *I*, 1939 *E*
Morgan, N (Newport) 1960 *S*, *I*, *F*
Morgan, P E J (Aberavon) 1961 *E*, *S*, *F*
Morgan, P J (Llanelli) 1980 *S* (R), *I*, *NZ* (R), 1981 *I*
Morgan, R (Newport) 1984 *S*
Morgan, T (Llanelli) 1889 *I*
Morgan, W G (Cambridge U) 1927 *F*, *I*, 1929 *E*, *S*, *F*, *I*, 1930 *I*, *F*
Morgan, W L (Cardiff) 1910 *S*
Moriarty, R D (Swansea) 1981 *A*, 1982 *I*, *F*, *E*, *S*, 1983 *E*, 1984 *S*, *I*, *F*, *E*, 1985 *S*, *I*, *F*, 1986 *Fj*, *Tg*, *WS*, 1987 [*I*, *Tg*, *C*(R), *E*, *NZ*, *A*]
Moriarty, W P (Swansea) 1986 *I*, *F*, *Fj*, *Tg*, *WS*, 1987 *F*, *E*, *S*, *I*, [*I*, *Tg*, *C*, *E*, *NZ*, *A*], *US*, 1988 *E*, *S*, *I*, *F*, *NZ* 1
Morley, J C (Newport) 1929 *E*, *S*, *F*, *I*, 1930 *E*, *I*, 1931 *E*, *S*, *F*, *I*, *SA*, 1932 *E*, *S*, *I*
Morris, G L (Swansea) 1882 *I*, 1883 *E*, *S*, 1884 *E*, *S*
Morris, H T (Cardiff) 1951 *F*, 1955 *I*, *F*
Morris, J I T (Swansea) 1924 *E*, *S*
Morris, M S (S Wales Police, Neath) 1985 *S*, *I*, *F*, 1990 *I*, *Nm* 1,2, *Bb*, 1991 *I*, *F*1, [*WS*(R)], 1992 *E*
Morris, R R (Swansea, Bristol) 1933 *S*, 1937 *S*
Morris, S (Cross Keys) 1920 *E*, *S*, *F*, *I*, 1922 *E*, *S*, *I*, *F*, 1923 *E*, *S*, *F*, *I*, 1924 *E*, *S*, *F*, *NZ*, 1925 *E*, *S*, *F*
Morris, W (Abertillery) 1919 *NZA*, 1920 *F*, 1921 *I*
Morris, W (Llanelli) 1896 *S*, *I*, 1897 *E*
Morris, W D (Neath) 1967 *F*, *E*, 1968 *E*, *S*, *I*, *F*, 1969 *S*, *I*, *F*, *E*, *NZ* 1,2, *A*, 1970 *SA*, *S*, *E*, *I*, *F*, 1971 *E*, *S*, *I*, *F*, 1972 *E*, *S*, *F*, *NZ*, 1973 *E*, *S*, *I*, *A*, 1974 *S*, *I*, *F*, *E*
Morris, W J (Newport) 1965 *S*, 1966 *F*
Morris, W J (Pontypool) 1963 *S*, *I*
Moseley, K (Pontypool, Newport) 1988 *NZ* 2, *R*, 1989 *S*, *I*, 1990 *F*, 1991 *F*2, [*WS*, *Arg*, *A*]
Murphy, C D (Cross Keys) 1935 *E*, *S*, *I*

Nash, D (Ebbw Vale) 1960 *SA*, 1961 *E*, *S*, *I*, *F*, 1962 *F*
Newman, C H (Newport) 1881 *E*, 1882 *I*, 1883 *E*, *S*, 1884 *E*, *S*, 1885 *E*, *S*, 1886 *E*, 1887 *E*
Nicholas, D L (Llanelli) 1981 *E*, *S*, *I*, *F*
Nicholas, T J (Cardiff) 1919 *NZA*
Nicholl, C B (Cambridge U, Llanelli) 1891 *I*, 1892 *E*, *S*, *I*, 1893 *E*, *S*, *I*, 1894 *E*, *S*, 1895 *E*, *S*, *I*, 1896 *E*, *S*, *I*
Nicholl, D W (Llanelli) 1894 *I*
Nicholls, E G (Cardiff) 1896 *S*, *I*, 1897 *E*, 1898 *I*, *E*, 1899 *E*, *S*, *I*, 1900 *S*, *I*, 1901 *E*, *S*, *I*, 1902 *E*, *S*, *I*, 1903 *I*, 1904 *E*, 1905 *I*, *NZ*, 1906 *E*, *S*, *I*, *SA*
Nicholls, F E (Cardiff Harlequins) 1892 *I*
Nicholls, H (Cardiff) 1958 *I*
Nicholls, S H (Cardiff) 1888 *M*, 1889 *S*, *I*, 1891 *S*
Norris, C H (Cardiff) 1963 *F*, 1966 *F*
Norster, R L (Cardiff) 1982 *S*, 1983 *E*, *S*, *I*, *F*, 1984 *S*, *I*, *F*, *E*, *A*, 1985 *S*, *I*, *F*, *E*, *Fj*, 1986 *Fj*, *Tg*, *WS*, 1987 *F*, *E*, *S*, *I*, [*I*, *C*, *E*], *US*, 1988 *E*, *S*, *I*, *F*, *NZ* 1, *WS*, 1989 *F*, *E*
Norton, W B (Cardiff) 1882 *I*, 1883 *E*, *S*, 1884 *E*, *S*, *I*

O'Connor, A (Aberavon) 1960 *SA*, 1961 *E*, *S*, 1962 *F*, *I*
O'Connor, R (Aberavon) 1957 *E*
O'Neill, W (Cardiff) 1904 *S*, *I*, 1905 *E*, *S*, *I*, 1907 *E*, *I*, 1908 *E*, *S*, *F*, *I*
O'Shea, J P (Cardiff) 1967 *S*, *I*, 1968 *S*, *I*, *F*
Oliver, G (Pontypool) 1920 *E*, *S*, *F*, *I*
Osborne, W T (Mountain Ash) 1902 *E*, *S*, *I*, 1903 *E*, *S*, *I*
Ould, W J (Cardiff) 1924 *E*, *S*
Owen, A (Swansea) 1924 *E*
Owen, G D (Newport) 1955 *I*, *F*, 1956 *E*, *S*, *I*, *F*
Owen, R M (Swansea) 1901 *I*, 1902 *E*, *S*, *I*, 1903 *E*, *S*, *I*, 1904 *E*, *S*, *I*, 1905 *E*, *S*, *I*, *NZ*, 1906 *E*, *S*, *I*, *SA*, 1907 *E*, *S*, 1908 *F*, *I*, *A*, 1909 *E*, *S*, *F*, *I*, 1910 *F*, *E*, 1911 *E*, *S*, *F*, *I*, 1912 *E*, *S*

Packer, H (Newport) 1891 *E*, 1895 *S*, *I*, 1896 *E*, *S*, *I*, 1897 *E*
Palmer, F (Swansea) 1922 *E*, *S*, *I*
Parfitt, F C (Newport) 1893 *E*, *S*, *I*, 1894 *E*, *S*, *I*, 1895 *S*, 1896 *S*, *I*
Parfitt, S A (Swansea) 1990 *Nm* 1(R), *Bb*
Parker, D S (Swansea) 1924 *I*, *F*, *NZ*, 1925 *E*, *S*, *F*, *I*, 1929 *F*, *I*, 1930 *E*
Parker, T (Swansea) 1919 *NZA*, 1920 *E*, *S*, *I*, 1921 *E*, *S*, *F*, *I*, 1922 *E*, *S*, *I*, *F*, 1923 *E*, *S*, *F*
Parker, W (Swansea) 1899 *E*, *S*
Parsons, G W (Newport) 1947 *E*
Pascoe, D (Bridgend) 1923 *F*, *I*
Pask, A E I (Abertillery) 1961 *F*, 1962 *E*, *S*, *F*, *I*, 1963 *E*, *S*, *I*, *F*, *NZ*, 1964 *E*, *S*, *I*, *F*, *SA*, 1965 *E*, *S*, *I*, *F*, 1966 *E*, *S*, *I*, *F*, *A*, 1967 *S*, *I*
Payne, G W (Army, Pontypridd) 1960 *E*, *S*, *I*
Payne, H (Swansea) 1935 *NZ*
Peacock, H (Newport) 1929 *S*, *F*, *I*, 1930 *S*, *I*, *F*
Peake, E (Chepstow) 1881 *E*
Pearce, G P (Bridgend) 1981 *I*, *F*, 1982 *I* (R)
Pearson, T W (Cardiff, Newport) 1891 *E*, *I*, 1892 *E*, *S*, 1894 *S*, *I*, 1895 *E*, *S*, *I*, 1897 *E*, 1898 *I*, *E*, 1903 *E*
Pegge, E V (Neath) 1891 *E*
Perego, M A (Llanelli) 1990 *S*, 1993 *F*, *Z*1, *Nm*(R), 1994 *S*, *I*, *F*, *E*, *Sp*
Perkins, S J (Pontypool) 1983 *S*, *I*, *F*, *R*, 1984 *S*, *I*, *F*, *E*, *A*, 1985 *S*, *I*, *F*, *E*, *Fj*, 1986 *E*, *S*, *I*, *F*
Perrett, F L (Neath) 1912 *SA*, 1913 *E*, *S*, *F*, *I*
Perrins, V C (Newport) 1970 *SA*, *S*
Perry, W (Neath) 1911 *E*
Phillips, A J (Cardiff) 1979 *E*, 1980 *F*, *E*, *S*, *I*, *NZ*, 1981 *E*, *S*, *I*, *F*, *A*, 1982 *I*, *F*, *E*, *S*, 1987 [*C*, *E*, *A*]
Phillips, B (Aberavon) 1925 *E*, *S*, *F*, *I*, 1926 *E*
Phillips, D H (Swansea) 1952 *F*
Phillips, H P (Newport) 1892 *E*, 1893 *E*, *S*, *I*, 1894 *E*, *S*
Phillips, H T (Newport) 1927 *E*, *S*, *F*, *I*, *A*, 1928 *E*, *S*, *I*, *F*
Phillips, K H (Neath) 1987 *F*, [*I*, *Tg*, *NZ*], *US*, 1988 *E*, *NZ* 1, 1989 *NZ*, 1990 *F*, *E*, *S*, *I*, *Nm* 1,2, *Bb*, 1991 *E*, *S*, *I*, *F*1, *A*
Phillips, L A (Newport) 1900 *E*, *S*, *I*, 1901 *S*
Phillips, R (Neath) 1987 *US*, 1988 *E*, *S*, *I*, *F*, *NZ* 1,2, *WS*, 1989 *S*, *I*
Phillips, W D (Cardiff) 1881 *E*, 1882 *I*, 1884 *E*, *S*, *I*
Pickering, D F (Llanelli) 1983 *E*, *S*, *I*, *F*, *R*, 1984 *S*, *I*, *F*, *E*, *A*, 1985 *S*, *I*, *F*, *E*, *Fj*, 1986 *E*, *S*, *I*, *F*, *Fj*, 1987 *F*, *E*, *S*
Plummer, R C S (Newport) 1912 *S*, *I*, *F*, *SA*, 1913 *E*
Pook, T (Newport) 1895 *S*
Powell, G (Ebbw Vale) 1957 *I*, *F*
Powell, J (Cardiff) 1906 *I*
Powell, J (Cardiff) 1923 *I*
Powell, R W (Newport) 1888 *S*, *I*
Powell, W C (London Welsh) 1926 *S*, *I*, *F*, 1927 *E*, *F*, *I*, 1928 *S*, *I*, *F*, 1929 *E*, *S*, *F*, *I*, 1930 *S*, *I*, *F*, 1931 *E*, *S*, *F*, *I*, *SA*, 1932 *E*, *S*, *I*, 1935 *E*, *S*, *I*
Powell, W J (Cardiff) 1920 *E*, *S*, *F*, *I*
Price, B (Newport) 1961 *I*, *F*, 1962 *E*, *S*, 1963 *E*, *S*, *F*, *NZ*, 1964 *E*, *S*, *I*, *F*, *SA*, 1965 *E*, *S*, *I*, *F*, 1966 *E*, *S*, *I*, *F*, *A*, 1967 *S*, *I*, *F*, *E*, 1969 *S*, *I*, *F*, *NZ* 1,2, *A*
Price, G (Pontypool) 1975 *F*, *E*, *S*, *I*, *A*, 1976 *E*, *S*, *I*, *F*, 1977 *I*, *F*, *E*, *S*, 1978 *E*, *S*, *I*, *F*, *A* 1,2, *NZ*, 1979 *S*, *I*, *F*, *E*, 1980 *F*, *E*, *S*, *I*, *NZ*, 1981 *E*, *S*, *I*, *F*, *A*, 1982 *I*, *F*, *E*, *S*, 1983 *E*, *I*, *F*
Price, M J (Pontypool, RAF) 1959 *E*, *S*, *I*, *F*, 1960 *E*, *S*, *I*, *F*, 1962 *E*
Price, R E (Weston) 1939 *S*, *I*
Price, T G (Llanelli) 1965 *E*, *S*, *I*, *F*, 1966 *E*, *A*, 1967 *S*, *F*

Priday, A J (Cardiff) 1958 *I*, 1961 *I*
Pritchard, C (Pontypool) 1928 *E, S, I, F*, 1929 *E, S, F, I*
Pritchard, C C (Newport, Pontypool) 1904 *S, I*, 1905 *NZ*, 1906 *E, S*
Pritchard, C M (Newport) 1904 *I*, 1905 *E, S, NZ*, 1906 *E, S, I, SA*, 1907 *E, S, I*, 1908 *E*, 1910 *F, E*
Proctor, W T (Llanelli) 1992 *A*, 1993 *E, S, Z*1,2, *Nm, C*, 1994 *I, C, Fj, WS, R, It, SA*, 1995 *S, I*
Prosser, D R (Neath) 1934 *S, I*
Prosser, G (Neath) 1934 *E, S, I*, 1935 *NZ*
Prosser, J (Cardiff) 1921 *I*
Prosser, T R (Pontypool) 1956 *S, F*, 1957 *E, S, I, F*, 1958 *A, E, S, I, F*, 1959 *E, S, I, F*, 1960 *E, S, I, F, SA*, 1961 *I, F*
Prothero, G J (Bridgend) 1964 *S, I, F*, 1965 *E, S, I, F*, 1966 *E, S, I, F*
Pryce-Jenkins, T J (London Welsh) 1888 *S, I*
Pugh, C (Maesteg) 1924 *E, S, I, F, NZ*, 1925 *E, S*
Pugh, J D (Neath) 1987 *US*, 1988 *S* (R), 1990 *S*
Pugh, P (Neath) 1989 *NZ*
Pugsley, J (Cardiff) 1910 *E, S, I*, 1911 *E, S, F, I*
Pullman, J J (Neath) 1910 *F*
Purdon, F T (Newport) 1881 *E*, 1882 *I*, 1883 *E, S*

Quinnell, D L (Llanelli) 1972 *F* (R), *NZ*, 1973 *E, S, A*, 1974 *S, F*, 1975 *E* (R), 1977 *I* (R), *F, E, S*, 1978 *E, S, I, F, A* 1, *NZ*, 1979 *S, I, F, E*, 1980 *NZ*
Quinnell, L S (Llanelli) 1993 *C*, 1994 *S, I, F, E, Pt, Sp, C, WS*

Radford, W J (Newport) 1923 *I*
Ralph, A R (Newport) 1931 *F, I, SA*, 1932 *E, S, I*
Ramsey, S H (Treorchy) 1896 *E*, 1904 *E*
Randell, R (Aberavon) 1924 *I, F*
Raybould, W H (London Welsh, Cambridge U, Newport) 1967 *S, I, F, E, NZ*, 1968 *I, F*, 1970 *SA, E, I, F* (R)
Rayer, M A (Cardiff) 1991 [*WS*(R), *Arg, A*(R)], 1992 *E*(R), A, 1993 *E, S, I, Z*1, *Nm, J*(R), 1994 *S*(R), *I*(R), *F, E, Pt, C, Fj, WS, R, It*
Rees, Aaron (Maesteg) 1919 *NZA*
Rees, Alan (Maesteg) 1962 *E, S, F*
Rees, A M (London Welsh) 1934 *E*, 1935 *E, S, I, NZ*, 1936 *E, S, I*, 1937 *E, S, I*, 1938 *E, S*
Rees, B I (London Welsh) 1967 *S, I, F*
Rees, C F W (London Welsh) 1974 *I*, 1975 *A*, 1978 *NZ*, 1981 *F, A*, 1982 *I, F, E, S*, 1983 *E, S, I, F*
Rees, D (Swansea) 1968 *S, I, F*
Rees, Dan (Swansea) 1900 *E*, 1903 *E, S*, 1905 *E, S*
Rees, E B (Swansea) 1919 *NZA*
Rees, H (Cardiff) 1937 *S, I*, 1938 *E, S, I*
Rees, H E (Neath) 1979 *S, I, F, E*, 1980 *F, E, S, I, NZ*, 1983 *E, S, I, F*
Rees, J (Swansea) 1920 *E, S, F, I*, 1921 *E, S, I*, 1922 *E*, 1923 *E, F, I*, 1924 *E*
Rees, J I (Swansea) 1934 *E, S, I*, 1935 *S, NZ*, 1936 *E, S, I*, 1937 *E, S, I*, 1938 *E, S, I*
Rees, L M (Cardiff) 1933 *I*
Rees, P (Llanelli) 1947 *F, I*
Rees, P M (Newport) 1961 *E, S, I*, 1964 *I*
Rees, T (Newport) 1935 *S, I, NZ*, 1936 *E, S, I*, 1937 *E, S*
Rees, T A (Llandovery) 1881 *E*
Rees, T E (London Welsh) 1926 *I, F*, 1927 *A*, 1928 *E*
Rees-Jones, G R (Oxford U, London Welsh) 1934 *E, S*, 1935 *I, NZ*, 1936 *E*
Reeves, F (Cross Keys) 1920 *F, I*, 1921 *E*
Reynolds, A (Swansea) 1990 *Nm* 1,2(R), 1992 *A*(R)
Rhapps, J (Penygraig) 1897 *E*
Rice-Evans, W (Swansea) 1890 *S*, 1891 *E, S*
Richards, B (Swansea) 1960 *F*
Richards, C (Pontypool) 1922 *E, S, I, F*, 1924 *I*
Richards, D S (Swansea) 1979 *F, E*, 1980 *F, E, S, I, NZ*, 1981 *E, S, I, F*, 1982 *I, F*, 1983 *E, S, I, R* (R)
Richards, E G (Cardiff) 1927 *S*
Richards, E S (Swansea) 1885 *E*, 1887 *S*
Richards, H D (Neath) 1986 *Tg* (R), 1987 [*Tg, E* (R), *NZ*]
Richards, I (Cardiff) 1925 *E, S, F*
Richards, K H L (Bridgend) 1960 *SA*, 1961 *E, S, I, F*
Richards, M C R (Cardiff) 1968 *I, F*, 1969 *S, I, F, E, NZ* 1,2, *A*
Richards, R (Aberavon) 1913 *S, F, I*
Richards, R (Cross Keys) 1956 *F*
Richards, T L (Maesteg) 1923 *I*
Richardson, S J (Aberavon) 1978 *A* 2 (R), 1979 *E*
Rickards, A R (Cardiff) 1924 *F*
Ring, J (Aberavon) 1921 *E*
Ring, M G (Cardiff, Pontypool) 1983 *E*, 1984 *A*, 1985 *S, I, F*, 1987 *I*, [*I, Tg, A*], *US*, 1988 *E, S, I, F, NZ* 1,2, 1989 *NZ*, 1990 *F, E, S, I, Nm* 1,2, *Bb*, 1991 *E, S, I, F*1,2, [*WS, Arg, A*]
Ringer, P (Ebbw Vale, Llanelli) 1978 *NZ*, 1979 *S, I, F, E*, 1980 *F, E, NZ*
Roberts, C (Neath) 1958 *I, F*
Roberts, D E A (London Welsh) 1930 *E*
Roberts, E (Llanelli) 1886 *E*, 1887 *I*
Roberts, E J (Llanelli) 1888 *S, I*, 1889 *I*
Roberts, G J (Cardiff) 1985 *F* (R), *E*, 1987 [*I, Tg, C, E, A*]
Roberts, H M (Cardiff) 1960 *SA*, 1961 *E, S, I, F*, 1962 *S, F*, 1963 *I*
Roberts, J (Cardiff) 1927 *E, S, F, I, A*, 1928 *E, S, I, F*, 1929 *E, S, F, I*
Roberts, M G (London Welsh) 1971 *E, S, I, F*, 1973 *I, F*, 1975 *S*, 1979 *E*
Roberts, T (Newport, Risca) 1921 *S, F, I*, 1922 *E, S, I, F*, 1923 *E, S*
Roberts, W (Cardiff) 1929 *E*
Robins, J D (Birkenhead Park) 1950 *E, S, I, F*, 1951 *E, S, I, F*, 1953 *E, I, F*
Robins, R J (Pontypridd) 1953 *S*, 1954 *F, S*, 1955 *E, S, I, F*, 1956 *E, F*, 1957 *E, S, I, F*
Robinson, I R (Cardiff) 1974 *F, E*
Rocyn-Jones, D N (Cambridge U) 1925 *I*
Roderick, W B (Llanelli) 1884 *I*
Rosser, M A (Penarth) 1924 *S, F*
Rowland, E M (Lampeter) 1885 *E*
Rowlands, C F (Aberavon) 1926 *I*
Rowlands, D C T (Pontypool) 1963 *E, S, I, F, NZ*, 1964 *E, S, I, F, SA*, 1965 *E, S, I, F*
Rowlands, G (RAF, Cardiff) 1953 *NZ*, 1954 *E, F*, 1956 *F*
Rowlands, K A (Cardiff) 1962 *F, I*, 1963 *I*, 1965 *I, F*
Rowles, G R (Penarth) 1892 *E*
Russell, S (London Welsh) 1987 *US*

Samuel, D (Swansea) 1891 *I*, 1893 *I*
Samuel, F (Mountain Ash) 1922 *S, I, F*
Samuel, J (Swansea) 1891 *I*
Scourfield, T (Torquay) 1930 *F*
Scrine, G F (Swansea) 1899 *E, S*, 1901 *I*
Shanklin, J L (London Welsh) 1970 *F*, 1972 *NZ*, 1973 *I, F*
Shaw, G (Neath) 1972 *NZ*, 1973 *E, S, I, F, A*, 1974 *S, I, F, E*, 1977 *I, F*
Shaw, T W (Newbridge) 1983 *R*
Shea, J (Newport) 1919 *NZA*, 1920 *E, S*, 1921 *E*
Shell, R C (Aberavon) 1973 *A* (R)
Simpson, H J (Cardiff) 1884 *E, S, I*
Skrimshire, R T (Newport) 1899 *E, S, I*
Skym, A (Llanelli) 1928 *E, S, I, F*, 1930 *E, S, I, F*, 1931 *E, S, F, I, SA*, 1932 *E, S, I*, 1933 *E, S, I*, 1935 *E*
Smith, J S (Cardiff) 1884 *E, I*, 1885 *E*
Sparks, B (Neath) 1954 *I*, 1955 *E, F*, 1956 *E, S, I*, 1957 *S*
Spiller, W J (Cardiff) 1910 *S, I*, 1911 *E, S, F, I*, 1912 *E, F, SA*, 1913 *E*
Squire, J (Newport, Pontypool) 1977 *I, F*, 1978 *E, S, I, F, A* 1, *NZ*, 1979 *S, I, F, E*, 1980 *F, E, S, I, NZ*, 1981 *E, S, I, F, A*, 1982 *I, F, E*, 1983 *E, S, I, F*
Stadden, W J W (Cardiff) 1884 *I*, 1886 *E, S*, 1887 *I*, 1888 *S, M*, 1890 *S, E*
Stephens, C J (Llanelli) 1992 *I, F, E, A*
Stephens, G (Neath) 1912 *E, S, I, F, SA*, 1913 *E, S, F, I*, 1919 *NZA*
Stephens, I (Bridgend) 1981 *E, S, I, F, A*, 1982 *I, F, E, S*, 1984 *I, F, E, A*
Stephens, Rev J G (Llanelli) 1922 *E, S, I, F*
Stephens, J R G (Neath) 1947 *E, S, F, I*, 1948 *I*, 1949 *S, I, F*, 1951 *F, SA*, 1952 *E, S, I, F*, 1953 *E, S, I, F, NZ*, 1954 *E, I*, 1955 *E, S, I, F*, 1956 *S, I, F*, 1957 *E, S, I, F*
Stock, A (Newport) 1924 *F, NZ*, 1926 *E, S*
Stone, P (Llanelli) 1949 *F*
Strand-Jones, J (Llanelli) 1902 *E, S, I*, 1903 *E, S*
Summers, R H B (Haverfordwest) 1881 *E*
Sutton, S (Pontypool, S Wales Police) 1982 *F, E*, 1987

F, E, S, I, [C, NZ (R), *A*]
Sweet-Escott, R B (Cardiff) 1891 *S*, 1894 *I*, 1895 *I*

Tamplin, W E (Cardiff) 1947 *S, F, I, A*, 1948 *E, S, F*
Tanner, H (Swansea, Cardiff) 1935 *NZ*, 1936 *E, S, I*, 1937 *E, S, I*, 1938 *E, S, I*, 1939 *E, S, I*, 1947 *E, S, F, I*, 1948 *E, S, F, I*, 1949 *E, S, I, F*
Tarr, D J (Swansea, Royal Navy) 1935 *NZ*
Taylor, A R (Cross Keys) 1937 *I*, 1938 *I*, 1939 *E*
Taylor, C G (Ruabon) 1884 *E, S, I*, 1885 *E, S*, 1886 *E, S*, 1887 *E, I*
Taylor, H T (Cardiff) 1994 *Pt, C, Fj, Tg, WS*(R), *R, It, SA*, 1995 *E, S*
Taylor, J (London Welsh) 1967 *S, I, F, E, NZ*, 1968 *I, F*, 1969 *S, I, F, E, NZ* 1, *A*, 1970 *F*, 1971 *E, S, I, F*, 1972 *E, S, F, NZ*, 1973 *E, S, I, F*
Taylor, M (Pontypool) 1994 *SA*, 1995 *F, E*
Thomas, A (Newport) 1963 *NZ*, 1964 *E*
Thomas, A G (Swansea, Cardiff) 1952 *E, S, I, F*, 1953 *S, I, F*, 1954 *E, I, F*, 1955 *S, I, F*
Thomas, Bob (Swansea) 1900 *E, S, I*, 1901 *E*
Thomas, Brian (Neath, Cambridge U) 1963 *E, S, I, F, NZ*, 1964 *E, S, I, F, SA*, 1965 *E*, 1966 *E, S, I*, 1967 *NZ*, 1969 *S, I, F, E, NZ* 1,2
Thomas, C (Bridgend) 1925 *E, S*
Thomas, C J (Newport) 1888 *I, M*, 1889 *S, I*, 1890 *S, E, I*, 1891 *E, I*
Thomas, D (Aberavon) 1961 *I*
Thomas, D (Llanelli) 1954 *I*
Thomas, Dick (Mountain Ash) 1906 *SA*, 1908 *F, I*, 1909 *S*
Thomas, D J (Swansea) 1904 *E*, 1908 *A*, 1910 *E, S, I*, 1911 *E, S, F, I*, 1912 *E*
Thomas, D J (Swansea) 1930 *S, I*, 1932 *E, S, I*, 1933 *E, S*, 1934 *E*, 1935 *E, S, I*
Thomas, D L (Neath) 1937 *E*
Thomas, E (Newport) 1904 *S, I*, 1909 *S, F, I*, 1910 *F*
Thomas, G (Llanelli) 1923 *E, S, F, I*
Thomas, G (Newport) 1888 *M*, 1890 *I*, 1891 *S*
Thomas, H (Llanelli) 1912 *F*
Thomas, H (Neath) 1936 *E, S, I*, 1937 *E, S, I*
Thomas, H W (Swansea) 1912 *SA*, 1913 *E*
Thomas, I (Bryncethin) 1924 *E*
Thomas, L C (Cardiff) 1885 *E, S*
Thomas, M C (Newport, Devonport Services) 1949 *F*, 1950 *E, S, I, F*, 1951 *E, S, I, F, SA*, 1952 *E, S, I, F*, 1953 *E*, 1956 *E, S, I, F*, 1957 *E, S*, 1958 *E, S, I, F*, 1959 *I, F*
Thomas, M G (St Bart's Hospital) 1919 *NZA*, 1921 *S, F, I*, 1923 *F*, 1924 *E*
Thomas, R (Pontypool) 1909 *F, I*, 1911 *S, F*, 1912 *E, S, SA*, 1913 *E*
Thomas, R C C (Swansea) 1949 *F*, 1952 *I, F*, 1953 *S, I, F, NZ*, 1954 *E, I, F, S*, 1955 *S, I*, 1956 *E, S, I*, 1957 *E*, 1958 *A, E, S, I, F*, 1959 *E, S, I, F*
Thomas, R L (London Welsh) 1889 *S, I*, 1890 *I*, 1891 *E, S, I*, 1892 *E*
Thomas, S (Llanelli) 1890 *S, E*, 1891 *I*
Thomas, W D (Llanelli) 1966 *A*, 1968 *S, I, F*, 1969 *E, NZ* 2, *A*, 1970 *SA, S, E, I, F*, 1971 *E, S, I, F*, 1972 *E, S, F, NZ*, 1973 *E, S, I, F*, 1974 *E*
Thomas, W G (Llanelli, Waterloo, Swansea) 1927 *E, S, F, I*, 1929 *E*, 1931 *E, S, SA*, 1932 *E, S, I*, 1933 *E, S, I*
Thomas, W H (Llandovery Coll, Cambridge U) 1885 *S*, 1886 *E, S*, 1887 *E, S*, 1888 *S, I*, 1890 *E, I*, 1891 *S, I*
Thomas, W J (Cardiff) 1961 *F*, 1963 *F*
Thomas, W L (Newport) 1894 *S*, 1895 *E, I*
Thomas, W T (Abertillery) 1930 *E*
Thompson, J F (Cross Keys) 1923 *E*
Thorburn, P H (Neath) 1985 *F, E, Fj*, 1986 *E, S, I, F*, 1987 *F*, [*I, Tg, C, E, NZ, A*], *US*, 1988 *S, I, F, WS, R* (R), 1989 *S, I, F, E, NZ*, 1990 *F, E, S, I, Nm* 1,2, *Bb*, 1991 *E, S, I, F*1, *A*
Titley, M H (Bridgend, Swansea) 1983 *R*, 1984 *S, I, F, E, A*, 1985 *S, I, Fj*, 1986 *F, Fj, Tg, WS*, 1990 *F, E*
Towers, W H (Swansea) 1887 *I*, 1888 *M*
Travers, G (Pill Harriers) 1903 *E, S, I*, 1905 *E, S, I, NZ*, 1906 *E, S, I, SA*, 1907 *E, S, I*, 1908 *E, S, F, I, A*, 1909 *E, S, I*, 1911 *S, F, I*
Travers, W H (Newport) 1937 *S, I*, 1938 *E, S, I*, 1939 *E, S, I*, 1949 *E, S, I, F*
Treharne, E (Pontypridd) 1881 *E*, 1883 *E*
Trew, W J (Swansea) 1900 *E, S, I*, 1901 *E, S*, 1903 *S*, 1905 *S*, 1906 *S*, 1907 *E, S*, 1908 *E, S, F, I, A*, 1909 *E, S, F, I*, 1910 *F, E, S*, 1911 *E, S, F, I*, 1912 *S*, 1913 *S, F*
Trott, R F (Cardiff) 1948 *E, S, F, I*, 1949 *E, S, I, F*
Truman, W H (Llanelli) 1934 *E*, 1935 *E*
Trump, L C (Newport) 1912 *E, S, I, F*
Turnbull, B R (Cardiff) 1925 *I*, 1927 *E, S*, 1928 *E, F*, 1930 *S*
Turnbull, M J L (Cardiff) 1933 *E, I*
Turner, P (Newbridge) 1989 *I* (R), *F, E*

Uzzell, H (Newport) 1912 *E, S, I, F*, 1913 *S, F, I*, 1914 *E, S, F, I*, 1920 *E, S, F, I*
Uzzell, J R (Newport) 1963 *NZ*, 1965 *E, S, I, F*

Vickery, W E (Aberavon) 1938 *E, S, I*, 1939 *E*
Vile, T H (Newport) 1908 *E, S*, 1910 *I*, 1912 *I, F, SA*, 1913 *E*, 1921 *S*
Vincent, H C (Bangor) 1882 *I*

Wakeford, J D M (S Wales Police) 1988 *WS, R*
Waldron, R (Neath) 1965 *E, S, I, F*
Walker, N (Cardiff) 1993 *I, F, J*, 1994 *S, F, E, Pt, Sp*, 1995 *F, E*
Waller, P D (Newport) 1908 *A*, 1909 *E, S, F, I*, 1910 *F*
Walters, N (Llanelli) 1902 *E*
Wanbon, R (Aberavon) 1968 *E*
Ward, W S (Cross Keys) 1934 *S, I*
Warlow, J (Llanelli) 1962 *I*
Waters, D R (Newport) 1986 *E, S, I, F*
Waters, K (Newbridge) 1991 [*WS*]
Watkins, D (Newport) 1963 *E, S, I, F, NZ*, 1964 *E, S, I, F, SA*, 1965 *E, S, I, F*, 1966 *E, S, I, F*, 1967 *I, F, E*
Watkins, E (Neath) 1924 *E, S, I, F*
Watkins, E (Blaina) 1926 *S, I, F*
Watkins, E (Cardiff) 1935 *NZ*, 1937 *S, I*, 1938 *E, S, I*, 1939 *E, S*
Watkins, H (Llanelli) 1904 *S, I*, 1905 *E, S, I*, 1906 *E*
Watkins, I J (Ebbw Vale) 1988 *E* (R), *S, I, F, NZ* 2, *R*, 1989 *S, I, F, E*
Watkins, L (Oxford U, Llandaff) 1881 *E*
Watkins, M J (Newport) 1984 *I, F, E, A*
Watkins, S J (Newport, Cardiff) 1964 *S, I, F*, 1965 *E, S, I, F*, 1966 *E, S, I, F, A*, 1967 *S, I, F, E, NZ*, 1968 *E, S*, 1969 *S, I, F, E, NZ* 1, 1970 *E, I*
Watkins, W R (Newport) 1959 *F*
Watts, D (Maesteg) 1914 *E, S, F, I*
Watts, J (Llanelli) 1907 *E, S, I*, 1908 *E, S, F, I, A*, 1909 *S, F, I*
Watts, W (Llanelli) 1914 *E*
Watts, W H (Newport) 1892 *E, S, I*, 1893 *E, S, I*, 1894 *E, S, I*, 1895 *E, I*, 1896 *E*
Weaver, D (Swansea) 1964 *E*
Webb, J (Abertillery) 1907 *S*, 1908 *E, S, F, I, A*, 1909 *E, S, F, I*, 1910 *F, E, S, I*, 1911 *E, S, F, I*, 1912 *E, S*
Webb, J E (Newport) 1888 *M*, 1889 *S*
Webbe, G M C (Bridgend) 1986 *Tg* (R), *WS*, 1987 *F, E, S*, [*Tg*], *US*, 1988 *F* (R), *NZ* 1, *R*
Webster, R E (Swansea) 1987 [*A*], 1990 *Bb*, 1991 [*Arg, A*], 1992 *I, F, E, S, A*, 1993 *E, S, I, F*
Wells, G T (Cardiff) 1955 *E, S*, 1957 *I, F*, 1958 *A, E, S*
Westacott, D (Cardiff) 1906 *I*
Wetter, H (Newport) 1912 *SA*, 1913 *E*
Wetter, J J (Newport) 1914 *S, F, I*, 1920 *E, S, F, I*, 1921 *E*, 1924 *I, NZ*
Wheel, G A D (Swansea) 1974 *I, E* (R), 1975 *F, E, I, A*, 1976 *E, S, I, F*, 1977 *I, E, S*, 1978 *E, S, I, F, A* 1,2, *NZ*, 1979 *S, I*, 1980 *F, E, S, I*, 1981 *E, S, I, F, A*, 1982 *I*
Wheeler, P J (Aberavon) 1967 *NZ*, 1968 *E*
Whitefoot, J (Cardiff) 1984 *A* (R), 1985 *S, I, F, E, Fj*, 1986 *E, S, I, F, Fj, Tg, WS*, 1987 *F, E, S, I*, [*I, C*]
Whitfield, J (Newport) 1919 *NZA*, 1920 *E, S, F, I*, 1921 *E*, 1922 *E, S, I, F*, 1924 *S, I*
Whitson, G K (Newport) 1956 *F*, 1960 *S, I*
Wilkins, G (Bridgend) 1994 *Tg*
Williams, A (Bridgend) 1990 *Nm* 2(R)
Williams, B (Llanelli) 1920 *S, F, I*
Williams, B L (Cardiff) 1947 *E, S, F, I, A*, 1948 *E, S, F, I*, 1949 *E, S, I*, 1951 *I, SA*, 1952 *S*, 1953 *E, S, I, F, NZ*, 1954 *S*, 1955 *E*
Williams, B R (Neath) 1990 *S, I, Bb*, 1991 *E, S*
Williams, C (Llanelli) 1924 *NZ*, 1925 *E*
Williams, C (Aberavon, Swansea) 1977 *E, S*, 1980 *F, E, S, I, NZ*, 1983 *E*

Williams, C D (Cardiff, Neath) 1955 *F*, 1956 *F*
Williams, D (Ebbw Vale) 1963 *E, S, I, F*, 1964 *E, S, I, F, SA*, 1965 *E, S, I, F*, 1966 *E, S, I, A*, 1967 *F, E, NZ*, 1968 *E*, 1969 *S, I, F, E, NZ* 1,2, *A*, 1970 *SA, S, E, I*, 1971 *E, S, I, F*
Williams, D B (Newport, Swansea) 1978 *A* 1, 1981 *E, S*
Williams, E (Neath) 1924 *NZ*, 1925 *F*
Williams, E (Aberavon) 1925 *E, S*
Williams, F L (Cardiff) 1929 *S, F, I*, 1930 *E, S, I, F*, 1931 *F, I, SA*, 1932 *E, S, I*, 1933 *I*
Williams, G (Aberavon) 1936 *E, S, I*
Williams, G (London Welsh) 1950 *I, F*, 1951 *E, S, I, F, SA*, 1952 *E, S, I, F*, 1953 *NZ*, 1954 *E*
Williams, G (Bridgend) 1981 *I, F*, 1982 *E* (R), *S*
Williams, G P (Bridgend) 1980 *NZ*, 1981 *E, S, A*, 1982 *I*
Williams, J (Blaina) 1920 *E, S, F, I*, 1921 *S, F, I*
Williams, J F (London Welsh) 1905 *I, NZ*, 1906 *S, SA*
Williams, J J (Llanelli) 1973 *F* (R), *A*, 1974 *S, I, F, E*, 1975 *F, E, S, I, A*, 1976 *E, S, I, F*, 1977 *I, F, E, S*, 1978 *E, S, I, F, A* 1,2, *NZ*, 1979 *S, I, F, E*
Williams, J L (Cardiff) 1906 *SA*, 1907 *E, S, I*, 1908 *E, S, I, A*, 1909 *E, S, F, I*, 1910 *I*, 1911 *E, S, F, I*
Williams, J P R (London Welsh, Bridgend) 1969 *S, I, F, E, NZ* 1,2, *A*, 1970 *SA, S, E, I, F*, 1971 *E, S, I, F*, 1972 *E, S, F, NZ*, 1973 *E, S, I, F, A*, 1974 *S, I, F*, 1975 *F, E, S, I, A*, 1976 *E, S, I, F*, 1977 *I, F, E, S*, 1978 *E, S, I, F, A* 1,2, *NZ*, 1979 *S, I, F, E*, 1980 *NZ*, 1981 *E, S*
Williams, L (Llanelli, Cardiff) 1947 *E, S, F, I, A*, 1948 *I*, 1949 *E*
Williams, L H (Cardiff) 1957 *S, I, F*, 1958 *E, S, I, F*, 1959 *E, S, I*, 1961 *F*, 1962 *E, S*
Williams, M (Newport) 1923 *F*
Williams, O (Bridgend) 1990 *Nm* 2
Williams, O (Llanelli) 1947 *E, S, A*, 1948 *E, S, F, I*
Williams, R (Llanelli) 1954 *S*, 1957 *F*, 1958 *A*
Williams, R D G (Newport) 1881 *E*
Williams, R F (Cardiff) 1912 *SA*, 1913 *E, S*, 1914 *I*
Williams, R H (Llanelli) 1954 *I, F, S*, 1955 *S, I, F*, 1956 *E, S, I*, 1957 *E, S, I, F*, 1958 *A, E, S, I, F*, 1959 *E, S, I, F*, 1960 *E*
Williams, S (Llanelli) 1947 *E, S, F, I*, 1948 *S, F*
Williams, S A (Aberavon) 1939 *E, S, I*
Williams, S M (Neath) 1994 *Tg*
Williams, T (Pontypridd) 1882 *I*
Williams, T (Swansea) 1888 *S, I*
Williams, T (Swansea) 1912 *I*, 1913 *F*, 1914 *E, S, F, I*
Williams, Tudor (Swansea) 1921 *F*
Williams, T G (Cross Keys) 1935 *S, I, NZ*, 1936 *E, S, I*, 1937 *S, I*
Williams, W A (Crumlin) 1927 *E, S, F, I*
Williams, W A (Newport) 1952 *I, F*, 1953 *E*
Williams, W E O (Cardiff) 1887 *S, I*, 1889 *S*, 1890 *S, E*
Williams, W H (Pontymister) 1900 *E, S, I*, 1901 *E*
Williams, W O G (Swansea, Devonport Services) 1951 *F, SA*, 1952 *E, S, I, F*, 1953 *E, S, I, F, NZ*, 1954 *E, I, F, S*, 1955 *E, S, I, F*, 1956 *E, S, I*
Williams, W P J (Neath) 1974 *I, F*
Williams-Jones, H (S Wales Police, Llanelli) 1989 *S*(R), 1990 *F*(R), *I*, 1991 *A*, 1992 *S, A*, 1993 *E, S, I, F, Z*1, *Nm*, 1994 *Fj, Tg, WS*(R), *It*(t), 1995 *E*(R)
Willis, W R (Cardiff) 1950 *E, S, I, F*, 1951 *E, S, I, F, SA*, 1952 *E, S*, 1953 *S, NZ*, 1954 *E, I, F, S*, 1955 *E, S, I, F*
Wiltshire, M L (Aberavon) 1967 *NZ*, 1968 *E, S, F*
Windsor, R W (Pontypool) 1973 *A*, 1974 *S, I, F, E*, 1975 *F, E, S, I, A*, 1976 *E, S, I, F*, 1977 *I, F, E, S*, 1978 *E, S, I, F, A* 1,2, *NZ*, 1979 *S, I, F*
Winfield, H B (Cardiff) 1903 *I*, 1904 *E, S, I*, 1905 *NZ*, 1906 *E, S, I*, 1907 *S, I*, 1908 *E, S, F, I, A*
Winmill, S (Cross Keys) 1921 *E, S, F, I*
Wintle, R V (London Welsh) 1988 *WS*(R)
Wooller, W (Sale, Cambridge U, Cardiff) 1933 *E, S, I*, 1935 *E, S, I, NZ*, 1936 *E, S, I*, 1937 *E, S, I*, 1938 *S, I*, 1939 *E, S, I*
Wyatt, M A (Swansea) 1983 *E, S, I, F*, 1984 *A*, 1985 *S, I*, 1987 *E, S, I*

Young, D (Swansea, Cardiff) 1987 [*E, NZ*], *US*, 1988 *E, S, I, F, NZ* 1,2, *WS, R*, 1989 *S, NZ*, 1990 *F*
Young, G A (Cardiff) 1886 *E, S*
Young, J (Harrogate, RAF, London Welsh) 1968 *S, I, F*, 1969 *S, I, F, E, NZ* 1, 1970 *E, I, F*, 1971 *E, S, I, F*, 1972 *E, S, F, NZ*, 1973 *E, S, I, F*

WELSH INTERNATIONAL RECORDS

Both team and individual records are for official Welsh international matches up to 31 March 1995.

TEAM RECORDS

Highest score

102 v Portugal (102-11) 1994 Lisbon
v individual countries
16 v Argentina (16-7) 1991 Cardiff
28 v Australia (28-3) 1975 Cardiff
40 v Canada (40-9) 1987 Invercargill
34 v England (34-21) 1967 Cardiff
49 v France (49-14) 1910 Swansea
40 v Fiji (40-3) 1985 Cardiff
34 v Ireland (34-9) 1976 Dublin
29 v Italy (29-19) 1994 Cardiff
55 v Japan (55-5) 1993 Cardiff
38 v Namibia (38-23) 1993 Windhoek
16 v N Zealand (16-19) 1972 Cardiff
102 v Portugal (102-11) 1994 Lisbon
16 v Romania (16-9) 1994 Bucharest
12 v S Africa (12-20) 1994 Cardiff
35 v Scotland (35-12) 1972 Cardiff
54 v Spain (54-0) 1994 Madrid
29 v Tonga (29-16) 1987 Palmerston North
46 v United States (46-0) 1987 Cardiff
32 v W Samoa (32-14) 1986 Apia
42 v Zimbabwe (42-13) 1993 Harare

Biggest winning points margin

91 v Portugal (102-11) 1994 Lisbon
v individual countries
9 v Argentina (16-7) 1991 Cardiff
25 v Australia (28-3) 1975 Cardiff
31 v Canada (40-9) 1987 Invercargill
25 v England (25-0) 1905 Cardiff
42 v France (47-5) 1909 Colombes
37 v Fiji (40-3) 1985 Cardiff
29 v Ireland (29-0) 1907 Cardiff

10 v Italy (29-19) 1994 Cardiff
50 v Japan (55-5) 1993 Cardiff
15 v Namibia (38-23) 1993 Windhoek
5 v N Zealand (13-8) 1953 Cardiff
91 v Portugal (102-11) 1994 Lisbon
7 v Romania (16-9) 1994 Bucharest
23 v Scotland { (35-12) 1972 Cardiff / (29-6) 1994 Cardiff
54 v Spain (54-0) 1994 Madrid
13 v Tonga (29-16) 1987 Palmerston North
46 v United States (46-0) 1987 Cardiff
22 v W Samoa (28-6) 1988 Cardiff
29 v Zimbabwe (42-13) 1993 Harare
No wins v South Africa

Longest winning sequence
11 matches – 1907-10

Highest score by opposing team
63 Australia (6-63) 1991 Brisbane
v individual countries
7 Argentina (16-7) 1991 Cardiff
63 Australia (6-63) 1991 Brisbane
26 Canada (24-26) 1993 Cardiff
34 England (6-34) 1990 Twickenham
36 France (3-36) 1991 Paris
15 Fiji (22-15) 1986 Suva
21 Ireland { (24-21) 1979 Cardiff / (7-21) 1980 Dublin / (9-21) 1985 Cardiff / (21-21) 1991 Cardiff
19 Italy (29-19) 1994 Cardiff
5 Japan (55-5) 1993 Cardiff
30 Namibia (34-30) 1990 Windhoek
54 N Zealand (9-54) 1988 Auckland
11 Portugal (102-11) 1994 Lisbon
24 Romania (6-24) 1983 Bucharest
35 Scotland (10-35) 1924 Inverleith
24 S Africa (3-24) 1964 Durban
0 Spain (54-0) 1994 Madrid
16 Tonga (29-16) 1987 Palmerston North
0 United States (46-0) 1987 Cardiff
34 W Samoa (9-34) 1994 Moamoa
13 Zimbabwe (42-13) 1993 Harare

Biggest losing points margin
57 v Australia (6-63) 1991 Brisbane
v individual countries
57 v Australia (6-63) 1991 Brisbane
2 v Canada (24-26) 1993 Cardiff
28 v England (6-34) 1990 Twickenham
33 v France (3-36) 1991 Paris
16 v Ireland (3-19) 1925 Belfast
49 v N Zealand (3-52) 1988 Christchurch
18 v Romania (6-24) 1983 Bucharest
25 v Scotland (10-35) 1924 Inverleith
21 v S Africa (3-24) 1964 Durban
25 v W Samoa (9-34) 1994 Moamoa
No defeats v Argentina, Fiji, Italy, Japan, Namibia, Portugal, Spain, Tonga, United States or Zimbabwe

---

Longest losing sequence
5 matches – 1989-90 and 1994-95

Most tries by Wales in an international
16 v Portugal (102-11) 1994 Lisbon

Most tries against Wales in an international
13 by England 1881 Blackheath

Most points by Wales in International Championship in a season – 102
in season 1975-76

Most tries by Wales in International Championship in a season – 21
in season 1909-10

INDIVIDUAL RECORDS

Most capped player
J P R Williams 55 1969-81
in individual positions
Full-back
J P R Williams 54(55)[1] 1969-81
Wing
I C Evans 51 1987-95
Centre
S P Fenwick 30[2] 1975-81
Fly-half
C I Morgan 29[3] 1951-58
Scrum-half
G O Edwards 53 1967-78
Prop
G Price 41 1975-83
Hooker
B V Meredith 34 1954-62
Lock
G O Llewellyn 37 1989-95
Flanker
W D Morris 32(34)[4] 1967-74
No 8
T M Davies 38[5] 1969-76

[1]*Williams won one cap as a flanker*
[2]*M R Hall, 39 caps, has won 29 as a centre and 10 on the wing*
[3]*M G Ring, 32 caps, won 27 at centre, 4 at fly-half and 1 as a full-back. P Bennett, 29 caps, played 25 times as a fly-half. N R Jenkins, 33 caps, has won 26 at fly-half, 6 at centre and 1 at full-back*
[4]*Morris won his first two caps as a No 8*
[5]*P T Davies, 46 caps, has won 26 as a No 8, 2 as a flanker and 18 as a lock*

Longest international career
W J Trew
14 seasons 1899-1900 to 1912-13
T H Vile
14 seasons 1907-08 to 1920-21
H Tanner
14 seasons 1935-36 to 1948-49

Most consecutive internationals – 53*
G O Edwards 1967-78
**entire career*

Most internationals as captain – 28
I C Evans 1991-95

Most points in internationals – 358
N R Jenkins (33 matches) 1991-95

Most points in International Championship in a season – 52
P H Thorburn (4 matches) 1985-86

Most points in an international – 24
N R Jenkins v Canada 1993 Cardiff
N R Jenkins v Italy 1994 Cardiff

Most tries in internationals – 21
I C Evans (51 matches) 1987-95

Most tries in International Championship in a season – 6
R A Gibbs (4 matches) 1907-08
M C R Richards (4 matches) 1968-69

Most tries in an international – 4
W M Llewellyn* v England 1899 Swansea
R A Gibbs v France 1908 Cardiff
M C R Richards v England 1969 Cardiff
I C Evans v Canada 1987 Invercargill
N Walker v Portugal 1994 Lisbon
**on first appearance*

Most conversions in internationals – 43
P H Thorburn (37 matches) 1985-91

Most conversions in International Championship in a season – 11
J Bancroft (4 matches) 1908-09

Most conversions in an international – 11
N R Jenkins v Portugal 1994 Lisbon

Most dropped goals in internationals – 13
J Davies (27 matches) 1985-88

Most dropped goals in an international – 2
J Shea v England 1920 Swansea
A Jenkins v Scotland 1921 Swansea
B John v England 1971 Cardiff
M Dacey v England 1984 Twickenham
J Davies v Ireland 1987 Wellington
J Davies v Scotland 1988 Cardiff

Most penalty goals in internationals – 85
N R Jenkins (33 matches) 1991-95

Most penalty goals in International Championship in a season – 16
P H Thorburn (4 matches) 1985-86

Most penalty goals in an international – 8
N R Jenkins v Canada 1993 Cardiff

Most points on major overseas tour – 89
N R Jenkins (6 matches) Africa 1993

Most points in a tour match – 28
M Rayer v N Region 1990 Namibia
P Bennett scored 34 points v Japan in Tokyo in 1975, but this was not on a major tour

Most tries in a tour match – 3
M C R Richards v Otago 1969 Dunedin, NZ
S Fealey v Welwitschia 1990 Swakopmund, Namibia
Several others have scored 3 in matches on non-major tours

OPTIMISM AND PESSIMISM

THE 1994-95 SEASON IN FRANCE

Bob Donahue *International Herald Tribune*

In France there used to be a feeling that English rugby ought to be strong, that their weakness was unnatural, bad for the world game. After some abject results during the 1970s, big England lost five times to France and drew once from 1983 to 1988. Something was obviously wrong on the northern side of the Channel.

Now, however, England are overdoing it. Eight consecutive defeats of France; a crushing score of 31-10 in 1995, with French possession conceded to deft English brawn 25 times; an English sweep of the Extra XV, University, Youth and Schoolboy fixtures... Some hopeful Frenchmen were saying at the end of this disappointing 1994-95 season that perhaps France and England would make it to the World Cup final, and then we would see what we would see. Others, though, found the prospect of meeting England again so soon frightening.

Optimists could point out that under coach Pierre Berbizier the French finally come right in the full-time training conditions of touring. It happened in South Africa in 1993 and again in New Zealand in 1994. So the 1995 World Cup campaign would see France soar again – bet on it. Pessimists laughed at this. A team which lost to Canada, England and Scotland and strained to beat Romania in the months leading up to the World Cup would be lucky to get past the quarter-final stage in South Africa. Optimists retorted that they didn't care about the fluke defeat in Ottawa in June on the way to New Zealand, or the boring chore in Bucharest in April. The season was too long; you could not expect top French players to be hungry enough on every occasion. Against England, France were tired and perhaps inhibited by the Merle and Cantona affairs. Against Scotland, they were arrogant and dazed as well as tired. But remember the Wales and Ireland matches during the winter after the defeat of Canada in Besançon in the autumn. Above all, remember New Zealand.

It was 3 July in Auckland. Defence and discipline had won the First Test handily in Christchurch, but the French now seemed unable to consolidate their success into a history-making series win. The score was 20-16 to New Zealand with three minutes left on the Eden Park clock. French captain Philippe Saint-André, as he himself later put it, 'counter-attacked from the end of the world', beginning a nine-man move which eventually put full-back Jean-Luc Sadourny across. A similar burst yielded the fourth of France's tries at Lansdowne Road in March. This time it was Saint-André who scored, wearing just one boot. It was his fourth try in the 1995 Championship, and France's tenth – one more than England's try tally in the tournament.

To all this the pessimists responded sadly that you don't win World

The French team which beat Ireland in Dublin. L-R, back row: J-M Gonzalez, C Califano, L Armary, M Cecillon, P Benetton, A Benazzi, O Merle, O Brouzet; front row: P Sella, F Mesnel, Y Delaigue, P Saint-André (capt), G Accoceberry, J-L Sadourny, E Ntamack.

Cups with desperate flashes of romance. Before the tournament England seemed to be doing everything right, while France were justifying that exasperating English cliché about their 'unpredictability'. After the wins in New Zealand, Berbizier said his goal was to win the World Cup. After the loss at home to Scotland, manager Guy Laporte had lowered the sights: he said the aim now was to get into a semi-final.

Despite six changes after that Scotland match, selection was fairly stable overall. Twenty-two of the 26 players named at the end of March for the World Cup squad had been on the Canada-New Zealand tour nine months earlier. The four other World Cup choices were Philippe Gallart, Marc de Rougemont, Arnaud Costes and Aubin Hueber. Berbizier named Benetton vice-captain in charge of tactics on the pitch. For the nine Tests from June to April, Berbizier used 14 forwards and 11 backs (not counting replacements).

Friction between top players and management about money was patched over well before the squad left for South Africa. At home, optimists and pessimists alike had their fingers crossed.

FRENCH CLUB CHAMPIONSHIP FINAL

6 May, Parc des Princes

Toulouse 31 (1G 7PG 1DG) **Castres 16** (1G 2PG 1DG)

Castres Olympique led 16-6 at half-time, but 25 points for reigning champions Stade Toulousain followed. The heavily forward-dominated final began violently, and Belot and Jeannard were sent off for ten minutes. Flowing play was rare from either side.

Séguier lost the ball while driving for the losers' try, but the referee was unsighted and allowed it. The Toulouse front five imposed themselves steadily as the Castres pack faded, their try coming from a pushover scrum and touched down by full-back Ougier. The popular Deylaud stood out for his kicking, driving Castres backwards and succeeding with all nine of his kicks at goal.

The match was the usual exuberant fête for good-humoured supporters, a gala occasion attended by President François Mitterand and both contenders for his succession in the second-round presidential election the next day. A 12th national championship since 1912 put Toulouse ahead of Béziers as the most successful club in French history.

Toulouse: S Ougier; E Ntamack, P Carbonneau, T Castaignède, D Berty; C Deylaud, J Cazalbou; C Califano, P Soula, C Portolan, H Miorin, F Belot, D Lacroix, A Cigagna (*capt*), R Sonnes *Replacements* E Artiguste for Cazalbou; R Castel for Lacroix
Scorers *Try:* Ougier *Conversion:* Deylaud *Penalty Goals:* Deylaud (7)
Dropped Goal: Deylaud
Castres: C Savy; P Escalle, A Hyardet, J-M Aué, C Lucquiaud; F Rui, F Séguier (*capt*); L Toussaint, C Batut, T Lafforgue, G Jeannard, J-F Gourragne, J Diaz, J-P Swiadek, G Pagès *Replacements* C Urios for Batut; C Gaston for Jeannard
Scorers *Try:* Séguier *Conversion:* Savy *Penalty Goals:* Savy (2)
Dropped Goal: Rui
Referee M Pascal (Limousin)

FRENCH INTERNATIONAL PLAYERS
(up to 31 March 1995)

ABBREVIATIONS

A – Australia; *Arg* – Argentina; *B* – British Forces and Home Union Teams; *C* – Canada; *Cz* – Czechoslovakia; *E* – England; *Fj* – Fiji; *G* – Germany; *I* – Ireland; *It* – Italy; *J* – Japan; *K* – New Zealand Services; *M* – Maoris; *NZ* – New Zealand; *R* – Romania; *S* – Scotland; *SA* – South Africa; *US* – United States of America; *W* – Wales; *Z* – Zimbabwe; (R) – Replacement; (t) – temporary replacement. Entries in square brackets [ ] indicate appearances in the World Cup.

Club Abbreviations: ASF – Association Sportive Française; BEC – Bordeaux Etudiants Club; CASG – Club Athlétique des Sports Généraux; PUC – Paris Université Club; RCF – Racing Club de France; SB – Stade Bordelais; SBUC – Stade Bordelais Université Club; SCUF – Sporting Club Universitaire de France; SF – Stade Français; SOE – Stade Olympien des Etudiants; TOEC – Toulouse Olympique Employés Club.

Note: Years given for Five Nations' matches are for second half of season, eg 1972 refers to season 1971-72. Years for all other matches refer to the actual year of the match. When a series has taken place, or more than one match has been played against a country in the same year, figures have been used to denote the particular matches in which players have featured. Thus 1967 *SA* 2,4 indicates that a player appeared in the second and fourth Tests of the 1967 series against South Africa. This list includes only those players who have appeared in FFR International Matches '*donnant droit au titre d'international*'.

Abadie, A (Pau) 1964 *I*
Abadie, A (Graulhet) 1965 *R*, 1967 *SA* 1,3,4, *NZ*, 1968 *S*, *I*
Abadie, L (Tarbes) 1963 *R*
Accoceberry, G (Bègles) 1994 *NZ* 1,2, *C* 2, 1995 *W*, *E*, *S*, *I*
Aguerre, R (Biarritz O) 1979 *S*
Aguilar, D (Pau) 1937 *G*
Aguirre, J-M (Bagnères) 1971 *A* 2, 1972 *S*, 1973 *W*, *I*, *J*, *R*, 1974 *I*, *W*, *Arg* 2, *R*, *SA* 1, 1976 *W*(R), *E*, *US*, *A* 2, *R*, 1977 *W*, *E*, *S*, *I*, *Arg* 1,2, *NZ* 1,2, *R*, 1978 *E*, *S*, *I*, *W*, *R*, 1979 *I*, *W*, *E*, *S*, *NZ* 1,2, *R*, 1980 *W*, *I*
Ainciart, E (Bayonne) 1933 *G*, 1934 *G*, 1935 *G*, 1937 *G*, *It*, 1938 *G* 1
Albaladejo, P (Dax) 1954 *E*, *It*, 1960 *W*, *I*, *It*, *R*, 1961 *S*, *SA*, *E*, *W*, *I*, *NZ* 1,2, *A*, 1962 *S*, *E*, *W*, *I*, 1963 *S*, *I*, *E*, *W*, *It*, 1964 *S*, *NZ*, *W*, *It*, *I*, *SA*, *Fj*
Alvarez, A-J (Tyrosse) 1945 *B* 2, 1946 *B*, *I*, *K*, *W*, 1947 *S*, *I*, *W*, *E*, 1948 *I*, *A*, *S*, *W*, *E*, 1949 *I*, *E*, *W*, 1951 *S*, *E*, *W*
Amand, H (SF) 1906 *NZ*
Ambert, A (Toulouse) 1930 *S*, *I*, *E*, *G*, *W*
Amestoy, J-B (Mont-de-Marsan) 1964 *NZ*, *E*
André, G (RCF) 1913 *SA*, *E*, *W*, *I*, 1914 *I*, *W*, *E*
Andrieu, M (Nîmes) 1986 *Arg* 2, *NZ* 1, *R* 2, *NZ* 2, 1987 [*R*, *Z*], *R*, 1988 *E*, *S*, *I*, *W*, *Arg* 1,2,3,4, *R*, 1989 *I*, *W*, *E*, *S*, *NZ* 2, *B*, *A* 2, 1990 *W*, *E*, *I*(R)
Anduran, J (SCUF) 1910 *W*
Araou, R (Narbonne) 1924 *R*
Arcalis, R (Brive) 1950 *S*, *I*, 1951 *I*, *E*, *W*
Arino, M (Agen) 1962 *R*
Aristouy, P (Pau) 1948 *S*, 1949 *Arg* 2, 1950 *S*, *I*, *E*, *W*
Armary, L (Lourdes) 1987 [*R*], *R*, 1988 *S*, *I*, *W*, *Arg* 3,4, *R*, 1989 *W*, *S*, *A* 1,2, 1990 *W*, *E*, *S*, *I*, *A* 1,2,3, *NZ* 1, 1991 *W*2, 1992 *S*, *I*, *R*, *Arg* 1,2, *SA* 1,2, *Arg*, 1993 *E*, *S*, *I*, *W*, *SA*1,2, *R*2, *A*1,2, 1994 *I*, *W*, *NZ* 1(t), 2(t), 1995 *I*
Arnal, J-M (RCF) 1914 *I*, *W*
Arnaudet, M (Lourdes) 1964 *I*, 1967 *It*, *W*
Arotca, R (Bayonne) 1938 *R*
Arrieta, J (SF) 1953 *E*, *W*
Arthapignet, P (see Harislur-Arthapignet)
Astre, R (Béziers) 1971 *R*, 1972 *I* 1, 1973 *E* (R), 1975 *E*, *S*, *I*, *SA* 1,2, *Arg* 2, 1976 *A* 2, *R*
Augé, J (Dax) 1929 *S*, *W*
Augras-Fabre, L (Agen) 1931 *I*, *S*, *W*
Averous, J-L (La Voulte) 1975 *S*, *I*, *SA* 1,2, 1976 *I*, *W*, *E*, *US*, *A* 1,2, *R*, 1977 *W*, *E*, *S*, *I*, *Arg* 1, *R*, 1978 *E*, *S*, *I*, 1979 *NZ* 1,2, 1980 *E*, *S*, 1981 *A* 2
Azarete, J-L (Dax, St Jean-de-Luz) 1969 *W*, *R*, 1970 *S*, *I*, *W*, *R*, 1971 *S*, *I*, *E*, *SA* 1,2, *A* 1, 1972 *E*, *W*, *I* 2, *A* 1, *R*, 1973 *NZ*, *W*, *I*, *R*, 1974 *I*, *R*, *SA* 1,2, 1975 *W*

Bader, E (Primevères) 1926 *M*, 1927 *I*, *S*
Badin, C (Chalon) 1973 *W*, *I*, 1975 *Arg* 1
Baillette, M (Perpignan) 1925 *I*, *NZ*, *S*, 1926 *W*, *M*, 1927 *I*, *W*, *G* 2, 1929 *G*, 1930 *S*, *I*, *E*, *G*, 1931 *I*, *S*, *E*, 1932 *G*
Baladie, G (Agen) 1945 *B* 1,2, *W*, 1946 *B*, *I*, *K*
Ballarin, J (Tarbes) 1924 *E*, 1925 *NZ*, *S*
Baquey, J (Toulouse) 1921 *I*
Barbazanges, A (Roanne) 1932 *G*, 1933 *G*
Barrau, M (Beaumont, Toulouse) 1971 *S*, *E*, *W*, 1972 *E*, *W*, *A* 1,2, 1973 *S*, *NZ*, *E*, *I*, *J*, *R*, 1974 *I*, *S*
Barrère, P (Toulon) 1929 *G*, 1931 *W*
Barrière, R (Béziers) 1960 *R*
Barthe, E (SBUC) 1925 *W*, *E*
Barthe, J (Lourdes) 1954 *Arg* 1,2, 1955 *S*, 1956 *I*, *W*, *It*, *E*, *Cz*, 1957 *S*, *I*, *E*, *W*, *R* 1,2, 1958 *S*, *E*, *A*, *W*, *It*, *I*, *SA* 1,2, 1959 *S*, *E*, *It*, *W*
Basauri, R (Albi) 1954 *Arg* 1
Bascou, P (Bayonne) 1914 *E*
Basquet, G (Agen) 1945 *W*, 1946 *B*, *I*, *K*, *W*, 1947 *S*, *I*, *W*, *E*, 1948 *I*, *A*, *S*, *W*, *E*, 1949 *S*, *I*, *E*, *W*, *Arg* 1, 1950 *S*, *I*, *E*, *W*, 1951 *S*, *I*, *E*, *W*, 1952 *S*, *I*, *SA*, *W*, *E*, *It*
Bastiat, J-P (Dax) 1969 *R*, 1970 *S*, *I*, *W*, 1971 *S*, *I*, *SA* 2, 1972 *S*, *A* 1, 1973 *E*, 1974 *Arg* 1,2, *SA* 2, 1975 *W*, *Arg* 1,2, *R*, 1976 *S*, *I*, *W*, *E*, *A* 1,2, *R*, 1977 *W*, *E*, *S*, *I*, 1978 *E*, *S*, *I*, *W*
Baudry, N (Montferrand) 1949 *S*, *I*, *W*, *Arg* 1,2
Baulon, R (Vienne, Bayonne) 1954 *S*, *NZ*, *W*, *E*, *It*, 1955 *I*, *E*, *W*, *It*, 1956 *S*, *I*, *W*, *It*, *E*, *Cz*, 1957 *S*, *I*, *It*
Baux, J-P (Lannemezan) 1968 *NZ* 1,2, *SA* 1,2
Bavozet, J (Lyon) 1911 *S*, *E*, *W*
Bayard, J (Toulouse) 1923 *S*, *W*, *E*, 1924 *W*, *R*, *US*
Bayardon, J (Chalon) 1964 *S*, *NZ*, *E*
Beaurin-Gressier, C (SF) 1907 *E*, 1908 *E*
Bégu, J (Dax) 1982 *Arg* 2 (R), 1984 *E*, *S*
Béguerie, C (Agen) 1979 *NZ* 1
Beguet, L (RCF) 1922 *I*, 1923 *S*, *W*, *E*, *I*, 1924 *S*, *I*, *E*, *R*, *US*
Behoteguy, A (Bayonne, Cognac) 1923 *E*, 1924 *S*, *I*, *E*, *W*, *R*, *US*, 1926 *E*, 1927 *E*, *G* 1,2, 1928 *A*, *I*, *E*, *G*, *W*, 1929 *S*, *W*, *E*
Behoteguy, H (RCF, Cognac) 1923 *W*, 1928 *A*, *I*, *E*, *G*, *W*
Belascain, C (Bayonne) 1977 *R*, 1978 *E*, *S*, *I*, *W*, *R*, 1979 *I*, *W*, *E*, *S*, 1982 *W*, *E*, *S*, *I*, 1983 *E*, *S*, *I*, *W*
Belletante, G (Nantes) 1951 *I*, *E*, *W*
Benazzi, A (Agen) 1990 *A* 1,2,3, *NZ* 1,2, 1991 *E*, *US*1(R),2, [*R*, *Fj*, *C*], 1992 *SA* 1(R),2, *Arg*, 1993 *E*, *S*, *I*, *W*, *A*1,2, 1994 *I*, *W*, *E*, *S*, *C* 1, *NZ* 1,2, *C* 2, 1995 *W*, *E*, *S*, *I*
Bénésis, R (Narbonne) 1969 *W*, *R*, 1970 *S*, *I*, *W*, *E*, *R*, 1971 *S*, *I*, *E*, *W*, *A* 2, *R*, 1972 *S*, *I* 1, *E*, *W*, *I* 2, *A* 1, *R*, 1973 *NZ*, *E*, *W*, *I*, *J*, *R*, 1974 *I*, *W*, *E*, *S*
Benetière, J (Roanne) 1954 *It*, *Arg* 1
Benetton, P (Agen) 1989 *B*, 1990 *NZ* 2, 1991 *US*2, 1992 *Arg* 1,2(R), *SA* 1(R),2, *Arg*, 1993 *E*, *S*, *I*, *W*, *SA*1,2, *R*2, *A*1,2, 1994 *I*, *W*, *E*, *S*, *C* 1, *NZ* 1,2, *C* 2, 1995 *W*, *E*, *S*, *I*
Benezech, L (RCF) 1994 *E*, *S*, *C* 1, *NZ* 1,2, *C* 2, 1995 *W*, *E*
Berbizier, P (Lourdes, Agen) 1981 *S*, *I*, *W*, *E*, *NZ* 1,2, 1982 *I*, *R*, 1983 *S*, *I*, 1984 *S* (R), *NZ* 1,2, 1985 *Arg* 1,2, 1986 *S*, *I*, *W*, *E*, *R* 1, *Arg* 1, *A*, *NZ* 1, *R* 2, *NZ* 2,3, 1987

W, *E*, *S*, *I*, [*S*, *R*, *Fj*, *A*, *NZ*], *R*, 1988 *E*, *S*, *I*, *W*, *Arg* 1,2, 1989 *I*, *W*, *E*, *S*, *NZ* 1,2, *B*, *A* 1, 1990 *W*, *E*, 1991 *S*, *I*, *W*1, *E*
Berejnoi, J-C (Tulle) 1963 *R*, 1964 *S*, *W*, *It*, *I*, *SA*, *Fj*, *R*, 1965 *S*, *I*, *E*, *W*, *It*, *R*, 1966 *S*, *I*, *E*, *W*, *It*, *R*, 1967 *S*, *A*, *E*, *It*, *W*, *I*, *R*
Berges, B (Toulouse) 1926 *I*
Berges-Cau, R (Lourdes) 1976 *E* (R)
Bergese, F (Bayonne) 1936 *G* 2, 1937 *G*, *It*, 1938 *G* 1, *R*, *G* 2
Bergougnan, Y (Toulouse) 1945 *B* 1, *W*, 1946 *B*, *I*, *K*, *W*, 1947 *S*, *I*, *W*, *E*, 1948 *S*, *W*, *E*, 1949 *S*, *E*, *Arg* 1,2
Bernard, R (Bergerac) 1951 *S*, *I*, *E*, *W*
Bernat-Salles, P (Pau) 1992 *Arg*, 1993 *R*1, *SA*1,2, *R*2, *A*1,2, 1994 *I*, 1995 *E*, *S*
Bernon, J (Lourdes) 1922 *I*, 1923 *S*
Bérot, J-L (Toulouse) 1968 *NZ* 3, *A*, 1969 *S*, *I*, 1970 *E*, *R*, 1971 *S*, *I*, *E*, *W*, *SA* 1,2, *A* 1,2, *R*, 1972 *S*, *I* 1, *E*, *W*, *A* 1, 1974 *I*
Bérot, P (Agen) 1986 *R* 2, *NZ* 2,3, 1987 *W*, *E*, *S*, *I*, *R*, 1988 *E*, *S*, *I*, *Arg* 1,2,3,4, *R*, 1989 *S*, *NZ* 1,2
Bertrand, P (Bourg) 1951 *I*, *E*, *W*, 1953 *S*, *I*, *E*, *W*, *It*
Bertranne, R (Bagnères) 1971 *E*, *W*, *SA* 2, *A* 1,2, 1972 *S*, *I* 1, 1973 *NZ*, *E*, *J*, *R*, 1974 *I*, *W*, *E*, *S*, *Arg* 1,2, *R*, *SA* 1,2, 1975 *W*, *E*, *S*, *I*, *SA* 1,2, *Arg* 1,2, *R*, 1976 *S*, *I*, *W*, *E*, *US*, *A* 1,2, *R*, 1977 *W*, *E*, *S*, *I*, *Arg* 1,2, *NZ* 1,2, *R*, 1978 *E*, *S*, *I*, *W*, *R*, 1979 *I*, *W*, *E*, *S*, *R*, 1980 *W*, *E*, *S*, *I*, *SA*, *R*, 1981 *S*, *I*, *W*, *E*, *R*, *NZ* 1,2
Berty, D (Toulouse) 1990 *NZ* 2, 1992 *R*(R), 1993 *R*2
Besset, E (Grenoble) 1924 *S*
Besset, L (SCUF) 1914 *W*, *E*
Besson, M (CASG) 1924 *I*, 1925 *I*, *E*, 1926 *S*, *W*, 1927 *I*
Besson, P (Brive) 1963 *S*, *I*, *E*, 1965 *R*, 1968 *SA* 1
Bianchi, J (Toulon) 1986 *Arg* 1
Bichindaritz, J (Biarritz O) 1954 *It*, *Arg* 1,2
Bidart, L (La Rochelle) 1953 *W*
Biemouret, P (Agen) 1969 *E*, *W*, 1970 *I*, *W*, *E*, 1971 *W*, *SA* 1,2, *A* 1, 1972 *E*, *W*, *I* 2, *A* 2, *R*, 1973 *S*, *NZ*, *E*, *W*, *I*
Biénès, R (Cognac) 1950 *S*, *I*, *E*, *W*, 1951 *S*, *I*, *E*, *W*, 1952 *S*, *I*, *SA*, *W*, *E*, *It*, 1953 *S*, *I*, *E*, 1954 *S*, *I*, *NZ*, *W*, *E*, *Arg* 1,2, 1956 *S*, *I*, *W*, *It*, *E*
Bigot, C (Quillan) 1930 *S*, *E*, 1931 *I*, *S*
Bilbao, L (St Jean de Luz) 1978 *I*, 1979 *I*
Billac, E (Bayonne) 1920 *S*, *E*, *W*, *I*, *US*, 1921 *S*, *W*, 1922 *W*, 1923 *E*
Billière, M (Toulouse) 1968 *NZ* 3
Bioussa, A (Toulouse) 1924 *W*, *US*, 1925 *I*, *NZ*, *S*, *E*, 1926 *S*, *I*, *E*, 1928 *E*, *G*, *W*, 1929 *I*, *S*, *W*, *E*, 1930 *S*, *I*, *E*, *G*, *W*
Bioussa, C (Toulouse) 1913 *W*, *I*, 1914 *I*
Biraben, M (Dax) 1920 *W*, *I*, *US*, 1921 *S*, *W*, *E*, *I*, 1922 *S*, *E*, *I*
Blain, A (Carcassonne) 1934 *G*
Blanco, S (Biarritz O) 1980 *SA*, *R*, 1981 *S*, *W*, *E*, *A* 1, 2, *R*, *NZ* 1,2, 1982 *W*, *E*, *S*, *I*, *R*, *Arg* 1,2, 1983 *E*, *S*, *I*, *W*, 1984 *I*, *W*, *E*, *S*, *NZ* 1,2, *R*, 1985 *E*, *S*, *I*, *W*, *Arg* 1,2, 1986 *S*, *I*, *W*, *E*, *R* 1, *Arg* 2, *A*, *NZ* 1, *R* 2, *NZ* 2,3, 1987 *W*, *E*, *S*, *I*, [*S*, *R*, *Fj*, *A*, *NZ*], *R*, 1988 *E*, *S*, *I*, *W*, *Arg* 1,2,3,4, *R*, 1989 *I*, *W*, *E*, *S*, *NZ* 1,2, *B*, *A* 1, 1990 *E*, *S*, *I*, *R*, *A* 1,2,3, *NZ* 1,2, 1991 *S*, *I*, *W*1, *E*, *R*, *US*1,2, *W*2, [*R*, *Fj*, *C*, *E*]
Blond, J (SF) 1935 *G*, 1936 *G* 2, 1937 *G*, 1938 *G* 1, *R*, *G* 2
Blond, X (RCF) 1990 *A* 3, 1991 *S*, *I*, *W* 1, *E*, 1994 *NZ* 2(R)
Boffelli, V (Aurillac) 1971 *A* 2, *R*, 1972 *S*, *I* 1, 1973 *J*, *R*, 1974 *I*, *W*, *E*, *S*, *Arg* 1,2, *R*, *SA* 1,2, 1975 *W*, *S*, *I*
Bonal, J-M (Toulouse) 1968 *E*, *W*, *Cz*, *NZ* 2,3, *SA* 1, 2, *R*, 1969 *S*, *I*, *E*, *R*, 1970 *W*, *E*
Bonamy, R (SB) 1928 *A*, *I*
Boniface, A (Mont-de-Marsan) 1954 *I*, *NZ*, *W*, *E*, *It*, *Arg* 1,2, 1955 *S*, *I*, 1956 *S*, *I*, *W*, *It*, *Cz*, 1957 *S*, *I*, *W*, *R* 2, 1958 *S*, *E*, 1959 *E*, 1961 *NZ* 1,3, *A*, *R*, 1962 *E*, *W*, *I*, *It*, *R*, 1963 *S*, *I*, *E*, *W*, *It*, *R*, 1964 *S*, *NZ*, *E*, *W*, *It*, 1965 *W*, *It*, *R*, 1966 *S*, *I*, *E*, *W*
Boniface, G (Mont-de-Marsan) 1960 *W*, *I*, *It*, *R*, *Arg* 1, 2,3, 1961 *S*, *SA*, *E*, *W*, *It*, *I*, *NZ* 1,2,3, *R*, 1962 *R*, 1963 *S*, *I*, *E*, *W*, *It*, *R*, 1964 *S*, 1965 *S*, *I*, *E*, *W*, *It*, *R*, 1966 *S*, *I*, *E*, *W*
Bonnes, E (Narbonne) 1924 *W*, *R*, *US*
Bonneval, E (Toulouse) 1984 *NZ* 2 (R), 1985 *W*, *Arg* 1, 1986 *W*, *E*, *R* 1, *Arg* 1,2, *A*, *R* 2, *NZ* 2,3, 1987 *W*, *E*, *S*, *I*, [*Z*], 1988 *E*
Bonnus, F (Toulon) 1950 *S*, *I*, *E*, *W*
Bonnus, M (Toulon) 1937 *It*, 1938 *G* 1, *R*, *G* 2, 1940 *B*
Bontemps, D (La Rochelle) 1968 *SA* 2
Borchard, G (RCF) 1908 *E*, 1909 *E*, *W*, *I*, 1911 *I*
Borde, F (RCF) 1920 *I*, *US*, 1921 *S*, *W*, *E*, 1922 *S*, *W*, 1923 *S*, *I*, 1924 *E*, 1925 *I*, 1926 *E*
Bordenave, L (Toulon) 1948 *A*, *S*, *W*, *E*, 1949 *S*
Boubée, J (Tarbes) 1921 *S*, *E*, *I*, 1922 *E*, *W*, 1923 *E*, *I*, 1925 *NZ*, *S*
Boudreaux, R (SCUF) 1910 *W*, *S*
Bouet, D (Dax) 1989 *NZ* 1,2, *B*, *A* 2, 1990 *A* 3
Bouguyon, G (Grenoble) 1961 *SA*, *E*, *W*, *It*, *I*, *NZ* 1,2, 3, *A*
Boujet, C (Grenoble) 1968 *NZ* 2, *A* (R), *SA* 1
Bouquet, J (Bourgoin, Vienne) 1954 *S*, 1955 *E*, 1956 *S*, *I*, *W*, *It*, *E*, *Cz*, 1957 *S*, *E*, *W*, *R* 2, 1958 *S*, *E*, 1959 *S*, *It*, *W*, *I*, 1960 *S*, *E*, *W*, *I*, *R*, 1961 *S*, *SA*, *E*, *W*, *It*, *I*, *R*, 1962 *S*, *E*, *W*, *I*
Bourdeu, J R (Lourdes) 1952 *S*, *I*, *SA*, *W*, *E*, *It*, 1953 *S*, *I*, *E*
Bourgarel, R (Toulouse) 1969 *R*, 1970 *S*, *I*, *E*, *R*, 1971 *W*, *SA* 1,2, 1973 *S*
Bourguignon, G (Narbonne) 1988 *Arg* 3, 1989 *I*, *E*, *B*, *A* 1, 1990 *R*
Bousquet, A (Béziers) 1921 *E*, *I*, 1924 *R*
Bousquet, R (Albi) 1926 *M*, 1927 *I*, *S*, *W*, *E*, *G* 1, 1929 *W*, *E*, 1930 *W*
Boyau, M (SBUC) 1912 *I*, *S*, *W*, *E*, 1913 *W*, *I*
Boyer, P (Toulon) 1935 *G*
Branca, G (SF) 1928 *S*, 1929 *I*, *S*
Branlat, A (RCF) 1906 *NZ*, *E*, 1908 *W*
Brejassou, R (Tarbes) 1952 *S*, *I*, *SA*, *W*, *E*, 1953 *W*, *E*, 1954 *S*, *I*, *NZ*, 1955 *S*, *I*, *E*, *W*, *It*
Brethes, R (St Sever) 1960 *Arg* 2
Bringeon, A (Biarritz O) 1925 W
Brouzet, O (Grenoble) 1994 *S*, *NZ* 2(R), 1995 *E*, *S*, *I*
Brun, G (Vienne) 1950 *E*, *W*, 1951 *S*, *E*, *W*, 1952 *S*, *I*, *SA*, *W*, *E*, *It*, 1953 *E*, *W*, *It*
Bruneau, M (SBUC) 1910 *W*, *E*, 1913 *SA*, *E*
Brunet, Y (Perpignan) 1975 *SA* 1, 1977 *Arg* 1
Buchet, E (Nice) 1980 *R*, 1982 *E*, *R* (R), *Arg* 1,2
Buisson, H (see Empereur-Buisson)
Buonomo, Y (Béziers) 1971 *A* 2, *R*, 1972 *I* 1
Burgun, M (RCF) 1909 *I*, 1910 *W*, *S*, *I*, 1911 *S*, *E*, 1912 *I*, *S*, 1913 *S*, *E*, 1914 *E*
Bustaffa, D (Carcassonne) 1977 *Arg* 1,2, *NZ* 1,2, 1978 *W*, *R*, 1980 *W*, *E*, *S*, *SA*, *R*
Buzy, C-E (Lourdes) 1946 *K*, *W*, 1947 *S*, *I*, *W*, *E*, 1948 *I*, *A*, *S*, *W*, *E*, 1949 *S*, *I*, *E*, *W*, *Arg* 1,2

Cabanier, J-M (Montauban) 1963 *R*, 1964 *S*, *Fj*, 1965 *S*, *I*, *W*, *It*, *R*, 1966 *S*, *I*, *E*, *W*, *It*, *R*, 1967 *S*, *A*, *E*, *It*, *W*, *I*, *SA* 1,3, *NZ*, *R*, 1968 *S*, *I*
Cabannes, L (RCF) 1990 *NZ* 2(R), 1991 *S*, *I*, *W*1, *E*, *US*2, *W*2, [*R*, *Fj*, *C*, *E*], 1992 *W*, *E*, *S*, *I*, *R*, *Arg* 2, *SA* 1,2, 1993 *E*, *S*, *I*, *W*, *R*1, *SA*1,2, 1994 *E*, *S*, *C* 1, *NZ* 1,2, 1995 *W*, *E*, *S*
Cabrol, H (Béziers) 1972 *A* 1 (R), *A* 2, 1973 *J*, 1974 *SA* 2
Cadenat, J (SCUF) 1910 *S*, *E*, 1911 *W*, *I*, 1912 *W*, *E*, 1913 *I*
Cadieu, J-M (Toulouse) 1991 *R*, *US*1, [*R*, *Fj*, *C*, *E*], 1992 *W*, *I*, *R*, *Arg* 1,2, *SA* 1
Cahuc, F (St Girons) 1922 *S*
Califano, C (Toulouse) 1994 *NZ* 1,2, *C* 2, 1995 *W*, *E*, *S*, *I*
Cals, R (RCF) 1938 *G* 1
Calvo, G (Lourdes) 1961 *NZ* 1,3
Camberabero, D (La Voulte, Béziers) 1982 *R*, *Arg* 1,2, 1983 *E*, *W*, 1987 [*R*(R), *Z*, *Fj*(R), *A*, *NZ*], 1988 *I*, 1989 *B*, *A* 1, 1990 *W*, *S*, *I*, *R*, *A* 1,2,3, *NZ* 1,2, 1991 *S*, *I*, *W*1, *E*, *R*, *US*1,2, *W*2, [*R*, *Fj*, *C*], 1993 *E*, *S*, *I*
Camberabero, G (La Voulte) 1961 *NZ* 3, 1962 *R*, 1964 *R*, 1967 *A*, *E*, *It*, *W*, *I*, *SA* 1,3,4, 1968 *S*, *E*, *W*
Camberabero, L (La Voulte) 1964 *R*, 1965 *S*, *I*, 1966 *E*, *W*, 1967 *A*, *E*, *It*, *W*, *I*, 1968 *S*, *E*, *W*
Cambré, T (Oloron) 1920 *E*, *W*, *I*, *US*
Camel, A (Toulouse) 1928 *S*, *A*, *I*, *E*, *G*, *W*, 1929 *W*, *E*, *G*, 1930 *S*, *I*, *E*, *G*, *W*, 1935 *G*
Camel, M (Toulouse) 1929 *S*, *W*, *E*
Camicas, F (Tarbes) 1927 *G* 2, 1928 *S*, *I*, *E*, *G*, *W*, 1929 *I*, *S*, *W*, *E*
Camo, E (Villeneuve) 1931 *I*, *S*, *W*, *E*, *G*, 1932 *G*
Campaes, A (Lourdes) 1965 *W*, 1967 *NZ*, 1968 *S*, *I*, *E*, *W*, *Cz*, *NZ* 1,2, *A*, 1969 *S*, *W*, 1972 *R*, 1973 *NZ*
Campan, O (Agen) 1993 *SA*1(R), 2(R), *R*2(R)
Cantoni, J (Béziers) 1970 *W*, *R*, 1971 *S*, *I*, *E*, *W*, *SA* 1,

2, *A* 1, *R*, 1972 *S*, *I* 1, 1973 *S*, *NZ*, *W*, *I*, 1975 *W* (R)
Capdouze, J (Pau) 1964 *SA*, *Fj*, *R*, 1965 *S*, *I*, *E*
Capendeguy, J-M (Begles) 1967 *NZ*, *R*
Capitani, P (Toulon) 1954 *Arg* 1,2
Capmau, J-L (Toulouse) 1914 *E*
Carabignac, G (Agen) 1951 *S*, *I*, 1952 *SA*, *W*, *E*, 1953 *S*, *I*
Carbonne, J (Perpignan) 1927 *W*
Carminati, A (Béziers) 1986 *R* 2, *NZ* 2, 1987 [*R*, *Z*], 1988 *I*, *W*, *Arg* 1,2, 1989 *I*, *W*, *S*, *NZ* 1(R),2, *A* 2, 1990 *S*
Caron, L (Lyon O, Castres) 1947 *E*, 1948 *I*, *A*, *W*, *E*, 1949 *S*, *I*, *E*, *W*, *Arg* 1
Carpentier, M (Lourdes) 1980 *E*, *SA*, *R*, 1981 *S*, *I*, *A* 1, 1982 *E*, *S*
Carrère, C (Toulon) 1966 *R*, 1967 *S*, *A*, *E*, *W*, *I*, *SA* 1, 3,4, *NZ*, *R*, 1968 *S*, *I*, *E*, *W*, *Cz*, *NZ* 3, *A*, *R*, 1969 *S*, *I*, 1970 *S*, *I*, *W*, *E*, 1971 *E*, *W*
Carrère, J (Vichy, Toulon) 1956 *S*, 1957 *E*, *W*, *R* 2, 1958 *S*, *SA* 1,2, 1959 *I*
Carrère, R (Mont-de-Marsan) 1953 *E*, *It*
Casaux, L (Tarbes) 1959 *I*, *It*, 1962 *S*
Cassagne, P (Pau) 1957 *It*
Cassayet-Armagnac, A (Tarbes, Narbonne) 1920 *S*, *E*, *W*, *US*, 1921 *W*, *E*, *I*, 1922 *S*, *E*, *W*, 1923 *S*, *W*, *E*, *I*, 1924 *S*, *E*, *W*, *R*, *US*, 1925 *I*, *NZ*, *S*, *W*, 1926 *S*, *I*, *E*, *W*, *M*, 1927 *I*, *S*, *W*
Cassiède, M (Dax) 1961 *NZ* 3, *A*, *R*
Castets, J (Toulon) 1923 *W*, *E*, *I*
Caujolle, J (Tarbes) 1909 *E*, 1913 *SA*, *E*, 1914 *W*, *E*
Caunègre, R (SB) 1938 *R*, *G* 2
Caussade, A (Lourdes) 1978 *R*, 1979 *I*, *W*, *E*, *NZ* 1,2, *R*, 1980 *W*, *E*, *S*, 1981 *S* (R), *I*
Caussarieu, G (Pau) 1929 *I*
Cayrefourcq, E (Tarbes) 1921 *E*
Cazals, P (Mont-de-Marsan) 1961 *NZ* 1, *A*, *R*
Cazenave, A (Pau) 1927 *E*, *G* 1, 1928 *S*, *A*, *G*
Cazenave, F (RCF) 1950 *E*, 1952 *S*, 1954 *I*, *NZ*, *W*, *E*
Cecillon, M (Bourgoin) 1988 *I*, *W*, *Arg* 2,3,4, *R*, 1989 *I*, *E*, *NZ* 1,2, *A* 1, 1991 *S*, *I*, *E* (R), *R*, *US*1, *W*2, [*E*], 1992 *W*, *E*, *S*, *I*, *R*, *Arg* 1,2, *SA* 1,2, 1993 *E*, *S*, *I*, *W*, *R*1, *SA*1,2, *R*2, *A*1,2, 1994 *I*, *W*, *NZ* 1(R), 1995 *I*
Celaya, M (Biarritz O, SBUC) 1953 *E*, *W*, *It*, 1954 *I*, *E*, *It*, *Arg* 1,2, 1955 *S*, *I*, *E*, *W*, *It*, 1956 *S*, *I*, *W*, *It*, *E*, *Cz*, 1957 *S*, *I*, *E*, *W*, *R* 2, 1958 *S*, *E*, *A*, *W*, *It*, 1959 *S*, *E*, 1960 *S*, *E*, *W*, *I*, *R*, *Arg* 1,2,3, 1961 *S*, *SA*, *E*, *W*, *It*, *I*, *NZ* 1,2,3, *A*, *R*
Celhay, M (Bayonne) 1935 *G*, 1936 *G* 1, 1937 *G*, *It*, 1938 *G* 1, 1940 *B*
Cessieux, N (Lyon) 1906 *NZ*
Cester, E (TOEC, Valence) 1966 *S*, *I*, *E*, 1967 *W*, 1968 *S*, *I*, *E*, *W*, *Cz*, *NZ* 1,3, *A*, *SA* 1,2, *R*, 1969 *S*, *I*, *E*, *W*, 1970 *S*, *I*, *W*, *E*, 1971 *A* 1, 1972 *R*, 1973 *S*, *NZ*, *W*, *I*, *J*, *R*, 1974 *I*, *W*, *E*, *S*
Chaban-Delmas, J (CASG) 1945 *B* 2
Chabowski, H (Nice, Bourgoin) 1985 *Arg* 2, 1986 *R* 2, *NZ* 2, 1989 *B*(R)
Chadebech, P (Brive) 1982 *R*, *Arg* 1,2, 1986 *S*, *I*
Champ, E (Toulon) 1985 *Arg* 1,2, 1986 *I*, *W*, *E*, *R* 1, *Arg* 1,2, *A*, *NZ* 1, *R* 2, *NZ* 2,3, 1987 *W*, *E*, *S*, *I*, [*S*, *R*, *Fj*, *A*, *NZ*], *R*, 1988 *E*, *S*, *Arg* 1,3,4, *R*, 1989 *W*, *S*, *A* 1,2, 1990 *W*, *E*, *NZ* 1, 1991 *R*, *US*1, [*R*, *Fj*, *C*, *E*]
Chapuy, L (SF) 1926 *S*
Charpentier, G (SF) 1911 *E*, 1912 *W*, *E*
Charton, P (Montferrand) 1940 *B*
Charvet, D (Toulouse) 1986 *W*, *E*, *R* 1, *Arg* 1, *A*, *NZ* 1,3, 1987 *W*, *E*, *S*, *I*, [*S*, *R*, *Z*, *Fj*, *A*, *NZ*], *R*, 1989 *E*(R), 1990 *W*, *E*, 1991 *S*, *I*
Chassagne, J (Montferrand) 1938 *G* 1
Chatau, A (Bayonne) 1913 *SA*
Chaud, E (Toulon) 1932 *G*, 1934 *G*, 1935 *G*
Chenevay, C (Grenoble) 1968 *SA* 1
Chevallier, B (Montferrand) 1952 *S*, *I*, *SA*, *W*, *E*, *It*, 1953 *E*, *W*, *It*, 1954 *S*, *I*, *NZ*, *W*, *Arg* 1, 1955 *S*, *I*, *E*, *W*, *It*, 1956 *S*, *I*, *W*, *It*, *E*, *Cz*, 1957 *S*
Chiberry, J (Chambéry) 1955 *It*
Chilo, A (RCF) 1920 *S*, *W*, 1925 *I*, *NZ*
Cholley, G (Castres) 1975 *E*, *S*, *I*, *SA* 1,2, *Arg* 1,2, *R*, 1976 *S*, *I*, *W*, *E*, *A* 1,2, *R*, 1977 *W*, *E*, *S*, *I*, *Arg* 1,2, *NZ* 1,2, *R*, 1978 *E*, *S*, *I*, *W*, *R*, 1979 *I*, *S*
Choy, J (Narbonne) 1930 *S*, *I*, *E*, *G*, *W*, 1931 *I*, 1933 *G*, 1934 *G*, 1935 *G*, 1936 *G* 2
Cimarosti, J (Castres) 1976 *US* (R)
Clady, A (Lezignan) 1929 *G*, 1931 *I*, *S*, *E*, *G*
Clarac, H (St Girons) 1938 *G* 1
Claudel, R (Lyon) 1932 *G*, 1934 *G*
Clauzel, F (Béziers) 1924 *E*, *W*, 1925 *W*
Clavé, J (Agen) 1936 *G* 2, 1938 *R*, *G* 2
Claverie, H (Lourdes) 1954 *NZ*, *W*
Clément, G (RCF) 1931 *W*
Clément, J (RCF) 1921 *S*, *W*, *E*, 1922 *S*, *E*, *W*, *I*, 1923 *S*, *W*, *I*
Clemente, M (Oloron) 1978 *R*, 1980 *S*, *I*
Cluchague, L (Biarritz O) 1924 *S*, 1925 *E*
Coderc, J (Chalon) 1932 *G*, 1933 *G*, 1934 *G*, 1935 *G*, 1936 *G* 1
Codorniou, D (Narbonne) 1979 *NZ* 1,2, *R*, 1980 *W*, *E*, *S*, *I*, 1981 *S*, *W*, *E*, *A* 2, 1983 *E*, *S*, *I*, *W*, *A* 1,2, *R*, 1984 *I*, *W*, *E*, *S*, *NZ* 1,2, *R*, 1985 *E*, *S*, *I*, *W*, *Arg* 1,2
Coeurveille, C (Agen) 1992 *Arg* 1(R),2
Cognet, L (Montferrand) 1932 *G*, 1936 *G* 1,2, 1937 *G*, *It*
Colombier, J (St Junien) 1952 *SA*, *W*, *E*
Colomine, G (Narbonne) 1979 *NZ* 1
Combe, J (SF) 1910 *S*, *E*, *I*, 1911 *S*
Combes, G (Fumel) 1945 *B* 2
Communeau, M (SF) 1906 *NZ*, *E*, 1907 *E*, 1908 *E*, *W*, 1909 *E*, *W*, *I*, 1910 *S*, *E*, *I*, 1911 *S*, *E*, *I*, 1912 *I*, *S*, *W*, *E*, 1913 *SA*, *E*, *W*
Condom, J (Boucau, Biarritz O) 1982 *R*, 1983 *E*, *S*, *I*, *W*, *A* 1,2, *R*, 1984 *I*, *W*, *E*, *S*, *NZ* 1,2, *R*, 1985 *E*, *S*, *I*, *W*, *Arg* 1,2, 1986 *S*, *I*, *W*, *E*, *R* 1, *Arg* 1,2, *NZ* 1, *R* 2, *NZ* 2,3, 1987 *W*, *E*, *S*, *I*, [*S*, *R*, *Z*, *A*, *NZ*], *R*, 1988 *E*, *S*, *W*, *Arg* 1,2,3,4, *R*, 1989 *I*, *W*, *E*, *S*, *NZ* 1,2, *A* 1, 1990 *I*, *R*, *A* 2,3(R)
Conilh de Beyssac, J-J (SBUC) 1912 *I*, *S*, 1914 *I*, *W*, *E*
Constant, G (Perpignan) 1920 *W*
Coscolla, G (Béziers) 1921 *S*, *W*
Costantino, J (Montferrand) 1973 *R*
Costes, A (Montferrand) 1994 *C* 2
Costes, F (Montferrand) 1979 *E*, *S*, *NZ* 1,2, *R*, 1980 *W*, *I*
Couffignal, H (Colomiers) 1993 *R*1
Coulon, E (Grenoble) 1928 *S*
Courtiols, M (Bègles) 1991 *R*, *US*1, *W*2
Crabos, R (RCF) 1920 *S*, *E*, *W*, *I*, *US*, 1921 *S*, *W*, *E*, *I*, 1922 *S*, *E*, *W*, *I*, 1923 *S*, *I*, 1924 *S*, *I*
Crampagne, J (Begles) 1967 *SA* 4
Crancee, R (Lourdes) 1960 *Arg* 3, 1961 *S*
Crauste, M (RCF, Lourdes) 1957 *R* 1,2, 1958 *S*, *E*, *A*, *W*, *It*, *I*, 1959 *E*, *It*, *W*, *I*, 1960 *S*, *E*, *W*, *I*, *It*, *R*, *Arg* 1, 3, 1961 *S*, *SA*, *E*, *W*, *It*, *I*, *NZ* 1,2,3, *A*, *R*, 1962 *S*, *E*, *W*, *I*, *It*, *R*, 1963 *S*, *I*, *E*, *W*, *It*, *R*, 1964 *S*, *NZ*, *E*, *W*, *It*, *I*, *SA*, *Fj*, *R*, 1965 *S*, *I*, *E*, *W*, *It*, *R*, 1966 *S*, *I*, *E*, *W*, *It*
Cremaschi, M (Lourdes) 1980 *R*, 1981 *R*, *NZ* 1,2, 1982 *W*, *S*, 1983 *A* 1,2, *R*, 1984 *I*, *W*
Crichton, W H (Le Havre) 1906 *NZ*, *E*
Cristina, J (Montferrand) 1979 *R*
Cussac, P (Biarritz O) 1934 *G*
Cutzach, A (Quillan) 1929 *G*

Daguerre, F (Biarritz O) 1936 *G* 1
Daguerre, J (CASG) 1933 *G*
Dal Maso, M (Mont-de Marsan) 1988 *R*(R), 1990 *NZ* 2
Danion, J (Toulon) 1924 *I*
Danos, P (Toulon, Béziers) 1954 *Arg* 1,2, 1957 *R* 2, 1958 *S*, *E*, *W*, *It*, *I*, *SA* 1,2, 1959 *S*, *E*, *It*, *W*, *I*, 1960 *S*, *E*
Darbos, P (Dax) 1969 *R*
Darracq, R (Dax) 1957 *It*
Darrieussecq, A (Biarritz O) 1973 *E*
Darrieussecq, J (Mont-de-Marsan) 1953 *It*
Darrouy, C (Mont-de-Marsan) 1957 *I*, *E*, *W*, *It*, *R* 1, 1959 *E*, 1961 *R*, 1963 *S*, *I*, *E*, *W*, *It*, 1964 *NZ*, *E*, *W*, *It*, *I*, *SA*, *Fj*, *R*, 1965 *S*, *I*, *E*, *It*, *R*, 1966 *S*, *I*, *E*, *W*, *It*, *R*, 1967 *S*, *A*, *E*, *It*, *W*, *I*, *SA* 1,2,4
Daudignon, G (SF) 1928 *S*
Dauga, B (Mont-de-Marsan) 1964 *S*, *NZ*, *E*, *W*, *It*, *I*, *SA*, *Fj*, *R*, 1965 *S*, *I*, *E*, *W*, *It*, *R*, 1966 *S*, *I*, *E*, *W*, *It*, *R*, 1967 *S*, *A*, *E*, *It*, *W*, *I*, *SA* 1,2,3,4, *NZ*, *R*, 1968 *S*, *I*, *NZ* 1,2,3, *A*, *SA* 1,2, *R*, 1969 *S*, *I*, *E*, *R*, 1970 *S*, *I*, *W*, *E*, *R*, 1971 *S*, *I*, *E*, *W*, *SA* 1,2, *A* 1,2, *R*, 1972 *S*, *I* 1, *W*
Dauger, J (Bayonne) 1945 *B* 1,2, 1953 *S*
Daulouede, P (Tyrosse) 1937 *G*, *It*, 1938 *G* 1, 1940 *B*
Decamps, P (RCF) 1911 *S*
Dedet, J (SF) 1910 *S*, *E*, *I*, 1911 *W*, *I*, 1912 *S*, 1913 *E*, *I*
Dedeyn, P (RCF) 1906 *NZ*
Dedieu, P (Béziers) 1963 *E*, *It*, 1964 *W*, *It*, *I*, *SA*, *Fj*,

R, 1965 *S*, *I*, *E*, *W*
De Gregorio, J (Grenoble) 1960 *S*, *E*, *W*, *I*, *It*, *R*, *Arg* 1,2, 1961 *S*, *SA*, *E*, *W*, *It*, *I*, 1962 *S*, *E*, *W*, 1963 *S*, *W*, *It*, 1964 *NZ*, *E*
Dehez, J-L (Agen) 1967 *SA* 2, 1969 *R*
de Jouvencel, E (SF) 1909 *W*, *I*
de Laborderie, M (RCF) 1921 *I*, 1922 *I*, 1925 *W*, *E*
Delage, C (Agen) 1983 *S*, *I*
de Malherbe, H (CASG) 1932 *G*, 1933 *G*
de Malmann, R (RCF) 1908 *E*, *W*, 1909 *E*, *W*, *I*, 1910 *E*, *I*
de Muizon, J J (SF) 1910 *I*
Delaigue, G (Toulon) 1973 *J*, *R*
Delaigue, Y (Toulon) 1994 *S*, *NZ* 2(R), *C* 2, 1995 *I*
Delque, A (Toulouse) 1937 *It*, 1938 *G* 1, *R*, *G* 2
de Rougemont, M (Toulon) 1995 *E* (t)
Descamps, P (SB) 1927 *G* 2
Desclaux, F (RCF) 1949 *Arg* 1,2, 1953 *It*
Desclaux, J (Perpignan) 1934 *G*, 1935 *G*, 1936 *G* 1,2, 1937 *G*, *It*, 1938 *G* 1, *R*, *G* 2, 1945 *B* 1
Deslandes, C (RCF) 1990 *A* 1, *NZ* 2, 1991 *W*1, 1992 *R*, *Arg* 1,2
Desnoyer, L (Brive) 1974 *R*
Destarac, L (Tarbes) 1926 *S*, *I*, *E*, *W*, *M*, 1927 *W*, *E*, *G* 1,2
Desvouges, R (SF) 1914 *W*
Detrez, P-E (Nîmes) 1983 *A* 2 (R), 1986 *Arg* 1(R),2, *A* (R), *NZ* 1
Devergie, T (Nîmes) 1988 *R*, 1989 *NZ* 1,2, *B*, *A* 2, 1990 *W*, *E*, *S*, *I*, *R*, *A* 1,2,3, 1991 *US*2, *W*2, 1992 *R* (R), *Arg* 2(R)
Deygas, M (Vienne) 1937 *It*
Deylaud, C (Toulouse) 1992 *R*, *Arg* 1,2, *SA* 1, 1994 *C* 1, *NZ* 1,2, 1995 *W*, *E*, *S*
Dintrans, P (Tarbes) 1979 *NZ* 1,2, *R*, 1980 *E*, *S*, *I*, *SA*, *R*, 1981 *S*, *I*, *W*, *E*, *A* 1,2, *R*, *NZ* 1,2, 1982 *W*, *E*, *S*, *I*, *R*, *Arg* 1,2, 1983 *E*, *W*, *A* 1,2, *R*, 1984 *I*, *W*, *E*, *S*, *NZ* 1,2, *R*, 1985 *E*, *S*, *I*, *W*, *Arg* 1,2, 1987 [*R*], 1988 *Arg* 1,2,3, 1989 *W*, *E*, *S*, 1990 *R*
Dizabo, P (Tyrosse) 1948 *A*, *S*, *E*, 1949 *S*, *I*, *E*, *W*, *Arg* 2, 1950 *S*, *I*, 1960 *Arg* 1,2,3
Domec, A (Carcassonne) 1929 *W*
Domec, H (Lourdes) 1953 *W*, *It*, 1954 *S*, *I*, *NZ*, *W*, *E*, *It*, 1955 *S*, *I*, *E*, *W*, 1956 *I*, *W*, *It*, 1958 *E*, *A*, *W*, *It*, *I*
Domenech, A (Vichy, Brive) 1954 *W*, *E*, *It*, 1955 *S*, *I*, *E*, *W*, 1956 *S*, *I*, *W*, *It*, *E*, *Cz*, 1957 *S*, *I*, *E*, *W*, *It*, *R* 1,2, 1958 *S*, *E*, *It*, 1959 *It*, 1960 *S*, *E*, *W*, *I*, *It*, *R*, *Arg* 1,2,3, 1961 *S*, *SA*, *E*, *W*, *It*, *I*, *NZ* 1,2,3, *A*, *R*, 1962 *S*, *E*, *W*, *I*, *It*, *R*, 1963 *W*, *It*
Domercq, J (Bayonne) 1912 *I*, *S*
Dorot, J (RCF) 1935 *G*
Dospital, P (Bayonne) 1977 *R*, 1980 *I*, 1981 *S*, *I*, *W*, *E*, 1982 *I*, *R*, *Arg* 1,2, 1983 *E*, *S*, *I*, *W*, 1984 *E*, *S*, *NZ* 1,2, *R*, 1985 *E*, *S*, *I*, *W*, *Arg* 1
Dourthe, C (Dax) 1966 *R*, 1967 *S*, *A*, *E*, *W*, *I*, *SA* 1,2, 3, *NZ*, 1968 *W*, *NZ* 3, *SA* 1,2, 1969 *W*, 1971 *SA* 2 (R), *R*, 1972 *I* 1,2, *A* 1,2, *R*, 1973 *S*, *NZ*, *E*, 1974 *I*, *Arg* 1,2, *SA* 1,2, 1975 *W*, *E*, *S*
Doussau, E (Angoulême) 1938 *R*
Droitecourt, M (Montferrand) 1972 *R*, 1973 *NZ* (R), *E*, 1974 *E*, *S*, *Arg* 1, *SA* 2, 1975 *SA* 1,2, *Arg* 1,2, *R*, 1976 *S*, *I*, *W*, *A* 1, 1977 *Arg* 2
Dubertrand, A (Montferrand) 1971 *A* 2, *R*, 1972 *I* 2, 1974 *I*, *W*, *E*, *SA* 2, 1975 *Arg* 1,2, *R*, 1976 *S*, *US*
Dubois, D (Begles) 1971 *S*
Dubroca, D (Agen) 1979 *NZ* 2, 1981 *NZ* 2 (R), 1982 *E*, *S*, 1984 *W*, *E*, *S*, 1985 *Arg* 2, 1986 *S*, *I*, *W*, *E*, *R* 1, *Arg* 2, *A*, *NZ* 1, *R* 2, *NZ* 2,3, 1987 *W*, *E*, *S*, *I*, [*S*, *Z*, *Fj*, *A*, *NZ*], *R*, 1988 *E*, *S*, *I*, *W*
Duché, A (Limoges) 1929 *G*
Duclos, A (Lourdes) 1931 *S*
Ducousso, J (Tarbes) 1925 *S*, *W*, *E*
Dufau, G (RCF) 1948 *I*, *A*, 1949 *I*, *W*, 1950 *S*, *E*, *W*, 1951 *S*, *I*, *E*, *W*, 1952 *SA*, *W*, 1953 *S*, *I*, *E*, *W*, 1954 *S*, *I*, *NZ*, *W*, *E*, *It*, 1955 *S*, *I*, *E*, *W*, *It*, 1956 *S*, *I*, *W*, *It*, 1957 *S*, *I*, *E*, *W*, *It*, *R* 1
Dufau, J (Biarritz) 1912 *I*, *S*, *W*, *E*
Duffaut, Y (Agen) 1954 *Arg* 1,2
Duffour, R (Tarbes) 1911 *W*
Dufourcq, J (SBUC) 1906 *NZ*, *E*, 1907 *E*, 1908 *W*
Duhard, Y (Bagnères) 1980 *E*
Duhau, J (SF) 1928 *I*, 1930 *I*, *G*, 1931 *I*, *S*, *W*, 1933 *G*
Dulaurens, C (Toulouse) 1926 *I*, 1928 *S*, 1929 *W*
Duluc, A (Béziers) 1934 *G*
Du Manoir, Y LeP (RCF) 1925 *I*, *NZ*, *S*, *W*, *E*, 1926 *S*, 1927 *I*, *S*
Dupont, C (Lourdes) 1923 *S*, *W*, *I*, 1924 *S*, *I*, *W*, *R*, *US*, 1925 *S*, 1927 *E*, *G* 1,2, 1928 *A*, *G*, *W*, 1929 *I*
Dupont, J-L (Agen) 1983 *S*
Dupont, L (RCF) 1934 *G*, 1935 *G*, 1936 *G* 1,2, 1938 *R*, *G* 2
Dupouy, A (SB) 1924 *W*, *R*
Duprat, B (Bayonne) 1966 *E*, *W*, *It*, *R*, 1967 *S*, *A*, *E*, *SA* 2,3, 1968 *S*, *I*, 1972 *E*, *W*, *I* 2, *A* 1
Dupré, P (RCF) 1909 *W*
Dupuy, J (Tarbes) 1956 *S*, *I*, *W*, *It*, *E*, *Cz*, 1957 *S*, *I*, *E*, *W*, *It*, *R* 2, 1958 *S*, *E*, *SA* 1,2, 1959 *S*, *E*, *It*, *W*, *I*, 1960 *W*, *I*, *It*, *Arg* 1,3, 1961 *S*, *SA*, *E*, *NZ* 2, *R*, 1962 *S*, *E*, *W*, *I*, *It*, 1963 *W*, *It*, *R*, 1964 *S*
Du Souich, C J (see Judas du Souich)
Dutin, B (Mont-de-Marsan) 1968 *NZ* 2, *A*, *SA* 2, *R*
Dutour, F X (Toulouse) 1911 *E*, *I*, 1912 *S*, *W*, *E*, 1913 *S*
Dutrain, H (Toulouse) 1945 *W*, 1946 *B*, *I*, 1947 *E*, 1949 *I*, *E*, *W*, *Arg* 1
Dutrey, J (Lourdes) 1940 *B*
Duval, R (SF) 1908 *E*, *W*, 1909 *E*, 1911 *E*, *W*, *I*

Echavé, L (Agen) 1961 *S*
Elissalde, E (Bayonne) 1936 *G* 2, 1940 *B*
Elissalde, J-P (La Rochelle) 1980 *SA*, *R*, 1981 *A* 1,2, *R*
Empereur-Buisson, H (Béziers) 1931 *E*, *G*
Erbani, D (Agen) 1981 *A* 1,2, *NZ* 1,2, 1982 *Arg* 1,2, 1983 *S* (R), *I*, *W*, *A* 1,2, *R*, 1984 *W*, *E*, *R*, 1985 *E*, *W*(R), *Arg* 2, 1986 *S*, *I*, *W*, *E*, *R* 1, *Arg* 2, *NZ* 1,2(R), 3, 1987 *W*, *E*, *S*, *I*, [*S*, *R*, *Fj*, *A*, *NZ*], 1988 *E*, *S*, 1989 *I*(R), *W*, *E*, *S*, *NZ* 1, *A* 2, 1990 *W*, *E*
Escaffre, P (Narbonne) 1933 *G*, 1934 *G*
Escommier, M (Montelimar) 1955 *It*
Esponda, J-M (RCF) 1967 *SA* 1,2, *R*, 1968 *NZ* 1,2, *SA* 2, *R*, 1969 *S*, *I*(R), *E*
Estève, A (Béziers) 1971 *SA* 1, 1972 *I* 1, *E*, *W*, *I* 2, *A* 2, *R*, 1973 *S*, *NZ*, *E*, *I*, 1974 *I*, *W*, *E*, *S*, *R*, *SA* 1,2, 1975 *W*, *E*
Estève, P (Narbonne, Lavelanet) 1982 *R*, *Arg* 1,2, 1983 *E*, *S*, *I*, *W*, *A* 1,2, *R*, 1984 *I*, *W*, *E*, *S*, *NZ* 1,2, *R*, 1985 *E*, *S*, *I*, *W*, 1986 *S*, *I*, 1987 [*S*, *Z*]
Etcheberry, J (Rochefort, Cognac) 1923 *W*, *I*, 1924 *S*, *I*, *E*, *W*, *R*, *US*, 1926 *S*, *I*, *E*, *M*, 1927 *I*, *S*, *W*, *G* 2
Etchenique, J-M (Biarritz O) 1974 *R*, *SA* 1, 1975 *E*, *Arg* 2
Etchepare, A (Bayonne) 1922 *I*
Etcheverry, M (Pau) 1971 *S*, *I*
Eutrope, A (SCUF) 1913 *I*

Fabre, E (Toulouse) 1937 *It*, 1938 *G* 1,2
Fabre, J (Toulouse) 1963 *S*, *I*, *E*, *W*, *It*, 1964 *S*, *NZ*, *E*
Fabre, L (Lezignan) 1930 *G*
Fabre, M (Béziers) 1981 *A* 1, *R*, *NZ* 1,2, 1982 *I*, *R*
Failliot, P (RCF) 1911 *S*, *W*, *I*, 1912 *I*, *S*, *E*, 1913 *E*, *W*
Fargues, G (Dax) 1923 *I*
Fauré, F (Tarbes) 1914 *I*, *W*, *E*
Fauvel, J-P (Tulle) 1980 *R*
Favre, M (Lyon) 1913 *E*, *W*
Ferrand, L (Chalon) 1940 *B*
Ferrien, R (Tarbes) 1950 *S*, *I*, *E*, *W*
Finat, R (CASG) 1932 *G*, 1933 *G*
Fite, R (Brive) 1963 *W*, *It*
Forestier, J (SCUF) 1912 *W*
Forgues, F (Bayonne) 1911 *S*, *E*, *W*, 1912 *I*, *W*, *E*, 1913 *S*, *SA*, *W*, 1914 *I*, *E*
Fort, J (Agen) 1967 *It*, *W*, *I*, *SA* 1,2,3,4
Fourcade, G (BEC) 1909 *E*, *W*
Foures, H (Toulouse) 1951 *S*, *I*, *E*, *W*
Fournet, F (Montferrand) 1950 *W*
Fouroux, J (La Voulte) 1972 *I* 2, *R*, 1974 *W*, *E*, *Arg* 1,2, *R*, *SA* 1,2, 1975 *W*, *Arg* 1, *R*, 1976 *S*, *I*, *W*, *E*, *US*, *A* 1, 1977 *W*, *E*, *S*, *I*, *Arg* 1,2, *NZ* 1,2, *R*
Francquenelle, A (Vaugirard) 1911 *S*, 1913 *W*, *I*
Furcade, R (Perpignan) 1952 *S*

Gabernet, S (Toulouse) 1980 *E*, *S*, 1981 *S*, *I*, *W*, *E*, *A* 1,2, *R*, *NZ* 1,2, 1982 *I*, 1983 *A* 2, *R*
Gachassin, J (Lourdes) 1961 *S*, *I*, 1963 *R*, 1964 *S*, *NZ*, *E*, *W*, *It*, *I*, *SA*, *Fj*, *R*, 1965 *S*, *I*, *E*, *W*, *It*, *R*, 1966 *S*, *I*, *E*, *W*, 1967 *S*, *A*, *It*, *W*, *I*, *NZ*, 1968 *I*, *E*, 1969 *S*, *I*
Galau, H (Toulouse) 1924 *S*, *I*, *E*, *W*, *US*
Galia, J (Quillan) 1927 *E*, *G* 1,2, 1928 *S*, *A*, *I*, *E*, *W*, 1929 *I*, *E*, *G*, 1930 *S*, *I*, *E*, *G*, *W*, 1931 *S*, *W*, *E*, *G*
Gallart, P (Béziers) 1990 *R*, *A* 1,2(R),3, 1992 *S*, *I*, *R*,

Arg 1,2, *SA* 1,2, *Arg*, 1994 *I*, *W*, *E*, 1995 *I*(t)
Gallion, J (Toulon) 1978 *E*, *S*, *I*, *W*, 1979 *I*, *W*, *E*, *S*, *NZ* 2, *R*, 1980 *W*, *E*, *S*, *I*, 1983 *A* 1,2, *R*, 1984 *I*, *W*, *E*, *S*, *R*, 1985 *E*, *S*, *I*, *W*, 1986 *Arg* 2
Galthié, F (Colomiers) 1991 *R*, *US*1, [*R*, *Fj*, *C*, *E*], 1992 *W*, *E*, *S*, *R*, *Arg*, 1994 *I*, *W*, *E*
Galy, J (Perpignan) 1953 *W*
Garuet-Lempirou, J-P (Lourdes) 1983 *A* 1,2, *R*, 1984 *I*, *NZ* 1,2, *R*, 1985 *E*, *S*, *I*, *W*, *Arg* 1, 1986 *S*, *I*, *W*, *E*, *R* 1, *Arg* 1, *NZ* 1, *R* 2, *NZ* 2,3, 1987 *W*, *E*, *S*, *I*, [*S*, *R*, *Fj*, *A*, *NZ*], 1988 *E*, *S*, *Arg* 1,2, *R*, 1989 *E*(R), *S*, *NZ* 1,2, 1990 *W*, *E*
Gasc, J (Graulhet) 1977 *NZ* 2
Gasparotto, G (Montferrand) 1976 *A* 2, *R*
Gauby, G (Perpignan) 1956 *Cz*
Gaudermen, P (RCF) 1906 *E*
Gayraud, W (Toulouse) 1920 *I*
Geneste, R (BEC) 1945 *B* 1, 1949 *Arg* 2
Genet, J-P (RCF) 1992 *S*, *I*, *R*
Gensane, R (Béziers) 1962 *S*, *E*, *W*, *I*, *It*, *R*, 1963 *S*
Gerald, G (RCF) 1927 *E*, *G* 2, 1928 *S*, 1929 *I*, *S*, *W*, *E*, *G*, 1930 *S*, *I*, *E*, *G*, *W*, 1931 *I*, *S*, *E*, *G*
Gerintes, G (CASG) 1924 *R*, 1925 *I*, 1926 *W*
Geschwind, P (RCF) 1936 *G* 1,2
Giacardy, M (SBUC) 1907 *E*
Gimbert, P (Bègles) 1991 *R*, *US*1, 1992 *W*, *E*
Gommes, J (RCF) 1909 *I*
Gonnet, C-A (Albi) 1921 *E*, *I*, 1922 *E*, *W*, 1924 *S*, *E*, 1926 *S*, *I*, *E*, *W*, *M*, 1927 *I*, *S*, *W*, *E*, *G* 1
Gonzalez, J-M (Bayonne) 1992 *Arg* 1,2, *SA* 1,2, *Arg*, 1993 *R*1, *SA*1,2, *R*2, *A*1,2, 1994 *I*, *W*, *E*, *S*, *C* 1, *NZ* 1,2, *C* 2, 1995 *W*, *E*, *S*, *I*
Got, R (Perpignan) 1920 *I*, *US*, 1921 *S*, *W*, 1922 *S*, *E*, *W*, *I*, 1924 *I*, *E*, *W*, *R*, *US*
Gourdon, J-F (RCF, Bagnères) 1974 *S*, *Arg* 1,2, *R*, *SA* 1,2, 1975 *W*, *E*, *S*, *I*, *R*, 1976 *S*, *I*, *W*, *E*, 1978 *E*, *S*, 1979 *W*, *E*, *S*, *R*, 1980 *I*
Gourragne, J-F (Béziers) 1990 *NZ* 2, 1991 *W*1
Goyard, A (Lyon U) 1936 *G* 1,2, 1937 *G*, *It*, 1938 *G* 1, *R*, *G* 2
Graciet, R (SBUC) 1926 *I*, *W*, 1927 *S*, *G* 1, 1929 *E*, 1930 *W*
Graou, S (Auch) 1992 *Arg*(R), 1993 *SA*1,2, *R*2, *A*2(R)
Gratton, J (Agen) 1984 *NZ* 2, *R*, 1985 *E*, *S*, *I*, *W*, *Arg* 1,2, 1986 *S*, *NZ* 1
Graule, V (Arl Perpignan) 1926 *I*, *E*, *W*, 1927 *S*, *W*, 1931 *G*
Greffe, M (Grenoble) 1968 *W*, *Cz*, *NZ* 1,2, *SA* 1
Griffard, J (Lyon U) 1932 *G*, 1933 *G*, 1934 *G*
Gruarin, A (Toulon) 1964 *W*, *It*, *I*, *SA*, *Fj*, *R*, 1965 *S*, *I*, *E*, *W*, *It*, 1966 *S*, *I*, *E*, *W*, *It*, *R*, 1967 *S*, *A*, *E*, *It*, *W*, *I*, *NZ*, 1968 *S*, *I*
Guelorget, P (RCF) 1931 *E*, *G*
Guichemerre, A (Dax) 1920 *E*, 1921 *E*, *I*, 1923 *S*
Guilbert, A (Toulon) 1975 *E*, *S*, *I*, *SA* 1,2, 1976 *A* 1, 1977 *Arg* 1,2, *NZ* 1,2, *R*, 1979 *I*, *W*, *E*
Guillemin, P (RCF) 1908 *E*, *W*, 1909 *E*, *I*, 1910 *W*, *S*, *E*, *I*, 1911 *S*, *E*, *W*
Guilleux, P (Agen) 1952 *SA*, *It*
Guiral, M (Agen) 1931 *G*, 1932 *G*, 1933 *G*

Haget, A (PUC) 1953 *E*, 1954 *I*, *NZ*, *E*, *Arg* 2, 1955 *E*, *W*, *It*, 1957 *I*, *E*, *It*, *R* 1, 1958 *It*, *SA* 2
Haget, F (Agen, Biarritz O) 1974 *Arg* 1,2, 1975 *SA* 2, *Arg* 1,2, *R*, 1976 *S*, 1978 *S*, *I*, *W*, *R*, 1979 *I*, *W*, *E*, *S*, *NZ* 1,2, *R*, 1980 *W*, *S*, *I*, 1984 *S*, *NZ* 1,2, *R*, 1985 *E*, *S*, *I*, 1986 *S*, *I*, *W*, *E*, *R* 1, *Arg* 1, *A*, *NZ* 1, 1987 *S*, *I*, [*R*, *Fj*]
Haget, H (CASG) 1928 *S*, 1930 *G*
Halet, R (Strasbourg) 1925 *NZ*, *S*, *W*
Harislur-Arthapignet, P (Tarbes) 1988 *Arg* 4(R)
Harize, D (Cahors, Toulouse) 1975 *SA* 1,2, 1976 *A* 1,2, *R*, 1977 *W*, *E*, *S*, *I*
Hauc, J (Toulon) 1928 *E*, *G*, 1929 *I*, *S*, *G*
Hauser, M (Lourdes) 1969 *E*
Hedembaigt, M (Bayonne) 1913 *S*, *SA*, 1914 *W*
Hericé, D (Begles) 1950 *I*
Herrero, A (Toulon) 1963 *R*, 1964 *NZ*, *E*, *W*, *It*, *I*, *SA*, *Fj*, *R*, 1965 *S*, *I*, *E*, *W*, 1966 *W*, *It*, *R*, 1967 *S*, *A*, *E*, *It*, *I*, *R*
Herrero, B (Nice) 1983 *I*, 1986 *Arg* 1
Heyer, F (Montferrand) 1990 *A* 2
Hiquet, J-C (Agen) 1964 *E*
Hoche, M (PUC) 1957 *I*, *E*, *W*, *It*, *R* 1
Hondagné-Monge, M (Tarbes) 1988 *Arg* 2 (R)
Hontas, P (Biarritz) 1990 *S*, *I*, *R*, 1991 *R*, 1992 *Arg*, 1993 *E*, *S*, *I*, *W*
Hortoland, J-P (Béziers) 1971 *A* 2
Houblain, H (SCUF) 1909 *E*, 1910 *W*
Houdet, R (SF) 1927 *S*, *W*, *G* 1, 1928 *G*, *W*, 1929 *I*, *S*, *E*, 1930 *S*, *E*
Hourdebaigt, A (SBUC) 1909 *I*, 1910 *W*, *S*, *E*, *I*
Hubert, A (ASF) 1906 *E*, 1907 *E*, 1908 *E*, *W*, 1909 *E*, *W*, *I*
Hueber, A (Lourdes, Toulon) 1990 *A* 3, *NZ* 1, 1991 *US*2, 1992 *I*, *Arg* 1,2, *SA* 1,2, 1993 *E*, *S*, *I*, *W*, *R*1, *SA*1,2, *R*2, *A*1,2
Hutin, R (CASG) 1927 *I*, *S*, *W*

Icard, J (SF) 1909 *E*, *W*
Iguiniz, E (Bayonne) 1914 *E*
Ihingoué, D (BEC) 1912 *I*, *S*
Imbernon, J-F (Perpignan) 1976 *I*, *W*, *E*, *US*, *A* 1, 1977 *W*, *E*, *S*, *I*, *Arg* 1,2, *NZ* 1,2, 1978 *E*, *R*, 1979 *I*, 1981 *S*, *I*, *W*, *E*, 1982 *I*, 1983 *I*, *W*
Iraçabal, J (Bayonne) 1968 *NZ* 1,2, *SA* 1, 1969 *S*, *I*, *W*, *R*, 1970 *S*, *I*, *W*, *E*, *R*, 1971 *W*, *SA* 1,2, *A* 1, 1972 *E*, *W*, *I* 2, *A* 2, *R*, 1973 *S*, *NZ*, *E*, *W*, *I*, *J*, 1974 *I*, *W*, *E*, *S*, *Arg* 1,2, *SA* 2 (R)
Isaac, H (RCF) 1907 *E*, 1908 *E*
Ithurra, E (Biarritz O) 1936 *G* 1,2, 1937 *G*

Janeczek, T (Tarbes) 1982 *Arg* 1,2, 1990 *R*
Janik, K (Toulouse) 1987 *R*
Jarasse, A (Brive) 1945 *B* 1
Jardel, J (SB) 1928 *I*, *E*
Jaureguy, A (RCF, Toulouse, SF) 1920 *S*, *E*, *W*, *I*, *US*, 1922 *S*, *W*, 1923 *S*, *W*, *E*, *I*, 1924 *S*, *W*, *R*, *US*, 1925 *I*, *NZ*, 1926 *S*, *E*, *W*, *M*, 1927 *I*, *E*, 1928 *S*, *A*, *E*, *G*, *W*, 1929 *I*, *S*, *E*
Jaureguy, P (Toulouse) 1913 *S*, *SA*, *W*, *I*
Jeangrand, M-H (Tarbes) 1921 *I*
Jeanjean, P (Toulon) 1948 *I*
Jérôme, G (SF) 1906 *NZ*, *E*
Joinel, J-L (Brive) 1977 *NZ* 1, 1978 *R*, 1979 *I*, *W*, *E*, *S*, *NZ* 1,2, *R*, 1980 *W*, *E*, *S*, *I*, *SA*, 1981 *S*, *I*, *W*, *E*, *R*, *NZ* 1,2, 1982 *E*, *S*, *I*, *R*, 1983 *E*, *S*, *I*, *W*, *A* 1,2, *R*, 1984 *I*, *W*, *E*, *S*, *NZ* 1,2, 1985 *S*, *I*, *W*, *Arg* 1, 1986 *S*, *I*, *W*, *E*, *R* 1, *Arg* 1,2, *A*, 1987 [*Z*]
Jol, M (Biarritz O) 1947 *S*, *I*, *W*, *E*, 1949 *S*, *I*, *E*, *W*, *Arg* 1,2
Judas du Souich, C (SCUF) 1911 *W*, *I*
Junquas, L (Tyrosse) 1945 *B* 1,2, *W*, 1946 *B*, *I*, *K*, *W*, 1947 *S*, *I*, *W*, *E*, 1948 *S*, *W*

Kaczorowksi, D (Le Creusot) 1974 *I* (R)
Kaempf, A (St Jean-de-Luz) 1946 *B*

Labadie, P (Bayonne) 1952 *S*, *I*, *SA*, *W*, *E*, *It*, 1953 *S*, *I*, *It*, 1954 *S*, *I*, *NZ*, *W*, *E*, *Arg* 2, 1955 *S*, *I*, *E*, *W*, 1956 *I*, 1957 *I*
Labarthete, R (Pau) 1952 *S*
Labazuy, A (Lourdes) 1952 *I*, 1954 *S*, *W*, 1956 *E*, 1958 *A*, *W*, *I*, 1959 *S*, *E*, *It*, *W*
Laborde, C (RCF) 1962 *It*, *R*, 1963 *R*, 1964 *SA*, 1965 *E*
Lacans, P (Béziers) 1980 *SA*, 1981 *W*, *E*, *A* 2, *R*, 1982 *W*
Lacassagne, H (SBUC) 1906 *NZ*, 1907 *E*
Lacaussade, R (Begles) 1948 *A*, *S*
Lacaze, C (Lourdes, Angoulême) 1961 *NZ* 2,3, *A*, *R*, 1962 *E*, *W*, *I*, *It*, 1963 *W*, *R*, 1964 *S*, *NZ*, *E*, 1965 *It*, *R*, 1966 *S*, *I*, *E*, *W*, *It*, *R*, 1967 *S*, *E*, *SA* 1,3,4, *R*, 1968 *S*, *E*, *W*, *Cz*, *NZ* 1, 1969 *E*
Lacaze, H (Périgueux) 1928 *I*, *G*, *W*, 1929 *I*, *W*
Lacaze, P (Lourdes) 1958 *SA* 1,2, 1959 *S*, *E*, *It*, *W*, *I*
Lacazedieu, C (Dax) 1923 *W*, *I*, 1928 *A*, *I*, 1929 *S*
Lacombe, B (Agen) 1989 *B*, 1990 *A* 2
Lacome, M (Pau) 1960 *Arg* 2
Lacoste, R (Tarbes) 1914 *I*, *W*, *E*
Lacrampe, F (Béziers) 1949 *Arg* 2
Lacroix, P (Mont-de-Marsan, Agen) 1958 *A*, 1960 *W*, *I*, *It*, *R*, *Arg* 1,2,3, 1961 *S*, *SA*, *E*, *W*, *I*, *NZ* 1,2,3, *A*, *R*, 1962 *S*, *E*, *W*, *I*, *R*, 1963 *S*, *I*, *E*, *W*
Lacroix, T (Dax) 1989 *A* 1(R), 2, 1991 *W*1(R), 2(R), [*R*, *C*(R), *E*], 1992 *SA* 2, 1993 *E*, *S*, *I*, *W*, *SA*1,2, *R*2, *A*1,2, 1994 *I*, *W*, *E*, *S*, *C* 1, *NZ* 1,2, *C* 2, 1995 *W*, *E*, *S*
Lafarge, Y (Montferrand) 1978 *R*, 1979 *NZ* 1, 1981 *I* (R)
Laffitte, R (SCUF) 1910 *W*, *S*
Laffont, H (Narbonne) 1926 *W*

Lafond, A (Bayonne) 1922 *E*
Lafond, J-B (RCF) 1983 *A* 1, 1985 *Arg* 1,2, 1986 *S, I, W, E, R* 1, 1987 *I* (R), 1988 *W*, 1989 *I, W, E*, 1990 *W, A* 3(R), *NZ* 2, 1991 *S, I, W*1, *E, R, US*1, *W*2, [*R*(R), *Fj, C, E*], 1992 *W, E, S, I*(R), *SA* 2, 1993 *E, S, I, W*
Lagisquet, P (Bayonne) 1983 *A* 1,2, *R*, 1984 *I, W, NZ* 1,2, 1986 *R* 1 (R), *Arg* 1,2, *A, NZ* 1, 1987 [*S, R, Fj, A, NZ*], *R*, 1988 *S, I, W, Arg* 1,2,3,4, *R*, 1989 *I, W, E, S, NZ* 1,2, *B, A* 1,2, 1990 *W, E, S, I, A* 1,2,3, 1991 *S, I, US*2, [*R*]
Lagrange, J-C (RCF) 1966 *It*
Lalande, M (RCF) 1923 *S, W, I*
Lane, G (RCF) 1906 *NZ, E*, 1907 *E*, 1908 *E, W*, 1909 *E, W, I*, 1910 *W, E*, 1911 *S, W*, 1912 *I, W, E*, 1913 *S*
Langlade, J-C (Hyères) 1990 *R, A* 1, *NZ* 1
Laporte, G (Graulhet) 1981 *I, W, E, R, NZ* 1,2, 1986 *S, I, W, E, R* 1, *Arg* 1, *A* (R), 1987 [*R, Z*(R), *Fj*]
Larreguy, P (Bayonne) 1954 *It*
Larribau, J (Périgueux) 1912 *I, S, W, E*, 1913 *S*, 1914 *I, E*
Larrieu, J (Tarbes) 1920 *I, US*, 1921 *W*, *1923 S, W, E, I*
Larrieux, M (SBUC) 1927 *G* 2
Larrue, H (Carmaux) 1960 *W, I, It, R, Arg* 1,2,3
Lasaosa, P (Dax) 1950 *I*, 1952 *S, I, E, It*, 1955 *It*
Lascubé, G (Agen) 1991 *S, I, W*1, *E, US*2, *W*2, [*R, Fj, C, E*], 1992 *W, E*
Lassegue, J-B (Toulouse) 1946 *W*, 1947 *S, I, W*, 1948 *W*, 1949 *I, E, W, Arg* 1
Lasserre, F (René) (Bayonne, Cognac, Grenoble) 1914 *I*, 1920 *S*, 1921 *S, W, I*, 1922 *S, E, W, I*, 1923 *W, E*, 1924 *S, I, R, US*
Lasserre, J-C (Dax) 1963 *It*, 1964 *S, NZ, E, W, It, I, Fj*, 1965 *W, It, R*, 1966 *R*, 1967 *S*
Lasserre, M (Agen) 1967 *SA* 2,3, 1968 *E, W, Cz, NZ* 3, *A, SA* 1,2, 1969 *S, I, E*, 1970 *E*, 1971 *E, W*
Laterrade, G (Tarbes) 1910 *E, I*, 1911 *S, E, I*
Laudouar, J (Soustons, SBUC) 1961 *NZ* 1,2, *R*, 1962 *I, R*
Lauga, P (Vichy) 1950 *S, I, E, W*
Laurent, A (Biarritz O) 1925 *NZ, S, W, E*, 1926 *W*
Laurent, J (Bayonne) 1920 *S, E, W*
Laurent, M (Auch) 1932 *G*, 1933 *G*, 1934 *G*, 1935 *G*, 1936 *G* 1
Lavail, G (Perpignan) 1937 *G*, 1940 *B*
Lavaud, R (Carcassonne) 1914 *I, W*
Lavergne, P (Limoges) 1950 *S*
Lavigne, B (Agen) 1984 *R*, 1985 *E*
Lavigne, J (Dax) 1920 *E, W*
Lazies, H (Auch) 1954 *Arg* 2, 1955 *It*, 1956 *E*, 1957 *S*
Le Bourhis, R (La Rochelle) 1961 *R*
Lecointre, M (Nantes) 1952 *It*
Le Droff, J (Auch) 1963 *It, R*, 1964 *S, NZ, E*, 1970 *E, R*, 1971 *S, I*
Lefevre, R (Brive) 1961 *NZ* 2
Lefort, J-B (Biarritz O) 1938 *G* 1
Le Goff, R (Métro) 1938 *R, G* 2
Legrain, M (SF) 1909 *I*, 1910 *I*, 1911 *S, E, W, I*, 1913 *S, SA, E, I*, 1914 *I, W*
Lemeur, Y (RCF) 1993 *R*1
Lenient, J-J (Vichy) 1967 *R*
Lepatey, J (Mazamet) 1954 *It*, 1955 *S, I, E, W*
Lepatey, L (Mazamet) 1924 *S, I, E*
Lescarboura, J-P (Dax) 1982 *W, E, S, I*, 1983 *A* 1,2, *R*, 1984 *I, W, E, S, NZ* 1,2, *R*, 1985 *E, S, I, W, Arg* 1, 2, 1986 *Arg* 2, *A, NZ* 1, *R* 2, *NZ* 2, 1988 *S, W*, 1990 *R*
Lesieur, E (SF) 1906 *E*, 1908 *E, W*, 1909 *E, W, I*, 1910 *S, E, I*, 1911 *E, I*, 1912 *W*
Leuvielle, M (SBUC) 1908 *W*, 1913 *S, SA, E, W*, 1914 *W, E*
Levasseur, R (SF) 1925 *W, E*
Levée, H (RCF) 1906 *NZ*
Lewis, E W (Le Havre) 1906 *E*
Lhermet, J-M (Montferrand) 1990 *S, I*, 1993 *R*1
Libaros, G (Tarbes) 1936 *G* 1, 1940 *B*
Lira, M (La Voulte) 1962 *R*, 1963 *I, E, W, It, R*, 1964 *W, It, I, SA*, 1965 *S, I, R*
Llari, (Carcassonne) 1926 *S*
Lobies, J (RCF) 1921 *S, W, E*
Lombard, F (Narbonne) 1934 *G*, 1937 *It*
Lombarteix, R (Montferrand) 1938 *R, G* 2
Londios, J (Montauban) 1967 *SA* 3
Loppy, L (Toulon) 1993 *R*2
Lorieux, A (Grenoble, Aix) 1981 *A* 1, *R, NZ* 1,2, 1982 *W*, 1983 *A* 2, *R*, 1984 *I, W, E*, 1985 *Arg* 1,2(R), 1986 *R* 2, *NZ* 2,3, 1987 *W, E*, [*S, Z, Fj, A, NZ*], 1988 *S, I, W, Arg* 1,2,4, 1989 *W, A* 2
Loury, A (RCF) 1927 *E, G* 1,2, 1928 *S, A, I*
Loustau, M (Dax) 1923 *E*
Lubin-Lebrère, M-F (Toulouse) 1914 *I, W, E*, 1920 *S, E, W, I, US*, 1921 *S*, 1922 *S, E, W*, 1924 *W, US*, 1925 *I*
Lubrano, A (Béziers) 1972 *A* 2, 1973 *S*
Lux, J-P (Tyrosse, Dax) 1967 *E, It, W, I, SA* 1,2,4, *R*, 1968 *I, E, Cz, NZ* 3, *A, SA* 1,2, 1969 *S, I, E*, 1970 *S, I, W, E, R*, 1971 *S, I, E, W, A* 1,2, 1972 *S, I* 1, *E, W, I* 2, *A* 1,2, *R*, 1973 *S, NZ, E*, 1974 *I, W, E, S, Arg* 1,2, 1975 *W*

Macabiau, A (Perpignan) 1994 *S, C* 1
Maclos, P (SF) 1906 *E*, 1907 *E*
Magnanou, C (RCF) 1923 *E*, 1925 *W, E*, 1926 *S*, 1929 *S, W*, 1930 *S, I, E, W*
Magnol, L (Toulouse) 1928 *S*, 1929 *S, W, E*
Magois, H (La Rochelle) 1968 *SA* 1,2, *R*
Majerus, R (SF) 1928 *W*, 1929 *I, S*, 1930 *S, I, E, G, W*
Malbet, J-C (Agen) 1967 *SA* 2,4
Maleig, A (Oloron) 1979 *W, E, NZ* 2, 1980 *W, E, SA, R*
Malquier, Y (Narbonne) 1979 *S*
Manterola, T (Lourdes) 1955 *It*, 1957 *R* 1
Mantoulan, C (Pau) 1959 *I*
Marcet, J (Albi) 1925 *I, NZ, S, W, E*, 1926 *I, E*
Marchal, J-F (Lourdes) 1979 *S, R*, 1980 *W, S, I*
Marchand, R (Poitiers) 1920 *S, W*
Marfaing, M (Toulouse) 1992 *R, Arg* 1
Marocco, P (Montferrand) 1986 *S, I, W, E, R* 1, *Arg* 1,2, *A*, 1988 *Arg* 4, 1989 *I*, 1990 *E*(R), *NZ* 1(R), 1991 *S, I, W*1, *E, US*2, [*R, Fj, C, E*]
Marot, A (Brive) 1969 *R*, 1970 *S, I, W*, 1971 *SA* 1, 1972 *I* 2, 1976 *A* 1
Marquesuzaa, A (RCF) 1958 *It, SA* 1,2, 1959 *S, E, It, W*, 1960 *S, E, Arg* 1
Marracq, H (Pau) 1961 *R*
Martin, C (Lyon) 1909 *I*, 1910 *W, S*
Martin, H (SBUC) 1907 *E*, 1908 *W*
Martin, J-L (Béziers) 1971 *A* 2, *R*, 1972 *S, I* 1
Martin, L (Pau) 1948 *I, A, S, W, E*, 1950 *S*
Martine, R (Lourdes) 1952 *S, I, It*, 1953 *It*, 1954 *S, I, NZ, W, E, It, Arg* 2, 1955 *S, I, W*, 1958 *A, W, It, I, SA* 1,2, 1960 *S, E, Arg* 3, 1961 *S, It*
Martinez, G (Toulouse) 1982 *W, E, S, Arg* 1,2, 1983 *E, W*
Mas, F (Béziers) 1962 *R*, 1963 *S, I, E, W*
Maso, J (Perpignan, Narbonne) 1966 *It, R*, 1967 *S, R*, 1968 *S, W, Cz, NZ* 1,2,3, *A, R*, 1969 *S, I, W*, 1971 *SA* 1,2, *R*, 1972 *E, W, A* 2, 1973 *W, I, J, R*
Massare, J (PUC) 1945 *B* 1,2, *W*, 1946 *B, I, W*
Massé, A (SBUC) 1908 *W*, 1909 *E, W*, 1910 *W, S, E, I*
Masse, H (Grenoble) 1937 *G*
Matheu-Cambas, J (Agen) 1945 *W*, 1946 *B, I, K, W*, 1947 *S, I, W, E*, 1948 *I, A, S, W, E*, 1949 *S, I, E, W, Arg* 1,2, 1950 *E, W*, 1951 *S, I*
Mauduy, G (Périgueux) 1957 *It, R* 1,2, 1958 *S, E*, 1961 *W, It*
Mauran, J (Castres) 1952 *SA, W, E, It*, 1953 *I, E*
Mauriat, P (Lyon) 1907 *E*, 1908 *E, W*, 1909 *W, I*, 1910 *W, S, E, I*, 1911 *S, E, W, I*, 1912 *I, S*, 1913 *S, SA, W, I*
Maurin, G (ASF) 1906 *E*
Maury, A (Toulouse) 1925 *I, NZ, S, W, E*, 1926 *S, I, E*
Mayssonnié, A (Toulouse) 1908 *E, W*, 1910 *W*
Mazas, L (Colomiers) 1992 *Arg*
Melville, E (Toulon) 1990 *I*(R), *A* 1,2,3, *NZ* 1, 1991 *US*2
Menrath, R (SCUF) 1910 *W*
Menthiller, Y (Romans) 1964 *W, It, SA, R*, 1965 *E*
Meret, F (Tarbes) 1940 *B*
Mericq, S (Agen) 1959 *I*, 1960 *S, E, W*, 1961 *I*
Merle, O (Grenoble, Montferrand) 1993 *SA*1,2, *R*2, *A* 1,2, 1994 *I, W, E, S, C* 1, *NZ* 1,2, *C* 2, 1995 *W, I*
Merquey, J (Toulon) 1950 *S, I, E, W*
Mesnel, F (RCF) 1986 *NZ* 2(R),3, 1987 *W, E, S, I*, [*S, Z, Fj, A, NZ*], *R*, 1988 *E, Arg* 1,2,3,4, *R*, 1989 *I, W, E, S, NZ* 1, *A* 1,2, 1990 *E, S, I, A* 2,3, *NZ* 1,2, 1991 *S, I, W*1, *E, R, US*1,2, *W*2, [*R, Fj, C, E*], 1992 *W, E, S, I, SA* 1,2, 1993 *E*(R), *W*, 1995 *I*
Mesny, P (RCF, Grenoble) 1979 *NZ* 1,2, 1980 *SA, R*, 1981 *I, W* (R), *A* 1,2, *R, NZ* 1,2, 1982 *I, Arg* 1,2
Meyer, G-S (Périgueux) 1960 *S, E, It, R, Arg* 2
Meynard, J (Cognac) 1954 *Arg* 1, 1956 *Cz*
Mias, L (Mazamet) 1951 *S, I, E, W*, 1952 *I, SA, W, E, It*, 1953 *S, I, W, It*, 1954 *S, I, NZ, W*, 1957 *R* 2, 1958

S, E, A, W, I, SA 1,2, 1959 *S, It, W, I*
Milliand, P (Grenoble) 1936 *G* 2, 1937 *G, It*
Minjat, R (Lyon) 1945 *B* 1
Mir, J-H (Lourdes) 1967 *R*, 1968 *I*
Mir, J-P (Lourdes) 1967 *A*
Modin, R (Brive) 1987 [*Z*]
Moga, A-M-A (Begles) 1945 *B* 1,2, *W*, 1946 *B, I, K, W*, 1947 *S, I, W, E*, 1948 *I, A, S, W, E*, 1949 *S, I, E, W, Arg* 1,2
Mommejat, B (Cahors, Albi) 1958 *It, I, SA* 1,2, 1959 *S, E, It, W, I*, 1960 *S, E, I, R*, 1962 *S, E, W, I, It, R*, 1963 *S, I, W*
Moncla, F (RCF, Pau) 1956 *Cz*, 1957 *I, E, W, It, R* 1, 1958 *SA* 1,2, 1959 *S, E, It, W, I*, 1960 *S, E, W, I, It, R, Arg* 1,2,3, 1961 *S, SA, E, W, It, I, NZ* 1,2,3
Monié, R (Perpignan) 1956 *Cz*, 1957 *E*
Monier, R (SBUC) 1911 *I*, 1912 *S*
Monniot, M (RCF) 1912 *W, E*
Montade, A (Perpignan) 1925 *I, NZ, S, W*, 1926 *W*
Montlaur, P (Agen) 1992 *E*(R), 1994 *S*(R)
Moraitis, B (Toulon) 1969 *E, W*
Morel, A (Grenoble) 1954 *Arg* 2
Morere, J (Toulouse) 1927 *E, G* 1, 1928 *S, A*
Moscato, V (Bègles) 1991 *R, US*1, 1992 *W, E*
Mougeot, C (Bègles) 1992 *W, E, Arg*
Mouniq, P (Toulouse) 1911 *S, E, W, I*, 1912 *I, E*, 1913 *S, SA, E*
Moure, H (SCUF) 1908 *E*
Moureu, P (Béziers) 1920 *I, US*, 1921 *W, E, I*, 1922 *S, W, I*, 1923 *S, W, E, I*, 1924 *S, I, E, W*, 1925 *E*
Mournet, A (Bagnères) 1981 *A* 1 (R)
Mouronval, F (SF) 1909 *I*
Muhr, A H (RCF) 1906 *NZ, E*, 1907 *E*
Murillo, G (Dijon) 1954 *It, Arg* 1

Namur, R (Toulon) 1931 *E, G*
Noble, J-C (La Voulte) 1968 *E, W, Cz, NZ* 3, *A, R*
Normand, A (Toulouse) 1957 *R* 1
Novès, G (Toulouse) 1977 *NZ* 1,2, *R*, 1978 *W, R*, 1979 *I, W*
Ntamack, E (Toulouse) 1994 *W, C*1, *NZ* 1,2, *C* 2, 1995 *W, I*

Olive, D (Montferrand) 1951 *I*, 1952 *I*
Ondarts, P (Biarritz O) 1986 *NZ* 3, 1987 *W, E, S, I*, [*S, Z, Fj, A, NZ*], *R*, 1988 *E, I, W, Arg* 1,2,3,4, *R*, 1989 *I, W, E, NZ* 1,2, *A* 2, 1990 *W, E, S, I, R*(R), *NZ* 1,2, 1991 *S, I, W*1, *E, US*2, *W*2, [*R, Fj, C, E*]
Orso, J-C (Nice, Toulon) 1982 *Arg* 1,2, 1983 *E, S, A* 1, 1984 *E* (R), *S, NZ* 1, 1985 *I* (R), *W*, 1988 *I*
Othats, J (Dax) 1960 *Arg* 2,3
Ougier, S (Toulouse) 1992 *R, Arg* 1, 1993 *E*(R)

Paco, A (Béziers) 1974 *Arg* 1,2, *R, SA* 1,2, 1975 *W, E, Arg* 1,2, *R*, 1976 *S, I, W, E, US, A* 1,2, *R*, 1977 *W, E, S, I, NZ* 1,2, *R*, 1978 *E, S, I, W, R*, 1979 *I, W, E, S*, 1980 *W*
Palat, J (Perpignan) 1938 *G* 2
Palmié, M (Béziers) 1975 *SA* 1,2, *Arg* 1,2, *R*, 1976 *S, I, W, E, US*, 1977 *W, E, S, I, Arg* 1,2, *NZ* 1,2, *R*, 1978 *E, S, I, W*
Paoli, R (see Simonpaoli)
Paparemborde, R (Pau) 1975 *SA* 1,2, *Arg* 1,2, *R*, 1976 *S, I, W, E, US, A* 1,2, *R*, 1977 *W, E, S, I, Arg* 1, *NZ* 1,2, 1978 *E, S, I, W, R*, 1979 *I, W, E, S, NZ* 1,2, *R*, 1980 *W, E, S, SA, R*, 1981 *S, I, W, E, A* 1,2, *R, NZ* 1,2, 1982 *W, I, R, Arg* 1,2, 1983 *E, S, I, W*
Pardo, L (Hendaye) 1924 *I, E*
Pardo, L (Bayonne) 1980 *SA, R*, 1981 *S, I, W, E, A* 1, 1982 *W, E, S*, 1983 *A* 1 (R), 1985 *S, I, Arg* 2
Pargade, J-H (Lyon U) 1953 *It*
Paries, L (Biarritz O) 1968 *SA* 2, *R*, 1970 *S, I, W*, 1975 *E, S, I*
Pascalin, P (Mont-de-Marsan) 1950 *I, E, W*, 1951 *S, I, E, W*
Pascarel, J-R (TOEC) 1912 *W, E*, 1913 *S, SA, E, I*
Pascot, J (Perpignan) 1922 *S, E, I*, 1923 *S*, 1926 *I*, 1927 *G* 2
Paul, R (Montferrand) 1940 *B*
Pauthe, G (Graulhet) 1956 *E*
Pebeyre, E-J (Fumel, Brive) 1945 *W*, 1946 *I, K, W*, 1947 *S, I, W, E*
Pebeyre, M (Vichy, Montferrand) 1970 *E, R*, 1971 *I, SA* 1,2, *A* 1, 1973 *W*
Pecune, J (Tarbes) 1974 *W, E, S*, 1975 *Arg* 1,2, *R*, 1976 *I, W, E, US*
Pedeutour, P (Begles) 1980 *I*
Pellissier, L (RCF) 1928 *A, I, E, G, W*
Penaud, A (Brive) 1992 *W, E, S, I, R, Arg* 1,2, *SA* 1,2, *Arg*, 1993 *R*1, *SA*1,2, *R*2, *A*1,2, 1994 *I, W, E*
Peron, P (RCF) 1975 *SA* 1,2
Perrier, P (Bayonne) 1982 *W, E, S, I* (R)
Pesteil, J-P (Béziers) 1975 *SA* 1, 1976 *A* 2, *R*
Petit, C (Lorrain) 1931 *W*
Peyrelade, H (Tarbes) 1940 *B*
Peyroutou, G (Périgueux) 1911 *S, E*
Phliponeau, J-F (Montferrand) 1973 *W, I*
Piazza, A (Montauban) 1968 *NZ* 1, *A*
Picard, T (Montferrand) 1985 *Arg* 2, 1986 *R* 1 (R), *Arg* 2
Pierrot, G (Pau) 1914 *I, W, E*
Pilon, J (Périgueux) 1949 *E*, 1950 *E*
Piqué, J (Pau) 1961 *NZ* 2,3, *A*, 1962 *S, It*, 1964 *NZ, E, W, It, I, SA, Fj, R*, 1965 *S, I, E, W, It*
Piquemal, M (Tarbes) 1927 *I, S*, 1929 *I, G*, 1930 *S, I, E, G, W*
Piquiral, E (RCF) 1924 *S, I, E, W, R, US*, 1925 *E*, 1926 *S, I, E, W, M*, 1927 *I, S, W, E, G* 1,2, 1928 *E*
Piteu, R (Pau) 1921 *S, W, E, I*, 1922 *S, E, W, I*, 1923 *E*, 1924 *E*, 1925 *I, NZ, W, E*, 1926 *E*
Plantefol, A (RCF) 1967 *SA* 2,3,4, *NZ, R*, 1968 *E, W, Cz, NZ* 2, 1969 *E, W*
Plantey, S (RCF) 1961 *A*, 1962 *It*
Podevin, G (SF) 1913 *W, I*
Poeydebasque, F (Bayonne) 1914 *I, W*
Poirier, A (SCUF) 1907 *E*
Pomathios, M (Agen, Lyon U, Bourg) 1948 *I, A, S, W, E*, 1949 *S, I, E, W, Arg* 1,2, 1950 *S, I, W*, 1951 *S, I, E, W*, 1952 *W, E*, 1953 *S, I, W*, 1954 *S*
Pons, P (Toulouse) 1920 *S, E, W*, 1921 *S, W*, 1922 *S*
Porra, M (Lyon) 1931 *I*
Porthault, A (RCF) 1951 *S, E, W*, 1952 *I*, 1953 *S, I, It*
Portolan, C (Toulouse) 1986 *A*, 1989 *I, E*
Potel, A (Begles) 1932 *G*
Prat, J (Lourdes) 1945 *B* 1,2, *W*, 1946 *B, I, K, W*, 1947 *S, I, W, E*, 1948 *I, A, S, W, E*, 1949 *S, I, E, W, Arg* 1, 2, 1950 *S, I, E, W*, 1951 *S, E, W*, 1952 *S, I, SA, W, E, It*, 1953 *S, I, E, W, It*, 1954 *S, I, NZ, W, E, It*, 1955 *S, I, E, W, It*
Prat, M (Lourdes) 1951 *I*, 1952 *S, I, SA, W, E*, 1953 *S, I, E*, 1954 *I, NZ, W, E, It*, 1955 *S, I, E, W, It*, 1956 *I, W, It, Cz*, 1957 *S, I, W, It, R* 1, 1958 *A, W, I*
Prevost, A (Albi) 1926 *M*, 1927 *I, S, W*
Prin-Clary, J (Cavaillon, Brive) 1945 *B* 1,2, *W*, 1946 *B, I, K, W*, 1947 *S, I, W*
Puech, L (Toulouse) 1920 *S, E, I*, 1921 *E, I*
Puget, M (Toulouse) 1961 *It*, 1966 *S, I, It*, 1967 *SA* 1,3,4, *NZ*, 1968 *Cz, NZ* 1,2, *SA* 1,2, *R*, 1969 *E, R*, 1970 *W*
Puig, A (Perpignan) 1926 *S, E*
Pujol, A (SOE Toulouse) 1906 *NZ*
Pujolle, M (Nice) 1989 *B, A* 1, 1990 *S, I, R, A* 1,2, *NZ* 2

Quaglio, A (Mazamet) 1957 *R* 2, 1958 *S, E, A, W, I, SA* 1,2, 1959 *S, E, It, W, I*
Quilis, A (Narbonne) 1967 *SA* 1,4, *NZ*, 1970 *R*, 1971 *I*

Ramis, R (Perpignan) 1922 *E, I*, 1923 *W*
Rancoule, H (Lourdes, Toulon, Tarbes) 1955 *E, W, It*, 1958 *A, W, It, I, SA* 1, 1959 *S, It, W*, 1960 *I, It, R, Arg* 1,2, 1961 *SA, E, W, It, NZ* 1,2, 1962 *S, E, W, I, It*
Rapin, A (SBUC) 1938 *R*
Raymond, F (Toulouse) 1925 *S*, 1927 *W*, 1928 *I*
Raynal, F (Perpignan) 1935 *G*, 1936 *G* 1,2, 1937 *G, It*
Raynaud, F (Carcassonne) 1933 *G*
Razat, J-P (Agen) 1962 *R*, *1963 S, I, R*
Rebujent, R (RCF) 1963 *E*
Revailler, D (Graulhet) 1981 *S, I, W, E, A* 1,2, *R, NZ* 1,2, 1982 *W, S, I, R, Arg* 1
Revillon, J (RCF) 1926 *I, E*, 1927 *S*
Ribère, E (Perpignan, Quillan) 1924 *I*, 1925 *I, NZ, S*, 1926 *S, I, W, M*, 1927 *I, S, W, E, G* 1,2, 1928 *S, A, I, E, G, W*, 1929 *I, E, G*, 1930 *S, I, E, W*, 1931 *I, S, W, E, G*, 1932 *G*, 1933 *G*
Rives, J-P (Toulouse, RCF) 1975 *E, S, I, Arg* 1,2, *R*, 1976 *S, I, W, E, US, A* 1,2, *R*, 1977 *W, E, S, I, Arg* 1,2, *R*, 1978 *E, S, I, W, R*, 1979 *I, W, E, S, NZ* 1,2, *R*, 1980 *W, E, S, I, SA*, 1981 *S, I, W, E, A* 2, 1982 *W, E, S, I, R*, 1983 *E, S, I, W, A* 1,2, *R*, 1984 *I, W, E, S*

Rochon, A (Montferrand) 1936 *G* 1
Rodrigo, M (Mauléon) 1931 *I, W*
Rodriguez, L (Mont-de-Marsan, Montferrand, Dax) 1981 *A* 1,2, *R, NZ* 1,2, 1982 *W, E, S, I, R,* 1983 *E, S,* 1984 *I, NZ* 1,2, *R,* 1985 *E, S, I, W,* 1986 *Arg* 1, *A, R* 2, *NZ* 2,3 1987 *W, E, S, I,* [*S, Z, Fj, A, NZ*], *R,* 1988 *E, S, I, W, Arg* 1,2,3,4, *R,* 1989 *I, E, S, NZ* 1,2, *B, A* 1, 1990 *W, E, S, I, NZ* 1
Rogé, L (Béziers) 1952 *It,* 1953 *E, W, It,* 1954 *S, Arg* 1,2, 1955 *S, I,* 1956 *W, It, E,* 1957 *S,* 1960 *S, E*
Rollet, J (Bayonne) 1960 *Arg* 3, 1961 *NZ* 3, *A,* 1962 *It,* 1963 *I*
Romero, H (Montauban) 1962 *S, E, W, I, It, R,* 1963 *E*
Romeu, J-P (Montferrand) 1972 *R,* 1973 *S, NZ, E, W, I, R,* 1974 *W, E, S, Arg* 1,2, *R, SA* 1,2 (R), 1975 *W, SA* 2, *Arg* 1,2, *R,* 1976 *S, I, W, E, US,* 1977 *W, E, S, I, Arg* 1,2, *NZ* 1,2, *R*
Roques, A (Cahors) 1958 *A, W, It, I, SA* 1,2, 1959 *S, E, W, I,* 1960 *S, E, W, I, It, Arg* 1,2,3, 1961 *S, SA, E, W, It, I,* 1962 *S, E, W, I, It,* 1963 *S*
Roques, J-C (Brive) 1966 *S, I, It, R*
Rossignol, J-C (Brive) 1972 *A* 2
Rouan, J (Narbonne) 1953 *S, I*
Roucaries, G (Perpignan) 1956 *S*
Rouffia, L (Narbonne) 1945 *B* 2, *W,* 1946 *W,* 1948 *I*
Rougerie, J (Montferrand) 1973 *J*
Rougé-Thomas, P (Toulouse) 1989 *NZ* 1,2
Roujas, F (Tarbes) 1910 *I*
Roumat, O (Dax) 1989 *NZ* 2(R), *B,* 1990 *W, E, S, I, R, A* 1,2,3, *NZ* 1,2, 1991 *S, I, W*1, *E, R, US*1, *W*2, [*R, Fj, C, E*], 1992 *W*(R), *E*(R), *S, I, SA* 1,2, *Arg,* 1993 *E, S, I, W, R*1, *SA*1,2, *R*2, *A*1,2, 1994 *I, W, E, C* 1, *NZ* 1,2, *C* 2, 1995 *W, E, S*
Rousie, M (Villeneuve) 1931 *S, G,* 1932 *G,* 1933 *G*
Rousset, G (Béziers) 1975 *SA* 1, 1976 *US*
Ruiz, A (Tarbes) 1968 *SA* 2, *R*
Rupert, J-J (Tyrosse) 1963 *R,* 1964 *S, Fj,* 1965 *E, W, It,* 1966 *S, I, E, W, It,* 1967 *It, R,* 1968 *S*

Sadourny, J-L (Colomiers) 1991 *W*2(R), [*C*(R)], 1992 *E*(R), *S, I, Arg* 1(R),2, *SA* 1,2, 1993 *R*1, *SA*1,2, *R*2, *A*1,2, 1994 *I, W, E, S, C* 1, *NZ* 1,2, *C* 2, 1995 *W, E, S, I*
Sagot, P (SF) 1906 *NZ,* 1908 *E,* 1909 *W*
Sahuc, A (Métro) 1945 *B* 1,2
Sahuc, F (Toulouse) 1936 *G* 2
Saint-André, P (Montferrand) 1990 *R, A* 3, *NZ* 1,2, 1991 *I*(R), *W*1, *E, US*1,2, *W*2, [*R, Fj, C, E*], 1992 *W, E, S, I, R, Arg* 1,2, *SA* 1,2, 1993 *E, S, I, W, SA*1,2, *A*1,2, 1994 *I, W, E, S, C* 1, *NZ* 1,2, *C* 2, 1995 *W, E, S, I*
Saisset, O (Béziers) 1971 *R,* 1972 *S, I* 1, *A* 1,2, 1973 *S, NZ, E, W, I, J, R,* 1974 *I, Arg* 2, *SA* 1,2, 1975 *W*
Salas, P (Narbonne) 1979 *NZ* 1,2, *R,* 1980 *W, E,* 1981 *A* 1, 1982 *Arg* 2
Saliné, R (Perpignan) 1923 *E*
Sallefranque, M (Dax) 1981 *A* 2, 1982 *W, E, S*
Salut, J (TOEC) 1966 *R,* 1967 *S,* 1968 *I, E, Cz, NZ* 1, 1969 *I*
Samatan, R (Agen) 1930 *S, I, E, G, W,* 1931 *I, S, W, E, G*
Sanac, A (Perpignan) 1952 *It,* 1953 *S, I,* 1954 *E,* 1956 *Cz,* 1957 *S, I, E, W, It*
Sangalli, F (Narbonne) 1975 *I, SA* 1,2, 1976 *S, A* 1,2, *R,* 1977 *W, E, S, I, Arg* 1,2, *NZ* 1,2
Sanz, H (Narbonne) 1988 *Arg* 3,4, *R,* 1989 *A* 2, 1990 *S, I, R, A* 1,2, *NZ* 2, 1991 *W*2
Sappa, M (Nice) 1973 *J, R,* 1977 *R*
Sarrade, R (Pau) 1929 *I*
Saux, J-P (Pau) 1960 *W, It, Arg* 1,2, 1961 *SA, E, W, It, I, NZ* 1,2,3, *A,* 1962 *S, E, W, I, It,* 1963 *S, I, E, It*
Savitsky, M (La Voulte) 1969 *R*
Savy, M (Montferrand) 1931 *I, S, W, E,* 1936 *G* 1
Sayrou, J (Perpignan) 1926 *W, M,* 1928 *E, G, W,* 1929 *S, W, E, G*
Scohy, R (BEC) 1931 *S, W, E, G*
Sébedio, J (Tarbes) 1913 *S, E,* 1914 *I,* 1920 *S, I, US,* 1922 *S, E,* 1923 *S*
Seguier, N (Béziers) 1973 *J, R*
Seigne, L (Agen, Merignac) 1989 *B, A* 1, 1990 *NZ* 1, 1993 *E, S, I, W, R*1, *A* 1,2, 1994 *S, C* 1, 1995 *E*(R), *S*
Sella, P (Agen) 1982 *R, Arg* 1,2, 1983 *E, S, I, W, A* 1,2, *R,* 1984 *I, W, E, S, NZ* 1,2, *R,* 1985 *E, S, I, W, Arg* 1,2, 1986 *S, I, W, E, R* 1, *Arg* 1,2, *A, NZ* 1, *R* 2, *NZ* 2,3, 1987 *W, E, S, I,* [*S, R, Z*(R), *Fj, A, NZ*], 1988 *E, S, I, W, Arg* 1,2,3,4, *R,* 1989 *I, W, E, S, NZ* 1,2, *B, A* 1,2, 1990 *W, E, S, I, A* 1,2,3, 1991 *W*1, *E, R, US*1,2, *W*2, [*Fj, C, E*], 1992 *W, E, S, I, Arg,* 1993 *E, S, I, W, R*1, *SA*1,2, *R*2, *A*1,2, 1994 *I, W, E, S, C* 1, *NZ* 1,2, *C* 2, 1995 *W, E, S, I*
Semmartin, J (SCUF) 1913 *W, I*
Senal, G (Béziers) 1974 *Arg* 1,2, *R, SA* 1,2, 1975 *W*
Sentilles, J (Tarbes) 1912 *W, E,* 1913 *S, SA*
Serin, L (Béziers) 1928 *E,* 1929 *W, E, G,* 1930 *S, I, E, G, W,* 1931 *I, W, E*
Serre, P (Perpignan) 1920 *S, E*
Serrière, P (RCF) 1986 *A,* 1987 *R,* 1988 *E*
Servole, L (Toulon) 1931 *I, S, W, E, G,* 1934 *G,* 1935 *G*
Sicart, N (Perpignan) 1922 *I*
Sillières, J (Tarbes) 1968 *R,* 1970 *S, I,* 1971 *S, I, E,* 1972 *E, W*
Siman, M (Montferrand) 1948 *E,* 1949 *S,* 1950 *S, I, E, W*
Simon, S (Bègles) 1991 *R, US*1
Simonpaoli, R (SF) 1911 *I,* 1912 *I, S*
Sitjar, M (Agen) 1964 *W, It, I, R,* 1965 *It, R,* 1967 *A, E, It, W, I, SA* 1,2
Skrela, J-C (Toulouse) 1971 *SA* 2, *A* 1,2, 1972 *I* 1 (R), *E, W, I* 2, *A* 1, 1973 *W, J, R,* 1974 *W, E, S, Arg* 1, *R,* 1975 *W* (R), *E, S, I, SA* 1,2, *Arg* 1,2, *R,* 1976 *S, I, W, E, US, A* 1,2, *R,* 1977 *W, E, S, I, Arg* 1,2, *NZ* 1,2, *R,* 1978 *E, S, I, W*
Soler, M (Quillan) 1929 *G*
Soro, R (Lourdes, Romans) 1945 *B* 1,2, *W,* 1946 *B, I, K,* 1947 *S, I, W, E,* 1948 *I, A, S, W, E,* 1949 *S, I, E, W, Arg* 1,2
Sorondo, L-M (Montauban) 1946 *K,* 1947 *S, I, W, E,* 1948 *I*
Soulié, E (CASG) 1920 *E, I, US,* 1921 *S, E, I,* 1922 *E, W, I*
Sourgens, J (Begles) 1926 *M*
Spanghero, C (Narbonne) 1971 *E, W, SA* 1,2, *A* 1,2, *R,* 1972 *S, E, W, I* 2, *A* 1,2, 1974 *I, W, E, S, R, SA* 1, 1975 *E, S, I*
Spanghero, W (Narbonne) 1964 *SA, Fj, R,* 1965 *S, I, E, W, It, R,* 1966 *S, I, E, W, It, R,* 1967 *S, A, E, SA* 1,2,3,4, *NZ,* 1968 *S, I, E, W, NZ* 1,2,3, *A, SA* 1,2, *R,* 1969 *S, I, W,* 1970 *R,* 1971 *E, W, SA* 1, 1972 *E, I* 2, *A* 1,2, *R,* 1973 *S, NZ, E, W, I*
Stener, G (PUC) 1956 *S, I, E,* 1958 *SA* 1,2
Struxiano, P (Toulouse) 1913 *W, I,* 1920 *S, E, W, I, US*
Sutra, G (Narbonne) 1967 *SA* 2, 1969 *W,* 1970 *S, I*
Swierczinski, C (Begles) 1969 *E,* 1977 *Arg* 2

Tachdjian, M (RCF) 1991 *S, I, E*
Taffary, M (RCF) 1975 *W, E, S, I*
Taillantou, J (Pau) 1930 *I, G, W*
Tarricq, P (Lourdes) 1958 *A, W, It, I*
Tavernier, H (Toulouse) 1913 *I*
Techoueyres, W (SBUC) 1994 *E, S*
Terreau, M-M (Bourg) 1945 *W,* 1946 *B, I, K, W,* 1947 *S, I, W, E,* 1948 *I, A, W, E,* 1949 *S, Arg* 1,2, 1951 *S*
Theuriet, A (SCUF) 1909 *E, W,* 1910 *S,* 1911 *W,* 1913 *E*
Thevenot, M (SCUF) 1910 *W, E, I*
Thierry, R (RCF) 1920 *S, E, W, US*
Thiers, P (Montferrand) 1936 *G* 1,2, 1937 *G, It,* 1938 *G* 1,2, 1940 *B,* 1945 *B,* 1,2
Tignol, P (Toulouse) 1953 *S, I*
Tilh, H (Nantes) 1912 *W, E,* 1913 *S, SA, E, W*
Tolot, J-L (Agen) 1987 [*Z*]
Tordo, J-F (Nice) *US*1(R), 1992 *W, E, S, I, R, Arg* 1,2, *SA* 1, *Arg,* 1993 *E, S, I, W, R*1
Torreilles, S (Perpignan) 1956 *S*
Tourte, R (St Girons) 1940 *B*
Trillo, J (Begles) 1967 *SA* 3,4, *NZ, R,* 1968 *S, I, NZ* 1,2,3, *A,* 1969 *I, E, W, R,* 1970 *E, R,* 1971 *S, I, SA* 1,2, *A* 1,2, 1972 *S, A* 1,2, *R,* 1973 *S, E*
Triviaux, R (Cognac) 1931 *E, G*
Tucoo-Chala, M (PUC) 1940 *B*

Ugartemendia, J-L (St Jean-de-Luz) 1975 *S, I*

Vaills, G (Perpignan) 1928 *A,* 1929 *G*
Vallot, C (SCUF) 1912 *S*
van Heerden, A (Tarbes) 1992 *E, S*
Vannier, M (RCF, Chalon) 1953 *W,* 1954 *S, I, Arg* 1,2, 1955 *S, I, E, W, It,* 1956 *S, I, W, It, E,* 1957 *S, I, E, W, It, R* 1,2, 1958 *S, E, A, W, It, I,* 1960 *S, E, W, I, It, R, Arg* 1,3, 1961 *SA, E, W, It, I, NZ* 1, *A*
Vaquer, F (Perpignan) 1921 *S, W,* 1922 *W*

Vaquerin, A (Béziers) 1971 *R*, 1972 *S*, *I* 1, *A* 1, 1973 *S*, 1974 *W*, *E*, *S*, *Arg* 1,2, *R*, *SA* 1,2, 1975 *W*, *E*, *S*, *I*, 1976 *US*, *A* 1(R), 2, *R*, 1977 *Arg* 2, 1979 *W*, *E*, 1980 *S*, *I*
Vareilles, C (SF) 1907 *E*, 1908 *E*, *W*, 1910 *S*, *E*
Varenne, F (RCF) 1952 *S*
Varvier, T (RCF) 1906 *E*, 1909 *E*, *W*, 1911 *E*, *W*, 1912 *I*
Vassal, G (Carcassonne) 1938 *R*, *G* 2
Vaysse, J (Albi) 1924 *US*, 1926 *M*
Vellat, E (Grenoble) 1927 *I*, *E*, *G* 1,2, 1928 *A*
Vergé, L (Bègles) 1993 *R* 1(R)
Verger, A (SF) 1927 *W*, *E*, *G* 1, 1928 *I*, *E*, *G*, *W*
Verges, S-A (SF) 1906 *NZ*, *E*, 1907 *E*
Viard, G (Narbonne) 1969 *W*, 1970 *S*, *R*, 1971 *S*, *I*
Viars, S (Brive) 1992 *W*, *E*, *I*, *R*, *Arg* 1,2, *SA* 1,2(R), *Arg*, 1993 *R*1, 1994 *C* 1(R), *NZ* 1(t), 1995 *E*(R)
Vigerie, M (Agen) 1931 *W*
Vigier, R (Montferrand) 1956 *S*, *W*, *It*, *E*, *Cz*, 1957 *S*, *E*, *W*, *It*, *R* 1,2, 1958 *S*, *E*, *A*, *W*, *It*, *I*, *SA* 1,2, 1959 *S*, *E*, *It*, *W*, *I*
Vigneau, A (Bayonne) 1935 *G*
Vignes, C (RCF) 1957 *R* 1,2, 1958 *S*, *E*
Vila, E (Tarbes) 1926 *M*
Vilagra, J (Vienne) 1945 *B* 2
Villepreux, P (Toulouse) 1967 *It*, *I*, *SA* 2, *NZ*, 1968 *I*, *Cz*, *NZ* 1,2,3, *A*, 1969 *S*, *I*, *E*, *W*, *R*, 1970 *S*, *I*, *W*, *E*, *R*, 1971 *S*, *I*, *E*, *W*, *A* 1,2, *R*, 1972 *S*, *I* 1, *E*, *W*, *I* 2, *A* 1,2
Viviès, B (Agen) 1978 *E*, *S*, *I*, *W*, 1980 *SA*, *R*, 1981 *S*, *A* 1, 1983 *A* 1 (R)
Volot, M (SF) 1945 *W*, 1946 *B*, *I*, *K*, *W*

Weller, S (Grenoble) 1989 *A* 1,2, 1990 *A* 1, *NZ* 1
Wolf, J-P (Béziers) 1980 *SA*, *R*, 1981 *A* 2, 1982 *E*

Yachvili, M (Tulle, Brive) 1968 *E*, *W*, *Cz*, *NZ* 3, *A*, *R*, 1969 *S*, *I*, *R*, 1971 *E*, *SA* 1,2, *A* 1, 1972 *R*, 1975 *SA* 2

Zago, F (Montauban) 1963 *I*, *E*

FRENCH INTERNATIONAL RECORDS

Both team and individual records are for official French international matches, up to 31 March 1995.

TEAM RECORDS

Highest score
70 v Zimbabwe (70-12) 1987 Auckland
v individual countries
37 v Argentina (37-3) 1960 Buenos Aires
34 v Australia (34-6) 1976 Parc des Princes
28 v Canada (28-9) 1994 Besançon
28 v Czechoslovakia (28-3) 1956 Toulouse
37 v England (37-12) 1972 Colombes
33 v Fiji (33-9) 1991 Grenoble
38 v Germany (38-17) 1933 Parc des Princes
44 v Ireland (44-12) 1992 Parc des Princes
60 v Italy (60-13) 1967 Toulon
30 v Japan (30-18) 1973 Bordeaux
24 v N Zealand (24-19) 1979 Auckland
59 v Romania (59-3) 1924 Colombes
28 v Scotland (28-22) 1987 Parc des Princes
29 v S Africa (29-16) 1992 Parc des Princes
41 v United States (41-9) 1991 Denver
36 v Wales (36-3) 1991 Parc des Princes
70 v Zimbabwe (70-12) 1987 Auckland

Biggest winning points margin
58 v Zimbabwe (70-12) 1987 Auckland
v individual countries
34 v Argentina (37-3) 1960 Buenos Aires
28 v Australia (34-6) 1976 Parc des Princes
19 v Canada (28-9) 1994 Besançon
25 v Czechoslovakia (28-3) 1956 Toulouse
25 v England (37-12) 1972 Colombes
24 v Fiji (33-9) 1991 Grenoble
34 v Germany (34-0) 1931 Colombes
32 v Ireland (44-12) 1992 Parc des Princes
47 v Italy (60-13) 1967 Toulon
12 v Japan (30-18) 1973 Bordeaux
14 v N Zealand (22-8) 1994 Christchurch
56 v Romania (59-3) 1924 Colombes
20 v Scotland (23-3) 1977 Parc des Princes
13 v S Africa (29-16) 1992 Parc des Princes
32 v United States (41-9) 1991 Denver
33 v Wales (36-3) 1991 Parc des Princes
58 v Zimbabwe (70-12) 1987 Auckland

Longest winning sequence
10 matches – 1931-37

Highest score by opposing team
49 Wales (14-49) 1910 Swansea
S Africa beat 'France' 55-6 at Parc des Princes on 3 January 1907, but it is not regarded as an official international match
by individual countries
27 Argentina (31-27) 1974 Buenos Aires
48 Australia (31-48) 1990 Brisbane
18 Canada (16-18) 1994 Ottawa
6 Czechoslovakia (19-6) 1968 Prague
41 England (13-41) 1907 Richmond
16 Fiji (31-16) 1987 Auckland
17 Germany { (16-17) 1927 Frankfurt; (38-17) 1933 Parc des Princes }

25 Ireland { (5-25) 1911 Cork / (6-25) 1975 Dublin
13 Italy (60-13) 1967 Toulon
18 Japan (30-18) 1973 Bordeaux
38 N Zealand (8-38) 1906 Parc des Princes
21 Romania (33-21) 1991 Bucharest
31 Scotland (3-31) 1912 Inverleith
38 S Africa { (5-38) 1913 Bordeaux / (25-38) 1975 Bloemfontein
17 United States (3-17) 1924 Colombes
49 Wales (14-49) 1910 Swansea
12 Zimbabwe (70-12) 1987 Auckland

Biggest losing points margin
42 v Wales (5-47) 1909 Colombes
The 6-55 defeat by S Africa in Paris in 1907 is regarded as unofficial
v individual countries
12 v Argentina (6-18) 1988 Buenos Aires
21 v Australia (3-24) 1993 Parc des Princes
2 v Canada (16-18) 1994 Ottawa
37 v England (0-37) 1911 Twickenham
3 v Germany (0-3) 1938 Frankfurt
24 v Ireland (0-24) 1913 Cork
30 v N Zealand (8-38) 1906 Parc des Princes
15 v Romania (0-15) 1980 Bucharest
28 v Scotland (3-31) 1912 Inverleith
33 v S Africa (5-38) 1913 Bordeaux
14 v United States (3-17) 1924 Colombes
42 v Wales (5-47) 1909 Colombes
No defeats v Czechoslovakia, Fiji, Italy, Japan or Zimbabwe

Longest losing sequence
18 matches – 1911-20

Most tries by France in an international
13 v Romania (59-3) 1924 Paris

INDIVIDUAL RECORDS

Most capped player
P Sella 106 1982-95
in individual positions
Full-back
S Blanco 81(93)[1] 1980-91
Wing
P Lagisquet 46 1983-91
Centre
P Sella 99(106)[2] 1982-95
Fly-half
J-P Romeu 33(34)[3] 1972-77
Scrum-half
P Berbizier 56 1981-91
Prop
R Paparemborde 55 1975-83
Hooker
P Dintrans 50 1979-90
Lock
J Condom 61[4] 1982-90
Flanker
J-P Rives 59[4] 1975-84
No 8
G Basquet 33[4] 1945-52

[1]*S Blanco won 12 caps as a wing*
[2]*Sella has won 6 caps as a wing and one as a full-back*
[3]*Romeu was capped once as a replacement full-back. F Mesnel, 53 caps, won 30 as a centre and 23 at fly-half. D Camberabero, 36 caps, won 30 at fly-half, 3 on the wing and 3 at full-back*
[4]*B Dauga and M Crauste, 63 caps each, are France's most-capped forwards. Dauga was capped as a lock and No 8; Crauste as a flanker and No 8*

Longest international career
F Haget 14 seasons 1974-87

Most consecutive Tests – 46
R Bertranne 1973-79

Most internationals as captain – 34
J-P Rives 1978-84

Most points in internationals – 354
D Camberabero (36 matches) 1982-93

Most points in International Championship in a season – 54
J-P Lescarboura (4 matches) 1983-84

Most points in an international – 30
D Camberabero v Zimbabwe 1987 Auckland

Most tries in internationals – 38
S Blanco (93 matches) 1980-91

Most tries in International Championship in a season – 5
P Estève (4 matches) 1982-83
E Bonneval (4 matches) 1986-87

Most tries in an international – 4
A Jauréguy v Romania 1924 Colombes
M Celhay v Italy 1937 Parc des Princes

Most conversions in internationals – 48
D Camberabero (36 matches) 1982-93

Most conversions in International Championship in a season – 7
P Villepreux (4 matches) 1971-72

Most conversions in an international – 9
G Camberabero v Italy 1967 Toulon
D Camberabero v Zimbabwe 1987 Auckland
Father and son

Most dropped goals in internationals – 15
J-P Lescarboura (28 matches) 1982-90

Most dropped goals in an international – 3
P Albaladejo v Ireland 1960 Paris
J-P Lescarboura v England 1985 Twickenham
J-P Lescarboura v New Zealand 1986 Christchurch
D Camberabero v Australia 1990 Sydney

Most penalty goals in internationals – 59
D Camberabero (36 matches) 1982-93

Most penalty goals in International Championship in a season – 10
J-P Lescarboura (4 matches) 1983-84

Most penalty goals in an international – 6
J M Aguirre v Argentina 1977 Buenos Aires

Most points on major tour – 112
S Viars (7 matches) 1992 Argentina

Most points in any match on tour – 28
P Lagisquet v Paraguayan XV 1988 Ascunción
P Estève scored 32 points against East Japan in 1984, but this was not on a major tour

---

Most tries in a tour match – 7
P Lagisquet v Paraguayan XV 1988 Ascunción
P Estève scored 8 tries v East Japan in 1984, but this was not on a major tour

---

A SEASON WITHOUT END

THE 1994 SEASON IN SOUTH AFRICA

Deon Viljoen

For some perverse reason, the rulers of South African rugby have chosen a helter-skelter programme of international commitments ever since the country's return to the world stage in 1992. Where a double round of Currie Cup games and the Lion Cup knock-out competition had served to reinforce South African rugby in isolation, they have now become a tremendous burden on the players, predictably leading to an outcry and, alas, to declining standards of play.

Viewed against this backdrop, the Transvaal players in particular excelled by winning a hat-trick of trophies, a repeat of their wonderful success in 1993, the unfortunate exception being their sorry capitulation in defence of the Super-10 trophy. Pienaar and his golden lions devoured the competition in the M-Net Night Series, the Lion Cup and the Currie Cup.

Transvaal at best stuttered to the Currie Cup climax, their leading players visibly fatigued after the punishing Test series in New Zealand. Awaiting them in the final were Free State, in their first Currie Cup final in almost two decades, by contrast rejuvenated by coach Nelie Smith. Free State's bravura performance helped them secure the coveted top-of-the-log position, ensuring home-ground advantage.

Limited ticket sales and the feeble venue contributed materially to a farcical final in which Transvaal, now coached solely by the competent Ray Mordt (his erstwhile partner, Kitch Christie, was in the stand in his new capacity of national mentor), triumphed 56-33. However, it must be said that the overall Currie Cup standard, always the benchmark of South African rugby, plummeted to an unparalleled low, if not consistently throughout the 1994 term, then certainly in the season's showpiece. Free State were, in a word, paralysed. Never before had the golden trophy been won by a bigger points margin, and never before – an unexpected discovery – had the winning team conceded as many points as Transvaal in the competition.

Much of the rest of the tournament was characterised by the same high-scoring, no-defence-to-speak-of trend. The most significant test of provincial strength was provided by the Super-10 competition, in which Natal reached the final only to succumb 21-10 to Queensland, with Michael Lynagh's generalship a vivid memory, in Durban. On the plus side, however, the monotony of the annual provincial parade was relieved by the vigorous nature of early Currie Cup competition when both Free State and Eastern Province set the pace against all expectations. The slow re-emergence of Western Province as a force on the local scene was another source of joy for many of their followers. In finishing among the top three places in the Currie Cup league table for the first time since 1989, they qualified for the Super-10 competition.

A lingering concern is the extent to which the domestic calendar was overshadowed by several negative aspects, including the demise of the annual National Club Championships. The rise of Louis Luyt as president of the SA Rugby Football Union promised at the very least a healthy shake-up of the old order, though the spring-cleaning exercise culminated in an unedifying public confrontation between the blunt, self-styled millionaire and Jannie Engelbrecht, the South African team manager. Their convoluted quarrel eventually saw Engelbrecht sacked after the tour to Scotland and Wales. The unerring television lens finally freeze-framed Johan le Roux's ear-biting escapades in New Zealand, but his subsequent suspension did little to placate those who believe that the primary problem in South African rugby is a lack of discipline.

James Small, too, helped to entrench this opinion. The South African wing, seemingly never far from trouble, was suspended for allegedly having thrown a punch in a Port Elizabeth bar.

Yet amid all the chaos, the overriding impression was that the lessons of the past two years were slowly beginning to sink in. Moreover, several talented young players were once again emerging from the morass of mediocrity, most strikingly the gifted Natal lock Mark Andrews. Chester Williams played such consistently good rugby on the wing for Western Province that he deserves a special mention, and Gavin Johnson (Transvaal) and Pieter du Randt (Free State) also had their moments, the latter coming through strongly in the Currie Cup final.

CURRIE CUP FINAL

Free State 33 (3G 3PG 1DG) **Transvaal 56** (6G 3PG 1T)

Free State: A Pawson (Technikon); H Truter (Oud Studente), H Müller (Technikon) (*capt*), B Venter (Free State U), C Badenhorst (Oud Studente); E Herbert (Old Greys), T Kirkham (Old Greys); P du Randt (Technikon), A H le Roux (Free State U), D Heymans (Oud Studente), A Venter (Technikon), R Opperman (Free State U), B Els (Oud Studente), J Beukes (Old Greys), J Coetzee (SAP) *Replacements* H Martens for Kirkham (38 mins); F Smith for Pawson (49 mins); N Drotské for Du Randt (temp)

Scorers *Tries:* A Venter (2), Badenhorst *Conversions:* Herbert (3) *Penalty Goals:* Herbert (3) *Dropped Goal:* Herbert

Transvaal: G Grobler (Wanderers); P Hendriks (Technikon), J Mulder (RAU), B Fourie (Alberton), G Johnson (Pirates); H le Roux (RAU), J Roux (Wanderers); B Swart (Roodepoort), U Schmidt (Wanderers), I Hattingh (Roodepoort), F Pienaar (RAU) (*capt*), K Wiese (Pirates), P Schutte (RAU), C Rossouw (Germiston-Simmer), G Combrinck (RAU) *Replacement* C Scholtz for Mulder (48 mins)

Scorers *Tries:* Hendriks, Le Roux, Rossouw, Roux, Schmidt, Grobler, pen try *Conversions:* Johnson (6) *Penalty Goals:* Johnson (3)

Referee S Neethling (Boland)

CURRIE CUP SECTION A	*P*	*W*	*D*	*L*	*F*	*A*	*Pts*
Free State	10	7	0	3	283	265	14
Transvaal	10	6	0	4	276	237	12
Western Province	10	5	0	5	267	190	10
Natal	10	4	0	6	231	208	8
Northern Transvaal	10	4	0	6	245	321	8
Eastern Province	10	4	0	6	236	317	8

LION CUP FINAL: Transvaal 29, Western Province 20
M-NET NIGHT SERIES FINAL: Transvaal 33, Eastern Province 3
SUPER-10 FINAL: Queensland 21, Natal 10
TOYOTA NATIONAL CLUB CHAMPIONSHIP FINAL: Crusaders 34, Oud Studente 2 (*kicks count for only two points in the competition*)

SOUTH AFRICAN INTERNATIONAL PLAYERS *(up to 31 March 1995)*

ABBREVIATIONS

A – Australia; *Arg* – Argentina; *BI* – British Isles teams; *Cv* – New Zealand Cavaliers; *E* – England; *F* – France; *I* – Ireland; *NZ* – New Zealand; *S* – Scotland; *S Am* – South America; *US* – United States of America; *W* – Wales; *Wld* – World Invitation XV; (R) – Replacement; (t) – temporary replacement.

PROVINCIAL ABBREVIATIONS

Bor – Border; Bol – Boland; EP – Eastern Province; GW – Griqualand West; N – Natal; NT – Northern Transvaal; OFS – Orange Free State; R – Rhodesia; SET – South East Transvaal; SWA – South West Africa; SWD – South West Districts; Tvl – Transvaal; WP – Western Province; WT – Western Transvaal; Z-R – Zimbabwe-Rhodesia

Note: When a series has taken place, figures denote the particular matches in which players featured. Thus 1968 *BI* 1,2,4 indicates that a player appeared in the first, second and fourth Tests of the 1968 series against the British Isles.

Ackermann, D S P (WP) 1955 *BI* 2,3,4, 1956 *A* 1,2, *NZ* 1,3, 1958 *F* 2
Albertyn, P K (SWD) 1924 *BI* 1,2,3,4
Alexander, E (GW) 1891 *BI* 1,2
Allan, J (N) 1993 *A* 1(R), *Arg* 1,2(R), 1994 *E* 1,2, *NZ* 1,2,3
Allen, P B (EP) 1960 *S*
Allport, P (WP) 1910 *BI* 2,3
Anderson, J A (WP) 1903 *BI* 3
Anderson, J H (WP) 1896 *BI* 1,3,4
Andrew, J B (Tvl) 1896 *BI* 2
Andrews, K S (WP) 1992 *E*, 1993 *F* 1,2, *A* 1(R),2,3, *Arg* 1(R),2, 1994 *NZ* 3
Andrews, M G (N) 1994 *E* 2, *NZ* 1,2,3, *Arg* 1,2, *S*, *W*
Antelme, M J G (Tvl) 1960 *NZ* 1,2,3,4, 1960-61 *F*
Apsey, J T (WP) 1933 *A* 4,5, 1938 *BI* 2
Ashley, S (WP) 1903 *BI* 2
Aston, F T D (Tvl) 1896 *BI* 1,2,3,4
Atherton, S (N) 1993 *Arg* 1,2, 1994 *E* 1,2, *NZ* 1,2,3
Aucamp, J (WT) 1924 *BI* 1,2

Baard, A P (WP) 1960-61 *I*
Babrow, L (WP) 1937 *A* 1,2, *NZ* 1,2,3
Badenhorst, C (OFS) 1994 *Arg* 2
Barnard, A S (EP) 1984 *S Am* 1,2, 1986 *Cv* 1,2
Barnard, J H (Tvl) 1965 *S*, *A* 1,2, *NZ* 3,4
Barnard, R W (Tvl) 1970 *NZ* 2(R)
Barnard, W H M (NT) 1949 *NZ* 4, 1951-52 *W*
Barry, J (WP) 1903 *BI* 1,2,3
Bartmann, W J (Tvl, N) 1986 *Cv* 1,2,3,4, 1992 *NZ*, *A*, *F* 1,2
Bastard, W E (N) 1937 *A* 1, *NZ* 1,2,3, 1938 *BI* 1,3
Bates, A J (WT) 1969-70 *E*, 1970 *NZ* 1,2, 1972 *E*
Bayvel, P C R (Tvl) 1974 *BI* 2,4, *F* 1,2, 1975 *F* 1,2, 1976 *NZ* 1,2,3,4
Beck, J J (WP) 1981 *NZ* 2(R), 3 (R), *US*
Bedford, T P (N) 1963 *A* 1,2,3,4, 1964 *W*, *F*, 1965 *I*, *A* 1,2, 1968 *BI* 1,2,3,4, *F* 1,2, 1969 *A* 1,2,3,4, 1969-70 *S*, *E*, *I*, *W*, 1971 *F* 1,2
Bekker, H J (WP) 1981 *NZ* 1,3
Bekker, H P J (NT) 1951-52 *E*, *F*, 1953 *A* 1,2,3,4, 1955 *BI* 2,3,4, 1956 *A* 1,2, *NZ* 1,2,3,4
Bekker, M J (NT) 1960 *S*
Bekker, R P (NT) 1953 *A* 3,4
Bergh, W F (SWD) 1931-32 *W*, *I*, *E*, *S*, 1933 *A* 1,2,3,4,5, 1937 *A* 1,2, *NZ* 1,2,3, 1938 *BI* 1,2,3
Bestbier, A (OFS) 1974 *F* 2(R)
Bester, J J N (WP) 1924 *BI* 2,4
Bester, J L A (WP) 1938 *BI* 2,3
Beswick, A M (Bor) 1896 *BI* 2,3,4
Bezuidenhoudt, C E (NT) 1962 *BI* 2,3,4
Bezuidenhoudt, N S E (NT) 1972 *E*, 1974 *BI* 2,3,4, *F* 1,2, 1975 *F* 1,2, 1977 *Wld*
Bierman, J N (Tvl) 1931-32 *I*
Bisset, W M (WP) 1891 *BI* 1,3
Blair, R (WP) 1977 *Wld*
Bosch, G R (Tvl) 1974 *BI* 2, *F* 1,2, 1975 *F* 1,2, 1976 *NZ* 1,2,3,4
Bosman, N J S (Tvl) 1924 *BI* 2,3,4
Botha, D S (NT) 1981 *NZ* 1
Botha, H E (NT) 1980 *S Am* 1,2, *BI* 1,2,3,4, *S Am* 3,4, *F*, 1981 *I* 1,2, *NZ* 1,2,3, *US*, 1982 *S Am* 1,2, 1986 *Cv* 1,2,3,4, 1989 *Wld* 1,2, 1992 *NZ*, *A*, *F* 1,2, *E*
Botha, J (Tvl) 1903 *BI* 3
Botha, J P F (NT) 1962 *BI* 2,3,4
Botha, P H (Tvl) 1965 *A* 1,2
Boyes, H C (GW) 1891 *BI* 1,2
Brand, G H (WP) 1928 *NZ* 2,3, 1931-32 *W*,*I*, *E*, *S*, 1933 *A* 1,2,3,4,5, 1937 *A* 1,2, *NZ* 2,3, 1938 *BI* 1
Bredenkamp, M (GW) 1896 *BI* 1,3
Breedt, J C (Tvl) 1986 *Cv* 1,2,3,4, 1989 *Wld* 1,2, 1992 *NZ*, *A*
Brewis, J D (NT) 1949 *NZ* 1,2,3,4, 1951-52 *S*, *I*, *W*, *E*, *F*, 1953 *A* 1
Briers, T P D (WP) 1955 *BI* 1,2,3,4, 1956 *NZ* 2,3,4
Brink, D J (WP) 1906 *S*, *W*, *E*
Brooks, D (Bor) 1906 *S*
Brown, C (WP) 1903 *BI* 1,2,3
Brynard, G S (WP) 1965 *A* 1, *NZ* 1,2,3,4, 1968 *BI* 3,4
Buchler, J U (Tvl) 1951-52 *S*, *I*, *W*, *E*, *F*, 1953 *A* 1,2,3,4, 1956 *A* 2
Burdett, A F (WP) 1906 *S*, *I*
Burger, J M (WP) 1989 *Wld* 1,2
Burger, M B (NT) 1980 *BI* 2(R), *S Am* 3, 1981 *US* (R)
Burger, S W P (WP) 1984 *E* 1,2, 1986 *Cv* 1,2,3,4
Burger, W A G (Bor) 1906 *S*, *I*, *W*, 1910 *BI* 2

Carelse, G (EP) 1964 *W*, *F*, 1965 *I*, *S*, 1967 *F* 1,2,3, 1968 *F* 1,2, 1969 *A* 1,2,3,4, 1969-70 *S*
Carlson, R A (WP) 1972 *E*
Carolin, H W (WP) 1903 *BI* 3, 1906 *S*, *I*
Castens, H H (WP) 1891 *BI* 1
Chignell, T W (WP) 1891 *BI* 3
Cilliers, G D (OFS) 1963 *A* 1,3,4
Claassen, J T (WT) 1955 *BI* 1,2,3,4, 1956 *A* 1,2, *NZ* 1,2,3,4, 1958 *F* 1,2, 1960 *S*, *NZ* 1,2,3, 1960-61 *W*, *I*, *E*, *S*, *F*, 1961 *I*, *A* 1,2, 1962 *BI* 1,2,3,4
Claassen, W (N) 1981 *I* 1,2, *NZ* 2,3, *US*, 1982 *S Am* 1,2
Clarke, W H (Tvl) 1933 *A* 3
Clarkson, W A (N) 1921 *NZ* 1,2, 1924 *BI* 1
Cloete, H A (WP) 1896 *BI* 4
Cockrell, C H (WP) 1969-70 *S*, *I*, *W*
Cockrell, R J (WP) 1974 *F* 1,2, 1975 *F* 1,2, 1976 *NZ* 1,2, 1977 *Wld*, 1981 *NZ* 1,2(R),3, *US*
Coetzee, J H H (WP) 1974 *BI* 1, 1975 *F* 2(R), 1976 *NZ* 1,2,3,4
Cope, D (Tvl) 1896 *BI* 2
Cotty, W (GW) 1896 *BI* 3
Crampton, G (GW) 1903 *BI* 2
Craven, D H (WP) 1931-32 *W*, *I*, *S*, 1933 *A* 1,2,3,4,5, 1937 *A* 1,2, *NZ* 1,2,3, 1938 *BI* 1,2,3
Cronje, P A (Tvl) 1971 *F* 1,2, A 1,2,3, 1974 *BI* 3,4
Crosby, J H (Tvl) 1896 *BI* 2
Crosby, N J (Tvl) 1910 *BI* 1,3
Currie, C (GW) 1903 *BI* 2

D'Alton, G (WP) 1933 *A* 1
Dalton, J (Tvl) 1994 *Arg* 1(R)
Daneel, G M (WP) 1928 *NZ* 1,2,3,4, 1931-32 *W*, *I*, *E*, *S*
Daneel, H J (WP) 1906 *S*, *I*, *W*, *E*

Davidson, M (EP) 1910 *BI* 1
De Bruyn, J (OFS) 1974 *BI* 3
De Jongh, H P K (WP) 1928 *NZ* 3
De Klerk, I J (Tvl) 1969-70 *E, I, W*
De Klerk, K B H (Tvl) 1974 *BI* 1,2,3(R), 1975 *F* 1,2, 1976 *NZ* 2(R),3,4, 1980 *S Am* 1,2, *BI* 2, 1981 *I* 1,2
De Kock, A (GW) 1891 *BI* 2
De Kock, J S (WP) 1921 *NZ* 3, 1924 *BI* 3
Delport, W H (EP) 1951-52 *S, I, W, E, F*, 1953 *A* 1,2,3,4
De Melker, S C (GW) 1903 *BI* 2, 1906 *E*
Devenish, C (GW) 1896 *BI* 2
Devenish, G St L (Tvl) 1896 *BI* 2
Devenish, M (Tvl) 1891 *BI* 1
De Villiers, D I (Tvl) 1910 *BI* 1,2,3
De Villiers, D J (WP, Bol) 1962 *BI* 2,3, 1965 *I, NZ* 1,3,4, 1967 *F* 1,2,3,4, 1968 *BI* 1,2,3,4, *F* 1,2, 1969 *A* 1,4, 1969-70 *E, I, W*, 1970 *NZ* 1,2,3,4
De Villiers, H A (WP) 1906 *S, W, E*
De Villiers, H O (WP) 1967 *F* 1,2,3,4, 1968 *F* 1,2, 1969 *A* 1,2,3,4, 1969-70 *S, E, I, W*
De Villiers, P du P (WP) 1928 *NZ* 1,3,4, 1931-32 *E*, 1933 *A* 4, 1937 *A* 1,2, *NZ* 1
Devine, D (Tvl) 1924 *BI* 3, 1928 *NZ* 2
De Vos, D J J (WP) 1965 *S*, 1969 *A* 3, 1969-70 *S*
De Waal, A N (WP) 1967 *F* 1,2,3,4
De Waal, P (WP) 1896 *BI* 4
De Wet, A E (WP) 1969 *A* 3,4, 1969-70 *E*
De Wet, P (WP) 1938 *BI* 1,2,3
Dinkelmann, E E (NT) 1951-52 *S, I, E, F*, 1953 *A* 1,2
Dirksen, C W (NT) 1963 *A* 4, 1964 *W*, 1965 *I,S*, 1967 *F* 1,2,3,4, 1968 *BI* 1,2
Dobbin, F J (GW) 1903 *BI* 1,2, 1906 *S, W, E*, 1910 *BI* 1, 1912-13 *S, I, W*
Dobie, J A R (Tvl) 1928 *NZ* 2
Dormehl, P J (WP) 1896 *BI* 3,4
Douglass, F W (EP) 1896 *BI* 1
Drotské, A E (OFS) 1993 *Arg* 2
Dryburgh, R G (WP) 1955 *BI* 2,3,4, 1956 *A* 2, *NZ* 1,4, 1960 *NZ* 1,2
Duff, B (WP) 1891 *BI* 1,2,3
Duffy, B A (Bor) 1928 *NZ* 1
Du Plessis, C J (WP) 1982 *S Am* 1,2, 1984 *E* 1,2, *S Am* 1,2, 1986 *Cv* 1,2,3,4, 1989 *Wld* 1,2
Du Plessis, D C (NT) 1977 *Wld*, 1980 *S Am* 2
Du Plessis, F (Tvl) 1949 *NZ* 1,2,3
Du Plessis, M (WP) 1971 *A* 1,2,3, 1974 *BI* 1,2, *F* 1,2, 1975 *F* 1,2, 1976 *NZ* 1,2,3,4, 1977 *Wld*, 1980 *S Am* 1,2, *BI* 1,2,3,4, *S Am* 4, *F*
Du Plessis, M J (WP) 1984 *S Am* 1,2, 1986 *Cv* 1,2,3,4, 1989 *Wld* 1,2
Du Plessis, N J (WT) 1921 *NZ* 2,3, 1924 *BI* 1,2,3
Du Plessis, P G (NT) 1972 *E*
Du Plessis, T D (NT) 1980 *S Am* 1,2
Du Plessis, W (WP) 1980 *S Am* 1,2, *BI* 1,2,3,4, *S Am* 3,4, *F*, 1981 *NZ* 1,2,3, 1982 *S Am* 1,2
Du Plooy, A J J (EP) 1955 *BI* 1
Du Preez, F C H (NT) 1960-61 *E, S*, 1961 *A* 1,2, 1962 *BI* 1,2,3,4, 1963 *A* 1, 1964 *W, F*, 1965 *A* 1,2, *NZ* 1,2,3,4, 1967 *F* 4, 1968 *BI* 1,2,3,4, *F* 1,2, 1969 *A* 1,2, 1969-70 *S, I, W*, 1970 *NZ* 1,2,3,4, 1971 *F* 1,2, *A* 1,2,3
Du Preez, J G H (WP) 1956 *NZ* 1
Du Preez, R J (N) 1992 *NZ, A*, 1993 *F* 1,2, *A* 1,2,3
Du Rand, J A (R, NT) 1949 *NZ* 2,3, 1951-52 *S, I, W, E, F*, 1953 *A* 1,2,3,4, 1955 *BI* 1,2,3,4, 1956 *A* 1,2, *NZ* 1,2,3,4
Du Randt, J P (OFS) 1994 *Arg* 1,2, *S, W*
Du Toit, A F (WP) 1928 *NZ* 3,4
Du Toit, B A (Tvl) 1938 *BI* 1,2,3
Du Toit, P A (NT) 1949 *NZ* 2,3,4, 1951-52 *S, I, W, E, F*
Du Toit, P G (WP) 1981 *NZ* 1, 1982 *S Am* 1,2, 1984 *E* 1,2
Du Toit, P S (WP) 1958 *F* 1,2, 1960 *NZ* 1,2,3,4, 1960-61 *W, I, E, S, F*, 1961 *I, A* 1,2
Duvenhage, F P (GW) 1949 *NZ* 1,3

Edwards, P (NT) 1980 *S Am* 1,2
Ellis, J H (SWA) 1965 *NZ* 1,2,3,4, 1967 *F* 1,2,3,4, 1968 *BI* 1,2,3,4, *F* 1,2, 1969 *A* 1,2,3,4, 1969-70 *S, I, W*, 1970 *NZ* 1,2,3,4, 1971 *F* 1,2, *A* 1,2,3, 1972 *E*, 1974 *BI* 1,2,3,4, *F* 1,2, 1976 *NZ* 1
Ellis, M (Tvl) 1921 *NZ* 2,3, 1924 *BI* 1,2,3,4
Engelbrecht, J P (WP) 1960 *S*, 1960-61 *W, I, E, S, F*, 1961 *A* 1,2, 1962 *BI* 2,3,4, 1963 *A* 2,3, 1964 *W, F*, 1965 *I, S, A* 1,2, *NZ* 1,2,3,4, 1967 *F* 1,2,3,4, 1968 *BI* 1,2, *F* 1,2, 1969 *A* 1,2
Erasmus, F S (NT, EP) 1986 *Cv* 3,4, 1989 *Wld* 2
Etlinger, T E (WP) 1896 *BI* 4

Ferreira, C (OFS) 1986 *Cv* 1,2
Ferreira, P S (WP) 1984 *S Am* 1,2
Ferris, H H (Tvl) 1903 *BI* 3
Forbes, H H (Tvl) 1896 *BI* 2
Fourie, C (EP) 1974 *F* 1,2, 1975 *F* 1,2
Fourie, T T (SET) 1974 *BI* 3
Fourie, W L (SWA) 1958 *F* 1,2
Francis, J A J (Tvl) 1912-13 *S, I, W, E, F*
Frederickson, C A (Tvl) 1974 *BI* 2, 1980 *S Am* 1,2
Frew, A (Tvl) 1903 *BI* 1
Froneman, D C (OFS) 1977 *Wld*
Froneman, I L (Bor) 1933 *A* 1
Fuls, H T (Tvl, EP) 1992 *NZ* (R), 1993 *F* 1,2, *A* 1,2,3, *Arg* 1,2
Fry, S P (WP) 1951-52 *S, I, W, E, F*, 1953 *A* 1,2,3,4, 1955 *BI* 1,2,3,4

Gage, J H (OFS) 1933 *A* 1
Gainsford, J L (WP) 1960 *S, NZ* 1,2,3,4, 1960-61 *W, I, E, S, F*, 1961 *A* 1,2, 1962 *BI* 1,2,3,4, 1963 *A* 1,2,3,4, 1964 *W, F*, 1965 *I, S, A* 1,2, *NZ* 1,2,3,4, 1967 *F* 1,2,3
Geel, P J (OFS) 1949 *NZ* 3
Geere, V (Tvl) 1933 *A* 1,2,3,4,5
Geffin, A O (Tvl) 1949 *NZ* 1,2,3,4, 1951-52 *S, I, W*
Geldenhuys, A (EP) 1992 *NZ, A, F* 1,2
Geldenhuys, S B (NT) 1981 *NZ* 2,3, *US*, 1982 *S Am* 1,2, 1989 *Wld* 1,2
Gentles, T A (WP) 1955 *BI* 1,2,4, 1956 *NZ* 2,3, 1958 *F* 2
Geraghty, E M (Bor) 1949 *NZ* 4
Gerber, D M (EP, WP) 1980 *S Am* 3,4, *F*, 1981 *I* 1,2, *NZ* 1,2,3, *US*, 1982 *S Am* 1,2, 1984 *E* 1,2, *S Am* 1,2, 1986 *Cv* 1,2,3,4, 1992 *NZ, A, F* 1,2, *E*
Gerber, M C (EP) 1958 *F* 1,2, 1960 *S*
Gericke, F W (Tvl) 1960 *S*
Germishuys, J S (OFS, Tvl) 1974 *BI* 2, 1976 *NZ* 1,2,3,4, 1977 *Wld*, 1980 *S Am* 1,2, *BI* 1,2,3,4, *S Am* 3,4, *F*, 1981 *I* 1,2, *NZ* 2,3, *US*
Gibbs, B (GW) 1903 *BI* 2
Goosen, C P (OFS) 1965 *NZ* 2
Gorton, H C (Tvl) 1896 *BI* 1
Gould, R L (N) 1968 *BI* 1,2,3,4
Gray, B G (WP) 1931-32 *W, E, S*, 1933 *A* 5
Greenwood, C M (WP) 1961 *I*
Greyling, P J F (OFS) 1967 *F* 1,2,3,4, 1968 *BI* 1, *F* 1,2, 1969 *A* 1,2,3,4, 1969-70 *S, E, I, W*, 1970 *NZ* 1,2,3,4, 1971 *F* 1,2, *A* 1,2,3, 1972 *E*
Grobler, C J (OFS) 1974 *BI* 4, 1975 *F* 1,2
Guthrie, F H (WP) 1891 *BI* 1,3, 1896 *BI* 1

Hahn, C H L (Tvl) 1910 *BI* 1,2,3
Hamilton, F (EP) 1891 *BI* 1
Harris, T A (Tvl) 1937 *NZ* 2,3, 1938 *BI* 1,2,3
Hartley, A J (WP) 1891 *BI* 3
Hattingh, H (NT) 1992 *A* (R), *F* 2 (R), *E*, 1994 *Arg* 1,2
Hattingh, L B (OFS) 1933 *A* 2
Heatlie, B H (WP) 1891 *BI* 2,3, 1896 *BI* 1,4, 1903 *BI* 1,3
Hendriks, P (Tvl) 1992 *NZ, A*, 1994 *S, W*
Hepburn, T (WP) 1896 *BI* 4
Heunis, J W (NT) 1981 *NZ* 3(R), *US*, 1982 *S Am* 1,2, 1984 *E* 1,2, *S Am* 1,2, 1986 *Cv* 1,2,3,4, 1989 *Wld* 1,2
Hill, R A (R) 1960-61 *W, I*, 1961 *I, A* 1,2, 1962 *BI* 4, 1963 *A* 3
Hills, W G (NT) 1992 *F* 1,2, *E*, 1993 *F* 1,2, *A* 1
Hirsch, J G (EP) 1906 *I*, 1910 *BI* 1
Hobson, T E C (WP) 1903 *BI* 3
Hoffman, R S (Bol) 1953 *A* 3
Holton, D N (EP) 1960 *S*
Honiball, H W (N) 1993 *A* 3(R), *Arg* 2
Hopwood, D J (WP) 1960 *S, NZ* 3,4, 1960-61 *W, E, S, F*, 1961 *I, A* 1,2, 1962 *BI* 1,2,3,4, 1963 *A* 1,2,4, 1964 *W, F*, 1965 *S, NZ* 3,4
Howe, B F (Bor) 1956 *NZ* 1,4
Howe-Browne, N R F G (WP) 1910 *BI* 1,2,3
Hugo, D P (WP) 1989 *Wld* 1,2

Immelman, J H (WP) 1912-13 *F*

Jackson, D C (WP) 1906 *I, W, E*
Jackson, J S (WP) 1903 *BI* 2
Jansen, E (OFS) 1981 *NZ* 1
Jansen, J S (OFS) 1970 *NZ* 1,2,3,4, 1971 *F* 1,2, *A* 1,2,3, 1972 *E*
Jennings, C B (Bor) 1937 *NZ* 1
Johnson, G K (Tvl) 1993 *Arg* 2, 1994 *NZ* 3, *Arg* 1
Johnstone, P G A (WP) 1951-52 *S, I, W, E, F*, 1956 *A* 1, *NZ* 1,2,4
Jones, C H (Tvl) 1903 *BI* 1,2
Jones, P S T (WP) 1896 *BI* 1,3,4
Jordaan, R P (NT) 1949 *NZ* 1,2,3,4
Joubert, A J (OFS, N) 1989 *Wld* 1 (R), 1993 *A* 3, *Arg* 1, 1994 *E* 1,2, *NZ* 1,2(R),3, *Arg* 2, *S, W*
Joubert, S J (WP) 1906 *I, W, E*

Kahts, W J H (NT) 1980 *BI* 1,2,3, *S Am* 3,4, *F*, 1981 *I* 1,2, *NZ* 2, 1982 *S Am* 1,2
Kaminer, J (Tvl) 1958 *F* 2
Kebble, G R (N) 1993 *Arg* 1,2, 1994 *NZ* 1(R),2
Kelly, E W (GW) 1896 *BI* 3
Kenyon, B J (Bor) 1949 *NZ* 4
Kipling, H G (GW) 1931-32 *W, I, E, S*, 1933 *A* 1,2,3,4,5
Kirkpatrick, A I (GW) 1953 *A* 2, 1956 *NZ* 2, 1958 *F* 1, 1960 *S, NZ* 1,2,3,4, 1960-61 *W, I, E, S, F*
Knight, A S (Tvl) 1912-13 *S, I, W, E, F*
Knoetze, F (WP) 1989 *Wld* 1,2
Koch, A C (Bol) 1949 *NZ* 2,3,4, 1951-52 *S, I, W, E, F*, 1953 *A* 1,2,4, 1955 *BI* 1,2,3,4, 1956 *A* 1, *NZ* 2,3, 1958 *F* 1,2, 1960 *NZ* 1,2
Koch, H V (WP) 1949 *NZ* 1,2,3,4
Kotze, G J M (WP) 1967 *F* 1,2,3,4
Krantz, E F W (OFS) 1976 *NZ* 1, 1981 *I* 1
Krige, J D (WP) 1903 *BI* 1,3, 1906 *S, I, W*
Kritzinger, J L (Tvl) 1974 *BI* 3,4, *F* 1,2, 1975 *F* 1,2, 1976 *NZ* 4
Kroon, C M (EP) 1955 *BI* 1
Kruger, P E (Tvl) 1986 *Cv* 3,4
Kruger, R J (NT) 1993 *Arg* 1,2, 1994 *S, W*
Kruger, T L (Tvl) 1921 *NZ* 1,2, 1924 *BI* 1,2,3,4, 1928 *NZ* 1,2
Kuhn, S P (Tvl) 1960 *NZ* 3,4 1960-61 *W, I, E, S, F*, 1961 *I, A* 1,2, 1962 *BI* 1,2,3,4, 1963 *A* 1,2,3, 1965 *I, S*

La Grange, J B (WP) 1924 *BI* 3,4
Larard, A (Tvl) 1896 *BI* 2,4
Lategan, M T (WP) 1949 *NZ* 1,2,3,4, 1951-52 *S, I, W, E, F*, 1953 *A* 1,2
Laubscher, T G (WP) 1994 *Arg* 1,2, *S, W*
Lawless, M J (WP) 1964 *F*, 1969-70 *E* (R), *I, W*
Ledger, S H (GW) 1912-13 *S, I, E, F*
Le Roux, A H (OFS) 1994 *E* 1
Le Roux, H P (Tvl) 1993 *F* 1,2, 1994 *E* 1,2, *NZ* 1,2,3, *Arg* 2, *S, W*
Le Roux, J H S (Tvl) 1994 *E* 2, *NZ* 1,2
Le Roux, M (OFS) 1980 *BI* 1,2,3,4, *S Am* 3,4, *F*, 1981 *I* 1
Le Roux, P A (WP) 1906 *I, W, E*
Little, E M M (GW) 1891 *BI* 1,3
Lochner, G P (WP) 1955 *BI* 3, 1956 *A* 1,2, *NZ* 1,2,3,4, 1958 *F* 1,2
Lochner, G P (EP) 1937 *NZ* 3, 1938 *BI* 1,2
Lockyear, R J (GW) 1960 *NZ* 1,2,3,4, 1960-61 *I, F*
Lombard, A C (EP) 1910 *BI* 2
Lötter, D (Tvl) 1993 *F* 2, *A* 1,2
Lotz, J W (Tvl) 1937 *A* 1,2, *NZ* 1,2,3, 1938 *BI* 1,2,3
Loubser, J A (WP) 1903 *BI* 3, 1906 *S, I, W, E*, 1910 *BI* 1,3
Lourens, M J (NT) 1968 *BI* 2,3,4
Louw, J S (Tvl) 1891 *BI* 1,2,3
Louw, M J (Tvl) 1971 *A* 2,3
Louw, M M (WP) 1928 *NZ* 3,4, 1931-32 *W, I, E, S*, 1933 *A* 1,2,3,4,5, 1937 *A* 1,2, *NZ* 2,3, 1938 *BI* 1,2,3
Louw, R J (WP) 1980 *S Am* 1,2, *BI* 1,2,3,4, *S Am* 3,4, *F*, 1981 *I* 1,2, *NZ* 1,3, 1982 *S Am* 1,2, 1984 *E* 1,2, *S Am* 1,2
Louw, S C (WP) 1933 *A* 1,2,3,4,5, 1937 *A* 1, *NZ* 1,2,3, 1938 *BI* 1,2,3
Luyt, F P (WP) 1910 *BI* 1,2,3, 1912-13 *S, I, W, E*
Luyt, J D (EP) 1912-13 *S, W, E, F*
Luyt, R R (WP) 1910 *BI* 2,3, 1912-13 *S, I, W, E, F*
Lyons, D (EP) 1896 *BI* 1
Lyster, P J (N) 1933 *A* 2,5, 1937 *NZ* 1

McCallum, I D (WP) 1970 *NZ* 1,2,3,4, 1971 *F* 1,2, *A* 1,2,3, 1974 *BI* 1,2
McCallum, R J (WP) 1974 *BI* 1
McCulloch, J D (GW) 1912-13 *E, F*
MacDonald, A W (R) 1965 *A* 1, *NZ* 1,2,3,4
Macdonald, D A (WP) 1974 *BI* 2
Macdonald, I (Tvl) 1992 *NZ, A*, 1993 *F* 1, *A* 3, 1994 *E* 2
McDonald, J A J (WP) 1931-32 *W, I, E, S*
McEwan, W M C (Tvl) 1903 *BI* 1,3
McHardy, E E (OFS) 1912-13 *S, I, W, E, F*
McKendrick, J A (WP) 1891 *BI* 3
Malan, A S (Tvl) 1960 *NZ* 1,2,3,4, 1960-61 *W, I, E, S, F*, 1962 *BI* 1, 1963 A 1,2,3, 1964 *W*, 1965 *I, S*
Malan, A W (NT) 1989 *Wld* 1,2, 1992 *NZ, A, F* 1,2, *E*
Malan, E (NT) 1980 *BI* 3(R),4
Malan, G F (WP) 1958 *F* 2, 1960 *NZ* 1,3,4, 1960-61 *E, S, F*, 1962 *BI* 1,2,3, 1963 *A* 1,2,4, 1964 *W*, 1965 *A* 1,2, *NZ* 1,2
Malan, P (Tvl) 1949 *NZ* 4
Mallett, N V H (WP) 1984 *S Am* 1,2
Mans, W J (WP) 1965 *I, S*
Marais, F P (Bol) 1949 *NZ* 1,2, 1951-52 *S*, 1953 *A* 1,2
Marais, J F K (WP) 1963 *A* 3, 1964 *W, F*, 1965 *I, S, A* 2, 1968 *BI* 1,2,3,4, *F* 1,2, 1969 *A* 1,2,3,4, 1969-70 *S, E, I, W*, 1970 *NZ* 1,2,3,4, 1971 *F* 1,2, *A* 1,2,3, 1974 *BI* 1,2,3,4, *F* 1,2
Maré, D S (Tvl) 1906 *S*
Marsberg, A F W (GW) 1906 *S, W, E*
Marsberg, P A (GW) 1910 *BI* 1
Martheze, W C (GW) 1903 *BI* 2, 1906 *I, W*
Martin, H J (Tvl) 1937 *A* 2
Mellett, T (GW) 1896 *BI* 2
Mellish, F W (WP) 1921 *NZ* 1,3, 1924 *BI* 1,2,3,4
Merry, J (EP) 1891 *BI* 1
Metcalf, H D (Bor) 1903 *BI* 2
Meyer, C du P (WP) 1921 *NZ* 1,2,3
Meyer, P J (GW) 1896 *BI* 1
Michau, J M (Tvl) 1921 *NZ* 1
Michau, J P (WP) 1921 *NZ* 1,2,3
Millar, W A (WP) 1906 *E*, 1910 *BI* 2,3, 1912-13 *I, W, F*
Mills, W J (WP) 1910 *BI* 2
Moll, T (Tvl) 1910 *BI* 2
Montini, P E (WP) 1956 *A* 1,2
Moolman, L C (NT) 1977 *Wld*, 1980 *S Am* 1,2, *BI* 1,2,3,4, *S Am* 3,4, *F*, 1981 *I* 1,2, *NZ* 1,2,3, *US*, 1982 *S Am* 1,2, 1984 *S Am* 1,2, 1986 *Cv* 1,2,3,4
Mordt, R H (Z-R, NT) 1980 *S Am* 1,2, *BI* 1,2,3,4, *S Am* 3,4, *F*, 1981 *I* 2, *NZ* 1,2,3, *US*, 1982 *S Am* 1,2, 1984 *S Am* 1,2
Morkel, A O (Tvl) 1903 *BI* 1
Morkel, D F T (Tvl) 1906 *I, E*, 1910 *BI* 1,3, 1912-13 *S, I, W, E, F*
Morkel, H J (WP) 1921 *NZ* 1
Morkel, H W (WP) 1921 *NZ* 1,2
Morkel, J A (WP) 1921 *NZ* 2,3
Morkel, J W H (WP) 1912-13 *S, I, W, E, F*
Morkel, P G (WP) 1912-13 *S, I, W, E, F*, 1921 *NZ* 1,2,3
Morkel, P K (WP) 1928 *NZ* 4
Morkel, W H (WP) 1910 *BI* 3, 1912-13 *S, I, W, E, F*, 1921 *NZ* 1,2,3
Morkel, W S (Tvl) 1906 *S, I, W, E*
Moss, C (N) 1949 *NZ* 1,2,3,4
Mostert, P J (WP) 1921 *NZ* 1,2,3, 1924 *BI* 1,2,4, 1928 *NZ* 1,2,3,4, 1931-32 *W, I, E, S*
Mulder, J C (Tvl) 1994 *NZ* 2,3, *S, W*
Muller, G H (WP) 1969 *A* 3,4, 1969-70 *S, W*, 1970 *NZ* 1,2,3,4, 1971 *F* 1,2, 1972 *E*, 1974 *BI* 1,3,4
Muller, H L (OFS) 1986 *Cv* 4 (R), 1989 *Wld* 1(R)
Muller, H S V (Tvl) 1949 *NZ* 1,2,3,4, 1951-52 *S, I, W, E, F*, 1953 *A* 1,2,3,4
Muller, L J J (N) 1992 *NZ, A*
Muller, P G (N) 1992 *NZ, A, F* 1,2, *E*, 1993 *F* 1,2, *A* 1,2,3, *Arg* 1,2, 1994 *E* 1,2, *NZ* 1, *S, W*
Myburgh, F R (EP) 1896 *BI* 1
Myburgh, J L (NT) 1962 *BI* 1, 1963 *A* 4, 1964 *W, F*, 1968 *BI* 1,2,3, *F* 1,2, 1969 *A* 1,2,3,4, 1969-70 *E, I, W*, 1970 *NZ* 3,4
Myburgh, W H (WT) 1924 *BI* 1

Naude, J P (WP) 1963 *A* 4, 1965 *A* 1,2, *NZ* 1,3,4, 1967 *F* 1,2,3,4, 1968 *BI* 1,2,3,4
Neethling, J B (WP) 1967 *F* 1,2,3,4, 1968 *BI* 4, 1969-70

S, 1970 *NZ* 1,2
Nel, J A (Tvl) 1960 *NZ* 1,2, 1963 *A* 1,2, 1965 *A* 2, *NZ* 1,2,3,4, 1970 *NZ* 3,4
Nel, J J (WP) 1956 *A* 1,2, *NZ* 1,2,3,4, 1958 *F* 1,2
Nel, P A R O (Tvl) 1903 *BI* 1,2,3
Nel, P J (N) 1928 *NZ* 1,2,3,4, 1931-32 *W, I, E, S*, 1933 *A* 1,3,4,5, 1937 *A* 1,2, *NZ* 2,3
Nimb, C F (WP) 1961 *I*
Nomis, S H (Tvl) 1967 *F* 4, 1968 *BI* 1,2,3,4, *F* 1,2, 1969 *A* 1,2,3,4, 1969-70 *S, E, I, W*, 1970 *NZ* 1,2,3,4, 1971 *F* 1,2, *A* 1,2,3, 1972 *E*
Nykamp, J L (Tvl) 1933 *A* 2

Ochse, J K (WP) 1951-52 *I, W, E, F*, 1953 *A* 1,2,4
Oelofse, J S A (Tvl) 1953 *A* 1,2,3,4
Oliver, J F (Tvl) 1928 *NZ* 3,4
Olivier, E (WP) 1967 *F* 1,2,3,4, 1968 *BI* 1,2,3,4, *F* 1,2, 1969 *A* 1,2,3,4, 1969-70 *S, E*
Olivier, J (NT) 1992 *F* 1,2, *E*, 1993 *F* 1,2, *A* 1,2,3, *Arg* 1
Olver, E (EP) 1896 *BI* 1
Oosthuizen, J J (WP) 1974 *BI* 1, *F* 1,2, 1975 *F* 1,2, 1976 *NZ* 1,2,3,4
Oosthuizen, O W (NT, Tvl) 1981 *I* 1(R),2, *NZ* 2,3, *US*, 1982 *S Am* 1,2, 1984 *E* 1,2
Osler, B L (WP) 1924 *BI* 1,2,3,4, 1928 *NZ* 1,2,3,4, 1931-32 *W, I, E, S*, 1933 *A* 1,2,3,4,5
Osler, S G (WP) 1928 *NZ* 1
Oxlee, K (N) 1960 *NZ* 1,2,3,4, 1960-61 *W, I, S*, 1961 *A* 1,2, 1962 *BI* 1,2,3,4, 1963 *A* 1,2,4, 1964 *W*, 1965 *NZ* 1,2

Parker, W H (EP) 1965 *A* 1,2
Partridge, J E C (Tvl) 1903 *BI* 1
Payn, C (N) 1924 *BI* 1,2
Pelser, H J M (Tvl) 1958 *F* 1, 1960 *NZ* 1,2,3,4, 1960-61 *W, I, F*, 1961 *I, A* 1,2
Pfaff, B D (WP) 1956 *A* 1
Pickard, J A J (WP) 1953 *A* 3,4, 1956 *NZ* 2, 1958 *F* 2
Pienaar, J F (Tvl) 1993 *F* 1,2, *A* 1,2,3, *Arg* 1,2, 1994 *E* 1,2, *NZ* 2,3, *Arg* 1,2, *S, W*
Pienaar, Z M J (OFS) 1980 *S Am* 2(R), *BI* 1,2,3,4, *S Am* 3,4, *F*, 1981 *I* 1,2, *NZ* 1,2,3
Pitzer, G (NT) 1967 *F* 1,2,3,4, 1968 *BI* 1,2,3,4, *F* 1,2, 1969 *A* 3,4
Pope, C F (WP) 1974 *BI* 1,2,3,4, 1975 *F* 1,2, 1976 *NZ* 2,3,4
Potgieter, H J (OFS) 1928 *NZ* 1,2
Potgieter, H L (OFS) 1977 *Wld*
Powell, A W (GW) 1896 *BI* 3
Powell, J M (GW) 1891 *BI* 2, 1896 *BI* 3, 1903 *BI* 1,2
Prentis, R B (Tvl) 1980 *S Am* 1,2, *BI* 1,2,3,4, *S Am* 3,4, *F*, 1981 *I* 1,2
Pretorius, N F (Tvl) 1928 *NZ* 1,2,3,4
Prinsloo, J (Tvl) 1958 *F* 1,2
Prinsloo, J (NT) 1963 *A* 3
Prinsloo, J P (Tvl) 1928 *NZ* 1
Putter, D J (WT) 1963 *A* 1,2,4

Raaff, J W E (GW) 1903 *BI* 1,2, 1906 *S, W, E*, 1910 *BI* 1
Ras, W J de Wet (OFS) 1976 *NZ* 1(R), 1980 *S Am* 2(R)
Reece-Edwards, H (N) 1992 *F* 1,2, 1993 *A* 2
Reid, A (WP) 1903 *BI* 3
Reid, B C (Bor) 1933 *A* 4
Reinach, J (OFS) 1986 *Cv* 1,2,3,4
Rens, I J (Tvl) 1953 *A* 3,4
Retief, D F (NT) 1955 *BI* 1,2,4, 1956 *A* 1,2, *NZ* 1,2, 3,4
Reynecke, H J (WP) 1910 *BI* 3
Richards, A R (WP) 1891 *BI* 1,2,3
Richter, A (NT) 1992 *F* 1,2, *E*, 1994 *E* 2, *NZ* 1,2,3
Riley, N M (ET) 1963 *A* 3
Riordan, C E (Tvl) 1910 *BI* 1,2
Robertson, I W (R) 1974 *F* 1,2, 1976 *NZ* 1,2,4
Rodgers, P H (NT, Tvl) 1989 *Wld* 1,2, 1992 *NZ, F* 1,2
Rogers, C D (Tvl) 1984 *E* 1,2, *S Am* 1,2
Roos, G D (WP) 1910 *BI* 2,3
Roos, P J (WP) 1903 *BI* 3, 1906 *I, W, E*
Rosenberg, W (Tvl) 1955 *BI* 2,3,4, 1956 *NZ* 3, 1958 *F* 1
Rossouw, D H (WP) 1953 *A* 3,4
Rousseau, W P (WP) 1928 *NZ* 3,4
Roux, F du T (WP) 1960-61 *W*, 1961 *A* 1,2, 1962 *BI* 1,2,3,4, 1963 *A* 2, 1965 *A* 1,2, *NZ* 1,2,3,4, 1968 *BI* 3,4, *F* 1,2, 1969 *A* 1,2,3,4, 1969-70 *I*, 1970 *NZ* 1,2,3,4
Roux, J P (Tvl) 1994 *E* 2, *NZ* 1,2,3, *Arg* 1
Roux, O A (NT) 1969-70 *S, E, I, W*, 1972 *E*, 1974 *BI* 3,4

Samuels, T A (GW) 1896 *BI* 2,3,4
Sauermann, J T (Tvl) 1971 *F* 1,2, *A* 1, 1972 *E*, 1974 *BI* 1
Schlebusch, J J J (OFS) 1974 *BI* 3,4, 1975 *F* 2
Schmidt, L U (NT) 1958 *F* 2, 1962 *BI* 2
Schmidt, U L (NT, Tvl) 1986 *Cv* 1,2,3,4, 1989 *Wld* 1,2, 1992 *NZ, A*, 1993 *F* 1,2, *A* 1,2,3, 1994 *Arg* 1,2, *S, W*
Schoeman, J (WP) 1963 *A* 3,4, 1965 *I, S, A* 1, *NZ* 1,2
Scholtz, C P (WP) 1994 *Arg* 1
Scholtz, H H (WP) 1921 *NZ* 1,2
Schutte, P J W (Tvl) 1994 *S, W*
Scott, P (Tvl) 1896 *BI* 1,2,3,4
Sendin, W D (GW) 1921 *NZ* 2
Serfontein, D J (WP) 1980 *BI* 1,2,3,4, *S Am* 3,4, *F*, 1981 *I* 1,2, *NZ* 1,2,3, *US*, 1982 *S Am* 1,2, 1984 *E* 1,2, *S Am* 1,2
Shand, R (GW) 1891 *BI* 2,3
Sheriff, A R (Tvl) 1938 *BI* 1,2,3
Shum, E H (Tvl) 1912-13 *E*
Sinclair, D J (Tvl) 1955 *BI* 1,2,3,4
Sinclair, J H (Tvl) 1903 *BI* 1
Skene, A L (WP) 1958 *F* 2
Slater, J T (EP) 1924 *BI* 3,4, 1928 *NZ* 1
Smal, G P (WP) 1986 *Cv* 1,2,3,4, 1989 *Wld* 1,2
Small, J T (Tvl, N) 1992 *NZ, A, F* 1,2, *E*, 1993 *F* 1,2, *A* 1,2,3, *Arg* 1,2, 1994 *E* 1,2, *NZ* 1,2,3(t), *Arg* 1
Smit, F C (WP) 1992 *E*
Smith, C M (OFS) 1963 *A* 3,4, 1964 *W, F*, 1965 *A* 1,2, *NZ* 2
Smith, C W (GW) 1891 *BI* 2, 1896 *BI* 2,3
Smith, D (GW) 1891 *BI* 2
Smith, D J (Z-R) 1980 *BI* 1,2,3,4
Smith, G A C (EP) 1938 *BI* 3
Smollan, F C (Tvl) 1933 *A* 3,4,5
Snedden, R C (GW) 1891 *BI* 2
Snyman, D S L (WP) 1972 *E*, 1974 *BI* 1,2(R), *F* 1,2, 1975 *F* 1,2, 1976 *NZ* 2,3, 1977 *Wld*
Snyman, J C P (OFS) 1974 *BI* 2,3,4
Sonnekus, G H H (OFS) 1974 *BI* 3, 1984 *E* 1,2
Spies, J J (NT) 1970 *NZ* 1,2,3,4
Stander, J C J (OFS) 1974 *BI* 4(R), 1976 *NZ* 1,2,3,4
Stapelberg, W P (NT) 1974 *F* 1,2
Starke, J J (WP) 1956 *NZ* 4
Starke, K T (WP) 1924 *BI* 1,2,3,4
Steenekamp, J G A (Tvl) 1958 *F* 1
Stegmann, A C (WP) 1906 *S, I*
Stegmann, J A (Tvl) 1912-13 *S, I, W, E, F*
Stewart, D A (WP) 1960 *S*, 1960-61 *E, S, F*, 1961 *I*, 1963 *A* 1,3,4, 1964 *W, F*, 1965 *I*
Stofberg, M T S (OFS, NT, WP) 1976 *NZ* 2,3, 1977 *Wld*, 1980 *S Am* 1,2, *BI* 1,2,3,4, *S Am* 3,4, *F*, 1981 *I* 1,2, *NZ* 1,2, *US*, 1982 *S Am* 1,2, 1984 *E* 1,2
Strachan, L C (Tvl) 1931-32 *E, S*, 1937 *A* 1,2, *NZ* 1,2,3, 1938 *BI* 1,2,3
Stransky, J (N) 1993 *A* 1,2,3, *Arg* 1, 1994 *Arg* 1,2
Straeuli, R A W (Tvl) 1994 *NZ* 1, *Arg* 1,2, *S, W*
Strauss, C P (WP) 1992 *F* 1,2, *E*, 1993 *F* 1,2, *A* 1,2,3, *Arg* 1,2, 1994 *E* 1, *NZ* 1,2, *Arg* 1,2
Strauss, J A (WP) 1984 *S Am* 1,2
Strauss, J H P (Tvl) 1976 *NZ* 3,4, 1980 *S Am* 1
Strauss, S S F (GW) 1921 *NZ* 3
Strydom, C F (OFS) 1955 *BI* 3, 1956 *A* 1,2, *NZ* 1,4, 1958 *F* 1
Strydom, J J (Tvl) 1993 *F* 2, *A* 1,2,3, *Arg* 1,2, 1994 *E* 1
Strydom, L J (NT) 1949 *NZ* 1,2
Styger, J J (OFS) 1992 *NZ*(R), *A, F* 1,2, *E*, 1993 *F* 2(R), *A* 3(R)
Suter, M R (N) 1965 *I, S*
Swart, J J N (SWA) 1955 *BI* 1
Swart, I S (Tvl) 1993 *A* 1,2,3, *Arg* 1, 1994 *E* 1,2, *NZ* 1,3, *Arg* 2(R)

Taberer, W S (GW) 1896 *BI* 2
Taylor, O B (N) 1962 *BI* 1
Theunissen, D J (GW) 1896 *BI* 3
Thompson, G (WP) 1912-13 *S, I, W*
Tindall, J C (WP) 1924 *BI* 1, 1928 *NZ* 1,2,3,4
Tobias, E G (SARF, Bol) 1981 *I* 1,2, 1984 *E* 1,2, *S Am*

1,2
Tod, N S (N) 1928 *NZ* 2
Townsend, W H (N) 1921 *NZ* 1
Trenery, W (GW) 1891 *BI* 2
Truter, D R (WP) 1924 *BI* 2,4
Truter, J T (N) 1963 *A* 1, 1964 *F*, 1965 *A* 2
Turner, F G (EP) 1933 *A* 1,2,3, 1937 *A* 1,2, *NZ* 1,2,3, 1938 *BI* 1,2,3
Twigge, R J (NT) 1960 *S*

Ulyate, C A (Tvl) 1955 *BI* 1,2,3,4, 1956 *NZ* 1,2,3
Uys, P de W (NT) 1960-61 *W*, *E*, *S*, 1961 *I*, *A* 1,2, 1962 *BI* 1,4, 1963 *A* 1,2, 1969 *A* 1(R),2

Van Aswegen, H J (WP) 1981 *NZ* 1, 1982 *S Am* 2(R)
Van Broekhuizen, H D (WP) 1896 *BI* 4
Van Buuren, M C (Tvl) 1891 *BI* 1
Van De Vyver, D F (WP) 1937 *A* 2
Van Den Berg, D S (N) 1975 *F* 1,2 1976 *NZ* 1,2
Van Den Berg, M A (WP) 1937 *A* 1, *NZ* 1,2,3
Van Den Bergh, E (EP) 1994 *Arg* 2(t & R)
Van Der Merwe, A J (Bol) 1955 *BI* 2,3,4, 1956 *A* 1,2, *NZ* 1,2,3,4, 1958 *F* 1, 1960 *S*, *NZ* 2
Van Der Merwe, A V (WP) 1931-32 *W*
Van Der Merwe, B S (NT) 1949 *NZ* 1
Van Der Merwe, H S (NT) 1960 *NZ* 4, 1963 *A* 2,3,4, 1964 *F*
Van Der Merwe, J P (WP) 1969-70 *W*
Van Der Merwe, P R (SWD, WT, GW) 1981 *NZ* 2,3, *US*, 1986 *Cv* 1,2, 1989 *Wld* 1
Vanderplank, B E (N) 1924 *BI* 3,4
Van Der Schyff, J H (GW) 1949 *NZ* 1,2,3,4, 1955 *BI* 1
Van Der Watt, A E (WP) 1969-70 *S* (R), *E*, *I*
Van Der Westhuizen, J C (WP) 1928 *NZ* 2,3,4, 1931-32 *I*
Van Der Westhuizen, J H (WP) 1931-32 *I*, *E*, *S*
Van Der Westhuizen, J H (NT) 1993 *Arg* 1,2, 1994 *E* 1,2(R), *Arg* 2, *S*, *W*
Van Druten, N J V (Tvl) 1924 *BI* 1,2,3,4, 1928 *NZ* 1,2,3,4
Van Heerden, A J (Tvl) 1921 *NZ* 1,3
Van Heerden, F J (WP) 1994 *E* 1,2(R), *NZ* 3
Van Heerden, J L (NT, Tvl) 1974 *BI* 3,4, *F* 1,2, 1975 *F* 1,2, 1976 *NZ* 1,2,3,4, 1977 *Wld*, 1980 *BI* 1,3,4, *S Am* 3,4, *F*
Van Jaarsveld, C J (Tvl) 1949 *NZ* 1
Van Jaarsveldt, D C (R) 1960 *S*
Van Niekerk, J A (WP) 1928 *NZ* 4
Van Reenen, G L (WP) 1937 *A* 2, *NZ* 1
Van Renen, C G (WP) 1891 *BI* 3, 1896 *BI* 1,4
Van Renen, W (WP) 1903 *BI* 1,3
Van Rensburg, J T J (Tvl) 1992 *NZ*, *A*, *E*, 1993 *F* 1,2, *A* 1, 1994 *NZ* 2
Van Rooyen, G W (Tvl) 1921 *NZ* 2,3
Van Ryneveld, R C B (WP) 1910 *BI* 2,3
Van Schoor, R A M (R) 1949 *NZ* 2,3,4, 1951-52 *S*, *I*, *W*, *E*, *F*, 1953 *A* 1,2,3,4
Van Vollenhoven, K T (NT) 1955 *BI* 1,2,3,4, 1956 *A* 1,2, *NZ* 3
Van Vuuren, T F (EP) 1912-13 *S*, *I*, *W*, *E*, *F*
Van Wyk, C J (Tvl) 1951-52 *S*, *I*, *W*, *E*, *F*, 1953 *A* 1,2,3,4, 1955 *BI* 1
Van Wyk, J F B (NT) 1970 *NZ* 1,2,3,4, 1971 *F* 1,2, *A* 1,2,3, 1972 *E*, 1974 *BI* 1,3,4, 1976 *NZ* 3,4
Van Wyk, S P (WP) 1928 *NZ* 1,2
Van Zyl, B P (WP) 1961 *I*
Van Zyl, C G P (OFS) 1965 *NZ* 1,2,3,4
Van Zyl, G H (WP) 1958 *F* 1, 1960 *S*, *NZ* 1,2,3,4, 1960-61 *W*, *I*, *E*, *S*, *F*, 1961 *I*, *A* 1,2, 1962 *BI* 1,3,4
Van Zyl, H J (Tvl) 1960 *NZ* 1,2,3,4, 1960-61 *I*, *E*, *S*, 1961 *I*, *A* 1,2
Van Zyl, P J (Bol) 1961 *I*
Veldsman, P E (WP) 1977 *Wld*
Venter, B (OFS) 1994 *E* 1,2, *NZ* 1,2,3, *Arg* 1,2
Venter, F D (Tvl) 1931-32 *W*, *S*, 1933 *A* 3
Versfeld, C (WP) 1891 *BI* 3
Versfeld, M (WP) 1891 *BI* 1,2,3
Vigne, J T (Tvl) 1891 *BI* 1,2,3
Viljoen, J F (GW) 1971 *F* 1,2, *A* 1,2,3, 1972 *E*
Viljoen, J T (N) 1971 *A* 1,2,3
Villet, J V (WP) 1984 *E* 1,2
Visagie, P J (GW) 1967 *F* 1,2,3,4, 1968 *BI* 1,2,3,4, *F* 1,2, 1969 *A* 1,2,3,4, 1969-70 *S*, *E*, 1970 *NZ* 1,2,3,4, 1971 *F* 1,2, *A* 1,2,3
Visagie, R G (OFS, N) 1984 *E* 1,2, *S Am* 1,2, 1993 *F* 1
Visser, J de V (WP) 1981 *NZ* 2, *US*
Visser, P J (Tvl) 1933 *A* 2
Viviers, S S (OFS) 1956 *A* 1,2, *NZ* 2,3,4
Vogel, M L (OFS) 1974 *BI* 2(R)

Wagenaar, C (NT) 1977 *Wld*
Wahl, J J (WP) 1949 *NZ* 1
Walker, A P (N) 1921 *NZ* 1,3, 1924 *BI* 1,2,3,4
Walker, H N (OFS) 1953 *A* 3, 1956 *A* 2, *NZ* 1,4
Walker, H W (Tvl) 1910 *BI* 1,2,3
Walton, D C (N) 1964 *F*, 1965 *I*, *S*, *NZ* 3,4, 1969 *A* 1,2, 1969-70 *E*
Waring, F W (WP) 1931-32 *I*, *E*, 1933 *A* 1,2,3,4,5
Wegner, N (WP) 1993 *F* 2, *A* 1,2,3
Wessels, J J (WP) 1896 *BI* 1,2,3
Whipp, P J M (WP) 1974 *BI* 1,2, 1975 *F* 1, 1976 *NZ* 1,3,4, 1980 *S Am* 1,2
White, J (Bor) 1931-32 *W*, 1933 *A* 1,2,3,4,5, 1937 *A* 1,2, *NZ* 1,2
Wiese, J J (Tvl) 1993 *F* 1
Williams, A E (GW) 1910 *BI* 1
Williams, A P (WP) 1984 *E* 1,2
Williams, C M (WP) 1993 *Arg* 2, 1994 *E* 1,2, *NZ* 1,2,3, *Arg* 1,2, *S*, *W*
Williams, D O (WP) 1937 *A* 1,2 *NZ* 1,2,3, 1938 *BI* 1,2,3
Williams, J G (NT) 1971 *F* 1,2, *A* 1,2,3, 1972 *E*, 1974 *BI* 1,2,4, *F* 1,2, 1976 *NZ* 1,2
Wilson, L G (WP) 1960 *NZ* 3,4, 1960-61 *W*, *I*, *E*, *F*, 1961 *I*, *A* 1,2, 1962 *BI* 1,2,3,4, 1963 *A* 1,2,3,4, 1964 *W*, *F*, 1965 *I*, *S*, *A* 1,2, *NZ* 1,2,3,4
Wolmarans, B J (OFS) 1977 *Wld*
Wright, G D (EP, Tvl) 1986 *Cv* 3,4, 1989 *Wld* 1,2, 1992 *F* 1,2, *E*
Wyness, M R K (WP) 1962 *BI* 1,2,3,4, 1963 *A* 2

Zeller, W C (N) 1921 *NZ* 2,3
Zimerman, M (WP) 1931-32 *W*, *I*, *E*, *S*

SOUTH AFRICAN INTERNATIONAL RECORDS

Both team and individual records are for official South African international matches, up to 31 March 1995.

TEAM RECORDS

Highest score
52 v Argentina (52-23) 1993 Buenos Aires
v individual countries
52 v Argentina (52-23) 1993 Buenos Aires
30 v Australia (30-11) 1969 Johannesburg

34 v B Isles (34-14) 1962 Bloemfontein
35 v England (35-9) 1984 Johannesburg
38 v France { (38-5) 1913 Bordeaux / (38-25) 1975 Bloemfontein }
38 v Ireland (38-0) 1912 Dublin
24 v N Zealand { (24-12) 1981 Wellington / (24-27) 1992 Johannesburg }
33 v NZ Cavaliers (33-18) 1986 Pretoria
50 v S America (50-18) 1982 Pretoria
44 v Scotland (44-0) 1951 Murrayfield
38 v United States (38-7) 1981 New York
24 v Wales (24-3) 1964 Durban

Biggest winning points margin
44 v Scotland (44-0) 1951 Murrayfield
v individual countries
29 v Argentina (52-23) 1993 Buenos Aires
25 v Australia (28-3) 1961 Johannesburg
20 v B Isles (34-14) 1962 Bloemfontein
26 v England (35-9) 1984 Johannesburg
33 v France (38-5) 1913 Bordeaux
38 v Ireland (38-0) 1912 Dublin
17 v N Zealand (17-0) 1928 Durban
15 v NZ Cavaliers (33-18) 1986 Pretoria
32 v S America (50-18) 1982 Pretoria
44 v Scotland (44-0) 1951 Murrayfield
31 v United States (38-7) 1981 New York
21 v Wales (24-3) 1964 Durban

Longest winning sequence
10 matches – 1949-53

Highest score by opposing team
33 England (16-33) 1992 Twickenham
by individual countries
26 Argentina { (29-26) 1993 Buenos Aires / (46-26) 1994 Johannesburg }
28 Australia (20-28) 1993 Brisbane
28 B Isles (9-28) 1974 Pretoria
33 England (16-33) 1992 Twickenham
29 France (16-29) 1992 Parc des Princes
15 Ireland (23-15) 1981 Cape Town
25 N Zealand (22-25) 1981 Auckland
19 NZ Cavaliers (18-19) 1986 Durban
21 S America (12-21) 1982 Bloemfontein
10 Scotland { (18-10) 1960 Port Elizabeth / (34-10) 1994 Murrayfield }
7 United States (38-7) 1981 New York
12 Wales (20-12) 1994 Cardiff

Biggest losing points margin
23 v Australia (3-26) 1992 Cape Town
v individual countries
23 v Australia (3-26) 1992 Cape Town
19 v B Isles (9-28) 1974 Pretoria
17 v England { (16-33) 1992 Twickenham / (15-32) 1994 Pretoria }
13 v France (16-29) 1992 Parc des Princes
3 v Ireland (6-9) 1965 Dublin
17 v N Zealand (3-20) 1965 Auckland
1 v NZ Cavaliers (18-19) 1986 Durban
9 v S America (12-21) 1982 Bloemfontein
6 v Scotland (0-6) 1906 Glasgow
No defeats v Argentina, United States or Wales

Longest losing sequence
7 matches – 1964-65

Most tries by South Africa in an international
10 v Ireland (38-0) 1912 Dublin

Most tries against South Africa in an international
5 { by B Isles (22-23) 1955 Johannesburg / by N Zealand (3-20) 1965 Auckland / by B Isles (9-28) 1974 Pretoria }

Most points on overseas tour (all matches)
753 in Australia/N Zealand (26 matches) 1937

Most tries on overseas tour (all matches)
161 in Australia/N Zealand (26 matches) 1937

INDIVIDUAL RECORDS

Most capped player
F C H du Preez } 38 { 1960-71
J H Ellis } 38 { 1965-76
in individual positions
Full-back
L G Wilson 27 1960-65
Wing
J P Engelbrecht 33 1960-69
Centre
J L Gainsford 33 1960-67
Fly-half
H E Botha 28 1980-92
Scrum-half
D J de Villiers 25 1962-70

Prop
J F K Marais 35 1963-74
Hooker
G F Malan 18 1958-65
Lock
F C H du Preez 31(38)[1] 1960-71
Flanker
J H Ellis 38 1965-76
No 8
D J Hopwood 22[2] 1960-65
[1]du Preez won 7 caps as a flanker
[2]T P Bedford, 25 caps, won 19 at No 8 and 6 as a flanker

Longest international career
J M Powell 13 seasons 1891-1903
B H Heatlie 13 seasons 1891-1903
D M Gerber 13 seasons 1980-1992/3
H E Botha 13 seasons 1980-1992/3
Gerber's and Botha's careers ended during a Northern Hemisphere season

---

Most consecutive internationals 25
S H Nomis 1967-72

Most internationals as captain
D J de Villiers 22 1965-70

Most points in internationals – 312
H E Botha (28 matches) 1980-92

Most points in an international – 22
G R Bosch v France 1975 Pretoria
G Johnson v Argentina 1993 Buenos Aires
J T Stransky v Argentina 1994 Port Elizabeth

Most tries in internationals – 19
D M Gerber (24 matches) 1980-92

Most tries in an international – 3
E E McHardy v Ireland 1912 Dublin
J A Stegmann v Ireland 1912 Dublin
K T van Vollenhoven v B Isles 1955 Cape Town
H J van Zyl v Australia 1961 Johannesburg
R H Mordt v New Zealand 1981 Auckland
R H Mordt v United States 1981 New York
D M Gerber v S America 1982 Pretoria
D M Gerber v England 1984 Johannesburg

Most conversions in internationals – 50
H E Botha (28 matches) 1980-92

Most conversions in an international – 7
A Geffin v Scotland 1951 Murrayfield

Most dropped goals in internationals – 18
H E Botha (28 matches) 1980-92

Most dropped goals in an international – 3
H E Botha { v S America 1980 Durban
v Ireland 1981 Durban }

Most penalty goals in internationals – 50
H E Botha (28 matches) 1980-92

Most penalty goals in an international – 6
G R Bosch v France 1975 Pretoria

Most points in international series – 69
H E Botha (4 appearances) v NZ Cavaliers 1986

Most points in international series on tour – 35
H E Botha (3 appearances) 1981 N Zealand

Most tries in international series on tour – 6
E E McHardy (5 appearances) 1912-13 B Isles/France

Most points on overseas tour – 190
G H Brand (20 appearances) 1937 Australia/N Zealand

Most tries on overseas tour – 22
J A Loubser (20 appearances) 1906-07 B Isles/France

Most points in a tour match – 38
A J Joubert v Swansea 1994 St Helen's

Most tries in a tour match – 6
R G Dryburgh v Queensland 1956 Brisbane

OFF THE STRAIGHT AND NARROW

THE 1994 SEASON IN NEW ZEALAND

Donald Cameron *New Zealand Herald*

It became typical of the uncertain direction of New Zealand rugby during 1994 that on an October night Zinzan Brooke, the Auckland and All Black back-row forward, became the New Zealand Personality of the Year and was 12 hours later suspended for two weeks for foul play in the First Division final against North Harbour.

The award was made in the memory of the late Kel Tremain, the legendary All Black loose forward, later a forceful administrator, at the first National Awards Dinner, staged by the NZRFU and backed by their brewery sponsor. The setting up of this event was typical of the rapacious attitude of the NZRFU, and especially of its main sponsor. They both ignored the 23-year-old National Rugby Player of the Year Award that the Ponsonby club had organised from Auckland with consistent and conspicuous success. The solution was typical of modern New Zealand rugby: Ponsonby threatened an injunction and the NZRFU settled out of court for about £16,000. This was perhaps the last time in 1994 that the NZRFU was caught with its public-relations pants down, but certainly not the first.

Similarly, the NZRFU's principal advertisement, the All Blacks, could move only hopefully along their six-Test path, losing the first two to France, the last to Australia, and thanking their lucky stars that a curiously ineffective South African side so ignored its winning opportunities that Laurie Mains' All Blacks scraped through with two wins and a draw.

Mains used 26 players in those six Tests, which showed that even after three years as the All Black coach, he has still to display consistency, especially among the backs. He started with Timu, Lomu (then a raw young flanker posted on the wing), Bunce, Kirwan, Cooper, Mannix and Forster. Five Tests later, all but Bunce and Timu had been axed, the latter retaining his place only by moving from full-back to wing.

The NZRFU broke new ground by staging their All Black coach election during rather than at the end of the season and Mains found himself opposed by John Hart, the former Auckland and All Black coach who had twice been spurned by the NZRFU and then tacked on to Alex Wyllie's World Cup coaching staff in 1991 – probably the biggest gaffe in NZRFU history, at least in recent years. Everything else in the country – politicians, unemployment, water shortages – took a back seat while the Mains-Hart battle was fought in the media.

The NZRFU appointed a screening committee to establish a pecking order before the ballot. The sub-committee could not make a finding. The council voted in favour of Mains and then retreated behind the secret-vote ballot box. Then, while the three National Championship divisions were bustling along in their spectacular, high-interest one-round contests, the NZRFU tried to persuade everyone that next winter there should be two rounds, the first early in the season to offer some publicity challenge to the launching of the Auckland Warriors in the New South Wales Rugby League Winfield Cup. The unions retorted that one round was quite enough, thank you, at a time when the NZRFU was busily putting up barriers against the four New Zealand provinces – North Harbour, Auckland, Canterbury and Otago – fielding full-strength sides in the Super-10 competition with South African, Australian and Tongan sides in March and April 1995.

At about the same time, the NZRFU was sending out its salesmen to try to revive interest in the commissioned survey on the reorganisation of the NZRFU and its workings. Out in the hinterland, the smaller unions can see this destroying their club competitions and themselves. Yet when they raise the question of when another survey recommendation can be put into effect – the trimming of the 19-man council to nine – the suggestion is that this idea remains in the too-hard basket.

From time to time, too, the NZRFU campaign against rough play, while totally commendable, has had the habit of coming up with the wrong legal definitions of the punishments and suspensions. At one stage the suspensions of Richard Loe from Canterbury, Blair Larsen and Mark Weedon from North Harbour and Zinzan Brooke from Auckland were all slightly out of kilter, adding to the lack of credibility within the NZRFU legal system.

NATIONAL CHAMPIONSHIP

Division 1	*P*	*W*	*D*	*L*	*F*	*A*	*Pts*
Auckland	8	7	0	1	319	164	29
North Harbour	8	7	0	1	294	165	28
Canterbury	8	6	0	2	230	194	24
Otago	8	4	0	4	241	205	18
Counties	8	4	0	4	179	166	17
Wellington	8	4	0	4	200	262	16
Waikato	8	3	0	5	191	202	13
King Country	8	1	0	7	136	324	4
Taranaki	8	0	0	8	153	261	4

Semi-finals: Auckland 33, Otago 16; North Harbour 59, Canterbury 27 **Final:** Auckland 22, North Harbour 16

Division 2	*P*	*W*	*D*	*L*	*F*	*A*	*Pts*
Hawke's Bay	8	8	0	0	399	172	32
Southland	8	7	0	1	284	177	28
Northland	8	6	0	2	343	166	24
Bay of Plenty	8	5	0	3	314	227	21
Manawatu	8	4	0	4	261	221	17
Nelson Bays	8	3	0	5	156	280	12
S Canterbury	8	2	0	6	217	275	10
Wairarapa-Bush	8	1	0	7	107	420	4
Horowhenua	8	0	0	8	155	274	1

Semi-finals: Southland 29, Northland 22; Hawke's Bay 65, Bay of Plenty 16 **Final:** Southland 20, Hawke's Bay 18

Division 3	*P*	*W*	*D*	*L*	*F*	*A*	*Pts*
Wanganui	8	8	0	0	310	121	32
Thames Valley	8	7	0	1	356	87	29
Poverty Bay	8	5	0	3	277	181	21
Mid-Canterbury	8	4	1	3	218	197	20
Marlborough	8	4	1	3	270	222	19
Buller	8	3	0	5	153	273	12
East Coast	8	2	0	6	142	234	9
West Coast	8	1	0	7	103	248	6
North Otago	8	1	0	7	168	425	4

Semi-finals: Poverty Bay 40, Thames Valley 20; Mid-Canterbury 22, Wanganui 13
Final: Mid-Canterbury 26, Poverty Bay 16

RANFURLY SHIELD

Waikato 74, Thames Valley 3; Waikato 26, Manawatu 11; Waikato 98, South Canterbury 22; Waikato 45, King Country 10; Canterbury 29, Waikato 26; Canterbury 42, Counties 16; Canterbury 22, Otago 20

NEW ZEALAND INTERNATIONAL PLAYERS *(up to 31 March 1995)*

ABBREVIATIONS

A – Australia; *Arg* – Argentina; *AW* – Anglo-Welsh; *BI* – British Isles teams; *C* – Canada; *E* – England; *F* – France; *Fj* – Fiji; *I* – Ireland; *It* – Italy; *R* – Romania; *S* – Scotland; *SA* – South Africa; *US* – United States; *W* – Wales; *Wld* – World Invitation XV; *WS* – Western Samoa; (R) – Replacement; (t) – temporary replacement. Entries in square brackets [ ] indicate appearances in the Rugby World Cup.

Note: When a series has taken place, figures denote the particular matches in which players featured. Thus 1959 *BI* 2,4 indicates that a player appeared in the second and fourth Tests of the 1959 series against the British Isles.

Abbott, H L (Taranaki) 1906 *F*
Aitken, G G (Wellington) 1921 *SA* 1,2
Allen, F R (Auckland) 1946 *A* 1,2 1947 *A* 1,2, 1949 *SA* 1,2
Allen, M R (Taranaki) 1993 *WS* (t)
Allen, N H (Counties) 1980 *A* 3, *W*
Alley, G T (Canterbury) 1928 *SA* 1,2,3
Anderson, A (Canterbury) 1983 *S*, *E*, 1984 *A* 1,2,3, 1987 [*Fj*]
Anderson, B L (Wairarapa-Bush) 1986 *A* 1
Archer, W R (Otago, Southland) 1955 *A* 1,2, 1956 *SA* 1,3
Argus, W G (Canterbury) 1946 *A* 1,2, 1947 *A* 1,2
Arnold, D A (Canterbury) 1963 *I*, *W*, 1964 *E*, *F*
Arnold, K D (Waikato) 1947 *A* 1,2
Ashby, D L (Southland) 1958 *A* 2
Asher, A A (Auckland) 1903 *A*
Ashworth, B G (Auckland) 1978 *A* 1,2
Ashworth, J C (Canterbury, Hawke's Bay) 1978 *A* 1,2,3, 1980 *A* 1,2,3, 1981 *SA* 1,2,3, 1982 *A* 1,2, 1983 *BI* 1,2,3,4, *A*, 1984 *F* 1,2 *A* 1,2,3, 1985 *E* 1,2, *A*
Atkinson, H (West Coast) 1913 *A* 1
Avery, H E (Wellington) 1910 *A* 1,2,3

Bachop, G T M (Canterbury) 1989 *W*, *I*, 1990 *S* 1,2, *A* 1,2,3, *F* 1,2, 1991 *Arg* 1,2, *A* 1,2, [*E*, *US*, *C*, *A*, *S*], 1992 *Wld* 1, 1994 *SA* 1,2,3, *A*
Bachop, S J (Otago) 1994 *F* 2, *SA* 1,2,3, *A*
Badeley, C E O (Auckland) 1921 *SA* 1,2
Baird, J A S (Otago) 1913 *A* 2
Ball, N (Wellington) 1931 *A*, 1932 *A* 2,3, 1935 *W*, 1936 *E*
Barrett, J (Auckland) 1913 *A* 2,3
Barry, E F (Wellington) 1934 *A* 2
Batty, G B (Wellington, Bay of Plenty) 1972 *W*, *S*, 1973 *E* 1, *I*, *F*, *E* 2, 1974 *A* 1,3, *I*, 1975 *S*, 1976 *SA* 1,2,3,4, 1977 *BI* 1
Batty, W (Auckland) 1930 *BI* 1,3,4, 1931 *A*
Beatty, G E (Taranaki) 1950 *BI* 1
Bell, R H (Otago) 1951 *A* 3, 1952 *A* 1,2
Bellis, E A (Wanganui) 1921 *SA* 1,2,3
Bennet, R (Otago) 1905 *A*
Berghan, T (Otago) 1938 *A* 1,2,3
Berry, M J (Wairarapa-Bush) 1986 *A* 3 (R)
Bevan, V D (Wellington) 1949 *A* 1,2, 1950 *BI* 1,2,3,4
Birtwistle, W M (Canterbury) 1965 *SA* 1,2,3,4, 1967 *E*, *W*, *S*
Black, J E (Canterbury) 1977 *F* 1, 1979 *A*, 1980 *A* 3
Black, N W (Auckland) 1949 *SA* 3
Black, R S (Otago) 1914 *A* 1
Blake, A W (Wairarapa) 1949 *A* 1
Boggs, E G (Auckland) 1946 *A* 2, 1949 *SA* 1
Bond, J G (Canterbury) 1949 *A* 2
Booth, E E (Otago) 1906 *F*, 1907 *A* 1,3
Boroevich, K G (Wellington) 1986 *F* 1, *A* 1, *F* 3 (R)
Botica, F M (North Harbour) 1986 *F* 1, *A* 1,2,3, *F* 2,3, 1989 *Arg* 1 (R)
Bowden, N J G (Taranaki) 1952 *A* 2
Bowers, R G (Wellington) 1954 *I*, *F*
Bowman, A W (Hawke's Bay) 1938 *A* 1,2,3
Braid, G J (Bay of Plenty) 1983 *S*, *E*
Bremner, S G (Auckland, Canterbury) 1952 *A* 2, 1956 *SA* 2
Brewer, M R (Otago, Canterbury) 1986 *F* 1, *A* 1,2,3, *F* 2,3, 1988 *A* 1, 1989 *A*, *W*, *I*, 1990 *S* 1,2, *A* 1,2,3, *F* 1,2, 1992 *I* 2, *A* 1, 1994 *F* 1,2, *SA* 1,2,3, *A*
Briscoe, K C (Taranaki) 1959 *BI* 2, 1960 *SA* 1,2,3,4, 1963 *I*, *W*, 1964 *E*, *S*
Brooke, R M (Auckland) 1992 *I* 2, *A* 1,2,3, *SA*, 1993 *BI* 1,2,3, *A*, *WS*, 1994 *SA* 2,3
Brooke, Z V (Auckland) 1987 [*Arg*], 1989 *Arg* 2 (R), 1990 *A* 1,2,3, *F* 1 (R), 1991 *Arg* 2, *A* 1,2, [*E*, *It*, *C*, *A*, *S*], 1992 *A* 2,3, *SA*, 1993 *BI* 1,2,3(R), *WS*(R), *S*, *E*, 1994 *F* 2, *SA* 1,2,3, *A*
Brooke-Cowden, M (Auckland) 1986 *F* 1, *A* 1, 1987 [*W*]
Brown, C (Taranaki) 1913 *A* 2,3
Brown, O M (Auckland) 1992 *I* 2, *A* 1,2,3, *SA*, 1993 *BI* 1,2,3, *A*, *S*, *E*, 1994 *F* 1,2, *SA* 1,2,3, *A*
Brown, R H (Taranaki) 1955 *A* 3, 1956 *SA* 1,2,3,4, 1957 *A* 1,2 1958 *A* 1,2,3, 1959 *BI* 1,3, 1961 *F* 1,2,3, 1962 *A* 1
Brownlie, C J (Hawke's Bay) 1924 *W*, 1925 *E*, *F*
Brownlie, M J (Hawke's Bay) 1924 *I*, *W*, 1925 *E*, *F*, 1928 *SA* 1,2,3,4
Bruce, J A (Auckland) 1914 *A* 1,2
Bruce, O D (Canterbury) 1976 *SA* 1,2,4, 1977 *BI* 2,3,4, *F* 1,2, 1978 *A* 1,2, *I*, *W*, *E*, *S*
Bryers, R F (King Country) 1949 *A* 1
Budd, T A (Southland) 1946 *A* 2, 1949 *A* 2
Bullock-Douglas, G A H (Wanganui) 1932 *A* 1,2,3, 1934 *A* 1,2
Bunce, F E (North Harbour) 1992 *Wld* 1,2,3, *I* 1,2, *A* 1,2,3, *SA*, 1993 *BI* 1,2,3, *A*, *WS*, *S*, *E*, 1994 *F* 1,2, *SA* 1,2,3, *A*
Burgess, G A J (Auckland) 1981 *SA* 2
Burgess, G F (Southland) 1905 *A*
Burgess, R E (Manawatu) 1971 *BI* 1,2,3, 1972 *A* 3, *W*, 1973 *I*, *F*
Burke, P S (Taranaki) 1955 *A* 1, 1957 *A* 1,2
Burns, P J (Canterbury) 1908 *AW* 2, 1910 *A* 1,2,3, 1913 *A* 3
Bush, R G (Otago) 1931 *A*
Bush, W K (Canterbury) 1974 *A* 1,2, 1975 *S*, 1976 *I*, *SA* 2,4, 1977 *BI* 2,3,4(R), 1978 *I*, *W*, 1979 *A*
Buxton, J B (Canterbury) 1955 *A* 3, 1956 *SA* 1

Cain, M J (Taranaki) 1913 *US*, 1914 *A* 1,2,3
Callesen, J A (Manawatu) 1974 *A* 1,2,3, 1975 *S*
Cameron, D (Taranaki) 1908 *AW* 1,2,3
Cameron, L M (Manawatu) 1980 *A* 3, 1981 *SA* 1(R),2,3, *R*
Carleton, S R (Canterbury) 1928 *SA* 1,2,3, 1929 *A* 1,2,3
Carrington, K R (Auckland) 1971 *BI* 1,3,4
Carter, M P (Auckland) 1991 *A* 2, [*It*, *A*]
Casey, S T (Otago) 1905 *S*, *I*, *E*, *W*, 1907 *A* 1,2,3, 1908 *AW* 1
Catley, E H (Waikato) 1946 *A* 1, 1947 *A* 1,2, 1949 *SA* 1,2,3,4
Caughey, T H C (Auckland) 1932 *A* 1,3, 1934 *A* 1,2, 1935 *S*, *I*, 1936 *E*, *A* 1, 1937 *SA* 3
Caulton, R W (Wellington) 1959 *BI* 2,3,4, 1960 *SA* 1,4 1961 *F* 2, 1963 *E* 1,2, *I*, *W*, 1964 *E*, *S*, *F*, *A* 1,2,3
Cherrington, N P (North Auckland) 1950 *BI* 1
Christian, D L (Auckland) 1949 *SA* 4
Clamp, M (Wellington) 1984 *A* 2,3
Clark, D W (Otago) 1964 *A* 1,2
Clark, W H (Wellington) 1953 *W*, 1954 *I*, *E*, *S*, 1955 *A* 1,2, 1956 *SA* 2,3,4
Clarke, A H (Auckland) 1958 *A* 3, 1959 *BI* 4, 1960 *SA* 1
Clarke, D B (Waikato) 1956 *SA* 3,4, 1957 *A* 1,2, 1958 *A* 1,3, 1959 *BI* 1,2,3,4, 1960 *SA* 1,2,3,4, 1961 *F* 1,2,3, 1962 *A* 1,2,3,4,5, 1963 *E* 1,2, *I*, *W*, 1964 *E*, *S*, *F*, *A* 2,3

Clarke, E (Auckland) 1992 *Wld* 2,3, *I* 1,2, 1993 *BI* 1,2, *S*(R), *E*
Clarke, I J (Waikato) 1953 *W*, 1955 *A* 1,2,3, 1956 *SA* 1,2,3,4, 1957 *A* 1,2 1958 *A* 1,3, 1959 *BI* 1,2, 1960 *SA* 2,4, 1961 *F* 1,2,3, 1962 *A* 1,2,3, 1963 *E* 1,2
Clarke, R L (Taranaki) 1932 *A* 2,3
Cobden, D G (Canterbury) 1937 *SA* 1
Cockerill, M S (Taranaki) 1951 *A* 1,2,3
Cockroft, E A P (South Canterbury) 1913 *A* 3, 1914 *A* 2,3
Codlin, B W (Counties) 1980 *A* 1,2,3
Collins, A H (Taranaki) 1932 *A* 2,3, 1934 *A* 1
Collins, J L (Poverty Bay) 1964 *A* 1, 1965 *SA* 1,4
Colman, J T H (Taranaki) 1907 *A* 1,2, 1908 *AW* 1,3
Connor, D M (Auckland) 1961 *F* 1,2,3, 1962 *A* 1,2,3, 4,5, 1963 *E* 1,2, 1964 *A* 2,3
Conway, R J (Otago, Bay of Plenty) 1959 *BI* 2,3,4, 1960 *SA* 1,3,4, 1965 *SA* 1,2,3,4
Cooke, A E (Auckland, Wellington) 1924 *I*, *W*, 1925 *E*, *F*, 1930 *BI* 1,2,3,4
Cooke, R J (Canterbury) 1903 *A*
Cooksley, M S B (Counties, Waikato) 1992 *Wld* 1, 1993 *BI* 2,3(R), *A*, 1994 *F* 1,2, *SA* 1,2, *A*
Cooper, G J L (Auckland, Otago) 1986 *F* 1, *A* 1,2, 1992 *Wld* 1,2,3, *I* 1
Cooper, M J A (Waikato) 1992 *I* 2, *SA*(R), 1993 *BI* 1(R), 3(t), *WS*(t), *S*, 1994 *F* 1,2
Corner, M M N (Auckland) 1930 *BI* 2,3,4, 1931 *A*, 1934 *A* 1, 1936 *E*
Cossey, R R (Counties) 1958 *A* 1
Cottrell, A I (Canterbury) 1929 *A* 1,2,3, 1930 *BI* 1,2, 3,4 1931 *A*, 1932 *A* 1,2,3
Cottrell, W D (Canterbury) 1968 *A* 1,2, *F* 2,3, 1970 *SA* 1, 1971 *BI* 1,2,3,4
Couch, M B R (Wairarapa) 1947 *A* 1, 1949 *A* 1,2
Coughlan, T D (South Canterbury) 1958 *A* 1
Creighton, J N (Canterbury) 1962 *A* 4
Crichton, S (Wellington) 1983 *S*, *E*
Cross, T (Canterbury) 1904 *BI*, 1905 A
Crowley, K J (Taranaki) 1985 *E* 1,2, *A*, *Arg* 1,2, 1986 *A* 3, *F* 2,3, 1987 [*Arg*], 1990 *S* 1,2, *A* 1,2,3, *F* 1,2, 1991 *Arg* 1,2, [*A*]
Crowley, P J B (Auckland) 1949 *SA* 3,4, 1950 *BI* 1,2,3,4
Cummings, W (Canterbury) 1913 *A* 2,3
Cundy, R T (Wairarapa) 1929 *A* 2(R)
Cunningham, G R (Auckland) 1979 *A*, *S*, *E*, 1980 *A* 1,2
Cunningham, W (Auckland) 1905 *S*, *I*, 1906 *F*, 1907 *A* 1,2,3, 1908 *AW* 1,2,3
Cupples, L F (Bay of Plenty) 1924 *I*, *W*
Currie, C J (Canterbury) 1978 *I*, *W*
Cuthill, J E (Otago) 1913 *A* 1, *US*

Dalley, W C (Canterbury) 1924 *I*, 1928 *SA* 1,2,3,4
Dalton, A G (Counties) 1977 *F* 2, 1978 *A* 1,2,3, *I*, *W*, *E*, *S*, 1979 *F* 1,2, *S*, 1981 *S* 1,2, *SA* 1,2,3, *R*, *F* 1,2, 1982 *A* 1,2,3, 1983 *BI* 1,2,3,4, *A*, 1984 *F* 1,2, *A* 1,2,3, 1985 *E* 1,2, *A*
Dalton, D (Hawke's Bay) 1935 *I*, *W*, 1936 *A* 1,2, 1937 *SA* 1,2,3, 1938 *A* 1,2
Dalton, R A (Wellington) 1947 *A* 1,2
Dalzell, G N (Canterbury) 1953 *W*, 1954 *I*, *E*, *S*, *F*
Davie, M G (Canterbury) 1983 *E*(R)
Davies, W A (Auckland, Otago) 1960 *SA* 4, 1962 *A* 4,5
Davis, K (Auckland) 1952 *A* 2, 1953 *W*, 1954 *I*, *E*, *S*, *F*, 1955 A 2, 1958 *A* 1,2,3
Davis, L J (Canterbury) 1976 *I*, 1977 *BI* 3,4
Davis, W L (Hawke's Bay) 1967 *A*, *E*, *W*, *F*, *S*, 1968 A 1,2, *F* 1, 1969 *W* 1,2, 1970 *SA* 2
Deans, I B (Canterbury) 1988 *W* 1,2, *A* 1,2,3, 1989 *F* 1,2, *Arg* 1,2, A
Deans, R G (Canterbury) 1905 *S*, *I*, *E*, *W*, 1908 *AW* 3
Deans, R M (Canterbury) 1983 *S*, *E*, 1984 *A* 1(R),2,3
Delamore, G W (Wellington) 1949 *SA* 4
Dewar, H (Taranaki) 1913 *A* 1, *US*
Diack, E S (Otago) 1959 *BI* 2
Dick, J (Auckland) 1937 *SA* 1,2, 1938 *A* 3
Dick, M J (Auckland) 1963 *I*, *W*, 1964 *E*, *S*, *F*, 1965 *SA* 3, 1966 *BI* 4, 1967 *A*, *E*, *W*, *F*, 1969 *W* 1,2, 1970 *SA* 1,4
Dixon, M J (Canterbury) 1954 *I*, *E*, *S*, *F*, 1956 *SA* 1,2,3,4, 1957 *A* 1,2
Dobson, R L (Auckland) 1949 *A* 1
Dodd, E H (Wellington) 1905 *A*
Donald, A J (Wanganui) 1983 *S*, *E*, 1984 *F* 1,2, *A* 1,2,3
Donald, J G (Wairarapa) 1921 *SA* 1,2
Donald, Q (Wairarapa) 1924 *I*, *W*, 1925 *E*, *F*
Donaldson, M W (Manawatu) 1977 *F* 1,2, 1978 *A* 1, 2,3, *I*, *E*, *S*, 1979 *F* 1,2, *A*, *S* (R), 1981 *SA* 3(R)
Dougan, J P (Wellington) 1972 *A* 1, 1973 *E* 2
Dowd, C W (Auckland) 1993 *BI* 1,2,3, *A*, *WS*, *S*, *E*, 1994 *SA* 1(R)
Dowd, G W (North Harbour) 1992 *I* 1(R)
Downing, A J (Auckland) 1913 *A* 1, *US*, 1914 *A* 1,2,3
Drake, J A (Auckland) 1986 *F* 2,3, 1987 [*Fj*, *Arg*, *S*, *W*, *F*], *A*
Duff, R H (Canterbury) 1951 *A* 1,2,3, 1952 *A* 1,2, 1955 *A* 2,3, 1956 *SA* 1,2,3,4
Duncan, J (Otago) 1903 *A*
Duncan, M G (Hawke's Bay) 1971 *BI* 3(R), 4
Duncan, W D (Otago) 1921 *SA* 1,2,3
Dunn, E J (North Auckland) 1979 *S*, 1981 *S* 1
Dunn, I T W (North Auckland) 1983 *BI* 1,4, *A*
Dunn, J M (Auckland) 1946 *A* 1

Earl, A T (Canterbury) 1986 *F* 1, *A* 1, *F* 3(R), 1987 [*Arg*], 1989 *W*, *I*, 1991 *Arg* 1(R), 2, *A* 1, [*E*(R), *US*, *S*], 1992 *A* 2,3(R)
Eastgate, B P (Canterbury) 1952 *A* 1,2, 1954 *S*
Elliott, K G (Wellington) 1946 *A* 1,2
Ellis, M C G (Otago) 1993 *S*, *E*
Elsom, A E G (Canterbury) 1952 *A* 1,2, 1953 *W*, 1955 *A* 1,2,3
Elvidge, R R (Otago) 1946 *A* 1,2, 1949 *SA* 1,2,3,4, 1950 *BI* 1,2,3
Erceg, C P (Auckland) 1951 *A* 1,2,3, 1952 *A* 1
Evans, D A (Hawke's Bay) 1910 *A* 2
Eveleigh, K A (Manawatu) 1976 *SA* 2,4, 1977 *BI* 1,2

Fanning, A H N (Canterbury) 1913 *A* 3
Fanning, B J (Canterbury) 1903 *A*, 1904 *BI*
Farrell, C P (Auckland) 1977 *BI* 1,2
Fawcett, C L (Auckland) 1976 *SA* 2,3
Fea, W R (Otago) 1921 *SA* 3
Finlay, B E L (Manawatu) 1959 *BI* 1
Finlay, J (Manawatu) 1946 *A* 1
Finlayson, I (North Auckland) 1928 *SA* 1,2,3,4, 1930 *BI* 1,2
Fitzgerald, J T (Wellington) 1952 *A* 1
Fitzpatrick, B B J (Wellington) 1953 *W*, 1954 *I*, *F*
Fitzpatrick, S B T (Auckland) 1986 *F* 1, *A* 1, *F* 2,3, 1987 [*It*, *Fj*, *Arg*, *S*, *W*, *F*], *A*, 1988 *W* 1,2, *A* 1,2,3, 1989 *F* 1,2, *Arg* 1,2, *A*, *W*, *I*, 1990 *S* 1,2, *A* 1,2,3, *F* 1,2, 1991 *Arg* 1,2, *A* 1,2, [*E*, *US*, *It*, *C*, *A*, *S*], 1992 *Wld* 1,2,3, *I* 1,2, *A* 1,2,3, *SA*, 1993 *BI* 1,2,3, *A*, *WS*, *S*, *E*, 1994 *F* 1,2, *SA* 1,2,3, *A*
Fleming, J K (Wellington) 1979 *S*, *E*, 1980 *A* 1,2,3
Fletcher, C J C (North Auckland) 1921 *SA* 3
Fogarty, R (Taranaki) 1921 *SA* 1,3
Ford, B R (Marlborough) 1977 *BI* 3,4, 1978 *I*, 1979 *E*
Forster, S T (Otago) 1993 *S*, *E*, 1994 *F* 1,2
Fox, G J (Auckland) 1985 *Arg* 1, 1987 [*It*, *Fj*, *Arg*, *S*, *W*, *F*], *A*, 1988 *W* 1,2, *A* 1,2,3, 1989 *F* 1,2, *Arg* 1,2, *A*, *W*, *I*, 1990 *S* 1,2, *A* 1,2,3, *F* 1,2, 1991 *Arg* 1,2, *A* 1,2, [*E*, *It*, *C*, *A*], 1992 *Wld* 1,2(R), *A* 1,2,3, *SA*, 1993 *BI* 1,2,3, *A*, *WS*
Francis, A R H (Auckland) 1905 *A*, 1907 *A* 1,2,3, 1908 *AW* 1,2,3, 1910 *A* 1,2,3
Francis, W C (Wellington) 1913 *A* 2,3, 1914 *A* 1,2,3
Fraser, B G (Wellington) 1979 *S*, *E*, 1980 *A* 3, *W*, 1981 *S* 1,2, *SA* 1,2,3, *R*, *F* 1,2, 1982 *A* 1,2,3, 1983 *BI* 1,2,3,4, *A*, *S*, *E*, 1984 A 1
Frazer, H F (Hawke's Bay) 1946 *A* 1,2, 1947 *A* 1,2, 1949 *SA* 2
Fryer, F C (Canterbury) 1907 *A* 1,2,3, 1908 *AW* 2
Fuller, W B (Canterbury) 1910 *A* 1,2
Furlong, B D M (Hawke's Bay) 1970 *SA* 4

Gallagher, J A (Wellington) 1987 [*It*, *Fj*, *S*, *W*, *F*], *A*, 1988 *W* 1,2, *A* 1,2,3, 1989 *F* 1,2, *Arg* 1,2, *A*, *W*, *I*
Gallaher, D (Auckland) 1903 *A*, 1904 *BI*, 1905 *S*, *E*, *W*, 1906 *F*
Gard, P C (North Otago) 1971 *BI* 4
Gardiner, A J (Taranaki) 1974 *A* 3
Geddes, J H (Southland) 1929 *A* 1
Geddes, W McK (Auckland) 1913 *A* 2
Gemmell, B McL (Auckland) 1974 *A* 1,2
George, V L (Southland) 1938 *A* 1,2,3
Gilbert, G D M (West Coast) 1935 *S*, *I*, *W*, 1936 *E*
Gillespie, C T (Wellington) 1913 *A* 2
Gillespie, W D (Otago) 1958 *A* 3

Gillett, G A (Canterbury, Auckland) 1905 *S*, *I*, *E*, *W*, 1907 *A* 2,3, 1908 *AW* 1,3
Gillies, C C (Otago) 1936 *A* 2
Gilray, C M (Otago) 1905 *A*
Glasgow, F T (Taranaki, Southland) 1905 *S*, *I*, *E*, *W*, 1906 *F*, 1908 *AW* 3
Glenn, W S (Taranaki) 1904 *BI*, 1906 *F*
Goddard, M P (South Canterbury) 1946 *A* 2, 1947 *A* 1,2, 1949 *SA* 3,4
Going, S M (North Auckland) 1967 *A*, *F*, 1968 *F* 3, 1969 *W* 1,2, 1970 *SA* 1(R),4, 1971 *BI* 1,2,3,4, 1972 *A* 1,2,3, *W*, *S*, 1973 *E* 1, *I*, *F*, *E* 2, 1974 *I*, 1975 *S*, 1976 *I* (R), *SA* 1,2,3,4, 1977 *BI* 1,2
Gordon, S B (Waikato) 1993 *S*, *E*
Graham, D J (Canterbury) 1958 *A* 1,2, 1960 *SA* 2,3, 1961 *F* 1,2,3, 1962 *A* 1,2,3,4,5, 1963 *E* 1,2, *I*, *W*, 1964 *E*, *S*, *F*, *A* 1,2,3
Graham, J B (Otago) 1913 *US*, 1914 *A* 1,3
Graham, W G (Otago) 1979 *F* 1(R)
Grant, L A (South Canterbury) 1947 *A* 1,2, 1949 *SA* 1,2
Gray, G D (Canterbury) 1908 *AW* 2, 1913 *A* 1, *US*
Gray, K F (Wellington) 1963 *I*, *W*, 1964 *E*, *S*, *F*, *A* 1,2,3, 1965 *SA* 1,2,3,4, 1966 *BI* 1,2,3,4, 1967 *W*, *F*, *S*, 1968 *A* 1, *F* 2,3, 1969 *W* 1,2
Gray, W N (Bay of Plenty) 1955 *A* 2,3, 1956 *SA* 1,2,3,4
Green, C I (Canterbury) 1983 *S*(R), *E*, 1984 *A* 1,2,3, 1985 *E* 1,2, *A*, *Arg* 1,2, 1986 *A* 2,3, *F* 2,3, 1987 [*It*, *Fj*, *S*, *W*, *F*], *A*
Grenside, B A (Hawke's Bay) 1928 *SA* 1,2,3,4, 1929 *A* 2,3
Griffiths, J L (Wellington) 1934 *A* 2, 1935 *S*, *I*, *W*, 1936 *A* 1,2, 1938 *A* 3
Guy, R A (North Auckland) 1971 *BI* 1,2,3,4

Haden, A M (Auckland) 1977 *BI* 1,2,3,4, *F* 1,2, 1978 *A* 1,2,3, *I*, *W*, *E*, *S*, 1979 *F* 1,2, *A*, *S*, *E*, 1980 *A* 1,2,3, *W*, 1981 *S* 2, *SA* 1,2,3, *R*, *F* 1,2, 1982 *A* 1,2,3, 1983 *BI* 1,2,3,4, *A*, 1984 *F* 1,2, 1985 *Arg* 1,2
Hadley, S (Auckland) 1928 *SA* 1,2,3,4
Hadley, W E (Auckland) 1934 *A* 1,2, 1935 *S*, *I*, *W*, 1936 *E*, *A* 1,2
Haig, J S (Otago) 1946 *A* 1,2
Haig, L S (Otago) 1950 *BI* 2,3,4, 1951 *A* 1,2,3, 1953 *W*, 1954 *E*, *S*
Hales, D A (Canterbury) 1972 *A* 1,2,3, *W*
Hamilton, D C (Southland) 1908 *AW* 2
Hammond, I A (Marlborough) 1952 *A* 2
Harper, E T (Canterbury) 1904 *BI*, 1906 *F*
Harris, P C (Manawatu) 1976 *SA* 3
Hart, A H (Taranaki) 1924 *I*
Hart, G F (Canterbury) 1930 *BI* 1,2,3,4, 1931 *A*, 1934 *A* 1, 1935 *S*, *I*, *W*, 1936 *A* 1,2
Harvey, B A (Wairarapa-Bush) 1986 *F* 1
Harvey, I H (Wairarapa) 1928 *SA* 4
Harvey, L R (Otago) 1949 *SA* 1,2,3,4, 1950 *BI* 1,2,3,4
Harvey, P (Canterbury) 1904 *BI*
Hasell, E W (Canterbury) 1913 *A* 2,3,
Hayward, H O (Auckland) 1908 *AW* 3
Hazlett, E J (Southland) 1966 *BI* 1,2,3,4, 1967 *A*, *E*
Hazlett, W E (Southland) 1928 *SA* 1,2,3,4, 1930 *BI* 1,2,3,4
Heeps, T R (Wellington) 1962 *A* 1,2,3,4,5
Heke, W R (North Auckland) 1929 *A* 1,2,3
Hemi, R C (Waikato) 1953 *W*, 1954 *I*, *E*, *S*, *F*, 1955 *A* 1,2,3, 1956 *SA* 1,3,4, 1957 *A* 1,2, 1959 *BI* 1,3,4
Henderson, P (Wanganui) 1949 *SA* 1,2,3,4, 1950 *BI* 2,3,4
Henderson, P W (Otago) 1991 *Arg* 1, [*C*], 1992 *Wld* 1,2,3, *I* 1
Herewini, M A (Auckland) 1962 *A* 5, 1963 *I*, 1964 *S*, *F*, 1965 *SA* 4, 1966 *BI* 1,2,3,4, 1967 *A*
Hewett, J A (Auckland) 1991 [*It*]
Hewson, A R (Wellington) 1981 *S* 1,2, *SA* 1,2,3, *R*, *F* 1,2, 1982 *A* 1,2,3, 1983 *BI* 1,2,3,4, *A*, 1984 *F* 1,2, *A* 1
Higginson, G (Canterbury, Hawke's Bay) 1980 *W*, 1981 *S* 1, *SA* 1, 1982 *A* 1,2, 1983 *A*
Hill, S F (Canterbury) 1955 *A* 3, 1956 *SA* 1,3,4, 1957 *A* 1,2, 1958 *A* 3, 1959 *BI* 1,2,3,4
Hines, G R (Waikato) 1980 *A* 3
Hobbs, M J B (Canterbury) 1983 *BI* 1,2,3,4, *A*, *S*, *E*, 1984 *F* 1,2, *A* 1,2,3, 1985 *E* 1,2, *A*, *Arg* 1,2, 1986 *A* 2,3, *F* 2,3
Holder, E C (Buller) 1934 *A* 2
Hook, L S (Auckland) 1929 *A* 1,2,3
Hooper, J A (Canterbury) 1937 *SA* 1,2,3
Hopkinson, A E (Canterbury) 1967 *S*, 1968 *A* 2, *F* 1,2,3, 1969 *W* 2, 1970 *SA* 1,2,3
Hore, J (Otago) 1930 *BI* 2,3,4, 1932 *A* 1,2,3, 1934 *A* 1,2, 1935 *S*, 1936 *E*
Horsley, R H (Wellington) 1960 *SA* 2,3,4
Hotop, J (Canterbury) 1952 *A* 1,2, 1955 *A* 3
Howarth, S P (Auckland) 1994 *SA* 1,2,3, *A*
Hughes, A M (Auckland) 1949 *A* 1,2, 1950 *BI* 1,2,3,4
Hughes, E (Southland, Wellington) 1907 *A* 1,2,3, 1908 *AW* 1, 1921 *SA* 1,2
Hunter, B A (Otago) 1971 *BI* 1,2,3
Hunter, J (Taranaki) 1905 *S*, *I*, *E*, *W*, 1906 *F*, 1907 *A* 1,2,3, 1908 *AW* 1,2,3
Hurst, I A (Canterbury) 1973 *I*, *F*, *E* 2, 1974 *A* 1,2

Ieremia, A I (Wellington) 1994 *SA* 1,2,3
Ifwersen, K D (Auckland) 1921 *SA* 3
Innes, C R (Auckland) 1989 *W*, *I*, 1990 *A* 1,2,3, *F* 1,2, 1991 *Arg* 1,2, *A* 1,2, [*E*, *US*, *It*, *C*, *A*, *S*]
Innes, G D (Canterbury) 1932 *A* 2
Irvine, I B (North Auckland) 1952 *A* 1
Irvine, J G (Otago) 1914 *A* 1,2,3
Irvine, W R (Hawke's Bay, Wairarapa) 1924 *I*, *W*, 1925 *E*, *F*, 1930 *BI* 1
Irwin, M W (Otago) 1955 *A* 1,2, 1956 *SA* 1, 1958 *A* 2, 1959 *BI* 3,4, 1960 *SA* 1

Jackson, E S (Hawke's Bay) 1936 *A* 1,2, 1937 *SA* 1,2,3, 1938 *A* 3
Jaffray, J L (Otago, South Canterbury) 1972 *A* 2, 1975 *S*, 1976 *I*, *SA* 1, 1977 *BI* 2, 1979 *F* 1,2
Jarden, R A (Wellington) 1951 *A* 1,2, 1952 *A* 1,2, 1953 *W*, 1954 *I*, *E*, *S*, *F*, 1955 *A* 1,2,3, 1956 *SA* 1,2,3,4
Jefferd, A C R (East Coast) 1981 *S* 1,2, *SA* 1
Jessep, E M (Wellington) 1931 *A*, 1932 *A* 1
Johnson, L M (Wellington) 1928 *SA* 1,2,3,4
Johnston, W (Otago) 1907 *A* 1,2,3
Johnstone, B R (Auckland) 1976 *SA* 2, 1977 *BI* 1,2, *F* 1,2, 1978 *I*, *W*, *E*, *S*, 1979 *F* 1,2, *S*, *E*
Johnstone, P (Otago) 1949 *SA* 2,4, 1950 *BI* 1,2,3,4, 1951 *A* 1,2,3
Jones, I D (North Auckland, North Harbour) 1990 *S* 1,2, *A* 1,2,3, *F* 1,2, 1991 *Arg* 1,2, *A* 1,2, [*E*, *US*, *It*, *C*, *A*, *S*], 1992 *Wld* 1,2,3, *I* 1,2, *A* 1,2,3, *SA*, 1993 *BI* 1,2(R),3, *WS*, *S*, *E*, 1994 *F* 1,2, *SA* 1,3, *A*
Jones, M G (North Auckland) 1973 *E* 2
Jones, M N (Auckland) 1987 [*It*, *Fj*, *S*, *F*], *A*, 1988 *W* 1,2, *A* 2,3, 1989 *F* 1,2, *Arg* 1,2, 1990 *F* 1,2, 1991 *Arg* 1,2, *A* 1,2, [*E*, *US*, *S*], 1992 *Wld* 1,3, *I* 2, *A* 1,3, *SA*, 1993 *BI* 1,2,3, *A*, *WS*, 1994 *SA* 3(R), *A*
Jones, P F H (North Auckland) 1954 *E*, *S*, 1955 *A* 1,2, 1956 *SA* 3,4, 1958 *A* 1,2,3, 1959 *BI* 1, 1960 *SA* 1
Joseph, H T (Canterbury) 1971 *BI* 2,3
Joseph, J W (Otago) 1992 *Wld* 2,3(R), *I* 1, *A* 1(R),3, *SA*, 1993 *BI* 1,2,3, *A*, *WS*, *S*, *E*, 1994 *SA* 2(t)

Karam, J F (Wellington, Horowhenua) 1972 *W*, *S*, 1973 *E* 1, *I*, *F*, 1974 *A* 1,2,3, *I*, 1975 *S*
Katene, T (Wellington) 1955 *A* 2
Kearney, J C (Otago) 1947 *A* 2, 1949 *SA* 1,2,3
Kelly, J W (Auckland) 1949 *A* 1,2
Kember, G F (Wellington) 1970 *SA* 4
Ketels, R C (Counties) 1980 *W*, 1981 *S* 1,2, *R*, *F* 1
Kiernan, H A D (Auckland) 1903 *A*
Kilby, F D (Wellington) 1932 *A* 1,2,3, 1934 *A* 2
Killeen, B A (Auckland) 1936 *A* 1
King, R R (West Coast) 1934 *A* 2, 1935 *S*, *I*, *W*, 1936 *E*, *A* 1,2, 1937 *SA* 1,2,3, 1938 *A* 1,2,3
Kingstone, C N (Taranaki) 1921 *SA* 1,2,3
Kirk, D E (Auckland) 1985 *E* 1,2, *A*, *Arg* 1, 1986 *F* 1, *A* 1,2,3, *F* 2,3, 1987 [*It*, *Fj*, *Arg*, *S*, *W*, *F*], *A*
Kirkpatrick, I A (Canterbury, Poverty Bay) 1967 *F*, 1968 *A* 1(R), 2, *F* 1,2,3, 1969 *W* 1,2, 1970 *SA* 1,2,3,4, 1971 *BI* 1,2,3,4, 1972 *A* 1,2,3, *W*, *S*, 1973 *E* 1, *I*, *F*, *E* 2, 1974 *A* 1,2,3, *I* 1975 *S*, 1976 *I*, *SA* 1,2,3,4, 1977 *BI* 1,2,3,4
Kirton, E W (Otago) 1967 *E*, *W*, *F*, *S*, 1968 *A* 1,2, *F* 1,2,3, 1969 *W* 1,2, 1970 *SA* 2,3
Kirwan, J J (Auckland) 1984 *F* 1,2, 1985 *E* 1,2, *A*, *Arg* 1,2, 1986 *F* 1, *A* 1,2,3, *F* 2,3, 1987 [*It*, *Fj*, *Arg*, *S*, *W*, *F*], *A*, 1988 *W* 1,2, *A* 1,2,3, 1989 *F* 1,2, *Arg* 1,2, *A*, 1990 *S* 1,2, *A* 1,2,3, *F* 1,2, 1991 *Arg* 2, *A* 1,2, [*E*, *It*, *C*, *A*, *S*],

1992 *Wld* 1,2(R),3, *I* 1,2, *A* 1,2,3, *SA*, 1993 *BI* 2,3, *A*, *WS*, 1994 *F* 1,2, *SA* 1,2,3
Kivell, A L (Taranaki) 1929 *A* 2,3
Knight, A (Auckland) 1934 *A* 1
Knight, G A (Manawatu) 1977 *F* 1,2, 1978 *A* 1,2,3, *E*, *S*, 1979 *F* 1,2, *A*, 1980 A 1,2,3, *W*, 1981 *S* 1,2, *SA* 1,3, 1982 *A* 1,2,3, 1983 *BI* 1,2,3,4, *A*, 1984 *F* 1,2, *A* 1,2,3, 1985 *E* 1,2, *A*, 1986 *A* 2,3
Knight, L G (Poverty Bay) 1977 *BI* 1,2,3,4, *F* 1,2
Koteka, T T (Waikato) 1981 *F* 2, 1982 *A* 3
Kreft, A J (Otago) 1968 *A* 2

Laidlaw, C R (Otago, Canterbury) 1964 *F*, *A* 1, 1965 *SA* 1,2,3,4, 1966 *BI* 1,2,3,4, 1967 *E*, *W*, *S*, 1968 *A* 1,2, *F* 1,2, 1970 *SA* 1,2,3
Laidlaw, K F (Southland) 1960 *SA* 2,3,4
Lambert, K K (Manawatu) 1972 *S*(R), 1973 *E* 1, *I*, *F*, *E* 2, 1974 *I*, 1976 *SA* 1,3,4, 1977 *BI* 1,4
Lambourn, A (Wellington) 1934 *A* 1,2, 1935 *S*, *I*, *W*, 1936 *E*, 1937 *SA* 1,2,3, 1938 *A* 3
Larsen, B P (North Harbour) 1992 *Wld* 2,3, *I* 1, 1994 *F* 1,2, *SA* 1,2,3, *A*(t)
Le Lievre, J M (Canterbury) 1962 *A* 4
Lendrum, R N (Counties) 1973 *E* 2
Leslie, A R (Wellington) 1974 *A* 1,2,3, *I*, 1975 *S*, 1976 *I*, *SA* 1,2,3,4
Leys, E T (Wellington) 1929 *A* 3
Lilburne, H T (Canterbury, Wellington) 1928 *SA* 3,4, 1929 *A* 1,2,3, 1930 *BI* 1,4, 1931 *A*, 1932 *A* 1, 1934 *A* 2
Lindsay, D F (Otago) 1928 *SA* 1,2,3
Lineen, T R (Auckland) 1957 *A* 1,2, 1958 *A* 1,2,3, 1959 *BI* 1,2,3,4, 1960 *SA* 1,2,3
Lister, T N (South Canterbury) 1968 *A* 1,2, *F* 1, 1969 *W* 1,2, 1970 *SA* 1,4, 1971 *BI* 4
Little, P F (Auckland) 1961 *F* 2,3, 1962 *A* 2,3,5, 1963 *I*, *W*, 1964 *E*, *S*, *F*
Little, W K (North Harbour) 1990 *S* 1,2, *A* 1,2,3, *F* 1,2, 1991 *Arg* 1,2, *A* 1, [*It*, *S*], 1992 *Wld* 1,2,3, *I* 1,2, *A* 1,2,3, *SA*, 1993 *BI* 1, *WS*(R), 1994 *SA* 2(R), *A*
Loader, C J (Wellington) 1954 *I*, *E*, *S*, *F*
Lochore, B J (Wairarapa) 1964 *E*, *S*, 1965 *SA* 1,2,3,4, 1966 *BI* 1,2,3,4, 1967 *A*, *E*, *W*, *F*, *S*, 1968 *A* 1, *F* 2,3, 1969 *W* 1,2, 1970 *SA* 1,2,3,4, 1971 *BI* 3
Loe, R W (Waikato, Canterbury) 1987 [*It*, *Arg*], 1988 *W* 1,2, *A* 1,2,3, 1989 *F* 1,2, *Arg* 1,2, *A*, *W*, *I*, 1990 *S* 1,2, *A* 1,2,3, *F* 1,2, 1991 *Arg* 1,2, *A* 1,2, [*E*, *It*, *C*, *A*, *S*], 1992 *Wld* 1,2,3, *I* 1, *A* 1,2,3, *SA*, 1994 *F* 1,2, *SA* 1,2,3, *A*
Lomu, J (Counties) 1994 *F* 1,2
Long, A J (Auckland) 1903 *A*
Loveridge, D S (Taranaki) 1978 *W*, 1979 *S*, *E*, 1980 *A* 1,2,3, *W*, 1981 *S* 1,2, *SA* 1,2,3, *R*, *F* 1,2, 1982 *A* 1,2,3, 1983 *BI* 1,2,3,4, *A*, 1985 *Arg* 2
Lucas, F W (Auckland) 1924 *I*, 1925 *F*, 1928 *SA* 4, 1930 *BI* 1,2,3,4
Lunn, W A (Otago) 1949 *A* 1,2
Lynch, T W (South Canterbury) 1913 *A* 1, 1914 *A* 1,2,3
Lynch, T W (Canterbury) 1951 *A* 1,2,3

McAtamney, F S (Otago) 1956 *SA* 2
McCahill, B J (Auckland) 1987 [*Arg*, *S*(R), *W*(R)], 1989 *Arg* 1(R), 2(R), 1991 *A* 2, [*E*, *US*, *C*, *A*]
McCaw, W A (Southland) 1951 *A* 1,2,3, 1953 *W*, 1954 *F*
McCool, M J (Wairarapa-Bush) 1979 *A*
McCormick, W F (Canterbury) 1965 *SA* 4, 1967 *E*, *W*, *F*, S, 1968 *A* 1,2, *F* 1,2,3, 1969 *W* 1,2, 1970 *SA* 1,2,3, 1971 *BI* 1
McCullough, J F (Taranaki) 1959 *BI* 2,3,4
McDonald, A (Otago) 1905 *S*, *I*, *E*, *W*, 1907 *A* 1, 1908 *AW* 1, 1913 *A* 1, *US*
Macdonald, H H (Canterbury, North Auckland) 1972 *W*, *S*, 1973 *E* 1, *I*, *F*, *E* 2, 1974 *I*, 1975 *S*, 1976 *I*, *SA* 1,2,3
McDowell, S C (Auckland, Bay of Plenty) 1985 *Arg* 1,2, 1986 *A* 2,3, *F* 2,3, 1987 [*It*, *Fj*, *S*, *W*, *F*], *A*, 1988 *W* 1,2, *A* 1,2,3, 1989 *F* 1,2, *Arg* 1,2, *A*, *W*, *I*, 1990 *S* 1,2, *A* 1,2,3, *F* 1,2, 1991 *Arg* 1,2, *A* 1,2, [*E*, *US*, *It*, *C*, *A*, *S*], 1992 *Wld* 1,2,3, *I* 1,2
McEldowney, J T (Taranaki) 1977 *BI* 3,4
MacEwan, I N (Wellington) 1956 *SA* 2, 1957 *A* 1,2, 1958 *A* 1,2,3, 1959 *BI* 1,2,3, 1960 *SA* 1,2,3,4, 1961 *F* 1,2,3, 1962 *A* 1,2,3,4
McGrattan, B (Wellington) 1983 *S*, *E*, 1985 *Arg* 1,2, 1986 *F* 1, *A* 1
McGregor, A J (Auckland) 1913 *A* 1, *US*
McGregor, D (Canterbury, Southland) 1903 *A*, 1904 *BI*, 1905 *E*, *W*
McGregor, N P (Canterbury) 1924 *W*, 1925 *E*
McGregor, R W (Auckland) 1903 *A*, 1904 *BI*
McHugh, M J (Auckland) 1946 *A* 1,2, 1949 *SA* 3
McIntosh, D N (Wellington) 1956 *SA* 1,2, 1957 *A* 1,2
McKay, D W (Auckland) 1961 *F* 1,2,3, 1963 *E* 1,2
McKechnie, B J (Southland) 1977 *F* 1,2, 1978 *A* 2(R),3, *W*(R), *E*, *S*, 1979 *A*, 1981 *SA* 1(R), *F* 1
McKellar, G F (Wellington) 1910 *A* 1,2,3
McKenzie, R J (Wellington) 1913 *A* 1, *US*, 1914 *A* 2,3
McKenzie, R McC (Manawatu) 1934 *A* 1, 1935 *S*, 1936 *A* 1, 1937 *SA* 1,2,3, 1938 *A* 1,2,3
McLachlan, J S (Auckland) 1974 *A* 2
McLaren, H C (Waikato) 1952 *A* 1
McLean, A L (Bay of Plenty) 1921 *SA* 2,3
McLean, H F (Wellington, Auckland) 1930 *BI* 3,4, 1932 *A* 1,2,3, 1934 *A* 1, 1935 *I*, *W*, 1936 *E*
McLean, J K (King Country, Auckland) 1947 *A* 1, 1949 *A* 2
McLeod, B E (Counties) 1964 *A* 1,2,3, 1965 *SA* 1,2,3,4, 1966 *BI* 1,2,3,4, 1967 *E*, *W*, *F*, *S*, 1968 *A* 1,2, *F* 1,2,3, 1969 *W* 1,2, 1970 *SA* 1,2
McMinn, A F (Wairarapa, Manawatu) 1903 *A*, 1905 *A*
McMinn, F A (Manawatu) 1904 *BI*
McMullen, R F (Auckland) 1957 *A* 1,2, 1958 *A* 1,2,3, 1959 *BI* 1,2,3, 1960 *SA* 2,3,4
McNab, J R (Otago) 1949 *SA* 1,2,3, 1950 *BI* 1,2,3
McNaughton, A M (Bay of Plenty) 1971 *BI* 1,2,3
McNeece, J (Southland) 1913 *A* 2,3, 1914 *A* 1,2,3
McPhail, B E (Canterbury) 1959 *BI* 1,4
Macpherson, D G (Otago) 1905 *A*
MacPherson, G L (Otago) 1986 *F* 1
MacRae, I R (Hawke's Bay) 1966 *BI* 1,2,3,4, 1967 *A*, *E*, *W*, *F*, *S*, 1968 *F* 1,2, 1969 *W* 1,2, 1970 *SA* 1,2,3,4
McRae, J A (Southland) 1946 *A* 1(R),2
McWilliams, R G (Auckland) 1928 *SA* 2,3,4, 1929 *A* 1,2,3, 1930 *BI* 1,2,3,4
Mackrell, W H C (Auckland) 1906 *F*
Macky, J V (Auckland) 1913 *A* 2
Maguire, J R (Auckland) 1910 *A 1,2,3*
Mahoney, A (Bush) 1935 *S*, *I*, *W*, 1936 *E*
Mains, L W (Otago) 1971 *BI* 2,3,4, 1976 *I*
Major, J (Taranaki) 1967 *A*
Manchester, J E (Canterbury) 1932 *A* 1,2,3, 1934 *A* 1,2, 1935 *S*, *I*, *W*, 1936 *E*
Mannix, S J (Wellington) 1994 *F* 1
Mason, D F (Wellington) 1947 *A* 2(R)
Masters, R R (Canterbury) 1924 *I*, *W*, 1925 *E*, *F*
Mataira, H K (Hawke's Bay) 1934 *A* 2
Matheson, J D (Otago) 1972 *A* 1,2,3, *W*, *S*
Max, D S (Nelson) 1931 *A*, 1934 *A* 1,2
Meads, C E (King Country) 1957 *A* 1,2, 1958 *A* 1,2,3, 1959 *BI* 2,3,4, 1960 *SA* 1,2,3,4, 1961 *F* 1,2,3, 1962 *A* 1,2,3,5, 1963 *E* 1,2, *I*, *W*, 1964 *E*, *S*, *F*, *A* 1,2,3, 1965 *SA* 1,2,3,4 1966 *BI* 1,2,3,4, 1967 *A*, *E*, *W*, *F*, *S*, 1968 *A* 1,2, *F* 1,2,3, 1969 *W* 1,2, 1970 *SA* 3,4, 1971 *BI* 1,2,3,4
Meads, S T (King Country) 1961 *F* 1,1962 *A* 4,5, 1963 *I*, 1964 *A* 1,2,3, 1965 *SA* 1,2,3,4, 1966 *BI* 1,2,3,4
Meates, K F (Canterbury) 1952 *A* 1,2
Meates, W A (Otago) 1949 *SA* 2,3,4, 1950 *BI* 1,2,3,4
Metcalfe, T C (Southland) 1931 *A*, 1932 *A* 1
Mexted, G G (Wellington) 1950 *BI* 4
Mexted, M G (Wellington) 1979 *S*, *E*, 1980 *A* 1,2,3, *W*, 1981 *S* 1,2, *SA* 1,2,3, *R*, *F* 1,2, 1982 *A* 1,2,3, 1983 *BI* 1,2,3,4, *A*, *S*, *E*, 1984 *F* 1,2, *A* 1,2,3, 1985 *E* 1,2, *A*, *Arg* 1,2
Mill, J J (Hawke's Bay, Wairarapa) 1924 *W*, 1925 *E*, *F*, 1930 *BI* 1
Milliken, H M (Canterbury) 1938 *A* 1,2,3
Milner, H P (Wanganui) 1970 *SA* 3
Mitchell, N A (Southland, Otago) 1935 *S*, *I*, *W*, 1936 *E*, *A* 2, 1937 *SA* 3, 1938 *A* 1,2
Mitchell, T W (Canterbury) 1976 *SA* 4(R)
Mitchell, W J (Canterbury) 1910 *A* 2,3
Mitchinson, F E (Wellington) 1907 *A* 1,2,3, 1908 *AW* 1,2,3, 1910 *A* 1,2,3, 1913 *A* 1(R), *US*
Moffitt, J E (Wellington)1921 *SA* 1,2,3
Moore, G J T (Otago) 1949 *A* 1
Moreton, R C (Canterbury) 1962 *A* 3,4, 1964 *A* 1,2,3, 1965 *SA* 2,3

Morgan, J E (North Auckland) 1974 *A* 3, *I*, 1976 *SA* 2,3,4
Morris, T J (Nelson Bays) 1972 *A* 1,2,3
Morrison, T C (South Canterbury) 1938 *A* 1,2,3
Morrison, T G (Otago) 1973 *E* 2(R)
Morrissey, P J (Canterbury) 1962 *A* 3,4,5
Mourie, G N K (Taranaki) 1977 *BI* 3,4, *F* 1,2, 1978 *I*, *W*, *E*, *S*, 1979 *F* 1,2, *A* , *S*, *E*, 1980 *W*, 1981 *S* 1,2, *F* 1,2, 1982 *A* 1,2,3
Muller, B L (Taranaki) 1967 *A*, *E*, *W*, *F*, 1968 *A* 1, *F* 1, 1969 *W* 1, 1970 *SA* 1,2,4, 1971 *BI* 1,2,3,4
Mumm, W J (Buller) 1949 *A* 1
Murdoch, K (Otago) 1970 *SA* 4, 1972 *A* 3, *W*
Murdoch, P H (Auckland) 1964 *A* 2,3, 1965 *SA* 1,2,3
Murray, H V (Canterbury) 1913 *A* 1, *US*, 1914 *A* 2,3
Murray, P C (Wanganui) 1908 *AW* 2
Myers, R G (Waikato) 1978 *A* 3
Mynott, H J (Taranaki) 1905 *I*, *W*, 1906 *F*, 1907 *A* 1,2,3, 1910 *A* 1,3

Nathan, W J (Auckland) 1962 *A* 1,2,3,4,5, 1963 *E* 1,2, *W*, 1964 *F*, 1966 *BI* 1,2,3,4, 1967 *A*
Nelson, K A (Otago) 1962 *A* 4,5
Nepia, G (Hawke's Bay, East Coast) 1924 *I*, *W*, 1925 *E*, *F*, 1929 *A* 1, 1930 *BI* 1,2,3,4
Nesbit, S R (Auckland) 1960 *SA* 2,3
Newton, F (Canterbury) 1905 *E*, *W*, 1906 *F*
Nicholls, H E (Wellington) 1921 *SA* 1
Nicholls, M F (Wellington) 1921 *SA* 1,2,3, 1924 *I*, *W*, 1925 *E*, *F*, 1928 *SA* 4, 1930 *BI* 2,3
Nicholson, G W (Auckland) 1903 *A*, 1904 *BI*, 1907 *A* 2,3
Norton, R W (Canterbury) 1971 *BI* 1,2,3,4, 1972 *A* 1,2,3, *W*, *S*, 1973 *E* 1, *I*, *F*, *E* 2, 1974 *A* 1,2,3, *I*, 1975 *S*, 1976 *I*, *SA* 1,2,3,4, 1977 *BI* 1,2,3,4

O'Brien, J G (Auckland) 1914 *A* 1
O'Callaghan, M W (Manawatu) 1968 *F* 1,2,3
O'Callaghan, T R (Wellington) 1949 *A* 2
O'Donnell, D H (Wellington) 1949 *A* 2
Old, G H (Manawatu) 1981 *SA* 3, *R*(R), 1982 *A* 1(R)
O'Leary, M J (Auckland) 1910 *A* 1,3, 1913 *A* 2,3
Oliver, C J (Canterbury) 1929 *A* 1,2, 1934 *A* 1, 1935 *S*, *I*, *W*, 1936 *E*
Oliver, D J (Wellington) 1930 *BI* 1,2
Oliver, D O (Otago) 1954 *I*, *F*
Oliver, F J (Southland, Otago, Manawatu) 1976 *SA* 4, 1977 *BI* 1,2,3,4, *F* 1,2, 1978 *A* 1,2,3, *I*, *W*, *E*, *S*, 1979 *F* 1,2, 1981 *SA* 2
Orr, R W (Otago) 1949 *A* 1
Osborne, W M (Wanganui) 1975 *S*, 1976 *SA* 2(R), 4(R), 1977 *BI* 1,2,3,4, *F* 1(R),2, 1978 *I*, *W*, *E*, *S*, 1980 *W*, 1982 *A* 1,3
O'Sullivan, J M (Taranaki) 1905 *S*, *I*, *E*, *W*, 1907 *A* 3
O'Sullivan, T P A (Taranaki) 1960 *SA* 1, 1961 *F* 1, 1962 *A* 1,2

Page, J R (Wellington)1931 *A*, 1932 *A* 1,2,3, 1934 *A* 1,2
Palmer, B P (Auckland) 1929 *A* 2, 1932 *A* 2,3
Parker, J H (Canterbury) 1924 *I*, *W*, 1925 *E*
Parkhill, A A (Otago) 1937 *SA* 1,2,3, 1938 *A* 1,2,3
Parkinson, R M (Poverty Bay) 1972 *A* 1,2,3, *W*, *S*, 1973 *E* 1,2
Paterson, A M (Otago) 1908 *AW* 2,3, 1910 *A* 1,2,3
Paton, H (Otago) 1910 *A* 1,3
Pene, A R B (Otago) 1992 *Wld* 1(R),2,3, *I* 1,2, *A* 1,2(R), 1993 *BI* 3, *A*, *WS*, *S*, *E*, 1994 *F* 1,2(R), *SA* 1(R)
Phillips, W J (King Country) 1937 *SA* 2, 1938 *A* 1,2
Philpott, S (Canterbury) 1991 [*It*(R), *S*(R)]
Pickering, E A R (Waikato) 1958 *A* 2, 1959 *BI* 1,4
Pierce, M J (Wellington) 1985 *E* 1,2, *A*, *Arg* 1, 1986 *A* 2,3, *F* 2,3, 1987 [*It*, *Arg*, *S*, *W*, *F*], *A*, 1988 *W* 1,2, *A* 1,2,3, 1989 *F* 1,2, *Arg* 1,2, *A*, *W*, *I*
Pokere, S T (Southland, Auckland) 1981 *SA* 3, 1982 *A* 1,2,3, 1983 *BI* 1,2,3,4, *A*, *S*, *E*, 1984 *F* 1,2, *A* 2,3, 1985 *E* 1,2, *A*
Pollock, H R (Wellington) 1932 *A* 1,2,3, 1936 *A* 1,2
Porter, C G (Wellington) 1925 *F*, 1929 *A* 2,3, 1930 *BI* 1,2,3,4
Preston, J P (Canterbury, Wellington) 1991 [*US*, *S*], 1992 *SA*(R), 1993 *BI* 2,3, *A*, *WS*
Procter, A C (Otago) 1932 *A* 1
Purdue, C A (Southland) 1905 *A*
Purdue, E (Southland) 1905 *A*
Purdue, G B (Southland) 1931 *A*, 1932 *A* 1,2,3
Purvis, G H (Waikato) 1991 [*US*], 1993 *WS*
Purvis, N A (Otago) 1976 *I*

Quaid, C E (Otago) 1938 *A* 1,2

Rangi, R E (Auckland) 1964 *A* 2,3, 1965 *SA* 1,2,3,4, 1966 *BI* 1,2,3,4
Rankin, J G (Canterbury) 1936 *A* 1,2, 1937 *SA* 2
Reedy, W J (Wellington) 1908 *AW* 2,3
Reid, A R (Waikato) 1952 *A* 1, 1956 *SA* 3,4, 1957 *A* 1,2
Reid, H R (Bay of Plenty) 1980 *A* 1,2, *W*, 1983 *S*, *E*, 1985 *Arg* 1,2, 1986 *A* 2,3
Reid, K H (Wairarapa) 1929 *A* 1,3
Reid, S T (Hawke's Bay) 1935 *S*, *I*, *W*, 1936 *E*, *A* 1,2, 1937 *SA* 1,2,3
Reside, W B (Wairarapa) 1929 *A* 1
Rhind, P K (Canterbury) 1946 *A* 1,2
Richardson, J (Otago, Southland) 1921 *SA* 1,2,3, 1924 *I*, *W*, 1925 *E*, *F*
Rickit, H (Waikato) 1981 *S* 1,2
Ridland, A J (Southland) 1910 *A* 1,2,3
Roberts, E J (Wellington) 1914 *A* 1,2,3, 1921 *SA* 2,3
Roberts, F (Wellington) 1905 *S*, *I*, *E*, *W*, 1907 *A* 1,2,3, 1908 *AW* 1,3, 1910 *A* 1,2,3
Roberts, R W (Taranaki) 1913 *A* 1, *US*, 1914 *A* 1,2,3
Robertson, B J (Counties) 1972 *A* 1,3, *S*, 1973 *E* 1, *I*, *F*, 1974 *A* 1,2,3, *I*, 1976 *I*, *SA* 1,2,3,4, 1977 *BI* 1,3,4, *F* 1,2, 1978 *A* 1,2,3, *W*, *E*, *S*, 1979 *F* 1,2, *A*, 1980 *A* 2,3, *W*, 1981 *S* 1,2
Robertson, D J (Otago) 1974 *A* 1,2,3, *I*, 1975 *S*, 1976 *I*, *SA* 1,3,4, 1977 *BI* 1
Robilliard, A C C (Canterbury) 1928 *SA* 1,2,3,4
Robinson, C E (Southland) 1951 *A* 1,2,3, 1952 *A* 1,2
Rollerson, D L (Manawatu) 1980 *W*, 1981 *S* 2, *SA* 1,2,3, *R*, *F* 1(R), 2
Roper, R A (Taranaki) 1949 *A* 2, 1950 *BI* 1,2,3,4
Rowley, H C B (Wanganui) 1949 *A* 2
Rutledge, L M (Southland) 1978 *A* 1,2,3, *I*, *W*, *E*, *S*, 1979 *F* 1,2, *A*, 1980 *A* 1,2,3
Ryan, J (Wellington) 1910 *A* 2, 1914 *A* 1,2,3

Sadler, B S (Wellington) 1935 *S*, *I*, *W*, 1936 *A* 1,2,
Salmon, J L B (Wellington) 1981 *R*, *F* 1,2(R)
Savage, L T (Canterbury) 1949 *SA* 1,2,4
Saxton, C K (South Canterbury) 1938 *A* 1,2,3
Schuler, K J (Manawatu, North Harbour) 1990 *A* 2(R), 1992 *A* 2
Schuster, N J (Wellington) 1988 *A* 1,2,3, 1989 *F* 1,2, *Arg* 1,2, *A*, *W*, *I*
Scott, R W H (Auckland) 1946 *A* 1,2, 1947 *A* 1,2, 1949 *SA* 1,2,3,4, 1950 *BI* 1,2,3,4, 1953 *W*, 1954 I, *E*, *S*, *F*
Scown, A I (Taranaki) 1972 *A* 1,2,3, *W*(R), *S*
Scrimshaw, G (Canterbury) 1928 *SA* 1
Seear, G A (Otago) 1977 *F* 1,2, 1978 *A* 1,2,3, *I*, *W*, *E*, *S*, 1979 *F* 1,2, A
Seeling, C E (Auckland) 1904 *BI*, 1905 *S*, *I*, *E*, *W*, 1906 *F*, 1907 *A* 1,2, 1908 *AW* 1,2,3
Sellars, G M V (Auckland) 1913 *A* 1, *US*
Shaw, M W (Manawatu, Hawke's Bay) 1980 *A* 1,2,3(R), *W*, 1981 *S* 1,2, *SA* 1,2, *R*, *F* 1,2, 1982 *A* 1,2,3, 1983 *BI* 1,2,3,4, *A*, *S*, *E*, 1984 *F* 1,2, *A* 1, 1985 *E* 1,2, *A*, *Arg* 1,2, 1986 *A* 3
Shelford, F N K (Bay of Plenty) 1981 *SA* 3, *R*, 1984 *A* 2,3
Shelford, W T (North Harbour) 1986 *F* 2,3, 1987 [*It*, *Fj*, *S*, *W*, *F*], *A*, 1988 *W* 1,2, *A* 1,2,3, 1989 *F* 1,2, *Arg* 1,2, *A*, *W*, *I*, 1990 *S* 1,2,
Siddells, S K (Wellington) 1921 *SA* 3
Simon, H J (Otago) 1937 *SA* 1,2,3
Simpson, J G (Auckland) 1947 *A* 1,2, 1949 *SA* 1,2,3,4, 1950 *BI* 1,2,3
Simpson, V L J (Canterbury) 1985 *Arg* 1,2
Sims, G S (Otago) 1972 *A* 2
Skeen, J R (Auckland) 1952 *A* 2
Skinner, K L (Otago, Counties) 1949 *SA* 1,2,3,4, 1950 *BI* 1,2,3,4, 1951 *A* 1,2,3, 1952 *A* 1,2, 1953 *W*, 1954 *I*, *E*, *S*, *F*, 1956 *SA* 3,4
Skudder, G R (Waikato) 1969 *W* 2
Sloane, P H (North Auckland) 1979 *E*
Smith, A E (Taranaki) 1969 *W* 1,2, 1970 *SA* 1
Smith, B W (Waikato) 1984 *F* 1,2, *A* 1
Smith, G W (Auckland) 1905 *S*, *I*
Smith, I S T (Otago, North Otago) 1964 *A* 1,2,3, 1965

SA 1,2,4, 1966 *BI* 1,2,3
Smith, J B (North Auckland) 1946 *A* 1, 1947 *A* 2, 1949 *A* 1,2
Smith, R M (Canterbury) 1955 *A* 1
Smith, W E (Nelson) 1905 *A*
Smith, W R (Canterbury) 1980 *A* 1, 1982 *A* 1,2,3, 1983 *BI* 2,3, *S*, *E*, 1984 *F* 1,2, *A* 1,2,3, 1985 *E* 1,2, *A*, *Arg* 2
Snow, E M (Nelson) 1929 *A* 1,2,3
Solomon, F (Auckland) 1931 *A*, 1932 *A* 2,3
Sonntag, W T C (Otago) 1929 *A* 1,2,3
Speight, M W (Waikato) 1986 *A* 1
Spencer, J C (Wellington) 1905 *A*, 1907 *A* 1(R)
Spiers, J E (Counties) 1979 *S*, *E*, 1981 *R*, *F* 1,2
Spillane, A P (South Canterbury) 1913 *A* 2,3,
Stanley, J T (Auckland) 1986 *F* 1, *A* 1,2,3, *F* 2,3, 1987 [*It*, *Fj*, *Arg*, *S*, *W*, *F*], *A*, 1988 *W* 1,2, *A* 1,2,3, 1989 *F* 1,2, *Arg* 1,2, *A*, *W*, *I*, 1990 *S* 1,2
Stead, J W (Southland) 1904 *BI*, 1905 *S*, *I*, *E*, 1906 *F*, 1908 *AW* 1,3
Steel, A G (Canterbury) 1966 *BI* 1,2,3,4, 1967 *A*, *F*, *S*, 1968 *A* 1,2
Steel, J (West Coast) 1921 *SA* 1,2,3, 1924 *W*, 1925 *E*, *F*
Steele, L B (Wellington) 1951 *A* 1,2,3
Steere, E R G (Hawke's Bay) 1930 *BI* 1,2,3,4, 1931 *A*, 1932 *A* 1
Stensness, L (Auckland) 1993 *BI* 3, *A*, *WS*
Stephens, O G (Wellington) 1968 *F* 3
Stevens, I N (Wellington) 1972 *S*, 1973 *E* 1, 1974 *A* 3
Stewart, A J (Canterbury, South Canterbury) 1963 *E* 1,2, *I*, *W*, 1964 E, *S*, *F*, *A* 3
Stewart, J D (Auckland) 1913 *A* 2,3
Stewart, K W (Southland) 1973 *E* 2, 1974 *A* 1,2,3, *I*, 1975 *S*, 1976 *I*, *SA* 1,3, 1979 *S*, *E*, 1981 *SA* 1,2
Stewart, R T (South Canterbury, Canterbury) 1928 *SA* 1,2,3,4, 1930 *BI* 2
Stohr, L B (Taranaki) 1910 *A* 1,2,3
Stone, A M (Waikato, Bay of Plenty) 1981 *F* 1,2, 1983 *BI* 3(R), 1984 *A* 3, 1986 *F* 1, *A* 1,3, *F* 2,3
Storey, P W (South Canterbury) 1921 *SA* 1,2
Strachan, A D (Auckland, North Harbour) 1992 *Wld* 2,3, *I* 1,2, *A* 1,2,3, *SA*, 1993 *BI* 1
Strahan, S C (Manawatu) 1967 *A*, *E*, *W*, *F*, *S*, 1968 *A* 1,2, *F* 1,2,3, 1970 *SA* 1,2,3, 1972 *A* 1,2,3, 1973 *E* 2
Strang, W A (South Canterbury) 1928 *SA* 1,2, 1930 *BI* 3,4, 1931 *A*
Stringfellow, J C (Wairarapa) 1929 *A* 1(R),3
Stuart, K C (Canterbury) 1955 *A* 1
Stuart, R C (Canterbury) 1949 *A* 1,2, 1953 *W*, 1954 *I*, *E*, *S*, *F*
Stuart, R L (Hawke's Bay) 1977 *F* 1(R)
Sullivan, J L (Taranaki) 1937 *SA* 1,2,3, 1938 *A* 1,2,3
Sutherland, A R (Marlborough) 1970 *SA* 2,4, 1971 *BI* 1, 1972 *A* 1,2,3, *W*, 1973 *E* 1, *I*, *F*
Svenson, K S (Wellington) 1924 *I*, *W*, 1925 *E*, *F*
Swain, J P (Hawke's Bay) 1928 *SA* 1,2,3,4

Tanner, J M (Auckland) 1950 *BI* 4, 1951 *A* 1,2,3, 1953 *W*
Tanner, K J (Canterbury) 1974 *A* 1,2,3, *I*, 1975 *S*, 1976 *I*, *SA* 1
Taylor, H M (Canterbury) 1913 *A* 1, *US*, 1914 *A* 1,2,3
Taylor, J M (Otago) 1937 *SA* 1,2,3, 1938 *A* 1,2,3
Taylor, M B (Waikato) 1979 *F* 1,2, *A*, *S*, *E*, 1980 *A* 1,2
Taylor, N M (Bay of Plenty, Hawke's Bay) 1977 *BI* 2, 4(R), *F* 1,2, 1978 *A* 1,2,3, *I*, 1982 *A* 2
Taylor, R (Taranaki) 1913 *A* 2,3
Taylor, W T (Canterbury) 1983 *BI* 1,2,3,4, *A*, *S*, 1984 *F* 1,2, *A* 1,2, 1985 *E* 1,2, *A*, *Arg* 1,2, 1986 *A* 2, 1987 [*It*, *Fj*, *S*, *W*, *F*], *A*, 1988 *W* 1,2
Tetzlaff, P L (Auckland) 1947 *A* 1,2
Thimbleby, N W (Hawke's Bay) 1970 *SA* 3
Thomas, B T (Auckland, Wellington) 1962 *A* 5, 1964 *A* 1,2,3
Thomson, H D (Wellington) 1908 *AW* 1
Thorne, G S (Auckland) 1968 *A* 1,2, *F* 1,2,3, 1969 *W* 1, 1970 *SA* 1,2,3,4
Thornton, N H (Auckland) 1947 *A* 1,2, 1949 *SA* 1
Tilyard, J T (Wellington) 1913 *A* 3
Timu, J K R (Otago) 1991 *Arg* 1, *A* 1,2, [*E*, *US*, *C*, *A*], 1992 *Wld* 2, *I* 2, *A* 1,2,3, *SA*, 1993 *BI* 1,2,3, *A*, *WS*, *S*, *E*, 1994 *F* 1,2, *SA* 1,2,3, *A*
Tindill, E W T (Wellington) 1936 *E*
Townsend, L J (Otago) 1955 *A* 1,3
Tremain, K R (Canterbury, Hawke's Bay) 1959 *BI* 2,3,4, 1960 *SA* 1,2,3,4, 1961 *F* 2,3, 1962 *A* 1,2,3, 1963 *E* 1,2, *I*, *W*, 1964 *E*, *S*, *F*, *A* 1,2,3, 1965 *SA* 1,2,3,4, 1966 *BI* 1,2,3,4, 1967 *A*, *E*, *W*, *S*, 1968 *A* 1, *F* 1,2,3
Trevathan, D (Otago) 1937 *SA* 1,2,3
Tuck, J M (Waikato) 1929 *A* 1,2,3
Tuigamala, V L (Auckland) 1991 [*US*, *It*, *C*, *S*], 1992 *Wld* 1,2,3, *I* 1, *A* 1,2,3, *SA*, 1993 *BI* 1,2,3, *A*, *WS*, *S*, *E*
Turner, R S (North Harbour) 1992 *Wld* 1,2(R)
Turtill, H S (Canterbury) 1905 *A*
Twigden, T M (Auckland) 1980 *A* 2,3
Tyler, G A (Auckland) 1903 *A*, 1904 *BI*, 1905 *S*, *I*, *E*, *W*, 1906 *F*

Udy, D K (Wairarapa) 1903 *A*
Urbahn, R J (Taranaki) 1959 *BI* 1,3,4
Urlich, R A (Auckland) 1970 *SA* 3,4
Uttley, I N (Wellington) 1963 *E* 1,2

Vincent, P B (Canterbury) 1956 *SA* 1,2
Vodanovich, I M H (Wellington) 1955 *A* 1,2,3

Wallace, W J (Wellington) 1903 *A*, 1904 *BI*, 1905 *S*, *I*, *E*, *W*, 1906 *F*, 1907 *A* 1,2,3, 1908 *AW* 2
Walsh, P T (Counties) 1955 *A* 1,2,3, 1956 *SA* 1,2,4, 1957 *A* 1,2, 1958 *A* 1,2,3, 1959 *BI* 1, 1963 *E* 2
Ward, R H (Southland) 1936 *A* 2, 1937 *SA* 1,3
Waterman, A C (North Auckland) 1929 *A* 1,2
Watkins, E L (Wellington) 1905 *A*
Watt, B A (Canterbury) 1962 *A* 1,4, 1963 *E* 1,2, *W*, 1964 *E*, *S*, *A* 1
Watt, J M (Otago) 1936 *A* 1,2
Watt, J R (Wellington) 1958 *A* 2, 1960 *SA* 1,2,3,4, 1961 *F* 1,3, 1962 *A* 1,2
Watts, M G (Taranaki) 1979 *F* 1,2, 1980 *A* 1,2,3(R)
Webb, D S (North Auckland) 1959 *BI* 2
Wells, J (Wellington) 1936 *A* 1,2
West, A H (Taranaki) 1921 *SA* 2,3
Whetton, A J (Auckland) 1984 *A* 1(R),3(R), 1985 *A*(R), *Arg* 1(R), 1986 *A* 2, 1987 [*It*, *Fj*, *Arg*, *S*, *W*, *F*], *A*, 1988 *W* 1,2, *A* 1,2,3, 1989 *F* 1,2, *Arg* 1,2, *A*, 1990 *S* 1,2, *A* 1,2,3, *F* 1,2, 1991 *Arg* 1, [*E*, *US*, *It*, *C*, *A*]
Whetton, G W (Auckland) 1981 *SA* 3, *R*, *F* 1,2, 1982 *A* 3, 1983 *BI* 1,2,3,4, 1984 *F* 1,2, *A* 1,2,3, 1985 *E* 1,2, *A*, *Arg* 2, 1986 *A* 2,3, *F* 2,3, 1987 [*It*, *Fj*, *Arg*, *S*, *W*, *F*], *A*, 1988 *W* 1,2, *A* 1,2,3, 1989 *F* 1,2, *Arg* 1,2, *A*, *W*, *I*, 1990 *S* 1,2, *A* 1,2,3, *F* 1,2, 1991 *Arg* 1,2, *A* 1,2, [*E*, *US*, *It*, *C*, *A*, *S*]
Whineray, W J (Canterbury, Waikato, Auckland) 1957 *A* 1,2, 1958 *A* 1,2,3, 1959 *BI* 1,2,3,4, 1960 *SA* 1,2,3,4, 1961 *F* 1,2,3, 1962 *A* 1,2,3,4,5, 1963 *E* 1,2, *I*, *W*, 1964 *E*, *S*, *F*, 1965 *SA* 1,2,3,4
White, A (Southland) 1921 *SA* 1, 1924 *I*, 1925 *E*, *F*
White, H L (Auckland) 1954 *I*, *E*, *F*, 1955 *A* 3
White, R A (Poverty Bay) 1949 *A* 1,2, 1950 *BI* 1,2,3,4, 1951 *A* 1,2,3, 1952 *A* 1,2, 1953 *W*, 1954 *I*, *E*, *S*, *F*, 1955 *A* 1,2,3, 1956 *SA* 1,2,3,4
White, R M (Wellington) 1946 *A* 1,2, 1947 *A* 1,2
Whiting, G J (King Country) 1972 *A* 1,2, *S*, 1973 *E* 1, *I*, *F*
Whiting, P J (Auckland) 1971 *BI* 1,2,4, 1972 *A* 1,2,3, *W*, *S*, 1973 *E* 1, *I*, *F*, 1974 *A* 1,2,3, *I*, 1976 *I*, *SA* 1,2,3,4
Williams, B G (Auckland) 1970 *SA* 1,2,3,4, 1971 *BI* 1,2,4, 1972 *A* 1,2,3, *W*, *S*, 1973 *E* 1, *I*, *F*, *E* 2, 1974 *A* 1,2,3, *I*, 1975 *S*, 1976 *I*, *SA* 1,2,3,4, 1977 *BI* 1,2,3,4, *F* 1, 1978 *A* 1,2,3, *I* (R), *W*, *E*, *S*
Williams, G C (Wellington) 1967 *E*, *W*, *F*, *S*, 1968 *A* 2
Williams, P (Otago) 1913 *A* 1
Williment, M (Wellington) 1964 *A* 1, 1965 *SA* 1,2,3, 1966 *BI* 1,2,3,4, 1967 *A*
Willocks, C (Otago) 1946 *A* 1,2, 1949 *SA* 1,3,4
Wilson, B W (Otago) 1977 *BI* 3,4, 1978 *A* 1,2,3, 1979 *F* 1,2, *A*
Wilson, D D (Canterbury) 1954 *E*, *S*
Wilson, H W (Otago) 1949 *A* 1, 1950 *BI* 4, 1951 *A* 1,2,3
Wilson, J W (Otago) 1993 *S*, *E*, 1994 *A*
Wilson, N A (Wellington) 1908 *AW* 1,2, 1910 *A* 1,2,3, 1913 *A* 2,3, 1914 *A* 1,2,3
Wilson, N L (Otago) 1951 *A* 1,2,3
Wilson, R G (Canterbury) 1979 *S*, *E*
Wilson, S S (Wellington) 1977 *F* 1,2, 1978 *A* 1,2,3, *I*, *W*, *E*, *S*, 1979 *F* 1,2, *A*, *S*, *E*, 1980 *A* 1, *W*, 1981 *S* 1,2, *SA* 1,2,3, *R*, *F* 1,2, 1982 *A* 1,2,3, 1983 *BI* 1,2,3,4, *A*, *S*, *E*
Wolfe, T N (Wellington, Taranaki) 1961 *F* 1,2,3, 1962 *A* 2,3, 1963 *E* 1

Wood, M E (Canterbury, Auckland) 1903 *A*, 1904 *BI*
Woodman, F A (North Auckland) 1981 *SA* 1,2, *F* 2
Wrigley, E (Wairarapa) 1905 *A*
Wright, T J (Auckland) 1986 *F* 1, *A* 1, 1987 [*Arg*], 1988 *W* 1,2, *A* 1,2,3, 1989 *F* 1,2, *Arg* 1,2, *A*, *W*, *I*, 1990 *S* 1,2, *A* 1,2,3, *F* 1,2, 1991 *Arg* 1,2, *A* 1,2, [*E*, *US*, *It*, *S*]
Wylie, J T (Auckland) 1913 *A* 1, *US*
Wyllie, A J (Canterbury) 1970 *SA* 2,3, 1971 *BI* 2,3,4, 1972 *W*, *S*, 1973 *E* 1, *I*, *F*, *E* 2

Yates, V M (North Auckland) 1961 *F* 1,2,3
Young, D (Canterbury) 1956 *SA* 2, 1958 *A* 1,2,3, 1960 *SA* 1,2,3,4, 1961 *F* 1,2,3, 1962 *A* 1,2,3,5, 1963 *E* 1,2, *I*, *W*, 1964 *E*, *S*, *F*

NEW ZEALAND INTERNATIONAL RECORDS

Both team and individual records are for official New Zealand international matches, up to 31 March 1995.

TEAM RECORDS

Highest score
74 v Fiji (74-13) 1987 Christchurch
v individual countries
60 v Argentina (60-9) 1989 Dunedin
38 v Australia { (38-13) 1936 Dunedin; (38-3) 1972 Auckland }
38 v B Isles (38-6) 1983 Auckland
29 v Canada (29-13) 1991 Lille
42 v England (42-15) 1985 Wellington
74 v Fiji (74-13) 1987 Christchurch
38 v France (38-8) 1906 Paris
59 v Ireland (59-6) 1992 Wellington
70 v Italy (70-6) 1987 Auckland
14 v Romania (14-6) 1981 Bucharest
27 v S Africa (27-24) 1992 Johannesburg
51 v Scotland (51-15) 1993 Murrayfield
51 v United States (51-3) 1913 Berkeley
54 v Wales (54-9) 1988 Auckland
35 v W Samoa (35-13) 1993 Auckland

Biggest winning points margin
64 v Italy (70-6) 1987 Auckland
v individual countries
51 v Argentina (60-9) 1989 Dublin
35 v Australia (38-3) 1972 Auckland
32 v B Isles (38-6) 1983 Auckland
16 v Canada (29-13) 1991 Lille
27 v England (42-15) 1985 Wellington
61 v Fiji (74-13) 1987 Christchurch
30 v France (38-8) 1906 Paris
53 v Ireland (59-6) 1992 Wellington
64 v Italy (70-6) 1987 Auckland
8 v Romania (14-6) 1981 Bucharest
17 v S Africa (20-3) 1965 Auckland
36 v Scotland (51-15) 1993 Murrayfield
48 v United States (51-3) 1913 Berkeley
49 v Wales (52-3) 1988 Christchurch
22 v W Samoa (35-13) 1993 Auckland

Longest winning sequence
17 matches – 1965-69

Highest score by opposing team
30 Australia (16-30) 1978 Auckland
by individual countries
21 Argentina (21-21) 1985 Buenos Aires
30 Australia (16-30) 1978 Auckland
20 B Isles (7-20) 1993 Wellington
13 Canada (29-13) 1991 Lille
16 England (10-16) 1973 Auckland
13 Fiji (74-13) 1987 Christchurch
24 France (19-24) 1979 Auckland
21 Ireland (24-21) 1992 Dunedin
21 Italy (31-21) 1991 Leicester
6 Romania (14-6) 1981 Bucharest
24 S Africa { (12-24) 1981 Wellington; (27-24) 1992 Johannesburg }
25 Scotland (25-25) 1983 Edinburgh
6 United States (46-6) 1991 Gloucester
16 Wales (19-16) 1972 Cardiff
13 W Samoa (35-13) 1993 Auckland

Biggest losing points margin
17 v S Africa (0-17) 1928 Durban
v individual countries
16 v Australia (10-26) 1980 Sydney
13 v B Isles (7-20) 1993 Wellington
13 v England (0-13) 1936 Twickenham
14 v France (8-22) 1994 Christchurch
17 v S Africa (0-17) 1928 Durban
5 v Wales (8-13) 1953 Cardiff
No defeats v Argentina, Canada, Fiji, Ireland, Italy, Romania, Scotland, United States or Western Samoa

Longest losing sequence
6 matches – 1949

Most tries by New Zealand in an international
13 v United States (51-3) Berkeley

Most tries against New Zealand in an international
5 by { S Africa (6-17) 1937 Auckland
Australia (16-30) 1978 Auckland
World XV (54-26) 1992 Wellington }

Most points on overseas tour (all matches)
868 in B Isles/France (33 matches) 1905-06

Most tries on overseas tour
215 in B Isles/France (33 matches) 1905-06

INDIVIDUAL RECORDS

Most capped player
J J Kirwan 63 1984-94
in individual positions
Full-back
D B Clarke 31 1956-64
Wing
J J Kirwan 63 1984-94
Centre (includes 2nd five-eighth)
B J Robertson 34 1972-81
1st five-eighth
G J Fox 46 1985-93
Scrum-half
S M Going 29 1967-77
Prop
S C McDowell 46 1985-92
Hooker
S B T Fitzpatrick 62 1986-94
Lock
G W Whetton 58 1981-91
Flanker
K R Tremain 36(38)[1] 1959-68
I A Kirkpatrick 36(39)[2] 1967-77
No 8
M G Mexted 34 1979-85

[1] *Tremain won 2 caps as a No 8*
[2] *Kirkpatrick won 3 caps as a No 8*

Longest international career

E Hughes	15 seasons	1907-21
C E Meads	15 seasons	1957-71

Most consecutive internationals – 60
S B T Fitzpatrick 1986-94

Most internationals as captain – 30
W J Whineray 1958-65

Most points in internationals – 645
G J Fox (46 matches) 1985-93

Most points in an international – 26
A R Hewson v Australia 1982 Auckland
G J Fox v Fiji 1987 Christchurch

Most tries in internationals – 35
J J Kirwan (63 matches) 1984-94

Most tries in an international – 4
D McGregor v England 1905 Crystal Palace
C I Green v Fiji 1987 Christchurch
J A Gallagher v Fiji 1987 Christchurch
J J Kirwan v Wales 1988 Christchurch

Most conversions in internationals – 118
G J Fox (46 matches) 1985-93

Most conversions in an international – 10
G J Fox v Fiji 1987 Christchurch

Most dropped goals in internationals – 7
G J Fox (46 matches) 1985-93

Most dropped goals in an international – 2
O D Bruce v Ireland 1978 Dublin
F M Botica v France 1986 Christchurch

Most penalty goals in internationals – 128
G J Fox (46 matches) 1985-93

Most penalty goals in an international – 7
G J Fox v W Samoa 1993 Auckland

Most points in international series – 46
A R Hewson (4 appearances) v B Isles 1983

Most points in international series on tour – 38
G J Fox (2 appearances) 1990 France

Most tries in international series on tour – 5
K Svenson (4 appearances) 1924-25
B Isles/France
Svenson scored in each match of the international series

Most points on tour – 230
W J Wallace (25 appearances) 1905-06
B Isles/France

Most tries on tour – 42
J Hunter (23 appearances) 1905-06
B Isles/France

Most points in a tour match – 43
R M Deans v South Australia 1984
Adelaide

Most tries in a tour match – 8
T R Heeps v Northern NSW 1962
Quirindi

Sean Fitzpatrick, New Zealand's most-capped hooker (62) and holder of the record for most consecutive internationals (60).

BURSTS OF BRILLIANCE BRIGHTEN THE MEDIOCRITY

THE 1994 SEASON IN AUSTRALIA
Greg Campbell

The Wallabies seem to have found a way to steady themselves away from the brink of disaster and remain in the pool of unbridled success. In a busy season of six domestic Tests, the Australians faced the humiliation of losing an international to Italy, yet by the end Bob Dwyer's team had once again completed another record year. It was almost shades of the 1991 World Cup, when Australia were nearly bounced out by Ireland before marching on to win the final against England. The good results may have indicated a year of consistency, but closer examination of the matches reveals that this was not the case with the performances. Ireland visited Australia for the first time in 15 years and were comfortably beaten 33-13 and 32-18 in each of the two Tests. While these victories suggest commanding Wallaby performances, the reality was spasmodic class overshadowed by mediocre passages.

Immediately after Ireland departed, Italy took centre stage, giving notice in the lead-up matches that they would play with greater enterprise than the Irish. The First Test at Ballymore, the first-ever Test played in Brisbane under lights, almost saw one of rugby's biggest-ever upsets, and one which would perhaps have rivalled Australia's 1973 loss to Tonga. Italy led 11-10 at half-time and 17-13 late into the second half before a try by Matthew Burke and the conversion and a penalty goal by replacement fly-half Tim Wallace rescued Australia from embarrassment.

A week later, Australia celebrated their Test return to Melbourne for the first time in 33 years when they maintained their perfect winning record with a dour, uninspiring 20-7 victory at Olympic Park. The lack of entertainment was exacerbated by the incessant whistling of South African referee Ian Rogers.

Against both Ireland and Italy, the Wallaby back line performed like a highly tuned six-cylinder engine misfiring on two cylinders. Tim Horan and Jason Little were sidelined and three different centre combinations were used in four Tests. Captain and fly-half Michael Lynagh was injured in the First Test against Italy and missed the remainder of the season. But the concerns raised during a gruelling four-week Test match campaign crumbled soon afterwards with breathtaking victories over Western Samoa and the All Blacks. Australia's record-breaking 73-3 win over the Samoans rocked the rugby world with the same force as the earthquake which shook Sydney during the match. A total of 11 tries were posted in the finest exhibition of attacking rugby ever seen on Australian soil.

Then, 11 days later, the Wallabies produced a devastating first-half blitz to lead the All Blacks 17-3 at the break before desperately hanging on to reclaim the Bledisloe Cup with a 20-16 win which will forever be remembered for the match-winning tackle by scrum-half George Gregan on All Black winger Jeff Wilson only minutes before full-time. The midweek night Test attracted a record crowd at the Sydney Football Stadium and broke rugby television ratings around the country. Gregan was undoubtedly the find of the season, while powerful No 8 Tim Gavin was adjudged the Australian Players' Player of the Year. Gregan made his Test debut during the season along with Matthew Pini, Daniel Herbert, Matthew O'Connor, Ryan Constable and Tim Wallace. Prop Tony Daly became Australia's most-capped Test prop, while his partnership with Phil Kearns and Ewen McKenzie broke the world record for most Tests as a front-row combination. After missing the entire 1993 season because of injury, lock John Eales and flanker Willie Ofahengaue both made successful Test comebacks.

At the conclusion of the domestic season, the Emerging Wallabies overcame a host of pre-tour unavailability disruptions by winning four of six games on their tour of southern Africa. The tour produced another potential star in the strongly built ACT threequarter Joe Roff, who scored 109 points in five appearances.

A new administration team took the helm of the Australian RFU. The roles of president and chairman were split for the first time and filled by Phil Harry and Leo Williams respectively, while executive director Bob Fordham resigned and was replaced by Bruce Hayman. Battles with Rugby League clubs resurfaced during the year. Wallaby lock Garrick Morgan accepted a lucrative contract and Emerging Wallabies Nathan Turner and Peter Jorgensen followed suit. Jason Little, however, rejected yet another mammoth offer to turn professional.

On the representative front, Queensland triumphed in the Super-10 championship with a 21-10 victory over Natal in Durban but later lost the inter-state series to New South Wales on points difference after it was levelled at 1-1. The NSW Rugby Union provided the season's most controversial issue when they refused to play Natal in Durban because player safety could not be guaranteed while a state of emergency existed. After a bitter and protracted dispute, Natal won the match on forfeit to qualify for a place in the final against Queensland.

The Australian sevens team showed signs of improvement in losing narrowly 10-5 to Western Samoa in the Digital International Sevens in Canberra before being outclassed by 32-20 against New Zealand at the Hong Kong Sevens. Australia also fielded their first-ever women's Test team against a highly experienced New Zealand side, losing 37-0.

MAJOR PROVINCIAL MATCHES: Queensland 22, NSW 20; NSW 38, Queensland 8; Queensland 36, ACT 15; ACT 44, NSW 28
SYDNEY GRAND FINAL: Randwick 36, Warringah 16
BRISBANE GRAND FINAL: Southern Districts 19, Sunnybank 8

AUSTRALIAN INTERNATIONAL PLAYERS *(up to 31 March 1995)*

ABBREVIATIONS

Arg – Argentina; *BI* – British Isles teams; *C* – Canada; *E* – England; *F* – France; *Fj* – Fiji; *I* – Ireland; *It* – Italy; *J* – Japan; *M* – Maoris; *NZ* – New Zealand; *S* – Scotland; *SA* – South Africa; *SK* – South Korea; *Tg* – Tonga; *US* – United States of America; *W* – Wales; *WS* – Western Samoa; (R) – Replacement; (t) – temporary replacement. Entries in square brackets [ ] indicate appearances in the Rugby World Cup.

STATE ABBREVIATIONS

ACT – Australian Capital Territory; NSW – New South Wales; Q – Queensland; V – Victoria; WA – Western Australia.

N.B. In the summer of 1986, the ARU retrospectively granted full Australian Test status to the five international matches played by the 1927-28 touring team to Europe. In 1988 Test status was extended to all those who played overseas in the 1920s.

Note: When a series has taken place, figures denote the particular matches in which players featured. Thus 1963 *SA* 2,4 indicates that a player appeared in the second and fourth Tests of the 1963 series against South Africa.

Abrahams, A M F (NSW) 1967 *NZ*, 1968 *NZ* 1, 1969 *W*
Adams, N J (NSW) 1955 *NZ* 1
Adamson, R W (NSW) 1912 *US*
Allan, T (NSW) 1946 *NZ* 1, *M*, *NZ* 2, 1947 *NZ* 2, *S*, *I*, *W*, 1948 *E*, *F*, 1949 *M* 1,2,3, *NZ* 1,2
Anlezark, E A (NSW) 1905 *NZ*
Armstrong, A R (NSW) 1923 *NZ* 1,2
Austin, L R (NSW) 1963 *E*

Baker, R L (NSW) 1904 *BI* 1,2
Baker, W H (NSW) 1914 *NZ* 1,2,3
Ballesty, J P (NSW) 1968 *NZ* 1,2, *F*, *I*, *S*, 1969 *W*, *SA* 2,3,4
Bannon, D P (NSW) 1946 *M*
Bardsley, E J (NSW) 1928 *NZ* 1,3, *M* (R)
Barker, H S (NSW) 1952 *Fj* 1,2, *NZ* 1,2, 1953 *SA* 4, 1954 *Fj* 1,2
Barnett, J T (NSW) 1907 *NZ* 1,2,3, 1908 *W*, 1909 *E*
Barry, M J (Q) 1971 *SA* 3
Barton, R F D (NSW) 1899 *BI* 3
Batch, P G (Q) 1975 *S*, *W*, 1976 *E*, *Fj* 1,2,3, *F* 1,2, 1978 *W* 1,2, *NZ* 1,2,3, 1979 *Arg* 2
Batterham, R P (NSW) 1967 *NZ*, 1970 *S*
Battishall, B R (NSW) 1973 *E*
Baxter, A J (NSW) 1949 *M* 1,2,3, *NZ* 1,2, 1951 *NZ* 1,2, 1952 *NZ* 1,2
Baxter, T J (Q) 1958 *NZ* 3
Beith, B McN (NSW) 1914 *NZ* 3
Bell, K R (Q) 1968 *S*
Bennett, W G (Q) 1931 *M*, 1933 *SA* 1,2,3
Bermingham, J V (Q) 1934 *NZ* 1,2, 1937 *SA* 1
Berne, J E (NSW) 1975 *S*
Besomo, K S (NSW) 1979 *I* 2
Betts, T N (Q) 1951 *NZ* 2,3, 1954 *Fj* 2
Biilmann, R R (NSW) 1933 *SA* 1,2,3,4
Birt, R (Q) 1914 *NZ* 2
Black, J W (NSW) 1985 *C* 1,2, *NZ*, *Fj* 1
Blackwood, J G (NSW) 1923 *NZ* 1,2,3, 1925 *NZ*, 1927 *I*, *W*, *S*, 1928 *E*, *F*
Blair, M R (NSW) 1928 *F*, 1931 *M*, *NZ*
Bland, G V (NSW) 1928 *NZ* 3, *M*, 1932 *NZ* 1,2,3, 1933 *SA* 1,2,4,5
Blomley, J (NSW) 1949 *M* 1,2,3, *NZ* 1,2, 1950 *BI* 1,2
Boland, S B (Q) 1899 *BI* 3,4, 1903 *NZ*
Bond, J H (NSW) 1921 *NZ*
Bonis, E T (Q) 1929 *NZ* 1,2,3, 1930 *BI*, 1931 *M*, *NZ*, 1932 *NZ* 1,2,3, 1933 *SA* 1,2,3,4,5, 1934 *NZ* 1,2, 1936 *NZ* 1,2, *M*, 1937 *SA* 1, 1938 *NZ* 1
Bosler, J M (NSW) 1953 *SA* 1
Bouffler, R G (NSW) 1899 *BI* 3
Bourke, T K (Q) 1947 *NZ* 2
Bowen, S (NSW) 1993 *SA* 1,2,3
Bowers, A J A (NSW) 1923 *NZ* 3, 1925 *NZ*, 1927 *I*
Boyce, E S (NSW) 1962 *NZ* 1,2, 1964 *NZ* 1,2,3, 1965 *SA* 1,2, 1966 *W*, *S*, 1967 *E*, *I* 1, *F*, *I* 2
Boyce, J S (NSW) 1962 *NZ* 3,4,5, 1963 *E*, *SA* 1,2,3,4, 1964 *NZ* 1,3, 1965 *SA* 1,2
Boyd, A (NSW) 1899 *BI* 3
Boyd, A F McC (Q) 1958 *M* 1
Brass, J E (NSW) 1966 *BI* 2, *W*, *S*, 1967 *E*, *I* 1, *F*, *I* 2, *NZ*, 1968 *NZ* 1, *F*, *I*, *S*
Breckenridge, J W (NSW) 1927 *I*, *W*, *S*, 1928 *E*, *F*, 1929 *NZ* 1,2,3, 1930 *BI*
Brial, M C (NSW) 1993 *F* 1(R), 2
Bridle, O L (V) 1931 *M*, 1932 *NZ* 1,2,3, 1933 *SA* 3,4,5, 1934 *NZ* 1,2, 1936 *NZ* 1,2, *M*
Broad, E G (Q) 1949 *M* 1
Brockhoff, J D (NSW) 1949 *M* 2,3, *NZ* 1,2, 1950 *BI* 1,2, 1951 *NZ* 2,3
Brown, B R (Q) 1972 *NZ* 1,3
Brown, J V (NSW) 1956 *SA* 1,2, 1957 *NZ* 1,2, 1958 *W*, *I*, *E*, *S*, *F*
Brown, R C (NSW) 1975 *E* 1,2
Brown, S W (NSW) 1953 *SA* 2,3,4
Bryant, H (NSW) 1925 *NZ*
Buchan, A J (NSW) 1946 *NZ* 1,2, 1947 *NZ* 1,2, *S*, *I*, *W*, 1948 *E*, *F*, 1949 *M* 3
Bull, D (NSW) 1928 *M*
Buntine, H (NSW) 1923 *NZ* 1(R)
Burdon, A (NSW) 1903 *NZ*, 1904 *BI* 1,2, 1905 *NZ*
Burge, A B (NSW) 1907 *NZ* 3, 1908 *W*
Burge, P H (NSW) 1907 *NZ* 1,2,3
Burge, R (NSW) 1928 *NZ* 1,2,3(R), *M* (R)
Burke, B T (NSW) 1988 *S* (R)
Burke, C T (NSW) 1946 *NZ* 2, 1947 *NZ* 1,2, *S*, *I*, *W*, 1948 *E*, *F*, 1949 *M* 2,3, *NZ* 1,2, 1950 *BI* 1,2, 1951 *NZ* 1,2,3, 1953 *SA* 2,3,4, 1954 *Fj* 1, 1955 *NZ* 1,2,3, 1956 *SA* 1,2
Burke, M (NSW) 1993 *SA* 3(R), *F* 1, 1994 *I* 1,2, *It* 1,2
Burke, M P (NSW) 1984 *E* (R), *I*, 1985 *C* 1,2, *NZ*, *Fj* 1,2, 1986 *It* (R), *F*, *Arg* 1,2, *NZ* 1,2,3, 1987 *SK*, [*US*, *J*, *I*, *F*, *W*], *NZ*, *Arg* 1,2
Burnet, D R (NSW) 1972 *F* 1,2, *NZ* 1,2,3, *Fj*
Butler, O F (NSW) 1969 *SA* 1,2, 1970 *S*, 1971 *SA* 2,3, *F* 1,2

Calcraft, W J (NSW) 1985 *C* 1, 1986 *It*, *Arg* 2
Caldwell, B C (NSW) 1928 *NZ* 3
Cameron, A S (NSW) 1951 *NZ* 1,2,3, 1952 *Fj* 1,2, *NZ* 1,2, 1953 *SA* 1,2,3,4, 1954 *Fj* 1,2, 1955 *NZ* 1,2,3, 1956 *SA* 1,2, 1957 *NZ* 1, 1958 *I*
Campbell, J D (NSW) 1910 *NZ* 1,2,3
Campbell, W A (Q) 1984 *Fj*, 1986 *It*, *F*, *Arg* 1,2, *NZ* 1,2,3, 1987 SK, [*E*, *US*, *J*(R), *I*, *F*], *NZ*, 1988 *E*, 1989 *BI* 1,2,3, *NZ*, 1990 *NZ* 2,3
Campese, D I (ACT, NSW) 1982 *NZ* 1,2,3, 1983 *US*, *Arg* 1,2, *NZ*, *It*, *F* 1,2, 1984 *Fj*, *NZ* 1,2,3, *E*, *I*, *W*, *S*, 1985 *Fj* 1,2, 1986 *It*, *F*, *Arg* 1,2, *NZ* 1,2,3, 1987 [*E*, *US*, *J*, *I*, *F*, *W*], *NZ*, 1988 *E* 1,2, *NZ* 1,2,3, *E*, *S*, *It*, 1989 *BI* 1,2,3, *NZ*, *F* 1,2, 1990 *F* 2,3, *US*, *NZ* 1,2,3, 1991 *W*, *E*, *NZ* 1,2, [*Arg*, *WS*, *W*, *I*, *NZ*, *E*], 1992 *S* 1,2, *NZ* 1,2,3, *SA*, *I*, *W*, 1993 *Tg*, *NZ*, *SA* 1,2,3, *C*, *F* 1,2, 1994 *I* 1,2, *It* 1,2, *WS*, *NZ*
Canniffe, W D (Q) 1907 *NZ* 2
Carberry, C M (NSW, Q) 1973 *Tg* 2, *E*, 1976 *I*, *US*, *Fj*

1,2,3, 1981 *F* 1,2, *I*, *W*, *S*, 1982 *E*
Cardy, A M (NSW) 1966 *BI* 1,2, *W*, *S*, 1967 *E*, *I* 1, *F*, 1968 *NZ* 1,2
Carew, P J (Q) 1899 *BI* 1,2,3,4
Carmichael, P (Q) 1904 *BI* 2, 1907 *NZ* 1, 1908 *W*, 1909 *E*
Carozza, P V (Q) 1990 *F* 1,2,3, *NZ* 2,3, 1992 *S* 1,2, *NZ* 1,2,3, *SA*, *I*, *W*, 1993 *Tg*, *NZ*
Carpenter, M G (V) 1938 *NZ* 1,2
Carr, E T A (NSW) 1913 *NZ* 1,2,3, 1914 *NZ* 1,2,3
Carr, E W (NSW) 1921 *NZ* 1 (R)
Carroll, D B (NSW) 1908 *W*, 1912 *US*
Carroll, J C (NSW) 1953 *SA* 1
Carroll, J H (NSW) 1958 *M* 2,3, *NZ* 1,2,3, 1959 *BI* 1,2
Carson, J (NSW) 1899 *BI* 1
Carson, P J (NSW) 1979 *NZ*, 1980 *NZ* 3
Carter, D G (NSW) 1988 *E* 1,2, *NZ* 1, 1989 *F* 1,2
Casey, T V (NSW) 1963 *SA* 2,3,4, 1964 *NZ* 1,2,3
Catchpole, K W (NSW) 1961 *Fj* 1,2,3, *SA* 1,2, *F*, 1962 *NZ* 1,2,4, 1963 *SA* 2,3,4, 1964 *NZ* 1,2,3, 1965 *SA* 1,2, 1966 *BI* 1,2, *W*, *S*, 1967 *E*, *I* 1, *F*, *I* 2, *NZ*, 1968 *NZ* 1
Cawsey, R M (NSW) 1949 *M* 1, *NZ* 1,2
Cerutti, W H (NSW) 1928 *NZ* 1,2,3, *M*, 1929 *NZ* 1,2,3, 1930 *BI*, 1931 *M*, *NZ*, 1932 *NZ* 1,2,3, 1933 *SA* 1,2,3,4,5, 1936 *M*, 1937 *SA* 1,2
Challoner, R L (NSW) 1899 *BI* 2
Chapman, G A (NSW) 1962 *NZ* 3,4,5
Clark, J G (Q) 1931 *M*, *NZ*, 1932 *NZ* 1,2, 1933 *SA* 1
Clarken, J C (NSW) 1905 *NZ*, 1910 *NZ* 1,2,3
Cleary, M A (NSW) 1961 *Fj* 1,2,3, *SA* 1,2, *F*
Clements, P (NSW) 1982 *NZ* 3
Clifford, M (NSW) 1938 *NZ* 3
Cobb, W G (NSW) 1899 *BI* 3,4
Cocks, M R (NSW, Q) 1972 *F* 1,2, *NZ* 2,3, *Fj*, 1973 *Tg* 1,2, *W*, *E*, 1975 *J* 1
Codey, D (NSW Country, Q) 1983 *Arg* 1, 1984 *E*, *W*, *S*, 1985 *C* 2, *NZ*, 1986 *F*, *Arg* 1, 1987 [*US*, *J*, *F*(R), *W*], *NZ*
Cody, E W (NSW) 1913 *NZ* 1,2,3
Coker, T (Q) 1987 [*E*, *US*, *F*, *W*], 1991 *NZ* 2, [*Arg*, *WS*, *NZ*, *E*], 1992 *NZ* 1,2,3, *W*(R), 1993 *Tg*, *NZ*
Colbert, R (NSW) 1952 *Fj* 2, *NZ* 1,2, 1953 *SA* 2,3,4
Cole, J W (NSW) 1968 *NZ* 1,2, *F*, *I*, *S*, 1969 *W*, *SA* 1,2,3,4, 1970 *S*, 1971 *SA* 1,2,3, *F* 1,2, 1972 *NZ* 1,2,3, 1973 *Tg* 1,2, 1974 *NZ* 1,2,3
Collins, P K (NSW) 1937 *SA* 2, 1938 *NZ* 2,3
Colton, A J (Q) 1899 *BI* 1,3
Colton, T (Q) 1904 *BI* 1,2
Comrie-Thomson, I R (NSW) 1928 *NZ* 1,2,3, *M*
Connor, D M (Q) 1958 *W*, *I*, *E*, *S*, *F*, *M* 2,3, *NZ* 1,2,3, 1959 *BI* 1,2
Constable, R (Q) 1994 *I* 2(t & R)
Cook, M T (Q) 1986 *F*, 1987 *SK*, [*J*], 1988 *E* 1,2, *NZ* 1,2,3, *E*, *S*, *It*
Cooke, B P (Q) 1979 *I* 1
Cooke, G M (Q) 1932 *NZ* 1,2,3, 1933 *SA* 1,2,3, 1946 *NZ* 2, 1947 *NZ* 2, *S*, *I*, *W*, 1948 *E*, *F*
Coolican, J E (NSW) 1982 *NZ* 1, 1983 *It*, *F* 1,2
Corfe, A C (Q) 1899 *BI* 2
Cornelsen, G (NSW) 1974 *NZ* 2,3, 1975 *J* 2, *S*, *W*, 1976 *E*, *F* 1,2, 1978 *W* 1,2, *NZ* 1,2,3, 1979 *I* 1,2, *NZ*, *Arg* 1,2, 1980 *NZ* 1,2,3, 1981 *I*, *W*, *S*, 1982 *E*
Cornes, J R (Q) 1972 *Fj*
Cornforth, R G W (NSW) 1947 *NZ* 1, 1950 *BI* 2
Cornish, P (ACT) 1990 *F* 2,3, *NZ* 1
Costello, P P S (Q) 1950 *BI* 2
Cottrell, N V (Q) 1949 *M* 1,2,3, *NZ* 1,2, 1950 *BI* 1,2, 1951 *NZ* 1,2,3, 1952 *Fj* 1,2, *NZ* 1,2
Cowper, D L (V) 1931 *NZ*, 1932 *NZ* 1,2,3, 1933 *SA* 1,2,3,4,5
Cox, B P (NSW) 1952 *Fj* 1,2, *NZ* 1,2, 1954 *Fj* 2, 1955 *NZ* 1, 1956 *SA* 2, 1957 *NZ* 1,2
Cox, M H (NSW) 1981 *W*, *S*
Cox, P A (NSW) 1979 *Arg* 1,2, 1980 *Fj*, *NZ* 1,2, 1981 *W*(R), *S*, 1982 *S* 1,2, *NZ* 1,2,3, 1984 *Fj*, *NZ* 1,2,3
Craig, R R (NSW) 1908 *W*
Crakanthorp, J S (NSW) 1923 *NZ* 3
Cremin, J F (NSW) 1946 *NZ* 1,2, 1947 *NZ* 1
Crittle, C P (NSW) 1962 *NZ* 4,5, 1963 *SA* 2,3,4, 1964 *NZ* 1,2,3, 1965 *SA* 1,2, 1966 *BI* 1,2, *S*, 1967 *E*, *I*
Croft, B H D (NSW) 1928 *M*
Cross, J R (NSW) 1955 *NZ* 1,2,3
Cross, K A (NSW) 1949 *M* 1, *NZ* 1,2, 1950 *BI* 1,2, 1951 *NZ* 2,3, 1952 *NZ* 1, 1953 *SA* 1,2,3,4, 1954 *Fj* 1,2, 1955 *NZ* 3, 1956 *SA* 1,2, 1957 *NZ* 1,2
Crossman, O C (NSW) 1925 *NZ*, 1929 *NZ* 2, 1930 *BI*
Crowe, P J (NSW) 1976 *F* 2, 1978 *W* 1,2, 1979 *I* 2, *NZ*, *Arg* 1
Crowley, D J (Q) 1989 *BI* 1,2,3, 1991 [*WS*], 1992 *I*, *W*, 1993 *C*(R)
Curley, T J P (NSW) 1957 *NZ* 1,2, 1958 *W*, *I*, *E*, *S*, *F*, *M* 1, *NZ* 1,2,3
Curran, D J (NSW) 1980 *NZ* 3, 1981 *F* 1,2, *W*, 1983 *Arg* 1
Currie, E W (Q) 1899 *BI* 2
Cutler, S A G (NSW) 1982 *NZ* 2(R), 1984 *NZ* 1,2,3, *E*, *I*, *W*, *S*, 1985 *C* 1,2, *NZ*, *Fj* 1,2, 1986 *It*, *F*, *NZ* 1,2,3, 1987 *SK*, [*E*, *J*, *I*, *F*, *W*], *NZ*, *Arg* 1,2, 1988 *E* 1,2, *NZ* 1,2,3, *E*, *S*, *It*, 1989 *BI* 1,2,3, *NZ*, 1991 [*WS*]

Daly, A J (NSW) 1989 *NZ*, *F* 1,2, 1990 *F* 1,2,3, *US*, *NZ* 1,2,3, 1991 *W*, *E*, *NZ* 1,2, [*Arg*, *W*, *I*, *NZ*, *E*], 1992 *S* 1,2, *NZ* 1,2,3, *SA*, 1993 *Tg*, *NZ*, *SA* 1,2,3, *C*, *F* 1,2, 1994 *I* 1,2, *It* 1,2, *WS*, *NZ*
D'Arcy, A M (Q) 1980 *Fj*, *NZ* 3, 1981 *F* 1,2, *I*, *W*, *S*, 1982 *E*, *S* 1,2
Darveniza, P (NSW) 1969 *W*, *SA* 2,3,4
Davidson, R A L (NSW) 1952 *Fj* 1,2, *NZ* 1,2, 1953 *SA* 1, 1957 *NZ* 1,2, 1958 *W*, *I*, *E*, *S*, *F*, *M* 1
Davis, C C (NSW) 1949 *NZ* 1, 1951 *NZ* 1,2,3
Davis, E H (V) 1947 *S*, *W*, 1949 *M* 1,2
Davis, G V (NSW) 1963 *E*, *SA* 1,2,3,4, 1964 *NZ* 1,2,3, 1965 *SA* 1, 1966 *BI* 1,2, *W*, *S*, 1967 *E*, *I* 1, *F*, *I* 2, *NZ*, 1968 *NZ* 1,2, *F*, *I*, *S*, 1969 *W*, *SA* 1,2,3,4, 1970 *S*, 1971 *SA* 1,2,3, *F* 1,2, 1972 *F* 1,2, *NZ* 1,2,3
Davis, G W G (NSW) 1955 *NZ* 2,3
Davis, R A (NSW) 1974 *NZ* 1,2,3
Davis, T S R (NSW) 1921 *NZ*, 1923 *NZ* 1,2,3
Davis, W (NSW) 1899 *BI* 1,3,4
Dawson, W L (NSW) 1946 *NZ* 1,2
Diett, L J (NSW) 1959 *BI* 1,2
Dix, W (NSW) 1907 *NZ* 1,2,3, 1909 *E*
Dixon, E J (Q) 1904 *BI* 3
Donald, K J (Q) 1957 *NZ* 1, 1958 *W*, *I*, *E*, *S*, *M* 2,3, 1959 *BI* 1,2
Dore, E (Q) 1904 *BI* 1
Dore, M J (Q) 1905 *NZ*
Dorr, R W (V) 1936 *M*, 1937 *SA* 1
Douglas, J A (V) 1962 *NZ* 3,4,5
Dowse, J H (NSW) 1961 *Fj* 1,2, *SA* 1,2
Dunbar, A R (NSW) 1910 *NZ* 1,2,3, 1912 *US*
Dunlop, E E (V) 1932 *NZ* 3, 1934 *NZ* 1
Dunn, P K (NSW) 1958 *NZ* 1,2,3, 1959 *BI* 1,2
Dunn, V A (NSW) 1921 *NZ*
Dunworth, D A (Q) 1971 *F* 1,2, 1972 *F* 1,2, 1976 *Fj* 2
Dwyer, L J (NSW) 1910 *NZ* 1,2,3, 1912 *US*, 1913 *NZ* 3, 1914 *NZ* 1,2,3

Eales, J A (Queensland) 1991 *W*, *E*, *NZ* 1,2, [*Arg*, *WS*, *W*, *I*, *NZ*, *E*], 1992 *S* 1,2, *NZ* 1,2,3, *SA*, *I*, 1994 *I* 1,2, *It* 1,2, *WS*, *NZ*
Eastes, C C (NSW) 1946 *NZ* 1,2, 1947 *NZ* 1,2, 1949 *M* 1,2
Egerton, R H (NSW) 1991 *W*, *E*, *NZ* 1,2, [*Arg*, *W*, *I*, *NZ*, *E*]
Ella, G A (NSW) 1982 *NZ* 1,2, 1983 *F* 1,2, 1988 *E* 2, *NZ* 1
Ella, G J (NSW) 1982 *S* 1, 1983 *It*, 1985 *C* 2 (R), *Fj* 2
Ella, M G (NSW) 1980 *NZ* 1,2,3, 1981 *F* 2, *S*, 1982 *E*, *S* 1, *NZ* 1,2,3, 1983 *US*, *Arg* 1,2, *NZ*, *It*, *F* 1,2, 1984 *Fj*, *NZ* 1,2,3, *E*, *I*, *W*, *S*
Ellem, M A (NSW) 1976 *Fj* 3(R)
Elliott, F M (NSW) 1957 *NZ* 1
Elliott, R E (NSW) 1921 *NZ*, 1923 *NZ* 1,2,3
Ellis, C S (NSW) 1899 *BI* 1,2,3,4
Ellis, K J (NSW) 1958 *NZ* 1,2,3, 1959 *BI* 1,2
Ellwood, B J (NSW) 1958 *NZ* 1,2,3, 1961 *Fj* 2,3, *SA* 1, *F*, 1962 *NZ* 1,2,3,4,5, 1963 *SA* 1,2,3,4, 1964 *NZ* 3, 1965 *SA* 1,2, 1966 *BI* 1
Emanuel, D M (NSW) 1957 *NZ* 2, 1958 *W*, *I*, *E*, *S*, *F*, *M* 1,2,3
Emery, N A (NSW) 1947 *NZ* 2, *S*, *I*, *W*, 1948 *E*, *F*, 1949 *M* 2,3, *NZ* 1,2
Erasmus, D J (NSW) 1923 *NZ* 1,2
Erby, A B (NSW) 1923 *NZ* 2,3
Evans, L J (Q) 1903 *NZ*, 1904 *BI* 1,3
Evans, W T (Q) 1899 *BI* 1,2

Fahey, E J (NSW) 1912 *US*, 1913 *NZ* 1,2, 1914 *NZ* 3
Fairfax, R L (NSW) 1971 *F* 1,2, 1972 *F* 1,2, *NZ* 1, *Fj*, 1973 *W*, *E*
Farmer, E H (Q) 1910 *NZ* 1
Farr-Jones, N C (NSW) 1984 *E*, *I*, *W*, *S*, 1985 *C* 1,2, *NZ*, *Fj* 1,2, 1986 *It*, *F*, *Arg* 1,2, *NZ* 1,2,3, 1987 *SK*, [*E*, *I*, *F*, *W*(R)], *NZ*, *Arg* 2, 1988 *E* 1,2, *NZ* 1,2,3, *E*, *S*, *It*, 1989 *BI* 1,2,3, *NZ*, *F* 1,2, 1990 *F* 1,2,3, *US*, *NZ* 1,2,3, 1991 *W*, *E*, *NZ* 1,2, [*Arg*, *WS*, *I*, *NZ*, *E*], 1992 *S* 1,2, *NZ* 1,2,3, *SA*, 1993 *NZ*, *SA* 1,2,3
Fay, G (NSW) 1971 *SA* 2, 1972 *NZ* 1,2,3, 1973 *Tg* 1,2, *W*, *E*, 1974 *NZ* 1,2,3, 1975 *E* 1,2, *J* 1, *S*, *W*, 1976 *I*, *US*, 1978 *W* 1,2, *NZ* 1,2,3, 1979 *I* 1
Fenwicke, P T (NSW) 1957 *NZ* 1, 1958 *W*, *I*, *E*, 1959 *BI* 1,2
Ferguson, R T (NSW) 1923 *NZ* 3
Fihelly, J A (Q) 1907 *NZ* 2
Finlay, A N (NSW) 1927 *I*, *W*, *S*, 1928 *E*, *F*, 1929 *NZ* 1,2,3, 1930 *BI*
Finley, F G (NSW) 1904 *BI* 3
Finnane, S C (NSW) 1975 *E* 1, *J* 1,2, 1976 *E*, 1978 *W* 1,2
FitzSimons, P (NSW) 1989 *F* 1,2, 1990 *F* 1,2,3, *US*, *NZ* 1
Flanagan, P (Q) 1907 *NZ* 1,2
Flett, J A (NSW) 1990 *US*, *NZ* 2,3, 1991 [*WS*]
Flynn, J P (Q) 1914 *NZ* 1,2
Fogarty, J R (Q) 1949 *M* 2,3
Forbes, C F (Q) 1953 *SA* 2,3,4, 1954 *Fj* 1, 1956 *SA* 1,2
Ford, B (Q) 1957 *NZ* 2
Ford, E E (NSW) 1927 *I*, *W*, *S*, 1928 *E*, *F*, 1929 *NZ* 1,3
Ford, J A (NSW) 1925 *NZ*, 1927 *I*, *W*, *S*, 1928 *E*, 1929 *NZ* 1,2,3, 1930 *BI*
Forman, T R (NSW) 1968 *I*, *S*, 1969 *W*, *SA* 1,2,3,4,
Fox, C L (NSW) 1921 *NZ*, 1928 *F*
Fox, O G (NSW) 1958 *F*
Francis, E (Q) 1914 *NZ* 1,2
Frawley, D (Q, NSW) 1986 *Arg* 2 (R), 1987 *Arg* 1,2, 1988 *E* 1,2, *NZ* 1,2,3, *S*, *It*
Freedman, J E (NSW) 1962 *NZ* 3,4,5, 1963 *SA* 1
Freeman, E (NSW) 1946 *NZ* 1 (R), *M*
Freney, M E (Q) 1972 *NZ* 1,2,3, 1973 *Tg* 1, *W*, *E* (R)
Furness, D C (NSW) 1946 *M*
Futter, F C (NSW) 1904 *BI* 3

Gardner, J M (Q) 1987 *Arg* 2, 1988 *E* 1, *NZ* 1, *E*
Gardner, W C (NSW) 1950 *BI* 1
Garner, R L (NSW) 1949 *NZ* 1,2
Gavin, K A (NSW) 1909 *E*
Gavin, T B (NSW) 1988 *NZ* 2,3, *S*, *It* (R), 1989 *NZ* (R), *F* 1,2, 1990 *F* 1,2,3, *US*, *NZ* 1,2,3, 1991 *W*, *E*, *NZ* 1, 1992 *S* 1,2, *SA*, *I*, *W*, 1993 *Tg*, *NZ*, *SA* 1,2,3, *C*, *F* 1,2, 1994 *I* 1,2, *It* 1,2, *WS*, *NZ*
Gelling, A M (NSW) 1972 *NZ* 1, *Fj*
George, H W (NSW) 1910 *NZ* 1,2,3, 1912 *US*, 1913 *NZ* 1,3, 1914 *NZ* 1,3
George, W G (NSW) 1923 *NZ* 1,2, 1928 *NZ* 1,2,3, *M*
Gibbons, E de C (NSW) 1936 *NZ* 1,2, *M*
Gibbs, P R (V) 1966 *S*
Gilbert, H (NSW) 1910 *NZ* 1,2,3
Girvan, B (ACT) 1988 *E*
Gordon, G C (NSW) 1929 *NZ* 1
Gordon, K M (NSW) 1950 *BI* 1,2
Gould, R G (Q) 1980 *NZ* 1,2,3, 1981 *I*, *W*, *S*, 1982 *S* 2, *NZ* 1,2,3, 1983 *US*, *Arg* 1, *F* 1,2, 1984 *NZ* 1,2,3, *E*, *I*, *W*, *S*, 1985 *NZ*, 1986 *It*, 1987 *SK*, [*E*]
Gourley, S R (NSW) 1988 *S*, *It*, 1989 *BI* 1,2,3
Graham, C S (Q) 1899 *BI* 2
Graham, R (NSW) 1973 *Tg* 1,2, *W*, *E*, 1974 *NZ* 2,3, 1975 *E* 2, *J* 1,2, *S*, *W*, 1976 *I*, *US*, *Fj* 1,2,3, *F* 1,2
Gralton, A S I (Q) 1899 *BI* 1,4, 1903 *NZ*
Grant, J C (NSW) 1988 *E* 1, *NZ* 2,3, *E*
Graves, R H (NSW) 1907 *NZ* 1 (R)
Greatorex, E N (NSW) 1923 *NZ* 3, 1928 *E*, *F*
Gregan, G (ACT) 1994 *It* 1,2, *WS*, *NZ*
Gregory, S C (Q) 1968 *NZ* 3, *F*, *I*, *S*, 1969 *SA* 1,3, 1971 *SA* 1,3, *F* 1,2, 1972 *F* 1,2, 1973 *Tg* 1,2, *W*, *E*
Grey, G O (NSW) 1972 *F* 2 (R), *NZ* 1,2,3, *Fj* (R)
Griffin, T S (NSW) 1907 *NZ* 1,3, 1908 *W*, 1910 *NZ* 1,2, 1912 *US*
Grigg, P C (Q) 1980 *NZ* 3, 1982 *S* 2, *NZ* 1,2,3, 1983 *Arg* 2, *NZ*, 1984 *Fj*, *W*, *S*, 1985 *C* 1,2, *NZ*, *Fj* 1,2, 1986 *Arg* 1,2, *NZ* 1,2, 1987 *SK*, [*E*, *J*, *I*, *F*, *W*]
Grimmond, D N (NSW) 1964 *NZ* 2

Gudsell, K E (NSW) 1951 *NZ* 1,2,3
Guerassimoff, J (Q) 1963 *SA* 2,3,4, 1964 *NZ* 1,2,3, 1965 *SA* 2, 1966 *BI* 1,2, 1967 *E*, *I*, *F*
Gunther, W J (NSW) 1957 *NZ* 2

Hall, D (Q) 1980 *Fj*, *NZ* 1,2,3, 1981 *F* 1,2, 1982 *S* 1,2, *NZ* 1,2, 1983 *US*, *Arg* 1,2, *NZ*, *It*
Hamalainen, H A (Q) 1929 *NZ* 1,2,3
Hamilton, B G (NSW) 1946 *M*
Hammand, C A (NSW) 1908 *W*, 1909 *E*
Hammon, J D C (V) 1937 *SA* 2
Handy, C B (Q) 1978 *NZ* 3, 1979 *NZ*, *Arg* 1,2, 1980 *NZ* 1,2
Hanley, R G (Q) 1983 *US* (R), *It* (R)
Hardcastle, P A (NSW) 1946 *NZ* 1, *M*, *NZ* 2, 1947 *NZ* 1, 1949 *M* 3
Hardcastle, W R (NSW) 1899 *BI* 4, 1903 *NZ*
Harding, M A (NSW) 1983 *It*
Hartill, M N (NSW) 1986 *NZ* 1,2,3, 1987 *SK*, [*J*], *Arg* 1, 1988 *NZ* 1,2, *E*, *It*, 1989 *BI* 1 (R), 2,3, *F* 1,2
Harvey, P B (Q) 1949 *M* 1,2
Harvey, R M (NSW) 1958 *F*, *M* 3
Hatherell, W I (Q) 1952 *Fj* 1,2
Hauser, R G (Q) 1975 *J* 1 (R), 2, *W* (R), 1976 *E*, *I*, *US*, *Fj* 1,2,3, *F* 1,2, 1978 *W* 1,2, 1979 *I* 1,2
Hawker, M J (NSW) 1980 *Fj*, *NZ* 1,2,3, 1981 *F* 1,2, *I*, *W*, 1982 *E*, *S* 1,2, *NZ* 1,2,3, 1983 *US*, *Arg* 1,2, *NZ*, *It*, *F* 1,2, 1984 *NZ* 1,2,3, 1987 *NZ*
Hawthorne, P F (NSW) 1962 *NZ* 3,4,5, 1963 *E*, *SA* 1,2,3,4, 1964 *NZ* 1,2,3, 1965 *SA* 1,2, 1966 *BI* 1,2, *W*, 1967 *E*, *I* 1, *F*, *I* 2, *NZ*
Hayes, E S (Q) 1934 *NZ* 1,2, 1938 *NZ* 1,2,3
Heinrich, E L (NSW) 1961 *Fj* 1,2,3, *SA* 2, *F*, 1962 *NZ* 1,2,3, 1963 *E*, *SA* 1
Heinrich, V W (NSW) 1954 *Fj* 1,2
Heming, R J (NSW) 1961 *Fj* 2,3, *SA* 1,2, *F*, 1962 *NZ* 2,3,4,5, 1963 *SA* 2,3,4, 1964 *NZ* 1,2,3, 1965 *SA* 1,2, 1966 *BI* 1,2, *W*, 1967 *F*
Hemingway, W H (NSW) 1928 *NZ* 2,3, 1931 *M*, *NZ*, 1932 *NZ* 3
Henry, A R (Q) 1899 *BI* 2
Herbert, A G (Q) 1987 *SK* (R), [*F* (R)], 1990 *F* 1(R), *US*, *NZ* 2,3, 1991 [*WS*], 1992 *NZ* 3(R), 1993 *NZ*(R), *SA* 2(R)
Herbert, D (Q) 1994 *I* 2, *It* 1,2, *WS*(R)
Herd, H V (NSW) 1931 *M*
Hickey, J (NSW) 1908 *W*, 1909 *E*
Hillhouse, D W (Q) 1975 *S*, 1976 *E*, *Fj* 1,2,3, *F* 1,2, 1978 *W* 1,2, 1983 *US*, *Arg* 1,2, *NZ*, *It*, *F* 1,2
Hills, E F (V) 1950 *BI* 1,2
Hindmarsh, J A (Q) 1904 *BI* 1
Hindmarsh, J C (NSW) 1975 *J* 2, *S*, *W*, 1976 *US*, *Fj* 1,2,3, *F* 1,2
Hipwell, J N B (NSW) 1968 *NZ* 1(R),2, *F*, *I*, *S*, 1969 *W*, *SA* 1,2,3,4, 1970 *S*, 1971 *SA* 1,2, *F* 1,2, 1972 *F* 1,2, 1973 *Tg* 1, *W*, *E*, 1974 *NZ* 1,2,3, 1975 *E* 1,2, *J* 1, *S*, *W*, 1978 *NZ* 1,2,3, 1981 *F* 1,2, *I*, *W*, 1982 *E*
Hirschberg, W A (NSW) 1905 *NZ*
Hodgins, C H (NSW) 1910 *NZ* 1,2,3
Hodgson, A J (NSW) 1933 *SA* 2,3,4, 1934 *NZ* 1, 1936 *NZ* 1,2, *M*, 1937 *SA* 2, 1938 *NZ* 1,2,3
Holt, N C (Q) 1984 *Fj*
Honan, B D (Q) 1968 *NZ* 1 (R), 2, *F*, *I*, *S*, 1969 *SA* 1,2,3,4
Honan, R E (Q) 1964 *NZ* 1,2
Horan, T J (Q) 1989 *NZ*, *F* 1,2, 1990 *F* 1, *NZ* 1,2,3, 1991 *W*, *E*, *NZ* 1,2, [*Arg*, *WS*, *W*, *I*, *NZ*, *E*], 1992 *S* 1,2, *NZ* 1,2,3, *SA*, *I*, *W*, 1993 *Tg*, *NZ*, *SA* 1,2,3, *C*, *F* 1,2
Horodam, D J (Q) 1913 *NZ* 2
Horsley, G R (Q) 1954 *Fj* 2
Horton, P A (NSW) 1974 *NZ* 1,2,3, 1975 *E* 1,2, *J* 1,2, *S*, *W*, 1976 *E*, *F* 1,2, 1978 *W* 1,2, *NZ* 1,2,3, 1979 *NZ*, *Arg* 1
How, R A (NSW) 1967 *I* 2
Howard, J (Q) 1938 *NZ* 1,2
Howard, J L (NSW) 1970 *S*, 1971 *SA* 1, 1972 *F* 1 (R), *NZ* 2, 1973 *Tg* 1,2, *W*
Howard, P W (Q) 1993 *NZ*, 1994 *WS*, *NZ*
Howell, M L (NSW) 1946 *NZ* 1 (R), 1947 *NZ* 1, *S*, *I*, *W*
Hughes, B D (NSW) 1913 *NZ* 2,3
Hughes, J C (NSW) 1907 *NZ* 1,3
Hughes, N McL (NSW) 1953 *SA* 1,2,3,4, 1955 *NZ*

1,2,3, 1956 *SA* 1,2, 1958 *W, I, E, S, F*
Humphreys, O W (NSW) 1921 *NZ*
Hutchinson, E E (NSW) 1937 *SA* 1,2
Hutchinson, F E (NSW) 1936 *NZ* 1,2, 1938 *NZ* 1,3

Ide, W P J (Q) 1938 *NZ* 2,3
Ives, W N (NSW) 1929 *NZ* 3

James, P M (Q) 1958 *M* 2,3
James, S L (NSW) 1987 *SK* (R), [*E* (R)], *NZ, Arg* 1,2, 1988 *NZ* 2 (R)
Jessep, E M (V) 1934 *NZ* 1,2
Johnson, A P (NSW) 1946 *NZ* 1, *M*
Johnson, B B (NSW) 1952 *Fj* 1,2, *NZ* 1,2, 1953 *SA* 2,3,4, 1955 *NZ* 1,2
Johnson, P G (NSW) 1959 *BI* 1,2, 1961 *Fj* 1,2,3, *SA* 1,2, *F*, 1962 *NZ* 1,2,3,4,5, 1963 *E, SA* 1,2,3,4, 1964 *NZ* 1,2,3, 1965 *SA* 1,2, 1966 *BI* 1,2, *W, S*, 1967 *E, I* 1, *F, I* 2, *NZ*, 1968 *NZ* 1,2, *F, I, S*, 1970 *S*, 1971 *SA* 1,2, *F* 1,2
Johnstone, B (Q) 1993 *Tg*(R)
Jones, G G (Q) 1952 *Fj* 1,2, 1953 *SA* 1,2,3,4, 1954 *Fj* 1,2, 1955 *NZ* 1,2,3, 1956 *SA* 1
Jones, H (NSW) 1913 *NZ* 1,2,3
Jones, P A (NSW) 1963 *E, SA* 1
Jorgensen, P (NSW) 1992 *S* 1(R), 2(R)
Joyce, J E (NSW) 1903 *NZ*
Judd, H A (NSW) 1903 *NZ*, 1904 *BI* 1,2,3, 1905 *NZ*
Judd, P B (NSW) 1925 *NZ*, 1927 *I, W, S*, 1928 *E*, 1931 *M, NZ*
Junee, D K (NSW) 1989 *F* 1(R), 2(R), 1994 *WS*(R), *NZ*(R)

Kahl, P R (Q) 1992 *W*
Kassulke, N (Q) 1985 *C* 1,2
Kay, A R (V) 1958 *NZ* 2, 1959 *BI* 2
Kay, P (NSW) 1988 *E* 2
Kearney, K H (NSW) 1947 *NZ* 1,2, *S, I, W*, 1948 *E, F*
Kearns, P N (NSW) 1989 *NZ, F* 1,2, 1990 *F* 1,2,3, *US, NZ* 1,2,3, 1991 *W, E, NZ* 1,2, [*Arg, WS, W, I, NZ, E*], 1992 *S* 1,2, *NZ* 1,2,3, *SA, I, W*, 1993 *Tg, NZ, SA* 1,2,3, *C, F* 1,2, 1994 *I* 1,2, *It* 1,2, *WS, NZ*
Kelaher, J D (NSW) 1933 *SA* 1,2,3,4,5, 1934 *NZ* 1,2, 1936 *NZ* 1,2, *M*, 1937 *SA* 1,2, 1938 *NZ* 3
Kelaher, T P (NSW) 1992 *NZ* 1, *I*(R), 1993 *NZ*
Kelleher, R J (Q) 1969 *SA* 2,3
Keller, D H (NSW) 1947 *NZ* 1, *S, I, W*, 1948 *E, F*
Kelly, A J (NSW) 1899 *BI* 1
Kelly, R L F (NSW) 1936 *NZ* 1,2, *M*, 1937 *SA* 1,2, 1938 *NZ* 1,2
Kent, A (Q) 1912 *US*
Kerr, F R (V) 1938 *NZ* 1
King, S C (NSW) 1927 *W, S*, 1928 *E, F*, 1929 *NZ* 1,2,3, 1930 *BI*, 1932 *NZ* 1,2
Knight, M (NSW) 1978 *W* 1,2, *NZ* 1
Knight, S O (NSW) 1969 *SA* 2,4, 1970 *S*, 1971 *SA* 1,2,3
Knox, D J (NSW) 1985 *Fj* 1,2, 1990 *US* (R), 1994 *WS, NZ*
Kraefft, D F (NSW) 1947 *NZ* 2, *S, I, W*, 1948 *E, F*
Kreutzer, S D (Q) 1914 *NZ* 2

Lamb, J S (NSW) 1928 *NZ* 1,2, *M*
Lambie, J K (NSW) 1974 *NZ* 1,2,3, 1975 *W*
Lane, T A (Q) 1985 *C* 1,2, *NZ*
Lang, C W P (V) 1938 *NZ* 2,3
Larkin, E R (NSW) 1903 *NZ*
Larkin, K K (Q) 1958 *M* 2,3
Latimer, N B (NSW) 1957 *NZ* 2
Lawton, R (Q) 1988 *E* 1, *NZ* 2 (R), 3, *S*
Lawton, T (NSW, Q) 1925 *NZ*, 1927 *I, W, S*, 1928 *E, F*, 1929 *NZ* 1,2,3, 1930 *BI*, 1932 *NZ* 1,2
Lawton, T A (Q) 1983 *F* 1 (R), 2, 1984 *Fj, NZ* 1,2,3, *E, I, W, S*, 1985 *C* 1,2, *NZ, Fj* 1, 1986 *It, F, Arg* 1,2, *NZ* 1,2,3, 1987 *SK*, [*E, US, I, F, W*], *NZ, Arg* 1,2, 1988 *E* 1,2, *NZ* 1,2,3, *E, S, It*, 1989 *BI* 1,2,3
Laycock, W M B (NSW) 1925 *NZ*
Leeds, A J (NSW) 1986 *NZ* 3, 1987 [*US, W*], *NZ, Arg* 1,2, 1988 *E* 1,2, *NZ* 1,2,3, *E, S, It*
Lenehan, J K (NSW) 1958 *W, E, S, F, M* 1,2,3, 1959 *BI* 1,2, 1961 *SA* 1,2, *F*, 1962 *NZ* 2,3,4,5, 1965 *SA* 1,2, 1966 *W, S*, 1967 *E, I* 1, *F, I* 2
L'Estrange, R D (Q) 1971 *F* 1,2, 1972 *NZ* 1,2,3, 1973 *Tg* 1,2, *W, E*, 1974 *NZ* 1,2,3, 1975 *S, W*, 1976 *I, US*
Lewis, L S (Q) 1934 *NZ* 1,2, 1936 *NZ* 2, 1938 *NZ* 1
Lidbury, S (NSW) 1987 *Arg* 1, 1988 *E* 2
Lillicrap, C P (Q) 1985 *Fj* 2, 1987 [*US, I, F, W*], 1989 *BI* 1, 1991 [*WS*]
Lindsay, R T G (Q) 1932 *NZ* 3
Lisle, R J (NSW) 1961 *Fj* 1,2,3, *SA* 1
Little, J S (Q) 1989 *F* 1,2, 1990 *F* 1,2,3, *US*, 1991 *W, E, NZ* 1,2, [*Arg, W, I, NZ, E*], 1992 *NZ* 1,2,3, *SA, I, W*, 1993 *Tg, NZ, SA* 1,2,3, *C, F* 1,2, 1994 *WS, NZ*
Livermore, A E (Q) 1946 *NZ* 1, *M*
Loane, M E (Q) 1973 *Tg* 1,2, 1974 *NZ* 1, 1975 *E* 1,2, *J* 1, 1976 *E, I, Fj* 1,2,3, *F* 1,2, 1978 *W* 1,2, 1979 *I* 1,2, *NZ, Arg* 1,2, 1981 *F* 1,2, *I, W, S*, 1982 *E, S* 1,2
Logan, D L (NSW) 1958 *M* 1
Loudon, D B (NSW) 1921 *NZ*
Loudon, R B (NSW) 1923 *NZ* 1 (R), 2,3, 1928 *NZ* 1,2,3, *M*, 1929 *NZ* 2, 1933 *SA* 2,3,4,5, 1934 *NZ* 2
Love, E W (NSW) 1932 *NZ* 1,2,3
Lowth, D R (NSW) 1958 *NZ* 1
Lucas, B C (Q) 1905 *NZ*
Lucas, P W (NSW) 1982 *NZ* 1,2,3
Lutge, D (NSW) 1903 *NZ*, 1904 *BI* 1,2,3
Lynagh, M P (Q) 1984 *Fj, E, I, W, S*, 1985 *C* 1,2, *NZ*, 1986 *It, F, Arg* 1,2, *NZ* 1,2,3, 1987 [*E, US, J, I, F, W*], *Arg* 1,2, 1988 *E* 1,2, *NZ* 1,3 (R), *E, S, It*, 1989 *BI* 1,2,3, *NZ, F* 1,2, 1990 *F* 1,2,3, *US, NZ* 1,2,3, 1991 *W, E, NZ* 1,2, [*Arg, WS, W, I, NZ, E*], 1992 *S* 1,2, *NZ* 1,2,3, *SA, I*, 1993 *Tg, C, F* 1,2, 1994 *I* 1,2, *It* 1

McArthur, M (NSW) 1909 *E*
McBain, M I (Q) 1983 *It, F* 1, 1985 *Fj* 2, 1986 *It* (R), 1987 [*J*], 1988 *E* 2 (R), 1989 *BI* 1 (R)
MacBride, J W T (NSW) 1946 *NZ* 1, *M, NZ* 2, 1947 *NZ* 1,2, *S, I, W*, 1948 *E, F*
McCabe, A J M (NSW) 1909 *E*
McCall, R J (Q) 1989 *F* 1,2, 1990 *F* 1,2,3, *US, NZ* 1,2,3, 1991 *W, E, NZ* 1,2, [*Arg, W, I, NZ, E*], 1992 *S* 1,2, *NZ* 1,2,3, *SA, I, W*, 1993 *Tg, NZ, SA* 1,2,3, *C, F* 1,2, 1994 *It* 2
McCarthy, F J C (Q) 1950 *BI* 1
McCowan, R H (Q) 1899 *BI* 1,2,4
McCue, P A (NSW) 1907 *NZ* 1,3, 1908 *W*, 1909 *E*
McDermott, L C (Q) 1962 *NZ* 1,2
McDonald, B S (NSW) 1969 *SA* 4, 1970 *S*
McDonald, J C (Q) 1938 *NZ* 2,3
Macdougall, D G (NSW) 1961 *Fj* 1, *SA* 1
Macdougall, S G (NSW, ACT) 1971 *SA* 3, 1973 *E*, 1974 *NZ* 1,2,3, 1975 *E* 1,2, 1976 *E*
McGhie, G H (Q) 1929 *NZ* 2,3, 1930 *BI*
McGill, A N (NSW) 1968 *NZ* 1,2, *F*, 1969 *W, SA* 1,2,3,4, 1970 *S*, 1971 *SA* 1,2,3, *F* 1,2, 1972 *F* 1,2, *NZ* 1,2,3, 1973 *Tg* 1,2
McIntyre, A J (Q) 1982 *NZ* 1,2,3, 1983 *F* 1,2, 1984 *Fj, NZ* 1,2,3, *E, I, W, S*, 1985 *C* 1,2, *NZ, Fj* 1,2, 1986 *It, F, Arg* 1,2, 1987 [*E, US, I, F, W*], *NZ, Arg* 2, 1988 *E* 1,2, *NZ* 1,2,3, *E, S, It*, 1989 *NZ*
McKenzie, E J A (NSW) 1990 *F* 1,2,3, *US, NZ* 1,2,3, 1991 *W, E, NZ* 1,2, [*Arg, W, I, NZ, E*], 1992 *S* 1,2, *NZ* 1,2,3, *SA, I, W*, 1993 *Tg, NZ, SA* 1,2,3, *C, F* 1,2, 1994 *I* 1,2, *It* 1,2, *WS, NZ*
McKid, W A (NSW) 1976 *E, Fj* 1, 1978 *NZ* 2,3, 1979 *I* 1,2
McKinnon, A (Q) 1904 *BI* 2
McKivat, C H (NSW) 1907 *NZ* 1,3, 1908 *W*, 1909 *E*
McLaughlin, R E M (NSW) 1936 *NZ* 1,2
McLean, A D (Q) 1933 *SA* 1,2,3,4,5, 1934 *NZ* 1,2, 1936 *NZ* 1,2, *M*
McLean, J D (Q) 1904 *BI* 2,3, 1905 *NZ*
McLean, J J (Q) 1971 *SA* 2,3, *F* 1,2, 1972 *F* 1,2, *NZ* 1,2,3, *Fj*, 1973 *W, E*, 1974 *NZ* 1
McLean, P E (Q) 1974 *NZ* 1,2,3, 1975 *J* 1,2, *S, W*, 1976 *E, I, Fj* 1,2,3, *F* 1,2, 1978 *W* 1,2, *NZ* 2, 1979 *I* 1,2, *NZ, Arg* 1,2, 1980 *Fj*, 1981 *F* 1,2, *I, W, S*, 1982 *E, S* 2
McLean, P W (Q) 1978 *NZ* 1,2,3, 1979 *I* 1,2, *NZ, Arg* 1,2, 1980 *Fj* (R), *NZ* 3, 1981 *I, W, S*, 1982 *E, S* 1,2
McLean, R A (NSW) 1971 *SA* 1,2,3, *F* 1,2
McLean, W M (Q) 1946 *NZ* 1, *M, NZ* 2, 1947 *NZ* 1,2
McMahon, M J (Q) 1913 *NZ* 1
McMaster, R E (Q) 1946 *NZ* 1, *M, NZ* 2, 1947 *NZ* 1,2, *I, W*
MacMillan, D I (Q) 1950 *BI* 1,2
McMullen, K V (NSW) 1962 *NZ* 3,5, 1963 *E, SA* 1
McShane, J M S (NSW) 1937 *SA* 1,2
Mackney, W A R (NSW) 1933 *SA* 1,5, 1934 *NZ* 1,2

Magrath, E (NSW) 1961 *Fj* 1, *SA* 2, *F*
Maguire, D J (Q) 1989 *BI* 1,2,3
Malcolm, S J (NSW) 1927 *S*, 1928 *E, F, NZ* 1,2, *M*, 1929 *NZ* 1,2,3, 1930 *BI*, 1931 *NZ*, 1932 *NZ* 1,2,3, 1933 *SA* 4,5, 1934 *NZ* 1,2
Malone, J H (NSW) 1936 *NZ* 1,2, *M*, 1937 *SA* 2
Malouf, B P (NSW) 1982 *NZ* 1
Mandible, E F (NSW) 1907 *NZ* 2,3, 1908 *W*
Manning, J (NSW) 1904 *BI* 2
Manning, R C S (Q) 1967 *NZ*
Mansfield, B W (NSW) 1975 *J* 2
Marks, H (NSW) 1899 *BI* 1,2
Marks, R J P (Q) 1962 *NZ* 4,5, 1963 *E, SA* 2,3,4, 1964 *NZ* 1,2,3, 1965 *SA* 1,2, 1966 *W, S*, 1967 *E, I* 1, *F, I* 2
Marrott, W J (NSW) 1923 *NZ* 1,2
Marshall, J S (NSW) 1949 *M* 1
Martin, G J (Q) 1989 *BI* 1,2,3, *NZ, F* 1,2, 1990 *F* 1,3 (R), *NZ* 1
Martin, M C (NSW) 1980 *Fj, NZ* 1,2, 1981 *F* 1,2, *W* (R)
Massey-Westropp, M (NSW) 1914 *NZ* 3
Mathers, M J (NSW) 1980 *Fj, NZ* 2 (R)
Maund, J W (NSW) 1903 *NZ*
Meadows, J E C (V, Q) 1974 *NZ* 1, 1975 *S, W*, 1976 *I, US, Fj* 1,3, *F* 1,2, 1978 *NZ* 1,2,3, 1979 *I* 1,2, 1981 *I, S*, 1982 *E, NZ* 2,3, 1983 *US, Arg* 2, *NZ*
Meadows, R W (NSW) 1958 *M* 1,2,3, *NZ* 1,2,3
Meagher, F W (NSW) 1923 *NZ* 3, 1925 *NZ*, 1927 *I, W*
Meibusch, J H (Q) 1904 *BI* 3
Meibusch, L S (Q) 1912 *US*
Melrose, T C (NSW) 1978 *NZ* 3, 1979 *I* 1,2, *NZ, Arg* 1,2
Messenger, H H (NSW) 1907 *NZ* 2,3
Middleton, S A (NSW) 1909 *E*, 1910 *NZ* 1,2,3
Miller, A R (NSW) 1952 *Fj* 1,2, *NZ* 1,2, 1953 *SA* 1,2,3,4, 1954 *Fj* 1,2, 1955 *NZ* 1,2,3, 1956 *SA* 1,2, 1957 *NZ* 1,2, 1958 *W, E, S, F, M* 1,2,3, 1959 *BI* 1,2, 1961 *Fj* 1,2,3, *SA* 2, *F*, 1962 *NZ* 1,2, 1966 *BI* 1,2, *W, S*, 1967 *I* 1, *F, I* 2, *NZ*
Miller, J M (NSW) 1962 *NZ* 1, 1963 *E, SA* 1, 1966 *W, S*, 1967 *E*
Miller, J S (Q) 1986 *NZ* 2,3, 1987 *SK*, [*US, I, F*], *NZ, Arg* 1,2, 1988 *E* 1,2, *NZ* 2,3, *E, S, It*, 1989 *BI* 1,2,3, *NZ*, 1990 *F* 1,3, 1991 *W*, [*WS, W, I*]
Miller, S W J (NSW) 1899 *BI* 3
Mingey, N (NSW) 1923 *NZ* 1,2
Monaghan, L E (NSW) 1973 *E*, 1974 *NZ* 1,2,3, 1975 *E* 1,2, *S, W*, 1976 *E, I, US, F* 1, 1978 *W* 1,2, *NZ* 1, 1979 *I* 1,2
Monti, C I A (Q) 1938 *NZ* 2
Moon, B J (Q) 1978 *NZ* 2,3, 1979 *I* 1,2, *NZ, Arg* 1,2, 1980 *Fj, NZ* 1,2,3, 1981 *F* 1,2, *I, W, S*, 1982 *E, S* 1,2, 1983 *US, Arg* 1,2, *NZ, It, F* 1,2, 1984 *Fj, NZ* 1,2,3, *E*, 1986 *It, F, Arg* 1,2
Mooney, T P (Q) 1954 *Fj* 1,2
Moran, H M (NSW) 1908 *W*
Morgan, G (Q) 1992 *NZ* 1(R), 3(R), *W*, 1993 *Tg, NZ, SA* 1,2,3, *C, F* 1,2, 1994 *I* 1,2, *It* 1, *WS, NZ*
Morrissey, C V (NSW) 1925 *NZ*
Morrissey, W (Q) 1914 *NZ* 2
Morton, A R (NSW) 1957 *NZ* 1,2, 1958 *F, M* 1,2,3, *NZ* 1,2,3, 1959 *BI* 1,2
Mossop, R P (NSW) 1949 *NZ* 1,2, 1950 *BI* 1,2, 1951 *NZ* 1
Moutray, I E (NSW) 1963 *SA* 2
Munsie, A (NSW) 1928 *NZ* 2
Murdoch, A (NSW) 1993 *F* 1
Murphy, P J (Q) 1910 *NZ* 1,2,3, 1913 *NZ* 1,2,3, 1914 *NZ* 1,2,3
Murphy, W (Q) 1912 *US*

Nasser, B P (Q) 1989 *F* 1,2, 1990 *F* 1,2,3, *US, NZ* 2, 1991 [*WS*]
Nicholson, F C (Q) 1904 *BI* 3
Nicholson, F V (Q) 1903 *NZ*, 1904 *BI* 1
Niuqila, A S (NSW) 1988 *S, It*, 1989 *BI* 1
Nothling, O E (NSW) 1921 *NZ*, 1923 *NZ* 1,2,3
Nucifora, D V (Queensland) 1991 [*Arg*(R)], 1993 *C*(R)

O'Brien, F W H (NSW) 1937 *SA* 2, 1938 *NZ* 3
O'Connor, J A (NSW) 1928 *NZ* 1,2,3, *M*
O'Connor, M (ACT) 1994 *I* 1
O'Connor, M D (ACT, Q) 1979 *Arg* 1,2, 1980 *Fj, NZ* 1,2,3, 1981 *F* 1,2, *I*, 1982 *E, S* 1,2
O'Donnell, C (NSW) 1913 *NZ* 1,2
O'Donnell, I C (NSW) 1899 *BI* 3,4
O'Donnell, J B (NSW) 1928 *NZ* 1,3, *M*
O'Donnell, J M (NSW) 1899 *BI* 4
O'Gorman, J F (NSW) 1961 *Fj* 1, *SA* 1,2, *F*, 1962 *NZ* 2, 1963 *E, SA* 1,2,3,4, 1965 *SA* 1,2, 1966 *W, S*, 1967 *E, I* 1, *F, I* 2
O'Neill, D J (Q) 1964 *NZ* 1,2
O'Neill, J M (Q) 1952 *NZ* 1,2, 1956 *SA* 1,2
Ofahengaue, V (NSW) 1990 *NZ* 1,2,3, 1991 *W, E, NZ* 1,2, [*Arg, W, I, NZ, E*], 1992 *S* 1,2, *SA, I, W*, 1994 *WS, NZ*
Osborne, D H (V) 1975 *E* 1,2, *J* 1
Outterside, R (NSW) 1959 *BI* 1,2
Oxenham, A McE (Q) 1904 *BI* 2, 1907 *NZ* 2
Oxlade, A M (Q) 1904 *BI* 2,3, 1905 *NZ*, 1907 *NZ* 2
Oxlade, B D (Q) 1938 *NZ* 1,2,3

Palfreyman, J R L (NSW) 1929 *NZ* 1, 1930 *BI*, 1931 *NZ*, 1932 *NZ* 3
Papworth, B (NSW) 1985 *Fj* 1,2, 1986 *It, Arg* 1,2, *NZ* 1,2,3, 1987 [*E, US, J* (R), *I, F*], *NZ, Arg* 1,2
Parker, A J (Q) 1983 *Arg* 1 (R), 2, *NZ*
Parkinson, C E (Q) 1907 *NZ* 2
Pashley, J J (NSW) 1954 *Fj* 1,2, 1958 *M* 1,2,3
Pauling, T P (NSW) 1936 *NZ* 1, 1937 *SA* 1
Pearse, G K (NSW) 1975 *W* (R), 1976 *I, US, Fj* 1,2,3, 1978 *NZ* 1,2,3
Penman, A P (NSW) 1905 *NZ*
Perrin, P D (Q) 1962 *NZ* 1
Perrin, T D (NSW) 1931 *M, NZ*
Phelps, R (NSW) 1955 *NZ* 2,3, 1956 *SA* 1,2, 1957 *NZ* 1,2, 1958 *W, I, E, S, F, M* 1, *NZ* 1,2,3, 1961 *Fj* 1,2,3, *SA* 1,2, *F*, 1962 *NZ* 1,2
Phipps, J A (NSW) 1953 *SA* 1,2,3,4, 1954 *Fj* 1,2, 1955 *NZ* 1,2,3, 1956 *SA* 1,2
Phipps, W J (NSW) 1928 *NZ* 2
Pilecki, S J (Q) 1978 *W* 1,2, *NZ* 1,2, 1979 *I* 1,2, *NZ, Arg* 1,2, 1980 *Fj, NZ* 1,2, 1982 *S* 1,2, 1983 *US, Arg* 1,2, *NZ*
Pini, M (Q) 1994 *I* 1, *It* 2, *WS, NZ*
Piper, B J C (NSW) 1946 *NZ* 1, *M, NZ* 2, 1947 *NZ* 1, *S, I, W*, 1948 *E, F*, 1949 *M* 1,2,3
Poidevin, S P (NSW) 1980 *Fj, NZ* 1,2,3, 1981 *F* 1,2, *I, W, S*, 1982 *E, NZ* 1,2,3, 1983 *US, Arg* 1,2, *NZ, It, F* 1,2, 1984 *Fj, NZ* 1,2,3, *E, I, W, S*, 1985 *C* 1,2, *NZ, Fj* 1,2, 1986 *It, F, Arg* 1,2, *NZ* 1,2,3, 1987 *SK*, [*E, J, I, F, W*], *Arg* 1, 1988 *NZ* 1,2,3, 1989 *NZ*, 1991 *E, NZ* 1,2, [*Arg, W, I, NZ, E*]
Pope, A M (Q) 1968 *NZ* 2 (R)
Potter, R T (Q) 1961 *Fj* 2
Potts, J M (NSW) 1957 *NZ* 1,2, 1958 *W, I*, 1959 *BI* 1
Prentice, C W (NSW) 1914 *NZ* 3
Prentice, W S (NSW) 1908 *W*, 1909 *E*, 1910 *NZ* 1,2,3, 1912 *US*
Price, R A (NSW) 1974 *NZ* 1,2,3, 1975 *E* 1,2, *J* 1,2, 1976 *US*
Primmer, C J (Q) 1951 *NZ* 1,3
Proctor, I J (NSW) 1967 *NZ*
Prosser, R B (NSW) 1967 *E, I* 1,2, *NZ*, 1968 *NZ* 1,2, *F, I, S*, 1969 *W, SA* 1,2,3,4, 1971 *SA* 1,2,3, *F* 1,2, 1972 *F* 1,2, *NZ* 1,2,3, *Fj*
Pugh, G H (NSW) 1912 *US*
Purcell, M P (Q) 1966 *W, S*, 1967 *I* 2
Purkis, E M (NSW) 1958 *S, M* 1

Ramalli, C (NSW) 1938 *NZ* 2,3
Ramsay, K M (NSW) 1936 *M*, 1937 *SA* 1, 1938 *NZ* 1,3
Rankin, R (NSW) 1936 *NZ* 1,2, *M*, 1937 *SA* 1,2, 1938 *NZ* 1,2
Rathie, D S (Q) 1972 *F* 1,2
Raymond, R L (NSW) 1921 *NZ*
Redwood, C (Q) 1903 *NZ*, 1904 *BI* 1,2,3
Reid, E J (NSW) 1925 *NZ*
Reid, T W (NSW) 1961 *Fj* 1,2,3, *SA* 1, 1962 *NZ* 1
Reilly, N P (Q) 1968 *NZ* 1,2, *F, I, S*, 1969 *W, SA* 1,2,3,4
Reynolds, L J (NSW) 1910 *NZ* 2 (R), 3
Reynolds, R J (NSW) 1984 *Fj, NZ* 1,2,3, 1985 *Fj* 1,2, 1986 *Arg* 1,2, *NZ* 1, 1987 [*J*]
Richards, E W (Q) 1904 *BI* 1,3, 1905 *NZ*, 1907 *NZ* 1 (R), 2
Richards, G (NSW) 1978 *NZ* 2 (R), 3, 1981 *F* 1
Richards, T J (Q) 1908 *W*, 1909 *E*, 1912 *US*

Richards, V S (NSW) 1936 *NZ* 1,2 (R), *M*, 1937 *SA* 1, 1938 *NZ* 1
Richardson, G C (Q) 1971 *SA* 1,2,3, 1972 *NZ* 2,3, *Fj*, 1973 *Tg* 1,2, *W*
Rigney, W A (NSW) 1925 *NZ*
Riley, S A (NSW) 1903 *NZ*
Roberts, B T (NSW) 1956 *SA* 2
Roberts, H F (Q) 1961 *Fj* 1,3, *SA* 2, *F*
Robertson, I J (NSW) 1975 *J* 1,2
Roche, C (Q) 1982 *S* 1,2, *NZ* 1,2,3, 1983 *US*, *Arg* 1,2, *NZ*, *It*, *F* 1,2, 1984 *Fj*, *NZ* 1,2,3, *I*
Rodriguez, E E (NSW) 1984 *Fj*, *NZ* 1,2,3, *E*, *I*, *W*, *S*, 1985 *C* 1,2, *NZ*, *Fj* 1, 1986 *It*, *F*, *Arg* 1,2, *NZ* 1,2,3, 1987 *SK*, [*E*, *J*, *W* (R)], *NZ*, *Arg* 1,2
Roebuck, M C (NSW) 1991 *W*, *E*, *NZ* 1,2, [*Arg*, *WS*, *W*, *I*, *NZ*, *E*], 1992 *S* 1,2, *NZ* 2,3, *SA*, *I*, *W*, 1993 *Tg*, *SA* 1,2,3, *C*, *F* 2
Rose, H A (NSW) 1967 *I* 2, *NZ*, 1968 *NZ* 1,2, *F*, *I*, *S*, 1969 *W*, *SA* 1,2,3,4, 1970 *S*
Rosenblum, M E (NSW) 1928 *NZ* 1,2,3, *M*
Rosenblum, R G (NSW) 1969 *SA* 1,3, 1970 *S*
Rosewell, J S H (NSW) 1907 *NZ* 1,3
Ross, A W (NSW) 1927 *I*, *W*, *S*, 1928 *E*, *F*, 1929 *NZ* 1, 1930 *BI*, 1931 *M*, *NZ*, 1932 *NZ* 2,3, 1933 *SA* 5, 1934 *NZ* 1,2
Ross, W S (Q) 1979 *I* 1,2, *Arg* 2, 1980 *Fj*, *NZ* 1,2,3, 1982 *S* 1,2, 1983 *US*, *Arg* 1,2, *NZ*
Rothwell, P R (NSW) 1951 *NZ* 1,2,3, 1952 *Fj* 1
Row, F L (NSW) 1899 *BI* 1,3,4
Row, N E (NSW) 1907 *NZ* 1,3, 1909 *E*, 1910 *NZ* 1,2,3
Rowles, P G (NSW) 1972 *Fj*, 1973 *E*
Roxburgh, J R (NSW) 1968 *NZ* 1,2, *F*, 1969 *W*, *SA* 1,2,3,4, 1970 *S*
Ruebner, G (NSW) 1966 *BI* 1,2
Russell, C J (NSW) 1907 *NZ* 1,2,3, 1908 *W*, 1909 *E*
Ryan, J R (NSW) 1975 *J* 2, 1976 *I*, *US*, *Fj* 1,2,3
Ryan, K J (Q) 1958 *E*, *M* 1, *NZ* 1,2,3
Ryan, P F (NSW) 1963 *E*, *SA* 1, 1966 *BI* 1,2

Sampson, J H (NSW) 1899 *BI* 4
Sayle, J L (NSW) 1967 *NZ*
Schulte, B G (Q) 1946 *NZ* 1, *M*
Scott, P R I (NSW) 1962 *NZ* 1,2
Scott-Young, S J (Q) 1990 *F* 2,3 (R), *US*, *NZ* 3, 1992 *NZ* 1,2,3
Shambrook, G G (Q) 1976 *Fj* 2,3
Shaw, A A (Q) 1973 *W*, *E*, 1975 *E* 1,2, *J* 2, *S*, *W*, 1976 *E*, *I*, *US*, *Fj* 1,2,3, *F* 1,2, 1978 *W* 1,2, *NZ* 1,2,3, 1979 *I* 1,2, *NZ*, *Arg* 1,2, 1980 *Fj*, *NZ* 1,2,3, 1981 *F* 1,2, *I*, *W*, *S*, 1982 *S* 1,2
Shaw, C (NSW) 1925 *NZ* (R)
Shaw, G A (NSW) 1969 *W*, *SA* 1 (R), 1970 *S*, 1971 *SA* 1,2,3, *F* 1,2, 1973 *W*, *E*, 1974 *NZ* 1,2,3, 1975 *E* 1,2, *J* 1,2, *W*, 1976 *E*, *I*, *US*, *Fj* 1,2,3, *F* 1,2, 1979 *NZ*
Sheehan, W B J (NSW) 1923 *NZ* 1,2,3, 1927 *W*, *S*
Shehadie, N M (NSW) 1947 *NZ* 2, 1948 *E*, *F*, 1949 *M* 1,2,3, *NZ* 1,2, 1950 *BI* 1,2, 1951 *NZ* 1,2,3, 1952 *Fj* 1,2, *NZ* 2, 1953 *SA* 1,2,3,4, 1954 *Fj* 1,2, 1955 *NZ* 1,2,3, 1956 *SA* 1,2, 1957 *NZ* 2, 1958 *W*, *I*
Sheil, A G R (Q) 1956 *SA* 1
Shepherd, D J (V) 1964 *NZ* 3, 1965 *SA* 1,2, 1966 *BI* 1,2
Simpson, R J (NSW) 1913 *NZ* 2
Skinner, A J (NSW) 1969 *W*, *SA* 4, 1970 *S*
Slack, A G (Q) 1978 *W* 1,2, *NZ* 1,2, 1979 *NZ*, *Arg* 1,2, 1980 *Fj*, 1981 *I*, *W*, *S*, 1982 *E*, *S* 1, *NZ* 3, 1983 *US*, *Arg* 1,2, *NZ*, *It*, 1984 *Fj*, *NZ* 1,2,3, *E*, *I*, *W*, *S*, 1986 *It*, *F*, *NZ* 1,2,3, 1987 *SK*, [*E*, *US*, *J*, *I*, *F*, *W*]
Slater, S H (NSW) 1910 *NZ* 3
Slattery, P J (Q) 1990 *US* (R), 1991 *W*(R), *E*(R), [*WS*(R), *W*, *I*(R)], 1992 *I*, *W*, 1993 *Tg*, *C*, *F* 1,2, 1994 *I* 1,2, *It* 1(R)
Smairl, A M (NSW) 1928 *NZ* 1,2,3
Smith, B A (Q) 1987 *SK*, [*US*, *J*, *I* (R), *W*], *Arg* 1
Smith, D P (Q) 1993 *SA* 1,2,3, *C*, *F* 2, 1994 *I* 1,2, *It* 1,2, *WS*, *NZ*
Smith, F B (NSW) 1905 *NZ*, 1907 *NZ* 1,2,3
Smith, L M (NSW) 1905 *NZ*
Smith, N C (NSW) 1923 *NZ* 1
Smith, P V (NSW) 1967 *NZ*, 1968 *NZ* 1,2, *F*, *I*, *S*, 1969 *W*, *SA* 1
Smith, R A (NSW) 1971 *SA* 1,2, 1972 *F* 1,2, *NZ* 1,2 (R), 3, *Fj*, 1975 *E* 1,2, *J* 1,2, *S*, *W*, 1976 *E*, *I*, *US*, *Fj* 1,2,3, *F* 1,2
Smith, T S (NSW) 1921 *NZ*, 1925 *NZ*
Snell, H W (NSW) 1928 *NZ* 3
Solomon, H J (NSW) 1949 *M* 3, *NZ* 2, 1950 *BI* 1,2, 1951 *NZ* 1,2, 1952 *Fj* 1,2, *NZ* 1,2, 1953 *SA* 1,2,3, 1955 *NZ* 1
Spragg, S A (NSW) 1899 *BI* 1,2,3,4,
Stanley, R G (NSW) 1921 *NZ*, 1923 *NZ* 1,2,3
Stapleton, E T (NSW) 1951 *NZ* 1,2,3, 1952 *Fj* 1,2, *NZ* 1,2, 1953 *SA* 1,2,3,4, 1954 *Fj* 1, 1955 *NZ* 1,2,3, 1958 *NZ* 1
Steggall, J C (Q) 1931 *M*, *NZ*, 1932 *NZ* 1,2,3, 1933 *SA* 1,2,3,4,5
Stegman, T R (NSW) 1973 *Tg* 1,2
Stephens, O G (NSW) 1973 *Tg* 1,2, *W*, 1974 *NZ* 2,3
Stewart, A A (NSW) 1979 *NZ*, *Arg* 1,2
Stone, A H (NSW) 1937 *SA* 2, 1938 *NZ* 2,3
Stone, C G (NSW) 1938 *NZ* 1
Stone, J M (NSW) 1946 *M*, *NZ* 2
Storey, G P (NSW) 1927 *I*, *W*, *S*, 1928 *E*, *F*, 1929 *NZ* 3 (R), 1930 *BI*
Storey, K P (NSW) 1936 *NZ* 2
Storey, N J D (NSW) 1962 *NZ* 1
Strachan, D J (NSW) 1955 *NZ* 2,3
Street, N O (NSW) 1899 *BI* 2
Streeter, S F (NSW) 1978 *NZ* 1
Stuart, R (NSW) 1910 *NZ* 2,3
Stumbles, B D (NSW) 1972 *NZ* 1 (R), 2,3, *Fj*
Sturtridge, G S (V) 1929 *NZ* 2, 1932 *NZ* 1,2,3, 1933 *SA* 1,2,3,4,5
Sullivan, P D (NSW) 1971 *SA* 1,2,3, *F* 1,2, 1972 *F* 1,2, *NZ* 1,2, *Fj*, 1973 *Tg* 1,2, *W*
Summons, A J (NSW) 1958 *W*, *I*, *E*, *S*, *M* 2, *NZ* 1,2,3, 1959 *BI* 1,2
Suttor, D C (NSW) 1913 *NZ* 1,2,3
Swannell, B I (NSW) 1905 *NZ*
Sweeney, T L (Q) 1953 *SA* 1

Taafe, B S (NSW) 1969 *SA* 1, 1972 *F* 1,2
Tabua, I (Q) 1993 *SA* 2,3, *C*, *F* 1, 1994 *I* 1,2, *It* 1,2
Tancred, A J (NSW) 1927 *I*, *W*, *S*
Tancred, J L (NSW) 1928 *F*
Tanner, W H (Q) 1899 *BI* 1,2
Tasker, W G (NSW) 1913 *NZ* 1,2,3, 1914 *NZ* 1,2,3
Tate, M J (NSW) 1951 *NZ* 3, 1952 *Fj* 1,2, *NZ* 1,2, 1953 *SA* 1, 1954 *Fj* 1,2
Taylor, D A (Q) 1968 *NZ* 1,2, *F*, *I*, *S*
Taylor, H C (NSW) 1923 *NZ* 1,2,3
Taylor, J I (NSW) 1971 *SA* 1, 1972 *F* 1,2, *Fj*
Teitzel, R G (Q) 1966 *W*, *S*, 1967 *E*, *I* 1, *F*, *I* 2, *NZ*
Thompson, C E (NSW) 1923 *NZ* 1
Thompson, E G (Q) 1929 *NZ* 1,2,3, 1930 *BI*
Thompson, F (NSW) 1913 *NZ* 1,2,3, 1914 *NZ* 1,2,3
Thompson, J (Q) 1914 *NZ* 1
Thompson, P D (Q) 1950 *BI* 1
Thompson, R J (WA) 1971 *SA* 3, *F* 2 (R), 1972 *Fj*
Thorn, A M (NSW) 1921 *NZ*
Thorn, E J (NSW) 1923 *NZ* 1,2,3
Thornett, J E (NSW) 1955 *NZ* 1,2,3, 1956 *SA* 1,2, 1958 *W*, *I*, *S*, *F*, *M* 2,3, *NZ* 2,3, 1959 *BI* 1,2, 1961 *Fj* 2,3, *SA* 1,2, *F*, 1962 *NZ* 2,3,4,5, 1963 *E*, *SA* 1,2,3,4, 1964 *NZ* 1,2,3, 1965 *SA* 1,2, 1966 *BI* 1,2, 1967 *F*
Thornett, R N (NSW) 1961 *Fj* 1,2,3, *SA* 1,2, *F*, 1962 *NZ* 1,2,3,4,5
Thorpe, A C (NSW) 1929 *NZ* 1 (R)
Timbury, F R V (Q) 1910 *NZ* 1,2
Tindall, E N (NSW) 1973 *Tg* 2
Toby, A E (NSW) 1925 *NZ*
Tolhurst, H A (NSW) 1931 *M*, *NZ*
Tombs, R C (NSW) 1992 *S* 1,2, 1994 *I* 2, *It* 1
Tonkin, A E J (NSW) 1947 *S*, *I*, *W*, 1948 *E*, *F*, 1950 *BI* 2
Tooth, R M (NSW) 1951 *NZ* 1,2,3, 1954 *Fj* 1,2, 1955 *NZ* 1,2,3, 1957 *NZ* 1,2
Towers, C H T (NSW) 1927 *I*, 1928 *E*, *F*, *NZ* 1,2,3, *M*, 1929 *NZ* 1,3, 1930 *BI*, 1931 *M*, *NZ*, 1934 *NZ* 1,2, 1937 *SA* 1,2
Trivett, R K (Q) 1966 *BI* 1,2
Turnbull, A (V) 1961 *Fj* 3
Turnbull, R V (NSW) 1968 *I*
Tuynman, S N (NSW) 1983 *F* 1,2, 1984 *E*, *I*, *W*, *S*, 1985 *C* 1,2, *NZ*, *Fj* 1,2, 1986 *It*, *F*, *Arg* 1,2, *NZ* 1,2,3, 1987 *SK*, [*E*, *US*, *J*, *I*, *W*], *NZ*, *Arg* 1 (R), 2, 1988 *E*, *It*, 1989 *BI* 1,2,3, *NZ*, 1990 *NZ* 1
Tweedale, E (NSW) 1946 *NZ* 1,2, 1947 *NZ* 2, *S*, *I*, 1948 *E*, *F*, 1949 *M* 1,2,3

Vaughan, D (NSW) 1983 *US*, *Arg* 1, *It*, *F* 1,2
Vaughan, G N (V) 1958 *E*, *S*, *F*, *M* 1,2,3
Verge, A (NSW) 1904 *BI* 1,2

Walden, R J (NSW) 1934 *NZ* 2, 1936 *NZ* 1,2, *M*
Walker, A K (NSW) 1947 *NZ* 1, 1948 *E*, *F*, 1950 *BI* 1,2
Walker, A S B (NSW) 1912 *US*, 1921 *NZ*
Walker, L F (NSW) 1988 *NZ* 2,3, *S*, *It*, 1989 *BI* 1,2,3, *NZ*
Walker, L R (NSW) 1982 *NZ* 2,3
Wallace, A C (NSW) 1921 *NZ*, 1927 *I*, *W*, *S*, 1928 *E*, *F*
Wallace, T M (NSW) 1994 *It* 1(R),2
Wallach, C (NSW) 1913 *NZ* 1,3, 1914 *NZ* 1,2,3
Walsh, J J (NSW) 1953 *SA* 1,2,3,4
Walsh, P B (NSW) 1904 *BI* 1,2,3
Walsham, K P (NSW) 1962 *NZ* 3, 1963 *E*
Ward, P G (NSW) 1899 *BI* 1,2,3,4
Ward, T (Q) 1899 *BI* 2
Watson, G W (Q) 1907 *NZ* 1
Watson, W T (NSW) 1912 *US*, 1913 *NZ* 1,2,3, 1914 *NZ* 1
Waugh, W W (NSW) 1993 *SA* 1
Weatherstone, L J (ACT) 1975 *E* 1,2, *J* 1,2, *S* (R), 1976 *E*, *I*
Webb, W (NSW) 1899 *BI* 3,4
Wells, B G (NSW) 1958 *M* 1
Westfield, R E (NSW) 1928 *NZ* 1,2,3, *M*, 1929 *NZ* 2,3
White, C J B (NSW) 1899 *BI* 1, 1903 *NZ*, 1904 *BI* 1
White, J M (NSW) 1904 *BI* 3
White, J P L (NSW) 1958 *NZ* 1,2,3, 1961 *Fj* 1,2,3, *SA* 1,2, *F*, 1962 *NZ* 1,2,3,4,5, 1963 *E*, *SA* 1,2,3,4, 1964 *NZ* 1,2,3, 1965 *SA* 1,2
White, M C (Q) 1931 *M*, *NZ*, 1932 *NZ* 1,2, 1933 *SA* 1,2,3,4,5
White, S W (NSW) 1956 *SA* 1,2, 1958 *I*, *E*, *S*, *M* 2,3
White, W G S (Q) 1933 *SA* 1,2,3,4,5, 1934 *NZ* 1,2, 1936 *NZ* 1,2, *M*
White, W J (NSW) 1928 *NZ* 1, *M*, 1932 *NZ* 1
Wickham, S M (NSW) 1903 *NZ*, 1904 *BI* 1,2,3, 1905 *NZ*
Williams, D (Q) 1913 *NZ* 3, 1914 *NZ* 1,2,3
Williams, I M (NSW) 1987 *Arg* 1,2, 1988 *E* 1,2, *NZ* 1,2,3, 1989 *BI* 2,3, *NZ*, *F* 1,2, 1990 *F* 1,2,3, *US*, *NZ* 1
Williams, J L (NSW) 1963 *SA* 1,3,4
Williams, S A (NSW) 1980 *Fj*, *NZ* 1,2, 1981 *F* 1,2, 1982 *E*, *NZ* 1,2,3, 1983 *US*, *Arg* 1 (R), 2, *NZ*, *It*, *F* 1,2, 1984 *NZ* 1,2,3, *E*, *I*, *W*, *S*, 1985 *C* 1,2, *NZ*, *Fj* 1,2
Wilson, B J (NSW) 1949 *NZ* 1,2
Wilson, C R (Q) 1957 *NZ* 1, 1958 *NZ* 1,2,3
Wilson, D J (Q) 1992 *S* 1,2, *NZ* 1,2,3, *SA*, *I*, *W*, 1993 *Tg*, *NZ*, *SA* 1,2,3, *C*, *F* 1,2, 1994 *I* 1,2, *It* 1,2, *WS*, *NZ*
Wilson, V W (Q) 1937 *SA* 1,2, 1938 *NZ* 1,2,3
Windon, C J (NSW) 1946 *NZ* 1,2, 1947 *NZ* 1, *S*, *I*, *W*, 1948 *E*, *F*, 1949 *M* 1,2,3, *NZ* 1,2, 1951 *NZ* 1,2,3, 1952 *Fj* 1,2, *NZ* 1,2
Windon, K S (NSW) 1937 *SA* 1,2, 1946 *M*
Windsor, J C (Q) 1947 *NZ* 2
Winning, K C (Q) 1951 *NZ* 1
Wogan, L W (NSW) 1913 *NZ* 1,2,3, 1914 *NZ* 1,2,3, 1921 *NZ*
Wood, F (NSW) 1907 *NZ* 1,2,3, 1910 *NZ* 1,2,3, 1913 *NZ* 1,2,3, 1914 *NZ* 1,2,3
Wood, R N (Q) 1972 *Fj*
Woods, H F (NSW) 1925 *NZ*, 1927 *I*, *W*, *S*, 1928 *E*
Wright, K J (NSW) 1975 *E* 1,2, *J* 1, 1976 *US*, *F* 1,2, 1978 *NZ* 1,2,3

Yanz, K (NSW) 1958 *F*

AUSTRALIAN INTERNATIONAL RECORDS

Both team and individual records are for official Australian international matches, up to 31 March 1995.

TEAM RECORDS

Highest score

73 v Western Samoa (73-3) 1994 Sydney
v individual countries
39 v Argentina (39-19) 1986 Brisbane
30 v British Isles (30-12) 1989 Sydney
59 v Canada (59-3) 1985 Sydney
40 v England (40-15) 1991 Sydney
52 v Fiji (52-28) 1985 Brisbane
48 v France (48-31) 1990 Brisbane
42 v Ireland (42-17) 1992 Dublin
55 v Italy (55-6) 1988 Rome
50 v Japan (50-25) 1975 Brisbane
30 v N Zealand (30-16) 1978 Auckland
37 v Scotland { (37-12) 1984 Murrayfield / (37-13) 1992 Brisbane
28 v South Africa (28-20) 1993 Brisbane
65 v South Korea (65-18) 1987 Brisbane
52 v Tonga (52-14) 1993 Brisbane
67 v United States (67-9) 1990 Brisbane
63 v Wales (63-6) 1991 Brisbane
73 v Western Samoa (73-3) 1994 Sydney

Biggest winning points margin

70 v Western Samoa (73-3) 1994 Sydney
v individual countries
26 v Argentina (26-0) 1986 Sydney
18 v British Isles (30-12) 1989 Sydney
56 v Canada (59-3) 1985 Sydney
25 v England (40-15) 1991 Sydney
24 v Fiji (52-28) 1985 Brisbane
21 v France (24-3) 1993 Parc des Princes
25 v Ireland (42-17) 1992 Dublin
49 v Italy (55-6) 1988 Rome
30 v Japan (37-7) 1975 Sydney
16 v N Zealand (26-10) 1980 Sydney
25 v Scotland (37-12) 1984 Murrayfield
23 v South Africa (26-3) 1992 Cape Town
47 v South Korea (65-18) 1987 Brisbane
38 v Tonga (52-14) 1993 Brisbane
58 v United States (67-9) 1990 Brisbane
57 v Wales (63-6) 1991 Brisbane
70 v Western Samoa (73-3) 1994 Sydney

Longest winning sequence
10 matches 1991-1992

Highest score by opposing team
38 { N Zealand (13-38) 1936 Dunedin
N Zealand (3-38) 1972 Auckland }
by individual countries
27 Argentina (19-27) 1987 Buenos Aires
31 British Isles (0-31) 1966 Brisbane
16 Canada (43-16) 1993 Calgary
28 England (19-28) 1988 Twickenham
28 Fiji (52-28) 1985 Brisbane
34 France (6-34) 1976 Paris
27 Ireland (12-27) 1979 Brisbane
20 Italy (23-20) 1994 Brisbane
25 Japan (50-25) 1975 Brisbane
38 { N Zealand (13-38) 1936 Dunedin
N Zealand (3-38) 1972 Auckland }
24 Scotland (15-24) 1981 Murrayfield
30 South Africa (11-30) 1969 Johannesburg
18 South Korea (65-18) 1987 Brisbane
16 Tonga (11-16) 1973 Brisbane
12 United States (47-12) 1987 Brisbane
28 Wales (3-28) 1975 Cardiff
3 { Western Samoa } { (9-3) 1991 Pontypool
(73-3) 1994 Sydney }

Biggest losing points margin
35 v N Zealand (3-38) 1972 Auckland
v individual countries
15 v Argentina (3-18) 1983 Brisbane
31 v British Isles (0-31) 1966 Brisbane
17 v England { (3-20) 1973 Twickenham
(6-23) 1976 Twickenham }
2 v Fiji { (15-17) 1952 Sydney
(16-18) 1954 Sydney }
28 v France (6-34) 1976 Paris
15 v Ireland (12-27) 1979 Brisbane
35 v New Zealand (3-38) 1972 Auckland
9 v Scotland (15-24) 1981 Murrayfield
25 v South Africa (3-28) 1961 Johannesburg
5 v Tonga (11-16) 1973 Brisbane
25 v Wales (3-28) 1975 Cardiff
No defeats v Canada, Italy, Japan, South Korea, United States or Western Samoa.

Longest losing sequence
10 matches { 1899-1907
1937-47 }

Most tries by Australia in an international
13 v South Korea (65-18) 1987 Brisbane

Most tries against Australia in an international
9 by N Zealand (13-38) 1936 Dunedin

Most points on overseas tour (all matches)
500 in B Isles/France (35 matches) 1947-48

Most tries on overseas tour (all matches)
115 in B Isles/France (35 matches) 1947-48

INDIVIDUAL RECORDS

Most capped player
D I Campese 86 1982-94
in individual positions
Full-back
R G Gould 25 1980-87
Wing
D I Campese 70(86)[1] 1982-94
Centre
A G Slack 39 1978-87
Fly-half
M P Lynagh 59(67)[2] 1984-94
Scrum-half
N C Farr-Jones 62(63)[3] 1984-93
Prop
A J Daly 39 1989-94
Hooker
P G Johnson 42 1959-71
P N Kearns 42 1989-94
Lock
S A G Cutler 40 1982-91
Flanker
S P Poidevin 59 1980-91
No 8
T B Gavin 34(36)[4] 1988-94
[1]*Campese has played 16 times as a full-back*
[2]*Lynagh has played 7 times as a centre and once as a replacement full-back*
[3]*Farr-Jones was capped once as a replacement wing*
[4]*Gavin has been capped twice as a lock. S N Tuynman, 34 caps, won 28 as a No 8 and 6 as a flanker.*

Longest international career
G M Cooke 16 seasons 1932-1947/8
A R Miller 16 seasons 1952-1967
Cooke's career ended during a Northern hemisphere season

Most consecutive internationals – 42
P N Kearns 1989-94

Most internationals as captain – 36
N C Farr-Jones 1988-92
Includes wins against the British Isles and all senior IB nations

---

Most points in internationals – 821
M P Lynagh (67 matches) 1984-94

Most points in an international – 24
M P Lynagh v France 1990 Brisbane
M P Lynagh v United States 1990 Brisbane

Most tries in internationals – 60
D I Campese (86 matches) 1982-94

Most tries in an international – 4
G Cornelsen v N Zealand 1978 Auckland
D I Campese v United States 1983 Sydney

Most conversions in internationals – 132
M P Lynagh (67 matches) 1984-94

Most conversions in an international – 8
M P Lynagh v Italy 1988 Rome
M P Lynagh v United States 1990 Brisbane

Most dropped goals in internationals – 9
P F Hawthorne (21 matches) 1962-67
M P Lynagh (64 matches) 1984-93

Most dropped goals in an international – 3
P F Hawthorne v England 1967 Twickenham

Most penalty goals in internationals – 159
M P Lynagh (67 matches) 1984-94

Most penalty goals in an international – 6
M P Lynagh v France 1986 Sydney
M P Lynagh v England 1988 Brisbane

Most points in international series on tour – 42
M P Lynagh (4 appearances) 1984 B Isles

Most tries in international series on tour – 4
G Cornelsen (3 appearances) 1978 N Zealand
M G Ella (4 appearances) 1984 B Isles
Ella scored in each match of the international series

Most points on overseas tour – 154
P E McLean (18 appearances) B Isles 1975-76

Most tries on overseas tour – 23
C J Russell B Isles 1908-09

Most points in a tour match – 26
A J Leeds v Buller (NZ) 1986 Westport

Most tries in a tour match – 6
J S Boyce v Wairarapa (NZ) 1962 Masterton

INTERNATIONAL MATCH APPEARANCES FOR BRITISH ISLES TEAMS (*up to 31 March 1995*)

*From 1910 onwards, when British Isles teams first became officially representative of the four Home Unions. (*Uncapped when first selected to play in a Test match for the British Isles.)*

ABBREVIATIONS

A – Australia; *NZ* – New Zealand; *SA* –South Africa; (R) – Replacement; (t) – temporary replacement.

CLUB ABBREVIATIONS

NIFC – North of Ireland Football Club; CIYMS – Church of Ireland Young Men's Society

Note: When a series has taken place, figures have been used to denote the particular matches in which players have featured. Thus 1962 *SA* 1,4 indicates that a player appeared in the first and fourth Tests of a series.

Aarvold, C D (Cambridge U, Blackheath and England) 1930 *NZ* 1,2,3,4, *A*
Ackerman, R A (London Welsh and Wales) 1983 *NZ* 1,4(R)
Ackford, P J (Harlequins and England) 1989 *A* 1,2,3
Alexander, R (NIFC and Ireland) 1938 *SA* 1,2,3
Andrew, C R (Wasps and England) 1989 *A* 2,3, 1993 *NZ* 1,2,3
Arneil, R J (Edinburgh Acads and Scotland) 1968 *SA* 1,2,3,4
Ashcroft, A (Waterloo and England) 1959 *A* 1, *NZ* 2

Bainbridge, S J (Gosforth and England) 1983 *NZ* 3,4
Baird, G R T (Kelso and Scotland) 1983 *NZ* 1,2,3,4
Baker, A M (Newport and Wales) 1910 *SA* 3
Baker, D G S (Old Merchant Taylors' and England) 1955 *SA* 3,4
Bassett, J (Penarth and Wales) 1930 *NZ* 1,2,3,4, *A*
Bayfield, M C (Northampton and England) 1993 *NZ* 1,2,3
Beamish, G R (Leicester, RAF and Ireland) 1930 *NZ* 1,2,3,4, *A*
Beattie, J R (Glasgow Acads and Scotland) 1983 *NZ* 2(R)
Beaumont, W B (Fylde and England) 1977 *NZ* 2,3,4, 1980 *SA* 1,2,3,4
Bebb, D I E (Swansea and Wales) 1962 *SA* 2,3, 1966 *A* 1,2, *NZ* 1,2,3,4
Bennett, P (Llanelli and Wales) 1974 *SA* 1,2,3,4, 1977 *NZ* 1,2,3,4
Bevan, J C (Cardiff Coll of Ed, Cardiff and Wales) 1971 *NZ* 1
Black, A W (Edinburgh U and Scotland) 1950 *NZ* 1,2
Black, B H (Oxford U, Blackheath and England) 1930 *NZ* 1,2,3,4, *A*
Blakiston, A F (Northampton and England) 1924 *SA* 1,2,3,4
Bowcott, H M (Cambridge U, Cardiff and Wales) 1930 *NZ* 1,2,3,4, *A*
Boyle, C V (Dublin U and Ireland) 1938 *SA* 2,3
Brand, T N (NIFC and *Ireland) 1924 *SA* 1,2
Bresnihan, F P K (UC Dublin and Ireland) 1968 *SA* 1,2,4
Brophy, N H (UC Dublin and Ireland) 1962 *SA* 1,4
Brown, G L (W of Scotland and Scotland) 1971 *NZ* 3,4, 1974 *SA* 1,2,3, 1977 *NZ* 2,3,4
Budge, G M (Edinburgh Wands and Scotland) 1950 *NZ* 4
Burcher, D H (Newport and Wales) 1977 *NZ* 3
Burnell, A P (London Scottish and Scotland) 1993 *NZ* 1
Butterfield, J (Northampton and England) 1955 *SA* 1,2,3,4

Calder, F (Stewart's-Melville FP and Scotland) 1989 *A* 1,2,3
Calder, J H (Stewart's-Melville FP and Scotland) 1983 *NZ* 3
Cameron, A (Glasgow HSFP and Scotland) 1955 *SA* 1,2
Campbell, S O (Old Belvedere and Ireland) 1980 *SA* 2(R), 3,4, 1983 *NZ* 1,2,3,4
Campbell-Lamerton, M J (Halifax, Army and Scotland) 1962 *SA* 1,2,3,4, 1966 *A* 1,2, *NZ* 1,3
Carleton, J (Orrell and England) 1980 *SA* 1,2,4, 1983 *NZ* 2,3,4
Carling, W D C (Harlequins and England) 1993 *NZ* 1
Chalmers, C M (Melrose and Scotland) 1989 *A* 1
Clarke, B B (Bath and England) 1993 *NZ* 1,2,3
Cleaver, W B (Cardiff and Wales) 1950 *NZ* 1,2,3
Clifford, T (Young Munster and Ireland) 1950 *NZ* 1,2,3, *A* 1,2
Cobner, T J (Pontypool and Wales) 1977 *NZ* 1,2,3
Colclough, M J (Angoulême and England) 1980 *SA* 1,2,3,4, 1983 *NZ* 1,2,3,4
Connell, G C (Trinity Acads and Scotland) 1968 *SA* 4
Cotton, F E (Loughborough Colls, Coventry and England) 1974 *SA* 1,2,3,4, 1977 *NZ* 2,3,4
Coulman, M J (Moseley and England) 1968 *SA* 3
Cove-Smith, R (Old Merchant Taylors' and England) 1924 *SA* 1,2,3,4
Cowan, R C (Selkirk and Scotland) 1962 *SA* 4
Cromey, G E (Queen's U, Belfast and Ireland) 1938 *SA* 3
Cunningham, W A (Lansdowne and Ireland) 1924 *SA* 3

Dancer, G T (Bedford) 1938 *SA* 1,2,3
Davies, C (Cardiff and Wales) 1950 *NZ* 4
Davies, D M (Somerset Police and Wales) 1950 *NZ* 3,4, *A* 1
Davies, D S (Hawick and Scotland) 1924 *SA* 1,2,3,4
Davies, H J (Newport and Wales) 1924 *SA* 2
Davies, T G R (Cardiff, London Welsh and Wales) 1968 *SA* 3, 1971 *NZ* 1,2,3,4
Davies, T J (Llanelli and Wales) 1959 *NZ* 2,4
Davies, T M (London Welsh, Swansea and Wales) 1971 *NZ* 1,2,3,4, 1974 *SA* 1,2,3,4
Davies, W G (Cardiff and Wales) 1980 *SA* 2
Davies, W P C (Harlequins and England) 1955 *SA* 1,2,3
Dawes, S J (London Welsh and Wales) 1971 *NZ* 1,2,3,4
Dawson, A R (Wanderers and Ireland) 1959 *A* 1,2, *NZ* 1,2,3,4
Dixon, P J (Harlequins and England) 1971 *NZ* 1,2,4
Dodge, P W (Leicester and England) 1980 *SA* 3,4
Dooley, W A (Preston Grasshoppers and England) 1989 *A* 2,3
Doyle, M G (Blackrock Coll and Ireland) 1968 *SA* 1
Drysdale, D (Heriot's FP and Scotland) 1924 *SA* 1,2,3,4
Duckham, D J (Coventry and England) 1971 *NZ* 2,3,4
Duggan, W P (Blackrock Coll and Ireland) 1977 *NZ* 1,2,3,4
Duff, P L (Glasgow Acads and Scotland) 1938 *SA* 2,3

Edwards, G O (Cardiff and Wales) 1968 *SA* 1,2, 1971 *NZ* 1,2,3,4, 1974 *SA* 1,2,3,4
Evans, G (Maesteg and Wales) 1983 *NZ* 3,4
Evans, G L (Newport and Wales) 1977 *NZ* 2,3,4
Evans, I C (Llanelli and Wales) 1989 *A* 1,2,3, 1993 *NZ* 1,2,3
Evans, R T (Newport and Wales) 1950 *NZ* 1,2,3,4, *A* 1,2
Evans, T P (Swansea and Wales) 1977 *NZ* 1

Evans, W R (Cardiff and Wales) 1959 *A* 2, *NZ* 1,2,3

Farrell, J L (Bective Rangers and Ireland) 1930 *NZ* 1,2,3,4, *A*
Faull, J (Swansea and Wales) 1959 *A* 1, *NZ* 1,3,4
Fenwick, S P (Bridgend and Wales) 1977 *NZ* 1,2,3,4
Fitzgerald, C F (St Mary's Coll and Ireland) 1983 *NZ* 1,2,3,4
Foster, A R (Queen's U, Belfast and Ireland) 1910 *SA* 1,2

Gibbs, I S (Swansea and Wales) 1993 *NZ* 2,3
Gibson, C M H (Cambridge U, NIFC and Ireland) 1966 *NZ* 1,2,3,4, 1968 *SA* 1(R),2,3,4, 1971 *NZ* 1,2,3,4
Giles, J L (Coventry and England) 1938 *SA* 1,3
Gravell, R W R (Llanelli and Wales) 1980 *SA* 1 (R),2,3,4
Graves, C R A (Wanderers and Ireland) 1938 *SA* 1,3
Greenwood, J T (Dunfermline and Scotland) 1955 *SA* 1,2,3,4
Grieve, C F (Oxford U and Scotland) 1938 *SA* 2,3
Griffiths, G M (Cardiff and Wales) 1955 *SA* 2,3,4
Griffiths, V M (Newport and Wales) 1924 *SA* 3,4
Guscott, J C (Bath and England) 1989 *A* 2,3, 1993 *NZ* 1,2,3

Hall, M R (Bridgend and Wales) 1989 *A* 1
Handford, F G (Manchester and England) 1910 *SA* 1,2,3
Harding, W R (Cambridge U, Swansea and Wales) 1924 *SA* 2,3,4
Harris, S W (Blackheath and England) 1924 *SA* 3,4
Hastings, A G (London Scottish, Watsonians and Scotland) 1989 *A* 1,2,3, 1993 *NZ* 1,2,3
Hastings, S (Watsonians and Scotland) 1989 *A* 2,3
Hay, B H (Boroughmuir and Scotland) 1980 *SA* 2,3,4
Hayward, D J (Newbridge and Wales) 1950 *NZ* 1,2,3
Henderson, N J (Queen's U, Belfast, NIFC and Ireland) 1950 *NZ* 3
Henderson, R G (Northern and Scotland) 1924 *SA* 3,4
Hendrie, K G P (Heriot's FP and Scotland) 1924 *SA* 2
Hewitt, D (Queen's U, Belfast, Instonians and Ireland) 1959 *A* 1,2, *NZ* 1,3,4, 1962 *SA* 4
Higgins, R (Liverpool and England) 1955 *SA* 1
Hinshelwood, A J W (London Scottish and Scotland) 1966 *NZ* 2,4, 1968 *SA* 2
Hodgson, J McD (Northern and *England) 1930 *NZ* 1,3
Holmes, T D (Cardiff and Wales) 1983 *NZ* 1
Hopkins, R (Maesteg and Wales) 1971 *NZ* 1(R)
Horrocks-Taylor, J P (Leicester and England) 1959 *NZ* 3
Horton, A L (Blackheath and England) 1968 *SA* 2,3,4
Howard, W G (Old Birkonians) 1938 *SA* 1
Howie, R A (Kirkcaldy and Scotland) 1924 *SA* 1,2,3,4

Irvine, A R (Heriot's FP and Scotland) 1974 *SA* 3,4, 1977 *NZ* 1,2,3,4, 1980 *SA* 2,3,4
Irwin, D G (Instonians and Ireland) 1983 *NZ* 1,2,4
Isherwood, G A M (Old Alleynians, Sale) 1910 *SA* 1,2,3

Jackson, P B (Coventry and England) 1959 *A* 1,2, *NZ* 1,3,4
Jarman, H (Newport and Wales) 1910 *SA* 1,2,3
Jeeps, R E G (Northampton and *England) 1955 *SA* 1,2,3,4, 1959 *A* 1,2, *NZ* 1,2,3, 1962 *SA* 1,2,3,4
Jenkins, V G J (Oxford U, London Welsh and Wales) 1938 *SA* 1
John, B (Cardiff and Wales) 1968 *SA* 1, 1971 *NZ* 1,2,3,4
John, E R (Neath and Wales) 1950 *NZ* 1,2,3,4, *A* 1,2
Johnson, M O (Leicester and England) 1993 *NZ* 2,3
Jones, B L (Devonport Services, Llanelli and Wales) 1950 *NZ* 4, *A* 1,2
Jones, D K (Llanelli, Cardiff and Wales) 1962 *SA* 1,2,3, 1966 *A* 1,2, *NZ* 1
Jones, E L (Llanelli and *Wales) 1938 *SA* 1,3
Jones, Ivor (Llanelli and Wales) 1930 *NZ* 1,2,3,4, *A*
Jones, J P (Newport and Wales) 1910 *SA* 1,2,3
Jones, K D (Cardiff and Wales) 1962 *SA* 1,2,3,4
Jones, K J (Newport and Wales) 1950 *NZ* 1,2,4
Jones, R N (Swansea and Wales) 1989 *A* 1,2,3
Jones, S T (Pontypool and Wales) 1983 *NZ* 2,3,4

Keane, M I (Lansdowne and Ireland) 1977 *NZ* 1
Kennedy, K W (CIYMS, London Irish and Ireland) 1966 *A* 1,2, *NZ* 1,4
Kiernan, M J (Dolphin and Ireland) 1983 *NZ* 2,3,4
Kiernan, T J (Cork Const and Ireland) 1962 *SA* 3, 1968 *SA* 1,2,3,4
Kininmonth, P W (Oxford U, Richmond and Scotland) 1950 *NZ* 1,2,4
Kinnear, R M (Heriot's FP and *Scotland) 1924 *SA* 1,2,3,4
Kyle, J W (Queen's U, Belfast, NIFC and Ireland) 1950 *NZ* 1,2,3,4, *A* 1,2

Laidlaw, F A L (Melrose and Scotland) 1966 *NZ* 2,3
Laidlaw, R J (Jedforest and Scotland) 1983 *NZ* 1(R), 2,3,4
Lamont, R A (Instonians and Ireland) 1966 *NZ* 1,2,3,4
Lane, M F (UC Cork and Ireland) 1950 *NZ* 4, *A* 2
Larter, P J (Northampton, RAF and England) 1968 *SA* 2
Leonard, J (Harlequins and England) 1993 *NZ* 2,3
Lewis, A R (Abertillery and Wales) 1966 *NZ* 2,3,4
Lynch, J F (St Mary's Coll and Ireland) 1971 *NZ* 1,2,3,4

McBride, W J (Ballymena and Ireland) 1962 *SA* 3,4, 1966 *NZ* 2,3,4, 1968 *SA* 1,2,3,4, 1971 *NZ* 1,2,3,4, 1974 *SA* 1,2,3,4
Macdonald, R (Edinburgh U and Scotland) 1950 *NZ* 1, *A* 2
McFadyean, C W (Moseley and England) 1966 *NZ* 1,2,3,4
McGeechan, I R (Headingley and Scotland) 1974 *SA* 1,2,3,4, 1977 *NZ* 1,2,3(R),4
McKay, J W (Queen's U, Belfast and Ireland) 1950 *NZ* 1,2,3,4, *A* 1,2
McKibbin, H R (Queen's U, Belfast and Ireland) 1938 *SA* 1,2,3
McLauchlan, J (Jordanhill and Scotland) 1971 *NZ* 1,2,3,4, 1974 *SA* 1,2,3,4
McLeod, H F (Hawick and Scotland) 1959 *A* 1,2, *NZ* 1,2,3,4
McLoughlin, R J (Gosforth, Blackrock Coll and Ireland) 1966 *A* 1,2, *NZ* 4
MacNeill, H P (Oxford U and Ireland) 1983 *NZ* 1,2, 4(R)
Macpherson, N C (Newport and Scotland) 1924 *SA* 1,2,3,4
Macrae, D J (St Andrew's U and Scotland) 1938 *SA* 1
McVicker, J (Collegians and Ireland) 1924 *SA* 1,3,4
Marques, R W D (Harlequins and England) 1959 *A* 2, *NZ* 2
Marsden-Jones, D (London Welsh and Wales) 1924 *SA* 1,2
Martin, A J (Aberavon and Wales) 1977 *NZ* 1
Martindale, S A (Kendal and England) 1930 *A*
Matthews, J (Cardiff and Wales) 1950 *NZ* 1,2,3,4, *A* 1,2
Maxwell, R B (Birkenhead Park) 1924 *SA* 1
Mayne, R B (Queen's U, Belfast and Ireland) 1938 *SA* 1,2,3
Meredith, B V (Newport and Wales) 1955 *SA* 1,2,3,4, 1962 *SA* 1,2,3,4
Meredith, C C (Neath and Wales) 1955 *SA* 1,2,3,4
Millar, S (Ballymena and Ireland) 1959 *A* 1,2, *NZ* 2, 1962 *SA* 1,2,3,4, 1968 *SA* 1,2
Milliken, R A (Bangor and Ireland) 1974 *SA* 1,2,3,4
Milne, K S (Heriot's FP and Scotland) 1993 *NZ* 1
Moore, B C (Nottingham, Harlequins and England) 1989 *A* 1,2,3, 1993 *NZ* 2,3
Morgan, C I (Cardiff and Wales) 1955 *SA* 1,2,3,4
Morgan, D W (Stewart's-Melville FP and Scotland) 1977 *NZ* 3(R),4
Morgan, G J (Clontarf and Ireland) 1938 *SA* 3
Morgan, H J (Abertillery and Wales) 1959 *NZ* 3,4, 1962 *SA* 2,3
Morgan, M E (Swansea and Wales) 1938 *SA* 1,2
Morley, J C (Newport and Wales) 1930 *NZ* 1,2,3
Morris, C D (Orrell and England) 1993 *NZ* 1,2,3
Mulcahy, W A (UC Dublin and Ireland) 1959 *A* 1, *NZ* 4, 1962 *SA* 1,2,3,4
Mullen, K D (Old Belvedere and Ireland) 1950 *NZ* 1,2, *A* 2

Mulligan, A A (Wanderers, London Irish and Ireland) 1959 *NZ* 4
Mullin, B J (London Irish and Ireland) 1989 *A* 1
Murphy, N A A (Cork Const and Ireland) 1959 *A* 2, *NZ* 1,2,4, 1966 *A* 1,2, *NZ* 2,3
Murray, P F (Wanderers and Ireland) 1930 *NZ* 1,2,4, *A*

Neale, M E (Bristol, Blackheath and *England) 1910 *SA* 1,2,3
Neary, A (Broughton Park and England) 1977 *NZ* 4
Nelson, J E (Malone and Ireland) 1950 *NZ* 3,4, *A* 1,2
Nicholson, B E (Harlequins and England) 1938 *SA* 2
Norris, C H (Cardiff and Wales) 1966 *NZ* 1,2,3
Norster, R L (Cardiff and Wales) 1983 *NZ* 1,2, 1989 *A* 1
Novis, A L (Blackheath and England) 1930 *NZ* 2,4, *A*

O'Donnell, R C (St Mary's Coll and Ireland) 1980 *SA* 1
O'Driscoll, J B (London Irish and Ireland) 1980 *SA* 1,2,3,4, 1983 *NZ* 2,4
O'Neill, H O'H (Queen's U, Belfast and Ireland) 1930 *NZ* 1,2,3,4, *A*
O'Reilly, A J F (Old Belvedere and Ireland) 1955 *SA* 1,2,3,4, 1959 *A* 1,2, *NZ* 1,2,3,4
Orr, P A (Old Wesley and Ireland) 1977 *NZ* 1
O'Shea, J P (Cardiff and Wales) 1968 *SA* 1

Parker, D (Swansea and Wales) 1930 *NZ* 1,2,3,4, *A*
Pask, A E I (Abertillery and Wales) 1962 *SA* 1,2,3, 1966 *A* 1,2, *NZ* 1,3,4
Patterson, C S (Instonians and Ireland) 1980 *SA* 1,2,3
Patterson, W M (Sale and *England) 1959 *NZ* 2
Paxton, I A M (Selkirk and Scotland) 1983 *NZ* 1,2,3,4
Pedlow, A C (CIYMS and Ireland) 1955 *SA* 1,4
Pillman, C H (Blackheath and England) 1910 *SA* 2,3
Piper, O J S (Cork Const and Ireland) 1910 *SA* 1
Poole, H (Cardiff) 1930 *NZ* 3
Popplewell, N J (Greystones and Ireland) 1993 *NZ* 1,2,3
Preece, I (Coventry and England) 1950 *NZ* 1
Prentice, F D (Leicester and England) 1930 *NZ* 2, *A*
Price, B (Newport and Wales) 1966 *A* 1,2, *NZ* 1,4
Price, G (Pontypool and Wales) 1977 *NZ* 1,2,3,4, 1980 *SA* 1,2,3,4, 1983 *NZ* 1,2,3,4
Price, M J (Pontypool and Wales) 1959 *A* 1,2, *NZ* 1,2,3
Prosser, T R (Pontypool and Wales) 1959 *NZ* 4
Pullin, J V (Bristol and England) 1968 *SA* 2,3,4, 1971 *NZ* 1,2,3,4

Quinnell, D L (Llanelli and *Wales) 1971 *NZ* 3, 1977 *NZ* 2,3, 1980 *SA* 1,2

Ralston, C W (Richmond and England) 1974 *SA* 4
Reed, A I (Bath and Scotland) 1993 *NZ* 1
Rees, H E (Neath and *Wales) 1977 *NZ* 4
Reeve, J S R (Harlequins and England) 1930 *NZ* 1,3,4, *A*
Reid, T E (Garryowen and Ireland) 1955 *SA* 2,3
Renwick, J M (Hawick and Scotland) 1980 *SA* 1
Rew, H (Blackheath, Army and England) 1930 *NZ* 1,2,3,4
Reynolds, F J (Old Cranleighans and England) 1938 *SA* 1,2
Richards, D (Leicester and England) 1989 *A* 1,2,3, 1993 *NZ* 1,2,3
Richards, D S (Swansea and Wales) 1980 *SA* 1
Richards, M C R (Cardiff and Wales) 1968 *SA* 1,3,4
Richards, T J (Bristol and Australia) 1910 *SA* 1,2
Rimmer, G (Waterloo and England) 1950 *NZ* 3
Ringland, T M (Ballymena and Ireland) 1983 *NZ* 1
Risman, A B W (Loughborough Colls and England) 1959 *A* 1,2, *NZ* 1,4
Robbie, J C (Greystones and Ireland) 1980 *SA* 4
Robins, J D (Birkenhead Park and Wales) 1950 *NZ* 1,2,3, *A* 1,2
Robins, R J (Pontypridd and Wales) 1955 *SA* 1,2,3,4
Rogers, D P (Bedford and England) 1962 *SA* 1,4
Rowlands, K A (Cardiff and Wales) 1962 *SA* 1,2,4
Rutherford, D (Gloucester and England) 1966 *A* 1
Rutherford, J Y (Selkirk and Scotland) 1983 *NZ* 3

Savage, K F (Northampton and England) 1968 *SA* 1,2,3,4
Scotland, K J F (Cambridge U, Heriot's FP and Scotland) 1959 *A* 1,2, *NZ* 1,3,4
Sharp, R A W (Oxford U, Redruth and England) 1962 *SA* 3,4
Slattery, J F (Blackrock Coll and Ireland) 1974 *SA* 1,2,3,4
Slemen, M A C (Liverpool and England) 1980 *SA* 1
Smith, A R (Edinburgh Wands, London Scottish and Scotland) 1962 *SA* 1,2,3
Smith, D F (Richmond and England) 1910 *SA* 1,2,3
Smith, D W C (London Scottish and Scotland) 1950 *A* 1
Smith, G K (Kelso and Scotland) 1959 *A* 1,2, *NZ* 1,3
Smith, I S (Oxford U, London Scottish and Scotland) 1924 *SA* 1,2
Smyth, T (Malone, Newport and Ireland) 1910 *SA* 2,3
Sole, D M B (Edinburgh Acads and Scotland) 1989 *A* 1,2,3
Spong, R S (Old Millhillians and England) 1930 *NZ* 1,2,3,4, *A*
Spoors, J A (Bristol) 1910 *SA* 1,2,3
Squire, J (Newport, Pontypool and Wales) 1977 *NZ* 4, 1980 *SA* 1,2,3,4, 1983 *NZ* 1
Squires, P J (Harrogate and England) 1977 *NZ* 1
Stagg, P K (Oxford U, Sale and Scotland) 1968 *SA* 1,3,4
Steele, W C C (Bedford, RAF and Scotland) 1974 *SA* 1,2
Stephens, I (Bridgend and Wales) 1983 *NZ* 1
Stephens, J R G (Neath and Wales) 1950 *A* 1,2
Stevenson, R C (St Andrew's U and Scotland) 1910 *SA* 1,2,3

Tanner, H (Swansea and Wales) 1938 *SA* 2
Taylor, A R (Cross Keys and Wales) 1938 *SA* 1,2
Taylor, J (London Welsh and Wales) 1971 *NZ* 1,2,3,4
Taylor, R B (Northampton and England) 1968 *SA* 1,2,3,4
Teague, M C (Gloucester, Moseley and England) 1989 *A* 2,3, 1993 *NZ* 2(t)
Telfer, J W (Melrose and Scotland) 1966 *A* 1,2, *NZ* 1,2,4, 1968 *SA* 2,3,4
Thomas, M C (Devonport Services, Newport and Wales) 1950 *NZ* 2,3, *A* 1, 1959 *NZ* 2
Thomas, R C C (Swansea and Wales) 1955 *SA* 3,4
Thomas, W D (Llanelli and *Wales) 1966 *NZ* 2,3, 1968 *SA* 3(R),4, 1971 *NZ* 1,2,4(R)
Thompson, R H (Instonians, London Irish and Ireland) 1955 *SA* 1,2,4
Travers, W H (Newport and Wales) 1938 *SA* 2,3
Tucker, C C (Shannon and Ireland) 1980 *SA* 3,4
Turner, J W C (Gala and Scotland) 1968 *SA* 1,2,3,4

Underwood, R (RAF, Leicester and England) 1989 *A* 1,2,3, 1993 *NZ* 1,2,3
Unwin, E J (Rosslyn Park, Army and England) 1938 *SA* 1,2
Uttley, R M (Gosforth and England) 1974 *SA* 1,2,3,4

Voyce, A T (Gloucester and England) 1924 *SA* 3,4

Waddell, G H (Cambridge U, London Scottish and Scotland) 1962 *SA* 1,2
Waddell, H (Glasgow Acads and Scotland) 1924 *SA* 1,2,4
Walker, S (Instonians and Ireland) 1938 *SA* 1,2,3
Wallace, W (Percy Park) 1924 *SA* 1
Waller, P D (Newport and Wales) 1910 *SA* 1,2,3
Ward, A J P (Garryowen and Ireland) 1980 *SA* 1
Waters, J A (Selkirk and Scotland) 1938 *SA* 3
Watkins, D (Newport and Wales) 1966 *A* 1,2, *NZ* 1,2,3,4
Watkins, S J (Newport and Wales) 1966 *A* 1,2,*NZ* 3
Webb, J (Abertillery and Wales) 1910 *SA* 1,2,3
Welsh, W B (Hawick and Scotland) 1930 *NZ* 4
Weston, M P (Richmond, Durham City and England) 1962 *SA* 1,2,3,4, 1966 *A* 1,2
Wheeler, P J (Leicester and England) 1977 *NZ* 2,3,4, 1980 *SA* 1,2,3,4
White, D B (London Scottish and Scotland) 1989 *A* 1
Whitley, H (Northern and *England) 1924 *SA* 1,3,4
Willcox, J G (Oxford U, Harlequins and England) 1962 *SA* 1,2,4
Williams, B L (Cardiff and Wales) 1950 *NZ* 2,3,4, *A* 1,2

Williams, C (Swansea and Wales) 1980 *SA* 1,2,3,4
Williams, D (Ebbw Vale and Wales) 1966 *A* 1,2, *NZ* 1,2,4
Williams, D B (Cardiff and *Wales) 1977 *NZ* 1,2,3
Williams, J J (Llanelli and Wales) 1974 *SA* 1,2,3,4, 1977 *NZ* 1,2,3
Williams, J P R (London Welsh and Wales) 1971 *NZ* 1,2,3,4, 1974 *SA* 1,2,3,4
Williams, R H (Llanelli and Wales) 1955 *SA* 1,2,3,4, 1959 *A* 1,2, *NZ* 1,2,3,4
Williams, S H (Newport and *England) 1910 *SA* 1,2,3
Williams, W O G (Swansea and Wales) 1955 *SA* 1,2,3,4
Willis, W R (Cardiff and Wales) 1950 *NZ* 4, *A* 1,2
Wilson, S (London Scottish and Scotland) 1966 *A* 2, *NZ* 1,2,3,4
Windsor, R W (Pontypool and Wales) 1974 *SA* 1,2,3,4, 1977 *NZ* 1
Winterbottom, P J (Headingley, Harlequins and England) 1983 *NZ* 1,2,3,4, 1993 *NZ* 1,2,3
Wood, B G M (Garryowen and Ireland) 1959 *NZ* 1,3
Wood, K B (Leicester) 1910 *SA* 1,3
Woodward, C R (Leicester and England) 1980 *SA* 2,3

Young, A T (Cambridge U, Blackheath and England) 1924 *SA* 2
Young, D (Cardiff and Wales) 1989 *A* 1,2,3
Young, J (Harrogate, RAF and Wales) 1968 *SA* 1
Young, J R C (Oxford U, Harlequins and England) 1959 *NZ* 2
Young, R M (Queen's U, Belfast, Collegians and Ireland) 1966 *A* 1,2, *NZ* 1, 1968 *SA* 3

Gavin Hastings, captain of the 1993 Lions in New Zealand, who retired this season.

RESULTS OF BRITISH ISLES MATCHES
(*up to 31 March 1995*)

From 1910 onwards – the tour to South Africa in that year was the first fully representative one in which the four Home Unions co-operated.

v SOUTH AFRICA

Played 30 British Isles won 8, South Africa won 18, Drawn 4

1910 *1* Johannesburg
South Africa 1G 3T (14) to 1DG 2T (10)

2 Port Elizabeth
British Isles 1G 1T (8) to 1T (3)

3 Cape Town
South Africa 3G 1PG 1T (21) to 1G (5)
South Africa won series 2-1

1924 *1* Durban
South Africa 1DG 1T (7) to 1T(3)

2 Johannesburg
South Africa 1G 1PG 3T (17) to 0

3 Port Elizabeth
Drawn 1T (3) each

4 Cape Town
South Africa 1DG 4T (16) to 1PG 2T (9)
South Africa won series 3-0, with 1 draw

1938 *1* Johannesburg
South Africa 4G 2PG (26) to 4PG (12)

2 Port Elizabeth
South Africa 2G 2PG 1T (19) to 1T (3)

3 Cape Town
British Isles 1G 1PG 1DG 3T (21)
to 2G 1PG 1T (16)
South Africa won series 2-1

1955 *1* Johannesburg
British Isles 4G 1T (23) to 2G 2PG 2T (22)

2 Cape Town
South Africa 2G 5T (25) to 1PG 2T (9)

3 Pretoria
British Isles 1PG 1DG 1T (9)
to 2PG (6)

4 Port Elizabeth
South Africa 2G 1DG 3T (22)
to 1G 1T (8)
Series drawn 2-2

1962 *1* Johannesburg
Drawn 1T (3) each

2 Durban
South Africa 1PG (3) to 0

3 Cape Town
South Africa 1G 1PG (8) to 1DG (3)

4 Bloemfontein
South Africa 5G 2PG 1T (34)
to 1G 1PG 2T (14)
South Africa won series 3-0, with 1 draw

1968 *1* Pretoria
South Africa 2G 4PG 1T (25)
to 1G 5PG (20)

2 Port Elizabeth
Drawn 2PG (6) each

3 Cape Town
South Africa 1G 2PG (11) to 2PG (6)

4 Johannesburg
South Africa 2G 1DG 2T (19) to 2PG (6)
South Africa won series 3-0, with 1 draw

1974 *1* Cape Town
British Isles 3PG 1DG (12) to 1DG (3)

2 Pretoria
British Isles 1G 1PG 1DG 4T (28)
to 2PG 1DG (9)

3 Port Elizabeth
British Isles 1G 2PG 2DG 2T (26)
to 3PG (9)

4 Johannesburg
Drawn British Isles 1G 1PG 1T (13)
South Africa 3PG 1T (13)
British Isles won series 3-0, with 1 draw

1980 *1* Cape Town
South Africa 3G 2T (26)
to 5PG 1DG 1T (22)

2 Bloemfontein
South Africa 2G 2PG 2T (26)
to 1G 3PG 1T (19)

3 Port Elizabeth
South Africa 1G 1PG 1DG (12)
to 2PG 1T (10)

4 Pretoria
British Isles 1G 1PG 2T (17)
to 3PG 1T (13)
South Africa won series 3-1

v NEW ZEALAND

Played 31 British Isles won 6, New Zealand won 23, Drawn 2

1930 *1* Dunedin
British Isles 2T (6) to 1T (3)

2 Christchurch
New Zealand 2G 1GM (13) to 2G (10)

3 Auckland
New Zealand 1G 1DG 2T (15) to 2G (10)

4 Wellington
New Zealand 2G 4T (22) to 1G 1PG (8)
New Zealand won series 3-1

1950 *1* Dunedin
Drawn 1PG 2T (9) each

2 Christchurch
New Zealand 1G 1T (8) to 0

3 Wellington
New Zealand 1PG 1T (6) to 1PG (3)

4 Auckland
New Zealand 1G 1DG 1T (11) to 1G 1PG (8)
New Zealand won series 3-0, with 1 draw

1959 *1* Dunedin
New Zealand 6PG (18) to 1G 1PG 3T (17)

2 Wellington
New Zealand 1G 2T (11) to 1G 1PG (8)

3 Christchurch
New Zealand 2G 1PG 1DG 2T (22) to 1G 1PG (8)

4 Auckland
British Isles 3T (9) to 2PG (6)
New Zealand won series 3-1

1966 *1* Dunedin
New Zealand 1G 2PG 1DG 2T (20) to 1PG (3)

2 Wellington
New Zealand 2G 1PG 1T (16) to 3PG 1DG (12)

3 Christchurch
New Zealand 2G 2PG 1T (19) to 2T (6)

4 Auckland
New Zealand 3G 1PG 1DG 1T (24) to 1G 1PG 1T (11)
New Zealand won series 4-0

1971 *1* Dunedin
British Isles 2PG 1T (9) to 1PG (3)

2 Christchurch
New Zealand 2G 1PG 3T (22) to 1PG 1DG 2T (12)

3 Wellington
British Isles 2G 1DG (13) to 1T (3)

4 Auckland
Drawn British Isles 1G 2PG 1DG (14) New Zealand 1G 2PG 1T (14)
British Isles won series 2-1, with 1 draw

1977 *1* Wellington
New Zealand 2G 1T (16) to 4PG (12)

2 Christchurch
British Isles 3PG 1T (13) to 3PG (9)

3 Dunedin
New Zealand 1G 2PG 1DG 1T (19) to 1PG 1T (7)

4 Auckland
New Zealand 2PG 1T (10) to 1G 1PG (9)
New Zealand won series 3-1

1983 *1* Christchurch
New Zealand 3PG 1DG 1T (16) to 3PG 1DG (12)

2 Wellington
New Zealand 1G 1PG (9) to 0

3 Dunedin
New Zealand 1G 3PG (15) to 2T (8)

4 Auckland
New Zealand 4G 2PG 2T (38) to 2PG (6)
New Zealand won series 4-0

1993 *1* Christchurch
New Zealand 5PG 1T (20) to 6PG (18)

2 Wellington
British Isles 4PG 1DG 1T (20) to 1G (7)

3 Auckland
New Zealand 3G 3PG (30) to 1G 2PG (13)
New Zealand won series 2-1

v AUSTRALIA

Played 10 British Isles won 8, Australia won 2, Drawn 0

1930 *1* Sydney
Australia 2T (6) to 1G (5)

1950 *1* Brisbane
British Isles 2G 2PG 1DG (19) to 2PG (6)

2 Sydney
British Isles 3G 1PG 2T (24) to 1T (3)
British Isles won series 2-0

1959 *1* Brisbane
British Isles 1G 2PG 1DG 1T (17) to 2PG (6)

2 Sydney
British Isles 3G 1PG 2T (24) to 1PG (3)
British Isles won series 2-0

1966 *1* Sydney
British Isles 1G 1PG 1T (11) to 1G 1PG (8)

2 Brisbane
British Isles 5G 1PG 1DG (31) to 0
British Isles won series 2-0

1989 *1* Sydney
Australia 4G 1PG 1DG (30) to 3PG 1DG (12)

2 Brisbane
British Isles 1G 2PG 1DG 1T (19) to 1G 2PG (12)

3 Sydney
British Isles 5PG 1T (19) to 1G 4PG (18)
British Isles won series 2-1

BRITISH ISLES RECORDS
(*up to 31 March 1995*)

From 1910 onwards – the tour to South Africa in that year was the first fully representative one in which the four Home Unions co-operated.

TEAM RECORDS

Highest score
31 v Australia (31-0) 1966 Brisbane
v individual countries
28 v S Africa (28-9) 1974 Pretoria
20 v New Zealand (20-7) 1993 Wellington
31 v Australia (31-0) 1966 Brisbane

Biggest winning points margin
31 v Australia (31-0) 1966 Brisbane
v individual countries
19 v S Africa (28-9) 1974 Pretoria
13 v New Zealand (20-7) 1993 Wellington
31 v Australia (31-0) 1966 Brisbane

Highest score by opposing team
38 New Zealand (6-38) 1983 Auckland
by individual countries
34 S Africa (14-34) 1962 Bloemfontein
38 New Zealand (6-38) 1983 Auckland
30 Australia (12-30) 1989 Sydney

Biggest losing points margin
32 v New Zealand (6-38) 1983 Auckland
v individual countries
20 v S Africa (14-34) 1962 Bloemfontein
32 v New Zealand (6-38) 1983 Auckland
18 v Australia (12-30) 1989 Sydney

Most tries by B Isles in an international
5 {
v Australia (24-3) 1950 Sydney
v S Africa (23-22) 1955 Johannesburg
v Australia (24-3) 1959 Sydney
v Australia (31-0) 1966 Brisbane
v S Africa (28-9) 1974 Pretoria
}

Most tries against B Isles in an international
7 by South Africa (9-25) 1955 Cape Town

Most points on overseas tour (all matches)
842 in Australia, New Zealand and Canada (33 matches) 1959
(includes 582 points in 25 matches in New Zealand)

Most tries on overseas tour (all matches)
165 in Australia, New Zealand and Canada (33 matches) 1959
(includes 113 tries in 25 matches in New Zealand)

INDIVIDUAL RECORDS

Most capped player
W J McBride 17 1962-74
in individual positions
Full-back
J P R Williams 8[1] 1971-74
Wing
A J F O'Reilly 9(10)[2] 1955-59
Centre
C M H Gibson 8(12)[3] 1966-71
Fly-half
P Bennett 8 1974-77
Scrum-half
R E G Jeeps 13 1955-62
Prop
G Price 12 1977-83
Hooker
B V Meredith 8 1955-62
Lock
W J McBride 17 1962-74
Flanker
N A A Murphy 8 1959-66
No 8
T M Davies 8[4] 1971-74

[1]*A R Irvine, 9 Tests, played 7 times at full-back and twice as a wing*
[2]*O'Reilly played once as a centre*
[3]*Gibson played 4 times as a fly-half. I R McGeechan, 8 Tests, played 7 times as a centre and once, as a replacement, on the wing*
[4]*Both A E I Pask and J W Telfer (8 Tests each), played 4 Tests at No 8 and 4 Tests at flanker*

Longest international career
W J McBride 13 seasons 1962-74

Most consecutive Tests – 15
W J McBride 1966-74

Most internationals as captain – 6
A R Dawson 1959

Most points in internationals – 66
A G Hastings (6 appearances) 1989-93

Most points in an international – 18
A J P Ward v S Africa 1980 Cape Town
A G Hastings v New Zealand 1993 Christchurch

Most tries in internationals – 6
A J F O'Reilly (10 appearances) 1955-59

Most tries in an international – 2
C D Aarvold v New Zealand 1930 Christchurch
J E Nelson v Australia 1950 Sydney
M J Price v Australia 1959 Sydney
M J Price v New Zealand 1959 Dunedin
D K Jones v Australia 1966 Brisbane
T G R Davies v New Zealand 1971 Christchurch
J J Williams v S Africa 1974 Pretoria
J J Williams v S Africa 1974 Port Elizabeth

Most conversions in internationals – 6
S Wilson (5 matches) 1966

Most conversions in an international – 5
S Wilson v Australia 1966 Brisbane

Most dropped goals in internationals – 2
D Watkins (6 matches) 1966
B John (5 matches) 1968-71
P Bennett (8 matches) 1974-77
C R Andrew (5 matches) 1989-93
(P F Bush also dropped 2 goals in Tests played by British teams prior to 1910)

Most dropped goals in an international – 2
P Bennett v S Africa 1974 Port Elizabeth

Most penalty goals in internationals – 20
A G Hastings (6 matches) 1989-93

Most penalty goals in an international – 6
A G Hastings v New Zealand 1993 Christchurch

Most points for B Isles on overseas tour – 188
B John (17 appearances) 1971 Australia/N Zealand
(including 180 points in 16 appearances in N Zealand)

Most tries for B Isles on overseas tour – 22*
A J F O'Reilly (23 appearances) 1959 Australia/N Zealand/Canada
(includes 17* tries in 17 appearances in N Zealand)
**Includes one penalty try*

Most points for B Isles in international series – 38
A G Hastings (3 appearances) 1993 New Zealand

Most tries for B Isles in international series – 4
J J Williams (4 appearances) 1974 S Africa

Most points for B Isles in any match on tour – 37
A G B Old v South Western Districts 1974 Mossel Bay, S Africa

Most tries for B Isles in any match on tour – 6
D J Duckham v West Coast-Buller 1971 Greymouth, N Zealand
J J Williams v South Western Districts 1974 Mossel Bay, S Africa
(A R Irvine scored 5 tries from full-back v King Country-Wanganui 1977 Taumarunui, N Zealand)

LEADING CAP-WINNERS
(up to 31 March 1995)

ENGLAND

R Underwood	73
C R Andrew	65
P J Winterbottom	58
B C Moore	58
W A Dooley	55
W D C Carling	55
A Neary	43
J V Pullin	42
D Richards	42
P J Wheeler	41
J Leonard	38
J A Probyn	37
D J Duckham	36
G S Pearce	36
D P Rogers	34
W B Beaumont	34
J P Scott	34
J C Guscott	34
J M Webb	33
P W Dodge	32
W W Wakefield	31
F E Cotton	31
M A C Slemen	31
E Evans	30
R Cove-Smith	29
C R Jacobs	29
M P Weston	29
P J Squires	29
R J Hill	29
J Butterfield	28
S J Smith	28
P A G Rendall	28
A T Voyce	27
J S Tucker	27
M C Teague	27
J Carleton	26
C N Lowe	25
J D Currie	25
M S Phillips	25
C B Stevens	25
W H Hare	25
M J Colclough	25

SCOTLAND

A G Hastings	56
S Hastings	53
J M Renwick	52
C T Deans	52
A R Irvine	51
A B Carmichael	50
A J Tomes	48
R J Laidlaw	47
A F McHarg	44
K W Robertson	44
I G Milne	44
D M B Sole	44
J McLauchlan	43
J Y Rutherford	42
D B White	41
C M Chalmers	41
J Jeffrey	40
H F McLeod	40
D M D Rollo	40
J MacD Bannerman	37
I Tukalo	37
A P Burnell	37
I A M Paxton	36
A G Stanger	36
K S Milne	36
F Calder	34
A R Smith	33
I S Smith	32
F A L Laidlaw	32
I R McGeechan	32
D G Leslie	32
D F Cronin	32
N S Bruce	31
I H P Laughland	31
G L Brown	30
G Armstrong	30
W I D Elliot	29
S R P Lineen	29
W M Simmers	28
P K Stagg	28
J W Y Kemp	27
K J F Scotland	27
P C Brown	27
J H Calder	27
D I Johnston	27
G R T Baird	27
G W Weir	27
W E Maclagan	26
D Drysdale	26
J C McCallum	26
G P S Macpherson	26
J B Nelson	25
J P Fisher	25
J R Beattie	25
J W Telfer	25

IRELAND

C M H Gibson	69
W J McBride	63
J F Slattery	61
P A Orr	58
T J Kiernan	54
D G Lenihan	52
M I Keane	51
B J Mullin	50
J W Kyle	46
K W Kennedy	45
M J Kiernan	43
G V Stephenson	42
N A A Murphy	41
W P Duggan	41
K D Crossan	41
N J Henderson	40
R J McLoughlin	40
M T Bradley	39
P M Matthews	38
S Millar	37
H P MacNeill	37
J R Kavanagh	35
W A Mulcahy	35
E O'D Davy	34
T M Ringland	34
D C Fitzgerald	34
P M Dean	32
A C Pedlow	30
G T Hamlet	30
W E Crawford	30
J D Clinch	30
J L Farrell	29
B G M Wood	29
A J F O'Reilly	29
N P J Francis	29
M Sugden	28
J S McCarthy	28
P P A Danaher	28
S P Geoghegan	28
N J Popplewell	28
A M Magee	27
A R Dawson	27
M G Molloy	27
J J Moloney	27
W A Anderson	27
J C Walsh	26
R M Young	26
J B O'Driscoll	26
G R Beamish	25
K D Mullen	25
F P K Bresnihan	25
A T A Duggan	25
B J McGann	25
T O Grace	25
S A McKinney	25
C F Fitzgerald	25
D G Irwin	25
S J Smith	25
B F Robinson	25

WALES

J P R Williams	55
G O Edwards	53
R N Jones	52
I C Evans	51
T G R Davies	46
P T Davies	46
K J Jones	44
G Price	41
M R Hall	39
T M Davies	38
P H Thorburn	37
G O Llewellyn	37
D Williams	36
R M Owen	35

England captain Will Carling, 55 caps for England plus one for the British Lions, celebrates his 50th cap, won in the first international of the season against Romania.

B V Meredith	34
D I E Bebb	34
W D Morris	34
A J Martin	34
R L Norster	34
E W Lewis	34
A Clement	34
W J Bancroft	33
N R Jenkins	33
B Price	32
J R G Stephens	32
G A D Wheel	32
M G Ring	32
M Griffiths	32
J J Williams	30
S P Fenwick	30
W J Trew	29
C I Morgan	29
P Bennett	29
J Squire	29
R W Windsor	28
R G Collins	28
A J Gould	27
W C Powell	27
M C Thomas	27
H J Morgan	27
A M Hadley	27
J Davies	27
R C C Thomas	26
A E I Pask	26
S J Watkins	26
J Taylor	26
G R Jenkins	26
G Travers	25
H Tanner	25
B John	25
N R Gale	25
W D Thomas	25
T D Holmes	25

FRANCE

P Sella	106
S Blanco	93
R Bertranne	69
M Crauste	63
B Dauga	63
J Condom	61
J-P Rives	59
P Berbizier	56
L Rodriguez	56
R Paparemborde	55
F Mesnel	53
A Domenech	52
J Prat	51
W Spanghero	51
J-L Joinel	51
M Celaya	50
P Dintrans	50
O Roumat	50
A Boniface	48
J-P Lux	47
J-C Skréla	46
D Erbani	46
P Lagisquet	46
M Vannier	43
L Armary	43
P Saint-André	43
J-P Garuet	42
E Champ	42
P Ondarts	42
M Cecillon	41
J Dupuy	40
C Darrouy	40
F Haget	40

J-M Aguirre	39
G Dufau	38
D Camberabero	36
J-B Lafond	36
G Boniface	35
E Cester	35
A Paco	35
E Ribère	34
J Bouquet	34
P Villepreux	34
J Iraçabal	34
J-P Romeu	34
L Cabannes	34
G Basquet	33
C Lacaze	33
C Dourthe	33
D Dubroca	33
J Gachassin	32
J-P Bastiat	32
A Benazzi	32
A Cassayet	31
A Jauréguy	31
M Prat	31
F Moncla	31
G Cholley	31
D Codorniou	31
P Albaladéjo	30
A Roques	30
R Bénésis	30
A Lorieux	30
R Biénès	29
L Mias	29
P Benetton	29
J Trillo	28
J-P Lescarboura	28
T Lacroix	28
H Rancoule	27
P Lacroix	27
J-C Berejnoi	27
C Carrère	27
J Fouroux	27
J Gallion	27
J-L Sadourny	27
B Chevallier	26
J Barthe	26
J-M Cabanier	26
A Gruarin	26
J-L Azarète	26
A Vaquerin	26
M Andrieu	26
R Martine	25
J Maso	25
J-L Averous	25
P Estève	25

SOUTH AFRICA

F C H Du Preez	38
J H Ellis	38
J F K Marais	35
J P Engelbrecht	33
J L Gainsford	33
J T Claassen	28
H E Botha	28
F du T Roux	27
L G Wilson	27
T P Bedford	25
D J de Villiers	25
P J F Greyling	25
S H Nomis	25
P J Visagie	25
L C Moolman	24
D M Gerber	24
D J Hopwood	22
A C Koch	22
M Du Plessis	22
J A du Rand	21
M T S Stofberg	21
J S Germishuys	20

NEW ZEALAND

J J Kirwan	63
S B T Fitzpatrick	62
G W Whetton	58
C E Meads	55
S C McDowell	46
G J Fox	46
R W Loe	44
A M Haden	41
I A Kirkpatrick	39
K R Tremain	38
B G Williams	38
I D Jones	37
G A Knight	36
A G Dalton	35
A J Whetton	35
M N Jones	35
B J Robertson	34
S S Wilson	34
M G Mexted	34
W J Whineray	32
D B Clarke	31
M W Shaw	30
T J Wright	30
S M Going	29
Z V Brooke	28
R W Norton	27
J T Stanley	27
M J Pierce	26
J K R Timu	26
B J Lochore	25
M R Brewer	25
W K Little	25
B E McLeod	24
K F Gray	24
I J Clarke	24
J C Ashworth	24
D S Loveridge	24
W T Taylor	24
R A White	23
B G Fraser	23
G T M Bachop	23
D J Graham	22
D Young	22
W T Shelford	22
F E Bunce	22
G N K Mourie	21
M J B Hobbs	21
K L Skinner	20
C R Laidlaw	20
I N MacEwan	20
P J Whiting	20
C I Green	20

AUSTRALIA

D I Campese	86
M P Lynagh	67
N C Farr-Jones	63
S P Poidevin	59
P G Johnson	42
P N Kearns	42
A R Miller	41
T A Lawton	41
S A G Cutler	40
G V Davis	39
A G Slack	39
A J Daly	39
A J McIntyre	38
E J A McKenzie	38
J E Thornett	37
J N B Hipwell	36
A A Shaw	36
B T Gavin	36
B J Moon	35
R J McCall	35
S N Tuynman	34
T J Horan	33
J S Little	31
N M Shehadie	30
P E McLean	30
M E Loane	28
S A Williams	28
K W Catchpole	27
G A Shaw	27
C T Burke	26
E E Rodriguez	26
J S Miller	26
R B Prosser	25
G Cornelsen	25
M G Ella	25
R G Gould	25
P C Grigg	25
M J Hawker	25
J K Lenehan	24
J P L White	24
J W Cole	24
G Fay	24
R Phelps	23
M P Burke	23
M C Roebuck	23
J A Eales	23
R A Smith	22
J E C Meadows	22
W A Campbell	22
D J Wilson	22
E T Bonis	21
P F Hawthorne	21
R J Heming	21
A N McGill	21
W H Cerutti	21
A S Cameron	20
B J Ellwood	20
C J Windon	20

WORLD'S LEADING CAP-WINNERS

(up to 31 March 1995)

The following list includes appearances for individual countries in major international matches.

P Sella	France	106
S Blanco	France	93
D I Campese	Australia	86
R Underwood	England	73
C M H Gibson	Ireland	69
R Bertranne	France	69
M P Lynagh	Australia	67
C R Andrew	England	65
M Crauste	France	63
W J McBride	Ireland	63
B Dauga	France	63
N C Farr-Jones	Australia	63
J J Kirwan	New Zealand	63
S B T Fitzpatrick	New Zealand	62
J Condom	France	61
J F Slattery	Ireland	61
J-P Rives	France	59
S P Poidevin	Australia	59
P A Orr	Ireland	58
G W Whetton	New Zealand	58
P J Winterbottom	England	58
B C Moore	England	58
L Rodriguez	France	56
P Berbizier	France	56
A G Hastings	Scotland	56
C E Meads	New Zealand	55
J P R Williams	Wales	55
R Paparemborde	France	55
W A Dooley	England	55
W D C Carling	England	55
T J Kiernan	Ireland	54
G O Edwards	Wales	53
S Hastings	Scotland	53
F Mesnel	France	53
A Domenech	France	52
J M Renwick	Scotland	52
C T Deans	Scotland	52
R N Jones	Wales	52
D G Lenihan	Ireland	52
J Prat	France	51
W Spanghero	France	51
A R Irvine	Scotland	51
M I Keane	Ireland	51
J-L Joinel	France	51
I C Evans	Wales	51
M Celaya	France	50
A B Carmichael	Scotland	50
P Dintrans	France	50
B J Mullin	Ireland	50
O Roumat	France	50

The following list incorporates appearances by home countries' players for British Isles teams (the Lions) in international matches against New Zealand, Australia and South Africa (up to 31 March 1995). The number of Lions appearances is shown in brackets.

P Sella	France	106	
S Blanco	France	93	
D I Campese	Australia	86	
C M H Gibson	Ireland	81	(12)
W J McBride	Ireland	80	(17)
R Underwood	England	79	(6)
C R Andrew	England	70	(5)
R Bertranne	France	69	
M P Lynagh	Australia	67	
J F Slattery	Ireland	65	(4)
P J Winterbottom	England	65	(7)
G O Edwards	Wales	63	(10)
J P R Williams	Wales	63	(8)
B C Moore	England	63	(5)
M Crauste	France	63	
B Dauga	France	63	
N C Farr-Jones	Australia	63	
J J Kirwan	New Zealand	63	
A G Hastings	Scotland	62	(6)
S B T Fitzpatrick	New Zealand	62	
J Condom	France	61	
A R Irvine	Scotland	60	(9)
T J Kiernan	Ireland	59	(5)
J-P Rives	France	59	
P A Orr	Ireland	59	(1)
S P Poidevin	Australia	59	
G W Whetton	New Zealand	58	
I C Evans	Wales	57	(6)
W A Dooley	England	57	(2)
W D C Carling	England	56	(1)
L Rodriguez	France	56	
P Berbizier	France	56	
R N Jones	Wales	55	(3)
S Hastings	Scotland	55	(2)
C E Meads	New Zealand	55	
R Paparemborde	France	55	
J M Renwick	Scotland	53	(1)
G Price	Wales	53	(12)
F Mesnel	France	53	
A Domenech	France	52	
C T Deans	Scotland	52	
J W Kyle	Ireland	52	(6)
M I Keane	Ireland	52	(1)
D G Lenihan	Ireland	52	
J Prat	France	51	
W Spanghero	France	51	
T G R Davies	Wales	51	(5)
J McLauchlan	Scotland	51	(8)
J-L Joinel	France	51	
R J Laidlaw	Scotland	51	(4)
B J Mullin	Ireland	51	(1)
M Celaya	France	50	
A B Carmichael	Scotland	50	
P Dintrans	France	50	
O Roumat	France	50	

Most appearances for the Lions are by W J McBride (Ireland) 17, R E G Jeeps (England) 13, C M H Gibson (Ireland) 12, G Price (Wales) 12, and A J F O'Reilly (Ireland), R H Williams (Wales), and G O Edwards (Wales) 10 each, up to 31 March 1995.

INTERNATIONAL REFEREES 1994-95

Leading Referees

Up to 31 March 1995, in major international matches. These include all matches for which senior members of the International Board have awarded caps, and also all matches played in the World Cup final stages.

12 or more internationals

W D Bevan	Wales	26	**F Palmade**	France	17
C Norling	Wales	25	**B S Cumberlege**	England	16
K D Kelleher	Ireland	23	**O E Doyle**	Ireland	16
D G Walters	Wales	23	**D I H Burnett**	Ireland	15
M Joseph	Wales	22	**C H Gadney**	England	15
R C Williams	Ireland	21	**S R Hilditch**	Ireland	15
K V J Fitzgerald	Australia	21	**I David**	Wales	14
F A Howard	England	20	**Dr I R Vanderfield**	Australia	14
J M Fleming	Scotland	20	**R G Byres**	Australia	13
D J Bishop	New Zealand	20	**J P Murphy**	New Zealand	13
A M Hosie	Scotland	19	**N R Sanson**	Scotland	13
Capt M J Dowling	Ireland	18	**K H Lawrence**	New Zealand	13
A E Freethy	Wales	18	**R F Johnson**	England	12
R C Quittenton	England	18	**T D Schofield**	Wales	12
J R West	Ireland	18	**T H Vile**	Wales	12
J B Anderson	Scotland	18	**W Williams**	England	12
R Hourquet	France	18	**A R MacNeill**	Australia	12
D P D'Arcy	Ireland	17	**E F Morrison**	England	12

Major international match appearances 1994-95

Matches controlled between 1 April 1994 and 31 March 1995.

1994

Pt v W	**B Leask** (Australia)
Sp v W	**D J Bishop** (New Zealand)
SA v E(2)	**C J Hawke** (New Zealand)
Arg v S(2)	***W J Erickson** (Australia)
C v F	**I Rogers** (South Africa)
A v I(2)	**J Dumé** (France)
C v W	**I Rogers** (South Africa)
Fj v W	**E Sklar** (Argentina)
A v It(2)	**I Rogers** (South Africa)
Tg v W	**E Sklar** (Argentina)
WS v W	**B Leask** (Australia)
NZ v F(2)	**W D Bevan** (Wales)
NZ v SA(2)	**B W Stirling** (Ireland)
NZ v SA	**R Yeman** (Wales)
A v WS	***G K Wahlstrom** (New Zealand)
A v NZ	**E F Morrison** (England)
R v W	***D T M McHugh** (Ireland)
SA v Arg(2)	**G K Wahlstrom** (New Zealand)
W v It	**K W McCartney** (Scotland)
I v US	***J-L Rolandi** (Argentina)
E v R	***S Neethling** (South Africa)
S v SA	**O E Doyle** (Ireland)
W v SA	***D Méné** (France)
E v C	**W J Erickson** (Australia)
F v C	**B Leask** (Australia)

1995

S v C	***C Thomas** (Wales)
F v W	***J J M Pearson** (England)
I v E	**P Thomas** (France)
E v F	**K W McCartney** (Scotland)
S v I	**W D Bevan** (Wales)
F v S	**D T M McHugh** (Ireland)
W v E	**D Méné** (France)
I v F	**C Thomas** (Wales)
S v W	***S Lander** (England)
E v S	**B W Stirling** (Ireland)
W v I	**R J Megson** (Scotland)

**Denotes debut in a major international*

Referees dismissing players in a major international

A E Freethy	E v NZ	1925	**R T Burnett**	A v E	1975
K D Kelleher	S v NZ	1967	**W M Cooney**	A v Fj	1976

N R Sanson (2)	W v I	1977
D I H Burnett	E v W	1980
C Norling	F v I	1984
K V J Fitzgerald	NZ v W	1987*
F A Howard	A v W	1987*
K V J Fitzgerald	Fj v E	1988
O E Doyle	Arg v F	1988
B W Stirling (2)	E v Fj	1989
F A Howard	W v F	1990
F A Howard	S v F	1990
F A Howard	Nm v W	1990
A J Spreadbury	A v F	1990
C Norling	A v F	1990
C J Hawke	E v Arg	1990
E F Morrison	R v F	1991
J M Fleming (2)	Arg v WS	1991*
S R Hilditch (2)	F v E	1992
D J Bishop	NZ v Wld	1992
E F Morrison	A v SA	1993
I Rogers (2)	C v F	1994
D Méné	W v E	1995

* *World Cup matches*

INTERNATIONAL REFEREES

The list which follows shows referees who have controlled major internationals (i.e. games for which a senior member country of the IB has awarded caps, or the final stages of the official World Cup) since 1876, when referees were first appointed, up to 31 March 1995.

ABBREVIATIONS

A – Australia; *Arg* – Argentina; *AW* – Anglo-Welsh; *B* – British Forces' and Home Union Teams; *Bb* – Barbarians; *BI* – British Isles; *C* – Canada; *Cv* – New Zealand Cavaliers; *Cz* – Czechoslovakia; *E* – England; *F* – France; *Fj* – Fiji; *GB* – Great Britain; *G* – Germany; *I* – Ireland; *It* – Italy; *J* – Japan; *K* – New Zealand Kiwis; *M* – New Zealand Maoris; *Nm* – Namibia; *NZ* – New Zealand; *NZA* – New Zealand Army; *P* – President's XV; *Pt* – Portugal; *R* – Romania; *S* – Scotland; *SA* – South Africa; *SAm* – South America; *SK* – South Korea; *Sp* – Spain; *Tg* – Tonga; *US* – United States of America; *W* – Wales; *Wld* – World XV; *WS* – Western Samoa; *Z* – Zimbabwe; (C) – Special Centenary Match; (R) – Replacement. Entries in square brackets [ ] indicate matches in the World Cup final stages.

N.B. The Australian Rugby Union now recognises the internationals played by the New South Wales touring teams of the 1920s as cap matches.

Ackermann, C J (South Africa) 1953 *SA v A* (2), 1955 *SA v BI*, 1958 *SA v F*

Acton, W H (Ireland) 1926 *W v E, E v S*

Adams, A (South Africa) 1991 *US v F* (2)

Alderson, F H R (England) 1903 *S v I*

Allan, M A (Scotland) 1931 *I v W, I v SA*, 1933 *E v I, I v W*, 1934 *I v E*, 1935 *E v I, I v W*, 1936 *I v E*, 1937 *I v W*, 1947 *I v E*, 1948 *I v W*

Allen, J W (Ireland) 1906 *W v S, S v E*

Anderson, C (Scotland) 1928 *I v F*

Anderson, I (South Africa) 1993 *Z v W*

Anderson, J B (Scotland) 1981 *W v E, I v A*, 1982 *R v F*, 1983 *I v E, A v NZ*, 1984 *E v W*, 1986 *W v F, NZ v A*, 1987 [*A v US, A v I, F v A*], 1988 *A v NZ*(2), 1989 *I v F, R v E, F v B*, 1991 [*E v It, Arg v WS*]

Anderson, J H (South Africa) 1903 *SA v GB*

Angus, A W (Scotland) 1924 *W v E*, 1927 *I v A*

Ashmore, H L (England) 1890 *S v I*, 1891 *S v W*, 1892 *S v I*, 1894 *I v S*, 1895 *S v I*

Austin, A W C (Scotland) 1952 *W v F*, 1953 *I v E*, 1954 *I v W*

Austry, R (France) 1972 *E v I*

Badger, Dr (England) 1900 *I v S*

Baise, M (South Africa) 1967 *SA v F* (2), 1968 *SA v BI* (2), 1969 *SA v A*, 1974 *SA v BI* (2)

Baise, S (South Africa) 1969 *SA v A*

Barnes, P (Australia) 1938 *A v NZ*

Baxter, J (England) 1913 *F v S, S v I*, 1914 *I v S*, 1920 *S v I*, 1921 *W v S, I v S*, 1923 *W v S*, 1925 *W v S, I v W*

Bean, A S (England) 1939 *W v S*, 1945 *W v F*, 1946 *F v W*, 1947 *F v W, W v A*, 1948 *S v F, W v F*, 1949 *S v I*

Beattie, R A (Scotland) 1937 *E v W*, 1938 *W v E*, 1945 *B v F*, 1947 *W v E, I v A*, 1948 *E v W*, 1949 *I v E*, 1950 *E v I, I v W*

Beattie, W H (Australia) 1899 *A v GB*, 1904 *A v GB*

Bell, T (Ireland) 1932 *S v W*, 1933 *E v W*

Bevan, W D (Wales) 1985 *E v R*, 1986 *F v E, NZ v A* (2), 1987 [*NZ v Fj, F v Z*], *A v NZ*, 1988 *I v WS*, 1990 *NZ v S*, 1991 *I v F*, [*F v Fj, S v WS, E v A*], 1992 *S v E, E v I, NZ v Wld* (2), 1993 *F v S, NZ v A, C v A, Arg v SA* (2), 1994 *S v F, NZ v F* (2), 1995 *S v I*

Beves, G (South Africa) 1896 *SA v GB*

Bezuidenhout, G P (South Africa) 1976 *SA v NZ* (3)

Bishop, D J (New Zealand) 1986 *Fj v W, R v F, I v R*, 1987 [*W v Tg, W v C*], 1988 *A v E* (2), *E v A, S v A*, 1990 *S v E, I v W*, 1991 *S v W, W v I*, [*A v Arg, F v E*], 1992 *NZ v Wld, SA v A*, 1993 *F v A* (2), 1994 *Sp v W*

Bisset, W M (South Africa) 1896 *SA v GB*

Bonnet, J-P (France) 1979 *W v E*, 1980 *S v E, SA v BI* (2), 1981 *I v E, Arg v E* (2), 1982 *W v S*

Bott, J G (Scotland) 1931 *W v S*, 1933 *W v S*

Boundy, L M (England) 1955 *S v I*, 1956 *W v S*, 1957 *F v S, I v F, S v I, R v F*, 1958 *S v F*, 1959 *S v I*, 1961 *S v SA*

Bowden, G (Scotland) 1910 *F v E*

Bowen, D H (Wales) 1905 *E v S*

Bradburn, T J (England) 1928 *F v A*, 1929 *F v G*

Bressy, Y (France) 1988 *W v S*

Brook, P G (England) 1963 *F v W*, 1964 *W v S*, 1965 *W v I, I v SA*, 1966 *F v I, It v F, R v F*

Brown, A (Australia) 1907 *A v NZ*

Brown, D A (England) 1960 *I v W, It v F*

Brunton, J (England) 1924 *W v NZ*

Buchanan, A (Scotland) 1877 *I v S*, 1880 *S v I*

Bullerwell, I M (England) 1988 *W v R*, 1990 *F v R*

Burger F (South Africa) 1989 *F v A* (2), 1990 *S v Arg*, 1992 *S v F, F v I, Arg v F* (2), 1993 *S v NZ, E v NZ*

Burmeister, R D (South Africa) 1949 *SA v NZ* (2), 1953 *SA v A*, 1955 *SA v BI* (2), 1960 *SA v NZ* (2), 1961 *SA v A*

Burnand, F W (England) 1890 *I v W*

Burnet, W (Scotland) 1932 *I v E*, 1934 *W v I*

Burnett, D I H (Ireland) 1977 *W v E*, 1979 *F v W*, 1980 *E v W*, 1981 *S v W, E v S*, 1982 *W v F, F v Arg*, 1983 *E v F*, 1984 *S v E, A v NZ*, 1985 *E v F, NZ v A*, 1986 *S v F*, 1987 [*S v Z, NZ v S*]

Burnett, R T (Australia) 1973 *A v Tg*, 1974 *A v NZ*,

1975 *A v E*, *A v J*, 1978 *A v W*
Burrell, G (Scotland) 1958 *E v I*, 1959 *W v I*
Burrell, R P (Scotland) 1966 *I v W*, 1967 *I v F*, *F v NZ*, 1969 *I v E*, *F v W*
Butt, C C (Australia) 1914 *A v NZ*
Byres, R G (Australia) 1976 *A v Fj*, 1978 *A v W*, 1979 *A v I* (2), *A v NZ*, 1980 *A v NZ*, 1981 *NZ v S*, 1982 *A v S* (2), 1983 *NZ v BI* (2), 1984 *I v W*, *W v F*

Calitz, M (South Africa) 1961 *SA v I*
Calmet, R (France) 1970 *E v W*
Calver, E W (England) 1914 *F v I*
Camardon, A (Argentina) 1960 *Arg v F*
Campbell, A (New Zealand) 1908 *NZ v AW* (2)
Carlson, K R V (South Africa) 1962 *SA v BI*
Cartwright, V H (England) 1906 *I v S*, 1909 *S v I*, 1910 *I v S*, *F v I*, 1911 *S v I*
Castens, H H(South Africa) 1891 *SA v GB*
Ceccon, A (France) 1991 *I v E*, *R v S*
Chambers, J (Ireland) 1888 *W v S*, *I v M*, 1890 *S v E*, 1891 *E v S*
Chapman, W S (Australia) 1938 *A v NZ* (2)
Charman, R (England) 1919 *W v NZA*
Chevrier, G (France) 1980 *I v S*
Chiene, Dr J (Scotland) 1879 *I v S*
Clark, K H (Ireland) 1973 *E v F*, 1974 *S v F*, 1976 *F v E*
Cochrane, C B (Australia) 1907 *A v NZ*
Coffey, J J (Ireland) 1912 *S v F*
Colati, L (Fiji) 1991 [*I v J*]
Coles, P (England) 1903 *W v I*, 1905 *S v I*
Collett C K (Australia) 1981 *NZ v S*
Combe, A (Ireland) 1876 *I v E*
Cook, H G (Ireland) 1886 *S v E*
Cooney, R C (Australia) 1929 *A v NZ*, 1930 *A v BI*, 1932 *A v NZ*, 1934 *A v NZ*
Cooney, W M (Australia) 1972 *A v F*, 1975 *A v E*, *A v J*, 1976 *A v Fj*
Cooper, Dr P F (England) 1952 *I v W*, 1953 *S v W*, *W v I*, *F v It*, *W v NZ*, 1954 *I v NZ*, *W v S*, *It v F*, 1956 *F v I*, *W v F*, *It v F*, 1957 *F v W*
Corley, H H (Ireland) 1906 *S v SA*, 1908 *S v E*
Corr, W S (Australia) 1899 *A v GB* (2)
Costello, J (Fiji) 1972 *Fj v A*
Craven, W S D (England) 1920 *F v W*
Crawford, S H (Ireland) 1913 *W v E*, *S v W*, 1920 *S v W*, 1921 *S v E*
Cross, W (Scotland) 1877 *S v E*
Crowe, K J (Australia) 1965 *A v SA*, 1966 *A v BI*, 1968 *A v NZ*, 1976 *A v Fj*
Cumberlege, B S (England) 1926 *S v I*, *W v I*, 1927 *S v F*, *I v S*, *I v W*, 1928 *S v I*, 1929 *F v I*, *S v F*, *I v S*, 1930 *I v F*, *S v I*, 1931 *I v S*, 1932 *S v SA*, *S v I*, 1933 *I v S*, 1934 *S v I*
Cunningham, J G (Scotland) 1913 *W v I*, 1921 *F v I*
Cuny, Dr A (France) 1976 *W v S*
Curnow, J (Canada) 1976 *US v F*
Currey, F I (England) 1887 *S v W*

Dallas, J D (Scotland) 1905 *W v NZ*, 1908 *I v W*, 1909 *W v E*, *I v E*, 1910 *E v W*, *I v W*, 1911 *I v E*, 1912 *I v W*
D'Arcy, D P (Ireland) 1967 *E v F*, *E v S*, *F v W*, *F v R*, 1968 *E v W*, *S v E*, *F v SA*, 1969 *E v F*, *W v E*, 1970 *W v S*, 1971 *W v E*, 1973 *F v NZ*, *F v W*, *F v R*, 1975 *E v S*, *F v Arg*, *W v A*
David, I (Wales) 1938 *E v S*, 1939 *S v E*, 1947 *E v S*, 1952 *S v F*, *I v S*, *E v I*, 1953 *S v I*, 1954 *S v F*, *E v NZ*, *S v NZ*, *F v NZ*, *F v E*, 1955 *I v F*, 1956 *F v E*
Davidson, I G (Ireland) 1911 *S v W*
Day, H L V (England) 1934 *S v W*
Day, P W (South Africa) 1903 *SA v GB*
Dedet, L (France) 1906 *F v NZ*, *F v E*
De Bruyn, C J (South Africa) 1969 *SA v A*, 1974 *SA v BI* (2)
Delany, M G (Ireland) 1899 *S v W*, 1900 *S v E*
Desclaux, M (France) 1992 *W v S*
Dickie, A I (Scotland) 1954 *F v I*, *E v I*, *W v F*, 1955 *I v E*, *W v I*, 1956 *E v I*, *I v W*, 1957 *W v E*, *I v E*, 1958 *W v A*, *W v F*
Dodds, J (Ireland) 1898 *S v E*
Domercq, G (France) 1972 *S v NZ*, 1973 *W v E*, 1976 *E v W*, 1977 *S v W*, 1978 *I v W*
Donaldson, S (Ireland) 1937 *S v E*
Donaldson, W P (South Africa) 1903 *SA v GB*

Don Wauchope, A R (Scotland) 1889 *W v I*, 1890 *E v I*, 1893 *I v E*
Doocey, T F (New Zealand) 1976 *NZ v I*, 1983 *E v S*, *F v W*
Douglas, W M (Wales) 1891 *I v E*, 1894 *E v I*, 1896 *S v E*, 1903 *E v S*
Doulcet, J-C (France) 1989 *S v W*
Dowling, M J (Ireland) 1947 *S v W*, 1950 *W v S*, *S v E*, *W v F*, 1951 *W v E*, *S v W*, *F v W*, *E v S*, *S v SA*, 1952 *W v S*, *F v SA*, *S v E*, 1953 *W v E*, *E v S*, 1954 *E v W*, 1955 *S v W*, 1956 *S v F*, *S v E*
Downes, A D (New Zealand) 1913 *NZ v A*
Doyle, O E (Ireland) 1984 *W v S*, *R v S*, *W v A*, 1987 *E v S*, 1988 *F v E*, *Arg v F* (2), *W v WS*, 1989 *F v S*, 1990 *F v E*, 1991 [*It v US*, *Fj v R*], 1992 *W v F*, 1993 *F v W*, *W v C*, 1994 *S v SA*
Drennan, V (Ireland) 1914 *W v S*
Duffy, B (New Zealand) 1977 *NZ v BI*
Dumé, J (France) 1993 *W v E*, *S v W*, 1994 *A v I* (2)
Duncan, J (New Zealand) 1908 *NZ v AW*
Durand, C (France) 1969 *E v S*, 1970 *I v S*, 1971 *E v S*

Eckhold, A E (New Zealand) 1923 *NZ v A*
Elliott, H B (England) 1955 *F v S*, *F v It*, 1956 *I v S*
Engelbrecht, Dr G K (South Africa) 1964 *SA v W*
Erickson, W J (Australia) 1994 *Arg v S* (2), *E v C*
Evans, F T (New Zealand) 1904 *NZ v GB*
Evans, G (England) 1905 *E v NZ*, 1908 *W v A*
Evans, W J (Wales) 1958 *I v A*, *F v E*

Farquhar, A B (New Zealand) 1961 *NZ v F* (3), 1962 *NZ v A* (2), 1964 *NZ v A*
Faull, J W (Wales) 1936 *E v NZ*, *S v I*, 1937 *E v I*
Ferguson, C F (Australia) 1963 *A v E*, 1965 *A v SA*, 1968 *A v F*, 1969 *A v W*, 1971 *A v SA* (2)
Ferguson, P (Australia) 1914 *A v NZ*
Findlay, D G (Scotland) 1895 *I v E*, 1896 *E v W*, *E v I*, 1897 *I v E*, 1898 *E v I*, 1899 *I v E*, 1900 *E v I*
Findlay, J C (Scotland) 1902 *I v W*, 1903 *I v E*, 1904 *E v W*, *I v W*, 1905 *I v NZ*, 1911 *I v F*
Finlay, A K (Australia) 1961 *A v Fj*, 1962 *A v NZ*
Fitzgerald, K V J (Australia) 1985 *I v F*, *W v I*, *NZ v E* (2), *Arg v NZ* (2), 1987 [*I v W*, *E v US*, *NZ v W*, *NZ v F*], 1988 *Fj v E*, 1989 *S v I*, *W v E*, *SA v Wld* (2), 1990 *A v US*, 1991 *F v W*, *S v I*, [*Fj v C*, *NZ v It*, *S v E*]
Fleming, G R (Scotland) 1879 *S v E*
Fleming, J M (Scotland) 1985 *I v E*, 1986 *A v Arg* (2), 1987 *E v F*, [*A v J*, *Fj v Arg*], *F v R*, 1989 *F v W*, 1990 *NZ v A*, 1991 *W v F*, [*E v NZ*, *Arg v WS* (R), *I v A*, *NZ v A*], 1992 *A v NZ*, 1993 *E v F*, *NZ v WS*, *F v R*, 1994 *F v I*, *E v W*
Fleury, A L (New Zealand) 1959 *NZ v BI*
Fong, A S (New Zealand) 1946 *NZ v A*, 1950 *NZ v BI*
Fordham, R J (Australia) 1986 *E v W*, *F v I*, *Arg v F* (2), 1987 [*NZ v It*, *F v R*]
Fornès, E (Argentina) 1954 *Arg v F* (2)
Forsyth, R A (New Zealand) 1958 *NZ v A*
Frames, P R (South Africa) 1891 *SA v GB*
Francis, R C (New Zealand) 1984 *E v A*, *I v A*, 1985 *Arg v F* (2), 1986 *W v S*, *S v E*, *WS v W*
Freeman, W L (Ireland) 1932 *E v SA*
Freethy, A E (Wales) 1923 *F v E*, 1924 *E v F*, *I v NZ*, *F v US*, 1925 *E v NZ*, *I v S*, *S v E*, *F v E*, 1926 *E v F*, 1927 *F v E*, 1928 *I v E*, *E v F*, 1929 *E v I*, *F v E*, 1930 *I v E*, *E v F*, 1931 *E v I*, *F v E*
Fright, W H (New Zealand) 1956 *NZ v SA* (2)
Frood, J (New Zealand) 1952 *NZ v A*
Fry, H A (England) 1945 *F v B*
Furness, D C (Australia) 1952 *A v Fj* (2), 1954 *A v Fj*

Gadney, C H (England) 1935 *S v NZ*, *W v NZ*, 1936 *S v W*, *W v I*, 1937 *W v S*, *I v S*, 1938 *S v W*, *S v I*, 1939 *I v S*, 1940 *F v B*, 1946 *F v B*, 1947 *F v S*, *S v I*, 1948 *F v A*, *I v S*
Games, J (Wales) 1909 *E v A*, 1913 *E v F*, 1914 *F v E*
Gardiner, F (Ireland) 1912 *S v E*, *I v SA*(R)
Gardner, J A (Scotland) 1884 *E v W*, 1887 *W v I*
Garling, A F (Australia) 1981 *A v NZ* (2)
Garrard, W G (New Zealand) 1899 *A v GB*
Gilchrist, N R (New Zealand) 1936 *M v A*
Gillespie, J I (Scotland) 1907 *W v E*, 1911 *W v E*
Gilliard, P (England) 1902 *W v S*
Gillies, C R (New Zealand) 1958 *NZ v A* (2), 1959 *NZ v BI* (2)

Gilliland, R W (Ireland) 1964 *It v F*, 1965 *S v W*, *E v F*, *F v W*, *F v R*, 1966 *E v W*, 1967 *F v A*
Gillmore, W N (England) 1956 *F v Cz*, 1958 *I v S*, *It v F*
Glasgow, O B (Ireland) 1953 *F v S*, *F v W*, 1954 *S v E*, 1955 *W v E*, *F v W*
Goulding, W J (Ireland) 1882 *I v W*
Gourlay, I W (South Africa) 1976 *SA v NZ*
Gouws, Dr J (South Africa) 1977 *SA v Wld*
Greenlees, Dr J R C (Scotland) 1913 *I v E*, 1914 *E v W*
Grierson, T F E (Scotland) 1970 *I v SA*, 1971 *F v R*, 1972 *F v E* , 1973 *W v I*, 1975 *E v F*
Griffin, Dr J (South Africa) 1891 *SA v GB*
Griffiths, A A (New Zealand) 1946 *M v A*, 1952 *NZ v A*
Guillemard, A G (England) 1877 *E v I*, 1878 *E v S*, 1879 *E v I*, 1880 *E v S*, 1881 *E v I*, *E v W*
Gurdon, E T (England) 1898 *I v S*, 1899 *S v I*

Hamilton, F M (Ireland) 1902 *S v E*
Harland, R W (Ireland) 1922 *F v W*, 1925 *W v F*, 1926 *F v W*, 1928 *W v E*, *S v W*, *F v W*, 1929 *E v W*, 1931 *W v F*
Harnett, G H (England) 1896 *W v S*, 1901 *S v I*, *W v I*
Harris, G A (Ireland) 1910 *S v F*
Harrison, G L (New Zealand) 1980 *Fj v A*, 1981 *A v F*, 1983 *A v US*, *F v A* (2), 1984 *Fj v A*
Harrison, H C (England) 1922 *F v S*
Hartley, A (England) 1900 *W v S*
Haslett, F W (Ireland) 1934 *W v E*, *E v S*, 1935 *E v W*, *W v S*, 1936 *W v E*
Hawke, C J (New Zealand) 1990 *I v Arg*, *E v Arg*, 1992 *A v S*, 1994 *SA v E* (2)
Haydon, N V (Australia) 1957 *A v NZ*
Helliwell, D (England) 1926 *S v W*, 1927 *W v A*, 1929 *W v S*, 1930 *F v S*, *W v I*, *G v F*, *F v W*
Herbert, D (Wales) 1883 *W v E*
Herck, M (Romania) 1938 *F v G*
High, C J (England) 1987 *F v W*, *W v US*, 1990 *NZ v S*
Hilditch, S R (Ireland) 1984 *S v A*, 1985 *W v Fj*, 1987 [*R v Z*, *S v R*], 1988 *E v W*, 1989 *E v F*, *NZ v A*, *S v R*, 1991 *E v S*, [*F v C*, *S v NZ*], 1992 *F v E*, *E v SA*, 1993 *SA v F*, 1994 *F v E*
Hill, A (England) 1902 *I v S*
Hill, E D (New Zealand) 1949 *NZ v A*
Hill, G R (England) 1883 *S v W*, 1884 *S v I*, *W v I*, 1885 *S v W*, 1886 *S v I*, 1887 *W v E*, *I v S*, 1888 *I v W*, 1889 *E v M*, 1891 *I v S*, 1893 *I v S*
Hill, W W (Australia) 1913 *US v NZ*
Hinton, W P (Ireland) 1921 *S v F*
Hodgson, J (England) 1892 *W v S*
Hofmeyr, E W (South Africa) 1949 *SA v NZ* (2), 1961 *SA v A*, 1963 *SA v A*
Hollander, S (New Zealand) 1930 *NZ v BI* (3), 1931 *NZ v A*
Hollis, M (England) 1931 *F v G*
Holmes, E (England) 1931 *W v SA*, 1932 *W v I*
Holmes, E B (England) 1892 *I v W*, 1894 *W v S*, 1895 *S v W*, *W v I*, 1896 *I v S*, *I v W*, 1897 *S v I*
Horak, A T (South Africa) 1938 *SA v BI*
Hosie, A M (Scotland) 1973 *I v E*, 1974 *F v I*, 1975 *W v E*, 1976 *E v I*, *F v A*, 1977 *F v W*, *I v F*, , 1979 *W v I*, *I v E*, 1980 *W v F*, *F v I*, 1981 *E v F*, *R v NZ*, 1982 *E v I*, *NZ v A* (2), 1983 *I v F*, *E v NZ*, 1984 *F v E*
Hourquet, R (France) 1983 *S v NZ*, 1984 *E v I*, *SA v E* (2), *SA v SAm* (2), 1985 *S v W*, 1987 *I v E*, [*E v J*, *W v E*], 1988 *I v E*, 1989 *A v BI* (2), 1990 *W v S*, *NZ v A* (2), 1991 [*W v Arg*, *Z v J*]
Howard, F A (England) 1984 *I v S*, 1986 *I v W*, *A v F*, *NZ v F*, 1987 [*F v S*, *I v C*, *A v W*], 1988 *W v F*, *A v NZ*, 1989 *NZ v F*(2), 1990 *W v F*, *S v F*, *Nm v W* (2), *W v Bb*, 1991 *A v W*, [*S v I*, *NZ v C*], 1992 *I v W*
Hughes, D M (Wales) 1965 *F v It*, 1966 *S v F*, *I v S*, 1967 *I v E*, *S v I*
Hughes, J (England) 1935 *I v S*
Hughes, P E (England) 1977 *F v R*, 1978 *I v S*
Humphreys, W H (England) 1893 *S v W*, *W v I*

Ireland, J C H (Scotland) 1938 *I v E*, *W v I*, 1939 *E v W*, *E v I*, *I v W*
Irving, A L C (Australia) 1934 *A v NZ*, 1937 *A v SA*

Jackson, W H (England) 1926 *F v M*, 1927 *W v S*, *W v F*, *F v G*, *G v F*
Jamison, G A (Ireland) 1972 *W v S*
Jardine, A (Scotland) 1906 *E v W*
Jeffares, R W (Ireland) 1930 *W v E*, *E v S*, 1931 *S v F*, 1935 *S v E*, *I v NZ*
Jeffares, R W (Sen) (Ireland) 1901 *S v W*, *E v S*, 1902 *E v W*, 1909 *S v W*
Jeffreys, M (England) 1920 *F v US*
Johns, E A (Wales) 1911 *E v F*
Johnson, R F (England) 1969 *F v R*, 1970 *F v I*, *E v W* (R), 1971 *W v I*, 1972 *I v F*, *W v NZ*, 1973 *I v F*, 1974 *W v S*, *I v NZ*, *F v SA*, 1975 *S v I*, *S v A*
Jones, A O (England) 1906 *W v SA*, 1907 *S v I*, 1911 *F v S*, 1912 *F v I*, *W v F*
Jones, T (Wales) 1947 *E v F*, 1948 *E v I*, *F v E*, 1949 *E v F*, 1950 *S v F*, 1951 *I v E*
Jones, W (Wales) 1984 *S v F*, *NZ v F* (2), 1988 *S v E*
Jones, W K M (Wales) 1968 *I v A*, 1970 *F v E*, 1971 *S v I*
Joseph, M (Wales) 1966 *S v A*, 1967 *I v A*, 1968 *I v S*, *E v I*, *R v F*, 1969 *S v I*, *S v SA*, 1970 *S v E*, 1971 *I v E*, *S v E*(C), 1972 *S v F*, *S v E*, 1973 *I v NZ*, *S v P*(C), *F v J*, 1974 *E v I*, 1975 *F v Arg*, 1976 *E v A*, *F v A*, 1977 *E v S*, *S v I*, *F v S*
Joynson, D C (Wales) 1955 *E v S*

Keenan, H (England) 1962 *It v F*, 1963 *I v NZ*
Kelleher, J C (Wales) 1973 *E v S*, 1974 *F v E*, 1976 *R v F*, 1977 *E v F*
Kelleher, K D (Ireland) 1960 *W v S*, 1961 *W v E*, *E v S*, 1962 *S v E*, *W v F*, 1963 *W v E*, *F v It*, 1964 *E v W*, *R v F*, 1965 *F v S*, *W v E*, 1966 *S v E*, *W v F*, *W v A*, 1967 *E v A*, *F v S*, *S v W*, *S v NZ*, 1968 *S v F*, 1969 *S v W*, *E v SA*, 1970 *W v F*, 1971 *F v S*
Kelly, H C (Ireland) 1881 *I v S*, 1883 *I v S*, *S v E*, 1885 *S v I*
Kemsley, H B (South Africa) 1896 *SA v GB*
Kennedy, G H B (Ireland) 1905 *S v W*, 1910 *W v S*, *S v E*
Kennedy, W (Ireland) 1905 *S v NZ*
Kilner, W F B (Australia) 1937 *A v SA*
King, J S (New Zealand) 1937 *NZ v SA* (2)
King, M H R (England) 1961 *S v I*
Kinsey, B (Australia) 1986 *Tg v W*, 1990 *Arg v E* (2), 1991 *Fj v E*, 1992 *F v SA* (2), 1993 *NZ v BI*
Knox, J (Argentina) 1949 *Arg v F*
Krembs, M (Germany) 1938 *G v F*

Lacroix, M (Belgium) 1962 *R v F*
Laidlaw, H B (Scotland) 1963 *I v E*, 1964 *W v F*, 1965 *I v E*, 1968 *F v E*, *W v F*
Lamb, G C (England) 1968 *F v I*, *W v S*, *F v SA*, 1969 *F v S*, *I v F*, 1970 *S v F*, *W v SA*, *I v W*, *R v F*, 1971 *I v F*, *F v A*
Lambert, N H (Ireland) 1947 *S v A*, 1948 *E v A*, *S v E*, 1949 *W v E*, *S v W*, *E v S*, *F v W*, 1950 *E v W*, *F v E*, 1951 *W v SA*, 1952 *E v W*
Lander, S (England) 1995 *S v W*
Lang, J S (Scotland) 1884 *I v E*
Larkin, F A (Australia) 1932 *A v NZ*
Lathwell, H G (England) 1946 *I v F*
Lawrence, K H (New Zealand) 1985 *A v C* (2), 1986 *A v It*, 1987 *F v S*, *S v W*, [*Fj v It*, *A v E*], *Arg v A* (2), 1989 *A v BI*, 1991 *A v E*, [*I v Z*, *W v A*]
Lawrie, A A (Scotland) 1924 *I v F*, 1925 *E v W*, 1926 *I v F*
Leask, B (Australia) 1993 *A v Tg*, 1994 *Pt v W*, *WS v W*, *F v C*
Lee, S (Ireland) 1904 *S v E*
Lefevre, C (Ireland) 1905 *W v E*, 1907 *S v W*
Leith, H S (New Zealand) 1928 *M v A*
Leslie, D (Scotland) 1990 *E v W*, 1993 *I v F*
Lewis, C P (Wales) 1885 *W v E*
Lewis, E M (Wales) 1971 *F v A*
Lewis, M S (Wales) 1975 *F v S*, 1976 *I v S*
Lewis, R (Wales) 1970 *E v I*, 1971 *E v F*, 1972 *F v I*, 1973 *S v I*, *E v A*, 1974 *Arg v F* (2)
Lieprand, M (Germany) 1934 *G v F*
Llewellyn, A (Wales) 1906 *E v I*
Llewellyn, V S (Wales) 1951 *E v F*
Llewellyn, W J (Wales) 1926 *F v S*, *I v E*, 1927 *S v A*
Lloyd, D M (Wales) 1975 *I v F*, 1976 *S v E*
Lloyd, R A (Ireland) 1922 *S v W*, *E v S*
Louw, L L (South Africa) 1953 *SA v A*
Luff, A C (England) 1963 *W v I*, 1964 *I v S*, *I v W*
Lyle, T R (Ireland) 1887 *E v S*
Lyne, H S (Wales) 1885 *E v I*

McAllister, E (Ireland) 1889 *S v W*, 1890 *W v S*
Macassey, L E (New Zealand) 1937 *NZ v SA*
McAuley, C J (New Zealand) 1962 *NZ v A*
McCartney, K W (Scotland) 1990 *F v I*, 1991 *NZ v A*, 1992 *F v R*, 1993 *Nm v W*, 1994 *W v It*, 1995 *E v F*
McDavitt, P A (New Zealand) 1972 *NZ v A*, 1975 *NZ v S*, 1977 *NZ v BI*
McEwan, M C (Scotland) 1892 *E v W*
McGill, J (Scotland) 1925 *F v I*, 1929 *I v W*
McGowan, J B (Ireland) 1923 *W v F*, 1924 *S v W*
McHugh, D T M (Ireland) 1994 *R v W*, 1995 *F v S*
McKenzie, E (New Zealand) 1921 *NZ v SA*
McKenzie, G (New Zealand) 1928 *NZ v A*
McKenzie, H J (New Zealand) 1936 *NZ v A*
McLachlan, L L (New Zealand) 1992 *A v S*, 1993 *A v SA*, 1994 *S v E*, *W v F*
MacLaren, J S (England) 1884 *W v S*, 1888 *S v I*
McMahon, D C J (Scotland) 1961 *W v I*, 1963 *E v F*, 1964 *E v NZ*, 1967 *E v NZ*, *W v E*, 1969 *W v I*
McMullen, R F (New Zealand) 1973 *NZ v E*
MacNeill, A R (Australia) 1988 *F v Arg* (2), 1989 *W v NZ*, *I v NZ*, 1990 *F v NZ* (2), 1991 [*C v R*], 1992 *NZ v I* (2), *SA v NZ*, 1993 *W v I*, *I v E*
Magee, J T (Ireland) 1897 *W v S*, *E v S*, 1898 *E v W*, 1899 *E v S*
Magrath, R M (Ireland) 1928 *F v S*
Mailhan, L (France) 1933 *F v G*, 1935 *F v G*, 1937 *F v G*
Malan, Dr W C (South Africa) 1970 *SA v NZ*, 1971 *SA v F* (2)
Marie, B (France) 1960 *Arg v F* (2), 1965 *F v W* (R), 1966 *E v I*
Marsh, F W (England) 1907 *W v I*
Martelli, E (Ireland) 1903 *S v W*
Martin, N B (Australia) 1910 *A v NZ* (2)
Matheson, A M (New Zealand) 1946 *NZ v A*
Maurette, G (France) 1987 *W v I*, [*J v US*, *I v Tg*], 1988 *NZ v W* (2), 1989 *E v S*
Mayne, A V (Australia) 1929 *A v NZ* (2), 1932 *A v NZ*
Megson, R J (Scotland) 1987 *W v E*, 1988 *I v W*, *I v It*, 1991 *W v E*, *A v NZ*, 1992 *E v W*, *F v Arg*, 1995 *W v I*
Méné, D (France) 1994 *W v SA*, 1995 *W v E*
Miles, J H (England) 1913 *F v W*, *I v F*, 1914 *W v F*
Millar, D H (New Zealand) 1965 *NZ v SA*, 1968 *NZ v F*, 1977 *NZ v BI* (2), 1978 *NZ v A* (3)
Millar, W A (South Africa) 1924 *SA v BI* (2)
Mitchell, R (Ireland) 1955 *E v F*, 1956 *E v W*, 1957 *E v S*
Moffat, F J C (Scotland) 1932 *W v E*
Moffitt, J (New Zealand) 1936 *NZ v A*
Moolman, Dr J (South Africa) 1972 *SA v E*
Moore, D F (Ireland) 1886 *E v W*, *W v S*
Moore, T W (Australia) 1947 *A v NZ*, 1950 *A v BI*, 1951 *A v NZ*, 1954 *A v Fj*, 1956 *A v SA*
Morgan, C E (Australia) 1907 *A v NZ*, 1910 *A v NZ*
Morgan, K (Wales) 1967 *F v It*
Morrison, D (USA) 1981 *US v SA*
Morrison, E F (England) 1991 *F v S*, *R v F*, [*S v J*, *A v WS*], 1992 *I v A*, 1993 *S v I*, *SA v F*, *A v SA*(2), *W v J*, 1994 *I v S*, *A v NZ*
Mortimer, S (England) 1888 *W v M*
Morton, D S (Scotland) 1893 *W v E*
Muller, F (South Africa) 1982 *SA v SAm*, 1988 *S v F*, *F v I*
Mullock, R (Wales) 1886 *I v E*
Muntz, J (France) 1924 *F v R*
Murdoch, W C W (Scotland) 1951 *W v I*, *I v SA*, 1952 *E v SA*, *F v E*
Murphy, J P (New Zealand) 1959 *NZ v BI*, 1963 *NZ v E*, 1964 *NZ v A* (2), 1965 *NZ v SA* (3), 1966 *NZ v BI* (3), 1968 *NZ v F*, 1969 *NZ v W* (2)
Myburgh, P A (South Africa) 1962 *SA v BI*, 1963 *SA v A* (3)

Neethling, S (South Africa) 1994 *E v R*
Neilson, A E (New Zealand) 1921 *NZ v SA* (2)
Neser, V H (South Africa) 1924 *SA v BI*, 1928 *SA v NZ* (4), 1933 *SA v A* (4)
Neville, Dr W C (Ireland) 1882 *I v E*
Nicholls, E G (Wales) 1909 *E v S*
Nicholls, F (England) 1904 *W v S*
Nicholson, G W (New Zealand) 1913 *NZ v A*
Noon, O (Argentina) 1949 *Arg v F*
Norling, C (Wales) 1978 *I v NZ*, 1979 *E v S*, 1980 *F v E*, 1981 *I v F*, *NZ v SA* (2), *F v NZ*, 1982 *I v S*, 1983 *A v Arg* (2), 1984 *F v I*, 1985 *E v S*, 1986 *E v I*, 1987 *I v F*, [*C v Tg*, *F v Fj*], 1988 *E v I*, *R v F*, 1989 *NZ v Arg* (2), 1990 *I v S*, *A v F* (2), 1991 *Nm v I* (2)
Nugent, G P (Ireland) 1880 *I v E*

Oakley, L D (South Africa) 1924 *SA v BI*
O'Callaghan, B J (Australia) 1959 *A v BI*
O'Leary, J (Australia) 1958 *A v M*

Palmade, F (France) 1973 *F v S* (R), *S v W*, 1974 *I v S*, 1975 *I v E*, 1977 *I v E*, 1978 *E v I*, 1979 *S v W*, 1980 *SA v BI* (2), 1981 *W v I*, *SA v I* (2), 1982 *E v W*, 1983 *NZ v BI* (2), 1985 *W v E*, 1986 *I v S*
Parfitt, V J (Wales) 1953 *E v F*, 1954 *I v S*
Parkes, Dr N M (England) 1958 *W v S*, *F v A*, *I v W*, *F v I*, 1959 *F v It*, *F v W*, 1960 *W v F*, 1961 *F v W*, 1962 *W v S*, *I v S*
Parkinson, F G M (New Zealand) 1955 *NZ v A*, 1956 *NZ v SA* (2)
Paton, R J (New Zealand) 1931 *M v A*
Pattinson, K A (England) 1973 *F v S*, *W v A*, 1974 *I v W*, *R v F*, 1975 *F v W*, 1976 *S v F*
Pattisson, A S (Scotland) 1883 *E v I*
Pauling, T G (Australia) 1904 *A v GB* (2), 1914 *A v NZ*
Peake, J F (New Zealand) 1923 *NZ v A*
Pearce, T N (England) 1948 *F v I*, *W v S*, 1949 *F v S*, *I v F*, *W v I*, 1950 *F v I*, *I v S*, 1951 *F v S*, *I v F*, *S v I*, 1952 *F v I*
Peard, L J (Wales) 1989 *I v E*, 1991 *E v F*, [*F v R*, *E v US*]
Pearson, J J M (England) 1995 *F v W*
Petrie, A G (Scotland) 1882 *S v I*
Phillips, T H (Wales) 1936 *E v S*
Phillips, W D (Wales) 1887 *I v E*, 1889 *I v S*
Pontin, A C (USA) 1976 *US v A*
Potter-Irwin, F C (England) 1909 *W v I*, 1911 *W v I*, 1912 *W v S*, *I v S*, *S v SA*, *I v SA*, *W v SA*, 1920 *F v S*, *W v I*
Pozzi, S (Italy) 1957 *F v R*, 1960 *R v F*
Pretorius, N F (South Africa) 1938 *SA v BI*
Price, F G (Wales) 1963 *I v F*
Prideaux, L (England) 1980 *W v S*, *I v W*, *SAm v SA* (2), 1981 *S v I*, *NZ v SA*, 1985 *F v S*
Priest, T E (England) 1952 *It v F*, 1953 *I v F*
Pring, J P G (New Zealand) 1966 *NZ v BI*, 1967 *NZ v A*, 1968 *NZ v F*, 1971 *NZ v BI* (4), 1972 *NZ v A*
Purcell, N M (Ireland) 1927 *S v E*

Quittenton, R C (England) 1977 *Arg v F* (2), 1978 *W v NZ*, 1979 *I v F*, *F v S*, *S v NZ*, 1981 *S v A*, 1982 *NZ v A*, 1983 *S v W*, *F v R*, 1984 *A v NZ* (2), 1986 *R v S*, 1987 *S v I*, [*Arg v It*, *NZ v Arg*], 1988 *I v S*, 1989 *W v I*

Rainie, R D (Scotland) 1890 *E v W*, 1891 *W v E*, 1894 *I v W*
Rea, M D M (Ireland) 1978 *R v F*, 1981 *S v R*, 1982 *F v E*
Reading, L S (England) 1912 *US v A*
Reilly, J R (Australia) 1972 *A v F*
Reordan, D (United States) 1991 [*S v Z*]
Richards, A (Wales) 1980 *R v F*, 1981 *A v F*, 1982 *E v A*, 1983 *F v S*
Richards, A R (South Africa) 1896 *SA v GB*
Robbertse, P (South Africa) 1967 *SA v F*, 1969 *SA v A*, 1970 *SA v NZ* (2)
Roberts, E (Wales) 1924 *F v S*
Roberts, R A (England) 1924 *F v W*
Robertson, W A (Scotland) 1920 *E v F*, *I v E*
Robin, P (France) 1988 *It v A*, 1989 *S v Fj*, 1990 *E v I*, 1991 [*W v WS*], 1992 *A v NZ* (2), 1993 *NZ v BI*(2), 1994 *W v S*
Robinson, H L (Ireland) 1882 *E v S*
Robson, C F (New Zealand) 1963 *NZ v E*
Roca, J (France) 1937 *F v It*
Rogers, I (South Africa) 1993 *Z v W*, 1994 *C v F*, *C v W*, *A v It* (2)
Rolandi, J-L (Argentina) 1994 *I v US*
Rowlands, K (Wales) 1980 *SA v SAm* (2), 1981 *F v S*, 1982 *S v E*, 1986 *SA v Cv* (4)
Rowsell, A (England) 1891 *W v I*
Royds, P M R (England) 1921 *W v F*, 1923 *F v I*
Rutherford, C F (Scotland) 1908 *F v E*
Rutter, A (England) 1876 *E v S*

St Guilhem, J (France) 1974 *S v E*, 1975 *W v I*

Sanson, N R (Scotland) 1974 *W v F, F v SA*, 1975 *I v P* (C), *SA v F* (2), *F v R*, 1976 *I v A, I v W*, 1977 *W v I*, 1978 *F v E, E v W, E v NZ*, 1979 *E v NZ*
Schoeman, J P J (South Africa) 1968 *SA v BI*
Schofield, T D (Wales) 1907 *E v S*, 1908 *E v I*, 1910 *E v I*, 1911 *E v S*, 1912 *E v I, F v E*, 1913 *E v S*, 1914 *E v I, S v E*, 1920 *E v S*, 1921 *E v I*, 1922 *S v I*
Schwoenberg, M (Germany) 1938 *R v F*
Scott, J M B (Scotland) 1923 *E v W*
Scott, R L (Scotland) 1927 *F v I, E v W*
Scriven, G (Ireland) 1884 *E v S*
Short, J A (Scotland) 1979 *F v R*, 1982 *I v W*
Simmonds, G (Wales) 1992 *E v C*
Simpson, J W (Scotland) 1906 *I v W*
Simpson, R L (New Zealand) 1913 *NZ v A*, 1921 *NZ v A*, 1923 *NZ v A*
Sklar, E (Argentina) 1991 [*NZ v US*], 1994 *Fj v W, Tg v W*
Slabber, M J (South Africa) 1955 *SA v BI*, 1960 *SA v NZ*
Smith, J A (Scotland) 1892 *E v I*, 1894 *E v W*, 1895 *W v E*
Spreadbury, A J (England) 1990 *A v F*, 1992 *I v S, W v A*, 1994 *I v W*
Stanton, R W (South Africa) 1910 *SA v GB* (3)
Steyn, M (Germany) 1932 *G v F*
Stirling, B W (Ireland) 1989 *E v Fj*, 1991 *Arg v NZ* (2), 1993 *E v S, R v F*, 1994 *NZ v SA* (2), 1995 *E v S*
Strasheim, Dr E A (South Africa) 1958 *SA v F*, 1960 *SA v S, SA v NZ*, 1962 *SA v BI* (2), 1964 *SA v F*, 1967 *SA v F*, 1968 *SA v BI*
Strasheim, Dr J J (South Africa) 1938 *SA v BI*
Strydom, S (South Africa) 1979 *Arg v A* (2), 1982 *SA v SAm*, 1985 *S v I, F v W*, 1986 *F v NZ* (2)
Sturrock, J C (Scotland) 1921 *E v W, F v E*, 1922 *W v I*
Sullivan, G (New Zealand) 1950 *NZ v BI*
Sutherland, F E (New Zealand) 1925 *NZ v A*, 1928 *NZ v A* (2), 1930 *NZ v BI*
Swainston, E (England) 1878 *I v E*

Taylor, A R (New Zealand) 1965 *NZ v SA* (R), 1972 *NZ v A*
Taylor, J A S (Scotland) 1957 *W v I*, 1960 *E v W, F v E, W v SA*, 1961 *F v It*, 1962 *E v W, F v I, I v W*
Tennent, J M (Scotland) 1920 *I v F*, 1921 *I v W*, 1922 *W v E, E v F, I v F, I v E*, 1923 *I v W*
Thomas, C (Wales) 1979 *S v I*, 1980 *E v I*
Thomas, C (Wales) 1995 *S v C, I v F*
Thomas, C G P (Wales) 1977 *F v NZ*, 1978 *S v F, F v I*
Thomas, P (France) 1994 *E v I*, 1995 *I v E*
Tierney, A T (Australia) 1957 *A v NZ*, 1958 *A v M*, 1959 *A v BI*
Tindill, E W T (New Zealand) 1950 *NZ v BI* (2), 1955 *NZ v A*
Titcomb, M H (England) 1966 *W v S*, 1967 *W v I, W v NZ*, 1968 *I v W, S v A*, 1971 *S v W, E v P* (C), 1972 *W v F*
Tognini, S (Italy) 1968 *Cz v F*
Tolhurst, H A (Australia) 1951 *A v NZ* (2)
Tomalin, L C (Australia) 1947 *A v NZ*, 1949 *A v M* (2) 1950 *A v BI*
Treharne, G J (Wales) 1960 *I v SA*, 1961 *E v SA, I v E, I v F*, 1963 *S v I*
Trigg, J A F (England) 1981 *F v R*, 1982 *S v F*, 1983 *W v I*
Tulloch, J T (Scotland) 1906 *I v SA, E v SA*, 1907 *I v E*, 1908 *E v W*, 1912 *E v W*, 1913 *E v SA*, 1914 *I v W*, 1920 *W v E*, 1924 *W v I*
Turnbull, A (Scotland) 1898 *I v W*, 1899 *W v E, W v I*, 1900 *E v W, I v W*, 1901 *W v E, I v E*

Vanderfield, Dr I R (Australia) 1956 *A v SA*, 1958 *A v M*, 1961 *A v Fj* (2), *A v F*, 1962 *A v NZ*, 1966 *A v BI*, 1967 *A v I*, 1968 *A v NZ*, 1970 *A v S*, 1971 *A v SA*, 1973 *A v Tg*, 1974 *A v NZ* (2)
Van der Horst, A W (South Africa) 1933 *SA v A*
Van der Merwe, A (Germany) 1936 *G v F*
Vile, T H (Wales) 1923 *S v F, E v I, I v S, S v E*, 1924 *I v E, S v I, E v S*, 1925 *E v I*, 1927 *E v I*, 1928 *E v A, E v S*, 1931 *F v I*

Wahlstrom, G K (New Zealand) 1994 *A v WS, SA v Arg* (2)
Waldron, C A (Australia) 1986 *F v R*, 1987 *A v SK*
Waldron, H (England) 1957 *F v It*
Walsh, L (New Zealand) 1949 *NZ v A*
Walters, D G (Wales) 1959 *F v S, I v E, E v S, I v F*, 1960 *S v F, E v I, I v S, F v I*, 1961 *F v SA, E v F*, 1962 *E v I, F v E*, 1963 *E v S, F v R*, 1964 *E v I, F v E, F v I, F v Fj*, 1965 *I v F, S v I, E v S, S v SA*, 1966 *F v E*
Warden, G (England) 1946 *F v K*
Warren, R G (Ireland) 1892 *S v E*
Warren, T H H (Scotland) 1928 *W v I*
Watson, D H (Scotland) 1881 *S v E*
Waugh, Dr R (Australia) 1903 *A v NZ*
Welsby, A (England) 1976 *F v I*, 1978 *W v F*, 1981 *F v W*, 1982 *F v I*
Welsh, R (Scotland) 1902 *E v I*, 1903 *W v E*, 1905 *I v E*
West, J R (Ireland) 1974 *E v W*, 1975 *S v W*, 1976 *W v F*, 1977 *F v NZ*, 1978 *W v S, S v E, S v NZ*, 1979 *E v F, NZ v F* (2), 1980 *S v F, SA v F, W v NZ*, 1981 *F v NZ, W v A*, 1982 *F v Arg*, 1983 *W v E*, 1984 *R v F*
Wheeler, Dr E de C (Ireland) 1925 *S v F*
Wheeler, Dr J R (Ireland) 1929 *S v E*, 1930 *S v W*, 1931 *E v W, S v E*, 1932 *E v S*, 1933 *S v E*
Whittaker, J B G (England) 1947 *I v F, W v I*
Wiesse, M (Germany) 1936 *G v F*
Wilkins, H E B (England) 1925 *F v NZ*, 1928 *G v F*, 1929 *W v F*
Wilkins, W H (Wales) 1893 *E v S*, 1894 *S v E*, 1895 *E v S*
Williams, J (New Zealand) 1905 *NZ v A*
Williams, R C (Ireland) 1957 *S v W, E v F*, 1958 *E v W, E v A, S v A, S v E*, 1959 *W v E, S v W, E v F*, 1960 *S v E*, 1961 *F v S, S v W, F v R*, 1962 *S v F*, 1963 *F v S, S v W, W v NZ*, 1964 *S v F, S v NZ, F v NZ, S v E*
Williams, T (Wales) 1904 *E v I*
Williams, W (England) 1904 *I v S*, 1905 *W v I*, 1907 *E v F*, 1908 *W v S, I v S, W v F*, 1909 *E v F, F v W, I v F*, 1910 *W v F*, 1911 *F v W*, 1913 *F v SA*
Wolstenholme, B H (New Zealand) 1955 *NZ v A*
Woolley, A (South Africa) 1970 *SA v NZ*
Wyllie, W D (Australia) 1949 *A v M*

Yché, J-C (France) 1983 *S v I, R v W, It v A*, 1985 *A v Fj* (2)
Yeman, R (Wales) 1993 *I v R*, 1994 *NZ v SA*
Young, J (Scotland) 1971 *F v W*, 1972 *E v W, R v F*, 1973 *E v NZ*

WORLD INTERNATIONAL RECORDS

Both team and individual records are for official cap matches played by senior members of the International Board, up to 31 March 1995.

TEAM RECORDS

Highest score – 102
Wales (102-11) v Portugal 1994 Lisbon

Biggest winning margin – 91
Wales (102-11) v Portugal 1994 Lisbon

Most tries by a team in an international – 16
Wales v Portugal 1994 Lisbon

Most conversions by a team in an international – 11
Wales v Portugal 1994 Lisbon

Most penalty goals in an international – 8
Wales v Canada 1993 Cardiff

Most consecutive international victories – 17
New Zealand between 1965 and 1969

Most consecutive internationals undefeated – 23
New Zealand between 1987 and 1990

Most points in an international series – 109
New Zealand v Argentina (2 matches) 1989 in New Zealand

Most tries in an international series – 18
New Zealand v Wales (2 matches) 1988 in New Zealand

Most points in Five Nations Championship in a season – 118
England 1991-92

Most tries in Five Nations Championship in a season – 21
Wales 1909-10

Most points on an overseas tour (all matches) – 868
New Zealand to B Isles/France (33 matches) 1905-06

Most tries on an overseas tour (all matches) – 215
New Zealand to B Isles/France (33 matches) 1905-06

Biggest win on a major tour (all matches)
117-6 New Zealand v S Australia 1974 Adelaide

INDIVIDUAL RECORDS

Including appearances for British Isles, shown in brackets.

Most capped player
P Sella (France) 106 1982-95
in individual positions
Full-back
S Blanco (France) 81[1] 1980-91
Wing
R Underwood (England) 79(6)[2] 1984-95
Centre (includes 2nd five-eighth)
P Sella (France) 99[3] 1982-95
Fly-half (includes 1st five-eighth)
C R Andrew (England) 69(5)[4] 1985-95
Scrum-half
G O Edwards (Wales) 63(10)[5] 1967-78
Prop
P A Orr (Ireland) 59(1) 1976-87
Hooker
B C Moore (England) 63(5) 1987-95
Lock
W J McBride (Ireland) 80(17) 1962-75

Flanker
J F Slattery (Ireland) 65(4) 1970-84
P J Winterbottom (England) 65(7) 1982-93
No 8
D Richards (England) 48(6)[6] 1986-95

[1] *Blanco also played 12 times as a wing*
[2] *D I Campese (Australia), 86 caps, has won 70 as a wing*
[3] *Sella has also played 6 times on the wing and once at full-back*
[4] *Andrew has also played once for England as a full-back. M P Lynagh (Australia), 67 caps in all, has played 59 times at fly-half, and 8 times in the centre*
[5] *N C Farr-Jones, 63 caps for Australia, won 62 as a scrum-half and one as a replacement wing*
[6] *Several French utility forwards won more caps than Richards, but none has played as frequently at No 8*

Most consecutive internationals for a country – 60
S B T Fitzpatrick (N Zealand) 1986-94

Most internationals as captain – 48
W D C Carling (England) 1988-95

Most points in internationals – 821
M P Lynagh (Australia) (67 matches) 1984-94

Most points in an international – 30
D Camberabero (France) v Zimbabwe 1987 Auckland
C R Andrew (England) v Canada 1994 Twickenham

Most tries in internationals – 60
D I Campese (Australia) (86 matches) 1982-94

Most tries in an international – 5
G C Lindsay (Scotland) v Wales 1887 Edinburgh
D Lambert (England) v France 1907 Richmond
R Underwood (England) v Fiji 1989 Twickenham

Most conversions in internationals – 132
M P Lynagh (Australia) (67 matches) 1984-94

Most conversions in an international – 11
N R Jenkins (Wales) v Portugal 1994 Lisbon

Most dropped goals in internationals – 20
C R Andrew (England) (65 matches) and (B Lions) (5 matches) 1985-95

Most dropped goals in an international – 3
P Albaladejo (France) v Ireland 1960 Paris
P F Hawthorne (Australia) v England 1967 Twickenham
H E Botha (South Africa) v S America 1980 Durban
H E Botha (South Africa) v Ireland 1981 Durban
J-P Lescarboura (France) v England 1985 Twickenham
J-P Lescarboura (France) v New Zealand 1986 Christchurch
D Camberabero (France) v Australia 1990 Sydney

Most penalty goals in internationals – 159
M P Lynagh (Australia) (67 matches) 1984-94

Most penalty goals in an international – 8
N R Jenkins (Wales) v Canada 1993 Cardiff

Fastest player to 100 points in internationals
G J Fox (New Zealand) in his 6th match

Fastest player to 200 points in internationals
G J Fox (New Zealand) in his 13th match

Fastest player to 300 points in internationals
G J Fox (New Zealand) in his 18th match

Fastest player to 400 points in internationals
G J Fox (New Zealand) in his 26th match

Most points in a Five Nations match – 24
S Viars (France) v Ireland 1992
C R Andrew (England) v Scotland 1995

Most points in Five Nations Championship in a season – 67
J M Webb (England) (4 matches) 1991-92

Most tries in Five Nations Championship in a season – 8
C N Lowe (England) (4 appearances) 1913-14
I S Smith (Scotland) (4 appearances) 1924-25

Tries in each match of a Five Nations Championship
H C Catcheside (England) 1923-24
A C Wallace (Scotland) 1924-25
P Estève (France) 1982-83
P Sella (France) 1985-86

Most penalty goals in Five Nations Championship in a season – 18
S D Hodgkinson (England) (4 matches) 1990-91

Most conversions in Five Nations Championship in a season – 11
J Bancroft (Wales) (4 appearances) 1908-09
J M Webb (England) (4 matches) 1991-92

Most dropped goals in Five Nations Championship in a season – 5
G Camberabero (France) (3 appearances) 1966-67
J-P Lescarboura (France) dropped a goal in each Championship match 1983-84, a unique feat

Most points on an overseas tour – 230
W J Wallace (NZ) (25 appearances) in B Isles/France 1905-06

Most tries on an overseas tour – 42
J Hunter (NZ) (23 appearances) in B Isles/France 1905-06

Most points in any match on tour – 43
R M Deans (NZ) v South Australia 1984 Adelaide

Most tries in any match on tour – 8
T R Heeps (NZ) v Northern NSW 1962
P Estève scored 8 for France v East Japan in 1984, but this was not on a major tour

PARTNERSHIP RECORDS

Centre threequarters
W D C Carling and J C Guscott (England) 34 (includes 1 Test for B Lions)
Half-backs
M P Lynagh and N C Farr-Jones (Australia) 47
Front row
A J Daly, P N Kearns and E J A McKenzie (Australia) 36
Second row
A J Martin and G A D Wheel (Wales) 27
Back row
J Matheu, G Basquet and J Prat (France) 22

OTHER INTERNATIONAL MATCH RECORDS

Up to 31 March 1995. These are included for comparison and cover performances since 1971 by teams and players in Test matches for nations which are not *senior members of the International Board.*

Most points in a match
By a team
164 Hong Kong v Singapore 1994 Kuala Lumpar
By a player
50 A Billington Hong Kong v Singapore 1994

Most tries in a match
By a team
26 Hong Kong v Singapore 1994 Kuala Lumpar
By a player
10 A Billington Hong Kong v Singapore 1994

Most conversions in a match
By a team
17 Hong Kong v Singapore 1994 Kuala Lumpar
By a player
17 J McKee Hong Kong v Singapore 1994

Most penalty goals in a match
By a team
8 Canada v Scotland 1991 St John
8 Italy v Romania 1994 Catania
8 Argentina v Canada 1995 Buenos Aires
By a player
8 M A Wyatt Canada v Scotland 1991 St John
8 D Dominguez Italy v Romania 1994 Catania
8 S E Meson Argentina v Canada 1995 Buenos Aires

Most dropped goals in a match
By a team
3 Argentina v SA Gazelles 1971 Pretoria
3 Argentina v Australia 1979 Buenos Aires
3 Argentina v New Zealand 1985 Buenos Aires
By a player
3 T A Harris-Smith Argentina v SA Gazelles 1971
3 H Porta Argentina v Australia 1979
3 H Porta Argentina v New Zealand 1985

Most points in matches
530 H Porta Argentina/South America
483 S Bettarello Italy

Most tries in matches
23 Marcello Cuttitta Italy

Most conversions in matches
54 H Porta Argentina/South America
46 S Bettarello Italy

Most penalty goals in matches
109 H Porta Argentina/South America
104 S Bettarello Italy

Most dropped goals in matches
25 H Porta Argentina/South America
17 S Bettarello Italy

Most matches as captain
43 H Porta Argentina/South America

Biggest win on a major tour
128-0 W Samoa v Marlborough (N Zealand) 1993 Blenheim

FROM STRENGTH TO STRENGTH

WOMEN'S RUGBY 1994-95
Alice Cooper

The home nations are now running their own unions. Discussions are well underway about staging a Triple Crown next season, upgrading to a Five Nations later, with women's fixtures expected to be played on the same weekend as the men's matches to maximise exposure and support.

ENGLAND

Following affiliation with the RFU, the new Rugby Football Union for Women started a new era for English rugby. One of the major differences was the welcome arrival of major sponsors – National Car Parks for the regional and divisional competitions, and Vladivar for the National Cup. It is to be hoped that these far-sighted companies will be followed by others for the Leagues and internationals.

On the club scene, the top three clubs changed places again: Richmond I decisively won Division 1 and comprehensively defeated Wasps in the Vladivar Cup final by 27-0. Saracens, the previous League champions, had a slow start due to the absence of some players but still managed second in the League. Wasps were third. Blackheath and Leeds are relegated, to be replaced by Novocastrians and Old Leamingtonians, who have scorched a path through Division 2 after promotion from Division 3 only this season. Eaton Manor and Alton win promotion to Division 2 as Sale and Wasps II are relegated.

Regular matches and tournaments are being held at youth level, attracting an increasing number of school and college sides. At student level, Loughborough emerged as the leading force, winning Division 1, the National Student Cup and the BUSA title. In the National Sevens, previous winners Saracens were surprisingly knocked out by an outstanding Clifton side who went on to win the tournament 5-0, the first club outside London to so so.

The NCP divisional title was won by the North, while in the international game England defeated Holland and Wales. England's performances were not much to write home about, considering their status as world champions, but nevertheless they won all their matches emphatically. Selector Steve Jew brought some new blood into the team, captained this season by Gill Burns, and there is talent in depth waiting in the wings in the A side and the Emerging England squad.

Vladivar National Cup: *9 April:* Richmond 27, Wasps 0 (Harlequins); **National Sevens:** *30 April:* Clifton 5, Wasps 0 (Marlow); **NCP Divisional Championship winners:** North
BUSA final: Loughborough 53, De Montfort, Bedford 11 (Twickenham);
Student National Cup: Loughborough 27, West London Institute 23

SCOTLAND

North of the border several new clubs joined the merit table, while a drive in youth development, masterminded by Sue Brodie, produced the 'Hands Up For Girls' Rugby' programme of open days which attracted hundreds of teenagers into the game.

On the club scene, Edinburgh Academicals were once again the winners of Division 1, while their second XV topped Division 2. In an interesting comparision of standards, the English winners, Richmond, comprehensively beat Accies in an Easter fixture. The name to watch is Heriot-Watt, who snatched the National Cup from under Accies' nose with a late score and also took the National Sevens title. Next season, Heriot's are to move to a new ground and will be renamed Edinburgh Wanderers.

At international level, Scotland fielded much the same squad as they did in the previous season's World Cup, a consistency which produced a narrow away win in their first fixture against Wales. Lisa O'Keefe was the new cap for the Italy game.

Scottish National Cup: Heriot-Watt (Lasmore); **Scottish National Plate:** West of Scotland

IRELAND

With five new clubs, bringing the total to 25, the expansion in the Irish game continued this season, culminating in the affiliation of the newly formed IWRFU with the RFU.

Blackrock College and Creggs emerged as the leading teams, Blackrock just edging the Division 1 title on points difference. In Division 2, newcomers Sligo defeated Shannon 5-0 in the play-offs between the two regions (Division 2 is divided geographically to minimise travelling) and gained promotion to Division 1.

At international level, the Irish have yet to win against the other Home Unions despite eight new caps and the return of centre Kim Donoghoe after having a baby.

O'Beirne Cup: Creggs 5, Blackrock 0 (*aet*)

WALES

Wales are settling into their new union, the WWRFU, and have developed a new combination in their national team. This mix of abilities was decisively beaten by an indifferent England performance, despite the energetic leadership of new captain Sue Butler.

In the domestic game, Cardiff continued to play in the RFUW First Division but narrowly missed relegation, while Swansea Uplands achieved a double in decisively winning both the new Welsh Division 1 and the Welsh Cup. Tymbl took Division 2.

National Welsh Cup: *30 April:* Aberystwyth Town 5, Swansea Uplands 22 (Ystradgynlais RFC)

EXILES MATCHES
Irish Exiles 16, Welsh Counties 5 (London Irish); Welsh Exiles 10, Welsh Counties 5 (London Welsh); Welsh Counties 0, Scottish Select 5 (Bridgend)

INTERNATIONALS
18 December: England 30, Holland 5 (Wasps); Wales 0, Scotland 5 (Bridgend)
22 January: Ireland 0, Nomads 5 (Blackrock)
12 February: England 25, Wales 0 (Sale); Scotland 20, Ireland 3 (Myreside)
5 March: Ireland 10, France 39 (Blackrock)
19 March: Wales 25, Ireland 0 (Cardiff)
30 April: Scotland 10, Italy 12 (Meggetland); Wales A 0, England A 29 (Abertillery)

Student Internationals: Welsh Students 0, English Students 5 (Cardiff); Welsh Universities 5, Scottish Universities 5 (Cardiff)

LEAGUE TABLES

RFUW National Division 1

	P	W	D	L	F	A	Pts
Richmond	14	14	0	0	464	26	28
Saracens	14	8	2	4	196	186	18
Wasps	14	8	1	5	204	111	17
Waterloo	14	7	0	7	137	180	14
Clifton	14	6	1	7	122	166	13
Cardiff	14	6	0	8	106	215	12
Leeds	14	3	0	11	64	183	6
Blackheath*	13	3	0	10	57	247	4

** 1 match defaulted*

RFUW National Division 2

	P	W	D	L	F	A	Pts
O Leams	10	9	0	1	221	42	18
Novocastrians	10	8	0	2	253	40	16
Richmond II	10	7	1	2	196	59	15
Cheltenham	10	2	1	7	57	197	5
Sale	10	2	0	8	55	130	4
Wasps II	10	2	0	8	47	361	4

RFUW Division 3 North

	P	W	D	L	F	A	Pts
Wharfedale	10	9	1	0	151	48	28
Whitchurch	10	6	0	4	162	93	22
Northern	10	5	1	4	129	94	21
Bury	10	3	0	7	79	281	16
York**	8	6	1	1	172	15	21
Manchester*	9	0	0	9	44	206	9

** 1 match defaulted   ** 2 matches defaulted*

RFUW Division 3 Midlands

	P	W	D	L	F	A	Pts
Selly Oak	10	10	0	0	247	55	30
N'pton	10	5	1	4	206	53	21
Sudbury	10	5	1	4	202	174	21
Notts C	10	3	3	4	126	118	19
Shelford	10	3	1	6	57	238	16
Sutton C'field*	9	1	2	6	54	254	13

** 1 match defaulted*

RFUW Division 3 South-West

	P	W	D	L	F	A	Pts
Hornets	8	7	0	1	138	56	22
Clifton II	8	6	1	1	72	27	22
Tavistock	8	3	0	5	55	141	14
Exeter	8	2	1	5	62	59	13
Supermarine*	4	1	3	0	42	86	6

** 4 matches defaulted*

RFUW Division 3 South-East

	P	W	D	L	F	A	Pts
Alton	10	8	1	1	346	36	27
Teddington A	10	7	1	2	343	40	25
Medway	10	6	1	3	249	62	23
Richmond III	10	4	1	5	203	172	19
Camberley	10	3	0	7	111	216	16
Staines	10	0	0	10	5	731	10

RFUW Division 3 Home Counties

	P	W	D	L	F	A	Pts
Eaton Manor	10	9	1	0	283	23	29
Wimbledon	10	6	2	2	143	115	24
St Albans	10	5	1	4	192	100	23
Saracens II	10	3	2	5	52	143	18
Blackheath II*	8	3	0	5	63	109	14
Southend**	7	1	0	6	5	248	9

** 2 matches defaulted   ** 3 matches defaulted*

Student League Winners: *Division 1:* Loughborough; *Division 2 London:* West London Institute; *Division 2 South-West:*

Bath University; *Division 2 South-East:* Canterbury Christ Church; *Division 2 North-West:* Salford University; *Division 2 West Midlands:* Birmingham University; *Division 2 East Midlands:* Bedford College

Scottish Division 1

	P	*W*	*D*	*L*	*F*	*A*	*Pts*
Edinburgh Acads	10	9	1	0	503	10	29
Heriot-Watt U	10	8	0	2	335	31	26
WO Scotland	10	6	1	3	265	104	23
Edinburgh U	10	3	1	6	77	351	17
Aberdeen U*	9	1	1	7	29	275	12
Glasgow U**	7	1	0	6	28	373	9

** 1 match defaulted ** 3 matches defaulted*

Scottish Division 2

	P	*W*	*D*	*L*	*F*	*A*	*Pts*
Edin Acads II	10	9	0	1	382	67	28
Biggar	10	7	1	2	252	95	25
WO Scotland II	10	5	1	4	132	94	21
Perthshire*	9	5	0	4	130	134	19
Stirling U*	9	3	0	6	66	162	15
St Andrew's U	8	0	0	8	10	420	8

** 1 match defaulted ** 2 matches defaulted*

Scottish Division 3

	P	*W*	*D*	*L*	*F*	*A*	*Pts*
Haddington	9	8	0	1	224	46	25
Clarkston	9	7	1	1	339	35	24
RDVC*	8	7	0	1	214	35	22
Kirkcaldy*	8	5	0	3	213	133	18
Dundee HSFP	9	4	1	3	63	66	18
Lismore	9	4	0	5	118	122	17
Mull	9	4	0	5	49	211	17
Inverness C D*	8	4	0	4	44	277	16
Peebles**	7	1	0	6	71	133	9
Dundee U†	5	0	0	5	10	287	5

** 1 match defaulted ** 2 matches defaulted*
† 4 matches defaulted

Irish Division 1 finishing order:
Blackrock College, Creggs, Cooke, Old Crescent, University College Dublin, University of Ulster Coleraine
Irish Division 2 finishing order:
Sligo, Shannon, Randalstown, Antrim, Athlone, Ballina, Ashbourne, Coolmine

Wales Division 1

	P	*W*	*D*	*L*	*F*	*A*	*Pts*
Swansea Uplands	6	6	0	0	231	10	18
Aberystwyth Tn	6	3	0	3	215	221	12
Blaenau Gwent*	6	3	0	2	123	105	11
Llangefni	6	0	0	6	15	298	6

Briton Ferry folded before completing all League fixtures
** 1 match conceded*

Wales Division 2

	P	*W*	*D*	*L*	*F*	*A*	*Pts*
Tymbl	11	9	0	2	209	42	29
Whitland	10	8	0	2	226	69	26
Newcastle E*	12	7	1	3	161	62	26
Ystradgynlais	11	6	1	4	186	50	24
Cefn Coed	11	1	0	4	25	434	13
Cardiff II*†	6	3	0	1	114	15	10
Taff's Well**†	11	1	0	7	35	284	10

** 1 match conceded **2 matches conceded*
† matches awarded to opposition due to unregistered players

CLUBS SECTION

Records of most-capped players are complete up to 31 March 1995.

ENGLAND

Bath

Year of formation 1865
Ground Recreation Ground, London Road, Bath Tel: Bath (01225) 425192
Colours Blue, white and black
Most capped player D M B Sole (Scotland) 44 caps
Captain 1994-95 J P Hall
Courage Leagues 1994-95 Div 1 2nd **Pilkington Cup 1994-95** *Winners* – beat Wasps 36-16 (final)

League Record 1994-95

Date	*Venue*	*Opponents*	*Result*	*Scorers*
10 Sept	H	Bristol	18-9	*T:* pen try, Lumsden *C:* Callard *PG:* Callard (2)
17 Sept	A	Northampton	32-16	*T:* Swift (2), Adebayo *C:* Callard *PG:* Callard (5)
24 Sept	H	Orrell	32-13	*T:* Clarke, De Glanville, Evans, Sleightholme *C:* Catt (3) *PG:* Catt (2)
1 Oct	A	Gloucester	15-10	*T:* Robinson, Sanders *C:* Catt *PG:* Catt
8 Oct	H	Wasps	12-9	*PG:* Callard (4)
15 Oct	A	West Hartlepool	20-18	*T:* Hall (2) *C:* Callard (2) *PG:* Callard *DG:* Catt
22 Oct	H	Leicester	20-20	*T:* Catt, Swift *C:* Callard (2) *PG:* Callard (2)
29 Oct	H	Harlequins	22-11	*T:* Geoghegan *C:* Callard *PG:* Callard (5)
5 Nov	A	Sale	19-3	*T:* Adebayo, De Glanville *PG:* Callard (3)
7 Jan	A	Bristol	10-9	*T:* Geoghegan *C:* Callard *PG:* Callard
14 Jan	H	Northampton	26-6	*T:* Geoghegan, Swift *C:* Callard (2) *PG:* Callard (4)
11 Feb	A	Orrell	6-6	*PG:* Callard (2)
4 Mar	H	Gloucester	19-19	*T:* Callard *C:* Callard *PG:* Callard (4)
25 Mar	A	Wasps	10-11	*T:* Butland *C:* Callard *PG:* Callard
8 Apr	H	West Hartlepool	53-17	*T:* Adebayo (2), Lumsden (2), Adams, De Glanville, Ubogu *C:* Butland (6) *PG:* Butland (2)
15 Apr	A	Leicester	21-31	*T:* Adebayo, Catt *C:* Callard *PG:* Callard (3)
22 Apr	A	Harlequins	25-19	*T:* Guscott, Sleightholme, Yates *C:* Butland (2) *PG:* Butland (2)
29 Apr	H	Sale	13-18	*T:* pen try *C:* Callard *PG:* Callard (2)

Bristol

Year of formation 1888
Ground Memorial Ground, Filton Avenue, Horfield, Bristol Tel: Bristol (0117) 9514448
Colours Navy blue and white
Most capped player J V Pullin (England) 42 caps
Captain 1994-95 D J Eves
Courage Leagues 1994-95 Div 1 6th **Pilkington Cup 1994-95** Lost 8-16 to Leicester (5th round)

League Record 1994-95

Date	*Venue*	*Opponents*	*Result*	*Scorers*
10 Sept	A	Bath	9-18	*PG:* Tainton (3)
17 Sept	H	Sale	44-22	*T:* Eves, Hull, John, Regan, G Sharp *C:* Tainton (2) *PG:* Tainton (5)

24 Sept	H	Harlequins	19-14	*T:* Eves *C:* Tainton *PG:* Tainton (4)
1 Oct	A	Northampton	18-15	*PG:* Tainton (6)
8 Oct	H	Orrell	20-9	*T:* Eves (2), Denney *C:* Tainton *PG:* Tainton
15 Oct	A	Gloucester	17-19	*T:* Eves *PG:* Tainton (4)
22 Oct	H	Wasps	24-25	*T:* Patten, Williams *C:* Tainton *PG:* Tainton (4)
29 Oct	A	West Hartlepool	11-47	*T:* G Sharp *PG:* Tainton (2)
5 Nov	H	Leicester	31-22	*T:* G Sharp *C:* Tainton *PG:* Tainton (7) *DG:* Tainton
7 Jan	H	Bath	9-10	*PG:* Tainton (3)
14 Jan	A	Sale	9-21	*PG:* Tainton (3)
11 Feb	A	Harlequins	10-9	*T:* Wring *C:* Tainton *PG:* Tainton
4 Mar	H	Northampton	13-24	*T:* Sharp *C:* Tainton *PG:* Tainton (2)
25 Mar	A	Orrell	16-20	*T:* Denney *C:* Tainton *PG:* Tainton (3)
8 Apr	H	Gloucester	21-17	*T:* John (2) *C:* Tainton *PG:* Tainton (2) *DG:* Tainton
15 Apr	A	Wasps	15-27	*PG:* Tainton (5)
22 Apr	H	West Hartlepool	12-17	*T:* Eves, Chudleigh *C:* Tainton
29 Apr	A	Leicester	3-17	*PG:* Tainton

Coventry

Year of formation 1874
Ground Coundon Road, Coventry Tel: Coventry (01203) 591274 or 593399
Colours Navy and white hoops
Most capped player D J Duckham (England) 36 caps
Captain 1994-95 B Evans
Courage Leagues 1994-95 Div 2 10th *relegated* **Pilkington Cup 1994-95** Lost 7-45 to Fylde (4th round)

League Record 1994-95

Date	*Venue*	*Opponents*	*Result*	*Scorers*
10 Sept	H	Wakefield	14-15	*T:* Douglas *PG:* Angell (3)
17 Sept	A	Nottingham	7-23	*T:* Horrobin *C:* Angell
24 Sept	H	Newcastle Gosforth	19-15	*T:* Douglas *C:* Angell *PG:* Angell (4)
1 Oct	A	London Scottish	0-30	
8 Oct	H	London Irish	36-30	*T:* Lakey, Powis *C:* Angell *PG:* Angell (5) *DG:* Lakey (2), Angell
15 Oct	A	Waterloo	5-26	*T:* Douglas
22 Oct	H	Fylde	17-21	*T:* Douglas *PG:* Angell (4)
29 Oct	H	Saracens	16-33	*T:* Douglas *C:* Quick *PG:* Quick (2), Angell
5 Nov	A	Moseley	8-19	*T:* Shepherd *PG:* Quick
7 Jan	A	Wakefield	14-19	*T:* Gulliver *PG:* Angell (3)
14 Jan	H	Nottingham	6-19	*PG:* Angell (2)
11 Feb	A	Newcastle Gosforth	22-38	*T:* Hancox *C:* Hart *PG:* Hart (5)
4 Mar	H	London Scottish	5-19	*T:* Caswell
25 Mar	A	London Irish	8-25	*T:* Shepherd *DG:* Hart
8 Apr	H	Waterloo	17-22	*T:* Shepherd *PG:* Angell (3) *DG:* Angell
15 Apr	A	Fylde	8-22	*T:* Shepherd *PG:* Angell
22 Apr	A	Saracens	0-38	
29 Apr	H	Moseley	11-22	*T:* Gee *PG:* Hart *DG:* Hart

Fylde

Year of formation 1919
Ground Woodlands Memorial Ground, Blackpool Road, Lytham St Annes
Tel: Lytham (01253) 734733
Colours Claret, gold and white
Most capped player W A Dooley (England) 55 caps
Captain 1994-95 B Hanavan
Courage Leagues 1994-95 Div 2 9th *relegated* **Pilkington Cup 1994-95** Lost 13-55 to Sale (5th round)

League Record 1994-95

Date	*Venue*	*Opponents*	*Result*	*Scorers*
10 Sept	H	Nottingham	33-14	*T:* Barclay (2), Ashton, Gough *C:* Parker (2) *PG:* Parker (2) *DG:* Barclay
17 Sept	A	Newcastle Gosforth	14-45	*T:* Hanavan *PG:* Parker (3)
24 Sept	H	London Scottish	10-31	*T:* Anderton *C:* Parker *PG:* Parker
1 Oct	A	London Irish	12-23	*PG:* Parker (3) *DG:* Barclay
8 Oct	H	Waterloo	12-16	*PG:* Parker (4)
15 Oct	A	Saracens	7-18	*T:* Hanavan *C:* Parker
22 Oct	A	Coventry	21-17	*T:* Anderton, Hanavan *C:* Parker *PG:* Parker (2) *DG:* Barclay
29 Oct	H	Moseley	10-6	*T:* Dixon *C:* Parker *PG:* Parker
5 Nov	A	Wakefield	13-24	*T:* O'Toole *C:* Parker *PG:* Parker (2)
7 Jan	A	Nottingham	10-9	*T:* Gough *C:* Gough *PG:* Gough
14 Jan	H	Newcastle Gosforth	6-12	*PG:* Parker (2)
11 Feb	A	London Scottish	3-28	*PG:* Parker
4 Mar	H	London Irish	27-12	*T:* Anderton, Barclay, Hanavan, Ashton *C:* Parker (2) *PG:* Parker
25 Mar	A	Waterloo	19-12	*T:* Anderton, Gough *PG:* Gough *DG:* Barclay (2)
8 Apr	H	Saracens	15-37	*T:* Gough, pen try *C:* Parker *PG:* Barclay
15 Apr	H	Coventry	22-8	*T:* Barclay, Gough, Hanavan *C:* Barclay, Parker *PG:* Parker
22 Apr	A	Moseley	8-6	*T:* Anderton *PG:* Gough
29 Apr	H	Wakefield	8-11	*T:* Greatorex *PG:* Barclay

Gloucester

Year of formation 1873
Ground Kingsholm, Kingsholm Road, Gloucester Tel: Gloucester (01452) 520901
Colours Cherry and white
Most capped player A T Voyce (England)/M C Teague (England) 27 caps
Captain 1994-95 V Wooley
Courage Leagues 1994-95 Div 1 7th **Pilkington Cup 1994-95** Lost 9-19 to Wakefield (4th round)

League Record 1994-95

Date	*Venue*	*Opponents*	*Result*	*Scorers*
10 Sept	A	Wasps	8-45	*T:* Morris *PG:* Mapletoft
17 Sept	H	West Hartlepool	48-12	*T:* Morris (3), Holford (2), Mapletoft, T Smith *C:* Mapletoft (5) *PG:* Mapletoft
24 Sept	A	Leicester	6-16	*PG:* Mapletoft *DG:* Kimber
1 Oct	H	Bath	10-15	*T:* T Smith *C:* Mapletoft *PG:* Mapletoft
8 Oct	A	Sale	14-16	*T:* T Smith *PG:* Mapletoft (2) *DG:* Kimber
15 Oct	H	Bristol	19-17	*T:* Sims *C:* Mapletoft *PG:* Mapletoft (4)
22 Oct	A	Northampton	6-9	*PG:* Mapletoft (2)
29 Oct	H	Orrell	9-6	*PG:* Mapletoft (2) *DG:* Kimber
5 Nov	A	Harlequins	14-10	*T:* Holford (2) *C:* Osborne (2)
7 Jan	H	Wasps	16-21	*T:* Mapletoft *C:* Mapletoft *PG:* Mapletoft (3)
14 Jan	A	West Hartlepool	21-22	*T:* Ashmead, Teague *C:* Mapletoft *PG:* Mapletoft (2) *DG:* Kimber
11 Feb	H	Leicester	9-3	*PG:* Osborne (3)
4 Mar	A	Bath	19-19	*T:* Holford *C:* Osborne *PG:* Osborne (2) *DG:* Kimber (2)
25 Mar	H	Sale	8-20	*T:* Holford *PG:* Osborne
8 Apr	A	Bristol	17-21	*T:* Holford (2), Teague *C:* Osborne
15 Apr	H	Northampton	14-13	*T:* Sims *PG:* T Smith (3)
22 Apr	A	Orrell	14-43	*T:* Ashmead *PG:* Osborne (3)
29 Apr	H	Harlequins	17-28	*T:* Devereux, Cornwell *C:* Osborne (2) *PG:* Osborne

Harlequins

Year of formation 1866
Ground Stoop Memorial Ground, Craneford Way, Twickenham, Middlesex
Tel: 0181-892 0822
Colours Light blue, magenta, chocolate, French grey, black and light green
Most capped player B C Moore & P J Winterbottom (England) 58 caps
Captain 1994-95 B C Moore
Courage Leagues 1994-95 Div 1 8th **Pilkington Cup 1994-95** Lost 13-31 to Bath (semi-final)

League Record 1994-95

Date	*Venue*	*Opponents*	*Result*	*Scorers*
10 Sept	A	Sale	20-19	*T:* O'Leary, Sheasby, Carling *C:* Bray *PG:* Bray
17 Sept	H	Wasps	26-57	*T:* Challinor, Moore, Sheasby *C:* Challinor *PG:* Challinor (3)
24 Sept	A	Bristol	14-19	*T:* Keyter *PG:* Challinor (2) *DG:* Challinor
1 Oct	H	West Hartlepool	20-10	*T:* Cassell *PG:* Challinor (5)
8 Oct	A	Northampton	23-16	*T:* Thompson (2), Cassell *C:* Challinor *PG:* Challinor, Greenwood
15 Oct	H	Leicester	13-40	*T:* Thompson *C:* Greenwood *PG:* Greenwood (2)
22 Oct	H	Orrell	6-8	*PG:* Greenwood (2)
29 Oct	A	Bath	11-22	*T:* Greenwood *PG:* Challinor *DG:* Challinor
5 Nov	H	Gloucester	10-14	*T:* Pinnock *C:* Bray *PG:* Bray
7 Jan	H	Sale	15-15	*PG:* Challinor (5)
14 Jan	A	Wasps	7-25	*T:* Mensah *C:* Staples
11 Feb	H	Bristol	9-10	*PG:* Challinor (3)
4 Mar	A	West Hartlepool	8-10	*T:* Mensah *PG:* Challinor
25 Mar	H	Northampton	10-9	*T:* Kitchin, Staples
8 Apr	A	Leicester	8-22	*T:* Wright *PG:* Challinor
15 Apr	A	Orrell	28-10	*T:* Mensah, Staples, Thresher *C:* Challinor (2) *PG:* Challinor (3)
22 Apr	H	Bath	19-25	*T:* Greenwood, Sheasby *PG:* Challinor (3)
29 Apr	A	Gloucester	28-17	*T:* Henderson, Mensah, pen try *C:* Staples (2) *PG:* Staples (2) *DG:* Staples

Leicester

Year of formation 1880
Ground Welford Road, Leicester Tel: Leicester (0116) 2540276 or 2541607
Colours Scarlet, green and white
Most capped player R Underwood (England) 73 caps
Captain 1994-95 D Richards
Courage Leagues 1994-95 Div 1 *Winners* **Pilkington Cup 1994-95** Lost 22-25 to Wasps (semi-final)

League Record 1994-95

Date	*Venue*	*Opponents*	*Result*	*Scorers*
10 Sept	H	Northampton	28-15	*T:* Hackney, T Underwood *PG:* Harris (6)
17 Sept	A	Orrell	6-0	*PG:* Harris (2)
24 Sept	H	Gloucester	16-6	*T:* Johnson *C:* Liley *PG:* Liley (3)
1 Oct	A	Wasps	23-18	*T:* T Underwood *PG:* Harris (5) *DG:* Harris
8 Oct	H	West Hartlepool	33-16	*T:* Murphy (2), Johnson, Liley *C:* Liley (2) *PG:* Liley (3)
15 Oct	A	Harlequins	40-13	*T:* Hackney (2), Kardooni, Liley *C:* Harris (4) *PG:* Harris (3) *DG:* Harris
22 Oct	A	Bath	20-20	*T:* Hamilton *PG:* Harris (5)
29 Oct	H	Sale	37-20	*T:* Hackney (2), T Underwood *C:* Harris (2) *PG:* Harris (5) *DG:* Harris

5 Nov	A	Bristol	22-31	*T:* Tarbuck *C:* Harris *PG:* Harris (4) *DG:* Harris
7 Jan	A	Northampton	20-18	*T:* Wigley, pen try *C:* Harris (2) *PG:* Harris *DG:* Harris
14 Jan	H	Orrell	29-19	*T:* Kilford, Tarbuck *C:* Harris (2) *PG:* Harris (5)
11 Feb	A	Gloucester	3-9	*PG:* Harris
4 Mar	H	Wasps	21-6	*T:* R Underwood (2) *C:* Liley *PG:* Liley (3)
25 Mar	A	West Hartlepool	12-6	*PG:* Harris (3) *DG:* Harris
8 Apr	H	Harlequins	22-8	*T:* T Underwood *C:* Liley *PG:* Liley (4) *DG:* Harris
15 Apr	H	Bath	31-21	*T:* R Underwood *C:* Liley *PG:* Liley (5) *DG:* Harris (3)
22 Apr	A	Sale	20-10	*T:* Liley *PG:* Liley (3) *DG:* Harris (2)
29 Apr	H	Bristol	17-3	*T:* Potter *PG:* Liley (3) *DG:* Harris

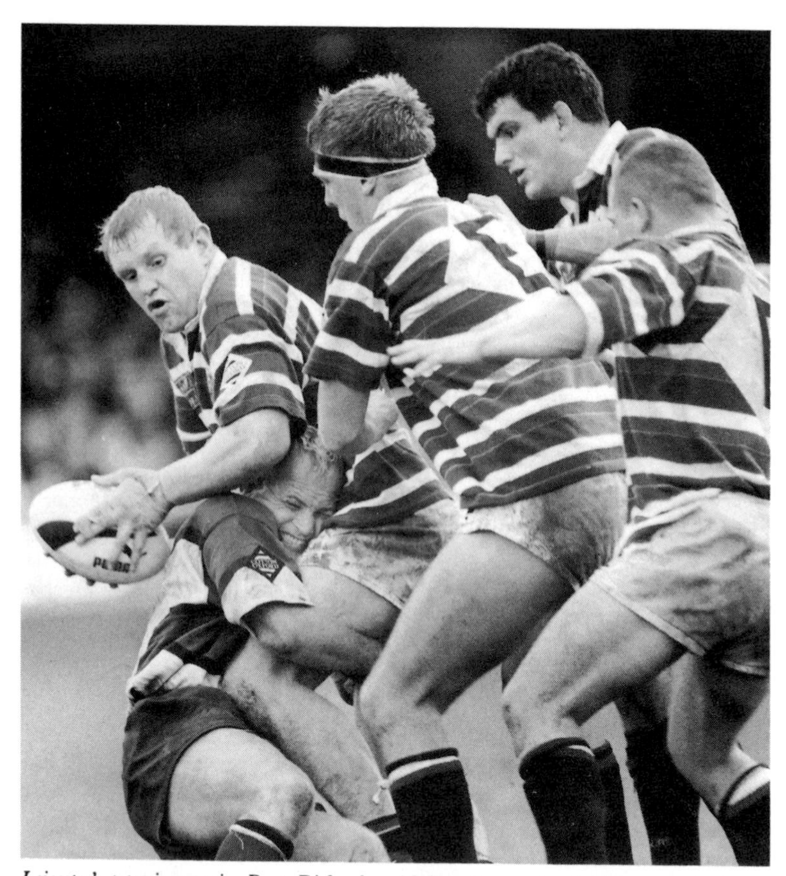

Leicester's totemic captain, Dean Richards, with Tom Smith, Martin Johnson and Richard Cockerill in support, is tackled by Andy Robinson of Bath in the 20-20 draw in October. The Tigers overcame Bath's stranglehold on the competition to take the League title for the first time since its inception in 1987-88.

London Irish

Year of formation 1898
Ground The Avenue, Sunbury-on-Thames, Middlesex Tel: Sunbury (01932) 783034
Colours Emerald green
Most capped player B J Mullin (Ireland) 50 caps
Captain 1994-95 P Bell
Courage Leagues 1994-95 Div 2 5th **Pilkington Cup 1994-95** Lost 15-40 to Harlequins (5th round)

League Record 1994-95

Date	*Venue*	*Opponents*	*Result*	*Scorers*
10 Sept	H	London Scottish	25-13	*T:* Walsh *C:* Corcoran *PG:* Corcoran (6)
17 Sept	A	Saracens	22-35	*T:* Halpin, Saunders, Short *C:* Corcoran (2) *PG:* Corcoran
24 Sept	A	Waterloo	19-22	*T:* Corcoran, Higgins *PG:* Corcoran (3)
1 Oct	H	Fylde	23-12	*T:* Henderson, pen try *C:* Corcoran (2) *PG:* Corcoran (3)
8 Oct	A	Coventry	30-36	*T:* Henderson, Hennessy *C:* Corcoran *PG:* Corcoran (6)
15 Oct	H	Moseley	47-19	*T:* Henderson (2), Hennessy (2), Corcoran, Jamieson, O'Sullivan *C:* Corcoran (3) *PG:* Corcoran (2)
22 Oct	A	Wakefield	3-25	*PG:* Corcoran
29 Oct	H	Nottingham	24-22	*T:* Henderson, O'Sullivan *C:* Corcoran *PG:* Corcoran (4)
5 Nov	A	Newcastle Gosforth	15-9	*T:* Corcoran, Verling *C:* Corcoran *PG:* Corcoran
7 Jan	A	London Scottish	27-15	*T:* Bishop, Street *C:* Cobbe *PG:* Cobbe (4) *DG:* Cobbe
14 Jan	H	Saracens	6-16	*PG:* Cobbe (2)
11 Feb	H	Waterloo	23-3	*T:* Bird (2), Henderson *C:* Cathcart *PG:* Cathcart (2)
4 Mar	A	Fylde	12-27	*T:* McEntegart, Bird *C:* Corcoran
25 Mar	H	Coventry	25-8	*T:* Hall, Irons, McEntegart *C:* Corcoran (2) *PG:* Corcoran (2)
8 Apr	A	Moseley	16-42	*T:* Hennessey, Street *PG:* Corcoran (2)
15 Apr	H	Wakefield	3-33	*PG:* Corcoran
22 Apr	A	Nottingham	11-22	*T:* Neary *PG:* Corcoran (2)
29 Apr	H	Newcastle Gosforth	32-22	*T:* Hennessey, pen try *C:* Corcoran (2) *PG:* Corcoran (5) *DG:* Corcoran

London Scottish

Year of formation 1878
Ground Richmond Athletic Ground, Richmond, Surrey Tel: 0181-332 2473
Colours Blue jersey with red lion crest
Most capped player A G Hastings (Scotland) 56 caps
Captain 1994-95 A P Burnell
Courage Leagues 1994-95 Div 2 4th **Pilkington Cup 1994-95** Lost 6-31 to Bath (4th round)

League Record 1994-95

Date	*Venue*	*Opponents*	*Result*	*Scorers*
10 Sept	A	London Irish	13-25	*T:* Troup *C:* Walker *PG:* Walker (2)
17 Sept	H	Waterloo	13-25	*T:* Millard, Wichary *PG:* Walker
24 Sept	A	Fylde	31-10	*T:* Troup (2), Signorini *C:* Carson (2) *PG:* Carson (4)
1 Oct	H	Coventry	30-0	*T:* Walker (2), Morrison *C:* Wichary (2), Russell *PG:* Russell, Wichary *DG:* Troup

8 Oct	A	Moseley	15-24	*T:* Walker, Johnston *C:* Walker *PG:* Walker
15 Oct	H	Wakefield	24-21	*T:* Millard (2) *C:* Walker *PG:* Walker (3) *DG:* Walker
22 Oct	A	Nottingham	8-23	*T:* Watson *PG:* Walker
29 Oct	H	Newcastle Gosforth	24-13	*T:* Eriksson (2) *C:* Wichary *PG:* Walker *DG:* Walker (2), Troup
5 Nov	A	Saracens	17-27	*T:* Harrold (2) *C:* Wichary, Walker *PG:* Walker
7 Jan	H	London Irish	15-27	*PG:* Walker (4) *DG:* Walker
14 Jan	A	Waterloo	9-17	*PG:* Russell (3)
11 Feb	H	Fylde	28-3	*T:* Clarke, Harrold, Holmes *C:* Steele (2) *PG:* Steele (3)
4 Mar	A	Coventry	19-5	*T:* Ferguson *C:* Steele *PG:* Steele (3) *DG:* Steele
25 Mar	H	Moseley	29-24	*T:* Harrold, Walker *C:* Steele (2) *PG:* Steele (4) *DG:* Steele
1 Apr	A	Newcastle Gosforth	18-10	*T:* Eriksson, Sly *C:* Steele *PG:* Steele (2)
8 Apr	A	Wakefield	19-42	*T:* Jackson *C:* Harrold *PG:* Harrold (4)
15 Apr	H	Nottingham	17-18	*T:* Clarke *PG:* Steele (3) *DG:* Steele
29 Apr	H	Saracens	22-7	*T:* Ferguson, Millard *PG:* Steele (3) *DG:* Steele

Moseley

Year of formation 1873
Ground The Reddings, Reddings Road, Moseley, Birmingham Tel: 0121-499 2149
Colours Red and black
Most capped player M C Teague (England) 27 caps
Captain 1994-95 S D Hodgkinson
Courage Leagues 1994-95 Div 2 6th **Pilkington Cup 1994-95** Lost 6-16 to Northampton (4th round)

League Record 1994-95

Date	*Venue*	*Opponents*	*Result*	*Scorers*
10 Sept	H	Saracens	9-11	*PG:* Kerr (3)
17 Sept	A	Wakefield	22-17	*T:* Robinson *C:* Hodgkinson *PG:* Hodgkinson (5)
24 Sept	H	Nottingham	19-12	*T:* Linnett *C:* Hodgkinson *PG:* Hodgkinson (3) *DG:* Hodgkinson
1 Oct	A	Newcastle Gosforth	10-37	*T:* Poll *C:* Hodgkinson *PG:* Hodgkinson
8 Oct	H	London Scottish	24-15	*T:* Bright (2) *C:* Hodgkinson *PG:* Hodgkinson (4)
15 Oct	A	London Irish	19-47	*T:* Mulraine *C:* Hodgkinson *PG:* Hodgkinson (4)
22 Oct	H	Waterloo	9-25	*PG:* Hodgkinson (3)
29 Oct	A	Fylde	6-10	*PG:* Hodgkinson (2)
5 Nov	H	Coventry	19-8	*T:* Dossett *C:* Hodgkinson *PG:* Kerr, Hodgkinson (3)
7 Jan	A	Saracens	15-17	*T:* Anderson, Kerr *C:* Kerr *PG:* Kerr
14 Jan	H	Wakefield	11-16	*T:* Anderson *PG:* Kerr (2)
11 Feb	A	Nottingham	9-9	*PG:* Hodgkinson (3)
18 Mar	H	Newcastle Gosforth	6-3	*PG:* Kerr (2)
25 Mar	A	London Scottish	24-29	*T:* Hanson, Bruce-Payne *C:* Kerr *PG:* Kerr (4)
8 Apr	H	London Irish	42-16	*T:* Matthews, Becconsall, Payne *C:* Hodgkinson (3) *PG:* Hodgkinson (5) *DG:* Hodgkinson (2)
15 Apr	A	Waterloo	27-12	*T:* Owen (2), Houston, Kerr *C:* Hodgkinson (2) *PG:* Hodgkinson
22 Apr	H	Fylde	6-8	*PG:* Hodgkinson (2)
29 Apr	A	Coventry	22-11	*T:* Robinson *C:* Hodgkinson *PG:* Hodgkinson (5)

Newcastle Gosforth

Year of formation 1877
Ground Kingston Park, Brunton Road, Kenton Bank Foot, Newcastle-upon-Tyne
Tel: 0191-214 0422
Colours Green and white
Most capped player R J McLoughlin (Ireland) 40 caps
Captain 1994-95 R Arnold
Courage Leagues 1994-95 Div 2 3rd **Pilkington Cup 1994-95** Lost 12-58 to Wasps (4th round)

League Record 1994-95

Date	*Venue*	*Opponents*	*Result*	*Scorers*
10 Sept	A	Waterloo	13-18	*T:* Corry *C:* Mason *PG:* Mason (2)
17 Sept	H	Fylde	45-14	*T:* Wilkinson (2), Archer, Arnold, Chandler *C:* Mason (4) *PG:* Mason (4)
24 Sept	A	Coventry	15-19	*T:* Wilkinson, Merritt *C:* Mason *PG:* Mason
1 Oct	H	Moseley	37-10	*T:* Casado, Long, Penn, Vanzandvliet, Wilkinson *C:* Mason (3) *PG:* Mason (2)
8 Oct	A	Wakefield	21-9	*T:* Archer, Penn *C:* Mason *PG:* Mason (3)
15 Oct	H	Nottingham	27-6	*T:* Corry, Mason *C:* Mason *PG:* Mason (5)
22 Oct	H	Saracens	11-17	*T:* Hetherington *PG:* Mason (2)
29 Oct	A	London Scottish	13-24	*T:* Penn *C:* Mason *PG:* Mason (2)
5 Nov	H	London Irish	9-15	*PG:* Mason (2) *DG:* Mason
7 Jan	H	Waterloo	33-16	*T:* Arnold, Douglas, Hetherington, Penn *C:* Mason (2) *PG:* Mason (3)
14 Jan	A	Fylde	12-6	*PG:* Mason (4)
11 Feb	H	Coventry	38-22	*T:* Arnold, Douglas, Penn, Hetherington, Tetlow, Vanzandvliet *C:* Mason *PG:* Mason (2)
18 Mar	A	Moseley	3-6	*PG:* Mason
25 Mar	H	Wakefield	15-15	*PG:* Mason (4) *DG:* Mason
1 Apr	H	London Scottish	10-18	*T:* Penn *C:* Mason *PG:* Mason
8 Apr	A	Nottingham	33-18	*T:* Cramb, Corry, Metcalfe *C:* Mason (3) *PG:* Mason (4)
15 Apr	A	Saracens	16-16	*T:* Whitfield *C:* Mason *PG:* Mason (3)
29 Apr	A	London Irish	22-32	*T:* Penn (2), Corry *C:* Mason (2) *PG:* Mason

Northampton

Year of formation 1888
Ground Franklins Gardens, Weedon Road, Northampton
Tel: Northampton (01604) 751543
Colours Black, green and gold
Most capped player G S Pearce (England) 36 caps
Captain 1994-95 T A K Rodber
Courage Leagues 1994-95 Div 1 10th *relegated* **Pilkington Cup 1994-95** Lost 6-26 to Bath (quarter-final)

League Record 1994-95

Date	*Venue*	*Opponents*	*Result*	*Scorers*
10 Sept	A	Leicester	15-28	*PG:* Grayson (5)
17 Sept	H	Bath	16-32	*T:* Grayson *C:* Grayson *PG:* Grayson (3)
24 Sept	A	Sale	6-41	*PG:* Grayson (2)
1 Oct	H	Bristol	15-18	*PG:* Grayson (5)
8 Oct	H	Harlequins	16-23	*T:* Hunter *C:* Grayson *PG:* Grayson (2) *DG:* Grayson
15 Oct	A	Orrell	10-13	*T:* Dawson *C:* Grayson *PG:* Grayson
22 Oct	H	Gloucester	9-6	*PG:* Grayson (3)

29 Oct	A	Wasps	21-27	*T:* Pountney, Rodber *C:* Grayson *PG:* Grayson (3)
5 Nov	H	West Hartlepool	25-14	*T:* Cassell *C:* Grayson *PG:* Grayson (6)
7 Jan	H	Leicester	18-20	*T:* Rodber, Seely *C:* Grayson *PG:* Grayson (2)
14 Jan	A	Bath	6-26	*PG:* Grayson (2)
11 Feb	H	Sale	9-22	*PG:* Grayson (3)
4 Mar	A	Bristol	24-13	*T:* Hunter, Dawson, Thorneycroft, Allen *C:* Grayson (2)
25 Mar	A	Harlequins	9-10	*PG:* Grayson (3)
8 Apr	H	Orrell	15-3	*PG:* Grayson (4) *DG:* Grayson
15 Apr	A	Gloucester	13-14	*T:* Dawson *C:* Grayson *PG:* Grayson (2)
22 Apr	H	Wasps	19-13	*T:* Seely *C:* Grayson *PG:* Grayson (4)
29 Apr	A	West Hartlepool	21-12	*T:* Allen, Seely *C:* Grayson *PG:* Grayson (2) *DG:* Hepher

Nottingham

Year of formation 1877
Ground Ireland Avenue, Beeston, Nottingham Tel: Nottingham (0115) 9254238
Colours White and green
Most capped player C R Andrew (England) 65 caps
Captain 1994-95 D West
Courage Leagues 1994-95 Div 2 7th **Pilkington Cup 1994-95** Lost 10-41 to Bristol (4th round)

League Record 1994-95

Date	*Venue*	*Opponents*	*Result*	*Scorers*
10 Sept	A	Fylde	14-33	*T:* Bygrave *PG:* Gallagher (3)
17 Sept	H	Coventry	23-7	*T:* Furley, Musto *C:* Gallagher (2) *PG:* Gallagher (3)
24 Sept	A	Moseley	12-19	*PG:* Gallagher (4)
1 Oct	H	Wakefield	29-25	*T:* Bradley, Smallwood *C:* Gallagher (2) *PG:* Gallagher (5)
8 Oct	H	Saracens	9-17	*PG:* Gallagher (3)
15 Oct	A	Newcastle Gosforth	6-27	*PG:* Stent (2)
22 Oct	H	London Scottish	23-8	*T:* Stent, pen try *C:* Stent (2) *PG:* Stent (3)
29 Oct	A	London Irish	22-24	*T:* West *C:* Stent *PG:* Stent (5)
5 Nov	H	Waterloo	28-11	*T:* Furley (2), pen try *C:* Stent (2) *PG:* Stent (3)
7 Jan	H	Fylde	9-10	*PG:* Stent (3)
14 Jan	A	Coventry	19-6	*T:* West *C:* Gallagher *PG:* Gallagher (3) *DG:* Carroll
11 Feb	H	Moseley	9-9	*PG:* Gallagher (3)
4 Mar	A	Wakefield	17-22	*T:* Passmore, Smallwood, pen try *C:* Gabriel
25 Mar	A	Saracens	7-32	*T:* Musto *C:* Gallagher
8 Apr	H	Newcastle Gosforth	18-33	*T:* Bees, Gabriel, Smallwood *PG:* Gallagher
15 Apr	A	London Scottish	18-17	*T:* Gallagher, West *C:* Stent *PG:* Stent (2)
22 Apr	H	London Irish	22-11	*T:* Gray, Stent *PG:* Stent (4)
29 Apr	A	Waterloo	14-11	*T:* Smallwood *PG:* Stent (3)

Orrell

Year of formation 1927
Ground Edge Hall Road, Orrell, Lancashire Tel: Upholland (01695) 623193
Colours Black and amber
Most capped player J Carleton (England) 26 caps
Captain 1994-95 C D Morris
Courage Leagues 1994-95 Div 1 5th **Pilkington Cup 1994-95** Lost 19-25 to Bath (5th round)

League Record 1994-95

Date	*Venue*	*Opponents*	*Result*	*Scorers*
10 Sept	A	West Hartlepool	19-17	*T:* Wynn *C:* Ainscough *PG:* Ainscough (3), Langford
17 Sept	H	Leicester	0-6	
24 Sept	A	Bath	13-32	*T:* Wynn (2) *PG:* Winstanley
1 Oct	H	Sale	22-19	*T:* Naylor *C:* Langford *PG:* Langford (5)
8 Oct	A	Bristol	9-20	*PG:* Langford (3)
15 Oct	H	Northampton	13-10	*T:* Bruce, Wynn *PG:* Langford
22 Oct	A	Harlequins	8-6	*T:* Morris *PG:* Langford
29 Oct	A	Gloucester	6-9	*PG:* Langford (2)
5 Nov	H	Wasps	10-16	*T:* Healey *C:* Hamer *PG:* Hamer
7 Jan	H	West Hartlepool	22-22	*T:* Hamer *C:* Langford *PG:* Langford (4) *DG:* Hamer
14 Jan	A	Leicester	19-29	*T:* Morris, Naylor *PG:* Langford (3)
11 Feb	H	Bath	6-6	*PG:* Langford (2)
4 Mar	A	Sale	8-8	*T:* Wynn *PG:* Langford
25 Mar	H	Bristol	20-16	*T:* Horrocks *PG:* Ainscough (5)
8 Apr	A	Northampton	3-15	*DG:* Taberner
15 Apr	H	Harlequins	10-28	*T:* Horrocks *C:* Ainscough *PG:* Ainscough
22 Apr	H	Gloucester	43-14	*T:* Ainscough (2), Wynn (2), Horrocks, Morris, Taberner *C:* Ainscough (4)
29 Apr	A	Wasps	25-53	*T:* Langford, Naylor *PG:* Ainscough (4), Langford

Sale

Year of formation 1861
Ground Heywood Road, Brooklands, Sale, Cheshire Tel: 0161-973 6348
Colours Blue and white
Most capped player F E Cotton (England) 31 caps
Captain 1994-95 M Kenrick
Courage Leagues 1994-95 Div 1 4th **Pilkington Cup 1994-95** Lost 12-14 to Leicester (quarter-final)

League Record 1994-95

Date	*Venue*	*Opponents*	*Result*	*Scorers*
10 Sept	H	Harlequins	19-20	*T:* Stocks, Ashurst, Vyvyan *C:* Turner (2)
17 Sept	A	Bristol	22-44	*T:* Mallinder *C:* Turner *PG:* Turner (4) *DG:* Turner
24 Sept	H	Northampton	41-6	*T:* Appleson (2), O'Grady (2), Mallinder *C:* Turner (5) *DG:* Turner, Mallinder
1 Oct	A	Orrell	19-22	*T:* Ashurst, O'Grady, Vyvyan *C:* Turner (2)
8 Oct	H	Gloucester	16-14	*T:* Verbickas (2) *PG:* Turner (2)
15 Oct	A	Wasps	22-52	*T:* Baldwin, Baxendell, Stocks *C:* Liley (2) *PG:* Liley
22 Oct	H	West Hartlepool	22-7	*T:* Verbickas, Vyvyan, Warr *C:* Turner (2) *PG:* Turner
29 Oct	A	Leicester	20-37	*T:* Baxendell, Vyvyan *C:* Turner (2) *PG:* Turner *DG:* Turner
5 Nov	H	Bath	3-19	*PG:* Liley
7 Jan	A	Harlequins	15-15	*T:* Baxendell, Fowler *C:* Turner *PG:* Turner
14 Jan	H	Bristol	21-9	*T:* Mallinder, Stocks *C:* Turner *PG:* Turner (3)
11 Feb	A	Northampton	22-9	*T:* Ashurst, Stocks, Yates *C:* Turner (2) *PG:* Turner
4 Mar	H	Orrell	8-8	*T:* Yates *PG:* Turner
25 Mar	A	Gloucester	20-8	*T:* Fowler, Mallinder, Turner *C:* Liley *PG:* Liley
8 Apr	H	Wasps	12-17	*PG:* Liley (4)
15 Apr	A	West Hartlepool	17-23	*T:* Yates (2), Mallinder *C:* Liley
22 Apr	H	Leicester	10-20	*T:* Stocks *C:* Liley *PG:* Liley
29 Apr	A	Bath	18-13	*T:* Appleson, Baldwin *C:* Liley *PG:* Liley (2)

Saracens

Year of formation 1876
Ground Bramley Sports Ground, Green Road, Southgate, London N14
Tel: 0181-449 3770
Colours Black with red star and crescent
Most capped player J Leonard (England) 38 caps
Captain 1994-95 B Davies
Courage Leagues 1994-95 Div 2 *Winners – promoted* **Pilkington Cup 1994-95** Lost 5-9 to Harlequins (4th round)

League Record 1994-95

Date	*Venue*	*Opponents*	*Result*	*Scorers*
10 Sept	A	Moseley	11-9	*T:* Harries *PG:* Tunningley *DG:* Lee
17 Sept	H	London Irish	35-22	*T:* Diprose, Green, Tunningley, Harries *C:* Tunningley (3) *PG:* Tunningley (2) *DG:* Lee
24 Sept	A	Wakefield	8-17	*T:* Diprose *DG:* Lee
1 Oct	H	Waterloo	27-5	*T:* Crawley, Green, Lee *C:* Tunningley (3) *PG:* Tunningley (2)
8 Oct	A	Nottingham	17-9	*T:* Butler *PG:* Tunningley (3) *DG:* Lee
15 Oct	H	Fylde	18-7	*PG:* Tunningley (6)
22 Oct	A	Newcastle Gosforth	17-11	*T:* Green *PG:* Tunningley (4)
29 Oct	A	Coventry	33-16	*T:* Buckton (2), Butler, Harries *C:* Tunningley (2) *PG:* Tunningley (3)
5 Nov	H	London Scottish	27-17	*T:* Harries, Tunningley *C:* Tunningley *PG:* Tunningley (3) *DG:* Lee (2)
7 Jan	H	Moseley	17-15	*T:* Gregory, Hill, Wilson *C:* Tunningley
14 Jan	A	London Irish	16-6	*T:* Buckton, Harries *PG:* Tunningley (2)
11 Feb	H	Wakefield	10-3	*T:* Green *C:* Tunningley *PG:* Tunningley
4 Mar	A	Waterloo	23-16	*T:* Diprose, pen try *C:* Tunningley (2) *PG:* Tunningley (3)
25 Mar	H	Nottingham	32-7	*T:* Botterman, Butler, Clark, Green *PG:* Lee (3), Tunningley
8 Apr	A	Fylde	37-15	*T:* Diprose, Hill, Green, Harries, Gregory *C:* Tunningley (3) *PG:* Tunningley (2)
15 Apr	H	Newcastle Gosforth	16-16	*T:* Clark (2) *PG:* Tunningley (2)
22 Apr	H	Coventry	38-0	*T:* Butler, Dooley, Green, Hill, Langley, Tunningley *C:* Tunningley (4)
29 Apr	A	London Scottish	7-22	*T:* pen try *C:* Tunningley

Wakefield

Year of formation 1901
Ground Pinderfields Road, College Grove, Wakefield Tel: Wakefield (01924) 372038
Colours Black and gold hoops
Most capped player M E Harrison (England) 15 caps
Captain 1994-95 M Jackson
Courage Leagues 1994-95 Div 2 2nd **Pilkington Cup 1994-95** Lost 8-13 to Harlequins (quarter-final)

League Record 1994-95

Date	*Venue*	*Opponents*	*Result*	*Scorers*
10 Sept	A	Coventry	15-14	*T:* Morley (2) *C:* Jackson *PG:* Jackson
17 Sept	H	Moseley	17-22	*T:* Morley *PG:* Jackson (4)
24 Sept	H	Saracens	17-8	*T:* Thompson (2) *C:* Jackson (2) *PG:* Jackson

1 Oct	A	Nottingham	25-29	*T:* Maynard *C:* Jackson *PG:* Jackson (6)
8 Oct	H	Newcastle Gosforth	9-21	*PG:* Jackson (3)
15 Oct	A	London Scottish	21-24	*T:* Stewart, Thompson *C:* Jackson *PG:* Jackson (2), Scully
22 Oct	H	London Irish	25-3	*T:* Garnett *C:* Jackson *PG:* Jackson (6)
29 Oct	A	Waterloo	19-18	*T:* Petyt, Maynard *PG:* Jackson (2) *DG:* Petyt
5 Nov	H	Fylde	24-13	*T:* Metcalfe, Scully *C:* Jackson *PG:* Jackson (4)
7 Jan	H	Coventry	19-14	*T:* White *C:* Jackson *PG:* Jackson (4)
14 Jan	A	Moseley	16-11	*T:* Thompson *C:* Jackson *PG:* Jackson (3)
11 Feb	A	Saracens	3-10	*PG:* Jackson
4 Mar	H	Nottingham	22-17	*T:* White *C:* Jackson *PG:* Jackson (5)
25 Mar	A	Newcastle Gosforth	15-15	*PG:* Jackson (5)
8 Apr	H	London Scottish	42-19	*T:* Jackson (2), Falkingham, White, Scully, Thompson *C:* Jackson (3) *PG:* Jackson (2)
15 Apr	A	London Irish	33-3	*T:* Thompson (2), Garnett, Maynard *C:* Jackson (2) *PG:* Jackson (3)
22 Apr	H	Waterloo	21-12	*T:* Holloway (2) *C:* Jackson *PG:* Jackson (3)
29 Apr	A	Fylde	11-8	*T:* Falkingham *PG:* Jackson (2)

Wasps

Year of formation 1867
Ground Repton Avenue (off Rugby Road), Sudbury, Middlesex Tel: 0181-902 4220
Colours Black with gold wasp on left breast
Most capped player C R Andrew (England) 65 caps
Captain 1994-95 D Ryan
Courage Leagues 1994-95 Div 1 3rd **Pilkington Cup 1994-95** Lost 16-36 to Bath (final)

League Record 1994-95

Date	*Venue*	*Opponents*	*Result*	*Scorers*
10 Sept	H	Gloucester	45-8	*T:* Andrew (2), Ufton, Dallaglio, Childs, D Hopley, Greenstock *C:* Andrew (2) *PG:* Andrew (2)
17 Sept	A	Harlequins	57-26	*T:* Greenstock (2), Hunter (2), Childs, Dallaglio, D Hopley, Ryan, Wilkins *C:* Andrew (3) *PG:* Andrew *DG:* Andrew
24 Sept	A	West Hartlepool	15-20	*T:* Greenwood, Dunston *C:* Gregory *PG:* Gregory
1 Oct	H	Leicester	18-23	*PG:* Andrew (5) *DG:* Andrew
8 Oct	A	Bath	9-12	*PG:* Andrew (3)
15 Oct	H	Sale	52-22	*T:* D Hopley (3), Childs, P Hopley, Kinsey *C:* Andrew (5) *PG:* Andrew (3) *DG:* Andrew
22 Oct	A	Bristol	25-24	*T:* pen try, Pilgrim, Ufton *C:* Andrew (2) *PG:* Andrew (2)
29 Oct	H	Northampton	27-21	*T:* Wilkins, Dallaglio, Delaney, P Hopley *C:* Andrew (2) *PG:* Andrew
5 Nov	A	Orrell	16-10	*T:* D Hopley *C:* Gregory *PG:* Gregory (3)
7 Jan	A	Gloucester	21-16	*T:* P Hopley, Bates, Dallaglio *PG:* Andrew (2)
21 Jan	H	Harlequins	25-7	*T:* Greenstock (2), Ufton *C:* Gregory (2) *PG:* Gregory (2)
11 Feb	H	West Hartlepool	33-22	*T:* Braithwaite (2), Childs, Dallaglio, Delaney *C:* Braithwaite (3), Ufton
4 Mar	A	Leicester	6-21	*PG:* Andrew (2)
25 Mar	H	Bath	11-10	*T:* Greenwood *PG:* Andrew (2)
8 Apr	A	Sale	17-12	*T:* P Hopley (2), Gomarsall *C:* Ufton
15 Apr	H	Bristol	27-15	*T:* P Hopley, Kinsey *C:* Gregory *PG:* Gregory (5)
22 Apr	A	Northampton	13-19	*T:* James *C:* Andrew *PG:* Andrew (2)
29 Apr	H	Orrell	53-25	*T:* Dunn, Greenstock, Greenwood, P Hopley, D Hopley, Kinsey, Ufton, White *C:* Andrew (4), P Hopley *PG:* Andrew

Waterloo

Year of formation 1882
Ground St Anthony's Road, Blundellsands, Liverpool Tel: 0151-924 4552
Colours Green, red and white
Most capped player H G Periton (England) 21 caps
Captain 1994-95 P Buckton
Courage Leagues 1994-95 Div 2 8th **Pilkington Cup 1994-95** Lost 13-54 to Wasps (5th round)

League Record 1994-95

Date	*Venue*	*Opponents*	*Result*	*Scorers*
10 Sept	H	Newcastle Gosforth	18-13	*PG:* Swindells (6)
17 Sept	A	London Scottish	25-13	*T:* White *C:* Swindells *PG:* Swindells (5) *DG:* Ryan
24 Sept	H	London Irish	22-19	*T:* Beeley, Northey *PG:* Ryan (2) *DG:* Ryan (2)
1 Oct	A	Saracens	5-27	*T:* Ryan
8 Oct	A	Fylde	16-12	*T:* Brennand, Ryan *PG:* Swindells (2)
15 Oct	H	Coventry	26-5	*T:* Buckton (2) *C:* Swindells (2) *PG:* Swindells (4)
22 Oct	A	Moseley	25-9	*T:* Bibby, Craig, Wright *C:* Swindells (2) *PG:* Swindells (2)
29 Oct	H	Wakefield	18-19	*PG:* Swindells (5) *DG:* Aitchison
5 Nov	A	Nottingham	11-28	*T:* Brennand *PG:* Swindells (2)
7 Jan	A	Newcastle Gosforth	16-33	*T:* Ryan, Wright *PG:* Swindells (2)
14 Jan	H	London Scottish	17-9	*T:* Greenhalgh *PG:* Ryan (2), Swindells (2)
11 Feb	A	London Irish	3-23	*PG:* Swindells
4 Mar	H	Saracens	16-23	*T:* Wright *C:* Swindells *PG:* Swindells (3)
25 Mar	H	Fylde	12-19	*PG:* Swindells (4)
8 Apr	A	Coventry	22-17	*T:* Allott *C:* Swindells *PG:* Swindells (4) *DG:* Wright
15 Apr	H	Moseley	12-27	*T:* Swindells, Wright *C:* Swindells
22 Apr	A	Wakefield	12-21	*PG:* Swindells (4)
29 Apr	H	Nottingham	11-14	*T:* Ryan *PG:* Swindells (2)

West Hartlepool

Year of formation 1881
Ground Brierton Lane, Hartlepool Tel: Hartlepool (01429) 272640
Colours Red, green and white hoops
Most capped player C D Aarvold (England) 16 caps
Captain 1994-95 P Hodder
Courage Leagues 1994-95 Div 1 9th **Pilkington Cup 1994-95** Lost 7-28 to Orrell (4th round)

League Record 1994-95

Date	*Venue*	*Opponents*	*Result*	*Scorers*
10 Sept	H	Orrell	17-19	*T:* G Evans *PG:* Oliphant (4)
17 Sept	A	Gloucester	12-48	*PG:* Oliphant (4)
24 Sept	H	Wasps	20-15	*T:* Emmerson, Stabler *C:* Oliphant (2) *PG:* Oliphant (2)
1 Oct	A	Harlequins	10-20	*T:* Hodder *C:* Oliphant *PG:* Oliphant
8 Oct	A	Leicester	16-33	*T:* Stabler *C:* Oliphant *PG:* Oliphant (3)
15 Oct	H	Bath	18-20	*T:* Cooke, Hodder, Watson *PG:* Stimpson
22 Oct	A	Sale	7-22	*T:* Stimpson *C:* Oliphant
29 Oct	H	Bristol	47-11	*T:* Watson (2), Brown, Elwine, O Evans, Hodder, Stimpson *C:* Stimpson (3) *PG:* Stimpson (2)
5 Nov	A	Northampton	14-25	*T:* Hodder, Whitaker *C:* Stimpson (2)
7 Jan	A	Orrell	22-22	*T:* Hodder *C:* Stimpson *PG:* Stimpson (5)

14 Jan	H	Gloucester	22-21	*T:* Elwine, Jones, D Mitchell *C:* Stimpson (2) *PG:* Stimpson
11 Feb	A	Wasps	22-33	*T:* Herbert *C:* Stimpson *PG:* Stimpson (5)
4 Mar	H	Harlequins	10-8	*T:* Brown, Jones
25 Mar	H	Leicester	6-12	*PG:* Stimpson (2)
8 Apr	A	Bath	17-53	*T:* Brown, Cook, Elwine *C:* Oliphant
15 Apr	H	Sale	23-17	*T:* Cook, O Evans, Jaques *C:* Stimpson *PG:* Stimpson (2)
22 Apr	A	Bristol	17-12	*T:* Cook, O Evans *C:* Stimpson (2) *PG:* Stimpson
29 Apr	H	Northampton	12-21	*T:* Cook, O Evans *C:* Stimpson

SCOTLAND

Biggar

Year of formation 1975
Ground Hartree Mill, Biggar Tel: Biggar (01899) 21219
Colours Black jersey with red collar and cuffs
Captain 1994-95 T Young
McEwan's 70/- National League: Div 2 4th

League Record 1994-95

Date	*Venue*	*Opponents*	*Result*	*Scorers*
10 Sept	H	Kelso	18-22	*T:* Harrison, Harvey *C:* Bruce *PG:* Bruce (2)
17 Sept	A	Wigtownshire	15-14	*T:* Cairns, Harvey *C:* Bruce *PG:* Bruce
24 Sept	H	Preston Lodge FP	13-13	*T:* Harvey *C:* Bruce *PG:* Bruce (2)
1 Oct	A	Selkirk	3-21	*PG:* Bruce
8 Oct	H	Edinburgh Wands	21-10	*T:* Harrison, Harvey, Lindsey *PG:* Bruce (2)
15 Oct	H	Kirkcaldy	24-19	*T:* Abernethy (2), Lindsey, R Young *C:* Harrison (2)
5 Nov	A	Grangemouth	16-19	*T:* Abernethy, Harrison *PG:* Harrison (2)
26 Nov	H	Glasgow Acads	17-9	*T:* Harvey, Watson *C:* Lavery (2) *PG:* Lavery
14 Jan	A	Gordonians	15-13	*T:* Harvey, Rose *C:* Lavery *PG:* Lavery
28 Jan	H	Musselburgh	8-6	*T:* S Jack *PG:* Lavery
11 Feb	A	Haddington	8-0	*T:* L Steele *PG:* Lavery
25 Feb	H	Corstorphine	13-13	*T:* Nisbet, T Young *PG:* Lavery
11 Mar	A	Peebles	9-14	*PG:* Lavery (2), W Steel

Boroughmuir

Year of formation 1919 (Boroughmuir FP until 1974)
Ground Meggetland, Colinton Road, Edinburgh EH14 1AS Tel: 0131-443 7571
Colours Blue and green quarters
Most capped player S R P Lineen (Scotland) 29 caps
Captain 1994-95 S J Reid
McEwan's 70/- National League Div 1 5th

League Record 1994-95

Date	*Venue*	*Opponents*	*Result*	*Scorers*
10 Sept	A	Glasgow High/K'side	16-36	*T:* McCallum *C:* Easson *PG:* Easson (3)
17 Sept	H	Stewart's-Melville FP	15-10	*PG:* Easson (4) *DG:* Easson
24 Sept	A	Gala	56-3	*T:* Cunningham, Easson, Hall, Lineen, Mardon, Reid, Stark *C:* Easson (6) *PG:* Easson (3)
1 Oct	A	Heriot's FP	9-15	*PG:* Easson (3)
8 Oct	H	West of Scotland	47-17	*T:* Finnie (2), Lineen, Stark (2), Tukalo (2) *C:* Easson (3) *PG:* Easson (2)
15 Oct	A	Dundee HSFP	15-35	*T:* Hall, Reid *C:* Easson *PG:* Easson
5 Nov	H	Jedforest	23-19	*T:* Laird, Stark (2), Tukalo *PG:* Reekie

26 Nov	A	Currie	30-13	*T:* Mardon (2), Reid, Tukalo *C:* Easson (2) *PG:* Easson (2)
14 Jan	H	Melrose	53-29	*T:* Burns (3), Hall, Jennings, Stark, Tukalo, Wright *C:* Easson (5) *PG:* Easson
28 Jan	A	Watsonians	26-9	*T:* Stark (2), Tukalo *C:* Easson *PG:* Easson (2) *DG:* Easson
11 Feb	H	Edinburgh Acads	8-9	*T:* Lineen *PG:* Easson
25 Feb	A	Stirling County	9-13	*PG:* Easson (3)
11 Mar	H	Hawick	18-18	*T:* Finnie, Knight, Reid *PG:* Easson

Corstorphine

Year of formation 1921
Ground Union Park, Carricknowe Parkway, Corstorphine, Edinburgh
Tel: 0131-334 8063
Colours Navy blue and scarlet quarters
Captain 1994-95 S R Maclean
McEwan's 70/- National League Div 2 10th

League Record 1994-95

Date	*Venue*	*Opponents*	*Result*	*Scorers*
10 Sept	A	Glasgow Acads	0-17	
17 Sept	H	Gordonians	18-9	*T:* Lillas, Robinson *C:* S R Maclean *PG:* S R Maclean (2)
24 Sept	A	Musselburgh	9-17	*PG:* Pollock (3)
1 Oct	H	Haddington	15-6	*PG:* S R Maclean (4) *DG:* Pollock
8 Oct	A	Kirkcaldy	22-20	*T:* Zavaroni *C:* S R Maclean *PG:* S R Maclean (4) *DG:* Pollock
15 Oct	A	Peebles	11-13	*T:* Zavaroni *PG:* S R Maclean (2)
5 Nov	H	Kelso	13-18	*T:* Dwyer *C:* Pollock *PG:* Pollock (2)
26 Nov	A	Wigtownshire	6-10	*PG:* Pollock (2)
14 Jan	H	Preston Lodge FP	12-18	*PG:* Pollock (3) *DG:* Pollock
11 Feb	H	Edinburgh Wands	19-0	*T:* S R Maclean *C:* S R Maclean *PG:* S R Maclean (3) *DG:* Donaldson
25 Feb	A	Biggar	13-13	*T:* M Maclean *C:* Pollock *PG:* S R Maclean, Pollock
11 Mar	H	Grangemouth	26-15	*T:* S R Maclean *PG:* Pollock (7)
25 Mar	A	Selkirk	16-58	*T:* Barry, McDonald *PG:* Pollock (2)

Currie

Year of formation 1970
Ground Malleny Park, Balerno, Edinburgh EH14 5HA Tel: 0131-449 2432
Colours Amber and black
Captain 1994-95 A Donaldson
McEwan's 70/- National League Div 1 13th

League Record 1994-95

Date	*Venue*	*Opponents*	*Result*	*Scorers*
10 Sept	A	Melrose	9-22	*PG:* Donaldson (2) *DG:* Donaldson
17 Sept	H	Watsonians	17-47	*T:* Dunn, Wilson *C:* Donaldson (2) *PG:* Donaldson
24 Sept	A	Edinburgh Acads	8-14	*T:* Plumb *PG:* Donaldson
1 Oct	H	Stirling County	7-13	*T:* Dickson *C:* Donaldson
8 Oct	A	Hawick	17-19	*T:* Wilson *PG:* Donaldson (3) *DG:* Donaldson
15 Oct	H	Glasgow High/K'side	20-6	*T:* Te Whaiti *PG:* Donaldson (4) *DG:* Plumb
5 Nov	A	Stewart's-Melville FP	12-21	*PG:* Donaldson (4)

26 Nov	H	Boroughmuir	13-30	*T:* Donaldson *C:* Donaldson *PG:* Donaldson (2)
14 Jan	A	Heriot's FP	11-22	*T:* Dickson *PG:* Donaldson (2)
25 Feb	H	Jedforest	28-32	*T:* Blair, Ellis, Wilson *C:* Donaldson (2) *PG:* Donaldson (3)
11 Mar	A	Gala	15-36	*T:* Keen, Robertson *C:* Donaldson *PG:* Donaldson
25 Mar	H	West of Scotland	9-3	*PG:* Donaldson (3)
1 Apr	A	Dundee HSFP	22-15	*T:* Donaldson *C:* Donaldson *PG:* Donaldson (4) *DG:* Donaldson

Dundee High School FP

Year of formation 1880
Ground Mayfield, Arbroath Road, Dundee Tel: Dundee (01382) 453517 (ground) and 451045 (clubhouse)
Colours Blue and red
Most capped player D G Leslie (Scotland) 32 caps
Captain 1994-95 W A Keys
McEwan's 70/- National League Div 1 12th

League Record 1994-95

Date	*Venue*	*Opponents*	*Result*	*Scorers*
10 Sept	A	Edinburgh Acads	9-9	*PG:* J R Newton (3)
17 Sept	H	Stirling County	18-19	*T:* Sandford (2) *C:* J R Newton *PG:* J R Newton (2)
24 Sept	A	Hawick	10-23	*T:* Langstaff *C:* J R Newtown *PG:* J R Newton
1 Oct	H	Glasgow High/K'side	6-9	*PG:* J R Newton (2)
8 Oct	H	Stewart's-Melville FP	24-20	*T:* Langstaff, Smith *C:* J R Newton *PG:* J R Newton (4)
15 Oct	H	Boroughmuir	35-15	*T:* Cousin, Hamilton, Jardine, Longstaff *C:* J R Newton (3) *PG:* J R Newton (3)
5 Nov	A	Heriot's FP	3-33	*PG:* J R Newton
26 Nov	H	West of Scotland	18-8	*T:* Cousin, pen try *C:* J R Newton *PG:* J R Newton (2)
14 Jan	A	Gala	10-32	*T:* Hamilton *C:* J R Newton *PG:* J R Newton
25 Feb	A	Melrose	20-23	*T:* Jardine, Smith *C:* J R Newton (2) *PG:* J R Newton (2)
11 Mar	A	Jedforest	21-24	*T:* Milne, Samson *C:* J R Newton *PG:* J R Newton (3)
25 Mar	H	Watsonians	11-27	*T:* Lamont *PG:* Tosh (2)
1 Apr	H	Currie	15-22	*PG:* J R Newton (5)

Edinburgh Academicals

Year of formation 1857
Ground Raeburn Place, Stockbridge, Edinburgh EH4 1HQ Tel: 0131-332 1070
Colours Blue and white hoops
Most capped player D M B Sole (Scotland) 44 caps
Captain 1994-95 D J McIvor
McEwan's 70/- National League Div 1 3rd

League Record 1994-95

Date	*Venue*	*Opponents*	*Result*	*Scorers*
10 Sept	H	Dundee HSFP	9-9	*PG:* Shepherd (2) *DG:* Shepherd
17 Sept	A	Jedforest	16-22	*T:* Russell *C:* Shepherd *PG:* Shepherd (3)
24 Sept	H	Currie	14-8	*T:* Newton *PG:* Shepherd (3)
1 Oct	A	Melrose	10-20	*T:* pen try *C:* Shepherd *PG:* Shepherd

8 Oct	H	Watsonians	25-26	*T:* Newton *C:* Shepherd *PG:* Shepherd (5) *DG:* Hay-Smith
15 Oct	H	Gala	0-0	
5 Nov	A	Stirling County	11-18	*T:* Burns *PG:* Shepherd (2)
26 Nov	H	Hawick	14-0	*T:* T A McVie *PG:* Hay-Smith, Shepherd *DG:* Hay-Smith
14 Jan	A	Glasgow High/K'side	25-20	*T:* Hoole, Newton *PG:* Shepherd (4) *DG:* Hay-Smith
28 Jan	H	Stewart's-Melville FP	30-0	*T:* Haslett, Hay-Smith, McIvor *PG:* Hay-Smith (4) *DG:* Burns
11 Feb	A	Boroughmuir	9-8	*PG:* Hay-Smith (3)
25 Feb	H	Heriot's FP	33-3	*T:* Hoole, Simmers, Swanson (2) *C:* Hay-Smith (2) *PG:* Hay-Smith (3)
1 Apr	A	West of Scotland	20-7	*T:* Fairbourne *PG:* Hay-Smith (4) *DG:* Hay-Smith

Edinburgh Wanderers

Year of formation 1868
Ground Murrayfield, Edinburgh EH12 5QG Tel: 0131-337 2196
Colours Red and black
Most capped player A R Smith (Scotland) 33 caps
Captain 1994-95 D Graham
McEwan's 70/- National League Div 2 11th

League Record 1994-95

Date	*Venue*	*Opponents*	*Result*	*Scorers*
10 Sept	H	Wigtownshire	30-15	*T:* Graham, Macrae, Rowley, Thomson, Waddell *C:* Bremner *PG:* Bremner
17 Sept	A	Preston Lodge FP	11-43	*T:* Melrose *PG:* Bremner (2)
24 Sept	H	Selkirk	23-25	*T:* Gillan (2) *C:* Bremner (2) *PG:* Bremner (3)
1 Oct	H	Kirkcaldy	23-10	*T:* Edwards, Lorrain-Smith, Melrose *C:* Bremner *PG:* Bremner *DG:* Bremner
8 Oct	A	Biggar	10-21	*T:* Melrose, Wilson
15 Oct	H	Grangemouth	20-19	*T:* Gillan, pen try *C:* Edwards (2) *PG:* Gillan (2)
5 Nov	A	Glasgow Acads	16-31	*T:* Boswell, Hepburn *PG:* Bremner (2)
26 Nov	H	Gordonians	18-12	*T:* Dunlop, Lorrain-Smith *C:* Gillan *PG:* Gillan (2)
14 Jan	A	Musselburgh	6-11	*PG:* Cropper (2)
11 Feb	A	Corstorphine	0-19	
25 Feb	H	Peebles	3-8	*PG:* Carnochan
11 Mar	A	Kelso	6-32	*PG:* Little (2)
25 Mar	H	Haddington	44-15	*T:* Boswell, Buttimer, Graham, Mason, Rowley, Wands *C:* Little (4) *PG:* Little *DG:* C C Docherty

Gala

Year of formation 1875
Ground Netherdale, Nether Road, Galashiels TD1 3HE Tel: Galashiels (01896) 755145
Colours Maroon
Most capped player P C Brown (Scotland) 27 caps
Captain 1994-95 M Dods
McEwan's 70/- National League Div 1 7th

League Record 1994-95

Date	*Venue*	*Opponents*	*Result*	*Scorers*
10 Sept	A	Stewart's-Melville FP	22-21	*T:* Corcoran, Hogg *PG:* Dods (4)

17 Sept	H	Melrose	27-50	*T:* Dalgleish, Turnbull, Weir *C:* Maitland (3) *PG:* Maitland (2)
24 Sept	H	Boroughmuir	3-56	*PG:* Maitland
1 Oct	A	Watsonians	11-22	*T:* Swan *PG:* Maitland (2)
8 Oct	H	Heriot's FP	5-3	*T:* M Changleng
15 Oct	A	Edinburgh Acads	0-0	
5 Nov	H	West of Scotland	22-6	*T:* Isaac, C Townsend (2) *C:* Dods (2) *PG:* Dods
26 Nov	A	Stirling County	20-26	*T:* Amos, Dods *C:* Dods (2) *PG:* Dods (2)
14 Jan	H	Dundee HSFP	32-10	*T:* Dalgleish, Dods (2) *C:* Dods *PG:* Dods (5)
11 Feb	H	Jedforest	14-13	*T:* Dalgleish *PG:* Dods, Townsend (2)
25 Feb	A	Glasgow High/K'side	25-12	*T:* Moncrieff (2), Swan, Townsend *C:* Townsend *PG:* Townsend
11 Mar	H	Currie	36-15	*T:* Corcoran (3), Moncrieff (2) *C:* Dods *PG:* Dods (3)
25 Mar	A	Hawick	9-11	*PG:* Dods (3)

Glasgow Academicals

Year of formation 1867
Ground New Anniesland, Helensburgh Drive, Glasgow Tel: 0141-959 1101
Colours Navy blue and white hoops
Most capped player W M Simmers (Scotland) 28 caps
Captain 1994-95 S M Simmers
McEwan's 70/- National League Div 2 6th

League Record 1994-95

Date	*Venue*	*Opponents*	*Result*	*Scorers*
10 Sept	H	Corstorphine	17-0	*T:* C G MacGregor, Stevens *C:* C G MacGregor (2) *PG:* C G MacGregor
17 Sept	A	Peebles	27-31	*T:* C G MacGregor (2), A Mason, Smith *C:* C G MacGregor (2) *PG:* C G MacGregor
24 Sept	H	Kelso	11-13	*T:* J F Mason *PG:* C G MacGregor (2)
1 Oct	A	Wigtownshire	20-18	*T:* I McAslan, C G MacGregor *C:* C G MacGregor (2) *PG:* C G MacGregor *DG:* C G MacGregor
8 Oct	H	Preston Lodge FP	8-20	*T:* G T MacGregor *PG:* C G MacGregor
15 Oct	A	Selkirk	17-42	*T:* G McAslan, G T MacGregor, Smith *C:* Smith
5 Nov	H	Edinburgh Wands	31-16	*T:* Hart, C G MacGregor, A Mason, Williams *C:* S M Simmers *PG:* C G MacGregor (3)
26 Nov	A	Biggar	9-17	*PG:* C G MacGregor (3)
14 Jan	H	Grangemouth	19-20	*T:* A Mason, S M Simmers *PG:* C G MacGregor *DG:* C G MacGregor (2)
25 Feb	H	Musselburgh	30-9	*T:* Barr, Davis, J F Mason, Williams *C:* C G MacGregor (2) *PG:* C G MacGregor (2)
11 Mar	A	Haddington	29-21	*T:* Barr, Halley (2), Williams *C:* C G MacGregor (3) *PG:* C G MacGregor
25 Mar	H	Kirkcaldy	35-16	*T:* Collins, S M Simmers, Williams, Winter *C:* C G MacGregor (3) *PG:* C G MacGregor (3)
1 Apr	A	Gordonians	46-16	*T:* Davis (4), Hart (2), Middleton (2) *C:* C G MacGregor (3)

Glasgow High/Kelvinside

Year of formation 1982 (on amalgamation of Glasgow High RFC and Kelvinside Academicals)
Ground Old Anniesland, 637 Crow Road, Glasgow Tel: 0141-959 1154
Colours Navy blue, green and white
Most capped player D S Munro (Scotland) 6 caps (before amalgamation J M Bannerman

[Glasgow HSFP] was capped 37 times and D M White [Kelvinside Academicals] 4 times, both for Scotland)
Captain 1994-95 W H Malcolm
McEwan's 70/- National League Div 1 9th

League Record 1994-95

Date	*Venue*	*Opponents*	*Result*	*Scorers*
10 Sept	H	Boroughmuir	36-16	*T:* Glasgow, Hawkes, C E Little, McIlwham, Peterson *C:* Hirini *PG:* Hirini (3)
17 Sept	A	Heriot's FP	21-9	*PG:* Hirini (7)
24 Sept	H	West of Scotland	17-6	*T:* Brown, Hawkes *C:* Bassi, Hirini *PG:* Hirini
1 Oct	A	Dundee HSFP	9-6	*PG:* Bassi (2) *DG:* Breckenridge
8 Oct	H	Jedforest	28-5	*T:* C E Little, Malcolm, Mellor, M I Wallace *C:* Hirini *PG:* Hirini *DG:* Breckenridge
15 Oct	A	Currie	6-20	*PG:* Hirini (2)
5 Nov	H	Melrose	9-16	*PG:* Hirini (3)
26 Nov	A	Watsonians	8-16	*T:* Hawkes *PG:* Hirini
14 Jan	H	Edinburgh Acads	20-25	*T:* Agnew, Hawkes (2) *C:* Breckenridge *PG:* Breckenridge
11 Feb	H	Hawick	17-17	*T:* Agnew, Watt, pen try *C:* Breckenridge
25 Feb	H	Gala	12-25	*PG:* Breckenridge (3) *DG:* Breckenridge
11 Mar	A	Stewart's-Melville FP	32-7	*T:* Breckenridge, Hawkes, F D Wallace *C:* Breckenridge *PG:* Breckenridge (3) *DG:* Breckenridge (2)
25 Mar	A	Stirling County	13-15	*T:* Bassi *C:* Breckenridge *PG:* Breckenridge (2)

Grangemouth

Year of formation 1929
Ground Glensburgh, Glensburgh Road, Grangemouth
Tel: Grangemouth (01324) 486142
Colours Red and black hoops
Captain 1994-95 G Rennie
McEwan's 70/- National League Div 2 9th

League Record 1994-95

Date	*Venue*	*Opponents*	*Result*	*Scorers*
10 Sept	H	Peebles	20-6	*T:* Crossan, Halliday *C:* Halliday (2) *PG:* Halliday (2)
17 Sept	A	Kelso	12-38	*PG:* Rennie (4)
24 Sept	H	Wigtownshire	18-6	*T:* Crossan, Rennie *C:* Rennie *PG:* Rennie (2)
1 Oct	A	Preston Lodge FP	22-25	*T:* Crossan *C:* Halliday *PG:* Halliday (4) *DG:* Halliday
8 Oct	H	Selkirk	17-27	*T:* Crossan, Lorenston *C:* Halliday (2) *PG:* Halliday
15 Oct	A	Edinburgh Wands	19-20	*T:* Lorenston, McNicol *PG:* Halliday (2) *DG:* Halliday
5 Nov	H	Biggar	19-16	*T:* Lorenston, McMillan, Penman *C:* Halliday (2)
26 Nov	H	Kirkcaldy	14-27	*T:* Jesty, Penman *C:* Halliday (2)
14 Jan	A	Glasgow Acads	20-19	*T:* Lorenston, Rutherford *C:* Halliday (2) *PG:* Halliday (2)
11 Feb	A	Musselburgh	13-30	*T:* Jesty, Penman *DG:* Halliday
25 Feb	H	Haddington	10-0	*T:* McFarlane *C:* Halliday *DG:* Halliday
11 Mar	A	Corstorphine	15-26	*PG:* Halliday (5)
25 Mar	H	Gordonians	26-6	*T:* Forsyth, Lyon *C:* Halliday (2) *PG:* Halliday (4)

Haddington

Year of formation 1911
Ground Neilson Park, Haddington EH41 4DB Tel: Haddington (01620) 823702
Colours Scarlet
Captain 1994-95 B A Craig
McEwan's 70/- National League Div 2 14th

League Record 1994-95

Date	*Venue*	*Opponents*	*Result*	*Scorers*
10 Sept	A	Gordonians	22-23	*T:* Cundy (2), Lees, Skea *C:* Murray
17 Sept	H	Musselburgh	15-21	*T:* Craig, Lees (2)
24 Sept	A	Kirkcaldy	23-31	*T:* Cundy, McGeary (2) *C:* Brownlee *PG:* Brownlee (2)
1 Oct	A	Corstorphine	6-15	*PG:* Brownlee (2)
8 Oct	H	Peebles	17-14	*T:* Cundy, Dickson *C:* Brownlee (2) *PG:* Brownlee
15 Oct	A	Kelso	14-26	*T:* McGeary *PG:* Brownlee (3)
5 Nov	H	Wigtownshire	12-13	*T:* Cringan, Kenny *C:* Brownlee
26 Nov	A	Preston Lodge FP	24-17	*T:* Craig, Kilmister *C:* Cringan *PG:* Cringan (3) *DG:* Craig
14 Jan	H	Selkirk	9-26	*PG:* Cringan (3)
11 Feb	H	Biggar	0-8	
25 Feb	A	Grangemouth	0-10	
11 Mar	H	Glasgow Acads	21-29	*T:* McGeary (2), McRaild *PG:* Cringan (2)
25 Mar	A	Edinburgh Wands	15-44	*T:* Chalmers, Craig, McGeary

Hawick

Year of formation 1873
Ground Mansfield Park, Mansfield Road, Hawick, Roxburghshire
Tel: Hawick (01450) 374291
Colours Dark green
Most capped player J M Renwick (Scotland)/C T Deans (Scotland) 52 caps
Captain 1994-95 J A Hay
McEwan's 70/- National League Div 1 4th

League Record 1994-95

Date	*Venue*	*Opponents*	*Result*	*Scorers*
10 Sept	H	Heriot's FP	13-21	*T:* Hughes, Suddon *PG:* Welsh
17 Sept	A	West of Scotland	25-26	*T:* Irvine, Stanger, Suddon *C:* Welsh (2) *PG:* Welsh (2)
24 Sept	H	Dundee HSFP	23-10	*T:* B L Renwick, Suddon *C:* B L Renwick, Welsh *PG:* Welsh (3)
1 Oct	A	Jedforest	6-15	*PG:* Welsh (2)
8 Oct	H	Currie	19-17	*T:* Murray, Suddon *PG:* Welsh (3)
15 Oct	A	Melrose	20-13	*T:* Grant, Suddon, C Turnbull *C:* Welsh *PG:* Welsh
5 Nov	H	Watsonians	21-19	*T:* Suddon, Welsh *C:* C W Turnbull *PG:* Welsh (3)
26 Nov	A	Edinburgh Acads	0-14	
14 Jan	H	Stirling County	14-10	*T:* Sharp *PG:* Welsh (3)
11 Feb	A	Glasgow High/K'side	17-17	*T:* Murray *PG:* Welsh (4)
25 Feb	H	Stewart's-Melville FP	28-10	*T:* Renwick (2), Stanger *C:* Welsh (2) *PG:* Welsh (3)
11 Mar	A	Boroughmuir	18-18	*PG:* Welsh (5) *DG:* Welsh
25 Mar	H	Gala	11-9	*T:* Murray *PG:* Welsh (2)

Heriot's FP

Year of formation 1890
Ground Goldenacre, Bangholm Terrace, Edinburgh EH3 5QN
Tel: 0131-552 4097 (groundstaff) and 0131-552 5925 (clubhouse)
Colours Blue and white horizontal stripes
Most capped player A R Irvine (Scotland) 51 caps
Captain 1994-95 S W Paul
McEwan's 70/- National League Div 1 6th

League Record 1994-95

Date	*Venue*	*Opponents*	*Result*	*Scorers*
10 Sept	A	Hawick	21-13	*T:* H R Gilmour (2) *C:* Glasgow *PG:* Glasgow (3)
17 Sept	H	Glasgow High/K'side	9-21	*PG:* Glasgow (2) *DG:* Glasgow
24 Sept	A	Stewart's-Melville FP	17-16	*T:* McRobbie *PG:* Glasgow (3) *DG:* Glasgow
1 Oct	H	Boroughmuir	15-9	*PG:* Glasgow (5)
8 Oct	A	Gala	3-5	*PG:* Glasgow
15 Oct	A	West of Scotland	6-18	*PG:* Glasgow (2)
5 Nov	H	Dundee HSFP	33-3	*T:* Aitken, H R Gilmour, Lawrie, Lee (2) *C:* Fowler *PG:* Glasgow (2)
26 Nov	A	Jedforest	22-16	*T:* Humphries, McRobbie, Milne *C:* Glasgow (2) *PG:* Glasgow
14 Jan	H	Currie	22-11	*T:* Lawrie, Milne *PG:* Hewitt (4)
11 Feb	H	Watsonians	9-15	*PG:* Hewitt (3)
25 Feb	A	Edinburgh Acads	3-33	*PG:* Hewitt
25 Mar	A	Melrose	28-26	*T:* Bryce, Glasgow, Watt, pen try *C:* Hewitt (4)
5 Apr	H	Stirling County	11-11	*T:* Murray *PG:* Hewitt (2)

Jedforest

Year of formation 1885
Ground Riverside Park, Jedburgh Tel: Jedburgh (01835) 862855
Colours Royal blue
Most capped player R J Laidlaw (Scotland) 47 caps
Captain 1994-95 K W Barrie
McEwan's 70/- National League Div 1 10th

League Record 1994-95

Date	*Venue*	*Opponents*	*Result*	*Scorers*
10 Sept	A	Watsonians	18-37	*T:* Kirkpatrick (2), McKechnie *PG:* Richards
17 Sept	H	Edinburgh Acads	22-16	*T:* A J Douglas *C:* Richards *PG:* Richards (5)
24 Sept	A	Stirling County	3-20	*PG:* McKechnie
1 Oct	H	Hawick	15-6	*PG:* Amos, Richards (4)
8 Oct	A	Glasgow High/K'side	5-28	*T:* J P Douglas
15 Oct	H	Stewart's-Melville FP	22-11	*T:* J P Douglas, Yule *PG:* Richards (3) *DG:* Richards
5 Nov	H	Boroughmuir	19-23	*T:* Amos, M Brown, J P Douglas *C:* Richards (2)
26 Nov	H	Heriot's FP	16-22	*T:* Kirkpatrick, Yule PG: Richards *DG:* Hogg
14 Jan	A	West of Scotland	7-13	*T:* Barrie *C:* Richards
11 Feb	A	Gala	13-14	*T:* K Armstrong, Kirkpatrick *PG:* Richards
25 Feb	A	Currie	32-28	*T:* Amos, Kirkpatrick, Richards *C:* Richards *PG:* Richards (4) *DG:* Richards
11 Mar	H	Dundee HSFP	24-21	*T:* Forster, Hogg *C:* Richards *PG:* Richards (4)
5 Apr	H	Melrose	25-17	*T:* Amos, Kirkpatrick, Pringle *C:* Richards (2) *PG:* Richards (2)

Kelso

Year of formation 1876
Ground Poynder Park, Bowmont Street, Kelso, Roxburghshire
Tel: Kelso (01573) 224300 or 223773
Colours Black and white
Most capped player J Jeffrey (Scotland) 40 caps
Captain 1994-95 S Bennet
McEwan's 70/- National League Div 2 *Winners – promoted*

League Record 1994-95

Date	*Venue*	*Opponents*	*Result*	*Scorers*
10 Sept	A	Biggar	22-18	*T:* Aitchison, Cowe *PG:* Aitchison (4)
17 Sept	H	Grangemouth	38-12	*T:* Baird, Bennet, J Thomson, pen try *C:* Aitchison (3) *PG:* Aitchison (4)
24 Sept	A	Glasgow Acads	13-11	*T:* J Thomson *C:* Aitchison *PG:* Aitchison (2)
1 Oct	H	Gordonians	42-0	*T:* Aitchison, Baird, Bennet (2), Cowe, Jeffrey *C:* Aitchison (3) *PG:* Aitchison (2)
8 Oct	A	Musselburgh	14-3	*T:* Cowe, R Laing *C:* Aitchison (2)
15 Oct	H	Haddington	26-14	*T:* J Thomson *PG:* Aitchison (7)
5 Nov	A	Corstorphine	18-13	*T:* G Laing, Roxburgh *C:* Lang *PG:* Lang (2)
26 Nov	H	Peebles	31-11	*T:* Roxburgh *C:* Tait *PG:* Tait (8)
14 Jan	A	Kirkcaldy	10-27	*T:* Jeffrey *C:* Aitchison *PG:* Aitchison
28 Jan	A	Wigtownshire	37-15	*T:* Millar, Tait, J Thomson *C:* Aitchison (2) *PG:* Aitchison (6)
11 Feb	H	Preston Lodge FP	22-12	*T:* Jeffrey *C:* Aitchison *PG:* Aitchison (5)
25 Feb	A	Selkirk	13-17	*T:* Lang *C:* Aitchison *PG:* Aitchison (2)
11 Mar	H	Edinburgh Wands	32-6	*T:* Bennet (2), Lang, J Thomson (2) *C:* Aitchison (2) *PG:* Aitchison

Kirkcaldy

Year of formation 1873
Ground Beveridge Park, Balwearie Road, Kirkcaldy Tel: Kirkcaldy (01592) 263470
Colours Royal blue
Most capped player D D Howie (Scotland)/R Howie (Scotland) 9 caps
Captain 1994-95 A D Henderson
McEwan's 70/- National League Div 2 3rd

League Record 1994-95

Date	*Venue*	*Opponents*	*Result*	*Scorers*
10 Sept	A	Musselburgh	20-18	*T:* Bonner, Brocklebank, M B Mitchell *C:* J R Mitchell *PG:* J R Mitchell
17 Sept	H	Selkirk	16-16	*T:* Reddick *C:* J R Mitchell *PG:* J R Mitchell (3)
24 Sept	H	Haddington	31-23	*T:* Ferguson, J R Mitchell, M B Mitchell, Thomson *C:* J R Mitchell (4) *PG:* J R Mitchell
1 Oct	A	Edinburgh Wands	10-23	*T:* Reddick *C:* J R Mitchell *PG:* J R Mitchell
8 Oct	H	Corstorphine	20-22	*T:* Carruthers, Brocklebank *C:* J R Mitchell (2) *PG:* J R Mitchell (2)
15 Oct	A	Biggar	19-24	*T:* Bonner *C:* J R Mitchell *PG:* J R Mitchell (4)
5 Nov	H	Peebles	27-16	*T:* Douglas, Melvin, J R Mitchell (2) *C:* J R Mitchell (2) *PG:* J R Mitchell
26 Nov	A	Grangemouth	27-14	*T:* Bonner, Carruthers *C:* J R Mitchell *PG:* J R Mitchell (5)
14 Jan	H	Kelso	27-10	*T:* Bonner, Douglas, McCormack, J R Mitchell *C:* J R Mitchell (2) *PG:* J R Mitchell
11 Feb	H	Wigtownshire	16-5	*T:* Brocklebank *C:* J R Mitchell *PG:* J R Mitchell (3)

25 Feb	A	Gordonians	22-6	*T:* Carruthers, J R Mitchell, Renton (2) *C:* J R Mitchell
11 Mar	H	Preston Lodge FP	20-18	*T:* Imrie, Macdonald, J R Mitchell *C:* J R Mitchell *PG:* J R Mitchell
25 Mar	A	Glasgow Acads	16-35	*T:* Henderson, J W Thomson *PG:* J R Mitchell (2)

Melrose

Year of formation 1877
Ground The Greenyards, Melrose, Roxburghshire TD6 9SA
Tel: Melrose (0189682) 2993 (office) and 2559 (clubrooms)
Colours Yellow and black hoops
Most capped player K W Robertson (Scotland) 44 caps
Captain 1994-95 C M Chalmers
McEwan's 70/- National League Div 1 8th

League Record 1994-95

Date	*Venue*	*Opponents*	*Result*	*Scorers*
10 Sept	H	Currie	22-9	*T:* Parker *C:* Parker *PG:* Parker (4) *DG:* Chalmers
17 Sept	A	Gala	50-27	*T:* R N C Brown, R R Brown, Chalmers, Joiner, Parker, B W Redpath, Scott, Weir *C:* Parker (5)
24 Sept	A	Watsonians	14-19	*T:* R R Brown, Kerr *C:* Parker (2)
1 Oct	H	Edinburgh Acads	20-10	*T:* Chalmers, Parker (2) *C:* Parker *PG:* Parker
8 Oct	A	Stirling County	15-22	*PG:* Parker (4) *DG:* Parker
15 Oct	H	Hawick	13-20	*T:* R R Brown *C:* Parker *PG:* Parker (2)
5 Nov	A	Glasgow High/K'side	16-9	*T:* Scott *C:* Parker *PG:* Parker (3)
26 Nov	H	Stewart's-Melville FP	37-6	*T:* Bain, R R Brown, Parker, Shiel (2) *C:* Parker (3) *PG:* Parker (2)
14 Jan	A	Boroughmuir	29-53	*T:* R N C Brown, Weir (2) *C:* Parker *PG:* Parker (4)
11 Feb	A	West of Scotland	26-13	*T:* Leighton, Parker *C:* Parker (2) *PG:* Parker (4)
25 Feb	H	Dundee HSFP	23-20	*T:* Shiel *PG:* Parker (6)
25 Mar	H	Heriot's FP	26-28	*T:* R R Brown, Redpath, Scott *C:* Parker *PG:* Parker (2) *DG:* Bain
5 Apr	A	Jedforest	17-25	*T:* Bain, R N C Brown *C:* Bain (2) *PG:* Bain

Musselburgh

Year of formation 1921
Ground Stoneyhill, Stoneyhill Farm Road, Musselburgh Tel: 0131-665 3435
Colours Navy blue with narrow white hoops
Captain 1994-95 A McLeod
McEwan's 70/- National League Div 2 8th

League Record 1994-95

Date	*Venue*	*Opponents*	*Result*	*Scorers*
10 Sept	H	Kirkcaldy	18-20	*T:* Bain, C Livingstone *C:* C Livingstone *PG:* C Livingstone, Lockhart
17 Sept	A	Haddington	21-15	*T:* Laidlaw, McLeod *C:* C Livingstone *PG:* C Livingstone (3)
24 Sept	H	Corstorphine	17-9	*T:* Pow *PG:* Lockhart (4)
1 Oct	A	Peebles	25-11	*T:* N Horsburgh *C:* C Livingstone *PG:* C Livingstone (6)
8 Oct	H	Kelso	3-14	*PG:* C Livingstone
15 Oct	A	Wigtownshire	15-29	*PG:* C Livingstone (5)

5 Nov	H	Preston Lodge FP	11-16	*T:* Monks *PG:* C Livingstone (2)
26 Nov	A	Selkirk	16-16	*T:* Pow, Talac *PG:* C Livingstone (2)
14 Jan	H	Edinburgh Wands	11-6	*T:* Bonthron *PG:* C Livingstone (2)
28 Jan	A	Biggar	6-8	*PG:* C Livingstone (2)
11 Feb	H	Grangemouth	30-13	*T:* Bain, Bonthron, Hawkins *C:* Lockhart (3) *PG:* Lockhart (3)
25 Feb	A	Glasgow Acads	9-30	*PG:* Lockhart (3)
11 Mar	H	Gordonians	21-9	*T:* Bonthron, Hawkins *C:* C Livingstone *PG:* C Livingstone (2) *DG:* C Livingstone

Peebles

Year of formation 1923
Ground Hay Lodge Park, Neidpath Road, Peebles EH45 8NN
Tel: Peebles (01721) 721600
Colours Red and white hoops
Captain 1994-95 J Currie
McEwan's 70/- National League Div 2 7th

League Record 1994-95

Date	*Venue*	*Opponents*	*Result*	*Scorers*
10 Sept	A	Grangemouth	6-20	*PG:* Knox (2)
17 Sept	H	Glasgow Acads	31-27	*T:* Beveridge, McIver (2) *C:* Wilson (2) *PG:* Nisbet, Wilson (3)
24 Sept	A	Gordonians	17-3	*T:* Farmer, Kerr *C:* Nisbet, Wilson *PG:* Nisbet
1 Oct	H	Musselburgh	11-25	*T:* Anderson *PG:* Nisbet (2)
8 Oct	A	Haddington	14-17	*T:* Gray *PG:* Wilson (3)
15 Oct	H	Corstorphine	13-11	*T:* Wilson *C:* Nisbet *PG:* Nisbet *DG:* Wilson
5 Nov	A	Kirkcaldy	16-27	*T:* Currie, Kerr *PG:* Mutch (2)
26 Nov	A	Kelso	11-31	*T:* Beveridge *PG:* Mutch (2)
14 Jan	H	Wigtownshire	15-3	*PG:* Mutch (5)
11 Feb	H	Selkirk	6-16	*PG:* Mutch (2)
25 Feb	A	Edinburgh Wands	8-3	*T:* Knox *PG:* Knox
11 Mar	H	Biggar	14-9	*T:* Clarke *PG:* Knox (3)
25 Mar	A	Preston Lodge FP	13-12	*T:* Nisbet *C:* Knox *PG:* Knox (2)

Selkirk

Year of formation 1907
Ground Philiphaugh, Ettrickhaugh Road, Selkirk Tel: Selkirk (01750) 20403
Colours Navy blue
Most capped player J Y Rutherford (Scotland) 42 caps
Captain 1994-95 R L Pow
McEwan's 70/- National League Div 2 2nd

League Record 1994-95

Date	*Venue*	*Opponents*	*Result*	*Scorers*
10 Sept	H	Preston Lodge FP	33-18	*T:* Jaffray, S A Nichol *C:* Brett *PG:* Pow (7)
17 Sept	A	Kirkcaldy	16-16	*T:* McConnell *C:* Pow *PG:* Pow (3)
24 Sept	A	Edinburgh Wands	25-23	*T:* Linton, Pow *PG:* Pow (5)
1 Oct	H	Biggar	21-3	*T:* Anderson, S A Nichol *C:* Brett *PG:* Brett, Pow (2)
8 Oct	A	Grangemouth	27-17	*T:* Jaffray (2), Lindores *PG:* Brett (4)
15 Oct	H	Glasgow Acads	42-17	*T:* Lindores, Linton (3), S A Nichol *C:* Brett (4) *PG:* Brett (3)
5 Nov	A	Gordonians	11-20	*T:* Linton *PG:* Brett (2)

26 Nov	H	Musselburgh	16-16	*T:* Hulme (2) *PG:* Hulme (2)
14 Jan	A	Haddington	26-9	*T:* Guntley, Lowrie (2) *C:* Pow *PG:* Pow (3)
11 Feb	A	Peebles	16-6	*T:* pen try *C:* Pow *PG:* Pow (2) *DG:* Smith
25 Feb	H	Kelso	17-13	*T:* Hunter *PG:* Pow (4)
11 Mar	A	Wigtownshire	30-12	*T:* Hunter, Minto, S A Nichol *C:* Pow (3) *PG:* Pow (3)
25 Mar	H	Corstorphine	56-16	*T:* Guntley, Hunter, Johnston (2), Nichol (2), Pow (3) *C:* Pow (4) *PG:* Pow

Stewart's-Melville FP

Year of formation 1973 (on amalgamation of Daniel Stewart's College FP and Melville College FP)
Ground Inverleith, Ferry Road, Edinburgh EH5 2DW Tel: 0131-552 1515
Colours Scarlet with broad black and narrow gold bands
Most capped player F Calder (Scotland) 38 caps
Captain 1994-95 D S Wyllie
McEwan's 70/- National League Div 1 14th

League Record 1994-95

Date	*Venue*	*Opponents*	*Result*	*Scorers*
10 Sept	H	Gala	21-22	*T:* Pollock, Rigby, Wyllie *PG:* Wyllie (2)
17 Sept	A	Boroughmuir	10-15	*T:* Wyllie *C:* Stirling *PG:* Stirling
24 Sept	H	Heriot's FP	16-17	*T:* Bull, Kittle *PG:* Thomson (2)
1 Oct	A	West of Scotland	7-27	*T:* Faulds *C:* Thomson
8 Oct	H	Dundee HSFP	20-24	*T:* Bull (2), Burns *C:* Thomson *PG:* Thomson
15 Oct	A	Jedforest	11-22	*T:* Hamilton *PG:* Thomson *DG:* Pollock
5 Nov	H	Currie	21-12	*T:* Pollock, Thomson *C:* Hodgson *PG:* Hodgson (3)
26 Nov	A	Melrose	6-37	*PG:* Hodgson (2)
14 Jan	H	Watsonians	16-28	*T:* Kittle *C:* Hodgson *PG:* Hodgson (3)
28 Jan	A	Edinburgh Acads	0-30	
11 Feb	H	Stirling County	13-17	*T:* Burns *C:* Thomson *PG:* Thomson (2)
25 Feb	A	Hawick	10-28	*T:* Kittle, Thomson
11 Mar	H	Glasgow High/K'side	7-32	*T:* Kittle *C:* Pollock

Stirling County

Year of formation 1904
Ground Bridgehaugh Park, Causewayhead Road, Stirling Tel: Stirling (01786) 474827
Colours Red, white and black
Most capped player K M Logan (Scotland) 15 caps
Captain 1994-95 J S Hamilton
McEwan's 70/- National League Div 1 *Winners*

League Record 1994-95

Date	*Venue*	*Opponents*	*Result*	*Scorers*
10 Sept	H	West of Scotland	17-9	*T:* Brough *PG:* M McKenzie (4)
17 Sept	A	Dundee HSFP	19-18	*T:* Turner *C:* M McKenzie *PG:* M McKenzie (4)
24 Sept	H	Jedforest	20-3	*T:* Ireland, K M Logan, Turner *C:* M McKenzie *PG:* M McKenzie
1 Oct	A	Currie	13-7	*T:* McGrandles *C:* M McKenzie *PG:* Williamson *DG:* M McKenzie
8 Oct	H	Melrose	22-15	*T:* Brough, K M Logan (2) *C:* Williamson (2) *DG:* M McKenzie
15 Oct	A	Watsonians	23-19	*T:* K M Logan (3) *C:* M McKenzie *PG:* M McKenzie (2)

5 Nov	H	Edinburgh Acads	18-11	*T:* Ireland, McGrandles *C:* M McKenzie *PG:* M McKenzie *DG:* M McKenzie
26 Nov	H	Gala	26-20	*T:* Crawford, Ireland, K M Logan *C:* M McKenzie *PG:* K M Logan, M McKenzie *DG:* M McKenzie
14 Jan	A	Hawick	10-14	*T:* Turner *C:* M McKenzie *PG:* M McKenzie
11 Feb	A	Stewart's-Melville FP	27-13	*T:* Flockhart, MacRobert *C:* M McKenzie *PG:* M McKenzie (5)
25 Feb	H	Boroughmuir	13-9	*T:* Turner *C:* K M Logan *PG:* K M Logan (2)
25 Mar	H	Glasgow High/K'side	15-13	*T:* Brough, Hamilton *C:* M McKenzie *PG:* M McKenzie
5 Apr	A	Heriot's FP	11-11	*T:* Mackay *PG:* A Logan, Sievwright

Watsonians

Year of formation 1875
Ground Myreside, Myreside Road, Edinburgh EH10 5DB Tel: 0131-447 5200
Colours Maroon and white hoops
Most capped player A G Hastings (Scotland) 56 caps
Captain 1994-95 J D MacDonald
McEwan's 70/- National League Div 1 2nd

League Record 1994-95

Date	*Venue*	*Opponents*	*Result*	*Scorers*
10 Sept	H	Jedforest	37-18	*T:* A G Hastings, S Hastings, F M Henderson, Hodge, Rudkin *C:* A G Hastings (3) *PG:* A G Hastings *DG:* Hodge
17 Sept	A	Currie	47-17	*T:* S Hastings (2), F M Henderson (2), Jessop, Kerr *C:* A G Hastings (4) *PG:* A G Hastings (3)
24 Sept	H	Melrose	19-14	*T:* A G Hastings *C:* A G Hastings *PG:* A G Hastings (4)
1 Oct	H	Gala	22-11	*T:* Kerr *C:* A G Hastings *PG:* A G Hastings (5)
8 Oct	A	Edinburgh Acads	26-25	*T:* F M Henderson, Hodge, Kerr *C:* A G Hastings *PG:* A G Hastings (3)
15 Oct	H	Stirling County	19-23	*T:* F M Henderson *C:* A G Hastings *PG:* A G Hastings (4)
5 Nov	A	Hawick	19-21	*T:* S Hastings *C:* A G Hastings *PG:* A G Hastings (4)
26 Nov	H	Glasgow High/K'side	16-8	*T:* Hodge *C:* A G Hastings *PG:* A G Hastings (3)
14 Jan	A	Stewart's-Melville FP	28-16	*T:* Hodge, Kerr (2) *C:* A G Hastings (2) *PG:* A G Hastings (3)
28 Jan	H	Boroughmuir	9-26	*PG:* A G Hastings (3)
11 Feb	A	Heriot's FP	15-9	*T:* Hodge, Inglis *C:* Hodge *PG:* Hodge
25 Feb	H	West of Scotland	12-13	*T:* Kerr (2) *C:* Hodge
25 Mar	A	Dundee HSFP	27-11	*T:* Garry, Inglis, Kerr (2) *C:* Hodge (2) *PG:* Hodge

West of Scotland

Year of formation 1865
Ground Burnbrae, Glasgow Road, Milngavie, Glasgow G62 6HX Tel: 0141-956 3116
Colours Red and yellow hoops
Most capped player A B Carmichael (Scotland) 50 caps
Captain 1994-95 J Lonergan
McEwan's 70/- National League Div 1 11th

League Record 1994-95

Date	*Venue*	*Opponents*	*Result*	*Scorers*
10 Sept	A	Stirling County	9-17	*PG:* Barrett (3)

17 Sept	H	Hawick	26-25	*T:* Barrett, M J A Craig, McVey, F H Stott *C:* Barrett (3)
24 Sept	A	Glasgow High/K'side	6-17	*PG:* Barrett (2)
1 Oct	H	Stewart's-Melville FP	27-7	*T:* Bulloch, F H Stott *C:* Barrett *PG:* Barrett (4) *DG:* Barrett
8 Oct	A	Boroughmuir	17-47	*T:* Service, F H Stott *C:* Barrett (2) *DG:* Barrett
15 Oct	H	Heriot's FP	18-6	*T:* Munro, F H Stott *C:* Hay *PG:* Williamson (2)
5 Nov	A	Gala	6-22	*PG:* Barrett, Williamson
26 Nov	A	Dundee HSFP	8-18	*T:* Munro *PG:* Barrett
14 Jan	H	Jedforest	13-7	*T:* F H Stott, Williamson *PG:* Barrett
11 Feb	H	Melrose	13-26	*T:* Hart, Munro *PG:* Barrett
25 Feb	A	Watsonians	13-12	*T:* Shaw *C:* Barrett *PG:* Barrett *DG:* Barrett
25 Mar	A	Currie	3-9	*PG:* Hart
1 Apr	H	Edinburgh Acads	7-20	*T:* Williamson *C:* Wallace

Wigtownshire

Year of formation 1922
Ground London Road Playing Fields, Ladies Walk, Stranraer
Tel: Stranraer (01776) 704133
Colours Royal blue
Captain 1994-95 R Stevenson
McEwan's 70/- National League Div 2 12th

League Record 1994-95

Date	*Venue*	*Opponents*	*Result*	*Scorers*
10 Sept	A	Edinburgh Wands	15-30	*T:* David Drysdale, Gemmell *C:* McHenry *PG:* McHenry
17 Sept	H	Biggar	14-15	*T:* J Drysdale *PG:* Corcoran (3)
24 Sept	A	Grangemouth	6-18	*PG:* Corcoran, Gibson
1 Oct	H	Glasgow Acads	18-20	*T:* Corcoran (2) *C:* Corcoran *PG:* Corcoran, Gibson
8 Oct	A	Gordonians	14-22	*T:* A Drysdale *PG:* Corcoran (3)
15 Oct	H	Musselburgh	29-15	*T:* A Drysdale, Dougie Drysdale, J L Parker *C:* Gibson *PG:* Gibson (4)
5 Nov	A	Haddington	13-12	*T:* H M Parker *C:* Corcoran *PG:* Louden (2)
26 Nov	H	Corstorphine	10-6	*T:* Alastair Hose, H M Parker
14 Jan	A	Peebles	3-15	*PG:* Gibson
28 Jan	H	Kelso	15-38	*T:* A Drysdale, Jessop *C:* Gibson *PG:* Gibson
11 Feb	A	Kirkcaldy	5-16	*T:* Dougie Drysdale
25 Feb	A	Preston Lodge FP	19-29	*T:* A Drysdale *C:* Gibson *PG:* Gibson (4)
11 Mar	H	Selkirk	12-30	*PG:* Gibson (3) *DG:* Louden

IRELAND
Ballymena

Year of formation 1922
Ground Eaton Park, Raceview Road, Ballymena   Tel: Ballymena 656746
Colours Black
Most capped player W J McBride (Ireland) 63 caps
Captain 1994-95 T McMaster
Insurance Corporation League Div 2 2nd *promoted* **First Trust Bank Ulster Senior Cup** Lost 11-18 to Dungannon (2nd round)

League Record 1994-95

Date	*Venue*	*Opponents*	*Result*	*Scorers*
17 Sept	A	Bective Rangers	6-18	*PG:* McAleese, Humphreys
24 Sept	H	Greystones	24-6	*T:* Smyth, Tweed, Humphreys *C:* McAleese (3) *PG:* McAleese
1 Oct	A	Bangor	20-12	*T:* Matchett, Smyth *C:* McAleese (2) *PG:* McAleese (2)
8 Oct	H	UC Dublin	9-9	*PG:* McAleese (2) *DG:* Humphreys
15 Oct	A	Wanderers	20-18	*T:* Matchett *PG:* McAleese (5)
7 Jan	H	Old Belvedere	11-13	*T:* Smyth *PG:* McAleese (2)
14 Jan	A	Terenure Coll	25-18	*T:* Humphreys, Tweed *PG:* McAleese (4) *DG:* McAleese
11 Feb	H	Dolphin	27-3	*T:* Tweed (3) *C:* McAleese (3) *PG:* McAleese *DG:* Humphreys
25 Mar	A	Old Crescent	20-6	*T:* J Topping (2), Matchett *C:* McAleese *PG:* McAleese
1 Apr	H	Malone	29-19	*T:* J Topping, D Topping, Matchett *C:* McAleese *PG:* McAleese (2) *DG:* Humphreys (2)

Bangor

Year of formation 1885
Ground Uprichard Park, Bloomfield Road South, Bangor Tel: Bangor 462670
Colours Old gold, royal blue and black
Most capped player J J McCoy (Ireland) 16 caps
Captain 1994-95 M McCall
Insurance Corporation League Div 2 11th *relegated* **First Trust Bank Ulster Senior Cup** Lost 10-39 to Instonians (semi-final)

League Record 1994-95

Date	*Venue*	*Opponents*	*Result*	*Scorers*
17 Sept	H	Terenure Coll	12-16	*PG:* McCall (4)
24 Sept	A	Malone	3-17	*PG:* McCall
1 Oct	H	Ballymena	12-20	*PG:* McCall (4)
8 Oct	A	Bective Rangers	6-15	*PG:* McCall (2)
15 Oct	H	Old Belvedere	10-16	*T:* Whittle *C:* McCall *PG:* McCall
7 Jan	A	Dolphin	17-26	*T:* Long (2) *C:* McCall (2) *PG:* McCall
14 Jan	H	Old Crescent	11-9	*T:* Kelly *PG:* McCall (2)
18 Feb	H	Greystones	3-22	*PG:* McCall
25 Mar	A	UC Dublin	9-20	*PG:* Wade (2) *DG:* Scott
1 Apr	A	Wanderers	7-44	*T:* Scott *C:* Wade

Bective Rangers

Year of formation 1881
Ground Donnybrook Dublin 4 Tel: Dublin 2693894
Colours Red, green and white hoops
Most capped player J L Farrell (Ireland) 29 caps
Captain 1994-95 M Mortell
Insurance Corporation League Div 2 5th **Aluset Leinster Senior Cup** Lost 6-16 to St Mary's Coll (semi-final)

League Record 1994-95

Date	*Venue*	*Opponents*	*Result*	*Scorers*
17 Sept	H	Ballymena	18-6	*T:* McQuilkin, McCaffrey *C:* Darcy *PG:* Darcy (2)
24 Sept	H	Wanderers	11-12	*T:* Cusack *PG:* Darcy (2)

1 Oct	A	Greystones	33-12	*T:* McQuilkin, Dwyer, Kealy *C:* Darcy (3) *PG:* Darcy (4)
8 Oct	H	Bangor	15-6	*T:* McQuilkin, Dwyer *C:* Darcy *PG:* Darcy
15 Oct	A	UC Dublin	8-28	*T:* Brennan *DG:* Darcy
14 Jan	A	Old Belvedere	10-11	*T:* Dwyer *C:* Darcy *PG:* Darcy
11 Mar	A	Malone	11-13	*T:* Whelan *PG:* Darcy (2)
25 Mar	A	Dolphin	17-17	*T:* Mortell, Whelan *C:* Darcy (2) *DG:* Darcy
1 Apr	H	Terenure Coll	20-5	*T:* Carville, McNamara, Mortell *C:* Darcy *PG:* Darcy
15 Apr	H	Old Crescent	38-25	*T:* Dwyer (4), Muldoon *C:* Darcy (5) *PG:* Darcy

Blackrock College

Year of formation 1882
Ground Stradbrook Road, Blackrock, Dublin Tel: Dublin 2805967
Colours Royal blue and white hoops
Most capped player J F Slattery (Ireland) 61 caps
Captain 1994-95 D Oswald
Insurance Corporation League Div 1 2nd **Aluset Leinster Senior Cup** Lost to Old Wesley 15-19 to (1st round)

League Record 1994-95

Date	*Venue*	*Opponents*	*Result*	*Scorers*
17 Sept	H	Garryowen	7-18	*T:* Rogers *C:* McGowan
24 Sept	A	Lansdowne	19-9	*T:* Mullin *C:* McGowan *PG:* McGowan (4)
1 Oct	H	Young Munster	28-3	*T:* Beggy, Rolland, Woods *C:* McGowan (2) *PG:* McGowan (3)
8 Oct	H	Dungannon	27-13	*T:* Assaf (2), Wallace, Beggy *C:* McGowan (2) *PG:* McGowan
15 Oct	A	Old Wesley	24-18	*T:* Mullin, Woods (2) *C:* McGowan (3) *DG:* McGowan
7 Jan	A	Cork Const	19-8	*T:* Rolland, Woods *PG:* McGowan (3)
14 Jan	H	Shannon	3-10	*PG:* McGowan
18 Feb	A	St Mary's	16-17	*T:* Mullin, Ridge *PG:* McGowan (2)
11 Mar	A	Instonians	56-17	*T:* Woods (2), Ridge, McGowan, Roland, Gavin, pen try *C:* McGowan (6) *PG:* McGowan (3)
1 Apr	H	Sunday's Well	29-22	*T:* Woods (4) *C:* McGowan (3) *PG:* McGowan

Cork Constitution

Year of formation 1892
Ground Temple Hill, Ballintemple, Cork Tel: Cork 292563
Colours White
Most capped player T J Kiernan (Ireland) 54 caps
Captain 1994-95 L Dineen
Insurance Corporation League Div 1 5th **Carling Munster Senior Cup** Lost 17-18 to Garryowen (semi-final)

League Record 1994-95

Date	*Venue*	*Opponents*	*Result*	*Scorers*
17 Sept	H	Lansdowne	25-23	*T:* Corkery, Burke, Howell *C:* Burke (2) *PG:* Burke (2)
24 Sept	A	Young Munster	14-10	*T:* Howell *PG:* Burke (3)
8 Oct	H	St Mary's Coll	12-16	*PG:* Burke (3) *DG:* K Murphy
15 Oct	A	Dungannon	20-13	*T:* Twomey *PG:* Burke (4) *DG:* Burke
7 Jan	H	Blackrock Coll	8-19	*T:* O'Mahony *PG:* Burke
14 Jan	A	Instonians	21-6	*T:* Murray, O'Mahony, Casey *PG:* O'Sullivan (2)
12 Feb	H	Shannon	6-8	*PG:* Burke (2)

25 Mar	A	Garryowen	6-13	*PG:* Burke (2)
1 Apr	H	Old Wesley	13-5	*T:* Twomey *C:* Burke *PG:* Burke (2)
8 Apr	H	Sunday's Well	23-16	*T:* Walsh, Soden *C:* Burke (2) *PG:* Burke (3)

Dolphin

Year of formation 1902
Ground Musgrave Park, Cork Tel: Cork 962435
Colours Navy blue, yellow and white
Most capped player M J Kiernan (Ireland) 43 caps
Captain 1994-95 B O'Neill
Insurance Corporation League Div 2 9th **Carling Munster Senior Cup** Lost 8-9 to UC Cork (2nd round)

League Record 1994-95

Date	*Venue*	*Opponents*	*Result*	*Scorers*
17 Sept	A	Greystones	6-21	*PG:* O'Neill (2)
24 Sept	H	Terenure Coll	12-18	*T:* O'Neill, Naylor *C:* O'Neill
8 Oct	A	Old Crescent	11-19	*T:* Clarke *PG:* Mahoney (2)
15 Oct	H	Malone	3-6	*PG:* O'Neill
7 Jan	H	Bangor	26-17	*T:* Waterman, O'Neill, Walsh *C:* Mahoney *PG:* Mahoney (3)
14 Jan	A	UC Dublin	6-3	*PG:* O'Neill (2)
11 Feb	A	Ballymena	3-27	*PG:* O'Neill
11 Mar	H	Wanderers	5-9	*T:* Waterman
25 Mar	H	Bective Rangers	17-17	*T:* Kingston, O'Shea *C:* Kelleher (2) *PG:* Kelleher
1 Apr	A	Old Belvedere	10-7	*T:* O'Neill, Cotter

Dungannon

Year of formation 1873
Ground Stevenson Park, Dungannon Tel: Dungannon 22387
Colours Blue and white hoops
Most capped player W A Anderson (Ireland) 27 caps
Captain 1994-95 Jeremy Hastings
Insurance Corporation League Div 1 11th *relegated* **First Trust Bank Ulster Senior Cup** *Winners* – beat Instonians 21-16 (final)

League Record 1994-95

Date	*Venue*	*Opponents*	*Result*	*Scorers*
17 Sept	A	Instonians	6-9	*PG:* McGarry (2)
24 Sept	H	Sunday's Well	13-3	*T:* Carey *C:* McGarry *PG:* McGarry *DG:* McGarry
1 Oct	A	Old Wesley	9-15	*PG:* McGarry (2) *DG:* Blair
8 Oct	A	Blackrock Coll	13-27	*T:* McCaughey *C:* Blair *PG:* Blair (2)
15 Oct	H	Cork Const	13-20	*T:* Beggs *C:* Blair *PG:* Blair (2)
14 Jan	H	Garryowen	11-15	*T:* McGarry *PG:* McGarry, Blair
18 Feb	H	Shannon	10-12	*T:* pen try *C:* McGarry *PG:* McGarry
11 Mar	H	Lansdowne	13-15	*T:* McDowell *C:* McGarry *PG:* Blair (2)
25 Mar	A	St Mary's Coll	9-13	*PG:* Blair (3)
1 Apr	A	Young Munster	17-12	*T:* John Hastings *PG:* McGarry (4)

Garryowen

Year of formation 1884
Ground Dooradoyle, Limerick Tel: Limerick 303099
Colours Light blue with white five-pointed star

Most capped player B G M Wood (Ireland) 29 caps
Captain 1994-95 P Hogan
Insurance Corporation League Div 1 4th **Carling Munster Senior Cup** *Winners* – beat Young Munster 23-3 (final)

League Record 1994-95

Date	*Venue*	*Opponents*	*Result*	*Scorers*
17 Sept	A	Blackrock Coll	18-7	*T:* Furlong, Wood *C:* Smith *PG:* Smith (2)
25 Sept	H	Shannon	10-15	*T:* Smith *C:* Smith *PG:* Smith
1 Oct	A	Instonians	17-5	*T:* Hogan *PG:* Smith (3) *DG:* Keane
9 Oct	A	Young Munster	24-3	*T:* Sheehan (2) *C:* Smith *PG:* Smith (3) *DG:* Larkin
15 Oct	H	Lansdowne	24-27	*T:* Smith, pen try *C:* Smith *PG:* Smith (4)
8 Jan	H	Sunday's Well	11-14	*T:* Wood *PG:* Smith (2)
14 Jan	A	Dungannon	15-11	*T:* Wallace, Costelloe *C:* Smith *PG:* Smith
11 Feb	H	Old Wesley	16-19	*T:* Wallace, Hogan *PG:* Smith (2)
11 Mar	A	St Mary's Coll	12-6	*PG:* Smith (4)
25 Mar	H	Cork Const	13-6	*T:* Wallace *C:* Smith *PG:* Smith (2)

Greystones

Year of formation 1937
Ground Dr J J Hickey Park, Delgany Road, Greystones, Co Wicklow
Tel: Dublin 2874640
Colours Green and white narrow hoops
Most capped player N J Popplewell (Ireland) 28 caps
Captain 1994-95 J Murphy
Insurance Corporation League Div 2 8th **Aluset Leinster Senior Cup** Lost 3-29 to St Mary's Coll (final)

League Record 1994-95

Date	*Venue*	*Opponents*	*Result*	*Scorers*
17 Sept	H	Dolphin	21-6	*T:* Harvey, Vance, Brennan *PG:* Harvey (2)
24 Sept	A	Ballymena	6-24	*PG:* Harvey (2)
1 Oct	H	Bective Rangers	12-33	*PG:* R Murphy (2), Harvey (2)
8 Oct	A	Old Belvedere	17-29	*T:* R Murphy *PG:* R Murphy (3) *DG:* R Murphy
29 Oct	A	Wanderers	21-6	*T:* McEntee, R Murphy *C:* R Murphy *PG:* R Murphy (3)
7 Jan	A	Old Crescent	12-19	*PG:* R Murphy (4)
14 Jan	H	Malone	19-9	*T:* J Murphy *C:* R Murphy *PG:* R Murphy (4)
18 Feb	A	Bangor	22-3	*T:* J Murphy, Power, Evans *C:* R Murphy (2) *PG:* R Murphy
11 Mar	A	Terenure Coll	17-33	*T:* Carney, McClean *C:* R Murphy (2) *DG:* Deady
1 Apr	H	UC Dublin	26-26	*T:* Deady, Dignam *C:* R Murphy (2) *PG:* R Murphy (4)

Instonians

Year of formation 1919
Ground Shane Park, Stockmans Lane, Belfast Tel: Belfast 660629
Colours Purple, yellow and black
Most capped player K D Crossan (Ireland) 41 caps
Captain 1994-95 G Bell
Insurance Corporation League Div 1 9th **First Trust Bank Ulster Senior Cup** Lost 16-21 to Dungannon (final)

League Record 1994-95

Date	*Venue*	*Opponents*	*Result*	*Scorers*
17 Sept	H	Dungannon	9-6	*PG:* Laing (2) *DG:* Nelson
24 Sept	A	St Mary's Coll	6-13	*PG:* Laing (2)
1 Oct	H	Garryowen	5-17	*T:* Hamilton
8 Oct	H	Sunday's Well	27-6	*T:* McCloskey, McCausland *C:* Laing *PG:* Laing (4) *DG:* Laing
7 Jan	A	Lansdowne	22-14	*T:* Hewitt, Burrowes *PG:* Russell (4)
14 Jan	H	Cork Const	6-21	*PG:* Laing *DG:* Laing
11 Feb	A	Young Munster	0-3	
18 Feb	A	Old Wesley	3-8	*PG:* Russell
11 Mar	H	Blackrock Coll	17-56	*T:* Irwin, Wilson *C:* Gray, O'Donnell *PG:* O'Donnell
1 Apr	A	Shannon	13-16	*T:* Wilson *C:* Laing *PG:* Laing *DG:* Laing

Lansdowne

Year of formation 1872
Ground Lansdowne Road, Dublin Tel: Dublin 6689300
Colours Red, yellow and black
Most capped player M I Keane (Ireland) 51 caps
Captain 1994-95 F Aherne
Insurance Corporation League Div 1 7th **Aluset Leinster Senior Cup** Lost 16-26 to Greystones (semi-final replay)

League Record 1994-95

Date	*Venue*	*Opponents*	*Result*	*Scorers*
17 Sept	A	Cork Const	23-25	*T:* White, Kearin, O'Shea *C:* O'Shea *PG:* O'Shea (2)
24 Sept	H	Blackrock Coll	9-19	*PG:* Kearin (3)
1 Oct	A	Shannon	0-39	
15 Oct	A	Garryowen	27-24	*T:* Glennon (2), Aherne *C:* O'Shea (3) *PG:* O'Shea (2)
7 Jan	H	Instonians	14-22	*T:* Bohan *PG:* O'Shea (3)
11 Mar	A	Dungannon	15-13	*T:* Glennon, Sharkey *C:* Elwood *PG:* Elwood
25 Mar	A	Sunday's Well	12-12	*PG:* O'Shea (4)
1 Apr	H	St Mary's Coll	24-13	*T:* O'Shea, Kearin *C:* O'Shea *PG:* O'Shea (2), Elwood *DG:* Glennon
8 Apr	H	Young Munster	0-30	
18 Apr	H	Old Wesley	26-28	*T:* Aherne *PG:* Elwood (5) *DG:* Elwood (2)

Malone

Year of formation 1892
Ground Gibson Park, Gibson Park Avenue, Belfast Tel: Belfast 451312
Colours White
Most capped player A Tedford (Ireland) 23 caps
Captain 1994-95 J McDonald
Insurance Corporation League Div 2 6th **First Trust Bank Ulster Senior Cup** Lost 16-21 to Dungannon (semi-final)

League Record 1994-95

Date	*Venue*	*Opponents*	*Result*	*Scorers*
17 Sept	A	Old Belvedere	24-30	*T:* Mackey, Porter, Rea, Harbinson *C:* Wilkinson (2)
24 Sept	H	Bangor	17-3	*T:* Harbinson, Porter *C:* Patterson, Wilkinson *DG:* Wilkinson

1 Oct	A	UC Dublin	12-5	*PG:* Wilkinson (4)
8 Oct	H	Terenure Coll	13-18	*T:* Harbinson, Rea *PG:* Wilkinson
15 Oct	A	Dolphin	6-3	*PG:* Wilkinson (2)
7 Jan	H	Wanderers	18-3	*T:* Wilkinson, Harbinson *C:* Cullen *PG:* Wilkinson, Cullen
14 Jan	A	Greystones	6-19	*PG:* Cullen *DG:* Bell
11 Feb	H	Old Crescent	12-20	*PG:* Strutt (4)
11 Mar	H	Bective Rangers	13-11	*T:* Harbinson *C:* Strutt *PG:* Strutt (2)
1 Apr	A	Ballymena	19-29	*T:* Harbinson, Willis *PG:* Strutt (3)

Old Belvedere

Year of formation 1930
Ground Angelsea Road, Ballsbridge, Dublin Tel: Dublin 6689748
Colours Black and white hoops
Most capped player A J F O'Reilly (Ireland) 29 caps
Captain 1994-95 G Dineen
Insurance Corporation League Div 2 *Winners – promoted* **Aluset Leinster Senior Cup** Lost 13-23 to St Mary's College (1st round)

League Record 1994-95

Date	*Venue*	*Opponents*	*Result*	*Scorers*
17 Sept	H	Malone	30-24	*T:* Francis, McDonnell, Dineen, O'Brien *C:* Murphy (2) *PG:* Murphy (2)
1 Oct	A	Wanderers	20-24	*T:* Gavin *PG:* Murphy (5)
8 Oct	H	Greystones	29-17	*T:* Norse, Gavin, McKenna *C:* Murphy *PG:* Murphy (4)
15 Oct	A	Bangor	16-10	*T:* Francis *C:* Murphy *PG:* Murphy (3)
7 Jan	A	Ballymena	13-11	*T:* O'Reilly *C:* Murphy *PG:* Murphy (2)
14 Jan	H	Bective Rangers	11-10	*T:* Gavin *PG:* Murphy (2)
11 Feb	H	UC Dublin	3-0	*PG:* Murphy
18 Feb	A	Terenure Coll	15-11	*T:* Feely, McDonnell *C:* Murphy *PG:* Murphy
11 Mar	A	Old Crescent	13-6	*T:* McDonnell, O'Reilly *PG:* Murphy
1 Apr	H	Dolphin	7-10	*T:* McDonnell *C:* Murphy

Old Crescent

Year of formation 1947
Ground Rosbrien, Limerick Tel: Limerick 228083
Colours Navy, blue and white stripes
Most capped player P Lane (Ireland) 1 cap
Captain 1994-95 J Forde
Insurance Corporation League Div 2 7th **Carling Munster Senior Cup** Lost 15-16 to Garryowen (1st round)

League Record 1994-95

Date	*Venue*	*Opponents*	*Result*	*Scorers*
17 Sept	A	Wanderers	12-12	*PG:* Begley (4)
24 Sept	H	UC Dublin	44-18	*T:* Madigan (2), Bowles, Reddan, O'Mara, Begley *C:* Begley (4) *PG:* Begley (2)
1 Oct	A	Terenure Coll	19-26	*T:* Reddan *C:* Begley *PG:* Begley (3) *DG:* Begley
8 Oct	H	Dolphin	19-11	*T:* Begley, Reddan *PG:* Begley (3)
7 Jan	H	Greystones	19-12	*T:* Madigan *C:* Begley *PG:* Begley (4)
14 Jan	A	Bangor	9-11	*PG:* Begley (3)
11 Feb	A	Malone	20-12	*T:* Madigan, Toland *C:* Begley (2) *PG:* Begley (2)
11 Mar	H	Old Belvedere	6-13	*PG:* Begley (2)

25 Mar	H	Ballymena	6-20	*PG:* Begley (2)
15 Apr	A	Bective Rangers	25-38	*T:* O'Dwyer *C:* Begley *PG:* Begley (6)

Old Wesley

Year of formation 1891
Ground Donnybrook, Dublin Tel: Dublin 6609893
Colours White with blue and red band
Most capped player P A Orr (Ireland) 58 caps
Captain 1994-95 C Younger
Insurance Corporation League Div 1 6th **Aluset Leinster Senior Cup** Lost 3-5 to Bective Rangers (2nd round)

League Record 1994-95

Date	*Venue*	*Opponents*	*Result*	*Scorers*
17 Sept	A	Sunday's Well	6-21	*PG:* Farren *DG:* Hawe
1 Oct	H	Dungannon	15-9	*T:* Younger, Gill *C:* Farren *PG:* Farren
8 Oct	A	Shannon	6-12	*PG:* Farren (2)
15 Oct	H	Blackrock Coll	18-24	*T:* Younger, Jackson *C:* Farren *DG:* Farren, Moloney
7 Jan	H	St Mary's Coll	3-25	*PG:* Hawe
11 Feb	A	Garryowen	19-16	*T:* Jackson *C:* Hawe *PG:* Hawe (4)
18 Feb	H	Instonians	8-3	*T:* Mooney *PG:* Hawe
11 Mar	H	Young Munster	23-22	*T:* Sexton, Jackson, Johnston *C:* Hawe *PG:* Hawe (2)
1 Apr	A	Cork Const	5-13	*T:* Jackson
18 Apr	A	Lansdowne	28-26	*T:* Moloney (2), Gill, Hoey *C:* Hawe *PG:* Hawe (2)

St Mary's College

Year of formation 1900
Ground Templeville Road, Templeogue, Dublin Tel: Dublin 4900440
Colours Royal blue with five pointed white star
Most capped player P M Dean (Ireland) 32 caps
Captain 1994-95 K Devlin
Insurance Corporation League Div 1 3rd **Aluset Leinster Senior Cup** *Winners* – beat Greystones 29-3 (final)

League Record 1994-95

Date	*Venue*	*Opponents*	*Result*	*Scorers*
17 Sept	A	Shannon	6-20	*PG:* Campion (2)
24 Sept	H	Instonians	13-6	*T:* Potts *C:* Barry *PG:* Barry (2)
1 Oct	A	Sunday's Well	21-13	*T:* Wall, Costello *C:* Barry *PG:* Barry (3)
8 Oct	A	Cork Const	16-12	*T:* Jameson *C:* Barry *PG:* Barry (3)
15 Oct	H	Young Munster	21-19	*T:* McEvoy, Browne *C:* Barry *PG:* Barry (3)
7 Jan	A	Old Wesley	25-3	*T:* Halpin, Wall, Costello, McEvoy *C:* McEvoy *PG:* McEvoy
18 Feb	H	Blackrock Coll	17-16	*T:* Halpin *PG:* Barry (2), McEvoy (2)
11 Mar	H	Garryowen	6-12	*PG:* McEvoy (2)
25 Mar	H	Dungannon	13-9	*T:* Lavin *C:* Barry *PG:* Barry (2)
1 Apr	A	Lansdowne	13-24	*T:* Lynch *C:* Barry *DG:* Campion (2)

Shannon

Year of formation 1884
Ground Thomond Park, Limerick Tel: Limerick 452350
Colours Black and blue hoops
Most capped player G A J McLoughlin (Ireland) 18 caps

Captain 1994-95 P Murray
Insurance Corporation League Div 1 *Winners* **Carling Munster Senior Cup** Lost 11-16 to Young Munster (1st round replay)

League Record 1994-95

Date	*Venue*	*Opponents*	*Result*	*Scorers*
17 Sept	H	St Mary's Coll	20-6	*T:* Murray, Kenny, Foley *C:* W O'Shea *PG:* W O'Shea
25 Sept	A	Garryowen	15-10	*T:* W O'Shea, Halvey *C:* W O'Shea *PG:* W O'Shea
1 Oct	H	Lansdowne	39-0	*T:* Galwey (2), Foley, Gallagher, W O'Shea, Thompson *C:* W O'Shea (2), Thompson *PG:* Thompson
8 Oct	H	Old Wesley	12-6	*PG:* Thompson (4)
16 Oct	A	Sunday's Well	10-6	*T:* Gallagher *C:* Thompson *PG:* Thompson
7 Jan	H	Young Munster	20-0	*T:* Thompson, W O'Shea, Halvey *C:* Thompson *PG:* Thompson
14 Jan	A	Blackrock Coll	10-3	*T:* W O'Shea *C:* Thompson *PG:* Thompson
12 Feb	A	Cork Const	8-6	*T:* Thompson *PG:* Thompson
18 Feb	A	Dungannon	12-10	*PG:* Thompson (4)
1 Apr	H	Instonians	16-13	*T:* N O'Shea *C:* Thompson *PG:* Thompson (3)

Sunday's Well

Year of formation 1923
Ground Musgrave Park, Tramore Road, Cork Tel: Cork 965735
Colours Red, green and white hoops
Most capped player J C Walsh (Ireland) 26 caps
Captain 1994-95 K O'Connell
Insurance Corporation League Div 1 10th *relegated* **Carling Munster Senior Cup** Lost 0-9 to Young Munster (2nd round)

League Record 1994-95

Date	*Venue*	*Opponents*	*Result*	*Scorers*
17 Sept	H	Old Wesley	21-6	*T:* Murphy, McCahill *C:* Daly *PG:* Daly (2) *DG:* Crotty
24 Sept	A	Dungannon	3-13	*PG:* Daly
1 Oct	H	St Mary's Coll	13-21	*T:* Roche, Cutriss *PG:* Daly
8 Oct	A	Instonians	6-27	*PG:* Daly *DG:* Crotty
16 Oct	H	Shannon	6-10	*PG:* Haly (2)
8 Jan	A	Garryowen	14-11	*T:* Daly *PG:* Daly (3)
14 Jan	A	Young Munster	6-13	*PG:* Daly (2)
25 Mar	H	Lansdowne	12-12	*PG:* Daly (3) *DG:* Crotty
1 Apr	A	Blackrock Coll	22-29	*T:* Daly, Whelehan, Cutriss, Roache *C:* Daly
8 Apr	A	Cork Const	16-23	*T:* McCahill, Gildea *PG:* Daly, Crotty

Terenure College

Year of formation 1940
Ground Lakelands Park, Greenlea, Terenure, Dublin Tel: Dublin 4907572
Colours Purple, black and white
Most capped player M L Hipwell (Ireland) 12 caps
Captain 1994-95 P Walsh
Insurance Corporation League Div 2 4th **Aluset Leinster Senior Cup** Lost 18-30 to Clontarf (1st round)

League Record 1994-95

Date	*Venue*	*Opponents*	*Result*	*Scorers*
17 Sept	A	Bangor	16-12	*T:* Larkin *C:* O'Farrell *PG:* O'Farrell (3)
24 Sept	A	Dolphin	18-12	*T:* Kenny, Browne, Coleman *PG:* Hennebry
1 Oct	H	Old Crescent	26-19	*T:* Coleman (2), Kenny *C:* P Walsh *PG:* P Walsh (3)
8 Oct	A	Malone	18-13	*T:* P Walsh, F Walsh *C:* P Walsh *PG:* P Walsh *DG:* Clarke
7 Jan	H	UC Dublin	31-24	*T:* Coleman (2), P Walsh *C:* P Walsh (2) *PG:* P Walsh (2) *DG:* Hennebry (2)
14 Jan	H	Ballymena	18-25	*PG:* Lynagh (3), P Walsh (3)
25 Jan	A	Wanderers	11-14	*T:* Hennebry *PG:* Lynagh (2)
18 Feb	H	Old Belvedere	11-15	*T:* Coleman *PG:* P Walsh *DG:* Hennebry
11 Mar	H	Greystones	33-17	*T:* P Walsh, Clarke, Hennebry, F Walsh *C:* P Walsh (2) *PG:* P Walsh (3)
1 Apr	A	Bective Rangers	5-20	*T:* F Walsh

University College Dublin

Year of formation 1910
Ground Belfield, Dublin Tel: Dublin 2834987
Colours St Patrick's blue and saffron
Most capped player W A Mulcahy (Ireland) 35 caps
Captain 1994-95 G McConkey
Insurance Corporation League Div 2 10th *relegated* **Aluset Leinster Senior Cup** Lost 0-29 to St Mary's College (2nd round)

League Record 1994-95

Date	*Venue*	*Opponents*	*Result*	*Scorers*
24 Sept	A	Old Crescent	18-44	*T:* Carey, Thorne *C:* Carey *PG:* Carey (2)
1 Oct	H	Malone	5-12	*T:* Murphy
8 Oct	A	Ballymena	9-9	*PG:* Carey (3)
15 Oct	H	Bective Rangers	28-8	*T:* Hogan, Carey, Flanagan *C:* Carey (2) *PG:* Carey (3)
7 Jan	A	Terenure Coll	24-31	*T:* O'Mahony (2) *C:* Buckley *PG:* Buckley (4)
14 Jan	H	Dolphin	3-6	*PG:* Buckley
11 Feb	A	Old Belvedere	0-3	
25 Feb	H	Wanderers	8-9	*T:* Carey *PG:* Carey
25 Mar	H	Bangor	20-9	*T:* O'Mahony (3) *C:* Buckley *PG:* Buckley
1 Apr	A	Greystones	26-26	*T:* Finn, Hickie *C:* Buckley (2) *PG:* Buckley (4)

Wanderers

Year of formation 1870
Grounds Lansdowne Road, Dublin Tel: Dublin 6689277
Colours Blue, black and white
Most capped player J R Kavanagh (Ireland) 35 caps
Captain 1994-95 P Brady
Insurance Corporation League Div 2 3rd **Aluset Leinster Senior Cup** Lost 3-13 to Lansdowne (2nd round)

League Record 1994-95

Date	*Venue*	*Opponents*	*Result*	*Scorers*
17 Sept	H	Old Crescent	12-12	*PG:* Wyse (3) *DG:* Whelan
24 Sept	A	Bective Rangers	12-11	*PG:* Whelan (4)
1 Oct	H	Old Belvedere	24-20	*T:* Garth, Leahy *C:* Whelan *PG:* Whelan (3) *DG:* Whelan

15 Oct	H	Ballymena	18-20	*T:* Finnegan, O'Callaghan *C:* Whelan *PG:* Whelan *DG:* Whelan
29 Oct	A	Greystones	6-21	*PG:* Whelan (2)
7 Jan	A	Malone	3-18	*PG:* Whelan
25 Jan	H	Terenure Coll	14-11	*T:* R Culliton *PG:* Wylie (3)
25 Feb	A	UC Dublin	9-8	*PG:* Wyse (3)
11 Mar	A	Dolphin	9-5	*PG:* Wyse *DG:* Wyse, L Mahon
1 Apr	H	Bangor	44-7	*T:* O'Callaghan (2), Moore, M Mahon, L Mahon, Spivack *C:* Wyse (4) *PG:* Wyse (2)

Young Munster

Year of formation 1895
Ground Tom Clifford Park, Greenfields, Limerick Tel: Limerick 228433
Colours Black and amber hoops
Most capped player T Clifford (Ireland) 14 caps
Captain 1994-95 M Fitzgerald
Insurance Corporation League Div 1 8th **Carling Munster Senior Cup** Lost 3-23 to Garryowen (final)

League Record 1994-95

Date	*Venue*	*Opponents*	*Result*	*Scorers*
24 Sept	H	Cork Const	10-14	*T:* P Clohessy *C:* A O'Halloran *PG:* A O'Halloran
1 Oct	A	Blackrock Coll	3-28	*PG:* A O'Halloran
9 Oct	H	Garryowen	3-24	*PG:* Benson
15 Oct	A	St Mary's Coll	19-21	*T:* Benson *C:* Benson *PG:* Benson (4)
7 Jan	A	Shannon	0-20	
14 Jan	H	Sunday's Well	13-6	*T:* McNamara, J Fitzgerald *DG:* Benson
11 Feb	H	Instonians	3-0	*PG:* Benson
11 Mar	A	Old Wesley	22-23	*T:* McNamara (2), McMahon *C:* Benson (2) *PG:* Benson
1 Apr	H	Dungannon	12-17	*PG:* Benson (4)
8 Apr	A	Lansdowne	30-0	*T:* O'Meara, Carey, M Fitzgerald *C:* A O'Halloran (3) *PG:* Benson (2) *DG:* Benson

WALES
Aberavon

Year of formation 1876
Ground Talbot Athletic Ground, Manor Street, Port Talbot, West Glamorgan Tel: Port Talbot (01639) 886038 and 882427
Colours Red and black hoops
Most capped player A J Martin (Wales) 34 caps
Captain 1994-95 B Shenton
Heineken Leagues 1994-95 Div 2 *Winners – promoted* **SWALEC Cup 1994-95** Lost 3-72 to Cardiff (quarter-final)

League Record 1994-95

Date	*Venue*	*Opponents*	*Result*	*Scorers*
27 Aug	A	Maesteg	23-14	*T:* P Horgan, B Shenton, G Richardson, G Thomas *PG:* D Davies
3 Sept	H	Penarth	19-0	*T:* B Shenton, R Diplock *PG:* D Davies (3)
7 Sept	A	S Wales Police	34-12	*T:* G Thomas, B Shenton, P Williams, J Jardine *C:* D Davies (4) *PG:* D Davies *DG:* D Davies

24 Sept	H	Llandovery	42-5	*T:* B Grabham (2), S Hutchinson, G Thomas, P Horgan, P Yardley, D Davies *C:* D Davies (2) *PG:* D Davies
1 Oct	A	Tenby Utd	31-3	*T:* S Hutchinson, A Bucknall, J Funnell, S Ford, P Horgan *C:* D Davies (3)
15 Oct	A	Ebbw Vale	18-29	*T:* J Thomas, G Thomas *C:* D Davies *PG:* D Davies *DG:* P Williams
29 Oct	H	Bonymaen	9-11	*PG:* D Davies (2) *DG:* P Williams
5 Nov	A	Cross Keys	32-9	*T:* M Watts, S Hutchinson, P Horgan *C:* M Watts *PG:* M Watts (5)
12 Nov	H	Abercynon	22-0	*T:* S Hutchinson, P Horgan *PG:* M Watts (4)
19 Nov	A	Narberth	17-10	*T:* C Young *PG:* S Holley (4)
3 Dec	H	Llanharan	16-10	*T:* P Horgan, B Grabham *PG:* M Watts (2)
10 Dec	H	Maesteg	23-6	*T:* B Shenton, J Jardine, G Thomas *C:* D Davies *PG:* D Davies (2)
21 Dec	A	Penarth	33-17	*T:* R Diplock, S Ford, J Davies, I Evans *C:* D Davies (2) *PG:* D Davies (3)
7 Jan	A	Llandovery	10-0	*T:* S Hutchinson *C:* M Watts *PG:* M Watts
4 Feb	H	Tenby Utd	11-10	*T:* C Kinsey *PG:* D Davies, M Watts
8 Feb	H	Ebbw Vale	10-6	*T:* C Kinsey *C:* M Watts *PG:* M Watts
11 Mar	H	Cross Keys	40-15	*T:* P Yardley (2), B Grabham, P Horgan, S Hutchinson *C:* D Davies (3) *PG:* D Davies (3)
1 Apr	A	Abercynon	13-18	*T:* C Young *C:* M Watts *PG:* M Watts (2)
4 Apr	H	S Wales Police	31-10	*T:* P Horgan, S Ford (2), D Davies *C:* D Davies *PG:* D Davies (3)
12 Apr	A	Bonymaen	30-29	*T:* B Grabham, M Watts *C:* M Watts *PG:* M Watts (5) *DG:* M Watts
15 Apr	H	Narberth	27-33	*T:* C Kinsey, G Thomas, J Funnell, P Matthews *C:* M Watts (2) *PG:* M Watts
29 Apr	A	Llanharan	15-16	*PG:* M Watts (4) *DG:* M Watts

Abercynon

Year of formation 1896
Ground Y Parc, Abercynon, Mid Glamorgan CF45 4RE Tel: Abercynon (01443) 740586
Colours Red and black
Captain 1994-95 A Haines
Heineken Leagues 1994-95 Div 2 3rd **SWALEC Cup 1994-95** Lost 24-58 to Swansea (5th round)

League Record 1994-95

Date	*Venue*	*Opponents*	*Result*	*Scorers*
27 Aug	H	Cross Keys	30-9	*T:* P Jones, M Morgan, A Roberts, S Pascoe *C:* M Pearce (2) *PG:* M Pearce *DG:* M Pearce
3 Sept	A	Tenby Utd	26-7	*T:* R Morgan, M Morgans *C:* M Pearce (2) *PG:* M Pearce (3) *DG:* M Pearce
8 Sept	A	Narberth	24-35	*T:* G Thomas, M Morgans, G Davies, D Pardoe *C:* M Pearce (2)
24 Sept	H	Llanharan	23-13	*T:* L Winder (2) *C:* M Pearce (2) *PG:* M Pearce (2) *DG:* M Pearce
1 Oct	A	Maesteg	13-9	*T:* G Thomas, J Edwards *PG:* M Pearce
15 Oct	H	Penarth	30-11	*T:* N Edwards, P Jones, R Morgan, A Keepings *C:* I Bebb, R Savage *PG:* R Savage *DG:* I Bebb
29 Oct	A	S Wales Police	3-23	*PG:* R Savage
5 Nov	H	Llandovery	21-9	*T:* R Savage, J Edwards *C:* R Savage *PG:* R Savage (3)
12 Nov	H	Aberavon	0-22	
19 Nov	H	Ebbw Vale	16-9	*T:* N Edwards *C:* R Savage *PG:* R Savage (3)
3 Dec	A	Bonymaen	3-23	*PG:* R Savage
10 Dec	A	Cross Keys	30-0	*T:* N Edwards, M Cotter, T Williams, A Keepings *C:* R Savage (2) *PG:* R Savage (2)
31 Dec	H	Narberth	20-0	*T:* J Pardoe, G Thomas *C:* R Savage (2) *PG:* R Savage (2)

7 Jan	A	Llanharan	11-10	*T:* A Keepings *PG:* R Savage (2)
4 Feb	H	Maesteg	16-6	*T:* J Edwards *C:* R Savage *PG:* R Savage (3)
7 Feb	A	Penarth	11-5	*T:* N Edwards *PG:* R Savage (2)
25 Feb	H	S Wales Police	10-10	*T:* G Thomas *C:* G Dixon *PG:* G Dixon
11 Mar	A	Llandovery	14-11	*T:* R Morgan *PG:* R Savage (3)
1 Apr	H	Aberavon	18-13	*PG:* R Savage (6)
8 Apr	H	Tenby Utd	22-3	*T:* G Davies *C:* R Savage *PG:* R Savage (5)
15 Apr	A	Ebbw Vale	15-17	*T:* S Reordon, S Pascoe *C:* R Savage *PG:* R Savage
29 Apr	H	Bonymaen	24-15	*T:* N Edwards, J Edwards, R Savage *C:* R Savage (3) *PG:* R Savage

Abertillery

Year of formation 1884
Ground The Park, Abertillery, Gwent Tel: Abertillery (01495) 212555
Colours Green and white quarters
Most capped player H J Morgan (Wales) 27 caps
Captain 1994-95 M Rossiter
Heineken Leagues 1994-95 Div 1 10th **SWALEC Cup 1994-95** Lost 6-29 to Abercynon (4th round)

League Record 1994-95

Date	*Venue*	*Opponents*	*Result*	*Scorers*
27 Aug	H	Newbridge	13-17	*T:* G Gladwyn, M Picton *PG:* M Williams
3 Sept	H	Llanelli	19-25	*T:* G Gladwyn, A Richards, M Picton *C:* R Roberts (2)
7 Sept	H	Newport	21-31	*PG:* M Williams (7)
24 Sept	A	Treorchy	20-61	*T:* B Corlett (2) *C:* M Williams (2) *PG:* M Williams (2)
1 Oct	H	Bridgend	17-19	*T:* M Griffiths *PG:* M Williams (4)
15 Oct	A	Pontypool	24-17	*T:* A Richards, G Gladwyn, R Lewis, J Williams *C:* A Price (2)
29 Oct	H	Pontypridd	20-42	*T:* G Gladwyn, R Roberts *C:* M Williams (2) *PG:* M Williams (2)
5 Nov	A	Cardiff	13-50	*T:* R Roberts *C:* A Price *PG:* A Price (2)
12 Nov	H	Neath	19-12	*T:* W Ford *C:* M Williams *PG:* M Williams (4)
19 Nov	A	Dunvant	15-16	*PG:* M Williams (5)
3 Dec	H	Swansea	12-10	*PG:* M Williams (4)
10 Dec	A	Newbridge	16-15	*T:* B Corlett *C:* M Williams *PG:* M Williams (3)
24 Dec	A	Llanelli	13-54	*T:* M Williams *C:* M Williams *PG:* M Williams (2)
2 Jan	A	Newport	10-19	*T:* M Williams, B Corlett
7 Jan	H	Treorchy	10-23	*T:* D John *C:* S Connors *PG:* S Connors
4 Feb	A	Bridgend	3-41	*PG:* K Price
8 Feb	H	Pontypool	15-3	*PG:* M Williams (4) *DG:* M Rossiter
25 Feb	A	Pontypridd	0-77	
11 Mar	H	Cardiff	9-16	*PG:* M Williams (3)
1 Apr	A	Neath	23-6	*T:* A Price, A Richards, B Corlett *C:* M Williams *PG:* M Williams (2)
15 Apr	H	Dunvant	22-21	*T:* R Roberts *C:* M Williams *PG:* M Williams (4) *DG:* K Price
29 Apr	A	Swansea	35-29	*T:* R McCorduck, A Harbison, A Richards, M Picton *C:* M Williams (3) *PG:* M Williams (3)

Bonymaen

Year of formation 1914
Ground Parc Mawr, Cefn Hengoed Road, Bonymaen, Swansea
Tel: Bonymaen (01792) 652859
Colours Red and black hoops

Captain 1994-95 M Clement
Heineken Leagues 1994-95 Div 2 5th **SWALEC Cup 1994-95** Lost 0-10 to Builth Wells (5th round)

League Record 1994-95

Date	*Venue*	*Opponents*	*Result*	*Scorers*
27 Aug	A	Narberth	11-15	*T:* D Howells *PG:* D Morgan *DG:* M Clement
3 Sept	H	Llanharan	18-12	*T:* D Morgan (2), P Roberts *PG:* D Morgan
8 Sept	A	Maesteg	7-12	*T:* N Davies *C:* D Morgan
24 Sept	H	Penarth	39-21	*T:* C Haste (2), M Hiles, C Lewis, G Evans, P Roberts *C:* M Dacey (3) *PG:* M Dacey
1 Oct	A	S Wales Police	3-24	*PG:* M Dacey
15 Oct	H	Llandovery	27-18	*T:* T Sturgess (2), M Clement, P Roberts *C:* P Rees (2) *PG:* P Rees
29 Oct	A	Aberavon	11-9	*T:* S Marney *PG:* P Rees (2)
5 Nov	H	Ebbw Vale	17-0	*T:* T Sturgess, G Evans *C:* P Rees (2) *PG:* P Rees
12 Nov	A	Tenby Utd	16-13	*T:* P Roberts *C:* P Rees *PG:* P Rees (3)
3 Dec	H	Abercynon	23-3	*T:* P Rees *PG:* P Rees (4) *DG:* P Rees, M John
10 Dec	H	Narberth	3-3	*PG:* P Rees
31 Dec	H	Maesteg	30-20	*T:* M Clement, S Marney, M Thomas, R Price *C:* P Rees (2) *PG:* P Rees (2)
7 Jan	A	Penarth	3-13	*PG:* P Rees
11 Feb	A	Llandovery	10-26	*T:* I Brown *C:* D Morgan *PG:* D Morgan
11 Mar	A	Ebbw Vale	3-13	*PG:* P Rees
25 Mar	A	Llanharan	7-11	*T:* A McFenton *C:* D Morgan
1 Apr	H	Tenby Utd	16-0	*T:* P Roberts *C:* D Morgan *PG:* D Morgan (3)
8 Apr	A	Cross Keys	25-12	*T:* P John, M Dacey, G Jenkins, G Evans *C:* D Morgan *PG:* D Morgan
12 Apr	H	Aberavon	29-30	*T:* A McFenton, M Clement *C:* P Roberts (2) *PG:* P Roberts (5)
15 Apr	H	Cross Keys	52-12	*T:* K Brookes (3), I Jones, D Morgan, P Roberts, N Sturgess, S Marney *C:* P Roberts (3) *PG:* P Roberts (2)
22 Apr	H	S Wales Police	5-21	*T:* R Price
29 Apr	A	Abercynon	15-24	*T:* M John (2) *C:* P Roberts *DG:* D Morgan

Bridgend

Year of formation 1878
Ground Brewery Field, Tondu Road, Bridgend, Mid Glamorgan
Tel: Bridgend (01656) 652707 and 659032
Colours Blue and white hoops
Most capped player J P R Williams (Wales) 55 caps
Captain 1994-95 R Howley
Heineken Leagues 1994-95 Div 1 5th **SWALEC Cup 1994-95** Lost 11-18 to Llanelli (quarter-final)

League Record 1994-95

Date	*Venue*	*Opponents*	*Result*	*Scorers*
27 Aug	A	Cardiff	20-50	*T:* M Back, A Williams *C:* M Lewis (2) *PG:* M Lewis *DG:* M Back
3 Sept	H	Dunvant	34-28	*T:* G Jones, G Webbe, C Bradshaw, S Bryant, pen try *C:* M Lewis (2), R Howley *PG:* R Howley
7 Sept	A	Newbridge	16-14	*T:* N Thomas *C:* M Lewis *PG:* M Lewis (3)
24 Sept	H	Newport	51-7	*T:* M Lewis, G Thomas, S Bryant, G Webbe, J Purnell, C Bradshaw, I Greenslade *C:* J Ball (3), M Lewis (2) *PG:* M Lewis, J Ball

1 Oct	A	Abertillery	19-17	*T:* C Bradshaw *C:* A Howells *PG:* A Howells (3), J Ball
5 Oct	A	Swansea	15-45	*T:* J Purnell, A Williams *C:* J Ball *PG:* J Ball
15 Oct	A	Pontypridd	6-22	*PG:* M Lewis (2)
21 Oct	H	Neath	20-20	*T:* R Howley, G Webbe *C:* M Lewis (2) *PG:* M Lewis (2)
2 Nov	H	Llanelli	16-3	*T:* G Thomas *C:* M Lewis *PG:* M Lewis (3)
19 Nov	A	Treorchy	12-8	*T:* G Thomas, I Greenslade *C:* J Ball
3 Dec	H	Pontypool	72-14	*T:* G Thomas (4), J Forster (2), G Jones (2), G Wilkins, C Bradshaw, M Lewis *C:* M Lewis (7) *PG:* M Lewis
10 Dec	H	Cardiff	10-34	*T:* M Back *C:* M Lewis *PG:* M Lewis
24 Dec	A	Dunvant	6-10	*PG:* G Ball (2)
2 Jan	H	Newbridge	15-12	*T:* G Wilkins, J Lewis *C:* M Lewis *PG:* M Lewis
7 Jan	A	Newport	22-15	*T:* M Back, R Howley *PG:* J Ball (4)
4 Feb	H	Abertillery	41-3	*T:* G Webbe (2), M Back, G Wilkins, S Gale *C:* J Ball (5) *PG:* J Ball (2)
8 Feb	H	Pontypridd	8-23	*T:* M Lewis *PG:* M Lewis
25 Feb	A	Neath	19-24	*T:* G Wilkins, J Forster, M Lewis *C:* J Ball (2)
11 Mar	H	Swansea	35-22	*T:* G Thomas, G Jones, G Wilkins, M Lewis *C:* M Lewis (3) *PG:* M Lewis (3)
1 Apr	A	Llanelli	13-26	*T:* J Ball *C:* M Lewis *PG:* M Lewis (2)
15 Apr	H	Treorchy	5-35	*T:* I Greenslade
29 Apr	A	Pontypool	63-19	*T:* G Jones (3), A Williams (3), R Howley (2), M Back, J Forster, I Greenslade *C:* M Back (3), I Greenslade

Cardiff

Year of formation 1876
Ground Cardiff Arms Park, Westgate Street, Cardiff CF1 1JA
Tel: Cardiff (01222) 383546
Colours Cambridge blue and black
Most capped player G O Edwards (Wales) 53 caps
Captain 1994-95 M R Hall
Heineken Leagues 1994-95 Div 1 *Winners* **SWALEC Cup 1994-95** Lost 9-16 (aet) to Swansea (semi-final)

League Record 1994-95

Date	*Venue*	*Opponents*	*Result*	*Scorers*
27 Aug	H	Bridgend	50-20	*T:* S Ford (2), M Bennett, J Humphreys, M Rayer, A Moore, J Hewlett *C:* A Davies (6) *PG:* A Davies
3 Sept	A	Pontypridd	12-6	*PG:* M Rayer (3) *DG:* M Rayer
8 Sept	H	Neath	37-9	*T:* H Bevan (2), M Rayer, S Hill, S Ford *C:* M Rayer (3) *PG:* M Rayer (2)
24 Sept	A	Swansea	13-17	*T:* S Ford *C:* M Rayer *PG:* M Rayer (2)
1 Oct	H	Llanelli	28-8	*T:* H Bevan, E Lewis, D Joseph, S Ford *C:* A Davies *PG:* M Rayer, A Davies
15 Oct	A	Treorchy	18-15	*T:* M Budd, A Moore *C:* M Rayer *PG:* M Rayer *DG:* A Davies
29 Oct	H	Pontypool	51-0	*T:* S Hill (2), E Lewis, H Bevan, A Booth, S Ford, C Laity *C:* A Davies (5) *PG:* A Davies (2)
5 Nov	H	Abertillery	50-13	*T:* S Hill (3), S Roy (2), J Wakeford, G John *C:* C John (6) *PG:* C John
12 Nov	A	Dunvant	27-10	*T:* M Hall (2) *C:* A Davies *PG:* A Davies (5)
19 Nov	H	Newbridge	45-8	*T:* S Ford (2), D Joseph (2), M Hall, A Lewis *C:* A Davies (3) *PG:* A Davies (3)
3 Dec	A	Newport	19-6	*T:* S Hill, O Williams *PG:* A Davies (3)
10 Dec	A	Bridgend	34-10	*T:* C John, M Hall, pen try *C:* A Davies (2) *PG:* A Davies (5)

Ian Jones (left) prepares to challenge the flying Nigel Walker in the match between Llanelli and eventual League champions Cardiff at Stradey Park, which Cardiff won 30-26.

22 Dec	H	Pontypridd	15-23	*PG:* A Davies (4) *DG:* A Davies
31 Dec	A	Neath	3-21	*PG:* A Davies
7 Jan	H	Swansea	16-3	*T:* S Ford *C:* A Davies *PG:* A Davies (3)
4 Feb	A	Llanelli	30-26	*T:* A Moore, N Walker, E Lewis *PG:* A Davies (4) *DG:* A Davies
8 Feb	H	Treorchy	17-11	*T:* S Hill, A Booth, C John *C:* A Davies
25 Feb	A	Pontypool	69-10	*T:* S Ford (5), C John (2), A Davies, A Lewis, S Hill, D Jones *C:* A Davies (7)
11 Mar	A	Abertillery	16-9	*T:* E Lewis *C:* A Davies *PG:* A Davies (3)
1 Apr	H	Dunvant	70-12	*T:* S Ford (4), A Moore (2), S Hill, M Budd (2), S Davies (2), J Westwood *C:* A Davies (5)
13 Apr	A	Newbridge	32-8	*T:* S Hill, H Taylor *C:* A Davies (2) *PG:* A Davies (6)
29 Apr	H	Newport	20-24	*T:* S Ford, M Budd *C:* C John (2) *PG:* C John (2)

Cross Keys

Year of formation 1885
Ground Pandy Park, Cross Keys, Gwent Tel: Cross Keys (01495) 270289
Colours Black and white hoops
Most capped player S Morris (Wales) 19 caps
Captain 1994-95 K Jones
Heineken Leagues 1994-95 Div 2 10th **SWALEC Cup 1994-95** Lost 5-80 to Bridgend (4th round)

League Record 1994-95

Date	*Venue*	*Opponents*	*Result*	*Scorers*
27 Aug	A	Abercynon	9-30	*PG:* G Thomas (3)
3 Sept	H	Narberth	19-10	*T:* J Powell *C:* G Thomas *PG:* G Thomas (3) *DG:* G Thomas

8 Sept	A	Llanharan	12-6	*PG:* G Thomas (4)
24 Sept	H	Maesteg	19-11	*T:* G Watkins, L Watkins *PG:* L Watkins (3)
1 Oct	A	Penarth	36-14	*T:* R Nicholls, S W Davies, M Wysocki, R Gladwyn *C:* G Thomas (2) *PG:* G Thomas (4)
15 Oct	H	S Wales Police	16-13	*T:* S Hanson *C:* L Watkins *PG:* L Watkins (3)
29 Oct	A	Llandovery	10-11	*T:* M Hassell *C:* L Watkins *PG:* L Watkin
5 Nov	H	Aberavon	9-32	*PG:* C Bushell (3)
12 Nov	A	Ebbw Vale	10-11	*T:* J Powell *C:* L Watkins *PG:* L Watkins
3 Dec	A	Tenby Utd	7-21	*T:* S Hanson *C:* C Bushell
10 Dec	H	Abercynon	0-30	
24 Dec	A	Narberth	32-13	*T:* L Watkins, S Barrett, R Nicholls *C:* L Watkins *PG:* L Watkins (4) *DG:* S Barrett
7 Jan	A	Maesteg	6-12	*PG:* L Watkins (2)
4 Feb	H	Penarth	21-18	*T:* S Hanson, pen try *C:* G Thomas *PG:* G Thomas (3)
7 Feb	A	S Wales Police	0-11	
25 Feb	H	Llandovery	17-27	*T:* R Nicholls, R Gladwyn, L Watkins *C:* C Bushell
11 Mar	A	Aberavon	15-40	*T:* M Price, D Edwards *C:* L Watkins *PG:* L Watkins
21 Mar	H	Llanharan	0-8	
1 Apr	H	Ebbw Vale	9-34	*PG:* C Bushell (3)
8 Apr	H	Bonymaen	12-25	*PG:* L Watkins (4)
15 Apr	A	Bonymaen	12-52	*T:* J Reid, E Wilson *C:* I Gladwyn
29 Apr	H	Tenby Utd	21-9	*T:* C Bushell, S Hanson *C:* C Bushell *PG:* C Bushell (3)

Dunvant

Year of formation 1888
Ground Broadacre, Killay, Swansea, SA2 7RU Tel: 01792 207291
Colours Red and green hoops
Captain 1994-95 D Evans
Heineken Leagues 1994-95 Div 1 11th *relegated* **SWALEC Cup 1994-95** Lost 8-29 to Llanelli (6th round)

League Record 1994-95

Date	*Venue*	*Opponents*	*Result*	*Scorers*
27 Aug	H	Newport	16-6	*T:* P Hopkins, W Lloyd *PG:* M Thomas (2)
3 Sept	A	Bridgend	28-34	*T:* D Niblo, I Callaghan, I Rowlands *C:* M Thomas (2) *PG:* M Thomas (3)
7 Sept	H	Pontypridd	17-15	*T:* N Lloyd *PG:* M Thomas (4)
24 Sept	A	Neath	11-11	*T:* P Morris *PG:* M Thomas (2)
1 Oct	H	Swansea	12-20	*PG:* W Booth (4)
15 Oct	A	Llanelli	19-22	*T:* P Morris, N Lloyd, I Callaghan *C:* M Thomas (2)
29 Oct	H	Treorchy	8-19	*T:* S Morgan *PG:* M Thomas
5 Nov	A	Pontypool	22-11	*T:* C Hutchings *C:* W Booth *PG:* W Booth (5)
12 Nov	H	Cardiff	10-27	*T:* R Greenwood, M Davies
19 Nov	H	Abertillery	16-15	*T:* D Evans (2) *PG:* W Booth (2)
3 Dec	A	Newbridge	15-16	*T:* G Davies (2) *C:* M Thomas *PG:* M Thomas
24 Dec	H	Bridgend	10-6	*T:* W Lloyd *C:* W Booth *PG:* D Evans
31 Dec	A	Pontypridd	3-54	*PG:* W Booth
7 Jan	H	Neath	13-17	*T:* I Callaghan *C:* M Thomas *PG:* W Booth, D Evans
4 Feb	A	Swansea	3-45	*PG:* M Thomas
8 Feb	H	Llanelli	3-36	*PG:* M Thomas
25 Feb	A	Treorchy	20-53	*T:* P Hopkins (2), W Lloyd *C:* W Booth *PG:* D Evans
11 Mar	H	Pontypool	29-3	*T:* P Hopkins, C Hutchings, W Lloyd *C:* M Thomas *PG:* M Thomas (4)

1 Apr	A	Cardiff	12-70	*T:* D Evans, M Jones *C:* M Thomas
15 Apr	A	Abertillery	21-22	*T:* C Davies, N Lloyd *C:* M Thomas *PG:* M Thomas (2) *DG:* M Thomas
22 Apr	A	Newport	13-30	*T:* M Davies, D Evans *PG:* M Thomas
29 Apr	H	Newbridge	32-10	*T:* P Morris (2), W Lloyd, C Davies *C:* M Thomas (3) *PG:* M Thomas (2)

Ebbw Vale

Year of formation 1880
Ground Eugene Cross Park, Ebbw Vale, Gwent Tel: Ebbw Vale (01495) 302995
Colours Red, white and green
Most capped player D Williams (Wales) 36 caps
Captain 1994-95 A Oliver
Heineken Leagues 1994-95 Div 2 2nd *promoted* **SWALEC Cup** Lost 11-14 to Old Illtydians (5th round)

League Record 1994-95

Date	*Venue*	*Opponents*	*Result*	*Scorers*
27 Aug	A	Llanharan	32-21	*T:* P Hudson (3), A Jewitt *C:* C Thomas (3) *PG:* C Thomas (2)
3 Sept	H	Maesteg	6-6	*PG:* C Thomas (2)
10 Sept	A	Penarth	17-12	*T:* M Mogford, D Harris, C Price *C:* C Thomas
24 Sept	A	S Wales Police	28-18	*T:* C Price, M Boys, M Thomas, C Thomas *C:* C Thomas *PG:* C Thomas (2)
1 Oct	A	Llandovery	9-19	*PG:* C Thomas (3)
15 Oct	H	Aberavon	29-18	*T:* D Davies, P Young, A Thomas, D Worgan *C:* C Thomas (3) *PG:* C Thomas
29 Oct	A	Tenby Utd	11-10	*T:* D Davies *PG:* C Thomas (2)
5 Nov	A	Bonymaen	0-17	
12 Nov	H	Cross Keys	11-10	*T:* P Young *PG:* C Thomas *DG:* M Boys
19 Nov	A	Abercynon	9-16	*PG:* C Thomas (3)
3 Dec	H	Narberth	33-10	*T:* N Chard (2), P Young, D Worgan *C:* C Thomas (2) *PG:* C Thomas (2) *DG:* M Boys
10 Dec	H	Llanharan	19-21	*T:* A Thomas, C Thomas *PG:* C Thomas (2) *DG:* M Boys
31 Dec	H	Penarth	27-13	*T:* C Thomas, D Harris, D Worgan, C Price, M Mogford *C:* C Thomas
8 Jan	H	S Wales Police	21-3	*T:* A Jewitt (2) *C:* C Thomas *PG:* C Thomas (3)
8 Feb	A	Aberavon	6-10	*PG:* D Worgan (2)
11 Mar	H	Bonymaen	13-3	*T:* A Jewitt *C:* C Thomas *PG:* C Thomas (2)
25 Mar	H	Llandovery	20-7	*T:* A Thomas (3), A Patey
1 Apr	A	Cross Keys	34-9	*T:* D Harris (2), D Davies, M Boys, P Hudson *C:* C Thomas (3) *PG:* C Thomas
15 Apr	H	Abercynon	17-15	*T:* A Jewitt *PG:* C Thomas (4)
17 Apr	H	Tenby Utd	27-18	*T:* A Thomas (2), D Harris, P Young, Watkins *C:* C Thomas
22 Apr	A	Maesteg	39-18	*T:* A Jewitt (2), C Thomas, A Thomas, P Hudson, D Davies, D Harris *C:* C Thomas (2)
29 Apr	A	Narberth	39-9	*T:* D Worgan (2), P Young, A Jewitt, N Chard, D Davies *C:* C Thomas (3) *PG:* C Thomas

Llandovery

Year of formation 1878
Ground Church Bank, Llandovery, Dyfed Tel: Llandovery (01550) 21389
Colours Red and white hoops
Most capped player C P Lewis (Wales) 5 caps
Captain 1994-95 H Thomas
Heineken Leagues 1994-95 Div 2 8th **SWALEC Cup 1994-95** Lost 3-32 to Cardiff Inst (4th round)

League Record 1994-95

Date	*Venue*	*Opponents*	*Result*	*Scorers*
27 Aug	H	Penarth	6-13	*PG:* D Lloyd-Jones *DG:* D Lloyd-Jones
3 Sept	H	S Wales Police	15-23	*T:* A Rowlands, S Richards *C:* D Lloyd-Jones *PG:* D Lloyd-Jones
10 Sept	A	Tenby Utd	8-18	*T:* S Richards *PG:* S Richards
24 Sept	A	Aberavon	5-42	*T:* G Bourne
1 Oct	H	Ebbw Vale	19-9	*T:* A Williams *C:* S Richards *PG:* S Richards (3) *DG:* D Lloyd-Jones
15 Oct	A	Bonymaen	18-27	*T:* A Williams, P Jones *C:* S Richards *PG:* S Richards (2)
29 Oct	H	Cross Keys	11-10	*T:* S Edwards *PG:* S Richards (2)
5 Nov	A	Abercynon	9-21	*PG:* S Richards (3)
12 Nov	H	Narberth	16-8	*T:* A Davies, A Williams *PG:* S Richards *DG:* A Davies
3 Dec	H	Maesteg	19-17	*T:* P Jones, A Davies, pen try *C:* C Jones (2)
24 Dec	A	S Wales Police	17-25	*T:* J Westgarth, G Bourne, P Jones *C:* C Williams
7 Jan	H	Aberavon	0-10	
14 Jan	H	Tenby Utd	23-3	*T:* P Jones, pen try *C:* S Richards (2) *PG:* S Richards (3)
28 Jan	A	Llanharan	11-18	*T:* C Williams *PG:* S Richards (2)
11 Feb	H	Bonymaen	26-10	*T:* P Jones (2), J Hughes *C:* S Richards *PG:* S Richards (3)
25 Feb	A	Cross Keys	27-17	*T:* S Doel (2), H James, Carwyn Jones *C:* S Richards (2) *PG:* S Richards
11 Mar	H	Abercynon	11-14	*T:* J Griffiths *PG:* S Richards (2)
25 Mar	A	Ebbw Vale	7-20	*T:* A Evans *C:* S Richards
1 Apr	A	Narberth	21-5	*T:* P Jones (2) *C:* S Richards *PG:* S Richards (3)
8 Apr	A	Penarth	27-24	*T:* P Jones (2), A Davies, pen try *C:* S Richards (2) *PG:* S Richards
15 Apr	H	Llanharan	6-9	*PG:* G Williams (2)
29 Apr	A	Maesteg	11-20	*T:* A Davies *PG:* C Jones (2)

Llanelli

Year of formation 1872
Ground Stradey Park, Llanelli, Dyfed SA15 4BT
Tel: Llanelli (01554) 774060 and 0891 660221
Colours Scarlet with white collar
Most capped player I C Evans (Wales) 51 caps
Captain 1994-95 R H StJ B Moon
Heineken Leagues 1994-95 Div 1 7th **SWALEC Cup 1994-95** Lost 14-20 to Pontypridd (semi-final)

League Record 1994-95

Date	*Venue*	*Opponents*	*Result*	*Scorers*
27 Aug	H	Swansea	35-23	*T:* I Evans (3), W Proctor, A Varney *C:* C Stephens (2) *PG:* C Stephens (2)
3 Sept	A	Abertillery	25-19	*T:* W Proctor (2), I Hemburrow, I Jones *C:* C Stephens *PG:* C Stephens
7 Sept	A	Treorchy	0-16	
24 Sept	H	Pontypool	20-32	*T:* S Davies, N Boobyer *C:* C Stephens (2) *PG:* C Stephens (2)
1 Oct	A	Cardiff	8-28	*T:* P Jones *PG:* C Stephens
15 Oct	H	Dunvant	22-19	*T:* H Harries, S John, I Jones *C:* C Stephens (2) *PG:* C Stephens
22 Oct	A	Newbridge	29-3	*T:* R Moon (2), I Jones, C Stephens, N Boobyer *C:* C Stephens (2)
5 Nov	H	Newport	15-12	*T:* R McBryde, M Wintle *C:* J Strange *PG:* J Strange

12 Nov	A	Bridgend	3-16	*PG:* J Strange
3 Dec	A	Neath	10-20	*T:* N Boobyer *C:* C Stephens *DG:* C Stephens
10 Dec	A	Swansea	16-23	*T:* I Jones *C:* J Strange *PG:* J Strange (2) *DG:* J Strange
24 Dec	H	Abertillery	54-13	*T:* W Proctor (4), G Evans (3), R Evans, P Davies *C:* C Stephens (2), J Strange *PG:* C Stephens
31 Dec	H	Treorchy	18-7	*T:* R Evans, A Lamerton, A McPherson *DG:* J Strange
7 Jan	A	Pontypool	13-22	*T:* I Jones, L Williams *PG:* J Strange
12 Jan	H	Pontypridd	3-11	*PG:* C Stephens
4 Feb	H	Cardiff	26-30	*T:* W Proctor, I Evans, N Davies, A Lamerton *C:* C Stephens (3)
8 Feb	A	Dunvant	36-3	*T:* H Williams-Jones, I Evans, N Boobyer, N Davies, W Proctor, R Moon *C:* C Stephens (3)
25 Feb	H	Newbridge	37-19	*T:* I Evans (2), M Wintle (2), W Proctor (2) *C:* C Stephens (2) *DG:* C Stephens
11 Mar	A	Newport	8-19	*T:* I Evans *PG:* C Stephens
1 Apr	H	Bridgend	26-13	*T:* C Quinnell, W Proctor, P Davies, G Evans *PG:* J Strange (2)
15 Apr	A	Pontypridd	22-26	*T:* G Evans, M Wintle, S Prenderville *C:* C Stephens (2) *DG:* C Stephens
29 Apr	H	Neath	33-35	*T:* S Davies (3), I Jones, H Harries *C:* J Strange (4)

Llanharan

Year of formation 1891
Ground Dairy Field, Bridgend Road, Llanharan, Mid Glamorgan
Tel: Llanharan (01443) 222209
Colours Black and sky blue hoops
Captain 1994-95 G Reffell
Heineken Leagues 1994-95 Div 2 9th **SWALEC Cup 1994-95** Lost 12-22 to Swansea (4th round)

League Record 1994-95

Date	*Venue*	*Opponents*	*Result*	*Scorers*
27 Aug	H	Ebbw Vale	21-32	*T:* P Hughes, M Harry, J Pick *PG:* J Morris (2)
3 Sept	A	Bonymaen	12-18	*PG:* J Morris (4)
8 Sept	H	Cross Keys	6-12	*PG:* W Jervis (2)
24 Sept	A	Abercynon	13-23	*T:* A Morgan, P Thompson *PG:* W Jervis
1 Oct	H	Narberth	11-14	*T:* A Morgan *PG:* J Morris (2)
15 Oct	H	Tenby Utd	17-20	*T:* M Harry *PG:* C Richards (4)
29 Oct	A	Maesteg	21-12	*T:* J Pick, S Jenkins *C:* J Morris *PG:* J Morris (3)
5 Nov	H	Penarth	34-6	*T:* W Merry, M Harry, J Morris, N Berbillion *C:* J Morris (4) *PG:* J Morris (2)
12 Nov	A	S Wales Police	13-22	*T:* D Martin *C:* J Morris *PG:* J Morris (2)
3 Dec	A	Aberavon	10-16	*T:* S Jenkins *C:* J Morris *PG:* J Morris
10 Dec	A	Ebbw Vale	21-19	*T:* S Jenkins, G Pritchard *C:* J Morris *PG:* J Morris (3)
7 Jan	H	Abercynon	10-11	*T:* A Donovan (2)
28 Jan	H	Llandovery	18-11	*T:* N Berbillion, J Morris *C:* J Morris *PG:* J Morris (2)
4 Feb	A	Narberth	0-19	
25 Feb	H	Maesteg	15-16	*T:* N Evans, M Griffiths *C:* J Morris *PG:* J Morris
11 Mar	A	Penarth	30-9	*T:* D Martin, G Pritchard, W Merry, N Berbillion *C:* J Morris (2) *PG:* J Morris (2)
25 Mar	H	Bonymaen	11-7	*T:* M Reynolds *PG:* S Hughes (2)
21 Mar	A	Cross Keys	8-0	*T:* N Berbillion *PG:* J Morris
1 Apr	H	S Wales Police	17-18	*T:* S Jenkins *PG:* S Hughes (4)
15 Apr	A	Llandovery	9-6	*PG:* S Hughes (3)
22 Apr	A	Tenby Utd	3-13	*PG:* D Emyr
29 Apr	H	Aberavon	16-15	*T:* W Merry *C:* W Jervis *PG:* W Jervis *DG:* W Jervis (2)

Maesteg

Year of formation 1877
Ground Old Parish Ground, Llynfi Road, Maesteg, Mid Glamorgan
Tel: Maesteg (01656) 732283
Colours Black and amber hoops
Most capped player G Evans (Wales) 10 caps
Captain 1994-95 H Lewis
Heineken Leagues 1994-95 Div 2 6th **SWALEC Cup 1994-95** Lost 9-14 to Ebbw Vale (4th round)

League Record 1994-95

Date	*Venue*	*Opponents*	*Result*	*Scorers*
27 Aug	H	Aberavon	14-23	*T:* C Stephens *PG:* M Watts (2) *DG:* M Watts
3 Sept	A	Ebbw Vale	6-6	*PG:* M Watts *DG:* M Watts
8 Sept	H	Bonymaen	12-7	*PG:* M Watts (4)
24 Sept	A	Cross Keys	11-19	*T:* P Davies *PG:* M Watts (2)
1 Oct	H	Abercynon	9-13	*PG:* M Watts (3)
15 Oct	A	Narberth	36-25	*T:* C Stephens (2), D Neill, M Richards, A Lloyd *C:* M Brown (4) *PG:* M Brown
29 Oct	H	Llanharan	12-21	*DG:* M Pearce (4)
5 Nov	H	Tenby Utd	20-21	*T:* C Stephens, Gwyn Lewis *C:* M Pearce (2) *PG:* M Pearce (2)
12 Nov	A	Penarth	27-18	*T:* M Richards, H Lewis, I Strang *C:* M Pearce (3) *PG:* M Pearce (2)
3 Dec	A	Llandovery	17-19	*T:* P Buckle *PG:* M Pearce (4)
10 Dec	A	Aberavon	6-23	*PG:* M Pearce (2)
31 Dec	A	Bonymaen	20-30	*T:* S Lewis, G Lewis, M Morgans *C:* M Brown *PG:* M Brown
7 Jan	H	Cross Keys	12-6	*T:* M Morgans (2) *C:* M Pearce
4 Feb	A	Abercynon	6-16	*PG:* M Brown (2)
25 Feb	A	Llanharan	16-15	*T:* M Morgans, B Davey *PG:* M Pearce (2)
6 Mar	H	S Wales Police	19-14	*T:* M Morgans, C Stephens *PG:* M Pearce (3)
11 Mar	A	Tenby Utd	10-22	*T:* B Davey *C:* M Pearce *PG:* M Pearce
1 Apr	H	Penarth	28-8	*T:* B Davey, D Neill, M Morgans, L Pagett *C:* M Pearce *PG:* M Pearce *DG:* M Pearce
8 Apr	H	Narberth	18-8	*T:* R Gregory, C Stephens *C:* M Pearce *PG:* M Pearce (2)
15 Apr	A	S Wales Police	28-24	*T:* B Davey, R Gregory, S Lewis, A Lloyd *C:* M Pearce *PG:* M Pearce (2)
22 Apr	H	Ebbw Vale	18-39	*T:* P Pincher, H Lewis *C:* M Pearce *PG:* M Pearce (2)
29 Apr	H	Llandovery	20-11	*T:* B Davey, A Lloyd *C:* M Pearce (2) *PG:* M Pearce (2)

Narberth

Year of formation 1882
Ground Lewis Lloyd Ground, Spring Gardens, Narberth, Dyfed
Tel: Narberth (01834) 860462
Colours Sky blue and navy hoops
Captain 1994-95 C Phillips
Heineken Leagues 1994-95 Div 2 11th *relegated* **SWALEC Cup 1994-95** Lost 10-15 to Mountain Ash (4th round)

League Record 1994-95

Date	*Venue*	*Opponents*	*Result*	*Scorers*
27 Aug	H	Bonymaen	15-11	*PG:* J Howells (5)

3 Sept	A	Cross Keys	10-19	*T:* G Williams *C:* J Howells *PG:* J Howells
8 Sept	H	Abercynon	35-24	*T:* P Middleton, R Dix, J Williams, A Phillips, P Anson *C:* R Dix (2) *PG:* R Dix *DG:* R Dix
24 Sept	H	Tenby Utd	16-21	*T:* A Young *C:* J Howells *PG:* J Howells (3)
1 Oct	A	Llanharan	14-11	*T:* M Roderick *PG:* J Howells (3)
15 Oct	H	Maesteg	25-36	*T:* S Gerrard (2), J Greggaine, S Davies *C:* J Howells *PG:* J Howells
29 Oct	A	Penarth	5-16	*T:* A Thomas
5 Nov	H	S Wales Police	22-22	*T:* C Phillips (3) *C:* J Howells (2) *PG:* J Howells
12 Nov	A	Llandovery	8-16	*T:* G Williams *PG:* J Howells
19 Nov	H	Aberavon	10-17	*T:* C Phillips *C:* J Howells *PG:* J Howells
3 Dec	A	Ebbw Vale	10-33	*T:* B Evans *C:* J Howells *PG:* J Howells
10 Dec	A	Bonymaen	3-3	*PG:* A Phillips
24 Dec	H	Cross Keys	13-32	*T:* L Anson *C:* R Dix *PG:* R Dix (2)
31 Dec	A	Abercynon	0-20	
7 Jan	A	Tenby Utd	14-15	*T:* C Phillips *PG:* R Dix (2) *DG:* R Dix
4 Feb	H	Llanharan	19-0	*T:* L Anson (2), S Gerard *C:* J Howells, A Phillips
25 Feb	H	Penarth	15-10	*T:* I Matthews, S Davies *C:* J Howells *PG:* J Howells
11 Mar	A	S Wales Police	10-35	*T:* L Anson, G Jones
1 Apr	H	Llandovery	5-21	*T:* C Phillips
8 Apr	A	Maesteg	8-18	*T:* M Roderick *PG:* J Howells
15 Apr	A	Aberavon	33-27	*T:* A Thomas (2), P Middleton, G Williams *C:* R Dix (2) *PG:* R Dix (3)
29 Apr	H	Ebbw Vale	9-39	*PG:* R Dix (3)

Neath

Year of formation 1871
Ground The Gnoll, Gnoll Park Road, Neath, West Glamorgan Tel: Neath (01639) 636547
Colours All black with white Maltese cross
Most capped player P H Thorburn (Wales)/G O Llewellyn (Wales) 37 caps
Captain 1994-95 G O Llewellyn
Heineken Leagues 1994-95 Div 1 4th **SWALEC Cup 1994-95** Lost 20-22 to Swansea (6th round)

League Record 1994-95

Date	*Venue*	*Opponents*	*Result*	*Scorers*
27 Aug	H	Treorchy	22-20	*T:* M Singer *C:* P Thorburn *PG:* P Thorburn (5)
3 Sept	H	Pontypool	18-12	*PG:* J Westwood (6)
8 Sept	A	Cardiff	9-37	*PG:* A Thomas (2) *DG:* A Thomas
24 Sept	H	Dunvant	11-11	*T:* J Davies *PG:* A Thomas (2)
1 Oct	A	Newbridge	10-8	*T:* S Williams *C:* A Thomas *PG:* A Thomas
15 Oct	H	Newport	23-25	*T:* L Davies, R Jones *C:* A Thomas (2) *PG:* A Thomas (2) *DG:* A Thomas
21 Oct	A	Bridgend	20-20	*T:* L Davies, S Williams, M Singer *C:* A Thomas *PG:* A Thomas
5 Nov	H	Pontypridd	6-27	*PG:* A Thomas (2)
12 Nov	A	Abertillery	12-19	*PG:* A Thomas (4)
19 Nov	A	Swansea	27-19	*T:* C Wyatt, H Woodland *C:* A Thomas *PG:* A Thomas (4) *DG:* A Thomas
3 Dec	H	Llanelli	20-10	*T:* H Woodland, M Morgan *C:* A Thomas (2) *PG:* A Thomas (2)
10 Dec	A	Treorchy	10-6	*T:* Barry Williams *C:* A Thomas *PG:* A Thomas
26 Dec	A	Pontypool	19-8	*T:* Andrew Thomas, J Davies *PG:* M McCarthy (3)
31 Dec	H	Cardiff	21-3	*T:* A Thomas, Richard Jones *C:* A Thomas *PG:* A Thomas (3)

7 Jan	A	Dunvant	17-13	*T:* C Wyatt *PG:* A Thomas (4)
4 Feb	H	Newbridge	27-15	*T:* D Llewellyn (2), L Davies, J Reynolds *C:* A Thomas (2) *PG:* A Thomas
8 Feb	A	Newport	9-27	*PG:* A Thomas (3)
25 Feb	H	Bridgend	24-19	*T:* P Thorburn, J Reynolds *C:* M McCarthy *PG:* M McCarthy (3), P Thorburn
11 Mar	A	Pontypridd	11-18	*T:* C Higgs *PG:* M McCarthy (2)
1 Apr	H	Abertillery	6-23	*PG:* M McCarthy (2)
15 Apr	H	Swansea	22-25	*T:* Richard Jones, H Woodland, C Scott *C:* M McCarthy (2) *PG:* M McCarthy
29 Apr	A	Llanelli	35-33	*T:* C Scott, M Morris, C Wyatt, Gareth Llewellyn, H Woodland *C:* M McCarthy (2) *PG:* M McCarthy *DG:* M McCarthy

Newbridge

Year of formation 1888
Ground The Welfare Ground, Bridge Street, Newbridge, Gwent
Tel: Newbridge (01495) 243247
Colours Blue and black hoops
Most capped player D Hayward (Wales) 15 caps
Captain 1994-95 P Crane
Heineken Leagues 1994-95 Div 1 9th **SWALEC Cup 1994-95** Lost 11-19 to Swansea (quarter-final)

League Record 1994-95

Date	*Venue*	*Opponents*	*Result*	*Scorers*
27 Aug	A	Abertillery	17-13	*T:* A Gibbs, S Fealey *C:* J Lloyd (2) *PG:* J Lloyd
3 Sept	A	Newport	15-6	*T:* S Fealey, P Crane *C:* J Lloyd *PG:* J Lloyd
7 Sept	H	Bridgend	14-16	*T:* C Crane, S Fealey *C:* J Lloyd (2)
1 Oct	H	Neath	8-10	*T:* P Pook *PG:* J Lloyd
15 Oct	A	Swansea	13-32	*T:* R Smith, W Taylor *PG:* W Taylor
22 Oct	H	Llanelli	3-29	*PG:* P Withers
5 Nov	A	Treorchy	6-13	*PG:* J Lloyd (2)
12 Nov	H	Pontypool	13-8	*T:* B Fisher *C:* P Withers *PG:* P Withers (2)
19 Nov	A	Cardiff	8-45	*T:* P Crane *PG:* P Withers
29 Nov	A	Pontypridd	6-30	*PG:* P Withers (2)
3 Dec	H	Dunvant	16-15	*T:* G Pugh, A Gibbs *PG:* P Withers *DG:* P Withers
10 Dec	H	Abertillery	15-16	*T:* G Pugh (2), S Hill
21 Dec	H	Newport	23-12	*T:* A Gibbs, P Withers *C:* P Withers (2) *PG:* P Withers *DG:* P Withers, W Taylor
2 Jan	A	Bridgend	12-15	*T:* S Reed, pen try *C:* P Withers
7 Jan	H	Pontypridd	13-9	*T:* P Withers *C:* P Withers *PG:* P Withers (2)
4 Feb	A	Neath	15-27	*T:* A Gibbs, J Hawker *C:* P Withers *PG:* P Withers
8 Feb	H	Swansea	27-22	*T:* P Crane, A Lucas *C:* P Withers *PG:* P Withers (4) *DG:* P Withers
25 Feb	A	Llanelli	19-37	*T:* P Edwards, A Gibbs, P Withers *C:* P Withers (2)
11 Mar	H	Treorchy	17-20	*T:* B Fisher, G Pugh, W Taylor *C:* P Withers
1 Apr	A	Pontypool	24-13	*T:* D Hooper, C Crane, W Taylor, pen try *C:* P Withers, W Taylor
13 Apr	H	Cardiff	8-32	*T:* G Pugh *PG:* P Withers
29 Apr	A	Dunvant	10-32	*T:* W Taylor *C:* P Withers *PG:* P Withers

Newport

Year of formation 1874
Ground Rodney Parade, Rodney Road, Newport, Gwent
Tel: Newport (01633) 258193 or 267410

Colours Black and amber
Most capped player K J Jones (Wales) 44 caps
Captain 1994-95 R Goodey
Heineken Leagues 1994-95 Div 1 8th **SWALEC Cup 1994-95** Lost 0-56 to Pontypridd (4th round)

League Record 1994-95

Date	*Venue*	*Opponents*	*Result*	*Scorers*
27 Aug	A	Dunvant	6-16	*PG:* B Hayward (2)
3 Sept	H	Newbridge	6-15	*PG:* B Hayward (2)
7 Sept	A	Abertillery	31-21	*T:* D Roberts *C:* B Hayward *PG:* B Hayward (7) *DG:* B Hayward
24 Sept	A	Bridgend	7-51	*T:* R Turner *C:* B Hayward
1 Oct	H	Pontypridd	3-10	*PG:* B Hayward
15 Oct	A	Neath	25-23	*T:* G Rees, M Voyle, S Enoch *C:* G Rees (2) *PG:* G Rees *DG:* G Rees
29 Oct	H	Swansea	9-16	*PG:* D Hughes (3)
5 Nov	A	Llanelli	12-15	*PG:* D Rees (4)
12 Nov	H	Treorchy	16-37	*T:* R Goodey, M Roderick *PG:* D Hughes (2)
19 Nov	A	Pontypool	29-17	*T:* D Roberts, N Jones *C:* M Jones (2) *PG:* M Jones (5)
3 Dec	H	Cardiff	6-19	*PG:* D Hughes *DG:* D Hughes
21 Dec	A	Newbridge	12-23	*T:* J Parfitt, J Lowry *C:* G Rees
2 Jan	H	Abertillery	19-10	*T:* I Jeffries *C:* G Rees *PG:* G Rees (4)
7 Jan	H	Bridgend	15-22	*PG:* G Rees (5)
4 Feb	A	Pontypridd	15-29	*T:* R Goodey, G Rees *C:* G Rees *PG:* G Rees
8 Feb	H	Neath	27-9	*T:* B Atkins (2), K Moseley, G Rees *C:* G Rees, D Hughes *PG:* G Rees
25 Feb	A	Swansea	9-10	*PG:* G Rees (3)
11 Mar	H	Llanelli	19-8	*T:* B Hayward, K Moseley *PG:* B Hayward (3)
1 Apr	A	Treorchy	13-33	*T:* R Rees *C:* B Hayward *PG:* B Hayward *DG:* B Hayward
15 Apr	H	Pontypool	33-16	*T:* R Goodey, M Roderick, D Hughes, S Enoch *C:* M Jones (2) *PG:* M Jones (3)
22 Apr	H	Dunvant	30-13	*T:* M Llewellyn, R Goodey, A Peacock, M Roderick *C:* M Jones (2) *PG:* M Jones (2)
29 Apr	A	Cardiff	24-20	*T:* R Rees (2) *C:* M Jones *PG:* M Jones (4)

Penarth

Year of formation 1880
Ground Athletic Field, Lavernock Road, Penarth, South Glamorgan
Tel: Penarth (01222) 708402
Colours Royal blue
Most capped player J A Bassett (Wales) 15 caps
Captain 1994-95 M Edwards
Heineken Leagues 1994-95 Div 2 12th *relegated* **SWALEC Cup 1994-95** Lost 8-19 to Ystrad Rhondda (4th round)

League Record 1994-95

Date	*Venue*	*Opponents*	*Result*	*Scorers*
27 Aug	A	Llandovery	13-6	*T:* M Liddiatt *C:* C Miller *PG:* C Miller *DG:* C Miller
3 Sept	A	Aberavon	0-19	
10 Sept	H	Ebbw Vale	12-17	*PG:* C Miller (4)
24 Sept	A	Bonymaen	21-39	*T:* T Crothers, J Aven *C:* C Miller *PG:* C Miller (2) *DG:* C Miller
1 Oct	H	Cross Keys	14-36	*T:* S Crothers *PG:* C Miller (3)
15 Oct	A	Abercynon	11-30	*T:* S Bell *PG:* C Howells (2)

29 Oct	H	Narberth	16-5	*T:* S Bell, J Allen *PG:* C Miller (2)
5 Nov	A	Llanharan	6-34	*PG:* C Miller (2)
12 Nov	H	Maesteg	18-27	*T:* M Liddiatt, R Phillips *C:* C Howells *PG:* C Howells (2)
19 Nov	H	Tenby Utd	7-13	*T:* M Liddiatt *C:* C Miller
3 Dec	A	S Wales Police	8-23	*T:* C Howells *PG:* C Howells
21 Dec	H	Aberavon	17-33	*T:* G Swaine, C Howells *C:* C Miller (2) *PG:* C Miller
31 Dec	A	Ebbw Vale	13-27	*T:* S Crothers *C:* C Howells *PG:* C Howells (2)
7 Jan	H	Bonymaen	13-3	*T:* I Fifield *C:* C Howells *PG:* C Howells (2)
4 Feb	A	Cross Keys	18-21	*T:* T Crothers, I Fifield *C:* C Miller *PG:* C Miller (2)
7 Feb	H	Abercynon	5-11	*T:* J Allen
25 Feb	A	Narberth	10-15	*T:* I Fifield *C:* C Miller *PG:* C Miller
11 Mar	H	Llanharan	9-30	*PG:* C Miller (3)
1 Apr	A	Maesteg	8-28	*T:* G Swaine *DG:* C Miller
8 Apr	H	Llandovery	24-27	*T:* C Lakin, G Swaine, I Roberts, M Jones *C:* C Miller (2)
15 Apr	A	Tenby Utd	27-12	*T:* C Miller, P Cousins, C Lakin *C:* C Miller (3) *PG:* C Miller (2)
29 Apr	H	S Wales Police	19-21	*T:* C Howells, A Rosser *PG:* C Miller (2) *DG:* C Miller

Pontypool

Year of formation 1868 (reconstituted 1901)
Ground The Park, Pontypool, Gwent Tel: Pontypool (01495) 763492
Colours Red, white and black hoops
Most capped player G Price (Wales) 41 caps
Captain 1994-95 M G Ring
Heineken Leagues 1994-95 Div 1 12th *relegated* **SWALEC Cup 1994-95** Lost 12-69 to Pontypridd (5th round)

League Record 1994-95

Date	*Venue*	*Opponents*	*Result*	*Scorers*
27 Aug	A	Pontypridd	25-30	*T:* M Ring, J Williams, M Taylor *C:* J Williams (2) *PG:* J Williams (2)
3 Sept	A	Neath	12-18	*T:* P Taylor, D Lynch *C:* J Williams
7 Sept	H	Swansea	21-20	*T:* pen try, W Morris *C:* J Williams *PG:* J Williams (3)
24 Sept	A	Llanelli	32-20	*T:* G Taylor (2), Mark Taylor, pen try *C:* J Williams (3) *PG:* J Williams (2)
1 Oct	H	Treorchy	13-12	*T:* W Morris *C:* J Williams *PG:* J Williams (2)
15 Oct	H	Abertillery	17-24	*T:* W Morris, B Taylor *C:* M Ring, J Williams *PG:* J Williams
29 Oct	A	Cardiff	0-51	
5 Nov	H	Dunvant	11-22	*T:* P Armstrong *PG:* M Ring *DG:* M Ring
12 Nov	A	Newbridge	8-13	*T:* M Ring *PG:* J Williams
19 Nov	H	Newport	17-29	*T:* M Ring *PG:* J Williams (4)
3 Dec	A	Bridgend	14-72	*T:* M Taylor, M Hayter *C:* J Williams (2)
10 Dec	H	Pontypridd	11-17	*T:* P Taylor *PG:* J Williams (2)
26 Dec	H	Neath	8-19	*T:* C Billen *DG:* M Ring
31 Dec	A	Swansea	10-31	*T:* Matthew Taylor, J Williams
7 Jan	H	Llanelli	22-13	*T:* M Hayter *C:* J Williams *PG:* J Williams (4) *DG:* J Williams
4 Feb	A	Treorchy	8-31	*T:* K Walker *PG:* J Williams
8 Feb	A	Abertillery	3-15	*PG:* Mark Taylor
25 Feb	H	Cardiff	10-69	*T:* W Morris *C:* Mark Taylor *PG:* Mark Taylor
11 Mar	A	Dunvant	3-29	*PG:* J Williams
1 Apr	H	Newbridge	13-24	*T:* W Morris *C:* N Humphreys *PG:* N Humphreys (2)
15 Apr	A	Newport	16-33	*T:* P Hewitt *C:* J Williams *PG:* J Williams (3)
29 Apr	H	Bridgend	19-63	*T:* W Morris (2), J Thomas *C:* J Williams (2)

Pontypridd

Year of formation 1876
Ground Sardis Road Ground, Pwllgwaun, Pontypridd
Tel: Pontypridd (01443) 405006 and 407170
Colours Black and white hoops
Most capped player N R Jenkins (Wales) 33 caps
Captain 1994-95 N Bezani
Heineken Leagues 1994-95 Div 1 2nd **SWALEC Cup 1994-95** Lost 12-17 to Swansea (final)

League Record 1994-95

Date	*Venue*	*Opponents*	*Result*	*Scorers*
27 Aug	H	Pontypool	30-25	*T:* G Prosser, Paul John *C:* N Jenkins *PG:* N Jenkins (5) *DG:* N Jenkins
3 Sept	H	Cardiff	6-12	*PG:* N Jenkins (2)
7 Sept	A	Dunvant	15-17	*T:* D McIntosh, L Lewis *C:* L Lewis *PG:* C Cormack
1 Oct	A	Newport	10-3	*T:* S Lewis *C:* C Cormack *PG:* C Cormack
15 Oct	H	Bridgend	22-6	*T:* Paul John *C:* N Jenkins *PG:* N Jenkins (5)
29 Oct	A	Abertillery	42-20	*T:* Paul John (2), C Thomas (2), J Lewis, O Robbins *C:* N Jenkins (3) *PG:* N Jenkins (2)
5 Nov	A	Neath	27-6	*T:* G Jones, S Lewis, O Robbins *C:* N Jenkins (3) *PG:* N Jenkins (2)
12 Nov	H	Swansea	32-10	*T:* D Manley, C Thomas, M Lloyd *C:* N Jenkins *PG:* N Jenkins (5)
29 Nov	H	Newbridge	30-6	*T:* C Jones, M Smith, M Lloyd *C:* N Jenkins (3) *PG:* N Jenkins (3)
3 Dec	H	Treorchy	39-13	*T:* D Manley, Phil John, Paul John, N Jenkins *C:* N Jenkins (2) *PG:* N Jenkins (5)
10 Dec	A	Pontypool	17-11	*T:* J Alvis, pen try *C:* N Jenkins (2) *PG:* N Jenkins
22 Dec	A	Cardiff	23-15	*T:* O Robbins *PG:* N Jenkins (5) *DG:* N Jenkins
31 Dec	H	Dunvant	54-3	*T:* D Manley (3), N Jenkins (2), G Jones, C Thomas, J Lewis, J Alvis *C:* N Jenkins (3) *PG:* N Jenkins
7 Jan	A	Newbridge	9-13	*PG:* N Jenkins (3)
12 Jan	A	Llanelli	11-3	*T:* D Manley *PG:* G Jones (2)
4 Feb	H	Newport	29-15	*T:* M Rowley, R Collins *C:* N Jenkins (2) *PG:* N Jenkins (5)
8 Feb	A	Bridgend	23-8	*T:* D Manley, Paul John *C:* N Jenkins (2) *PG:* N Jenkins (3)
25 Feb	H	Abertillery	77-0	*T:* D Manley (4), L Lewis (2), J Lewis (2), N Jenkins, K Jones, Paul John, P Thomas *C:* N Jenkins (7) *PG:* N Jenkins
11 Mar	H	Neath	18-11	*T:* Paul John, N Jenkins *C:* N Jenkins *PG:* N Jenkins (2)
1 Apr	A	Swansea	6-22	*PG:* N Jenkins (2)
15 Apr	H	Llanelli	26-22	*T:* J Alvis, L Lewis, O Robbins *C:* L Jarvis *PG:* L Jarvis (3)
29 Apr	A	Treorchy	9-14	*PG:* L Jarvis (3)

South Wales Police

Year of formation 1969
Ground Waterton Cross, Bridgend, Mid Glamorgan
Tel: Bridgend (01656) 655555 ext 218
Colours Red, white and royal blue with blue shorts
Most capped player R G Collins (Wales) 28 caps
Captain 1994-95 J Apsee

Heineken Leagues 1994-95 Div 2 4th **SWALEC Cup 1994-95** Lost 3-20 to Old Penarthians (5th round)

League Record 1994-95

Date	*Venue*	*Opponents*	*Result*	*Scorers*
27 Aug	H	Tenby Utd	15-11	*T:* S Pritchard, J Williams *C:* G Jones *PG:* G Jones
3 Sept	A	Llandovery	23-15	*T:* S Evans, S Pritchard, A Flowers *C:* J Price *PG:* J Price (2)
7 Sept	H	Aberavon	12-34	*T:* J Williams, N Davies *C:* A Hughes
24 Sept	H	Ebbw Vale	18-28	*T:* A Flowers, A Davies *C:* S Pritchard *PG:* S Pritchard (2)
1 Oct	H	Bonymaen	24-3	*T:* J Griffiths, J Williams *C:* M Cox *PG:* M Cox (4)
15 Oct	A	Cross Keys	13-16	*T:* pen try *C:* J Price *PG:* J Price (2)
29 Oct	H	Abercynon	23-3	*T:* D Thomas (2), pen try *C:* J Price *PG:* J Price (2)
5 Nov	A	Narberth	22-22	*T:* J Apsee, I Hemburrow, S Legge *C:* J Price (2) *PG:* J Price
12 Nov	H	Llanharan	22-13	*T:* I Hemburrow, J Williams *PG:* J Price (4)
3 Dec	H	Penarth	23-8	*T:* D Thomas, A Davies, J Price *C:* J Price *PG:* J Price (2)
10 Dec	A	Tenby Utd	26-27	*T:* D Thomas, A Flowers, J Price *C:* J Price *PG:* J Price (3)
24 Dec	H	Llandovery	25-17	*T:* A Flowers (2), M Poole *C:* G Jones (2) *PG:* G Jones (2)
8 Jan	A	Ebbw Vale	3-21	*PG:* J Price
7 Feb	H	Cross Keys	11-0	*T:* R James *PG:* J Price (2)
25 Feb	A	Abercynon	10-10	*T:* G Hiscocks *C:* J Price *PG:* J Price
6 Mar	A	Maesteg	14-19	*T:* M Cox, R James *C:* J Price (2)
11 Mar	H	Narberth	35-10	*T:* I Hemburrow (2), S Legge, N Davies, J Price *C:* J Price (2) *PG:* J Price (2)
1 Apr	A	Llanharan	18-17	*T:* D Thomas, A Phillips *C:* J Price *PG:* J Price (2)
4 Apr	A	Aberavon	10-31	*T:* J Price, I Thomas
15 Apr	H	Maesteg	24-28	*T:* M Cox, J Williams, S Legge, W Matthews *C:* J Price (2)
22 Apr	A	Bonymaen	21-5	*T:* N Davies, D Thomas *C:* J Price *PG:* J Price (3)
29 Apr	A	Penarth	21-19	*T:* S Legge, J Williams, I Hemburrow *PG:* J Price (2)

Swansea

Year of formation 1873
Ground St Helen's Ground, Bryn Road, Swansea, West Glamorgan SA2 0AR
Tel: Swansea (01792) 466593
Colours All white
Most capped player R N Jones (Wales) 52 caps
Captain 1994-95 A Clement
Heineken Leagues 1994-95 Div 1 6th **SWALEC Cup 1994-95** *Winners* – beat Pontypridd 17-12 (final)

League Record 1994-95

Date	*Venue*	*Opponents*	*Result*	*Scorers*
27 Aug	A	Llanelli	23-35	*T:* S Marshall, Simon Davies *C:* A Williams (2) *PG:* A Williams (3)
3 Sept	H	Treorchy	21-16	*T:* A Williams (2) *C:* A Williams *PG:* A Williams (3)
7 Sept	A	Pontypool	20-21	*T:* Robbie Jones, R Appleyard, D Weatherley *C:* A Williams *PG:* A Williams

24 Sept	H	Cardiff	17-13	*T:* Simon Davies *PG:* A Williams (4)
1 Oct	A	Dunvant	20-12	*T:* R Boobyer *PG:* A Williams (5)
5 Oct	H	Bridgend	45-15	*T:* D Weatherley (2), Simon Davies, I Jones, C McDonald, M Thomas, A Williams *C:* A Williams (5)
15 Oct	H	Newbridge	32-13	*T:* D Weatherley, A Reynolds, C McDonald, M Thomas *C:* A Williams (3) *PG:* A Williams (2)
29 Oct	A	Newport	16-9	*T:* R Boobyer *C:* A Williams *PG:* A Williams (3)
12 Nov	A	Pontypridd	10-32	*T:* Simon Davies *C:* A Williams *PG:* A Williams
19 Nov	H	Neath	19-27	*T:* Iwan Jones *C:* A Williams *PG:* A Williams (4)
3 Dec	A	Abertillery	10-12	*T:* S Marshall *C:* A Williams *PG:* A Williams
10 Dec	H	Llanelli	23-16	*T:* D Weatherley, G Jenkins *C:* A Williams (2) *PG:* A Williams (2) *DG:* A Williams
31 Dec	H	Pontypool	31-10	*T:* A Harris (2), Stuart Davies, A Reynolds, Simon Davies *PG:* A Williams (2)
7 Jan	A	Cardiff	3-16	*PG:* A Williams
4 Feb	H	Dunvant	45-3	*T:* R Appleyard (2), A Harris (2), D Weatherley, R Jones *C:* A Williams (3) *PG:* A Williams (3)
8 Feb	A	Newbridge	22-27	*T:* A Harris (2), Simon Davies, Robin Jones *C:* A Williams
25 Feb	H	Newport	10-9	*T:* A Reynolds *C:* A Williams *PG:* A Williams
11 Mar	A	Bridgend	22-35	*T:* A Clement, G Jenkins, A Williams *C:* A Williams (2) *PG:* A Williams
1 Apr	H	Pontypridd	22-6	*T:* R Boobyer, A Williams *PG:* L Griffiths (4)
15 Apr	A	Neath	25-22	*T:* R Boobyer, Simon Davies, D Weatherley *C:* L Griffiths (2) *PG:* L Griffiths (2)
25 Apr	A	Treorchy	10-16	*T:* M Thomas *C:* L Griffiths *PG:* L Griffiths
29 Apr	H	Abertillery	29-35	*T:* A Harris (3), G Jenkins *C:* A Williams (3) *PG:* A Williams

Tenby United

Year of formation 1901
Ground Heywood Lane, Tenby, Dyfed Tel: Tenby (01834) 842909 and 843501
Colours Black and scarlet hoops
Captain 1994-95 M Evans
Heineken Leagues 1994-95 Div 2 7th **SWALEC Cup 1994-95** Lost 3-6 to Aberavon (5th round)

League Record 1994-95

Date	*Venue*	*Opponents*	*Result*	*Scorers*
27 Aug	A	S Wales Police	11-15	*T:* M Evans *PG:* D Bowen (2)
3 Sept	H	Abercynon	7-26	*T:* D Bowen *C:* B Childs
10 Sept	H	Llandovery	18-8	*T:* M Evans, S Wake *C:* B Childs *PG:* B Childs (2)
24 Sept	A	Narberth	21-16	*T:* M Evans, S Wake *C:* B Childs *PG:* B Childs (2) *DG:* B Childs
1 Oct	H	Aberavon	3-31	*PG:* B Childs
15 Oct	A	Llanharan	20-17	*T:* D Subbiani *PG:* B Childs (2) *DG:* B Childs (3)
29 Oct	H	Ebbw Vale	10-11	*T:* M Evans *C:* B Childs *PG:* B Childs
5 Nov	A	Maesteg	21-20	*T:* R Jenkins, R Thomas *C:* H Evans *PG:* H Evans (3)
12 Nov	H	Bonymaen	13-16	*T:* S Williams *C:* H Evans *PG:* H Evans, D Bowen
19 Nov	A	Penarth	13-7	*T:* D Bowen, S Wake *PG:* D Bowen
3 Dec	H	Cross Keys	21-7	*T:* C Harts, D Hadley *C:* H Evans *PG:* H Evans (3)

10 Dec	H	S Wales Police	27-26	*T:* S Wake, pen try *C:* H Evans *PG:* H Evans (5)
7 Jan	H	Narberth	15-14	*PG:* H Evans (5)
14 Jan	A	Llandovery	3-23	*PG:* H Evans
4 Feb	A	Aberavon	10-11	*T:* E Lewis *C:* H Evans *PG:* H Evans
11 Mar	H	Maesteg	22-10	*T:* E Lewis (2), C Evans, P May *C:* H Evans
1 Apr	A	Bonymaen	0-16	
8 Apr	A	Abercynon	3-22	*PG:* D Bowen
15 Apr	H	Penarth	12-27	*T:* C Harts, N Truman *C:* H Evans
17 Apr	A	Ebbw Vale	18-27	*T:* S Wake, D Balkwill *C:* H Evans *PG:* H Evans (2)
22 Apr	H	Llanharan	13-3	*T:* S Wake *C:* D Bowen *PG:* D Bowen (2)
29 Apr	A	Cross Keys	9-21	*PG:* D Bowen (3)

Treorchy

Year of formation 1886
Ground The Oval, Treorchy, Rhondda Tel: Treorchy (01443) 434671
Colours Black and white hoops
Most capped player W Cummins (Wales)/D Jenkins (Wales) 4 caps
Captain 1994-95 K Orrell
Heineken Leagues 1994-95 Div 1 3rd **SWALEC Cup 1994-95** Lost 10-25 to Newbridge (4th round)

League Record 1994-95

Date	*Venue*	*Opponents*	*Result*	*Scorers*
27 Aug	A	Neath	20-22	*T:* A Lewis, L Gilbey *C:* L Evans (2) *PG:* D Evans (2)
3 Sept	A	Swansea	16-21	*T:* L Gilbey *C:* L Evans *PG:* D Evans (3)
7 Sept	H	Llanelli	16-0	*T:* L Davies *C:* D Evans *PG:* D Evans (3)
24 Sept	H	Abertillery	61-20	*T:* D Evans (2), L Davies (2), D Hughes, A Gwilym, D Lloyd, A Lewis *C:* D Evans (6) *PG:* D Evans (3)
1 Oct	A	Pontypool	12-13	*PG:* D Evans (3), L Evans
15 Oct	H	Cardiff	15-18	*PG:* D Evans (3), L Evans (2)
29 Oct	A	Dunvant	19-8	*T:* J Riggs *C:* L Evans *PG:* D Evans (2), L Evans (2)
5 Nov	H	Newbridge	13-6	*T:* A Gwilym *C:* D Lloyd *PG:* D Evans, D Lloyd
12 Nov	A	Newport	37-16	*T:* K Orrell (2), A Lewis (2) *C:* A Harries, L Evans (3) *PG:* A Harries, L Evans *DG:* A Harries
19 Nov	H	Bridgend	8-12	*T:* A Jones *PG:* L Evans
3 Dec	A	Pontypridd	13-39	*T:* A Harries *C:* A Harries *PG:* A Harries (2)
10 Dec	H	Neath	6-10	*PG:* A Harries (2)
31 Dec	A	Llanelli	7-18	*T:* K Orrell *C:* A Harries
7 Jan	A	Abertillery	23-10	*T:* A Harries (2), L Evans *C:* A Harries *PG:* A Harries (2)
4 Feb	H	Pontypool	31-8	*T:* A Lewis (2), L Evans, L Gilbey *C:* D Evans *PG:* D Evans (2), L Evans
8 Feb	A	Cardiff	11-17	*T:* A Jones *PG:* L Evans (2)
25 Feb	H	Dunvant	53-20	*T:* A Jones (2), O Lloyd (2), C Bridges, J Riggs, G Owen, A Lewis *C:* D Lloyd (4), L Evans *PG:* D Lloyd
11 Mar	A	Newbridge	20-17	*T:* D Evans, K Jones *C:* D Lloyd (2) *PG:* D Lloyd (2)
1 Apr	H	Newport	33-13	*T:* K Jones, A Dibble, A Lewis *C:* D Lloyd (3) *PG:* D Lloyd (4)
15 Apr	A	Bridgend	35-5	*T:* J Burnell, D Evans, A Jones, A Lewis, O Lloyd *C:* D Lloyd (5)
25 Apr	H	Swansea	16-10	*T:* J Riggs *C:* D Lloyd *PG:* D Lloyd (3)
29 Apr	H	Pontypridd	14-9	*T:* G Owen *PG:* D Lloyd (3)

OBITUARY 1994-95 (*up to 1 May 1995*)

Arthur Rex ALSTON (Bedford, Rosslyn Park) died at Ewhurst on 8 September 1994, aged 93. As a young man, he won an athletics Blue at Cambridge, where he was a contemporary of Harold Abrahams, and captained Bedford Rugby Club. Later he became a distinguished all-round sports broadcaster whose experience of first-class rugby brought insight to his commentaries on international matches in the 1950s. He also reported on various sports for the *Daily Telegraph*.

John Jeffries BEST (Marlborough, Waikato, Bay of Plenty) was a back-row member of Jack Manchester's Third All Blacks to Britain in 1935-36. He was an automatic choice for the visit after impressing the selectors at the trials, yet he was a disappointment on tour, playing only six matches and failing to win a Test place. He died at Blenheim on 25 May 1994 at the age of 80.

Georges BRUN (Vienne), who died in 1994, appeared in the first French wins at Twickenham (1951) and Murrayfield (1952). A versatile back, he won 14 caps as a full-back, wing and centre between 1950 and 1953. In the early years of his sporting career he was also a noted athlete and a skilful basketball player.

Lochlann Gerard BUTLER (Blackrock College) was Ireland's hooker against Wales in Dublin in 1960 and toured Australia as understudy to Ken Kennedy with the 1967 Irish team. More recently he was better known for the efficient manner in which he acted as liaison officer to incoming tour teams in Ireland. Last summer he toured Australia as assistant manager of the Ireland side and he was involved with the visit of François Pienaar's South Africans only a month before his death, on 6 January, 1995. He was 59.

Roderick Henry CHESTER, who died of cancer at his Auckland home on 6 June 1994, aged 57, was Rugby Union's foremost statistician. He and his co-author, Nev McMillan, produced a succession of carefully compiled volumes on the history and records of New Zealand rugby. Rod's meticulous research set high standards for others to follow, and his patience as a reliable correspondent was particularly valued by the compilers of this Yearbook.

Peter CRANMER (Oxford U, Moseley) played 16 consecutive internationals for England as a centre from 1934 to 1938. His midfield vision helped the national side to two Triple Crowns and a famous victory over the 1936 All Blacks. Although that match was remembered for Prince Obolensky's two tries, it was Peter who gave the flying Russian the crucial passes. He also dropped a goal early in the second half. An England captain in 1938, he also captained Warwickshire at cricket. He died on 29 May 1994, aged 79.

Donald Brian DEVEREUX (Neath), who died at Resolven on 8 February 1995 at the age of 62, won three caps for Wales as a prop in 1958 before joining Huddersfield Rugby League Club. When he returned to south Wales as a teacher in 1963, he built a sound reputation as a schoolboy coach. Eventually he became coach to the Welsh Secondary Schools squad, but objections to his former League connections forced him to relinquish the position.

Ronald Leslie DOBSON (Auckland), who died in Auckland on 26 October 1994, was a second five-eighth who toured Britain with the popular 1945-46 NZEF team known as the Kiwis. He won his only cap for the All Blacks in Wellington against the 1949 Wallabies. He was 71.

Steve FEALEY (Newbridge) was unlucky to find himself in competition with Robert Jones for the Wales scrum-half berth in the early 1990s, and narrowly failed to win a full cap. He did travel, however, with the 1990 Welsh side to Namibia, and scored a record-equalling hat-trick of tries in the match against Welwitschia on that tour. He died on 21 September 1994, aged 30, after a freak accident while working on the Cardiff Barrage.

Charles FORTUNE, the English-born schoolmaster who became the voice of South African rugby, died in Johannesburg on 22 November 1994. He was 89.

Adam Kelso FULTON (Edinburgh U, Dollar Academy), a retired GP, died on 27 August 1994, aged 65. He was Scotland's scrum-half against France in 1952 and 1954. On both occasions he was partnered by his university fly-half colleague, Norman Davidson.

Geremia GUGLIELMO (Petrarca), the businessman who was for 45 years connected with his beloved Petrarca club, died at the age of 63 on 7 January 1995. 'Memo' had been player, captain, coach and manager of the club before becoming its president in 1985. He won one cap for Italy as a prop in 1956 and was, for a brief spell in 1971, national coach.

Robert GORDON (Edinburgh Wanderers) made a memorable debut for Scotland in 1951, scoring two tries at Murrayfield in the 19-0 massacre of a then unbeaten Welsh team packed with British Lions. The Edinburgh wing went on to win six caps before a knee injury brought his international career to a premature end. He died on 21 March 1995, aged 64, in Edinburgh, where he was the senior partner in a chartered accountancy firm.

Gerbrand GROBLER (Transvaal), who died on 7 November 1994 in Pretoria after a car accident, scored a try in Transvaal's Currie Cup win against Orange Free State a month before his death. He had also been nominated as reserve full-back for the South Africans' visit to Britain last November. He was 32.

Philip Francis HAWTHORNE (New South Wales) was first capped for Australia as a teenager in New Zealand in 1962. A quick-witted fly-half, he formed an effective partnership with Ken Catchpole and appeared in 21 Tests before turning professional in 1968. Arguably his finest match was at Twickenham in 1967, when he steered the Wallabies to a then record 23-11 win against England, dropping three goals. He died at the age of 51 on 18 September 1994 after a brave fight against leukaemia.

Elwyn JONES (Penarth), a former Penarth captain who played as the Barbarians' uncapped player in the 1964 tour finale against Wilson Whineray's All Blacks, died in April 1995, aged 59.

Huw JONES, who died on 21 November 1994 after a short illness, was the producer of BBC Television's *Rugby Special* in the 1980s.

Peter Frederick JONES (North Auckland) was the outstanding New Zealand loose forward of the late 1950s. His 11 Tests included the games against England and Scotland on the 1953-54 tour of Britain, but he is chiefly remembered for his performances at home in 1956, when the All Blacks took a rubber off the Springboks for the first time. In the final Test of that series he sprinted 30 yards along the Eden Park touchline to score a decisive try. He was famous for commenting in a radio interview after the match that he was 'absolutely buggered'. He died in Waipapakauri on 7 June 1994, aged 62.

Raymond Bark JONES (Cambridge U, Waterloo), who died on 2 February 1995 at the age of 83, was a lock in the 1933 Wales team which, at the tenth attempt, finally broke the Twickenham bogey, beating England 7-3. Bark Jones, a solicitor, was one of seven new caps in that side, but he played only once more for Wales: against Scotland a fortnight later.

William John KIRWAN-TAYLOR (Cambridge U, Blackheath) was a member of the 1928 England side which defeated the Waratahs and took the Five Nations Grand Slam. Business demands prevented him from playing serious rugby thereafter, and his international career ended with five wins in five games before he was 23. He died in Lausanne, Switzerland, on 28 August 1994, aged 89.

Richard LANGHORN (Harlequins), the popular Harlequins forward who played in both internationals on the England A tour of Canada in 1993, died of a heart attack during a routine back operation on 25 November 1994 at the age of 29.

Thomas Hope Brendan LAWTHER (Old Millhillians) was Scotland's full-back against South Africa and Wales in 1932. Unusually, he was capped direct from his school's old boys' club, but professional duties as an engineer took precedence over his rugby career. He died on 12 December 1994, aged 85.

Thomas William LEWIS (Cardiff), who died in Cardiff on 31 May 1994 at the age of 91, was a forward who won three caps for Wales in 1926 and 1927. A collier turned policeman, like so many of the Welsh forwards of that era, he captained Cardiff in 1932-33, his last season in the first-class game.

Neil James McPHAIL (Canterbury), who died in Christchurch on 7 November 1994, aged 81, was a Canterbury prop between 1935 and 1939. The war almost certainly deprived him of All Black honours. In 1945-46, he visited Britain and France with the Kiwis, playing in the 'Victory' internationals against Wales and Scotland. He was appointed a New Zealand selector in 1961 and returned to Britain in 1963-64 as coach to Wilson Whineray's successful team.

Dr Ronald Ormiston MURRAY, MBE (Cambridge U), the distinguished clinical radiologist, died on 5 March 1995, aged 82. He was capped twice for Scotland as a forward in 1935. While he was an undergraduate at Cambridge, he won two rugby Blues.

John Robert NOTLEY (Wanderers) was an outside-half who won two caps for Ireland in 1952. He toured Argentina with Ireland later the same year and skippered his club from 1951 to 1953. Jack Notley's death was announced on 21 December 1994. He was 68.

Frederick Ernest OLIVER, OBE (Leicester), better known as a former chairman of George Oliver (Footwear), died on 7 September 1994, aged 93. He played once as a scrum-half for Leicester in 1923.

Richard Langhorn.

Henry O'Hara O'NEILL (Queen's U, UC Cork), a stocky prop who won six caps in the Irish packs of the early 1930s, died in November 1994 at the age of 87. In the summer of 1930 he was an immovable obstacle to the All Blacks and Wallabies in the five Tests of the Lions tour Down Under. After completing his studies, he sacrificed his rugby interests to pursue a career in the civil service.

David PROTHEROUGH (Moseley, Cheltenham), a no-nonsense hooker who later became a respected club and county coach, was killed in a road accident on 14 October 1994, aged 53. At the time of his death he was the rugby administrator at Cheltenham, the club he had captained early in his senior playing career.

Alan Robin REID (Waikato), who died in Morrinsville on 16 November 1994, aged 65, was, at 5ft 3, one of the smallest scrum-halves to play Test rugby. Although he toured Australia with the 1951 All Blacks, he did not win a regular Test place until 1956, when he also inspired Waikato to defeat the touring Springboks. 'Ponty' Reid appeared in three of the four Tests of New Zealand's first winning series against South Africa that season. A year later he captained the All Blacks team which won all 13 games of their tour of Australia.

Johnstone RICHARDSON (Otago, Southland). The 1924-25 New Zealand Invincibles are always referred to as Cliff Porter's team, yet their captain in the wins against Ireland, Wales and England – there was no match against Scotland – was loose forward 'Jock' Richardson. He was the last survivor of the team and the oldest living All Black at the time of his death in Nowra, Australia on 28 October 1994. He was 95.

Augustus John RISMAN (Army), the legendary Rugby League player who died in Workington on 17 October 1994, aged 83, paraded his all-round rugby talents as a Union player during the Second World War, when exponents of both codes united in a series of service internationals. Gus Risman learned the game in the Tiger Bay area of Cardiff before moving north as a teenager, and captained Wales in five wartime Union matches. His son, Bev, played Rugby Union for England eight times between 1959 and 1961.

Arthur James ROWLEY (Coventry) was a back-row forward who won his only cap for England against South Africa at Twickenham in 1932. He helped Warwickshire to reach their first County Championship final in 1931 and was instrumental in building Coventry into a force to be reckoned with on the Midlands club circuit. He died on 11 April 1995, aged 86, after a long illness.

Stephen John SCOTT (Canterbury), who died on 16 June 1994, aged 38, made a sensational All Black debut in Australia in 1980, scoring four tries against Queensland Country. A replacement for Mark Donaldson on that tour, he played in four games but failed to break into the Test side.

Noel Henry STANLEY, a former president of the NZRFU who managed the All Black teams which toured Ireland in 1974 and South Africa in 1976, died at the age of 75 in Opunake on 11 August 1994.

Surg Vice-Admiral Sir Derek STEELE-PERKINS (Royal Navy), the former medical director of the Navy and Queen's honorary surgeon, died on 9 December 1994, aged 86. He played lock for the Rest against England at Twickenham in the final international trial of 1933-34.

Michael STEVENSON, the former Cambridge cricket Blue who died at Colwyn Bay on 19 September 1994, aged 67, was a schoolmaster who wrote on cricket and rugby football for a number of publications. For the previous seven years he had contributed to the Youth, Colts and Schools sections of this Yearbook.

Alan TAYLER, CBE, fellow and tutor in mathematics at St Catherine's College, Oxford, who died on 29 January 1995 at the age of 63, was the president of the OURFC. For more than 30 years he gave Oxford rugby backbone and, as befits a mathematician, provided outstanding service to the club as its treasurer.

Brigadier George TAYLOR, CBE (Waterloo, Army), the distinguished Second World War battalion commander who died on 17 July 1994, aged 88, was a well-known forward in the 1930s. He played for the Barbarians and regularly turned out for Lancashire and the Army at a time when the latter dominated the Inter-Services tournament.

Air Commodore John Marlow THOMPSON, CBE (RAF), a Battle of Britain pilot who became AOC military traffic operations, was a threequarter in the RAF XVs of the 1930s. 'Tommy' Thompson was 79 when he died in Brighton on 23 July 1994.

Anthony Lawley WARR (Oxford U), who won two caps in the England Triple Crown team of 1934, died on 29 January 1995, aged 81. He scored a try on his debut against Wales at Cardiff but was dropped after playing against Ireland three weeks later. For 30 years 'Tim' Warr was a master at Harrow School.

Gordon Thomas WELLS (Neath, Cardiff) was a threequarter who won seven caps for Wales between 1955 and 1958, scoring a try against Scotland in his last international. As an athlete he briefly held the British AAA triple jump record and was a successful sprinter considered unlucky to have been overlooked for the British athletics team in the 1952 Olympics. An executive with Shell Chemicals, he died in April 1995, aged 67.

T P WILLIAMS, whose death in Cornwall at the age of 93 was announced in February 1995, was for more than 30 years the rugby master at Llandovery College. In the years leading up the Second World War, his college products filled all of the positions in the Welsh senior international back division.

Michael WILLIMENT (Wellington) scored 70 points in nine Tests for New Zealand in the mid-1960s, when the All Blacks were the best international team in world rugby. He established himself as a reliable full-back after Don Clarke's retirement, but just as his career seemed set to take off he was dropped in favour of Fergie McCormick for the 1967 All Blacks tour to Britain. He died in Wellington on 5 September 1994, aged 54.

Michael John YANDLE (Swansea, Leicester), whose death in Peru at the age of 49 was announced in April 1995, was a member of the Llanelli GS sides which dominated the Rosslyn Park sevens tournament in the early 1960s. After leaving university, he played regularly for Leicester. Shortly before being transferred to South America by his company, he scored the only try of Swansea's 9-9 draw with the 1973 Wallabies.

FIXTURES 1995-96

Venues and fixtures are understood to be correct at the time of going to press, but are subject to alteration. We should like to thank all those who have assisted in the compilation of this list, especially those at the various headquarters of the Home Unions.

Saturday, 2 September

SOUTH AFRICA v WALES
(Johannesburg)

SRU Tennent's Leagues
Premier League
Division 1
Boroughmuir v Edinburgh Acads
Gala v Watsonians
Heriot's FP v Melrose
Stirling County v Hawick
Division 2
Currie v Kelso
Dundee HSFP v Stewart's-Melville FP
Jedforest v Glasgow High/Kelvinside
Selkirk v West of Scotland
Division 3
Corstorphine v Peebles
Glasgow Acads v Musselburgh
Grangemouth v Kirkcaldy
Preston Lodge FP v Biggar
Division 4
Ayr v Wigtownshire
Clarkston v Haddington
Edinburgh Wands v Langholm
Gordonians v Kilmarnock

SRU Tennent's 1556 Cup:
Preliminary round

WRU Heineken Leagues
Division 1
Abertillery v Newbridge
Bridgend v Cardiff
Newport v Aberavon
Pontypridd v Ebbw Vale
Swansea v Llanelli
Treorchy v Neath
Division 2
Cross Keys v Abercynon
Dunvant v Maesteg
Llandovery v Caerphilly
Pontypool v Llanharan
Tenby Utd v S Wales Police
Ystradgynlais v Bonymaen

Bath v Garryowen
Bedford v Rosslyn Park
Blackheath v Ards
Fylde v Kendal
Gloucester v Wakefield
Hull Ionians v Nottingham
Leicester v Northampton
London Irish v Richmond
London Scottish v Rugby
Malone v Instonians
Morley v Leeds
Newcastle Gosforth v West Hartlepool
Orrell v Harrogate
Penzance-Newlyn v Bristol
Plymouth Albion v Clifton
Sale v Coventry
St Mary's Coll v Sunday's Well
Terenure Coll v Lansdowne
Wasps v Moseley
Wharfedale v Otley

Sunday, 3 September

Cornwall v Bristol (Penryn)
Brixham v Clifton
Shannon v Saracens

Tuesday, 5 September

Crynant v Aberavon
Northampton v Met Police
Penarth v Ebbw Vale
Treorchy v Tredegar

Wednesday, 6 September

Newcastle Gosforth v Morpeth
Richmond v Ealing
Terenure Coll v St Mary's Coll

Saturday, 9 September

RFU Courage Leagues
Division 1
Gloucester v Sale
Leicester v Saracens
Orrell v Harlequins
Wasps v Bristol
West Hartlepool v Bath
Division 2
London Irish v Northampton
Moseley v Newcastle Gosforth
Nottingham v Blackheath
Wakefield v Bedford

Waterloo v London Scottish
Division 3
Harrogate v Coventry
Otley v Reading
Richmond v Morley
Rosslyn Park v Rotherham
Rugby v Fylde
Division 4
Clifton v London Welsh
Leeds v Liverpool St Helens
Plymouth Albion v Havant
Redruth v Aspatria
Walsall v Exeter

SRU Tennent's Leagues
Premier League
Division 1
Edinburgh Acads v Gala
Hawick v Heriot's FP
Melrose v Boroughmuir
Watsonians v Stirling County
Division 2
Glasgow High/Kelvinside v Currie
Kelso v Dundee HSFP
Stewart's-Melville FP v Selkirk
West of Scotland v Jedforest
Division 3
Biggar v Grangemouth
Kirkcaldy v Glasgow Acads
Musselburgh v Corstorphine
Peebles v Preston Lodge FP
Division 4
Haddington v Gordonians
Kilmarnock v Edinburgh Wands
Langholm v Ayr
Wigtownshire v Clarkston

SRU Tennent's 1556 Cup: *1st round*

WRU Heineken Leagues
Division 1
Aberavon v Bridgend
Cardiff v Pontypridd
Ebbw Vale v Neath
Llanelli v Abertillery
Newbridge v Newport
Treorchy v Swansea
Division 2
Abercynon v Tenby Utd
Caerphilly v Dunvant
Llanharan v Bonymaen
Maesteg v Pontypool
S Wales Police v Llandovery
Ystradgynlais v Cross Keys

RFU Pilkington Cup: *1st round*
RFU Pilkington Shield: *1st round*
Ballymena v Malone
Instonians v City of Derry
Lansdowne v Wanderers
St Mary's Coll v Greystones

Tuesday, 12 September

Aberavon v Bonymaen
Blaina v Pontypridd
Crynant v Llanelli

Wednesday, 13 September

SRU Tennent's Leagues
Premier League
Division 1
Boroughmuir v Gala
Heriot's FP v Watsonians
Melrose v Hawick
Stirling County v Edinburgh Acads
Division 2
Currie v Dundee HSFP
Glasgow High/Kelvinside v West of Scotland
Jedforest v Stewart's-Melville FP
Selkirk v Kelso
Division 3
Biggar v Peebles
Corstorphine v Kirkcaldy
Grangemouth v Glasgow Acads
Preston Lodge FP v Musselburgh
Division 4
Ayr v Kilmarnock
Clarkston v Gordonians
Edinburgh Wands v Haddington
Wigtownshire v Langholm

Abertillery v Penarth

Saturday, 16 September

RFU Courage Leagues
Division 1
Bath v Gloucester
Bristol v West Hartlepool
Harlequins v Wasps
Sale v Leicester
Saracens v Orrell
Division 2
Bedford v Waterloo
Blackheath v Wakefield
London Scottish v London Irish
Newcastle Gosforth v Nottingham
Northampton v Moseley

Division 3
Coventry v Rugby
Fylde v Rotherham
Morley v Otley
Reading v Harrogate
Rosslyn Park v Richmond
Division 4
Aspatria v Clifton
Exeter v Leeds
Havant v Redruth
Liverpool St Helens v Plymouth Albion
London Welsh v Walsall
Division 5 South
Camborne v Berry Hill
Cheltenham v Askeans
Henley v Met Police
High Wycombe v Lydney
North Walsham v Camberley
Weston-super-Mare v Barking
Division 5 North
Broughton Park v Sheffield
Preston Grasshoppers v Lichfield
Sandal v Birmingham Solihull
Stourbridge v Kendal
Winnington Park v Nuneaton
Worcester v Stoke

SRU Tennent's Leagues
Premier League
Division 1
Gala v Stirling County
Edinburgh Acads v Heriot's FP
Hawick v Boroughmuir
Watsonians v Melrose
Division 2
Dundee HSFP v Selkirk
Kelso v Jedforest
Stewart's-Melville FP v Glasgow High/Kelvinside
West of Scotland v Currie
Division 3
Glasgow Acads v Corstorphine
Kirkcaldy v Preston Lodge FP
Musselburgh v Biggar
Peebles v Grangemouth
Division 4
Gordonians v Edinburgh Wands
Haddington v Ayr
Kilmarnock v Wigtownshire
Langholm v Clarkston

IRFU Insurance Corporation Leagues
Division 1
Ballymena v Old Wesley
Garryowen v Instonians
Lansdowne v Shannon
St Mary's Coll v Old Belvedere
Young Munster v Blackrock Coll
Division 2
Bective Rangers v Greystones
Dungannon v Clontarf
Malone v NIFC
Old Crescent v Terenure Coll
Sunday's Well v Wanderers
Division 3
Bangor v City of Derry
Bohemians v Buccaneers
Skerries v Highfield
UC Cork v Monkstown
UC Dublin v De La Salle Palmerston
Waterpark v Galwegians
Division 4
Ballina v Dublin U
Corinthians v Ards
Portadown v Armagh
Queen's U, Belfast v CIYMS
Sligo v Collegians

WRU Heineken Leagues
Division 1
Bridgend v Newbridge
Llanelli v Treorchy
Neath v Cardiff
Newport v Abertillery
Pontypridd v Aberavon
Swansea v Ebbw Vale
Division 2
Abercynon v Ystradgynlais
Bonymaen v Maesteg
Cross Keys v Llanharan
Dunvant v S Wales Police
Llandovery v Tenby Utd
Pontypool v Caerphilly

Monday, 18 September

Cornwall v Crawshay's (Camborne)

Tuesday, 19 September

Aberavon v Llanharan
London Welsh v Wasps
Treorchy v Cross Keys

Saturday, 23 September

RFU Courage Leagues
Division 1
Bristol v Harlequins
Leicester v Bath
Orrell v Sale
Wasps v Saracens
West Hartlepool v Gloucester

Division 2
Bedford v Blackheath
Moseley v London Scottish
Nottingham v Northampton
Wakefield v Newcastle Gosforth
Waterloo v London Irish
Division 3
Coventry v Reading
Harrogate v Morley
Otley v Rosslyn Park
Richmond v Fylde
Rugby v Rotherham
Division 4
Aspatria v Havant
Clifton v Walsall
Leeds v London Welsh
Plymouth Albion v Exeter
Redruth v Liverpool St Helens
Division 5 South
Askeans v Camborne
Barking v Cheltenham
Berry Hill v High Wycombe
Camberley v Weston-super-Mare
Met Police v North Walsham
Tabard v Henley
Division 5 North
Birmingham Solihull v Winnington Park
Kendal v Worcester
Lichfield v Broughton Park
Nuneaton v Stourbridge
Sheffield v Sandal
Wharfedale v Preston Grasshoppers

SRU Tennent's Leagues
Premier League
Division 1
Boroughmuir v Stirling County
Hawick v Watsonians
Heriot's FP v Gala
Melrose v Edinburgh Acads
Division 2
Currie v Selkirk
Glasgow High/Kelvinside v Kelso
Jedforest v Dundee HSFP
West of Scotland v Stewart's-Melville FP
Division 3
Biggar v Kirkcaldy
Grangemouth v Corstorphine
Peebles v Musselburgh
Preston Lodge FP v Glasgow Acads
Division 4
Ayr v Gordonians
Clarkston v Edinburgh Wands
Langholm v Kilmarnock
Wigtownshire v Haddington

IRFU Insurance Corporation Leagues
Division 1
Blackrock Coll v Lansdowne
Cork Const v Young Munster
Instonians v St Mary's Coll
Old Belvedere v Ballymena
Shannon v Garryowen
Division 2
Clontarf v Bective Rangers
Dolphin v Old Crescent
Greystones v Sunday's Well
NIFC v Dungannon
Terenure Coll v Malone
Division 3
Bangor v Monkstown
Buccaneers v Skerries
City of Derry v Waterpark
De La Salle Palmerston v UC Cork
Galwegians v Bohemians
Highfield v UC Dublin
Division 4
Ards v Queen's U, Belfast
Collegians v Corinthans
Dublin U v Armagh
Portadown v Sligo
UC Galway v Ballina

WRU Heineken Leagues
Division 1
Aberavon v Neath
Abertillery v Treorchy
Cardiff v Swansea
Ebbw Vale v Llanelli
Newbridge v Pontypridd
Newport v Bridgend
Division 2
Caerphilly v Bonymaen
Llandovery v Dunvant
Llanharan v Abercynon
Maesteg v Cross Keys
S Wales Police v Pontypool
Tenby Utd v Ystradgynlais

WRU SWALEC Cup: *1st round*

Tuesday, 26 September

Aberavon v Glam Wands
Pontypridd v S Wales Police

Wednesday, 27 September

Harlequins v Barking

Thursday, 28 September

CLOB v Oxford U

Saturday, 30 September

RFU Courage Leagues
Division 1
Bath v Orrell
Gloucester v Leicester
Harlequins v West Hartlepool
Sale v Wasps
Saracens v Bristol
Division 2
Blackheath v Waterloo
London Irish v Moseley
London Scottish v Nottingham
Newcastle Gosforth v Bedford
Northampton v Wakefield
Division 3
Fylde v Otley
Morley v Coventry
Reading v Rugby
Rosslyn Park v Harrogate
Rotherham v Richmond
Division 4
Exeter v Redruth
Havant v Clifton
Liverpool St Helens v Aspatria
London Welsh v Plymouth Albion
Walsall v Leeds
Division 5 South
Camborne v Barking
Cheltenham v Camberley
High Wycombe v Askeans
Lydney v Berry Hill
North Walsham v Tabard
Weston-super-Mare v Met Police
Division 5 North
Broughton Park v Wharfedale
Sandal v Lichfield
Stoke v Kendal
Stourbridge v Birmingham Solihull
Winnington Park v Sheffield
Worcester v Nuneaton

SRU Tennent's Leagues
Premier League
Division 1
Boroughmuir v Watsonians
Edinburgh Acads v Hawick
Gala v Melrose
Stirling County v Heriot's FP
Division 2
Currie v Stewart's-Melville FP
Dundee HSFP v Glasgow High/Kelvinside
Kelso v West of Scotland
Selkirk v Jedforest
Division 3
Corstorphine v Preston Lodge FP
Glasgow Acads v Biggar
Grangemouth v Musselburgh
Kirkcaldy v Peebles
Division 4
Clarkston v Kilmarnock
Edinburgh Wands v Ayr
Gordonians v Wigtownshire
Haddington v Langholm

IRFU Insurance Corporation Leagues
Division 1
Ballymena v Instonians
Garryowen v Blackrock Coll
Lansdowne v Cork Const
Old Wesley v Old Belvedere
St Mary's Coll v Shannon
Division 2
Dolphin v Greystones
Dungannon v Bective Rangers
Malone v Sunday's Well
Old Crescent v Wanderers
Terenure Coll v Clontarf
Division 3
Bohemians v De La Salle Palmerston
Monkstown v Buccaneers
Skerries v Galwegians
UC Cork v Bangor
UC Dublin v City of Derry
Waterpark v Highfield
Division 4
Armagh v Ards
Ballina v Collegians
Corinthians v CIYMS
Dublin U v UC Galway
Sligo v Queen's U, Belfast

WRU Heineken Leagues
Division 1
Bridgend v Abertillery
Llanelli v Cardiff
Neath v Newbridge
Pontypridd v Newport
Swansea v Aberavon
Treorchy v Ebbw Vale
Division 2
Abercynon v Maesteg
Bonymaen v S Wales Police
Cross Keys v Caerphilly
Dunvant v Tenby Utd
Pontypool v Llandovery
Ystradgynlais v Llanharan

Tuesday, 3 October

Newport v Barbarians
Aberavon v S Wales Police
Cambridge U v Cambridge City
Tredegar v Abertillery

Wednesday, 4 October

Surrey v Sussex (Met Police)
Harlequins v Brunel U
Newcastle Gosforth v Ashington
Rosslyn Park v Oxford U
West Hartlepool v Durham U

Saturday, 7 October

RFU Courage Leagues
Division 1
Bristol v Sale
Harlequins v Saracens
Orrell v Gloucester
Wasps v Bath
West Hartlepool v Leicester
Division 2
Bedford v Northampton
Blackheath v Newcastle Gosforth
Nottingham v London Irish
Wakefield v London Scottish
Waterloo v Moseley

SRU Tennent's Leagues
Premier League
Division 1
Hawick v Gala
Heriot's FP v Boroughmuir
Melrose v Stirling County
Watsonians v Edinburgh Acads
Division 2
Glasgow High/Kelvinside v Selkirk
Jedforest v Currie
Stewart's-Melville FP v Kelso
West of Scotland v Dundee HSFP
Division 3
Biggar v Corstorphine
Musselburgh v Kirkcaldy
Peebles v Glasgow Acads
Preston Lodge FP v Grangemouth
Division 4
Ayr v Clarkston
Kilmarnock v Haddington
Langholm v Gordonians
Wigtownshire v Edinburgh Wands

IRFU Insurance Corporation Leagues
Division 1
Blackrock Coll v Cork Const
Instonians v Lansdowne
Old Belvedere v Garryowen
St Mary's Coll v Old Wesley
Young Munster v Shannon
Division 2
Dolphin v Sunday's Well
Malone v Dungannon
NIFC v Greystones
Old Crescent v Bective Rangers
Terenure Coll v Wanderers
Division 3
Bohemians v UC Cork
City of Derry v De La Salle Palmerston
Highfield v Galwegians
Skerries v Monkstown
UC Dublin v Buccaneers
Waterpark v Bangor
Division 4
Ards v Ballina
CIYMS v Dublin U
Portadown v UC Galway
Queen's U, Belfast v Armagh
Sligo v Corinthians

WRU Heineken Leagues
Division 1
Aberavon v Llanelli
Abertillery v Ebbw Vale
Bridgend v Pontypridd
Cardiff v Treorchy
Newbridge v Swansea
Newport v Neath
Division 2
Caerphilly v Abercynon
Dunvant v Pontypool
Llandovery v Bonymaen
Maesteg v Ystradgynlais
S Wales Police v Cross Keys
Tenby Utd v Llanharan

RFU Pilkington Cup: *2nd round*
RFU Pilkington Shield: *2nd round*

Sunday, 8 October

Cornwall v Devon (Redruth)

Tuesday, 10 October

Aberavon v Llandovery
Cambridge U v Rosslyn Park
Cross Keys v Crumlin
Nottingham v Loughborough U
Oxford U v Bedford
Pontypridd v Pontypool
Treorchy v Glam Wands

Wednesday, 11 October

Harlequins v Exeter U
Newcastle Gosforth v Durham U
Rugby v HM Prison Service
Saracens v Brunel U

Saturday, 14 October

RFU Courage Leagues
Division 1
Bath v Bristol
Gloucester v Wasps
Leicester v Orrell
Sale v Harlequins
Saracens v West Hartlepool
Division 2
London Irish v Wakefield
London Scottish v Bedford
Moseley v Nottingham
Newcastle Gosforth v Waterloo
Northampton v Blackheath
Division 3
Coventry v Rosslyn Park
Harrogate v Fylde
Otley v Rotherham
Reading v Morley
Rugby v Richmond
Division 4
Aspatria v Exeter
Clifton v Leeds
Havant v Liverpool St Helens
Plymouth Albion v Walsall
Redruth v London Welsh
Division 5 South
Askeans v Lydney
Barking v High Wycombe
Camberley v Camborne
Henley v North Walsham
Met Police v Cheltenham
Tabard v Weston-super-Mare
Division 5 North
Birmingham Solihull v Worcester
Lichfield v Winnington Park
Nuneaton v Stoke
Preston Grasshoppers v Broughton Park
Sheffield v Stourbridge
Wharfedale v Sandal

SRU Tennent's Leagues
Premier League
Division 1
Edinburgh Acads v Boroughmuir
Hawick v Stirling County
Melrose v Heriot's FP
Watsonians v Gala
Division 2
Glasgow High/Kelvinside v Jedforest
Kelso v Currie
Stewart's-Melville FP v Dundee HSFP
West of Scotland v Selkirk
Division 3
Biggar v Preston Lodge FP
Kirkcaldy v Grangemouth
Musselburgh v Glasgow Acads
Peebles v Corstorphine
Division 4
Haddington v Clarkston
Kilmarnock v Gordonians
Langholm v Edinburgh Wands
Wigtownshire v Ayr

IRFU Insurance Corporation Leagues
Division 1
Cork Const v Instonians
Garryowen v Ballymena
Old Belvedere v Young Munster
Shannon v Blackrock Coll
Division 2
Bective Rangers v Dolphin
Dungannon v Old Crescent
Greystones v Clontarf
Sunday's Well v Terenure Coll
Wanderers v NIFC
Division 3
Bangor v UC Dublin
Buccaneers v Waterpark
De La Salle Palmerston v Highfield
Galwegians v City of Derry
Monkstown v Bohemians
UC Cork v Skerries
Division 4
Armagh v CIYMS
Ballina v Sligo
Collegians v Portadown
Dublin U v Ards
UC Galway v Queen's U, Belfast

WRU Heineken Leagues
Division 1
Ebbw Vale v Cardiff
Llanelli v Newbridge
Neath v Bridgend
Pontypridd v Abertillery
Swansea v Newport
Treorchy v Aberavon
Division 2
Abercynon v S Wales Police
Bonymaen v Dunvant
Cross Keys v Llandovery
Llanharan v Maesteg

Pontypool v Tenby Utd
Ystradgynlais v Caerphilly

Corinthians v St Mary's Coll

Sunday, 15 October

IRFU Insurance Corporation Leagues
Division 1
Old Wesley v Lansdowne

Tuesday, 17 October

Cambridge U v Crawshay's
Blaina v Abertillery
Cardiff v Penarth
Cross Keys v Pontypridd
Llanharan v Treorchy
New Dock Stars v Llanelli
Oxford U v London Welsh

Friday, 20 October

Pontypridd v Abercynon

Saturday, 21 October

Wales A v Fijians (Bridgend)

RFU Courage Leagues
Division 1
Bristol v Gloucester
Harlequins v Bath
Orrell v West Hartlepool
Saracens v Sale
Wasps v Leicester
Division 2
Bedford v London Irish
Blackheath v London Scottish
Newcastle Gosforth v Northampton
Nottingham v Waterloo
Wakefield v Moseley
Division 3
Fylde v Coventry
Morley v Rugby
Richmond v Otley
Rosslyn Park v Reading
Rotherham v Harrogate
Division 4
Exeter v Havant
Leeds v Plymouth Albion
Liverpool St Helens v Clifton
London Welsh v Aspatria
Walsall v Redruth
Division 5 South
Berry Hill v Askeans
Camborne v Met Police
Cheltenham v Tabard
High Wycombe v Camberley
Lydney v Barking
Weston-super-Mare v Henley
Division 5 North
Kendal v Nuneaton
Sandal v Preston Grasshoppers
Stoke v Birmingham Solihull
Stourbridge v Lichfield
Winnington Park v Wharfedale
Worcester v Sheffield

SRU Tennent's Leagues
Premier League
Division 1
Boroughmuir v Melrose
Gala v Edinburgh Acads
Heriot's FP v Hawick
Stirling County v Watsonians
Division 2
Currie v Glasgow High/Kelvinside
Dundee HSFP v Kelso
Jedforest v West of Scotland
Selkirk v Stewart's-Melville FP
Division 3
Corstorphine v Musselburgh
Glasgow Acads v Kirkcaldy
Grangemouth v Biggar
Preston Lodge FP v Peebles
Division 4
Ayr v Langholm
Clarkston v Wigtownshire
Edinburgh Wands v Kilmarnock
Gordonians v Haddington

IRFU Insurance Corporation Leagues
Division 1
Ballymena v St Mary's Coll
Instonians v Young Munster
Lansdowne v Old Belvedere
Old Wesley v Garryowen
Shannon v Cork Const
Division 2
Clontarf v Wanderers
Dolphin v Dungannon
NIFC v Sunday's Well
Old Crescent v Malone
Terenure Coll v Bective Rangers
Division 3
Bangor v Bohemians
Buccaneers v UC Cork
De La Salle Palmerston v Skerries
Galwegians v UC Dublin
Highfield v City of Derry
Waterpark v Monkstown
Division 4
Ards v Sligo

Collegians v Armagh
Portadown v Ballina
Queen's U, Belfast v Corinthians
UC Galway v CIYMS

WRU SWALEC Cup: *2nd round*
Llanelli v Cambridge U
Maesteg v Aberavon
Newbridge v Cross Keys
Oxford U v Loughborough U
Swansea v Neath
Treorchy v Pontypool

Tuesday, 24 October

Bedford v Western Province
Aberavon v Penarth
Oxford U v Wasps
Tredegar v Cross Keys

Wednesday, 25 October

Neath v Fijians

Saturday, 28 October

Cardiff v Fijians
Leinster v Western Province (Dublin)

RFU Courage Leagues
Division 1
Bath v Saracens
Gloucester v Harlequins
Leicester v Bristol
Orrell v Wasps
West Hartlepool v Sale
Division 2
London Irish v Blackheath
London Scottish v Newcastle Gosforth
Moseley v Bedford
Nottingham v Wakefield
Waterloo v Northampton
Division 3
Coventry v Rotherham
Harrogate v Richmond
Morley v Rosslyn Park
Otley v Rugby
Reading v Fylde
Division 4
Aspatria v Walsall
Havant v London Welsh
Liverpool St Helens v Exeter
Plymouth Albion v Clifton
Redruth v Leeds
Division 5 South
Barking v Berry Hill
Camberley v Lydney
Henley v Cheltenham
North Walsham v Weston-super-Mare
Met Police v High Wycombe
Tabard v Camborne
Division 5 North
Birmingham Solihull v Kendal
Broughton Park v Sandal
Lichfield v Worcester
Preston Grasshoppers v Winnington Park
Sheffield v Stoke
Wharfedale v Stourbridge

SRU Tennent's Leagues
Premier League
Division 1
Edinburgh Acads v Stirling County
Gala v Boroughmuir
Hawick v Melrose
Watsonians v Heriot's FP
Division 2
Dundee HSFP v Currie
Kelso v Selkirk
Stewart's-Melville FP v Jedforest
West of Scotland v Glasgow High/Kelvinside
Division 3
Glasgow Acads v Grangemouth
Kirkcaldy v Corstorphine
Musselburgh v Preston Lodge FP
Peebles v Biggar
Division 4
Gordonians v Clarkston
Haddington v Edinburgh Wands
Kilmarnock v Ayr
Langholm v Wigtownshire

WRU Heineken Leagues
Division 1
Aberavon v Ebbw Vale
Abertillery v Cardiff
Bridgend v Swansea
Newbridge v Treorchy
Newport v Llanelli
Pontypridd v Neath
Division 2
Caerphilly v Llanharan
Dunvant v Cross Keys
Llandovery v Abercynon
Pontypool v Bonymaen
S Wales Police v Ystradgynlais
Tenby Utd v Maesteg

Instonians v Banbridge
Loughborough U v Cambridge U

Malone v Portadown
St Mary's Coll v NIFC

Sunday, 29 October

UC Dublin v Lansdowne

Tuesday, 31 October

Northampton v Oxford U
Swansea v Cross Keys
Wasps v Cambridge U

Wednesday, 1 November

French Barbarians v New Zealanders (Toulon)
Treorchy v Fijians
Ulster v Western Province (Belfast)
Surrey v Middlesex (Met Police)
Percy Park v Newcastle Gosforth

Saturday, 4 November

French Selection v New Zealanders (Béziers)
Pontypridd v Fijians
Munster v Western Province

RFU Courage Leagues
Division 1
Bristol v Orrell
Harlequins v Leicester
Sale v Bath
Saracens v Gloucester
Wasps v West Hartlepool
Division 2
Bedford v Nottingham
Blackheath v Moseley
Newcastle Gosforth v London Irish
Northampton v London Scottish
Wakefield v Waterloo

SRU Tennent's Leagues
Premier League
Division 1
Boroughmuir v Hawick
Heriot's FP v Edinburgh Acads
Melrose v Watsonians
Stirling County v Gala
Division 2
Currie v West of Scotland
Glasgow High/Kelvinside v Stewart's-Melville FP
Jedforest v Kelso
Selkirk v Dundee HSFP
Division 3
Biggar v Musselburgh
Corstorphine v Glasgow Acads
Grangemouth v Peebles
Preston Lodge FP v Kirkcaldy
Division 4
Ayr v Haddington
Clarkston v Langholm
Edinburgh Wands v Gordonians
Wigtownshire v Kilmarnock

WRU Heineken Leagues
Division 1
Cardiff v Aberavon
Ebbw Vale v Newbridge
Llanelli v Bridgend
Neath v Abertillery
Treorchy v Newport
Division 2
Abercynon v Dunvant
Bonymaen v Tenby Utd
Cross Keys v Pontypool
Llanharan v S Wales Police
Maesteg v Caerphilly
Ystradgynlais v Llandovery

RFU Pilkington Cup: *3rd round*
RFU Pilkington Shield: *3rd round*
Armagh v Malone
Fylde v Winnington Park
Otley v Tynedale
Preston Grasshoppers v Harrogate
St Mary's Coll v Terenure Coll

Sunday, 5 November

Lansdowne v Greystones

Tuesday, 7 November

French Selection v New Zealanders (Bayonne)
Llanelli v Fijians
Cardiff v Western Province
Abercynon v Treorchy
Cambridge U v Northampton
Cross Keys v Blaina
Mountain Ash v Pontypridd
Neath v Oxford U

Wednesday, 8 November

Edinburgh Districts v Western Samoa (Inverleith)
Army v Civil Service
Sale v Loughborough U

Friday, 10 November

Bridgend v Western Province
Abertillery v Cross Keys

Cardiff v Cambridge U
Newport v Maesteg
Treorchy v Ystradgynlais

Saturday, 11 November

FRANCE v NEW ZEALAND (Toulouse)
WALES v FIJI (Cardiff)

RFU Courage Leagues
Division 1
Bath v West Hartlepool
Bristol v Wasps
Harlequins v Orrell
Sale v Gloucester
Saracens v Leicester
Division 2
Bedford v Wakefield
Blackheath v Nottingham
London Scottish v Waterloo
Newcastle Gosforth v Moseley
Northampton v London Irish
Division 3
Coventry v Richmond
Fylde v Morley
Harrogate v Otley
Rotherham v Reading
Rugby v Rosslyn Park
Division 4
Clifton v Exeter
Leeds v Aspatria
London Welsh v Liverpool St Helens
Plymouth Albion v Redruth
Walsall v Havant
Division 5 South
Askeans v Barking
Berry Hill v Camberley
Camborne v Henley
Cheltenham v North Walsham
High Wycombe v Tabard
Lydney v Met Police
Division 5 North
Kendal v Sheffield
Nuneaton v Birmingham Solihull
Stoke v Lichfield
Stourbridge v Preston Grasshoppers
Winnington Park v Broughton Park
Worcester v Wharfedale

SRU Tennent's Leagues
Premier League
Division 1
Edinburgh Acads v Melrose
Gala v Heriot's FP
Stirling County v Boroughmuir
Watsonians v Hawick
Division 2
Dundee HSFP v Jedforest
Kelso v Glasgow High/Kelvinside
Selkirk v Currie
Stewart's-Melville FP v West of Scotland
Division 3
Corstorphine v Grangemouth
Glasgow Acads v Preston Lodge FP
Kirkcaldy v Biggar
Musselburgh v Peebles
Division 4
Edinburgh Wands v Clarkston
Gordonians v Ayr
Haddington v Wigtownshire
Kilmarnock v Langholm

CIYMS v Malone
Old Wesley v Lansdowne
Skerries v St Mary's Coll
Toulouse U v Oxford U

Sunday, 12 November

Scotland A v Western Samoans (Hawick)

Monday, 13 November

Glasgow Districts v Western Province (Glasgow)

Tuesday, 14 November

French Selection v New Zealanders (Nancy)
Scottish North & Midlands v Western Samoans (Perth)
Connacht v Fijians (Galway)
Devon v Somerset (Exeter)
Aberavon v Mountain Ash
Berry Hill v Penarth
Gloucester v Cheltenham

Wednesday, 15 November

Oxford U v Major R V Stanley's XV
Hampshire v Royal Navy (US Portsmouth)
Coventry v Northampton
Pontypool v Abertillery

Friday, 17 November

South of Scotland v Western Province (Gala)
Clifton v Cheltenham

Saturday, 18 November

ENGLAND v SOUTH AFRICA (Twickenham)
FRANCE v NEW ZEALAND (Paris)
SCOTLAND v WESTERN SAMOA (Murrayfield)
IRELAND v FIJI (Lansdowne Road)
RFU CIS Divisional Championship
Midlands Division v London Division
South & South-West Division v Northern Division

RFU CIS County Championship
Midlands Division Pool 1
Leicestershire v Warwickshire
Midlands Division Pool 2
Staffordshire v East Midlands (Burton-on-Trent)
Northern Division
Durham v Cumbria
Lancashire v Yorkshire
Northumberland v Cheshire

WRU Heineken Leagues
Division 1
Abertillery v Aberavon
Bridgend v Treorchy
Neath v Swansea
Newbridge v Cardiff
Newport v Ebbw Vale
Pontypridd v Llanelli
Division 2
Bonymaen v Cross Keys
Dunvant v Ystradgynlais
Llandovery v Llanharan
Pontypool v Abercynon
S Wales Police v Maesteg
Tenby Utd v Caerphilly

WRU SWALEC Cup: *3rd round*
Bath v Coventry
Bristol v Northampton
Cambridge U v Harlequins
Clontarf v Lansdowne
Fylde v Leeds
Gloucester v Bedford
Harrogate v Driffield
Instonians v Portadown
Kendal v Sale
Leicester v Loughborough U
London Irish v Met Police
London Welsh v Saracens
Malone v City of Derry
Moseley v Rosslyn Park
Newcastle Gosforth v Middlesbrough
Nottingham v Morley
Otley v Huddersfield
Preston Grasshoppers v Rugby
Richmond v Blackheath
Wakefield v West Hartlepool
Wasps v London Scottish

Sunday, 19 November

SRU Tennent's Leagues
Premier League
Division 1
Hawick v Edinburgh Acads
Heriot's FP v Stirling County
Melrose v Gala
Watsonians v Boroughmuir
Division 2
Glasgow High/Kelvinside v Dundee HSFP
Jedforest v Selkirk
Stewart's-Melville FP v Currie
West of Scotland v Kelso
Division 3
Biggar v Glasgow Acads
Musselburgh v Grangemouth
Peebles v Kirkcaldy
Preston Lodge FP v Corstorphine
Division 4
Ayr v Edinburgh Wands
Kilmarnock v Clarkston
Langholm v Haddington
Wigtownshire v Gordonians

SRU Tennent's 1556 Cup: *2nd round*

Monday, 20 November

Leicester v Western Province

Tuesday, 21 November

Oxford U v Western Samoans
Blaina v Aberavon
Northampton v London Welsh

Wednesday, 22 November

High Wycombe v RAF
Rugby v Nuneaton

Saturday, 25 November

Cambridge U v Western Samoans

RFU CIS Divisional Championship
Northern Division v London Division (Wakefield)

South & South-West Division v Midlands Division

RFU CIS County Championship
Midlands Division Pool 1
Warwickshire v Notts, Lincs & Derbys
Midlands Division Pool 2
East Midlands v North Midlands
Northern Division
Cheshire v Yorkshire (New Brighton)
Durham v Northumberland
Lancashire v Cumbria
Southern Division Pool 1
Dorset & Wilts v Berkshire
Southern Division Pool 2
Devon v Oxfordshire
Hertfordshire v Gloucestershire
Southern Division Pool 3
Middlesex v Hampshire
Sussex v Kent
Southern Division Pool 4
Somerset v Eastern Counties (Taunton)
Surrey v Cornwall (Richmond)

IRFU Provincial Championship
Irish Exiles v Connacht
Ulster v Munster

SRU Tennent's Leagues
Premier League
Division 1
Boroughmuir v Heriot's FP
Edinburgh Acads v Watsonians
Gala v Hawick
Stirling County v Melrose
Division 2
Currie v Jedforest
Dundee HSFP v West of Scotland
Kelso v Stewart's-Melville FP
Selkirk v Glasgow High/Kelvinside
Division 3
Corstorphine v Biggar
Glasgow Acads v Peebles
Grangemouth v Preston Lodge FP
Kirkcaldy v Musselburgh
Division 4
Clarkston v Ayr
Edinburgh Wands v Wigtownshire
Gordonians v Langholm
Haddington v Kilmarnock

WRU Heineken Leagues
Division 1
Aberavon v Newbridge
Cardiff v Newport
Ebbw Vale v Bridgend
Llanelli v Neath
Swansea v Abertillery
Treorchy v Pontypridd
Division 2
Abercynon v Bonymaen
Caerphilly v S Wales Police
Cross Keys v Tenby Utd
Llanharan v Dunvant
Maesteg v Llandovery
Ystradgynlais v Pontypool

Bath v Loughborough U
Blackheath v Fylde
Bristol v Leinster
Coventry v Exeter
Durham U v Oxford U
Lansdowne v De La Salle Palmerston
Leicester v Rugby
London Irish v Wasps
London Scottish v Richmond
London Welsh v Bedford
Morley v Hull Ionians
Newcastle Gosforth v Harrogate
Northampton v Gloucester
Otley v Wakefield
Rosslyn Park v Saracens
Sale v Moseley
St Mary's Coll v Wanderers
West Hartlepool v Nottingham

Tuesday, 28 November

Army v Bristol
Boroughmuir v Edinburgh Wands
Pontypool v Cardiff
Pontypridd v Maesteg
Richmond v Brunel U
S Wales Police v Aberavon

Wednesday, 29 November

London & South-East Division v Western Samoans (Twickenham)
Cambridge U v M R Steele-Bodger's XV

Saturday, 2 December

Midlands Division v Western Samoans (Leicester)

RFU CIS Divisional Championship
London Division v South & South-West Division

RFU CIS County Championship
Midlands Division Pool 1
Notts, Lincs & Derbys v Leicestershire

Midlands Division Pool 2
North Midlands v Staffordshire
Northern Division
Cheshire v Durham (Wilmslow)
Cumbria v Yorkshire (Aspatria)
Northumberland v Lancashire
Southern Division Pool 1
Berkshire v Buckinghamshire
Southern Division Pool 2
Devon v Hertfordshire
Oxfordshire v Gloucestershire (Banbury)
Southern Division Pool 3
Kent v Hampshire
Sussex v Middlesex
Southern Division Pool 4
Cornwall v Eastern Counties (Camborne)
Surrey v Somerset (Met Police)

IRFU Provincial Championship
Connacht v Ulster
Irish Exiles v Leinster

WRU Heineken Leagues
Division 1
Aberavon v Newport
Cardiff v Bridgend
Ebbw Vale v Pontypridd
Llanelli v Swansea
Neath v Treorchy
Newbridge v Abertillery
Division 2
Abercynon v Cross Keys
Bonymaen v Ystradgynlais
Caerphilly v Llandovery
Llanharan v Pontypool
Maesteg v Dunvant
S Wales Police v Tenby Utd

RFU Pilkington Shield: *4th round*
Alnwick v Kelso
Ballymena v Stewart's-Melville FP
Bath v Nottingham
Bedford v Wasps
Cambridge U v Leicester
Clifton v London Scottish
Dundee HSFP v Gala
Edinburgh Acads v Biggar
Fylde v Sheffield
Glasgow High/Kelvinside v Boroughmuir
Gloucester v Val-Triangle
Grangemouth v Kilmarnock
Harlequins v London Irish
Hawick v Tynedale
Jedforest v Stirling County
Lansdowne v St Mary's Coll
London Welsh v Rosslyn Park
Lydney v Blackheath
Malone v Queen's U, Belfast
Melrose v Glasgow Acads
Moseley v Bristol
Musselburgh v Currie
Newcastle Gosforth v Rotherham
Northampton v Loughborough U
Otley v Kendal
Oxford U v Sydney U
Preston Lodge FP v Heriot's FP
Richmond v Newbury
Rugby v Leeds
Saracens v Waterloo
Selkirk v Langholm
Wakefield v Morley
Watsonians v Kirkcaldy
West Hartlepool v Hull Ionians

Sunday, 3 December

SRU District Championship
Scottish Exiles v South of Scotland (London)

Tuesday, 5 December

Northern Division v Western Samoans (Huddersfield)
Berry Hill v Abertillery
Cross Keys v Treorchy
Narberth v Aberavon

Wednesday, 6 December

SRU District Championship
Scottish Exiles v Edinburgh District (London)
Scottish North & Midlands v Glasgow District (Kirkcaldy)

Army v NZ Army
Bedford v RAF
Clifton v Bristol U

Saturday, 9 December

South & South-West Division v Western Samoans (Gloucester)

RFU CIS Divisional Championship
Midland Division v Northern Division

RFU County Championship
Midland Division semi-finals
Winners Pool 1 v Runners-up Pool 2
Winners Pool 2 v Runners-up Pool 1

Northern Division
Cumbria v Cheshire (Workington)
Durham v Lancashire
Yorkshire v Northumberland
Southern Division Pool 1
Buckinghamshire v Dorset & Wilts (Aylesbury)
Southern Division Pool 2
Gloucestershire v Devon
Hertfordshire v Oxfordshire
Southern Division Pool 3
Hampshire v Sussex (Havant)
Middlesex v Kent
Southern Division Pool 4
Eastern Counties v Surrey (Bury St Edmund's)
Somerset v Cornwall

IRFU Provincial Championship
Leinster v Connacht
Munster v Irish Exiles

SRU Tennent's Regional Leagues
Division East 1
Biggar v Boroughmuir
Edinburgh Wands v Currie
Musselburgh v Haddington
Watsonians v Preston Lodge FP
Division East 2
Corstorphine v Edinburgh Acads
Dundee HSFP v Grangemouth
Gordonians v Heriot's FP
Stewart's-Melville FP v Kirkcaldy
Division West
Ayr v West of Scotland
Clarkston v Glasgow High/Kelvinside
Glasgow Acads v Wigtownshire
Stirling County v Kilmarnock
Division South
Gala v Jedforest
Langholm v Kelso
Peebles v Melrose
Selkirk v Hawick

WRU Heineken Leagues
Division 1
Abertillery v Llanelli
Bridgend v Aberavon
Neath v Ebbw Vale
Newport v Newbridge
Pontypridd v Cardiff
Swansea v Treorchy
Division 2
Bonymaen v Llanharan
Cross Keys v Ystradgynlais
Dunvant v Caerphilly
Llandovery v S Wales Police
Pontypool v Maesteg
Tenby Utd v Abercynon

Bedford v Richmond
Bristol v Rugby
Clontarf v St Mary's Coll
Exeter v Blackheath
Fylde v Wharfedale
Harlequins v Rosslyn Park
Lansdowne v Dublin U
Leicester v London Welsh
Liverpool St Helens v Sale
London Scottish v Bath
Malone v Ballymena
Morley v Sheffield
Moseley v Gloucester
Newcastle Gosforth v Leeds
Nottingham v Harrogate
Orrell v Wakefield
Reading v Clifton
Saracens v London Irish
Wanderers v Coventry
Wasps v Northampton
West Hartlepool v Otley

Sunday, 10 December

SRU District Championship
Glasgow District v Scottish Exiles (Glasgow)
South of Scotland v Scottish North & Midlands (Kelso)

Tuesday, 12 December

England A v Western Samoans
Oxford U v Cambridge U (Twickenham)

RFU CIS County Championship
Northern Division
Lancashire v Cheshire

Wednesday, 13 December

Bedford v RAF

Friday, 15 December

Bath v Exeter
Bristol v Clifton
Coventry v Gloucester
Rugby v Nottingham

Saturday, 16 December

ENGLAND v WESTERN SAMOA (Twickenham)

RFU CIS County Championship
Northern Division
Northumberland v Cumbria
Yorkshire v Durham

IRFU Provincial Championship
Munster v Leinster
Ulster v Irish Exiles

SRU Tennent's Regional Leagues
Division East 1
Boroughmuir v Musselburgh
Currie v Watsonians
Haddington v Edinburgh Wands
Preston Lodge FP v Biggar
Division East 2
Edinburgh Acads v Stewart's-Melville FP
Grangemouth v Corstorphine
Heriot's FP v Dundee HSFP
Kirkcaldy v Gordonians
Division West
Glasgow High/Kelvinside v Ayr
Kilmarnock v Glasgow Acads
West of Scotland v Stirling County
Wigtownshire v Clarkston
Division South
Hawick v Gala
Jedforest v Langholm
Kelso v Peebles
Melrose v Selkirk

SWALEC Cup: *4th round*
Ards v Malone
Bedford v Barking
Harlequins v Royal Navy
Harrogate v Leicester
Havant v Blackheath
Liverpool St Helens v Fylde
London Irish v London Welsh
NIFC v Lansdowne
Northampton v West Hartlepool
Orrell v Otley
Richmond v Moseley
Rosslyn Park v Lydney
Saracens v London Scottish
Wakefield v Sale
Wasps v Newcastle Gosforth
Waterloo v Morley

Sunday, 17 December

SRU District Championship
Edinburgh District v South of Scotland
Scottish North & Midlands v Scottish Exiles (Aberdeen)

Wednesday, 20 December

Army v Territorial Army

Saturday, 23 December

RFU Pilkington Cup: *4th round*
RFU Pilkington Shield: *5th round*

SRU Tennent's Regional Leagues
Division East 1
Biggar v Musselburgh
Edinburgh Wands v Boroughmuir
Preston Lodge FP v Currie
Watsonians v Haddington
Division East 2
Corstorphine v Heriot's FP
Gordonians v Dundee HSFP
Kirkcaldy v Edinburgh Acads
Stewart's-Melville FP v Grangemouth
Division West
Ayr v Stirling County
Clarkston v Kilmarnock
Glasgow Acads v West of Scotland
Glasgow High/Kelvinside v Wigtownshire
Division South
Gala v Melrose
Jedforest v Hawick
Langholm v Peebles
Selkirk v Kelso

IRFU Provincial Championship
Connacht v Munster
Leinster v Ulster

WRU Heineken Leagues
Division 1
Aberavon v Pontypridd
Abertillery v Newport
Cardiff v Neath
Ebbw Vale v Swansea
Newbridge v Bridgend
Treorchy v Llanelli
Division 2
Caerphilly v Pontypool
Llanharan v Cross Keys
Maesteg v Bonymaen
S Wales Police v Dunvant
Tenby Utd v Llanharan
Ystradgynlais v Abercynon

Dromore v Malone
Fylde v Vale of Lune
Lansdowne v Monkstown
Morley v Bradford & Bingley
Richmond v High Wycombe
Sheffield v Harrogate

Sunday, 24 December

SRU District Championship
Edinburgh District v Scottish North & Midlands
South of Scotland v Glasgow District (Selkirk)

Tuesday, 26 December

Bedford v Bedfordshire
Cardiff v Pontypridd
Currie v Boroughmuir
Ebbw Vale v Abertillery
Gala v Melrose
Glasgow High/Kelvinside v Glasgow Acads
Gloucester v Lydney
Llanelli v London Welsh
London Irish v Old Millhillians
Moseley v Coventry
Newport v Bristol
Northampton v Stirling County
Northern v Newcastle Gosforth
Otley v Leeds
Preston Grasshoppers v Fylde
Preston Lodge FP v Musselburgh
Sale v Broughton Park
Treorchy v Penygraig
West Hartlepool v Hartlepool Rovers

Wednesday, 27 December

Leicester v Barbarians

Thursday, 28 December

Cornish President's XV v Penzance-Newlyn (Penzance)

Saturday, 30 December

Ireland Trial (Lansdowne Road)

RFU Courage Leagues
Division 1
Gloucester v Bath
Leicester v Sale
Orrell v Saracens
Wasps v Harlequins
West Hartlepool v Bristol
Division 2
London Irish v London Scottish
Moseley v Northampton
Nottingham v Newcastle Gosforth
Wakefield v Blackheath
Waterloo v Bedford

SRU Tennent's Regional Leagues
Division East 1
Boroughmuir v Watsonians
Currie v Biggar
Haddington v Preston Lodge FP
Musselburgh v Edinburgh Wands
Division East 2
Dundee HSFP v Corstorphine
Edinburgh Acads v Gordonians
Grangemouth v Kirkcaldy
Heriot's FP v Stewart's-Melville FP
Division West
Kilmarnock v Glasgow High/Kelvinside
Stirling County v Glasgow Acads
West of Scotland v Clarkston
Wigtownshire v Ayr
Division South
Hawick v Langholm
Kelso v Gala
Melrose v Jedforest
Peebles v Selkirk

WRU Heineken Leagues
Division 1
Bridgend v Newport
Llanelli v Ebbw Vale
Neath v Aberavon
Pontypridd v Newbridge
Swansea v Cardiff
Treorchy v Abertillery
Division 2
Abercynon v Llanharan
Bonymaen v Caerphilly
Cross Keys v Maesteg
Dunvant v Llandovery
Pontypool v S Wales Police
Ystradgynlais v Tenby Utd

Clifton v Weston-super-Mare
Coventry v Warwickshire XV
Fylde v Lichfield
Harrogate v Bradford & Bingley
London Welsh v Richmond
Otley v Sandal
Rugby v Birmingham Solihull
St Mary's Coll v Terenure Coll

Sunday, 31 December

SRU District Championship
Glasgow District v Edinburgh District

Monday, 1 January 1996

Fylde v Blackburn
Hawick v Heriot's FP
Maesteg v Aberavon

Newcastle Gosforth v Novocastrians

Tuesday, 2 January

Boroughmuir v Musselburgh
Gala v Selkirk
Glasgow High/Kelvinside v Melrose
Haddington v Preston Lodge FP
Jedforest v Alnwick
Penarth v Cardiff

Saturday, 6 January

Italy v Scotland A
Italy Under-21s v Scotland Under 21s

RFU Courage Leagues
Division 1
Bath v Leicester
Gloucester v West Hartlepool
Harlequins v Bristol
Sale v Orrell
Saracens v Wasps
Division 2
Blackheath v Bedford
London Irish v Waterloo
London Scottish v Moseley
Newcastle Gosforth v Wakefield
Northampton v Nottingham
Division 3
Morley v Rotherham
Otley v Coventry
Reading v Richmond
Rosslyn Park v Fylde
Rugby v Harrogate
Division 4
Aspatria v Plymouth Albion
Clifton v Redruth
Exeter v London Welsh
Havant v Leeds
Liverpool St Helens v Walsall
Division 5 South
Camberley v Askeans
Henley v High Wycombe
Met Police v Berry Hill
North Walsham v Camborne
Tabard v Lydney
Weston-super-Mare v Cheltenham
Division 5 North
Broughton Park v Stourbridge
Lichfield v Kendal
Preston Grasshoppers v Worcester
Sandal v Winnington Park
Sheffield v Nuneaton
Wharfedale v Stoke

SRU Tennent's Regional Leagues
Division East 1
Biggar v Edinburgh Wands
Currie v Haddington
Preston Lodge FP v Boroughmuir
Watsonians v Musselburgh
Division East 2
Edinburgh Acads v Grangemouth
Gordonians v Corstorphine
Kirkcaldy v Heriot's FP
Stewart's-Melville FP v Dundee HSFP
Division West
Ayr v Glasgow Acads
Clarkston v Stirling County
Glasgow High/Kelvinside v West of Scotland
Wigtownshire v Kilmarnock
Division South
Gala v Peebles
Hawick v Melrose
Jedforest v Kelso
Langholm v Selkirk

WRU Heineken Leagues
Division 1
Aberavon v Swansea
Abertillery v Bridgend
Cardiff v Llanelli
Ebbw Vale v Treorchy
Newbridge v Neath
Newport v Pontypridd
Division 2
Caerphilly v Cross Keys
Llandovery v Pontypool
Llanharan v Ystradgynlais
Maesteg v Abercynon
S Wales Police v Bonymaen
Tenby Utd v Dunvant

De La Salle Palmerston v Malone
St Mary's Coll v Bective Rangers
UC Cork v Lansdowne

Wednesday, 10 January

RAF v Civil Service
Royal Navy v CLOB

Saturday, 13 January

RFU Courage Leagues
Division 3
Coventry v Morley
Harrogate v Rosslyn Park
Otley v Fylde
Richmond v Rotherham
Rugby v Reading

Division 4
Aspatria v Redruth
Exeter v Walsall
Havant v Plymouth Albion
Liverpool St Helens v Leeds
London Welsh v Clifton
Division 5 South
Askeans v Met Police
Barking v Camberley
Berry Hill v Tabard
Camborne v Weston-super-Mare
High Wycombe v North Walsham
Lydney v Henley
Division 5 North
Birmingham Solihull v Sheffield
Kendal v Wharfedale
Nuneaton v Lichfield
Stoke v Preston Grasshoppers
Stourbridge v Sandal
Worcester v Broughton Park

SRU Tennent's Regional Leagues
Division East 1
Boroughmuir v Currie
Edinburgh Wands v Watsonians
Haddington v Biggar
Musselburgh v Preston Lodge FP
Division East 2
Corstorphine v Stewart's-Melville FP
Dundee HSFP v Kirkcaldy
Grangemouth v Gordonians
Heriot's FP v Edinburgh Acads
Division West
Glasgow Acads v Clarkston
Kilmarnock v Ayr
Stirling County v Glasgow High/
Kelvinside
West of Scotland v Wigtownshire
Division South
Kelso v Hawick
Melrose v Langholm
Peebles v Jedforest
Selkirk v Gala

WRU Heineken Leagues
Division 1
Ebbw Vale v Abertillery
Llanelli v Aberavon
Neath v Newport
Pontypridd v Bridgend
Swansea v Newbridge
Treorchy v Cardiff
Division 2
Abercynon v Caerphilly
Bonymaen v Llandovery
Cross Keys v S Wales Police
Llanharan v Tenby Utd
Pontypool v Dunvant
Ystradgynlais v Maesteg

Bedford v Loughborough U
Bristol v London Irish
Gloucester v London Scottish
Instonians v Terenure Coll
Lansdowne v Dolphin
Malone v Collegians
Northampton v Bath
Nottingham v Harlequins
Orrell v Blackheath
Saracens v Moseley
Wakefield v Wasps
Waterloo v Sale
West Hartlepool v Newcastle Gosforth

Tuesday, 16 January

Tredegar v Abertillery

Wednesday, 17 January

Cambridge U v RAF
Newcastle Gosforth v Durham City
Royal Navy v Oxford U

Friday, 19 January

Ireland A v Scotland A
Ireland Under-21s v Scotland Under-21s
Alnwick v Melrose
Askeans v Cambridge U
Bath v Moseley
Bristol v Exeter
Clarkston v Dundee HSFP
Clifton v Stroud
Edinburgh Wands v Glasgow High/
Kelvinside
Kelso v Boroughmuir
Langholm v Jedforest
Lansdowne v Heriot's FP
Leicester v Bedford
Northampton v Wasps
Portadown v Musselburgh
Preston Lodge FP v Stewart's-Melville FP
Stirling County v Grangemouth
West of Scotland v Kirkcaldy

Saturday, 20 January

IRELAND v SCOTLAND (Dublin)
FRANCE v ENGLAND (Paris)
WRU SWALEC Cup: *5th round*
Blackheath v Harlequins
Harrogate v Leeds
London Irish v Rosslyn Park

London Welsh v London Scottish
Newport v Cross Keys
Richmond v Saracens
Rugby v Orrell
Sale v Newcastle Gosforth
Wakefield v Coventry
Waterloo v Gloucester
West Hartlepool v Fylde

Sunday, 21 January

Dolphin v St Mary's Coll

Tuesday, 23 January

WRU Heineken Leagues
Division 1
Swansea v Pontypridd

Maesteg v Treorchy

Wednesday, 24 January

Surrey v PS Wands (Met Police)
Newport v Glam Wands
Oxford U v RAF

Saturday, 27 January

RFU Pilkington Cup: *5th round*
RFU Pilkington Shield: *6th round*

SRU Tennent's Regional Leagues
Division East 1
Currie v Musselburgh
Haddington v Boroughmuir
Preston Lodge FP v Edinburgh Wands
Watsonians v Biggar
Division East 2
Edinburgh Acads v Dundee HSFP
Grangemouth v Heriot's FP
Kirkcaldy v Corstorphine
Stewart's-Melville FP v Gordonians
Division West
Clarkston v Ayr
Glasgow High/Kelvinside v Glasgow Acads
Kilmarnock v West of Scotland
Wigtownshire v Stirling County
Division South
Gala v Langholm
Hawick v Peebles
Jedforest v Selkirk
Melrose v Kelso

IRFU Provinces Cups: *1st round*
Aberavon v Abercynon
Abertillery v Pontypool
Cambridge U v Richmond
Cardiff v Newport
Clifton v Basingstoke
Coventry v Bedford
Exeter v Moseley
Fylde v Broughton Park
Gloucester v Rugby
Harlequins v Northampton
Hull Ionians v Sale
Leeds v Wakefield
Liverpool St Helens v Harrogate
Llanelli v Dunvant
London Irish v Reading
Maesteg v Pontypridd
Morley v Northern
Newcastle Gosforth v Otley
Oxford U v Dublin U
S Wales Police v Treorchy
Swansea v Bridgend
Walsall v Rosslyn Park
Wasps v Waterloo

Tuesday, 30 January

Abercynon v Pontypridd
Bath v Cardiff
Gloucester v New South Wales
Llandovery v Aberavon
Wasps v Loughborough U

Wednesday, 31 January

CLOB v RAF
Civil Service v Royal Navy
Oxford U v Oxford

Thursday, 1 February

Ayr v Glasgow High/Kelvinside

Friday, 2 February

Scotland A v France A (Myreside)
England Students v Wales Students
Scotland Under-21s v France Under-21s
Abertillery v Blaina
Bedford v Saracens
Blackheath v Harrogate
Boroughmuir v Stewart's-Melville FP
Cambridge U v Sale
Cross Keys v Tredegar
Edinburgh Acads v Grangemouth
Gala v Kelso
Gloucester v Pontypool
Hillhead Jordanhill v West of Scotland
Jedforest v Melrose
Langholm v Hawick
Leicester v Coventry
London Irish v S Wales Police

Moseley v Bridgend
Musselburgh v Dunfermline
Newport v Loughborough U
Pontypridd v Bristol
Stourbridge v Nottingham
Swansea v Bath
Treorchy v Cheltenham
Wasps v Bridgend

Saturday, 3 February

ENGLAND v WALES (Twickenham)
SCOTLAND v FRANCE (Murrayfield)
IRFU Provinces Cups: *2nd round*

Edinburgh Acads v Montpellier
Fylde v Waterloo
Harlequins v Rugby
London Scottish v Reading
London Welsh v Cardiff
Newcastle Gosforth v Morley
Richmond v Met Police
Rosslyn Park v Clifton
Sheffield v Otley
Wakefield v Orrell

Saturday, 3 February

ENGLAND v WALES (Twickenham)
SCOTLAND v FRANCE (Murrayfield)
IRFU Provinces Cups: *2nd round*
Edinburgh Acads v Montpellier
Fylde v Waterloo
Harlequins v Rugby
London Scottish v Reading
London Welsh v Cardiff
Newcastle Gosforth v Morley
Richmond v Met Police
Rosslyn Park v Clifton
Sheffield v Otley
Wakefield v Orrell

Tuesday, 6 February

Maesteg v Llanelli
Swansea v S Wales Police

Wednesday, 7 February

Cambridge U v Royal Navy
Oxford U v Army

Saturday, 10 February

RFU Courage Leagues
Division 1
Bristol v Saracens
Leicester v Gloucester
Orrell v Bath
Wasps v Sale
West Hartlepool v Harlequins
Division 2
Bedford v Newcastle Gosforth
Moseley v London Irish
Nottingham v London Scottish
Wakefield v Northampton
Waterloo v Blackheath
Division 3
Fylde v Harrogate
Morley v Reading
Richmond v Rugby
Rosslyn Park v Coventry
Rotherham v Otley
Division 4
Clifton v Aspatria
Leeds v Exeter
Plymouth Albion v Liverpool St Helens
Redruth v Havant
Walsall v London Welsh
Division 5 South
Cheltenham v Camborne
Henley v Berry Hill
Met Police v Barking
North Walsham v Lydney
Tabard v Askeans
Weston-super-Mare v High Wycombe
Division 5 North
Broughton Park v Stoke
Lichfield v Birmingham Solihull
Preston Grasshoppers v Kendal
Sandal v Worcester
Wharfedale v Nuneaton
Winnington Park v Stourbridge

Ayr v Heriot's FP
Bonymaen v Aberavon
Brunel U v Cambridge U
Clarkston v Preston Lodge FP
Cross Keys v Newbridge
Dundee HSFP v Grangemouth
Gala v Stewart's-Melville FP
Glasgow Acads v Jedforest
Hawick v Glasgow High/Kelvinside
Kirkcaldy v Edinburgh Wands
Llanelli v Swansea
Maesteg v Newport
NIFC v Malone
Old Crescent v Lansdowne
Oxford U v Bristol U
Selkirk v Melrose
St Mary's Coll v UC Dublin
Watsonians v Kelso
West of Scotland v Boroughmuir
Ystradgynlais v Treorchy

Monday, 12 February

Royal Navy v Devon

Tuesday, 13 February

Cardiff v Swansea
S Wales Police v Pontypridd
Treorchy v Abercynon

Wednesday, 14 February

Oxford U v Anti-Assassins

Friday, 16 February

Wales A v Scotland A (Newport)
Wales Under-21s v Scotland Under-21s (Newport)
Wales Students v Scotland Students (Glam Wands RFC)
Abertillery v Glam Wands
Blaina v Cross Keys
Cardiff v Watsonians
Edinburgh Acads v Kelso
Edinburgh Wands v West of Scotland
Instonians v Dungannon
Kirkcaldy v Selkirk
Langholm v Gala
Llanelli v Boroughmuir
Musselburgh v Stewart's-Melville FP
Newport v Glasgow High/Kelvinside
Pontypridd v Dundee HSFP
Swansea v Pontypool
Treorchy v Bonymaen

Saturday, 17 February

WALES v SCOTLAND (Cardiff)
FRANCE v IRELAND (Paris)

RFU Courage Leagues
Division 1
Bath v Wasps
Gloucester v Orrell
Leicester v West Hartlepool
Sale v Bristol
Saracens v Harlequins
Division 2
London Irish v Nottingham
London Scottish v Wakefield
Moseley v Waterloo
Newcastle Gosforth v Blackheath
Northampton v Bedford
Division 3
Coventry v Fylde
Harrogate v Rotherham
Otley v Richmond
Reading v Rosslyn Park
Rugby v Morley
Division 4
Exeter v Plymouth Albion
Havant v Aspatria
Liverpool St Helens v Redruth
London Welsh v Leeds
Walsall v Clifton
Division 5 South
Askeans v Henley
Barking v Tabard
Berry Hill v North Walsham
Camberley v Met Police
High Wycombe v Cheltenham
Lydney v Weston-super-Mare
Division 5 North
Birmingham Solihull v Wharfedale
Kendal v Broughton Park
Nuneaton v Preston Grasshoppers
Sheffield v Lichfield
Stoke v Sandal
Worcester v Winnington Park

St Mary's Coll v De La Salle Palmerston

Sunday, 18 February

Skerries v Lansdowne

Tuesday, 20 February

S Wales Police v Abertillery
Treorchy v Maesteg

Wednesday, 21 February

Cambridge U v Army
Newport v Pontypool
Nottingham v RAF
Oxford U v Penguins

Saturday, 24 February

RFU Pilkington Cup: *Quarter-finals*
RFU Pilkington Shield: *Quarter-finals*

RFU Courage Leagues
Division 3
Fylde v Reading
Richmond v Harrogate
Rosslyn Park v Morley
Rotherham v Coventry
Rugby v Otley
Division 4
Aspatria v Liverpool St Helens
Clifton v Havant
Leeds v Walsall
Plymouth Albion v London Welsh
Redruth v Exeter

Division 5 South
Camborne v High Wycombe
Cheltenham v Lydney
Henley v Barking
North Walsham v Askeans
Tabard v Camberley
Weston-super-Mare v Berry Hill
Division 5 North
Broughton Park v Nuneaton
Preston Grasshoppers v Birmingham Solihull
Sandal v Kendal
Stourbridge v Worcester
Wharfedale v Sheffield
Winnington Park v Stoke

SRU Tennent's 1556 Cup: *3rd round*
WRU SWALEC Cup: *6th round*
Abertillery v Maesteg
Boroughmuir v Newcastle Gosforth
Bridgend v Gloucester
Bristol v Waterloo
Currie v Preston Lodge FP
Dundee HSFP v Stirling County
Dungannon v Malone
Edinburgh Acads v Glasgow High/Kelvinside
Gloucester v London Irish
Harlequins v Bedford
Kelso v Grangemouth
Lansdowne v Bangor
Llanelli v Wasps
Moseley v Newport
Musselburgh v Heriot's FP
Northampton v Leicester
Nottingham v Sale
Old Crescent v St Mary's Coll
Penarth v Aberavon
Stewart's-Melville FP v Melrose
Treorchy v Llanharan
Wakefield v Saracens
Watsonians v Glasgow Acads
West of Scotland v Gala

Tuesday, 27 February

Aberavon v Blaina
Cardiff v Bridgend
Lydney v RAF
Pontypridd v Cross Keys

Wednesday, 28 February

Royal Navy v Surrey (US Portsmouth)
Cambridge U v Anti-Assassins
Nuneaton v Rugby
Swansea U v Oxford U

Friday, 1 March

Ireland A v Wales A
Ireland Under-21s v Wales Under-21s
Ireland Students v Wales Students
Scotland Students v England Students
Bath v Newbridge
Boroughmuir v Waterloo
Bristol v Newport
Clarkston v Grangemouth
Clifton v Berry Hill
Currie v Heriot's FP
Gala v Northampton
Gloucester v Swansea
Hawick v Haddington
Jedforest v Rugby
Kelso v Bedford
Kirkcaldy v Dundee HSFP
Langholm v Melrose
Leicester v Nottingham
Musselburgh v Glasgow High/Kelvinside
Pontypool v Treorchy
St Mary's Coll v Llanelli
Wasps v Coventry

Saturday, 2 March

SCOTLAND v ENGLAND (Murrayfield)
IRELAND v WALES (Lansdowne Road)
Bective Rangers v Lansdowne
Bradford & Bingley v Otley
Cambridge U v Blackheath
Fylde v Stourbridge
Hull Ionians v Harrogate
London Irish v Saracens
London Welsh v Moseley
Orrell v Newcastle Gosforth
Richmond v Harlequins
Rosslyn Park v Bridgend
Sale v Morley
Watsonians v London Scottish
West Hartlepool v Wakefield

Tuesday, 5 March

Bristol v Royal Navy
Gloucester v Army
Mountain Ash v Aberavon

Wednesday, 6 March

Cambridge U v Penguins
Clifton v RAF
Gala v Newcastle Gosforth
Oxfordshire v Oxford U

Saturday, 9 March

RFU CIS County Championship:
Semi-finals

WRU Heineken Leagues
Division 1
Aberavon v Treorchy
Abertillery v Pontypridd
Bridgend v Neath
Cardiff v Ebbw Vale
Newbridge v Llanelli
Newport v Swansea
Division 2
Caerphilly v Ystradgynlais
Dunvant v Bonymaen
Llandovery v Cross Keys
Maesteg v Llanharan
S Wales Police v Abercynon
Tenby Utd v Pontypool

Bath v London Irish
Bedford v Bristol
Blackheath v London Welsh
Blaydon v Selkirk
Boroughmuir v Ayr
Coventry v Sale
Dundee HSFP v Heriot's FP
Exeter v Gloucester
Gala v Kirkcaldy
Grangemouth v Jedforest
Glasgow High/Kelvinside v Biggar
Hawick v Hartlepool Rovers
Kelso v Langholm
Lansdowne v Sunday's Well
London Scottish v Rosslyn Park
Malone v Instonians
Melrose v Harrogate
Middlesbrough v Otley
Moseley v Leicester
Newcastle Gosforth v Fylde
Northampton v Richmond
Orrell v Morley
Peebles v Clarkston
Rotherham v West Hartlepool
Rugby v Clifton
Saracens v Watsonians
St Mary's Coll v Dublin U
Stewart's-Melville FP v Glasgow Acads
Stirling County v Musselburgh
Wakefield v Harlequins
Wasps v Nottingham
West of Scotland v Preston Lodge FP

Tuesday, 12 March

Abercynon v Aberavon
Bristol v Cardiff
Clifton v Army
Llanelli v Maesteg
Pontypool v Pontypridd
Tredegar v Treorchy
Wasps v Royal Navy

Wednesday, 13 March

Army v Lydney
Alnwick v Newcastle Gosforth
Nuneaton v Coventry

Friday, 15 March

Wales Under-21s v France Under-21s (Cardiff)
Wales Students v France Students (Cardiff)

Saturday, 16 March

ENGLAND v IRELAND (Twickenham)
WALES v FRANCE (Cardiff)
SRU Tennent's 1556 Cup: *4th round*

Sunday, 17 March

St Mary's Coll v Monkstown

Tuesday, 19 March

Bath & Army
Lydney v Gloucester
Maesteg v Abertillery
Northampton v RAF

Wednesday, 20 March

Royal Navy v Cornwall (Devonport)
Surrey v Kent (Met Police)

Saturday, 23 March

RFU Pilkington Cup: *Semi-finals*
RFU Pilkington Shield: *Semi-finals*

RFU Courage Leagues
Division 3
Morley v Fylde
Otley v Harrogate
Reading v Rotherham
Richmond v Coventry
Rosslyn Park v Rugby
Division 4
Exeter v Aspatria
Leeds v Clifton
Liverpool St Helens v Havant
London Welsh v Redruth
Walsall v Plymouth Albion

IRFU Insurance Corporation Leagues
Division 1
Blackrock Coll v St Mary's Coll
Cork Const v Garryowen
Instonians v Old Wesley
Shannon v Ballymena
Young Munster v Lansdowne
Division 2
Bective Rangers v NIFC
Dungannon v Terenure Coll
Malone v Dolphin
Sunday's Well v Clontarf
Wanderers v Greystones
Division 3
Buccaneers v Bangor
City of Derry v Skerries
Highfield v Bohemians
Monkstown v De La Salle Palmerston
UC Cork v Galwegians
Waterpark v UC Dublin
Division 4
Armagh v UC Galway
CIYMS v Ards
Corinthians v Portadown
Queen's U, Belfast v Collegians
Sligo v Dublin U

WRU SWALEC Cup: *Quarter-finals*

Tuesday, 26 March

Glam Wands v Treorchy

Saturday, 30 March

Cathay Pacific-Hong Kong Bank Sevens
Royal Navy v Army (Twickenham)

RFU Courage Leagues
Division 1
Bristol v Bath
Harlequins v Sale
Orrell v Leicester
Wasps v Gloucester
West Hartlepool v Saracens
Division 2
Bedford v London Scottish
Blackheath v Northampton
Nottingham v Moseley
Wakefield v London Irish
Waterloo v Newcastle Gosforth
Division 3
Coventry v Otley
Fylde v Rosslyn Park
Harrogate v Rugby
Richmond v Reading
Rotherham v Morley
Division 4
Aspatria v London Welsh
Clifton v Liverpool St Helens
Havant v Exeter
Plymouth Albion v Leeds
Redruth v Walsall
Division 5 South
Askeans v Weston-super-Mare
Barking v North Walsham
Berry Hill v Cheltenham
Camberley v Henley
Lydney v Camborne
Met Police v Tabard
Division 5 North
Birmingham Solihull v Broughton Park
Kendal v Winnington Park
Lichfield v Wharfedale
Nuneaton v Sandal
Sheffield v Preston Grasshoppers
Stoke v Stourbridge

SRU Tennent's Cup: *5th round*

IRFU Insurance Corporation Leagues
Division 1
Ballymena v Blackrock Coll
Garryowen v Young Munster
Old Belvedere v Instonians
Old Wesley v Shannon
St Mary's Coll v Cork Const
Division 2
Clontarf v Dolphin
Greystones v Old Crescent
NIFC v Terenure Coll
Sunday's Well v Dungannon
Wanderers v Malone
Division 3
Bangor v De La Salle Palmerston
Bohemians v City of Derry
Buccaneers v Galwegians
Monkstown v UC Dublin
Skerries v Waterpark
UC Cork v Highfield
Division 4
Ards v Portadown
Armagh v Ballina
CIYMS v Collegians
Corinthians v UC Galway
Queen's U, Belfast v Dublin U

WRU Heineken Leagues
Division 1
Cardiff v Abertillery
Ebbw Vale v Aberavon
Llanelli v Newport
Neath v Pontypridd

Swansea v Bridgend
Treorchy v Newbridge
Division 2
Abercynon v Llandovery
Bonymaen v Pontypool
Cross Keys v Dunvant
Llanharan v Caerphilly
Maesteg v Tenby Utd
Ystradgynlais v S Wales Police

Sunday, 31 March

Cathay Pacific-Hong Kong Bank Sevens

Tuesday, 2 April

WRU Heineken Leagues
Division 1
Aberavon v Cardiff

Saturday, 6 April

Cardiff v Barbarians

RFU Courage Leagues
Division 1
Bath v Harlequins
Gloucester v Bristol
Leicester v Wasps
Sale v Saracens
West Hartlepool v Orrell
Division 2
London Irish v Bedford
London Scottish v Blackheath
Moseley v Wakefield
Northampton v Newcastle Gosforth
Waterloo v Nottingham
Division 3
Coventry v Harrogate
Fylde v Rugby
Morley v Richmond
Reading v Otley
Rotherham v Rosslyn Park
Division 4
Clifton v Plymouth Albion
Exeter v Liverpool St Helens
Leeds v Redruth
London Welsh v Havant
Walsall v Aspatria

Gala Sevens

IRFU Insurance Corporation Leagues
Division 1
Blackrock Coll v Old Wesley
Cork Const v Ballymena
Lansdowne v Garryowen
Shannon v Old Belvedere
Young Munster v St Mary's Coll
Division 2
Bective Rangers v Sunday's Well
Dolphin v NIFC
Dungannon v Wanderers
Malone v Greystones
Old Crescent v Clontarf
Division 3
City of Derry v UC Cork
De La Salle Palmerston v Buccaneers
Galwegians v Bangor
Highfield v Monkstown
UC Dublin v Skerries
Waterpark v Bohemians
Division 4
Ballina v CIYMS
Collegians v Ards
Dublin U v Corinthians
Portadown v Queen's U, Belfast
UC Galway v Sligo

WRU Heineken Leagues
Division 1
Abertillery v Neath
Bridgend v Llanelli
Newbridge v Ebbw Vale
Newport v Treorchy
Pontypridd v Swansea
Division 2
Caerphilly v Maesteg
Dunvant v Abercynon
Llandovery v Ystradgynlais
Pontypool v Cross Keys
S Wales Police v Llanharan
Tenby Utd v Bonymaen

Monday, 8 April

Aberavon v Narberth
Fylde v Preston Grasshoppers
Newport v London Welsh
Penygraig v Treorchy

Wednesday, 10 April

Army v Royal Air Force (Twickenham)

Saturday, 13 April

RFU Courage Leagues
Division 1
Bristol v Leicester
Harlequins v Gloucester
Sale v West Hartlepool
Saracens v Bath
Wasps v Orrell
Division 2
Bedford v Moseley

Blackheath v London Irish
Newcastle Gosforth v London Scottish
Northampton v Waterloo
Wakefield v Nottingham
Division 3
Harrogate v Reading
Otley v Morley
Richmond v Rosslyn Park
Rotherham v Fylde
Rugby v Coventry
Division 4
Aspatria v Leeds
Exeter v Clifton
Havant v Walsall
Liverpool St Helens v London Welsh
Redruth v Plymouth Albion

Melrose Sevens

IRFU Insurance Corporation Leagues
Division 1
Ballymena v Young Munster
Instonians v Shannon
Old Belvedere v Blackrock Coll
Old Wesley v Cork Const
St Mary's Coll v Lansdowne
Division 2
Clontarf v Malone
Greystones v Dungannon
NIFC v Old Crescent
Terenure Coll v Dolphin
Wanderers v Bective Rangers
Division 3
Bangor v Skerries
Bohemians v UC Dublin
Buccaneers v Highfield
De La Salle Palmerston v Galwegians
Monkstown v City of Derry
UC Cork v Waterpark
Division 4
Ards v UC Galway
CIYMS v Portadown
Corinthians v Ballina
Collegians v Dublin U
Sligo v Armagh

WRU SWALEC Cup: *Semi-finals*

Tuesday, 16 April

Crumlin v Cross Keys
Glam Wands v Aberavon

Wednesday, 17 April

Royal Navy v Royal Air Force (Twickenham)
CLOB v Surrey (Old Walcountians)
Coventry v Moseley

Saturday, 20 April

RFU CIS County Championship: *Final* (Twickenham)
Hawick Sevens

IRFU Insurance Corporation Leagues
Division 1
Blackrock Coll v Instonians
Cork Const v Old Belvedere
Garryowen v St Mary's Coll
Lansdowne v Ballymena
Young Munster v Old Wesley
Division 2
Bective Rangers v Malone
Clontarf v NIFC
Greystones v Terenure Coll
Sunday's Well v Old Crescent
Division 3
City of Derry v Buccaneers
De La Salle Palmerston v Waterpark
Galwegians v Monkstown
Highfield v Bangor
Skerries v Bohemians
UC Dublin v UC Cork
Division 4
Armagh v Corinthians
Ballina v Queen's U, Belfast
Dublin U v Portadown
CIYMS v Sligo
UC Galway v Collegians

WRU Heineken Leagues
Division 1
Aberavon v Abertillery
Cardiff v Newbridge
Ebbw Vale v Newport
Llanelli v Pontypridd
Swansea v Neath
Treorchy v Bridgend
Division 2
Abercynon v Pontypool
Caerphilly v Tenby Utd
Cross Keys v Bonymaen
Llanharan v Llandovery
Maesteg v S Wales Police
Ystradgynlais v Dunvant

Sunday, 21 April

SRU Tennent's 1556 Cup: *Quarter-finals*

IRFU Insurance Corporation Leagues
Division 2
Wanderers v Dolphin

Tuesday, 23 April

Cardiff v Pontypool

Saturday, 27 April

RFU Courage Leagues
Division 1
Bath v Sale
Gloucester v Saracens
Leicester v Harlequins
Orrell v Bristol
West Hartlepool v Wasps
Division 2
London Irish v Newcastle Gosforth
London Scottish v Northampton
Moseley v Blackheath
Nottingham v Bedford
Waterloo v Wakefield
Division 3
Fylde v Richmond
Morley v Harrogate
Reading v Coventry
Rosslyn Park v Otley
Rotherham v Rugby
Division 4
London Welsh v Exeter
Leeds v Havant
Plymouth Albion v Aspatria
Redruth v Clifton
Walsall v Liverpool St Helens

Jedforest Sevens
IRFU Provinces Cups: *Semi-finals*

WRU Heineken Leagues
Division 1
Abertillery v Swansea
Bridgend v Ebbw Vale
Neath v Llanelli
Newbridge v Aberavon
Newport v Cardiff
Pontypridd v Treorchy
Division 2
Bonymaen v Abercynon
Dunvant v Llanharan
Llandovery v Maesteg
Pontypool v Ystradgynlais
S Wales Police v Caerphilly
Tenby Utd v Cross Keys

Sunday, 28 April

SRU Tennent's 1556 Cup: *Semi-finals*

Saturday, 4 May

RFU Pilkington Cup: *Final* (Twickenham)
RFU Pilkington Shield: *Final* (Twickenham)
Langholm Sevens
Connacht Senior Cup: *Final*
Leinster Senior Cup: *Final*
Munster Senior Cup: *Final*
Ulster Senior Cup: *Final*
WRU SWALEC Cup: *Final* (Cardiff)

Saturday, 11 May

Middlesex Sevens: *Finals* (Twickenham)
SRU Tennent's 1556 Cup: *Final* (Murrayfield)

MAJOR TOURS 1995-96

FIJIANS TO WALES AND IRELAND

October

21 **Wales A** (Bridgend)
25 **Neath** (Neath)
28 **Cardiff** (Cardiff)

November

1 **Treorchy** (Treorchy)
4 **Pontypridd** (Pontypridd)
7 **Llanelli** (Llanelli)
11 **WALES** (Cardiff)
14 **Connacht** (Galway)
18 **IRELAND** (Dublin)

WESTERN SAMOANS TO ENGLAND AND SCOTLAND

November

8 **Edinburgh District** (Inverleith)
12 **Scotland A** (Hawick)
14 **Scottish North & Midlands** (Perth)
18 **SCOTLAND** (Murrayfield)
21 **Oxford U** (Oxford)
25 **Cambridge U** (Cambridge)
29 **London and South-East Division** (Twickenham)

December

2 **Midlands Division** (Leicester)
5 **Northern Division** (Huddersfield)
9 **South & South-West Division** (Gloucester)
12 **England A**
16 **ENGLAND** (Twickenham)

NEW ZEALANDERS TO FRANCE
(all dates & venues provisional)

November

1 **French Barbarians** (Toulon)
4 **French Selection** (Béziers)
7 **French Selection** (Bayonne)
11 **FRANCE** (Toulouse)
14 **French Selection** (Nancy)
18 **FRANCE** (Paris)

MAJOR FIXTURES 1995-96

September

2 **SOUTH AFRICA v WALES** (Johannesburg)

October

21 **Wales A v Fijians** (Bridgend)

November

11 **FRANCE v NEW ZEALAND** (Toulouse)
WALES v FIJI (Cardiff)
12 **Scotland A v Western Samoans** (Hawick)
18 **ENGLAND v SOUTH AFRICA** (Twickenham)
SCOTLAND v WESTERN SAMOA (Murrayfield)
IRELAND v FIJI (Lansdowne Road)
FRANCE v NEW ZEALAND (Paris)

December

12 **England A v Western Samoans**
Oxford U v Cambridge U (Twickenham)
16 **ENGLAND v WESTERN SAMOA** (Twickenham)
30 **Ireland Trial** (Lansdowne Road)

January

6 **Italy v Scotland A**
19 **Ireland A v Scotland A**
20 **IRELAND v SCOTLAND** (Lansdowne Road)
FRANCE v ENGLAND (Paris)

February

2 **Scotland A v France A** (Myreside)
3 **ENGLAND v WALES** (Twickenham)
SCOTLAND v FRANCE (Murrayfield)
16 **Wales A v Scotland A** (Newport)
17 **WALES v SCOTLAND** (Cardiff)
FRANCE v IRELAND (Paris)

March

1 **Ireland A v Wales A**
2 **IRELAND v WALES** (Lansdowne Road)
SCOTLAND v ENGLAND (Murrayfield)
16 **ENGLAND v IRELAND** (Twickenham)
WALES v FRANCE (Cardiff)
30 **Hong Kong Sevens**
Royal Navy v Army (Twickenham)
31 **Hong Kong Sevens**

April

10 **Army v Royal Air Force** (Twickenham)
17 **Royal Navy v Royal Air Force** (Twickenham)
20 **RFU County Championship Final** (Twickenham)

May

4 **RFU Pilkington Cup Final** (Twickenham)
SWALEC Cup Final (Cardiff)
11 **SRU Tennent's 1556 Cup Final** (Murrayfield)
Middlesex Sevens Finals (Twickenham)